A Call to Arms

A
CALL TO
ARMS

. . .

MOBILIZING AMERICA
FOR WORLD WAR II

MAURY KLEIN

BLOOMSBURY PRESS
New York   London   New Delhi   Sydney

Published by Bloomsbury Press, New York

All papers used by Bloomsbury Press are natural, recyclable products made
from wood grown in well-managed forests. The manufacturing processes
conform to the environmental regulations of the country of origin.

LIBRARY OF CONGRESS CATALOGING-IN-PUBLICATION DATA

Klein, Maury, 1939–
A call to arms : mobilizing America for World War II / Maury Klein.—First
U.S. edition.

pages cm

ISBN 978-1-59691-607-4 (hardback)
1. Industrial mobilization—United States—History—20th century.
2. United States—Armed Forces—Mobilization—History—20th century.
3. World War, 1939–1945—Economic aspects—United States.   4. United
States—Economic policy—1933–1945.   I. Title.
D769.2.K54 2013
940.53'73—dc23

First U.S. Edition 2013

1 3 5 7 9 10 8 6 4 2

Typeset by Westchester Book Group
Printed and bound in the U.S.A. by Thomson-Shore, Inc., Dexter, Michigan

For Kim and Shannon, and Joan and Stephanie:
the bookends of my life.

CONTENTS

ACKNOWLEDGMENTS

As always, special thanks go to those people who helped this project along at every step of the way. At the University of Rhode Island library, Emily Greene deserves lavish praise for the cheerful and efficient manner in which she ran down and obtained source materials for me. Mary Anne Sumner performed a variety of tasks that made my life in the library far easier. My friend T. J. Stiles read a portion of a crucial chapter and proffered his usual sage advice. Marian Young has long since graduated to good friend and counselor as well as agent. At Bloomsbury Pete Beatty provided invaluable help and was always ready with an answer to any question. India Cooper once again provided her expert copyediting. Jerry Strahan cheerfully provided two important photographs of the Higgins family and plant, which Dawn Higgins Murphy gave permission for me to use.

My editor, Peter Ginna, deserves special thanks for the enlarged role he played. Apart from his expert editing, he first advanced the idea for this book as something he had long wished to see done. I visited the project with him once, decided against it, and revisited it several years later with a more positive response. He was correct in his vision, and I am deeply grateful for his persistence.

Finally, my wife, Kim, once again sustained me through a long and difficult project with her good cheer and encouragement.

Beyond the usual acknowledgements I would like to pay special tribute to the large number of writers who filled the magazines and journals of the 1940s with their observations and insights. Only a handful of them received the dignity of a byline; the rest remain anonymous to readers then and now. From their work I have gleaned much of the material used in this book, and I am profoundly grateful for their work and their unwitting assistance.

ABBREVIATIONS

AAR	Association of American Railroads
ACF	American Car & Foundry
AFL	American Federation of Labor
ANMB	Army-Navy Munitions Board
AP	Associated Press
ASF	Army Service Forces
ASP	Army Supply Program
ASTP	Army Specialized Training Program
AWPC	Aircraft War Production Council
BCR	Bureau of Construction and Repair
BEW	Board of Economic Warfare
BRS	Bureau of Research and Statistics
BS	Bureau of Ships
CARD	Committee to Abolish Racial Discrimination
CCC	Civilian Conservation Corps
CIO	Congress of Industrial Organizations
CMP	Controlled Materials Plan
CPA	Civilian Production Administration
CPI	Committee on Public Information
CTC	Centralized Traffic Control
DPC	Defense Plant Corporation
DSC	Defense Supplies Corporation
DSRP	Defense Supplies Rating Plan
ERC	Enlisted Reserve Corps
FPC	Federal Power Commission
FSA	Federal Security Agency
HUAC	House Un-American Activities Committee
IMP	Industrial Mobilization Plan
JCS	Joint Chiefs of Staff
JPSC	Joint Production Survey Committee
MED	Manhattan Engineer District

MPC	Military Policy Committee
NACA	National Advisory Committee for Aeronautics
NAM	National Association of Manufacturers
NDAC	National Defense Advisory Commission
NDMB	National Defense Mediation Board
NDRC	National Defense Research Committee
NLRB	National Labor Relations Board
NRA	National Recovery Administration
NYA	National Youth Administration
OCD	Office of Civilian Defense
OCS	Office of Civilian Supply
ODT	Office of Defense Transportation
OEM	Office of Emergency Management
OES	Office of Economic Stabilization
OFF	Office of Facts and Figures
OGR	Office of Government Reports
OPA	Office of Price Administration
OPACS	Office of Price Administration and Civilian Supply
OPM	Office of Production Management
OP&M	Office of Procurement and Material
OSRD	Office of Scientific Research and Development
OSS	Office of Strategic Services
OWI	Office of War Information
OWM	Office of War Mobilization
OWMR	Office of War Mobilization and Reconversion
PAC	Political Action Committee
PAW	Petroleum Administration for War
PEC	Production Executive Committee
PRP	Production Requirements Plan
RAF	Royal Air Force
RFC	Reconstruction Finance Corporation
RRC	Rubber Reserve Company
SPAB	Supply Priorities and Allocations Board
SWOC	Steel Workers Organizing Committee
SWPA	Surplus War Property Administration
UAW	United Auto Workers of America
UMW	United Mine Workers of America
USES	United States Employment Service
WAAC	Women's Army Auxiliary Corps
WAVES	Women Accepted for Volunteer Emergency Service
WFA	War Food Administration

WIB	War Industries Board
WLB	War Labor Board
WMC	War Manpower Commission
WPB	War Production Board
WRA	War Resources Administration
WRB	War Resources Board
WSA	War Shipping Administration

PREFACE:
THE UNLUCKIEST
GENERATION

THIS BOOK EXPLORES A DIMENSION of World War II that is often mentioned but rarely explained in detail. It describes how Americans at home mobilized for what became the first truly global war in history. The scale of their effort was epic, their task a stupendous one. The story of how it all got done is both complex and convoluted, which is why it has been so difficult to tell. Yet it is unquestionably one of the most important stories in our history for several reasons. Most obviously, the combined effort of so many diverse Americans won this gigantic war, the stakes of which were for the nation matched only by those of the Civil War. Beyond this great achievement, the outcome of their labors, and the process by which it was accomplished, have shaped American history since 1945. Their influence still resonates deeply in our lives and institutions today.

Consider just this short list of its impact. Military spending for preparedness ended the decade-long Great Depression, and wartime outlays laid the foundation for an unprecedented period of postwar prosperity and the flowering of the consumer economy. The war created the industrial-military complex and fostered the rise of Big Science. It introduced the world to the most destructive weapons in human history and thereby set the stage for the Cold War and its lethal arms race. For the first time the military remained a large and continuing presence in American life. For the first time, too, the United States, like it or not, assumed the leading role in world affairs. Even more than in 1918 it was the only major power left standing.

Technologies developed during the war moved to the center of American life in a burgeoning consumer economy. Jet planes, radar, magnetic tape recording, early computers, and a host of electronic innovations are but a few of the military products that found their way into consumer goods. Long-range bombers morphed into a new breed of commercial airliners. The revitalized automobile industry poured out more cars than ever before, including a civilian version of the ubiquitous jeep. A new generation of appliances incorporated improvements developed originally for military use. The Space Age has deep roots in wartime developments.

Big government became a way of life much more than during the New Deal of the 1930s. The modern system of taxation, reaching down into the ranks of low incomes, made its appearance. New Deal programs such as Social Security and unemployment insurance became staples of an expanding social welfare system. The GI Bill of Rights provided education, training, and a fresh start in life to veterans instead of merely dumping them onto a shrinking job market as happened after World War I. Unions became an enduring part of the workplace. The world of Big Business, Big Government, and Big Labor had arrived. Oh yes, and the democratic system of government was preserved from the gravest threat it had ever known.

The war changed the face of America. Plants, airfields, military bases, testing ranges, and other installations created new towns or enlarged existing ones beyond recognition. Sleepy villages mushroomed into dynamic towns. The war transformed the West from an economic colony of the East to a vibrant, fast-growing section with new industries that moved it toward economic self-sufficiency. Millions of Americans migrated westward to find jobs and a better life. The war also injected new energy into the long-moribund South's economy even as tens of thousands of its people, black and white, moved to the North or West to earn the highest pay they had ever seen. In the process they rewrote the demography of their destination cities, creating social and racial tensions that sometimes exploded into violence.

Black Americans and Hispanics found some of the best job opportunities they had ever seen. The war's urgent need for manpower helped spur the rise of a civil rights movement that began with modest gains but grew into an irresistible force over the years. Women flocked to jobs in war plants or elsewhere in record numbers, and their critical role in mobilization changed not only their individual lives but their place in American society as well. Children's lives were shaped and often scarred by wartime deprivations and losses. Juvenile delinquency became a staple of American life, not only in cities but in fast-growing suburbs as well.

How did all of this happen? Too often America's mobilization has been portrayed as a smoothly flowing process in which patrotic Americans rose to the challenge and performed what has often been called "miracles of production." While some of the results might seem miraculous in scope, nothing about the process was smooth or flowing. It was rather an arduous, chaotic, contentious grind that exacted a high physical and psychic toll. A curious reversal of fortune took place in that more Americans died in industrial and work-related accidents at home than in combat overseas.

Three factors have blurred our understanding of what happened during those tumultuous years. The first is a tendency to forget that the war began twenty-seven months before the United States entered the fighting. During that time a fierce struggle took place over what position the country should take in the conflict and how fast it should prepare for the possibility that it might become involved. As a result, American mobilization took place in two distinct phases, preparedness (1939–41) and wartime (1942–45). The first proved the more crucial and did much to shape the direction, nature, and timing of the second. It was complicated by the fact that no one knew for certain whether we would go to war, when, where, or with whom. Asking the people to prepare for a war that might or might not involve us could not help but produce conflict and disagreement.

A second factor, easily overlooked, is the extent to which the American experience in World War I loomed over nearly every aspect of mobilization. The bitter, wholly unsatisfying outcome of that experience deeply scarred the memories of that generation, many of whom were leaders in every field of American life by 1939. Many if not most of them wanted no more of war, bailing out Europe from its eternal conflicts, or "blood profits" for bankers and munitions makers. Generals are far from the only ones who tend to fight the last war.

A third factor involves the way in which the nation's response to this crisis has been portrayed in retrospect. Over the years some writers have enshrined those who lived through the depression and war period as somehow different, even better than Americans of other eras. While the sentiment is understandable, it also clouds efforts to get at a clear story of the mobilization process. The time has come to deflate the "Greatest Generation" myth.

Myth is a powerful force and a major obstacle in trying to understand the past. Every nation's history is glazed with myths, and America is no exception. Apart from often being incomplete or simply wrong, they get in the way of grasping what really happened. The problem is less one of forgetting the past and its meaning than of remembering the wrong things about it and drawing the wrong lessons from it. The characterization of "Greatest Generation" is a good example of a myth that, in Walter Lippmann's phrase, is well meaning but unmeaning. Tom Brokaw and others meant well in heaping such lavish tribute on this group of Americans, but the phrase is both misleading and meaningless.

To take one example, how is the generation that fought World War II any "greater" than the one that fought the Civil War? The Civil War lasted slightly longer than American involvement in World War II. Some 620,000 Americans died in it, more than in all other American wars combined, the large majority of them from noncombat causes. The war was fought entirely at home, on

American soil, devastating large parts of the country and leaving the losing section in ruins. Southerners endured the ordeal, not experienced by any Americans since, of suffering military occupation for eleven years afterward. More than 3 million Americans were slaves who gained their freedom, if not equality. Yet that generation cannot claim the "greatest" title either.

A generation consists of people born in a particular span of years. It is an accident of history over which they have neither choice nor control. The difference between one generation and another lies in the situations they have to confront. Their range of responses will be similar down through the ages even though the circumstances that confront them may vary widely. The generation discussed in this book had to deal with two of the worst crises in our history: the Great Depression and World War II. As always, each crisis affected different people in a wide variety of ways. Some were deeply scarred by the experience; others scarcely knew its presence. Like it or not, many (but not all or even most) of those in the service literally invested and sacrificed their very lives to the task. Others used the crises to turn a profit or improve their fortunes or simply rode it out with as little disturbance to their lives as possible.

How is one even to know the extent or depth to which these crises affected different people? For some—who knows how many?—the basic stuff of their life, emotional, situational, and otherwise, may have far transcended or overshadowed the impact of these larger events. Most people have all they can handle just to deal with whatever is in front of them. When the larger world intrudes, many try to escape or avoid or simply deny its presence for as long as possible. A depression is no big deal to those who have always been poor. For professional soldiers war is an opportunity. When the war came, some men rushed to enlist in a burst of patriotism; many more did not or tried actively to evade military service. However great or small their sense of patriotism, thousands of people flocked to jobs in defense plants because they could earn more money than they ever had in their lives. Whatever else the war did, it lifted huge numbers of Americans out of poverty and hard times and gave them a better life than they had ever had.

No generation is greater than any other for the simple reason that there is no way to measure or define what they did in comparison with other generations. On what basis can you even compare one generation to another? What is being measured or evaluated, and how? If the criterion is accomplishment, then it is a false one because individuals and groups, not generations, get things done. Knowing the modern fetish for statistics and measurement, someone may well come along one day and claim, with elaborate charts and formulas, that 79.3 percent of the Greatest Generation made contributions compared to an average of only 52.7 percent in other generations. Don't believe a word (or figure) of it. While you ponder that absurdity, consider also the enormous difficulty involved in defining or measuring what constitutes a contribution or accomplishment.

The generation that fought World War II set prodigious new production records in both farm and factory. While this is an undeniable achievement, how can it be compared to the accomplishments of earlier generations that lacked the tools, techniques, organizations, technology, and resources present in 1940? How do we measure it against the achievements of the Civil War generation with its radically different context? It was, after all, the work of earlier generations that created the basis for the productivity of their successors. In this sense history is a process of accretion and accumulation in which succeeding generations build upon or undo the work of their predecessors. The old cliché of standing on the shoulders of giants applies in varying degrees to every generation and its legacy.

In every war, on every battlefield, there are heroes and cowards, stalwarts and shirkers, mainstays and misfits. The same holds just as true at home as at the front. Some people did their part, others did more than their share, and some did little if anything at all or tried to get what they could personally from the times. World War II differed from other wars in scale and scope but not in its diversity of human behavior and responses. History never repeats itself but historical patterns do, especially those centered in human behavior. In radically changing contexts across the centuries the same range of basic emotions and responses can be seen: love and hate, generosity and greed, sacrifice and selfishness, openness and bigotry, vision and small-mindedness, commitment and indifference, hope and fear, patriotism and profiteering.

Does "greatness" refer to what people had to endure or how they responded to the crises confronting them? If measured by what they had to endure, the term becomes meaningless. No generation gets to choose its fate; its members have no choice but to face whatever circumstances await them. If measured by performance, the record is far more complex and uneven than the Tom Brokaws of the world would have you believe. A better argument can be made that this generation had more to deal with than most others, although that too cannot be measured. But if this is indeed the case, then it would be far more accurate to describe them as the unluckiest generation.

The people of this unluckiest generation, if it is that, had to face first a broken economy that threatened the very essence of the American dream, and then a broken world that threatened to destroy individual freedom. That they survived both challenges is a tribute to the grit, hardiness, and persistence of the best of them. To them, separately and as individuals, belong our hymns of praise and thanks, not to an abstraction called a generation. This book tells the stories of some of them, as well as some of those who contributed little, and tries to show how they managed to get the job done. It is a tale that, with its frustrating yet fascinating mixture of the heroic, routine, and dishonorable, could not be more American or, for that matter, more human.

Maury Klein
Saunderstown, Rhode Island

PROLOGUE:
THE WORLD
UNRAVELING—AGAIN

*Some day the survivors of this generation will tell their grand-
children what it meant to live through a critical week in the
world's history. They will tell of the newspapers bought, edition
after edition, each with its record of new disasters. About the
perfect May weather . . . the shudder as an airplane passed overhead . . . About turning the radio knob for news, and instead
getting sales plugs and dance music—till a new voice broke in to
announce that Antwerp had fallen, or St. Quentin, so that the
war seemed to be fought in one's living room . . . About the sense
of absolute dehumanization rising from these stories of dive
bombers and tanks . . . What the radio suggests is a world of
machines for reducing human flesh to shreds and cinders . . .
But worst of all, they will say, was the feeling of helplessness.*
—FREDA KIRCHWEY, *NEW REPUBLIC*, MAY 27, 1940 [1]

A NICKEL RIDE ON THE SUBWAY OR a dime on the Long Island Railroad
brought one to the gates of the future, that place of promise so enticing to
depression-ravaged Americans in 1939. The future happened to be located in
Flushing Meadows, where, on April 30, President Franklin D. Roosevelt presided over the opening of the New York World's Fair with its theme, "Building the World of Tomorrow." After paying 75 cents admission, the visitor
stepped into a wonderland of exhibits dominated by examples of tomorrow's
technologies. The most imposing sight, the signature emblems of the fair,
loomed up like the discarded toys of some giant. The 610-foot-tall Trylon
connected to the 180-foot-wide Perisphere by a graceful bridge on which long
lines of people waited patiently for their turn inside the huge ball. [2]

Once past the entrance they stepped into one of two rings revolving in opposite directions. Beneath them lay Democracity, a huge diorama depicting 11,000 square miles of a future city and suburbs interwoven with stretches of parks and farmland, all tied together with expressways and parkways. After a six-minute show the audience left by descending the Helicline, a spiraling 950-foot ramp that took them back to ground level. Impressive as it was, Democracity was not even the largest diorama at the fair. That honor belonged to the City of Light, a scale replica of New York City's skyline that stretched a city block and stood three stories high. Shifting, brightly colored lights flashed the city through a twenty-four-hour cycle in twelve minutes with factories that hummed, subways and elevators that operated, and other machines powered by underground lines.

Another long line snaked along the General Motors building that housed the fair's most popular exhibit, Futurama. Visitors slipped into 552 tall, plush seats, each pair with its own speakers, that revolved around a 36,000-square-foot model of a highway system in 1960 featuring seven-lane expressways monitored by radio control towers that enabled speeds as high as 100 miles an hour. The highways were the arteries of a city delightfully free of pollution and congestion, brimming with parks and civic buildings, model homes, and farms through which traffic flowed unobtrusively. Next door the Ford building offered a half-mile spiral Road of Tomorrow and a stunning 100-foot turntable with eighty-seven animated groups depicting every step in the building of an automobile from extracting ore to the finished vehicle.

Machines, the servants of tomorrow's good life, dominated many of the exhibits. The General Electric building presented a kitchen with talking appliances; the Westinghouse building featured Elektro, a seven-foot robot, and his mechanical dog Sparko, as well as a duel between "Mrs. Drudge," who washed a stack of dishes by hand, and "Mrs. Modern," who did them in an electric dishwasher. The highlight of the RCA building was a fabulous new device called television, set in a handsome cabinet, its picture seen not directly but reflected off a mirror in the lid. A host of other corporations had their own wonders on display. At every turn could be found new marvels, machines that promised an easier, more gracious lifestyle if only one could afford them.

But today's and tomorrow's technology had another, much darker side that was about to be unleashed on an unsuspecting world. The first people to suffer its wrath were the Poles, one of the nations with an exhibit at the fair. Its staff would not return home at the season's end because their home no longer existed as such.

*   *   *

On September 1, while the fair was still in session, tomorrow's technology crashed down on Poland with sudden and swift brutality. Without warning German warplanes rained bombs on the town of Wielun, destroying most of it and killing more than a thousand civilians. German tanks and troops poured across the Polish border from the north, northwest, and south while more than 200 Stuka dive-bombers and other planes terrorized Polish cities, creating a panic among civilians and cutting communication lines. While the three German forces looked to converge on Warsaw and surround the valiant but fragmented Polish army, the Luftwaffe created mass confusion and destruction, driving inhabitants of attacked cities onto the roads, clogging defense efforts and escalating the sense of panic.[3]

Although the Poles fought stubbornly and managed small victories, they were no match for the Wehrmacht and its air cover. By September 7 lead elements of the German Tenth Army, led by the Fourth Panzer, approached Warsaw. Thousands of Polish soldiers and civilians died in the attacks; many more were executed by the advancing Germans, who had been told by Hitler to show no mercy. In Warsaw alone about 40,000 civilians died from air and artillery fire before the defenders surrendered on September 27. More than 10 percent of the city's buildings were completely destroyed and another 40 percent heavily damaged. Polish resistance collapsed quickly after the Soviet Union invaded the country from the east on September 17.

On September 3 Great Britain and France declared war on Germany in response to the invasion but could offer no significant military help. So rapidly had the Germans overrun Poland with their juggernaut of planes, tanks, and motorized troops that shocked observers were convinced a new style of warfare had emerged. A journalist called it "blitzkrieg," lightning war, but he was only half right. Only part of the attack managed to utilize the full impact of a mobile, disruptive mechanized force; much of the short campaign amounted to more conventional fighting. But Poland was an ominous harbinger of things to come, a new type of warfare that drew its inspiration and its strength from factories and scientific laboratories.

The bells that rang in the New Year on December 31, 1939, tolled a tune of celebration despite a week of cold, dreary weather across the nation. People eager to forget their cares jammed restaurants, theaters, and bars to welcome a year they hoped would be kinder to them than the departing one. Instead they would encounter what Donald Nelson, then a Sears, Roebuck executive in Chicago, called "one of the saddest, most confused, and perilous years in the annals of our nation."[4]

The country was closing out a decade of the longest and worst depression in its history. A sharp recession in 1938 had crushed hopes for recovery and delivered a devastating blow to Franklin D. Roosevelt's fading New Deal. Unemployment hovered around 17 percent with more than 9 million people seeking work, and nothing on the horizon promised any improvement. Roosevelt entered the eighth and presumed final year of his presidency as the lamest of lame ducks. The depression would not go away despite every effort to banish it, Congress had turned against him, and the once bright hopes of the administration for continued social and economic reform seemed all but extinguished. The New Deal was played out and under increasing attack from its many enemies, who hoped to roll back some of its main achievements.[5]

It was small consolation that the rest of the world was in even worse shape. In August Nazi Germany and Communist Russia, the most implacable of ideological enemies, had shocked everyone by signing a nonaggression treaty. Two months after Germany's revitalized armies rolled across the Polish border and conquered that hapless nation, Russia invaded Finland. On the other side of the globe Japan continued its undeclared but merciless invasion of China, having boasted on Christmas Day that it had killed more than 1.2 million Chinese troops with a loss of only 27,000 Japanese soldiers. More than half the world's people were at war with no end in sight.[6]

Amid this first truly global conflict the United States remained the only major power not fighting somewhere, and most Americans were determined to keep things that way. The sour outcome of the First World War had left them bitterly disillusioned and determined never to repeat the experience. Woodrow Wilson had led the nation into the European bloodbath as a "crusade for democracy" that promised to be the "war to end all wars." Instead it sowed the seeds for an even greater conflict that erupted only twenty-one years later. Congress tried to ensure that no future president could lead the United States on a similar fool's errand. Between 1935 and 1939 it passed a series of Neutrality Acts that throttled any effort to lend aid or comfort to foreign combatants. The idea was to keep American companies from selling munitions to nations at war, thereby squelching the profiteers that in the public's mind had drawn the country into the earlier war.

But the world had changed greatly since 1918. The war shattered four imperial regimes, leaving Europe in the throes of instability and revolution. In Russia the inept czarist government gave way to a Communist leadership bent on world revolution. The Ottoman Empire collapsed, leaving a troubled collection of new states struggling to define themselves. The disintegrated Austro-Hungarian Empire created a dangerous vacuum in central Europe as a number of new countries—the product of freshly drawn maps—fought to define their new identities. Then there was Germany, exhausted and starving from the war, crushed by the burden of the onerous Versailles Treaty that sought to keep it from ever posing a threat again but instead made it even more determined to do so.[7]

Germany had risen from the ashes of defeat and humiliation to become a relentlessly efficient war machine. Italy under its fascist regime had grown giddy with pretensions of power and glory. Over all of Europe loomed the huge, enigmatic shadow of the Soviet Union with its Communist ideology. In Asia Japan, the most westernized power, doggedly pursued its obsession for empire and expansion. The differences between these ambitious countries and the democracies of Europe, most notably England and France, bore little if any resemblance to the clashes leading up to World War I. A toxic element in the form of conflicting ideologies had come to infuse their thinking. While not new, never had it played so dominant and lethal a role in international relations.

Franklin Delano Roosevelt understood better than most the threat these beliefs posed. Eighty years earlier Abraham Lincoln had defined the American democratic republic as the last best hope of earth. The threat then had been internal, the splintering of the world's one shining example of self-rule. It was averted by what remains the bloodiest war in American history—made so by the fact that the casualties on both sides were Americans. In Roosevelt's time the danger had become external in the form of aggressive authoritarian governments driven not only by the ancient fuel of national or ethnic pride but also by the seductive dogmas of competing ideologies in the form of fascism, Nazism, and Communism. The age of imperial dynasties gave way to one of dictatorial and managerial dynasties.

The rise of these regimes met little resistance from the weary democracies. England and France, the supposed victors, emerged from World War I weakened, broke, and lacking the resources to support their enlarged responsibilities. One major ally, Russia, had grown hostile and isolated itself from the rest of Europe. Their key supporter, the United States, turned its back on the new order in Europe by refusing to join the League of Nations and pursuing its own brand of unilateralism. The new republics created by the war struggled to overcome ethnic, economic, and political tensions that undermined stability. In Germany the Kaiser had abdicated, but his military and administrative regime remained largely intact and influential. The new Weimar government had little chance of planting democracy in such hostile soil, especially after the ruinous inflation of 1922–23 and economic collapse of 1929–30.

Especially was it helpless against the Freikorps, the militant, right-wing veterans described by historian Michael Adams as "self-appointed violent defenders of German honor." Their goals were to subvert the Versailles Treaty, destroy Communism at home, and bring all German-speaking peoples back into the motherland. The latter included some provinces ceded to France, the

Polish corridor with its port of Danzig, which had been given to Poland, the Sudeten region made part of Czechoslovakia, and the Germans living in Austria. "People told us that the War was over," said one veteran. "That made us laugh. We ourselves are the War. Its flame burns strongly in us. It envelops our whole being and fascinates us with the urge to destroy."[8]

The rise to power of Adolf Hitler gave the Freikorps veterans the leader they craved: a strong man committed to their entire program and more. By 1939 Hitler had restored German pride through a hypnotic blend of rhetoric and pageantry coupled with sheer brutality, military strength, and the reacquisition of nearly all the coveted territories. Germany had again become the major power of Europe, partly by default but largely through its own demonic commitment to rearming and rebuilding its military. Thanks to its continued scientific and technological superiority, the new Third Reich enjoyed the finest and most advanced weaponry even though the country lacked thirty-three of thirty-five raw materials needed for industrial production.[9]

While Germany rebuilt its military at lightning speed, a similar pattern unfolded on the other side of the world. Since the late nineteenth century Japan had developed a Western-style business and industrial base handicapped by its lack of raw materials. It sought to overcome this shortcoming through creation of a new order in Asia dominated by a Japanese empire and by trade with the United States, which provided several key materials such as oil, gasoline, and scrap iron for making steel. Gradually, however, extreme elements of the Japanese military rose to power in the political system, especially after the onset of depression severely reduced the nation's exports and lowered its standard of living. A better solution, insisted the militarists, was to achieve self-sufficiency through expansion and conquest. Moderates who opposed this policy were silenced by intimidation or assassination.

Thus did the depression, striking different nations at different times, feed the rise of extremism in both Germany and Japan even as it weakened the democracies, which let their armed forces slide into obsolescence while they struggled to solve their economic woes. In 1931 Japan invaded Manchuria and converted it to a puppet state called Manchukuo. Three years later Benito Mussolini revived Italian fantasies of empire by invading Abyssinia (Ethiopia). Between 1936 and 1939 Germany and Italy helped right-wing forces led by Francisco Franco overthrow the Spanish republic in a bitter civil war that became a proving ground for newly developed weapons. In 1936, too, Hitler took his first major gamble by occupying and remilitarizing the Rhineland, the buffer zone between Germany and France. Already he had begun a campaign of intimidation to undermine the government of Austria; in 1938 German troops marched into that country.

The acquisition of Austria, with its resources and financial reserves, greatly strengthened Germany's position. That same year Hitler demanded the return of the Sudetenland, the mountainous northern portion of Czechoslovakia that, if lost, would leave the rest of the country unprotected. This demand led in the summer of 1938 to the infamous Munich Conference at which England and France yielded to Hitler's demand despite Czechoslovakia's pleas. The two nations believed themselves utterly unready to fight Hitler alone, and they knew the United States had no interest in providing military support. Only the Soviet Union offered to guarantee Czech borders, but neither England nor France trusted Joseph Stalin's intentions. Nor did Poland want Russian troops crossing its borders, lest they decide to remain in the country. Instead the Russians contented themselves with occupying the three small Baltic countries of Latvia, Lithuania, and Estonia.

Having gained the Sudetenland, Hitler promised yet again that it would be his last territorial demand in Europe. Six months later, in March 1939, German troops occupied the remainder of defenseless Czechoslovakia. A month later Mussolini invaded Albania. England and France responded by extending guarantees to Poland, vowing to declare war if Germany crossed its borders. Then, in August, came the stunning nonaggression treaty between Germany and the Soviet Union. With his eastern front secure for the time being, Hitler unleashed his troops on Poland. Once again Europe found itself engulfed in a war of the most desperate kind.

After the fall of Poland, however, autumn gave way to winter without any further overt moves by the Germans. Blitzkrieg turned into "sitzkrieg," what observers called the "phony war" even as they tried to fathom Hitler's intentions. Some hoped that his appetite for expansion had finally been satisfied; others viewed the pause as the lull before the storm.

AMERICAN OPINION REMAINED divided at every level from the president and his cabinet on down. "Our government has information . . . that Germany now has a total of eighty divisions on the Belgium and Holland frontier," noted Harold Ickes, the secretary of the interior, on January 27, 1940. "This is about sixty per cent of the total of Germany's troops. Just what this may mean, anyone may guess." Franklin Roosevelt did not like anything he was hearing, least of all the reports coming in from Poland. He told the cabinet that "probably nothing in all history exceeds the sadistic cruelty that Germany is responsible for in Poland . . . The Jews are receiving the worst treatment."[10]

Most Americans were not privy to these reports and cared little about what was happening in Europe. The long ordeal of the depression, coupled with disillusionment over the previous war, left most people far more concerned with events at home. The belief was widespread that the so-called merchants of death had dragged the country into the war. During the 1920s reports circulated that the war had created some 23,000 new millionaires who had grown rich by selling munitions to the belligerents and then to our own government. In their bitterness many people found a convenient scapegoat in the war industries and vowed never to repeat that mistake. The crash and depression had already thrown businessmen into disrepute; war profiteering added a glaze of shame and disgrace to their image.[11]

This determination to let Europe stew in its own malign juices fostered the revival of an old American attitude. Popularly known as isolationism, it was more accurately unilateralism. The object was not to sever contact with the rest of the globe, especially in matters of trade and commerce, but rather to ensure that only Americans decided what the nation would and would not do overseas. Opposition to the League of Nations arose from the fact that it might have the power to send American troops to fight abroad whether Americans liked it or not. No international body was going to dictate policy to the United States or decide the fate of its soldiers. On that basis the Senate rejected the League, and with it the opportunity for America to play a major role in the new organization.

During the 1920s nearly all Americans agreed that American soldiers should not be sent to fight another foreign war unless the nation was directly attacked. The growing threat of another European war during the 1930s only strengthened this attitude. As Hitler's mounting belligerence deepened tensions, most Americans made no secret of their sympathies for England and France but stopped short of favoring any form of aid that risked involving the nation in a war. The first three Neutrality Acts, 1935–37, tried to guarantee that there would be no repeat of the process that led the United States into World War I. The acts forbade the shipment of arms to warring nations, barred American ships from carrying war materials to belligerents, prohibited all loans to belligerents, and created a National Munitions Board to put the armament industry under federal control. Some isolationists even demanded a complete embargo on trade with warring nations but failed to get their way.[12]

According to the isolationist argument, nations went to war for territorial or economic gain or to defend their boundaries, trade, or principles. None of these reasons applied to America's position during the 1930s, so its proper course was to avoid getting entangled in foreign affairs and mind its own business. Others embraced what historian Charles A. Beard called the "devil theory of war," which held that the bankers and business interests had drawn the United States into the war through their manipulations. A special Senate committee chaired by Gerald P. Nye of North Dakota held nearly two years of hearings that condemned the role of munitions makers and bankers in pushing weak-willed politicians into going to war. Of this lengthy witch hunt

Senator Harry Truman later wrote, "The Nye Committee did more damage to the morale and welfare of this country than any other Committee that held Hearings in the Senate."[13]

Americans would not let go of the belief that bankers and munitions makers had dragged the nation into war. Between 1918 and April 1942 no less than 170 bills and resolutions to reduce or eliminate war production profits were introduced into Congress. To many people greed was simply one more dimension to the devil theory of war.[14]

Congress hoped the Neutrality Acts would cage the devil before he got loose to work his mischief. It also wanted to handcuff Franklin Roosevelt, who did not share this narrow view of America's role in the world. An obscure Indiana congressman named Louis Ludlow thrust himself into the limelight with an even more drastic proposal, sponsoring a constitutional amendment that would require a referendum of the American people before war could be declared. "It changes the Constitution," said Ludlow, "so that the trigger that starts the war machinery will be pulled, not by a little group subject to being cajoled and bullied by selfish special interests, but by all the people." Here was the devil theory writ large, but it failed despite the support of many prominent people and groups.[15]

Some Americans took the practical view that Hitler was going to win and that the United States, like it or not, had to learn to do business with him. Others marveled at the technological achievements of Hitler's Germany and thought his leadership represented the wave of the future. Their numbers included Charles A. Lindbergh, hero of the first transatlantic flight, who became the celebrity hero of the isolationist cause. Lindbergh had lived for several years in Europe and had seen firsthand the air forces of the warring powers. He was as impressed by the strength and efficiency of Germany's Luftwaffe as he was by the weakness of England and France. He concluded logically that the democracies were no match for the regimented power of Germany, and that the United States must avoid giving them any aid while strengthening its own military.[16]

The isolationists in Congress posed a special problem. They not only occupied a forum for influencing the public but could also block or delay the president's legislative efforts. Most believed that the United States should fight a war only if attacked, and that it should do so alone by avoiding any entangling alliances. Roosevelt thought it made much more sense to fight as far from home as possible and enlist as many allies as possible to help share the burden. But the isolationists could not shake free of their hangover from the legacy of World War I. Robert Bruce Lockhart, a witty Scot lecturing in the United States early in 1939, offered his impression of the average American's attitude toward the British:

We Americans went into the last war to save democracy. We pulled
you out of a hole and we received very grudging thanks. At Versailles
and after Versailles you trampled on democratic ideals. Now, largely
through your own fault, you are in trouble again and you want our
help. Well, we've learned our lesson.[17]

Against this tide of opposition Roosevelt made little headway. In October
1937 he had delivered what became known as the Quarantine Speech in which
he portrayed a growing "epidemic of world lawlessness" that would spread like
a contagious disease unless contained by the international community, including the United States. "The very foundations of civilization" were threatened, he warned, and the United States could not escape if the rest of the world
plunged into war. It was a trial balloon that went nowhere and drew heavy
criticism for its "war mongering" message. Most Americans rejected it as the
wrong medicine for the wrong problem. One resident of Albany, New York,
wrote the White House to voice his adamant refusal to go to war for "trade or
munitions makers or international bankers." Others declared that the nation
had more than enough problems at home without seeking them overseas.[18]

The heart of those problems remained the depression. The recession of
1938 cost Roosevelt dearly, not only in his hopes for recovery but also in the
off-year elections that fall. Republicans scooped up eighty-two seats in the
House, eight in the Senate, and a dozen governorships. Roosevelt's abortive
attempt to purge the worst southern conservatives had boomeranged and
earned him even greater opposition in the solidly Democratic South. Although Democrats still had a majority in Congress, Republicans joined with
conservative southerners to oppose Roosevelt, the New Deal, and any policy
that smacked of aid to England and France. The master politician seemed to
have lost his touch and to be destined for the political irrelevance accorded
lame duck presidents.

However, veteran politicians knew better than to underestimate Roosevelt. No other president since Andrew Jackson had aroused so broad a spectrum of primal emotions, from unrestrained love to seething, irrational
hatred. He saw the need not only to strengthen the nation's own military but
even more to help those opposing Hitler's aggressions. Most isolationists approved building up American defense but strongly objected to offering aid
abroad. After the Munich Conference events increasingly thrust foreign policy onto the political table despite all efforts by the isolationists to keep it at
bay. "The issue, now rapidly taking shape," observed Kiplinger's *Washington
Letter* on January 28, 1939, "is over whether we shall give active economic
support to the democracies in advance of any overt and demonstrable threat
to U.S. The President is definitely steering toward such a policy."[19]

A week later Kiplinger's added another twist to the debate. *"Now a new element appears—suspicion of President's motives,"* it reported. *". . .* Many members of Congress, in BOTH of the parties, suspect the President of *welcoming a war crisis for third-term reasons."* Would Roosevelt defy the time-honored, two-term tradition established by George Washington and run again? In mid-May Kiplinger's declared flatly that "the 'draft' Roosevelt movement is about to start . . . Politicians who know how to interpret the intentions behind actions have no doubt that *Roosevelt is a definite behind-the-scenes candidate."* The president remained silent about his intentions and said repeatedly that the country would remain aloof from any European war, but none of his detractors believed him. "The Executive branch . . . is putting up a front of intention-talk about staying out of the war," predicted Kiplinger's shortly after the Nazi invasion of Poland, "but is actually preparing to go into it."[20]

Intervention had little public support. A Roper poll in September 1939 showed that 30 percent of Americans wanted nothing at all to do with the warring nations. Another 37 percent were willing to sell arms to belligerents on a cash-and-carry basis but also wished to "take no sides and stay out of the war entirely." With two thirds of the people opposed to giving aid of any kind to the Allies, Roosevelt had no illusions about the uphill struggle facing him. "It's a terrible thing," he told Samuel Rosenman, one of his closest advisers, "to look over your shoulder when you are trying to lead—and find no one there." But lead he would because he believed the stakes were so high and the time short. Seven controversial years in office had done much to immunize him from the acrimony, insults, and slander heaped on him by those who feared and loathed him.[21]

However, an astute politician like Roosevelt also knew better than to get too far out in front. When war erupted in Europe, his public response was tame enough to satisfy even diehard isolationists. On September 8, 1939, after issuing a Proclamation of Limited Emergency, Roosevelt said during a press conference:

> There is no intention and no need of doing all those things that could be done . . . There is no thought in any shape, manner or form, of putting the Nation, either in its defenses or in its internal economy, on a war basis. That is one thing we want to avoid. We are going to keep the Nation on a peace basis, in accordance with peacetime authorizations.[22]

Robert Sherwood called these "probably the weakest words that Roosevelt ever uttered." They outraged his supporters, and his enemies doubted that he meant them. But Roosevelt had a limited palette of choices. "I am almost literally walking on eggs," he admitted. To get anything done he needed support in Congress, which had so far given him precious little. On September 21, three weeks after the war began, he called for a repeal of the arms embargo and a return to traditional American neutrality. Congress obliged by replacing the embargo with a cash-and-carry provision that allowed belligerents to buy war goods in the United States if they paid cash and hauled them away in their own ships. This was something, at least; the British and French lost no time placing orders and coordinating their purchases.[23]

To gain even this concession, however, required every ounce of his political clout. He had practically begged Congress to go this modest step while calling in chits from friendly congressmen, governors, mayors, businessmen, and even sympathetic Republicans to get them to exert their influence. The debate occupied six weeks, during which the isolationists unleashed their battalions of familiar rhetoric. Old Senator William E. Borah, who had coined the phrase "phony war," warned yet again in a failing voice that if the repeal passed, "You will send munitions without pay, and you will send your boys back to the slaughter pens of Europe."[24]

One modest step at a time was all the president felt he could manage. On January 12, 1939, he requested $525 million as a "minimum program for the necessities of defense," which Congress granted grudgingly. In May Secretary of State Cordell Hull asked Congress to repeal the arms embargo; a bill was put forth but defeated 214–173 amid charges that munitions makers would "look forward to again reaping unrestricted profits" while American mothers might "well shudder at the likely prospect of again sending their sons across the sea to die in the attempt to collect the debts owed these warlords." In July Roosevelt again urged Congress to act, but the Senate ignored his request.[25]

However, in April 1939 the president did get something he wanted very badly. After a two-year struggle Congress finally passed the Administrative Reorganization Act, thanks in large part to the guiding hand of Roosevelt's close friend and ally Senator James F. Byrnes of South Carolina. The innocuous title of this act masked its potential for revolutionizing the executive wing of the government; some later scholars called it the beginning of the modern presidency. Under its authority dozens of agencies and bureaus, including the Bureau of the Budget, the National Resources Planning Board, the Office of Government Reports, the Army-Navy Munitions Board, the Joint Economy Board, the Joint Chiefs, and the White House Office, moved from congressional oversight or semiautonomy to a newly created Executive Office of the President. The arrangement gave the president adequate machinery to administer the government. It also enlarged the Budget Bureau's activities to include research in developing "improved plans of administrative management."[26]

Prior to the act the president had no actual executive organization. White House aides were considered part of the presidential household and not part of any administrative command. All the lines of authority that converged on the White House—cabinet members, agency heads, mission heads, and others—flowed directly to the president, and conflicts between them had to be resolved by him personally. As Robert Sherwood observed, "It was a system which could not have existed in any well-ordered big business organization."[27]

The executive order creating the internal divisions of the Executive Office also contained a provision for establishing an Office of Emergency Management (OEM), which created a legal basis for setting up any special agency the president deemed necessary for defense, war, or any other emergency. It was a logical inclusion and, as events revealed, a crucial one that Roosevelt intended to exploit to the fullest. If there was one thing the future promised, it was more emergencies.[28]

THE LONGER THE phony war dragged on, the bolder and more shrill grew the isolationists, who insisted that the European war was of no concern to Americans. Their opponents, the so-called interventionists, insisted that a British victory over the Nazis was crucial to American security. Both camps included in their ranks improbable mixes of strange bedfellows that ignored conventional divisions such as liberal-conservative, Democrat-Republican, Catholic-Protestant, and management-labor. Isolationism drew together fascists, Communists, pacifists, anti-Semites, racists, some Italian Americans, Irish Americans, Anglophobes, and a host of others who sincerely believed America should pursue its own destiny free of European influence. The interventionist camp was equally mixed, which meant that both sides disagreed among themselves on any specific issue almost as much as they did with their adversaries.[29]

Many people in both camps agreed on one issue, albeit for different reasons: that the United States should move quickly to strengthen its own defenses. Interventionists pointed out that the contracts for armaments signed by the British and French led to the construction of new factories, which would strengthen American production. The diehards in Congress, however, remained unconvinced. On January 3, 1940, Roosevelt declared in his annual message, "I am asking the Congress for Army and Navy increases which are based not on panic but on common sense. They are not as great as enthusiastic alarmists seek. They are not as small as unrealistic persons claiming superior private information would demand." The House Appropriations Committee dawdled over the request until April and imposed cuts totaling

10 percent. Where the president asked for 496 new airplanes, the committee approved only 57. By the time the Senate applied its wisdom to the measure, the phony war had ended.[30]

When Americans awoke on the morning of April 9, Appomattox Day, they learned that Hitler's troops had seized control of Denmark and Norway. With the conquest of Denmark came a claim to Greenland, the exercise of which would put Hitler within dangerous reach of North America. For the next month the United States and the rest of the world watched and waited for the next blow. It came on May 10 when Hitler's legions stormed across the borders into Belgium, the Netherlands, France, and Luxembourg. On that same day Prime Minister Neville Chamberlain resigned and was replaced by Winston Churchill, who could hardly have inherited a worse situation. During the phony war Churchill said pointedly of Europe's neutral nations that tried to avoid invasion by appeasing Hitler, "Each one hopes that if he feeds the crocodile enough, the crocodile will eat him last."[31]

Now the crocodile was loose and voracious of appetite. Where Poland had been the dress rehearsal, the real blitzkrieg arrived, and it aimed for quick, devastating victories. A date would be set for launching the attack, and the target country hit with overwhelming force at a speed never before thought possible. No quarter would be given or concern shown for collateral damage to civilians. Indeed, the blitzkrieg targeted them as part of the plan to demoralize and confuse the enemy. There would be no repeat of the endless trench warfare that had turned World War I into a slaughterhouse. This would be butchery of a much different kind, featuring new, greatly improved weapons and a mobility never before seen in warfare. "The Germans under Hitler," observed Robert Sherwood, "had accomplished in eleven days what they had failed to do in the four years of bitter fighting in the First World War."[32]

The Dutch lasted only five days before surrendering; King Leopold of Belgium managed to hold out until May 28. The German juggernaut rolled through the Belgian Ardennes, crushed the befuddled French Ninth Army at Sedan, and by May 21 had the Allied armies in full retreat across Flanders. The shattered British Expeditionary Force, having lost more than 60,000 men, piled up in a chaotic heap at Dunkirk on the coast, where more than 300,000 Allied troops awaited their doom from the onrushing Germans. Then, on May 24, for reasons never fully explained, Hitler ordered the Wehrmacht's panzers to halt their advance for three days. During that respite the English threw together an improbable armada of every type of ship that could float, crossed the strait to Dunkirk, and for nine days heroically carried troops back to England amid air attacks, fire, and high seas. Nearly 340,000 troops escaped in a rescue that became the stuff of legend.[33]

The audacity of the rescue could not conceal the harsh fact that, as Churchill admitted, "what has happened in France and Belgium is a colossal military disaster." In its desperate retreat the BEF had been forced to abandon virtually all its equipment, including 680 of 700 tanks, 82,000 scout cars and motorcycles, 90,000 rifles and even more machine guns, and 8,000 field telephones. During the evacuation 10 of England's 74 destroyers had been sunk and 177 Royal Air Force planes lost, leaving it with only 283 aircraft and 362 pilots in the entire country. The scene at Dunkirk itself defied imagination. The ruined town was littered with corpses of soldiers and civilians, and clogged beyond belief with wrecked vehicles of all kinds. "Over a distance of several miles," observed a reporter on the scene, "the highway was lined with thousands of Allied trucks and other motorized vehicles. Immense numbers of these had been driven into ditches to prevent their use by the enemy." The docks were so jammed with trucks and other vehicles that the "final jam was completely impossible to disentangle."[34]

Nor was the nightmare over. On June 5 the German divisions turned their full fury against France. In one of the great follies of modern warfare, the French had placed their faith for defending themselves from Germany in the gigantic series of fortifications known as the Maginot Line. Evidently no French leader gave enough thought to two basic facts: German planes could simply fly over the Maginot Line, and the Wehrmacht could repeat—this time successfully—the strategy used in World War I of sweeping through the Lowland countries and attacking France from the north. As one reporter noted, the Germans were "following their 1914 route but on a triple-quick timetable." Having already subdued the Lowland countries, the Wehrmacht pushed relentlessly through France as the latter's armies crumbled in the wake of combined air and ground attacks. By June 10 the Germans were within thirty-five miles of Paris; four days later they reached the city, which was deliberately left undefended to avoid its destruction. That same day Italy declared war on France and attacked it from the south.[35]

With its once proud and vastly overrated army shattered and demoralized, the French surrendered on June 22. "A sense of terror swept through the civilized world as a result of these incredible achievements of mechanical barbarism," noted Sherwood. ". . . It was the supreme triumph of what Edmond Taylor has correctly called the 'Strategy of Terror.'" Hitler now stood astride most of western Europe, greatly increasing the resources at his disposal and giving him air bases near enough to England for sustained attacks by the Luftwaffe. England lacked almost every weapon in quantity, especially aircraft, to mount an effective defense. It was too late to save France; the question was whether England could hold out. "Never," admitted Churchill, "has a nation been so naked before her foes."[36]

"Even the Nazis did not know how little Britain had left," recalled Donald

Nelson. "There were hardly enough tanks to fight a regiment of well armed Boy Scouts. There were few small arms, and almost no ammunition. Practically the entire arsenal of the nation had been lost in the valiant effort to save France."[37]

Nor was the crisis limited to Europe. The fall of France and the Lowland countries left their overseas colonies in a perilous state. From the Dutch West Indies the Germans could threaten the Gulf Coast of the United States and the Panama Canal. Japan might well be emboldened to seize the Dutch East Indies and British colonies in Asia, giving it huge amounts of oil, rubber, tin, and other resources while cutting off the United States from its supply of rubber and other minerals. The new state of Europe threatened trouble for the United States not only there but on the other side of the globe as well. And who knew what other ambitions Hitler held? Surely he would attack England, and possibly the remaining small nations of Europe as well.

The threat was real. Since the 1920s the Germans had worked slavishly to invent what one military critic called "timetable" war. It was the closest thing to total war yet seen. Donald Nelson described it this way:

> It was mapped out in complete, scientific detail . . . The fundamental requirements were the drilling of a mass army and the militarizing of the entire economy, determining the synthesis of weapons which could be most effectively used to smash the powers backward in military affairs, and accumulating an armament beyond anything ever before imagined, besides organizing raw materials, manpower, food production—in fact, every item on the national balance sheet— for the sole purpose of making war. This was probably the first completely and coldly scientific conception of totalitarian war . . . It was utterly ruthless and pragmatic, as devoid of ethics and humanitarian principle as an exercise in higher mathematics.[38]

In less than six weeks the world as it was passed into oblivion, replaced by a new order that, its creator boasted, would last a thousand years. Suddenly, improbably, Americans found themselves in a position where distance and two oceans no longer offered the same protection and security they once did. They had assumed that the war would at least be a long one regardless of who won; instead Germany had marched to victory in breathtaking fashion. New and unpleasant questions arose. What effect would a Hitler-controlled Europe have on American business, trade, commerce, travel, and foreign policy? How grave a threat did he pose to America's own security? How prepared was the nation to meet that threat?

Changes were coming, big changes that could no longer be avoided. "The great argument of the last nine months—Isolation vs. Intervention—fell suddenly to unimportance," observed *Life* magazine even before the fall of France. ". . . Left behind was a decade of economic experimentation, for armament on this new scale means active business and wide employment. Left behind was the coddling of labor, for the U.S. cannot afford to repeat the mistake of France in allowing its plane-building program to bog down in labor disputes. Left behind was the bitter antagonism of Business and Government, for both are now united with the same objective. Ahead lay years of gigantic effort, of heavy taxes, perhaps of a lower standard of living."[39]

1940: The Year of Denial

CHAPTER 1

THE MAN AND THE HOUR

Many French soldiers are reported to have fought through the epic battle of France in the late spring of 1940 without seeing a German. All they saw were airplanes, tanks, and guns. The human enemy seemingly was absent ... Many observers testify that the individual French soldier ... was just as courageous as the German soldier, but he couldn't fight mechanized juggernauts with his bare hands or with obsolete and inferior equipment.

—BURNHAM FINNEY [1]

The United States was probably in the most precarious position in its history. Yet to many of us the peril seemed remote ... We continued with unabated zest our political feuds even though these internal cleavages affected our ability to react quickly to changes in the international environment.

—BUREAU OF THE BUDGET [2]

The President never "thinks"! He decides.

—ELEANOR ROOSEVELT [3]

AT 11:00 P.M. ON THE NIGHT OF May 9, 1940, the phone call that Franklin Roosevelt most dreaded came to him. John Cudahy, the ambassador to Belgium, told the president that Hitler's armies were pouring into Holland, Belgium, France, and Luxembourg. Bombs were falling on Brussels, Amsterdam, Rotterdam, Dunkirk, Calais, and Metz, killing hundreds of civilians, clogging the roads with others fleeing in terror, and creating exactly the kind of panic and confusion the Nazis wanted. The phony war was over, and with it the hope that it might buy the United States time to prepare for whatever was to come. For Roosevelt it meant, among other things, that decisions he had hoped to defer could no longer be delayed. So much had to be done, and no one knew how much time there would be to do it all.[4]

He sat in the presidential study on the second floor of the White House, leaning against the high back of his favorite red leather chair, modeled after one designed by Thomas Jefferson. General Edwin "Pa" Watson, his appointments secretary, responded to his call, and shortly after midnight Stephen Early, the press secretary, joined them to monitor the swelling tide of incoming messages. After another short talk with Cudahy, Roosevelt made his first decision: He called Secretary of the Treasury Henry Morgenthau Jr. and ordered him to freeze all Belgian, Dutch, and Luxembourg assets before the market opened to keep them out of German hands. Not until 2:40 A.M. did Roosevelt go to bed. He shifted heavily to an armless and backless wheelchair that, according to one reporter, looked like a typewriter table and rolled himself into his bedroom adjoining the study.[5]

Going to bed was itself a ritual for Roosevelt. Unable to use his legs since a devastating attack of polio in 1921, he relied on his valet, a black man named Irvin McDuffie, to lift him from the wheelchair into his narrow bed, straighten out his withered legs, and help him undress and get into pajamas. Once settled into bed, Roosevelt usually slept soundly regardless of how much tension and turmoil the day had inflicted on him. This night was no exception. He awoke refreshed at his usual hour of 8:00 A.M. and pressed the button for McDuffie to come help him to the bathroom, after which he did what he had done virtually every morning since entering the White House in 1933. Throwing his worn blue cape over his pajamas, he had his usual breakfast in bed of orange juice, eggs, toast, and coffee while scanning the morning papers from Washington, New York, Philadelphia, and Baltimore. Afterward he reviewed his day's schedule with Early and Watson, making whatever adjustments were needed.[6]

He was by far the most familiar face and voice in the nation, the best-known and yet most unknowable figure in American life—an attribute he shared with Abraham Lincoln. Physically the two men could not have been more different. Lincoln was tall, thin, and gangly, with ugly, oversized features that often wore a melancholy air. Roosevelt had in effect two bodies thanks to his affliction—a powerful upper torso with long arms set on undersized legs shrunken by years of paralysis. Both men had large heads. Roosevelt's features were more regular and pleasing, though at fifty-eight brown shadows lay beneath his deep, narrow-set blue eyes, and two creases framed his mouth.

Both men liked to laugh and tell stories; humor was for them catharsis and a tool for deflecting or evading. Although Lincoln was even better than Roosevelt at reading other men (but not women), both excelled at concealing their innermost selves. Lincoln managed this by wearing an impenetrable air of mystery, Roosevelt by displaying so many contradictory elements in his nature that no one could add them up satisfactorily. They shared a genius for politics and may well have been the two greatest politicians in presidential history. Lincoln came from humble origins and pulled himself up by his own bootstraps; Roosevelt was the product of old-line American aristocracy that carried very different burdens. Lincoln spoke with the twang of the West, Roosevelt with the cultured accent of an upstate New York aristocrat. Yet both men possessed an uncanny ability to connect with that most familiar yet elusive American, the common man.

"Although," observed *Time*, "his every facial grimace, the tone of his voice, each mannerism, the dark mole over his left eyebrow, the mole on his right cheek—although all these were public property, intimate to every U.S. citizen, still there was no man in the U.S. who could answer the question: Who is Franklin Roosevelt?" Even those closest to him despaired of penetrating what Robert Sherwood called his "heavily forested interior." One theory portrayed him as "the Great Improviser, impetuously patching up the irremediable, a dextrous three-shell manipulator." Another theory, advanced by newspaperman Marquis W. Childs, viewed Roosevelt as "a sad man, having seen through the illusions and futilities of his time. Nevertheless, he has the courage to be cheerful and to do good in the sight of God." This version made Roosevelt "a sitting Lincoln, streamlined for 1940, wearing a club tie instead of a shawl."[7]

Conservative by nature, the two presidents relished the wisdom of eternal verities. They rarely attended church but often invoked the Almighty in their speeches and writings. One had to overcome a physical handicap, the other the more subtle but no less real disadvantage of being a nobody with no formal education. Where Roosevelt was a Harvard man who had held a variety of offices at the state and national levels, Lincoln came to the presidency with an absurdly thin résumé that included only a lone term in the House of Representatives and time in the Illinois state legislature. Both men aroused deep emotions in others ranging from undying devotion to blind hatred. They shared a gift for language and metaphor as a way to get their message understood.

Most pertinent of all, both men had come to office at a moment of crisis. Lincoln had triumphed over his crisis, the gravest in American history, but not survived it. Roosevelt had failed to triumph over the Great Depression and had now to face yet another, potentially greater threat. Both men had hoped fervently to keep the nation out of war. Lincoln had failed in this task for reasons that went beyond his ability to control. The great question confronting Roosevelt was whether or not he could keep the United States out of the war that had already begun to devour Europe.

THE WORSENING WORLD crisis posed an intolerable dilemma for Roosevelt. As he followed its deterioration, the conviction grew ever stronger that the nation's own security required giving whatever support was needed to the Western democracies. Congress had shown a contrary opinion with the Neutrality Acts, and the response to his Quarantine Speech demonstrated how uphill the struggle to convince the American people of his views would be. It would have to be done step by painful, often halting step. An obvious first step would be to fortify the country's own defenses by strengthening its military, but even that goal faced strong opposition. The legacy of World War I hung like an albatross over the nation and would not budge from its memory.

The heart of that legacy lay in the War Industries Board (WIB), a body created to organize and direct the American wartime economy. Created in July 1917, it limped along with inadequate authority and direction until it was reorganized in March 1918 under the chairmanship of financier Bernard M. Baruch. Given full authority, Baruch transformed a stumbling, chaotic effort into an efficient war machine with shrewd, effective leadership. The key to his success, Baruch concluded, lay in the centralization of authority. "The great principle followed throughout the Board's dealings with industry," declared one appraisal of the WIB, "was that of voluntary co-operation with the big stick in the closet. The biggest problem was to increase production so as to raise the output of industry up somewhere nearer the tremendous demands of the government."[8]

When the war ended in November 1918, however, the WIB was dismantled along with virtually the entire American war apparatus. In 1920 Congress did pass the National Defense Act, which emphasized the importance of peacetime planning for mobilizing industry in wartime. From it flowed a series of studies and reports culminating in the Industrial Mobilization Plan (IMP), later known popularly as the M-day Plan. First published in 1931, it was revised in 1933, 1936, and 1939. Although Roosevelt gave it lip service, he found it too full of defects to take seriously and largely ignored it. Among other shortcomings, it showed little grasp of the sensitive relationship between society and the military in a major war. There also existed authority from wartime statutes for a Council of National Defense composed of six cabinet secretaries, for which the president could appoint an advisory council.[9]

The challenge facing Roosevelt transcended all these earlier efforts. It was as much political as organizational. He was trying to alert the American people to a danger most of them did not believe existed. If war broke out in Europe, he wanted both to strengthen American armaments and lend aid to those opposing Hitler. But how to do this in the face of a hostile Congress, an indifferent and fearful public, and disarray within his own administration? He was notorious for being an erratic administrator who liked to keep the reins in his own hands. He was familiar with the WIB from his service as assistant secretary of the navy during the World War, and he had known Baruch for a long time. Here was an ego and an ambition not far from his own, one who basked in his reputation as the hero of American mobilization in the World War.

Like Roosevelt, Baruch had long believed that America must arm itself and lend support to England and France against the aggressions of Hitler. "In the modern world," he later wrote, "neutrality is a delusion. Carried to its ultimate end of refusing commercial intercourse with belligerents, it can amount to economic sanctions—which are, in effect, acts of war." In 1937 he returned from a trip abroad and told reporters that he thought Europe was a tinderbox. The following summer, while Hitler seized Austria and demanded the Sudetenland, he went to Europe again to gather information on French, German, and English armaments. The Nazi war machine he saw as sleek and powerful; by contrast English defenses were sketchy at best, the French army and especially its air force a joke. Alarmed, Baruch called Roosevelt from Scotland on August 19 and said emphatically that the democracies were in no shape to stop Hitler.[10]

Roosevelt was noncommittal on the phone but invited Baruch to a private dinner at the White House shortly after his return. Time was running out, Baruch warned the president. It was necessary to expand the military, modernize and mechanize it, create a two-ocean navy, build airplanes—lots of airplanes—and pay for it all with increased taxes. Roosevelt agreed but thought the public wasn't ready, that it needed educating. Although politics still stayed his hand, he did pull off one major surprise earlier in August 1939 by appointing a War Resources Board (WRB). It marked the beginning of a new alphabet soup fully equal to the outpouring of New Deal agencies and legislation. Journalist Eliot Janeway called it "an essay in manipulation." Most other people called it a mistake.[11]

The purpose of the new board was to help the assistant secretary of war deal with mobilization issues and in particular undertake another revision of IMP, the third version of which had gone public that summer. Roosevelt appointed as chairman Edward R. Stettinius Jr., the son of a Morgan partner and chairman of United States Steel, who had earned a reputation as a progressive businessman by admitting a labor union into his plants. Stettinius in turn named three other well-known corporate figures to the board as well as the presidents of MIT and the Brookings Institution. Conspicuously absent were any representatives of two major pressure groups in American politics, labor and agriculture. Technically the new board advised the Army-Navy Munitions Board (ANMB), which was about to move under the control of the executive branch.[12]

The new board had a short, unhappy life of only six weeks. New Dealers and labor complained about its being dominated by Wall Street, isolationists howled about warmongering, and Roosevelt himself disliked both IMP and the changes suggested by the WRB. The president stunned everyone by announcing at a press conference that the WRB would file its report and then disband—but the report would not be published. It was, he explained, a war plan; since the country was not going to war, the public would have no interest in it. The timing of this fiasco could not have been worse. Between the creation and disbanding of the board, Hitler had invaded and conquered Poland, plunging Europe into war. The situation had changed.[13]

But there was more to the story. Baruch had authored the original IMP, which among other things called for a single administrator to oversee government policy and organization on the model of the WIB. Although he indicated otherwise, Baruch had himself in mind for the position. The plan also presumed an immediate transition from peace to war and made no provision for the situation in which the United States found itself—a sort of limbo in which the country might or might not be drawn into the war. Roosevelt persuaded Baruch to revise the original plan, incorporating some of the president's suggestions. This improved version became the report of the WRB, much of it done by Baruch's longtime associate John Hancock.[14]

Baruch and Hancock did their work well, correcting flaws in the earlier version and accommodating most of Roosevelt's suggestions. They supplied what Eliot Janeway called "a really workable blueprint of mobilization" that "might have been written by Roosevelt himself." However, the president was not yet ready to push hard for mobilization. He did not merely ignore the report and its recommendations; he ordered it suppressed and locked away. At one point he explained that the earlier plan's call for a single administrator impinged on his own authority, and that he "would simply be abdicating the presidency to some other person." Roosevelt had no intention of abdicating power to anyone, and he neglected to add that the revised version had retracted this recommendation. "Because the President had decided to do nothing," concluded Janeway, "a year was to be lost."[15]

The whole affair underscored a basic quandary underlying mobilization: how to organize the economy while still preserving the essential machinery of democratic government. Nazi Germany had created its military machine through brute force and harsh restrictions on its people. Roosevelt wanted none of that for Americans, but some degree of central authority was needed to get the job done. To his mind the process posed two distinct threats: militarism and domination by big business. Experience had led Roosevelt to distrust both of them for different reasons. Someone had to maintain a balance by operating at a level above them, and he determined to be that someone. This was a responsibility he could not delegate; the problem was finding a suitable mechanism or organization to get it done. Roosevelt had to figure out not only what to do but how best to do it within the constraints in which he operated.[16]

Those constraints included the iron maiden of politics. Here too part of Roosevelt's task was maintaining some sort of delicate balance among the conflicting interest groups, but this was becoming increasingly difficult. He had erred in allowing Stettinius to fill the WRB with representatives of big business while ignoring labor and agriculture. New Dealers in the administration protested the WRB and its desire to replicate the centralized WIB model of World War I but offered only vague and unrealistic alternatives to it. Roosevelt added fuel to the controversy with his September executive order creating the OEM. The result was a running battle within the administration over how to mobilize the economy for defense or war that continued well into 1940.[17]

Distrust clouded every move by any group. New Dealers viewed any action by big businessmen as an effort to roll back the social and economic reforms of the past eight years. Business interests suspected any move by Roosevelt or New Dealers of trying to extend what they deemed a social revolution. Organized labor was determined to preserve its gains of recent years; unions had finally won legal status only four years earlier, in 1935. Agricultural interests were concerned only about the effect of a given issue on them. The military, having languished in postwar limbo since 1918, sensed new opportunities in the growing crisis and calls for rearmament. Then there were the government bureaucrats, many of whom had been pushing paper since the administration of William McKinley and regarded their place as a sinecure until death or retirement did them part. They were hardly the stuff of bold new actions and programs.

Problems within his official family also constrained Roosevelt. Cordell Hull, the courtly but rigid secretary of state, could not abide his talented and energetic undersecretary, Sumner Welles, and their frosty relationship cast a chill over activities there. Secretary of War Harry Woodring was utterly incompetent and an isolationist to boot; his bumbling infuriated the capable assistant secretary, Louis Johnson, a strong interventionist who openly coveted the top job. Navy Secretary Claude A. Swanson died in July 1939 and was not replaced by his assistant secretary, Charles Edison, son of the inventor, until January 2, 1940. Edison showed more interest in running for governor of New Jersey than in the navy. Interior Secretary Harold Ickes was able but overbearing, with strong views that he did not hesitate to advance. He had long disliked Henry Wallace, the secretary of agriculture, even though Wallace was an unabashed New Dealer and an original thinker.[18]

Treasury Secretary Henry Morgenthau was close to the president, a strong interventionist, energetic, and a good administrator as well as a neighbor of the Roosevelts in Hyde Park. Attorney General Robert H. Jackson was thoughtful and a loyal New Dealer, as was Labor Secretary Frances Perkins, the first woman to hold a cabinet post. She had been with Roosevelt since his days as governor of New York. Postmaster General James A. Farley was a longtime New Deal and Roosevelt supporter who handled patronage for the Democratic Party with a masterful hand. As 1940 neared, however, Farley developed a strong case of presidential fever on the assumption that Roosevelt would not seek a third term. The newest member of the cabinet, Secretary of Commerce Harry Hopkins, was also the man closest to Roosevelt and therefore viewed with suspicion by many of his colleagues.[19]

No one outside his family rivaled Hopkins in Roosevelt's affections. He was not only the president's closest personal and political friend but his alter ego as well. In 1938 columnist Raymond Clapper wrote this astute description of their relationship:

> Many New Dealers have bored Roosevelt with their solemn earnestness. Hopkins never does. He knows instinctively when to ask, when to keep still, when to press, when to hold back; when to approach Roosevelt direct, when to go at him roundabout . . . Quick, alert, shrewd, bold, and carrying it off with a bright Hell's bells air, Hopkins is in all respects the inevitable Roosevelt favorite.

Another observer thought Hopkins had "an almost 'feminine' sensitivity to Roosevelt's moods. He seems to know precisely when Roosevelt wants to consider affairs of State and when he wants to escape from the awful consciousness of the Presidency."[20]

But Hopkins was also a very sick man. In 1937, the same year his wife died of cancer, he had undergone a secret operation for the same disease. The cancer did not return, but the surgery left his body unable to process proteins and fats properly. For the rest of his life Hopkins endured constant bouts of sickness that sometimes kept him abed for months. In July 1939 he had to quit work entirely and return to the Mayo Clinic for another round of treatment. "The doctors have given Harry up for dead," Roosevelt told friends that fall, but the president did not. He had Hopkins brought back to Washington and placed under the care of the navy's surgeon general, a specialist in tropical diseases. Hopkins survived but remained too weak to work for months.[21]

For the cabinet as well as the president, the great unanswered question was whether Roosevelt would dare violate the venerated tradition set by George Washington of no more than two terms in office. Eleanor's uncle Teddy Roosevelt had, to his lasting regret, gone to great lengths to honor it. If Franklin did likewise, the Democratic nomination in 1940 would be as wide open as that of the Republican Party, and more than one cabinet member had his eye on that prize. Roosevelt himself revealed nothing on the subject. Eight years in office had worn him down; both his health and his finances needed repairing. But the outbreak of war in Europe posed major problems for the nation that required strong leadership, and who else but Roosevelt had the stature and experience to provide it?

"His outstanding characteristic," observed the shrewd journalist W. M. Kiplinger, "is an air of supreme self-confidence. He always gives the impression that to him nothing is impossible, that everything will turn out all right . . . He is always 'the boss.' Without saying it, he imparts the impression that he knows he has had broader experience in public office, borne heavier burdens, and made graver decisions than any other living American citizen." Which he had. Also left unsaid was another crucial intangible: Roosevelt loved being president, loved the challenges it posed, and had mastered the art not only of surviving but thriving under its pressures. However much he might long for rest and leisure, no one knew how well he would do without the huge responsibilities he had borne for so long.[22]

As the election year of 1940 opened, Harold Ickes observed that "all of us are more or less convinced now that the President will not run this year if the European war has come to an end and there are only domestic questions with which to grapple." Sam Rosenman agreed. "I was absolutely convinced," he admitted, "during the spring months of 1940 that the President—at least up to April 9, the day that Norway was invaded—was absolutely determined not to seek a third term." As late as June Rexford Tugwell, an ardent New Dealer, predicted flatly that the president would not be a candidate. Missy LeHand, Roosevelt's secretary, who had devoted nearly twenty years of her life to serving him, admitted he was very tired and looking forward to retirement even though she wanted him to run again. Grace Tully, his other utterly devoted secretary, sent Roosevelt a pointed little poem about who would be her boss next year.[23]

By mid-February, however, Ickes sensed that "the movement to renominate the President is growing stronger and deeper." Roosevelt himself remained silent on the issue, but he took care to examine the third-term question carefully, Robert Sherwood thought, "and most of all in relation to his own position in history, a subject of supreme importance to him and one of which he was rarely forgetful." He realized that victory would by no means be certain if domestic issues dominated the campaign, but events since the Munich Conference had caused a seismic shift in American politics.[24]

Ickes had foreseen this possibility that same summer of 1938. While in Europe enjoying a honeymoon with his young second wife, he talked to the leaders of England and France and found that they all thought war was inevitable. On the voyage home Ickes surveyed the list of potential candidates for 1940 and concluded that Roosevelt alone had the ability to manage the looming crisis. "When I got home, I came out for a third term," he told Sherwood, "and I went right on urging it at every opportunity. The President did not give me one word of encouragement on this. But he also did not tell me to stop. I was then the only one in the Cabinet for Roosevelt." Hopkins publicly urged a third term in June 1939 despite strong opposition from Eleanor Roosevelt, who wanted the president to retire. In January 1940 Hopkins said he was nearly certain that the president would decide to run.[25]

Hopkins once had strong hopes of his own to succeed Roosevelt, but his illness and near-death experience cured him of that ambition. The cabinet member most eager to get the nomination was Jim Farley, who also had the largest network of political connections as well as the support of the vice president, John Nance Garner. The crusty Texan, notorious for his remark that the vice presidency wasn't worth a bucket of spit, had his own aspirations for the office and was willing to help Farley in any move to keep the nomination from Roosevelt. What neither of them could have foreseen was the sudden and shocking outcome of the phony war.

On March 13 Finland came reluctantly to terms with Russia. Less than a month later, Germany occupied Denmark and Norway, and on May 10 her troops unleashed the blitzkrieg against the Lowland countries. Although Roosevelt never admitted as much, the events following May 10 did more to convince him to run than any other factor. At the cabinet meeting the next day he said that he expected Italy to come into the war on Germany's side whenever the timing seemed right. No one was impressed with Italy's military prowess. At dinner that night Ickes said scornfully, "To the victor belongs Mussolini."[26]

Throughout the nation the news had a galvanizing effect. "To many a U.S. citizen," reported *Time*, "the screaming headlines of the German smash through Belgium and down into France came like an unremitting, seven-day Orson Welles broadcast of an invasion from Mars." In Jeannette, Pennsylvania, a gun club prepared to shoot down Nazi paratroopers, while in Kirkland,

Washington, a coffee shop changed its hamburgers to "liberty steaks." The *New York Herald Tribune*, a Republican paper, said bluntly that "the least costly solution in both life and welfare would be to declare war on Germany at once." Isolationists tried to stem the rising tide of indignation. "Our danger in America," insisted Charles Lindbergh, "is an internal danger. We need not fear a foreign invasion unless American peoples bring it on through their own quarreling and meddling with affairs abroad." The *New York Times* responded by calling Lindbergh "a blind young man if he really believes that we can live on terms of equal peace and happiness 'regardless of which side wins this war' in Europe."[27]

Even isolationist newspapers called for massive defense spending, and some even wanted to render Britain all possible aid. Frank Knox, publisher of the *Chicago Daily News* and a Republican interventionist, wrote a scorching editorial demanding that the United States "help in every way short of war itself, those who are now fighting the bestial monster that is making a shambles of Europe." A Scripps Howard reporter rediscovered the 1925 warning of General Billy Mitchell, who had been court-martialed for accusing the high command of incompetence in refusing to see the growing importance of air power: "In future wars it will be too late to organize an air force after the contest begins."[28]

Editor Felix Morley of the *Washington Post* struck the note Roosevelt wanted to hear. "Neutrality has no meaning when such a merciless military machine is in full operation," he wrote. ". . . No country can possibly be indifferent . . . Nor can it be said realistically that the U. S. is any longer neutral." A Gallup poll released on that fateful May 10 showed overwhelming support for staying out of the war, but two thirds of respondents said they favored a candidate who would give more aid to Britain and France. This margin was virtually identical for members of both political parties. The *New York Times* viewed the attacks as "a moral to put our house in order, to strengthen our defenses, to prepare ourselves against the consequences of German success which might spread war across the Atlantic or Pacific to our own hemisphere."[29]

Fortified by this response, Roosevelt drove through a gray rain to appear before Congress on May 16. "These are ominous days," he began in a solemn voice. ". . . The clear fact is that the American people must recast their thinking about national protection." He shocked everyone by calling for the production of 50,000 planes in a year and an increase in the standing air forces of the army and navy to 50,000. At the time the industry could produce only about 15,000 planes a year tops, and the cost of 50,000 would be phenomenal. He also asked to add nearly $1.2 billion to the $1.7 billion already appropriated for military purposes. Nine days later Roosevelt, using his newly created authority, established OEM, which was to become the home base for other organizations. On May 29 he resurrected the National Defense Advisory Commission (NDAC).[30]

The "advisers" chosen by Roosevelt showed that he had learned his lesson from the failure of the WRB. Three of the seven came from the business world: Edward Stettinius Jr., William S. Knudsen, and Ralph Budd; Chester Davis represented farm interests, and Harriet Elliott consumer protection; Sidney Hillman was a labor leader and Leon Henderson a New Deal economist. Revival of the NDAC signaled a clear rejection of IMP, which vanished into irrelevancy. Still sensitive to the political barometer, however, Roosevelt hedged his position. "This is not complete, immediate national mobilization," he said. "We are not talking at the present time about a draft system, either to draft money or men or women or all three." During May he also reassured the American people by saying, "I do not believe that there is an awful lot of Government action that is needed at the present time . . . We have got surpluses in almost everything. The shelves are well stocked."[31]

But the dispatches from Europe continued to echo disaster after disaster. Although the White House had a general rule not to do radio broadcasts on Sundays, Roosevelt chose to deliver one of his fireside chats on Sunday, May 26, when he would be assured of a large audience. Harry Hopkins and Sam Rosenman worked on the speech. At dinner before the broadcast, the usual levity and small talk was absent. A White House usher brought Roosevelt more dispatches, which he read and handed to his wife, muttering all the while, "All bad, all bad." Gloom engulfed the room. "The President was worried," recalled Rosenman. "But he was not scared; he could not give the impression that he was scared. In fact I do not ever recall seeing the President scared at any time."[32]

In his fireside chat that evening Roosevelt explained to his radio audience what was needed for defense and how the money was being spent. At the same time he stressed that there must be "no breakdown or cancellation of any of the great social gains we have made in these past years." The forty-hour workweek should remain intact and labor standards such as the minimum wage maintained, along with Social Security and unemployment insurance. There would be no new generation of war millionaires. However, at a press conference two days later he offered reassurance that "we are not going to upset, any more than we have to, a great many of the normal processes of life." To the female reporters he quipped that "this delightful lady will not have to forego cosmetics, lipsticks, ice-cream sodas."[33]

This form of double-talk had become typical for Roosevelt through the long months of trying to nudge the American people into more awareness of the crisis at hand. But the time for nudging had passed. The Dunkirk evacuation and the swift fall of France stunned people across the nation. "All of a sudden the old world, and the old pattern of thought, ceased to exist," wrote Bruce Catton. ". . . The war *was* going to a decision and it was going with unbelievable speed, and the decision looked as if it would be one we could not live with." Donald Nelson recalled that "in my part of the country the war . . . was a nuisance—exciting perhaps, but not conducive to public confidence or the normal progress of business. It was not until the fall of France became inevitable that the shock registered in the Middle West."[34]

After Dunkirk Roosevelt ordered every spare rifle and fieldpiece and as much ammunition as possible sent to Britain as quickly as possible. "I am adopting the 'thought,'" he explained to a friend, "that the more effective immediately usable materiel we can get to the other side will mean the destruction of an equivalent amount of German materiel—thereby aiding American defense in the long run." But stripping American arsenals to aid the British carried an enormous risk if it backfired. It violated the spirit if not the letter of the Neutrality Acts, and what if Britain fell to the Nazis anyway? Nevertheless, most of the cabinet supported his action, and the two military chiefs, General George C. Marshall and Admiral Harold R. Stark, cooperated willingly. Marshall declared the weapons to be surplus at a time when there was no surplus, while Stark managed to procure ships for transporting them. Morgenthau and other cabinet members scrambled to find a legal basis for the transactions.[35]

Roosevelt realized that he still had to tread a cautious political path. Hardcore isolationists were quick to regain their voices, while interventionists in Congress began to wonder whether Roosevelt might prove to be another Neville Chamberlain, the champion of appeasement. Others suspected that the prospect of a third term was influencing the president's course. Suspicion also clouded the ranks of the cabinet. On that fateful evening of May 10 a still unwell Harry Hopkins dined at the White House. Roosevelt persuaded him to spend the night. Hopkins borrowed some pajamas and settled in for the night; he did not leave for more than three years. His presence in the White House nettled Ickes and others, who resented the influence Hopkins exerted by having constant access to the president.[36]

The prickly Ickes had a running feud with Hopkins dating back to early New Deal days when they competed for funds as heads of two government agencies with very different philosophies and goals. "The most disturbing thing about Harry's situation," grumbled Ickes privately, "is that he not only reaches the President directly but reaches him through 'Missy,' to whom he is playing up for all that he is worth." Missy had long loved Roosevelt and saw herself as a sort of surrogate wife. "There's no doubt," observed Raymond Moley, who had once been close to Roosevelt, "that Missy was as close to being a wife as he ever had—or could have." Those in the White House understood that an order from Missy would always be supported by the president.[37]

Ickes also feared that Roosevelt might be "throwing away everything we have gained during the past seven years." To make matters worse, Roosevelt was in a foul mood, which was not like him. The White House staff whispered anxiously about the bad state of his temper. "Apparently," noted Ickes, "he is taking absolutely nobody into his confidence."[38]

The president had good reasons for his ill temper. The rapid pace of events had sharpened the dilemma that tortured him and had left him helpless to manage the timing of his response in a manner that suited him. The nation had to mobilize for war but was interested primarily in strengthening its defenses even though it was clear American security could no longer depend entirely on its two oceans of separation. He needed huge sums of money, which Congress was willing to provide, but even more he needed efficient agencies to oversee the expenditures. Both the War and Navy departments suffered from weak, ineffectual leadership that he continued to tolerate because one of his greatest weaknesses was an inability to fire anybody. The undisguised hostility between Woodring and Louis Johnson drove everyone in the War Department to despair and made life miserable for the most competent and commanding presence, Army Chief of Staff George C. Marshall.[39]

No one in the official family liked or respected Woodring. After one cabinet meeting at the end of May, as members filed out of the room, an aide walking behind Woodring bellowed indiscreetly to waiting reporters, "Has Woodring resigned yet?" Roosevelt realized that something had to be done about the squabbles and inefficiencies within the administration if the armed services were to be upgraded. Marshall had tried all winter and spring to open Woodring's eyes to the military's lack of preparedness, but the doggedly isolationist secretary wanted no part of the European conflict. If this were not enough, the president had also to contend with the growing speculation about a third term. Although he remained a sphinx on the subject, he could hardly ignore the impact his every action would have on his chances for reelection if he chose to run.[40]

Then, on June 10, Mussolini delivered a belligerent rant in which he declared war on an already prostrate France. Roosevelt heard the news as he was about to board a train for Charlottesville, Virginia, where he had agreed to speak at the University of Virginia's commencement while attending the graduation of his son Franklin Jr. from law school. Mussolini's blatant attempt to snatch some spoils of the war infuriated Roosevelt. He had tried repeatedly to persuade Il Duce to stay out of the war only to receive a reply described as "cutting and hostile." At the request of Sumner Welles, who also hoped to keep Italy out of the war, Roosevelt had cut a particularly sharp phrase from his prepared text. On the ride to Charlottesville, however, he discussed the matter with Eleanor and decided to restore the sentence that got more attention than anything else he said.[41]

"On this tenth day of June, 1940," he told an audience of several thousand in Memorial Gymnasium, "the hand that held the dagger has struck it into the back of his neighbor." Democratic politicos listening to the address on the radio immediately worried about the impact on Italian voters, but Roosevelt did not stop there. In the strongest language he had yet used, he went on to denounce the dictators and American isolationists alike while pledging to use "the material resources of this nation" to aid the Allies. Already he had announced that 275 army and 90 navy warplanes would be made available to beleaguered Britain and France, along with $50 million in surplus World War I arms. The twin goals of aid to the Allies and a speeding up of defense preparations at home, he emphasized, were "two obvious and simultaneous courses."[42]

"It was a fighting speech," declared *Time*, "more powerful and more determined than any he had delivered since the war began. It was a speech of decision, with none of the ambiguities that had marked his words on neutrality . . . The U.S. had taken sides. Ended was the myth of U.S. neutrality . . . Ended was the vacillating talk about the value of aiding the Allies; nothing remained now but to get on with the job."[43]

Ten days later Roosevelt startled the nation with another announcement. He had shuffled his cabinet by replacing Woodring with Henry Stimson and Charles Edison with Frank Knox. That the changes were long overdue only underscored their surprising suddenness. The fact that both newcomers were conservative Republicans threw both parties into confusion. Democrats wondered whether Roosevelt had lost his political bearings, while the Republican National Committee chairman foolishly read the two turncoats out of the party. Both men were strong interventionists as well as longtime critics of the New Deal. If nothing else their appointment revealed something about Roosevelt's priorities.[44]

Both men had impeccable credentials. Now seventy-three years old, Stimson had been an active Republican since the 1890s and worked in the law firm of Elihu Root, his lifelong idol. He had run for governor in New York, served as secretary of war under Taft and secretary of state under Hoover, and had been a friend of Teddy Roosevelt. Frank Knox had been an actual Rough Rider and a veteran of San Juan Hill. He became a Bull Mooser in 1912 and was Alf Landon's running mate in 1936. A longtime newspaper publisher, he had always been a staunch Republican. Both men had served in World War I.[45]

For weeks most of Roosevelt's inner circle—Missy LeHand, Pa Watson, and Dr. Ross McIntire, his physician—had been after him to make the changes, especially in the War Department. Finally, on June 19, Roosevelt penned a letter to Woodring asking for his resignation. As a sop he offered him the post of governor of Puerto Rico, which Woodring declined. Stimson agreed to take the position on condition that he be allowed to choose his assistant secretary. He chose Robert P. Patterson, a circuit court judge who had risen to the rank of major during the World War and won the Distinguished Service Cross for "extraordinary heroism." He would soon earn a reputation as "the Toughest Man in Washington."[46]

The choice of Stimson posed another problem for Roosevelt in the form of Louis Johnson, who had fully expected to get the post once Woodring was ousted. His indignation mounted steadily as Roosevelt tried to explain his reasons until he finally burst out in an unsteady voice, "But Mr. President, you promised me not once but many times . . ." Bernard Baruch happened to be in Roosevelt's office at the time. "Reaching over with my foot," he recalled, "I gave Louis a gentle kick to tell him to shut up. He did." Johnson left the department along with the boss he had cordially despised. His forced resignation did not sit well with many in the administration. Although able, Johnson could not begin to match the prestige, experience, and political clout Stimson brought to the post.[47]

Knox was another matter entirely. After elevating Edison in February, Roosevelt wrote Knox that Edison had been promoted with an understanding that he would resign whenever Knox was willing to accept the job. Ickes liked Knox because he was one of a few men outside Washington who understood the implications of a German victory and the need to prepare defenses without losing any more time. Like Stimson he chose a first-rate assistant secretary, James V. Forrestal, giving both the War and Navy departments good management teams for the first time in Roosevelt's presidency. Forrestal left the presidency of Dillon, Read, a top Wall Street house, to take the government position.[48]

Two days after Roosevelt's announcement of the cabinet changes, France surrendered. Hitler now held sway over most of Europe, and no one doubted that he would turn his war machine toward England. On June 19 Lord Lothian, the British ambassador to the United States, treated a group of Yale alumni to a pointed message that he would repeat frequently in the coming weeks. America's security had long rested on its domination with the British of the seas, but that situation had changed drastically. Hitler was nearing control of the French fleet and coveted that of Britain as well. If he succeeded, America would have no ally to protect it from Hitler's growing web of air and sea bases. Britain was the last bastion of democracy in the world, Lothian stressed, and "if Britain goes it will be difficult to preserve it for long . . . anywhere else." Any assistance the United States could render could mean the difference between victory or defeat and should come as quickly as possible. Aid to Britain offered, among other things, the best protection for America.[49]

Roosevelt agreed entirely. He knew from Churchill that the British would not surrender a single ship to Germany and vowed to muster as much aid as possible to the defense of Britain. Churchill too emphasized that the United States needed Britain to survive as a base to counter Hitler's growing inventory of conquered assets. Without the British fleet to protect them, the entire Mediterranean along with the Suez Canal and all of North Africa could fall into German hands, and the British colonies in Asia would be at the mercy of the Japanese. Hitler already had at his disposal not only the resources of Germany but those of Italy, France, and other occupied domains.

"This, then, was Roosevelt's first tremendous wartime decision," wrote Sherwood, "to back the seemingly hopeless cause of Britain with everything that he could possibly offer in the way of material and moral encouragement." Although he did not say so publicly, Roosevelt had also made another crucial decision: He would defy tradition and seek a third term. Late in June the Republican convention witnessed a rare revolution in which the old-line leaders lost control and a political novice in the form of Wendell Willkie seized the nomination. President of a giant utility company, Willkie had been a Democrat until 1939. He infuriated Republican professionals by being not only an outsider but a liberal and internationalist as well.[50]

Willkie's nomination posed an unexpected dilemma for the Democrats. Although he opposed the New Deal, he did not call for repeal of its main achievements and actually had supporters in the labor movement. Nor could he be attacked as an isolationist or appeaser. Even before his nomination Willkie published a short article calling for Roosevelt to run again so that voters could take a clear stand on the New Deal. "Nothing so extraordinary has ever happened in American politics," marveled Ickes. ". . . No one doubts Willkie's ability. He is an attractive, colorful character, bold and resourceful, and, I believe, utterly unscrupulous." The Democrats had no potential candidate to counter Willkie's appeal except, of course, the president, who revealed nothing of his plans until the eve of the Democratic convention in mid-July.[51]

Hopkins took upon himself the task of going to Chicago to represent Roosevelt at the convention. The president's supporters begged him to go in person, but he flatly refused. The only written instructions Hopkins carried consisted of three short paragraphs scrawled by Roosevelt on a sheet of ruled yellow paper and addressed to the temporary chairman, Senator William B. Bankhead. It asked him to tell the convention that "I have not today and have never had any wish or purpose to remain in the office of President, or indeed anywhere in public office after next January. You know and all my friends know that this is a simple and sincere fact. I want you to repeat this simple and sincere fact to the Convention."[52]

No one believed a word of it. The party pros conceded grudgingly that no other candidate stood a ghost of a chance against Willkie and that their own futures depended on Roosevelt remaining in office. On the first ballot Roosevelt received 946 votes to 72 for Farley and 61 for Garner. However, the regulars balked when Roosevelt insisted on having Henry Wallace as his vice presidential candidate. Their reaction was so disorderly and vulgar that Roosevelt began work on a statement declining the nomination. Into the breach stepped Hopkins, who displayed enough toughness and political ruthlessness to impress even the ward heelers who regarded him as an amateur. Without a whimper of complaint Hopkins absorbed the hatred and resentment unleashed, and Wallace got the nomination on the first ballot.[53]

In a thirty-two-minute acceptance speech broadcast from the dungeon-like radio room in the basement of the White House, Roosevelt perpetuated the fiction that he was responding to the call of a draft like any good citizen asked to serve the country in an hour of need. He would not have time to campaign in the conventional sense but added that "I shall never be loath to call the attention of the nation to . . . falsifications of fact which are sometimes made by political candidates." As to the larger issue, Roosevelt framed it in unmistakable terms: "We face one of the great choices of history . . . It is the continuance of civilization as we knew it versus the ultimate destruction of all we have held dear—religion against Godlessness; the ideal of justice against the practice of force, moral decency versus the firing squad."[54]

The nomination was his, and with it another restraint on his actions. Ahead lay three and a half months of campaigning wrapped around pushing the work of mobilization and coping with whatever new crises flared up. As a candidate Roosevelt scheduled only five speeches, along with a radio address from Hyde Park on the eve of the election. Although the tempo of mobilization would speed up, Roosevelt still had to walk a fine line to avoid doing anything that might cost him the election. To some extent this meant more double-talk, more saying one thing and doing another. This could not be avoided if aid to the Allies and the nation's own mobilization were to be expedited. It helped greatly that the president was a past master of the art.

CHAPTER 2

THE WHEREWITHAL
OF WAR

*My experience in two world wars, the aftermaths, and the en-
deavors to make a lasting peace, makes me marvel at the regu-
larity with which errors are repeated. One of the errors that
most frequently recurs is failure to study and understand the
records of the past.*

—BERNARD BARUCH [1]

*The country in 1940 was altogether unprepared for the age of
crisis that had begun—unprepared politically, economically,
and above all emotionally . . . It was a country whose people
were as unready to fight a war as its economy was to win it . . . It
was a country, in short, in which the economy had not yet been
mobilized for security, social or national.*

—ELIOT JANEWAY [2]

The cold truth is, in summary, that Germany prepared for this
war; France prepared for the last *war; Britain prepared for* no
war. To-day we stand somewhere between France and Britain.

—HANSON W. BALDWIN [3]

BERNARD BARUCH WAS AN ANOMALY wrapped in a bundle of contradic-
tions. Born amid the ashes of the Lost Cause, he lived to see the Atomic Age.
He was a Jew from South Carolina who moved to New York at an early age
but never lost his southern roots. His father was a doctor who hated war yet
found himself a surgeon in the Confederate Army. Both his parents belonged
to families rooted in East Prussia who had migrated to Camden, South Carolina, where Bernie was born in 1870, five years after the Confederacy's defeat.
In 1881 Simon Baruch moved his family to New York to give himself a wider

field of opportunities for employment and his children schooling they could not get in the impoverished South.[4]

Once accustomed to this new and very different world, Bernie looked to find his place in it. He developed an early fascination with gambling, but not as a reckless habit. His approach was cautious, studied, and calculating—fueled by an excellent memory and a willingness to learn. Gradually he found his way to the ultimate casino, Wall Street, where he learned the art of finance and speculation at the elbows of such masters as James R. Keene, Thomas Fortune Ryan, and William Whitney. From this education Baruch accumulated a fortune through a mixture of bold moves and shrewd, careful appraisals.

Although he never hesitated to strike unexpectedly, Baruch was anything but a plunger. He had that rarest of financial gifts, a keen nose for knowing when it was time to get out of an investment. Never did he buy at the bottom and get out at the top, he admitted freely. Most of the time he sold out well before the top, content to take a smaller and surer profit. Believing in the immutability of certain economic laws, he formulated a set of rules by which he played the speculative game and tended to lose only on those rare occasions when he overrode them. In 1900, when his father turned sixty, Baruch set him up with a yearly income so that Simon could retire from general practice and devote his time to research he had longed for years to do.

Having become a wealthy man on Wall Street, Baruch graduated into larger deals in commodities like copper, rubber, and sulfur while pondering the question of what to do with his money and the rest of his life. In 1912 he fell under the spell of a new kind of politician, Woodrow Wilson. Meeting Wilson for the first time that October, only weeks before his election to the presidency, Baruch said the next day, "I have met one of the great men of the world." Decades later he described the meeting as "one of the great events of my life." Biographer Margaret Coit agreed that "it was Wilson of the New Freedom who released Baruch's talents, who gave the world the future statesman. With the one exception of his father, Woodrow Wilson was the greatest influence on Baruch's life."[5]

For all his reputation as a speculator, there resided in Baruch a streak of idealism similar to that in Wilson. He longed for some larger purpose in his life and found at least the doorway to that hope in his connection to Wilson and the Democratic Party. He became a financial angel and insider during the Wilson administration. Wilson came to admire Baruch for his intellect, his devotion to facts, and his willingness to speak his mind even if his point was unpopular. Gradually Baruch made himself an encyclopedia of American industry and an indispensable source of wisdom and advice to Wilson and others in the administration. It was this growing recognition of his ability and sagacity that led to his appointment as head of the WIB.

Baruch's presence in the inner circle of government aroused controversy. Admirers portrayed him as a man who, having made his fortune, now wished to devote himself to public service. Detractors, apart from the inevitable anti-Semites, could not let go of his previous career and Wall Street background. "That man," said a friend to scholar and journalist Alvin Johnson, "is the biggest menace in America. Big capitalist, ruthless speculator, he leads the flock of big business cormorants that has settled down on Washington." Others told Johnson that Baruch was a menace, but to big business interests. Everyone agreed he was smart and a clear thinker. A naval purchasing officer described him as "a man who knew so damn many things I didn't even know were problems."[6]

His performance as head of the WIB won Baruch a wide circle of respect and a reputation for sagacity and competence. He remained calm under pressure and talked easily. His aristocratic appearance contrasted with his democratic manners that put people at ease. His was a self-contained ego that never boasted or shouted but demanded recognition in more subtle ways. He accepted philosophically the irony that critics denounced him as a Wall Street predator even as Wall Street cursed him for being a turncoat. His old friend Thomas Fortune Ryan provided some cheer by telling him, "You're doing a good job. All our friends here are kicking." His management style was hardly that of a dictator. Secretary of War Newton D. Baker described it this way:

> When [Baruch] wanted, for instance, to fix prices in an industry or to divert the capacity of an industry from one occupation to another, the way he did it was to send for the leaders of that industry, seat them around the table with him, tell them the national need, lay out the economics of the situation to them with experts in their own field at his elbow, and, at the end of the conference, they were not only informed of what was to be done but they knew why it was to be done, and they were enthusiastic for doing it.[7]

After the war Baruch remained active in the Democratic Party, taking care to make friends from both wings and not push himself forward for any office. He supported all three losing Democratic candidates during the 1920s and tried to stay aloof from intraparty squabbles. With his usual caution Baruch sensed that the financial and economic climates were growing unhealthy. As early as 1928 he began getting out of the stock market and liquidating other investments, all the while urging his friends to do likewise. However, even Baruch was unprepared for the depth and duration of the depression that followed the crash of the stock market. He avoided taking sides at the Democratic convention in 1932 but supported Roosevelt fully during the campaign.[8]

Franklin Roosevelt was no stranger to Baruch. They had known each other since Roosevelt's political debut as a state senator in New York, through his Washington days as assistant secretary of the navy and vice presidential candidate in 1920, and later as governor of New York. Once Roosevelt was elected, Baruch was rumored to be in line for a cabinet post, but none was offered; later Baruch insisted that he would not have accepted an offer. He remained loyal to the Democratic Party but was not entirely comfortable with the New Deal. "Far from being a power behind the scenes," he said later, "my role during the New Deal was largely that of observer and critic. There was much in the New Deal that I applauded. But there was also much that disturbed me, and moved me to protest."[9]

Not everyone admired Baruch. Young economist John Kenneth Galbraith called him a "self-accredited sage" but conceded the power of his influence. "Public deference was universal," Galbraith later wrote. "At the same time private skepticism was also nearly obligatory. A number of New Dealers held that he was a highly accomplished fraud but none ever said so in public." Hopkins did not like him, and Sam Rosenman thought he used his influence with Roosevelt against Baruch. However, Eleanor Roosevelt regarded Baruch as "one of the wisest and most generous people I have ever known, and he never forgets or neglects a friend." Those who liked and admired him often sought his counsel at his suite in the Carlton Hotel or his favorite bench number six in Lafayette Park, where he held court. Rosenman called him "a kind of Mecca for troubled officials."[10]

Journalist I. F. Stone was convinced that much of this image of Baruch was crafted by the old master himself. "Why do so many people consult Baruch?" he asked. "He has been around for a long time and knows the ropes. He has sense. He is *simpatico*. He has a capacity for smoothing out ruckuses, a valuable talent in a town as full of them as Washington. He knows how to handle the press. The picture he has built up of himself is that of a contented old man feeding the squirrels from a bench in the park opposite the White House and occasionally running into old friends who stop to chat a while with him. This is a masterpiece of public relations."[11]

Baruch did not hesitate to disagree with Roosevelt but was always careful to do so in a manner that did not ruin their relationship. Seventy years old in 1940, he settled comfortably into the role of Elder Statesman, a man of influence rather than of power. His relationship with Roosevelt would always remain complicated, the scraping of two enormous egos that deeply respected and liked but never fully trusted one another. "They are too much alike; both are charmers," observed Stone, adding, "It is my impression that Mr. Roosevelt does not like Baruch . . . Mr. Roosevelt feels about Baruch as a young married woman does when her mother tries to help her by showing her the right way to handle a maid or a baby." Roosevelt would never cut himself off from Baruch's sound, clear-eyed advice with its vast reservoir of experience, but neither would he allow it to impinge on his own powers. The preparedness dilemma was an especially sensitive issue because of the way Baruch's shadow and that of the WIB loomed over every aspect of it.[12]

No one had brooded at greater length over the issue than Baruch. Later he claimed that "from the end of World War One, the problem of preparedness, particularly those of its economic and industrial aspects, had been foremost in my mind . . . In this fight, as in others I have undertaken, I was espousing an unpopular cause." Through the 1920s and 1930s he won few converts until the Nazi menace swelled to frightening proportions. After the Munich Conference in 1938 he returned from Europe, reported to the president, and said afterward on the White House steps, "The condition of American defense is unknown only to Americans. Every foreign power knows what we are doing and exactly what we lack." By 1940 preparedness was on the minds of many people, and Baruch remained the symbol for what was widely acclaimed as the successful approach to it during the last war.[13]

Tall (nearly six-four) and lean with unrevealing blue eyes, his thick mane of snowy hair parted in the middle, Baruch dressed impeccably but still wore old-fashioned high-laced shoes. His patrician face with its benign expression was accented by the pince-nez he wore and by the hearing aid in his left ear, which he often turned off to discourage interruption. The Elder Statesman had long since renewed his South Carolina roots by putting together a huge estate called Hobcaw, a composite of seven former rice plantations six miles from Georgetown. There, in what he called his "Garden of Eden," Baruch entertained lavishly, rested, refreshed himself between trips to Washington or New York, and awaited the call to duty that he thought must surely come. After all, who knew more about the subject or had done more to deal with it?[14]

THE WHEREWITHAL OF war seemed deceptively simple on paper. Building up the military required manpower and productive capacity. The latter in turn needed factories, raw materials, machine tools, skilled workers, adequate transportation, fuel, good designs, and an efficient organization. Each of these components had its own requirements, and putting them together in an effective manner could be fiendishly difficult. The United States had by far the greatest industrial production capacity in the world, yet it was almost completely unprepared for the challenges posed by mobilization. As Eliot Janeway observed, "The fall of France had found the American economy unprepared even to become prepared."[15]

Germany held an enormous lead on everyone else. For seven years her economy had been ruthlessly harnessed to the production of armaments. Having been stripped of nearly her entire war machine by the Versailles Treaty, she had only the newest and latest weapons. The blitzkrieg provided another huge advantage. "The conquest of continental Europe," wrote economist and military authority Fritz Sternberg, "served to improve to an almost staggering extent the productive capacity of Germany's heavy industries." Coal, oil, steel, bauxite, aircraft factories, shipyards, and armament and other factories all fell under German rule. The coal available to the Nazi regime leaped from 186 to 327 million tons a year, steel-making capacity from 25 million to 42 million tons compared to 17 million tons for England. Petroleum and refining capacity increased tenfold.[16]

The United States was not yet an economic or military superpower. It had no allies and wanted none, was divided internally, and lacked the political will to make its presence felt in the unfolding global catastrophe. Its economic and military strength was measured not in output but in potential. In 1938, for example, America produced 26.4 million tons of steel compared to Germany's 20.7 million, Russia's 16.5 million, and Japan's 6 million. But the latter three steel industries were all working at full capacity while the depressed American industry was operating at barely one third of capacity. For a decade the American economy had been shackled by depression, unemployment, and the rise of ghost towns created by factories and mills gone silent. No one knew what heights it might reach if operating at full potential, and no one expected to find out anytime soon.[17]

Much of the problem lay in the legacy of World War I. Paul von Hindenburg, the German army chief of staff during the war, paid tribute to American productive might, saying that its industrialists "understood war" and that their machinery was "brilliant if pitiless." Many corporations supplied war goods to the Allies in large part by building new facilities for their production. After the war, however, the tax laws did not allow companies to write off equipment that was neither obsolete nor worn out. Rather than maintain idle war plants and pay taxes on them, they chose to demolish them. The casualties included Remington's Eddystone, Pennsylvania, plant, then the biggest rifle manufacturer in the world.[18]

The abrupt termination of wartime contracts by the government, coupled with the attack on "blood profits" and "merchants of death," spurred companies to dismantle a once formidable munitions industry. In November 1918 the United States led the world in the production of explosives. By 1940 the government's entire supply of small-arms powder came from only two plants operated by DuPont and Hercules and a small army arsenal near Dover, New Jersey, which was little more than a laboratory. Mobilization meant rebuilding the munitions and weapons capacity that had been scrapped, but hardly any companies cared to invest in new factories that promised orders only during the short shelf life of wartime.[19]

Events in recent months reinforced this reluctance. The outbreak of war raised hopes that the depression might finally be ending as foreign war orders poured into American firms. Then came the sitzkrieg, and during the winter of 1940 the infant war boom evaporated as quickly as it had come. "Almost everyone expected 1939 to pick us up exactly where 1919 dropped us," observed Eliot Janeway. "There was a sinister excitement in the autumn air . . . and grocers and directors of the Steel Corporation both began muttering 'War boom' under their breath . . . Notices went out to domestic consumers that they had better lay in stocks for future use at once if they did not want their orders lost in the scramble to export that was surely coming . . . And then it was over."[20]

Many American firms, fearful of price rises and slow deliveries, followed this advice and expanded their inventories between September and December 1939 only to find that the expected rush did not materialize. No one cared to revisit the demoralizing recession of 1937–38, when excessive inventories were thought to be the reason behind the economic falloff. Hitler's march through the Lowland countries and France triggered a sharp renewal of war orders but also brought fresh uncertainties, most notably in the derangement of foreign trade and probable loss of major overseas markets. Promise and peril seemed to be inseparable in the fast-changing economic landscape, along with the resolve to heed the lessons of World War I. But what exactly were those lessons?[21]

The first time around had witnessed an economic boom for two years before the United States entered the fighting—one that erased a recession, eliminated unemployment, generated fat profits for "war baby" corporations, and distorted price levels. Once into the war, however, the nation lacked a plan for organizing its productive effort and bumbled its way along. It did not help that President Wilson held moral objections to war and had been outraged at hearing that the general staff was preparing a plan in the event of hostilities with Germany. When told about war games played at the War College, Wilson said to his secretary of war, "That seems to me a very dangerous occupation. I think you had better stop."[22]

Despite energetic efforts, production floundered in a sea of problems. Orders were placed for 20,000 guns of all calibers, along with ammunition for them, yet only 133 guns and 600 shells of a single caliber reached the front in time to be used; 20 million hand grenades were ordered, but General John Pershing ended up buying grenades from the British, along with rifles and machine guns. Huge outlays went to aircraft production, but not a single American plane flew at the front. Supply purchases turned into a comedy of errors. For the military's 86,000 horses, orders were placed for 945,000 saddles, a million horse covers, 2 million feed bags, and 2.8 million halters. During the five months and five days the Packard Motor Car Company worked on an airplane engine, it was forced to make over a thousand changes to the design.[23]

The war effort did not stabilize until authority was centralized. General George Washington Goethals took charge of army purchasing and fixed its breakdowns. When the railroad system bogged down in a hopeless traffic jam on the Eastern Seaboard, Wilson nationalized the roads. For industry as a whole the solution proved to be the WIB, which thrust Baruch to prominence and erased much of his earlier reputation as a speculator. Although the board had only vague powers, Baruch utilized them cleverly. As chairman he had ultimate authority for all decisions except the determination of prices, and all government agencies were ordered to submit their orders to the WIB. He surrounded himself with experts in each area, delegated authority freely, and dressed every order as a request for voluntary action from patriotic firms and industries.[24]

But Baruch also kept an iron fist in his velvet glove. When he presented plans to limit severely the output of automobiles, the three leading manufacturers flatly refused to comply. One automaker barked that he didn't want any "Wall Street son of a bitch" telling him how to run his business. Baruch responded by informing the manufacturers that their supplies of coal, iron, and other key materials would be diverted to war manufacturers. Later the automaker apologized for his name-calling to George Peek, vice president of Deere Plow Co., who also worked for the WIB. "Oh hell," Peek replied. "Everybody calls the Chief that these days."[25]

The WIB did its job by organizing, coordinating, and standardizing production. It devised a system for clearing orders to avoid duplication and took charge of allocating resources through a priorities system that, once developed, became the board's most important instrument of control. A Division of Planning and Statistics was created to help determine the industries most suitable for conversion to war work. Congress stopped short of giving the WIB power to control prices, which made it difficult to harness the inevitable inflationary effect of wartime purchasing except indirectly through priorities and commandeering. Standardization became a key instrument to increase output and save resources. The board slashed the number of steel plow models from 312 to 76, tire sizes from 287 to 9, and types of wooden coffins by 85 percent. It also took on the task of curbing nonessential construction and other use of resources despite protests from those eager to build, and began reducing the variety and output of consumer goods.[26]

In all this work Baruch leaned heavily on corporate executives, especially promising younger men like Peek at the vice president level. They were, after all, the people who knew how to produce things. If, as Frederick Lewis Allen declared, the nation in 1940 was "confronted with the necessity of yielding to Washington vast and dictatorial powers" to expedite mobilization, it made sense to get business executives involved and to create an entity similar to the WIB to oversee the process. For that matter, it also made sense to many influential people to put Baruch back in charge of such a board. Who knew better what needed to be done and how to go about it?[27]

Baruch certainly thought as much. Less than two months after the nation entered World War I he had submitted a plan to Wilson for a single, all-powerful board headed by one individual to oversee purchasing, priorities, production, and other functions. Although created in July 1917, WIB floundered under lack of authority and effective leadership until March 1918, when Wilson put Baruch in charge with more authority. The board achieved its impressive record in only eight months before the war's end. Nobody knew how well it would have performed in a more prolonged conflict. In 1940 Baruch remained convinced that his model was the right one.[28]

Roosevelt could not help but feel the pressure to heed the lessons of 1917–18 and create a replica of the WIB, possibly with Baruch in charge. He agreed entirely that the defense effort needed a leader, but that leader would be himself. He welcomed Baruch's counsel but did not trust him fully, and he trusted most businessmen even less. His greatest fear was that mobilization would end up in the hands of big business and the military, neither of which he thought was equipped to run it. Their domination would pose a grave threat to the social reforms of his administration, would curb or reverse rather than extend them. "If war does come," he had vowed, "we will make it a New Deal war." Yet he also realized that, like it or not, the defense effort could not do without the expertise of business executives and the military. Nor could the model of the WIB be ignored entirely.[29]

How then to reconcile these conflicting goals and needs with time running out? Britain needed all the help she could get, and at home events had finally set the stage for speeding up mobilization. For Roosevelt, delivering on his promises had to take priority over just about everything else, even though some of them blatantly contradicted other ones.

THE WHEREWITHAL OF war required money, lots of it, and Congress was slow to loosen the purse strings. Since 1934 the military had spent more than $7.6 billion, and economy-minded congressmen demanded to know what the taxpayers had got for their money. The navy clamored for more ships, arguing that it had to defend America on two oceans. The army was undersized, underequipped, and lacking modern weapons. In his January budget message Roosevelt asked Congress for $1.8 billion in defense expenditures and new taxes to pay for them. Republicans—and some Democrats—bristled at once. None of them wanted new taxes in an election year, and what was the money needed for, anyway? Some Republicans like Senator Robert A. Taft suspected the president of trying to sneak money for other pet projects under the guise of defense. Concern also arose over what *Newsweek* called "the President's never very-well-concealed tendency to identify the interests of Britain and France with our own."[30]

"I should like to make it perfectly clear," Admiral Harold R. Stark, the chief of naval operations, told the House Naval Affairs Committee, "that what we have asked for . . . is not sufficient to defend our home waters, the Monroe Doctrine, our possessions, and our trade routes, against a coalition of Japan, Russia, Germany, and Italy." The committee responded by whacking $112.7 million from the more than $1 billion naval bill and by paring the funds for eighty-one navy planes from another bill. In the Senate a strong midwestern bloc led by Senator Alva B. Adams of Colorado called for diverting a proposed $460 million in new taxes from defense to farm benefits. "We can make the savings," argued Adams, "by reducing appropriations for a war which is not coming."[31]

The reasoning of those opposing the outlays was old school. The United States had no business getting involved in the European war, Hitler posed no immediate threat to America, and the oceans still provided our first line of defense, which meant that the navy might need money but only the barest minimum need be spent on the army, which had no one to fight. In February Congress grudgingly passed a $252.3 million bill for emergency defense measures, and the House sent to the Senate a $965.8 million naval appropriation. The army fared even worse, leaving George Marshall frustrated and discouraged. To renew his appeal, he asked his old friend Bernard Baruch to arrange a meeting with key congressmen. Baruch, who had pressed both Roosevelt and Congress for larger appropriations, agreed readily.[32]

On the evening of April 10 Marshall and Baruch joined a dozen or so senators, including Alva Adams, for a meeting that lasted past two in the morning. Baruch opened with a statement on the army's needs, then gave way to Marshall, who outlined the overall situation with eloquence and clarity. When he had finished, Marshall said, "My job as Chief of Staff is to convince you of our needs and I have utterly failed. I don't know what to do." Adams, who had followed Marshall's argument closely, snorted. "You came before the committee without even a piece of paper," he said, "and you got every damn thing you asked for." Afterward Baruch described the outcome as "a turning point in convincing such critics of preparedness as Senator Adams of the urgent need for speeding the rebuilding of our defenses."[33]

The startling end of the phony war did even more to convince skeptics of the need for speed. Unhappy with Woodring's chronic inertia, Henry Morgenthau asked Marshall to brief him on the army's needs with a proposal he could take to Roosevelt and Congress. "Just remember," he cautioned Marshall, "it is all new to me." Marshall poured out his shopping list: more regular army troops, enough planes to build a modern air force, plants to manufacture munitions, reserve equipment, better pay, shelter, rations, clothing, and maintenance for the army, more rifles, artillery, antiaircraft guns, and all types of ammunition. Altogether Marshall figured it would cost about $650 million and said apologetically, "It makes me dizzy."

"It makes me dizzy," countered Morgenthau, "if we don't get it."[34]

On May 13 Morgenthau and Marshall took their case to the White House. They knew the argument would be uphill; the navy was Roosevelt's pet, and just then he was also deeply interested in airplanes. Woodring, Johnson, and budget director Harold Smith joined the meeting. As the debate heated up, Roosevelt remained unconvinced. Predictably Woodring offered no support, and even Johnson differed with Marshall on some points. The president resorted to his usual technique of dominating the conversation to avoid dealing with the issue. When he signaled an end to the meeting with no decision, Marshall asked for three minutes to make his case. In blunt terms he poured out the army's crucial requirements and concluded hotly, "If you don't do something . . . and do it right away, I don't know what is going to happen to this country." If five German divisions landed at any point on the East Coast, he added glumly, they could go anywhere they wished.[35]

His blunt appeal impressed Roosevelt enough that he asked him to return the next day with a detailed list of his requirements. At that meeting the president agreed to seek immediate funds for buying 200 B-17 bombers, for pilot training, and for essential supplies to upgrade existing units. Marshall prepared the draft of the message asking Congress for the money. On May 16 Roosevelt requested an immediate appropriation of $896 million and another $286 million in authorized military contract funds. "The clear fact," said the president, "is that the American people must recast their thinking about national protection . . . We have had the lesson before us over and over again—nations that were not ready and were unable to get ready found themselves overrun by the enemy."[36]

Fifteen days later he asked Congress for another $1.3 billion for defense purposes, saying, "The almost incredible events of the past two weeks in the Europe conflict, particularly as a result of the use of aviation and mechanized equipment . . . necessitate another enlargement of our military program." By early June Congress had passed two bills totaling nearly $3.3 billion to upgrade the army and navy. This figure equaled the entire amount spent on the

Civil War by both sides and was half the total outlay for the military from 1934 to 1940. Modern war was incredibly expensive, in large part because it was more than ever before a war of machines. "The machine has won," conceded Raymond Moley, a former New Dealer turned harsh critic. "The future has already been determined in the laboratories and machine shops of the world."[37]

On July 10 Roosevelt dispatched his third extraordinary defense message to Congress, calling for "total defense" and asking for the largest sum yet, more than $4.8 billion. The money was to push the creation of a two-ocean navy; complete the equipping of an army of 1.2 million men; procure tanks, guns, artillery, ammunition, and other equipment; help underwrite manufacturing facilities needed to produce ordnance, equipment, and other critical items; and buy 15,000 more planes for the army and 4,000 for the navy, along with spare engines and other supplies. For eight weeks Congress wrestled with these requests before approving slightly over $4 billion along with $1.1 billion for the navy.[38]

Getting Congress to loosen the purse strings was one side of the problem; finding ways to raise the funds was quite another. From the beginning the New Deal had run a steady string of deficits, which deeply offended the orthodoxies of Republicans and the conventional wisdom of many economists. By June 1940 the national debt stood at $43 billion and showed no signs of shrinking. The cost of defense mobilization was certain to send it soaring if steps were not taken to raise more revenue. The obvious danger was that heavy defense spending would not only give the economy a jolt but pose the threat of inflation. Increased taxes offered a logical tool for raising revenue and curbing inflation, but the political price could be high.[39]

Taxes paid for only 36 percent of the cost of World War I, during which wholesale prices rose 81 percent and the cost of living 83 percent even though American involvement lasted only twenty months. Both Roosevelt and Henry Morgenthau wanted taxation to support as much of the defense effort as possible. Congress seemed reasonably agreeable and barely flinched at a tax bill totaling $656 million early in June even though it realized that more was to come. The bill raised excise taxes on gasoline, beer, automobiles, cigarettes, and movie tickets, among other items. More important, it lowered exemptions and thereby embraced nearly 2.2 million individuals who never before had to pay federal income taxes. The lack of serious opposition led Robert L. "Muley" Doughton of North Carolina, chairman of the House Ways and Means Committee, to explain blandly that "everybody is so patriotic."[40]

Roosevelt signed the bill into law on July 1. That same day he asked Congress to enact a "steeply graduated excess profits tax, to be applied to all individuals and all corporate organizations without discrimination." The object was not only to raise revenue but also to show the public that there would be no new war millionaires. A similar, crudely done version during World War I was called "one of the most unpopular taxes . . . since the Boston Tea Party" and cost the Democrats dearly in the 1918 elections. To ensure its passage, Roosevelt decided to attach it to a bill with two provisions that the business community wanted: a 20 percent depreciation allowance on new defense plants, and repeal of a provision limiting profits on aircraft and shipbuilding to 8 percent.[41]

Unfortunately, this tactic backfired. The excess profits tax was by nature a difficult thing to define. Attempts to clarify it produced a complicated bill that by September had swollen from 96 to 480 pages and, in the words of a journalist, "had progressed from intricacy to metaphysics." Liberals thought it coddled profiteers instead of taxing them; conservatives resented having the other two provisions shackled to the excess profits debate. *Time* called it "the most mismanaged bill of the 76th Congress. . . . Few Senators understood it." Congress and the Treasury Department fell into an extended wrangle over how much revenue would be produced and other issues. Meanwhile, manufacturers continued to put off expansion until they knew the outcome. Senator Pat Harrison of Mississippi admitted that drawing up the bill was the worst thing he had ever tackled.[42]

When the bill finally passed, many observers expected it to be no more than a stopgap. Columnist Ralph Robey, a New Deal critic, dismissed it as "the worst hodgepodge of legalistic muddleheadedness and confused political compromises ever to go on the statute books." Henry Stimson, who had urged Roosevelt not to combine the excess profits bill with the other two provisions, took a more philosophical view of the mess. "If you are going to try to go to war, or to prepare for war in a capitalist country," he observed, "you have got to let business make money out of the process or business won't work, and there are a great many people in Congress who think that they can tax business out of all proportion and still have business men work diligently and quickly. That is not human nature."[43]

With funds for serious mobilization finally beginning to materialize, the question became how quickly industry could adjust to producing the goods needed and how far along the military was in adapting to the new warfare. In both cases the answer was far from encouraging.

BRIGADIER GENERAL C. T. HARRIS, assistant to the chief of ordnance, admitted freely that "the army is as dependent upon industry as it is upon soldiers." But the United States no longer had a munitions industry. "Germany has its Krupp factories," observed Burnham Finney, editor of *American*

Machinist, "France her Schneider-Creusot plants, Czechoslovakia her Skoda works, and Britain her Vickers organization, all of them devoted to the art of producing military equipment. Nothing has existed in this country comparable with any one of those semi-government companies." During World War I the country built up a sizable munitions industry, though not in time to contribute much equipment before the Armistice. Now it was long gone, thanks largely to government policy.[44]

Bethlehem Steel, among other companies, had built a formidable arsenal, but after the war the government continued to impose heavy taxes on its machinery that had use only in wartime. In desperation Bethlehem offered to give the facilities to the government, which politely declined the offer. Rather than pour more money into unused equipment, Bethlehem brought in gigantic hammers and smashed the machines into scrap iron and steel to sell for whatever it would bring. For a time the nation had led the world in production of smokeless powder, but those factories too shut down under the twin blows of taxes and relentless criticism of those who viewed them as merchants of death.[45]

Surveying the industrial landscape, Burnham concluded that the United States, long a master of mass production, would have to start from scratch in rebuilding a munitions industry. Everywhere he looked, bottlenecks loomed on the horizon. Smokeless powder, a staple of modern warfare, seemed to be the worst bottleneck of all. In a sizable battle every soldier consumed about half a pound a day. The current output of government arsenals would barely equip an army of 100,000 men. Airplane engines were in critically short supply, as were the aircraft themselves. Hardly anyone made tanks, and the military did not have a single model suitable for modern warfare. Armor plate, especially for warships, was made only by a few mills and was difficult to produce. The shortage of machine tools and gages was hardly a secret. On and on the list went, extending to key raw materials and skilled labor as well.[46]

Less obvious but equally discouraging was the lack of what William Knudsen called the "terrible urgency of the situation." To eliminate the bottlenecks the government and industry would have to work together, but businessmen and New Dealers had disliked and distrusted each other for several years and could not simply drop those feelings. Nor could managers and labor easily shed their mutual animosity and bitterness of recent years. In itemizing what was needed to mobilize America's defenses, Burnham was not alone in wondering how these and other bottlenecks could possibly be overcome in a short time.[47]

DURING LATE MAY, while Hitler's troops rolled through the Low Countries, some 68,000 army regulars assembled on the Sabine River between

Louisiana and Texas to conduct war games. The exercises had the sounds and smells of modern war—the roar of truck and tank engines, the rush of troops toward an objective, guns belching smoke from fired blanks—but little else. Few planes took part, and no antiaircraft practice took place. Nor were there any paratroopers, which the army did not yet officially recognize. The tanks involved were small and medium units that would be helpless against German 80-ton panzers. One cavalry brigade was completely mechanized, but another consisted of horses with trucks to haul them on long marches. The games cost taxpayers about $2.4 million and resulted in twelve deaths and 200 injuries. No one summed up the overall impression better than a *Time* reporter: "Against Europe's total war, the U.S. Army looked like a few nice boys with BB guns."[48]

Since 1919 the army had endured its usual peacetime ritual of neglect to the point where it had become a standing joke. Frugality had become a way of life for its officers, who had to beg Congress for scraps from the budgetary table. The 1939 appropriation of $646 million, for example, sounded generous, but nearly a third of it went to indirect military needs such as the Panama Canal, rivers, and harbors. Current needs for essential equipment being so pressing, less than 1 percent went to research and development of new weapons. Army chiefs learned to ask Congress not for what they needed but rather for what they thought they could get.[49]

The status of the military in peacetime could be inferred from its headquarters. From 1888 until the summer of 1939 the State, War, and Navy departments had shared the same ancient building next to the White House. That summer the army moved into the ramshackle Munitions Building on Constitution Avenue, one of the decaying wooden "temporaries" left over from World War I. By then, complained an unhappy Marshall, years of lean budgets and neglect "had reduced the army to the status of a third-rate power." Privates in the all-volunteer army earned $21 a month; a first sergeant with twenty years' experience took home $105.[50]

By the summer of 1940 the army had about 280,000 men, with plans to increase the ranks to 375,000. The National Guard added another 250,000 potential troops, nearly all of whom lacked training. Among the world's armies America's ranked eighteenth, trailing such military powers as Spain, Portugal, Switzerland, Holland, and Belgium. Thanks to years of compulsory military training, Germany boasted an army estimated at between 5 million and 6 million, with another half million in the Luftwaffe. At best the American army could put five or six fully equipped divisions in the field; Hitler already had 136 divisions in action and was said to have around 200 in all. The army needed not only more manpower but also the camps, equipment, uniforms, and weapons to arm and train them. Already some recruits were obliged to use wooden sticks instead of rifles in drills.[51]

The arsenals housed about 900,000 of the old reliable Springfield rifles of the World War along with 1.2 million Enfields. Mass production of a new model, the semiautomatic Garand, was bogged down in controversy over whether it was actually superior to a rival design, the Johnson. Only a few thousand troops had the Garand; the rest made do with Springfields. Infantrymen still wore the flat pan helmets of World War I. The supply of fresh powder totaled about 50 million pounds, with another 48 million pounds left over from the war. Automatic rifles, machine guns, and mortars were in short supply. No antitank guns existed beyond some obsolete 37 mm models, and few in the military knew much about antiaircraft guns. The light artillery consisted of 75 mm pieces of World War vintage and only a handful of newer and superior 105 mm guns. Ammunition was lacking for every type of weapon.[52]

The few hundred tanks in the army were older versions that, in Bob Patterson's words, were "scarcely more formidable than trucks." The "hell buggies," as the troops called them, couldn't begin to compare to the German tanks. Lightly armored and windowless, they depended for sight and direction on the commander sitting in the turret and issuing orders by kicking the driver's back and shoulder. Two kicks meant straight ahead; a kick to the right or left shoulder signaled a turn in that direction. Verbal commands were useless because of the incessant noise, which one wag described as "ten robots tap dancing inside a cement mixer." Shooting the exposed commander or spotter rendered the driver completely blind.[53]

One key element of the army, the cavalry, was staffed with officers who could not bear the thought of giving up their horses for tanks or other mechanical vehicles. On the day the Louisiana maneuvers ended, the two generals in charge of the army's lone tank brigade met secretly with other sympathetic officers, including Colonel George Patton, to put together a case for an independent armored force. Taking care not to invite the heads of the cavalry and infantry, they completed their recommendation and forwarded it directly to Marshall, who gave his approval. But the horse-drawn army still had its dogged adherents. Old army hands sneered at motor transport as unnecessary and even harmful because it softened the infantry's spirit as well as its leg muscles.[54]

The shortage of aircraft was even more disheartening. As of June 30, 1940, the Army Air Corps had only 2,755 planes in its inventory, most of them trainers or obsolete combat models. Large orders had been placed to update and increase the supply, but they were slow in arriving. Nothing resembling mass production had yet been devised for aircraft, and most of the planes coming out of the factories had been ordered by the British and French. Mindful of the debacle after the last war, manufacturers hesitated to expand capacity unless the buyers paid for it or offered guarantees in contracts. Patterson asked General Henry "Hap" Arnold, head of the Army Air Corps, how many planes he could throw into combat against a nation with a modern air force and was stunned when Arnold said only 300. None of them had such important improvements as leakproof gas tanks, armor plate to protect motor and pilot, or power-operated gun turrets.[55]

Pilots were also in short supply. The country had about 37,500 pilots of all ages, but fewer than 8,000 of them had military training, and 78 percent of those were already on active duty in the armed services. Roosevelt asked Congress for $32 million to provide training for 50,000 men and refresher courses for lapsed licenses. Planes also needed mechanics, who required at least seven months of training. No provision yet existed for increasing their number; the military had only 8,500 airplane mechanics, and another 10,200 people were certified civilian mechanics. Then there was the matter of airports. Germany boasted 650 first-class airports with all the facilities needed for military operations; the United States had 20 military air bases. Of the nation's 2,174 civilian airports, only 200 were suitable for military use, and only 31 could be converted quickly into bomber bases.[56]

Marshall also faced the thankless task of overhauling the army's fossilized leadership, which meant displacing long-standing traditions, overriding seniority, and offending old friends. During the years between the wars, most military officers did what they had always done for ages past: They thought and planned in terms of the last war, the fount of their experience. Too often this led to disaster, as it had in World War I when thousands upon thousands of troops went to the slaughterhouse because their leaders had not adapted to the constantly changing nature of war. Too many colonels were already in their sixties and nearing retirement. They scarcely understood modern war, let alone had the ability to command troops and make split-second decisions under its enormous pressures. In a process that scarred Marshall and everyone involved, he retired senior officers and promoted younger men over those who remained.[57]

The navy was in no better shape. It too suffered from an antiquated organization and sclerotic leadership that still looked back to the last war. When Frank Knox took office, his staff included only a military aide and some secretaries. The navy had six bureaus but no central procurement authority and hardly any knowledge of or statistics on the proposed expansion program. Nor did it have any inventory of existing stocks or catalog of facilities or any semblance of long-range production planning. Its contracting machinery was primitive and glacial. James Forrestal, occupying the new position of undersecretary, had neither office nor staff nor defined duties. He and Knox would have to start from scratch, often butting heads with an entrenched officer corps.[58]

Neither service had any idea how much raw material or other goods would be required for their needs because they had no way of knowing what those needs were. They had virtually no data on these matters because no one had ever asked them for any such thing. Forecasting military needs for several years of war was a hopeless task, if only because neither service knew what role it was expected to play. The fundamental axiom was that needs depended on what the service was expected to do. Was the navy limited to defending the coasts or convoying an army overseas? Was it to fight a war in the Atlantic or Pacific, or both at the same time? Would the army be based entirely at home or overseas as well?[59]

The need for answers was imperative. World War I had raised the stakes by introducing the world to the deadly possibilities of war in the industrial age, where new machines and technologies elevated the arts of killing and destruction to a scale never before imagined. It posted a warning flag to the modern age that war would never be the same, and that thinking in terms of the last war would be more than ever a colossal error. Industrialization created new weapons that were constantly evolving, and with them came new possibilities for how best to exploit them. Mechanized warfare moved at an ever faster pace, as did industrial and scientific innovation. It made killing and destruction a more impersonal process. Most American military leaders were slow to grasp the nature and implications of this sea change in warfare until the Nazi onslaught opened their eyes.

The new face of war placed a premium on production. Germany had been the first nation to grasp this truth, and Japan was not far behind. Both had geared their society and their economy to a state of maximum war effort. Both also realized that the United States possessed far more of the wherewithal of war than the two of them combined, but until the spring of 1940 America remained little more than a sleeping giant slow to stir and reluctant to act. "German production capacity is the highest in the world," boasted Adolf Hitler. ". . . Germany today, in any case, is, together with her Allies, strong enough to oppose any combination of powers in the world."[60]

CHAPTER 3

THE POSSIBILITIES OF PRODUCTION

Perhaps there was once a time when courage, daring, imagination and intelligence were the hinges on which wars turned. No longer. The total wars of modern history give the decision to the side with the biggest factories. The economically inferior may win battles; they do not win the all-out wars.

—GEOFFREY PERRETT [1]

Our danger never has been that we couldn't do the job. It always has been that we were slow in waking up to what had to be done. Now again, that is our chief danger.

—RAYMOND CLAPPER, AUGUST 26, 1940 [2]

Orators, columnists, professors, preachers, and propagandists performed magnificently with the theme that World War II was a war between two ideologies. But whatever inflamed people's minds in warring countries, victory was on the side of the heaviest-armed battalions. The conflict became one of two systems of production.

—CHARLES E. SORENSEN [3]

REGARDLESS OF WHAT WAS BUILT and how, everything started with machine tools. They were the cradle of production, the machines that built other machines: lathes, milling machines, automatic screw machines, precision grinders, iron planers, and other metalworking machinery. Without them no plant could turn out the thousands of parts that went into planes, tanks, rifles, field guns, trucks, shells, and every other implement of war. As the foundation of the production process, the machine-tool industry was usually the first to feel the effects of every swing in the economic climate. During the depression decade it languished as manufacturing output dropped and firms stopped ordering new equipment. Then the outbreak of war in Europe hit the industry with a sudden wave of frantic buying orders from European countries.[4]

The term "machine tool" covered any power-driven machine that automatically cut identical shapes into metal passed through it. They could be grouped into six basic types by function: drilling and boring; turning; milling; planing; grinding; and shearing and pressing. Some were bench tools the size of a typewriter that could be made in quantity. Larger models cost as much as $100,000 each and could take a year or two to build. Many if not most of the machines needed for defense purposes fell into the latter category. The automobile industry was the largest civilian customer for machine tools, using about $100–150 million worth on its assembly lines and in its shops. Exports provided another outlet. One eager customer, Japan, bought $63 million worth between 1936 and 1940.[5]

"Toolmakers," declared historian Francis Walton, "are the master builders of the machine age." They could transform a 200-pound inert lump of metal into a 75-pound propeller shaft, precisely turned, rounded and gleaming. The shaft was but one of 17,000 parts of an air-cooled aircraft engine, and a relatively simple one at that. Forming the cylinder barrels alone in 1940 required no less than eighty-eight separate machine tools.[6]

Machine tools made mass production possible. To build airplane engines, for example, the manufacturer sent a machine-tool company blueprints of every part of the motor he wished to mass-produce. The toolmaker informed him what machines he would need and in what order to use them, then built the necessary equipment. Ironically, this process could not be reversed. Machine tools themselves could not be mass-produced because they were so specialized and had to be custom built.[7]

The Germans understood the crucial role of machine tools from the outset. An American commercial attaché in Berlin reported in December 1939 that "the adjustment of the machinery industry in Germany to war conditions is based to a large degree on the efficiency and versatility of the German machine-tool industry . . . It is estimated that the production of German machine-tool industry in 1938 was eight times the volume of 1933." By contrast the British and French allowed their machine-tool industries to slide during the depression and showed no urgency in reviving them as the threat of war loomed. Another American commercial attaché, this one in London, reported only four months before Hitler invaded Poland that "the British machine-tool-importing fraternity does not contemplate that the present crisis . . . will cause any substantial increase in the volume of British machine-tool imports." Their attitude, he added, was that war was unlikely and that

"British machine-tool builders are already in a position, without increased imports, to supply machine tools in sufficient quantity and variety to permit not only the armament program . . . but also of its vast expansion."[8]

Within a few months this tune changed and buying commissions from Britain, France, and Russia, among others, descended on the United States seeking vast quantities of machine tools. In 1939 half the output of American manufacturers went to foreign customers; the figure for 1940 was estimated to exceed 75 percent unless curbs were placed on the outflow. American companies weren't buying because they didn't have enough business to justify replacing older machines with newer ones. As a result, factories in other countries were acquiring newer, more efficient machinery than that in American plants. One expert estimated that more than 50 percent of the metalworking machinery in American industry was obsolete and needed replacing—a steep hill to climb in the face of a huge spike in demand. A survey in September 1939 revealed that 85 percent of the machinery was over ten years old. Much of it predated the 1900s; some had been installed before the Civil War.[9]

One knowledgeable observer described the American machine-tool industry as "ultraconservative if not actually reactionary." Along with a handful of larger firms like Warner & Swasey and Cincinnati Milling Machine Company, it consisted of several hundred small, mostly family-owned firms that also bore scars from World War I, when overexpansion followed by canceled contracts left them with excess capacity. Unable to pay taxes or get depreciation allowances, many went bankrupt and left the industry during the decade after 1918. The survivors then saw their ranks thinned by the depression decade and clung desperately to what little business remained. None cared to expand even when business picked up, because taxes ate up much of their profits and no way existed to amortize the extra cost of new facilities and machinery.[10]

The number of tools needed could be staggering. Mobilization created the greatest industrial expansion in modern history, and with it an enormous demand for machine tools. Two of three war factories built by the government and operated by Studebaker, for example, each required 3,488 pieces of equipment; the third needed 13,000 machines. To produce more machine tools meant growing the industry, which in turn required more of the very tools and materials so urgently needed elsewhere. The problem was compounded by the tendency of American plants to use not multipurpose tools but specialized ones designed to stamp out a particular product quickly and cleanly in one operation. These could not be converted easily to other tasks. In an average year the entire industry turned out about 25,000 tools; during the depression output sank to fewer than 7,000 a year.[11]

Expanding the industry posed other problems as well, most notably a serious shortage of skilled mechanics. Machine-tool building required a considerable degree of skill. Unlike in high-output industries like automobiles, the machines that produced parts were not automated but manually controlled. An automobile manufacturer could train someone in a few days to tend a machine; the machine-tool worker required specialized skills and a degree of individual judgment that often took years to develop. The quantities produced were consequently small, ruling out the possibility of mass output. The depression took its toll on the ranks, leaving the industry with an aging workforce and no apprentice program turning out younger replacements. Competent foremen and manufacturing executives were also in short supply. As a result, most plants lacked the means to operate more than the standard forty-hour week even when the rush of new orders began pouring in.[12]

By the spring of 1940 the price of machine tools had climbed sharply as shiploads of them headed overseas. The end of the phony war jarred the larger manufacturers into changing their policy to one favoring American firms first, with only excess output going abroad. American orders got shorter delivery times and more favorable terms as well. However, with yet another spike in demand sure to come thanks to the nation's increased defense outlays, the limited output of the industry made it a potentially dangerous bottleneck for production at home, if not overseas. As the editor of the *Saturday Evening Post* observed, "There is no large armament factory in the world, nor a machine-tool industry behind it, that has not machines from Cincinnati, Cleveland, Springfield, New England, Pennsylvania, Indiana and Michigan."[13]

At the same time, the machine tools in many small plants without prime defense contracts fell silent. In December 1940 the National Association of Manufacturers surveyed 16,000 manufacturing plants and discovered that more than 400,000 machines in them stood idle an average of fourteen hours a day, and that the situation was likely to get worse as the defense program ramped up. Here was an impressive reservoir of equipment; the problem was finding the best way to tap into it.[14]

"AMERICA'S SUPPLY OF airplanes for the Allies," noted *Life*, "may be the vital factor which will tip the balance of the war against Germany." But the planes were slow in coming. Between September 1939 and March 1940 American manufacturers delivered 177 planes to the army and navy, 311 to Britain, and 459 to France, an average of 178 a month. In January 1940 the manufacturers managed to turn out 300 planes; to reach Roosevelt's fantastic goal of 50,000 planes a year, 4,167 would have to be produced every month. Of the 84 American plants making planes, only 23 produced military models. "Hence the one great factor needed to make the U.S. airplane industry burgeon," concluded *Life*, "is orders, orders, orders with assurance that those orders will continue at least until the cost of plant expansion is paid off, or with advance payment of expansion cost by the buyers."[15]

Like other munitions firms, the infant American aircraft industry had been burned in World War I. It had managed to turn out planes at an annual rate of 21,000 only to have the Allies pull the plug on orders three days after the Armistice, forcing many companies out of business and 175,000 workers into unemployment. "The memory of this burst bubble," said a reporter, "has acted as a red light to American aircraft makers in negotiations for orders from the belligerents in the present hostilities." Despite having $700 million worth of orders on their books, they balked at expansion lest it leave them saddled with excess capacity. Instead they made plans to farm out part of the work to other plane makers who had not booked war orders and to lean heavily on subcontracting for parts and accessories.[16]

Other problems kept the industry from stepping up production as well. As Charles Sorensen, William Knudsen, and other old Ford men well knew, mass production of anything consisted of a few well-defined principles. The first step was to break the product down into as many interchangeable parts as possible. Those parts could then be manufactured in quantity and fitted together on an assembly line where the machines were arranged in proper order. If each part was uniform and each subassembly identical, every finished product would function the same way. In this process speed mattered less than accuracy at every stage. If the accuracy was there, it would create its own brand of speed.

None of this was present in the aircraft industry. In 1940 building planes was strictly a boutique operation. It had only modest standardization of parts and nothing resembling mass production. A bomber, for example, contained 5,000 to 10,000 distinct parts, each of which had to be fabricated from a blueprint or specification and then put together using hundreds of thousands of rivets into a complex series of subassemblies and assemblies "to the accompaniment of the banshee din of air-riveting hammers and the high-pitched swearing of tortured souls." The military wanted their planes yesterday, but they had to be made precisely and carefully, and the military did not hesitate to pile on design changes in midstream. Hurd Barrett, who worked at several different jobs in three aircraft factories for seven years, drew two conclusions from his experience: Americans built the world's finest airplanes, and the manner of their building was "strictly screwball."[17]

The process was long, tedious, and endlessly frustrating. Sometimes 500,000 man-hours went into the design stage alone to create the experimental model. Another 30,000 or so man-hours were then needed to build each replica, depending on how many engineering changes were imposed along the way. In that sense no two finished planes of the same model were exactly alike. About twenty weeks were devoted to fashioning the experimental model, and another eight weeks to the army's testing it against other models from competing firms at Wright Field in Dayton, Ohio. If the bomber survived that stage, it then ran a gauntlet of more suggested changes from army engineers and test pilots. Every change often begat several more to accommodate it.

While the company's procurement department scrambled to lay in the materials needed for a plane that didn't yet exist in final form, the lofting department—a term borrowed from the shipbuilding industry—constructed a full-sized wooden model of the bomber into which was fitted real machinery, piping, guns, and flight instruments to ensure that the design had no hidden gaffes. Finally it went to the production department, where the machine tools and special jigs and dies alone might cost $20,000 a unit on a 100-plane run. Despite working against deadlines imposed by the military, the production schedule was rarely complete because of changes introduced along the way. The production people were allotted a given number of man-hours to build the plane but had to use them within an elapsed period of time, say sixteen weeks. Barrett likened it to "cramming a toy balloon through a keyhole."

The schedule might be possible if the plane was fully engineered, the necessary tools ready, and the materials on hand, but this rarely occurred. Weeks passed waiting for one or more of these. The lack of castings and forgings especially haunted production foremen. About 90 percent of the plane's structural parts were made of sheet metal and usually farmed out to machine shops that were often miles away. Inevitably there would be some faulty work and rejections. Key items often arrived last, in part because the engineers, for reasons of their own, drew them last. "Engineers do not release the hardest parts first," said a resigned Barrett. "They just don't."

The plant itself was seldom laid out for efficient production. It lacked anything resembling an assembly line, and most companies were slow to rearrange their space for straight-line production with raw materials at one end and final assembly at the other. The rush of orders finally compelled many companies to rethink how they made their product. When at last the first completed bomber emerged from the plant for its first flight, the entire workforce turned out to cheer. Once it soared into the air, they turned and walked slowly back into the plant. Only ninety-nine more to go.

THE ORDERS WERE coming. By the eve of Hitler's May onslaught, foreign buyers had ordered $650 million worth of American aircraft, more than twice the total value of airplane exports to world markets in the past eighteen years. The Allies also advanced funds to American firms for plant expansion to expedite production. Most of the orders went to a handful of companies with existing warplanes: Curtiss, Douglas, Bell, Lockheed, Consolidated, Martin, Grumman, Boeing, and North American. A mere thirteen plants produced significant aircraft frames. None of them built the component that posed the greatest potential bottleneck to production: engines. Only three American companies built aircraft engines large enough for combat use: Wright Aeronautical, Pratt & Whitney, and Allison. Wright and Pratt featured air-cooled models, while Allison had developed a liquid-cooled version it claimed to be superior to the others. Allison was a fully owned subsidiary of General Motors, which also owned 30 percent of North American Aviation.[18]

In 1940 the aviation industry was barely a generation old. The army bought its first plane in 1909 from the Wright brothers—a concoction of bamboo, cloth, and wire that sped along at 42 miles an hour. Current models included the Bell Airacobra (top speed 400 miles an hour), the twin-engine Lockheed P-38 Lightning, the Curtiss P-40, and Boeing's constantly evolving B-17 Flying Fortress. Although every company had its own story of survival since World War I, Lockheed typified the pattern. Its founder, Allan Loughead, a California barnstormer and designer, figured out how to make sturdy fuselages out of plywood and set up shop in Hollywood in 1926 and Burbank in 1927. His early models, the Vega, Altair, and Sirius, became the darlings of every prominent pilot from Lindbergh to Amelia Earhart.[19]

In 1929 control of Lockheed passed to Detroit Aircraft Corporation, one of the many conglomerations spawned by the holding-company mania of the 1920s. Three years later the parent company dragged the still profitable Lockheed down into bankruptcy. It survived only because a small group of investors paid $40,000 for its name and assets and nursed the company through the lean years of the depression. Operating on a shoestring, Lockheed in 1934 produced the Electra, an all-metal ten-passenger plane faster than the renowned Douglas DC-2. Two more refined models followed, yet between 1932 and 1938 Lockheed manufactured only 300 planes, all custom-built for a few customers at a leisurely pace. Then, in the spring of 1938, it received an order from the British Air Ministry for 250 bombers of a special new type for $25 million, one of the largest contracts ever made by an American manufacturer.[20]

Suddenly Lockheed had to revamp its thinking and move from a boutique manufacturer to producing on a larger scale. It raised $750,000 for expansion, increased its workforce from 2,500 to 7,200, and acquired adjacent buildings alongside a busy highway opposite a string of cheap lunch joints and a revivalist billboard warning, "Except ye Repent ye shall all likewise perish." When development of the advanced P-38 required still more space in the summer of 1939, Lockheed took over a neighboring distillery building and allowed whiskey to be stored on the top floor. Even more important, management began developing techniques for speeding up production. For the Hudson bomber ordered by the British, it skipped the experimental model stage entirely while pushing redesigning and tooling simultaneously. During the first six months of 1939 it turned out 48 of the bombers but still had to produce another 200 in the next seven months.[21]

In building the Hudson, Lockheed devised a production line centered around sixteen stations where the fuselage remained for eight hours at each stop while parts were installed. If the parts were not available, the fuselage moved on to the next station anyway. The first Hudson off the line cost the company $119,100, the later ones only $63,000 because direct labor costs fell by 70 percent and overhead dropped as well. The more planes it built, the faster grew the tempo of production. Development of the P-38, scheduled to fly in the summer of 1940, followed a similar pattern. It featured the most radical design of any American warplane and used the Allison engines that had caused such a row in the industry. The immediate problem for Lockheed, as for other manufacturers, was simply getting enough engines to keep production on schedule. In January Henry Morgenthau had toured the factories making engines and concluded that more such facilities were needed. Six months later the situation had grown worse because of the flood of orders.[22]

The two manufacturers of air-cooled engines, Pratt & Whitney and Wright Aeronautical, both hoped to be turning out 900 engines a month by December 1940. Allison was lucky to ship four or five engines a day but was doubling its plant and looked to produce 400 a month by November. Although many people assumed that GM's ownership of Allison meant that mass production of the engines would soon be forthcoming, the problem was more complicated. Many more parts of an aircraft engine required closer micrometric attention than did automobile engines. However, the liquid-cooled Allison offered significant advantages over air-cooled engines. Besides being lighter, it lowered air resistance or drag, could maintain top speed for a longer period of time, and did not have to be placed directly behind the propeller. The engine used ethylene glycol rather than water for cooling.[23]

Similar progress in production could be seen at most of the other aircraft factories as well, but many of them still blanched at the scale of the task. By the summer of 1940 the aircraft, engine, and instrument industries had increased their workforce to about 100,000. However, the Germans were estimated to have around 400,000 aircraft workers, as well as entire factories devoted to training more of them. The Nazis had also decided to freeze model designs in order to turn out large numbers of planes as quickly as possible. The German aviation program was already five years old, while the American version was just getting started. The public was hardly reassured when Captain Eddie Rickenbacker published an article that August stating baldly that the nation needed 250,000 planes and 500,000 pilots to protect it from invasion.[24]

Henry Ford boasted that if needed he could turn out a thousand aircraft engines a week. His son Edsel was summoned to Washington and asked to produce Rolls-Royce liquid-cooled engines desperately needed by the British for their Spitfire and Hurricane fighters. "Sure, we can do it," he replied, and hurried back to Detroit. A short time later, he called Morgenthau to say sheepishly that his father did not want to make engines for the British. A fervent isolationist, Ford offered to make engines for American defense but not for Britain or any foreign government. Not even a flying visit from William Knudsen could budge the old man; after their meeting Knudsen stalked off in a rage. Packard then agreed to build a new $30 million plant to make 6,000 of the engines for the British and half that number for the United States, but getting the operation up and running would take time. Meanwhile, the backlog of orders continued to pile up for aircraft manufacturers. By October 28 airplane, engine, and parts makers exceeded $2.5 billion in unfilled orders.[25]

Packard learned early the difference between American and British ways of making engines. The blueprints it received from Rolls-Royce were more a guideline for craftsmen than exact specifications. Expert workmen cut out the pieces and, after careful milling and machining, fitted them together into a fine engine. To mass-produce the engines, Packard had to take apart an engine, weigh and measure each piece, compare them to the original blueprints, then draw up a new set of blueprints with a precise set of specifications down to Detroit's standard of one ten-thousandth of an inch. Once this was done, the engines could roll off an assembly line.[26]

When the British put in another large order on top of the planes already ordered, Henry Stimson observed that it would "prolong the industrial activity of our airplane factories for quite a while." Critics wondered whether the industry had bitten off more than it could chew. Columnist Ernie Pyle toured the giant Curtiss-Wright plant in Buffalo and found that expansion had not changed the hand-tailored methods used to make the planes. "It is," he said, "almost like building a house." Nobody had yet found a way to bring mass-production techniques to airplane building, and prospects for doing so did not look promising.[27]

AT SEVEN O'CLOCK in the morning, six days a week, Albin Schuck left his home in Hamilton, Maryland, a suburb of Baltimore, and drove seven miles to the Glenn Martin aviation plant to take up his duties as first-shift foreman of the spot-welding department. Once at the sprawling plant, he oversaw a crew of forty-five men who spent the day at eleven spot-welding machines tapping out countless invisible welds joining Alclad skin (a thin aluminum-alloy sheet) to the framework of various subassemblies. Spot welding pressed and fused the aluminum sheathing of two pieces of Alclad together to support the riveting at major joints. The subassemblies came in all sizes and shapes, each one requiring a different technique. They arrived with the Alclad skin temporarily attached to the supporting metal framework with spring pins.[28]

Each cumbersome subassembly, be it a curved piece of engine cowling or a section of bomb-bay door, had to be fitted between the pencillike points of the spot welder. Schuck and his men had to know the reactions of various metals to stress and heat as well as the functions of every part that came his way. Nearly all of the subassemblies passed through his department, which meant that any stoppage or delay brought production to a halt. Schuck worked an eight-hour day, averaging another hour and a half overtime during the week, and got time and a half for his eight-hour Saturday as well. For his efforts he took home about seventy dollars a week.

Schuck wore a business suit to work, having graduated from the overalls that were his uniform for eleven years. After four years of vocational training at the Maryland Institute, he had worked as a carpenter and draftsman for his father's contracting business until, in 1930 at the age of twenty-two, he landed a job at Martin. He dreamed of becoming a foreman and started willingly at the bottom of the metalworking ladder as a tool clerk for 40 cents an hour. From there he moved to the power shears, which sliced the thin, pliable sheets of Alclad into different sizes for machining, and then to the power brake, a press that bent and shaped the Alclad pieces into simple curves and angles.

In 1932 he married his boyhood sweetheart just as the depression pushed the aviation industry to the brink of insolvency. While Martin struggled to survive, Schuck found himself laid off for two months and then for another four months that year. He supported himself and his bride by doing odd contracting jobs until February 1933, when Martin took him back. In 1935 he was promoted to leader overseeing six brakes with a raise in pay. Two years later he was transferred to the punch presses and began taking courses at the factory. Once a week after work, he spent an hour taking three one-year courses in foremanship, spot welding, and work simplification. Gradually he moved into supervisory positions until by 1940 he had become foreman of the spot-welding department and could shed his overalls.

Schuck had the job he had always wanted, and life seemed good. He lived with his wife, Florence, and their four children in a ten-room house he had helped design and build. They occupied the lower six rooms and rented out the four rooms on the upper floor. In time the tenants would be gone and the family could spread out into the entire house. Martin gave him two weeks' vacation with pay every year and was delighted to have him. Good men were already becoming hard to find. The company was hiring any worker over eighteen who showed some mechanical ability. It figured that the average young worker, trained in shop practice, would take six months to start earning his pay of 50 cents an hour.

TO MOST PEOPLE the navy consisted of warships such as battleships, cruisers, aircraft carriers, and destroyers, but that fleet could not stay in action for very long without a second important fleet, the merchant marine that supplied it with food, fuel, ammunition, and other goods. Both had languished during the interwar years and were sorely in need of reviving. The problems facing shipbuilders had much in common with those confronting aircraft manufacturers: lack of facilities, painfully slow construction techniques, changing technology, and, above all, lack of orders to keep the industry vibrant. Shipbuilding had no rival as a feast-or-famine industry, and for private shipyards the famine had lasted for a decade and a half. However, in 1940 the pendulum was swinging back toward feast to the point where, like the aircraft industry, the issue became not lack of orders but ability to handle the incoming flood of them.

After the shipbuilding orgy spawned by World War I, the United States let both its fleets slide into obsolescence. The Washington Naval Treaty of 1922 limited the number of capital naval ships and discouraged further upgrading of the fleet. As for the merchant marine, American shipyards built not a single vessel for transoceanic trade between 1922 and 1928 even as it sold off many of the ships built for wartime use. In 1930 the Maritime Commission, which had charge of the merchant marine, still had 129 obsolete ships from the war tied up in ports at taxpayer expense. Then, in 1936, Roosevelt induced Congress to pass the Merchant Marine Act providing a subsidy to shipowners and spurring a new shipbuilding program. During the next four years forty-six ships were launched and thirty-seven put into service.[29]

The shipbuilding industry consisted of both public and private facilities. The navy had eight shipyards of its own scattered along the nation's three coastlines. These yards totaled nineteen ways (the structure on which ships were built and launched) and did about half of the navy's building. Another twenty-two yards belonged to private owners and had a total of eighty-three ocean ways. Two of the private yards worked exclusively for the navy, but only three of them could build any size vessel from a trawler to a battleship. The biggest of the three, Bethlehem Shipbuilding (owned by Bethlehem Steel), was the newest and most profitable. Newport News Shipbuilding & Dry Dock, the largest independent yard, had been built by rail magnate Collis P. Huntington in 1886 and turned out everything from ocean liners to aircraft carriers and battleships. New York Shipbuilding, smallest of the three with only five ways, changed hands in 1938 but had produced three battleships and the carrier *Saratoga*, among other vessels.[30]

The surge of shipbuilding soon filled these yards, and the $4 billion naval expansion bill passed in July 1940 overwhelmed their capacity. Even before the bill's passage the yards had 80 ships worth about $750 million under construction along with 118 cargo ships ordered by the Maritime Commission at a cost of another $300 million. The private yards had another thirty-seven partially dismantled ways that could be restored to use, but beyond that the only alternatives were to expand existing yards, build new ones, put back into service old ones, or work longer hours at the yards with extra shifts. During World War I yard employees averaged sixty hours a week and sometimes worked seventy hours, but a labor movement that had fought hard for years to get the forty-hour workweek would fight to retain it. As the preparedness drive intensified, so did the clash over extending the workweek even on a temporary basis.[31]

The strain of rapid expansion extended well beyond the shipyard, since less than half the cost of a vessel was spent there. As with aircraft, large sums went for materials and equipment—steel, lumber, turbines, pumps, electrical apparatus, and armaments. This ripple effect would do wonders for the economy but would also create labor and supply problems. Like airplanes, too, the building of ships was a slow, methodical process that had never needed or known the methods of mass production. *Time* even borrowed Ernie Pyle's metaphor in explaining that "building a ship is like building a house where putting up the walls must wait laying the foundation and the roof must wait on the walls." After completing their specialized task, workers were laid off until needed for the same job on another ship. Some were unwilling to wait and found work at another yard.[32]

In June one new shipyard at Pascagoula, Mississippi, unveiled a new way of building ships. Instead of the traditional practice of building from the keel up, Ingalls Shipbuilding laid decks on shored-up timbers and attached the framework, stern assemblies, bow sections, and others by swinging them into place with giant gantry cranes that could hoist as much as 75 tons. These sections were assembled separately on platforms thanks to what Ingalls claimed was a revolutionary innovation: The parts were welded together instead of riveted. Although Germany used welding on her pocket battleships, she kept the process secret. The only American ships that used welding instead of riveting were tankers. When the first welded cargo ship, the aptly named *Exche-quer,* slid into the water in June for her first trial run off Guantánamo, Cuba, officials watched anxiously to see if their expectations would be fulfilled.[33]

If successful, welding offered huge advantages in cost, time, and speed. A single welder could replace an entire four-man riveting team for big savings in labor, which constituted 40 percent of a ship's cost. If built the traditional way, the *Exchequer* would have required 1.25 million rivets as well as overlapping steel plates at the seams. Eliminating the overlap alone saved an estimated 16 percent of the steel required for the ship. Welding also enabled different sections of the ship to be constructed simultaneously and kept crews on the job with no layoffs or delays. Robert I. Ingalls, the crusty president of the company, believed strongly that riveted ships were destined for the museum. Having kept his firm alive during the famine years by building river craft, he had gambled in 1938 by building the big new yard at Pascagoula in order to get some of the Maritime Commission's new orders for cargo ships.[34]

Welding proved its worth but did not spread immediately to other yards. Meanwhile, the crush of business on American yards received another jolt in the form of desperate orders from the British for cargo ships. By November 1940 the British had lost about 2.5 million tons of its merchant marine fleet, mostly to submarine attacks. Although the country had the largest merchant marine in the world—about 18 million tons—British shipbuilders could replace only about a third of that rate of losses a year. But the British shipping commission found American yards jammed with enough orders to keep them busy for a year or more. Instead the commission resorted to buying 168 used ships from American owners, including 36 left over from the last war. This stopgap could not suffice if the sinkings continued, and no one expected them to stop.[35]

"EVERYTHING IS RAW materials until I get ready to cut it up," said William Knudsen, to which a general added, "The ultimate bottleneck is raw materials. In the final analysis, that is what will decide how much munitions we can produce." The basic stuff of production tended to be taken for granted until it was needed. In normal times, and especially during a depression, raw materials were plentiful and often cheap. War changed the formula drastically, transforming surpluses into scarcities and unmasking shortages of essential ingredients. The United States had more of these materials than almost any other nation, yet it lacked some of them entirely and had only small amounts of others. As soon as the war broke out, the question arose as to how it would disrupt the importation of raw materials. The problem was truly global, affecting not only the Atlantic world but the Pacific nations as well, where Japan was at war with China and growing more aggressive in Southeast Asia.[36]

America possessed large quantities of two key materials, petroleum and iron ore, but it lacked adequate amounts of seventeen strategic materials: aluminum, antimony, chromium, coconut-shell char (used for gas masks), high-grade manganese, manila fiber, mica, nickel, optical glass, quartz crystal, quicksilver, quinine, rubber, silk, tin, tungsten, and wool. Some of these were easy to obtain; Canada had ample supplies of nickel and Mexico of antimony. Others could pose serious problems if the United States got into a war. Russia supplied manganese, and South Africa, New Caledonia, and the Philippines furnished chromium; rubber and tin came from British Malaya and the Dutch East Indies, and silk from Japan. All of these and many others depended on long, unbroken supply lines across the ocean as well as continued good relations with their producers. What if those vital links were severed?[37]

In May 1940 Harry Hopkins warned the cabinet that the country had only a five- or six-month supply of tin and rubber. To avoid shortages, some industries had already taken to stockpiling key raw materials. Within the government the Army-Navy Munitions Board and secretary of war had tried in vain for years to get funds for stockpiling strategic materials. In 1938 Congress finally gave the navy $3.5 million to acquire manganese and some other materials. The following June, after much prodding, Congress passed the Strategic Materials Act authorizing the ANMB to stockpile a broader list of materials. The ANMB argued that $200 million to $700 million was needed for the job; by March 1940 it had received only $13 million, and little progress had been made despite repeated warnings from industrialists and economists. Shortly after the Germans invaded the Lowland countries, Roosevelt asked Congress for $60 million for stockpiling.[38]

Seeking another approach to the problem, the ANMB in June got Congress to authorize the Reconstruction Finance Corporation (RFC) to create subsidiaries for buying up to $300 million in materials. The RFC then organized four entities: the Rubber Reserve Company, the Metals Reserve Company, the Defense Plant Corporation, and the Defense Supplies Corporation. Swift action depended on the head of the RFC, Jesse Jones, a Texan included by Raymond Clapper in his list of the ten most powerful people in Washington. *Fortune* rated him even higher, calling him "certainly the second most powerful in the government." A socially shy, lumbering giant of six foot three and 220 pounds, Jones relished power and knew how to wield it. Under his rule the RFC became one of the most potent agencies in Washington. The crafty Jones ruled it as his personal fiefdom; some said he distributed more patronage than the president. He knew his way around Capitol Hill and had long since mastered the political game.[39]

"So vast are Jesse's powers," wrote Samuel Lubell in a profile of Jones, "so tricky the techniques of financial control that it is virtually impossible for anyone short of a congressional investigating committee to check the RFC's operations. That, perhaps, is the most important fact about the RFC."[40]

Jones was regarded as honest, reliable, and smart even though he lacked much of a formal education. He was as brilliant with figures as he was help-less with language, and savvy in the ways of business, having made a fortune the old-fashioned way. At twenty-three he bought a lumberyard and in nine years owned sixty-five yards worth $1 million. Over time he piled up a fortune in lumber, office buildings, hotels, and other enterprises, endured a nervous breakdown through sheer self-control, and in 1932 was appointed a director of the RFC by Herbert Hoover despite being a lifelong Democrat. A year later he became chairman.[41]

Jones commanded respect because he was said to be close to the president and had long since ingratiated himself with Congress and most of the cabinet. "There is nothing of shyness or modesty about Jesse Jones," observed Harold Ickes, "but he is a likeable fellow notwithstanding and I always enjoy him, even if he is not a New Dealer." In 1939 Jones took on the added job of federal loan administrator. When Harry Hopkins felt obliged to resign as secretary of commerce in August 1940, Roosevelt offered the post to Jones. He accepted on condition that Congress allow him to keep his other jobs as well. No one else in the administration held so many important posts at the same time. The hope was that if anyone could use the RFC's loan power to boost the preparedness effort, Jones could. He was not only a master power broker but a consummate horse trader as well.[42]

Each material posed its own problem. More than a quarter of America's prodigious supply of iron ore came from the huge Mesabi range in Minnesota. A mile-wide string of mines stretched for a hundred miles northwest of Duluth, part of a complex expected to produce 100 million tons of the ore a year for as long as the war lasted. Calvin Coolidge, while president, once visited a Mesabi mine complex. After staring down into a vast pit three miles long, a mile wide, and 375 feet deep, he said with typical understatement, "That's a pretty big hole." During the past year the pretty big hole alone had produced 22 million tons of ore. To handle the enlarged shipping load, the government provided $58 million to build new port facilities at Escanaba, Michigan, on Lake Michigan.[43]

Manganese was crucial to making steel, which required about fourteen pounds of it for every ton of steel produced, or 850,000 tons if the industry ran at 90 percent capacity. The United States had no native high-grade manganese, but it did have the world's largest supply of low-grade manganese near Butte, Montana. In ordinary times it was not profitable to mine, but during World War I it had provided 35 percent of the nation's supply. In August 1940 Anaconda Copper signed a contract with the new Metals Reserve

Company to deliver 80,000 tons a year for three years. Claiming that it had a new process to turn the ore into high-grade manganese, Anaconda started work on a new $1.5 million plant.[44]

Americans used 75,000 tons of tin a year, 99 percent of which came from Europe and British Malaya. Although Bolivia had large deposits in this hemisphere, it lacked refineries to process the ore and sent most of it to Britain. The United States had only a couple of small, experimental smelters, but efforts were under way to expand smelting facilities in this country. Tin was essential for cans, solder, bronze, and bearing metals, among other things, yet the nation's reserve supply was low. Chromium, derived from chromite ore, was necessary for making steel alloys and other uses. Americans used about 350,000 tons a year, most of it from overseas sources. The industry had about 165,000 tons in reserve and was stepping up purchases to increase that amount. Silk was vital for parachutes and bags for powder charges; it was the only material that burned away completely when a cannon was fired. The United States had virtually no native supply, but during the past year DuPont had unveiled a promising new synthetic substitute called nylon, which had already become the rage in women's hosiery.[45]

Rubber posed the gravest dilemma of all. In normal times the nation used about 525,000 tons a year, 98 percent of it imported from the Far East over a 12,000-mile route that took more than two months to travel. By 1939 it had become the largest single commodity in dollar value imported into the United States. Motor vehicles, civilian and military, depended on rubber for tires, hoses, gaskets, wire insulation, and innumerable other uses, as did industry in general. Efforts to grow rubber trees in South America and Africa proved disappointing; new attempts offered no immediate help because rubber trees took seven years to mature. No supply of a raw material was more vulnerable or its loss more devastating than that of rubber. The need to accumulate a large stockpile was pressing. Jesse Jones knew it and was expected to respond accordingly. By 1940, however, another possibility loomed in the form of synthetic rubber.[46]

The Germans had pioneered in the development of synthetic rubber as early as World War I, when the British blockade throttled her supply of imported natural rubber and other vital materials. Nearly all of Hitler's vaunted blitzkrieg units and aircraft rolled on tires that never saw a rubber tree. The fall of Holland threw the fate of the Dutch East Indies into uncertainty. With the Germans and Japanese allied, the blow against both British and Dutch holdings in the Far East could come at any time and cut the United States off from its supply. Two options existed to counter this threat. Americans could start stockpiling as much rubber as possible, and they could follow the German example of investing heavily in the production of synthetic rubber.[47]

Stockpiling made a lot of sense. American manufacturers had long resented the violent fluctuation of rubber prices by the international cartel that controlled the market. Ridding the nation of dependence on overseas suppliers by developing a synthetic rubber industry made even more sense. Although the effort was already under way on a small scale, familiar obstacles could not be ignored. A synthetic rubber plant was a highly specialized facility requiring large quantities of alloy steel, special machinery, and skilled workmen. "To throw up huge plants now," concluded one writer, "diverting men and materials from sorely needed aircraft, munitions, and guns, would be a major blunder." By most estimates it would take two years to get the industry off the ground. No one knew when the emergency might come, if it came at all, or how long the war would last, and no manufacturer wanted to be stuck with large, nonsustaining plants if they were not definitely needed. Synthetic rubber products cost three to five times more to make than the natural product, especially when made in small quantities.[48]

Attempts had been made to grow the real thing elsewhere. Henry Ford started a rubber plantation in Brazil, Firestone in Liberia, and Goodyear in the Philippines. Thomas A. Edison tried to produce latex from milkweed, and rubber trees were planted in Florida. None of these projects succeeded for various reasons, leaving synthetic rubber as the only viable option. A few American companies, most notably Standard Oil of New Jersey, DuPont, and B. F. Goodrich, had been experimenting in the field for several years. In 1939 they turned out 2,000 tons of synthetic rubber and hoped to increase that output to 10,000 tons—still a superficial bump on the overall national needs. For Jesse Jones the message was plain: The country needed to buy as much rubber as possible as fast as possible, and it needed to invest in synthetic rubber plants using funds provided by the RFC's Rubber Reserve subsidiary.[49]

Unlike rubber, the steel industry was already the second largest in the nation behind automobiles. United States Steel dominated an oligopoly of thirteen integrated firms that controlled more than one third of total capacity. It too had absorbed the painful lessons of the depression. The word "expansion" was not in its vocabulary after a decade of surplus capacity and profit-devouring price wars. The fact that it was the most vital material for the preparedness drive did not alter the conviction of steel executives that they could meet any demand with the facilities they had. But in February 1940 U.S. Steel departed from its usual role by announcing that for the first time it would sell iron ore from its fabulous Mesabi range to competitors and that it would cut prices on the ore. That spring it declared the first dividend on its common stock since 1937 even though industry production had fallen to 60.7 percent of capacity after the surge generated by the abortive wartime boom.[50]

No one knew what to make of the steel situation. American firms owned about half the world's capacity, but not all of it was directly suitable for war needs. About 90 percent of its output came from open hearth furnaces and only 2 percent from electric furnaces, which were hotter and more precisely controlled and could turn out ingots of the highest grade. Many airplane parts, components of internal combustion engines, light armor plate for tanks, and machine tools needed the greater precision of electric furnaces. Republic Steel, run by Tom Girdler, led the nation in electric furnaces but could not begin to meet the growing preparedness demand. It planned to add two new giant electric furnaces to raise its capacity by 50 percent. At the same time, Bethlehem Steel, second only to U.S. Steel in size, declared that it would also add two new electric furnaces to triple its capacity. Bethlehem also planned to increase its capacity for making heavy armor plate, as did the only other three plants that made this product.[51]

Suddenly the notoriously unstable industry found itself running at 89.7 percent of capacity in August and 93 percent in September. The usual practice was to keep the furnaces running and defer all maintenance or repairs until the boom gave out, which it always did. But this boom looked different to steel executives. The defense contracts created a demand for heavy types of steel used in construction and capital goods work rather than the lighter steel sheets and strips for consumer goods. Naval vessels, forging steel for arsenals, and new locomotive orders, among others, all required heavy steel, and their demand showed no sign of slowing. Pittsburgh's Jones & Laughlin, the nation's number-four steel firm in size, specialized in heavy steel and had limped along until the surge propelled it to nearly 95 percent capacity. By mid-September the steel mills were doing so well that pig-iron production began to lag behind them and long-dormant coke ovens were being fired up again.[52]

Still the steel executives harbored grave doubts about how long the boom would last. Edward Stettinius, the U.S. Steel chairman who had moved on to NDAC, agreed with them that the industry had more than enough capacity to handle whatever was asked of it. After all, the United States produced nearly 67 million net tons of steel compared to 28.2 million for Germany, 21.8 million for Russia, and 15 million for Great Britain. The situation with manganese was bothersome but solvable despite what pessimists had to say, and more electric furnaces were coming online. If there was a problem, it could wait for another day.[53]

ONE KIND OF raw material posed the most sensitive and complex problem of all: manpower. It involved getting not only enough men for the military but also enough skilled workers for crucial industries. Beyond this obvious level it involved getting the right people—and the right number of people—in the right places. People could not be moved around like iron ore, and any plan drawn up to rationalize their use had to reckon with a host of outside influences. Politics would most certainly play a role, businesses and unions would have their say, and individuals would demand a voice in their own future. Freedom of choice was a core value of democracy, but in wartime it had to yield to national needs. The problem always was to find a balance point between them, which made democracies by their very nature less efficient than totalitarian governments.

In his July 10 message to Congress, Roosevelt called for funds to supply an army of 1.2 million men with another 800,000 in reserve, taking care to hedge the request by saying that "this total of men would not be in the Army in time of peace." Recruiting alone could not provide that many men, and certainly not in a hurry. The obvious solution was conscription, but that posed huge problems. There had never been a peacetime draft in the nation's history, and Congress would surely balk at passing one in the midst of an election campaign. Roosevelt favored conscription and had tried to get it written into the Democratic platform. When this effort failed, he mentioned the need for it in his acceptance speech. George Marshall understood the political danger and also wondered whether the army could even handle a large buildup in a short time.[54]

The strongest advocate turned out to be Henry Stimson, the new secretary of war, who was sworn into office that same July 10. At Roosevelt's request he had reviewed the president's message the day before and was disappointed to find no mention of a compulsory service bill. He called Roosevelt and said some mention had to be made of compulsory service; Roosevelt asked him to draw something up. Stimson got together with Marshall at the War Department and hurriedly put together a reference to a bill that had been introduced in Congress. Roosevelt added it to his message with some changes. The bill in question had caught everyone by surprise. Without consulting the president or the War Department, two conservative congressmen, Senator Edward R. Burke of Nebraska and Representative James W. Wadsworth Jr. of New York, introduced a bill calling for a national selective service system.[55]

Burke was a Democrat, Wadsworth a Republican who as a senator had helped shape the National Defense Act of 1920. Since neither could be called a New Dealer, the bill eased Roosevelt's efforts by lifting much of the onus from him. It also aroused unexpected support; a Gallup poll reported that 67 percent of those questioned favored a peacetime draft even though it was unprecedented. The basic provision called for immediate registration of about 42 million males between the ages of eighteen and sixty-four, with those between twenty-one and thirty called first for a year of military service. Those physically unfit would be exempted, and agricultural and industrial workers engaged in vital defense jobs would be deferred. Conscientious objectors would be exempted from combat but assigned to noncombat duty.[56]

The fight began at once. Roosevelt and Stimson both heard on good authority that the isolationists in Congress were confident of defeating the bill. Marshall began a string of pilgrimages to Capitol Hill to testify for it. Using Europe as his example, he warned that the nation faced "a tragic shortage of time" and would be in grave danger if it followed the fallen countries' example of preparing "too late and too little." Journalist Hanson W. Baldwin denied that the current situation necessitated a draft and advocated instead a well-trained professional army of 500,000 to 750,000. Longtime antiwar senator Burton K. Wheeler of Montana denounced the bill as "a step toward totalitarianism." Some liberal congressmen, most notably the venerable George W. Norris of Nebraska, announced that they would oppose the bill.[57]

To everyone's surprise, the bill generated some congressional and newspaper support. However, Roosevelt stayed mum on endorsing it, unwilling to roil the political waters. Until he spoke out, Stimson and Knox could not come before Congress to support the bill. The normally tactful Stimson gritted his teeth in frustration at the delay until he could stand it no longer. "God, Wadsworth," he blurted out to the congressman, "we ought to start it! Look what's going on in the world!" Roosevelt waited until after both the Republican nominating convention and his own nomination to break his silence. At a press conference on August 2, he wound up a somewhat convoluted explanation by saying, "That is why I have made it perfectly clear that I am in favor of a selective training bill . . . and consider it essential to adequate national defense."[58]

Still the fight raged on. As with isolationism, the opposing forces gathered strange bedfellows crossing party, economic, social, and political lines. Labor leader John L. Lewis, who was an isolationist and despised Roosevelt, identified conscription with dictatorship. The American Communist Party opposed the bill, as did the American Youth Congress. To the surprise of many, Eleanor Roosevelt wrote in her daily column, "The general feeling I encounter is that we should remain, where military service is concerned, on a voluntary basis." However, Wendell Willkie came out in favor of the draft, which neutralized the issue in the presidential campaign. When Stimson finally got before one of the congressional committees, he suffered their quibbling for a time, then barked, "All this talk of wait, wait, wait, and we're confronted by an enemy who does not wait!"[59]

Some weeks earlier Roosevelt had asked Congress for authority to call out the National Guard should an emergency arise when it was not in session. On July 29 he upped the ante by asking for power to place the Guard into service for a year to provide immediate training. Congress gave him the authority on August 27, by which time the Selective Service Act had gained momentum. Events were developing rapidly. The air battle over Britain began on August 8, and nine days later Germany declared a total blockade of Great Britain. On September 7 the Nazis switched tactics to the blitz—an unrelenting night bombing of London. Six days later Italian troops invaded Egypt, widening the Mediterranean conflict. As the war news grew gloomier, Congress passed the Selective Service Act on September 14, and Roosevelt signed it two days later. Work began at once on setting up the machinery to implement the draft.[60]

A second army was needed to implement the growing preparedness program, this one of skilled workers. Although the ranks of the unemployed still bulged with workers of all kinds, many were not in the right place with the right skills—or any skills at all. "An ironic commentary on our contemporary economic difficulties," said one writer in July, "is that, with more than ten million unemployed, there is even now in an increasing number of fields of activity shortage of skilled labor."[61]

To create this army, what was needed was not a draft but a massive training program, for which there would be eager volunteers. In July the New York City Board of Education announced its desire to recruit 10,000 men with some mechanical experience to undergo ten weeks of brush-up courses for work in armament plants. On the first day 5,000 applicants showed up at the recruiting desks, many having waited in line all night; within a week the total reached nearly 20,000, 4,000 of them mechanics. These men were sent to a dozen schools that ran two separate shifts, one for those working days and one for the unemployed. Similar programs were launched in a hundred other cities with the goal of turning out 150,000 trained machinists, lathe operators, welders, aviation mechanics, electricians, and radio technicians.[62]

On the national level Roosevelt had put forward the notion of conscripting 1.5 million trainees for "industrial defense," but that plan went nowhere. The American Federation of Labor (AFL) disputed whether a shortage of mechanics even existed given the number of unemployed. Already several potential sources were available for training industrial workers. Public vocational schools turned out half a million machinists a year, and the Civilian Conservation Corps (CCC) and National Youth Administration (NYA) had facilities for training those enrolled in their programs. A few large companies had their own apprentice programs, and the army its technical schools. The challenge was to find ways of coordinating and augmenting these efforts. This task belonged largely to Sidney Hillman, labor's representative on the NDAC.[63]

Like his corporate cohorts, Hillman was a dollar-a-year man living on his presidential salary of $12,500 from the Amalgamated Clothing Workers

Union. He operated out of an office so unadorned, noted one visitor, that "it has a perpetual untenanted look." As head of the Labor Division he took on a job that most observers regarded as somewhere between formidable and hopeless. He enlisted the help of Owen D. Young, the legendary retired chairman of General Electric, who had experience in organizing such training projects in World War I. In a concise memorandum, Young surveyed the problem and proposed a system of training within industries to be coordinated by the government's defense agencies. By late summer the plan was approved and implementation under way, despite protests from the AFL metal and machinery unions, which did not welcome the creation of thousands of new workers.[64]

The industrial workforce of America consisted of about 20 million people, 75 percent of them men and only 7 percent of them black. Hillman and Young tried to create a schema of the workers by occupation and location arranged in four tiers. The top level contained about 900,000 men skilled but unemployed and presumably available for work. Level two included an unknown number of people with misplaced skills, who had, for example, been trained as a machinist but forced to take some other job; they would require only refresher courses. Hillman was convinced that this pool was much larger than suspected. "It is a maldistribution of skilled labor, not a shortage that we face," he declared. "The real problem is the highly skilled machinist who— due to lack of work in his own trade—has been unemployed or forced to do something else."[65]

The lower tiers comprised differing types of vocational training. Level three embraced the large number of men being trained in company programs for work at a higher skill level. The fourth level included what Hillman called a "reservoir of assurance": 2 million men and women in vocational schools and another million in National Youth Administration and Civilian Conservation Corps programs. He also managed to rouse the U.S. Employment Service (USES) from its bureaucratic slumber to perform its first major task: an inventory by occupation and experience of the 5.7 million unemployed persons registered at the 1,500 public employment offices across the country. "There's nothing we need that we can't have," Hillman said early in his work. He soon found to his regret that in fact there was much he didn't have that was sorely needed.[66]

CHAPTER 4

THE ONUS OF ORGANIZATION

The President . . . must have talked for about an hour straight, and I was reminded of other occasions when he was developing a new idea . . . The plans that he outlined for the members of the commission were nebulous and inchoate . . . The commission was not to be executive so much as co-ordinating, and yet it appeared to be given certain executive powers . . . The whole session became more and more depressing, so far as I was concerned.

—HAROLD ICKES[1]

The New Deal has never prepared its own mind for preparedness. Its brilliant mentality has been dominated always by a silly prejudice . . . that preparedness meant profits for the munitions makers, whereas, in fact, the ablest advocates of preparedness were at the same time the strongest advocates of keeping profit out of it. Nor has the Government yet prepared either its own mind or that of the country.

—SATURDAY EVENING POST, JUNE 29, 1940[2]

The primary theme in industrial mobilization is that it is impossible to regulate or control the operation of one segment of our industrial economy without the concomitant supervision of all of the other factors with which that segment is joined.

—HARPER'S, JULY 1940[3]

WASHINGTON WAS NOTORIOUS FOR its awful weather, especially its sweltering summers that drove many natives elsewhere to escape the heat. The federal bureaucracy lumbered even slower than usual, and Congress took care to adjourn so that its members could flee the furnace during the summer months along with the army of lobbyists and other political camp followers. However, even veteran Washingtonians cringed at the stifling heat of July 1940. The venerable Henry Stimson, who had been around the city since the Taft administration, complained that July had witnessed "one of the longest and most severe hot periods that I can remember in Washington." Like many others, he was moved to install newfangled air-conditioning units in his home.[4]

Roosevelt did not follow suit. Although air-conditioning had recently been placed in six White House rooms, the president rarely used the unit in his study because it seemed to aggravate his chronic sinus problem, an affliction common to the city. Nor did he resort to an electric fan except for a small one in a distant corner. Instead he shed his coat and tie, unbuttoned his collar, rolled up his sleeves, and mopped his brow constantly as he worked. Sometimes he permitted himself the luxury of a short-sleeve shirt. His shirt and seersucker trousers soon lost their shape as the sweat flowed, but Sam Rosenman thought he actually enjoyed it.[5]

The heat was on Roosevelt in every sense that summer. In trying to mesh the urgency of the preparedness work with the practical needs of the presidential campaign, he did even more backing and filling than usual. Isolationists demanded that he stand down the effort and stop leading the nation toward war. All-outers pushed him to speed up the defense effort and create some mechanism like the WIB to direct and oversee the process. Bernie Baruch stood waiting in the wings, ready and eager to assume a role comparable to that he played in the First World War. Roosevelt was not about to let Baruch usurp the role that he intended for himself. Nor did he intend to let the businessmen starting to infiltrate Washington, or the military with its growing sense of importance, seize the reins of running the war effort.

Yet he had to do something. So far his only response had been to create the seven-member NDAC, which raised more questions than it answered. The advisory commission was neither fish nor fowl. Its stated purpose was "to translate the defense program from blueprints into action." In announcing its formation Steve Early told reporters that Roosevelt wanted to keep it flexible so that "it can be modified in the light of changing conditions." However, he added that the members "will not supersede anyone in the government but will work with them." One reporter took this to mean that "the board might be one in name only, the strings of operation being pulled by Administration overseers." The members were to coordinate procurement and expand industrial production. Each one oversaw a particular area: William Knudsen took charge of industrial production, Edward Stettinius industrial materials, Sidney Hillman labor and employment issues, Leon Henderson price stabilization, Chester Davis farm products, Ralph Budd transportation, and Harriet Elliott consumer protection.[6]

Put another way, NDAC's role was to translate defense appropriations into actual factory operations as quickly as possible, preferably within six months. At first only Knudsen, Stettinius, and Hillman served full-time. Although they were expected to coordinate their activities, Roosevelt appointed no one as chairperson. At the end of the first meeting Knudsen asked Roosevelt, "Who is boss?" Roosevelt replied with a laugh, "I guess I am." The president intended to chair the weekly sessions when possible. William H. McReynolds served as secretary to the commission, which had no office or home base. Nor did it receive any authority to carry out its mission other than the prestige of its members. Despite its vague structure and lack of power, the commission tried vigorously to exert operational influence in production and procurement.[7]

The three leading figures on the commission could not have been more different from each other in personality and background. Bill Knudsen enjoyed enormous prestige and respect as one of the nation's foremost developers of mass production. The big, burly, amiable Dane had migrated to America at the age of twenty and worked his way through a variety of horny-handed jobs to the presidency of General Motors in 1937. He left that $300,000-a-year post to come to the NDAC at a dollar a year because he was an ardent patriot. "I am most happy," he wrote Roosevelt after being appointed, "you've made it possible for me to show my gratitude to my country for the opportunity it has given me to acquire home, family and happiness in abundant measure." Knudsen loathed red tape, publicity, and politics. A man of simple tastes, he spoke with a soft Danish accent and impressed everyone with his honest, direct manner.[8]

Production was Knudsen's passion and his genius. He had been present at the creation of mass production, working as one of Henry Ford's bright young men who did their part to bring the first moving assembly line into existence at the Highland Park plant in 1913. From this experience he absorbed several valuable lessons he later put to good use: the critical role of interchangeable parts; the necessity of continuous flow on the production line; the importance of arranging machines in the best possible way to expedite that flow; the value of a moving line to increase output; and the virtue of simplicity of design. In its quest for efficiency, Ford's men managed in six months to cut the assembly time for an engine from 9 hours and 56 minutes to 5 hours and 56 minutes. On this base of experience Knudsen built a sterling reputation for production, first at Ford and then at General Motors.[9]

Edward Stettinius Jr. was the son of a J. P. Morgan partner who had served as assistant secretary of war during World War I. Starting at General Motors as a mechanic, he became assistant to President Alfred Sloan and a vice president before moving briefly to a post in the Roosevelt administration. In 1934 he joined U.S. Steel and became chairman four years later. Tall and handsome with silver hair, he married into a prominent Virginia family and spent his leisure time on a 500-acre stock farm there. That he was ambitious no one doubted; whether his ability matched his ambitions remained an open question.[10]

Like Knudsen, Sidney Hillman was an immigrant made good. A native of Zagare, Lithuania, he spent ten months in jail during the country's abortive 1905 uprising and afterward fled to the United States via England. After finding his way to Chicago he became an apprentice cutter at Hart, Schaffner & Marx. His part in a 1910 labor dispute launched his career in the labor movement. Hillman organized 95 percent of the men's clothing industry and in 1915 assumed the presidency of the Amalgamated Clothing Workers of America. In that position he created a number of innovative social programs for his workers. Amid the labor turmoil following passage of the Wagner Act, he helped organize the Congress of Industrial Organizations (CIO) in 1937. Slight of figure with curly hair and spectacles, Hillman looked more like a professor than a labor leader. Unlike his rival and nemesis, John L. Lewis, he was cautious, diplomatic, and undramatic. He was a devout supporter of Roosevelt and preferred quiet negotiations to histrionic displays.[11]

Hillman's ability shone through his earliest days as an American labor leader and negotiator. Joseph Schaffner of Hart, Schaffner & Marx said of him, "That man Hillman is a wonderful genius . . . Beyond his supreme talent in leading men he has a quality that is even more remarkable. That is his absolute integrity. He is the squarest labor leader I have ever known." Those qualities would be put to a severe test during the years after 1939.[12]

Knudsen's job was to facilitate the production of munitions not usually manufactured. His division gathered or estimated military requirements, figured out how much of each kind of goods the economy could produce, and decided whether new plants or equipment were needed to produce them. It got involved in negotiating contracts, locating and building new factories, and ensuring timely delivery. In these tasks Knudsen worked more closely with the military than did the other divisions. Predictably, most of his staff came from the corporate world as dollar-a-year men who left their companies to help with the defense effort. They were, after all, the men who knew most about production, but their presence made longtime New Dealers uneasy.[13]

Stettinius's Materials Division did work with raw materials similar to that Knudsen's group performed for production. The dividing line between them revolved around fabrication; Stettinius had charge of covered steel and armored plate, for example, while Knudsen handled ships and tanks. His work also included stockpiling essential materials and inevitably drew him into what became one of the most critical areas of concern: priorities. Like Knudsen, Stettinius drew heavily on the business world for his staff, especially trade associations and their officials. Conflicts of interest, real and suspected, emerged more commonly here than in any other division. At one point Leon Henderson, an ardent New Dealer, complained that some of the people under Stettinius "do not know who their client is."[14]

The deep, often bitter animosity between the New Dealers and businessmen created tensions that were hard to dispel. Creation of the NDAC and the growing importance of the War Department disturbed many New Dealers. "He started out with the firm announcement that he was not going to have a supergovernment," Ickes said of the president, "that the people whom he would bring to Washington would have to work through the regular establishments. But, all at once, apparently he gave a clearance to Knudsen and Stettinius and they have already gone far toward creating a supergovernment." Ickes, William O. Douglas, Archibald MacLeish, Ben Cohen, and Tommy Corcoran all worried that the whole New Deal accomplishment had been placed in jeopardy. Others had more parochial concerns. William Green, head of the AFL, complained most bitterly about Sidney Hillman being on the commission.[15]

Hillman's work was no less important or difficult. The three sections of his division had very different assignments. Labor Relations sought to keep labor peace in defense plants and avoid any interruption of production. Labor Supply and Training took on the job of increasing the supply of skilled labor, especially by promoting vocational training in state schools and within companies. The third section, Labor Requirements and Employment Standards, tried to estimate how many of which kinds of workers were needed where. It also worked to standardize wages and hours across geographic and industrial areas and to protect labor standards from erosion. The ancient tensions between business and labor hampered Hillman's relationship with those divisions dominated by corporate officials. He also had to mediate labor disputes, and the unions put constant pressure on him to withhold contracts from companies that ignored the nation's labor laws. Nor did it help that Hillman's health was fragile.[16]

The other divisions took a back seat to these three. Henderson's Price Stabilization Division was charged with monitoring prices and recommending steps to prevent inflation. While doing this job, Henderson extended his influence through sheer force of personality. A blunt-speaking, cigar-smoking bear of a man, he became a driving force within NDAC for centralizing mobilization programs and getting the agency to act as a unified body rather than as separate divisions. Unlike many ardent New Dealers, he understood the nuances of power and the need for compromise. Davis's Agricultural Division performed a number of useful studies but did little else. Budd took a crabbed view of his role as facilitator of transportation coordination and accomplished little, and Elliott's Consumer Division left little imprint.[17]

A more significant contribution came from a man who joined the NDAC as head of the Office for Coordination of National Defense Purchases. In this role quiet, unassuming Donald Nelson made a lasting impact and a reputation that elevated him into someone worth watching.

AS A BOY in his native Hannibal, Missouri, Don Nelson grew up in the shadow of Mark Twain's fictional world. He swam in the Mississippi and played on the same islands as Tom Sawyer and Huck Finn, knew the man on whom Injun Joe was supposed to be modeled, and took piano lessons in the house where Samuel Clemens lived as a boy. Once during a lesson the great man himself stopped by to reminisce with the piano teacher about the house. When Clemens was in town, Nelson sometimes saw him sitting in a straight-backed chair on the veranda of the Kettering Hotel, rocking back against the wall and talking to old cronies or anyone passing by. He was, Nelson thought, "as common ... as an old shoe." He didn't know why Clemens was considered a great man, but the old man's white flannel suit and shock of white hair fascinated him.[18]

Although Nelson was born—by his own admission—on the "wrong side of Bear Creek," Hannibal was for him "a great town, probably the sort of place where all American boys should be born." In that all-American town he enjoyed a pleasant if unexceptional childhood. His father was an engineer on the Katy railroad, and his mother died when he was three, leaving her mother the task of raising the boy. He played baseball, took a shine to chemistry in high school, and went on to get a degree in chemical engineering at the University of Missouri. After graduating in 1911 he hoped to go on to Harvard for a doctorate but first had to earn the money to do so. In April 1912 he took a temporary job at Sears, Roebuck and stayed for thirty years. He received schooling and an apprenticeship in textile manufacturing before returning to Chicago to organize a pioneer textile-testing laboratory for Sears.[19]

During the World War Nelson got a brief taste of the WIB. Julius Rosenwald, the president of Sears, sat on the board and sent a steady stream of textile samples for testing to Nelson's laboratory. After the war Nelson received what he considered the "very odious assignment" of obtaining scientific descriptions of merchandise for the Sears catalog that were 100 percent accurate. This work made him unpopular with virtually every buyer the company had. During the 1920s he rose through the ranks by managing a variety of clothing departments until 1930, when he became vice president in charge of merchandising and a director of the company. In 1939 he was made executive vice president and chairman of the executive committee with a salary of $70,000 a year. He had arrived at what he deemed "the very best job I had ever had in my life. I was more comfortable in material benefits and prospects for the future than I had ever expected to be."[20]

To most people Nelson seemed the very model of the modern corporate executive. His round, smooth-featured face with its owlish glasses radiated pleasantness and good cheer. Tall, rotund, and slow moving, with a thoughtful, soft-spoken manner that never shouted for attention, he made friends easily and was quick with praise even while demanding more effort from subordinates. While puffing on his omnipresent pipe he seemed lost in thought, yet no one doubted that he knew his stuff and got things done in a quiet, efficient manner. He had a voracious appetite for work. In 1934 Nelson got his first taste of Washington with an appointment to the National Recovery Administration (NRA). Later he referred to it as "my first sentence in the chain gang of bureaucracy." After returning to Chicago he told a reporter, "I would not take a million dollars for my experience in Washington, and I wouldn't give five cents for another day of it."[21]

Early in May 1940 Henry Morgenthau telephoned the chairman of Sears, General Robert E. Wood, to ask for the services of his vice president in charge of factories. The man was not immediately available, Wood replied, and suggested Nelson instead—provided the assignment lasted no more than two months. When Morgenthau agreed, Wood broke the news to Nelson by saying he had sold him down the river—but for two months only. Nelson arrived at Morgenthau's office on May 17 and was told that an acting director of procurement was needed to help handle all the requests by foreign governments for raw materials and manufactured products. Nelson agreed to stay for two or three months to help set up the operation. Thus began his second sentence in Washington, one that gave him "a grandstand seat . . . at the most stupendous and dramatic show in history."[22]

Morgenthau impressed him deeply with his "extraordinary insight into the currents of world affairs." He made Nelson realize that his private interests no longer mattered as they once did and that "within a relatively few months the kind of world in which we could live might collapse." Even before the fall of France Morgenthau convinced him that war with Germany was inevitable. On his third day in office Nelson met with a Canadian member of the British Purchasing Commission, who awakened him not only to the gravity of the crisis but to the acute Allied need for planes, tanks, and guns. After a meeting hosted by Morgenthau the army and navy launched a mad scramble to gather enough planes to aid the beleaguered French while Nelson's staff concocted a legal argument for the transfer. The frantic effort succeeded, and the planes were transferred to a French aircraft carrier in Quebec. Shortly after the carrier left harbor, however, the French surrendered, and the carrier sailed instead to Martinique, where it remained for most of the war.[23]

A few days later Morgenthau called Nelson into his office and introduced him to Louis Renault, the French automobile manufacturer, who had come to negotiate a rush order for tanks. While they talked, Nelson's secretary handed him a note saying that France had surrendered. He showed the note to Renault, who burst into tears and fled the room. Immediately Morgenthau and Nelson set to work transferring the large French orders for machine tools, tanks, planes, guns, bombs, and other items to the British, who were sorely in need of everything. Some of the material was already waiting in warehouses and on piers. Again some legal sleight-of-hand was needed to effect the transfer, but Morgenthau and his assistants got it done. Less than a week later came Dunkirk with its horrific loss of men and equipment.[24]

For Don Nelson the war was no longer a distant event but a stark and terrifying reality. His second sentence in Washington would be much more prolonged than he imagined. Unlike many businessmen, Nelson was comfortable around New Dealers and often talked the same language. His first sentence in Washington with the NRA had toughened him to the devious and often vicious ways of politics there. Having no political ambitions of his own, he could concentrate on doing his job as well as possible. The new coordinator's office, created in June, made him an equal of the other seven advisers. No man had better credentials for purchasing work. At Sears, Nelson had overseen the legendary catalog and dealt in 100,000 items provided by more than six thousand suppliers. He had some lessons to teach those procurement officers of the military who regarded change as a disease to be avoided at all costs.[25]

NELSON WAS STILL on Morgenthau's staff when the NDAC was created, but within a short time he was asked to sit in on a meeting and discuss purchasing. Most of the members were old friends of his, and they talked freely about their confusion over who was to do what. Nelson directed the Procurement Division of the Treasury Department, which had authority to make purchases for all government departments except the army and navy. The armed services were adamant in not wanting civilians involved in their procurement work. Roosevelt was equally determined not to let the military gain control of the nation's economy. At NDAC's suggestion he appointed a committee to look into the problem. On June 28 the committee reported that serious gaps existed in the purchasing procedures of both civilian and military authorities. It proposed several steps to improve a badly flawed system.[26]

Although no one could know it at the time, the recommendations proved remarkably prescient in pinpointing problems that were to plague the procurement effort throughout the war. The committee wanted purchasing coordinated to avoid competition between federal agencies for both materials and finished products. To that end it asked that all federal materials requirements, present and future, be compiled in one list. Wherever the combined requirements exceeded the available supply, some system of priorities and/or allocations should be devised. The purchasing function should be assigned to whatever agency was best qualified to perform it within existing legal restraints, and any current delays in purchasing should be eliminated by corrective legislation.[27]

Roosevelt accepted the report and asked the commissioners for someone to serve as coordinator of purchasing. They suggested Nelson, who was preparing to return home as his sentence neared its end. Roosevelt summoned him to his office and, in his inimitable way, persuaded him to take the job. When Nelson joined the commission, its relations with the military were relatively cordial. Nelson himself declared that his "number one job" was to "help the Army to get what it wants when it wants it." Most of the army's procurement was done by the Ordnance and Quartermaster departments, with the rest divided among five smaller departments. Their pattern in peacetime had been to solicit bids and award contracts to large suppliers whose work was familiar and reliable. Given their small scale of operations, this approach posed few problems; however, the sheer size of the mobilization drive quickly created bottlenecks and confusion.[28]

The War Department inherited by Henry Stimson was in poor shape to preside over a major military buildup. The National Defense Act of 1920 authorized the assistant secretary of war to handle procurement and planning on his own rather than under direction of the secretary of war. It was this fact, among other things, that led to the constant fights between Woodring and Louis Johnson. In December 1940 Stimson got Congress to amend the law by changing the assistant secretary to an undersecretary who did procurement and planning at the bidding of the secretary. Even before that change occurred, Bob Patterson organized his activities in close cooperation with Stimson, who gladly delegated authority to him. Together they built the most powerful executive department in the federal government. Patterson was tough, dedicated, and a soldier at heart. He occupied a desk used by William Tecumseh Sherman and wore combat boots to the office with his suit.[29]

Since 1921 the assistant secretary had had in his office a procurement division with two branches, one for current procurement and the other a planning branch. Between 1921 and 1940 the planning branch grew into a large organization that dominated peacetime procurement efforts. From it emerged the Army-Navy Munitions Board, the Army Industrial College, planning sections of the supply arms and services, and the development of IMP. Although created in October 1922 to coordinate the needs of the two services, ANMB did little for a decade because the navy showed little interest. In peacetime the navy was considered the first line of defense and managed to get appropriations for ships while the army went begging for even basic equipment. In July 1939 Roosevelt moved ANMB to the Executive Office, placing the assistant secretary directly under himself at a time when Woodring showed no interest in rearmament. As the mobilization effort increased, ANMB's role expanded.[30]

Even in peacetime military procurement was a complicated business. In World War I the army's catalog of needed goods exceeded 700,000 items. By the end of 1940 the list of major components had been whittled down to 7,400 items classified into three categories: those easily obtained; those relatively easy to obtain and requiring only minor advance planning; and those difficult to obtain and needing formal planning. In times of war requirements could change drastically because of unforeseen developments in strategy, tactics, shift of theaters of operation, weaponry design, and other causes. To cope with these and other variables, planners concluded that "the best preparation appears to be a thorough knowledge of past procurement efforts in war to insure that past mistakes will not be repeated."[31]

But this was fiendishly difficult to do in an environment where the instruments and tactics of war changed so rapidly. To complicate matters, military planning assumed that there would be an "M-day" when the nation shifted from peace to war. Nothing in their plans envisioned the state of limbo that existed during 1940–41 in which the country might go to war at some unknown date in the future. The notion of an M-day had been a crucial part of every version of IMP. "On M-Day, the day on which this country enters a state of war," observed a writer, "the entire military machine of the nation comes to life." Mobilizing for an uncertain role at an unknown date against one or more possible enemies on both sides of the globe posed a whole different set of problems. Procurement officers also had to deal with a hopelessly dense tangle of laws, regulations, court decisions, and other rulings that had grown up around the process to prevent "blood profits," labor abuse, and other problems.[32]

These legal obstacles ranged from special interest and special purpose restrictions to procedural requirements that bound public contracts in red tape. Whatever their other merits, the restrictions slowed procurement to a crawl. Contracts also presented a challenge. During World War I each of the six existing supply branches had its own contracts, requiring a total of 400 different forms. A permanent War Contract Board, created in 1922, resolved most of the difficulties encountered during the war. Four basic contract forms were devised to meet most needs. The War Department preferred fixed-price contracts for most situations but resorted to other forms when the need arose.[33]

The military's procurement planning also included an allocation system "designed to earmark and prepare specific plants for particular tasks so that a minimum of time would be lost in getting emergency production under way." For those products that were difficult to make and/or required large amounts of key raw materials, the goal was to spread the load over those companies able to manufacture them. A flexible measuring system was created and more than 10,000 plants listed as key to productive capacity. Predictably, they were the largest corporations; the military had no practical way in an emergency to make direct contracts with the 250,000 firms that comprised American industry. Both military planners and industrialists realized that a war emergency would require massive adjustments of any plans they made.[34]

Twenty years of planning, however flawed, had given the military a lead over the civilian agencies in the mobilization process. Despite the veneer of cordiality, the military was as suspicious of civilians as labor was of businessmen, and vice versa. Yet Stimson came to like and admire Knudsen for his ability and no-nonsense approach. "My impression of Mr. Knudsen's ability and his tact grows with each time I see him," he noted. "He is doing very well." Knudsen's tact had ample room for growth. A public relations man got a taste of his style when he introduced himself. Without looking up from his desk Knudsen asked, "Can you build a tank?" Startled, the man said no. "Then I won't be seeing much of you," replied Knudsen in a tone that ended the conversation.[35]

Along with planes, tanks, and ships, a construction boom was under way. Powder plants had to be built and other facilities expanded. Once new plants were located, housing for workers would be needed as well. The army needed storehouses, barracks, hangars, repair shops, and other buildings, while the navy looked to construct dry docks, airfields, and other shore installations. The $5 billion already appropriated by July amounted to spending $13.7 million every day, and Congress authorized another $4 billion to create a two-ocean navy and still had before it Roosevelt's request for another $5 billion.[36]

To expedite this work Knudsen got authority from Roosevelt to approve most contracts totaling $500,000 or more. Nelson also had the job of clearing contracts. To avoid overlap Knudsen oversaw contracts for ordnance and other "hard goods" while Nelson took charge of quartermaster supplies and "soft goods." That summer NDAC and the War Department thrashed out a nine-point guideline for military contracting that tried to recognize such factors as protection of labor, use of negotiated contracts, and avoiding congestion caused by awarding too many contracts to one firm or region. The military paid little attention to the guidelines. Adamant in its rejection of civilian interference in contracting, it continued to emphasize two primary factors: reliability of the contractor and speed of delivery. Contracts were submitted to NDAC for clearance only after negotiations on them were virtually complete, leaving Knudsen the option only of vetoing them and thereby delaying the work. Even when NDAC cleared contracts, the military did not hesitate to modify them later.[37]

Nelson had better luck, partly because he dealt with goods that, unlike munitions, were produced by a wide variety of existing firms. Where Knudsen's concern was chiefly production, Nelson's was almost entirely procurement. Since the military claimed no special expertise in such goods, its officers were more amenable to learning new tricks from a master buyer like Nelson. Lieutenant General Edmund B. Gregory, the quartermaster general, welcomed the help of Nelson and his staff, all of whom were experienced buyers of goods in quantity. Nelson emphasized two key approaches to the task of supplying an army that was about to mushroom in size. The first was to utilize a broad network of firms, large and small and spread across the country, in order not to clog a few companies trying to fill orders for both the military and civilians. The second was to time orders so that they reached manufacturers during their slow season.[38]

Clothing, for example, was a seasonal industry that responded well to the old trick of off-season buying. The rush to produce blankets occurred from August through October as retailers anticipated winter demand. The army needed 1.2 million blankets but couldn't order them until the July 1 appropriation. Placing the whole order at once would have congested the mills and spurred a rise in price. Nelson persuaded the army to feed the order in gradually through the slow winter months. His staff also got the Quartermaster Corps to centralize its procurement of meat and produce and thereby eliminate middlemen. Above all, they sold the army on the concept of "distributive buying": spreading contracts according to the availability of facilities, workforce, and materials as well as the prospect of continued production and stable prices.[39]

The army had long relied on sealed bids, a slow but reliable way of buying goods in normal times. Mobilization changed the game radically, however, through the sheer quantity and speed of its demands. Businesses rarely bought through sealed bids but used negotiated contracts. Nelson persuaded Gregory to give this method a try even though many of his officers opposed changing the familiar way of doing things. Nelson's approach had two major advantages: It spread the business over a much larger number of firms and in the process gave hundreds of smaller companies some experience with war contracts that might prove useful later. Gregory agreed to try Nelson's methods and was pleased with the results. Gradually they worked out a set of principles for buying soft goods that won approval from the military, the president, and Congress.[40]

WHILE NELSON SUCCEEDED in establishing a rapport with the military, Knudsen struggled mightily with the much larger task of pushing the production of hard goods and coping with an intractable Ordnance Department. Between June and December 1940 the military awarded over $11 billion in contracts, of which 60 percent went to only twenty corporations and 86.4 percent to a hundred companies. The finalizing of these contracts got bogged down in a quagmire of issues. Foremost among them was the dispute over the expansion of facilities to produce war goods. New plants had to be built and existing ones expanded. How was this to be done and on what basis? During its short life NDAC helped to promote $9 billion in facilities expansion, but the process proved painful.[41]

Every contract, whether for planes, engines, tanks, ships, barracks, guns, or other goods, had to run a gauntlet of issues, each of which caused frustrating delays while they were resolved. Who would erect the new or expanded plant, government or private industry? How would it be financed? What would be done with it once the emergency ended? These questions alone held up negotiations for a new engine plant near Cincinnati for more than six weeks. Would the tax laws allow faster amortization of private investment? This prolonged debate delayed a deal for Packard to manufacture airplane engines and several other pending contracts. Most corporations hesitated to act until these questions were answered. As a result, large numbers of contracts dangled in limbo through the summer and early fall of 1940.[42]

Prior to the creation of NDAC, the government included in its early defense contracts the cost of facility expansion with a proviso that when the contract ended, the company would own the addition. Morgenthau and others adamantly opposed this arrangement as unfair to both the government and competing firms lacking such contracts. The government could simply build and own the plants, leasing them to private companies during the emergency, but Congress allotted only $750 million to the military for building new facilities of all kinds in the last half of 1940. This left the Roosevelt administration with two choices. It could persuade private enterprise to underwrite new facilities or it could concoct some new approach to the problem.[43]

Few companies were eager to make the investment. Many still shuddered at their World War I experience, when the government sued them to recover funds advanced to expand their plants. They also feared being stuck with excess capacity once the emergency ended, and who knew when that would be? After all, the country wasn't at war, and the president kept insisting that it would not be. Manufacturers wanted new facilities if they could be had on good terms, and bankers sniffed fresh opportunities for financing. Recalling the disastrous financial aftermath of the last war, they demanded two concessions before underwriting expansion: a 20 percent (five-year) depreciation allowance on new defense plants, and repeal of a provision limiting profits on aircraft and shipbuilding to 8 percent. NDAC sponsored the amortization bill; however, the decision to link these provisions to Roosevelt's bill seeking an excess profits tax left the whole package stalled in Congress.[44]

New Dealers sneered at what they deemed selfish motives on the part of industrialists. "Our defense program is still being held up while certain 'patriotic' manufacturers of airplanes and other war materials haggle about the pending tax bill," grumbled Harold Ickes in early September. He had long protested the government's building and equipping plants at its own expense "while permitting private individuals and corporations to make excessive profits at practically no risk to themselves." But the businessmen had a point. Their "patriotism" had been badly burned the last time around, and their amortization request in particular seemed a reasonable protection in so uncertain an environment. Nevertheless, I. F. Stone ridiculed what he called "the sitdown strike of capital."[45]

Morgenthau told Roosevelt bluntly that it was "a lousy bill" that contained "the very kinds of discrimination that the President and the Treasury have for so many years opposed." Eleanor Roosevelt said much the same thing, not only to her husband but in her column as well. But the president would not be swayed. Sitting in his rocker on the back porch at Hyde Park that summer, he told Morgenthau over and over, "I want a tax bill; I want one damned quick; I don't care what is in it; I don't want to know . . . The contracts are being held up and I want a tax bill."[46]

Stettinius presented a sunnier picture for his Materials Division. Six weeks into his work he issued a progress report assuring the nation of "adequate supplies of critical and strategic materials." He had no kind words for three anti–New Deal congressmen who blocked a $25 million appropriation for a Tennessee Valley Authority (TVA) dam because they hated the agency. Stettinius reminded them that more TVA power was essential for producing aluminum, which was coming to be in short supply. Rubber was the most sensitive and worrisome commodity, but the report claimed that a solution was in sight through the building of plants to produce synthetic versions.

Tin, which came from Bolivia and the Far East but was smelted in Britain, was being stockpiled. The output of 100-octane gasoline for airplanes was being stepped up, and other key materials were being accumulated.[47]

By August complaints of bottlenecks and delays filled the media. An exasperated Stimson told two congressional committees that contracts had been let for only 33 of the 4,000 planes authorized since June because of uncertainty over amortization and future taxation. Some critics charged that presidential politics had also poisoned the process. *Fortune* assessed the overall defense effort and concluded that "it is no exaggeration to say that nine months of preparation were partially lost." Nor did it help that southern and western congressmen did not hesitate to buttonhole War Department and NDAC officials seeking plants, camps, and other facilities for their undeveloped states. Senator Pat Harrison of Mississippi importuned Stimson to place a military camp in his state. However, the general in charge of the Construction Division assured Stimson that, after close investigation, Mississippi, Georgia, Alabama, and Louisiana had "absolutely no people capable of building as promptly as we need to get it done before cold weather, construction of the size as is required in these camps."[48]

Stimson and Patterson were beside themselves over the delays. As a first step Stimson tried to persuade Roosevelt and Sidney Hillman to let him put the government arsenals on a temporary forty-eight-hour week to boost production. Roosevelt balked on the grounds that the longer workweek might become permanent. When, to his surprise, Hillman agreed because it meant hiring nearly 20,000 more men altogether, the president relented. The arsenals went to three eight-hour shifts six days a week instead of five days. But nothing seemed to move the tax bill forward. As the complaints over delays in the airplane program grew louder, Stimson resented his department taking heat for a problem that belonged entirely to Congress.[49]

Early in September Stimson invited Knudsen to his office and raised the question of getting the automobile manufacturers to stop making their annual model changes while a shortage of machine tools continued. Knudsen thought the move premature because the delay in facilities expansion meant that more tools were not immediately needed, and the automobile industry didn't begin preparing for their new models until December. But Knudsen had his own requests. He suggested that all models for munitions or military equipment be frozen to avoid the delays inherent in constant design changes, and he wanted the location of all new plants frozen to get rid of the political pressure on those agencies choosing sites. The next morning Stimson had to endure the protest of a Kentucky contingent led by Senator Alben Barkley against the mechanization of a National Guard horse regiment.[50]

Two days later Stimson received the shocking news that a huge explosion had swallowed up the Hercules powder plant in Kenvil, New Jersey, killing forty-three and injuring 200 people. It was the only plant making the special powder used in antiaircraft guns, leading Stimson to suspect sabotage. This left only the DuPont plant capable of making small-arms powder until two new plants under construction opened and Hercules reopened. On top of that came word that Thurman Arnold of the Justice Department's Antitrust Division was threatening to bring suits against some major defense corporations at this critical juncture. There seemed no end of aggravations at a time when Stimson was struggling to take hold of his department and weed out the dead wood to improve its efficiency. "If I was not overworked and could sleep," he complained to his friend Felix Frankfurter, "and were younger and a few other things I might get through, as it is I don't know."[51]

Knudsen managed to persuade some aircraft manufacturers to begin expanding even though the tax bill had not passed, but he too was frustrated by the commission's lack of authority and piecemeal approach to solving problems. "It is one vast bottleneck," he admitted. Stettinius agreed that "Until we really get rolling, everything is apt to be a bottleneck." On the key expansion issue the commission remained a house divided. Stettinius supported industry's reluctance to expand, as did Knudsen to some degree. Nelson, Henderson, and Hillman favored maximizing output through immediate expansion, while Budd, Davis, and Elliott seemed more interested in where facilities got located and their impact on local communities. Hillman also insisted that all contracts contain provisions protecting workers.[52]

A broader split also complicated their work. The New Dealers wanted control of the preparedness effort to remain within existing agencies, while the military demanded a temporary superagency like the WIB manned by "patriotic business leaders." On this and other issues NDAC was not only powerless but a house divided against itself. Baruch came to speak to the commission and laid out his ideas about organization. He emphasized the importance of priorities, which he called the "synchronizing force" of all war production, and the need for price controls. Predictably, he repeated his familiar call for centralizing all requirements in one agency that could oversee all activity, headed by someone like himself.[53]

Late in August Roosevelt took a break from these intramural squabbles to see for himself how the army was faring. He spent two days observing troop maneuvers and came away more discouraged than ever. "Anybody who knows anything about the German methods of warfare would know that that army would have been licked by thoroughly trained and organized forces of a similar size within a day or two," he wrote a friend privately. The soldiers lacked many kinds of modern equipment and were not well trained to use the arms they had. Even worse, he added, "the men themselves are soft...It would take a good long time to accomplish for them what the German armies are capable of doing." If this was any indication, the road ahead was going to be a lot longer and tougher than most people realized.[54]

THE MOBILIZATION OF American resources for the war effort extended to one of the most crucial yet elusive of all: brainpower. Trying to identify, organize, and utilize the talents of scientists, inventors, engineers, and other technical people posed a unique challenge to a government that had little knowledge and even less experience of how to go about it. Yet the need was urgent. "This is the most technical of all wars in history," declared *Fortune*. ". . . The U.S., therefore, can hardly win total victory unless it bends and coordinates its highest technology to the task everywhere." Physicist Arthur H. Compton was even more blunt. "In modern warfare," he insisted, "one hundred trained physicists may be more valuable than one million infantrymen."[55]

American brainpower was even more widely scattered than America's farmers. Basic scientific research took place mostly in universities with a smattering in a handful of industrial laboratories. Applied science and product research could be found throughout industry, which had gone heavily into the field after World War I. Development engineering ranged through universities, research foundations, industrial laboratories, and countless facilities of individual inventors. Pockets of technological research honeycombed a host of government agencies from the Department of Agriculture to the Bureau of Mines to the Bureau of Standards to TVA. The military had its own technical subdivisions doing work in aviation, ordnance, engineering, medicine, and other areas. No clearinghouse existed to locate and coordinate all this work; nor had the government ever developed a strong technical civil service.[56]

By early 1941 the problem of cataloging brainpower had grown more intense as manufacturers began pirating each other's technical people. Two federal agencies were compiling a National Roster of Scientific and Specialized Personnel, but it was flawed and incomplete. A group of engineers in Detroit devised a plan to compile a local inventory of brainpower by going directly to all the employers in the state with a questionnaire. Distributed through 2,200 employers, the questionnaire divided technicians into nine occupational groups and asked each respondent to list a major and minor field. It was a start but did not extend beyond Michigan.[57]

When the war began, only one integrated technical body existed. The National Advisory Committee for Aeronautics (NACA) had been founded in 1915 to conduct and supervise basic research in aviation, using government money. It had achieved an impressive safety and performance record in commercial aviation but until recently had neither funds nor incentive to keep up with the rapid development of military aircraft elsewhere in the world. The National Academy of Sciences traced its origins to 1863, but its members came together on a volunteer basis to deal with specific problems. The military, steeped in tradition, viewed innovation in weaponry with dark suspicion and refused steadfastly to share its research with civilians. As a result, the nation lagged far behind the Germans not only in military strength but in quality of weapons.[58]

Physicist Isidor Rabi got a firsthand taste of the military's obsession with secrecy when the navy asked for some black boxes to be developed with certain voltages and other features. When Rabi asked what they were for, he was told, "We prefer to talk about that in our swivel chairs in Washington." Rabi did not reply and did nothing about the request, continuing instead his work to develop short-distance radar. Six months later the navy officials returned with the same request. "Now, look," said Rabi, "let's stop kidding. Bring your man who understands aircraft, and we'll talk about your problems." This time the navy did so, and Rabi learned that they needed a shipborne, height-finding radar to supplement and guide equipment already in their carrier-based planes. "We made an agreement with the Navy," Rabi added. "We'll develop that if you and we can do the whole thing together—a partnership. We are in this war together. We can talk about the whole thing, whatever it is, and then our side will do its best to develop the appropriate radar. Which it did."[59]

The experience impressed an important lesson on Rabi. "As time went on," he said, "we set up an effective pattern of interdependence with the military . . . After we learned to get along with the military men, we grew to have a deep respect for them. Respect for their devotion and hard work. We got along with them once they saw we were not there to take anything away from them but actually to help them."[60]

The mechanism for forging this odd-couple relationship was the brainchild of Vannevar (Vun-NEE-ver) Bush, who was as much entrepreneur as engineer. The son of a Massachusetts minister, Bush survived a sickly childhood to display a gift for mathematics. After earning a doctorate in electrical engineering at MIT, he carved out a vigorous career that moved easily between academia and business. His homespun manner belied a brilliant mind, assertive style, and ambitious personality. While on the MIT faculty he won acclaim by inventing a mathematics instrument, the differential analyzer, as well as a reputation for arrogance. His restless energy and quick mind inspired some even as it led others to fear or resent him. Always in a hurry, Bush perpetually scanned his horizon for the next world to conquer.[61]

The arrival of Karl T. Compton as president of a floundering MIT in 1930 forged an enduring bond between the two men. While rescuing the institution from its doldrums, Compton made Bush his vice president in 1932. A year later, as part of his effort to revive the nation from the depression, Roosevelt named Compton chief of the new Science Advisory Board. Futile attempts to get funds from the administration for scientific research—and employ idle researchers in the process—turned both Compton and Bush against the New Deal. Both men charged that the government's own technical services were disorganized and second-rate, which was true. Agriculture alone had eighteen bureaus, ten of them scientific, with no means of coordinating their overlapping activities. A climate of suspicion existed between government agencies and researchers, born partly of the New Deal's negative view of business and corporations. At the same time, Bush disapproved of the increasingly conservative nature of the major industrial research laboratories. He still held as his ideal the ruggedly independent inventor with his gift for novelty and willingness to take risks.[62]

On January 1, 1939, Bush launched a decisive career shift when he became president of the Carnegie Institution in Washington. Once in the capital he worked diligently at mastering the bewildering maze of politics. In August he was appointed to NACA, giving him a direct insight into the arcane mixture of politics and military technology. Bush thrived on the pulse and glamour of Washington life even as he put his personal stamp on the sclerotic Carnegie Institution. As war swept over Europe, confirming fears he had long held, Bush searched for ways to pull the disparate research efforts of industry, government, and the military together in some coordinated way. He became more active in NACA as the war demonstrated the growing importance of airpower, seeking ways to mesh the military and civilian interests in joint activities. By early 1940 he was convinced that the nation would be drawn into the war at some point.[63]

The obstacles were formidable. The military was suspicious of civilians and scientists alike; the National Academy of Sciences distrusted the government, and its own members were deeply divided. Bush found one kindred spirit in Hap Arnold, head of the Army Air Corps, who desperately wanted to modernize the air force and recognized the important role that scientists and engineers had to play in the process. He had another in James B. Conant, the president of Harvard and an outspoken internationalist. Karl Compton also supported his efforts, as did Alfred Loomis, a retired investment banker, generous patron of major physicists such as E. O. Lawrence, and a cousin of Henry Stimson. Loomis became a powerful supporter of Bush. "Of the men whose death in the summer of 1940 would have been the greatest calamity for America," he once observed, "the President is first, and Dr. Bush would be second or third."[64]

During that summer Bush concocted his own plan for injecting scientists into the defense effort by getting the government to sponsor promising research that the military ignored. In May he tried to wangle an appointment with Roosevelt through the influence of the president's uncle, Frederic Delano. "I knew that you couldn't get anything done," Bush said later, ". . . unless you organized under the wing of the President." He prepared a one-page memo for the president to read in advance; it advocated a new agency devoted to military research. The timing could hardly have been better. On May 25 Nazi armies were rolling toward Paris, and Roosevelt asked Congress for more defense money and the creation of OEM. Early in June Bush got a meeting with Hopkins, who was already interested in the matter. They hit it off at once. Both were lean, intense, no-nonsense men with quick minds who said what they thought in salty language and did not let convention bind their thinking.[65]

Hopkins liked new ideas that were big and daring. He read Bush's succinct memo and agreed to arrange an appointment with Roosevelt. On the afternoon of June 12 Bush met with the president and Hopkins to discuss the memo with its six points for mobilizing military technology. Bush expected to answer all sorts of questions and defend his proposal. Instead Roosevelt said he had already gone over the memo with Hopkins. He uttered a pleasantry or two and scribbled on it, "OK—F.D.R." The meeting was over in minutes. Bush drafted a letter that Roosevelt signed on June 15, the day after Paris fell, making him head of the new National Defense Research Committee (NDRC). The eight-man committee included Compton, Conant, and Frank Jewett, president of both Bell Telephone Laboratories and the National Academy of Sciences.[66]

Later Bush wrote that "there were those who protested that the action of setting up NDRC was an end run, a grab by which a small company of scientists and engineers, acting outside established channels, got hold of the authority and money for the program of developing new weapons. That, in fact, was exactly what it was." The only way to get the job done, he insisted, was to operate outside the usual channels.[67]

Roosevelt had one possibility already in mind. He had recently appointed a special committee to "study into the possible relationship to national defense of recent discoveries in the field of atomistics, notably the fusion of uranium. I will now request that this committee report directly to you, as the function of your Committee includes this special matter." The June 15 letter also noted that NDRC was not meant to replace research done by the military but to supplement it "by extending the research base and enlisting the aid of scientists who can effectively contribute to the more rapid improvement of important devices, and by study determine where new effort on new instrumentalities may be usefully employed."[68]

The charge was all that Bush could have asked for, and Conant was stunned at his accomplishment. "I shall never forget my surprise at hearing about this revolutionary scheme," he recalled. "Scientists were to be mobilized for the defense effort in their own laboratories." Bush moved quickly to get lists from the services of what research they wanted done. He assured Marshall and Admiral Stark that his mission was to help them do what they needed done. Conant thought the committee would have to build and staff new laboratories, but Bush had a better idea. "We will write contracts with universities, research institutes and industrial laboratories," he said. The contract would become NDRC's prime instrument for getting things done. Farming the work out would benefit all parties and keep yet another federal bureaucracy from arising. Researchers could continue to work in their own facilities.[69]

NDRC marked a sea change not only in the relationship between the government and the scientific community but also in the basis of scientific research. It opened the door to the development of Big Science and to increasing dependence of scientists on government funding for their work even though Bush insisted that contracts made them less subservient. It also provided the first framework for enlisting the talents of scientists and engineers in the war effort on an organized basis. Within a year one out of every four physicists in the country would be working on war projects, leading Conant to observe that "all research in physics, except on war problems, has ceased." Industry followed suit. General Electric stopped all its research on commercial radio and television to devote its full attention to defense projects.[70]

Bush was unabashed in relishing his new position of power and prestige. "At no time in history," declared *Time*, "has one man held the reins of so much scientific research." At no time in history had there ever been so much scientific research, but in Bush's view the surge was woefully late in coming to America. "If we had been on our toes in war technology ten years ago," he growled, "we would probably not have had this damn war."[71]

DESPITE ITS FLAWS, the National Roster of Scientific and Specialized Personnel was a unique inventory of highly trained and professional practitioners in seven major categories: biological and agricultural sciences; physical sciences; engineering sciences; management and administration; social sciences; architecture and planning; and languages. Eventually it succeeded in registering some 690,000 men and women in these and other fields, placing their data on IBM punch cards that could be machine sorted to find possible specialists for any needed project.[72]

Those who registered filled out carefully devised questionnaires that revealed not only major discipline but secondary skills, interests, and hobbies.

Each run of the sorting machine isolated one characteristic requested by whoever was seeking talent. A request for an unmarried aeronautical engineer who spoke French would trigger separate runs for each characteristic. It could provide a list of potential candidates but had no way to determine which was the best one for a given job. In one case the army came looking for men with ham radio experience for communications and radar operations. Later it returned seeking ham operators who spoke French to reach the underground in France. For its bombing runs the air force wanted men familiar with French railroads. The navy sought female mathematicians and physicists to commission for radar work. Industry also came calling. A U.S. Rubber plant needed a first-rate metallurgist.

In time more than 50,000 placements were arranged, and the military offered commissions to another 10,000 registrants. The roster was far from complete, but it was a daring and unique start, the first attempt to create an American brain bank. Over time it was to pay handsome dividends.

CHAPTER 5

MAKING HASTE SLOWLY

It was necessary to induce manufacturers to accept defense contracts. Only recently, businessmen who had manufactured munitions in the first World War had been subjected to investigations . . . The War and Navy Departments, accustomed to small-scale, meticulous, and slow-moving procedures, had to be shocked into altering their practices to meet the necessities of larger-scale operation.

—BUREAU OF THE BUDGET[1]

We have arrived at what is in effect an Anglo-American military alliance; and the only people in the world who do not know it are the American people. By measures short of war we have arrived at the verge of total participation, still without looking at it. One more act would oblige us to take the plunge. A single symbolic act is wanting.

—SATURDAY EVENING POST[2]

Since June of 1940 the administration had been busy doing one thing and saying that it was doing another. This was a matter of necessity . . . Everything was being done for defense, and since that meant so many different things to so many different people, it had to be done most delicately; which meant that most of it was done badly.

—BRUCE CATTON[3]

SLOWLY, HALTINGLY, PROGRESS WAS being made. Even the gloomiest pessimist in 1940 could see the roots of what might blossom into a mighty machine of production as the economy showed impressive gains. Automobile sales boomed in June, and the manufacturers anticipated an even better

second half of the year. Packard was hardly alone in trying to combine civilian and defense production. Once a maker of hand-tooled, expensive cars, it
had moved to mass production under Max Gilman. But it had also produced
Liberty aircraft engines during World War I and continued to sell them to the
government until 1925. Packard also turned out high-quality marine engines
and already had a $2 million contract from the navy for more of them. After
some waffling, its directors struck a deal to produce the Rolls-Royce engines
for British fighters that Henry Ford declined to make.[4]

"Honest Bill Knudsen," as *Time* called him, did his best to give Americans
the straight story on the defense effort. "What may seem to some as unnecessary delay is almost always, in reality, a period of basic preparation," he told a
press conference. ". . . Few people realize that before actual production can
start, months of effort must be expended upon design alone." As an example
he pointed to the light tank, which required about 2,400 individual drawings
before actual work could begin. Putting machine tools in place was another
problem that did not make headlines but was a crucial step. Asked why he did
not simply put more factories to work on defense production, Knudsen quoted
Charles Kettering's remark that "two hens sitting on the eggs do not produce
the chicks in half the time."[5]

All the necessary work was going forward, Knudsen assured the reporters.
He didn't need more authority, and he didn't feel bound by red tape. "People
might have thought we had red tape in General Motors, because we did
things in a definite way," he added. "Here, too, there are certain definite ways
to proceed. I propose to proceed by those ways just as long as I can get results
by them." But Knudsen found the ways of government work strange and frustrating. "You could not spend a dollar unless you actually had it," he said of
appropriations, "and after you had the dollar you could not spend it excepting
for the things the dollar was appropriated for." He had scarcely arrived in
Washington before critics demanded action on getting planes built. "Everybody was talking about airplanes," he said. ". . . We had no money for plants,
and we did not know what kind of plants were needed. But they wanted action, although nobody knew just what 'action' meant."[6]

Washington politics presented its own challenge. As Knudsen began
building a production staff, he received a visit from a member of the Democratic National Committee who wanted some "good Democrats" placed in
the key jobs. Knudsen protested that he had already discussed this with Roosevelt. "To get production, I have picked production men. As for their politics, I don't give a damn how they vote." When the man persisted, Knudsen
asked him to send along a list of names. Hardly any of them had production
experience. Knudsen replied that the names were not satisfactory and added

that the key positions paid only a dollar a year. Nothing more was heard from the committee member.[7]

Speculation persisted that Roosevelt would have to appoint a chairman for the commission but would put off doing so until after the election. "Meanwhile," declared *Newsweek*, "the general Washington feeling is that the commission 'is a screwy setup which is somehow working well.'" Much of the credit for coordinating its efforts went to Nelson.[8]

Some companies improvised as best they could to get into defense production. American Car & Foundry's (ACF) plant in Berwick, Pennsylvania, had languished for want of equipment orders from the railroads, which had a surplus of unused cars. The army awarded the plant a $6 million "educational" order for 329 12-ton tanks for its new armored force. When the plant proved it could turn out tanks of high quality at a suitable speed, the army doubled its order. A separate order from the Allies for $12 million in shells prompted ACF to build three additions to the plant. A Pullman subsidiary tooled up its Butler, Pennsylvania, plant to handle an Allied order for shell forgings (everything except the cap and powder). Pittsburgh Pressed Steel Car Company did likewise for an American government shell-forging order, as did a Dallas company that usually made cottonseed oil machinery.[9]

Casual observers expected major tank orders to go to a company like Caterpillar Tractor, since many of its tractors ran on similar cleat-studded belts. But the country and the military needed tractors as badly as it needed tanks, and nothing else in tank construction resembled that of tractors. Tanks used different tracks, suspension systems, engine designs, and ratios of weight to horsepower. Tractors used diesel motors, while those of tanks, which needed higher speeds, were more like airplane engines. Since tanks needed armor, building them was a heavy-steel fabricating job requiring the kind of huge stamping tools used in locomotive and railway car shops. To manufacture them Caterpillar would have to start from scratch, much as automobile manufacturers had to do when they switched to airplane engines. Moreover, Caterpillar turned out another crucial product for both civilians and defense: It operated the nation's biggest assembly line for diesel engines.[10]

The tank orders went instead to firms like ACF and Marmon-Herrington, a truck maker. Republic Steel prepared to turn out armor plate for tanks. Textile mills awoke from their doldrums to feast on orders for uniforms and other goods. A Buffalo company went to work on an experimental order of parachutes made from DuPont's new nylon fabric in hopes of ending dependence on Japanese silk. By the end of September American business output rose 12 percent above the level of 1929, and some industries, notably steel, were approaching capacity. Copper firms strained to meet British orders for brass and sheets, which triggered a domestic buying wave as well. But even with the mills running full, companies hesitated to undertake more than modest expansion.[11]

Revere Copper & Brass allocated $1.5 million for expansion of plant and equipment but stopped there. "We cannot take the business risk of going further than this," explained its president, "because first, if we built a new plant it would not be in production for over a year, and we do not know whether at the end of that time we would have any orders for it or not; second, if we did have orders, we know in advance that profits made would be largely taken by taxes, and at the end of the emergency we might have to borrow money . . . besides having a plant which was a white elephant on our hands."[12]

Washington planned to put about $3 billion into new plants through either direct construction of facilities it would lease to private firms or through RFC loans to private companies willing to build for defense production. These efforts touched off a dispute over plant locations as midwestern representatives demanded more factories in their states rather than on the two seaboards, which already housed most of American war industry. About 40 percent of all manufacturing wage jobs were centered within thirteen industrial areas, and 75 percent were located within 200 industrial counties. Inland plants would be safer from enemy attack while also helping to diversify the economies of primarily agricultural states. However, many plants went instead into areas served by major power sources such as TVA. Congress granted NDAC authority to approve the location and plans for facilities financed by the government, only to trigger a running dispute with the military.[13]

The military had statutory authority over contracting, which in its view included site location of plants. It insisted that NDAC could suggest projects to the army and navy and veto their proposals but nothing more. The commissioners split among themselves over how broadly to interpret their congressional mandate, but in practice the military simply ignored or bypassed them. The War Department created a plant site board to deal with NDAC; it provided the commissioners with little information and with done deals that could not be undone without causing construction delays. As a result NDAC had little impact on plant location, and midwesterners continued to cry for more plants in their region.[14]

To expedite financing of new facilities, NDAC came up with the emergency plant facilities contract, while some of the more liberal staff members at RFC devised the Defense Plant Corporation. Although complicated, both arrangements helped underwrite plant expansion after a slow start. Still, the delay over amortization and excess profits stalled progress, especially on airplanes. "The reduction in . . . profit . . . has made it very difficult for the aircraft manufacturer to place subcontracts," complained Admiral John Towers.

Under its limitations subcontractors earned only about 5 percent net profit, which did not interest them. "The other and major reason, however," added Towers, "is the lack of definite legal provisions under which they can... carry out this contract. They do not know where they stand." Hap Arnold of the Air Corps echoed the theme that "the industry feels that there are so many uncertainties, unknown quantities that they have to contend with."[15]

Standardization posed another obstacle. Despite efforts to reduce and simplify its inventory of war materials, the army still had more than 125 different makes and models of motor vehicles. Together the two services used thirty-four different airplanes and fourteen sizes and types of guns. Standardizing and simplifying designs would not only enable mass production but also reduce the number of mechanics and parts needed. NDAC pushed the services to standardize the basic features of airplane design, simplify them, and sharply curb the number of changes that delayed production and required retooling. However, the military feared that freezing designs would cause them to miss improvements and the development of new types, especially for weapons still in their early stages of evolution such as antiaircraft and anti-tank guns.[16]

NDAC could not compel the military to do anything, and its own members divided on many issues. Each commissioner had his or her own interest and staff, but the group lacked a center to integrate or coordinate their activities. The defense effort made strange bedfellows within and without the commission. Nelson, Henderson, Hillman, Davis, and Elliott tended to be all-outers who thought the defense work should take priority even at the expense of producing civilian goods. Stimson and Patterson of the War Department shared this view even though they did not care for New Dealers. Knudsen and Stettinius accepted Roosevelt's vague prescription that the economy could afford guns and butter and that the boat should not be rocked too hard. Most of the business community agreed.[17]

"The situation is abnormal," declared the *Saturday Evening Post*. "The country is neither at war nor at peace. Not being at war, it is reluctant to embrace a war economy; and yet, on the other hand, an emergency defense program in which time is the crucial factor, a program, moreover, that entails imperative expenditures comparable in magnitude to wartime expenditures, cannot be carried through successfully under a peace economy."[18]

FOR ROOSEVELT THE dilemma of how to make haste less slowly was but one of many problems piling up in his lap. The war was going badly for Britain. Between September 7 and November 3 London endured fifty-seven consecutive nights of bombing by an average of 250 planes, while the shrinking

Royal Navy fought gallantly to keep supplies coming despite repeated German U-boat attacks. On September 27 Japan allied itself with Germany and Italy in the Tripartite Pact, which made it clear that the United States would face enemies across both oceans if it got into the war. A month later Italy invaded Greece. Even before these grim events the British faced a crisis in trying to defend their waterways. Roosevelt learned that the Royal Navy had only 68 destroyers fit for service—a far cry from the 450 it possessed in 1917. On July 31 Winston Churchill cabled the president that the British had lost 4 destroyers and had 7 others damaged within the past ten days. He asked that Roosevelt "ensure that 50 or 60 of your oldest destroyers are sent to me at once."[19]

The United States had plenty of destroyers—more than the combined navies of the world, including 140 World War I ships that had been put back into service. But giving some of them to Britain would raise a political firestorm. The naval appropriations bill passed in June contained a clause forbidding the sale of "surplus military material" unless the chief of naval operations certified that it was not essential to national defense. The isolationists would pounce on any such move, and the presidential campaign was in full swing. But Roosevelt determined to find some way to get the destroyers to Churchill. On August 2 he thrashed out the matter in what Stimson called "one of the most serious and important debates that I have ever had in Cabinet meeting." The cabinet agreed that the ships should go to Britain and suggested sounding Willkie on supporting such a move. To Roosevelt's surprise, Willkie favored the move and agreed not to make an issue of it. In so doing he did what was best for the nation and worst for his campaign.[20]

To help sway public opinion, Roosevelt also asked General John J. Pershing, the heroic leader of American troops in World War I, to make a radio speech in support of giving the ships to Britain. Nearing eighty years old, still lean and ramrod straight though in poor health, Pershing went on the air August 4 to tell Americans that the British were in desperate need, that we had an "immense reserve" of old destroyers, and that helping the Royal Navy might "save us from the danger and hardship of another war." That same night, by coincidence, Charles Lindbergh spoke to a partisan crowd at Soldier Field in Chicago urging cooperation with Germany if she won the war. All-outers pounced on this juxtaposition; Senator Claude Pepper declared that the American people had to decide who to follow, General Pershing or "the chief of the fifth column in this country, Colonel Lindbergh."[21]

A legal rationale was hurriedly put together, part of which involved turning the gift of fifty destroyers into a trade for American use of British bases in the Atlantic for its own defense. Through an involved chain of reasoning this avoided having to seek legislation from Congress, where isolationists could sink it with a filibuster. On September 3 Roosevelt informed Congress of the terms of the deal. To appease all sides, Britain donated use of its bases in Bermuda and Newfoundland and exchanged use of six other bases for the fifty overage destroyers. The deal, said Roosevelt, was "an epochal and far-reaching act of preparation for continental defense in the face of grave danger." A public opinion poll in mid-August revealed that 62 percent of those questioned favored the transfer of destroyers. Even the isolationist *Chicago Tribune* approved the deal because it regarded the bases as important for hemispheric defense.[22]

Although the focus remained on Europe, steps had also been taken to deal with the Japanese, whose intentions remained as murky as ever. In July Congress passed a bill limiting the export of munitions and critical materials. Later that month Stimson alerted Roosevelt to information he had received that Japan was buying immense quantities of American aviation oil. Roosevelt placed both petroleum and scrap iron on the list of articles that could be exported only under license, giving the government control over how much or little Japan could buy. When Japan moved troops into Indochina in September, Roosevelt embargoed the shipment of steel and scrap iron to Japan, and the cabinet discussed whether to add gasoline to the list as well. It bothered Stimson that the embargo applied only to aviation gasoline and not to aviation lubricating oil or other types of gasoline.[23]

Stimson, like Knudsen, was trying to push the airplane contracts forward while still feeling his way into his new position. Patterson suggested executing contracts on the basis of cost plus a fixed fee, which the manufacturers would accept. Then the aircraft companies balked over the tax and amortization uncertainties. A new plan was devised whereby the manufacturer would build the plant and be reimbursed by the government in five annual installments. At the end of five years the company could buy the plant at an appraised valuation or the government would retain it. Still the companies hesitated. "All our manufacturers are holding back on account of their uncertainty as to what the tax law will be," Stimson complained late in August. The media railed against the delays. The NDAC itself was divided over how best to proceed; Stimson derided it as "a typical New Deal performance."[24]

In mid-September Stimson had to contend with what he called "the rampage that Thurman Arnold is raising under the anti-trust laws . . . Coming just now, when we have all been trying to encourage industry to exert itself and . . . that the administration is not its enemy, why this is a serious threat." When a mangled version of the tax bill finally passed late in September, the aviation bottleneck began to loosen, but other problems persisted. Stimson wanted to curtail the production of commercial airplanes and enlist the automobile manufacturers by eliminating the annual model change, thereby keeping the die makers free for defense work. Roosevelt told him to see what he could do.[25]

Knudsen persuaded the automobile makers to sign an agreement placing their toolmaking capacity and extra time used for designing new models at the disposal of national defense. The old production warrior proposed having dies made to stamp out in mass production numerous parts of airplanes currently being made by hand. He planned to try this approach first on B-17 and B-25 bombers. If successful, it would remove one of the largest bottlenecks to aircraft production, the lack of mass-production techniques. Getting rid of another major obstacle, politics, was a problem utterly beyond Knudsen and difficult even for a master magician like the president.[26]

POLITICS WAS ALWAYS in the mix, as Knudsen found out to his disgust when the Democratic committeeman came calling. Congress wasted three months bickering over and ultimately mutilating the tax bill, and the isolationists had their knives ready for anything that looked to nudge the country toward war. Above all, the election campaign left its imprint on every move the administration made. That a third term was unprecedented mattered less to Roosevelt than his belief—and that of many others—that in such troubled and uncertain times he had to be the man to lead the nation through them. "There is no doubt that this war situation is likely to make or break the President," observed Ickes. ". . . The international situation is looming ahead of everything else in the minds of the voters."[27]

Not quite everything else. For some the issue was Roosevelt himself—the hubris of wanting a third term to perpetuate the changes he had wrought in American life and his obvious love of power centralized in the office of the president. Kiplinger's tracked some of these attitudes in its forecasts through the summer and fall. "*Some sort of highly integrated economy, national planning*, national control, regimentation under government, is probably expectable for a period of years ahead," it declared in June. A week later it warned, "*Democracy in the U.S.* will be threatened, perhaps permanently, by putting the U.S. into foreign war." In August it stressed that "*American expeditionary forces* abroad are foreseen . . . eventually. Our government is not being candid with its people." By September the newsletter concluded that "*practically we are already a nonbelligerent ally* of Britain . . . Thus we are already in the war . . . *Roosevelt's election* undoubtedly would expedite the trend." The election, it predicted in October, was "retarding many formal steps toward war and activity will be far greater after elections . . . if Roosevelt wins."[28]

The fear of expanded presidential power, rooted in the New Deal itself, galvanized Roosevelt haters. The Reorganization Act had already provided a basis for augmenting his control over the military. An amendment to the Selective Service Act authorized the president to take over and operate any existing plant or facility "necessary for national defense" that refused to accept military contracts. Willkie blasted it as a move to "socialize and sovietize our system of free enterprise." Ralph Robey warned that "it confers greater power upon the President than anything we have ever done before even in wartime." The destroyer-for-bases deal enhanced this fear. "The President did this as an act of his own will," complained the *Saturday Evening Post*, "without the knowledge of Congress, and presented it to the Congress as a *fait accompli*."[29]

The anti-Roosevelt elements included people in his own party as well. After the Democratic convention Roosevelt privately lamented the strength of what he privately called "The Hater's Club," which consisted of "strange bedfellows like Wheeler and McCarran and Tydings and Glass and John J. O'Connor and some of the wild Irishmen from Boston, et cetera." Although largely indifferent to personal attacks, he faced real and self-imposed limitations in campaigning. He had pledged to interrupt his presidential work with only five political speeches; the first would not be delivered until October 23; the last would be a radio address from Hyde Park on election eve, November 4.[30]

Physical limitations hampered his campaigning as well. He despised flying and had done so only once, going to Chicago to accept his first nomination for president in 1932. "The thought of flying is impossible," he explained to a friend, "because with my large group it would take a whole squadron of planes to move me. As President, I simply have to be within twelve hours by rail of the capital. I am like the man who had to stay at the fire house when his family was sick."[31]

True to his word, Roosevelt remained silent for weeks while Willkie barnstormed across the country giving several speeches a day, shouting himself hoarse in the most vigorous and aggressive campaign since William Jennings Bryan's crusade in 1896. Overall Willkie's entourage traveled 18,789 miles through thirty-one states to deliver a message that seemed as aimless as it was sincere. Since he mostly agreed with Roosevelt on what should be done, he could only criticize how it was being done by going after the president and his administration personally. The major issues before the nation had to do with foreign policy, and Willkie could not direct his attack there except in marginal ways. The Republican old guard was of no help to him. They were tired, dispirited, and obsolete in their unrelenting negativism, and they couldn't get past their conviction that Willkie wasn't a real Republican. Willkie was fresh blood, a dynamic personality that alone among them stood any chance of winning, but after a few weeks it became clear that he had little chance of beating Roosevelt.[32]

Nevertheless, the GOP poured huge sums into the campaign, so desperate were they to dethrone Roosevelt. The press was overwhelmingly in Willkie's corner. Even papers once friendly to Roosevelt such as the *New York Times*, the *New York Daily News*, and the Scripps Howard chain joined the Republican press in lionizing Willkie through headlines, columns, editorials, and cartoons. Willkie persisted in talking night and day in all kinds of weather despite a failing voice, enduring a shower of boos and eggs from union members in Detroit and Pontiac without flinching, and ignoring the pleas of party pros to drop his fatal notion of bipartisan foreign policy. He wanted to engage Roosevelt directly and was furious at being ignored. His organization was amateurish and disorganized. "Seldom has there been more chaos in a presidential campaign," concluded Raymond Clapper.[33]

With their cause seemingly hopeless, the Roosevelt haters turned to fanning the flames of fear already loose in the country. Insurance companies informed their policyholders that Roosevelt's election would render their policies worthless; doctors warned that it would lead to socialized medicine; bank directors urged their depositors to protect their funds by voting for Willkie. Above all, Willkie stung Roosevelt by blaming him and his "socialistic" administration for the nation's military weakness. Reports poured into Democratic national headquarters and the White House begging the president to "give solemn promise to the mothers of America that you will not send their sons into any foreign wars. If you fail to do this, we lose the election!"[34]

It was, of course, a promise no president could realistically make, but as the campaign turned nasty and Willkie grew more aggressive, Roosevelt found himself on the defensive. His speeches became equivocal, although in Madison Square Garden on October 30 he electrified the crowd by concluding a list of congressional isolationists with the euphonious names of "Martin, Barton, and Fish." The second time he repeated their names, the large crowd joined happily in, and the phrase stuck, tying Willkie to three old-guard Republican dinosaurs. At his next major speech in Boston, however, Roosevelt yielded to pleas that he address the fear-of-war hysteria by saying, "And while I am talking to you mothers and fathers, I give you one more assurance. I have said this before, but I shall say it again and again and again: Your boys are not going to be sent to any foreign wars."[35]

It did not help that once close allies had also turned against Roosevelt. Al Smith, who never got over losing the Democratic nomination in 1932, began campaigning for Willkie. Senator Hiram Johnson of California also threw his support to Willkie. Labor leader John L. Lewis, in a national radio address, heaped scorn on Roosevelt for playing "a game that may make cannon fodder of your sons" and for an "overweening, abnormal and selfish craving of increased power." Lewis had come to despise Roosevelt. Originally he had backed isolationist senator Burton K. Wheeler; now he urged the large membership of the CIO to vote for Willkie. Since labor had always been a critical part of Roosevelt's support, Lewis's desertion posed a major threat if the members took his advice. To reinforce his seriousness of purpose, Lewis declared that he would resign as president of the CIO if Roosevelt won. Robert Sherwood labeled the speech a "Hymn of Hate" against the president.[36]

Both candidates began swinging wildly. As his poll numbers started slipping, Willkie lost his scruples and followed the old guard's advice to echo the isolationist line. He charged in a nationally broadcast speech that Roosevelt had made secret agreements that would commit the nation to war. If the president's "promise to keep our boys out of foreign wars is no better than his promise to balance the budget," Willkie cried, "they're already almost on the transports." The scare tactics boosted Willkie's poll ratings but also soured some of his supporters. It also alarmed Democrats, who begged Roosevelt to take off the gloves and start hitting harder. "I am fighting mad," the president admitted. An alarmed Harold Ickes wrote privately that "I desperately want the President to win. I am horribly afraid of Willkie. I believe him to be unscrupulous, unfair, reckless to the point of daring, and greedy for power. If he should be elected, I would honestly fear for the future of my country."[37]

Roosevelt's last major speech took place in Cleveland on the Saturday before the election. It proved to be his best one, delivered to a vociferous crowd. At lunch on the train the day before, he shocked his speechwriting aides by looking careworn and gray, but as soon as they started work he perked up and went at the speech for six hours, pausing only to put on his leg braces and walk out on the platform when the train stopped to greet the crowd. Richard Ketchum called the speech "an almost poetic evocation of America's future." The president's radio address at 11:00 P.M. on election eve was, as it had been twice before, brief and upbeat. "No mere politician, and certainly no mere ghost writer," observed Sherwood, "could put into [the speeches] the same degree of conviction and the same deep spiritual quality that he conveyed."[38]

It was the sort of message at which Roosevelt excelled, and for which Willkie had no reply. Roosevelt won thirty-eight states and swept the electoral vote 449–82, but Willkie received 22.3 million popular votes to Roosevelt's 27.3 million. No Republican candidate had ever garnered that many votes, and none would before Dwight Eisenhower in 1952. Republicans picked up five Senate seats and two governorships in the election. Roosevelt took pleasure in winning his staunchly Republican home district of Hyde Park by a 367–302 margin, the best showing he had ever made there. In his first campaign speech at Philadelphia he had said, "I am an old campaigner and I love a good fight." But not this one. It had been not only tough but distasteful, as both candidates assumed personas that made them cringe privately. Roosevelt kept his office, but at a steep and unpalatable price.[39]

Eight days after the election Roosevelt wrote Sam Rosenman in disgust that "there were altogether too many people in high places in the Republican campaign who thought in terms of appeasement of Hitler . . . In affairs at home, I live, as you know, in constant dread that the national security might, under remote circumstances, call for quick and drastic action . . . I am certain that if the other crowd had won there would have been many more probabilities of drastic action by the government. Those newspapers . . . which most loudly cried dictatorship against me would have been the first to justify the beginnings of dictatorship by somebody else."[40]

Despite all the ugliness preceding it, the election marked a turning point. Rosenman saw the difference in the president at once. "He was now no longer a President whose term was about to expire," he observed. ". . . He had just been elected for four more years, and he was now in a position to lay long-term plans."[41]

THE SELECTIVE SERVICE Act signed by Roosevelt on September 16 contained an amendment authorizing him to seize and operate industrial plants if necessary. It also required a large administrative apparatus to organize the registration of men scheduled to occur on October 16. A director of selective service was needed, but Roosevelt didn't appoint one right away. Instead he sent Harold Smith, director of the Budget Bureau, to sound out Stimson on the subject. A perplexed Stimson regarded it as "a typical instance of the President's haphazard way of hopping about from one Department to another to do another Department's work." Colonel Lewis B. Hershey did much of the work setting up the registration system, but Roosevelt wanted a civilian for the post to mitigate the opposition among labor and others to a peacetime draft. Stimson offered the job to the president of the University of California, who wasted five days before declining it. Stimson then created an order giving Hershey interim powers, but the president, who had not met Hershey, balked at giving any army officer authority to act on so political a business as the appointment of local boards.[42]

With time running out before registration day, the cabinet prevailed on Roosevelt to approve Stimson's order. The setting up of boards went forward while Stimson found a director in Clarence A. Dykstra, president of the University of Wisconsin. Hershey continued as executive officer and was promoted to brigadier general. Registration day went smoothly, although twenty Union Theological Seminary students refused to register even though they would be exempted once on the rolls. Mohawk and Seneca Indians in New York also declined to register but said they would volunteer if war came. Conscription also brought the racial issue to the surface. Black leaders urged Roosevelt to tear down the segregated barriers in the military.[43]

During the summer thousands of blacks flocked to recruiting stations when the army began its expansion, only to encounter familiar obstacles. The regular army of half a million men had only 4,700 black soldiers, two black officers, and three black chaplains. Only one of the four black units was getting combat training. The Marine Corps, Armored Corps, Signal Corps, and Army Air Corps had not a single black in the ranks. The navy had some 4,000 blacks enlisted, but they served only in menial roles with no hope of advancement. The defense movement helped spark a growing revolt against segregation in the military under the cry of "the right to fight." When fifteen black sailors protested their treatment and were summarily handed dishonorable discharges, a smoldering wave of protest burst into the open.[44]

The new Selective Service System offered blacks a chance, however slim, of improving their lot in the army. After Eleanor Roosevelt pressured her husband to address the issue, he held a meeting on September 27 with three civil rights leaders, Frank Knox, and Patterson. Stimson was too busy to attend and dubious about the whole business. He recalled the last war when Woodrow Wilson yielded to similar demands and sent black officers with several of the divisions that went to France. "The poor fellows made perfect fools of themselves," he thought, "and one at least of the Divisions behaved very badly. The others were turned into labor battalions." The aristocratic Stimson saw nothing but disaster in an integrated military. "Colored troops do very well under white officers," he wrote privately, "but every time we try to lift them a little bit beyond where they can go, disaster and confusion follows . . . I hope for Heaven's sake they won't mix the white and the colored troops together in the same units for then we shall certainly have trouble."[45]

In October the White House persuaded Stimson to appoint a black civilian aide, William H. Hastie, a graduate of Harvard Law School who was then a dean at Howard University. General Marshall said he planned to organize a brigade of cavalry with two black regiments and to train some black pilots for the Air Corps. "As to this last," Stimson wrote privately, "I have very grave doubts as to their efficiency. I don't think they will have the initiative to do well in the air." However, he regarded Hastie as "a rather decent negro." Although the black press and civil rights organizations raised a loud protest, the army and navy remained staunchly committed to their policy of segregation. At the September 27 meeting Frank Knox told the black leaders bluntly, "We have a factor in the Navy that is not so in the Army, and that is that these men live aboard ship. And in our history we don't take Negroes into a ship's company."[46]

The manpower problem had another awkward dimension plaguing Stimson. With Selective Service in place, the army had nowhere near enough housing for a large number of draftees. Under the act's provisions, it could not take men unless it could furnish quarters for them. Although Congress had passed the Selective Service Act, it did not provide funds for new camps until September. Bad weather and other problems delayed construction, as did the sheer scale of new work thrust upon the small Construction Division of the Quartermaster Corps. General Charles D. Hartman tried diligently to handle the difficult task of choosing contractors on so many projects. Cautious and careful, he was a poor organizer and soon fell hopelessly behind in the work. In December Marshall replaced him with a far more dynamic officer, Lieutenant Colonel Brehon Somervell, but more precious time had been lost.[47]

Relations between the military and the NDAC over contracts remained tense. At a White House meeting on October 16 Stimson got drawn into a debate with the commissioners that turned into what he called "a full dress parade argument . . . I rolled up my shirt sleeves and went for them and their doctrinaire methods full blast." It was bad business, he told Roosevelt, to have two bodies signing contracts with divided authority. Ordnance had prepared contracts for $70 million worth of badly needed shell casings only to have the commission hold them up. Leon Henderson and others barked back about the military's high-handed way of dropping contracts on NDAC and expecting them to be signed without a murmur, but Stimson would not budge from his view that contracting authority belonged to the military. To his mind the NDAC was merely another layer of red tape slowing the production process.[48]

"The Defense Commission," declared *Time* scornfully, "is still as naked as the day it was born . . . of all but 'advisory power.'" Meanwhile debate continued over whether prices should be allowed to rise. Henderson concluded that "today the price level is lower than it ever was when wheels of industry were turning fast. This I regard as the healthiest sign of our industrial well-being."[49]

As the year drew down, dissatisfaction over the lagging state of production increased. Knox complained that the big industrialists still clung to the notion of guns and butter and were not moving forward on the defense program. Baruch paid Stimson a visit and talked at length about what he thought needed to be done. Stimson told him frankly what he thought the problems were. The NDAC lacked a responsible head, and industry wasn't working as hard as he thought it should. Nor would it, Stimson argued, until the commission developed what he called a "war psychosis—until the people of the country and the people in industry in particular realize that they are up against a great danger just as much as if they were in war and were willing to buckle down and meet it."[50]

Baruch agreed that the commission needed a head, but he had an alternative to offer. The problem with NDAC was that it was merely an advisory body; its members oversaw spheres of activity without having any power of decision. Knudsen and the others should discuss issues, but in the end Knudsen needed the authority to make his own decisions in his own way. Baruch also advised Stimson to get a "conspectus," a term used by Woodrow Wilson to describe Baruch's set of flow charts that showed the rate of production of every munition and its components compared with the original program and estimated dates. As an example he showed Stimson how to draw one up so that he could track every part of an airplane, which ones were on schedule or behind, so he would know who to hurry along. As soon as he left, Stimson summoned his aides and asked them to prepare one for him.[51]

Already Stimson was pushing to get more people and manufacturers to change their thinking to guns *or* butter. Charles E. Wilson, who replaced Knudsen as president of General Motors, helped with a speech arguing that "the defense program . . . can be successfully completed only by improving efficiency . . . and by sacrifice." If people were willing to pay higher taxes, do more work, and buy fewer nonessential goods, he stressed, "then we probably can get the job done without sowing the seeds of future depression." Stimson came down even harder by announcing that henceforth nonmilitary planes would be classified as pure butter. He cited a report showing that American airlines hoped to double their total fleet of 322 planes in two years. "Which is more vital to the nation right now," he challenged, "increased military and naval strength in the air or increased business for the commercial airlines?"[52]

The normally reticent Knudsen also let loose with some blasts of his own. "The defense job," he told the National Association of Manufacturers, ". . . has not been sufficiently sold to Industry and Labor as yet." The public believed in its necessity, but not the two groups most vital to it. Plants were overflowing with defense and foreign orders but not expanding to meet them. Labor insisted on preserving its forty-hour week despite the need for longer workweeks. Knudsen railed against what he called "this blackout, this lack of production from Friday to Monday" and asked, "Isn't it possible to put the defense job on a war basis even if we are at peace?" The military came in for its own share of blame as well. Fingers pointed at the lack of camps and other facilities that forced the army to postpone calling up 96,000 National Guardsmen. Some of the army's outmoded procurement efforts became a joke. One recent order called for $300,000 worth of 1917-type underwear that could not be made on 1940 machines.[53]

By December it had become obvious that NDAC could do little to rectify these shortcomings. "It is becoming very clear," observed Stimson, "that the country is getting restive under the present lack of organization and there is a great deal of criticism of the delays that are occurring." The primary cause seemed obvious to him: "Five months work here has convinced me and has convinced Bob Patterson that the trouble arises primarily from the fact that the President has never made a proper organization of that Commission and that it has no Head, all of the seven members being independent and merely advisory. No man has now the right to *decide* what shall be done in regard to production." Stimson conferred with Knox and James Forrestal, who agreed with him as to what should be done.[54]

Somehow the president had to be disabused of his belief that a strong commission with a head would create a supergovernment in peacetime. The election was over, and pressure was mounting on Roosevelt to speed up the defense program. Much of corporate America still favored the IMP, as did some congressmen like Robert A. Taft. Willkie had campaigned for an organization with a strong head. The economy had begun to feel the effects of the procurement program in the form of general or regional shortages of materials, plants, skilled labor, housing, and other facilities. Nearly everyone agreed that NDAC was inadequate to the tasks facing it.[55]

Stimson and Knox took their case to Morgenthau and found him amenable to the idea of approaching Roosevelt with the suggestion of giving Knudsen more power "yet leaving the responsibility to the two Secretaries intact." In effect a three-man board would direct the mobilization effort. They went to see Jesse Jones and got his support. Jones telephoned William Green of the AFL and brought him on board as well; Stimson called Felix Frankfurter, who saw Sidney Hillman and found him receptive. At noon the next day, December 18, Hillman met with Stimson and Knox and said he had doubts about Knudsen's ability to push hard for things, but he agreed to go along with the plan. At 2:45 Stimson, Knox, Patterson, and Forrestal went to make their pitch to Roosevelt.[56]

"Conferences with the President are difficult matters," Stimson sighed. "His mind does not follow easily a consecutive chain of thought but he is full of stories and incidents and hops about in his discussion from suggestion to suggestion and it is very much like chasing a vagrant beam of sunshine around a vacant room." The Roosevelt style of coming at an issue made Stimson nervous, but eventually the president settled into the discussion. He had, of course, been thinking about the problem and searching for a solution. After expressing concern about the threat of inflation during the current expansion, he agreed that more concentration of authority was needed to eliminate the delays in production. Harold Smith of the Budget Bureau had called his attention to an obscure statute that might be broad enough to cover such a change, which Roosevelt wanted to announce by December 22.[57]

Stimson's first idea was to create a triumvirate with Knudsen and the two secretaries, but he realized that labor would object to being left out. The solution, he thought, was a collateral board headed by Hillman, who would have direct access to the president, leaving Knudsen clearly as the man in charge.

When they returned to see the president on Friday, December 20, however, Roosevelt had gone a step beyond them. He wanted Hillman made an associate director with Knudsen. Stimson had no objection—he had come to trust and respect Hillman as a labor representative. Knudsen balked somewhat at the idea but agreed to give it a try. The Big Three would instead be the Big Four.[58]

That same day Roosevelt summoned a special press conference to announce the new arrangement. The whole affair wore an air of improvisation. The president dismissed the call for what he called a "'Czar' or 'Poobah' or 'Akhoond of Swats'" to oversee the defense program, saying that "you cannot, under the Constitution, set up a second President of the United States." Pointing to the provision in the Reorganization Act that created the Office for Emergency Management, he invoked it as the basis for setting up a new organization he called the Office of Production Management (OPM). "From now on," he declared, "the responsibility for turning out this production and purchasing, and priorities, those are the three important things . . . will be in the Office of Production Management." It would be a four-man board consisting of Knudsen, Hillman, Stimson, and Knox.[59]

Asked about NDAC, Roosevelt said its members would continue doing their jobs. Details remained to be worked out and would be forthcoming in the next few weeks. Although he left the relationship between Knudsen and Hillman somewhat vague, he expected unanimous agreement on most issues among the four members. "They will agree," he stressed. "They won't vote. I don't think you will ever find a vote taken." He applauded Knudsen for saying earlier that the airplane program was 30 percent behind schedule. The object, he admitted off the record, "was to get the people in this country a bit scared." Although no one yet knew what OPM would do or how it would function, one point was clear: The reins of control remained firmly in Roosevelt's hands. At the same time, the new arrangement brought business and the military closer together.[60]

Next day the four newly appointed OPM members met for the first time. Stimson told Knudsen that he had earned the right to be the "chief figure" and that he (Stimson) and Knox were there to "push behind him and help him." Knox agreed that Knudsen should be the leader, and Hillman took what Stimson hailed as "a very fine position as to labor's loyal support of production and realization of the true issue." They agreed that speedy production was the paramount issue and that they would meet only when summoned by Knudsen. Harmony reigned, at least for the moment, but there was plenty of trouble elsewhere. Labor problems were already plaguing some aircraft plants, and a spat erupted between Knudsen and Hillman over awarding big defense contracts to Ford despite its refusal to honor the law guaranteeing workers the right to organize.[61]

"Since the inception of the defense program," observed *Newsweek*, "the public has been told that the armaments production would be superimposed upon 'business as usual'—that it would cause little or no disturbance of regular peacetime production. But with Britain entering a crucial stage of the war and the public demanding that our aid be stepped up, it becomes increasingly obvious that peacetime production must give way at some points to arms output."[62]

PRODUCTION LAGS AND bottlenecks, strikes, the ineffectiveness of NDAC, aid to Britain, airplane output, fleet bases, and taxes, always taxes—these were the stuff of table talk throughout the nation as the year drew to its dreary close. "All talk, all possible hope of leadership came down to one man, Franklin Roosevelt," said *Time*. ". . . The people wanted facts—no matter how hard, cold, disillusioning. In every way they knew how, Americans asked last week—how grave the peril? How great the sacrifices? How heavy the burden? Franklin Roosevelt was the man they wanted the answer from." The man himself was just returning from a ten-day cruise in the Caribbean aboard the USS *Tuscaloosa* to recharge his batteries and do some uninterrupted thinking. He took along only Hopkins, Pa Watson, and Dr. McIntire, although reporters followed his ship aboard a destroyer without knowing either the itinerary or length of the trip.[63]

His blithe departure in the midst of so many crises shocked and infuriated many people, including his own cabinet. William Bullitt, the ambassador to France, told Ickes that Roosevelt was terribly tired and might not physically be able to do expeditiously all the things that needed to be done. "The tragic thing," thought Ickes, "is that the President, as tired as he is, is isolating himself more and more." Even Missy LeHand, who was herself frail, did not offer her usual advice unless she saw Roosevelt about to make a major mistake. "Harry Hopkins, who is in the invalid class," grumbled Ickes, "is the only other person close to the President and his role is to play up to him all the time."[64]

The reason given for the cruise was for Roosevelt to inspect some of the bases in the West Indies included in the recent deal with Great Britain, but knowing observers viewed it more as a vacation. The president loafed, talked, fished, entertained guests at the various stops, and in the evenings enjoyed two of his favorite pastimes, playing poker and watching movies. Along the way seaplanes delivered mail to the president. On December 9 a letter arrived from Churchill that the prime minister deemed one of the most important he had ever written. He outlined the grim details of the war picture, stated Britain's financial woes in plain terms, and asked for more destroyers. "Only the

United States," Churchill emphasized, "could supply the additional shipping capacity so urgently needed as well as the crucial weapons of war."[65]

The letter moved Roosevelt deeply and set him to thinking about how best to fulfill Churchill's requests. Churchill said candidly that "the moment approaches where we shall no longer be able to pay cash for shipping and other supplies" and added that "I believe you will agree that it would be wrong in principle and mutually disadvantageous in effect if, at the height of this struggle Great Britain were to be divested of all saleable assets so that after the victory was won with our blood, civilization saved and the time gained for the United States to be fully armed against all eventualities, we should stand stripped to the bone." Roosevelt did agree; the problem was how to send aid to Britain legally without receiving payment in return.[66]

After the *Tuscaloosa* docked at Charleston, South Carolina, on Sunday, December 15, a refreshed and tanned Roosevelt went first to Warm Springs, Georgia, where he ate turkey dinner with ninety polio patients. He told them, "I hope to be down here in March, without any question, if the world survives," then boarded a train for Washington and arrived the next morning. "Diplomats, military men, economists, production bosses; capital, labor— all were ready for orders," intoned *Time*. ". . . Unimportant, at the moment, were . . . the controversies, vexations and misunderstandings of ordinary times. Mr. Roosevelt had asked for the job of dealing with just such a situation, and the U.S. had given him the job. Now the U.S. wanted to know what he was going to do about it."[67]

The first answer came the next day when Roosevelt held the 702nd press conference of his presidency and announced an expansion of aid to Britain. His plan was to take over all the British orders and then lease the munitions in one form or another back to Great Britain, which would pay for or replace them at the end of the war. "Now, what I am trying to do is to eliminate the dollar sign," he said, and proceeded to use one of his brilliantly homey analogies to make the point: "Suppose my neighbor's home catches fire, and I have a length of garden hose four or five hundred feet away. If he can take my garden hose and connect it up with his hydrant, I may help him to put out his fire. Now, what do I do? I don't say to him before that operation, 'Neighbor, my garden hose cost me $15; you have to pay me $15 for it' . . . I don't want $15—I want my garden hose back after the fire is over . . . Suppose it gets smashed up—holes in it—during the fire . . . He says, 'All right, I will replace it.' Now, if I get a nice garden hose back, I am in pretty good shape."[68]

Stimson thought it a good way to avoid the delays inherent in going to Congress for authority, but Roosevelt regarded it only as a first step. Somehow he had to convey the full gravity of the situation to the public. To do this he resorted to the vehicle that had served him so well in the past: the fireside chat. Before starting work on his speech, however, he allowed himself the brief pleasure of celebrating Christmas. As Robert Sherwood observed, the holiday for Roosevelt "was always a real, old-fashioned family festival in the White House, with aunts and uncles, children and grandchildren, stockings and packages galore, and invariably a highly dramatic reading by the President of *A Christmas Carol*." In his message to the people he urged them "to make this Christmas a merry one for the little children in our midst. For us of maturer years it cannot be merry."[69]

On the day after Christmas Sherwood and Sam Rosenman joined Hopkins at the White House to work on the fireside chat speech. It went through seven drafts. An early version went to Knudsen for his comments; the sixth draft was sent to Cordell Hull for the State Department's input. At each stage Roosevelt, working at the long table in the cabinet room, went through the suggestions in his usual way, adding and subtracting material. Occasionally he would glance up at the portrait of Woodrow Wilson over the mantelpiece. "The tragedy of Wilson was always somewhere within the rim of his consciousness," said Sherwood. "Roosevelt could never forget Wilson's mistakes, which had been made with the noblest will in the world." Nothing moved Roosevelt more than the determination not to repeat those mistakes.[70]

At 9:20 on Sunday evening, December 29, Roosevelt was wheeled down to the little oval broadcasting room and a desk filled with seven microphones, two glasses of water, two newly sharpened pencils, a notepad, and an open pack of Camel cigarettes. The room was jammed with wobbly gilt chairs to hold an invited audience that included Cordell Hull; Sara Roosevelt, the president's mother; other cabinet members and their wives; Senator Alben Barkley; and, in the front row, Clark Gable and his wife, Carole Lombard. The crowded room was hot, forcing Roosevelt to mop his brow repeatedly with a large white handkerchief. He wore a dark blue suit with a black bow tie as if to emphasize the solemnity of his talk.[71]

Promptly at 9:30 more than 500 radio stations across the nation tuned to receive his talk, as did shortwave stations that would carry his words around the globe. Attendance at movies fell off sharply that evening. It was his fifteenth fireside chat. "In barrooms, farmhouses, trains, planes and ships, people waited, listening," reported *Time*. "His words might mark a turning point in history."[72]

"This is not a fireside chat on war," he began. "It is a talk on national security." In the midst of this global crisis, he said, his thoughts traveled back eight years to the banking crisis of 1933, when disaster seemed to threaten the entire national economy. Sitting in his study then, preparing to speak on the subject, there had flashed before his eyes a panorama of his apprehensive audience. "I saw the workmen in the mills, the mines, the factories," he recalled, "the girl behind the counter, the small shopkeeper; the farmer doing his spring plowing; the widows and the old men wondering about their life's savings." He had tried then to explain what it all meant to them, and in the present crisis he hoped to do the same thing for his apprehensive listeners.[73]

"Never before since Jamestown and Plymouth Rock has our American civilization been in such danger as now," he said gravely. In his inimitable way the president laid out the depth and extent of the perils posed by the three signees of the Tripartite Pact. The intent of the Axis powers was clear: They sought nothing less than world domination. The Germans were trying to subdue the last major European power opposing them, Great Britain; the Japanese were occupied in fighting China. With the American fleet stationed in the Pacific, the nation relied, as it had for decades, on the British navy to protect the Atlantic.

"If Great Britain goes down," he warned, "the Axis powers will control the continents of Europe, Asia, Africa, Australasia, and the high seas—and they will be in a position to bring enormous military and naval resources against this hemisphere. It is no exaggeration to say that all of us, in all the Americas, would be living at the point of a gun—a gun loaded with explosive bullets, economic as well as military . . . To survive in such a world, we would have to convert ourselves permanently into a militaristic power on the basis of war economy."

Many people had written the president about what they wanted him to say. A small minority poured their fears into telegrams that said in effect, "Please, Mr. President, don't frighten us by telling us the facts." But Roosevelt wanted them to know the facts: "Frankly and definitely there is danger ahead—danger against which we must prepare. But we well know that we cannot escape danger, or the fear of danger, by crawling into bed and pulling the covers over our heads." Step by step he laid out the threat to the western hemisphere and ridiculed the "American appeasers" who insisted that the country could make peace with Germany. The fate of those conquered nations that had had agreements of one kind or another with Germany "tells us what it means to live at the point of a Nazi gun." Today Belgium was being used as a base to attack Britain; what would the Germans do if they occupied a South American country?

"The experience of the past two years has proven beyond doubt that no nation can appease the Nazis," he stressed. "No man can tame a tiger into a kitten by stroking it. There can be no appeasement with ruthlessness . . . We know now that a nation can have peace with the Nazis only at the price of total surrender."

The way to avoid going to war, he insisted, was to lend all possible assistance to the gallant resistance of Great Britain. "We are planning our own defense with the utmost urgency," he assured, "and in its vast scale we must integrate the war needs of Britain and the other free nations which are resisting aggression . . . This effort requires great sacrifice." Business, labor, and government were working together to get the job done.

"But all our present efforts are not enough," Roosevelt exhorted. "We must have more ships, more guns, more planes—more of everything. This can only be accomplished if we discard the notion of 'business as usual' . . . Our defense efforts must not be blocked by those who fear the future consequences of surplus plant capacity. The possible consequences of failure of our defense efforts now are much more to be feared." Lest anyone doubt his resolve, the president declared, "I want to make it clear that it is the purpose of the nation to build now with all possible speed every machine, every arsenal, every factory that we need to manufacture our defense material . . . I am confident that if and when production of consumer or luxury goods in certain industries requires the use of machines and raw materials that are essential for defense purposes, then such production must yield, and will gladly yield, to our primary and compelling purpose."

The mission was clear if not entirely welcome. "We must be the great arsenal of democracy," he said in a phrase that would endure. "For us this is an emergency as serious as war itself. We must apply ourselves to our task with the same resolution, the same sense of urgency, the same spirit of patriotism and sacrifice as we would show were we at war . . . There will be no 'bottlenecks' in our determination to aid Great Britain." Near the end of his talk Roosevelt made a remarkable statement. "I believe that the Axis powers are not going to win this war," he said. "I base that belief on the latest and best information." That he had no such information to justify the belief did not trouble him in the least. He closed by calling on all Americans to "put forth a mightier effort than they have ever yet made to increase our production of all the implements of defense."

By one estimate 100 million people around the nation and the world heard these words. Although reactions varied, the response was largely positive even from some Republican leaders. Senator Arthur Capper of Kansas dissented, saying that the speech "left me feeling that we are pretty close to war." At the War Department Stimson didn't get a copy of the speech until the next morning, when he read it aloud to his aides. "We were all delighted with his forthright and outright analysis," he said, ". . . and his coming out flatly that life would be insupportable unless Britain won and therefore we must give all possible aid to Britain." Germany responded by subjecting London to its heaviest bombing of the war, one that demolished a large part of the old city. "London has nothing to smile about at the moment," wrote propaganda minister Joseph Goebbels in his diary.[74]

Despite the severe bombardment, thousands of Londoners found their way to radios to hear Roosevelt's words even though it was 3:30 in the morning. Churchill thanked Roosevelt the next day for instilling hope and confidence in the British people. "When I visited the still-burning ruins today," he wrote, "the spirit of the Londoners was as high as in the first days of the indiscriminate bombing in September."[75]

Roosevelt had set the tone for the effort to come. As the new year opened, he had much more to say and do. "The sequel to what may well come to be regarded as one of the greatest speeches in history," observed *Newsweek*, "will come Jan. 6, when the President addresses the joint session of the 77th Congress." Ahead too lay the inauguration on January 20, which Roosevelt wanted to be as simple and inexpensive as possible. Still, it would feature a two-hour military parade that would include a mechanized unit from Fort Knox. While the parade would impress many of the visitors to the city, it would remind more knowing spectators of how far the American war machine had to go before it reached combat readiness.

Despite the criticism heaped on NDAC, it had provided an impressive beginning to the mobilization effort. During its first six months it had approved more than $10 billion in contracts, set up the first crude system of priorities to minimize bottlenecks, developed purchasing policies to hold down inflation, started worker training programs, and begun the task of stockpiling strategic raw materials. In the past two months alone a million unemployed workers had been rehired, mostly for defense production, and ghost towns where the primary industry had been long dormant were springing to life again. The "arsenal of democracy" had been launched, but no one yet realized even remotely how enormous it would have to become.[76]

1941: The Year of Turmoil

CHAPTER 6

A HOUSE DIVIDED

[1941] will go down in history, I believe, as the year when we almost lost the war before we ever got into it.
—DONALD NELSON[1]

Total defense means more than weapons. It means an industrial capacity stepped up to produce all the materiel for defense with the greatest possible speed. It means people of health and stamina, conscious of their democratic rights and responsibilities. It means an economic and social system functioning smoothly and geared to high-speed performance.
—FRANKLIN D. ROOSEVELT, JANUARY 3, 1941[2]

You know the history of labor is division, and every time there is division it destroys everything we have built.
—SIDNEY HILLMAN[3]

THE NEW YEAR OPENED WITH A flurry of activity. At a January 3 press conference Roosevelt announced that he was authorizing $36 million as a first step toward building 200 new merchant ships, the first of which he hoped to get within a year. That same day he submitted his annual budget message to Congress requesting nearly $28.5 billion for the defense program and called for higher taxes to help pay for it. Three days later he stood before Congress to deliver his annual message. It was, he said, "a moment unprecedented in the history of the Union . . . because at no previous time has American security been as seriously threatened from without as it is today." Near the end Roosevelt spelled out what he called "four essential freedoms": of speech and worship, and from want and fear. Against the dictators' new order of tyranny he proposed "the greater conception—a moral order."[4]

On the next day, January 7, Roosevelt unveiled at a press conference the executive and administrative orders defining the new OPM. The four top men would fix the policy, which Knudsen and Hillman would carry out. Asked if they were equals, Roosevelt danced around the issue by saying they were like law partners and would act as a firm. When a reporter asked why he didn't want a single, responsible head, the president replied, "I have a single, responsible head; his name is Knudsen & Hillman." Nelson got the message. "The President's announcement . . . informed us that he was going to run the new show just as he had run the headless NDAC," he wrote. ". . . The new machine was to operate with co-pilots." Before reporters could fully digest this conundrum, a bill went into the congressional hopper on January 10 that received, at the suggestion of Felix Frankfurter, the fitting designation of HR 1776. Within days it became more popularly known as the Lend-Lease bill.[5]

Although Treasury Department officials did most of the drafting, the bill's origins traced back to a brainstorm of Roosevelt's during his cruise. Whether the inspiration was Churchill's letter or something else, it gave Roosevelt a clear vision of the mechanism for providing unlimited aid to Britain. He knew that it would also trigger an acrimonious debate and a firestorm of criticism from his enemies. It would be what Sherwood called a "revolutionary law" and amounted to one of the greatest risks of the president's career. "No bill like it had ever been introduced," warned *Time*. "Under the bill, powers would go to Franklin Roosevelt such as no American has ever before even asked for."[6]

By its provisions almost anything became a defense article if the president said it was. He could order the manufacture of any defense article for use by any other country "notwithstanding the provisions of any other law." He could sell, exchange, transfer, lease, or loan any defense article to any other country without regard to existing laws, and give technical information about defense articles to any country as well. To pay for such articles, he received what amounted to a blank-check authorization from any unappropriated funds in the treasury. Among other things the law would allow British ships to be repaired in American yards at American expense. "Its sweeping language," declared *Newsweek*, "entrusted the nation's future to Franklin D. Roosevelt more completely than it had ever been entrusted to George Washington or Abraham Lincoln."[7]

Roosevelt expected an ugly fight with the isolationists over the bill, but he expected to win. The center of organized opposition came from America First, formed in September 1940 to spearhead the fight against American intervention. Its impressive roster of celebrity supporters included Lindbergh, General Robert E. Wood, who served as chairman, and Alice Roosevelt Longworth, Theodore Roosevelt's feisty daughter. The chairman of Sears, Roebuck, Wood was Donald Nelson's boss. Within Congress the isolationists were well outnumbered but not outshouted. Their leader, Senator Wheeler of Montana, coined a particularly nasty phrase by declaring that Lend-Lease was "the New Deal's triple 'A' foreign policy—it will plow under every fourth American boy." The normally thick-skinned Roosevelt bristled at this remark; at a press conference he labeled it "the most untruthful . . . dastardly, unpatriotic thing that has ever been said . . . Quote me on that. That really is the rottenest thing that has been said in public life in my generation."[8]

Wood announced that America First would oppose Lend-Lease "with all the vigor it can exert . . . The President is not asking for a blank check, he wants a blank check book with the power to write away your manpower, our laws and our liberties." But Roosevelt had the votes in Congress, and public support for the bill grew steadily. Wendell Willkie went to England to see the devastation for himself and flew home to testify in favor of the bill despite howls of outrage from Republican Party regulars. Outside the Capitol the cries of protest grew ever more shrill; Henry Ford suggested that the United States give both England and the Axis "the tools to keep on fighting until they both collapse." None of it slowed the bill's momentum. It passed the House 260–165 on February 8 and the Senate 60–31 on March 8. A smiling Roosevelt signed it on March 11 and the next day asked Congress for $7 billion to finance the Lend-Lease program. Sam Rosenman called it "one of the most brilliantly conceived and important contributions President Roosevelt made to ultimate victory."[9]

Although Lend-Lease passed with seeming ease after fifty-eight days of debate, the nation remained deeply divided over both American aid to Britain and the possibility of intervention in the war. A poll of Congress in January revealed that 73 percent still thought the nation would not go to war with Germany and 79 percent thought it would avoid war with Japan. Only 26 percent believed the Neutrality Act would be amended to allow American ships in war zones, but 71 percent agreed the United States should defend the entire western hemisphere. Among the broader population, aid to Britain had strong support so long as American troops did not get sent into battle. For the defense program, however, popular support meant full speed ahead and continued public dissatisfaction with the delays that had so far stalled progress on production.[10]

JANUARY 20 DAWNED clear and cold. Shortly after noon, Roosevelt and his new vice president, Henry Wallace, took their oaths of office and the president delivered his third inaugural speech. It was short, more philosophical than his stirring earlier efforts, and aroused little public response. Afterward he was driven back to the White House, where, after lunch, he borrowed a fur-lined overcoat to wear while watching the inaugural parade. At its head rode General Marshall on his bay horse with six aides and a troop of cavalry. To some eyes they presented a nostalgic image, the ghosts of wars past. Behind them came a stream of West Point cadets, Annapolis midshipmen, a procession of Fords bearing governors and other dignitaries, marching CCC boys in green uniforms, NYA girls in blue and white dresses, and a black WPA contingent.[11]

As these units passed from view the road remained clear for about five minutes. Then came a procession of armored cars and soldiers on motorcycles, followed by three tanks, more armored cars, forty-two light tanks, eighteen medium tanks, still more armored cars, trucks carrying pontoon bridges, kitchen trucks, trucks hauling 6-inch guns, and eight truckloads of antiaircraft guns. Unlike the leisurely pace of their predecessors, they moved past the reviewing stand quickly, shaking the pavement and leaving the air thick with gasoline fumes. They were the ghosts of war at present and, as everybody knew, there were not nearly enough of them.[12]

THE PRESIDENT'S GUIDE to speedy production was as clear and simple as it was wishful thinking. "The nation expects our defense industries to continue operation without interruption by strikes or lockouts," he said. "It expects and insists that management and workers will reconcile their differences by voluntary or legal means." He also expected companies to expand their capacity without hesitation over tax issues or fear of future surplus capacity. Instead he confronted a defense program stumbling repeatedly over exactly those problems.[13]

Isolation versus intervention was not the only issue dividing the house. Far more threatening to defense production were the acrimonious splits between management and labor and those within the ranks of the labor movement. During 1941 these divisions erupted into a wave of strikes in defense industries just at the time when Roosevelt was calling for unity of effort. In most of these conflicts public opinion lined up against the unions. Strikes received wide publicity from the press, while management's activities occurred mostly behind the scenes and seldom made news. Nor did it help that several major unions and their leaders were engaged in a savage brawl with each other, and one of them, John L. Lewis, had long been at war with the president as well as his peers.

Although racked by internal conflicts, the labor movement had come into its own by 1940. The minimum wage and maximum hours imposed gradually by the Fair Labor Standards Act of 1938 decreed that the forty-hour workweek would become permanent by October 1940, just as mobilization was heating up. Some 700,000 workers in defense industries already worked more than forty hours but received time-and-a-half pay for overtime. The unions, anxious to protect this hard-won privilege, found themselves under siege from business and other spokesmen who insisted that the national emergency called for more hours and a six- or even seven-day week at regular pay. Labor leaders suspected with justification that many of these demands were using mobilization as a smoke screen for their desire to roll back gains made by labor during the 1930s. "The hard difficulty now," observed the *Saturday Evening Post*, "is to reconcile our newly conceived national labor policy with the imperatives of an unlimited defense program."[14]

In these struggles Sidney Hillman found himself at an enormous disadvantage. He was supposed to be labor's voice in NDAC and OPM, but Lewis despised him as a rival, while William Green of the AFL considered him a renegade. Lee Pressman, general counsel of the CIO, dismissed Hillman as "a Government representative in the ranks of labor, rather than a representative of the ranks of labor in the field of Government." He had no base of support from the two major unions and no real power within either NDAC or OPM. Nearly all his responsibilities overlapped those of Labor Secretary Frances Perkins, who resented him as an intruder on her turf. He came from a union that to most eyes had no direct involvement in defense work. In effect he was spokesman for groups that refused to recognize him as such.[15]

The AFL and CIO were at war with each other as well as management. Both organizations had a shortage of capable leaders, a fear of losing members, and a pressing need to gather more workers into their fold. They also had to deal with constant charges that their ranks were filled with radicals, especially Communists, and riddled with racketeering. Although the CIO's United Auto Workers (UAW) finally succeeded in organizing General Motors in April 1940, many large corporations remained openly defiant of the Wagner Act. Newly expanding defense industries also became prime targets for organization, leading to jurisdictional clashes between competing unions. And there remained the problem of the still large army of unemployed, although the defense boom was helping to reduce its ranks.[16]

The hostility of the unions left Hillman without a base of support. Within NDAC he tried in vain to get the commission and the military to place contracts only with firms that honored federal, state, and local labor laws. The biggest battle raged over contracts awarded to Ford and Bethlehem Steel, both of which blatantly ignored the Wagner Act's stipulations. Stimson liked Hillman and appreciated his conservative instincts, but the War Department would not budge from its belief that the needs of production trumped all other considerations. When the CIO's Steel Workers Organizing Committee (SWOC) threatened to strike Bethlehem Steel in October 1940, Hillman joined with Stimson and Knox to avoid a stoppage of work. "Hillman is showing up very well in all these matters," observed Stimson.[17]

Attorney General Robert Jackson then ruled that any company judged by the National Labor Relations Board (NLRB) to be guilty of unfair labor practices should be denied government contracts. Columnist Raymond Moley denounced the ruling as "a perfect example of bureaucratic oppression" and warned that it "really authorizes a black list of American industry." Some congressmen declared that it sabotaged the entire defense program. Walter Lippmann went even further. "To roast pigs we must burn down the barn," he said acidly; "to strengthen the Wagner Act we must weaken the National Defense." Next day Jackson backtracked by saying he had made a ruling on an administrative matter and not on "whether violators should or should not be awarded contracts." With the election looming, Roosevelt remained discreetly above the fray.[18]

After the election Hillman and the CIO looked for Lewis to honor his pledge to resign if Roosevelt won again. The CIO annual meeting took place in Atlantic City, the AFL gathering in New Orleans, a symbolic 1,400 miles apart. "C.I.O. was itself divided in a fight over Communist leaders," reported *Time*, "A.F. of L. similarly split in a fight over racketeers." With his usual dramatic flair Lewis resigned as president of the CIO and nominated in his place Philip Murray, the moderate, well-respected leader of SWOC, but not before delivering a scathing speech that denounced William Green as a "traitor" and "poltroon." Earlier Murray had refused to take the post unless the convention passed a resolution condemning fascism, Nazism, and Communism, which it did. Hillman seconded Murray's nomination and rejoiced at his election. Like Hillman, Murray was cautious and diplomatic, preferring negotiations to bombast. Observers hoped he would stabilize the perpetually turbulent CIO. Lewis departed the presidency but remained a force on the labor scene as head of the large and influential United Mine Workers (UMW), whose product was crucial to national defense.[19]

In New Orleans Green of the AFL said, "There is harmony and tranquility here" compared to the "hate, enmity, division, and discord" at the other convention. But not entirely. The main event to reporters proved to be a fistfight in a hotel barroom between David Dubinsky of the Garment Workers Union and Joseph Fay of the Operating Engineers Union. Dubinsky, who had earned a withering blast from Lewis for moving his union from the CIO to the AFL, had introduced a resolution giving the federation's executive council power to remove any official guilty of corrupt practices or "moral turpitude." Fay spotted Dubinsky in the bar and denounced it as "the dirtiest, lousiest resolution" he had ever seen. A fight followed in which Dubinsky's daughter was knocked to the floor. At the convention Green got the resolution quashed and brushed aside the fight, but it was hardly the image the AFL wished to convey to a public already deeply suspicious of corruption and racketeering within unions.[20]

Nothing aroused public resentment toward labor more than a wave of strikes that ensued against firms engaged in defense production. They created an awkward dilemma for Roosevelt, who had befriended labor and relied on its political support. "Some friends of labor in the Administration are very deeply troubled," wrote Raymond Clapper, ". . . and I think with good reason indeed, over the fact that labor is working itself into a role of irresponsible obstruction to war production." Clapper blamed the problem not on workers but on certain labor leaders "bent upon playing union politics, bent upon gaining power" and "using this situation in irresponsible ways that ignore the urgent needs of the nation." He also criticized managements at companies like Ford, Bethlehem Steel, and Allis-Chalmers for their ruthlessly antiunion policies.[21]

Mediating disputes became one more major task for Hillman. The War Department had a long-standing policy of staying out of labor conflicts while working through other government agencies, usually the Department of Labor, for a settlement. The mobilization effort posed a new challenge to this policy because strikes in many companies stalled defense production, but Stimson was content to rely on Hillman to handle labor conflicts. In November 1940, however, a strike against Vultee Aircraft turned into an embarrassment for Hillman and the War Department.[22]

The UAW, a CIO union, had entered the aircraft industry and complained that Vultee's workers averaged only 73.8 cents an hour compared to 94.9 cents for automobile workers. When negotiations went nowhere, the union threw pickets around the plant, idling more than 5,000 men and $80 million worth of airplane construction. Patterson persuaded Hillman to let one of his staff, Major Sidney Simpson, mediate the dispute. In August Simpson had joined an NDAC mediator in avoiding a strike threat at Boeing Aircraft in Seattle, then the only producer of the B-17 bomber. Their success convinced Patterson that Simpson was the man to handle the conflict at Vultee. Stimson was dubious. His impression of Simpson had dropped, especially after Felix Frankfurter warned him that the major had a drinking problem. Although Stimson passed this information along, Patterson decided to send Simpson anyway.[23]

Once in Los Angeles, Simpson found what he described as a very bad situation. "My impression," he reported, "is that Hillman's office is sissy on this one. I am going to take drastic action if I have to." After several days of bargaining Simpson produced a proposed contract pleasing to the company but not to the union, which also found Simpson objectionable. Faced with a deadlock, Simpson went on an embarrassing drinking binge that drew loud attention in the press and prolonged the contract dispute. A chagrined Patterson had to relieve Simpson of duty while Hillman worked feverishly to patch up the situation. After twelve days of idleness the workers returned to work with a new agreement including a pledge not to strike for sixteen months. Stimson called it "a victory probably justifiably to be laid at the door of Sidney Hillman."[24]

More strikes followed, and with them the first trickle of antistrike bills in Congress. After his election as president Murray had proclaimed boldly that "C.I.O. assumes complete jurisdiction over every major defense industry in the U.S.," which only fanned public fears about union power and radicalism. But Murray was neither a radical nor a hothead. An Irishman born in Scotland, he entered the mines at ten and gradually worked his way up to a place on the board of the UMW. In 1936 he took on the thankless task of trying to organize the steel industry, which had been racked by bloody strikes for years. Despite the depression, SWOC succeeded in bringing giant United States Steel into a contract, and dozens of smaller companies soon followed. Only the so-called Little Steel firms—Bethlehem, Youngstown, Republic, and Inland—continued to resist unionization.[25]

A thoughtful executive, Murray took a broader view than most of his peers. Although he made it clear that labor wanted not only jobs but a larger share of the defense-boom profits, he also understood the perils of inflation and technological unemployment. To deal with these problems he proposed the creation of industry councils for each vital industry with members from management, labor, and government. He also helped formulate Walter Reuther's plan to speed up automobile production and made his own survey of the steel industry that claimed to show how production could be improved 30 percent without building new facilities. Even steel executives came to respect his forthright approach and ability. "He handles his own crowd better than most steel company presidents handle theirs," admitted one.[26]

"I was struck again," observed Ickes, "as I frequently am when I am with members of the labor group, with their intelligence." However, outside observers saw only the disruptions in production caused by the strikes. In the Northwest, the AFL and CIO put aside their rivalry long enough to join forces in closing down logging camps and sawmills. As the number and severity of strikes increased during 1941, pressure grew on the administration to devise a solution to the labor situation. Roosevelt also had to deal with the belief of Frank Knox and others that the labor troubles in government shipyards and arsenals were the work of what Stimson called "Communists and other suspected bad eggs in the labor forces."[27]

Hillman then got into a squabble with his OPM associates over a contract awarded to Ford even though the National Labor Relations Board had upheld a CIO protest that Ford had violated existing labor law. Stimson and Patter-son disagreed, arguing that labor violations had their own legal remedies. More important, stressed Stimson, "in this case Ford was the lowest bidder and the one who agreed to finish the contract in the shortest possible time, far less than any of the others. It would be making a serious setback to the Government's speed program to take away this contract." Giving it up, said Patterson, amounted to the government "cutting off its nose to spite its face." Stimson took the case to Roosevelt, who agreed to let him work things out with Hillman. Let this issue go by, the president added, and try to get Ford to play fair with labor in the future. Knudsen also acquiesced in this approach.[28]

Ford kept his contract, and Hillman turned to dealing with a wave of fresh strikes that mounted steadily during the winter of 1941. During 1940 a total of 2,500 strikes had created 6.7 million idle labor days; in 1941 the number of strikes soared to 4,300 and the idle labor days to 23.1 million. Many of the dis-putes were over money. The average wage earner in 1941 made about 74 cents an hour. Auto workers averaged $1.04 an hour, tire workers almost as much, and steel workers about 95 cents. Coal miners made 99 cents but worked ten fewer hours a week than factory workers. Manufacturing workers took home an aver-age of $1,479 a year, nearly $220 more than in 1940 but still a good distance from the $2,000 projected by standardized budgets that an average family needed to live without frills.[29]

As the blight of depression and unemployment lifted, most workers were better off than they had been in years, but still not well off. In 1940 nearly a third of American homes had no running water or indoor toilets. Two fifths lacked bathtubs or showers, nearly 60 percent had no central heating, and more than 25 percent did without mechanical or ice refrigeration. But 65 per-cent of median wage earners did have cars, the one possession that had al-ready grown most precious to Americans. Widely perceived as a symbol of freedom, the automobile also served as a major drain on personal and family resources.[30]

Contrary to widespread public opinion, most of the working class had not been radicalized. A poll in the spring of 1941 revealed that 84 percent of lower-income respondents thought union leaders actually had too much power. They firmly supported the efforts of the House Un-American Activi-ties Committee (HUAC) and overwhelmingly believed that the constitutional rights of Communists should be curtailed. But factory workers also had en-dured more than their share of abuse from employers who fought unionization, imposed arbitrary rules, practiced favoritism, and fired people with impu-nity. As one UAW activist said bluntly, "My boss was an S.O.B . . . No one had the right to talk back, the right to question decisions, the right to dissent." Despite the inroads made by the New Deal, most executives still believed that a company was theirs to run without interference and that employees had nothing to say that was worth hearing.[31]

Although wages were rising, other issues divided the workplace. Workers in many industries wanted a greater say in what went on, arguing that they knew more about the nuts and bolts of production than anyone else and that their input could increase output. The more enlightened managements who shared this view usually found it to be true when put into practice, but for most executives the old authoritarian attitude was hard to shake. Jurisdictional fights also plagued many industries as competing unions fought each other as well as management to gain the right to organize a workplace. Working conditions grew steadily more important as the pressure to produce increased. Above all, labor leaders feared that the union movement would recede instead of advance, not only from public hostility and management pressure but also from worker indifference.[32]

The winter of discontent began with trouble in some California aircraft plants, where danger of a strike threatened to shut down a small San Diego company that made crucial parts for the much larger Consolidated factory. Hillman fell ill and was hospitalized, leaving Stimson and Knudsen to deal with it on their own. A rash of smaller strikes followed along with more serious conflicts at Bethlehem Steel, Allis-Chalmers in Milwaukee, and three International Harvester plants. OPM's leadership, waggishly dubbed "Knudsenhillman" by *Time*, struggled to put out the fires. "If we could get across to labor and industry how vital this program is to our future," Knudsen told a congressional committee almost wistfully, but nobody seemed in a mood to cooperate and critics pounced acidly on every misstep.[33]

"Where is the big strong Government that is supposed to assert the national will and make it effective above the selfish interests of management and labor alike?" asked Raymond Clapper. ". . . The Government is lying down on the job. It is being defied and ignored with impunity by both sides . . . Where is the new Defense Mediation Board? It is hiding under the table."[34]

The UAW moved on to North American Aviation, while at Boeing a faction of the AFL threatened to secede and join the CIO. In mid-March some 400 UAW workers at Harvill Aircraft Die Casting went on strike and shut down production. Although a small company, Harvill had developed a superior new method of making alloy castings used by nearly every aircraft manufacturer on the West Coast. If the strike went on, it could shut down the production of military aircraft. Hillman labeled it "the country's No. 1 strike" and sent a strong team of mediators, who managed to get a settlement on March 24. Three weeks later the UAW opened negotiations with North American Aviation, which produced 20 percent of all military planes in the nation. The weeks dragged on with little progress, and a strike loomed.[35]

Hillman fell ill again, and Knudsen had grown tired and discouraged over the constant work stoppages. Stimson took his message to a cabinet meeting and told Roosevelt "how serious and hard it was on him and what a great handicap it was to have Sidney Hillman away." Knudsen wanted the president to create a mediation board similar to one used in World War I, but Roosevelt had resisted the suggestion so far. Rumors surfaced that a coterie of New Deal advisers were scheming to take control of the mobilization effort, and that part of their plot was to demolish the myth that Knudsen was "a great man, competent to handle defense." Knudsenhillman succeeded in settling the bitter Bethlehem Steel strike, but conflict raged on at Allis-Chalmers, and a new problem erupted at Wright Field in Ohio, where electrical workers went on strike for two weeks.[36]

Since Wright Field was home to a major air force installation, Stimson asked Roosevelt to let the War Department intervene directly. Patterson telegraphed the AFL local in Dayton that if they did not return to work, the government would bring in outside employers. The union assured him that its men would return to work. Roosevelt had also given Stimson and Knox the nod to wade into the strike at Allis-Chalmers, which posed a very different problem. By late March it had been going on for eight weeks with no end in sight. The production delays there affected both the army and navy. Among other things the strike delayed work on three turbines needed by a Virginia ordnance works that produced smokeless powder, as well as machine tools used in building ships.[37]

Stimson viewed the dispute as at bottom an "interdepartmental row" aggravated by misunderstandings, but some observers argued that neither side really wanted a quick settlement. The local UAW head was reputed to be a "Communist fellow traveler," while Max Babb, the president of Allis-Chalmers, was fiercely antiunion and said frankly that he was "thoroughly in accord with the principles of the America First Committee." Stimson wanted the navy to seize the plant and run it, but the law was unclear on whether the military could do so. Roosevelt agreed to let Stimson and Knox try to rush an amendment through Congress giving them the power to take over plants. At the same time, the president bowed to another hope of the War Department by creating the National Defense Mediation Board (NDMB). Composed of four representatives from business, four from labor, and three from the public, the new board, in typical Roosevelt style, was given a charge but no power to enforce its actions other than the harsh glare of publicity.[38]

Critics complained that "the new body will have no more legal power than the United States Conciliation Service or the OPM labor experts who are attempting to clean up the situation now without any great success." A Gallup poll indicated that 72 percent of the respondents believed strikes should be forbidden in defense industries, but the strikes continued. In Bethlehem, Pennsylvania, police charged a picket line at the steel plant; fighting broke out at the International Harvester plant in Richmond, Indiana; and strikers milled about and jeered at the gates of the International Harvester factory in Chicago on the site of the legendary Haymarket Riot of 1886. At Allis-Chalmers Hillman tried in vain to convince Stimson and Knox that a union would calm rather than inflame worker militancy. On March 27 the two sec-retaries ordered Babb to reopen his plant. Babb invited the workers back, but only 15 percent returned to work. On April Fool's Day fighting broke out on the picket lines and raged for three days. The governor of Wisconsin tele-graphed Roosevelt that the situation was "absolutely out of control" and asked for help because the state's National Guard had already been called up and was unavailable.[39]

After talking with Attorney General Jackson, Stimson and Knox con-cluded that the president did have the power to intervene with federal troops. The cabinet agreed with Stimson that "if we took it over—the plant—and operated it, we must treat both management and labor pretty rough, so that no other plants will be anxious to be taken over by the Government." Stim-son also made it clear to Roosevelt that if the army sent troops in, the presi-dent had to back the action to the end. "The reputation of the Army," added Stimson, "and the prestige in the coming emergency that we are facing de-mands that nothing be done to put any troops at any time in a humiliating position." Roosevelt agreed to stand firm but still wanted to give mediation another chance.[40]

On April 4 Stimson warned both sides publicly that "nobody makes a greater mistake than to construe Uncle Sam's patience for weakness." He hinted that the army might seize the plant. Next day Roosevelt called the strike the most serious obstacle to the defense program and threatened direct action. The NDMB then sat down with both sides for nineteen hours of nego-tiation that finally produced a settlement. But that same week the tinderbox at Ford's huge River Rouge plant exploded into violence, the culmination of a four-year campaign by the UAW to organize the most antilabor automobile manufacturer. At seventy-seven Henry Ford continued to maintain that he would never allow unions in his factories, but this vow was becoming more difficult to keep. When the company fired eight union spokesmen on April 1, the sprawling 1,200-acre Rouge and its 85,000 employees endured their first-ever strike. Within two days thirty-four other Ford plants dependent on the Rouge stopped work as well.[41]

A racial element clouded the strike. An estimated 6,000 to 10,000 blacks worked at the Rouge and were grateful to Henry Ford for the jobs. About 1,200 of them refused to leave the Rouge when the walkout occurred, saying they felt safer inside. Union officials claimed they had been hired as strike-breakers and were trying to muddy the dispute by injecting a racial issue. Then, to the surprise of most observers, Ford agreed to negotiate with the union and to reinstate all but three of the fired men. Two months later he astonished everyone even more by signing the most liberal union contract of any automaker, one that gave the UAW almost everything it had asked for but never expected to get. "No half measures will be effective," said Henry Ford's son Edsel, ". . . so we have decided to go the whole way." He added the hope that the settlement "has eliminated every possible source of friction that can hamper or delay national defense production."[42]

Peace at Ford did not extend to the beleaguered aircraft industry. Fewer than half the industry's 200,000 workers had been organized, and the flood of new orders meant that more workers would be streaming into plants. For union organizers the industry emerged as a mother lode. The worst confrontation arose at North American, where a complicated dispute thwarted prolonged efforts to reach a settlement. Two competing unions, the CIO's UAW and the AFL's International Association of Machinists, fought to organize the company. Early in 1941 the UAW won a narrow victory, but the company dragged out negotiations for a new contract. The Communist-leaning elements of the CIO and UAW were strongest on the West Coast, and their role in organizing defense companies like North American became a controversial political issue both within and outside the unions.[43]

Late in May North American's workers grew impatient with the stalled negotiations and authorized a strike. The timing could not have been worse. On May 26 one of Stimson's top aides, Robert A. Lovett, returned from a survey of West Coast aviation plants and reported that the manufacturers wanted more protection from strikes. Stimson held a meeting with the attorney general and others to explore ways of "stopping the subversive elements which are getting into labor." He suggested using a neglected section of an old conspiracy statute. Next day Roosevelt went on the radio to proclaim an unlimited national emergency that required "the strengthening of our defense to the extreme limit of our national power and authority." At the end of April he had sent a public letter to Knudsen and Hillman urging that critical machine tools be operated seven days a week and twenty-four hours a day, pausing only for necessary repairs. In a press conference he backtracked from the ongoing "guns and butter" debate by saying Americans would have to give up some things. "That is the message to give to the American people," he told reporters. " 'You can't eat your cake and have it too.' "[44]

Under these circumstances the last thing UAW national officials wanted was a strike in a major defense plant. They changed organizers at the plant, but local unionists moved ahead of their national leaders. Some 4,000 new workers had come to North American since the union was certified six months earlier, putting pressure on the local leaders to deliver a strong contract. On June 5, convinced that mediation was getting nowhere, UAW members picketed the plant. Next day Stimson summoned a meeting of OPM and others to deal with what he considered "a flagrantly unnecessary strike" called by a "band of subversive agitators whom we suspect to be in the pay of Germany and who are calling strike after strike on the Coast at the places where we are most vulnerable." Fed up with the parade of strikes, Stimson wanted to get tough. Afterward he considered the outcome of the meeting as part of "*one of the most important days of my service here.*"[45]

The animated cabinet discussion over labor agitators aroused even the normally placid Cordell Hull, who declared that the Justice Department should make an example of the labor agitators, that German consulates should be closed, and that it might be well even to recall the American staff in Berlin and close the German embassy in Washington. The passion with which he spoke astonished everyone. After the meeting Ickes quipped to Stimson that "someone must have told him there was a war on."[46]

After a long conference they agreed to recommend to the president that the government take over the North American plant. Hillman took a strong stand in favor of doing so and later warned UAW officials about what would happen if the strike continued. At the cabinet meeting later that day everyone, including the president, accepted the recommendation. UAW officials, acting on Hillman's warning, spent four frantic days trying to persuade the strikers to stand down, going so far as to suspend the local leadership. Their efforts were drowned out by boos and heckling, and only a third of the men obeyed the order to return to work. Patterson and Assistant Secretary John McCloy hired a seaplane and flew to see Roosevelt, who was relaxing on his yacht. After hearing their report he signed an order to seize the plant.[47]

On June 9 some 2,500 troops marched into the plant with fixed bayonets and broke the strike. Determined to handle this precedent carefully, Stimson consulted with Hillman and Jackson, then went with them to brief the president. North American would continue to operate the plant as agent of the government; Stimson was anxious to avoid anything that resembled the government taking over actual operation. Patrol cars had been sent to protect the families of workers from "so-called goon cars who were going around to try to fight them." But Stimson also wanted to keep control of the plant long enough to weed out all subversive elements. "I am drawing the line sharply," he insisted, "between legitimate labor controversies and subversive action by men who have ulterior motives against our defense."[48]

A strange situation had evolved. Labor leaders of varying political stripes denounced the takeover for using force against labor, but the troops were acting on behalf of the NDMB and the UAW itself, which had condemned the strike, as well as Hillman, who supported the takeover wholeheartedly. Stimson himself told reporters only that "we want to get this plant . . . to producing ten planes a day again . . . All the rest is mere detail." A new group of local UAW leaders resumed negotiations that on July 2 produced a new contract with substantial wage increases, whereupon Stimson ordered the army to stand down and leave North American in charge of the plant.[49]

"It is generally agreed," observed *Fortune*, "that the strike at North American represented a convulsive turning point in U.S. industrial labor relations. But what kind of turning point? . . . The fact is that when a government takes over a struck plant it inherits a labor problem; it does not solve it. The solution of our labor problem cannot lie at the bayonet point. It lies in our achieving a production efficiency superior to that of Germany while still maintaining the core of democratic procedures." A handful of labor leaders like Hillman and Murray thought they had an answer to this dilemma, but the deep divisions within their ranks made it hard to sell any one approach to the membership. And in the end labor would be measured by one criterion alone: how well it produced.[50]

During the summer Hillman mounted a campaign to standardize wages in the aircraft plants. Having brought Ford and Bethlehem Steel into the union fold, labor gained another major triumph in July when Tom Girdler of Republic Steel, who had once said, "I'll go back to the farm and dig potatoes before I sign with the C.I.O.," signed a contract with the CIO and kept producing steel. For the union the triumph was second only to the conquest of Ford. Still the strikes kept coming. In August the navy seized a private shipbuilding firm with $450 million in contracts after workers walked out when its management refused to accept an NDMB settlement proposal. A month later it took over some ships stranded when the AFL's seamen's union struck. Hillman got embroiled in a controversial dispute between AFL building unions and a company manufacturing prefabricated housing that undercut the unions' construction domination.[51]

Strikes were not the only problem during these tumultuous months. Workers in some plants resorted to slowdown tactics that delayed output. At Boeing workers used a clause in their contract that provided for discussion of grievances on company time to formulate vague disputes that took hours of argument and negotiation to resolve and kept supervising personnel from their jobs. At Continental Motors, which made airplane parts, more than a hundred instances of deliberate work slowdowns were reported in a single month. One employee, who at the management's request had devised a method for increasing the output of certain machines, was rewarded by having his clothes slashed as a warning against any speed-up of work. Gear cutters were broken and machine parts intentionally damaged. Some union shop stewards resisted every attempt by management to improve production.[52]

By the year's end one out of every twelve workers had gone out on strike, the highest percentage since 1919. Only two other years, 1919 and 1937, had witnessed more strikes. Stimson and Knox wanted legislation from Congress to prevent strikes, and both their departments resorted to strike statistics as part of a public relations campaign to sway public opinion against walkouts. During March and April the War Department distributed a bulletin showing the man days lost at Vultee, Allis-Chalmers, and other companies, along with a list of the defense products affected. The navy did the same and continued doing so into the fall. Roosevelt questioned this approach. "I notice that the Navy is still giving out strike information based on the number of man-days lost," he told Steve Early. ". . . Tell the Navy that no layman knows what 109,000 man-days constitute."[53]

Meanwhile, Congress and the public grew more restive about the labor imbroglio. "I am sad today," said Texas representative Hatton W. Sumners, "to see my nation walking in the footsteps of France, walking toward the common doom of the democracies of the world . . . These strikes are not the things of fundamental trouble . . . These strikes are an indication of the unfitness of the American people to win . . . We are flirting with defeat . . . It has never gotten through the egotistical hide of the average American that there is at this very time a chance of America being licked."[54]

EVERY STRIKE TOOK its toll on both labor and management, but some exacted a larger price as well. None did more damage or dragged out longer than that of soft-coal miners under their enigmatic leader, John L. Lewis. No single figure loomed larger in the labor movement of the 1930s. As leader of the UMW's 600,000 members he presided over not only coal miners but carpenters, electricians, transport workers, and laborers employed at mine sites. He had broken with the AFL to help found the CIO in 1935–36 and served as its president. His UMW was the CIO's strongest, most stable union and contributed $30,000 a month to its coffers, often more than half its revenue. Lewis had helped create SWOC, which organized Big Steel, a major triumph for the fledgling CIO. The monthly $30,000 provided much of SWOC's funding, along with paying the salaries of many CIO organizers and Washington staff.[55]

By 1937 the CIO had emerged as a clear rival to the AFL, and their rivalry intensified. As the leader of the CIO Lewis grew steadily more erratic and secretive. He added his brother, daughter, and brother-in-law to its staff and showed little interest when its membership growth slowed to a crawl. The

UMW remained his chief concern, yet so closely identified was he with the CIO that some wondered whether the organization could achieve its own identity apart from Lewis. Dues collection remained so chronic a problem as to leave the CIO heavily dependent on contributions from the UMW. A few unions drifted back to the AFL, while others, like the UAW, wrestled with political struggles between leftist and moderate leaders. By 1940 the CIO was a divided, floundering organization.[56]

The steadily escalating feud between Lewis and Hillman inflamed these divisions, especially after they chose different sides in the 1940 presidential election. Lewis's belligerent isolationism had the effect of isolating him from the mainstream of the CIO, which continued to support Roosevelt. No other labor leader identified more closely with the administration's foreign policy than Hillman. His selection to represent labor on the NDAC convinced Lewis that the president was using Hillman to co-opt the labor movement and push it in another direction. Lewis hurled a steady stream of invective at most of what NDAC did or didn't do. The election's outcome sealed his fate in the CIO. At its convention two weeks after the election, some delegates made a concerted effort to keep Lewis in power. Hillman helped defuse it with a shrewd speech that praised Lewis and regretted his departure from power while promoting Murray as his replacement.[57]

During 1941 the change from Lewis to Murray brought the CIO the growth and stability lacking earlier. Boosted by the rise of defense production, union membership surged as the CIO fought tough battles to bring into the fold such resistant companies as Ford, Bethlehem, Republic, Westinghouse, International Harvester, and Goodyear, as well as shipyards, aircraft plants, and even some southern textile mills. The CIO emerged as a powerful institution led by two men, Hillman and Murray, who were close to the administration as well as capable, moderate leaders. But Lewis remained head of the influential UMW and continued his vendetta against Hillman. For Murray the problem was more subtle: how to emerge from Lewis's shadow without alienating him. The more Lewis attacked the administration's policies, the more of an embarrassment he became to the CIO's moderate leaders. The coal strike became one more test of this increasingly strained relationship.[58]

In April the UMW struck southern commercial bituminous mine operators, seeking not only better pay but recognition of the union shop. At one point Lewis actually called Roosevelt to suggest an increase in the minimum price of coal. "If they don't get together pretty soon on a price," noted Ickes, "there will be a real shortage of coal. Perhaps this is what . . . Lewis wants." Ickes regarded Lewis as an appeaser "willing to do anything . . . that will sabotage our preparedness program and our aid to England. There is absolutely no excuse for this coal strike." But it went on, forcing some industries two weeks later to shut down and threatening to take blast furnaces offline and cripple railroads as the nation's supply of coal dwindled to about two weeks' worth. Finally the operators gave in and conceded the union shop issue, but the captive mines—those owned by steel companies, railroads, and utilities—refused to accept the settlement.[59]

Through the summer Lewis and UMW worked to extend the union shop guarantee to the captive mines, which were located near Pittsburgh with smaller groups in West Virginia and near Birmingham. By September it had become clear that the union shop had become as crucial an issue to the unions as wages. Unhappy with the lack of progress, Lewis pulled the 53,000 employees of the captive mines off the job on September 15. Five days later the UMW agreed to reopen the mines for thirty days while negotiations took place. The talks dragged on without success. As the deadline neared, Roosevelt made two pleas for the miners to keep working while negotiations continued. With his appeals came three separate plans for a settlement from the NDMB. Lewis responded by summoning newsmen to the UMW's boardroom, where he delivered a haughty rejection of the president's appeals. Along the way he blasted the NDMB as being "casual and lackadaisical to the point of indifference" and denounced Hillman as being "responsible for the fantastic procedure which has been followed."[60]

Although annoyed, Roosevelt brushed aside the insult inherent in Lewis's defiance and offered a third appeal. The threat to defense industries was major; the companies served by the captive mines produced 80 percent of the nation's steel. Moreover, the captive mines were already 95 percent organized, but Lewis wanted the other 5 percent, and the owners balked at guaranteeing them to him. Relishing center stage as always, he emerged as the symbol for labor unrest even as other disputes and strikes occurred during the same period. Indignant congressmen vented their anger with another rash of anti-strike bills, and political cartoonists had a field day flogging Lewis. Senator Tom Connally of Texas called him "the fourth member of the Axis."[61]

On November 10 the NDMB, which had tended to favor labor's position in its decisions, surprised everyone by ruling against Lewis's demand for a closed shop. Only two board members, Murray and Thomas Kennedy of the UMW, had supported it; the four employer and three public representatives voted against it, as did the two AFL members. Outraged at the finding, the two CIO representatives promptly resigned from the board, and the union withdrew all of its cases awaiting consideration by the NDMB. Hastily Roosevelt and Stimson put together a program of what to do if the strike went forward and the mines had to be seized. With resumption of the strike looming on November 15, Roosevelt summoned Lewis, Murray, and Kennedy to the White House the day before to meet with steel company executives Eugene Grace of Bethlehem, Benjamin Fairless of U.S. Steel, and Frank Purnell of Youngstown Sheet & Tube. In stern tones he impressed on them the importance of steel to the defense effort and warned that Congress was ready to pass legislation to keep the mines running.[62]

Before his visitors could digest this warning, Roosevelt stunned them with another message. "I tell you frankly," he said, "that the Government of the United States will not order, nor will Congress pass legislation ordering a so-called closed shop." The administration would not compel the unorganized 5 percent of miners to join because "that would be too much like the Hitler method toward labor." He asked them to confer at length and report back to him on Monday, the seventeenth. Next day the six men filed into the Wardman Park Hotel to bargain. Purnell and Fairless were thought to be flexible, but bad blood had long existed between Lewis and Grace, who was notorious for his antilabor attitude. *Time* described their clash as one between "the smooth, hard-boiled man whose income has averaged about $600,000 a year for 23 years" and "the huge, hard-boiled man who has seldom been down a mine in the last 20 years, who lives luxuriously on $25,000 a year (and perquisites) squeezed out of the $35-a-week earnings of 400,000 very poor men."[63]

The bargaining sessions went nowhere. At 4:30 P.M. on Sunday Lewis walked out of the conference room and told reporters tersely, "The conversations are terminated. No conclusions have been reached." The miners went back out on strike and received the reluctant support of the CIO, which resented the position Lewis had put them in but saw no other alternative. By November 21 some 175,000 workers from the commercial mines had joined the strike. During that week the cabinet agreed that the army might have to seize the mines but flailed around over how best to do it. Stimson was adamant that if the army was called in, it must be allowed to finish the job with full support from the president. Roosevelt agreed but backtracked at the cabinet meeting next day. Stimson was furious. "We had the hardest and hottest debate at Cabinet that we have ever had," he recorded, "and I really talked out to the President more than I ever have."[64]

The debate went on for a full hour. Stimson's argument did not convince Ickes, who admitted to being "discouraged not only by Stimson's attitude but by his slowness in grasping what the President had in mind. His mind seemed to be far from alert. He was tenacious of his own position to that degree that the president exhibited some impatience." But Stimson had a point to make: There was a crucial difference between using the army to break the strike by closing the mines and merely using it as a police force to deal with sporadic episodes, which ought to be handled by local authorities. Roosevelt finally agreed with him, but before the troops were assembled Lewis abruptly reversed course and called off the strike. On November 22 the president announced that both sides had agreed to arbitration by a three-man board. Stimson congratulated Roosevelt for using an approach that "gradually fenced Lewis into a corner from which he can't get out."[65]

Nevertheless, Lewis got his closed shop. The board handed down its decision on December 7, a day on which another event completely dominated the news. The arbitration agreement relieved Roosevelt of one nagging labor dispute, but others remained. During November an ugly strike at Air Associates in Bendix, New Jersey, compelled the president to send in troops for the third time. For months the threat had also loomed of a major railroad strike, the first since 1922. By November plans were outlined for what *Time* called "the most daring, gigantic, inconceivable strike in all U.S. history." The rail unions were hardly hotheaded radicals. As the nation's oldest unions, the brotherhoods had become the aristocrats of American labor. But the cumbersome strike-prevention machinery created by the Railway Labor Act had produced wage increases far below what the unions had demanded. The planned, carefully orchestrated strike, which would paralyze the entire American rail system, was scheduled to begin on December 7.[66]

The major casualty of the coal strike proved to be the NDMB. The resignation of Murray and Kennedy left the board in limbo, alive but inactive until its status was clarified. Despite widespread criticism that it favored labor, the board had done an effective job. During the ten months of its existence it had adjusted 96 of the 118 cases on its docket. Much of the credit for its record belonged to the chairman, William H. Davis, a strong advocate of mediation and voluntary collective bargaining. With the board no longer functioning, the status of labor relations remained unsettled. Although the coal strike was settled, Roosevelt had by no means heard the last of John L. Lewis.[67]

CHAPTER 7

TO HAVE AND HAVE NOT

The old talk of "business as usual" *is being abandoned. The new talk is of "deprivations ahead." It's not a new tune but it's a new emphasis . . . The WHOLE economy is to be geared to defense (or war) efforts.*

—KIPLINGER'S [1]

The hardest lesson for us to learn in 1941 was that a lot of money wasn't enough . . . It was no substitute for rubber . . . or for much of manganese . . . for chrome or nickel or copper alloys.

—DONALD NELSON [2]

This spring, after one year of total verbal defense, we are producing mechanical luxuries that compete with defense not merely in normal but in boom quantities. He [Roosevelt] has encouraged this country to remain asleep and to dream that it could defeat Hitler without sacrifice or even without inconvenience.

—LIFE [3]

THE AUDIENCE THIS TIME WAS ESTIMATED at more than 65 million, with another 10 million listening overseas from Greenland to French Equatorial Africa. "Had so many human beings ever before in history hung on the words of one man?" asked a reporter. Seated in the East Room of the White House on Tuesday night, May 27, 1941, at 9:30 P.M., the president cast a sidelong glance at Gilbert Stuart's portrait of George Washington, then went on the air to proclaim a state of unlimited national emergency. Experts disagreed on what new powers it actually gave the executive but thought it allowed him to suspend the eight-hour provision in government contracts; requisition American ships; regulate Reserve bank and foreign transactions; suspend or take over radio facilities; increase the armed forces; take over power plants, dams, and reservoirs; expand credit; regulate imports and exports; take over industrial plants; and seize transportation facilities for the movement of troops. Small wonder that Alf Landon declared the speech to be "the end of democratic government in the United States, at least temporarily."[4]

In a calm but determined voice Roosevelt laid out his planned course of action. The nation would defend the Americas against all attacks, protect the freedom of the seas, produce more goods faster for the nations resisting aggression, and deliver them faster. It would forcibly resist any Axis attempt to grab such Atlantic stepping-stones as Iceland, Greenland, Labrador, the Cape Verdes, the Canaries, Madeira, and the Azores. To do this work more planes and ships would be added to those already patrolling the Atlantic, and they would not hesitate to use force to repel any attack. More ships would be sent to the British, and the whole mobilization program would be stepped up. Only the day before, Roosevelt had signed into law a bill giving the government legal authority to subordinate all civilian needs completely to defense production.[5]

Why was all this being done? "The first and fundamental reason," he stressed, "is that what started as a European war has developed, as the Nazis always intended it should develop, into a world war for world domination . . . It is unmistakably apparent to all of us that, unless the advance of Hitlerism is forcibly checked now, the Western Hemisphere will be within range of the Nazi weapons of destruction." Why did the United States have to help the British? "Every dollar of material that we send helps to keep the dictators away from our own hemisphere, and every day that they are held off gives us time to build more guns and tanks and planes and ships."[6]

Listening to the speech from the front row, Eleanor Roosevelt sensed the "suppressed and intense excitement" in the room. "Diplomats are trained to observe the amenities, no matter what they feel," she wrote in her column, "but everybody's face showed some emotion as the evening progressed." As for herself, she watched her husband's face until a thought suddenly overwhelmed her. "What a weight of responsibility this one man at the desk, facing the rest of the people, has to carry. Not just for this hemisphere alone but for the world as a whole!"[7]

Afterward a flood of letters and telegrams descended on the White House, the largest outpouring ever after a presidential speech. An astounding 95 percent approved Roosevelt's stand, as did most of the newspaper editorials. Wendell Willkie lent his support, along with a host of organizations ranging from the American Legion to the National League of Women Voters. A poll taken that week showed 62 percent of respondents convinced that Germany would attack the United States within ten years if Britain went down, and a like number believing that America should go into the war rather than let that happen. America First and the congressional isolationists pledged not to give up their fight to keep the country out of a "shooting war." At a mass meeting Charles Lindbergh accused Roosevelt of seeking "world domination" and asked, "Is it not time for us to turn to . . . new leadership?"[8]

Raymond Clapper regarded the new edict as a requiem to the days of business as usual. "We say good-bye now to the land we have known," he said in his radio broadcast that evening. "Like lovers about to be separated by a long journey, we sit in this hour of mellow twilight, thinking fondly of the past, wondering . . . It's been a grand life in America. We have had to work hard. But usually there was a good reward . . . Man has gained steadily in security and dignity, in hours of leisure, in those things that made his family comfortable and gave lift to his spirit. Under his feet, however rough the road, he felt the firm security of a nation fundamentally strong, safe from any enemy, able to live at peace by wishing to. In every one of us lived the promise of America. Now we see the distant fire rolling toward us . . . It is still some distance away, but the evil wind blows it toward us."[9]

Two weeks later the fire nudged even closer when news dribbled in from survivors that an American freighter, the *Robin Moor*, had been sunk in the South Atlantic by a German submarine—whether by accident or design, no one knew. Although the *Robin Moor* was no *Lusitania*, the incident invoked instant memories of the manner in which submarine warfare had dragged the United States into World War I. Roosevelt responded by closing all twenty-five German consulates in the United States and ordering their personnel out of the country by July 10. Nevertheless, the question hovered over the nation, as it had a quarter century earlier: How far would the United States go to protect its freedom of the seas in the Atlantic?[10]

BY MAY 1941 government officials estimated that conquered France alone was providing Germany more armaments from her repaired and reconstructed factories than the United States was supplying to Britain. This dismal fact underscored the nonstop criticism heaped on the American mobilization effort from all sides. The four key objectives of the defense effort—procurement, production, purchasing, and priorities—continued to defy every attempt to harness them through a concerted, organized campaign. OPM, like its predecessor, faced a huge task without the authority or plan of attack it needed to be successful. It was supposed to expedite production by involving itself in requirements, procurement, facilities, equipment, and raw materials, but its charge allowed it only to plan, survey, advise, coordinate, and encourage. Knudsenhillman served as policy formulators but had little more authority than they had in NDAC.[11]

OPM featured three main divisions: Production, Priorities, and Purchasing. John Biggers, Knudsen's second-in-command in NDAC, headed production, Nelson handled purchasing, and Stettinius oversaw priorities. For various reasons Hillman's Labor Division did not move from NDAC to OPM until mid-March and never played a significant role in production activity. Two key staff members joined the new agency: Herbert Emmerich as executive secretary and John Lord O'Brian as general counsel. Both proved to be valuable additions. The Production Division had two main functions, to oversee the construction or conversion of facilities and to ensure the supply of critical materials. During 1940 the guns-and-butter mentality discouraged restrictions on the output of civilian goods even as defense production grew. As a result, shortages of materials began to appear by the winter of 1941, which put increased pressure on OPM to develop an effective system of priorities. By March four materials—aluminum, nickel, magnesium, and neoprene (a synthetic rubber)—had been placed under priorities along with machine tools.[12]

Left unsaid in Roosevelt's announcement creating OPM was what it still could *not* do. It had no power to determine military and other requirements, place contracts, or purchase supplies. The military still decided its own needs on an arbitrary basis utterly lacking statistical support or rationale. OPM had no more power over priorities than its predecessor and therefore no control over the delivery of materials. For the first six months of its existence the three divisions operated independently of each other, as they had under NDAC. Each one had its own contacts with the military and other agencies. Anyone seeking a contract often had to approach each division separately, which made for a slow, cumbersome process. Most of OPM's personnel moved over from NDAC; the commission was never formally dissolved but its functions were gradually siphoned off.[13]

Statistical services remained a weak and controversial element in the whole mobilization process. The military utterly lacked adequate data on its needs and had no interest in developing any, preferring instead to operate as it had always done. Individual industries had data, but no government agency possessed the authority or information to create an overview of defense needs. Each of OPM's three divisions had its own statistical staff, and the Bureau of Research and Statistics (BRS) under the capable Stacy May was moved over from NDAC to OPM to serve as clearinghouse for all the divisions. However, most businessmen regarded the BRS as a bastion of New Dealers and academics bent on stepping up defense production at the expense of civilian output. In general they were leery of any influence by fuzzy-headed statisticians, economists, and "perfessors" on policymakers, a prejudice rooted deep in their dislike of the New Deal itself.[14]

This statistical vacuum meant that at bottom nobody knew who needed how much of what, or how those needs fit the available supply of anything. No single problem bedeviled the mobilization process more than this inability to match needs with available supply and its inevitable consequence, the difficulty of coordinating the flow of materials to the right sectors of production. "We had vast arrays of statistics," concluded one study. "But no one could say how good they were, or how complete. No one knew how they could be used effectively. Above all, no one could use them . . . to control and appraise the effectiveness of the implementation of policy decisions."[15]

This shortcoming reflected a deeper problem in the entire mobilization effort, one inherent in the notion of business as usual. The military had its ways of doing things and took pride in going by the book. So did the dollar-a-year businessmen who flocked to Washington. They came from corporations with established procedures and operating techniques for getting things done, a managerial structure that had evolved over time. As executives they were accustomed to making policy and having their organizations carry it out, just as the military and existing government agencies operated through their bureaucracies. They naturally assumed that their role was to make policy decisions, which would be implemented by existing bureaus, organizations, and especially the procurement divisions of the army and navy.[16]

This proved to be a fatal assumption because no such administrative machinery existed to handle the scale of defense production. Industrial war output grew at so explosive a rate that it deranged the functioning of the entire economy. None of the routine systems created to provide profit-and-loss accounting in private firms or to account for normal expenditures by government agencies yielded the kind of information needed by a central agency trying to determine the feasibility of military programs, their impact on the rest of the economy, how much plant expansion was needed for any given weapons program to meet future production schedules, and a host of other questions. Although the need for more and better data soon became obvious, the need for effective administrative machinery to interpret it and carry out policy decisions based on it was not yet recognized.[17]

Here especially did the legacy of World War I continue to haunt the mobilization process. As one study observed, echoing the sentiments of Bernard Baruch, "Many of the mistakes in the administration of controls in 1917 and 1918 were repeated in 1941 and 1942. Each new production or material-control problem was approached as if there were no fund of experience on which to draw. Time after time, the administrative and procedural blunders of the earlier years were reproduced in new settings." Some people openly scorned the experience. Baruch was taken aback when Hillman dismissed his lessons from the past by saying, "I don't want to hear about that old World War One stuff."[18]

PRIORITIES EMERGED EARLY as a weakness in the mobilization effort, one that could shape the entire process. Until June 1940 the slack in the American economy enabled it to absorb all the demands placed on it. Then the flood of orders from both the American and foreign governments began overloading contractors, who responded by competing for raw materials and hoarding goods. "As early as midsummer 1940, we detected the loud storm signals of the priorities issue," recalled Nelson, who was charged with studying the question and making recommendations to the president. To Nelson, a priorities system was at bottom a system of traffic control, and the traffic was increasing faster than anyone imagined. Late in June Congress gave the president authority to grant priority to orders for military goods over those for private or foreign buyers.[19]

On October 21, acting on Nelson's recommendation, Roosevelt created a Priorities Board and named Nelson as its head, with Knudsen, Stettinius, and Henderson as members. Almost at once a turf war began with the military. The ANMB had in June set up its own Priorities Committee, which was intent on gaining independent priority power. Nelson understood that priorities served three constituencies: the military, civilians, and foreign buyers. He learned quickly that hardly any military officers, in his tactful words, "realized how necessary it is to keep a civilian economy operating efficiently and in good health." Most of them embraced the dogma of Bob Patterson: "Everything else must be subordinated to defense. There can be no exceptions."[20]

It took only a few meetings for harmony to vanish. Douglas and Lockheed were making commercial airliners as well as transport planes for the army. In November 1940, with its orders increasing steadily, the army asked the Priorities Board to cancel the commercial work by both companies. The two firms insisted they could handle both obligations without difficulty, but Stimson was adamant that Douglas "was making 12 big commercial airplanes a month" while "in default on the 186 bombers which it ought to have been busy for us." A war of words commenced in the newspapers. One member of the priorities staff said unequivocally that the companies were right and the army wrong, but Patterson would not budge. He demanded that a "stop" order be issued and got his way.[21]

Disgusted by the episode, Nelson concluded that a priorities board with only advisory powers could not work. He went to see the president, eager to go home and determined this time to quit. Once again he encountered a fog of Rooseveltian charm. Before he could say anything, the president regaled him with one story after another until his hour had expired. "Don, I didn't really get a chance to hear what you had to say," Roosevelt said graciously as he waved his next appointment in, "but I have decided that I very much want you to stay. I'll be seeing you later." Only later did Nelson realize that "this was one of his most crafty and engaging characteristics: this method of talking you out of doing something which you firmly intended to do, of changing the subject at just the right moment, of seeing to it that you left his office charmed but baffled."[22]

Earlier Nelson had inexplicably authorized the ANMB to decide which items would be subject to preference ratings, leaving his board the right to approve any changes involving priorities. The ANMB began operating independently but never managed to extend its control over the army and navy supply bureaus, which left procurement officers free to operate on their own. By December 1940 the military had issued so many preference orders that the priorities system became a joke. Once NDAC gave way to OPM, Nelson took charge of the Purchasing Division, while Stettinius headed a new Priorities Division. By then the torrent of orders from home and abroad had begun to produce shortages of some materials as well as overload the capacity of many firms. Under Stettinius the Priorities Division and its committees floundered while the military gained increasing dominance. The original system under NDAC concentrated on 200 items the military listed as most important to its needs. Gradually the military expanded the list to a wide variety of materials, parts, and equipment until it became virtually useless.[23]

The preference ratings ranged from A-1 to B-10 and soon required subsets such as A-1-a to A-1-j. As the volume of requests increased, a technique used in World War I was dusted off and put into service. The first general preference order, P-1, issued on March 12, 1941, listed a variety of items as eligible for preference ratings, including electric motors, switches, steel bars, plates, forgings, and castings. Order P-2 covered machine tool parts, and P-3 airframes. Another series, beginning with M-1, aimed to conserve supplies of strategic materials such as aluminum, tungsten, and neoprene. With these orders came an enormous increase in the amount of paperwork as well as a tendency to inflate ratings, especially after the passage of Lend-Lease that same March. The most basic problem, however, was the ancient one of supply and demand; manufacturers wanted more of key raw materials than could be provided for them. The military and private manufacturers alike took to hoarding materials, which, as Eliot Janeway observed, "turned OPM's priorities orders into so many rubber checks."[24]

* * *

THE M-1 ORDER TRIED to rationalize the distribution of aluminum, which had already grown hard to obtain. In the Aviation Age aluminum had emerged as a strategically important material. It was a third lighter than steel, durable, and never rusted, making it ideal for planes. Aluminum was derived from alumina, a substance that made up about 8 percent of the earth's crust. The best source for alumina was a clay called bauxite. Four pounds of high-grade bauxite yielded two pounds of alumina, which made one pound of aluminum. Decent quantities of high-grade bauxite existed only in British and Dutch Guiana and in a small area of Arkansas. The conversion process required enormous amounts of electricity, 10 to 12 kilowatt-hours for every pound of aluminum. Producing the metal required access to a large supply of water power.[25]

When Roosevelt issued his call for 50,000 planes, it exposed the first of two serious problems concerning aluminum. Nobody—not the aircraft makers, the military, or Alcoa—knew just how much aluminum went into any of the airplanes being manufactured. As a result, nobody knew how much was needed or had any way to measure whether existing output matched foreseeable demand. Neither the army nor the navy could come up with gross figures on what alloy or type of aluminum was required for sheet, forgings, extrusions, or tubing. Neither did anyone care to admit ignorance. In 1939 Alcoa had produced a record high of 327 million pounds of raw aluminum, nearly all of which went into commercial products. It had a capacity of about 335 million pounds, but its output depended on the reliability of its water power, which could be reduced by drought.[26]

Producing aluminum was but the first of several steps. The basic metal had to be alloyed, then shaped into sheets, castings, and forgings for each of its many products. An airplane wing strut might require one kind of tubing, the landing gear another, and the rudder a third. A shortage in aluminum, therefore, might be of the basic metal or any one of its fabricated forms. When a bottleneck arose, locating its real source took time and patience, since it was as likely to be at some fabricating stage as with the supply of raw aluminum. In this area, as in the creation of the metal itself, Alcoa had cornered most of the facilities for preliminary fabrication.[27]

The second problem was Alcoa itself. For all the nation's furor through the years about monopoly, no major company had ever achieved complete control of its field—except Alcoa. Having started the industry in 1888, it had produced every pound of raw aluminum made in the country. It controlled the mines that produced high-grade bauxite and the sources of electric power needed to convert it into aluminum. When Niagara Falls was first exploited for electric power in 1895, Alcoa supplied its own generators and got the utility company to agree never to sell power to any other aluminum company. It did the same with the rivers feeding into the rapids of the St. Lawrence River in Quebec. For years it resisted efforts by the Roosevelt administration and others to develop more use of the St. Lawrence for power.[28]

"There never was a monopoly as tight and as agile as ALCOA," said Arthur Goldschmidt, who worked for Ickes. "First they had patent control, then they moved to control power, then mining. Everything they did was calculated to keep supply down and prices up. They even kept the auto industry—no mean feat—from having scrap, fearing it would lower prices." Ickes himself, after hearing a report by Thurman Arnold of the Justice Department, called Alcoa "one of the worst monopolies that has ever been able to fasten itself upon American life." In 1937 the federal government launched an antitrust suit, but four years later it had still not been decided. Part of the problem was finding experts knowledgeable about aluminum who did not work for Alcoa.[29]

The lack of reliable information did not deter Stettinius from assuring the country that the supply of aluminum was ample. In October 1940, while still head of NDAC's Materials Division, he told the press that the supply was sufficient for both military and civilian needs. On November 28 he went even further, declaring that a "surplus" of aluminum existed. When near the year's end Northrop complained that it was cutting its work shifts by 20 percent because of a lack of aluminum, Stettinius looked into the matter and reported that these were "mere temporary delays." Although General Marshall reported a similar situation at the Martin plant near Baltimore, Stettinius waxed indignant that "public anxiety over our national defense preparations should be based upon reports of shortages which do not exist." Northrop's peeved chairman of the board snapped back, "If a delay in the receipt of raw materials of nearly half a year is not a shortage, I don't know what one is."[30]

Richard S. Reynolds saw the seriousness of the problem earlier than most. A nephew of the cigarette manufacturer R. J. Reynolds, he got out of the business in 1912 and eventually drifted into making tinfoil for cigarette packs. Reynolds bought aluminum from Alcoa and also imported ingots from France. During the summer of 1939 he was alarmed to hear that Germany was buying large amounts of bauxite from France. He asked a French aluminum company official who visited him that summer why, with war looming, the French were selling key airplane material to Germany. The Frenchman assured him that the Germans were using the aluminum "for making things like window frames and doorknobs." A few months later the bauxite was bombing France and his visitor was managing a French aluminum plant for the Nazis.[31]

After the blitzkrieg began, Reynolds went to see Senator Lister Hill of Alabama and warned him that this war would not be in the trenches but in the air, which made aluminum critical. Hill asked him to visit Arthur Vining

Davis, Alcoa's chairman, to assess American output of the metal. Reynolds urged Davis to ask the government for funds to triple Alcoa's output, along with safeguards to protect its monopoly. Davis saw no reason to be alarmed. There would be more than enough aluminum for all purposes, he assured Reynolds. Possibly Reynolds did not know that the government's suit against Alcoa had charged the company with trying to restrict the supply of aluminum and that Alcoa had informed the federal court that the nation had plenty of aluminum. Yet by June OPM had launched a publicity campaign to collect scrap aluminum because a shortage loomed.[32]

Unimpressed by Davis, Reynolds decided on a bold move: By mortgaging eighteen of his factories he obtained $20 million in loans from the RFC to build an ingot factory at Listerhill, Alabama, and another plant at Longview, Washington, where it could draw power from the Bonneville Dam. For the first time Alcoa would have a competitor, small as it was, and Davis was not pleased. Alcoa wanted power from Bonneville for a plant and pressed the government hard for it. Patterson recognized the need for expansion of aluminum output and argued that Alcoa was best suited to accomplish it. Ickes opposed giving the company a monopoly of power in the Northwest. Frank Knox found that a major cause of the shortage was the lack of workmen who knew how to process aluminum pig because Alcoa had been careful not to let its workers know all the secrets of final processing. Attempts had been made to import some aluminum workers from Switzerland, but Germany brought pressure on the Swiss government to deny passports.[33]

After hearing Thurman Arnold give "a very complete and very black picture" of Alcoa's endeavors, Ickes determined to deny the company access to Bonneville power if at all possible. He resented having been misled by Stettinius's earlier assurances of a plentiful supply. "This is so far from the truth," he growled, "that recently these same people have had to admit not only that there is a present shortage but that there would be a greater shortage." Still Patterson persisted in favoring Alcoa, arguing that the national emergency should override all other considerations. "I believe that he would turn over every kilowatt of power if Alcoa wanted it," grumbled an unimpressed Ickes. When a contract was negotiated in February 1941 for Reynolds to build his mill at Bonneville, Ickes held it up until he could talk to another rising star in the defense effort, Henry J. Kaiser.[34]

A few days later Jesse Jones surprised Ickes by urging him to go with Reynolds and deny any more power to Alcoa. Jones had already agreed to provide funding for the plant. Ickes promptly executed the contract, pleased that "we are really setting up a rival to Alcoa." Later, however, Alcoa gained access to Bonneville power because the aluminum shortage continued to mount, forc-

ing the government to spend $250 million in financing new plants to be oper-
ated by Alcoa, Reynolds, and Bohn Aluminum & Brass. A decision to increase
the output of bombers added to the already strong demand for aluminum. By
July Davis had changed his tune and told Baruch he was willing to do whatever the government wanted in expanding aluminum output.[35]

Davis kept his word and got at least part of what he wanted. In August
Alcoa agreed to build three new government-owned plants capable of producing 400 million pounds a year, increasing the nation's current capacity by 40
percent. The government put up $52 million for construction and leased the
plants to Alcoa for five years. Alcoa would pocket only 15 percent of the profits, the rest going to the government. One of the plants would draw power
from the Bonneville dam along with the Reynolds facility. At the same time,
Alcoa announced a price cut effective October 1 from 17 to 15 cents a pound.
Yet even more aluminum was needed. Reynolds agreed to build another
plant, and OPM recommended that the government add another 600 million
pounds of capacity to Alcoa's plant in Arkansas.[36]

Ickes had wanted to accept Kaiser's proposal for an aluminum plant because he regarded him as "one of the biggest contractors in the country. I
have had dealings with him and have found him to be a man of imagination
and great driving energy." He preferred Kaiser to Reynolds because "he is not
afraid of the Aluminum Company of America and will stand up to that concern." Thwarted in aluminum, Kaiser turned to competing with Alcoa on
another front. Magnesium was even lighter than aluminum by about a third,
almost as strong when alloyed, and could be produced about as cheaply. After
World War I Alcoa bought up all the American producers of magnesium except Dow Chemical. The two companies formed a patent pool and marketing
agreement with Germany's IG Farben to control output and prices. During
the late 1930s Germany's production far exceeded that of the United States; in
1940 Germany turned out 80,000 tons compared to America's paltry 4,000
tons.[37]

Despite Dow's assurances that it could handle all defense needs, Kaiser
began looking for ways to produce magnesium that skirted the Dow-Alcoa
patent wall. Learning of a different process developed by an Austrian expatri-
ate, he borrowed a total of $22 million from the RFC to build a magnesium
plant adjacent to his giant Permanente Cement plant near Palo Alto, California. The plant opened in August but got off to a stumbling start with two accidents that claimed five lives and a flawed process that took months to fix.
"It's a thrilling achievement," said Harry Davis, Permanente's manager, "to
take a raw material worth four bits a ton and turn it into a metal worth five
hundred and forty dollars a ton to the United States Government." But the

transformation had not yet occurred, and Kaiser began to wonder if it ever would.[38]

STEEL POSED A drearily similar problem. Having undergone a miserable decade where production averaged only 48 percent of capacity, the industry rejoiced at the steep demand created by mobilization. At the same time, it was wary of any attempt to increase its existing capacity. Steel executives were adamant in their belief that existing plants could handle any and all defense needs as well as those of the civilian economy. Part of the problem lay in the inadequate requirement figures from the military. For 1940 the ANMB had projected that the armed forces would need at most no more than 17 percent of steel's existing capacity; by March 1941 defense orders had swallowed 30 percent of capacity. The army agreed with the steelmakers that no expansion was needed; the navy thought otherwise.[39]

By late 1940 a stormy battle was under way between steel's leaders and New Dealers who insisted that the industry had to expand. NDAC split on the issue as well. "If everything in this country was in as good shape as steel to supply the national defense program and England," asserted Tom Girdler of Republic Steel, "there would be nothing to worry about." But William L. Batt, Stettinius's deputy in NDAC and head of a ball-bearing company, said he was convinced "that the steel industry must enlarge its capacity, and I see indications that the industry realizes it too." Roosevelt summoned Stettinius and told him he wanted less talk and more steel. Apart from the rising tide of foreign orders, what would happen if the long-dormant railroads started ordering new equipment? A few companies had begun modest increases in their capacity, but serious expansion would require eighteen months to install new blast furnaces and rolling mills.[40]

One allegation charged that the tightening supply had led some steel companies to hold back orders from Britain in order to satisfy the needs of old customers at home. In December Roosevelt had asked Gano Dunn, president of an engineering firm, to study the problem and make a report. Dunn was supposed to be a disinterested party, but his findings astonished even the steel executives. On February 28 he reported that not only was steel capacity sufficient for emergency needs but that there existed excess capacity for 1941 of 10 million to 14 million tons. Roosevelt doubted the findings but had to endorse them to avoid triggering panic buying of steel. Leonard Ayres, chief statistician for the War Department, declared that in most cases the building of new plants or additions should be avoided. Columnist Ralph Robey chided steel's critics for being "wrong on their facts. Our steel industry can meet any demand made upon it by the defense program." The major steel companies reported record earnings for 1940, yet continued to insist that expansion was unnecessary. Walter S. Tower, the steel consultant for both NDAC and OPM, happened also to be president of the American Iron and Steel Institute. He recommended that the agencies accept Dunn's findings.[41]

This chorus of assurances won few converts. I. F. Stone marveled at Dunn's "remarkable ingenuity at arithmetic." *Time* dissected Dunn's report and concluded that "if any of the numerous Dunn 'ifs' break down, there will be a real steel shortage soon." *Fortune* also analyzed the eighty-page report and found that its "fatal weakness . . . is not in what it says. It is in what it left unsaid. In its cozy assumptions it ignores what is actually happening in steel *now*, and what will inevitably happen if the nation ever goes full out on a war program." With steel output already running at 97 percent of capacity, no margin remained for the unexpected. Deliveries were being pushed back, and in an emergency controls and curtailment of civilian use would certainly be imposed. Within weeks circumstances laid bare the absurdity of Dunn's conclusions.[42]

Between January and June defense production doubled, spurred not only by soaring military budgets but also by the passage of Lend-Lease in March. Spot shortages began turning into large ones, leading to more delays. By March the output of structural steel was already two months behind schedule, and new orders faced a delay of five months or more. Shipyards could not get enough steel plate because munitions plants were claiming so much of it. The manufacture of railroad cars halted, and shortages plagued heavy forgings, tool steel, and other alloys. Civilian consumption also continued to rise, and the steel men continued to favor their longtime customers, especially the booming automobile industry. By May shortages had become acute in some areas, yet the industry continued to resist expansion. "What would we do with 30,000,000 tons more?" asked Knudsen, of all people. "That's too much for me . . . Let's keep our feet on the ground."[43]

On May 22 Dunn issued a second report with revised figures suggesting that 1941 would see a shortage of 1.4 million tons rather than a surplus. "Mr. Dunn had to eat his own words," wrote an unconvinced Stone, "but he ate them very gingerly." Roosevelt asked OPM to study a proposal for expanding steel production by 15 million tons, with the government financing the work through the Defense Plant Corporation (DPC). The steelmakers, in not-so-secret meetings with Jesse Jones, James Forrestal, and two OPM men, agreed to start plans for a 10-million-ton expansion, but this would take time. Meanwhile, Leon Henderson and the War Department agreed on at least one thing: Something had to be done to curtail civilian consumption of steel.[44]

*   *   *

STIMSON AND OTHERS liked to call OPM's leadership the "Big Four." Although the other remnants of NDAC languished, Leon Henderson kept his imposing presence in the forefront of activity. The man some called "FDR's tough guy" was too loud, too brash, and too energetic to dwell in the shadows. "Leon has an almost religious willingness to fight for what he thinks is right," observed a White House intimate. "That's what the President likes in him." Although he stood only five foot seven, everything about him seemed oversized. His burly, restless 200-pound frame made a shambles of everything he wore. He chewed gum, chomped cigars, liked his whiskey, and boasted of being the best no-trump bridge player in Washington. Above all, he liked to trample the toes of those he thought held wrong or outmoded ideas or who blocked action he deemed necessary. To refined eyes he looked more like a truck driver than a former professor, and he swore as vigorously as one.[45]

To an amused John Kenneth Galbraith, Henderson seemed always to be tugging at his belt, and his loose pants, struggling in vain to climb over his belly, flopped when he walked. "The rest of Leon's attire was somewhat more disorderly," Galbraith added. "He shaved regularly but without precision. His face alternated between an expression of unconvincing belligerence and one of shocked, unbelieving innocence, and sometimes he favored both at the same time." But Galbraith admired Henderson's powerful intellect and retentive mind. "After a few minutes' study of a paper on any subject, however complex," he wrote, "he not only had absorbed it for all needed use but could give convincingly the impression that he had written it himself."[46]

Like Baruch, Henderson believed in the power of persuasion and patriotism to move industrialists, as well as judicious use of publicity when all else failed. Although he could be a rampaging bull and often was, he also practiced the art of sweet talk. His economic ideas were unorthodox to both classical and New Deal economists, and he loved to argue them. He had also come to believe that it was imperative for the country to plan for a long war and that the key to victory was to swamp the enemy with overwhelming production.[47]

His energy and drive were legendary, as was his capacity for working long hours. During the early years of the New Deal he held as many as six positions at a time, which was about half the number he had while putting himself through college. Alone among the leading New Dealers he frequented the Press Club and became popular among newsmen. On weekends he retreated to his summer cottage near Annapolis, pulled on a pair of shorts, grabbed a bottle of whiskey, and took his boat out to fish and sing hymns with great gusto. Friends and enemies alike tagged him as a card-carrying character but one of immense intelligence and ability. Even more, he was fearless in marching toward his objectives with the subtlety of a bull elephant. Ickes, who had known Henderson for years, admitted that he was "a man whom I just don't like personally. I never have and I doubt if I ever will be able to care for him."[48]

A product of Millville, New Jersey, Henderson endured a rugged childhood, working constantly at a host of jobs while going to school and playing three sports. He wangled a scholarship to Swarthmore, where he continued to work at several jobs while taking classes and playing baseball. His teachers marveled at his persistence but saw nothing special in his ability; one admitted later to being dumbfounded at his success. He left Swarthmore in 1917 to join the army and advanced to the rank of captain while holding a desk job in Washington. In the fall of 1919 he returned to Swarthmore, got his degree, and taught economics at Pennsylvania and Carnegie Tech, an experience that led him to dispute many of the classical economic theories. He left teaching to work for Governor Gifford Pinchot of Pennsylvania, then took a job at the Russell Sage Foundation. Along the way he married the daughter of a railroad engineer and had three children.[49]

A meeting with General Hugh Johnson in 1933 landed Henderson a position with the National Recovery Administration, where he soon earned a reputation not only as a bright economist and indefatigable worker but also as an uncanny prophet. Shunning the usual measurements employed by orthodox economists, he had called the stock market collapse in 1929 (but not its severity) and England's departure from the gold standard. During the New Deal era he had a knack for predicting surges and falls in business. Most famously, during the recovery year of 1937 he wrote a memorandum predicting another depression within a year. No one took him seriously; most New Dealers were convinced the recovery would continue. When the recession of 1938 hit, Henderson's star in the administration rose as sharply as the economy fell. He was made executive secretary of the Temporary National Economic Committee, called by some the great antimonopoly crusade, and then head of the Securities and Exchange Commission as well.[50]

Both positions gave Henderson a fine grounding for his post at NDAC. One of his first acts was to order his staff to read and digest everything they could find on America's experience in the last war. Curiously, he was the only NDAC commissioner to consult Bernard Baruch. Henderson began meeting regularly with him and soon won the old man over as a warm supporter. He also grew close to Donald Nelson, and the two of them formed an alliance opposing Knudsen and Stettinius on many issues. When OPM was created, Henderson's power over priorities was moved elsewhere, leaving him in charge only of prices. His furious work pace had aggravated his weak back and made him physically ill. When the president told him to take a month off, Henderson fled to Florida until Roosevelt recalled him for yet another position.[51]

The winter of 1941 brought creeping shortages and with them a rise in prices that, coupled with growing demands for wage increases, threatened to bloom into an inflationary spiral. By spring the threat could no longer be ignored. Between May 1940 and February 1941 industrial production rose 24 percent, but the wholesale price index climbed only 3 percent. The shortages and wage demands had not yet affected the entire economy, and Roosevelt was determined to keep them at bay. On April 11 he announced the creation of yet another new agency, the Office of Price Administration and Civilian Supply (OPACS), and put Henderson at its head. The new organization combined the two NDAC units led by Henderson and Harriet Elliott. Its task was to stabilize prices, hold down the cost of living, guard against profiteering and hoarding, and protect consumers by maximizing the output of materials and goods for civilian use once the military's needs had been met. Rising prices of key commodities had raised public concern over the possibility of inflation.[52]

Henderson lost no time making his presence felt. The steel manufacturers, having given their workers a wage increase of 10 cents per hour, announced that they would pass the expense on via a price increase. This posed a major inflationary threat; iron and steel products comprised nearly 12 percent of all manufactures. Within a week of his appointment Henderson slapped a price ceiling on all iron and steel products. The manufacturers cried in protest even though the industry's profits had increased by nearly 99 percent in 1940. By August he had issued formal price ceilings for pig iron, brass and nickel scrap, hides, combed cotton yarn, and a few other textile products. Letters were sent to firms in other industries urging them to hold their prices in line voluntarily. Through these actions nearly a quarter of the wholesale price structure came under formal or informal controls. At the end of August the Civilian Allocation Division was transferred back to OPM, and OPACS was renamed OPA, the Office of Price Administration.[53]

By then OPM and OPACS had already locked horns, in part because their responsibilities overlapped but even more because of a dispute that erupted between Knudsen and Henderson. With aluminum, magnesium, zinc, and other metals already running short and steel heading in the same direction, Henderson argued that civilian production was doing too much business as usual and consuming too large a share of key commodities. OPM had imposed mandatory priorities on aluminum and steel with little effect. Henderson wanted cutbacks in production of certain civilian goods, most notably the biggest consumer of raw materials. In 1939 the automobile industry swallowed 80 percent of all rubber consumed in the nation, 51 percent of malleable iron, 34.2 percent of lead, 18.1 percent of steel, 23 percent of nickel, 13.7 percent of copper, 11.4 percent of tin, and 9.7 percent of aluminum.[54]

In July 1940 Kiplinger's had predicted that "Automobiles will be cut way down . . . perhaps 70%. New cars by this time next year will be really SCARCE." Instead production ran at record levels during 1941, thanks in large part to the defense boom that put more money in people's pockets. The manufacturers made few design changes in the '41 models, preferring to load them up with what *Time* called "a superabundance of 'gingerbread'" in the form of nickel, chromium, and golden bronze. Air-conditioning had become almost standard on sedans, and power-operated tops on convertibles. All the mechanical improvements and adornments consumed more raw materials than ever, which is what aroused Henderson's wrath.[55]

The growing shortages of key materials and some skilled labor in the spring of 1941 affected the automobile manufacturers no less than other industries. Knudsen met with leaders of the industry and on April 17 announced that all the manufacturers had agreed to a voluntary 20 percent reduction of production of next year's models, scheduled to begin August 1, "to make available more man power, materials, facilities, and management for the defense load." For all-outers this concession was not enough. Many thought the manufacturers agreed only because they couldn't get enough raw materials anyway. I. F. Stone pointed out that auto production of 1940 models, which ended in June, was running at a record level. In fact, the industry's output was the second highest in its history at a time when resources were urgently needed elsewhere.[56]

"Walter Lippmann suggests that we ought to take over the Azores," said Stone. "I think we ought to take over Detroit . . . We cannot fight a war with convertible coupes or overawe a Panzer division with a brigade of statistics on automobile sales. The problem is to turn existing mass-production facilities as rapidly as possible to the production of armament. We are fumbling the problem." Since production of the 1940 model was running 20 percent above the previous year, he added, the so-called reduction amounted only to going back to the more normal 1940 level. Stone was not alone in calling for Knudsen's resignation because he was seen as protecting his own industry at the expense of the defense effort.[57]

For months rumors had floated that a cadre of New Dealers were plotting to seize control of production. "One very necessary preliminary to the whole plan," reported *Time*, "the U. S. public must be disabused of its belief that . . . Knudsen is a great man, competent to handle defense." Already some gossip columnists friendly to the New Deal had begun overtures of criticism. Stimson too was undergoing a change of heart. In May Ickes had expressed his own reservations about Knudsen and those of others. Stimson agreed that Knudsen tended to be slow and somewhat lacking in initiative, but he still thought he was the best man for the job and was doing pretty well. But Stimson grew increasingly unhappy about the "enormous auto industry which is consuming so much skilled labor and so much facilities and yet is going on at a tremendous rate on what is really now a luxury . . . I am afraid that Knudsen is too soft and slow because of his connections with the automobile industry."[58]

Stimson was right in thinking that a showdown loomed. Henderson demanded a 50 percent cut in auto production; Knudsen insisted that such a move would create economic disorder. Interrupting a record production year would throw thousands of workers out of jobs while factories were converted to defense output, and who knew how long that would take? Walter Reuther of the UAW insisted that enough excess machine equipment existed in Detroit to build and equip new plants for airplane engines and frames while keeping the automobile assembly lines running. Knudsen and many others disagreed, insisting that the transition was better done gradually, thereby minimizing disruptions in both the factories and the economy.[59]

Part of the difficulty lay in what was meant by conversion. Months earlier Knudsen had explained to Roosevelt that curbing civilian production of cars meant shutting down plants for months to install new machines and tools. Most of the toolmakers would likely scatter to other jobs such as the airplane plants, and it would be hard to get them back. Charles E. Wilson of General Motors and other auto executives emphasized that there was no such thing as "partial conversion" of automobile facilities. It had to be done all the way or not at all. "When you convert one of our factories," said Wilson, "you move everything out and start with blank space . . . The production line will necessarily consist mainly of new, special-purpose machines along with any of the old machines that can be rebuilt for the new manufacturing process."[60]

Back in October 1940 Knudsen had held a secret meeting in Detroit of everyone involved in automobile manufacturing: the primary producers, the parts makers, and the tool and die makers. So many people attended that the meeting had to be moved from the directors' room to a closed fancy meat market downstairs, with chairs provided by a nearby undertaker. Knudsen showed the men numerous parts of airframes and aircraft engines; Major Jimmy Doolittle asked whether they could produce any or all of them. After inspecting and measuring the parts, nearly everyone concluded that they could reproduce them in their own plants. The lone dissenter was Charles E. Sorensen, Ford's legendary production man, who said Ford would not make parts for outside manufacturers who might complain that they didn't fit or were made improperly. Ford would produce entire planes or nothing.[61]

On January 8, 1941, Sorensen, Edsel Ford, his sons Benson and Henry Ford II, and two production men met in San Diego to inspect a Consolidated Aircraft factory where the new B-24 bomber was being assembled. "I liked neither what I saw nor what I heard," Sorensen wrote later. Consolidated hoped to produce a bomber a day, but to his eye the company had neither the right plant nor production methods. The scene reminded him of his early days of building the Model N Ford before Walter Flanders had created the assembly line and mass production. "Here was a custom-made plane," he said, "put together as a tailor would cut and fit a suit of clothes."[62]

The chaos of the scene appalled him: men crawling over fuselages, getting in each other's way, working and shouting with no apparent rhyme or reason. The final assembly took place outside in the heat of the California sun, where temperature changes distorted the metal and required adjustments on every plane. It was, he concluded, the epitome of what mass production was not. Asked what he would do instead, Sorensen promised an answer the next morning. He took his copious notes back to his hotel room and spent the entire night dashing off piles of sketches for a layout that could turn out a bomber an hour. It was, he wrote later, "the biggest challenge of my production career ... planning the layout for building not only something I had never put together before, but the largest and most complicated of all air transport and in numbers and at a rate never before thought possible." From this experience later arose the most gargantuan and controversial aircraft plant of the war: Willow Run.[63]

Still the pressure on the automobile industry mounted. Even as the manufacturers celebrated their near-record production year, Knudsen warned that the earlier 20 percent cut "doesn't mean a damn thing now." In August Knudsen decreed that production had to be cut 26.5 percent for the next four months with an eye to a 50 percent reduction for the year. Beginning September 15, new quotas would be set three months in advance for the rest of the year, with each cut deeper than the last. A 50 percent reduction would bring output down to the level of 1934. Some 90,000 to 200,000 people would be thrown out of work pending transfer to defense production. Dealers would suffer, and a growing demand for fewer cars would likely drive prices up, giving Henderson another headache.[64]

Nothing better illustrated the change in emphasis than the annual August preview of its new models that Chrysler hosted for newsmen. During the six-hour tour Chrysler officials led the reporters to inspect production lines building M-3 medium tanks, B-26 bomber fuselages, antitank guns, and army trucks. Half of Dodge's daily output consisted of 250 army trucks. New space had been leased and new facilities built to handle the company's $400 million worth of defense orders. "Here, just a year ago, stood a corn field," observed one guide. Chief test driver Frenchy Raes gave the newsmen a demonstration of a truck and small command car, speeding them through a sea of mud, whipping through thick underbrush, and cruising up and down a 45-degree grade. Near the end of the tour a Chrysler official asked the reporters if they would also like a peek at its new cars. "Yeah," replied one, "we might as well have a look at the by-product."[65]

Other auto manufacturers followed the Chrysler example when their turn came. General Motors staged an exhibit showing samples of defense products being made at sixty divisional plants in thirty-five cities, including Allison and Pratt & Whitney aircraft engines, aircraft machine guns, antiaircraft guns, ball bearings, diesel engines, and army trucks. Ford displayed its Navy Service School at River Rouge, which trained enlisted men as technicians, a nearly completed aircraft engine plant, also at River Rouge, and the early construction stages of the giant Willow Run bomber facility near Ypsilanti. Hudson had a new naval ordnance plant near Detroit that was already turning out antiaircraft guns and was preparing to make rear fuselages for B-26 bombers. Briggs showed off its new arms factory at Detroit that was mass-producing plane subassemblies.[66]

The Federal Reserve Board imposed a restriction of its own by limiting installment sales terms to eighteen months with a required down payment of at least one third. Price increases on the new models ranged from 7 to 23 percent. Already manufacturers were scrambling to find substitute materials for those made scarce by defense needs. Even before the crunch Henry Ford had developed an all-plastic-bodied automobile that he predicted would be mass-produced in one to three years. Some people expressed vague concerns about ersatz materials being put in cars; others wondered how the drop in production would affect needed replacements. Of the nearly 26.5 million cars on American roads in 1940, nearly half were more than five years old and more than 6.1 million were nine or more years old. About 4 million of them belonged to the government or commercial fleets; the rest were driven by individuals, most of whom depended on them to get to work. What would happen if they could no longer replace their old cars or get parts for them?[67]

THE POPULATION OF Astoria, Oregon, had declined by half over the past two decades to about 10,000, but the city's automobile dealers still managed to do a thriving business. Many of their customers were Finnish fishermen—the town was one-third Finnish—or lumberjacks who came down from the coastal logging camps. On Duane Street, the town's automobile row, the recent decrees emanating from distant Washington filled the dealers with concern about their future. With more potential buyers than ever and fewer cars (and who knew how low the supply would eventually go?), they worried about how to keep their business going. Already a few had let a salesman or other worker go to save expenses. "They want to make a whipping boy of this industry," grumbled Chrysler/Plymouth dealer E. C. Probst, who in September had dropped a salesman and a cleanup man from his staff. "We've got a President in this country that would stop making autos tonight."[68]

Two kinds of dealers inhabited Duane Street. A half-dozen older, established agencies had built their businesses around repair shops as well as car sales. The second group consisted of newcomers trying to cash in on the recent boom in auto sales. They concentrated on selling new cars and had little or no service capacity. Probst belonged to the latter group, who were the most vulnerable to any curtailment of new cars. Members of the first group were less worried. If the supply of new cars dwindled, they expected a brisk business in repairing older cars, tuneups, and parts sales. The factories had assured them that they could always get mechanical parts but that fancy accessories were not to be had.

Studebaker dealer Julius Johnson was deemed a maverick by his peers because he argued that production should be cut by two thirds. "There's nothing I love better than to see production curtailed," he said. "It's going to put the business on a sounder basis." Johnson had always bridled against the way the big manufacturers forced product on their dealers. He remembered a time when Ford, in liquidating old stock to raise cash, shipped $7,500 worth of unordered parts to an Astoria dealer and forced him to take $4,000 of them to keep his franchise. Johnson himself had lost his Chrysler/Plymouth dealership in 1939 when he flatly refused to take one leftover 1939 model with each new 1940 model shipped by the factory. There would be no more of this nonsense, at least for a while.

Sherman Lovell had the honor of being Astoria's oldest, biggest, and most successful dealer, having started his business in 1909 with a handful of Reo touring cars. He sold Buicks and Chevrolets, and his shop did a steady business. In September 1940 he pocketed $2,694 in bonus money for selling 229 Chevrolets and 93 Buicks. He projected a gross of $600,000 for 1941, which would yield a net profit of about $50,000 if all went well. More income would flow from the shop and the sale of parts and tires, unless tires were rationed. Sherman expected a good year despite the curtailments and credit restrictions. The city had five Ford and five Plymouth dealers competing for business. "The poor Plymouth dealers are the ones who're getting hell," he said. "It's not going to be hard on us. It'll make a nice, clean business. We can pick our deals."

Others disagreed, predicting that a shortage of new cars would revive the old practice of cutthroat deals in what one practitioner labeled "the dirtiest, most unethical of all large-volume businesses." The dealers of both camps knew all the tricks of the trade. They knew how to lure even uninterested buyers into a deal by offering them more for their used car than it was worth.

The reduction in output was spread proportionally. Since the Big Three of General Motors, Ford, and Chrysler produced 90 percent of all cars, they were cut an average of 52 percent, while the six smaller companies—Studebaker, Packard, Nash, Willys, Hudson, and Crosley—lost only 15 percent. None of them could load their reduction on one line or model; it had to be spread evenly according to a formula. The problem was how to apportion the remaining output among dealers. If Henderson's 50 percent reduction actually happened, dealer mortality could not be avoided. Not only the small dealers would be affected. Thirty percent of the dealers sold two thirds of the cars, and those who depended on the combination of volume and narrow margins would probably be the first to suffer.

The uncertainty of it all kept Astoria's dealers on edge. Older heads like Sherm Lovell took comfort in the strength of his repair shop; those without so reliable a standby had little to fall back on if the supply was curtailed even more. And further cuts were a real possibility. The manufacturers already realized that the 1942 model was probably the last new design that would be built until after the emergency. Frank Knox wanted the government to tell the manufacturers that no more passenger cars could be made. "Certainly we haven't cut down automobile production as we should," observed Ickes. "The result has been a greatly delayed war preparedness program."[69]

Spring brought more bad news to the desk of a weary president. Early in April the Germans invaded Greece and Yugoslavia, inflicting wholesale slaughter on the latter and forcing a surrender in eleven days. Greece held out for four weeks. On May 10 and 11 London endured its heaviest bombing yet. On the other side of the globe the Japanese subjected Chungking to a heavy bombing early in June. British forces were suffering reverses in North Africa, and German submarines were sinking British merchant ships almost at will in the North Atlantic. The British economy was in shambles and desperate for more aid. Stimson and Knox urged Roosevelt to ask Congress for power to convoy British ships across the Atlantic, but the president hesitated. He wanted to use convoys and figured he would eventually do so, but the time was not yet ripe. "Convoys mean shooting," he told a visitor, "and shooting means war." The issue soon turned into yet another political dogfight.[70]

While ducking the convoy issue, Roosevelt made other important moves. In April he signed an agreement placing Greenland under American protection for the duration of the war, thereby thwarting possible German access to an ideal location for an air base and submarine haven. He also removed the southern entrance to the Red Sea from the list of combat zones, allowing American merchant ships to carry supplies through the Suez Canal to neutral Egypt. A Gallup poll released early in May revealed an intriguing split of public opinion. Asked whether the navy should convoy British ships, the respondents said no by a 50 to 41 percent margin. However, asked whether the navy should convoy if British defeat seemed certain without this help, 71 percent said yes. A similar split occurred over whether the nation should go to war against Germany and Italy. An overwhelming 81 percent said the country should not, but when asked whether the United States should enter the war if there was no other way to defeat the Axis nations, 68 percent said yes.[71]

The president understood that the nation remained divided, that the defense program was far from shipshape, and that criticism continued to be heaped on him for its administrative shortcomings. By late spring the season of discontent was coming into full bloom even as the war itself grew more complex and uncertain.

CHAPTER 8

GETTING SHIPSHAPE

This emergency is so dire, so immediate and so pressing that no effort we could conceivably make would be more than just enough. The very best we can possibly do . . . will be just good enough, with nothing to spare.

—DONALD NELSON [1]

If you want fast ships, fast shipbuilding, fast women, or fast horses, you pay through the nose.

—ADMIRAL EMORY SCOTT "JERRY" LAND [2]

You find your key men by piling work on them. They say, "I can't do any more," and you say, "Sure you can." So you pile it on and they're doing more and more. Pretty soon you have men you can rely on absolutely.

—HENRY KAISER [3]

THEY CALLED IT THE "EMERGENCY program," and never was a name more apt. During 1941 three waves of new contracts were laid on top of an already accelerated shipbuilding program. In January the United States contracted for 200 more transport vessels and the British for 60. Then came Lend-Lease with its provision for transferring merchant and other ships to Britain. A third wave rolled in more gradually through the remainder of the year as orders poured in on already overworked shipyards. While the regular navy with its Bureau of Ships struggled to commission and build the vessels that would give it fleets in both oceans, the Maritime Commission improvised to tame the chaos that was fast becoming the merchant marine shipbuilding program. [4]

The task of overseeing this mad scramble fell to Jerry Land, who had become chairman of the Maritime Commission in April 1937. Lean, intense, athletic, and suitably profane as befits a sailor, Land owned a distinguished career and an impressive resume. He graduated from Annapolis in 1902 ranking sixth in his class and tops in half a dozen sports; two years earlier his touchdown on a trick play had enabled Navy to beat Army. After postgraduate work at MIT he served many years with the navy's Bureau of Construction and Repair (BCR), eventually becoming its head for four years. At fifty he got involved in aeronautics and qualified for a pilot's license. Sailors called him "the busiest guy in the Navy" and were stunned when at age fifty-eight he asked to be put on the retirement list. The reason became clear a few days after his retirement when Roosevelt appointed him to the new Maritime Commission under its first chairman, Joseph Kennedy. When Roosevelt sent Kennedy to London as ambassador in 1938, he made Land chairman of the commission.[5]

The president and Land had been friends since Roosevelt's days as assistant secretary of the navy. They had served together on the Guggenheim Fund for the Promotion of Aeronautics, and it was Roosevelt who in March 1933 promoted Land to chief of the BCR. Land had many qualities that appealed to the president. He insisted on loyalty at every level, moved and thought with a speed that galvanized those around him, and knew how to cut through red tape with a trenchant remark or act. Not overly modest, he liked to say that "I got my start in life by working from sunrise to sunset, with my hands, for $10.00 a month and keep." He claimed to prefer bureaus to commissions, saying on one occasion, "You know, I don't believe in the commission form of government; I think you ought to have a one-man show and shoot him at sunrise if he doesn't run it right." But beneath his tough veneer Land had a shrewd, practical bent that knew how to work with the material at hand.[6]

The job at hand was formidable. The existing merchant marine was not only small but dangerously old; by 1942 an estimated 92 percent of the ships built for the last war would be obsolete. Most of the shipping lines serving the foreign trade were family or privately owned. They were being asked to take over some routes vacated by the British and to accept a voluntary system of priorities to ensure delivery of vital defense materials. Land's mandate was clear: turn out ships and more ships, and turn them out fast. The navy had its own $4 billion shipbuilding program under way, and it also needed auxiliary ships to supplement the fighting vessels. Another key objective was keeping each program from getting in the other's way.[7]

Here too World War I offered an instructive lesson in the form of the Hog Island experience. In 1917 German submarines were sending ungodly amounts of British tonnage to the bottom, and a depleted American merchant marine had a puny eighty-one ships in foreign trade. The fleet relied on foreign bottoms for coal and other necessities, many of which were no longer available. To help the Allies, the United States embarked on a program to build a "bridge of ships" carrying supplies and ultimately troops to Europe. Hog Island, located in the Delaware River just below Philadelphia, became the site of the world's largest shipyard: 250 buildings, fifty ways, twenty-eight outfitting berths, and eighty miles of railroad track. At Hog Island ships were not so much built as assembled from parts fabricated at inland steel mills and shipped to the yard.[8]

The Hog Islanders had a standard design adapted from an old British tramp and could be produced relatively fast. They were 7,500-ton vessels that could do 11 knots. During a twenty-two-month period beginning in February 1918 Hog Island turned out a total of 122 ships; at its peak in 1919 a new keel was laid every five and a half days. Ironically, Hog Island didn't furnish a bridge of ships because the government didn't receive its first contribution until two months after the Armistice. Nevertheless, the lesson remained vivid in both Britain and the United States. As German submarines took their appalling toll on British ships, sinking 274 merchant vessels totaling 1.4 million tons in the five months between June and October 1940 alone, Churchill wrote Roosevelt in December 1940 that "it would seem that production on a scale comparable to that of the Hog Island scheme of the last war ought to be faced for 1942." At a press conference on January 3 Roosevelt announced that 200 such ships would be built, most of them in new facilities since existing ones were already booked solid. Hog Island itself would not be included; it had long since been dismantled and abandoned.[9]

"Nobody that loves ships can be very proud of them," admitted the president. But they could be turned out six to eight months faster than a conventional merchant ship. Jerry Land did not like having to build a fleet of "ugly ducklings," as *Time* labeled them. His conceit was to consider their construction an emergency program, which it was, for the benefit of the British, while the Maritime Commission devoted its main energies to the standard types. He preferred more ships built to standard designs, the sleek, speedy freighters that would restore American merchant marine supremacy. "The last thing I want to do," he wrote Roosevelt, "is to repeat the mistakes of the last war and have a lot of obsolete vessels on our hands unless the emergency is so great as to make this an absolute necessity."[10]

But Land recognized that the standard freighter types had no place in the emergency program. They took too long to build. In November 1940 he had written Knudsen that "the proper procedure for the production of ships in quantities is to settle on the *type* of ship . . . for quick delivery." It would be a "simple type of cargo ship with reciprocating engines, boiler pressure of 200 to 220 lbs., with all steam auxiliaries." Turbine engines improved speed but took longer to build, cost more, and would overload manufacturers already struggling to turn out enough of them for naval vessels. The old-fashioned diesel reciprocating engines would do for ships turned out as quickly as possible. Speed of production trumped speed of performance.[11]

When the commission was organized, it received a quota of 500 ships ranging from tankers to luxury liners. By March 1941 it had delivered 71 vessels to ship lines operating with government subsidies under the watch of Captain Howard Vickery, Land's key subordinate, who had charge of ship construction. Part of its task became hauling rusted old Hog Islanders out of dry dock and refitting them for duty as well as building new ones. Every available ship was needed because the emergency program kept growing. In April Roosevelt added another 112 ugly ducklings and 100 standard-design ships, including 72 tankers, to the list of emergency orders. He also issued an edict requisitioning idle foreign ships sitting in American ports. The foreign vessels belonged to belligerent nations or countries taken over by the Nazis.[12]

The new programs changed the geography of American shipbuilding. Where 92 of 133 existing ways in 1939 fronted the Atlantic Ocean, 70 of a projected 121 new ways went up on the Gulf and Pacific coasts. The decisions on where to locate new sites were, as always, charged with political pressure. Land kept several key criteria uppermost: adequate transportation, labor supply, and quality of management. The Northeast already had most of the existing shipyards and could not furnish much more labor. The South had plenty of labor but lacked engineers, naval architects, draftsmen, managers, foremen—what Land called "white collar brains." The West Coast was already busy with ship and aircraft production and had no steel industry to support shipbuilding. Despite its lack of management talent, the Gulf Coast appealed because of its mild climate, abundant labor supply, and low cost of living. Land decided to spread the load. Early in 1941 9 yards with a total of 65 ways were chosen to build the 260 ugly ducklings ranging from South Portland, Maine, to Portland, Oregon.[13]

The selection process involved not only where ships would be built but who would build them. Two of the nine new emergency yards were operated by familiar companies, Bethlehem and Newport News. Two others went to relative newcomers, American Shipbuilding, a company transplanted to New Orleans from the Great Lakes, and Alabama Dry Dock & Shipbuilding, a Mobile repair company. The other five sites were managed by a combine headed by a new team from Todd Shipyards, a large concern that had built ships in World War I and one of the two biggest operators on the West Coast. Founded twenty-five years earlier by William H. Todd, the company had made its reputation in repair work rather than construction. Late in 1939, it acquired the Seattle-Tacoma Shipbuilding Corporation and entered the construction lists.[14]

After Todd's death in 1932, his protégé, John D. Reilly, took command of the company. The tall, heavyset, blustery Reilly loved to throw big parties at the Waldorf but also knew how to get things done. In winning contracts for the emergency ships he relied heavily on associates, especially William S. "Pete" Newell of the Bath Iron Works, Jack McEachern, a tough Seattle contractor, and Roscoe Jay "Jim" Lamont, president of Seattle-Tacoma Shipbuilding. It was McEachern who brought the others together with a consortium of western contractors who had earned an impressive reputation for building the massive Boulder, Bonneville, and Grand Coulee dams. Known as the Six Companies, the consortium was dominated by a man fast gaining a reputation as one who got things done when others hesitated. *Fortune* called Henry J. Kaiser a man "whose Napoleonic dreams are hitched to a driving spirit."[15]

No one yet suspected how far or how fast Kaiser would drive the craft of shipbuilding. "Whether Kaiser and his coterie of dam builders have bitten off more than they can chew remains to be seen," added *Fortune*, "although the presumption is that they can get away with it."[16]

LITTLE IN HENRY Kaiser's background hinted at great achievements. Born in 1882 in a small farmhouse in upstate New York, he quit school at thirteen and embarked on the usual round of low-paying jobs endured by any hardworking adolescent intent on working his way up in the world. He developed a love for photography and at age twenty acquired his own small studio. He fell in love with the daughter of a well-to-do lumberman who imposed some tough terms for their courtship. Before Kaiser could marry Bess Fosburgh, he was told to go west, establish himself in a stable business, earn at least $125 a month, and build a house for her. In the summer of 1906 Kaiser boarded a train and headed west with no particular destination in mind. He landed in Spokane, Washington, and in ten months fulfilled the requirements demanded by Edgar Fosburgh.[17]

After his marriage Kaiser managed a hardware store, then became a salesman for a construction company while he learned the business. Beginning in 1914, he spent thirty years paving roads, laying pipelines, digging tunnels, erecting jetties, building sand and gravel facilities, and constructing dams. His boundless energy and enthusiasm made him an outstanding salesman, but he also earned a reputation for completing contracts well ahead of schedule. From building roads he developed an uncanny knack for coordinating the flow of workers and materials. He embraced new technologies, developed several inventions, and used his ebullient personality to charm men who later proved instrumental in his career. One of them, Warren A. Bechtel, became a mentor of sorts and drew Kaiser into a variety of new opportunities.[18]

The onset of depression in 1930 sent the construction industry into freefall. Kaiser escaped disaster by joining the Six Companies consortium to make what proved to be the winning bid to build Hoover Dam. It was a daring and colossal undertaking. The dam was 660 feet wide at the base, 726 feet high, and 45 feet across at the top. It required an estimated 4.5 million cubic yards of concrete, more than the Bureau of Reclamation had used in all its past projects combined, as well as 19 million pounds of reinforcing steel. The logistics were staggering and the political pressure for progress intense. A small town had to be built to house the workers who flocked to the desert in search of jobs. The consortium's progress and its clean handling of federal funds impressed even Ickes, who watched the project closely.[19]

When the work began, the consortium decided to make Kaiser their key figure in Washington. This experience opened the door to Kaiser's education in the ways of political and bureaucratic machinations, and the techniques of landing government contracts. He grew familiar with New Dealers and bureaucrats and mastered the art of gaining access to influential people. Success with the Hoover Dam helped him win the Bonneville and later the Grand Coulee contracts, although he lost the bid on the latter's preliminary work. Grand Coulee proved to be Kaiser's last major construction project. Begun in 1938 and finished in 1942, it was at the time the largest single structure ever built. After failing to win the contract for the Shasta Dam, Kaiser turned his attention to a business that had long intrigued him: manufacturing cement. From this decision arose the Permanente Cement Company, which produced its first bag in December 1939. It became the world's largest cement plant and knocked the price of cement down by 11 percent.[20]

That he knew nothing about running a cement plant did not faze him. Neither did the fact that five companies owned by very influential men dominated the West Coast cement industry and did not take kindly to his presence. Kaiser had a simple explanation for his decision. "It used to anger me to see the cement companies gouge the little contractor," he said. "Cement represented a major part of his costs, but there was nothing he could do about it." In a daring move he underbid the powerful West Coast combine to provide $6.9 million in cement for the Shasta Dam. The contractor had become an industrialist and once again demonstrated his talent for finding novel solutions to tough problems. Kaiser could tap sand and gravel pits situated only ten miles from Shasta, but the local railroad wanted what he deemed an exorbitant price of 27 cents a ton to haul the materials. His engineers proceeded to devise an amazing ten-mile-long conveyor system that moved thousands of tons 24/7 at a cost of 18 cents a ton. The "rubber railroad" became a marvel to journalists and spectators alike.[21]

The move to shipbuilding was hardly a stretch for Kaiser. During his boyhood, spent within eyesight of the Erie Canal, he developed a fascination for boats. As early as 1937 two of his associates in Six Companies argued that building ships was "about ripe to become big volume business," largely because of the Merchant Marine Act of 1936 that authorized the building of 500 merchant ships over ten years. The other partners showed little interest, but a year later Kaiser became a convert and was constructing ways for Jim Lamont's Seattle-Tacoma Shipbuilding Company. Lamont introduced Kaiser to John Reilly of Todd Shipyards, who wanted more construction contracts spread to West Coast shipbuilders rather than to the dominant Atlantic seaboard companies.[22]

In the summer of 1939 Reilly and Kaiser went to Washington and offered the Maritime Commission an audacious proposal. They would build a group of new yards to turn out ships on a quasi-mass-production basis if each yard were given a contract for not fewer than twenty nor more than fifty ships. When the commission declined their offer, Reilly and Kaiser enlisted Pete Newell and Steve Bechtel, Warren's son, and won a contract for five C-1 cargo ships. None of the Six Companies men, including Kaiser, had shipbuilding experience; they built the ways and went to school while Todd's workers constructed the ships. Late in 1940 the besieged British sent a commission to the United States to place an order for sixty ships. Todd and the Six Companies pursued the contract aggressively and won it even though some doubted whether they could handle it.[23]

Two new companies were formed to do the work. Todd–Bath Iron Shipbuilding built ships on the East Coast while Todd-California did the same on the West Coast in new yards paid for by the British. These contracts marked Kaiser's first direct entry into shipbuilding, though his role remained largely financial. He dwelled in the shadow of Reilly and Todd Shipbuilding, who were the known names in the industry, but he would not long remain there. Even as construction went forward on the new yards, Roosevelt announced the program to build 200 more ships. The news sent Kaiser's imagination soaring. Here, as in his other endeavors, he longed to become the biggest and best, turning out ships in some form of mass production yet to be devised.[24]

BUILDING SHIPS WAS a painstaking and arcane craft that did not lend itself to rush orders. A heavy cruiser could tie up a way for more than three years, a light cruiser only a year less, which is why so many new shipyards and ways were needed. The major shipyards were crammed with orders for naval vessels and had neither time, workers, materials, nor space for merchant ships. This desperate need was what galvanized Kaiser, Todd, and other shipbuilders. Success depended on speeding up the process, which in turn required fresh thinking, new techniques, and standardization of the type of ship to be built. The process began with design work and detailed drawings for engine makers and other vendors who supplied components. The big shipbuilders had their own design and engineering staffs; the smaller fry had to go usually to one of the two leading naval architects, William Francis Gibbs or George G. Sharp.[25]

The lanky, eccentric Gibbs, once described by a reporter as looking as though he had just stepped out of a coffin, did more than half the nation's independent ship-designing business. He owned a law degree from Columbia, but ship design became his passion. After a few years on his own Gibbs partnered with a well-known yacht designer, Daniel Hargate Cox. Married to the socialite daughter of famed lawyer Paul Cravath, he was anything but a bon vivant. He affected a lack of social graces, insisted he was a rank amateur at design, and when asked about his business would reply, "You never heard a waiter say the fish was poor."[26]

"Gibbs is a very peculiar man, you see," explained an associate. "I mean, he is like an artist. He likes his work." He was also meticulous and thorough, and his shrewd mind saw early the demand for more ships coming after the long drought of the 1930s. He responded by increasing his workforce from 750 to 1,000. It was to Gibbs that Todd–Six Companies came for design work after securing the British contract for sixty ships. When America announced its program of 200 ships, Gibbs was ready to play a role there as well.[27]

Gibbs liked to say that ships were built primarily by making decisions. The British wanted ships that were cheap to build and operate, and that could be built as quickly as possible. They envisioned a modified version of one of their old northeast-coast tramps with a length of about 440 feet, speed of 11 knots, carrying capacity of 10,000 tons, and reciprocating engines because turbines were too expensive and impossible to get, thanks to the flood of naval orders. Two Maritime Commission engineers ransacked the files and came up with an alternative design to the British model with about the same cost and deadweight. It was based on the Los Angeles class, a World War I type of which 238 were mass-produced along with 110 Hog Islanders. The two designs were thrashed out at a meeting on January 8 presided over by Land. Gibbs argued persuasively that the alternative design would delay the construction process. After another meeting five days later, Land decided to go with the British version.[28]

The task of preparing the plans and blueprints fell to the firm of Gibbs & Cox, which found translation of the British versions more difficult than they expected. Gradually the drawings incorporated several changes that made the American version distinct from its British prototype. From this tinkering emerged the infamous ugly duckling, which desperately needed a new name.

Land suggested calling them "Emergency Ships." In May 1941 they received the designation EC2. Although some persisted in calling them ugly ducklings, a Maritime commissioner insisted on referring to them collectively as the "Liberty fleet." As publicity about the new breed of freighters spread across the country, reporters and others began referring to them simply as "Liberty ships."[29]

A typical Liberty ship had deadweight tonnage of 10,419, measured 441 feet in length, stored cargo in five holds, and carried gun turrets fore and aft. Over time an already simple design was simplified even more. Don Nelson called it the "'Model T' . . . of the seaways." It did not cause an immediate sensation; during 1941 only seven were actually completed, five of them for the British, but the groundwork had been laid for output on a scale never before seen. The entire merchant ship program turned out 136 ships between July 1, 1940, and the end of 1941, far short of needs. It too had to compete for crucial materials such as steel plates and engine machinery as these grew scarcer. The navy enjoyed more pull and prestige among manufacturers; the Maritime Commission did not even get a seat on the ANMB until the spring of 1941.[30]

Like the Model T, the Liberty ship was basic to a fault, designed to be built as cheaply as possible. A host of items standard on most American vessels were omitted to save space and money. No fewer than thirty-five deviations from the Maritime Commission's own standards for fireproofing and crew comfort were made. The crew's lockers and rooms were made smaller; skylights and ventilator cowls had to be operated manually. The holds, engine and boiler rooms, and officers' and crew quarters all lacked mechanical ventilation. The galley made do with oil lamps instead of electricity, and many areas of the ship used combustible instead of noncombustible materials. Several navigation aids, including a gyrocompass and radio direction finder, were left out. For crews the Liberty ship was anything but a luxury liner.[31]

One innovation promised to expedite the construction work. Like the aircraft manufacturers, the shipbuilders were discovering the many virtues of welding over riveting. The navy still insisted on rivets, although it had managed to reduce their number from 2 million to 70,000 on some ships. On freighters and tankers, however, welding proved a godsend once the techniques were perfected. It involved melting at extremely high temperatures the beveled edges of two plates and a piece of welding rod into one solid mass. Little scientific knowledge existed about how steel reacted under the intense heat of an electric arc or what sorts of strains might cause the finished plate to crack after cooling. Nevertheless, three yards were already making heavy use of welding, one had already built an all-welded tanker, and two had developed automatic welding machinery.[32]

The advantages of welding were enormous. A riveting operation required four men, welding only two, saving labor and reducing the chances of human error. It took five or six months to train a riveter, only two or three months for welders. Tack welding, the first phase, could even be done by beginners. A hard blow to a riveted plate often caused the holes to tear or the rivets to shear, where a welded plate merely absorbed a harmless dent. Riveting required the use of supporting angle bars, I-beams, H-bars, bulb angles, and the like, adding extra tonnage to the vessel. An all-welded ship was lighter, had more room for cargo, and could go faster on less fuel. It could also be built much faster; a welded ship could be assembled on what resembled a mass-production basis.[33]

One of the welding innovators, Sun Shipbuilding & Dry Dock Co. of Chester, Pennsylvania, which built the first all-welded tanker, had invested $800,000 in a huge automatic welding machine and was hurriedly adding twelve new ways to its existing eight along the Delaware River. Sun's goal was to produce seventy-two tankers in two years, a tanker every ten days. "Hell," snorted Vickery, who had charge of merchant ship construction, "we're not *building* ships." What the commission was building for its second navy was in effect an almost complete new shipping industry parallel to the existing one, partly in new yards and partly in the expansion of existing yards. No other type of defense work required so much lead time to get under way, and too much time had already been wasted. As Vickery bemoaned, the age of craftsmanship in shipbuilding had passed, at least for the time being.[34]

CLAY BEDFORD WAS in Corpus Christi, Texas, helping to build a naval air station when his boss called. "Clay," said Henry Kaiser, "you're going to build a shipyard." Bedford knew nothing about shipyards, but he knew his boss. "Where?" was all he asked. "Richmond," replied Kaiser. A short time later Kaiser sent his other young associate and son, Edgar Kaiser, to the Portland/Vancouver area to build shipyards there as well.[35]

Richmond, California, stood on the eastern shore of San Francisco Bay. In 1940 it was a sleepy town of 23,642 souls, many of whom worked for a Standard Oil refinery, a Ford plant, or a smattering of small companies along the shoreline. It was a blue-collar town with a main drag, Macdonald Avenue, and neighborhoods of modest bungalows. Local residents welcomed the new shipyard and barely noticed the first trickle of engineers and construction men. Bedford took care to recruit mostly Bay Area workers and by the summer of 1941 had 4,500 workers on the payroll. But the first yard got off to an unpromising start. On a dreary, rainy day the first tractor lumbered onto the marshy terrain to clear a service road and sank. Experienced engineers shook their heads and predicted it would take six months to produce solid ground with fill.

Bedford was a young but seasoned construction man who knew his stuff and Kaiser's way of working. His father had worked for Kaiser in California, and Clay impressed his boss with his work hacking through thick jungle in Cuba to build major roads. Although most of the other engineers were senior to Bedford, who was not yet twenty-five, Kaiser so appreciated his attitude and ability that he put the young man in charge of the entire project. Bedford did not disappoint him. He became one of Kaiser's bright young men who, it was said, "keep the promises Kaiser makes." Richmond was only the latest test of his talents.[36]

Toiling around the clock for three weeks, Bedford's crews dumped 300,000 cubic yards of rock on the 80-acre site, then started building ways even before they had plans. On April 14, 1941, less than four months after Kaiser signed the contract for British ships, his men laid the keel for the first of what would ultimately be 747 vessels. Two days later plans were approved for construction of a second Richmond yard to build ships for the Maritime Commission. Local merchants rejoiced in the surge of business. Unlike local industries, however, the shipyard worked around the clock, and residents soon noticed that streets and stores remained busy at all hours. Changes were coming to Richmond, vast changes that no one could yet even imagine. Within three years this small town would be transformed into a city of 150,000, and it was only one of many that would undergo this metamorphosis.[37]

Edgar got the Portland yard under way a month behind Richmond. When the first keel was laid on May 19, Vickery was on hand to exhort the workers to "roll ships out of here at the rate of 45 a year. I know you can do it."

"Boys, you've heard what they told us," said Edgar. "It's our job and we're going to put this ship out and do it fast. Let's go."[38]

On August 16 the first completed freighter at Richmond was ready for launching. Jerry Land was on hand for the occasion along with his wife, who did the honors with a bottle of champagne. Portland followed suit on September 27, a day the Maritime Commission officially designated as Liberty Fleet Day to dramatize the shipbuilding program. Roosevelt gave a nationwide radio talk on its importance. After appropriate ceremonies the wife of Oregon's governor christened the new freighter. Many more would soon follow.[39]

Earlier, on July 16, Lord Halifax, the British ambassador to the United States, had toured Richmond in the company of Henry Kaiser and Clay Bedford, and afterward delivered a rousing speech to about half of the yard's 4,700 workers. "What has been done here in the last six months is as near a miracle as any other human thing I've ever seen," he said. "It's wonderful . . .

No job in the whole war effort is more important than what you are doing here."[40]

THE PRESSURE CONTINUED to mount on Jerry Land, in large part because the war was taking so ghastly a toll of British shipping. By May nearly all the British merchant marine had been withdrawn from their regular routes for war duty, and the undersized American merchant fleet struggled to take over the abandoned trade routes. Where only seventeen American ships sailed to Africa in 1939, fifty-one now covered the journey. The number of ships going to the Far East jumped from twelve to eighty-two, to India from twelve to twenty-five; American President Lines upped its around-the-world sailings from twenty-six to thirty-nine. Every vessel that could float was being hauled out of dry dock and put to work. In Australia and New Zealand tons of butter and cheese desperately needed in Britain piled up waiting for ships; 840,000 bales of Australian wool couldn't find passage to the United States.[41]

The American merchant marine, which boasted nearly 8.18 million tons when the war started, had dwindled to 5.5 million tons due to sales to Britain, the Lend-Lease transfer of some 900,000 tons of old bottoms, a million tons diverted to a ship-aid pool formed after passage of Lend-Lease, and another million tons requisitioned by the military, including every passenger ship operated by the United States Lines.[42]

At the same time, Land had to preside over a construction program that kept raising the stakes. The original 1937 program to build 500 ships in ten years was accelerated in 1939 to five years. Then came the British order for 60 ships in December 1940 and Roosevelt's call for 200 vessels the next month. In April 227 more ships were ordered as part of the Lend-Lease program. Before this addition was fully digested, July brought the biggest order of all: 541 more cargo ships and tankers, and 25 seagoing tugs along with 48 new ways. Altogether the programs totaled 13.5 million deadweight tons of new vessels. In addition, the commission was asked to build 25 small coasters, 25 Great Lakes ore boats, and 100 reinforced-concrete oil barges. The commission was underwriting 32 yards with 234 ways, but they would not turn out new ships until sometime in 1942. Still Land remained optimistic. In September he declared that by 1942 the United States would be turning out more tonnage than the Germans were currently sinking.[43]

Or so he hoped. The wild card in his reckoning remained the flow of materials and skilled workers. Delays in steel deliveries left some shipyards standing idle for a time, and shortages of gears, steel valves, and other parts hampered progress as well. As more new ways came online, they required more equipment that also had to scratch for steel and other raw materials. Two Morgan cranes were needed to hoist a 30-ton tanker bulkhead into place; they took eight months to build. The cost of a way ran about $500,000 with another $30,000 needed for its two cranes. Everything, it seemed, needed steel, and steel was in short supply.[44]

AS THE NAVY learned the hard way, Andrew Jackson Higgins was not a man to trifle with. Standing an inch under six feet, he had a boyish face with blue eyes that belied a strong, rugged frame and masked an explosive Irish temper. He wore no airs, spoke his mind bluntly, loved his bourbon, and despised red tape or any obstacle that got in his way. The navy's Bureau of Ships considered him an arrogant know-it-all because he insisted that he knew more about building certain types of boats than its own designers did. As it happened, he was right. Higgins was also a charismatic figure who inspired his workers, a gifted salesman like Henry Kaiser, and a hell of a storyteller. Like Kaiser, too, he knew how to get things done; unlike Kaiser, he developed a passion for boats.[45]

In 1940 Higgins was fifty-four years old and already at war with the navy. His only military experience had been a youthful stint in the Nebraska National Guard before he moved south at the age of twenty. He tried farming, got married, switched to the lumber business, and moved to New Orleans, where he found a partner to stake him in a lumber import-export business. During the 1920s he drifted into building small boats until that activity pushed the lumber business into the background. He specialized in sturdy, reliable workboats that could operate in shallow waters. The great flood of 1927 gave his boats an opportunity to show their worth in rescuing marooned farm equipment along the Ohio and Mississippi rivers. He devised a ramped platform set between two boats for hauling tractors and other large equipment that became one inspiration for a type of boat that later became his specialty: the landing craft.

In September 1930, amid hard times, he formed Higgins Industries to manufacture and sell a variety of boats. Despite some setbacks he weathered the depression and managed to hire talented engineers. He continued to focus on dependable workboats that could navigate the shallow swamps and marshes of Louisiana. During the early 1930s Higgins displayed his sales genius by first selling his Wonderboat to the Coast Guard as a patrol craft to catch rumrunners during Prohibition, and then persuading the rumrunners to buy a faster version from him. By 1937 he had the Coast Guard, Army Corps of Engineers, and Biological Survey Agency as customers, but he could not interest the navy's BCR, which preferred to design its own boats. Thus began his lengthy battle with the navy bureaucracy.

Although the boat designed by the BCR proved a dismal failure in tests, the navy steadfastly refused to consider a Higgins craft that others found clearly superior. Finally, in May 1938 Higgins got his first navy contract to build an experimental 30-foot landing boat. Although he considered the required length too short for the beam, his version performed extremely well in tests and led to a contract for four more experimental 30-footers. In response to his complaints over the length, the navy replied that some of its transport vessels already had davits capable of handling a 30-foot boat and they had decided to standardize the length. "To hell with designing a boat to fit the davits," growled Higgins. "They should design their davits to fit a proper size boat." The navy did not appreciate his views.

Part of the problem involved a difference of views between the navy and the Marine Corps. The navy saw little need for landing craft. Looking chiefly at Europe, it assumed that friendly ports would be available to off-load troops and supplies, as had occurred in the last war. Military planners paid virtually no attention to the possible need for large-scale amphibian operations. The marines thought otherwise; General Holland M. Smith considered Japan to be the ultimate enemy and recognized the need posed by island warfare for good landing craft. In 1936 the Marine Corps had asked for a five-year plan that would produce 120 landing craft; by 1939 only 19 had been built. That year, after a competition, the BCR decided to have two new landing craft built, both designed by its own staff. It also solicited bids to build patrol torpedo (PT) boats. Relying on his experience with building fast boats during Prohibition, Higgins came up with a model constructed at his own expense because the navy balked at giving him specifications for the 81-foot boats. Nevertheless, he submitted a low bid to win the contract for two boats.

Through 1939 and 1940 Higgins continued to do battle with the navy over both the PT boats and landing craft. Although his models were clearly superior in tests, the BCR kept favoring its own inferior boats in hopes that they would be improved enough to match the Higgins versions. Naval inspectors forced Higgins to make modifications that detracted from rather than improved his boat. When the navy belatedly gave him an order to build two more experimental 30-foot landing craft, an exasperated Higgins built a 36-foot version at his own expense and sent it to Norfolk with a demand that it be tested. The marines applauded. In September a competitive trial was held for three boats: the Higgins model, a metal BCR boat, and one built by Chris-Craft Corporation. The Higgins boat won so decisively that in November Higgins received a contract for 335 of the 36-foot boats. "Through the unfathomable process whereby the official mind finally emerges from darkness into light," recalled a pleased Holland Smith, "the Navy eventually decided to standardize on the 36-foot Higgins boat." But the fight was far from over.

By the end of 1940 Higgins had nearly $3.1 million in navy contracts, and his workforce had grown from 50 to 691. With the depression winding down, commercial sales were coming back as well. Higgins had always treated his workers well, but rapid growth led the AFL to try organizing his plant. Higgins fought hard to persuade his men to accept a company union. When the fight was lost, he accepted the verdict and became a model employer who worked with the union. Working with the navy proved more difficult. Joint exercises in the Caribbean during February 1941 widened the split between the navy and the Marine Corps. At one point Admiral Ernest J. King, commander of the Atlantic fleet, roared at Smith, "I'm getting sick and tired of hearing the word 'beachhead.' It's beach, I tell you, not beachhead. Why don't you Marines get it straight?" During the exercise King had aerial photographs of the beach where the marines were to land but did not bother to give them to Smith.

Higgins did no better with the navy. In one memorable meeting he told Admiral S. M. "Mike" Robinson that "there are no officers, whether present in this room or otherwise in the Navy who know a goddamn thing about small boat design, construction or operation—but, by god, I do."[46]

In these squabbles Higgins unabashedly favored the Marine Corps, which had always supported his efforts. The marines still lacked a suitable lighter for carrying tanks. The navy's version, in Smith's words, "would have got us nowhere in combat, except killed." He considered the task of getting artillery, tanks, and heavy equipment ashore under combat conditions so important that he sent aides to ask Higgins to come up with a modified version of his Eureka landing boats. Unable to fulfill the marines' needs with a design of its own, the BCR hoped that Higgins could deliver. Asked to design a 45-foot tank lighter, Higgins replied that he would have not a design but a workable craft when the navy's representatives arrived in three days. He also stipulated that he would build the lighter only under oversight by the Marine Corps. Reluctantly the navy agreed.

Earlier Higgins had begun constructing a combination towboat and dredge tender for the Corps of Engineers for a contract that never materialized. Using the incomplete vessel as a base, Higgins and his team worked tirelessly to modify and improvise their way to a finished lighter. The boat was designed, built, and floated in only sixty-one hours. It passed all tests, and Higgins received an order for fifty lighters, with ten to be delivered by June 15. With his usual manic energy Higgins scrounged engines and steel for the work; at one point he even persuaded the Southern Railway to haul some of the steel he needed on flatcars hitched to one of its passenger trains. In need of bronze shafting, he had workers steal it from an oil well storage depot and apologized later for their "mistake." He closed off an entire block adjacent to his plant, covered it with canvas to protect the workers, and turned it into a makeshift fabrication yard and warehouse. Assembly took place in an old nearby stable Higgins had bought. Before June 15 he had twenty-six craft on their way to Norfolk.

By June Higgins's workforce had grown to 1,600, he was building PT boats for three countries, and his landing craft had proven their worth. As his biographer Jerry Strahan observed, "This was a man who could quickly grasp an idea, translate it into a practical design, and have his workers construct a prototype while others were still pondering the problem." Nobody knew small boats better than Higgins or had the ability to create whatever type was needed. That same month the navy combined two agencies, the BCR and the Bureau of Engineering, into a single new entity, the Bureau of Ships, which included a small-boat division. The change did not improve the agency's attitude toward Higgins. He was still resented as an outsider who somehow posed a threat to its bureaucrats. Their clash found its way in June to the ears of a new congressional committee formed to look closely into the national defense program.[47]

No one appreciated Higgins's gifts more than Holland Smith, who wrote the industrialist, "Often I ponder the question 'Where the Hell would the Amphibious Force have been without you and your boats?'" The letter was dated December 6, 1941.[48]

CHAPTER 9

THE SEASON OF
DISCONTENT

It is safe to predict that it will not be the OPM that will win the battle of America, nor any of the essentially conventional men of business whose thinking is as unadapted to our present realities as is the thinking in most of our armed forces.

—FORTUNE[1]

The great bottleneck, as everyone knows, everyone but the President himself, is the President's own desk . . . This crisis . . . is one of administration.

—GARET GARRETT[2]

The President is a profound student of naval strategy, a genius at political maneuver. But he does not delegate authority. He is not at home in the realm of industry and production. Above all, he does not call forth the national will to action . . . Part of the difficulty is that the dollar-a-year managers do not exercise the authority necessary to do a satisfactory job of management.

—TIME[3]

"SUMMER ALWAYS SEEMS TO CATCH Washington unawares," complained the debonair Noël Coward after visiting the president at the White House, "to break over it like an awesome seventh wave, flooding it with sudden, sweltering discontent. There is air-conditioning, of course, and there are iced drinks and sun-blinds and electric fans, but even those fail to dispel . . . a feeling that such breathless oppressiveness must herald a cosmic disaster, that some feckless star has changed its course and we are all about to frizzle, curl up and die."[4]

The president himself had been ill during the spring and into the summer, bedraggled by one of his more interminable colds as well as the heat. He saw few people and told Stimson by phone that he had no pep and could not get his temperature down. Cordell Hull too was ill for most of June and took refuge at Hot Springs, Arkansas. Hopkins was under the weather again, but some observers regarded that as almost normal. Senator Pat Harrison of Mississippi, chairman of the Finance Committee, died on June 22, casting a pall over an already gloomy Washington summer.[5]

While Washington sweltered, sports fans enjoyed a bonanza summer dampened only by the death of Lou Gehrig in June. That same month boxing fans were treated to a magnificent slugfest between heavily favored Joe Louis and a brash, quick Irishman named Billy Conn, who came within a whisker of one of the great upsets in the sport's history before being knocked out. Baseball fans got to see the once hapless Brooklyn Dodgers win their first pennant since 1920 and follow two great players who set records for the ages. Beginning in May, Joe DiMaggio put together a hitting streak of fifty-six consecutive games that has never been approached. At the same time, Ted Williams was spraying hits on his way to a season's batting average of .406, the first player to reach .400 since 1930 and the last one to do so. The enthusiasm for these feats moved William Allen White to observe sourly that "two-fifths of our people are more interested in the baseball scores than they are in foreign news."[6]

Certainly the midyear scorecard for defense did not impress many people. As production lagged behind goals, shortages mounted, and labor strife intensified, critics on all sides voiced their displeasure. In particular they blamed Roosevelt for dispersing the mobilization effort among a slew of agencies and not appointing one person to oversee the whole process. Garet Garrett pointed to no less than sixteen key defense agencies in the Washington telephone directory, all of them under the Executive Office of the President, and the list did not include three other agencies too new to have made the book. *Fortune* itemized how OPM had to share its authority over priorities with OPACS, ANMB, and several other agencies. "The result," it concluded, "is an unparalleled complexity." The military got no better reviews. "Quite naturally," quipped *Fortune*, "the army clings to those principles that successfully subjugated the Indians in the Black Hawk War (1831)."[7]

Complaints came from within as well as without the agencies. "In light of the emergency with which the world is desperately confronted," said William L. Batt, Knudsen's deputy, in May, "we are doing a terribly inadequate job. We should be producing twice the 1,400 airplanes that were produced in April." That same month Stimson warned, "At least a year will pass before we can have an Army and an air force adequate to meet the air and ground forces which could be brought against us." In February he had conceded that of the

Air Corps's 4,000 planes, only 650 were first-line, and none could match the battle standards of the current war. Bob Patterson doubted "that more than 15% of America's productive endeavor is devoted to defense work." For its part the navy had blundered, as Frank Knox admitted, by failing to provide protection for antiaircraft gun crews on its ship decks and was scrambling to rectify that oversight.[8]

In July Leon Henderson published an article in *Fortune* entitled "We Only Have Months" in which he reminded Americans that "it took Hitler more than five years to get ready for this war. We've got months, not years, in which to prepare . . . This battle for human dignity can be won only if this nation produces more and faster than any nation has ever produced before." To do that required an all-out effort and strict priorities on the allocation of raw materials. Henderson conceded that "today there is no central planning, no central purchasing, and as yet no clear statement of requirements and resources," but he foresaw them coming once Americans accepted the gravity of the crisis. Both government and business people were already sick of priorities, but they would ultimately work because they were inescapable.[9]

Ralph Robey thought that American industry was producing well but lacked balance between its defense and civilian output. The reasons were several: No overall plan or program had been formulated; no central flow sheet existed to show progress of the individual parts; the strike-plagued labor situation imposed needless obstacles; the price situation was messy; and the public had yet to be convinced that the emergency was real "and not just the long-awaited opportunity to feather their own nests." The solution, he argued along with many others, was to put one man in charge of the entire operation, preferably one experienced in business and "not in the field of oratory, party machines, and politics." Raymond Clapper summed up his feelings by saying bluntly, "Affairs are frankly in an appalling state."[10]

Clapper conceded that production was moving along well, in stark contrast to the utter inadequacy of planning. "The mistakes have been in thinking and programming in Washington," he wrote, the result of "a planning eye that has been looking through the wrong end of the telescope." The United States was a peaceful nation, he thought, that did not think in terms of war. "When we begin to think of war," he added, "our imagination flattens out."[11]

The *Saturday Evening Post*, that last bastion of the nostalgic world of Norman Rockwell and Horatio Alger, despised the New Deal but observed that "every day the Office of Production Management is saying our sights are too low, that we are not doing enough by half, that we are living too much as usual; all of which, we believe, is true," adding that "the Office of Production Management, divided in its own mind on principles, and without power, is itself a bottleneck." *Fortune* scolded Americans by reminding them, "There is no history, no record of a nation emerging victorious from a war that it entered leaden-hearted and unconvinced . . . Yet, in a world of war, the U.S. yearns for peace—tomorrow morning. Too many of us believe the oceans are barriers, that you can do business with Hitler, that it's not our war, that our ideals are shoddy."[12]

The world had changed, *Fortune* insisted, and America's destiny with it. "Confronted with the blood lust of Hitler's Germany," the nation "still wishes it could continue to dream about colored bathtubs, longer wheel bases, and quicker-freezing cubes. It would like to run the war, but with automatic overdrive and finger-tip control . . . America has yet to learn that it may never go home again. Largely as a reflection of this national psychology the U.S. war effort to date remains grimly unimpressive." Blame for this condition tracked directly to the president, whose "failure to establish a truly forceful high War Policy Board is the major scandal of the war effort."[13]

The administration lacked a rational plan and a rational organization. Businessmen who came to Washington to see what they might make for the war effort were shuffled from one agency to another in search of guidance. Production was in one division, priorities in another, purchasing in a third. "It is a bastard mixture of functional organization and specific commodity administration," admitted a high OPM official. "It leaves policy administration horizontally scattered. It is, in short, a mess."[14]

THE PRESIDENT HAD been far from his best since the spring. On May 2 he went to Staunton, Virginia, to dedicate Woodrow Wilson's birthplace. His stomach bothered him, and a fever developed. He managed to get through the ceremony, but the scheduled pleasantries afterward were canceled. A reporter on the scene observed that he "had looked about as bad as a man can look and still be about." His physician, Dr. Ross McIntire, diagnosed an intestinal disorder and severe anemia. Roosevelt was sent to bed for a prolonged rest and given transfusions as well as iron injections. For nearly two weeks he remained secluded in his bedroom, seeing only Missy LeHand and Harry Hopkins even though his illness had passed. Robert Sherwood was invited to have a long chat with him and said to Missy afterward, "The President seems in fine shape to me." Smiling, Missy replied, "What he's suffering from most of all is a case of sheer exasperation."[15]

His absence heightened the suspicions and wrangling within the cabinet. Shortly before the president's illness Ickes had grumbled that "the blind side of the President, when his personal friends are involved, seems to be growing blinder." Hopkins in particular aroused his ire. Their differences traced back to the early New Deal days when Ickes headed the PWA and Hopkins the WPA, during which they competed for funds as well as attention. Ickes resented Hopkins being made head of Lend-Lease, to say nothing of his living in the White House and having such easy access to Roosevelt. Missy reminded him that the president was tired and naturally tended to rely more on the people closest to him.[16]

The press was quick to pick up on the turmoil within the cabinet. A *Time* reporter portrayed the elder members of the group, most notably Hull and Stimson, as tired, ineffective old men. Hull was depicted as lost in paper-shuffling and out of touch, Stimson as notorious for dozing off in meetings. The article infuriated Stimson, who asked Felix Frankfurter whether he should sue for libel. "I am getting pretty sick of this sort of thing," he growled. ". . . It is about time to give some of these people a lesson, as I have been in particularly good health all through this year and have never been asleep in a conference in my life." Both men found refuge after work in sports, Hull in croquet and Stimson in deck tennis or lawn bowling. Knox was faulted for constantly putting his foot in his mouth, Morgenthau for being "cautious, slow, well-meaning."[17]

The criticism extended to the president as well. "The worst executive management could be traced to Franklin Roosevelt," declared the reporter. "To solve his problem of management, the President had done little except to create new jobs and new agencies, overlapping and ineffectual." Privately Ickes told John J. McCloy that if he had known how uninspiring and inactive Roosevelt was going to be, he would never have supported the third term. When the president returned for his first cabinet meeting in three weeks, Ickes thought he still looked tired. "I wonder," he mused, "if he is going to have the physical stamina to lead us during these next critical years."[18]

THE TENSION WITHIN the administration did derive in part from the president himself. On one hand, Roosevelt had, as Frances Perkins observed, a "serene belief that his whole administration should work like a team and that his associates should find ways of addressing their problems." On the other hand, he once told Perkins that "there is something to be said for having a little conflict between agencies. A little rivalry is stimulating, you know. It keeps every body going to prove that he is a better fellow than the next man. It keeps them honest too." He got his wish and more. By 1941 the different parts of the administration had become seedbeds of conflict both within themselves and with each other, giving the media plenty of rumors, innuendo, and sniping on which to feast.[19]

"The inside struggle for power in the White House," reported *Time* in

March, "is a struggle as thick with political intrigue as the palace politics of a French court." All around the president, who seemed to be aloof from it all, "could be heard the ratlike sounds of politics, the scurrying and the whispers."[20]

The central struggle continued to be between the New Dealers, most of whom were all-outers, and the business representatives, most of whom favored a gradual transition from civilian to defense production. The New Dealers considered the business executives, especially the dollar-a-year men, as opportunists seeking to protect and extend their private interests under the guise of patriotic service. Where the New Dealers regarded themselves as neutral participants defending the public interest, businessmen in their eyes sought only profits. For their part, business executives dismissed the New Dealers as woolly-haired academics, economists, and bureaucrats who dwelled in a land of theories and knew nothing about the realities of production or running a business. They had never met a payroll or organized a production line. The industrialists, after all, owned and operated the plants that made everything; who knew more about the process and its needs than they did?

Somewhere between these two adversaries stood the military, steeped in its own needs and prejudices. The war had elevated both major services from their usual peacetime obscurity into a position of prominence. It had revived their traditional arrogance but done little to modify their archaic thinking. Stimson, Patterson, Knox, and Forrestal worked diligently along with a nucleus of forward-thinking officers to shake the cobwebs of tradition off both branches, but they all shared the belief that the military knew what was best for the country. They remained suspicious of New Dealers and businessmen alike and believed strongly that the military's needs transcended all others and should govern decisions regarding output and allocation of resources. Put bluntly, they alone should determine their needs and dictate their priorities, with civilian needs consigned to the status of leftovers.

Not that the two services agreed on priorities between themselves. After Hitler invaded Russia on June 22, the president wanted tank production doubled and then doubled again to help the Soviet Union. Knudsen reminded him that any increase required higher priorities for the tools necessary to produce tanks. The navy bitterly opposed raising the priorities on tanks to the level of A-1-a, just as they had fought any increase of priorities for the tooling of four-engine bombers. Priorities had turned into a game of sorts anyway because everyone wanted an A-1-a priority, which rendered the whole system useless.[21]

"In many respects," observed *Fortune*, "the army has no conception of the nature, abilities, or limitations of mass production. Nevertheless, the army insists on acting as if it had." It showed no interest in technical advice or guidance from those who knew the process, leaving manufacturers confused and irritated at the military. Chrysler, for example, received an order to produce tanks and, as an automotive company, had good suggestions for improvements, to which the army turned a deaf ear. "The result," concluded a reporter, "is an engine of war that, at the very start of its production, is already militarily obsolete."[22]

Roosevelt was determined above all else not to let either business or the military take over the economy. But only the businessmen knew how to produce things, and only the military understood what it needed for whatever assignment was handed it. The fact that the country was not actually at war complicated both ends of this equation; the military was not sure who or what it was to prepare for, and industrialists had only a general notion of what was required from them or the urgency for producing it, let alone how long the emergency might last. All sides suffered from an excessive diet of ambiguity and lack of precedent. The dilemma for Roosevelt was how to keep everyone working toward goals that were murky and on timetables that were guesstimates at best. Small wonder, then, that the course he steered seemed erratic and contradictory.

During 1941 the agencies fumbled their way along this rocky, uncertain path, pausing only to argue over who should take the lead. "In Washington, or out of it," chided *Fortune* in April, "the fact that national defense is in pretty bad shape is too familiar to be alarming. Government men swap the latest and most shocking stories of government bungling. Each has his favorite bungler, not counting the Quartermaster Corps, which is everybody's favorite." OPM ranked high on many lists, with its endless internal clashes and difficulty in defining who exactly did what. In April and again in June it underwent reorganizations designed to eliminate duplication of effort and clarify the role of its industry advisory committees. Corporate and trade association officials dominated these committees, which grew more influential after the reorganizations. OPM had little choice since it depended on voluntary cooperation from industry in carrying out its orders.[23]

Business leaders were willing to cooperate with OPM in part to prevent further extension of priorities and avoid mandatory regulations. As shortages grew more critical, however, priorities became the major concern. OPM and industrialists worked to keep them voluntary or at least limited in application. When these efforts did not suffice, the industrialists also dominated the committees that helped write and administer the priorities system. In this struggle New Dealers found an ally in OPM's chief counsel, John Lord O'Brian, who worked with Attorney General Jackson in writing rules that defined and limited the role of the advisory committees. The goal was to make the committees useful without suspending the antitrust laws or giving them authority that more properly belonged to the public. During the last half of 1941, however, the committees ignored or violated the rules as much as they honored them.[24]

OPM began life with a thousand employees inherited from NDAC; by the year's end it had 7,600 employees and had become a very different organization, though still beset with its original problems. The creation of OPACS in April set in motion the friction between it and OPM over the amount of civilian output, especially automobiles. Debate raged over what exactly was meant by the terms "defense" and "essential," Distinguishing between civilian and defense facilities or materials proved almost impossible as existing stockpiles dwindled and more factories produced both civilian and military goods at the same time. Everyone agreed that the production of "nonessentials" should be cut, but how quickly? And what constituted a nonessential? Defense production had originally meant only military hardware, but it had expanded to include such things as machine tools and some metals as well as construction materials.[25]

The April reorganization did improve Nelson's authority over purchasing. He had watched in disgust as the army, needing lumber to build camps for its flood of draftees, put its order in "as naively as if it were buying a plank" and wondered why the price doubled. The Quartermaster Corps ordered cots based on specifications from the last war requiring a kind of wire that mills no longer made. For uniforms it insisted on horn or ivory buttons that had to be imported even though Nelson pointed out that a Rochester company made fine celluloid buttons. The army's intransigence forced the button manufacturer to dust off obsolete machinery and hire extra workers "until such time as the army is convinced that plastics are here to stay."[26]

To eliminate this archaic approach, Nelson devised a plan to reorganize army procurement methods and sent it to OPM. Knudsen approved it and passed it along to the army, which rejected it and moved to curtail his purchasing powers. That was when Nelson told some columnists he was stepping down as of May 1. Roosevelt then met with Nelson and persuaded him to stay on with increased authority, giving him veto power over all army and navy orders for merchandise but not engineered equipment. The army had its own grievances against OPM, which lacked the staff and experience to clear the contracts and cases forwarded to it. In one instance Patterson complained to Knudsen about eighteen cases sent to OPM between January and March 15 that were not acted on until May 9.[27]

The June reorganization tried to eliminate some red tape by making OPM more vertical than horizontal, creating thirty commodity sections that would handle the entire process for each one. Under the existing setup all three main divisions had sections covering the same commodity, which drove manufacturers and suppliers to distraction in seeking materials and gave OPM much of its reputation as the land of red tape. John D. Biggers's Production Division took charge of aircraft, ordnance, machine tools, shipbuilding, construction, and some industrial materials; Nelson's Purchasing Division became responsible for areas like food, clothing, textiles, leather, and drugs, where purchasing was the chief activity. The Priorities Division under Stettinius was assigned those commodities such as tin, rubber, nickel, chromium, copper, and zinc, where importation and allocation were most important.[28]

The reorganizations helped somewhat but the delays and friction continued, as did the growing shortages of materials. A survey in May of over 500 defense manufacturers revealed their major obstacle to be materials shortages. Some were already under priority orders; others were headed there. For certain key materials the lines were already forming, especially for manufacturers of nonessential civilian goods. To make matters worse, a southern drought reduced the power output from TVA dams, prompting a voluntary effort to cut electricity usage by 20 to 30 percent. Southern textile mills depended heavily on TVA for power, as did plants that turned out more than half of the nation's aluminum. The Federal Power Commission (FPC), invoking emergency authority under the 1935 Federal Power Act, ordered the immediate construction of links between TVA and power companies in seventeen states. But priorities would be required for the materials needed to build the links.[29]

Still the complaints continued that progress was too slow, that Roosevelt was overburdened and needed to appoint some one person to oversee the defense effort. Congress pondered a bill to scrap OPM in place of a new War Resources Administration, but it died. More sparks arose between OPM and OPACS when Henderson went over Knudsen's head and ordered a 50 percent cut in automobile production for the next model year. Publicly Knudsen admitted only that there was "a little dispute," but Henderson had also challenged OPM's Priorities Division under Stettinius over the question of whether it or OPACS controlled priorities. When the FPC announced an ambitious five-year program to expand the nation's power capacity by one third, Ickes trashed it as "ill-advised" and "carelessly prepared." The program had come from OPM's young and aggressive new power coordinator, Julius A. Krug, a rising star in the defense bureaucracy.[30]

By midsummer priorities had emerged as the single most important defense problem. At stake was the power of putting delivery of materials or goods to the military before the claims of civilian or export buyers. Everybody agreed that the existing system was broken. "You put a red ticket on a job which has to be done by yesterday," said Knudsen. "That's all right for a week, maybe. Then, after a week, every job in the shop has a red ticket. And your red ticket doesn't mean anything." Nelson complained of the "inde-scribable confusion, arising out of the increase in all sorts of demands, many of them conflicting."[31]

The unanswered question remained whether steps would be taken to give OPM complete responsibility for procurement rather than continue as an advisory body. Baruch, among others, was still pressing for some form of one-man rule. He told the president that Knudsen was not the man for the job, and Roosevelt was inclined to agree. On a visit to Bob Patterson's upstate New York place, Baruch told the undersecretary that someone had to step forward and assume leadership. It could not be himself, he added quickly, despite all the gossip to the contrary, because he was simply too old and a Jew to boot. However, he thought Patterson had the stuff to be such a man and urged him to let Baruch advance his name. Patterson made it clear that he had "neither time nor inclination to play politics."[32]

Altogether some fourteen federal agencies supervised the economic and civilian aspects of preparedness, and their authority often overlapped. Four days after Roosevelt declared a state of unlimited national emergency on May 27, Congress extended priority controls to cover essential civilian production and also gave the president power to allocate materials, enabling him to de-cide what materials were vital to national defense. This new grant of authority intensified the friction between OPM and OPACS, both of which hoped to administer it. Roosevelt did not give either agency new powers, but by August the clash between them and complaints over the lack of direction in the de-fense effort could no longer be ignored. Roosevelt asked Sam Rosenman to look at the problem and come up with a new organizational plan. Then he went off to sea in a veil of mystery for the Argentia Conference, his first face-to-face meeting with Winston Churchill. From it would come the Atlantic Charter and the first bonds of an indelible friendship.[33]

"This was probably the most difficult of any of the administrative reorga-nizations on which I worked," admitted Rosenman. He had to deal with com-peting demands and conflicting personalities, as well as the conundrum of imposing tough priorities on a nation not actually at war. No plan existed and no basic decisions had been made on how to allocate resources among civil-ians, the military, Lend-Lease, and other claimants. But Roosevelt had great faith in the ability of the loyal adviser he liked to call "Sammy the Rose." Rosenman dutifully commenced long rounds of meetings with agency heads and other officials, trying to sense their concerns and needs, drawing out their likes and dislikes, and enlisting them in the task of finding a better or-ganization. By mid-August he had the general outlines of a proposal.[34]

On August 18 Harold Smith of the Budget Bureau presented Roosevelt with several alternative plans, which the president turned over to Rosenman.

They agreed that the solution required the creation of yet another board. Ten days later the president issued an executive order redefining OPM and creating the Supply Priorities and Allocations Board (SPAB). The order surprised most observers, who expected a reorganization that put one individual in charge of the defense program. Bernard Baruch had been meeting more or less weekly with the president to offer his advice. Upon hearing of the new board he dismissed it as "a faltering step forward" while standing on the White House steps after meeting with Roosevelt. Shortly afterward his invitations to the White House ceased. "It looks to me," grumbled Ickes, "as if he has taken the Baruch proposal and . . . put it in some form that would be satisfactory to Harry Hopkins . . . I think that the President has given Bernie a particularly rotten deal."[35]

The new arrangement, Rosenman told Stimson confidentially, amounted only to a first step toward a proper solution, which would be concentration of authority in one person. Until Roosevelt was ready to take that step, Rosenman added, the burden of making final decisions when disputes arose remained with the president. No one expected Roosevelt to relinquish that role anytime soon.[36]

Despite loud complaints about another dose of alphabet soup, the reorganization brought with it significant changes. SPAB took charge of priorities as a top-level policymaking and coordinating center for the whole defense program with Vice President Henry Wallace as chairman. Four of its seven members—Wallace, Hopkins, Henderson, and Hillman—were all-outers, giving them a majority over the business and military representatives, Stimson, Knox, and Knudsen. Nelson was made executive director of the new board; in addition, he moved from his job as purchasing chief of OPM to director of its Priorities Division, replacing the much-maligned Stettinius. The change put him in an odd position in which he was both over and under Knudsen. "As Executive Director of the new board I gave orders to OPM," he said wryly; "as Director of Priorities I received orders from OPM." Stettinius was shuffled over to Lend-Lease and exclaimed, "I got the plum." The ailing Hopkins cheerfully turned the post over to his friend, realizing that Lend-Lease policy would still come from the White House and that Roosevelt would rely on Hopkins in shaping it.[37]

At the same time, the civilian supply function of OPACS moved to OPM as the Division of Civilian Supply, but Henderson remained in charge of both it and the renamed Office of Price Administration. OPM also got a separate Division of Materials with hard-charging Bill Batt as its head. John Biggers, Knudsen's assistant and chief of production, long considered an obstacle by the all-outers, was dropped from OPM and replaced by William Henry Harrison, an AT&T vice president. When the smoke cleared, OPM remained in conservative hands, while SPAB was clearly dominated by the all-outers. SPAB assumed the task of formulating broad policy, leaving OPM to focus on production. However, SPAB had to rely on OPM in carrying out its tasks because it had no operating structure.[38]

Although the arrangement looked awkward, it worked reasonably well during its short life. Despite the constant criticism, Roosevelt did not yet want to appoint a single individual to preside over the mobilization program. All sides agreed that priorities had become the central problem and that some form of planning held the key to solving the priorities riddle. The question was how best to go about it. The struggle between OPM and OPACS demonstrated that priorities had to be determined and administered by a single agency. Rosenman persuaded the president that it had to be a new entity. Patterson had urged that an expanded version of the OPM council do the job. Henderson and the Budget Bureau opposed his recommendation and regarded a new board, however makeshift, as the best solution.[39]

Among other advantages, the reorganization allowed Nelson, who had emerged as the golden boy of the defense effort, to show what he could do. *Time* praised him as "one of the most far-sighted defense managers" who had been one of the first to argue that mobilization could not simply be imposed on top of the normal economy. He had allied himself with Henderson at the low point in the latter's reputation, and together they understood the gigantic scale of the defense effort better than anyone else. "Informed Washingtonians," reported *Newsweek*, "are coming more and more to expect big things from Donald Nelson as SPAB director." He wasted no time in getting the new board launched. At its first meeting on September 2 he won agreement on a statement of purpose and general policy, then started the tough task of fleshing it out.[40]

The board had before it an imperfect set of figures for the supply of thirty-three basic commodities that revealed a large gap between projected needs and estimated supply. Two problems were obvious: Demand for most items exceeded supply, and no one had any real sense of how much of what materials were needed by the three competing constituencies, the military, civilian, and Lend-Lease. The starting point was clear to Nelson. "No housewife can tell how many cakes she can make," he observed later, "unless she knows, first, how many cups of flour she has, and, second, how many cups of flour it takes to make a cake. That shows exactly the position we were in; we knew neither how much 'flour' we had nor how much we needed." The lack of reliable statistics on both needs was glaring. It was a major source of the dispute over curtailing production of civilian goods, and it was also a moving target in that the demand for military goods kept escalating.[41]

Three important decisions emanated from this first session. The board concluded that reliable data had to be assembled. It also agreed to set up an allocations system instead of one based on priorities. The difference was significant. A priorities system merely specified the order in which companies' applications for raw materials were filled; an allocation system earmarked a specific quantity of materials for them. Finally, the board concluded that enforcement of its policies could best be done by existing agencies such as the FBI, Treasury Department, and Federal Trade Commission. Nelson saw no reason to create duplicate entities for work that was the specialty of existing agencies.[42]

By the time the group met again a week later, the demand for aluminum, magnesium, copper, zinc, and brass had jumped sharply. The board reached a decision that Nelson regarded as "one of the most important and far-reaching actions taken in the entire pre-war defense program." It directed him to report at the next meeting on the maximum amount of these materials and steel that could be obtained by expansion and to make recommendations on the best methods of obtaining such expansion. To Nelson it marked the first time any official government agency had decided on an all-out program. "The die was cast," he noted happily; "*all* of America's tremendous strength was to be applied to the job at hand, instead of just that portion . . . which could be spared conveniently."[43]

But what exactly was that strength? What were the requirements and the resources available to meet them? Finding the answer required an exhaustive survey of civilian and military needs, including the procurement schedules of all the armed forces, as well as whatever goods were to go overseas under Lend-Lease and other programs. This was a stupendous task, made even more difficult by the military's utter lack of useful statistics and disdain toward compiling them. Nevertheless, SPAB's staff undertook the challenge of a systematic review of raw materials needs; it would take more than nine months to come up with a complete survey. ANMB was asked to estimate the quantities and delivery dates of raw materials needed by the military, but its initial figures proved worthless. The services literally did not know how much they needed of which items, let alone the amount of raw materials required to produce them.[44]

The complexities of the task were staggering. It was not enough merely to translate guns into tons of steel or ammunition into pounds of copper. The amount of steel needed for airplane engines had to jibe with the amount of aluminum needed for airframes. Warships required huge amounts of materials of many kinds; a single shortage could delay or scuttle production. No one had a clue as to the requirements for an all-out program if the nation should get into the war. SPAB undertook an inventory to determine what already existed in both resources and capacity, then launched a survey designed to answer two basic questions: What did the nation have to produce to defend itself and to provide needed aid to Britain, Russia, China, and Latin America, as well as satisfy its own minimum civilian needs; and how much raw materials, machinery, and manpower did these needs require?[45]

If that were not enough, SPAB tackled two other enormous and controversial challenges: initiating increases in supply to meet demands, and dividing the available supply of resources among the military, civilian, and export claimants for them. Lend-Lease complicated this assignment, as did the Nazi invasion of Russia, by greatly increasing the foreign demand for aid. Opposition arose from many quarters to shipping anything to the Soviets. Militant anti-Communists, church groups, patriotic societies, and other groups protested on ideological grounds, Polish Americans and Finnish Americans on the Soviet presence in their native lands. Some practical minds, including many in the military, doubted the Russians could survive and didn't want American goods wasted on a losing effort. Knox, for one, fought hard against releasing any materials to the Russians.[46]

Roosevelt disagreed. He understood, as did many others, that the Russian front was draining German resources on a grand scale, especially if the Soviets could hold out until their greatest ally, Father Winter, came to their aid. To that end he dispatched an ailing Hopkins to visit Joseph Stalin as his personal representative. After a tortuous flight via Archangel, Hopkins saw Stalin and asked what he needed in the form of aid. Antiaircraft guns, rifles, and large machine guns at once, Stalin replied; high-octane aviation fuel and aluminum later. "Give us anti-aircraft guns and the aluminum and we can fight for three or four years," Stalin added. The message conveyed by Hopkins, along with his impression of the dictator, reinforced Roosevelt's desire to speed aid to the Russians despite opposition to it.[47]

But the going was exasperatingly slow. At the cabinet meeting on August 1 the president unleashed his dissatisfaction with the delays in a forty-five-minute tirade that stunned the secretaries. He gave both Hull and Stimson what Ickes called "one of the most complete dressings down that I have witnessed," accusing them of giving the Russians a runaround. "I am sick and tired of hearing that they are going to get this and they are going to get that," growled Roosevelt. In particular he wanted 150 pursuit planes and a smaller number of bombers sent to them. "Get the planes off with a bang next week," he barked, adding, "I want to do all of this at once, to help their morale." Stimson looked into the matter and found that only forty planes could be spared and that the best solution was to have the British send some planes they had in storage.[48]

Most of the president's wrath had been directed at Stimson, who confided his hurt and anger to his diary. "This Russian munitions business thus far has shown the President at his worst," he complained. "He has no system. He goes haphazard and he scatters responsibility among a lot of uncoordinated men and consequently things are never done. This time I got very angry over it for he had no business to talk that way in Cabinet about a run-around and indicate that it was the War Department. I am the only man in the whole Government that is responsible for the difficult decision on whether we can give up planes or other munitions with safety to our own defense. All of these other people are just hell-bent to satisfy a passing impulse or emotion to help out some other nation . . . and they have no responsibility over whether or not our own army and our own forces are going to be left unarmed or not."[49]

While the drama over Russian aid played itself out, SPAB went about its business with a decisiveness rare for a government agency. Its job, explained Henry Wallace, involved "cutting off the fat and hardening the muscles" of the defense program. Efforts were made to wean the armed services off their dependence on big firms by spreading orders among more companies. A survey revealed that only 6,657 of 11,819 plants deemed useful for arms production actually had contracts. SPAB also put Lend-Lease and civilian requirements on a mandatory rather than voluntary priority basis, making them equal with military needs. Henderson won the battle over who should determine quotas for the automobile industry and other durable goods such as refrigerators, stoves, and washing machines. SPAB also began curbing construction work on nondefense projects that consumed steel or other scarce materials; defense housing received priority over civilian home construction. In issuing priorities for building materials, it also applied the same standards to public works, giving it a potential veto power over congressional pork projects.[50]

At the board's first meeting Wallace made a crucial distinction between "more essential" and "less essential" production rather than "essential" or "nonessential." Everything was needed, but choices had to be made. Giving civilian output priority was important because repair parts for everything from automobiles to farm machinery were urgently needed. This mattered greatly because, as Nelson observed, "we were not going to be able to make many new things," so older machines had to keep working. Attention also went to major elements of agriculture, such as the dairy industry. On becoming vice president Wallace had yielded his post as secretary of agriculture to Claude Wickard, but he never lost interest in the field. SPAB took steps to expand dairy output and to ensure the continued production of farm equipment where needed. In the process it demonstrated that food production was no less important than any other critical need.[51]

On October 7 Nelson submitted a report showing that nearly half of the steel ingots used in private and public construction went to nondefense projects, mostly private and commercial buildings. SPAB laid down a policy that materials would be authorized only for projects needed for defense or public health and safety. It also ordered the steel industry to expand its ingot output by another 10 million tons but met the usual resistance from the companies. Loud protests also rose from the $11.2 billion construction industry with its 2.4 million employees. To these objections SPAB could offer little resistance. It lacked any administrative machinery to enforce its policy and failed to provide a clear definition of "essential" construction. As a result the policy had little impact.[52]

Critics had mixed reactions to SPAB. Eliot Janeway mocked its organization as "a Rube Goldberg cartoon" but admitted that "with all its shortcomings and all its overtones of musical comedy, [it] represented a bold step forward and an historic one. For the first time a central agency was empowered to determine the requirements of our armed forces, our civilian economy, and our Allies-to-be." Bruce Catton called it "an organizational nightmare . . . but it did serve a good purpose." Nelson concluded that SPAB "did a far better job than most people ever gave it credit for." Above all else, it had launched the vital task of compiling data on requirements and supplies. It had also protected the civilian economy even as it pushed for an all-out defense effort.[53]

In mid-November the Army and Navy departments tried to get the board restructured to give the conservative elements the same control they exerted in OPM. If successful the army and navy would be in a position to dictate mobilization policy and determine how much aid went to Russia and other nations. Stimson was not alone in thinking this largesse to others wasteful; in his mind the goal was not to help other nations but to make America invincible. On one occasion he referred to such aid as "raids on our munitions." But Roosevelt thwarted the move. As the year wound down, SPAB's research teams worked diligently at what came to be known as the Victory Program, which was an estimation of the overall munitions output needed to defeat potential enemies if the United States lent aid to the Allies as either a belligerent or nonbelligerent.[54]

IT WAS EASY to underestimate Bill Knudsen. He never shouted for attention or played the bureaucratic game. "I don't understand this political nonsense," he admitted to Baruch over lunch. "I'll work for you or the President, but nobody else." Baruch thought he was miscast at OPM. Knudsen confided that at the agency he felt like an old cat trying to scramble across a highly polished floor. Ickes doubted whether the Dane was up to handling so huge and diverse an assignment. He was "good at turning out one particular product," but he would be "at sea when he has to cover too much ground." It amazed

Ickes that Knudsen went to the trouble of making his own handwritten notes."[55]

In his earnest, straightforward way Knudsen plodded toward the goals set for him by those who knew little or nothing about the intricacies of production. Unlike many of his colleagues, he was willing to suffer some fools as a necessary part of their education and to endure the constant barrage of criticism and insinuation heaped on him. His way was not to repay sarcasm or abuse in like coinage but simply to set people straight if he could. Patterson got a dose of this treatment during his early days as undersecretary when he shoved a pile of papers at Knudsen during a meeting, saying, "There, Bill, is your small arms program." While the others went on talking, Knudsen put on his glasses, pulled a pencil stub from his pocket, and did some figuring. Satisfied, he removed his glasses, returned the stub to his pocket, and said, "These figures are cock-eyed. Carry them out for two years and they call for making things in the trillions."[56]

On another occasion Patterson presented Knudsen with some figures on the number of typewriters needed by the army. Knudsen went through the same ritual with his glasses and pencil stub, then said, "Mr. Secretary, sometimes it is confusing to know just where to put the decimal point." Patterson asked what was wrong. "Well," Knudsen replied, "on these figures you've given me somebody in your department has put the decimal point in the wrong place. As they stand, they call for one typewriter for every four soldiers in the whole Army. I don't think we need quite that many."[57]

He had his moments with Stimson as well. Early in August the secretary learned that OPM had awarded an entire contract to produce 18,000 jeeps, which Stimson called "Bantam cars," to the Willys-Overland company. Two other firms, Ford and American Bantam, which had created the car, had also bid for the contract. Although Bantam had designed the original version, it lost out as the highest bidder and was also a relatively small company. Stimson thought the contract should have gone to Ford because it was "by far the most responsible manufacturer and this is a car which I am very anxious for certain early deliveries," but Willys had submitted the low bid. Nor was he pleased that Knudsen, in awarding the contract, had gone directly against Bob Patterson's advice.[58]

A delegation from the War Department descended on Knudsen in hopes of persuading him to change his mind. They explained that they had more confidence in Ford, which was a big manufacturer with more know-how, and they wanted the jeeps made properly. After hearing them out, Knudsen said, "Now, you gentlemen have been kind enough to say that I know something about production. If I know anything about production at all, I know about producing motor cars. Is that right?" They nodded agreement. "Well, gentlemen," Knudsen continued, "*this jeep is a motor car.* And I say Willys can make it." The discussion ended as quickly as it had begun.[59]

Knudsen knew how to make cars and how to organize production. What he could not do was make OPM work, for reasons that had little to do with his own abilities. Its lack of authority continued to undermine much of what it did, especially with the military. Although the military worked more closely with OPM than it had with NDAC, it still went its own way in procurement and elsewhere. The army and navy had statutory authority to do their own procurement and jealously guarded that privilege even though their methods were obsolete and utterly inadequate to the scale of the defense program. OPM's three fields of activity, production, purchasing, and priorities of munitions, completely overlapped those of ANMB and the separate agencies of the armed services. Patterson realized this early in his tenure and struggled to formulate a working relationship, but he also believed strongly that the military should be the one defining goals and economic output.[60]

In retrospect Nelson thought that OPM was "ready for the oxygen tent" by midsummer and that it faltered because of its inability to deal with the nexus of materials, priorities, and allocations that grew ever more severe and intertwined. A reorganization in September added two new divisions to the existing four, but lines of authority within the agency remained too tangled to work well. After SPAB was created, Knudsen found that he had more educational work to do. At the first meeting, while he, Knox, and Stimson were discussing the effect of copper on brass, Wallace leaned across the table and asked, "Mr. Knudsen, what is brass?" At first Knudsen thought he was joking. When it became clear that he wasn't, Knudsen explained that it was an alloy of copper and zinc. A few minutes later Wallace leaned over the table again and asked, "Mr. Knudsen, how many gallons are there in a barrel of oil?" Forty-two, replied Knudsen, who left the meeting discouraged that so high ranking an official knew so little about the basic stuff of production.[61]

THE SEASON OF discontent grew hotter in part because the mobilization effort gained a powerful new watchdog as of March 1. On that date the Senate authorized a new ad hoc committee to make a full and complete study of the defense program with a less than bountiful budget of $15,000. Within a short time it became known as the Truman Committee after its chairman, the hitherto obscure senator from Missouri, Harry Truman. Since January Truman had been receiving letters complaining about waste and favoritism in the construction of Fort Leonard Wood. He had noticed the same thing in other camps he had visited as a member of the Senate's military subcommittee, and he wondered how extensive fraud and waste in the overall program had grown. It did not help his suspicions that so many war contracts were concentrated in so few companies and in relatively few areas of the country.[62]

This concentration bothered Truman, who had been a small businessman himself, as much as graft or waste. "The little manufacturer, the little contractor, and the little machine shop have been left entirely out in the cold," he said. "The policy seems to be to make the big man bigger and to put the little man completely out of business . . . I am reliably informed that from 70 to 90 per cent of the contracts let have been concentrated in an area smaller than England." Despite its small budget, the committee received broad powers, but it had to walk a delicate line. Nobody, least of all Truman himself, wanted anything resembling a repeat of the notorious Joint Committee on the Conduct of the War that had meddled in almost every aspect of the Civil War and made life miserable for Lincoln. Truman intended to make it a straightforward investigatory body untainted by political meddling. "If nothing is wrong, there will be no harm done," he declared. "If something is wrong, it ought to be brought to light."[63]

The small, feisty Truman, with his thick glasses, flat features, and even flatter Missouri twang, had just won reelection to a second Senate term as a New Dealer who supported the administration's every move. Although he had come to office through the support of the notorious Pendergast machine in Kansas City, no one doubted his personal honesty or strength of character. Neither did he impress anyone as a man of unusual talents or abilities. He had little formal education, but his active mind developed a powerful appetite for facts and for learning. Only a few people yet knew of his strong will and streak of personal courage that led him to brook no obstacle in his quest to get at the facts and act on them. Unlike so many of his colleagues, he never played to the gallery or the press.[64]

Truman asked Attorney General Jackson to recommend the best investigator he knew for the committee's chief counsel. Jackson responded by sending Hugh Fulton to see Truman. At thirty-five Fulton had already made a reputation with several high-profile investigations and prosecutions, but he did not make a strong first impression on Truman. "He came in wearing a derby hat," Truman recalled, "a big fat fellow with a squeaky voice. I said to myself, 'Oh shucks!' However, I paid him more than half the money I had, $8,500." He also promised Fulton that no political pressure or other interference would be exerted on him or his staff, and that promise was kept. Fulton demanded high standards of work and conduct from his staff, and the result turned out to be one of the most important and productive congressional committees ever created. A student of history, Truman had pored over the old joint committee's hearings, having recalled a statement by Robert E. Lee that the committee was worth two divisions to him. Never did the Truman Committee involve itself in military strategy or tactics.[65]

Nor did Truman want the committee to second-guess the agencies responsible for defense programs. The committee, he said on radio, "does not seek to substitute its judgment for that of other governmental departments or agencies of defense. They have their own jobs to do. However, we can and will and do ascertain the facts about what they are doing and why they are doing it." Another member, Joseph Ball of Minnesota, made this goal even more plain when he declared, "We decided that we did not want to make it either a smear committee or a whitewash committee." Most of the complaints came to the committee, usually by mail but sometimes by phone or in person, from private citizens who did not like what they saw about projects going on around them or at work. At one point, the committee received a host of letters about the mysterious Manhattan Project. Truman inquired about it to Stimson, who told him it was a project racing to beat a similar one undertaken by the Germans. The first one to succeed, Stimson added, would probably win the war. Truman dropped the matter, little suspecting how it would come back to him a few years later.[66]

The committee held its first hearings on April 15 with Stimson, Patterson, Knox, Knudsen, and Hillman as the first witnesses on the state of the defense program. It then turned to the camp construction program, the aluminum shortage, and the shipbuilding program. Along the way it developed a keen interest in defense contracts and their distribution. Truman kept his focus on the plight of small businesses that lacked access to defense contracts. "If you should see my correspondence," he told a witness, "you would think that every little businessman in the country is going out of business." In scrutinizing the intricacies of the defense program, and the work of OPM in particular, the committee found little that it liked. In its first annual report, read to the Senate in January 1942, Truman blasted the agency's performance.[67]

"Its record has not been impressive," he read in a quiet voice that drew an increasing ring of senators closer to him. "Its mistakes of commission have been legion; and its mistakes of omission have been even greater . . . The disappointing record of the Office of Production Management is not so much due to its lack of power as to its failure to perform the functions for which it was created . . . The failure has not been due so much to the lack of power as to the ineptness of the officials . . . and their unwillingness to use the weapon which they had." Truman followed this indictment with a blast at the dollar-a-year men who "continued to act for their companies, publicly announcing that their Government work was part-time only." They approved all important procurement contracts and may have done so honestly and conscientiously. However, Truman added, "it is not their intentional acts that the

committee fears, but their subconscious tendency . . . to judge all matters before them in the light of their past experience and convictions."[68]

Nelson was not much kinder in his appraisal of the agency. He concluded
that "it was baffled by the priorities problem, the materials problem, and, not
least, by the . . . lack of adequate definition of its own goals." Having noted
the need for a single person to direct the overall program, the Truman Committee suggested that perhaps the time had come to create yet another new
agency or program to oversee the entire production process. Step by step the
mobilization effort was stumbling toward a better way of doing its job.[69]

Recalling the president's clarion call in 1936, "This nation has a rendezvous
with destiny," a *Fortune* reporter thought the time had come to update and
reinforce its import. "One basic fault in the war effort," he concluded, "is that
not enough Americans have yet been *asked* to do things for their country, to
perform for it any of the patriotic acts that the vast majority are anxious to
perform."[70]

One troubled episode that sweaty summer underscored this conclusion.
The Selective Service Act of 1940 obligated draftees to serve for only twelve
months; their term would expire in October unless the act was renewed. If an
extension did not occur, some 987,000 draftees, National Guardsmen, and
reserve officers would be eligible to go home, slicing the size of the army in
half and undoing most of what had been done during the past year to build its
strength. Their departure would gut the battle-worthiness of nearly every
American division, a prospect that appalled George Marshall. He had been
trying since March to get legislation introduced to extend the term of service,
but neither the president nor Congress wanted to touch the subject.[71]

The issue was a political hot potato. Critics insisted that the administration had made a solemn promise to let the boys go home after their year of
service. Talk of reneging on that promise touched off a firestorm of controversy and sent the morale of the men plummeting. Where was the emergency,
anyway? It was one thing to arm the nation, quite another to prepare troops
for a foreign war. Congressional leaders warned Roosevelt that an extension
bill had no chance of passage. The matter drifted until June, when Marshall
suggested to Stimson that they give out a statement that the War Department
intended to extend the length of service if presidential and congressional approval could be obtained. Roosevelt was still ill at the time, but Stimson informed Hopkins of their plan to make the announcement and asked him to
explain it to the president.[72]

By pushing his staff hard, Marshall managed to complete in five days his
first annual report as chief of staff, including a detailed summary on the army's growth during the past year, what had been accomplished, and what
would happen if it were decimated by the loss of so many men at a time when

the Nazis continued to gain strength. Boldly he recommended removal of "legal restrictions" that tended to "hamstring the development of the Army into a force immediately available for whatever defensive measure may be necessary." Still a novice in the wiles of Capitol Hill, he neglected to brief congressional leaders, who bridled at being blindsided by requests for a bill they thought could not be passed. Several of them had already declared themselves in favor of letting the boys go back home and resume their normal lives. "That has produced a situation which is always difficult," admitted Stimson, "namely, of trying to get them to reverse themselves." He and Marshall could not budge the congressional leaders, who kept insisting that in getting the original bill passed they had promised to hold the men for a year only.[73]

While the controversy gathered steam, some distressing facts came out about the draftees. A thorough survey revealed that nearly half the men who reported to draft boards had been rejected as unfit. The main reasons included bad teeth (20.9 percent), poor eyesight (13.7 percent), heart and circulatory problems, (10.6 percent), and venereal diseases (6.3 percent). Another 10 percent failed to measure up to fourth-grade educational standards; Stimson thought most of these were southern blacks. The cabinet and other advisers debated these astonishing figures early in July. Former Indiana governor Paul McNutt argued that men with remediable diseases should be taken in and treated, but Stimson countered that the modernizing army wanted only men in perfect condition. Ickes thought it "perfectly absurd that a man should be rejected because he needs the services of a dentist." Finally Stimson and Marshall persuaded a reluctant Roosevelt to get behind an extension bill. On July 21 the president asked Congress for authority to extend the term of service.[74]

Much of the opposition derived from bitter opposition to Roosevelt himself. America Firsters mobilized to fight any extension, convinced that it marked the next step in pushing the nation into the European war. In going before Congress to testify on behalf of the bill, Marshall realized that its members were far more willing to listen to him than to the president. This revelation discouraged him, but he decided to make the most of it. "Is there an emergency?" he said to a Senate committee. "I say there is, and the War Department says there is. You gentlemen will have to settle it." He reminded a House committee of the dismal failure of the volunteer system in the War of 1812, Mexican War, and Civil War. Aware that some Republican votes would be needed, he went so far as to meet with forty Republican House members. After hearing his plea, one of them growled, "You put the case very well, but I will be damned if I am going along with Mr. Roosevelt." The remark infuriated Marshall, who fired back, "You are going to let plain hatred of the personality dictate to you to do something that you realize is very harmful to the interest of the country."[75]

After seven days of tough debate the Senate passed the bill 45–30. Seven Republicans joined the majority, while sixteen Democrats and one Progressive opposed the bill. Of the thirty opponents, twenty-three were diehard isolationists who had voted against Lend-Lease and nearly every other Roosevelt foreign policy measure. The bill passed only when the majority accepted an amendment to boost the pay of army men $10 a month to $40 for privates after a year's service. The fight was even more bitter in the House. Marshall's plea induced a handful of Republicans to support the bill even if it cost them reelection, but forty-five Democrats stood opposed and another thirty-five were uncertain. On August 12, beneath packed galleries and amid fiery exchanges of rhetoric, the House voted to extend the terms of service by eighteen months. The margin of victory could not have been smaller; the final vote was 203–202.[76]

Nothing revealed the depth of division and discontent in the nation more succinctly than this vote count. America First hailed it as a victory of sorts. The venomous Senator Wheeler proclaimed that it served "notice to the War Department that the Congress does not approve of their breaking faith with the draftees. It is also served notice that the Congress does not take seriously the cry of the Administration that the so-called emergency is greater now than it was a year ago." Elsewhere the news of the tally carried a very different and dampening effect. A few days later a war-weary Londoner told an American radio commentator, "The Americans are a curious people. I can't make them out. One day they're announcing they'll guarantee freedom and fair play for everybody everywhere in the world. The next day they're deciding by only one vote that they'll go on having an Army."[77]

CHAPTER 10

MATERIAL GAINS AND LOSSES

We in America, the richest country on earth, had never really stopped to consider if we might ever be faced with serious shortages in anything ... War changed this easy arrangement.

—DONALD NELSON [1]

We have used so far only our surplus strength, and not all of that ... It is not enough. Now begins the grunt of real and earnest.

—GARET GARRETT [2]

No task is easier than to assemble a list of materials you need and haven't got. We had the list and did nothing about it ... When we suddenly woke up to our defenselessness, practically the only reserves of strategic materials we possessed were the stores, inadequate to the need, held by private corporations for their own use.

—FORTUNE [3]

BY LATE SUMMER IT HAD BECOME fashionable among the press to draw up a summary of where the defense program stood compared to where it had been before the war. September was, after all, the second anniversary of the war that had spread across the whole of Europe like a plague and gone on to infect other continents as well. The end was nowhere in sight, especially after the Nazi invasion of Russia, and the scale of mobilization kept ramping up. As of June 30, 1941, Congress had authorized an astounding $46.9 billion for defense programs, but contracts had been let for only $21 billion of that amount, and only $7 billion had actually been disbursed for goods received. Of that figure only about $100 million went for materials to aid Britain. The consensus among the armchair experts of the press centered on one major theme: "National defense has been marked by a good job of production but a shoddy demonstration of planning."[4]

Nowhere did this seem to be more true than in the crucial realm of raw materials. In August *Fortune* published a survey outlining the status of nineteen key materials under the title "The Crisis in Materials." Among other things, the charts revealed "the appalling degree to which men have failed to conceive the magnitude of mechanized war." Steel was projected to fall short of needs by 8 million tons in 1941 and 27 million tons the following year, thanks in large part to the industry's resistance to expansion. Petroleum faced a different problem. In 1940 the nation produced more than twenty times the output of all the Axis nations in Europe, but transport had become a problem because of rising demand coupled with the transfer of fifty tankers to Britain. Rubber, with its dependence on East Indies imports, was becoming an endangered species because of the war, increased consumption, and the lack of ships to bring it to American shores.[5]

The aluminum supply remained desperate. "There is not a scrap of aluminum for civilian needs the rest of the year and next," declared the reporter, "nor is there any aluminum for indirect military needs." Production of magnesium had ramped up from 13 million pounds annually to 30 million pounds, with another 44 million pounds on the way. But OPM pleaded for a staggering output of 400 million pounds by the end of 1942. Zinc supplies were decent, but soaring demand threatened to swallow them unless output increased by about 40 percent. Copper, which had faced problems of surplus supply a short time earlier, was overwhelmed by rising demand despite a large domestic output and sizable imports from South America. Brass, a vital component of cartridges, was a mixture of 70 percent copper and 30 percent zinc; military demands had already forced it out of the civilian economy. No one cared to contemplate what would happen if the country got into a shooting war.

The supply of tungsten was holding up, but nickel was in desperately short supply because of the rush of war orders. Most of the nation's chromite came from Rhodesia and New Caledonia, where tons of the material piled up at docks awaiting ships. Existing inventories of manganese remained adequate, but lead was becoming scarce because so much of it was being used as a substitute for even scarcer metals. The vast majority of America's tin came from the Far East, where both the supply and shipping had become problems. Most silk came from Japan, putting it in deep peril, while Australian and New Zealand wool suffered from the shipping shortage along with cork, which was in short supply. Kapok was obtained from the Philippines and Ecuador; here too lack of ships posed a problem. Toluene, a critical component of TNT, was a by-product of coke ovens. The Nazis, with their stranglehold on Europe, had nearly five times the coke oven capacity of England.

Each one of these materials played vital roles in industrial output. Magnesium made a tough alloy vital to airplanes; zinc was needed for making brass, dry-cell batteries, and a number of other products; copper was used in a wide variety of military products as well as plumbing and electrical goods. Brass was needed for bullets and other military supplies, and scrap brass did not work in cartridges. Tungsten was irreplaceable in mass-producing cutting tools and carbide tool bits, while nickel was vital in making armor plate, projectiles, and a wide range of armaments. Chromite went into ferrochrome, the master alloy in stainless and chrome steels. Manganese acted as a desulfurizer and deoxidizer, making it indispensable in producing steel. Lead played innumerable roles as a substitute and key ingredient in many products, while tin saw heavy usage in cans, solder, and other goods. Silk went into not only parachutes but also powder bags that held the propelling charge in large guns. Wool had a great variety of uses for uniforms, blankets, and cold weather gear. Cork was needed for insulation and marine goods, kapok for life preservers and upholstery, pillow and mattress stuffing. In addition to these vital materials, another list existed in the form of chemical products such as polyvinyl chloride, chlorine, ammonia, methanol, and the fast-growing family of plastics that were finding more and more usages in manufacturing. In February OPM put Society of the Plastics Industry people together with military and government officials to explore ways of using plastics in defense and industrial output.[6]

Copper posed a peculiar problem in that American mines were the world's largest producers but their output still fell short of the soaring demand. Good supplies of zinc existed, but the entire western hemisphere lacked smelter capacity. Petroleum also had no supply problem but groaned under the demand for 100-octane aviation gasoline, the miracle blend that enabled the RAF to hold off the swarm of Nazi planes attacking England. Coal production was rising steadily but subject to the perpetual threat of labor disturbances. Lumber seemed to be an inexhaustible resource, with output not having yet reached the 1929 level of 35 billion board feet. The aluminum squeeze sent manufacturers searching for substitutes. By March Maytag was replacing aluminum washing-machine tubs with enameled steel, while General Electric saved 4 million pounds of aluminum by switching to plastics and steel for ice cube trays. Westinghouse dropped two refrigerator models from its line to save aluminum.[7]

So desperate were some small manufacturers for aluminum, nickel, and zinc scrap that they paid junk dealers higher prices for it than for the new metal coming from the mills. A few defense contractors added to their bottom line by procuring more of the new metals than they needed and selling the surplus to junk dealers. The plastics industry grew so rapidly that it too suffered from a lack of capacity to fill the growing demands on it. Although some attempts to use them in munitions production turned out badly, the army kept looking for new applications that would replace scarce metals. OPM encouraged companies to push the search for new uses. Pullman redesigned its rail cars and coaches to save nearly 3.4 million pounds of aluminum and 180,000 pounds of nickel. To save nickel and chrome, OPM asked eleven bicycle manufacturers to reduce the average weight of their models by 10 percent and to limit their lines to a maximum of ten models each.[8]

Some of the new cars rolling off the production lines contained what one report called "the most radical innovation in metallurgy since the Bronze Age." GM cars had twenty-five parts, and Chrysler vehicles thirty, that began life not as molten metal but as metallic powder that was pressed into solid shapes. Engineers predicted that most cars would soon have a hundred pounds of the cheaper, lighter, more porous metallic powders. Subsidiaries of both companies scrambled to supply other manufacturers with powdered metal gears, bearings, parts of airplane engines, guns, ships, and household items—anything with wheels that turned and levers that moved. Work also went forward on more efficient methods to process low-grade manganese, of which the nation had abundant supplies, into the high-grade version. By October, however, even paper was in short supply. Only two months earlier OPM had declared that no paper shortage was in sight, but the defense effort consumed an estimated 30 percent of the available supply.[9]

Another resource vital to steel production had the dubious honor of being the only metal of which the United States produced more than 85 percent of the world's total. Molybdenum, which the steel industry called "moly" and its miners "mollie-be-damned," went mostly to foreign markets until rising steel production and the defense program kept more of it at home. For six other metals, however, the gap between demand and supply was stunning. The nation consumed about 1.125 million long tons of manganese but produced less than 75,000 long tons; it used more than 60,000 tons of nickel but produced only about 500 tons, and used 700,000 tons of chrome against production of about 2,600 tons. More than 12,000 tons of antimony got consumed but only 2,500 tons produced; of 9,000 tons of tungsten used, only 5,000 were produced. Tin had the sorriest record of all, with more than 90,000 tons consumed and less than 50 tons produced.[10]

To close these gaps, Americans fell back on their history. By the fall of 1941 a new kind of gold rush was on. Unlike its predecessor, this one was far more orderly and organized, dominated by prospectors working in collaboration with the government. Their impulse was the same: chuck a routine job for the chance of striking it rich, not with gold but with one of the scarce metals that were fast becoming as good as gold. Not only grizzled prospectors but filling station attendants, mechanics, clerks, cowboys, and small businessmen headed west to try their luck along with representatives from the Bureau of Mines and the Bureau of Metallurgy. Most of them landed in the broad expanses between the Continental Divide and the Sierra Nevadas, seeking their fortune in what was called the poor man's metals.

COTTONWOOD CANYON IN the White Mountain range of California boasted a decent trout stream along with several enticing seams of free-milling gold quartz that were being ignored by half a dozen hopefuls living in small cabins. Farther down the grade at Deep Springs Valley, Pete Cherooty, who was part Shoshone, parked his flashy new car with its two big search-lights. A former jackhammer operator, he had come in search of white talc, which contained magnesite that had many defense uses. He had found one good seam and sold it on option for $25,000. The Lemke brothers had also found a seam and done well with it, while Lyle Donohue and his partner were mining scheelite, one of the tungsten ores, and hauling it thirty-five miles to a homemade mill. "Way I figure it," said Lyle, "we're making thirty-five dol-lars a day and better. And we have got a real mine."[11]

Another prospector crossed the Humboldt range into the Antelope dis-trict seeking quicksilver. His wife had taken in sewing to help raise money to build a retort. After finding a shallow deposit, he put together a homemade firebox and used sagebrush for fuel. Before long he had two other men work-ing for him, taking out about a hundred dollars' worth day after day until he sold the property and used the money to buy a resort. Ed Allen had his own quicksilver mine up Dunlap Canyon outside Mina, Nevada. Now in his early sixties, he had wandered the mineral wilderness in seven western states and Alaska before trying his luck in Dunlap Canyon. He led a visitor through the narrow twists and turns of his shaft and up a couple of ladders before reaching a rock wall. Shining his carbide lamp on it, he said proudly, "I made pretty nigh six thousand dollars here in less than eighteen feet." Half a dozen other small mines lay scattered within a mile of Allen's shaft, with many more in California and Arizona and the greatest concentration in Nevada.

Tungsten City became the mecca for A. L. Crowthers. It had sprung to life near the end of World War I in the Sierra Nevada foothills behind Bishop, California, and consisted of some bunkhouses, a few pine shacks, a mill, a mine, and a tailings dump below the mill that extended nearly half a mile down the canyon. After the war the demand for tungsten dropped, and

Tungsten City became a classic western ghost town. A contractor in Bishop, Crowthers knew about the tailings dump and in the spring drove out to it with a fluorescent lamp. When he shined the lamp on the dump, the tailings glowed like the show window of a drugstore. He and two partners leased the dump on a 10 percent royalty basis and invested $25,000 to extract tungsten from it. Crowthers bought out his partners and began netting more than $3,000 a month from the dump, which had about half a million tons of tailings. The dump yielded not only tungsten but garnet, which aircraft factories used in sandblasting.

Within a short time Bishop became a hotbed of tungsten mining. U.S. Vanadium reached a huge low-grade deposit by blasting a road through granite ledges. Its new mine worked 600 men and operated a mill that processed 1,200 tons of ore a day. The company also built a tramway to move the ore quickly down the high ridge. Elsewhere another company, Utah Copper, had been tearing down a mountain in Bingham Canyon and smelting its low-grade ore, which was thick with molybdenum. The company had grumbled at spending so much money to get rid of the molybdenum until the Bureau of Mines found that molybdenum could sometimes be used as a substitute for tungsten. Utah Copper then searched for methods of saving the molybdenum.

Government agencies played a crucial role in the new gold rush. The Bureau of Mines tended to getting ore out of the ground, while the Bureau of Metallurgy devoted its attention to the next phase, getting the metal out of the ore. The former set up headquarters in Tucson, the latter in Salt Lake City, where it built a large plant for its crew of 200 geologists, engineers, and metallurgists. Substations were set up across the West to assist both the large companies that were moving into the business and the small operators who were also growing in numbers. The RFC advanced money to anyone in either group who could show proof of sufficient ore holdings. Government metallurgists not only helped prospectors solve problems but also did experimental work on issues that were too big for private interests to tackle. It was a government experimental station that made the crucial discovery of using electrolysis to recover 95 percent of the manganese in low-grade deposits compared to only 6 to 20 percent with existing methods.

For all the differences in the modern gold rush, the basic transaction remained the same: a prospector looking for the big strike that he could sell to some large company capable of exploiting it. Jim Logan was one such hopeful. Sitting on the steep flank of a small mountain near the California-Nevada border, he waited patiently for dusk to arrive before getting out his fluorescent lamp, a gadget that looked like the receiver of a cradle telephone and was attached by two wires to a dry battery. Several versions were advertised in mining journals, and Jim had sent $20 to a company back east to get his model. When it was dark enough, he turned on the ultraviolet rays and pointed them into a shallow trench where he had scraped away the loose dirt and rock to expose a brownish gray outcrop. As he swept the light across it, small streaks and flecks of white, so vivid that they seemed to move, leaped from the blue background.

"Scheelite, all right!" he said with satisfaction. "And boy! She sure looks rich!"

A prudent man, Logan ran a small eating house in a small town and lived a quiet life, but he had long had the itch to prospect. From time to time he had wandered into the desert and returned with small bags of rock that he displayed on every windowsill of his house until his wife put her foot down. The morning after returning from his find, Logan spotted Lute Gregg coming out of the butcher shop. "Want to go prospecting?" he asked. Gregg knew nothing of ores but could handle a single jack. They went out to the site, trenched vigorously with picks and shovels, and traced the outcrop, which ran for nearly a mile at a width of ten feet. Logan sent a sample to the Mackay School of Mines, which did free assays for Nevada prospectors. The results showed 4 percent in concentrates, which translated to about a hundred dollars a ton for the ore.

"High grade," said Logan. "That lamp didn't lie. I bet she's richer lower down." After talking things over with his wife, he rented out the eating house and, with Gregg, recorded their claims and drove a tunnel into the vein at a lower level. One day an engineer from the Bureau of Mines turned up and stayed several days, walking the ground and taking samples. Two weeks later another engineer arrived with a crew of twenty men. Logan and Gregg allowed the government to explore their claims; the men collected samples above ground and below while others worked on maps. Two men from the Geological Survey flew over the site taking photographs to reveal fault lines or other characteristics. Samples and cores from boring went into separate bags for shipment to Washington, Salt Lake City, Reno, and Tucson.

Once completed, the project would give Logan and Gregg a factual analysis of their holdings, a basis for coming up with figures to show any company that wanted to lease or buy out their property. For its part the government got reliable data on the potentialities of the new district, one more piece of a larger mosaic being assembled to indicate where key materials could be found for the mobilization effort.

THE MOST DOMINANT mineral in the American arsenal proved to be the most important one of all. Petroleum and its by-products constituted 40 percent of the nation's total mineral production, and they had fast become the heart and soul of modern warfare. "Had there been no such thing as oil," mused Harold Ickes, "I doubt if there would have been a global war." Apart from its crucial role as a lubricant and ingredient in numerous products, oil had become the fuel of choice for every kind of moving vehicle. By the time Hitler invaded Poland, more than 60 percent of American transportation and 65 percent of the world's oceanic transportation ran on oil. It had become the life blood of modern civilization.[12]

Oil leaped to prominence with almost frightening speed during the twentieth century. In World War I the United States supplied more than 90 percent of the petroleum used by the Allies, shipping more than 29.3 million barrels between January and October 1918. Although this amount seemed huge at the time, it was soon dwarfed by America's growing dependence on machines that ran on oil. Between 1914 and 1940 automobiles increased from 1.6 million to 27.4 million, trucks from 85,000 to nearly 4.6 million, tractors from 17,000 to nearly 1.57 million, and buses from virtually none to 142,000. Nor was that all. Oil was used to power ships, airplanes, manufacturing plants, and utilities and to heat homes, factories, and stores. Both naval and merchant ships switched almost entirely to fuel oil; diesel locomotives used oil. The most striking change occurred in commercial and home heating as owners abandoned coal furnaces in favor of oil burners. Between 1927 and 1940 commercial use of oil soared from 15.8 million to 44.8 million barrels and domestic heating use from 11.7 million to a stunning 115.5 million barrels.[13]

Despite this soaring demand, the petroleum industry on the eve of the war found itself awash in oil. The yield from a barrel of crude oil increased steadily as chemists discovered better techniques. Thanks largely to the Great Depression, consumption remained static or fell slightly during the 1930s even as new sources of oil were found. Like other industries, oil companies fretted over maintaining prices and avoiding excess capacity. By May 1940 their gasoline inventory exceeded 102.4 million barrels, an increase of 44 percent over the previous September. Illinois, where new fields had elevated the state to the nation's third-largest producer behind Texas and California, had no mechanisms in place to regulate its output, and the scramble to produce was fast eroding the props under crude oil prices.[14]

Unlike with most other materials, the problem with oil was not lack of it but getting it where the need existed. For many years the United States had been an exporter of oil except for residual fuel oil, the longtime shortage of which had been covered by imports from the Caribbean. Within the country, however, large imbalances complicated supply. The Pacific Coast and Rocky Mountain region produced and refined enough oil to meet their demands, which amounted to about 18 percent of the nation's total. The midwestern states had adequate refining capacity but not enough crude oil, and their production was dwindling. The East Coast consumed about 40 percent of the nation's total but had hardly any crude oil production and only half the refinery capacity needed. Most of its crude and half of its refined products came from the giant Gulf Coast oil fields and refineries, as well as foreign imports. The system of supply depended utterly on a well-choreographed transportation system relying mostly on tankers and pipelines.[15]

The petroleum industry was the second largest in the nation, and the war greatly complicated its extensive overseas operations. It was highly competitive and utterly dependent on complex technologies. Few plants looked more daunting or intricate than a refinery, yet its operation was delicately balanced. Its products could be stored only for a few weeks, which meant that the flow of materials had to be carefully scheduled from producing well to point of consumption. It was also an industry with a checkered history and a poor public image born of its early days when Standard Oil and John D. Rockefeller became public emblems for all that was evil in big business. A strong streak of mutual distrust existed between the industry and the government. In 1911 an antitrust suit broke up the original Standard Oil into thirty-four separate companies. Since then the larger firms had continued to grow and integrate their operations.[16]

During 1940 the Justice Department prepared to bring another suit to atomize their power by separating production from transportation just at the time when the need to increase output from the industry was becoming apparent to more people. Leon Henderson tried to get Justice to delay the suits long enough to get the defense program going. At the same time, the industry found itself again face-to-face with one of its worst nemeses, Harold Ickes. On May 28, 1941, the day after proclaiming a state of unlimited national emergency, Roosevelt appointed Ickes to a new post, petroleum coordinator for national defense. The title brought a smile to Ickes's face as he recalled a definition then current in Washington: "A coordinator is a man who can tell you the time if you show him your watch."[17]

The problems given Ickes to solve were formidable: rationalize the production and utilization of crude oil and natural gas reserves; reduce or eliminate the cross-hauling of petroleum and its products; develop more efficient use of transportation and storage facilities; balance refining operations, making the most economical use of raw materials; improve the efficiency of production and distribution; and eliminate the drilling of unnecessary wells and other unneeded activity that consumed scarce resources. The president's letter of appointment pleased Ickes greatly. It was, he thought, "both very sweeping and very specific. This is what I wanted it to be. If I am to have power, I do not want any doubt to exist that I have it . . . Just how the oil people will take this order I do not know. I suspect that some will like it and some won't."[18]

Most did not like it. One industry figure recalled that the creation of the new position "came as a complete surprise to those engaged in the petroleum industry" and that the appointment of Ickes aroused "considerable alarm." Since coming to the administration in 1933 Ickes had fought for an oil conservation policy even though the industry was drowning in cheap oil at the time. As administrator under the Connally Hot Oil Act of 1935 he had constantly antagonized oil executives who hated federal interference in their industry. As secretary of the interior he had reversed past policy of giving away public lands, minerals, oil, water rights, power sites, and timber. At one point he compelled Standard Oil of California to return to the government the 1,232-acre Elks Hill naval oil reserve and pay more than $7.1 million for the oil it had extracted. Columnist Raymond Moley, a disaffected New Dealer, assured readers that "there is little power in Mr. Ickes' job."[19]

Ickes understood the industry's suspicions, but he was also fully alive to the emergency. More than a year earlier he had tried to awaken interest in creating an oil committee but got no response. As a shrewd first step Ickes named as his deputy administrator Ralph K. Davies, a vice president of Standard Oil of California and one of the rare oilmen who believed strongly in oil conservation. Disgruntled oilmen predicted that Ickes's appointment meant "a virtual Federal dictatorship over the industry." Instead the combination of Ickes and Davies proved to be one of the most successful and productive teams within the administration. Ickes was pleasantly surprised when Baruch told him that William Farish, the president of Standard Oil of New Jersey, was entirely satisfied with the appointment because he thought Ickes had been a good administrator who dealt fairly with people. The praise especially gratified him because some oilmen had described Farish as a man "always trying to get more than he is entitled to."[20]

Few industries needed a coordinator more desperately than petroleum. The big companies waged perpetual war with small, independent operators and with producers. States like California and Illinois, which had no regulations, produced to excess, creating what Ickes and others considered a waste of valuable resources. Price-fixing and other abuses also stained the industry. An investigation by Senator William P. Cole Jr. of Maryland, begun in November 1939, led to his introducing a bill to regulate the industry. Just when the oilmen thought they had killed the bill, Cole released correspondence in April 1940 showing that Roosevelt had asked him for the bill and fully supported its objectives. The president wanted production regulated by Washington if the states failed to do so. Thurman Arnold followed with an announcement of fifteen proposed investigations of the oil industry, and a House committee opened an inquiry into the transportation of oil and its products.[21]

The oilmen countered by assuring everyone that they could meet any demand placed on it. Reserves were three times as great as in 1917, refinery capacity had been quadrupled, and stocks of key products were ten times larger. Early in 1940 the big companies spent $30 million to increase output of high-octane aviation fuel and tripled their inventories to 6 million barrels, only to have the army and navy buy just a million barrels during the first half of 1941. Rather than foot huge storage bills, some companies converted their aviation fuel into high-test gasoline for automobiles by blending it with low-test fuels. By the summer of 1941 a peculiar situation had evolved: There seemed to be plenty of oil but not in the right places. Transportation emerged as the bottleneck, partly due to the fifty tankers sent to England to replace its losses in submarine attacks. With fewer tankers available, more oil would have to be moved by pipeline or rail car. However, the cost of shipping by tanker was only a third of that by pipeline and a tenth of that by rail.[22]

Ickes found himself in a quandary, thanks to an improbable conjoining of circumstances. Oil was cheap and plentiful, yet scarce in some places, especially the Eastern Seaboard. At the same time the nation was still selling oil to Japan, a policy that rankled Ickes. Between March 15 and May 31 nearly 4.7 million barrels went to Japan, including nearly 1.4 million barrels of high-octane crude that could be made into aviation gasoline. More tankers were being built, but transportation remained a problem. To ease the crunch, the oilmen wanted to build two new pipelines, one for crude oil and one for gasoline, from East Texas to the Philadelphia–New York area. They were willing to finance the projects but fearful of being slapped with an antitrust suit if they collaborated on them. One department of the government urged them to cooperate in the defense effort, while another threatened them with suits if they undertook joint action. The Cole bill included a provision granting rights-of-way for pipelines, which the railroad interests vehemently opposed.[23]

Never one to seek the easy way out, Ickes plunged into all these issues at once. At a cabinet meeting on June 6 he brandished a collection of editorials and political cartoons "raising hell about continuing to ship oil and gasoline to Japan while talking of rationing our own people on the Atlantic Coast." True, the problem was not one of supply but one of transportation, Ickes admitted, but people who could not get oil to heat their homes next winter would not understand or care about that distinction. It would be easier to grasp, he added, if the American record of supplying Japan had not been so bad for years prior to the outbreak of war. Roosevelt asked him to give Hull three or four more days to resolve the matter. "If Hull moves that fast," Ickes muttered to his diary, "it will be a new speed record for him." As for the president, it annoyed Ickes no end that he could "always find some good reason for not moving, while uttering threats from time to time."[24]

Roosevelt and Hull were playing a delicate game of diplomacy, hoping to prevent an open break with Japan as long as possible. "Japan's willingness to make war," observed Hull in his memoirs, "plus her far greater state of military preparedness, provide full explanation for holding off as long as we did on applying embargoes on the shipment of petroleum, scrap iron, and other strategic materials to Japan. The President and I saw eye to eye on this policy." Ickes had other ideas. When a Philadelphia manufacturer telegraphed him on June 16 that oil needed by his company to produce defense materials was being loaded aboard a Japanese tanker, Ickes promptly ordered the shipment held up. To Steve Early he explained that the action was taken "not because it was headed for Japan but because it was headed away from the Atlantic seaboard, where oil and gasoline will undoubtedly be scarce this summer and winter." Ickes also sent telegrams to every oil supplier on the Atlantic Coast asking them not to ship any oil to Japan without first consulting his office.[25]

Roosevelt was furious. At lunch on June 11 Ickes found the president "in probably the worst humor that I have ever seen him in. Certainly he was angrier with me than at any other previous time." The source of his wrath was a column he suspected Ickes of inspiring, which Ickes denied. On June 18 Roosevelt ordered Ickes not to issue any more holding directives on oil shipments without first clearing them with himself or Hull. Ickes considered it "the most peremptory and ungracious communication that I have ever received from him . . . It certainly was intended to pin my ears back." He responded with a lengthy explanation of what he had done and why; his reasons were sound but did not move Roosevelt, who was more concerned about maintaining control of American policy toward Japan at a difficult time.[26]

A day after Ickes wrote his letter, the stunning news arrived that Hitler had invaded Russia. "It now remains to be seen," Ickes noted acidly, "whether Japan will go in on the Axis side. If so, she will do so with an ample supply of American oil and gasoline." While Roosevelt and Hull scrambled to absorb this development and recalibrate their diplomacy accordingly, Ickes wrote the president that the invasion presented a great opportunity to stop shipping oil to Japan altogether. Roosevelt replied by reminding him that "this is a matter not of oil conservation but of foreign policy, a field peculiarly entrusted to the President and under him to the Secretary of State. The considerations in this particular situation are peculiarly delicate and peculiarly confidential." Ickes promptly offered his resignation as petroleum coordinator, confident that it would not be accepted. "I have not attempted to interfere with the policy of the State Department," he insisted, "but I did not know that I am not supposed to have an opinion with respect to it and some of its policies." Privately he observed that "I am at or near the parting of the ways with the President."[27]

Roosevelt knew well the Ickes temperament with its penchant for drama. "There you go again!" he answered while dismissing the resignation. "There ain't nothing unfriendly about me, and I guess it was the hot weather that made you think there was a lack of a friendly tone . . . You are doing a grand job as Petroleum Coordinator—so much so that it looks to me as if you will have to take unto your manly bosom the coordination of the whole power situation if things get any worse. That would include, of course, coal—hard and soft—water power, and domestic consumption of all of them." The letter was vintage Roosevelt in its conciliatory tone and the dangling of possible increased powers that he knew Ickes wanted badly. Ickes knew the game and regarded the letter as "more than a little disingenuous," but it cleared the air for the time being. To Ickes's surprise and pleasure, the State Department decided on the same policy Ickes had advocated, the licensing of all oil exports from American ports. On August 1 Roosevelt stopped the export of aviation gasoline entirely.[28]

The pipeline issue was another matter. Here too Ickes saw the danger early. In March 1940 he had urged the building of a pipeline from the Gulf through Georgia to the major refineries in New Jersey. "If there should be a real emergency involving the Atlantic Seaboard," he stressed, "we would lack transportation facilities to get enough oil and gasoline to our Eastern Seaboard." However, the railroads in Georgia and the rail unions opposed the plan, and the state legislature defeated a bill to permit such a pipeline. A year later the emergency was fast approaching, and the pipeline issue crackled with controversy. A pipeline of that length would take at least a year to build, and critics agreed with Raymond Moley that "the pipeline would be costly, it would divert precious materials from more urgent uses and it would be a long while building. Even its ultimate necessity is not clear." Others claimed that 19,000 rail tank cars were sitting idle and could be pressed into service.[29]

Stimson's attitude reflected much of the opposition to the pipeline. At a SPAB meeting he listened to Davies explain why the pipeline was needed but remained convinced that the "alleged shortage of gasoline" in the Northeast was exaggerated. "Everybody is afraid of the howl which will come up from a shortage of gasoline," he observed, "but as a matter of fact we are at the peak of a luxury demand for pleasure cars. Pleasure cars have increased tremendously during the summer. Nobody is willing to give them up. I finally stated my views and carried the situation that we should not waste good munitions on this pipe line for the present."[30]

Four pipeline projects were on the table, but only one—running from Montreal to Portland, Maine—was under way. The Cole bill finally passed and was signed by Roosevelt on July 30, 1941. By then Ickes was convinced that the new pipelines were urgently needed and that the Northeast faced potentially severe shortages by winter. He stunned oilmen by asking them to turn another 100 tankers over to the British, 25 of them at once, which would cut the coastal tanker fleet by 40 percent. Although he knew this would badly hurt deliveries to the East Coast, he hoped it would expedite gaining approval for the pipelines. At the same time he asked motorists in sixteen Atlantic states to cut their gasoline consumption by one third. Predictably, protests rained down on Ickes from all sides.[31]

When his voluntary approach to reducing consumption did not work, Ickes imposed curfews on gas stations in the East. Patriotic drivers responded by filling up earlier and more often; gas consumption actually rose 8 percent. Ickes then worked up a plan to have Leon Henderson order suppliers to cut their deliveries to filling stations by 10 percent. Rationing looked to be just around the corner. Ickes found another ally in Jesse Jones, who agreed with him on the need for a pipeline and was willing to have the RFC advance $60 million to build it. The oil companies produced a plan to build the largest pipeline in the world at a cost of $80 million. The Cole bill authorized the government to build pipelines or lend money to private companies for the work. By August the project for a major pipeline could at last go forward, but it would not be finished in time to relieve the threatened winter shortage of oil in the East.[32]

The furor grew louder when the Senate created a committee to investigate the alleged shortages. John J. Pelley, president of the Association of American Railroads, and Ralph Budd of NDAC assured the committee that the railroads had enough tank cars to move 200,000 gallons a day eastward when needed. The committee concluded that "unnecessary alarm was created" by Ickes's handling of the situation and that no transportation shortage existed. A peeved Ickes demanded to appear before the committee, where he blasted the members for their shallow investigation and produced evidence of a shortage of tank cars. But the fall weather proved to be unusually warm, leaving heating oil stocks higher than normal in the East. The railroads managed to scrounge enough tank cars to haul 140,000 gallons eastward a day, and the British surprised everyone by returning twenty-five of the borrowed tankers while promising forty more in the coming weeks.[33]

In October Farish of Standard Oil of New Jersey (Jersey Standard) and two other oil presidents urged Ickes to lift the restrictions in the East. If oil stocks were not drawn down as usual, they stressed, there would be no storage space to fill with gasoline for the coming summer. Ickes saw little choice. "It was up to us to beat a graceful retreat as rapidly as possible," he admitted. He could hardly insist there was a shortage of oil when the heads of three major oil companies said otherwise, or a shortage of transportation when tankers were being returned from England. Still he remained convinced that "we have gotten out of a very dangerous situation and in doing so have not only saved our faces but have bettered our position." However, the experience left a sour taste. He informed his staff that "there won't be any more restrictions on the sale of gasoline until people drive their cars to the filling stations and find empty pumps. I am not going to kid myself ever again that the dear American people will voluntarily ration themselves or even cut out waste in the public interest."[34]

Through these difficult months Ickes also stewed over his distancing from Roosevelt. They had always fought over this or that issue but saw each other often enough to reconcile their differences. But even in the early New Deal days the president had never been as busy as he was now or beset with so many problems, many if not most of them in the realm of foreign policy that left Ickes in the dark. New agencies filled with new faces and a shrinking circle of intimates around the president left him less time for seeing Ickes except at cabinet meetings. Ickes began to feel like an outsider, which increased his dislike of Hopkins, the quintessential insider with the president. When SPAB was created, Ickes interpreted it as a rejection not only of Baruch but of himself as well. Neither had Roosevelt carried out his suggestion of putting Ickes in charge of hard fuels such as coal and power. He took the neglect to mean "that I had been pushed back again on the side lines as far as possible."[35]

Once again, while on vacation with his young wife, he blamed his enemies, especially Hopkins, for keeping him down and pondered whether to resign. He agreed with Baruch that Hopkins had become in effect assistant president and dreaded his return to Washington. In pondering his relationship with Roosevelt, he decided, "I was determined that I had to come to grips with him, if possible, because the personal situation between us had become intolerable." But when Ickes lunched with the president the next day, he was astonished to find him "entirely friendly and cordial. I hadn't seen him like that for a longer time than I could remember." It was like old times, he thought, adding wryly, "It was like old times also in that I could not come to grips with him." Nevertheless, Ickes came away with his mind eased and determined to "refrain from beating my wings against the cage because I am having nothing worth while to do in connection with the defense program."[36]

He struggled mightily and often in vain to keep this resolution. In October he had Ralph Davies prepare a memorandum and sent it to Roosevelt with a note saying it was one of the most important he had ever sent him. But that same day news came that the Japanese cabinet had fallen and been replaced by one much more militaristic and chauvinistic. The president canceled a scheduled cabinet meeting and met instead with his war council—Hull, Stimson, Knox, Marshall, Stark, and, Ickes noted sourly, "the inevitable Harry Hopkins, without whose wise counsel we cannot resolve anything."

Ickes's memorandum was indeed important, and prescient as well. It called the president's attention to "how our own oil reserves have been shrinking since 1928 and how important, consequently, it is that we should be looking abroad with a view to acquiring oil reserves elsewhere."[37]

ELECTRICITY WAS NOT, strictly speaking, a material, but it was vital to the production of nearly every other material as well as the products made from them. The United States led the world in power generation, yet by 1941 the available supply was struggling to keep up with the soaring demands made on it. Two huge public projects in the Northwest were just coming online to increase the supply of hydroelectric power: the Bonneville Dam (capacity 518,400 kilowatts) and PWA Project No. 9, better known as the Grand Coulee Dam, with a projected output of 1,890,000 kilowatts. Grand Coulee started up its first two smaller generators on March 22, nearly two years ahead of schedule. Towering 550 feet above the Columbia River, it spanned nearly a mile from bank to bank. The lake piling up behind its massive wall would eventually stretch 151 miles to the Canadian border.[38]

During the seven years and seven months of its construction the Grand Coulee had claimed seventy-two lives. It proved to be Henry Kaiser's last major construction project before his move into manufacturing and defense work. The first two 10,000-kilowatt generators sent power 266 miles to ship-yards in Tacoma and 260 miles to Boeing's bomber plant in Seattle. They were dwarfs compared to the giant 108,000-kilowatt generators being built by Westinghouse that would soon follow. The parts for each one weighed nearly 2.4 million pounds and required thirty-eight freight cars to haul them. Once online, they figured to generate about one twelfth of all the power then produced in the nation.[39]

Every bit of it would be needed. As impressive as the American power system was, it already strained to meet the growing demands of the defense effort. The drought that spring in the Southeast, home of the TVA dam complex, created a severe shortage. The region got only half its normal rainfall, leaving some TVA reservoirs 60 percent lower than usual. Federal Power Commission Chairman Leland Olds predicted a shortfall of a million kilowatts by year's end. He brought together TVA officials and executives of private power companies, who agreed to link their facilities and form a power pool covering seventeen states. Even before the drought Olds had warned that a shortage loomed because of rising defense demands. The drought succeeded in thrusting the power issue into the limelight, and with it came a political dogfight even as the FPC and southern utilities worked out a rationing system for the emergency.[40]

The irrepressible Ickes waded in by asserting bluntly that "there is a power shortage now and a greater one in prospect." OPM's Bill Batt estimated that an additional million kilowatts would be needed for expanded aluminum output alone. To these warnings Charles W. Kellogg, president of the Edison Electric Institute and a dollar-a-year man for OPM, countered that existing generating capacity had a 20 percent margin of safety and was adequate for all defense and civilian needs. At a press conference Ickes accused Kellogg of "misrepresenting the facts to the people" and snapped, "He's worth all of the $1 a year he's being paid." The construction of new facilities for aluminum and magnesium required huge amounts of power, an estimated 10 to 12 kilowatts per pound of aluminum alone. Producing enough aluminum for a single bomber consumed enough electricity to supply the town of Tupelo, Mississippi, for a week; the steel for a 10,000-ton cruiser used enough current to heat all the electric irons in the nation.[41]

Although output was expanding, the problem went beyond mere capacity. By the year's end the total available generating capacity was estimated to be just under 45 million kilowatts, plus another 10 million kilowatts installed in private industrial plants. About a third came from hydroelectric sources, a number that was reduced by the drought. New generating capacity could not be created quickly. It took at least two years to construct new equipment and put it online even if the necessary materials were given priority. To make matters worse, the existing infrastructure was aging. Thanks largely to the depression, which slashed capital spending, steam turbines and generators were wearing out and needed replacing along with a host of other electrical equipment. They were old and tired, hardly in condition to withstand the pressures of increased emergency service. The problem was not merely expanding capacity but also playing catch-up in replacing obsolete and worn-out existing plant at a time when materials were in short supply.[42]

At a meeting with Roosevelt, Olds, and others, Ickes advanced a plan to spend $1.5 billion to develop more power in the West. Roosevelt assured him that Congress would never agree to that sum. It might accept $200 million, he added, if provision was made to use the money only to expand existing public and private plants and build no new ones without authorization from Congress. After the meeting Olds announced to reporters a plan of his own to spend $2.3 billion over five years for adding 13.44 million kilowatts to the power system. Already private utilities had agreed to underwrite two thirds of a projected 6.4-million-kilowatt expansion program scheduled for completion by December 1942. In reporting this scheme *Time* cut to what it thought was its heart. "In undertaking to embellish the Administration program," it noted, "Olds seems to be undertaking something else: a race with his ex-sponsor Ickes for the job of U.S. energy tsar."[43]

Ickes wanted even more to be made coordinator of power as well as of solid fuels; he believed strongly that the same person should be in charge of both areas as well as petroleum. He also suspected Olds of being among those seeking to prevent this from happening. "He is a good technical man," Ickes conceded, "but he has no ability or effectiveness as an executive." A few days later he secured an appointment with Roosevelt and asked bluntly to be made power coordinator. He also told the president what he thought of Olds and was pleased to learn that Roosevelt had not even read Olds's report and plan. As chairman of the National Power Policy Committee, Ickes argued, he was the logical man to coordinate all power. Roosevelt observed that opposition to the move existed, most notably from eighty-year-old Senator George Norris, considered by many the founding father of TVA. Norris had already urged the president not to make the appointment because he believed ardently in the regional form of authority such as TVA had.[44]

Roosevelt had also long opposed centralizing control in Washington, but he seemed more amenable to a compromise. While Rosenman was working on the plan that became SPAB, Ickes let him know of his desire to be power coordinator even though he didn't know Rosenman all that well. Finally, on November 5 Roosevelt signed an order making Ickes coordinator of hard fuels, but he still held off on power. The press played up images of a savage clash between Ickes and Norris; *Time* described it as "months of close in-fighting and wire-pulling" and labeled it "one of the fiercest and most important struggles for power in the history of the New Deal."[45]

The conflict did pit longtime New Deal liberals against one another but did not create a fatal breach between them. Ickes liked Norris and on November 25 had him in for lunch, after which the old warriors talked for two hours. Ickes feared that making Julius Krug power administrator for OPM delivered its management into the hands of the private interests. Norris lamented that so many men from the utility companies were on Krug's staff. He wondered aloud whether the country might win the war while losing everything the New Dealers had fought for during the past eight years. Throughout his long career he had fought for the principle of public power, and now it seemed in greater peril than ever. He mourned the passing of the old liberal vanguard in the Senate, which included himself since he had already decided not to run for reelection. They agreed that the war was hastening its departure and parted on terms much more friendly than those portrayed in the media.[46]

The power situation was, as Norris observed, in bad shape, but some new developments offered hope for the future. An experimental new turbine installed at South Bend, Indiana, operated at an initial steam pressure of 2,300 pounds per square inch, more than 900 pounds above the highest existing conventional turbine. It also converted 1 pound of soft Indiana coal into 1 kilowatt of electricity, reducing coal usage by 40 percent; in 1901 it took 6 to 8 pounds of coal to generate 1 kilowatt-hour. Steam plants, mostly owned by private utilities, converted an average of only 30 percent of coal's energy into current compared to the 75 to 90 percent conversion rate of hydroelectric plants. And in remote Vermont an old technology was taking on new life. Atop Grandpa's Knob in the Green Mountains near Hubbardton stood a 110-foot windmill with blades like airplane wings, ready to generate 1,000 kilowatts of power, or enough to light 2,000 homes. Unlike a lone windmill, this tower was connected to Vermont's utility company to supplement its supply.[47]

THE SOLUTION TO the rubber shortage was as obvious as it was difficult: More rubber had to be acquired, and current usages had to be reduced. The obvious way to cut rubber use meant wading into the same thicket that snarled efforts to reduce gasoline usage. Drivers had to drive less, thereby using less gas and prolonging the life of their tires. If voluntary means did not work, then rationing was the logical sequel. Ickes discovered quickly the futility of trying to get Americans to drive less. Getting them to see the big picture in gasoline was hard enough; it was even more difficult with rubber. The larger problem was getting more rubber either through buying or through the manufacture of synthetic versions.

Stockpiling seemed a logical first step. Congress had provided the means with the $100 million fund for strategic raw materials in July 1939, yet during the next year only $13 million was spent on acquiring all materials. During 1940 rubber consumption rose to 648,500 tons and reserves fell below 130,000 tons. Late in May, as France was falling, Hopkins mentioned to Jesse Jones that the president wanted him to stockpile some rubber and tin. Jones had legislation prepared that led to the creation of the Rubber Reserve Company (RRC) on June 25. In acquiring rubber, however, he had to coordinate with buyers from American rubber companies as well as compete with foreign governments seeking to stockpile it. Since a British-Dutch cartel controlled the flow of raw rubber, bidding up prices became a serious problem. A bid of even a few cents above market price could induce the cartel to withhold supplies in hopes of even higher bids. It took diplomatic intervention with the British to get an agreement for buying additional supplies.[48]

Still the buying went slowly. Later Jones claimed that by December the United States had accumulated "the largest stock of rubber that had ever been accumulated at any time in any country." Even if true, this claim missed the point. The stockpile of 533,344 long tons barely amounted to a year of average peacetime consumption. Eliot Janeway accused the tight-fisted Jones of using the "stock-pile fund for bargain-hunting in a war-inflated market that offered no bargains." When the market was fluctuating between 18 and 20 cents a pound, Jones held out for a lower price, only to have Japan bid it up to 20 cents and take the rubber. "On the eve of the great rubber famine," said Janeway, "Jesse Jones did not regard rubber as a sound investment at 20 cents."[49]

Newsman Marquis Childs thought he understood Jones. "All his life he has been a shrewd trader," he wrote, "and how he could have been expected to have thrown overboard at sixty-eight the values of a lifetime is difficult to see. He thinks in terms of money and the amassing and saving of money. He will dicker over a loan or a purchase until he obtains what he considers the greatest advantage for the government. In normal times his shrewdness might have been an important asset. But the war was not a war of money. It was a war of things."[50]

Even a large stockpile of natural rubber would vanish quickly in an emergency that cut already fragile shipping lines in the Pacific. The only viable alternative was to push the development of synthetic rubber as rapidly as possible. A variety of synthetics already existed or were in the experimental stage. No one of them duplicated all the qualities of natural rubber, but several of them outdid it in specific areas. For all its versatility, natural rubber had three major weaknesses. It tended to swell and weaken in oil, deteriorate at high temperatures, and gradually crack under the glare of sunlight. Most of the synthetics improved on solving these problems, but none had the special bounce, flexibility, or versatility of natural rubber.[51]

Since no one synthetic could do all the things rubber did, different kinds had to be developed. Several already existed that could replace natural rubber in many of its uses, but not the one that counted most. Tires accounted for 75 percent of all the rubber used in the nation. Every major tire company was researching the problem, and one or two had what they thought were solutions. The Nazis found their answer in two compounds known as Buna-N and Buna-S, both of which were derived from butadiene. American companies, especially Jersey Standard, were familiar with these compounds, and some were eager to develop a synthetic rubber industry, but they faced an uphill climb that had more to do with politics than with science.[52]

Congress showed no interest in synthetic rubber. On June 14, 1940, executives from Jersey Standard and other companies testified before a Senate committee and suggested immediate production of 100 tons of synthetic rubber a day from new plants. Nothing came of their appearance. Stettinius and Batt of NDAC were more receptive, and a committee was formed to study the matter. After soliciting the views of all the rubber manufacturers, the committee on July 17 tentatively agreed to recommend a production program of 100,000 tons a year. Jersey Standard, which had been working on Buna rubber since November 1939, then stopped to await the government's decision on what role it would play.[53]

Stettinius and Batt urged Roosevelt to have the government invest $100 million in plants to produce synthetic rubber. When he showed no interest, they went to Jones, who met with the president the next day. Roosevelt shrugged the matter off, saying that if necessary the plants could always be built within a year's time. Earlier Jersey Standard had warned the government that even under the most favorable circumstances it would take at least eighteen to thirty months to complete a construction program and get quantity production of synthetic rubber under way. Evidently this warning had not reached Roosevelt. Jones thought he was "woefully ignorant of the problem," but he knew the president well enough to realize that he could not be budged. In September Jones and Stettinius tried to nudge the president again but got approval only for $25 million instead of the $100 million they sought. "These wealthy rubber companies," said Roosevelt, "ought to build their own plants."[54]

A strange reversal of roles occurred in the case of rubber. Where in other cases the government had to prod industries to expand their output of a strategic material, it neglected to pursue synthetic rubber production and left several key corporations to push ahead on their own initiative. A *Fortune* reporter thought this approach made sense. "A synthetic-rubber plant is a highly specialized industrial mechanism," he wrote, "needing quantities of alloy steels, special machinery, and skilled labor in its construction. To throw up huge plants now, diverting men and materials from sorely needed aircraft, munitions and guns, would be a major blunder. And huge, non-self-sustaining plants, for a shadowy emergency that might be five years in coming, would jeopardize the U.S. defense position . . . The first line of defense, therefore, is the U.S. natural rubber reserves."[55]

The rubber companies, like their peers in other industries, did not welcome the prospect of expanding their facilities overnight, but they agreed it could be done should the need arise. With government financing and priority in materials, they could tool up in about twenty months to fill normal rubber needs. The cost would be high, but not excessively so as an emergency measure. Nearly everyone agreed that it would cost less to build the synthetic plants than to buy a year's supply of rubber for the stockpile—assuming it could even be had. The result would also carry a lasting bonus in the form of a new industry that freed the nation from dependence on Far Eastern rubber supplies. As always, the major unanswered questions were how long the emergency would last, and how much time the industry had to get a construction program under way.[56]

The private sector had made some progress on its own. DuPont introduced its neoprene in 1931; it was suitable for a wide variety of rubber products but not for tires. Thiokol Chemical Company made a liquid polymer sealant under its company name. B. F. Goodrich produced its own synthetic, Koroseal, and in June 1940 introduced a new synthetic called Ameripol or "Liberty Rubber." With a flair for the dramatic, the company gave a party at the Waldorf-Astoria to unveil its new product. President John L. Collyer pulled open plush blue curtains to reveal a map of the world with green neon lights tracing the tortuous route of natural rubber from the Far East to Akron, Ohio. A small cardboard boat moved slowly along the route, then suddenly exploded. This was Collyer's way of announcing that Ameripol would be used to make tires. In August Goodrich put the tires on the market with a massive advertising campaign.[57]

With much less fanfare, Jersey Standard announced in April 1940 that it would build a plant in Baton Rouge to produce Buna rubber by the year's end. Although its first product would be Buna-N, Jersey Standard also held the American rights for Buna-S, the best hope for synthetic tires. Buna-S was 20 to 30 percent longer wearing than natural rubber but also cost four times as much at present. However, Jersey Standard had one huge advantage it hoped to exploit. The Buna in Germany's synthetic tires had been made from coal; Jersey Standard was developing the means to produce it in much larger quantities from petroleum gases. In 1939 the company decided on a three-pronged strategy. It would erect a plant for making butadiene to demonstrate that it was practical to produce it from oil. The plant would be large enough to fulfill all the Buna-N demand and also serve as a model for a future Buna-S plant. Jersey Standard also offered to license Buna-N to any of the rubber companies if they would agree to experiment with Buna-S should the government so wish.[58]

Two companies, Firestone and United States Rubber, accepted the third proposal at once. Goodyear hung back, and Goodrich went its own way with Ameripol. Firestone began manufacturing Buna in February 1940, staged a demonstration of how to make synthetic rubber at the New York World's Fair that summer, and started construction on a $50 million plant. Jersey Standard also pushed research on another synthetic, Butyl, and pursued negotiations on who was to manufacture how much of the two key ingredients in Buna, butadiene and styrene. Meanwhile, the RFC assumed responsibility in October for the government's role in advancing the synthetic program. A month later Stettinius informed Jones that NDAC was "not now considering itself responsible for developments in this matter."[59]

Jones met with Harvey Firestone and the president of Humble Oil, a Jersey Standard affiliate, in November and asked bluntly what they thought could be done with $30 million, which soon shrank to $25 million. With suitable cooperative arrangements, they replied, it would be enough to build four 10,000-ton Buna plants and provide the butadiene and styrene needed for them. The president wouldn't approve any higher figure, Jones added, and the future was too dim to gamble larger sums on an untried field. He then asked which kind of synthetic each plant was going to make. "Let each company make any kind it chooses," suggested Firestone, "but require each one to use that rubber in its own tires." Everyone liked this idea and agreed to it. Firestone, U.S. Rubber, and Jersey Standard believed strongly that Buna-S was the only option, but Goodyear and Goodrich continued to pursue a different approach.[60]

Formal requests for proposals did not come from the RFC until December 9, 1940. By then Jersey Standard had agreed to build its butadiene plant in Baton Rouge only to learn in February 1941 that the RFC's rubber program was in "a state of suspended animation." For reasons never made clear, it was decided to reassess whether the government should invest money in laying the foundation for a large new synthetic rubber industry. Jones asked W. L. Clayton, his deputy loan administrator, to look into the matter. On February 20 Clayton circulated a memorandum saying in essence, "It may be safely assumed therefore that we have in sight now, even if cut off at once from any further supply, a sufficient supply of rubber to carry us for three years." It was entirely fitting that this incredible conclusion appeared during the same month as Gano Dunn's infamous appraisal of the steel supply. Both were flights of fancy unmarred by the facts, let alone any broad view of what needs the war might impose even if the United States did not become a belligerent.[61]

Appalled at the news, William Farish of Jersey Standard had Frank Howard, one of his top executives, write a five-page letter to Clayton explaining the facts of the case. Firestone and F. B. Davis Jr. of U.S. Rubber learned that the 40,000-ton program had been definitely abandoned, but they continued to press the RFC for some kind of action. In March they secured a "shadow plan" to finance construction of four plants capable of producing only 2,500 tons each. Clayton then asked Jersey Standard to waive all patent royalties and infringement claims that might arise from the program. Howard agreed to do so in support of what he called Clayton's "very modest program." But he also reminded Clayton, "It is our conviction that the synthetic tire rubber program is essential to the national defense, and an important development in the postwar economy." At the time Howard wrote this letter, no means of producing butadiene from petroleum in large quantities yet existed, even though Jersey Standard's Baton Rouge plant was nearing completion.[62]

Jersey Standard's plant was designed to produce a mere 5 tons a day of Buna-N rubber, the only type then commercially competitive with natural rubber. With the government program in limbo, the company decided on its own to build a second, larger butadiene plant at Baton Rouge. Meanwhile, its officers tried to convince OPM officials of the necessity for a larger synthetic rubber program. An entire year had been frittered away with little to show for it, and opposition to such a program remained strong. "It did not seem possible," recalled a disgusted Howard, "that a world which in peace consumed more than a million tons a year of natural rubber could wage war on an unprecedented scale of mechanization and still get along for three years without any natural rubber save what it got out of the Brazilian jungles and without any advance preparation for the large-scale manufacture of a synthetic substitute."[63]

Jersey Standard and Firestone continued to push for revival of the 40,000-ton plan, reminding OPM officials that establishing a new synthetic industry on a vast scale would require at least eighteen to thirty months. The OPM officials were more sympathetic to the idea, and Knudsen saw the necessity at once. On May 9 he wrote Jones urging immediate approval of the 40,000-ton program "with the idea that we may want to multiply this production to 100,000 or even 200,000 tons." A week later the program was back on track, but five months had been lost since its conception. Not until mid-September was ground broken for the first of the four plants by U.S. Rubber at Naugatuck, Connecticut. Once completed, the plants would give four different companies experience in producing synthetic rubber and evaluating one type against another. Until then, the rubber riddle remained unsolved.[64]

CHAPTER 11

THE BUSINESS OF WAR

The use of this crisis as an excuse either to extort unjustifiable profits or to pursue partisan political objectives is not only indefensible and dangerous but reprehensible morally.
— NATIONAL ASSOCIATION OF MANUFACTURERS[1]

The U. S. defense program ... suffered from elephantiasis ... Defense was too big to be seen whole ... Many a "lag" was in fact no lag in actual production or planning, but a confession that somebody had promised the impossible.
— TIME[2]

Mass production is the way to make a lot of something at minimum time per unit, and ... the American nation has that trick down finer than any other nation on earth ... The only thing that might spoil the national defense program was that the public didn't know how long you have to work on the make-ready before you can make a lot of anything.
— CHARLES F. KETTERING[3]

FEW CITIES UNDERSTOOD THE BUSINESS of war better than Bridgeport, Connecticut. In 1917–18 it had been called "the Essen of America" for its prolific outpouring of war goods. Remington Arms produced bayonets for the British, rifles for the Russians, and cartridges for the American Expeditionary Force. The Locomobile Company turned out trucks; the Lake Torpedo Boat Company, submarines. Despite the tribulations of wartime dislocations, the city thrived as its population jumped from 114,000 to 166,000. Toolmakers raked in as much as $16 a day and flaunted their new prosperity by appearing in $15 striped silk shirts on Main Street or at Seaside Park. Then came the government's abrupt cancellation of war contracts. Remington, a DuPont subsidiary, handed dismissal notices to 7,000 workers on Christmas Eve, two days before the season's first major snowstorm.[4]

The experience left a bitter, lingering distrust of war orders in the city. When a fresh batch of them appeared in November 1940, its leaders naturally feared a repeat of their past letdown. A reporter called the city "schizophrenic about the war" and described it as looking on war orders as if they were "forbidden fruit, tasty but fatal." Nearly every one of its 400 companies proceeded with the same caution; yes, they would produce, but only if the government shouldered the financial risks. This was, after all, the hometown of Phineas T. Barnum, and its businessmen were determined not to be made suckers by what might prove to be fool's gold.

Bridgeport had a most unusual mayor in Jasper McLevy, a Socialist by party but also a Yankee Scot who believed in business-dominated government, balanced budgets, and pay-as-you-go city financing. A roofer by trade, he drove a Ford to work and his own tractor on his Litchfield County farm. No one ever saw him in a dress suit. He regarded himself as the representative of the city's 26,000 small-home owners. Where New Dealers warned of the menace presented by Hitler, McLevy insisted that the war was "going to end overnight." His city comptroller, a tough former boxer and concert pianist, agreed that the war would end that very winter. McLevy remembered all too well how Bridgeport had prospered during the last war and borrowed freely for roads, schools, sewers, and, fittingly, an extension of the poorhouse.

He remembered too the boom of the late twenties that collapsed in disaster, leaving the city burdened with debt and dwindling tax revenues from falling land prices and a real estate market that remained dormant through the thirties. During the war the city, with some government help, had built enough housing to absorb the new workers flooding into the factories. But after Remington and the other munitions factories shut down in 1918–19, much of the housing stood empty and remained so amid a wave of mortgage foreclosures. By 1922 Bridgeport had 37,750 people on its relief rolls. A few large companies like General Electric kept the local economy afloat with their production of consumer goods, but the lingering effects of the postwar shrinkage could still be seen around the city in 1941.

By 1939 prosperity seemed to be creeping back into town as its factories churned out a smorgasbord of consumer goods from sewing machines to lipstick to brassieres. When the war orders began, business leaders remained wary of an increase in plant capacity that would come back to bite them. "What are we supposed to live on after the war?" they asked. But the city still possessed a wide variety of industries with a good supply of machinery and skilled workers to man them. It was a preeminently metalworking town that could not help but play an important role in the defense effort. By 1941 the city had already received $1.5 billion in war orders, most of it to the larger firms like Remington Arms, General Electric, Vought-Sikorsky (a subsidiary of United Aircraft), Bridgeport Brass, and Bullard. The smaller companies got plenty of subcontracts to keep them almost as busy as the major companies.

Yet the fears remained. A local chamber of commerce official likened the situation to "a cat that is being choked on cream." Workers, especially skilled ones, rejoiced in their good fortune but worried that it would end soon and leave them in the lurch. Some spent their newfound money on the goods denied them through the depression years; others salted their earnings away for "the evil day when peace breaks out again." Housing had again grown tight, especially for families, petty crime was on the rise, and both schools and the sewage system were strained by the influx of newcomers. The mayor, having pushed the tax rate down from $34.10 per $1,000 to $28.30, cringed at the thought of new bond issues; neither did he want New Deal largesse. But he saw little choice in pleading for federal funds that he had rejected during the early 1930s.

"What's happening now," said one official, "is almost identical with the last war. It's insane. But what is sane about war?"

WAR HAD LONG been thought to be good for business, whatever its other baleful effects. Conventional wisdom shared the belief of crafty speculator Daniel Drew that "it's good fishing in troubled waters." The first generation of great American entrepreneurs used the Civil War years to build their fortunes and business experience in a tough, volatile, and hugely profitable arena. During that tumultuous era John D. Rockefeller built his first oil refinery, Philip D. Armour pulled off a lucrative speculation in pork, Jay Gould cut his teeth in Wall Street, John Wanamaker launched his career in clothing with a windfall in uniforms, and J. P. Morgan acquired the worst stain attached to his career with reputed profits from a sale of rifles to the government. Bankers like Morgan, George F. Baker, Jay Cooke, and Harris C. Fahnestock accelerated their careers in the vibrant environment of wartime finance.[5]

World War I placed this belief under a cloud of disrepute. Although the war created more than its share of profits for bankers, businessmen, and industrialists, it also left ugly scars on their reputations. The government's abrupt cancellation of wartime contracts left many companies with excess capacity and a wariness of repeating that mistake. Even more painful, the investigations of the Nye Committee between September 1934 and February 1936 tainted the profits of bankers and the munitions manufacturers with the label "blood money." In 1936 Roosevelt himself declared, "If war should break out again in another continent, let us not blink the fact that we would find in this country thousands of Americans who, seeking immediate riches—fool's gold—would attempt to break down or evade our neutrality."[6]

When war did come and the American defense program began, concern arose at once over the possibility of companies earning "blood profits." By 1940 the mantra that "American industry hates war" was widespread. McGraw-Hill included in all its business and industrial publications a message beginning, "Business stands against war. Let us take a clear-eyed look at this thing we call war. War is a political tool for domination of suppression, a device of futility." In 1940 popular writer Garet Garrett published an article entitled "War Has Lost Its Pocket," in which he proclaimed that "American business . . . makes this original declaration—that it has neither heart nor stomach for war profits." However, once the defense contracts began to flow freely, some politicians, labor leaders, and New Dealers were quick to accuse big business of refusing to cooperate with the government and demanding huge profits for their work.[7]

One businessman, James S. Knowlson, head of Stewart-Warner Corporation, grew tired of the yelping and lashed back. In a letter to his employees Knowlson pointed out that the company had bid on $10 million worth of government work and won contracts for about $2 million. "Prices at which they were taken," he added, "were such that up to July 31, we lost $60,000 on what we shipped. This loss represents what we have paid out of our own pockets to learn how to do our job. That is not profiteering." The company had also bought or ordered $450,000 worth of machinery without government aid in anticipation of government business. Other firms reported a similar experience of paying a price to learn the ropes of defense work. Hardly anyone had much experience with the products demanded by the military, many of which hardly resembled those of the last war and were constantly evolving.[8]

Taxes also swallowed their share of profits. In July 1941 Roosevelt informed Henry Morgenthau that "I am ready to make a strong statement to Congress on the tax bill whenever you think the time is appropriate. I would lay particular emphasis on the excess profits tax." Six weeks later he handed Congress an unexpected set of proposed changes to produce another $463 million in revenue, citing the need to curb inflation as well as get more money. The two revenue acts of 1940 had put the normal tax on corporations at 22–35 percent and excess profits tax at 25–50 percent. Given the huge expenditures for defense, the president wanted to bump these rates up as well as impose new or increased excise taxes on a wide range of activities. Congress proved more responsive than it had in 1940, enabling the president to sign the Revenue Act of 1941 on September 20. For corporations it hiked the normal rate to 24–37 percent and the excess profits rate to 35–60 percent.[9]

The new tax law set corporate taxes at a record high while lowering exemptions on individuals to a record low, thereby compelling 2.3 million more Americans to pay income taxes. Other changes in the excess profits tax provisions made it even more stringent than its World War I predecessor even though the rates remained somewhat lower. There would be no "blood money" profits in the defense effort if the administration had its way. Morgenthau went even further, proposing that all profits above 6 percent be taxed at 100 percent, but Congress balked at that proposition.[10]

Businessmen shuddered at the notion. Many already thought it not worth the effort to do defense work, let alone expand their facilities, if most of what the company made went to the government. Some never cared for it under any circumstances. As *Fortune* observed, "A great many businessmen look upon defense orders with an ancient mistrust of government work in general compounded with a dread of Army red tape in particular." They longed for the days of business as usual, but who knew when they would come again?[11]

WALL STREET FOUND little comfort in the war. Since its glory days of the 1920s the stock market had languished in the limbo of economic depression, the opprobrium attached to it by the scandals following the Great Crash, and the restrictions clamped on it by New Deal legislation. In March 1940 *Newsweek* labeled the securities business the nation's "sickest industry" with good reason. Between October 1939 and March 1940 the Dow Jones Industrial Average fluctuated within a range of only twelve points, the first time in the New York Stock Exchange's history that such a thing occurred. "Instead of following or anticipating the business trend during these six months," observed columnist Ralph Robey, "the market has simply stood still for variations of six or eight points."[12]

Wall Street was not only changing but shriveling as well. The Glass-Steagall Act of 1933, which separated investment from commercial banking, changed the face and leadership of the Street, as did the disrepute into which bankers had fallen during the parade of scandals exposed during the 1930s. In June 1940 the most powerful and familiar name on the Street severed its last ties with the New York Stock Exchange. Junius S. Morgan III, the eldest son of J. P. Morgan Jr., sold the family's last seat on the Exchange, leaving it without a Morgan for the first time since 1871. During the frenzied summer of 1929 an Exchange seat had sold for $625,000; Morgan let his go for $40,000 and was lucky to get that. Two months later two discouraged brokers sold their seats for $35,000, and in December two more went for $33,000. The Exchange itself lost nearly $1.15 million in 1939 and $981,348 in 1940.[13]

Trading in 1940 reached a low not seen since 1921. The Street had 200,000 fewer employees than in 1929, and the ranks kept dwindling. Office vacancies in 1939 totaled 4.4 million square feet, 800,000 more than existed at the bottom of the depression in 1932. By June the slumping Dow Jones Industrial Average had dropped to 114.75, and volume continued to shrink. A month later volume touched a twenty-two-year low of 226,580 shares for one day; the week's volume of 1.6 million shares averaged out to only 216 shares a day for each of the Exchange's 1,375 members. During July and August daily trades averaged 280,000, the lowest figure for any month since 1918 and well below the 700,000 needed by an average commission house to stay in business. Bargains went begging even among the best stocks, and clerks moaned about their "Scotch Weeks" (forced leaves).[14]

Despite an improving economy fueled by defense spending, the stock market remained sluggish throughout 1941 as well. Between November 1940 and February 1941 it declined gradually, then marked time for several months. For five months the average level of prices varied only five points north or south of 120. In July Robey marveled that he had had nothing to say about the market for more than eight months. Even though fears of inflation grew stronger during the year, the market remained comatose through the fall. The driving engine of American capitalism had run out of steam, and the war boom had yet to refuel it. Like other businessmen, Wall Streeters still bore the scarlet letter of their past sins in the minds of many Americans.[15]

Why had the market been moribund for so long? Robey advanced several reasons. The economic recovery had been fueled by British and defense spending and would last only as long as the war continued. The outlook for business profits remained grim because companies were not making much money off their defense orders. "All the evidence we have," he noted, "indicates that this is the nearest thing to a profitless recovery that we have ever had." Taxes were sure to go higher given the level of government spending, and the market itself had gone nowhere since the war began. The public usually jumped into the market only when it saw a definite upward trend, but in October 1941 prices remained below what they had been in September 1939. As the Street liked to say, it had cost the public nothing to stay out of the market for two years.[16]

PUNDITS OF THE economy were no less baffled by what they saw than those of the market. The outbreak of war had promised to lift the American economy, but the phony war gave rise to a phony boom and the return of pessimism that not even the surge of war orders in the summer of 1940 could banish. When shortages began to mount, fears arose that the lack of materials would force nondefense firms, especially smaller ones, to shut down and throw their workers on the street. A new term, "priority okies," was coined to describe them. "If the workers live in one-industry towns, whose factories cannot be adapted easily and readily to defense," warned one writer, "their plight can become even more critical. Priority 'ghost towns' may result." By the fall of 1941 reports mounted of companies on the brink of closing because they couldn't get materials. In small towns their distress would spread quickly to small shopkeepers and other merchants dependent on their business. "The next three months," predicted one official, "are going to be pure misery."[17]

The sharp upturn in business after Hitler's invasion of the Lowland countries gave rise to hopes of a solid recovery and drop in unemployment. New jobs were opening up not only in defense plants but in supporting industries as well. During June and July 1940 alone, textile mills hired 21,500 new workers, shoe factories added 15,000, railroads and public utilities took on 65,000, the construction trades put on 136,000, and steel mills employed another 41,000. Overall employment rose by 1.8 million over that in July 1939, but there remained another 8.2 million workers still without jobs. Serious gaps persisted, especially in rural America. A partner in the world's largest cotton firm observed that "we have in the United States a surplus of at least 2,000,000 farm families and 75,000,000 to 100,000,000 acres of farm land." How were they to survive now that the war had deprived them of their overseas markets? No sector of the economy depended more on exports than agriculture.[18]

In October 1940 industrial output reached new all-time highs, boosted by not only defense goods but by record sales of refrigerators, vacuum cleaners, and other appliances. Department and chain stores reported record earnings, but overall gains did not touch those regions like the Southwest and parts of the Midwest that had yet to receive defense orders or new facilities. By the winter of 1941 talk had turned from surpluses to shortages not only of materials but of some transportation facilities. Railroads groaned under an enormous wheat crop. In February carloadings soared 19.2 percent above 1940. However, the realization gradually dawned on businessmen that what lay ahead was not the usual recovery or boom but a war mobilization, which brought with it drastic controls and restrictions that could cause dislocations and unemployment. Business as usual was fast becoming an endangered species along with fat profit margins.[19]

Corporate returns in the third quarter of 1941 reflected the new realities of business in the defense era. The combined profits of 200 top companies reached $374 million, the highest since 1929 and 40 percent higher than 1940. However, for the first time in American financial history the government's tax collectors got a larger share of the profits (55 percent) than shareholders (45 percent). Oil companies, automobile manufacturers, and toolmakers did exceptionally well. A 25 percent jump in freight traffic rewarded railroads with their highest net income in a decade. The New York Central earned $21.8 million in profits, a whopping 698 percent over 1940. The pace of business in general was estimated to be a full 50 percent above 1929's record level, but no one knew how long it would continue.[20]

"Signs multiply that the economic system is in for heavy weather," warned one pundit in November 1941. "Has the defense program produced a real depression," he wondered, "or is it merely going through an unpleasant phase as a prelude to prosperity?" *Business Week* saw the economy entering a third phase. It had come through an expansion period in which armament and related industries had grown rapidly, and a second one of tooling up to fit the need for more capacity. A third period had begun, one of restrictions that hit consumer and nondefense production hard. "The next several months," it warned, "are bound to be disruptive and painful to business men, workers, and the consuming public alike." A *Washington Post* article quoted OPM officials as saying that the "swiftly mounting impact of priorities will assume perfectly appalling proportions before many weeks." Another official predicted gloomily that the irony of a depression arising from the boom in defense production "may shift interest from the 'Battle of the Atlantic' to the 'Battle of the Stomach.'"[21]

Business leaders remained steeped in doubt. *Fortune*'s quarterly management poll revealed in November 1941 that 75.6 percent of those polled believed the administration was using the national emergency as a pretext for advancing the more radical social and economic aims of the New Deal. They had mixed views about the quality and effectiveness of the dollar-a-year men in Washington but agreed that the best businessmen in government lacked enough authority to do their jobs well. The manufacturers among them, nearly half their number, expressed concerns about being strapped by priorities, having to lay off more people, watching their inventories decline, and enduring more agitation from unions for closed shops. Yet only 35 percent of them had assigned somebody to keep a close watch on priorities. Small businessmen felt the crunch even more severely. A chamber of commerce survey revealed that 90 percent of small nondefense manufacturers thought they would soon have to "cut their operations to the bone." Two thirds of executives in small Illinois plants expected to be forced out of business within a year.[22]

An OPM official went even further, predicting that one third of American industry might soon shut down for lack of business. Ten industries, he added, already faced eclipse because of defense priorities. Small businesses would take the hardest hit. "It is one of the profound ironies of our defense effort," he said, "that its total effect may well be to obliterate smaller enterprises." Die casting offered a prime example. Although essential to many defense industries, defense orders (which carried priorities) comprised less than 15 percent of the industry's business. Die casters required about 15,000 tons of aluminum a year to stay in business, and already the metal was in short supply. It was a small industry of 125 independent companies and fewer than 25,000 workers, yet its product was crucial to hundreds of consumer goods.[23]

Some kept going by resorting to a new and inevitable supplier, the metal bootlegger, who furnished scarce materials to small companies and even some larger ones in a pinch. A Cleveland manufacturer despaired of locating 20,000 pounds of brass to finish a defense order. One day he received a call from a bootlegger offering to provide the material at twice the government's price. To get the brass, the manufacturer had to send his own trucks, carefully disguised to avoid recognition, to an appointed site in Chicago, where he picked up the material and paid cash for it. When offenders got caught, the penalty was light. A Chicago foundry that delivered 41,449 pounds of aluminum parts for civilian goods despite regulations restricting the metal to defense uses, and also bought 25,605 pounds of aluminum scrap for which it lacked preference ratings, became the first to be reprimanded. Donald Nelson, OPM's priorities director, could do no more than suspend the company from the aluminum business for five months. The company's president responded by saying, "I believe the Government is all wet."[24]

BENEATH ITS MASTHEAD the *Bradford County Telegraph* claimed to serve the "Home of the Sweetest Strawberries This Side of Heaven." There was truth to this boast, which was read mostly by the citizens of Starke, Florida, a sleepy rural village of 1,500 souls some forty-eight miles by car from Jacksonville. Life revolved around the strawberry crop in a town where everybody knew everybody else and little traffic tested its two traffic lights. In the summer families found relief by renting one of the little cabins on Lake Kingsley for fishing and swimming. The Rotary Club brought the town's merchants and businessmen together, and rarely did they pass an unfamiliar face on the street. Then, between October 1940 and March 1941, life as they knew it was swept away, never to return. As a reporter marveled, " "The town filled up as if some hidden dam of humanity had been dynamited."[25]

The seeds of change were sown in 1939 when Jacksonville bought a Florida National Guard camp in its own county and sold it to the navy for a big naval air station. Needing a new camp, it chose an area surrounding Kingsley Lake, seven miles from Starke and connected to Jacksonville by a narrow highway.

Early in the summer of 1940 the War Department assigned National Guard units from four southern and four New England states to train at the small camp along with some artillery regiments. The infantry units bivouacked at Jacksonville Municipal Airport for a year while training at Camp Blanding, as the place was named. Hardly any of this activity had much impact on Starke until the War Department decided to construct an even larger camp to train 40,000 soldiers. A New York firm took a $10 million contract to build the new Camp Blanding in three months. For this work they needed 7,000 workers, mostly carpenters, at once.

News of the jobs triggered a migration of hopeful workers into the area. Starke's residents awoke one day to find steady streams of jalopies clogging the streets in every direction. Already the camp's construction quartermaster had bought up every handsaw in town. The contractors demanded still more workers, and they came from all parts of the country; one batch of 300 workers arrived from Boston and were hired on the spot. The overburdened labor compound, which had been hiring 500 men a day, increased its yield to 1,600 a day. Blanding's labor force climbed to 21,000 men with a monthly payroll of $2.5 million. For the first time in ages thousands of them had money in their pocket, and they spent it freely. Walter McFashion, the bootblack at the Three Friends barber shop, exclaimed happily, "Business am busted loose!"

What most of the workers didn't have was a place to sleep or bathe or even eat. Available rooms filled up at once, eventually with two or three shifts of workers sharing the same bed left warm by its previous occupant. Evelyn Stephens, a shrewd, handsome women with an easy manner, had come to Starke from Oklahoma in the summer of 1940 and become secretary of a virtually nonexistent chamber of commerce. Having lived near Fort Sill in Oklahoma, she anticipated what the future held for Starke. Doggedly she visited those housewives who refused to take in boarders and told them it was their patriotic duty to give the men shelter. Her appeals found beds for some 5,000 men, but much more was needed. A thousand workers commuted from Jacksonville on a train that every morning deposited them in Starke and every evening took them back again. Others parked their ancient cars or trucks somewhere off the highway and lived in them, while still others survived in lean-tos, tarpaulin shelters, cardboard box huts, or brush piles hollowed out for sleeping.

Local families did their part, putting cots in garages and every spare room while moving themselves down to the first floor. Apartments that once rented for $18 or $20 now went for $50 to $60; a waitress in a local restaurant paid $5 a week for the privilege of sleeping on a cot in the kitchen. As many as thirty people had to use the same bathroom. Camp Blanding created its own hellhole, euphemistically called "craftsmen's barracks," for 2,000 workmen and a "white-collar" hotel for 150 civil service employees. Wives and families fared worst of all and usually had to be content with whatever they could find in nearby towns. Privacy became even more scarce than rooms as houses bulged with boarders and the streets overflowed with humanity, especially during shift changes.

Prosperity washed over Starke, but at a steep price. Local merchants reported huge leaps in sales and services. Joe Alvarez, who had run a men's clothing store since 1890, did eleven times as much business in November 1940 as he had the previous year. Deposits and clearings at the local bank doubled. A host of new buildings went up all over town, turning it into a place the locals no longer recognized. The already crowded county schools groaned beneath the influx of new students. Raw sewage overwhelmed the town's aging septic tanks and flowed into a nearby creek. Behind the workers and later the soldiers came the usual camp-following army of musicians, fortune-tellers, three-for-a-dime photographers, con men, prostitutes, gamblers, and proprietors of bowling alleys, dart games, and shooting galleries. Juke joints sprouted overnight along the highway, now crowded with traffic and hitchhikers. Drunks and rowdies overflowed the town's tiny four-man jail.

Working in her one-room madhouse, Evelyn Stephens operated as the town's welfare, social, and charity agencies rolled into one, badgering state and federal officials for help in a situation created by them. She and Mayor Newman "Noon" Wainwright both envisioned a bright future for the town if it could get the new hospital, schools, water wells, sewage disposal plant, and wider streets they sought. The wild card always was how long the emergency would last and what would happen when the workers and the military went away. Meanwhile, the town had to cope with a new way of life that showed no signs of slowing down, and a lot of locals detested the changes. "Lives?" grumbled one resident. "We don't have lives any more."

THE STARKE EXPERIENCE played out again and again throughout the South, where a renaissance was under way. The combination of a mild climate and cheap land made it the ideal location for the big new camps required by the draft-driven expansion of the army. Some 60 percent of the more than 100 large camps went up in southern states. New towns sprang up out of wilderness, and small villages like Starke mushroomed into good-sized towns. Farmers and farmhands deserted the land to work for good wages in construction, sometimes earning more in a month than they had in a year. During 1940 alone new construction totaled more than $1.5 billion, an all-time record that would not last long. The section that Roosevelt once called "the Nation's No. 1 economic problem" seemed to be racing toward prosperity.[26]

The signs were everywhere. Alexandria, Louisiana, a town of 27,066 on the Red River, welcomed five army camps that employed some 25,000 workers and jumped its population to somewhere between 45,000 and 60,000. Shipyards along the southern coasts bulged with new orders for naval or merchant vessels. Even the textile mills underwent a resurgence of business. The steel mills in Birmingham, the South's leading industrial site, operated at full capacity and were expanding; Sloss-Sheffield Steel & Iron Company planned to reopen eighty-seven old beehive ovens that had sat unused for more than twenty years. The Republic Steel plant at Gadsden planned a $6 million addition to produce artillery shells. Tennessee Coal & Iron, preparing to make 140-inch plate for ships, built seventy-three new ovens to ease a coke bottleneck. At Muscle Shoals in Alabama, Reynolds Metals was erecting a $23.5 million aluminum plant and a $17.5 million rolling mill.[27]

Childersburg, a village of only 515 people, was about to get a $48 million powder plant and a $15 million powder-bag loading plant. Its mayor pleaded with the governor for help, complaining that "our resources are totally inadequate . . . If we aren't prepared for it, this thing can ruin us instead of helping us." His plea was echoed across the South, where the joy of good times was tempered by the fear of what would happen when the boom passed. Once the camps were completed, the workers would leave as quickly as they had come. Many of them had left farms to earn better wages; Donald Comer of Birmingham's Avondale Mills expressed the hope that tenant farmers would use the money to buy the land they worked. Despite its hoary reputation as a backward rural region, the South was already changing before the defense boom; its factories produced 260 percent more wealth than did its farms. The defense effort, however long it lasted, merely accelerated an existing trend.[28]

By mid-1941 a reaction to the boom-town phenomenon had emerged. Instead of embracing army camps or facilities, many small towns opposed them vehemently. They did not want their way of life transformed, their economy turned upside down, and thousands of acres of land moved to nontaxable status. The army was in fact gobbling up land at a prodigious rate, and not only for new camps. It swallowed 360,000 acres near Hinesville, Georgia, for antiaircraft practice ground and an enormous 1.5 million acres in Utah for an air force bombing range. The new style of war, it seemed, required huge testing grounds. New and existing camps expanded their share of acreage as well, including 154,000 at Fort Ord, 51,000 at Fort Bliss, 39,500 for Camp Joseph T. Robinson in Arkansas, and 19,400 for Fort Sill.[29]

Prior to the war the army had maintained quarters for about 225,000 troops at its 320 military posts; now it prepared to accommodate an army of 1.4 million men at a staggering cost. Not surprisingly, the camp construction program became one of the earliest subjects of investigation by the Truman

Committee. Its ninety-eight-page report in August 1941 blasted the process for waste and inefficiency. Failing to heed the lessons of World War I, the army lacked coherent plans for the camps and squandered at least $100 million of the $828 million spent on 229 projects. "We used that $100,000,000 figure," explained Truman in an aside, "because the Army admitted that much. It will run two and a half times that much, easily." The report also emphasized that "there were very few officers in the quartermaster corps or in the engineering corps who were at all fit to cope with the problems involved in the camp-construction program."[30]

The committee recommended that army construction be removed from the Quartermaster Corps and given to a new organization of qualified specialists. General Edmund B. Gregory, head of the Quartermaster Corps, admitted that mistakes had been made but pointed out that the army had demanded maximum speed of construction. "It's axiomatic," he said, "that you can't save time and money at the same time." Gregory proved to be a capable and flexible leader who had been trying to upgrade the Quartermaster Corps way of doing things, but the corps had long been poorly structured and unable to operate efficiently. Among other problems, its operating and planning units had never merged but performed as separate, unrelated entities.[31]

The business of war created another pitfall that became painfully apparent when shortages began to emerge during 1941. The construction program, whether for plants or shipyards or military facilities, competed with the production program for materials. In determining priorities decisions had to be made as to what was most needed: steel for tanks or for plants to build tanks, for ships or for the equipment to make ships. The equation also had to include a long list of civilian needs that supported the war indirectly. The nondefense plants pleading for raw materials did not make munitions, but many made products that sustained the people who made munitions. In the realm of construction, what about new housing, schools, hospitals, and other public facilities?

In the public mind the key to output lay in mass production, an easy phrase that most people knew although they had no real understanding of what it meant. Detroit and the automobile industry had long been the heart and soul of American mass production, and the public expected miracles from its companies doing defense work. But few people realized how much preliminary work was required to set up mass production of anything. "Guns aren't windshield wipers," growled Charles F. Kettering, the master of research at General Motors. He recalled being asked, "You fellows know how to make eight thousand automobiles a day, don't you? Well, then, why can't you make one thousand tanks a day without all this stalling around?"[32]

The obvious answer was that tanks were nothing at all like cars or any other civilian vehicle. The nation had virtually no experience with them, having manufactured a mere sixty-four tanks during World War I. Prior to 1939 the army would get a pittance from Congress to spend on a dozen or two tanks, which were made virtually by hand at the Rock Island Arsenal. Nothing even remotely approaching volume production was attempted until 1939, when American Car & Foundry received a contract for several hundred light tanks to be made at its Berwick, Pennsylvania, factory. Even then the transition to a production line was halting at best.[33]

While debate raged among producers of aircraft engines over the merits of liquid-cooled versus air-cooled engines, manufacturers at least had the power plants of existing planes to use as a starting point. No prototype engine existed for tanks, let alone the variety of types used in modern warfare. Designers had to improvise off existing engines to find workable power plants. As the aircraft industry was learning so painfully, it took time to develop the techniques and machinery to mass-produce a new implement of war. It was said that getting a tank into production required 186 pounds of blueprints. The figure didn't surprise Kettering; several hundred pounds of blueprints had to be shipped to every assembly plant when a new-model car went into production.[34]

Mass production required two stages: the time-consuming process of designing, adjusting, and tooling up the assembly line, and then the actual output of the product. The first stage was as glacial as the second was speedy, which was why the mobilization process seemed so slow. Detroit got so much defense business because it understood this process better than almost anybody. But making implements of war, except for trucks and jeeps, was vastly different from an annual model change. It usually required one of two approaches: either stripping the machine tools from existing plants and replacing them with new ones or building a new plant altogether to produce the desired weapon. For tanks Chrysler chose the second option. When Bill Knudsen called K. T. Keller, head of Chrysler, and asked if his company could make tanks, Keller said he didn't know why not. What was a tank, he asked, and where could he see one?[35]

No one on the team of engineers and technicians Keller took to the Rock Island Arsenal had ever seen a tank before. They took apart a tank at the arsenal, left the pieces for the local mechanics to reassemble, and returned to Detroit laden with blueprints. Patternmakers took the blueprints and made exact wooden models of each part, then assembled them into a full-sized dummy tank. The model could then be examined for flaws and possible improvements, and the cost of every piece estimated. Keller went to Washington with cost estimates, which the government accepted. The government provided funds to build and equip a new plant. Chrysler leased it for $1 and agreed to produce 28-ton tanks at so much per tank for the first 1,000. The contract totaled $53.2 million.[36]

Then the problems began. The army decided that the tank used as a model was already obsolete. The latest intelligence from the warfront dictated a need for heavier armor, bigger guns, more speed. The army agreed to take the first thousand tanks under the current design while an improved model was put together. Keller turned the project over to Edward J. Hunt, a genius of machine craft of whom an admirer said, "His feeling for machines is such as some men have for horses." He could read a blueprint like a conductor read a musical score, seeing not merely what was on it but what was in it. Hunt cleared the top floor of an existing facility and filled it with a monster pile of blueprints and the tank model. The tank had 3,500 parts, some simple and others requiring as many as fifteen operations. Some could be made on standard machines; for others special machines had to be designed and built. By calculating how many machines of what size were needed altogether, Hunt could figure the size of the building required to house them, along with assembly lines, railroad track, receiving station, and other essentials. The building turned out to be a quarter mile long and a tenth of a mile wide.[37]

The blueprints found their way to an experienced contractor, who began transforming a Michigan cornfield into a building. While it went up, the tool and production engineers spread a floor plan of the plant on a large table and filled it with tiny cardboard machines and tanks built exactly to scale so they could determine how many would fit on the assembly lines. The machine pieces got shoved back and forth amid arguments over the best arrangement. Although the engine would arrive whole, the thousands of other parts had to be choreographed to flow to the right place at the right moment even though some required more machining than others. The key to the whole process lay in getting the right machines at the right places in the right order. Known as tool engineering, this art held the key to the success of mass production. It was in essence a ballet of imagined precision. To Hunt's practiced eyes the bits of cardboard *were* the machines and tanks. He could see and hear them moving along the assembly line, could walk around them in his mind's eye and find the trouble spots.[38]

Through the harsh winter of 1940–41, as the building slowly rose from the frozen ground, the precious machines began arriving by flatcar to be tuned and tested while operators were trained to use them. Once the concrete floor was in place, the position of each machine was marked on it. Meanwhile, a special crew painstakingly put together a pilot tank, the final mock-up for poking and testing to find any flaws in the design and ensure that the tolerances were perfect. The engineers and army inspectors examined, measured, and tested every part, after which the army took the pilot and tried to wreck it. The marvel of the process was that prior to the contract virtually none of the engineers had ever seen a tank, yet they knew what they had built. They concluded, for example, that it would be tougher and safer if the body was cast in a single mold rather than built up with pieces of armor plate that had to be riveted at the edge. Casting would also speed up the production process.[39]

Once in operation, the plant slowly gathered momentum. By November 1941 eight tanks a day rolled off its assembly line; another seven a day were expected by Christmas. In August 1942 the War Department awarded Chrysler a second contract worth $74.6 million for 1,600 more tanks of a later design. By August 1941 American Car & Foundry was producing 200 13-ton light tanks a month and was about to start work on an improved 18-ton model. American Locomotive (ALCO) and Baldwin Locomotive turned out medium tanks along with Chrysler, but in smaller numbers. The engines were air-cooled, unlike the liquid-cooled engines of the European powers, a blessing in the parched deserts of North Africa, where many of the tanks went on Lend-Lease. Where the British preferred metal treads, the Americans used rubber treads that they claimed were far more durable.[40]

Tanks came in three basic types: light tanks of 8 to 14 tons; medium tanks of 15 to 30 tons, and heavy tanks weighing anywhere from 30 to 100 tons. The differences were striking. Light tanks reached 25 miles an hour in combat, could hit 60 miles an hour, and were sure-footed even on rugged terrain, but they were lightly armed and armored. Medium tanks reached 50 miles an hour on roads and 15 to 20 in combat. Their heavier armor and guns made them a better match for the formidable German panzers. The American army had never ordered heavy tanks because it could see no use for them. They were heavily armed but slow and cumbersome in battle, making them easy targets for mobile artillery. Russia had some good monster tanks, but Germany was considered the leader in every category and had already demonstrated its prowess in armored warfare with its blitzkrieg campaign. The army was rumored to have a secret project developing a new heavy tank at Baldwin Locomotive. That fall, as Ford and General Motors prepared to join the producers, Roosevelt announced that tank production would be doubled.[41]

American light tanks used by the British in North Africa took a beating in part because their 37 mm guns proved no match for German 50 mm and 75 mm pieces. A heavier gun was needed not only for tanks but also for use as an antitank gun. The standard American antitank weapon was the same 37 mm gun. The Ordnance Department refused to concede its inadequacies for stopping tanks even as it scrambled to come up with a more powerful piece. Attention focused on a heavy but mobile "tank destroyer," a self-propelled half-track with a 75 mm gun mounted on it. Although development of it was rushed during 1941, Ordnance had no choice but to keep buying

37 mm guns until it had something better. *Time* lampooned the army for continuing to acquire an obsolete weapon, but the pattern had already become a familiar one. Here, as elsewhere, the army was trying to overcome years of neglect in weapons research.[42]

ONE OF MANY shortcomings suffered by tanks in combat was their inability to fire accurately while bouncing along rough terrain at full speed. What they needed was a device that would hold the gun stable while firing independent of the motion caused by the tank's movement. In short, they required some kind of stabilizer. Another problem was their fixed guns, a defect Eliot Janeway blamed on army engineers "who designed tanks able to shoot in only one direction." During 1941 a new, eagerly awaited medium model solved the second problem by mounting a 75 mm gun in a revolving turret set atop an armored hull that was partly cast and partly welded. The attempt to stabilize mobile guns began in 1939 when Captain D. J. Crawford of the Ordnance Department visited the Westinghouse Research Laboratories in Pittsburgh as part of a yearly tour of American research facilities in search of new ideas. While there he happened upon a device called a "Silverstat" invented by Clinton Hanna, head of the electromechanical department. It consisted of two clusters of copper strips with silver contacts between them. From their meeting eventually arose a tank-stabilizer program that supplied $80 million worth of control equipment to the Allied forces.[43]

The two men began discussing gyroscopes and their little-known property to respond instantly to changes in rotational speeds at right angles to their own axis. Hanna had devised a clever method of stabilizing rotational speed by using a gyro frame to apply pressure to either one of the Silverstat's clusters. "Do you suppose you could apply something like this to our tank guns?" Crawford asked. "It would . . . make the gunners independent of the motion of the tank itself. Then we could advance and fire at the same time." Hanna agreed to try, and in June 1939 he submitted an outline of a system utilizing two gyros. It was ingenious in its simplicity, but Ordnance had no funds for a development contract. Neither guns nor tanks were available for experimental work, which would have to be done entirely on mock-ups. Despite the lack of a contract, Hanna persuaded his superiors to let him go ahead on his own.[44]

After rigging up a machine that would pitch and roll like a tank, Hanna tested his device and concluded that the principle was sound. The army learned of his success and invited another proposal, insisting that it be kept top secret. A contract finally materialized in June 1940 along with an actual 37 mm gun for testing. In October the device underwent its first trials at the Aberdeen Proving Ground. After six weeks of grueling tests Hanna refined the model by eliminating one of the gyros. Although the improvement in performance was obvious, Ordnance insisted that both gyros be included in the device. The tests revealed that even an experienced gunner scored no hits on a target while moving at 15 miles an hour but could manage 70 hits out of 100 with the new device installed. Ordnance was convinced, and the stabilizer went into production. Secrecy was so great that the preliminary blueprints for the trials had been cut into small sections and issued piecemeal so that no workman would see the entire plan.

Once the device was approved for production, Ordnance sent a crate with a complete gun turret to Westinghouse's East Springfield, Massachusetts, plant. A wall was opened up to put it in a special room where no one could see its contents; the room was padlocked, with a guard at the foot of the stairs. Problems arose first with the reciprocating oil pump and then with the tiny electric motors used to spin the gyros. Others emerged as these were solved, dragging the process out for more weeks. When the army stipulated that the unit could not exceed a certain weight, the engineers found to their dismay that the stabilizer was six ounces too heavy and had to be streamlined. It took a full year to work out all the development bugs and get tooled up for production. The army promised a contract for a thousand units but did not sign contracts for them until May 1941. A new order for 13,000 more units hung fire through the summer, and the company's request for $350,000 worth of machine tools was rejected.

In June Westinghouse committed to produce 55 stabilizers a day by January 1942. Then came word of the decision to expand tank production to 1,800 a month, which would require 125 stabilizers a day. The British were reluctant to use the stabilizers until a delegation of their officers took part in a test with an actual tank and came away convinced that every tank should have a stabilizer. As the fall dwindled down, Springfield braced for yet another increase in output while still struggling to obtain adequate machine tools. Despite these obstacles, a crucial improvement had been devised. As one general observed, "A tank that must come to a dead stop to fire accurately itself becomes an excellent target . . . Since American tanks can be always in motion, they make difficult targets."[45]

The Westinghouse experience with stabilizers exemplified the relationship of business and the military in the uncertain atmosphere of the defense era. For all the grief heaped on large corporations about making "blood profits" and hogging most of the defense contracts, many of them accepted a high degree of risk in pursuing projects and research that looked promising even though the military had yet to underwrite them. The battlefield classroom dictated constant and rapid changes in existing weaponry and demanded the development of new, improved versions. American manufacturers knew well the annual-model syndrome and were gradually learning to apply it to the arti-facts of war as well. As Charles Kettering liked to say, "War is Horsepower."[46]

The gruff Kettering had his own view of the matter, as he did of most things. "The idea of war production," he declared, "is to make something the other fellow doesn't want and didn't order, and deliver it at the time he least expects it, in a form he doesn't expect either. It is just inverse economics . . . That is why special plants are being built as fast as possible in Detroit and elsewhere, to apply mass production to planes and tanks and aviation engines and the other crying needs among defense items."[47]

Small businesses continued to complain that they got too small a piece of the defense pie. The army, navy, OPM, and big defense contractors still had deep pockets of resistance to subcontracting, preferring to deal with the larger, more experienced firms. The latter used many subcontractors but en-countered problems of their own in the process. As an automobile manufac-turer explained, he had fifty subcontractors on one deal alone, and most of them had trouble getting their necessary materials on time. The automobile company had to send its own purchasing agent out to place orders, handle shipments, and trace their movement. Every problem meant delays in the production line, and the smaller companies lacked the experience and pres-tige to get such things done. Some smaller firms resorted to bootlegging sup-plies to fulfill their contracts.[48]

By November 1941 large corporations felt the squeeze of shortages no less than smaller companies. In Detroit the sense was widespread that its domi-nant industry had entered a strange and unpredictable new world. The re-cord production year had come and gone, no new models graced the drawing boards, key materials were hard to get, and no one knew how many cars would roll off its assembly lines during the next year. New plants were rising all around the city, and existing ones were being retooled to turn out a grow-ing menu of defense items. The automakers had long been accustomed to re-tooling for a new model, but most of the defense product was strange to them and, as Charles Wilson had emphasized, incompatible with their existing tools. Many of them were big, single-purpose machines like the Bullard Mult-Au-Matic that could bore out the cylinder blocks of a Ford V-8 engine in a single operation. Some machine tools were flexible enough to be adapted to making other products, but even that took time.[49]

THE IMPACT OF the defense program on small businesses had long been a concern for Roosevelt. As early as February 1940 he asked, "On our next 500 planes can we give a large part of engine orders to the smaller companies and not to the three big ones? This to spread the load." That October Congress created a special committee to investigate the plight of small businesses. Truman's committee, once established, also took a keen interest in the problem. However, as the pressure of priorities, schedules, and shortages mounted, the squeeze on smaller companies grew worse. In his usual blunt fashion Charles Wilson of General Motors declared that "this defense program is big business. We might as well make up our minds to that. It is big business and it isn't going to be handled by thousands of small businesses alone. Small plants can't make tanks, airplanes or other large complex armaments."[50]

Even a sympathetic Donald Nelson admitted that "the war production program was not a form of WPA, and could not be used as one. The real problem was not how to keep the small business firm alive but how to make use of it in a war economy." Roosevelt had his own ideas on the subject. On September 4, 1941, without even notifying OPM, he issued an executive order replacing that agency's Defense Contract Service with a new Division of Contract Distribution headed by Floyd B. Odlum. His charge was an ambitious one: assist small businesses, develop programs for converting industries from civilian to defense production, distribute defense contracts as widely as possible, and maximize subcontracting.[51]

Odlum seemed an odd choice for the job. The president of a $100 million investment trust, he was known as the "Wall Street Wolf," with a gift for "swallowing businesses as a whale does fish." But Odlum took his responsibility seriously and threw his demonic energy and bravura into the task, burning out three assistants in short order. His findings indicated that of 184,000 industrial enterprises in the country, about 133,000 were small firms employing twenty or fewer workers. Of that number, only 45,000 were deemed suitable for conversion to defense production. Odlum focused on this group and came up with a scheme that became known as "Odlum's circus." It consisted of three special exhibit trains, painted red, white, and blue, carrying samples of defense equipment and parts to show small manufacturers what they might make if they could. For those firms unable to convert to defense, Odlum asked that 2 percent of scarce raw materials be set aside for their use.[52]

Small businesses did not have to await their fate stoically or depend on the government for handouts to keep them going. A select few took the initiative of moving aggressively to get contracts. When pundits wished to make this point, they raised the example of York, Pennsylvania, a town of 57,000 people, and its approach that became known as the York Plan. William S. Shipley, chairman of the York Ice Machinery Corporation, persuaded his fellow members of the Manufacturers Association to organize a Defense Program Committee in the fall of 1940. They created a local office at the Defense Contract Service and began promoting the virtues of farming out business under the motto "Do what you can with what you have." Local companies pooled their bids for defense contracts as if they were one big firm, enabling them to go after larger contracts than would otherwise be possible. By November 1941 they had secured $130 million worth of defense business and become a model for how small businesses could survive and even flourish.[53] To get that business, the committee cataloged the town's supply of machine tools and operators, enlarged its vocational-training program, and pumped up civic enthusiasm. Facing a shortage of mechanics thanks to the loss of men from depression cuts, manufacturers combed their payrolls for ten to fifteen years back and compiled a list of all competent former employees. The committee then tracked down as many of them as possible, offered them refresher courses at night school, and lured them back to the workbench. In one case a skilled craftsman was languishing in jail for drunkenness; the committee secured his release on the plea of his importance to national defense.[54]

Shipley did his part in spreading the work. His company owned a large horizontal boring mill that it used only about 350 hours a year. Beginning in September 1940, the company made it available for use by other producers. The machine was quickly booked solid through the following year. Part of the time went to another York firm that was making powder presses for DuPont. The survey of machines enabled such time-sharing to take place on a broad scale.[55]

The York Plan seemed to work wonders. By the end of June 1941 industrial consumption of electricity had risen 63 percent over the previous year, industrial payrolls were up 75 percent, and industrial employment was 40 percent higher. The number of people on relief rolls had dropped by more than two thirds and was still falling. A closer look at York's success revealed that it also owed much to an individual who had nothing to do with either the plan or the Manufacturers Association. S. Forry Laucks was a crotchety martinet in his early seventies who had been head of the York Safe and Lock Company since 1890. He was everything his peers were not: the anti-Rotarian and Democrat in a staunchly Republican town who had resigned from both the National Association of Manufacturers and the U.S. Chamber of Commerce because of their anti–New Deal leanings. His roots and loyalties lay rather with the strongly Democratic Pennsylvania Dutch farmers on the land surrounding York.[56]

When Laucks took charge of York Safe and Lock, the company had a mortgage for $45,000 and owed another $40,000 to banks, and its stock was worthless. Although reserved, self-centered, and "as jovial as an iced haddock" in the words of one reporter, he was a superb salesman who somehow got bank presidents to believe in his ability to deliver a superior vault even though he had no experience at it. When his plant burned down, Laucks had a new one up and running in sixty days. During that time he learned the art of subcontracting by farming out his unfilled orders to neighboring shops and maintaining his reputation for meeting deadlines. The new plant soon sprawled across 10 acres, employed 600 workers, and earned what one admirer called "a Tiffany reputation in the vault business."[57]

York Safe and Lock earned a global reputation for making custom vaults large and small, including the massive vaults of most federal reserve banks and the largest vault in the world at the Bank of Japan in Tokyo. In a sense Laucks did his work too well. The business that had made him a multimillionaire came to an abrupt halt with the epidemic of bank failures during the late 1920s and early 1930s. Laucks got little repeat business because his vaults were so good that they lasted for years. During the 1930s his company lost $2 million and stayed afloat only because Laucks dug into his own pockets to sustain it, but he could not keep doing that forever.[58]

Age and illness made Laucks even more meticulous, controlling, and inflexible. No change, however small, took place at the office without his express permission. He still signed every check and requisition. His subordinates feared him, yet admired his ability to rise from the sickbed to run the business. He had little choice; his only son had no interest in it and moved away. To his employees he was a benevolent despot with a tough veneer. York was a highly specialized company with a corps of skilled machinists who, Laucks insisted, were happy in their work. "This plant is fully organized and it works well," he told a *New York Times* reporter. "There aren't any labor problems. These Pennsylvania Dutchmen are good workers who can't be driven. I understand them—I'm one myself. They don't ask the unreasonable. We get along without friction. Once in a while they ask me to their union parties, and whenever I can, I go—and for the reason that I always have a better time than I do when I'm out with the stuffed shirts."[59]

The stuffed shirts of York did not appreciate this dismissal, but they were accustomed to it. What they could not fathom was Laucks's habit of doing things his own way. He was not a team player, but he was an old dog who knew how to learn new tricks. Weary of the depression and recalling his conversion experience in World War I, Laucks and his general manager, Charles Sioberg, toured some army arsenals in 1938 and came away convinced that the worsening situation in Europe would soon spark a demand for munitions that could not be met with current facilities. In September he went to Washington and met with the Ordnance Department. He wanted a government contract; he had no particular product in mind but told them that if his workers could build something as massive as a bank vault and as delicate as the lock on a safe-deposit box, "Well, I guess they can turn out not only a gun carriage but the breechblock of the gun and the firing mechanism as well."

A few days later he returned to York with a contract to produce 138 mounts for a new 3-inch antiaircraft gun for $1.6 million. It was the first contract given to a private company for ordnance equipment since the last war. At first the Ordnance Department wanted to give him only two thirds of the order— the other third going to General Electric—because it did not think his small company could turn out the whole amount in the allotted twenty-two months. Laucks went straight to the budget director and persuaded him otherwise; he got the whole contract. York's business leaders shook their heads at his audacity. A gun mount had 6,000 individual parts, and Laucks had not yet even bought new machine tools for the job. But Sioberg had earlier made a survey of the town's resources and found plenty of idle machine capacity. York was a hotbed of small machine shops. No less than 45 percent of the machining operations for that first order was farmed out to shops all over town.

Laucks had made an important discovery that became his major contribution to York's revival. Even a small firm like his own could subcontract much of the work and still make deadlines otherwise unreachable. He convinced army skeptics that small firms could do this as well as large ones. As a result he procured contracts for eighteen different items from both the army and navy, including not only gun mounts but the gun itself. His workforce that September of 1938 totaled 325 men; three years later it was marching toward 5,000 with a new plant about to open. Other local shops feasted as well on his orders. The Floorola company, which made floor-waxing and -polishing machines, had struggled through the lean years of the depression and was hungry for work. It had lathes, drill presses, and a small planing mill and grinder along with the skilled workers to man them. By providing Laucks with a variety of parts, it salvaged its own future in the process.

Charley Coffey at the City Market finished tool heads for Safe and Lock's planing machines. Harry Dusman, an old harness maker, used his shop to make leather pads for the shoulder guards of antiaircraft guns. The largesse spread beyond York's borders. Forty miles west of York, on the Emmitsburg Road near the Gettysburg battlefield, another old Pennsylvania Dutchman named Barge Donmoyer toiled over bushings and steel spindles for 37 mm antitank guns. Donmoyer had spent fifteen years as a machinist at the Washington Navy Yard before coming back to live an easier life. He had built four tourist cabins that he hoped would support him, but after Laucks came along he boarded up three of them and used the fourth as a machine shop. His thirteen-year-old son served as an apprentice, and his wife helped out by packing the product for delivery to Safe and Locks.

The stuffed shirts of York were justifiably proud of their town's role in the defense effort and its ability to keep the local economy booming in hard times. However, they didn't talk much about Forry Laucks and his contribution to this effort, let alone his pioneering role as a model for getting war orders and filling them. The most visible sign of York's changing role could be found at City Market, the lofty brick building where for years farmers had brought their produce to sell to the city dwellers. It still teemed with counters of vegetables and fruits in season, but a new partition rose at one end of the building to create a space with a concrete floor for lathes, drill presses, and a boring mill. This was Charley Coffey's machine shop, the likes of which could be found in almost every corner of the town. Of such stuff was the arsenal of democracy made, even though the vast majority of it escaped the eyes of bureaucrats in Washington and *Newsweek* opined that such pools "rarely have been found practical."[60]

CHAPTER 12

THE RUSH OF EVENTS

The weakness of the American undertaking is moral, not physical. . . . Save only those who have been drafted for military service, who has made any sacrifices to defend the American way of life?

—SATURDAY EVENING POST [1]

I doubt that more than 15% of America's productive endeavor is devoted to defense work.

—ROBERT PATTERSON [2]

In a world of war, the U. S. yearns for peace—tomorrow morning. Too many of us believe the oceans are barriers, that you can do business with Hitler, that it's not our war, that our ideals are shoddy . . . But once Americans accept this war as their job, the entire trend of our time will be reversed. That is the clue to victory.

—FORTUNE [3]

TIME WAS THE UNKNOWN FACTOR in the equation. Nearly every element of the defense effort had its own timetable—so many guns, tanks, planes, ships, or parts by this or that date. The timetables had to be mapped out on a blank slate because no one knew how long the war would last or if and when the United States would get drawn into it. For this reason alone it was impossible to determine whether enough of any given item was being produced, whether it was being produced fast enough, and whether it was the right item in the first place. While some people had their suspicions, only a select few within the government sensed that time was slipping away much faster than they had hoped and that the worst pressure point lay in the Pacific rather than in the European war. But nearly everyone agreed that things were not getting done fast enough.

"We invented mass production," declared the *Saturday Evening Post*. "Quantity is our principle . . . Time was only money. Now time is life, and the measure of it . . . is not fixed. It is relative and variable, because the clock is quantity." For months the magazine hammered away at this theme of urgency still unrecognized. "Liberty is fighting for its life," it warned in June. "If the aggressor be not destroyed, he will devour the world. America is in peril. Only by heroic and self-sacrificing exertions may we hope to save ourselves. There is no time to spare."[4]

Time was the enemy and delay its chief agent, abetted by conflicts at every level. The army and navy fought with each other, and both battled civilian administrators. New Dealers fought with business interests and dollar-a-year men, who themselves differed over at what speed to pursue defense work. Civilians accused the army of being slower than slow to calculate what it needed and of still operating with the starvation mentality of prewar years. "In a real world," went the argument, "the real question is how quickly can one obtain the equipment needed to give superiority?" The military countered that "while Germany had six years to prepare, civilians are trying to force them to accomplish a like miracle in one year." How, the services asked, could they plan what equipment they might need when they did not know where or against whom they might have to fight?[5]

Knudsen encountered this dilemma early when he asked army procurement officials, "What do you want?" They replied that they needed to arm 400,000 men within three months of M-day and another 800,000 men within three months. "That's not what I want," said Knudsen. "I want to know what kind of equipment you need for these men—and how many pieces of each kind. Please tell me *how many pieces*." They could not say and had no way of knowing. How then could the necessary equipment be produced?[6]

Economist Robert R. Nathan encountered the same problem. When he asked the army and navy for their military requirements, they responded by asking whether it was for a land war, sea war, air war, or defensive war on American soil. "You must have some assumptions and some lists of quantities of weaons and planes and ships needed under various assumptions," Nathan persisted. No, we don't, came the reply. Well, then, said Nathan, give me your requirements for an army of 1 million, 5 million, and 10 million men. "We are not going to do all of that work," said the spokesman, "unless we have some indication of what kind of prospective hostilities we will face."[7]

Time had not yet cured the well-publicized shortcomings of the defense program or solved the riddle of its organization. A *Newsweek* editor concluded in September that "the nation is still a long way from being equipped to fight a war efficiently or to supply anywhere near the amount of weapons needed to lick the Nazis." Mobilization still lacked leadership and coherent planning, a blueprint for the overall program. An overworked president insisted on keeping control in his own hands rather than appointing a single executive to oversee things. Congress bungled the draft issue, first by limiting service to one year, against the army's advice, and then by creating a major morale problem with its reluctance to extend the term. Labor hampered production with its strikes and absenteeism, and the government's failure to curb the output of consumer goods created severe shortages of key materials. The military compounded delays by insisting on repeated changes in the weapons being produced; the army, for example, imposed a whopping 30,000 design changes on Lockheed's P-38 fighter between its receipt of the prototype and the start of mass production.[8]

Shortages created odd scenes of confusion. A plant making motors for the Anaconda Copper Company couldn't finish the job because it could not get enough copper for them. A Newark manufacturer of slide zippers fasteners had to lay off more than 400 of its 1,700 workers because it could not obtain enough metal, leaving the garment trade in chaos. If slide zippers fasteners left the market, garment makers would likely not be able to get machinery to make buttonholes, which were already scarce because of a lack of silk thread. Rayon thread could not do the job, and substituting the old snap fasteners required more metal, the lack of which was the source of the original problem. None of it made any sense to the people in the plants who faced the loss of their jobs.[9]

Machine tool production declined late in 1941 despite a survey that revealed the need for three times the output of that year. Summoned to a meeting in Washington, the leading toolmakers attributed the decline to a lack of orders and inadequate financing. Munitions manufacturers hesitated to place orders until they had signed contracts; some held off in hopes of using the priority authority to seize tools already made. The toolmakers were prepared to go to three shifts, seven days a week, and increased subcontracting once the orders arrived, but they lacked the financial strength to expand on their own.[10]

"Enormous waste, great bungling, afterthinking, alphabetical confusion, free wheeling, conflict of authority, all that is true and very serious and has yet to be dealt with," concluded writer Garet Garrett in the *Saturday Evening Post*. "In their anxiety to see it dealt with, many are saying . . . that America is failing. The program is bogged down." But what program? "There has never been a program," he added. "There is not now a program for which it is possible to make any definite outline. In place of a program there has been a progressive intention, bounded only by the unknown." However, he thought, the sleeping giant was at last awakening to the scale and scope of the task.[11]

"The time is the extraordinary present," intoned *Time*, ". . . the remarkable, violent, inescapable, exhilarating, blundering, stirring, terrible Present, short of chromite, full of nonsense—the elusive, mysterious, future-destroying Now." But time was also a battery of unknown strength being steadily drained. How long before it died? Projections of output tended to estimate how much of a given item would be produced or available by 1942, but who knew what 1942 would bring in the shifting landscape of war?[12]

In the five giant aircraft plants that ringed Los Angeles, some so large that company regulations forbade women to walk from one part to another unless accompanied by a male chaperone, apathy and disenchantment had begun to sap production rates. So rapidly had the workforce grown that it overwhelmed facilities, turning every basic function or chore outside work into an ordeal. One plant that already had 40,000 workers kept hiring about 200 men a day with the goal of doubling its force. They came from all over the country, men without jobs or with jobs that didn't pay as much compared to the promised land of the defense plants. They waited interminably for job interviews and the filling out of forms, then got assigned to crews working on some part of the giant bombers. The work was repetitive and tedious, one small step in a seemingly endless chain of steps on the road to a finished plane.[13]

The lack of decent living conditions made the work even more intolerable. At lunchtime some 8,000 workers streamed out in search of food and respite. A few found refuge in one of the few restaurants near the plant; most made do with the beaneries or hot-dog stands outside the gates, screaming their orders and taking their dogs to a nearby curb to sit and eat. Across the street stood three credit jewelry stores waiting to take their money; aircraft workers liked to splurge on jewelry for themselves or their girl friends. Inside the plant men were constantly on edge, and fights often broke out. Both participants would be sent home for a few days, or, in some cases, the instigator would be fired. Others were buying clothes, cars, furniture, even homes, going into hock for a few thousand dollars that they could never repay even on their good earnings.

In time, many of them grew listless, weary of the work and uneasy at what would happen when the emergency ended. The war was not their war, and appeals to their patriotism only made them suspicious. They were transients in an uncertain world that was changing too fast for them, loners away from home with no USO to ease their loneliness. As one observer noted, they wanted to give a damn but couldn't find anything to give a damn about. They were not unpatriotic or cynical but simply lost in the present and uncertain about the future. To their mind they were not doing America's work but simply holding temporary jobs in an alien place called an airplane factory.

THE FOCUS OF diplomats, politicians, and citizens alike tended to be toward Europe and the Atlantic. When a German submarine sank the *Robin Moor* without warning on May 21, it was the first time the Nazis had attacked an American merchant vessel. The passengers and crew were left afloat for more than two weeks before being accidentally discovered. In a message to Congress, an indignant Roosevelt denounced it as "total disregard for the most elementary principles of international law and of humanity." It was, he emphasized, "a warning to the United States not to resist the Nazi movement of world conquest" and "a warning that the United States may use the high seas of the world only with Nazi consent . . . We are not yielding and we do not propose to yield." In the final revision of this message Roosevelt had penciled in this last sentence.[14]

That same month a *Fortune* poll revealed that more than two thirds of respondents thought that Hitler wanted to dominate the United States and that nearly 72 percent believed a German victory in the war would have "very serious" effects on the nation's well-being. When asked about aid to Great Britain, 21 percent favored giving all our war materials being manufactured, while 38 percent preferred sending only half, and only 7 percent wanted none sent at all. By August more than 72 percent of those polled said that if Britain was defeated, Hitler would not be satisfied until he had conquered the Americas, and 76 percent thought the United States should back Britain and help defeat Hitler. In October 73 percent of those polled favored helping Russia beat Hitler even though they despised Communism. At the same time, nearly 47 percent of respondents thought the country should not get excited about Japan unless she attacked the United States or interfered with American shipping.[15]

Public opinion seemed as gloomy as that of the administration. In July a *New York Daily News* poll asked whether the United States should enter the war to help Great Britain. A surprising 30 percent said yes, the country should go to war at once. Less than a month later a third of newspaper editors gave the same response, and two thirds favored seizure of strategic bases owned by foreign powers. Except for rabid anti–New Dealers, Americans seemed to be growing increasingly resigned to the fact that the nation could not escape the war in one form or another. Nazism resembled a disease that, left untreated, would spread until it became too virulent to control. Long-suffering workers welcomed the economic boom spawned by defense spending but hated the dislocations it brought and worried over how long it would last and what would follow it.[16]

Congress had its own views of the key issues. A poll taken in June revealed that 30 percent of the members thought the country would go to war with Germany, 6 percent answered "probably," and 3 percent believed the nation was already at war. Only 15 percent thought the United States would go to war with Japan, and another 6 percent answered "probably." A mere 20 percent approved of American convoys to England, and no less than 85 percent believed that some part of the defense program was being mishandled, with labor strife and strikes getting half that vote. The divisions within its ranks reflected deeper splits among their constituents. Above all, there loomed a sense of dread, a feeling of helplessness that, like it or not, the nation was being sucked into the whirlpool of war.[17]

The rush of events during 1941 unsettled opinions and beliefs before they could get seated. During April the Nazis conquered Greece despite stubborn resistance from the Greek and British contingents, and soon afterward the battle for North Africa began. In June the stunning German invasion of Russia bewildered the administration and public alike. Both came quickly to the conclusion that the enemy of their enemy was their friend, though aid to the Soviet Union remained controversial among many Americans. The invasion changed America's relations with Russia and threw Japan's diplomacy into utter confusion. It had treaties with both countries and had to formulate a new strategy. On July 16 the cabinet resigned and was re-formed two days later minus its most controversial and pro-German member, Yosuke Matsuoka.[18]

"The Japs are having a real drag-down and knock-out fight among themselves and have been for the past week," Roosevelt wrote Ickes, "trying to decide which way they are going to jump—attack Russia, attack the South Seas (thus throwing in their lot definitely with Germany) or whether they will sit on the fence and be more friendly with us. No one knows what their decision will be." He told the cabinet that it would not surprise him if Japan invaded Indochina the next day; a few days later truckloads of Japanese troops rolled into Saigon. Roosevelt responded by signing the orders cutting off shipments of gasoline to Japan and freezing Japanese assets in the United States. A week later Japanese planes damaged an American warship anchored in the Yangtze River off Chungking. Although the Japanese ambassador offered an apology, tensions mounted steadily in the Pacific.[19]

During the first half of the year the long-smoldering tensions with Japan had remained mostly on the back burner of American foreign policy. The Nazi invasion of Russia, which at first glance seemed to affect only the European war, escalated friction in the Pacific arena as well by forcing Japanese policy into hard new choices. That worsening situation framed Roosevelt's dilemma in even bolder relief. Despite the progress made by the defense program, he realized that the United States was in no position to fight a war on three continents and two oceans with a one-ocean navy and token army. Nor did it help that the nation remained bitterly divided on what course it should pursue. He could not force his own vision of what should be done on the people. They had to be persuaded to see the danger and accept what must be done to prevent it. But persuasion took time, and time was running out.

"Ten years of mutual shoving, glowering, apologizing and more shoving had put the U.S. and Japan dangerously close to war," said *Time*. Of the other front Ickes observed in September that "the Russians have done enormously better than anyone gave them any credit in advance for being able to do, and if they keep on fighting, even if they have to fall back, Hitler cannot win in the end." But the Germans kept advancing, and Leningrad remained under a fearful siege. Nobody cared to speculate on what would happen if the Russians broke and Germany managed to win the war before the onset of winter.[20]

OF ALL THE unsung heroes in the Washington bureaucracy, Stacy May ranked among the most improbable. A plump, balding, bespectacled statistician, he looked to be the very model of a bureaucratic functionary. Never happier than when immersed in his charts and graphs, he had left the Rockefeller Foundation to become the first head of NDAC's Bureau of Research and Statistics because he thought the country might be going to war and he wanted to do his part to help. As his bureau moved from NDAC to OPM, May's job remained that of generating useful data to show the real extent of the overall defense production program. He agreed with the Frenchman Jean Monnet, who argued vigorously that it was imperative for the British and Americans to coordinate their military and industrial planning in order to estimate who needed how much of what. "We knew that the British wanted all they could get of everything," May said, "but we had no way of knowing what came first, what they could do for themselves, and what their long-range planning was like."[21]

The problem was persuading both the British and American military to provide reliable data on their future needs. May agreed to undertake the task and had his staff compile an enormous ledger with comprehensive categories and tabs, and then fill in the American columns with best estimates on total industrial and raw-material capacities and potentials. The British hesitated to furnish their own figures, fearing that they would inevitably find their way into the newspapers. Stimson arranged for May to fly to London with his big book as a representative of the War Department. For two months during the late summer and early fall of 1941 he met with the British war cabinet and chiefs of staff to complete his tabulation of British and American resources and production potential. It was a fiendishly complex task, compounded by the tendency of each country to use different terms for the same thing. May had to devise a glossary of common terms and measurements to make sense of his figures.[22]

May's encyclopedic volume, which he called his balance sheet, listed requirements in terms of troop units: how many tanks, small arms, artillery, ammunition, food, clothing, and other supplies were needed for so many troops of every kind. From these figures could be projected how much wool, cotton, steel, copper, and other materials would be needed to provide the supplies, and how much of every resource, material, and facility each nation had to meet these needs. What May had done was compile the first useful measuring stick for determining army and navy orders as well as overall needs. The data was priceless and would have been invaluable to Hitler if it had fallen into his hands. To get his thirty-five pounds of precious cargo home, May boarded a plane at Manchester, only to have bad weather force him to land in Dublin, then a hotbed of German spies.[23]

Since the Irish Republic did not allow foreign planes to fly across its territory, May had to lug his material in a taxicab from Dublin to Foynes. There he boarded a British bomber bound for America. He had no military or other escort, and his only companion on the flight was a reticent British general. "We had room to play polo in the plane," May recalled. He took the precaution of locating the plane's bomb release so as to ditch his portfolio in the ocean if the plane were attacked. The plane landed safely in Baltimore where, May quipped, "I might have been met at the airport and escorted to Washington by an armed guard equipped with at least 45's and submachine guns." But no one was there to meet him. May flagged a cab and rode to Washington alone with what he considered "the most important batch of papers in the world," and delivered them to the War Department.[24]

May's compilation overjoyed the planners. It gave them an inside view of British requirements and methods of war, based on their considerable experience in two years of fighting. These could be compared to the American military's estimated needs and used as leverage in finding the best level of production output for any given weapon or supply. Shortly after May's return, a mission headed by W. Averell Harriman and William Batt went to Moscow to obtain the same kind of information from the Russians. The Russians were even more wary than the British in revealing their needs, armaments, and battlefield experience, but they provided enough data to make the effort worthwhile. An earlier mission to London in July had furnished complete schedules of airplane production for both nations and an agreement to pool patents and share secret data on planes and their performance. Among other data the British sent along drawings of their first jet engines.[25]

Together these three missions proved invaluable in coordinating resources and production, as well as understanding what each nation was doing. They emerged as some of the most important work done by the much-maligned OPM, unappreciated because the public knew little or nothing about them. Knowing the full extent of what was required—even though the figures shifted constantly—mattered greatly in trying to plan production for 1942. As Knudsen's assistant, John Biggers, told him in January, OPM didn't "want to start out at a 100-yard pace" if it turned out they would "have to run four miles." Don Nelson thought that May's mission in particular "revolutionized our production, and it may very well have been a decisive turning point. It enabled us to get a pretty good line on what we would have to take out of the economy in order to proceed with either a defense or a war production program."[26]

On September 17 Nelson had written to the War and Navy departments, the Maritime Commission, and the Lend-Lease administrator asking for "estimates of requirements over the next two years based on military objectives as determined by the reporting agencies." When combined with data from the missions, these figures provided a basis for what would be needed by September 30, 1943, if by then a sustained offensive were launched against the Axis. Put another way, it answered the question: How much have we got to make to beat the enemy? It was hardly a final answer, but at least it offered a first rational one, and it led to a second, even more difficult question: Can it be done? Finding the answer to that query fell to Bob Nathan of the Planning Division, a bright, abrasive authority on national income figures.[27]

Nathan was a formidable figure. The *New Republic* described him as "a huge hulk of a man with a kettledrum voice. He is no dreamy brain-truster. Rather, he is more like a wrestler than a thinker and talks more like a barker than a savant. Yet when faced with a thorny problem, his mind can slip to the solution with the ease of a rabbit slipping through briar." Nathan had a first-draft mind, unfettered by details, and a gift for getting at the main point of an argument succinctly and directly. Asked to evaluate the production process at a factory, his report said, "The only trouble with that plant is the guy running it. Fire him."[28]

To find an answer, Nathan had to translate the statements of requirements into raw materials, component parts, man-hours, energy, and dollars and then match them against the nation's known resources. He also had to factor in the most critical component of all, the time factor—not only how much of what could be made but by when. This involved creating incredibly elaborate algebraic formulas that factored in all the thousands of component parts for any given weapon and the availability of the materials from which they were made. It matched what *had* to be done against what *could* be done within given time, resource, and production-level frameworks. From this complex exercise emerged figures that underlay the so-called Victory Program, which assumed an all-out production effort.[29]

Completed in late November 1941, the study was an impressive achievement. At the time existing production schedules for all defense items totaled $27 billion for 1942 and $34 billion for 1943. May and Nathan concluded that these figures could be raised to $40–45 billion for 1942 and $60–65 billion for 1943 without harming the economy or crippling crucial consumer goods and services. But it all rested on estimates and assumptions. No one in the government or the military had actually tried to formulate firm production schedules based on real wartime needs. After all, the nation was not at war. The report reached Nelson on December 4.[30]

The Victory Program was an important analytical tool but not an action program. It matched the combined war requirements of the United States and its allies against the nation's productive capacity in a sort of grand balance sheet. What Nathan and May found was a sizable gap between existing production schedules and potential output. While they pondered the question of how to close this gap, others disputed its existence. Their work also emphasized the need for creating procedures to keep the programs up to date.[31]

Although neither OPM nor the War Department gave the Victory Program a warm welcome, Bruce Catton called it "about as useful a set of tabulations as America ever obtained in an hour of dire need." But the economy was not yet going all out for defense production, even though it had come a long way during the year. Time, as always, was a crucial unknown factor, one that could not be evaded by the most ingenious of mathematical formulations, and for that Nathan had no more of an answer than anyone else.[32]

A SECOND UNKNOWN, no less elusive but almost as important as time, was the nation's morale. Polls and pundits alike tried to track it with indifferent success. "There's a great disparity between the public attitude out around the country and the attitude of Washington officialdom," reported Kiplinger's in May. "Out around the country there's much talk that Washington is hysterical, and our officials know they are so regarded, but they say they are NOT. They retort hotly that the country is 'asleep,' and too much 'unaware' and consequently 'unprepared' for the rigid government controls which must be imposed 'soon.' They say 'business-as-usual is out,' and they are amazed businessmen do not yet understand." Roosevelt thought he knew a major reason. "The lessons of this war," he wrote that same month, "constitute relatively such a complete change from older methods that less than 1% of our people have understood."[33]

Morale in the army suffered greatly from the uncertainty surrounding the draft extension. A *Life* reporter, after talking to 400 privates from five different regiments at Fort McClellan, Alabama, found their morale to be very low, thanks in large part to the uncertainty. They were also disgusted at the lack of equipment that forced them to train with ersatz goods in lieu of real weapons. "We came here to learn how to fight a blitzkrieg," said one. "Instead we get close-order drill and kitchen police." The reporter also detected a larger concern. "As far as the men can see," he wrote, "the Army has no goal. It does not know whether it is going to fight, or when or where." Scattered across the camp could be found the initials "OHIO," which stood for "Over the Hill in October," if their year's term was extended.[34]

Stimson was aware of their discontent. "The absence of any concrete war objective," he informed the president that same month, "coupled with delays in getting their weapons and lack of energy and imagination here and there among their instructors, are being reflected in the spirit of the men and I am seeing letters on the subject." But the problem extended beyond the troops. Raymond Moley was struck by the "apathetic attitude, or 'low morale,' with which the American people approach the hardships now being so freely forecast at the end of the second year of the war." A newspaper columnist, in an article entitled "How Bad Is U.S. Morale?," observed that "this is the year when every military expert agrees that modern war is war between economies. Yet where are the base hospitals to take care of the economic casualties? . . . Our small businessmen are in greater danger at this moment than our soldiers."[35]

"Morale has fallen off because the public has not been told enough," declared writer Bernard DeVoto. "It has not been kept informed about developments in foreign relations or about the progress of national defense. So it has tended to believe the worst of both . . . You don't get public support by treating the public as children." Journalist Samuel T. Williamson found fault with the public itself. "The really bad morale is among us home folks," he argued. "Few of us have done more than to hand a couple of worn out aluminum saucepans over to the Girl Scouts or fork out a dollar or two for the U.S.O. or do a bit of knitting or tie a bundle for Britain or roll up tin foil . . . Some of America's half-hearted morale comes from the wish for a last fling at pleasure before more serious things start. The last drink before the bar closes . . . We Americans outside the armed forces want to wait for our miracles, and we want lollipops as usual while we wait—how we suffer when we can't get them!"[36]

Neither DeVoto nor Williamson nor anyone else cared to speculate on the great unanswered question: When would the serious things start, where, and with whom?

* * *

"AT LEAST A year will pass before we can have an Army and an air force adequate to meet the air and ground forces which could be brought against us," declared Henry Stimson in May. That same month Raymond Moley insisted that "we must be mentally prepared for total war, with all that it implies, and for a long war." The *Saturday Evening Post* grumbled in July that "for all we have done and spent, the fact is that there is hardly one feature of the armament program that is not now enveloped in doubt and anxiety." Even as defense factories complained of labor shortages, dire warnings of shutdowns and massive unemployment because of material shortages filled the air. The connection between them was obvious but complex; no pipeline existed to funnel workers from one plant or line of work to another, let alone from one region to another. A hotbed of defense contracts like Detroit discouraged unskilled workers from migrating there because it feared that the shutdown of automobile production would create a surplus of labor for defense projects.[37]

One long-standing bottleneck showed signs of progress. Shell and bomb forgings could be mass-produced, but no machinery existed in private plants for the delicate job of loading them with the explosive TNT. A construction program was launched to build facilities capable of turning out the finished product in large quantity. The first plant went into production July 13 at Elmwood, Illinois. A second, larger complex opened a month later at Burlington, Iowa, with two more nearing completion in Tennessee and Ohio. The Burlington plant was a huge compound of 500 buildings with seventy-five miles of railroad track and a hundred miles of road enclosed by twenty-five miles of seven-foot wire fence and fully illuminated at night by floodlights. The facilities were the latest design in maximizing safety for 7,000 workers while speeding the production of a dangerous product.[38]

The operation featured power-operated production lines modeled after automobile assembly lines. Empty shells went onto revolving machines that carried them through paint spray booths, after which overhead tongs picked them up and deposited them in jiggleproof tote boxes for conveying to the melt-loading building. There, on an upper floor, TNT, which resembled brown sugar, was melted on fireless steam-heated stoves and piped downstairs into ladles for pouring by hand into the shells. Once it cooled, special safety drills powered by compressed air bored holes into the solidified TNT for the detonator. It was a prime example of slow, dangerous work made as fast as possible by new techniques, and a contribution about which the public knew virtually nothing. The plants were government owned but privately managed, like so many other defense facilities.[39]

What the public did know and feel was the lengthening parade of changes in daily life, most of them resulting from the shortages that grew steadily worse during the fall, and the price increases that inevitably followed. Ickes's futile attempt to curb gasoline use in the Northeast was followed by restrictions on the manufacture of silk stockings, which led to a feeding frenzy at hosiery counters. Ickes tried also to save gasoline by restricting deliveries; department stores obliged by asking customers to carry small purchases out with them. The production of whitewall tires, which required two pounds more rubber than all-black tires, was banned. Restrictions on steel use imposed the most potential hardship on the manufacture of everything from appliances to automobiles to tin cans as well as private construction. SPAB flatly banned all nondefense plant expansion. In November Frank Knox suggested that all passenger car production be banned, and Ickes agreed with him, but that drastic step had not yet been taken. Most observers thought it was only a matter of time.[40]

SEPTEMBER TURNED INTO an unusually difficult month for the president. On the seventh his regal, strong-willed mother died. Not five minutes after her death at Hyde Park, the largest oak tree on the estate simply crashed to the ground, untouched by wind or storm. The symbolism did not escape Roosevelt, who went out to observe the fallen tree. During the next few days, according to the *New York Times*, the distraught president "shut himself off from the world more completely than at any time since he assumed his present post." Eleanor shouldered the burden of making all the arrangements and tending to the myriad of details concerning Sara's belongings. At one point, coming across a box of his childhood memorabilia lovingly preserved by Sara, Roosevelt broke down and wept. An embarrassed Grace Tully left the room; no one on the staff had ever seen the president shed tears.[41]

Events left Roosevelt little time to mourn. Three days before his mother's death a German submarine had attacked but did not hit an American destroyer, the *Greer*. Within a five-day period three merchant ships were also attacked and two of them sunk, and the survivors of another, earlier sinking were found at sea. On September 11, a black armband around the sleeve of his gray seersucker suit, the president held another of his fireside chats with the nation. Although the facts of the *Greer* attack were somewhat muddy, he denounced it as "piracy—legally and morally." It was, he emphasized, "the Nazi design to abolish the freedom of the seas, and to acquire absolute control and domination of these seas for themselves." Recalling Germany's unlimited submarine warfare of World War I, he promised that "no matter what it takes, no matter what it costs, we will keep open the line of legitimate commerce in these defensive waters . . . When you see a rattlesnake poised to strike, you do not wait until he has struck before you crush him. These Nazi submarines and raiders are the rattlesnakes of the Atlantic."[42]

Since July Roosevelt had been gradually extending the American reach over the North Atlantic as far as he dared. He had sent American troops to occupy Iceland to prevent Germany from doing so, putting them more than a thousand miles closer to Berlin than to New York. He not only froze Japanese assets in the United States but closed the Panama Canal to her ships. Even Senator Wheeler admitted that "the President did the right thing. You may say for me that I agree with him—for the first time." After his rendezvous at sea with Churchill in August, Roosevelt returned to Washington with renewed energy and enthusiasm. At a press conference on the nineteenth he pointedly read to the reporters an excerpt of a statement by Abraham Lincoln to a group of visiting women in 1862: "The fact is the people have not yet made up their minds that we are at war with the South. They have not buckled down to the determination to fight this war through; for they have got the idea into their heads that we are going to get out of this fix somehow by strategy!"[43]

Two days later he told a convention of young Democrats that "against naked force the only possible defense is naked force." In a Labor Day speech he went even further, vowing that "we shall do everything in our power to crush Hitler and his Nazi forces." *Time* called it "the most far-reaching pledge the President had yet made." On October 9 he asked Congress to revise the Neutrality Act and authorize the arming of merchant ships. Although a Gallup survey showed his popularity at 73 percent, down only 3 percent from June, Roosevelt still faced an uphill climb to arouse the public to the menace facing them and the need for vigorous action. "A great many observers feel that the American people simply will not undergo even the home-front hardships and privations of war so long as they are technically at peace," concluded *Newsweek*. "This, then, is Mr. Roosevelt's dilemma: how to create a war economy in a nation at peace."[44]

The Japanese continued to blow hot and cold, offering peace gestures in one breath and belligerent warnings with the next. Then, in mid-October, the cabinet of venerable diplomat Prince Fumimaro Konoye fell and was replaced by one with General Hideki Tojo as its head, the first army general to hold the position. For months the cabinet had been wrangling over foreign policy, its split aggravated by the Nazi invasion of Russia. Konoye had opposed any break with the United States and was supported by the navy, while the army had long called for a more aggressive policy and an alliance with Germany. Then the navy changed positions, and the fragile Konoye cabinet had no choice but to resign. The belligerent, outspoken Tojo, nicknamed "Razor," promised strengthened ties with the Axis and a forceful push for Japanese dominance in the Pacific.[45]

After hearing the news, Roosevelt canceled a cabinet meeting and met instead with his war advisers. "This is a military and undoubtedly a chauvinistic Cabinet," said Ickes of the change. "Japan is again rattling her sword in the sheath . . . For a long time I have believed that our best entrance into the war would be by way of Japan. Undoubtedly we are nearer that eventuality than ever before . . . If we go to war against Japan, it will inevitably lead us to war against Germany." An American destroyer, the *Kearny*, was torpedoed and managed to make it safely to port, but eleven lives were lost. The bill allowing the Neutrality Act to be amended passed the House but still faced the usual opposition in the Senate; meanwhile, two more freighters went to the bottom.[46]

Back in May, his eye ever fixed on history and on Lincoln in particular, Roosevelt had declared near the end of a cabinet meeting, "I am not willing to fire the first shot." But the rush of events had outraced his ability to control them. In his Navy Day speech on October 27 he said of the *Kearny* incident, "We have wished to avoid shooting. But the shooting has started. And history has recorded who fired the first shot." Three days later a Nazi submarine sank an American destroyer, the *Reuben James*, killing ninety-seven of her crew. To American protests Germany sneered that "anybody walking along the railroad tracks at night should not be surprised if he gets run over by an express train" and heaped insults on Roosevelt personally for his Navy Day speech. To reinforce patrols of the Atlantic shipping lanes, the president transferred the entire Coast Guard from Treasury Department jurisdiction to that of the navy, a step normally taken only in time of war.[47]

Many remained unconvinced. Columnist Ernest K. Lindley, normally a strong administration supporter, decried the Navy Day speech as a "scaremongering election-eve type, indicative that the moment for grave decision is near." However, a London paper regarded the sinking of the *Reuben James* as a sign that America was "marching down the last miles to a declaration of war." In Moscow *Pravda* agreed that the United States had "taken its fighting post." As the fighting in Russia grew more desperate, Roosevelt did what he could to speed weapons and supplies to the Soviet Union, giving it planes ahead even of the United States. A special emissary, Saburo Kurusu, arrived from Japan on November 15 to join Admiral Kichisaburo Nomura, the ambassador already engaged in long and futile negotiations with Hull. A suave diplomat comfortable in many languages, including English, Kurusu was thought to be as anti-Axis as his American wife. But the stumbling block remained what it had been for decades: the Japanese desire to create a great Far Eastern empire by force and American insistence that this plan be abandoned.[48]

November brought an even harsher winter than usual to Russia as the Germans launched a desperate offensive to break through to Moscow or Leningrad before the weather stalled them. Reports indicated that the campaign had bled the Nazi army dearly. Japan's new foreign minister, Shigenori Togo, warned bluntly that "there is naturally a limit to our conciliatory attitude . . . There is no necessity of spending much time on negotiations hereafter." Premier Tojo declared that Japan would not tolerate interference in its plans to erect a Pacific empire. Congress responded by passing the bill gutting the Neutrality Act, but only by the narrow vote of 212–194 with fifty-three Democrats voting against it. The threat of crippling coal and railroad strikes got entangled in the issue, and the administration gained a majority only by promising to act sternly against either threat. "Many Democrats, whose own views are changing," observed Lindley, "are troubled by pledges made in the 1940 election. They told their constituents that the President's foreign policy was intended to keep us out of war and promised not to vote for war and in some cases even for repeal of the Neutrality Act." *Newsweek* referred to the latter as a "legislative Maginot Line."[49]

PROTESTING AGAINST SHORTAGES, the jewelry industry warned that 60,000 workers, 35,000 of them in Massachusetts and Rhode Island alone, would be thrown out of work unless they received a small supply of scarce copper and zinc. Sperry Corporation, maker of instruments, revealed that more than half of its $250 million backlog in defense orders was farmed out to more than a thousand firms. Leon Henderson, after a three-hour session with automobile executives, announced that no cars made in 1942 would contain nickel, chromium, or aluminum in nonfunctional parts such as trim and hubcaps. Timken Roller Bearing Company rebuked its largest customers with a full-page ad in twenty-three major newspapers urging railroads to ease freight congestion by converting their freight cars from friction bearings to roller bearings.[50]

Nomura and Kurusu continued their earnest but futile talks with Hull in search of a compromise that did not exist, their every message from Tokyo read secretly by American officials in advance thanks to cryptographers who broke the Japanese diplomatic code. Tojo demanded three things that the United States would not concede: abandonment of China, lifting of the trade embargo, and a free hand to create Japan's new order in Asia. Roosevelt had American troops occupy Dutch Guiana to keep it out of Axis hands and protect its bauxite mines. To his surprise two longtime isolationist senators, Robert A. Taft of Ohio and Guy Gillette of Iowa, announced that they would support the president's foreign policy as long as it was covered by congressional enactments. *Time* described Roosevelt as "waging the first great undeclared war in U.S. history." On November 8 Kiplinger's reported, "*War with Japan.* Opinion here is SLIGHTLY that it will not be."[51]

At a meeting on November 25 Hull showed Stimson and Knox a proposal for a three-month truce that he was going to offer the Japanese. No one expected them to accept it. At noon they joined General Marshall and Admiral Stark for a meeting with the president. In going over the Japanese situation Roosevelt remarked that the nation might well be attacked within the week. The Japanese were notorious for attacks without warning, he added, and the key question was how to get them to fire the first shot while putting Americans in as little jeopardy as possible. "It was," Stimson conceded, "a difficult proposition." Once back in his office, Stimson learned that a Japanese expedition of thirty to fifty ships had been sighted south of Formosa. No one knew where they were headed, but Stimson relayed the information to the president. On the twenty-seventh Stark advised the president that "the most essential thing now . . . is to gain time."[52]

Earlier that morning Stimson called Hull to see what he had done about the truce proposal. Hull said he had not delivered it. "I have washed my hands of it," he added, "and it is now in the hands of you and Knox—the Army and Navy." Stimson called the president, who said Hull had in fact given the Japanese a statement of position the United States had long demanded. On the twenty-eighth he went early to see Roosevelt, who said while still sitting on his bed that he saw three options: do nothing; present some sort of ultimatum, a point beyond which the country would go to war; or fight at once. Stimson replied that there were really only two options; doing nothing was not possible. Of the others, he preferred fighting at once. A noontime meeting of the war cabinet agonized over where the Japanese expedition might strike. Roosevelt wanted to make a special appeal to the emperor but was persuaded to do so in a secret letter.[53]

That same day, to Stimson's chagrin, Roosevelt left for Warm Springs, Georgia, to enjoy his annual turkey dinner with fellow polio sufferers. The trip had been twice postponed by the growing crisis and the coal strike, but the latter had been settled. He hoped to remain for ten days to rest and visit Missy LeHand, who was convalescing from a stroke. Arriving at Newnan, Georgia, on the morning of the twenty-ninth, the weather encouraged him to ride the last forty miles by car, waving happily to farmers attracted by the sound of his motorcycle escort. At Warm Springs the corps of newsmen set themselves up in two cottages, enjoyed a few drinks, and then joined the president at the cottage of Canadian minister Leighton McCarthy for a cocktail party in the afternoon. Roosevelt arrived, seated himself, and, tired and careworn as he was, put everyone at ease by growling, "Well, get me a drink— that's what I came for!"[54]

From there he adjourned to the dining hall and feasted happily on roast turkey, oyster-corn stuffing, pumpkin pie, and cider. Afterward he gave a short talk to 116 polio victims, then shook hands and patted backs all around. His remarks included a brief, pointed comment that American boys now training in the service academies might actually be fighting by next Thanksgiving. The reporters picked up on it and made a mad dash for the telephones. The next morning, after a telephone conversation with Hull, Roosevelt hurried back to Washington, where a showdown seemed to be looming. Arriving on the morning of December 2, he met at once with Hull for an update. The Japanese expedition seemed to be landing in Indochina, but a belligerent speech by Tojo called on his people to purge Asia of British and American exploitation. All American forces in the Far East were put on alert. Then, abruptly, the Japanese cabinet instructed Nomura and Kurusu to continue the talks even as more of their troops massed on the border of Thailand.[55]

Harry Hopkins, back in the hospital, left to have lunch with Roosevelt. Afterward he assured Stimson that the president remained firm and had not been swayed by the appeasers. Stimson fretted again over Roosevelt being "so irregular in his habits of consultations. He has a regular group . . . who are his official advisers, Hull, Knox and myself, and the two military men, and here . . . suddenly he stops and makes his decisive decision without calling us into conference again. It was probably a right decision for the time being but it is not the right way to do it." As for the Japanese, Stimson thought they had "evidently made up their minds to attack as soon as they get what they deem a favorable opportunity."[56]

Elsewhere the war seemed to be going well. At November's end the Russians were still holding, and the British had launched an offensive in Libya while lifting the siege of Tobruk. The last Italian garrison in Ethiopia surrendered, freeing that country. "The prospects are much more cheerful than they have been for a long time," wrote a satisfied Harold Ickes. "Now if we can only get busy in the Pacific and smash Japan." Stimson was far less sanguine. "The atmosphere indicated that something was going to happen," he wrote on December 6. That afternoon he went home for lunch and afterward took a horseback ride, "for I thought it might be the last one I would get for some time." That night Roosevelt sent a private, personal appeal to Emperor Hirohito. Although his views of the Japanese had long waffled, they appeared to have hardened early in this difficult year. "They hate us," he told journalist Quentin Reynolds in mid-March. "They come to me and they hiss between their teeth and they say: 'Mr. President, we are your friends. Japan wants nothing but friendship with America,' and then they hiss between their teeth again, and I know they're lying. Oh, they hate us, and sooner or later they'll come after us."[57]

*   *   *

TO THE PUBLIC the White House was simply one more public monument in a city of monuments. People could enter the grounds without showing a pass or answering any questions. Thousands of visitors milled through the formal rooms every day with no more admonition than being asked to leave their cameras and packages at the checkroom. None of the four gates had guardhouses or sentry boxes; the police at each gate served chiefly to direct official traffic. Reporters filing into the president's office for a press conference did not have to show any identification unless they were complete strangers. The Secret Service guarded the president, but no one guarded the White House until that first clear, sunny Sunday in December, when police rushed to secure the entrances against entry by anyone except those with reason to go inside. Never again would the place enjoy so casual and informal an atmosphere.[58]

Hull was to meet with the Japanese emissaries at one o'clock that afternoon of December 7 to receive their reply to his statement. It had been coming in over the Japanese diplomatic code, which among other things instructed Kurusu and Nomura to meet with Hull at precisely one o'clock and no later. Hull saw Stimson and Knox at 10:30 and remained in conference with them until noon. Roosevelt had lunch with Hopkins at his desk in the Oval Room and was chatting with him when Knox called at about 1:40 to say that a radio message from the commander in Honolulu said that Pearl Harbor was under attack. Hopkins thought it must be a mistake, that the Japanese would never attack Hawaii. No, said Roosevelt, it was just the kind of unexpected thing they would do: discuss peace at the very time they were plotting to overthrow it. He gave instructions to Hull and notified Stimson of what had happened. A meeting of the war cabinet was hastily called for 3:00 P.M. and one for the full cabinet at 8:30 that evening.[59]

At 2:22 Steve Early broke the news to the three press associations, and reporters scrambled to get to the White House. A crowd began gathering outside the gates. Many officials and reporters had to be summoned by loudspeaker from the Eagles-Redskins game at Griffith Stadium. By five o'clock a record crowd of reporters, radio men, photographers, newsreel photographers, and others were trying to wedge themselves into a press room where normally a dozen reporters gathered. "In a space of four hours I handled four flashes and eight bulletin stories," recalled Merriman Smith. ". . . Men spend an entire lifetime in press association work without ever handling one flash story. I had four in four hours." The growing crowd outside the gates remained quiet and orderly, shifting in the cold and warming themselves by singing "God Bless America" and "My Country, 'Tis of Thee."[60]

John Kenneth Galbraith was lying down at home when a call came around three o'clock informing him of the attack. Henderson was in New York and unavailable. The senior defense officials hastily arranged to meet at the Social Security Building south of the Mall, where both OPM and SPAB had offices. Galbraith felt honored to attend in Henderson's place. Men filed in wearing the uniforms of their Sunday afternoon activities—some in tennis shoes, golf pants, and other casual garb. Knudsen arrived and sat on a couch without removing his hat. Nelson was there, and Bill Batt. Someone left to phone Knox's office for the latest news and returned with the message that things were worse than expected. After some milling around, discussion began on what to do.[61]

"It was soon evident that the gathering would be a major disaster," Galbraith concluded. "That was because there was nothing to decide . . . So important were the people attending that none could speak firmly about a needed course of action lest it be a decision." Batt saw the drift and conspicuously asked Knudsen, "Bill, what are the marching orders for tomorrow?" Knudsen looked up and said, "I expect we will be worrying about copper shortages just as we are today." Someone retrieved an enormous stock book listing alphabetically the inventories and sources of all essential materials. An aimless debate arose over which materials now under enemy control were really essential. Disillusioned, Galbraith left the meeting and went home. On the way he saw crowds assembled at the White House and in front of the Japanese embassy on Massachusetts Avenue.[62]

Harold Ickes had hosted a luncheon for several guests that afternoon, including Don Nelson, Senator Tom Connally, and Justice Hugo Black. It was the first time he had met Nelson, whom he described as "energetic and forceful but lacking somewhat in background." He too was lying down when a friend called to tell him the news. Promptly at 8:30 that evening he joined the other cabinet members in the president's study, along with Hopkins, who still looked pale and ill. Chairs had been arranged in a semicircle around Roosevelt's desk. The president looked uncharacteristically solemn; there were no jokes or wisecracks and scarcely a smile. "His reaction to any event was always to be calm," observed Eleanor, who had watched him absorb one gloomy dispatch after another that day. "If it was something that was bad, he just became almost like an iceberg, and there was never the slightest emotion that was allowed to show." He admitted to her that he never wanted to fight the war on two fronts at once. "We haven't got the Navy to fight in both the Atlantic and the Pacific . . . so we will have to build up the Navy and the Air Force and that will mean that we will have to take a good many defeats before we can have a victory."[63]

"I don't think he spoke to anyone who came in that night," recalled Frances Perkins. "He was living off in another area. He wasn't noticing what went on on the other side of the desk. He was very serious. His face and lips were pulled down, looking quite gray." She noticed too that he had trouble accepting that the navy—his pride and joy—had been caught unawares. Twice he told Knox, "Find out, for God's sake, why the ships were tied up in rows." Knox answered, "That's the way they berth them!"[64]

It was, Roosevelt told them, probably the most serious situation any cabinet had faced since 1861. Then he ran down the litany of reports that had come in all afternoon and were still arriving, each one more grim than the last. The fleet had been caught flatfooted, the battleships tied up "snugly side by side" with no steam up and only a small guard. Four were fully or completely sunk, and two of the other four seriously damaged, along with three light cruisers and three destroyers. Four warships in dry dock were also badly hit and the dry dock heavily damaged. Fortunately, the three carriers—the prime Japanese target—were all at sea. The army airfields also took a pounding. Most of the planes were destroyed on the ground. The total number of casualties was not yet known; the deaths would reach 3,500. Hull was livid at the Japanese for meeting with him even as their planes were bombing Pearl Harbor. Roosevelt read a short message he had prepared to give at a joint session of Congress the next day. Hull kept insisting on a longer message conveying all the background details leading up to the attack until Roosevelt grew impatient with him. Others argued that the message should at least be broader, but the president was intent on a short, direct text.[65]

At 8:45 the congressional leaders joined the meeting. They sat in stunned silence while Roosevelt repeated the details of what Ickes called "the worst naval disaster in American history." When Tom Connally asked sharply how the fleet had been caught sitting like "lame ducks," an embarrassed Frank Knox held his tongue. "I don't know, Tom," the president replied wearily. "I just don't know." The congressmen agreed to receive Roosevelt at a joint session on Monday even though he refused to tell them in advance what he would say. Too much might happen overnight, he explained. When his contingent left at 10:40 Connally told the crowd of reporters, "Japan has started this war in treachery; we will end it in victory."[66]

The cabinet filed out behind them. Stimson admitted feeling relieved "that the indecision was over and that a crisis had come in a way which would unite all our people . . . For I feel that this country united has practically nothing to fear while the apathy and divisions stirred up by unpatriotic men have been hitherto very discouraging." Knox thought the president must feel the same way. "You know," he whispered to Perkins, "I think the boss must have a great load off his mind. I thought the load on his mind was just going to kill him, going to break him down. This must be a great sense of relief to him. At least we know what to do now."[67]

At noon the next day Roosevelt headed up Pennsylvania Avenue in his closed car, Secret Service men perched on both running boards and their cars flanking it on both sides. The crowd sprawled across the length of the Plaza. Scattered throughout the street could be found police, marines, and plain-clothesmen. Once inside the Capitol he was greeted with long, lingering applause by the packed crowd, including the cabinet and Supreme Court. His message, beginning with "Yesterday, December 7, 1941—a date which will live in infamy," took less than seven minutes to deliver. Not only Pearl Harbor but the Philippines, Guam, Wake Island, Midway, Hong Kong, and Malaya had been attacked. Thirty-three minutes after Roosevelt finished, both houses passed declarations of war against Japan, the Senate 82–0 and the House 388–1, with only a forlorn Jeannette Rankin of Montana casting a negative vote as she had in 1917. On the morning of December 11 Germany and Italy declared war on the United States, which replied in kind.[68]

In one stroke the Japanese had resolved Roosevelt's dilemma, albeit at heavy cost. They had fired the first shot, and in a manner bound to unite the American people behind the war effort. Critics would later charge him with maneuvering the country into war, but no one could doubt that the United States had to fight once attacked. The America First Committee folded up almost overnight after pledging its support to the war effort on the evening of December 7. Pearl Harbor also resolved the differences between the all-outers and the gradualists over the speed of conversion to war production. On December 9 Roosevelt held his first wartime news conference and later delivered a fireside chat to explain the crisis to the American people. That morning he attended a SPAB meeting in which it was agreed to speed up the existing production program and to increase the plant expansion program. Knudsen had been asked whether the nation's productive capacity could achieve the Victory Plan estimates. Yes, he told Stimson, if the completion date were moved from June 1943 to June 1944.[69]

About $3 billion in new facilities would be needed, Knudsen added. Total cost of production, which hit $12.7 billion in 1941, he estimated at $33 billion for 1942, $44 billion for 1943, and $30 billion for 1944. Given these figures at the meeting, Roosevelt told Knudsen to go ahead with estimates for the $3 billion in new facilities; the rest would be requested portion by portion. They discussed priorities, the possibility of a seven-day workweek, curtailing civilian consumption, streamlining procurement procedures, and other issues. Stimson got the president's approval to merge Lend-Lease into army and navy production schedules. Already Patterson had alerted the army's supply chiefs to shift every operation into high gear: "You are directed to take all necessary steps to boost munitions manufacture to the highest possible level . . . Our production must be quickly put on a 24 hour a day basis."[70]

After more than two years of uncertainty, hesitation, debate, and delays, the path was clear. Time had run out. The need was immediate and urgent, the task winnowed down to logistics on a colossal scale. In this war as in the last, the strength of the United States lay not in its military, which needed time to develop, but in its productive might. Here too what was desperately needed was an organization capable of maximizing that strength. On one point the debate would renew with increased vigor: whether the experience of World War I should be duplicated and a body created with one man at its head to oversee the essentials of the war effort.

1942: THE YEAR OF DESPAIR

CHAPTER 13

FIRST REACTIONS

I was only ten on December 7, 1941 . . . Like millions of other Americans I heard about the attack on the radio—in the middle of a Chicago Bears football game, I believe . . . I remember running out of the house and meeting my next-door pal Robert Riggs, who had burst out looking for me as if galvanized by a telepathic alarm bell. We gazed at each other blankly, not knowing what to say. This was too scary, too vast. Something was coming, we knew it, something like a storm . . . Thus the war began in my tiny sector of the Home Front . . . Crawfordsville, Indiana.

—RICHARD LINGEMAN[1]

The popular idea—popular in 1942—of a man with a big stick cracking down on innumerable other government officials and compelling them to carry out his orders, always struck me as unrealistic. The job was too big for such tactics.

—DONALD NELSON[2]

No one else . . . could have launched the industrial phase of the program so brilliantly as Bill Knudsen did. He was invested with only the shadow of actual authority. He moved mountains through his own prestige and persuasiveness, and strength of character. Tooling up had to start with him . . . and tooling up for war manufacture proved to be one of the biggest jobs ever done in this world . . . Speed was a recognized necessity. The catch was that Knudsen had been told to perform this magic without upsetting the civilian economy . . . He knew considerable grief would be part of his job.

—DONALD NELSON[3]

ON THE MORNING OF DECEMBER 8 it was natural for Americans to think that everything had changed, even though they knew nothing as yet of what the changes might be. As their first reactions of anger, outrage, and patriotic fervor subsided, they began to speculate on how their lives might change, what might be gained or lost. War was no stranger to Americans, but they had never fought one like this before, on so colossal a scale in so many places around the globe. As always, the most obvious and immediate impact fell upon the generation of young men who would march off to battle, but those who stayed behind would have no end of adjustments to make as well. The war was no longer something "out there," and it would leave few lives untouched.

Roosevelt pulled no punches in his fireside chat Tuesday night. "We are now in this war," he said. "We are all in it—all the way. Every single man, woman, and child is a partner in the most tremendous undertaking of our American history. We must share together the bad news and the good news, the defeats and the victories—the changing fortunes of war. So far, the news has been all bad . . . It will not only be a long war but a hard war. That is the basis on which we now lay all our plans." There would be shortages and hardships, but he was sure the American people would "cheerfully give up those material things that they are asked to give up."[4]

Would the United States fall prey to the ravages of bombing and invasion that blighted so much of the rest of the world? The possibility was slim but it existed, and precautions had to be taken. On the West Coast the first reaction quickly morphed into a frenzy of fear that Japanese planes would soon appear over California, and Japanese ships in West Coast harbors. Three times that first morning of war, sirens sounded an alarm in San Francisco. Since they were fire engine sirens, the city having no air raid sirens, no one knew what to do. Rumors of strange planes over the city led General John L. DeWitt, commander of the Fourth Army and Western Defense Command, to declare, "I don't think there's any doubt that planes came from a carrier." Fifteen huge searchlights around the bay and the Presidio scanned the sky but found no planes.[5]

The blackout that followed threw drivers into confusion as police ordered all vehicles to use parking lights only. Huge traffic jams developed, along with a string of accidents. An unimpressed General DeWitt blasted those who suggested that it had all been a false alarm. "There are more damned fools in this locality than I have ever seen," he proclaimed. "Death and destruction are likely to come to this city at any moment. Those planes were over our community for a definite period. They were enemy planes. I mean Japanese planes. They were tracked out to sea. Why bombs were not dropped, I do not know. It might have been better if some bombs had dropped to awaken this city."

When the alert reached Seattle, a mob of a thousand people gathered downtown, intent on enforcing a blackout. Most lights were out except for one glaring neon sign. While police stood idly by, the mob began throwing anything they could find at the sign. Its leader, a woman of nineteen and the wife of a sailor, later explained, "We've got to show them they can't leave their lights burning. This is war. They don't realize one light in the city might betray us. That's my patriotism." The mob then began targeting other lights and shifted their patriotism to looting stores. Before the police broke them up, they had trashed a six-block area. By Tuesday night the ghostly enemy planes were reported over the Los Angeles area, but the response was more orderly. Lacking sirens, police, firemen, a handful of air raid wardens and even Boy Scouts roamed the city turning off lights.

By nine o'clock the city was dark, yet the fear persisted. Much later, concerned at the extent to which some movie studios resembled nearby aircraft plants, Jack Warner of Warner Bros. demonstrated his patriotism by having workmen paint a twenty-foot arrow on the roof of a soundstage along with giant letters stating, LOCKHEED—THATAWAY. Presumably his hopes rested on the Japanese pilots being able to read English.[6]

On the East Coast, New York endured its share of false alarms and sporadic violence against Japanese citizens. The FBI rounded up 200 Japanese deemed dangerous and deposited them on Ellis Island after questioning. Police turned back all Japanese trying to leave the city by plane. Attorney General Francis Biddle, who had succeeded Robert Jackson after the latter's promotion to the Supreme Court, assured reporters that "procedures are being established to provide a fair hearing for all." In Washington helmeted men with fixed bayonets guarded the Capitol doors and corridors. A reporter going from the Senate entrance to the House press gallery had to show his credentials a dozen times. The White House replaced its friendly demeanor with the look of a fortress. Sentry boxes appeared at all the gates, and only those with official appointments were allowed inside. The White House guard was doubled, identity cards were issued to those working there or needing access, and bulletproof glass was installed halfway up the three south windows of the Oval Office. To Eleanor's disgust, long, heavy blackout curtains were hung on every window and drawn tight every night. Fireplace use was banned lest the smoke attract enemy bombers.[7]

Roosevelt rejected a long list of other proposed security measures but agreed to the construction of a temporary shelter in the Treasury Department connected to the White House by a tunnel running under the street. When Morgenthau tried to persuade him to visit the facility, however, the president balked. "Henry," he said, "I will not go down into the shelter unless you allow me to play poker with all the gold in your vaults." Eleanor grew so exasperated at the precautions that she asked whether the Washington Monument would be dismantled because an enemy could measure the distance between it and the White House. The social season at the White House was canceled for 1941–42, never to resume while the war lasted.[8]

DURING THE DREARY days of December after Pearl Harbor, confronted by the most stupendous tasks facing any president since Lincoln, Roosevelt moved briskly on several fronts. On the eleventh, the same day he asked Congress to declare war on Germany and Italy, he invited representatives of management and labor to a conference that would draft a wartime labor policy. Four days later he sent Congress a history of the nation's relations with Japan and followed on the eighteenth with a commission to investigate the attack on Pearl Harbor. That same day he created the Office of Defense Transportation and later named Joseph B. Eastman, chairman of the Interstate Commerce Commission (ICC), to head it. On the nineteenth he established the Office of Censorship to deal with the delicate task of deciding what information should be withheld to prevent aiding the enemy. Three days later, with obvious relish, he announced the arrival of Churchill, who had come to America aboard a new battleship along with Lord Beaverbrook, his minister of supply, and several military officers.[9]

Churchill stayed a week, thoroughly demolishing the White House routine with his odd habits and hours while savoring the entire experience. From this so-called Arcadia Conference emerged several crucial decisions. The first appeared on New Year's Day under the title "Declaration by United Nations"; in it, twenty-six countries at war with the Axis pledged their unity and support of the program and principles agreed upon by Roosevelt and Churchill. The president was the driving force behind this document that echoed something more than the usual alliance. Privately the two new best friends agreed that, notwithstanding Pearl Harbor, Hitler constituted the greater menace. The European war would get priority while the Pacific remained a holding action until more resources could be built up. Finally, after some tough bargaining, General Marshall won agreement that the two nations should have a unified command structure in the Pacific.[10]

Still another product of Arcadia was an agreement to pool all munitions and provide for a free exchange of information. Part of this effort involved creating production goals for the coming year and beyond. Parallel meetings for this purpose took place at the Mayflower Hotel between Lord Beaverbrook, Averell Harriman, and their staffs of experts. "We had all agreed that it had taken the British too many years to get full war production," recalled Harriman, "and Hopkins had the idea, I think with Roosevelt's full approval, that this time could be shortened if we set our sights high at once." High they were, thanks in part to Roosevelt taking the large numbers given him and raising them even higher. When Hopkins questioned the figures, the president replied, "Oh, the production people can do it if they really try."[11]

Roosevelt had asked the production people to provide their most exact estimates of raw materials, facilities, and production potential. Before their hurried efforts were completed, the president summoned Nelson to a meeting that included Churchill, Beaverbrook, Hopkins, and Knudsen. "I have been thinking about the munitions which this country must produce in order to lick the Germans and the Japs as quickly as possible," Roosevelt said, "and by my usual rule-of-thumb method I have arrived at the following figures." Nelson blanched at the numbers he mentioned. "These figures are high," Roosevelt admitted, "because they represent what we simply *have* to produce. I have absolute confidence that the country can do the job." When someone suggested that the figures be kept secret to prevent the enemy from learning them, Roosevelt replied, "I believe these figures will tell our enemies what they are up against." A few days later he went public with them.[12]

The original estimates called for 28,600 aircraft, 20,400 tanks, 6,300 antiaircraft guns, and 6 million deadweight tons of merchant ships. In his State of the Union address on January 6 Roosevelt stunned listeners with the figures he rolled out: 60,000 planes (45,000 combat) for 1942 and 125,000 (100,000 combat) for 1943; 45,000 tanks for 1942 and 75,000 for 1943; 20,000 antiaircraft guns for 1942 and 35,000 for 1943; 6 million deadweight tons of merchant ships for 1942 and 10 million for 1943. Shortly afterward the president raised the merchant ship totals to 9 million for 1942 and 15 million for 1943. The figures, observed Sherwood, "were so astronomic that they were greeted with derision and, in some cases, despair by military and civilian authorities alike," even though Congress cheered them. "The President has gone in for the 'numbers racket'!" muttered some officers in the War Department. Many blamed Hopkins and the New Dealers like Henderson for deluding Roosevelt, but the inflated figures all came from the president.[13]

In a press conference Roosevelt explained his reasoning. He had been appalled at the amount of productive capacity still going into civilian use. Steel, for example, devoted only about 25 percent of its output to war production, compared to 75 percent for the British. He asked the Maritime Commission, then making just over a million tons of steel a year, how much it could increase output. Five million tons, he was told. "Not enough," Roosevelt countered, and the estimate went up to six million. What about 1943? he asked. Can you reach ten million tons? They agreed to try. When the president gave his figure for airplanes to Knudsen and Nelson, he chuckled, "I nearly took their breath away." After some waffling, they agreed it could be done.[14]

But not with the existing structure of things. Two days after Pearl Harbor Roosevelt summoned Knudsen and the other members of SPAB to the White House and told them he wanted production stepped up, especially of aircraft. In particular he wanted 30,000 planes in 1942 and an increase in bomber output from 500 to 1,000 a month. Knudsen said it could be done. Then came Arcadia and the British observation that the United States, being four times larger than Great Britain, should produce four times as much. Roosevelt asked Knudsen again how many planes he could make. With new facilities, Knudsen replied, 44,600. As for tanks, he thought 20,000 with a chance of 25,000. Hearing Roosevelt's final figures left OPM officials astounded and distraught. "I presume this is done for propaganda purposes," said Merrill Meigs, who asked the obvious question: Where would the machine tools and raw material come from?[15]

In his dogged manner Knudsen offered no complaint and set out to make the figures come true. But something was in the air. Meigs and John Lord O'Brian warned him that, in the latter's words, "there is a strong movement under way to get you out of OPM." Never a political animal, Knudsen made little effort to defend himself. At a SPAB meeting on January 13, a messenger handed Vice President Wallace a note. He and Nelson then excused themselves, saying they were needed at the White House. After the meeting ended, Knudsen returned to his office. An hour later one of the staff handed him an item torn off the news ticker. Knudsen read it and walked into O'Brian's office, a dazed expression on his face. "Look here, Judge," he said. "I've been fired!"[16]

Of course, it was not that direct; Roosevelt rarely fired anyone. For three months Roosevelt had been wrestling with the question of how best to push production. Stimson, who applauded Roosevelt's State of the Union address as "the best speech that I ever heard him make," drafted at Hopkins's request a letter to the president urging him not to appoint any "industry dictator" unless he was convinced the man had two things: sufficient character and initiative for the job, and enough experience in industrial methods to win the confidence of the industrialists with whom he had to work. Hearing rumors that William Douglas would be the man, he groaned privately that it would be "a hideous appointment."[17]

Roosevelt had reached the point of bowing to the incessant demand for a single head to oversee the whole process but could not decide on the best man for the job. Everyone seemed to agree that Knudsen was not suitable; he knew production but had little imagination and no political instincts. He had thought first of plucking Bill Douglas from the Supreme Court to take the job and actually talked to him about it, but Douglas showed little interest. One weekend in January, while relaxing at Hyde Park, he mentioned to Hopkins the possibility of a three-man committee composed of Nelson, Douglas, and Willkie. Hopkins strongly opposed it because neither Douglas nor Willkie knew anything about production. Later, when Roosevelt brought the idea up again, Hopkins again argued against it. Instead, he suggested, better to appoint Nelson alone to the job. He was, after all, the only one of the three who understood production.[18]

"The amusing part of the whole business," recalled Hopkins, "was that everybody was a candidate. Wallace, I am sure, hoped the President would ask him. Bernie Baruch was in a hotel room in Washington spreading propaganda for himself. A great many of my friends were pushing Bill Douglas. Morgenthau wanted it worse than anything in the world. So did Jesse Jones, and, of course, Knudsen."[19]

After their return to Washington Roosevelt told Hopkins that he thought Nelson was the right man. Make the appointment at once, Hopkins urged, because once the news got out the president would be besieged by people giving reasons for not doing it. Roosevelt asked Hopkins to get together with Senator James Byrnes and Harold Smith to plan an announcement, then summoned Wallace and Nelson from their meeting. Neither man knew what was up; on the ride to the White House they continued their discussion about ways to increase copper production.[20]

A visit to the president's office had its own ritual. After scrutiny by the guard at the gate and Secret Service men at the entrance, visitors were greeted by the keeper of the outer door to the president's office. He took hats and coats, hung them up, and escorted the visitors into the outer office, where Pa Watson presided. Watson would normally ask them to take a seat and wait until the president concluded his present business. On this day, however, no one else was waiting and the president was alone, so Watson ushered them to the door of the inner office and opened it with his own special flourish. To Nelson's awed eyes the Oval Office was a magnificent sea of pictures and models of ships about a desk overflowing with "astonishing collections of gimcrackery," the latest display from the endless souvenirs sent to Roosevelt. Not surprisingly for a Democratic president, donkeys prevailed.[21]

Roosevelt's typical greeting was a big smile and hearty handshake, but on this occasion he struck Nelson as more detached and thoughtful, his face strained with lines of fatigue. "He was a strong man," Nelson reflected, "but obviously he was operating upon his almost superhuman reserve of strength, and the time was bound to come when there would be no reserve left." Nor did Roosevelt open the conversation with his usual quip or pleasantry. Instead he motioned Wallace and Nelson to chairs and filled them in on where the war effort stood, followed by an impressive recital of the available resources for each of the warring countries. Then he shifted mood again and talked of democracy, its strength and virtues in meeting great crises. "It was almost as if I were listening to another Gettysburg Address, delivered to an audience of two," thought Nelson.

The president shifted abruptly to a review of the government's organization for war and its shortcomings. For more than half an hour he ran down the list of individuals, meting out praise while itemizing deficiencies. Not only the agencies but the army, navy, and Maritime Commission, as well as generals and admirals, were evaluated in frank terms. "I have given the matter great thought," Roosevelt said at last, "and I have come to the conclusion that American war production should be placed under the direction of one man." Someone was needed who could bring all the discordant elements together, ramp production up to unheard-of volumes, and do it quickly. Speed, speed, and more speed was needed, he repeated, drumming his knuckles on the desk for emphasis. The faster the war was won, the more American lives would be spared.

A new board was needed, one that would combine long-range vision and managerial skills with the will and—most important—legal authority to get the job done. It would include the secretaries of War and Navy along with seasoned government and business executives. "I'm going to form the new board immediately," Roosevelt said. "And I'm going to appoint a chairman who will have complete and absolute control over the production of all implements of war and over all related activities." To illustrate his point, the president told the story of the time Lincoln polled his cabinet on a controversial issue that most of them opposed. After finishing the poll Lincoln said, "All in favor say 'Aye.' *I* vote 'Aye.' The 'Ayes' have it." Roosevelt chuckled at the story, then said, "That's the kind of board I want, and that's the kind of chairman I want, to run it."

Itching to say something, Nelson asked what the new board would be called. Roosevelt smoked awhile in silence, then waved his cigarette holder and said, "War Production Administration," before remembering that the New Deal already had a WPA that had aroused plenty of controversy. "Oh no, that won't do," he laughed, and thought some more. "I think I've got it," he said finally. "Just move the last initial one notch downward in the alphabet and you get WPB—the War Production Board." He asked Nelson what he thought, and Nelson said the name was fine. "I'm glad you approve," replied Roosevelt, "because you are the Chairman of the War Production Board, a new government agency which has just been named . . . I want you to do the job, Don."

In discussing the scope of the new board, Nelson reminded the president that earlier boards had foundered because their functions and powers had not been adequately defined. Roosevelt told him to write out the order himself and he would sign it. "I want the authority vested in you," he added with a twinkle in his eye, "but please make the Executive Order reasonable—or, I should say, workable." Nelson took the problem to John Lord O'Brian, who huddled with his assistant and returned with a draft that Nelson called "a model of brevity and soundness." The key phrase authorized the chairman to "exercise the powers, authority, and discretion conferred upon him . . . in such a manner as he may determine; and his decisions shall be final." The president did not hesitate to sign it.[22]

"The maneuvers which finally installed Nelson as production czar deflated Knudsen-Hillman into a pair of pathetic victims of political persecution," complained Eliot Janeway. "Every headline proclaimed their failure." The news spread at once and was on the ticker tape Knudsen read in his office that evening. Deeply distressed, the Great Dane, as he was affectionately known, wanted to call Roosevelt at once, but O'Brian talked him out of it. Hopkins called Jesse Jones, told him that the handling of Knudsen had been brutal, and asked him to urge Knudsen to accept another offer as a general in the army charged with overseeing production. Jones went at once to Knudsen's house and found him steeped in gloom. The president, said Knudsen, had kicked him out, and he was going home to Detroit.[23]

They talked all through dinner, but Knudsen would not budge. More hurt than bitter, he sat at the piano after dinner, playing and humming sad tunes, firm in his resolve to leave Washington. On his own initiative Jones called Hopkins at the White House around midnight and said that Knudsen would accept a position as an army general. It had to be a lieutenant general, Jones insisted, to give him clout over other generals in production conflicts, and because he deserved the highest possible distinction. Hopkins agreed and persuaded Roosevelt to invite Knudsen to lunch, where the president turned on the full wattage of his personal charm. When he had finished, the ever loyal Knudsen thanked him and said he would do whatever was asked of him. Thus did the president soothe the old Dane's wounded pride and put him in a post where his expertise could perform at its best. No other civilian had ever received so high a rank; nevertheless, Jones thought Knudsen never got over the slight and was never quite happy again.[24]

Whatever his feelings, Knudsen took up his new role vigorously. Beginning on February 1, he flew 55,000 miles to visit 350 plants in more than 100 cities and towns in six months. At every plant he received a warm welcome as he strolled up and down assembly lines, sometimes stopping to show a workman how to handle a tool more smoothly and sometimes rearranging an entire production line. The men loved his unassuming manner and ability to find flaws small or large that cut efficiency. In one southern shell plant he found conveyor lines running lengthwise so that when shells reached the end of one, they had to be carried by truck to the start of the next line. Knudsen revised the lines to make one start where the other one ended and told management, "Now throw your trucks out the window." A Nash-Kelvinator plant sent him a telegram saying that propeller production had jumped by more than 50 percent. "This is a new high," it added, "a tribute to 'Knudsen month' after your visit." In such work Knudsen was at home, doing what he loved best and making an invaluable contribution.[25]

On January 16 an executive order established the new WPB and abolished SPAB, transferring its staff and records to the new agency. Eight days later OPM was dismantled as well. The press gushed approval of the new arrangement. "A Single Boss At Last," proclaimed the *Baltimore Sun*. "One-Man Control of Production Clears Way for All-Out Effort," headlined *Newsweek*. "Nelson Given the Authority to Slash Red Tape and Overrule Whims of the Brass Hats." The magazine praised Nelson as both efficient and diplomatic. Nelson had once said he noticed that people who lost their temper usually lost arguments as well, and that he strove to keep his "30 seconds longer than the other fellow." Roosevelt emphasized that Nelson's decisions on procurement and production would be final. The order expressly gave him authority over the ANMB and curbed the military's authority to make and change specifications.[26]

Nelson also inherited control of civilian production and priorities from the defunct SPAB. The new board, which included Knudsen, Jones, Stimson, Knox, Henderson, Hillman, and Hopkins, remained an advisory body without power to overrule Nelson's decisions. In effect, Nelson was viewed as the long-needed Baruch of 1918 and the American Lord Beaverbrook. Roosevelt was praised for his "unrivaled sense of timing." The new board undercut a recent scathing report on OPM by the Truman Committee and a forthcoming speech by Willkie calling for a single production head to "end debating-society methods." Hearing the news, Willkie hastily deleted the references from his speech.[27]

The president did not stop with WPB. The management-labor conference, meeting on December 17, agreed to avoid strikes or lockouts for the duration of the war and to settle disputes by peaceful means. For that purpose Roosevelt established the National War Labor Board (WLB) on January 12 to succeed the NDMB. Its twelve members—four each representing management, labor, and the public—had the power to impose arbitration and to adjust wage levels. Its jurisdiction extended to all nongovernment employees except railroad and agricultural workers and covered all issues subject to collective bargaining. In practice it worked closely with the Labor Department's Conciliation Service, which adjudicated many disputes before referring them to the board. By the war's end the new board closed 17,650 dispute cases involving 12.2 million workers and had to refer only 46 unresolved cases to the president.[28]

During January Roosevelt also received from Congress a flawed but vital piece of legislation he had long wanted. Signed on January 30, the Emergency Price Control Act empowered Henderson's dogged fight against inflation. As both he and Roosevelt quipped, it made an honest woman of him. Henderson could now fix maximum prices and control rents rather than merely jawbone them. He could also stimulate production of strategic raw materials by paying subsidies to domestic producers—a little-noticed provision that later assumed great importance. However, a major defect marred the act. Powerful lobbying by pressure groups removed wages and agricultural prices from Henderson's control. Without authority over those two sectors Henderson could hardly expect to manage inflation.[29]

Roosevelt hailed the act as "an important weapon in our armory . . . Nothing could better serve the purposes of our enemies than that we should become the victims of inflation." But he also lamented its shortcomings. Two days after Pearl Harbor, with commodity prices rising steadily, Henderson had urged a Senate committee for a strong price control law. He cited the horrors of the inflation-deflation cycle that plagued the nation during and after the last war. "All wars in this country," he added, "have produced an inflationary period followed by a deflation which paralyzed recovery." Price stabilization could be achieved only if the price administrator could manage wages and farm prices, but the unions and the powerful American Farm Bureau Federation, the stronghold of agribusiness, played a clever game of political Ping-Pong, each one emphasizing that the other was not included in the bill.[30]

To get the bill passed, Henderson had to back down on wages and accept the farm bloc's demand for price ceilings only on agricultural commodities that reached a lofty 110 percent of parity. Having already been battered and bruised in the House, the bill became in the Senate's hands "a bill to push up prices, a bill to promote inflation," according to the New York Times. Senator Alben Barkley called it "this farm-relief measure." But at least it gave the OPA some legislative teeth, and, as Roosevelt emphasized, it placed authority in the hands of a single administrator.[31]

Amid these major changes Roosevelt joined with Churchill to set up three joint boards to coordinate raw materials, munitions assignments, and shipping adjustments. He also found time to proclaim that professional baseball should continue in wartime but added that players eligible for military service should be taken. "Even if the actual quality of the teams is lowered by the greater use of older players," he observed, "this will not dampen the popularity of the sport." During the first week of February he established by executive order the War Shipping Administration (WSA), which placed control of all shipping vessels in the hands of a single administrator. Stimson tried to have the army and navy share in the responsibility, but Roosevelt insisted on keeping control in civilian hands. The new WSA relieved the Maritime Commission of these duties and soon found itself doing work of critical importance. Admiral Jerry Land, chairman of the Maritime Commission, became head of the WSA as well.[32]

Through this series of moves Roosevelt hoped not only to refine his administration of the war but to set the tone for the hard months of struggle to come. Never mind that production had faltered during the fourth quarter of 1941 as shortages and labor disputes mounted, or that the task of fighting a war on so many fronts at once while supplying the Allies at the same time was a stupendous one. All hands were now on deck and ready to do their duty. Authority had been granted to key managers to expedite the production process, and much was expected of the new arrangements. Not even an occasional dose of hard reality could dampen the president's belief in the nation's ability to perform miracles.

A few days after the State of the Union speech Nelson met again with Roosevelt, Churchill, Beaverbrook, Hopkins, and Knudsen to review production possibilities. Churchill, dressed in his siren suit that reminded Nelson of the overalls Sears sold in great quantities to mechanics, sat puffing nonstop on his favorite mammoth cigars. At one point Beaverbrook congratulated Roosevelt on the excellent state of the nation's synthetic rubber situation. Nelson objected at once, saying that stockpiles were much lower than Beaverbrook imagined and the synthetic rubber program was barely in its infancy. "I think we are going to be in terrible straits before another year rolls round," he warned.[33]

"Well, that's an interesting difference of opinion," said Roosevelt. "Who's right?"

After Nelson offered a mass of data, an astonished and annoyed Beaverbrook said, "Well, perhaps I was misinformed about rubber, but I'm glad I have a right to be happy about the 100-octane gasoline situation. That is, after all, our biggest need for the kind of air warfare that we must develop . . . It looks to me as if your new 100-octane plants will save the day for us all." Not so, countered Nelson. "We are in terrible shape on 100-octane gasoline, and I think you ought to know that unless we do a lot better than we are doing now, the Allies are going to be in a lot of trouble."

Roosevelt looked quizzically at them both but said nothing. A smiling Churchill settled deeper into his easy chair beneath a cloud of smoke and said, "You aren't doing as well as you thought you were, are you, Franklin?"

*   *   *

DURING THE FIRST dreary months of America's war, bad news continued to flow into Washington. The Germans, stalled in their assault on Leningrad and Moscow, shifted fronts and launched an offensive toward the Crimea in the south. In the Pacific the Japanese stunned everyone with the strength and efficiency of their offensive. Guam was overwhelmed in half an hour, and Wake Island fell despite heroic resistance by the small contingent of 500 marines and some construction workers. In the Philippines the Japanese knocked out most of the American planes on the ground while troops began landing at Luzon. In China, Shanghai offered little resistance compared to Hong Kong, but both were bludgeoned into surrender. As Japanese troops poured into Malaya, the empire gained control of the sea and air by sinking the only Allied battleship and battle cruiser in the region west of Hawaii, the *Prince of Wales* and *Repulse*. By New Year's Day columns of Japanese troops were converging on Singapore; they also advanced in Burma and landed in Java. On February 15 Singapore, once thought to be invincible, surrendered.[34]

The news was demoralizing to both Americans and the British, and seemed to get worse every day. The three great strongholds of Western presence in the Far East, Hong Kong, Singapore, and Manila, all fell to the Japanese by mid-February. In the Philippines American and native troops fought a heroic but losing battle against overwhelming odds. The crippled Pacific Fleet was patching its wounds and helpless to offer any support. As the Japanese web spread across the region, Australia braced for the worst, aware that neither Great Britain nor the United States was in position to offer much help. In North Africa, a sharp counterattack by General Erwin Rommel reversed recent British gains and sent them reeling backward to Tobruk, where they languished for months.[35]

Still the Japanese pressed onward. As early as mid-January they held a firm grip on northern Borneo and the northeast tip of Celebes. By seizing Rabaul in New Britain and Bougainville in the Solomon Islands, they threatened the vital sea route between the United States and Australia. Within another six weeks the Japanese occupied the capitals of both Borneo and Celebes, gained control of southern Sumatra, and occupied both Timor and Bali, thereby isolating Java. The Dutch East Indies were lost. On February 26 Japanese planes sank an American carrier headed for Java with thirty-five planes aboard. During the next three days the first major sea battle raged in which superior Japanese forces utterly crushed a combined British and Dutch fleet that included one American ship. The Battle of the Java Sea proved to be the worst Allied naval defeat of the war and gave the Japanese undisputed control of the southwest Pacific. A week earlier, the same carrier force that had struck Pearl Harbor delivered a similar blow to Port Darwin on Australia's

northern coast, inflicting hundreds of casualties while sinking eleven transports, supply ships, and an American destroyer.[36]

In January the war came to American shores when German submarines
began prowling the Eastern Seaboard in search of tankers and merchant
ships. Their presence not only alarmed Americans but threatened to disrupt
the flow of supplies headed overseas, as well as shipments of crude oil to refineries on the coast and heating oil to the Northeast. Within two months, operating at night using the light cast by large American cities from New York to
Miami, they sank 132 ships against wholly inadequate defenses. It was, said
historian Samuel Eliot Morison, "as much a national disaster as if saboteurs
had destroyed half a dozen of our biggest war plants."[37]

Ships moved along the coast without lights but were outlined against the
backdrop of bright coastal cities, which outraged Morison. "Miami and its
luxurious suburbs," he wrote acidly, "threw up six miles of neon-light glow,
against which the southbound shipping that hugged the reefs to avoid the
Gulf Stream was silhouetted. Ships were sunk and seamen drowned in order
that the citizenry might enjoy business and pleasure as usual." As the carnage
grew worse, Americans were treated to the sight of oil-slicked flotsam, equipment, and bodies washing ashore along the coast. Given the fact that nearly
everything moved by sea in this global war, nothing posed a graver threat to
the war effort than the submarine attacks in the Atlantic and along the coast.[38]

The American military had not witnessed such dark days since the winter
at Valley Forge and that of 1862–63 following the Union rout at Fredericks-
burg. American morale, so filled with rage and pledges of unity after Pearl
Harbor, plummeted with the news of each defeat. For the first time, or so it
seemed, American forces were being whipped by what many if not most
Americans regarded as an inferior people. The bravado so often expressed
earlier about disposing of the Japanese quickly turned to frustration and bewilderment over how this could happen. The thin veneer of unity behind the
war effort gave way to querulous demands for explanations, a search for scapegoats, and a resurgence of old differences. Many former isolationists demanded to know why the European war had priority when American boys in
the Pacific so desperately needed the supplies and equipment going to England and, of all places, the Soviet Union.[39]

Polls showed a sharp drop in Roosevelt's popularity among both the press
and the public. General Hugh Johnson, another New Deal defector turned
conservative critic, blamed Hopkins and his "palace janissariat" for the flaws
in war production and grumbled that nobody had elected him to any office.
Through all the bluster and whining Roosevelt remained a pillar of determination. He knew the war would be long and hard, and that it would not go
well for some time. He also realized that the American people were impa-

tient, but he believed ardently in their essential goodness and willingness to do whatever was needed to achieve victory. On Washington's Birthday he delivered a fireside address, having asked the American people in advance to spread a map of the world before them as they listened so they could locate the unfamiliar places he would be mentioning. The request triggered a bonanza in map sales throughout the country. When he went on the air at 10:00 P.M., more than 61 million Americans tuned in their radios, nearly 80 percent of the nation's entire adult audience.[40]

After invoking the ordeal of George Washington and the Continental Army, the president declared, "This war is a new kind of war . . . not only in its methods and weapons but also in its geography. It is warfare in terms of every continent, every island, every sea, every air lane in the world." Everything had to travel vast distances, which is why the enemy sought to isolate the Allies from each other. He explained what each of America's allies was doing to help the cause, and what would happen if American aid no longer reached them. American ships traveled four crucial routes: the North Atlantic, South Atlantic, Indian Ocean, and South Pacific. They carried troops and munitions outward and returned with critical raw materials. Roosevelt dispelled the more outrageous rumors about losses at Pearl Harbor and explained why the Japanese offensive could not have been stopped even if the American fleet had remained intact.[41]

"Your Government has unmistakable confidence in your ability to hear the worst, without flinching or losing heart," Roosevelt stressed. The losses would continue until the United States tipped the balance in "our special task of production." The enemy was very near their peak in output, while the United States had only begun to utilize its full productive capacity. For that purpose he asked three things of Americans: Do not stop work even for a single day; do not demand special gains or privileges or advantages for any one group or occupation; and willingly give up conveniences and modify routines and habits when asked to do so. Enemy propagandists described Americans as weaklings and playboys, he said, pausing for emphasis.

> Let them repeat that now!
> Let them tell that to General MacArthur and his men.
> Let them tell that to the sailors who today are hitting hard in the far waters of the Pacific.
> Let them tell that to the boys in the Flying Fortresses.
> Let them tell that to the Marines!

In closing he outlined the sacrifices being made by other peoples, such as the Dutch and Chinese, and recalled again those made by Washington and his men. He closed with words written by Tom Paine that Washington had ordered read to all his troops: "Tyranny, like hell, is not easily conquered; yet we have this consolation with us, that the harder the sacrifice, the more glorious the triumph."

The talk was a brilliant success and earned wide praise from the media and listeners alike. Sam Rosenman thought it even more effective than the first fireside chat back in the gloomy days of 1933. Some friends urged Roosevelt to give such chats more often, but he feared rightly that too many talks would undercut their effectiveness. Moreover, preparing each one required four or five days of long hours and tough work, time that he could ill afford.[42]

"The speeches as finally delivered were his—and his alone—no matter who the collaborators were," emphasized Rosenman, who worked on the drafts along with Robert Sherwood and sometimes Hopkins. "He had gone over every point, every word, time and again. He had studied, reviewed, and read aloud each draft, and had changed it again and again . . . The preparation of some of the speeches or messages took as many as ten days, and very few took less than three . . . Sometimes a speech went through as many as twelve or thirteen drafts before the President was finally satisfied."[43]

Although the reaction to the speech pleased him, Roosevelt held no illusions about how long the impact would last. In the long run only victories would win real approval, and victories depended on production. During the winter of 1942 military victories were not likely, which put the burden on the nation's ability to crank out the wherewithal of war. To lighten the intolerable load he carried, Roosevelt resorted as always to his sense of humor. He liked to repeat to friends Elmer Davis's comment on the fireside chat: "Some people want the United States to win so long as England loses. Some people want the United States to win so long as Russia loses. And some people want the United States to win so long as Roosevelt loses."[44]

ALTHOUGH THE RADIO and papers talked endlessly about production having a czar at last, Nelson felt like anything but a dictator. The task before him was as clear as it was gigantic: convert the economy to a full wartime basis. The obvious starting point was the automobile industry, which was ordered on January 29 to cease all production of civilian cars and trucks. The huge amounts of steel and other strategic materials it consumed were desperately needed elsewhere, as was the industry's enormous productive capacity. Nelson set up a WPB office in Detroit to oversee the conversion process. Ernest Kanzler, a former Ford executive, took charge of the work. The 450,000 cars in company inventories and the 250,000 still on assembly lines were not to be sold through dealers but rationed out to high-priority users such as doctors and police.[45]

Nelson asked the existing staffs of SPAB and OPM to remain while the organization sorted itself out. In effect WPB absorbed the two other agencies with only a few major changes. Knudsen was gone, but the other members of the advisory boards remained; the key difference was that Nelson could make decisions with or without their advice. Hillman, who learned of the new agency through the newspaper, lost his status as codirector. He remained head of the Labor Division, and there was talk of creating a new manpower agency with Hillman at its head. However, two other entities, the Labor Department and the United States Employment Service, the latter part of Paul McNutt's Federal Security Agency (FSA), fell at once into a dispute over who should have charge of mobilizing the civilian workforce.[46]

By January 21 Nelson had WPB's organization in place. The Production Division, under William Harrison of AT&T, carried over from OPM its mission of working with the military to expand munitions production. The Division of Industry Operations, headed by James Knowlson of Stewart-Warner, emerged as a crucial component with three major functions. It would direct the conversion of industry to war production while maintaining adequate capacity for civilian needs, direct and control the flow of raw materials and equipment to manufacturers, and oversee all the industry branches and their advisory committees—giving them a clear point of contact with WPB. Eventually this new division centralized control over industry to an unprecedented degree.[47]

The Materials Division under Bill Batt continued to oversee the fourteen commodity branches as it had in OPM. Leon Henderson's Civilian Supply Division gradually lost ground as the war effort ramped up. So did Hillman's Labor Division, thanks in large part to the growing squabble over who had authority over what sectors of manpower. Stacy May remained in charge of the Statistics Division and O'Brian of the Legal Division. The Purchasing Division was left with little of substance to do. Nelson also created a new Planning Committee chaired by Bob Nathan, the brilliant statistician who had worked for the evolving agencies since NDAC. Its main job was long-range planning to help shape a feasible, balanced production program. Joining Nathan on the committee were economist Thomas C. Blaisdell Jr., and Fred Searls Jr., a conservative mining engineer who served as a consultant for the Ordnance Department. All three men were tough-minded professionals who knew their way around the corridors of Washington.[48]

Nelson conceded that this arrangement was far from perfect but insisted that "we had to get going fast and did not have the time to figure out and put

together an ideal organization." Time was still the enemy, as it had been before Pearl Harbor, and compromises would have to be made. For the first
time someone was in a position to dictate, but Nelson was at heart a diplomat
rather than a dictator. In practice he could accomplish little without support
from the Army and Navy departments, which would not hesitate to run crying to Roosevelt over decisions they opposed. Congress too wanted a voice in
the process. Already two committees were looking over Nelson's shoulder.
Truman's group had earlier launched an investigation into the use of dollar-
a-year men and the conflicts of interest they posed. A House committee
chaired by John H. Tolan of California was poking around the manpower
question.[49]

No illusions clouded Nelson's view of his task. "It wasn't up to me or to
WPB to *tell* industry how to do its job," he explained; "it was our function to
show industry what had to be done, and then to do everything in our power
to enable industry to do it . . . We had to get our nation's tremendous productive machine harnessed . . . but we had to do it *within the framework of
American tradition*. Merely to inflict defeat on our enemies was not enough.
We had to do it *in our own way*." Democracy could not use the methods of
tyrants.[50]

Procurement offered a major challenge to this approach. It had long been a
tug-of-war among agencies, and between them and the military, which insisted that it had—and should have—absolute control over the process for its
needs. Critics complained that the army and navy, by placing all contracts for
and doing the actual buying of military goods, controlled the process, and
with it the economy as well. None of the earlier agencies had the power to
interfere with this arrangement; now it appeared that Nelson did have the
authority to take over or at least oversee both functions. He agreed with
the widespread criticism of the existing system. Later he would write that
"the cause of almost all these disputes was perfectly simple: the Army always
wished to assume greater control over war production and civilian economy
than the War Production Board deemed it prudent for it to have."[51]

From the outset Roosevelt emphasized his concern that in wartime the
military tended to acquire too much power and that it was vital to keep control of the economy in civilian hands. But another voice had Nelson's ear as
well. On the evening of his very first day in the WPB Nelson had dinner with
Baruch, whom he was to see often in the coming weeks. Wednesday night
dinners became a ritual at which Baruch listened sympathetically and offered
advice on whatever problems Nelson brought to him. Nelson had not been
Baruch's first choice to head WPB; he had suggested to Roosevelt five other
names headed by Bill Douglas and James F. Byrnes. Once Nelson had been
named, however, Baruch was as quick to offer his aid and comfort as Nelson

THE WINNING TEAM: The president and his cabinet in 1945. From left: Claude Wickard (agriculture), Frances Perkins (labor), Henry Wallace (commerce), unidentified, Harold Ickes (interior), unidentified but possibly James Forrestal (navy), Henry Stimson (army), Edward R. Stettinius (state), Franklin Roosevelt, Henry Morgenthau (treasury), Francis Biddle (attorney general), unidentified but possibly Frank Comerford Walker (postmaster general). (*Harry S. Truman Library*)

MAJOR PLAYERS: Clockwise from top left: THE SAGE. Bernard Baruch, whose shadow and reputation loomed over the entire war effort. THE QUINTESSENTIAL OLD PRO. The aristocratic Henry Stimson. THE LIGHT THAT FAILED. Donald Nelson, the man whose reputation rose and fell in painful trajectories. THE ROOSEVELT LOYALIST. Sidney Hillman, the labor leader who remained steadfastly loyal to the president. (*Library of Congress*)

LOST EXPERTISE: (Top) Dorothea Lange took this picture of a greenhouse at a nursery in San Leandro, California, operated by Japanese Americans before their relocation. (*National Archives*) (Bottom) Japanese Americans file aboard a train for relocation in April 1942. (*National Archives*)

BRITAIN BOUND: (Top) Two lines of Vengeance bombers being built for the RAF at Vultee's Downey, California, plant. (*National Archives*) (Bottom) Work proceeds on A-20 attack bombers at the Douglas Aircraft plant in Long Beach, California. Many of these bombers also went to the British. (*FDR Library*)

COMING TOGETHER: (Top) A mating operation on a C-87 transport plane just before it reaches the pre-assembly line at Consolidated's Fort Worth plant. (*Library of Congress*) (Bottom) Workers assemble a B-24 Liberator bomber at Consolidated's Fort Worth plant. (*Library of Congress*)

THE SUM OF THE PARTS: (Top) A completed B-17 bomber gets a going over by inspectors prior to flight tests at the Douglas Long Beach plant. (*FDR Library*) (Bottom) The overflowing stockroom of the Douglas Aircraft Company at Long Beach. (*FDR Library*)

WOMEN AT WORK: (Top) Two women work inside the cramped space of a B-24 section. (*Library of Congress*) (Bottom) A group of women welders pause long enough to pose for a picture. (*National Archives*)

APPRENTICES: (Top) Oyida Peaks practices riveting as part of her NYA training to become a mechanic at the Naval Air Base in Corpus Christi, Texas. (*Library of Congress*) (Bottom) A group of female trainees learn the work behind protective goggles. (*National Archives*)

FIND YOUR WAR JOB
In Industry – Agriculture – Business

This poster exhorts workers, especially women, to find their place in the war production effort. (*Library of Congress*)

Ansel Adams captured this scene of farm workers at the Manzanar War Relocation Center in California, one of the sites housing dispossessed Japanese Americans. Mt. Williamson is in the background. (*Library of Congress*)

STILL LIFE: A rare view of Richmond Shipyard No. 3 at rest. From left to center, the forge shop, machine shop, general warehouse, and riggers loft/paint shop/sheet metal shop. Five ship basins are to the right. (*Library of Congress*)

UGLY DUCKLING: A Liberty ship under construction, 1942. (*Library of Congress*)

MASTER BUILDER: The smiling, ever restless countenance of Henry J. Kaiser. (*Kaiser Permanente*)

FAMILY BUSINESS: Andrew Jackson Higgins lays out plans with his four sons, (from left) Ed, Andrew Jr., Andrew Sr., Frank, and Roland. (*Courtesy Dawn Higgins Murphy*)

PUSHING THE WORK: A catchy slogan (THE GUY WHO RELAXES IS HELPING THE AXIS!) exhorts Higgins workers to turn out more landing craft. (*Courtesy Dawn Higgins Murphy*)

SERIOUS WORKERS: (Top) These two men worked fifteen hours each day, seven days a week, to produce 18,000 steel flanges for war equipment in eighteen months. (*FDR Library*) DOING THEIR PART: (Bottom) Two grandmothers maintain the production schedule at the La Roe family shop in Eustis, Florida. (*FDR Library*)

LUNCH BREAK: (Top) Work on a nearly completed 37mm antiaircraft gun carriage pauses at a Pennsylvania plant while workers snatch a quick meal from the company lunch cart. (*FDR Library*) AT DAY'S END: (Bottom) The La Roe family of Eustis, Florida, enjoys some leisure time after a long day's work in the family shop. From left: Mrs. La Roe, her granddaughter, Clarence La Roe's son Eugene, and Mr. La Roe. (*FDR Library*)

ALL ABOARD: (Top left) Franklin Roosevelt and his secretary, Grace Tully, settle into their seat during the president's tour of defense and military facilities in September 1942. (*FDR Library*) THE GOOD SOLDIER: (Top right) William Knudsen in his military garb. (Automobile *magazine*) CLASHING AMBITIONS: (Bottom left) Edward R. Stettinius, the man of many positions and master of none. (*Library of Congress*) (Bottom right) The ambitious Paul McNutt mulls matters over (*Library of Congress*)

DELIVERING THE GOODS: (Top left) Cargo ships wait to be loaded with war materials. (*National Archives*) (Top right) A line of landing ships await their cargo of tanks at a French naval base in Tunisia just before the invasion of Sicily, July 1943. (*National Archives*) (Bottom left) A trainload of armored trucks on their way to the West Coast for shipment. (*Union Pacific Museum*) (Bottom right) The Manitowoc Company, in Wisconsin, launches a new submarine. (*National Archives*)

THE HOME FRONT: (Top left) Price controls make their presence felt. (*FDR Library*) (Top right) People wait in line to get their ration of sugar. (*National Archives*) (Bottom) Carloads of scrap metal await their journey to an open-hearth furnace at a steel mill in Brackenridge, Pennsylvania. The overhead magnet deposited the steel in a loader for the trip. (*Library of Congress*)

was eager to receive it. The WPB, after all, was the closest Roosevelt had yet come to emulating the model of the WIB.[52]

One of Baruch's earlier admonitions had stuck with Nelson. Civilians should never sign Army contracts, he had warned; it should be done only by authorized contracting officers. "This advice sank into and anchored itself in my mind," Nelson recalled, "and I never deviated from it." The contracting power gave whoever held it immense influence over the economy; it was the force that set the economic machine in motion. Both the House and Senate committees made it clear that they wanted to see procurement handled by one central agency under civilian control. Nelson had no doubt that the president and Congress would have supported such an arrangement and provided any necessary legislation, but after mulling the matter over he thought it the wrong thing to do.[53]

To create a separate buying organization, Nelson figured, would take at least six weeks, probably much longer. He didn't have six weeks to spare. The cry everywhere was for speed, fast action, quick response to needs. Every day lost meant not simply delays in production but more American lives lost. And how would civilians do at the crucial job of inspecting military equipment that had been bought? Contracting also involved the purchasing agency in questions of design and specifications, which would involve them in strategic issues. "It was never part of my job," insisted Nelson, ". . . to tell the military people what they wanted in the way of weapons. But if I had taken over the production function in its entirety I would have come very close to having such a job."[54]

Even if the changeover could have occurred quickly, Nelson would also have to wade into the legal thicket involved in transferring the contracting power from military agencies that had long held it. The military's procurement authority rested on thousands of statutory provisions, court rulings, decisions by the comptroller general, and a mountain of precedents, all of which would have to be reversed. Even assuming that Congress would enact the necessary legislation, how long would it take to pass and be implemented? If the military challenged the process, months could be squandered in court proceedings. An executive order by the president would have to be challenged because legally a military officer who signed a contract became responsible for it and could not waive that responsibility, and there were thousands of such contracts.[55]

Nelson concluded that his only realistic option was to follow Baruch's admonition and leave contracting with the military. It was his first major decision, and one that probably could not have been otherwise in practical terms. "I have gone even to the point of being over-zealous in seeing that the contract powers were kept within the Army and Navy," he told the Truman

Committee. But doing so gave away part of the authority vested in his new position and, as Bruce Catton observed, it was "to fly up and hit him in the face, just the same, and in the end it had a profound effect on the shape of events." Nelson never doubted that he had made the right choice. "If I had the same decision to make over again," he said, "I would do exactly the same thing."[56]

Critics pounced on his position. No one was more unsparing than Eliot Janeway, who thought Nelson had given away the store. "Nelson announced immediately that he had no intention of imposing a system of mandatory priorities upon the economy," he wrote. "Instead he compounded the confusion he was appointed to bring under control. He delegated the Presidential power vested in him over military priorities to the Army-Navy Munitions Board, which he resented and opposed . . . The military's use of this power quickly demonstrated their own need of civilian control . . . The enormity of this initial blunder of Nelson's is magnified by his own insistence that he understood he was committing it." A trio of experts added after the war that surrendering this authority was "a deliberate, conscious policy which could have been formulated only as a result of the failure to grasp the fundamental importance of the power . . . The heart of the control problem is in the contracting function."[57]

THE MILITARY DID have civilian oversight, of course, in the form of the president as commander-in-chief and the secretaries of War and Navy, but the president had too much else to do and the secretaries became by the very nature of their duties advocates for their services. Although both branches tended to resent civilian influence, the navy grew more sensitive to its needs in large part because Knox and Forrestal fought hard to maintain its prerogatives. Stimson and Patterson were both all-outers who argued that the army should have anything and everything it wanted to do its job, and nothing should stand in the way. Unfortunately, neither service was even remotely prepared to handle the enormous procurement requirements suddenly thrust on it after Pearl Harbor. Like the civilian agencies, the military required a drastic organizational overhaul.[58]

No one recognized the army's obsolete organization more clearly than George Marshall. He had under him no less than 30 major and 350 smaller commands, and some sixty-one officers had direct access to him. Within hours after Pearl Harbor he launched a whirlwind campaign for what he called "a drastically complete change, wiping out Civil War institutions" and the time-encrusted prerogatives of many offices and officers who had built fiefdoms over the years. Using a core of younger officers headed by General

Joseph T. McNarney, he set them to devising a new structure that would be lean and efficient, give him more time for strategic planning, and eliminate the maze of red tape that delayed decisions interminably. The resulting plan could hardly have been more drastic. It downgraded the General Staff divisions and chiefs of services and abolished General Headquarters entirely. A host of officers would lose their prerogatives and power over their domains.[59]

The plan was executed efficiently before opposition to it could coalesce. After winning approval from Stimson and Roosevelt, who signed the executive order on February 28, the most drastic reorganization of the army since the days of Elihu Root went into effect on March 9. Three commands replaced the myriad of agencies and commands: the Army Ground Forces, the Army Air Forces, and the Army Services of Supply, later renamed Army Service Forces (ASF). Except for the development and procurement of aviation equipment, which the Air Forces handled, the Services of Supply took charge of all procurement. To head it, Marshall named General Brehon Somervell. It was an inspired if risky choice. An engineer with a reputation for being as ruthless as he was efficient, Somervell was a tough, unyielding officer of the sort Marshall needed for a difficult and thankless job. Despite his abrasive personality and tendency toward empire building, Somervell suited Marshall's needs well. "He was efficient," the general said later; "he shook the cobwebs out of their pants."[60]

Born in Little Rock, Arkansas, the son of a doctor and grandson of a wealthy Tennessee planter, Somervell showed his spirited personality in high school, where the yearbook labeled him "The Irrepressible One" and declared him to be "about the liveliest one we have come across lately and no one knows what he is going to do next." What he did next was gain entry to the West Point class of 1914. For four years he remained near the top of his class in every major area of study as well as excelling in horsemanship, marksmanship, and swordsmanship. He finished sixth in a class of 107, with a final fitness report that described him as "excellent as far as general abilities for an officer in the army," and received a commission in the Corps of Engineers.[61]

After his graduation Somervell pursued a varied and unusual career. He served in France during the World War, then did river-navigation survey work for the League of Nations and an economic survey for the Turkish government. Between these assignments he served on river-and-harbor boards in New York and Washington before becoming president of the Mississippi River Commission. Much of his energy went toward flood-control projects. He directed work on the controversial Florida Ship Canal but shifted career gears in 1936 by becoming a WPA administrator in New York. From this experience he learned something of management-labor relations as well as the nature of the political game as played outside the military. He also acquired a reputation as a first-rate manager. Late in 1940 he took charge of the army's Construction Division and spent a year racked with controversies overhauling its operation and overseeing a variety of projects, including the army's new Pentagon building. Few officers brought so varied a résumé to their next assignment.[62]

Somervell had a temper, and his style was to run roughshod over those who got in his way. He had no qualms about dumping officers who failed to perform, and he pursued his objectives relentlessly. He rejoiced in the motto "We do the impossible immediately. The miraculous takes a little longer" and reveled in driving through projects where time and results mattered more than costs. Despite his gift for making enemies, he knew how to manage large systems effectively and put together a solid staff. While the Purchasing Division received the most attention, Somervell created an innovative and controversial new Control Division that sought to impose business practices on supply operations. Staffed chiefly with civilian management experts, its drive for standardizing and simplifying procedures and forms resulted in the elimination of 2,900 reports and records within a year. It also improved statistical analysis, long a glaring weakness in the army, and provided Somervell with a useful management tool in the form of a monthly progress report.[63]

The reorganization put Somervell in charge of the army's entire machinery for procurement, economic mobilization, and supply. The Army Supply Program (ASP) received top priority and gradually developed a complex organization for equipping and supplying the army. It formulated immediate and long-term material needs and translated them into programs, contracts, production schedules, procurement deliveries, and their distribution to troops in the field. ASP, and therefore Somervell, became the army's authoritative voice for requirements and procurement. Its statements were used by Congress and by the agencies charged with establishing production schedules, creating priorities, determining raw material requirements, and allocating materials. It was also Somervell's baby. In a lengthy January memo, he had advocated its creation two months before the reorganization handed him the opportunity to realize it.[64]

Somervell struggled to give technical services an organization that satisfied him. The Ordnance Department, Quartermaster and Signal Corps, Engineers Corps, and other bureaus had long histories, close ties to the president and Congress, and their own budgets that together accounted for half the War Department's appropriations. Somervell managed to move construction from Ordnance to the Engineers and to set up a new bureau, the Transportation Corps, but he could not budge their almost haphazard relationships to one another. Nor could he harness the independence of the air force, which was determined to establish itself as a separate service. The air force had developed its own supply system that differed sharply from those of the technical services. It was expanding rapidly and would consume a third of the War Department's total budget by the war's end.[65]

The navy also underwent a major reorganization by March. Guided largely by Forrestal, the new arrangement centered supply responsibilities in the Office of Procurement and Material (OP&M). Forrestal also brought greater unity to the navy's inspection system and reformed its contracting system. The Procurement Branch of OP&M excelled under the direction of Frank M. Folsom, who had been a Nelson assistant at WPB. Over time it managed to lower prices for the goods it acquired but never succeeded in creating an effective system of inventory control. Admiral Samuel M. Robinson, head of OP&M, proved to be a smooth, capable leader with a far more genial style that that of Somervell. However, it was Forrestal who drove the revamping of the navy's supply system even as he strengthened civilian control of the Navy Department.[66]

On March 12, three days after the approval of Marshall's reorganization plan, Nelson signed an agreement with the War Department defining the relationship between it and WPB. A similar agreement with the navy followed on April 22, and together the two set the ground rules for procurement. What Nelson called "a fundamental concept" stated that "the war supply organizations should be viewed by all participants as a single integrated system operating under the general direction of the Chairman of the War Production Board in a unified effort to win the war and not as a group of autonomous or semiautonomous organizations acting in mere liaison with one another." The agreement also contained lists of specific duties that each agency was to perform with regard to facilities, priorities, materials, and production. It was a noble statement but could not possibly cover all the jurisdictional disputes and overlaps that would arise in the coming months. Nevertheless, Nelson told the Truman Committee in April that the War Department agreement was "the Magna Carta of our operation."[67]

Three veterans of the WPB who later wrote a detailed study of wartime production controls concluded that Nelson's two agreements with the military amounted to "specific abdication of direct authority over military procurement . . . Following this concordat, the military was relatively unrestrained in its placement of contracts."[68]

The agreement did not move Somervell, who steadfastly refused to acknowledge any degree of subordination to the WPB and worked tirelessly to extend his own jurisdiction at the WPB's expense. Nor did it include the ANMB, which was undergoing its own transformation. Wall Street banker Ferdinand Eberstadt, who had been asked to investigate the activities of ANMB in the fall of 1941, became the board's chairman on December 7 and tackled the question of how it fit into the overall mobilization scheme. A staunch defender of the military, Eberstadt viewed his role as being an advocate for its demands before the civilian agencies. A revision of ANMB's authority, approved by Roosevelt on February 21 at Eberstadt's suggestion, gave it power to coordinate the procurement plans of the two services, locate bottlenecks in the production of military items, and suggest solutions for them.[69]

However, the revision also required ANMB to report to the chairman of WPB and remain subject to his orders, directives, and instructions. In effect the ANMB, like the earlier civilian boards, had administrative duties but no powers. Nelson remedied that shortcoming by giving away another part of his own authority. He delegated to ANMB priority powers over contracts of the army, the navy, the Maritime Commission, and foreign governments under the Lend-Lease Act. James Knowlson persuaded Nelson to do this on the conviction that WPB lacked the staff and organization to perform this function. Within a short time experience revealed an enormous amount of overlap, duplication, and confusion between the functions of WPB and ANMB. The stage had been set for precisely the kinds of conflicts and infighting that Nelson had hoped to avoid.[70]

Nelson welcomed debate and discussion within WPB. As he explained to the Truman Committee, he had "purposely set up the War Production Board so that there are all shades of opinion in it . . . from businessmen who are conservative, businessmen who are liberal, professors, economists, public servants, people of all kinds, because this job of conversion, this job of shutting off civilian production is not an easy thing, sir, nor is it to be toyed with lightly . . . Only time will tell, and only history can record, whether we have been too slow or too rapid."[71]

Diversity of views helped Nelson formulate policy. What he did not grasp at first was the extent to which everything he tried to do lay at the mercy of the dynamics within and among agencies. He had a firm understanding of the big picture but not of the countless small forces that served to undermine the best of intentions in a bureaucracy. Their restless, unceasing presence was about to impose some harsh lessons on him.

CHAPTER 14

A SEA OF TROUBLES

From one great crisis we have lunged into another. The 1941 crisis of production and materials has been succeeded by the 1942 crisis of shipping, and the most urgent problem facing the nation today is to move the war goods that are now being produced faster than ships can be built to transport them.

—FORTUNE[1]

When we finished one of these beautiful ships, it was inspiring and thrilling. Once it . . . withstood the test of water your whole body thrilled because you'd done something worthwhile.

—WOMAN WORKER IN PORTLAND, OREGON[2]

We are in a war of transportation, primarily water transportation—a war of ships.

—ADMIRAL JERRY LAND[3]

EUGENIO GALLEGO OF HOUSTON, Texas, couldn't decide whether he was just plain lucky or unlucky. As a crewman on a tanker he had been torpedoed twice in the space of three weeks, but he survived both sinkings. His second ship had been heading south when struck at 3:45 A.M. on a beautiful night. Although conceding that his wife might be worried about him after this second brush with death, he refused to be intimidated. "You get, you get," he said. "I sign on again."[4]

"I was in my bunk," said George W. Bill, the chief mate on the ship. He had just checked his watch when a terrific shock jolted the ship like an earthquake, followed by a flash of flame. Bill was fully dressed except for his shoes; the crews slept with their clothes on these days. "We expected shells, or at least another torpedo," he said, "but that was all. The men were fine. We got all four boats away. Two men were lost—an assistant engineer and a wiper, trapped below. That's the most dangerous part of the ship when it happens. There was an oiler down there who got out somehow. How, I don't know."

The oiler, twenty-eight-year-old Tony Barboza of Fall River, Massachusetts, had been working thirty-three iron steps below the main deck when he heard a buzzing sound and then felt a terrible shock. "You don't hear an explosion," he said. "Everything sort of rushes in and squeezes you. The lights went out. In a couple of seconds I was up to my knees in water and fuel oil from the bunker."

Barboza groped his way to the steps and managed to climb one flight before losing his sense of direction in the darkness. He wandered in a blind alley behind the boilers, looking for some handhold to resist the swirling water pouring in. "The water really washed me out," he said. "It raised me up to a short ladder I couldn't have reached otherwise, and I squeezed through a place between the corner of the boiler and the footwalk grating. The hole wasn't nearly as big as me."

Only after getting pulled aboard a lifeboat did Barboza realize that he had cut himself badly in forcing his way through the opening. He too was ready to sign on again. George Bill had already done so after saying good-bye once again to his wife and two children in Yonkers. "It's his job," said his wife with a resigned shrug. "I can't tell him what to do." Bill knew the sea and its risks; he was a navy veteran. He also knew that he was luckier than most in surviving. In March 1942 Sydney Wayland was the second mate standing watch when his tanker was hit. He sounded the alarm, all four boats were lowered, and the crew rushed to them. But the weather was fierce and a near-gale wind was blowing. The boats on the weather side of the ship got crushed by the sea. Eighteen men made it off the ship, fourteen of them in one boat. They were barely a hundred yards from the tanker when she sank in a bowl of flames.

With the seas running thirty to forty feet high, the survivors got out a sea anchor to keep the boat headed into the waves. "Like Coney Island, isn't it?" Wayland yelled to the captain as the boat coasted down a roller. He was lucky in being warmly dressed because he had been on watch; most of the others had only shirts and trousers in the bitter cold. Sparks, the young radioman who had chosen to send an SOS instead of throwing on more clothes, was the first to die. "He was only a boy," said Wayland. "He went quietly to sleep and never woke up again." The boat drifted for five days, and one by one the men drifted slowly into the torpor that precedes death by exposure. At first the survivors tried to hoist the dead overboard, but soon they lacked the strength to do even that. The most they could do was bail desperately.

By the fifth day Wayland was the only man left alive. He grew light-headed and was preparing for his fatal sleep when the rescue boat found him. The crew checked quickly for any other survivors. Finding none and fearing a submarine attack, they left the boat of corpses and moved away with a full head of steam. Later Wayland learned that the other boat with four men had been found with only one man still alive; he died aboard the ship that picked him up.

These were tough men, the tanker crews. They manned ships that were prime targets and sitting ducks, and they rarely got to fight back. Nobody would give them medals or even praise in most cases, yet they kept coming back to the work. But Wayland did not. A naturalized American who hailed from Southampton, England, he had had enough of tanker duty. Instead he joined the navy.

DURING 1941 GERMAN U-boats sank 432 ships, slightly fewer than in 1940, sending more than 2,000 tons of capacity to the bottom, while losing 35 of their submarines. Having failed to push submarine construction early in the war, the Germans were by 1941 rushing expansion of the fleet. Once the United States entered the war, the need grew even more urgent as the American East Coast lay exposed and virtually unprotected. During the first five months of 1942 the U-boats sank 362 Allied merchant ships, exceeding their entire total for the previous year. In that same period the overstretched navy managed to sink only one submarine and a Coast Guard cutter sank another one. The submarines were hunting in what the Germans called "wolf packs," a tactic that proved lethally effective. By October 1942 Admiral Karl Dönitz had 196 front-line boats at his command, and German shipyards were turning out 20 more every month. In the last six months of 1942 the Allies lost a staggering 575 ships totaling 3 million tons to the U-boats. Altogether the Allies had since 1939 lost 14 million tons of merchant shipping to all causes and had replaced less than half of it.[5]

Nelson called it "a life-or-death race with destruction." During the first days of the war, naval and merchant ships emerged as the front rank of the most desperately needed equipment. Planes, tanks, and other goods would be of little use unless the means existed to get them safely across the oceans. Nor could they receive needed fuel if the supply of crude oil to northeastern refineries was cut off. As the sinkings from submarine attacks mounted, the demand soared for more tankers and merchant ships to replace the losses. So did the navy's need for warships to fight the submarines, which put the two classes of vessels in competition for raw materials. Already the shortages had begun to mount; by February petroleum, sugar, and coffee were in short supply because ships were lacking to deliver them. Half a dozen major eastern sugar refineries shut down. Land's vice chairman, Howard Vickery, promoted to rear admiral February 12, declared that the production time of Liberty ships had been cut to 105 days, provided enough steel plate was available for them.[6]

But ships could not be built without gears, engines, valves, and other components. Amid the clamor for these materials and parts, the Maritime Commission operated at a severe disadvantage. After December 17, 1941, the ANMB ceased to grant merchant vessels a priority equal to naval construction. The ongoing shortage of steel and other materials forced the Maritime Commission to wait in line behind the other services. Attempts to gain equal status for it failed; the harsh truth was that within ANMB the army and navy could simply outvote the commission. Protests from the Planning Committee of the WPB proved futile. Land found himself helpless to push construction of merchant vessels because of continued shortages and lack of priority standing.[7]

Land and Vickery made an impressive tag team. "Land whittles us down," said one shipbuilder, "and then Vickery tears us apart. Either one alone is bad enough—together they're sheer murder." Vickery had an acid tongue and a gift for finding a shipbuilder's weak spot. "He found out the only thing in the world that can bother me," admitted one, "and he goes after it. He never uses an ax—just a needle. He never draws blood, but he sure makes it sting." While at launching festivities in one yard, Vickery as principal speaker said, "I have never seen such a beautiful launching in my whole life—the way the ship came sliding down the ways, so slowly, so slowly, so slowly—just like the way you build ships in this yard."[8]

The son of a Cleveland judge, Vickery excelled at mathematics at the Naval Academy, then spent time at the Boston Navy Yard, in Haiti, and in the Philippines. He had been to the naval yard at Danzig and saw how the Germans built their ships. The navy put him through the Army Industrial College, assigned him to the board investigating the *Morro Castle* disaster, and made him head of the secret war-plans section of the BCR. When Land was made head of the Maritime Commission, he was quick to seek Vickery as his assistant. They worked flawlessly together and became known as the Siamese Twins of Washington. Together they pushed, prodded, and bullied the revival of American shipping. It was Vickery who learned about Henry Kaiser and got him interested in building ships. They developed a close friendship grounded in mutual abuse. Kaiser called Vickery one of the greatest men in America, and the first man he intended to strangle with his bare hands once the war ended. Vickery used his patented needle to perfection on Kaiser's usually thick hide, goading him to ever shorter times for turning out Liberty ships and then using his record to taunt other builders into better performances.[9]

In January 1942 the average time to build a Liberty ship was 210 days. By

May it had dropped to 156 days, then 106 days in July. Nevertheless, criticism continued to be heaped on the Maritime Commission for the lag in shipbuilding. Improved convoying had reduced losses in the North Atlantic only to see them mount steadily along the Atlantic Coast. In May *Fortune* labeled the lack of merchant ships "the No. 1 Bottleneck." Jerry Land agreed. The repeated increases in output demanded of him had swollen his job to unprecedented proportions. He was charged with building 2,000 Liberty ships right away as well as barges, tenders, and tugs. Instead of 46 ways he now presided over nearly 300 that would soon employ 700,000 men compared to 100,000 only a short time earlier. Workers he had aplenty, but not enough with shipbuilding experience. The challenge, said Vickery, "gives you a feeling like a hand grenade after removing the pin."[10]

To increase production, Land hit on the idea of enlisting Andrew Jackson Higgins. In February Vickery and some of his staff members visited New Orleans and tried to persuade Higgins to build Liberty ships. At first Higgins declined until Vickery cleverly posed the issue as a challenge. Never one to refuse a dare, Higgins agreed but imposed some stiff demands. The government had to furnish the capital for plant expansion, guarantee a large enough order to make an assembly-line technique worthwhile, and assure him that all necessary materials would be delivered to him on the dates specified. He needed these guarantees because he had in mind a shipyard unlike any in existence, one that when fully operational would launch a Liberty ship every day as long as production remained uninterrupted.[11]

The contract, approved on March 13, called for construction of 200 Liberty ships, only 5 in 1942 and the rest in 1943. It was the largest ever awarded and made Higgins even more the toast of New Orleans. His design called for two major assembly lines separated by a giant machine and fabricating shop. One line would be manned by white workers, the other by black workers. Each race would have a trade school to train workers. "Yes, we are going to build ships, by the strength of Americans," he wrote, "and we are going to tap that great reservoir of unskilled Negro labor, and by such educational training as we can give, equip him to do the job, with equal pay for the same work, and equal opportunity for advancement." Amid great fanfare Higgins began work on the yard at a site on the eastern edge of New Orleans. Union locals pledged no work stoppages, and public officials stood ready to lend any support needed. To the excited citizens of New Orleans it seemed like one of the greatest events in their city's illustrious history.[12]

" 'It can't be done,' some told Higgins," reported Raymond Moley. " 'The hell it can't!' was the answer. And don't bet against Higgins."[13]

* * *

AT THE LARGE shipyard on the Maine coast, lines of workers streamed out of a long building shaped like a shoe box, its oblong windows stained dark blue. The morning shift was punching out, a sea of men and women dressed alike in visored caps, thick clothes bunched at the waist under coveralls or woolen trousers tucked into arctics or lumberjack's boots. All had identification badges pinned to their caps or shirts, and their faces all wore similar coatings of grime. They were building freighters even though only about 10 percent of them had ever worked in a shipyard before. This yard boasted the two great changes in shipbuilding: the use of assembly-line methods made possible by welding instead of riveting, and the heavy use of women.[14]

"These Maine women have so much stuff," said the personnel director, a woman. They surprised everyone by proving to be first-rate welders, but they also ran lathes and drill presses, dressed tools in the blacksmith shop, and could be found in every other department. About a third were wives of men in the service; a great many were wives of farmers or millhands at the textile and shoe factories. A corps of tough, hard-faced dance hall girls proved to be ace welders. "And let me tell you," said the personnel director, "that it takes stuff to handle a welding arc all day long—stuff and skill." Many men shrank from the noise and sputter and fumes, but the women fastened steel plates together as calmly as if they were sewing a hem on a dress.

Along the coast, too, could be found smaller yards that built barges, tugs, and minesweepers out of wood, a skill that had all but vanished in recent years except for fishing boats and yachts. Shaping oak timbers with an adze took both strength and a very special skill. Some grizzled old ship carpenters were lured from other jobs to the work, and most of the other men picked it up fast because they were handy with an ax and had done lumbering or carpentry. The workforce of one yard had 900 men and 40 women and desperately needed 500 more. The women, perched on the scaffolding alongside the men, painted and sewed on pipe covering and spun oakum for caulking and drove in the wooden bungs covering the bolt heads that held the joints together. The muffled whirr of buzz saws from the sawmill on a nearby hill provided counterpoint to the ringing crack of adzes on timber.

Unlike in days past, it was no big deal when a new ship was launched because there were so many of them even in the smaller yards. At the big yard, noted writer John Dos Passos, "speed of production has reached such a point that you can see a steel ship grow before your eyes as the huge sections are put together. The whole process to a layman seems strangely simple, like putting models together out of children's construction toys . . . In a shipyard you can see what you are producing."

* * *

By spring the lack of ships had become even more widely labeled as the number one bottleneck in the war effort. It didn't take a genius to notice that munitions were being produced faster than they could be transported. Inevitably the search began for reasons and scapegoats. Ralph Robey listed five common explanations—short-sighted planning by Washington officials, poor allocation of materials, inefficient production by shipyards, shortage of steel plates, and submarine sinkings—and concluded that none of them held water except the sinkings. Since the government refused to give out figures of losses lest it aid and comfort the enemy, no one knew for sure how much tonnage was going to the bottom. Nevertheless, it seemed obvious that the amount of tonnage lost exceeded that being built. By July the unofficial number of sinkings was reported as 323, and the navy appealed to fishermen and yachtsmen for 1,000 more small craft to join the 1,200 others already pressed into service.[15]

More shipyards were needed to turn out Liberty ships at a record pace. Jerry Land found himself in the position of a CEO operating a huge business empire on the premise that speed mattered more than cost. "My job," he said tersely, "is ships—building them, operating them." To do that job he was spending $178 million on shipyards and a whopping $7 billion on ships with 31 million deadweight tonnage. He had in effect enlisted the nation's private shipyards for this gigantic task. Roosevelt's original call for 6 million tons of shipping in 1942 had been revised to 8 million and then 9 million tons. Everybody knew these were impossible figures under the circumstances, but Land was under pressure to deliver something close to them despite the limitations of facilities, materials, and skilled labor. Already cries for his scalp had been raised by those ignorant of the obstacles facing him. "Damn it," Land growled, "a man can't do any more than his best."[16]

Land's best was far better than most. Originally asked to build 500 ships by 1947, he was now ordered to turn out 2,000 as fast as possible, not even counting tugs, barges, and tenders. Where peak output had once been a ship a week, Land's new goals looked to produce a ship a day and hopefully three a day by year's end. In reaching that goal he had to fight the navy for facilities. "We started this job with only five real yards—Newport News, Fore River, New York Shipbuilding, Federal, and Sun," he said. "The navy has taken over the first two, has always had the third, has taken most of Federal. Now it is crowding us in new yards we created ourselves—in Tampa, Pascagoula, Tacoma, and Moore in Oakland." The Puget Sound area had seven yards, but only one built ships for the Maritime Commission.[17]

However, new yards were going up, and Land counted on them to produce ships as never before. Henry Kaiser had already taken up the challenge in a big way. While Clay Bedford built up the Richmond yard, Henry sent his son

Edgar to Portland, Oregon, to build a yard for the Oregon Shipbuilding Corporation at an 87-acre site on the Columbia River. When Kaiser dissolved his alliance with Todd Shipbuilding in 1942, he gave Edgar full rein to run the Portland operation. Like Bedford, Edgar showed the ability and initiative to get large jobs done fast. He too built yards before the blueprints were even complete and got production going, partly by recruiting workers from lumber camps, paper mills, fish hatcheries, orchards, and other local businesses. He realized that the faster he added ways, the more business he could attract. After Pearl Harbor, Edgar opened two new yards at Swan Point and across the river at Vancouver, Washington; Richmond got two more yards as well. Edgar began a friendly but fierce rivalry with Bedford to see who could turn out more ships faster.[18]

The results were impressive. Richmond No. 1 turned out a Liberty ship in 111 days and looked to cut that time sharply. For the Portland-area yards Edgar laid down a schedule of 55 days from keel to launching. By contrast Bethlehem-Fairchild in March took pride in reducing its time from 270 to 150 days and aimed for 95 days. To ease the shortage of steel plate, the Maritime Commission had in November 1941 recommended a change in specifications allowing the use of strip-mill steel in place of the wider sheared steel plate. A typical yard used steel plate in 435 different shapes and innumerable sizes. The strip-mill steel required more welding or riveting but could be had more easily from plants that had made it for the automobile industry. No such substitute existed for the lack of experienced shipbuilders. Training programs took time, and meanwhile the yards coped with outbreaks of absenteeism and labor discontent.[19]

Techniques of prefabrication and subassembly were known but seldom used because so few vessels had been built in recent years. The war created a unique opportunity: a demand for hundreds of ships and new yards paid for by the government. Subassembly was an innovation that came almost simultaneously to several yards. Building a complete ship in a way or basin clogged it for too long and produced indescribable confusion as workers swarmed over the hulls with each other trying to get the ship finished. The obvious solution was to build as much of the vessel as possible on dry land and then assemble the parts as if putting a huge puzzle together. The only limitation lay in the hoisting power of the cranes that lifted the final subassemblies into place. Prefabrication had another great advantage: Unlike traditional shipbuilding, it could be carried on at night within the shop.[20]

Older yards, mostly those on the East Coast, expanded their ways within whatever limited space they had and added fabrication plants. The Bethlehem-Fairchild yard in Baltimore, unable to secure enough steel-fabricating machinery, bought some old shops two and a half miles away that once repaired Pullman railroad cars to cut, roll, furnace, and drill or punch steel before welding or riveting it into sections as large as freight cars could handle for the trip to the yard. Port and starboard innerbottom units, weighing about 10 tons each, were joined with the vertical keep and rider plate to make a complete innerbottom unit weighing 22 tons. Subassemblies as large as a 48.8-ton forepeak were stored near the ways until needed. At each way every bottom plate and double-bottom section was stacked and numbered for the sequence in which it was to be hoisted and the position it was to occupy in the ship.[21]

While traditional yards improvised, Kaiser's men came up with new techniques to speed production. Aware of the cramped space of most older yards, they built yards in open, uncluttered areas to allow room for spreading out subassemblies. By using giant cranes previously seen only in construction work such as his dams, Kaiser could prefabricate larger sections. His men used welding on 90 percent of a ship and built parts of the superstructure upside down to permit downward welding rather than the slower and more tiring overhead work. Welding itself was not only faster and cheaper but less tiring as well; downward welding let gravity do some of the work. In one yard Kaiser increased speed by constructing ships in basins below water level instead of on ways. Once the ship was finished, the basin was flooded and the ship floated out into the bay.[22]

Seventeen yards worked on Liberty ships, using the same standardized parts. To avoid having them compete with 600 subcontractors, the Maritime Commission created a central purchasing pool that did all the buying and then allocated materials to the yards. Labor posed a more difficult problem. With so many new workers, the shipbuilders had to break down complicated operations into simpler components for learning. Bedford had visited a Ford plant assembly line late in 1940 and noticed that workers there learned many jobs in hours, while apprentices in eastern shipyards required weeks to master complex jobs. Although many tasks were simplified, shipfitters still needed two or three months of intensive training to understand blueprints and the fitting together of certain parts. Gradually supervisors discovered that women made excellent welders.[23]

The rivalry among the Kaiser yards shortened production times but also aroused controversy. Boasting a new $3 million subassembly plant at Portland, Edgar decided to stage a show that fall. The mammoth new building had eleven enormous baylike structures, each one with two bridge cranes that together could hoist 35 tons of prefabricated parts. On signal an army of waiting workers gave a shout and scrambled to the task of laying the keel in huge sections. As it took shape, the cranes lifted numbered, prefabricated sections of the ship into place to be attacked by welders and riveters. More than half the ship had been prebuilt in the subassembly plant. Ten days later the *Joseph N. Teal* slid into the water ready for service—two weeks faster than

Kaiser's earlier all-time record set in August and 202 days faster than the best performance in World War I.[24]

Edgar's ten-day feat gained national attention. The day before the launching he called Clay Bedford and asked him to come to Portland for the ceremony. When Clay said he was too busy, Edgar replied, "Do you want me to call my father and have him order you to be here?" Clay agreed to come and was glad he did. Just before the launching President Roosevelt's special train pulled into the yard. At the ceremony the president surprised Clay by saying, "I remember you from Grand Coulee when you were one of the men who showed me around there."[25]

Impressed by Edgar's feat, Bedford accepted the challenge by carefully lining up men and materials to halve that time. Working eight-hour shifts around the clock, his men produced a ship in only four days, fifteen hours, and twenty-six minutes. Critics denounced both feats as cheap publicity stunts, but Henry Kaiser defended them. Bedford likened his approach to a laboratory experiment that taught his men about moving far heavier parts than usual and other technical insights. Kaiser reported that after Edgar's ten-day accomplishment, workers came up with 250 suggestions for producing ships even faster. Bedford added that officials from other yards had come to watch his performance and learn improved methods from it. Most observers were impressed. Jerry Land observed in November that Kaiser's prefabrication and assembly techniques had cut construction time of Liberty ships in all yards to 64.4 days, compared with 227.8 days in March. "Kaiser is to shipbuilding," declared *Time*, "what the late Knute Rockne was to football: both introduced a revolutionary shift."[26]

Kaiser drew even more fire from critics for his habit of evading regulations to get the materials he needed. He became a frequent guest of the Truman Committee to explain his nonconforming ways. At one point in the fall the OPA charged him with paying black market prices to get the steel he needed for his shipyards. Amid the uproar that ensued, Raymond Clapper defended Kaiser in terms that spoke for many Americans. While others talked and carped, Kaiser built ships and built them fast. "If it is a stunt it's the kind of stunt we can watch without ever becoming tired of it," Clapper said. ". . . If you have to be a scofflaw to get steel out of the arsenal of bureaucracy, then that's okay with me. If that's the way Old Man Kaiser has to get his steel to build ships to carry American forces to the fighting fronts, then I hope the old fellow breaks every law in the books."[27]

DURING 1940 AND 1941 William Francis Gibbs and his firm had done more than anyone else to organize the emergency shipbuilding program. As naval architects for the British they had drawn up the plans for Liberty ships, made all the necessary adjustments to the specifications, solved technical problems, and handled procurement from the vendors to coordinate the flow of materials. Their work embraced not only the original British order of 60 ships but later orders of 112 and 200 for the United States as well. Then, as the program swelled in size, it became clear that the government would have to assume the ordering and other functions. A dispute arose over the fee paid Gibbs & Cox as the number of ships increased. When the two sides could not agree, they parted company in June 1942. "We felt that we paid plenty for it and they felt that we did not pay enough," said Land, "so we just split business with them and said, 'Good-bye boys,' and kissed each other on both cheeks, and we are running our own show now."[28]

The split hardly eased the workload for Gibbs, who had a huge lot of navy business as well. His firm designed not only merchant ships but destroyers, cruisers, and tankers. A destroyer alone required 20,000 tracings for construction. Every day Gibbs & Cox cranked out 8,000 to 10,000 blueprints, or 26 acres' worth a month. One multiple order of ships might require them to issue 6,700 purchase orders daily; rarely did a day pass without the company contracting for at least $1 million worth of materials. Kaiser got credit for applying mass-production techniques to shipbuilding, but it was Gibbs who first attacked the problem of reducing the amount of labor that went into the work by designing parts that were easier to make and devising easier methods of fitting them together. Spreading operations over the whole shipyard meant more men could work at once on different parts rather than being crammed together in the tight interior of a ship under construction on a way.[29]

Naval vessels did not lend themselves as easily to these techniques, but construction time there shortened impressively as well. Destroyers that once took twenty-eight months to build began sliding into the water in slightly more than eight months. A new carrier was launched a year ahead of schedule. Gibbs & Cox found itself responsible for nearly 70 percent of the ships under construction. The challenge for its 2,000 employees sprawled across thirteen floors of a Manhattan building was to mass-produce plans, specifications, and purchase orders. Chief engineers and architects roamed through the rows of drafting tables urging the work on and checking its progress. Special attention went to the floor where exact scale models of each ship were built to catch any flaws in design before they infiltrated production.[30]

The destroyer program launched Gibbs's close relationship with the navy. In submitting designs for a new class of the vessel, Gibbs had proposed a new high-pressure, high-temperature steam propulsion system that he had worked out with General Electric, Westinghouse, and three other firms. The navy cast a dubious eye on the radical change but agreed to give it a try. By 1942 more than a few naval officers conceded that if the system had not been adopted, they would be fighting the war with outmoded warships. The cadaverous Gibbs, dressed in his shiny, patched suits, enjoyed his reputation as a prophet but remained leery of success. "As soon as a man thinks himself successful," he observed, "he gets to thinking he is so goddamn bright that it just paralyzes him."[31]

"THE KAISER YARDS look like something out of Disney," reported Alistair Cooke, who was touring the country to get a sense of how the war effort was going. "They are absurdly clean and neat. The elements of a ship are divided into separate piles all the way from the administration building down to the ways. Innumerable cranes . . . clutch precisely at the piles, deposit them at the plate shop, heave them down to the ways, where small armies of Disney characters rush forth with welding guns and weld the parts into a ship as innocently as a child fits A into B on a nursery floor."[32]

Cooke was amazed by the simplicity of Kaiser's methods. Construction consisted of three elements: the piles, the cranes, and the assembly bay. He counted fifty "unvarying automatic processes" between the piles and the finished ship. That the workers were not experienced shipmakers didn't matter. Sheets of steel were "marked VK2 and MQ3, to indicate to a moron where they fit on a ship." Cranes hoisted the sheets fifty yards to the yard floor, where a plywood template dropped down on them and thirty men traced the template onto the steel. Then another crane lifted the marked sheet to another place where drills and files cut it into the traced parts. Yet another crane carried each part off to the plate shop, where they were welded together.[33]

"This is the precision work," added Cooke, "and to Mr. Kaiser it is a niggling but necessary evil." The solid work took place in the lofts, where whole forepeaks and sterns were prefabricated. At the assembly bay an entire bulkhead would be put into place and sent out onto the launching skids. To Kaiser, building a ship was not an ancient craft but simply another construction problem to be solved. Cooke had been warned that it was bad taste to mention Kaiser's name to traditional shipbuilders in the Bay Area. He did so to one old shipbuilder, who "rolled his eyes to the ceiling, coughed, and shared a reproving sneer with his manager." After all, what to make of a man who insisted on calling the bow of a ship the "front end?"[34]

"THIS IS NO Henry Kaiser outfit," proclaimed Charles Cameron West. "This is just a hell of a swell team, and we're carrying the ball. That's all."[35]

The "team" belonged to the improbable Manitowoc Shipbuilding Company. Located in Manitowoc, Wisconsin, on the shores of Lake Michigan, it had the distinction of being the only inland builder of submarines. A slim, ruddy-cheeked six-footer, West had earned an engineering degree at Cornell before going to work for American Shipbuilding in Chicago to learn the business. After two years he quit to buy a small, run-down shipyard at Manitowoc that had begun life building clipper ships in 1847 but never done well. As a first step he recruited a savvy, alert engineering staff and set up a large machine shop that made boilers, engines, and most other parts for his ships. World War I brought him prosperity, then hard times when the ship orders vanished. The machine shop kept the company alive during the lean years by turning out industrial cranes, dredges, and machines for paper mills and cement plants.

When World War II broke out, West turned happily back to his first love and landed a navy contract worth $32.8 million for ten submarines in the summer of 1940. To build them he not only had to convert his own plant but had to persuade sixty subcontractors to do so as well. To avoid the harsh Wisconsin winter, West built the submarines piecemeal indoors and assembled them in fifteen sections weighing from 38 to 65 tons each. When he launched the first submarine eight months ahead of schedule, impressed naval officials gave him a contract for invasion barges. West promptly drew up the necessary plans, farmed out the work, and delivered the entire lot only eight months after the order was signed. His 6,200 employees, secured by a closed AFL shop and a twenty-year-old collective bargaining plan, worked three eight-hour shifts seven days a week.

Although some of the workers were old-timers who had been with the company from the start, most were refugees from dairy and other farms in the region. West trained them in a tough apprentice course that turned the survivors into shipbuilders. An impressed naval inspector said of them, "We lovingly call them cheese makers and cherry pickers, but lord what beautiful work they do."

COMPANIES LIKE MANITOWOC came new to the navy, but the larger corporations had been working with the military for decades. In particular the navy relied heavily on the two electrical giants, General Electric and Westinghouse, with whom they had been doing business since early in the century. The reason for their relationship was simple: The two companies not only made much of the critical equipment the navy needed but in many cases had invented or developed it. The army too depended heavily on a wide variety of electrical equipment that only the giant firms could develop and manufacture in large quantities. GE and Westinghouse, along with other big companies, also had the research staffs and facilities to solve the endless problems brought to them by the military. They dominated the age of electricity, and electricity had become as vital to warfare as it was to the consumer society.[36]

From the start of the electrical age the two companies had provided most of the turbines that generated power. In 1909 GE engineer W. L. R. Emmet made the radical suggestion of using electric drive for large naval vessels in place of reciprocating steam engines. Earlier the company had demonstrated the worth of electricity aboard ship by installing an experimental system of motors and controls for operating gun turrets on a cruiser. The striking success of the trial opened the door to widening use of electricity on naval ships. In 1913 the first trial runs of a ship with turbine-electric propulsion proved so successful that the navy adapted it to a battleship then under construction. The main drawback remained a lack of speed-reducing gears large and strong enough to step down the rapid rotation of the turbine to the slower rotation of the propeller.[37]

The hiatus in shipbuilding after World War I proved beneficial in one sense. During that time the art of gear making advanced enough to overcome this obstacle. When the navy decided in the early 1930s to build some new destroyers, it accepted a GE proposal for a compact, high-pressure, high-speed steam turbine geared directly to the propeller shaft. The first vessel so equipped went into service in 1936 and showed a 25 percent decrease in fuel consumption thanks to the greater power generated by a smaller power plant. Naval Secretary Charles Edison hailed it as the greatest engineering progress the navy had made in a generation. Thereafter all the navy's major ships featured turbine-gear drives. Fortunately, the innovation arrived on the eve of an enormous naval expansion program that nobody had foreseen.[38]

A single destroyer used two 30,000-horsepower turbine drives. Building the turbines, especially for capital ships, posed as great a challenge as designing them. Steam entered a turbine at a pressure of 700 pounds per square inch with a velocity far exceeding that of a hurricane, only to emerge less than a second later at less than atmospheric pressure. The turbine wheels whizzed at 10,000 revolutions per minute, with their outer edges racing at 600 miles an hour. Harnessing one of them to a propeller shaft required gears as large as 200 inches in diameter and weighing up to 70,000 pounds in which the tooth spacing could not vary more than three tenths of a mil. Manufacturing them required almost a watchmaker's precision, which in turn gave American warships unrivaled reliability in combat. The construction of one large turbine needed some 700 working drawings and more than 4,000 engineers and workmen.[39]

The use of electricity aboard ship only began with the drive system. A large ship might have as many as 2,000 individual meters, instruments, and control devices, all of which had to be not only reliable but sturdy enough to withstand the shocks of combat. The British experience in battle revealed a glaring need for completely new lines of shockproof meters and controls. In response to hurried orders from the navy, GE designed new versions, revamped factories to produce them, and began deliveries only a few months after Pearl Harbor. Ships also needed lots of lighting—a battleship could have some 20,000 bulbs, plus twice that number for replacements—and electric refrigeration to preserve food, store plasma and other temperature-sensitive goods, and perform one function unique to the American navy, making ice cream for the crew. All this equipment in turn needed specially designed ship fittings to house switches, fuses, circuit breakers, relays, and other items in waterproof boxes that could withstand the stress of battle and storms at sea.[40]

Electricity also powered radio and radar units, steering gear, ventilating fans, fire control equipment, ammunition hoists, searchlights, X-ray machines, welding sets, cooking ranges, laundry machines, and a wide array of cranes, winches, and windlasses. General Electric supplied more than 23,000 motors ranging from ½ to 250 horsepower to run ventilating systems alone. Within a short time repairs aboard damaged ships became an urgent user of electric power. The first taste of this work came with salvaging the broken fleet at Pearl Harbor. A hurried call to experts in several GE factories brought together a team of fifty-eight men in Los Angeles for the trip to Hawaii. To reclaim the sunken battleships *California* and *West Virginia*, the men toiled in three eight-hour shifts seven days a week underwater, breathing air pumped from abovedecks.[41]

The motors were fouled with thick oil and muck, and some were corroded by the saltwater. Tons of electric-propulsion apparatus, located deep within the hull, had to be removed by men walking single file on narrow companionways through four decks. Special techniques had to be devised to repair the giant 12-foot motors that drove the battleships. The *Oklahoma* posed an even more difficult problem; it had capsized with nothing but keel and part of the bottom above water. For seventy-two hours expert crews worked at the delicate task of using cables and pulleys attached to twenty-one electric winches on shore with special controls to turn the ship over gently without breaking her apart. Only then could the massive job of repairing the ship begin.[42]

Auxiliary vessels crucial to the war effort also needed power equipment. In 1920 GE introduced a form of diesel-electric propulsion that became widely used on such ships as fleet tugs, harbor tugs, salvage vessels, minesweepers, and net tenders, which raised and lowered the heavy submarine nets guarding the entrances to major harbors. Submarines also used diesel-electric drives; during the 1930s GE developed a small, high-speed electric motor that connected directly to the propeller shaft through reduction gears. The navy adopted it as a way of conserving weight and space aboard this most cramped of vessels. From 1935 until the end of the war, GE had a hand in the construction of every new submarine ordered by the navy.[43]

From Westinghouse the navy needed some of the same equipment but also very different specialty items. Like GE, the company was already deep into defense work before Pearl Harbor. Besides its involvement in the navy's ordnance plants, it was making gun mounts. The Springfield, Massachusetts, factory worked on gun-position regulators, radar-antenna stabilizers, and fire control equipment as well as its main project, the tank-gun stabilizers. Baltimore took on military radio and radar equipment, while Lima turned out aircraft generators and a variety of small motors. Mansfield was preparing to handle forty different war jobs, including bomb fuzes, binoculars, and parts for airplanes and their engines. The Meter Division at Newark specialized in aircraft instruments of many designs, and Bloomfield produced radio and radar tubes as well as a mysterious, secret project dealing with the mass production of uranium. No less than three plants—Bridgeport, Sharon, and Springfield—collaborated on a special project of intense interest to the navy: the electric torpedo.[44]

The standard torpedo was propelled by compressed air and the combustion of highly volatile fuel that drove its propellers through turbines. Its weakness was a white wake of bubbles left by exhaust gases that warned the target of its approach. An electric drive would leave no wake but required a motor of several hundred horsepower that could power slow-turning propellers yet be small enough to fit into the torpedo body. The Germans had developed one and used it exclusively since 1939. When the Allies recovered one that washed ashore unexploded, the navy asked Westinghouse to design a motor capable of driving an American version. A team of Westinghouse engineers examined the captured German motor in January 1942; two months later the navy gave them the assignment of developing not just the motor but the entire torpedo. "You are to do everything your way," declared Admiral Ted Ruddock of the Ordnance Bureau. "We want a production of 300 complete electric torpedoes a month and the first sample by mid-summer."[45]

In only 104 days the Sharon factory shipped its first electric "fish" to Newport for testing, but it had serious design gaps. The navy's own people were to produce the most delicate component, the control gear that kept the torpedo on target and beneath the water. The mechanical artists at the Newport Torpedo Station in Rhode Island crafted this complex mechanism lovingly by hand, with no two parts interchangeable. It took them fifteen hours to assemble one unit, a production rate that would keep electric fish from ever being mass-produced. The Bureau of Ordnance asked Westinghouse to turn out control gear in quantity or find a firm that could do so. None of its own factories were suitable for the job, and all were busy with other war orders. Finally, Westinghouse approached the Bryant Electric Company in Bridgeport, Connecticut, a subsidiary that specialized in household switches, electric wiring devices, and plastic dishes. "Torpedo controls?" said its manager, Harry Seim. "Sure! Why not?"

It was a bold gesture. Seim had no engineering department or skilled toolmakers or suitable machinery for the job. Nevertheless, his staff went first to Newport, where the skeptical craftsmen instructed them on how the units were made, then to Alexandria, Virginia, where torpedoes were assembled. Seim devised a tooling layout that included ninety-one machines and 1,147 special jibs and fixtures, then waded into the priorities arena to get what he needed. While waiting, he started a training program to indoctrinate a group of supervisors and mechanics in the art of extreme accuracy. He asked the navy for 200 complete sets of control gear parts for practice purposes but did not get them. In July he still did not have the materials needed for the job.

The supervisors made repeated pilgrimages to Newport, struggling to learn the art from teams of fathers and sons who had over the years devised their own methods. No two did the job the same way. The supervisors studied them all and tried to boil down what they saw into standard procedures that could be reduced to drawings with exact tolerances for every part. This proved impossible in some of the most delicate work, where they were forced to compile "butcher books" of notes describing in detail how it was done. Not until January 1943 did Bryant finally turn out its first fifteen complete units, only to have them rejected because by then the specifications at Newport had been tightened due to changes in the war situation. With something between a curse and a sigh, Seim and his men went back to the drawing board.

THINGS LARGE AND small challenged the Westinghouse engineers, as they did in many other firms. After Pearl Harbor the navy's demands grew more strict and demanding in almost everything they requested. A tiny ⅛-horsepower motor, used to drive an air pump, had to perform while soaking wet; another small motor had to resist the action of salt spray. A third motor had to operate on either 50 or 60 cycles with only one winding. At the other end of the spectrum, two 1,000-horsepower engines had to be designed for delivering 1.4 million gallons of water a minute in the navy's secret model-test basin at Carderock, Maryland. Few projects rivaled the difficulty posed by a radical new deck elevator created for aircraft carriers.[46]

The seven existing carriers had two huge platforms, one fore and one aft, for raising planes from the hangar deck to the flight deck, both operated by hydraulic rams. In 1940 a German bomb plunged down an elevator shaft and exploded on the hangar deck of a British carrier, immobilizing every plane on board. Design officers at the Navy's Bureau of Ships recognized from this incident that the elevators with their yawning crevices made inviting targets for enemy planes. One of them came up with the idea of installing a third elevator amidships that hung over the side above only water. In battle the two regular elevators could be secured, removing the wells, while the third unit brought planes up. A hit on it would limit damage to the elevator itself, leaving the other elevators intact.

When the bureau brought the idea to the Westinghouse Elevator Company in January 1941, a new class of carriers pioneered by the *Essex* was still on the drawing boards. Westinghouse was asked to design, develop, and produce a type of elevator that did not yet exist for a very large new type of carrier. It was the kind of impossible problem that appealed to James Dunlop, the company's chief design engineer. The elevator had to be 34 feet by 60 feet and would probably weigh about 50 tons. It had to lift 18,000 pounds of plane and crew from hangar to flight deck in just under thirteen seconds, automatically level itself with the deck, and complete a round trip in forty-five seconds. It also had to be made operable by hand cranks in case the hoisting gear was disabled in battle. And it must be able to fold upward on hinges to stow against the ship's side without extending more than two feet beyond the outboard gun platforms; otherwise the ship could not get through the Panama Canal.

Of necessity Dunlop had to discard the cumbersome power system used by the two conventional elevators. Instead he conceived an elevator going up and down on steel ropes running over pulleys and connected to two sides of a piston moving in a single hydraulic cylinder. A 300-horsepower pump would operate the cylinder, supplying oil through control valves. The platform structure would ride up and down on heavy steel guide rails set in the side of the ship, using specially hardened rollers to reduce friction. A locking system would automatically keep the platform from falling overboard if the cables were shot away. It was a bold vision, unlike anything in existence, and Dunlop started work on it in the spring of 1941.

Problems came in flocks. No one in the engineering department or shop had any experience to guide them, and the plant's machinery limited what they could do. The heavy 60-foot guide rails, for example, had to be cut into four sections to fit onto the shop's biggest planers. The big hydraulic cylinder had to be built in three sections, then welded into a single assembly—something that had never been done before. The platform itself had to be constructed in many pieces so that the flatcars carrying them could get around the numerous curves on the rail line between Jersey City and Newport News.

Through 1941 Dunlop toiled at the problem. Then came Pearl Harbor and a parade of design changes that followed. Navy studies of the Pacific concluded that high-speed carriers would have to endure fierce poundings from giant seas that submerged the deck edge. New designs were needed that would enable the mechanism to withstand being dragged through the water at 33 knots or slammed abruptly down on its surface and then lifted just as suddenly with tons of water still on the platform. Undaunted, Dunlop scrapped his existing version and started over. To reduce water resistance, he decided to use steel tubing in place of standard beams for the platform skeleton. This required 400 separate units, every one of which had to be fully calculated for stresses under sixteen different conditions, a total of 6,400 separate stress analyses. Doing them would occupy four engineers steadily for six months.

Dunlop had neither the men nor the time. The first carrier of the new class, the *Essex*, was due to be commissioned in December. The navy had serious doubts as to whether Dunlop could get the job done and made plans for the ship to sail without a third deck elevator. But Dunlop persisted. The elevator company chose five young women and sent them to Newark College of Engineering for a three-month course in stress analysis. Once finished, they were put to work on the calculations and came up with the answers within the allotted time. Their figures showed that the elevator had to withstand overall stresses of a million pounds while dragged through the water at more than 30 knots. Vanadium steel, the strongest known metal tubing, would have to be used but was hard to get. Welding it was even more difficult and could only be done by experts. The company scoured the labor market for skilled welders and found enough to do the job by working long hours.

The main guides for holding the elevator to the ship posed another problem because of the enormous stresses they would have to endure on the rollers and guide rails. Dunlop and his men came up with special steels to line them and to fashion the rollers so that they would not crush each other or throw the whole unit out of alignment. Here too so little engineering data on such stress problems existed that the men had to find their way by setting up actual structures in the shop and testing them with full-sized loads. Despite all obstacles, the first elevator reached Newport News during Christmas week, and crews worked around the clock to install it on the *Essex* by December 29.

Still the navy had its doubts. Engineering officers accepted nothing until it passed exhaustive tests. "Whatever is done will have to be completed in the next twelve hours," they declared on December 30. "If it doesn't meet all tests, we shall not be able to use it."

*   *   *

FOR TWO WEEKS Don Magnuson worked on destroyers in the Seattle-Tacoma Shipbuilding yard, earning $8.36 a day for a shift of seven and a half hours. During his brief stay he watched what was going around him more closely than most. Watching was his main purpose; he was actually a reporter for the *Seattle Times* interested in doing a story on shipyard work. What he found surprised him as much as it did his readers.[47]

"Never during my time in the yard did I put in an honest day's work," he reported in his series of articles. "I do not think I averaged one hour of labor each shift . . . Some nights I was engaged usefully for no more than ten minutes." Looking down from the superstructure of a destroyer, he once saw a group of thirteen men of whom only one was working while the others talked or smoked or lolled against the railings. A friendly welder advised him to "just keep a wrench or something in your hand. Then you'll be okay." Once he arrived three minutes late for work, which meant losing a half hour's pay. When he started into the yard, the gateman said, "There's no sense doing anything you don't get paid for. Get smart. Go over and have a cup of coffee for 25 minutes."

Magnuson estimated that at no time were more than 70 percent of the men in the yard actually working, yet he did not blame them. "They were idle," he wrote, "but not from choice. They want to work." Before printing the series, the *Times* showed it to the head of the shipyard, who was infuriated. "Your whole God-damned bunch ought to be ashamed of themselves," he raged. "You are giving the company, the men and the war effort a stab in the back. How in the hell can you call yourselves Americans? . . . How the hell do you suppose the boys overseas will feel?" Once he cooled down, he was quick to point out that the yard was several months ahead of schedule.

CHAPTER 15

THE MANPOWER MUDDLE

Manpower is the No. 1 raw material of war—the only resource for which no substitute can be found—and it has to be utilized accordingly.

—FORTUNE [1]

No man or woman is free to place his personal preference or convenience ahead of the public interest.

—PAUL V. McNUTT [2]

The day is not far distant when men may say, "All troubles lead to Paul McNutt."

—TIME [3]

IN WARTIME AS IN GOOD TIMES AND the depression, numbers filled the air. Those struggling to grasp the totality of what was happening sought answers, or at least clues, in swirls of figures that sometimes grew so large as to be incomprehensible. Bureaucrats and economists dwelled in a world of numbers, using them not only to understand but as arguments or armor. The sheer scale of a global war produced numbers that once belonged only to astronomers and were no more fathomable than a light-year. Sometimes, however, even the numbers seemed inadequate to the need and downright misleading. On such occasions judgments had to be rendered that cut through the fog of figures or simply ignored them altogether.

Thus it was on New Year's Day 1942 that Ferdinand Eberstadt, a prominent lawyer and investment banker, surveyed an area of interest to him and concluded, "To date, every aspect of the manpower problem—labor supply, labor relations, wages, etc.—has been badly handled. The fact is that it is being and has been treated as a wholly political matter, with emphasis on social gains rather than on the immediate mobilization of our entire labor resources for successful prosecution of a war."[4]

Manpower was the glue of the entire mobilization and war effort, without which nothing got done. On the surface it was very much a numbers game. The United States in 1942 had nearly 133.9 million people, of whom 6.9 million were over the age of sixty-five, 3.9 million were characterized as disabled, 8.4 million were between fourteen and seventeen years old, and 30.7 million were children under fourteen. The labor force was estimated at 71.7 million, or 54 percent, not including 10.7 million mothers with children under ten. However, it did include 400,000 working mothers with children under ten, 1.3 million boys and girls under eighteen who worked or were seeking jobs, and 2.1 million people over sixty-five who either had jobs or wanted them. In the spring of 1942 some 16 million people remained unemployed for whatever reasons, and the census included a mystery group of nearly 1.8 million souls classified simply as "unknown."[5]

Once past these surface numbers, the manpower maze grew more involved. The army already had 1.7 million men, and Stimson projected that it would reach 3.6 million by the year's end. Filling the ranks marked only the first step because the rule of thumb was that each fighting man required the labor of ten other workers to supply him. Even more, it needed these workers to be in the right jobs and places at the right time. Their labors occupied two broad fields, industry and agriculture. Some jobs required little more than muscle and persistence; others demanded varying levels of skill. The great logistical puzzle was how to achieve and maintain a balance between these fields and among the different tasks within each one. In a static environment this feat would have been difficult enough; it grew diabolically complex in a world where workers moved from one job to another or simply dropped out, and where the ranks were depleted by men leaving for the military.[6]

One of the privileges of living in a free society was the right to move anywhere at any time and to better one's lot by changing jobs. However, a nation fighting the new kind of war needed to stabilize and balance its workforce to maximize production. Inevitably competition arose for skilled labor and even for untrained workers. Companies raided the workforce of their rivals, and thousands of workers simply left one job or the farm or menial labor in search of better-paying positions. The explosion of new defense plants accelerated this process and turned normal labor markets upside down. Increasingly the location of new plants came to be dictated by the availability of a labor supply. "The present organization of manpower in the war effort," declared *Fortune* in April, "is a chart maker's nightmare. It is incomplete, inefficient, uncoordinated, planless, short of authority, and lacking the confidence of both labor and management."[7]

Somehow order had to be imposed on the process, but virtually any approach meant curtailing individual freedom of movement. From the start, then, the question of compulsion versus voluntarism emerged as a potent political issue, raising hackles over the old debate as to whether a free society should employ what many regarded as dictatorial tactics to achieve its ends, and whether doing so ultimately destroyed freedom. The struggle over this issue grew steadily more intense as the war proceeded and the manpower situation became more chaotic.

Stimson and Patterson had no doubts on the subject. They assumed that all able-bodied Americans would be ready if not eager for service, that the size of the fighting force would be determined chiefly by the number of young men available for combat, and that controls would be implemented to assure the civilian manpower pool would perform necessary tasks in a timely manner. Grenville Clark held no illusions on the subject. "The magnitude of the required manpower mobilization for production," he wrote Nelson in January, "is so great (along with military mobilization) that it cannot . . . be left to the operation of the law of supply and demand . . . We can't afford to take risks any longer . . . We may lose this war . . . Time is of the essence." Two months later he warned the president that "to cope successfully with the vast forces against us in this war, nothing less than a comprehensive system of national service will be adequate."[8]

Here too the shadow of World War I darkened the memories of many officials. Severe labor shortages created by the rapid expansion of industry, the abrupt cutting off of European immigration, and the need for soldiers had forced the tapping of new sources. Women went to work in factories, and labor agents swarmed the South recruiting more than 400,000 blacks to migrate northward. Some 20,000 Mexicans were allowed across the border, and 2,500 Bahamian blacks were imported to do work. To discourage job hopping among shipyard workers on the West Coast, uniform wages were established. In Illinois 21,000 boys were recruited to harvest crops. Interned enemy aliens were put to work on roads, as were thousands of tramps. Congress approved the use of prison labor to produce supplies for the military. In June 1918 General Enoch Crowder set about executing the War Department's "work or fight" rule, which many viewed as the first step toward drafting labor. Three months later President Wilson added a Labor Priorities Section to the WIB, but the war ended soon afterward.[9]

Early in this war no one suspected that virtually all these expedients would be resorted to again. The first challenge was simply to get a grip on manpower because authority over it was scattered across so many hands and agencies. Secretary of Labor Perkins had lost most of what little authority she possessed. Paul McNutt's Federal Security Agency included the Bureau of Employment Security and USES, but neither had the power to plan or execute labor policy. Neither did the National Labor Supply Committee or the new WLB or any of the thirty-three federal agencies reportedly involved in collecting and processing manpower data. Lewis Hershey's Selective Service System presided over the draft of manpower for the military and was not inclined to share power with anyone. The process remained, as *Fortune* labeled it, a "headless hodgepodge."[10]

The obvious place to look for leadership was the WPB and Nelson, who had been given full authority to mobilize industry and labor. But Nelson thought overseeing war production was a big enough job and willingly surrendered his authority over manpower. Within WPB the logical candidate was Sidney Hillman. He was not only a diehard Roosevelt loyalist but had done good work in dealing with labor disputes, and especially in overseeing the worker training programs that by the end of 1941 had produced nearly 2.3 million people ready to be employed and another 557,060 enrolled in classes. Hillman made no secret of his desire for the job. Even before Roosevelt announced the formation of WPB, Hillman had asked to see him about "the whole labor situation." His labor division in OPM simply moved over to WPB, but the worsening manpower muddle made it clear that something more had to be done.[11]

Discussions within the administration indicated that the something would be the creation of a separate commission to oversee manpower. After his meeting with Roosevelt on January 27 Hillman came away convinced that he would be appointed head of the new commission. He saw Nelson and got his approval for delegating oversight of manpower to a separate agency. Nelson then drafted a letter to that effect recommending Hillman as the man to head such a body, but for reasons unknown it was never sent. Both Philip Murray and William Green asked to see Roosevelt on possible commission appointments. Paul McNutt raised the issue early in December, prompting Roosevelt to appoint three cabinet members to look into the whole question. McNutt, who wanted the responsibility located in his FSA, submitted the cabinet members' report on the thirty-first. It proposed creating a new Manpower Mobilization Board but remained vague on what authority it would have over the welter of existing agencies.[12]

The dilemma was how best to centralize so diffuse a function in one agency amid all the rival claimants and intramural jealousies. Should the new body have direct responsibility for recruiting and placing workers, or should it simply make policy and issue instructions to existing agencies? Those who favored compulsory controls over the labor market in the British fashion favored a strong operating organization; those who disliked such regimentation wanted a policy board that left operating responsibility in the hands of the FSA. Some opposed the creation of a new agency altogether. "I fought tooth and nail," Frances Perkins said later. "I was so disturbed about it and was [so] sure that it was going to be such a failure that I enlisted the assistance of Claude Wickard, Ickes, Jones, and others . . . There was a pretty general assault on the idea . . . It was one of the silliest things that Roosevelt did."[13]

Hillman did not care for the idea of a new agency, but he continued to assume that he would be made its head if it were created. However, the Bureau of the Budget prepared a compromise plan that Harold Smith and McNutt discussed with Roosevelt on February 7. The president approved the idea in principle but did not sign an order because he wanted to hear the views of the affected agencies. Their negative response was loud and clear, along with those of Perkins and Hillman. For weeks the pressures mounted steadily until an exasperated Roosevelt appointed Sam Rosenman, Smith, Justice William O. Douglas, and Anna Rosenberg to a committee to come up with a manpower organization and recommend someone to head it. They produced a plan closely resembling the February 7 proposal.[14]

While their deliberations proceeded, it became clear that Hillman's position was being undermined. He lacked a reliable constituency outside his own union. His refusal to act as labor's puppet in the administration had alienated Murray and Green, and he had made enemies among businessmen and in Congress despite his moderation. While Roosevelt delayed a final decision, gossip swirled that Hillman was about to be demoted. In February Hillman sent Roosevelt a memo pleading that he receive full authority over manpower or be allowed to resign. No reply was forthcoming. On March 2 a Michigan congressman charged Hillman with diverting military clothing contracts to his own union; radio commentator Fulton Lewis Jr. echoed the charges in a series of attacks. Patterson had the charges investigated and reported that "Hillman had nothing whatever to do with those contracts."[15]

As the web of bureaucratic intrigue on the manpower question continued to spread, labor's leaders continued to fight each other more than their adversaries in management. None rose to Hillman's defense. The longer Roosevelt left Hillman dangling in uncertainty, the more tormented he grew. The president neither returned his calls or made himself available to be seen. On March 22 Hillman penned a long memo to Roosevelt begging him to make up his mind, but the memo was never sent. Then, on April 14, he suffered a serious heart attack and was hospitalized. Just before his collapse, word had reached him—not from Roosevelt—that the president had decided to create a new War Manpower Commission (WMC) to be headed by McNutt.[16]

The whole transaction was vintage Roosevelt. Having groped his way to a decision, he lacked the heart to tell Hillman personally. In search of a way to let his old friend down easily, he dispatched a telegram to Hillman four days after his heart attack asking him to become "special adviser" to the president on labor matters after his recovery. Hillman said no thanks and left government service. "If a man has the support and full confidence of his chief he can go ahead and do anything," he told John Lord O'Brian, who had come to visit him, "but once he feels that the chief's confidence is weakening, then it's time to get out." After six weeks in the hospital he returned to New York and his union presidency, disappointed but no less loyal to Roosevelt despite all he had endured.[17]

THE NEW COMMISSION seemed to be modeled on the WPB. Its chairman had the power to "issue such policy and operating directives as may be necessary." He was required to consult the commission but could act without its consent. However, its reach was limited. Selective Service remained independent, and USES stayed within the FSA. The labor supply functions of the WPB moved to the new commission, but its training functions went to FSA. In effect the new arrangement amounted to a loose canopy over the operating agencies rather than a central manpower authority. Its members included representatives from the War, Navy, Agriculture, and Labor departments, WPB, Selective Service, and Civil Service Commission. Whatever powers it possessed had been drained from the WPB. As *Newsweek* observed, "McNutt's new job obviously raises him to parity with Donald M. Nelson in direction of the war production effort."[18]

Unlike Nelson, McNutt was a politician with well-advertised aspirations to succeed Roosevelt. Tall and broad-shouldered, his full round face topped with a thatch of white hair above thick, jet black eyebrows, he flashed a ready smile and enjoyed being called the "Adonis of American politics." New Dealers distrusted him as an opportunist but respected his shrewd, skillful ways. Before taking over the FSA in July 1939 he had been governor of Indiana and U.S. high commissioner to the Philippines. As governor he had outraged the unions in 1935 by calling out the militia to quell rioting strikers. Since then, however, he had fought to save the forty-hour week and other New Deal social gains, thereby winning back some support from labor.[19]

The task facing McNutt was daunting. He had to find some way to stop the serious problem of employers pirating skilled labor from each other. War contracts had to be steered toward regions that still had a surplus of labor rather than those with shortages. Skilled workers had to be directed into the most essential work, and discrimination against black and alien workers had to be eased. Everyone agreed that the war effort would require more women in the workforce, but their presence meant major adjustments of both attitudes and facilities in plants. Turnover rates remained high as workers left to take a higher-paying job or simply quit. The "quit rate" had risen steadily from 0.66 per 100 employees in January 1940 to 1.31 in January 1941 and 2.36 in January 1942. The supply was there. A WPA survey disclosed that, apart from 3.6 million people still unemployed, the nation had 45.2 million persons of working age (fourteen and over). Of these, 31.9 million consisted of housewives or unemployables, but the other 13.3 million, mostly women, were willing to take any full- or part-time job within their community.[20]

Some officials advocated registering women much as the draft had done with men, but Roosevelt squelched the idea. McNutt thought it unnecessary but favored doing it on a voluntary basis in communities where labor was short. On May 27 the WMC issued an order to stop pirating in industry, allowing workers to change jobs only for good reason. "In 1942, the United States will need 13,000,000 additional skilled and semiskilled workers," proclaimed McNutt in an article urging people to seek war jobs. "For every skilled tool designer available," he added, "51 are needed. There are 25 jobs for every toolmaker, 7 for every ship carpenter, 22 for every marine machinist, 4 for every aircraft riveter." Farms would also suffer shortages, especially at harvest time, because of the mass exodus to military and defense plants. McNutt emphasized that the scale of the war effort demanded the recruiting of women, the elderly, the handicapped, untrained young people, and skilled workers held down by discrimination.[21]

As the pool of unemployed and readily available workers shrank, USES emerged as the most important agency handling labor supply. It consisted of a nationwide network of public employment offices operated by the states with federal funding. In June 1940 it had 1,500 full-time and 3,100 part-time offices with 18,000 employees, and remained at that level throughout the war even though its placement work increased greatly. The number of placements soared from 4.5 million in 1940 to more than 8 million in 1942. Since the quality of facilities and personnel varied widely from state to state, the offices were put under direct federal control after Pearl Harbor. However, efforts to strengthen the weaker ones by importing personnel from other states made only modest gains, and local officials still took their cues from state capitols rather than Washington.[22]

Apart from the unevenness of local operations, USES suffered from other handicaps. It had developed during the depression and served mainly to steer the unemployed toward public works projects. Private employers made little use of it and regarded it as part of the relief effort. The performance of many offices justified the low esteem in which USES was held by most military and

Selective Service officials. USES adjusted slowly from its origins in a time when jobs were scarce and applicants plentiful to one where the reverse was true. It also had a manpower problem of its own in struggling to find capable personnel for interviewing, testing, hiring, and other functions. Many of its best people left to take better-paying jobs, hampering efforts to strengthen its personnel.[23]

Finding enough capable workers to fill critical jobs—and keeping them there—was hard enough, but McNutt also had to confront another dimension of his task. Even as plants competed with each other for skilled or semiskilled labor, and agriculture competed with industry, the entire civilian workforce competed with the military for bodies. The armed services needed not only a huge number of men for combat and supply work but also civilians to perform a myriad of jobs. The awarding of contracts by the military also had an impact on labor distribution, which raised yet another controversy. Few knowledge-able people expected these differences to be resolved easily, if at all.

WHILE MCNUTT GRAPPLED with getting the new agency up and running, the War Department fought its own battle over manpower. During January the General Staff proposed and Roosevelt agreed to increase the army from 1.6 million to 3.6 million men. The existing 27 infantry and 6 armored divisions would be augmented with 32 more infantry and 4 more armored divisions, while the Air Forces' 54 groups would be more than doubled to 115. The number of candidates in the Officers Training Schools would jump from 14,000 to 90,000. The question was where and how to get these men. In February Selective Service enrolled another 9 million men, but only 1.65 million of them were twenty or twenty-one years old; the rest were older men between thirty-six and forty-four. Since Pearl Harbor, enlistments in the navy had passed the 100,000 mark, and that service did not expect to need a draft. However, the army anticipated needing another 7 million men in 1943. "These demands," Patterson told Stimson, "together with the demands for manpower in war industries, will severely tax the resources of the country in respect to men of military age."[24]

Nowhere did the numbers game prove more perplexing than in trying to square the military's needs with those of the civilian sector. One major controversy raged around the age of draftees. As the pool of men aged twenty to twenty-six dried up, Stimson and Patterson pressed to have the draft age lowered to include men eighteen and nineteen, ages they deemed excellent for military service. Roosevelt agreed, but Congress did not want to touch the issue until after the November elections even though polls showed strong public support for lowering the age. Roosevelt set April 27 as the enrollment date for men between forty-five and sixty-four, a group that hardly excited the War Department. Most observers took it to be a census for skills that might be tapped to replace men eligible for combat duty. Many of the new enrollees were veterans from the last war. One New Yorker, a machinist named Monroe Fisher who had lost his right leg in the Argonne, said with a grin, "I have a clear mind, two good hands, and one good leg."[25]

A second, more strenuous controversy erupted over the question of deferments. The 1940 Selective Service Act allowed draft boards to defer men of draft age whose occupations were deemed necessary to the national health, safety, or interest. Prior to Pearl Harbor most boards filled their quotas with little trouble, but the war's sudden demands for more men pushed them hard to find enough able bodies even as requests for occupational deferments soared because of the increase in war orders. On March 21 Lewis Hershey instructed local boards to reconsider all cases of occupational deferment. If predictions held, the boards would reach the bottom of their barrels by May unless some serious reclassification took place. Hershey announced that inductions of men up to the age of forty-four would begin in June.[26]

Men rejected in the earlier drafts for physical defects, illiteracy, or other reasons got another look as well. Those with minor shortcomings would be taken for "limited" military service to replace fully qualified men in noncombat jobs. Pressure mounted to reclassify men with dental problems or medical problems such as venereal disease by treating their ailments, and illiterates by teaching them to read and write. The nation had 1.6 million men between eighteen and fifty who were illiterate; in February the army began accepting some of them into segregated training battalions modeled on the Civilian Conservation Corps that taught them to read and write as well as drill. A special "Soldier's Primer" was commissioned to instruct them. Sergeant Alvin York, the celebrated hero of World War I, proudly registered during the "senior" draft call and offered to recruit a regiment of crack Tennessee riflemen from the ranks of hillbillies who had been rejected because of illiteracy. Patterson liked the idea. "The ability to read and write does not make a good soldier," he told Stimson. "I had fine soldiers in my company in the last war who signed their names with an 'X.'"[27]

The debate over what to do about draftees rejected for medical reasons had been going on for nearly a year. Roosevelt was perturbed to learn that nearly half the nation's youth were being rejected for physical shortcomings, most of them for bad teeth or venereal diseases. McNutt argued that they should be taken into the army and treated; Stimson disagreed vigorously and thought only those in perfect physical condition should be accepted. "I do not see any reason in the world," countered Ickes, "why men who need the attention of a dentist should be rejected." Stimson was adamant, but the growing shortage of manpower forced him to reconsider.[28]

The deferment dilemma surfaced as early as January when the chemical industry protested that the loss of chemists and engineers called to duty as reserve officers threatened the output of synthetic rubber, toluene, ammonia, and other key products. The chiefs of the army's Supply Services voiced their own complaints over loss of civilian personnel from arsenals, laboratories, and factories. After creation of the WMC, occupational deferment evolved into something between a firefight and a tug-of-war. Early on the commission announced that it would defer not only men in essential occupations but also those qualified for such posts though not actually in them. One major controversy emerged over what constituted an "essential" occupation. WMC kept expanding its list until Patterson complained that "the value of such a list is destroyed when the list is packed with so many dispensable services."[29]

A second controversy erupted over dependency deferments, the decisions on which rested in the hands of 6,443 local draft boards across the nation. Some considered all wives as dependents, others only those unable to work. Every board had its own standards as to who constituted a legitimate Class B (not wife or children) dependent. After Pearl Harbor a marriage mill developed for men hoping to escape the draft. Senator Robert A. Taft of Ohio offered a plan to eliminate dependency as a test and replace it with a classification according to family status and age. Ernest Lindley argued that another test was needed—usefulness to war production—and added that the whole process should be nationalized rather than left in the hands of local boards whose approach ranged from tough to easy. Members of the local boards insisted that only they knew the draftees and their situations.[30]

The boards consisted of unpaid volunteers who had the time to shoulder the enormous workload involved. Each one had a quota to meet and had to square that need with all the factors involved in granting deferments. "We're way short of our quota now," moaned one member after his board granted two deferments. "Lord, but this thing gets tougher and tougher." The average board had to process nearly 3,000 registrants, with some going as high as 6,000. After a slow start, most of the boards had done well until Pearl Harbor expanded their workload as well as the age of their registrants. By midwinter the typical board had sent only 240 of those 3,000 men into the armed services. Another 300 were in various stages of examinations as to whether they were fit for duty. Of the remainder, 480 were placed into Class II (men necessary to the community's welfare, such as firemen and policemen) or Class IV (unfit for various reasons), 120 had yet to be classified, and a startling 1,860, or 62 percent, received Class III deferrals for dependents.[31]

Clearly this pattern would allow few boards to make their quotas, especially when coupled with occupational deferments. Nor could they possibly balance local concerns against overall national needs in the labor market. In

June McNutt asked USES to classify all registrants by occupation and WPB to list war plants in order of their urgency. A presidential order tried to clarify the dependents dilemma by directing draft boards to take men in this order: 1) those without dependents; 2) those with Class B dependents; 3) those with wives; and 4) those with wives and children. To skirt the marriage mill, men had to have married before December 8, 1941. Stimson then issued an order making those in Class 1-B (men with minor physical defects) eligible for "limited" military service to release 1-A men for combat duty. A fifth draft registration on June 30 included men eighteen to twenty years old, but those under twenty still could not be drafted.[32]

Yet another controversy revolved around deferments for college students. The draft hit hard at the age group of male students, prompting calls from educators for laws that would defer men preparing for essential occupations or research. Harvard president James B. Conant reminded the country that institutions of higher learning provided a critical flow of scientific and technical talent as well as research. Patterson disagreed strongly with the idea of deferring any students except those training in specific fields crucial to the war effort. "The 'seed corn' people worry about the next war," he grumbled. "Our worry should be about this war." Nevertheless, in May the War Department established an Enlisted Reserve Corps (ERC), which allowed some 215,000 male students to pursue their studies without fear of the draft. It amounted to an empty vessel that provided no training or military experience. Patterson loathed the ERC as catering to the privileged class, while many academics disliked its piecemeal approach to the problem.[33]

By midsummer the manpower situation seemed as muddled as ever. The WMC had made little impact, partly because McNutt relied on a voluntary approach to the difficult issues facing the commission. Highly skilled workers remained in short supply, and new areas, such as copper mining, developed shortages as workers fled to higher-paying jobs elsewhere. A host of industries ranging from aluminum to logging complained of a shortfall of workers. By summer the crunch had spread to geographical regions as well. In July Baltimore had the dubious honor of being designated the first "critical labor area" in the nation; by October sixty-five other regions joined it. Job jumping and labor pirating had grown worse instead of better. WMC's list of "critical occupations" totaled nearly 3,000, a number Patterson thought absurd. On one side the draft drained major industries, especially aircraft plants, of irreplaceable workers, while on the other Patterson wondered "where the Army will get its men."[34]

In July Congress tried to clarify the standards of selection by revising the draft law. Three separate grounds for deferment were listed: family relationship, financial dependency, and occupational necessity. Selective Service then replaced the old classifications with seven rule-of-thumb classes ranging from single men without dependents to married men with children. Despite these changes and a 150-page book of regulations along with a steady stream of mimeograph releases, local boards continued to follow their own paths. As *Time* put it, "6,443 local draft boards have interpreted the law 6,443 ways." For the nation this meant more uncertainty in the flow of manpower; for the men involved it prolonged their inability to make any plans for their own future. "Some day soon," said *Time* wistfully, "the U.S. Government may be able to perform a major service for its male citizens: to tell them if & when they will be drafted."[35]

THE PROLONGED AND often heated debate over manpower included only passing consideration of resources that were hardly being utilized. Women got their fair share of attention, if grudgingly at times, as did older people, the disabled, aliens, and blacks. So strong was the prejudice against one group, however, that its potential contribution to the war effort was stifled from the very beginning. Long the subject of discrimination, especially on the West Coast, Japanese Americans found themselves in a hopeless position after Pearl Harbor. Twin fears, coupled with outrage over the sneak attack, combined to inflame public wrath against them: the traditional prejudice against Asiatic peoples and widespread alarm that a Japanese invasion might be coming. Against these rampant emotional forces reason and tolerance had no way to prevail.

In 1940 the census counted 126,948 Japanese Americans in the continental United States, less than a tenth of 1 percent of the population. Nearly 90 percent of them lived on the West Coast, 75 percent in California. But even in Los Angeles County, where the highest density resided, they accounted only for sixteen out of every thousand people. Their ranks included three generations: the immigrant Issei; their American-born children, the Nisei; and the latter's children, the Sansei. The Issei tended to be elderly, the last of them having entered the country before the Immigration Act of 1924 barred their entry and made the 47,000 already here ineligible for citizenship. Some states also denied them the right to vote or own land. Most of them came from Japan's countryside and drifted naturally into agriculture, as did many of their children. Where the Issei, like other first-generation immigrants, clung to many of their native traditions, the Nisei tended to be thoroughly Americanized despite the bigotry displayed against them.[36]

Those Issei who went to the cities found work as laborers, servants, and commercial fishermen. Excluded from trade unions, many saved their earnings and opened small businesses. They lived in segregated neighborhoods; Los Angeles had its own "Little Tokyo." Mindful of the prejudices against them, many Nisei worked hard to be better Americans than their white counterparts. As tensions grew in the Pacific, so did their anxiety. One Nisei student at the University of California asked in 1937, "What are we going to do if war does break out between United States and Japan? . . . Even if the Nisei wanted to fight for America, what chances? Not a chance! . . . Our properties would be confiscated and most likely [we would be] herded into prison camps." After Pearl Harbor, his nightmare vision became a reality for all Japanese Americans.[37]

The problem that emerged was twofold: how to respond to the frantic demands for protection against sabotage or subversion while also protecting Japanese Americans from the growing intolerance against them. General John DeWitt, who headed the Western Defense Command, was utterly unequal to the task. A cautious, conservative bureaucrat of sixty-one, he had spent most of his career in supply and never saw combat. He also harbored a long-standing prejudice against people of color, though in this crisis he seemed moved more by fear of invasion than by bias. The last thing he wanted as a capstone to his undistinguished career was disgrace for not taking an invasion threat seriously. Already he had shown his mettle by fanning the hysteria over imaginary air raids against major coastal cities. At the very time General Marshall was working to overhaul the army's organization by pruning it of senior officers who were unproductive and unimaginative, one such general found himself at the center of the Japanese American dilemma.[38]

"We have a very difficult problem on the west coast," admitted Stimson, who found himself in a quandary. DeWitt was pressing him to remove all Japanese from the major cities and Puget Sound, where so many aircraft plants and shipyards were located. He claimed to have evidence that Japanese spies were communicating regularly with submarines off the coast to assist their attacks on ships. Stimson had his own prejudice on the subject. The Issei might be aliens, but he considered the younger Nisei as "less staunch in their character than the older ones and . . . probably a more dangerous element at the present time." To remove the Issei as aliens would not affect the Nisei, who were his prime target, but to evacuate all of them would be difficult because "we cannot discriminate among our citizens on the ground of racial origin," which, of course, was exactly what he and others did.[39]

After poring over maps of the West Coast, Stimson remained uncertain as to the best approach. He considered it a fact that "their racial characteristics are such that we cannot understand or trust even the citizen Japanese," but he thought that removing them on such grounds would "make a tremendous hole in our constitutional system." However, he also believed that if the Japanese gained naval dominance in the Pacific, they might well attempt an invasion that would be hard to counter. DeWitt continued to press for evacuation, saying, "We know that they are communicating at sea." Actually he knew no such thing, but he also resorted to an argument that California attorney general Earl Warren advanced: The fact that not even sporadic attempts at sabotage had occurred was proof that someone was in control and orchestrating the fifth-column effort. In other words, absence of activity was proof that activity existed.[40]

Attorney General Francis Biddle had been in office only three months when the United States entered the war. "I was determined to avoid mass internment, and the persecution of aliens that had characterized the First World War," he wrote later, but as the cabinet newcomer he deferred especially to Stimson, whom he called "a heroic figure of sincerity and strength." In the West Coast crisis Biddle had to deal mostly with John J. McCloy, one of Stimson's top assistants. "McCloy was the man who handled everything that no one else happened to be handling," noted McGeorge Bundy, Stimson's official biographer. ". . . His energy was enormous, and his optimism almost unquenchable. He became so knowing in the ways of Washington that Stimson sometimes wondered whether anyone in the administration ever acted without 'having a word with McCloy.'"[41]

By the end of January most California officials, as well as a number of citizens groups, had joined DeWitt in calling for mass evacuation. At a meeting on February 1, Biddle said flatly that his department would have nothing to do with a mass evacuation that included American citizens. "You are putting a Wall Street lawyer in a helluva box," replied McCloy, "but if it is a question of the safety of the country [and] the Constitution. . . . Why the Constitution is just a scrap of paper to me." For his part DeWitt declared blandly, "Hell, it would be no job as far as the evacuation is concerned to move 100,000 people." Stimson thought otherwise. "The moving and relocating of some 120,000 people including citizens of Japanese descent," he noted, ". . . is one of those jobs that is so big that, if we resolved on it, it just wouldn't be done."[42]

But it was done. During February pressures from all sides mounted on Roosevelt to take action. Biddle made a last attempt to prevent a mass evacuation in a memo to Roosevelt, but it was in vain. The president had already yielded to the "military necessity" argument and told Stimson to go ahead along the line that he thought best. On February 19 Roosevelt signed an executive order for the mass evacuation. "I do not think he was much concerned with the gravity or implications of this step," Biddle wrote later. "He was never theoretical about things. What must be done to defend the country must be done."[43]

The order was shocking in its scope. It suspended the right of habeas corpus and all other constitutional protections against search and seizure and authorized the army to round up more than 110,000 American citizens—men, women, and children—and relocate them in what even Roosevelt admitted later were concentration camps. They had committed no crime or broken any law; the sole reason for their incarceration was their Japanese ancestry. When Eleanor complained to her husband about the racist nature of the order, he told her curtly not to mention the subject to him again. "This decision was easy," wrote Kenneth Davis, "made so by the priorities that the war imposed upon his compartmentalizing collector's mind." In that hierarchy military necessity came first, and there was, after all, historical precedent. Had not Lincoln suspended habeas corpus in dealing with the Copperheads during the Civil War?[44]

"There was at the core of him," added Davis, "a curious icy coldness that, streaking the general warmth of his nature, enabled him to turn off or on at will, seemingly, his remarkably empathic sensitivities, enabling him to bear with equanimity, if not wholly without guilt feelings, human suffering he might have prevented." In retrospect Averell Harriman thought that Roosevelt "always enjoyed other people's discomfort. I think it fair to say that it never bothered him very much when other people were unhappy." Possibly this coldness stemmed from the lessons taught him by his bout with polio, which imbued him with both an appreciation of suffering and the need for a steeliness of purpose to overcome it. For all his warmth, he was not a man to whom empathy came naturally. And did Lincoln not possess this same steely will when it was needed?[45]

Once passed on March 21, the new act put the onus of enforcement on Biddle and his department, all of whom agreed that it was blatantly unconstitutional. By then Roosevelt had created the War Relocation Authority, with Milton Eisenhower as its head, to exercise civilian control over the evacuation. Eisenhower hoped to make the process as voluntary and humane as possible, but the zeal and bigotry of many local officials undid his good intentions.[46]

The bewildered but compliant Japanese Americans were herded into a motley assortment of assembly points at racetracks, fairgrounds, and parking lots with little consideration for their personal comfort or needs. The vast majority were cooperative, believing that their loyalty to the United States was best expressed by submission to authority. Most of them lost nearly everything they had accumulated through years of hard work, including their homes, stores, and farms. Issei assets were frozen, and rapacious neighbors, along with what one federal official called "commercial buzzards," pounced on the opportunity to acquire land, homes, and goods cheaply. "The Japanese, angry but helpless, sold their dearly purchased possessions because they didn't know what to do," said writer Bill Hosokawa, "... and because they sensed the need for all the cash they could squirrel away." For an estimated $200 million worth of lost property the federal government ultimately repaid only about $38 million.[47]

In one stroke the nation not only committed its most appalling mass violation of civil rights but also deprived the war effort of one of its most productive minority groups. Japanese American farmers controlled over 450,000 acres of agricultural land. They produced nearly 40 percent of California's total crop and 22 percent of the national total even though this acreage amounted to only 1 percent of the state's land under cultivation. Historian Masakazu Iwata outlined their contribution: "As independent farm operators, the Japanese with their skill and energy helped to reclaim and improve thousands of acres of worthless lands throughout the State, lands which the white man abhorred, and made them fertile and immensely productive. They pioneered the rice industry, and planted the first citrus orchards in the hog wallow lands of the San Joaquin Valley. They played a vital part in establishing the present system of marketing fruits and vegetables, especially in Los Angeles County, and dominated in the field of commercial truck crops."[48]

Once the evacuation began, members of the white-dominated Western Growers Protective Association and others swooped in to grab this land at eviction prices or rent it for a song. In the ugliest display of irony, the governor of California asked the War Department to hold up the relocation of Japanese in July and keep them in temporary quarters so that they might be hired as laborers at harvest time—perhaps on the very land they once owned. This was too much even for Stimson, who protested it vigorously and conveyed his feelings to Roosevelt. "After the Californians have been hellbent to get the poor Japs away from California and into other States," he grumbled, "now they are turning around and trying to stop them and keep them in temporary and unsanitary quarters for their own convenience for the period of the harvest."[49]

During the months to come, the nation would sorely miss their contribution to its food and labor supply. Nor was it only farmers that were lost. The evacuation crushed but did not destroy the spirit and energy of Japanese Americans in many fields. "Can this be the same America we left a few weeks ago?" asked Ted Nakashima, a young architectural draftsman from Seattle. His father was an editor, his oldest brother an architect, and his middle brother a doctor. All four of them had been forced to abandon flourishing careers for internment in an alien wilderness. "The senselessness of all of the inactive manpower," he noted gloomily. "Electricians, plumbers, draftsmen, mechanics, carpenters, painters, farmers—every trade—men who are able and willing to do all they can to lick the Axis . . . What really hurts is the constant reference to we evacuees as 'Japs.' 'Japs' are the guys we are fighting. We're on this side and we want to help. Why won't America let us?"[50]

* * *

"WASHINGTON IS GENUINELY worried about the Negro problem," noted *Newsweek* in mid-March. "The last war was marked by race riots, and those most familiar with the situation are alarmed at the steadily growing friction between Negroes and whites today." In fact, Washington had been worried about the race situation for some time. Official concern grew as the manpower crunch grew worse and highlighted a pressing dilemma. Both industry and the military urgently needed more men, yet both resisted taking on blacks in any significant numbers. Black people comprised 10 percent of the American population and were more American than the white majority. Of the 12,865,500 blacks counted in the 1940 census, 99.4 percent were of purely native parentage compared to less than 70 percent of the white population. Yet they could not get good jobs or serve in the military except in menial roles.[51]

"When we are supposed to be making our maximum efforts," wrote an outraged Harold Ickes, "here are ten per cent of our people who are not even considered for defense jobs while, at the same time, the color line is pretty rigidly drawn in the Army." George Derrick could attest to that fact. A light-skinned black engineer living in Washington, he answered a request to be interviewed for a position of radio engineer in the Signal Corps. His training and ability so impressed the War Department officials that they offered him a better post with higher pay. As he was leaving the interview, a personnel officer asked him what nationality he was. "I am an American Negro," Derrick replied. A week later he received a letter from the War Department stating that he lacked sufficient qualifications for the position.[52]

Despite its pressing need for more workers, the aircraft industry shunned blacks. Martin and Vultee refused to hire them, and J. H. Kindelberger, president of North American Aviation, was quoted as saying, "Negroes will be considered only as janitors and in other similar capacities . . . It is the company policy not to employ them as mechanics and aircraft workers." The shipyards were more amenable, thanks in part to the stances taken by Higgins and Kaiser, but stiff resistance continued in many yards. A representative of the Bethlehem shipyard in San Pedro, California, assured a reporter that "we do not intend to practice discrimination against any race, creed, or color." But only 2 of its more than 2,800 workers were black, and both were in menial jobs even though they were skilled workmen. The South posed the most difficult problem because it had the largest supply of available black labor and the most opposition to using it, but it had no monopoly on segregated workplaces.[53]

A survey by the Bureau of Employment Security in September 1941 revealed that of 282,245 prospective job openings, 51 percent were barred to blacks as a matter of policy. For the aircraft industry the figure was 58 percent, for the electrical industry 50 percent, for chemicals 69 percent, and for iron and steel

61 percent. Shipbuilding recorded only 28 percent of jobs beyond the reach of blacks. The discrimination was not confined to skilled positions. Overall 42 percent of unskilled jobs were declared unavailable for blacks. Neither was it strictly a southern phenomenon. In Texas 52 percent of war industry jobs were closed to blacks, compared to 82 percent in Michigan, 94 percent in Indiana, and 84 percent in Ohio. The difference stemmed in part from the stronger role of unions in the North and their own bias against integrating workplaces.[54]

Most unions hindered more than they helped because of their own blatant discriminatory practices. The CIO and its affiliates tried to foster equal treatment of blacks but could not budge the segregation stance of its southern locals. "Where minority group workers are employed," conceded a CIO statement, "the union's job is often more difficult." The AFL did not even pretend to make a widespread effort at equal treatment. More than twenty-five of its affiliates excluded blacks from membership; others admitted a token few while discriminating tacitly or created a separate but not equal local for blacks. The Machinists and the Boilermakers, who together represented nearly 40 percent of aircraft workers, followed this pattern. The Machinists simply excluded blacks, while the Boilermakers placed them in segregated locals with no voice in union policies. Altogether thirty-one national unions discriminated by rules or practice against blacks, including the nineteen railroad brotherhoods, even though 20 percent of the country's 1.5 million rail workers were black.[55]

The CIO at least made an effort to end discrimination, partly to contrast its treatment of blacks with that of the AFL. During 1942 it accepted the United Transportation Service Employees, a union of primarily black baggage handlers and railway terminal employees, as an affiliate, giving CIO its first black officer on the executive board. At its November convention the CIO formed the Committee to Abolish Racial Discrimination (CARD) after realizing that more black workers were doing industrial work and demanding equality of treatment. With racial tensions in the automobile industry growing steadily, Walter Reuther urged the CIO to put racial discrimination "on top of the list with union security and other major union demands" in contract negotiations and "get this message down to the people in the factories."[56]

Some companies made progress on their own. Once Lockheed-Vega decided to hire black labor, it pressed supervisors and foremen to make sure the effort succeeded and got their agreement. Every employee received a notice of management's intention to carry out this policy based on Roosevelt's executive order. New black hires were brought gradually into the plant. Boxer Joe Louis was on hand to introduce the hundredth black worker; the white workers cheered his presence. Within months several hundred blacks held jobs at Lockheed-Vega. Elsewhere Wright Aeronautical in Cincinnati hired more than a thousand black workers without incident. Western Electric brought blacks into its

Kearny, New Jersey, plant and put them alongside skilled white employees. The factory, which made complicated instruments, had no separate cafeterias or restrooms and reported no problems or decline in the quality of work.[57]

No such progress tainted the War Department, which became the largest single employer of civilian labor after the March reorganization. It had long been a bastion of segregation and was not likely to change much under the patronizing, aristocratic direction of Stimson. Only 600 of its 13,000 employees in Washington were black, while in Army arsenals only 690 blacks filled the ranks of its 32,280 workers. Roosevelt's executive order against discrimination in the workplace had so far been honored in the breach. In June 1942 a Department of Labor survey estimated that more than half a million blacks available for war production remained idle because of discriminatory hiring practices and that the talents of an untold number of others were being wasted by their being confined to menial and unskilled tasks. Altogether blacks accounted for only 4.2 percent of the workforce in war industries.[58]

At the plant level the basic problem remained one of getting people to overcome lifelong prejudices and habits. Even white women, who also had to overcome biases to enter the workforce, protested against working with black women. "I still don't like to be near them," admitted one. "My mother is the same way. I can't say that the way I feel is right. I suppose it isn't, but I have been taught that way." Another woman told a reporter, "It don't make me no difference how hard I try. I just can't get used to working with niggers. I'll be so glad when this war is over and we don't have to do it no more." Some came to terms with their feelings. "At first I thought I just couldn't do it," said a Texas woman, "but I wouldn't want to work with nicer people. If every white man could be as nice and polite as that colored man who works with me, he'd have something to be proud of."[59]

Apart from the welter of social issues, the practical problem of production overrode all other considerations. The large, deep pool of black labor with its eagerness to find good jobs and a new life was scarcely being tapped despite the urgent need for it. Too often that very desire created conflicts that became one more rationalization against hiring more black workers. In June several thousand white workers at Hudson Naval Ordnance in Detroit instigated a wildcat strike because eight black employees were by seniority assigned to machines formerly operated by white men. A manager explained his dilemma this way: "You can't expect the plant to adopt a missionary attitude concerning its colored employees. We can't buck the whole system. This is a plant and we are forced to produce. We can't produce if our employees are going to hold up production while they fight out the race question."[60]

*   *   *

ALTHOUGH WOMEN fared much better in their quest for war jobs, they faced their own backlog of prejudices and preconceptions in entering the workforce. They were by far the largest pool of potential workers. In 1940 about 36 million women were not in the labor force and another 2 million were unemployed but seeking work. Of the latter group some 860,000 found jobs by March 1942. By the end of 1941 most women engaged in war production worked in government arsenals or naval shipyards. Only about 4,000 had jobs in the aircraft plants, and hardly any toiled in private shipyards.[61]

Private firms had all sorts of reasons for not wanting to hire women for factory and other work. They had less physical strength than men, got sick more often, and created problems of health and safety. New washroom and rest facilities had to be installed. Machinery, tools, and workbenches had to be retrofitted for them, training programs had to be revised, and sometimes new counseling services provided—to say nothing of day care areas for working mothers. All these things cost time and money. The unions did not want them, and some refused to accept them as members. Many states had laws restricting women from doing heavy work or working more than eight hours a day. Male workers objected to women moving into fields that were their domain. Above all, no one really knew what and how much they could or could not do, although most men had their own preconceptions on the subject.[62]

Yet the need was urgent and the desire among many women intense. After Pearl Harbor the surge of patriotism caught them up no less than men, but they had almost nowhere to go to fulfill the desire to serve. Representative Edith Nourse Rogers of Massachusetts understood this dilemma. She had served overseas as a nurse in World War I, acted as the president's personal representative in the care of disabled veterans, and helped in the aircraft spotting service. In the summer of 1941 she introduced a bill seeking $25 million to create a volunteer Women's Army Auxiliary Corps (WAAC) 25,000 strong. The bill languished until January 1942, when Stimson urged that it go forward with the dollar amount and number of women left indefinite. He thought that women could perform many duties that would release men for combat duty. Women swamped Rogers with letters of support. One New Jersey enthusiast said, "Let the men slackers stay home and knit sweaters for us—we look better in them anyway."[63]

The bill passed the House in March despite tough opposition. A South Carolina representative called it the most ridiculous bill he had ever seen; a colleague from New York echoed the sentiment. To these views Charles A. Plumley of Vermont replied tersely, "You cannot win this war without these women." When the bill finally passed in May, the eager women who flocked to recruiting offices ranged all the way from the daughter of Governor Leverett Saltonstall of Massachusetts to Laughing Eyes, a Creek Indian who showed up at the New York office in full tribal dress. The response exceeded all expectations. Most of the women were over twenty-five years old, half of them were married, and nearly 90 percent already had jobs. By July the first 770 recruits had arrived in Fort Des Moines, Iowa, to undergo basic training—eight weeks for the 440 officer candidates and four weeks for the 330 auxiliaries or privates, who might face eight more weeks of work if selected for specialist school. The navy did not get its women's corps until August.[64]

The push by women to get into war work encountered more obstacles. McNutt did not help by asserting on April 21 that there were "far more women workers who want and are available for jobs than there are job openings for them." A few days later Roosevelt said in a news conference that no immediate need existed to recruit women for industrial work. The first flood of applications that descended on USES offices was fueled by the surge of patriotism after Pearl Harbor. "To hell with the life I have had," declared a fashion designer. ". . . This war is too damn serious, and it is too damn important to win it." However, many of the applicants met the response, "No defense jobs unless you are a trained machinist or assembler." Those who were turned away and went home disillusioned proved harder to lure back later when the need became glaring.[65]

McNutt and the WMC continued to downplay the recruitment of women well into the fall, convinced that it was futile to recruit them if employers didn't want to hire them. But many firms were taking on women in various roles. A California aircraft plant was hiring fifty women a day, a Wisconsin tanning corporation employed 125 women for jobs once held by men, and sugar mills in Louisiana were training young women as chemical analysts. Joan Eskri, a twenty-one-year-old Pennsylvania farm girl, was painting chinaware in a small Brooklyn shop before entering a new class for shop training. After passing her bench-assembly examination, she went to work at an electrical-assembly plant for twice the pay. Of the 775 women who completed the same course, 80 percent transferred into war work.[66]

Some companies that did take on women underwent a startling conversion. Dubious supervisors discovered that women were more nimble with their hands, more patient with detail, more capable of enduring repetitive jobs without their attention straying, more willing to take direction and learn in general. At a Consolidated Aircraft plant in Texas one supervisor revealed that the production rate shot up at once in departments with a large percentage of women. Frances De Witt got a job operating a lathe at Consolidated after three weeks of craft school training. "I never did anything more mechanical than replace a blown-out fuse," she admitted. "But after the war broke out I wasn't satisfied with keeping house and playing bridge. The foreman asked if I could run a lathe. I said, 'I can, if you'll show me how.' He did, and I've been at it ever since."[67]

De Witt was one of about 20,000 women then employed in the aircraft industry. Alice "Alphie" Wagner of Montana worked at the Vega Aircraft plant in Burbank, California, as part of a five-person crew—two men, three women—that made bomb doors. Her team assembled the doors and riveted the frame and its "skin" of sheet metal. She worked forty-eight hours a week and took home $39 compared to the $16 a week she had earned working in a laundry. Having no family in the area, she had to buy her own tools, which cost $35, and paid $10 a week for a small room with a folding bed and board. At the plant the women all chipped in for a supply of hand lotion, of which they used a gallon a month. Alphie and most of her colleagues loved the independent lives they were leading and talked wistfully of continuing them after the war.[68]

Inez Sauer's life revolved around country-club luncheons, bridge parties, and golf until she abandoned it to work on an assembly line at Boeing. "My mother was horrified," she said. "She said no one in our family has ever worked in a factory . . . You don't know what kind of people you're going to be associated with . . . My father was horrified. He said no daughter of his could work in a factory. My husband thought it was utterly ridiculous." But Inez persisted even though her mother warned her that she would never go back to the life of a housewife. On that point Mother knew best. The job changed Inez's life entirely. She joined a union, marched in a labor demonstration, and encountered black people for the first time. She came to respect those who worked with their hands and had to earn their own living. Inez divorced her husband and moved with her three children into her parents' small house in West Seattle. Her former life was gone forever.[69]

By June women were not merely replacing men in western aircraft plants but competing for jobs on an even and sometimes preferred basis. At Vultee they manned the entire final assembly line except for engines and wing sections, which were too heavy for them to lift. James Kindelberger of North American, who had such a low opinion of black workers, had no qualms about women. "Employment of women has proved a boon to the aircraft industry," he admitted, calling them "well-trained, conscientious, and thorough workers." One Consolidated executive was more blunt. "I'll deny it to the end of my days if you use my name," he confided to a bemused reporter. "Listen, girl, I'll deny that I ever saw you. But if you want to know how I feel . . . If I had my way now, I'd say 'to hell with the men. Give me the women.'"[70]

CHAPTER 16

INTRAMURAL WARS

Intense, often brutal bureaucratic brawling took place throughout a good part of 1942 over adopting and implementing policies for feasibility, materials, allocations and production scheduling. While winning the battles, Nelson and the Planning Committee lost the war.
—PAUL A. C. KOISTINEN[1]

The power given Nelson . . . was greater than he ever dared use. Instead, he lived in mortal fear of having to use it. Inevitably, his failure gutted the concept of WPB and scrapped the Executive Order creating it . . . Nor could he see the simple, single problem of problems—the problem of gauging requirements and allocating capacities to meet them.
—ELIOT JANEWAY[2]

The civilian, no less than the military officers of government, chafed under the restraints which were necessarily imposed on their operations by WPB . . . The heads of agencies outside WPB did not discourage the bringing of pressure against WPB through Congress, through the press, and through other channels . . . The Chairman . . . was in the unhappy position of not being able to satisfy everybody. He was battered, abused, and cajoled by other agencies of the Government.
—BUREAU OF THE BUDGET[3]

WE ARE FIGHTING THE AXIS, NOT EACH OTHER
—PLACARD IN WPB OFFICES[4]

"NELSON'S EXECUTIVE HONEYMOON Clouded by Inter-Bureau Rows."[5] So read a headline only a month after Don Nelson assumed his new position.

The challenge facing him dwarfed anything that other executives or administrators had ever had to face. He was expected to speed the conversion process, expedite production on all fronts, rationalize the tangled priorities and allocation process, and somehow get all parties involved to pull together in the task. Public expectations could not have been more inflated; people had long craved a czar, and now it appeared they had one. But he did not have absolute power and could not wield the power he did have absolutely. As an observer noted later, "It was naïve to suppose that the Chairman of a War Production Board could sit at a table with the top officials of other agencies and determine the strategy for utilization of our economic resources. That job required the collaboration of literally thousands of men."[6]

Other agencies resisted the new arrangement. No bureaucrat, however patriotic, was about to let even a morsel of authority slip from his clutch if it could be avoided. To his credit, Nelson recognized the limitations to his power even as he freely gave some of it away to others. He also had a clear-eyed vision of what was needed. He had accepted an invitation to deliver a speech in Vincennes, Indiana, on January 14 and wrote it just before being asked to head WPB. Although not given by him personally, the speech went on as scheduled and became his first pronouncement as WPB head. In it he emphasized that the time had come to try anything and everything that would expedite production. Conversion had to come as quickly as possible. As to methods, the gauge would be whatever produced the greatest output in a given industry.[7]

"It may, in fact," he stressed, "and probably very often will, call for utterly revolutionary changes in the method of operating that industry and the whole network of relationships as between government, management, suppliers, and workers. But what of it? The one thing that counts is to get the stuff out and get it out quickly. We cannot waste three months—or three weeks, for that matter—in wrangling and discussion; we cannot compromise this demand for all-out production, or accept a formula which gives us anything less than the absolute maximum of production, just because someone's toes are going to be stepped on."[8]

What Nelson failed to grasp entirely was the extent to which direct American participation in the war changed the game. For more than two years he had sided with the all-outers in their campaign to get more production of war goods, while most industrialists continued to insist on business as usual. The all-outers fought to convert more manufacturing output from civilian to military goods. After Pearl Harbor, the push for conversion continued, but in time it forced the players to change sides. The all-outers, Nelson, and others felt obliged to maintain an adequate production of civilian goods, while industrialists and especially the military demanded that civilian output be stripped to the bone. Together these factors promised nonstop conflicts among all sides, especially as resources of all kinds grew scarce. The WPB became the cockpit in which these struggles got played out.[9]

"We have just one job to do," Nelson wrote Bob Patterson on the day WPB's creation was announced, ". . . to make enough war material to lick Hitler and the Japs, and to do it in the shortest possible time." Patterson agreed heartily; the question was how best to go about it, and what role everyone should play in the process.[10]

The assumption was widespread that one of Nelson's first decisions would be to remove the contracting power from the two services. Instead he left it intact. A second controversy had been brewing over what some critics deemed as excessive reliance on dollar-a-year men. During 1942 their number increased from 310 to a wartime high of 805 as WPB's total staff soared from 13,626 to 22,591. The Truman Committee's first report on January 15 criticized the role of dollar-a-year men and obliged Nelson to testify in defense of using them. The committee distrusted their role in making decisions that affected their own industries and wanted to do away with them altogether. Nelson disagreed and defended them as indispensable but agreed to enforce the rules against conflicts of interest.[11]

Nelson's argument was simple. "On this job we must get the maximum results from American industry," he declared. "To do that we must have down here men who understand and can deal with industry's intricate structure and operations. In other words, we must have men with expert business and technical knowledge." The committee did not like the fact that the dollar-a-year men continued to receive salaries from their companies, but Nelson countered that in most cases it was not possible to put them on the government payroll. Most were highly paid specialists with financial obligations who were asked to suspend their careers and take temporary positions with no future. Nelson himself had severed all connection with the company that had been his business life for thirty years. "No one who has not gone through it," he wrote later, "can appreciate the wrench which comes when a man resigns a job on which he has spent a lifetime . . . to take a job with the government."[12]

But Nelson also understood the need for acquiring business talent on more than a temporary basis. On February 10 he sent the Truman Committee a set of revised rules for dollar-a-year men. After a review of existing appointments, 105 such men were released and another 24 transferred to salaried status. But the dollar-a-year men hardly disappeared from the administration. Reluctantly the committee accepted Nelson's argument, although it continued to scrutinize the dollar-a-year men.[13]

Business and industrial interests continued to dominate WPB. As Catton observed, the alternative would have been "an entirely different kind of war effort. Almost inevitably, it would have turned out to be deeply and permanently revolutionary ... The decision Nelson made was fundamental, a decision to bank on the existing order—and ... to preserve it." Despite the fears of conservatives that the growing role of government in the economy portended a social and economic revolution, business remained firmly in control of WPB just as the military continued to hold the reins on procurement. Ironically, those who most felt power slipping from their hands were the original all-outers: the New Dealers. They watched sullenly as business and the military took charge of the war effort.[14]

WHEN WPB's TEXTILE Unit began life in March 1941, it had two people sharing one office and telephone in the huge Social Security Building that sprawled across an entire block. Other agencies began moving in as well, and the Textile Unit expanded to nine people. Desks, chairs, and telephones became prized commodities as the unit moved first to another floor and then, when it numbered twenty-five employees, to a floor with no partitions that was called the "broad open spaces." The entire room, a block long and a hundred feet wide, was soon jammed with so many desks that people could hardly move between them. As the unit morphed into the Textile and Fiber Section, it acquired a large table with a dozen chairs that became notorious as the "Textile Round Table," which hosted meetings of all kinds amid the jangling of telephones and streams of people moving about the room. Other meetings took place around desks, with people crammed so close together that occasionally they found themselves involved in the wrong meeting.[15]

The round table reached a tipping point when the government summoned fourteen major textile mill executives to Washington, each of whom was to organize a new unit in the section to handle that segment of the industry from which he had come. They expected to find nice offices, a secretary, and one or two telephones; instead they walked into the broad open spaces to the round table, which had chairs only for twelve. They were told that offices, desks, and secretaries would be provided "shortly," but meanwhile they had no place to hang hats or coats and no place to sit but the round table or a windowsill. Not one of them betrayed his feelings at this discovery. By noon that first day the twelve chairs were filled, and the executives began to get acquainted. When the last two wandered in, they were lucky to get a chair behind the others, there being no room at the table for them.

A system quickly developed whereby the first men to arrive put their briefcases on the table in front of a chair and thereby claimed it as their own. The last two to arrive took back seats or stood around. After three weeks desks finally arrived, but only enough to accommodate two or three men at each one. All had to share a single telephone perched on a nearby windowsill. Secretaries were hard to get, and there was no place to put them anyway. The executives got accustomed to writing their own correspondence with pencil and paper and to using outside pay phones at their own expense. It was an abrupt comedown from their past experience, but they stuck to it, most of them for two years or more even though they had been asked to come for only three months. Ultimately, the Textile, Clothing, and Leather Division (later Bureau) consisted of 10 operating branches with 525 employees and 77 dollar-a-year men that handled more than 3,500 different commodities produced in some 50,000 plants. It also had more than 110 industry committees with about 1,200 total members.

When the ranks passed 100 people, the unit moved to yet another floor. After Pearl Harbor it soared to 300 people and migrated this time across the street to another building. A few months later the ranks totaled 500, some of whom had to sit in the hallways. The unit moved again, this time to what amounted to the garage of the Ford Motor Building across town. Chairs remained prized possessions that had a habit of disappearing as if in a constant game of musical chairs. None of it fazed the faithful; this was Washington in wartime during what some called the "cuss and debate" period. No one yet knew how far to go or how quickly anything could be done, which produced much cussing over delays and debate over programs.

DURING HIS EIGHT years as president Roosevelt had shown himself to be a master of communication. He had revolutionized the art of talking to the American people through his fireside chats, demonstrating how effective radio could be in reaching even those in the most remote of locations. His frequent press conferences won the trust and respect of reporters even though most of them worked for papers hostile to the administration. He had no illusions about the lords of journalism, if only because so many of them despised him. "The more I see of American newspapers," he observed in 1940, "the more I am convinced that they represent, in nine cases out of ten, the personal slant or point of view . . . of the fellow who owns the paper!"[16]

During its first two terms the administration had worked hard to sell the New Deal to the American people. The coming of war in Europe and the growing defense program posed a different problem of communication: how to coordinate the flow of information from different agencies as well as the executive office. Here too World War I offered a model in the form of the Committee on Public Information (CPI) headed by newspaperman George

Creel with the secretaries of State, War, and Navy as ex officio members. Under Creel's energetic direction the CPI not only coordinated information from the various agencies but manipulated it as well, becoming the propaganda arm of the government. Repulsed by the measured hysteria the CPI aroused with its campaign of fear and hate, Roosevelt wanted nothing resembling it for the American government. Several of his supporters disagreed. Ickes, for one, wondered "why the President has set his face so against anything in the way of straightforward propaganda. All other countries use propaganda and it can be a very formidable weapon."[17]

However strong his dislike of hyperbole, Roosevelt had to do something. The dissemination of information, like so many other functions, was a mess. By the fall of 1941 the government had some twenty-six information offices employing more than 3,000 workers at a cost of $20 million a year. The voice of most agencies tended to advocate as well as inform. No mechanism existed to coordinate or control their output, which was often contradictory. The line between information and propaganda could be thin in ordinary times, but it grew especially precarious during the period of feverish debate over what role the country should play in the European war. There was also the matter of military security in a time of rapid mobilization. Someone had to decide what information should be withheld or deferred lest it aid the nation's enemies.[18]

A start had been made in July 1939 when the Office of Government Reports (OGR) was created to "distribute information concerning the purposes and activities of the executive departments and agencies." Two years later Roosevelt appointed Colonel William J. Donovan as coordinator of information to collect and assemble all information bearing on national security. Already in May 1941 he had established the Office of Civilian Defense (OCD), which was to sustain morale and provide a clearinghouse for information on defense activities. OCD would handle domestic morale, while Donovan took control of broadcasts dealing with overseas propaganda. Five months later, pressured by Eleanor Roosevelt and other advisers, Roosevelt created yet another agency, the Office of Facts and Figures (OFF), and charged it with "the dissemination of factual information . . . on the progress of the defense effort and on the defense policies and activities of the Government."[19]

OCD's efforts to boost morale had, in Sam Rosenman's delicate phrase, a "stormy life." To head OFF, Roosevelt chose poet Archibald MacLeish, the librarian of Congress and sometime speechwriter for the president. "In this war the Administration is very strongly determined to have the departments speak through their own mouthpieces," MacLeish said a few days after being appointed; ". . . hence, the problem of a common information policy does very decidedly come up." He promised to give the American people "the fullest possible statement of facts and figures bearing upon conditions." But in short order the agency was labeled the "Office of Fuss and Feathers." News-men complained that the different agencies were slow and inefficient, prac-ticed censorship, and sometimes contradicted one another. Where the WPB wanted to release production data to boost morale, the army and navy sup-pressed it as being helpful to the enemy.[20]

Pearl Harbor then thrust a huge new and different responsibility on the agencies. The Axis stepped up its propaganda efforts, while the Americans floundered about in search of a coherent policy. Pearl Harbor itself presented the first crisis; the public did not learn the full extent of losses for weeks, to prevent the Japanese from discovering how much damage they had done. However, when rumors of catastrophic losses began to circulate, Roosevelt felt obliged to deny them in his fireside chat of February 23. Early in 1941 the military had provided him with a plan for censorship in time of war. On De-cember 19, 1941, the president established the Office of Censorship with Byron Price, executive news editor of the Associated Press, as its director. Codes of wartime practices were to be developed in consultation with the military de-partments as well as other agencies. The new agency had two primary goals: prevent useful information from reaching the enemy and intercept informa-tion that might be helpful to the war effort.[21]

The new agency, while performing an important function, compounded the already muddled news situation. Early in January it was decided that the Censorship Office would not censor information released by other govern-ment agencies and that the principles governing the release of information should be developed by OFF. The army and navy continued to stonewall efforts to pry even basic information from them. The navy in particular exas-perated the press and public alike by refusing to release details of ship sink-ings until casualty lists had been verified and next of kin notified. Reporters charged that the navy was simply afraid of giving out bad news. Even Roose-velt was disgusted by his beloved navy, which he thought was sclerotic at the top. "He understands that under its method of organization the old men are in control," observed Stimson, who was shocked to hear Roosevelt speak so frankly on the subject. "They are very crusty and bigoted and arrogant and he is having a very hard time to get through the crust."[22]

The fact that Allied forces were suffering severe, repeated defeats on every front did not help. The press complained that the military did not disclose news fully or frankly and provided too little human-interest material. Mac-Leish tried to provide the facts, but many newspapers, especially those hostile to the administration, put their own spin on them to portray what they con-sidered the mess in Washington: faltering production, bungling agencies, botched policies, bloated bureaucracies, coddled labor, and other grievances. Radio went its own way in part because MacLeish, himself a wordsmith, and his senior staff long considered it as "distinctly minor, not to say silly." Advertisers still defined the content, especially of the immensely popular soap operas, to which war news took a back seat. "The war," one critic lamented, "was handled as if it were a Big Ten football game, and we were hysterical spectators."[23]

At bottom the issue of information dissemination revolved around the question of whether its purpose was simply to provide the facts or to improve public morale. Was it to be news, public relations, or propaganda? If all of the above, what agencies were to perform which functions? Apart from the agencies already mentioned and the information offices of numerous others, there also existed the Division of Information. Created in March 1941, it was first a part of OPM and then moved to OEM. Robert W. Horton, its director, believed strongly that in a democracy the people should be given the plain, unvarnished facts. So did Lowell Mellett, the head of OGR and Horton's boss, who also harbored a distaste for public relations and the massaging of information. Three powerful constituencies, the military, the industrialists, and the New Dealers, did not share their faith in the people. They preferred "spokesmen" who explained their activities carefully and selectively according to script and who were happiest when the press simply accepted their statements at face value.[24]

Horton built up a large staff and indoctrinated them with his approach, which Bruce Catton described this way: "We are working for the people. They are footing the bill for this defense program, and if it comes to fighting they are the ones who will have to carry the guns, and they have a right to know exactly what is being done, how it's being done, and why it's being done. It's up to us to enable them to find out. We are not supposed to cover up any mistakes that may be made, we're not supposed to build or to protect anybody's good reputation, we're not supposed to try to make something look good when it isn't good. That's not what we're being paid for; we are neither salesmen nor promoters."[25]

Both Knudsen and Nelson shared this philosophy. In his kindly, awkward way, Knudsen embodied it in his utter disdain for Washington rumor-mongering. During the fall of 1940, rumors began circulating that Knudsen would resign because Roosevelt was seeking a third term. When Horton approached him on the subject, Knudsen grew indignant. "Me quit the President?" he roared. "Why—why, *he calls me Bill!*" Why was such nonsense printed? Knudsen asked, then brushed aside the explanation and said in his brogue, "Dis job—dis is not politics! Dis is *defense!*" But Knudsen had been displaced in a rather callous manner, and the shooting war did come. Nelson too never knew what the papers would print and didn't care. He understood that opinions would differ, that they *should* differ, and he had no interest in trying to manage the flow of information in a way that made WPB look good. But Knudsen and Nelson were rarities in a city that thrived on rumors, discontents, and backstabbing.[26]

In a bureaucracy with so many agencies working on the same or similar problems and often at cross-purposes, it was only natural for intramural wars to develop, and for each group to want its own information office and spokesmen on the grounds that only they were in a position to explain what the agency was *really* doing. After Pearl Harbor the workload for both Horton's group and OFF increased sharply, as did its intensity. The two agencies did not cooperate well, and MacLeish soon became aware of the flawed nature of the order creating OFF, which gave him little authority. On February 20 he wrote a letter urging that OFF be abolished in favor of a stronger agency that would control all others in the information field. The need for some level of wartime censorship, coupled with the growing conflicts among agencies, left all parties unhappy for different reasons. The problem of "leaks" compounded the difficulties.[27]

"I note the article by Hanson W. Baldwin in . . . the New York Times of today, which gives away some of our most secret information," a perturbed Roosevelt wrote on November 2, 1941. "Obviously, this newspaperman had access either to a report which had been published, or to some individuals in the government who gave him secret information."[28]

The leak was a time-honored tradition in modern American journalism. Catton called it "one of the most important elements in our whole democratic system of government; one of those roundabout but effective devices by which the operation of the bureaucracy is kept in line." It relied on the willingness of some official in the know to convey inside information so long as his name wasn't attached to it, and on the integrity of the reporter to keep the bargain. During the weeks after Pearl Harbor official Washington was a sieve leaking information on all sides despite efforts to curb the outflow. As Catton observed wryly, "The heads of all government agencies are bitterly opposed to leaks—except when they themselves indulge in leaking."[29]

The Victory Program offered a prime example. It had never been mentioned officially in a press release, but reporters had no trouble finding out about it through Robert Nathan and other of its authors. One result was a blatant contradiction in production figures that did much to sink OPM. At a time when OPM reluctantly boosted its predicted maximum output for 1942 to $33 billion worth of war goods, Nathan and Stacy May presented data showing that the number ought to be $45 billion. In effect they were rebuking their own agency, which did not accept or reveal their report. Both men might have been cashiered for their impudence, but Henry Wallace and Don Nelson believed their analysis and took it to Roosevelt. At the same time, news of the discrepancy leaked to the press. On December 23, 1941, a series of articles written by reporter Albert Friendly began in the *Washington Post* under the title "Wanted: A Director of Supply." Friendly warned that "America's military potential is being wasted" and charged that it was then "left unorganized, unrealized, only one-third used."[30]

For his articles Friendly ignored official OPM releases and talked instead to Nelson, Henderson, Nathan, and Bill Batt. On Christmas Day, for example, Batt told him that neither the army nor OPM believed that the Victory Program could be achieved. The series brimmed with specific data hitherto unreleased and which could not easily be denied or ignored. Its impact on officialdom was terrific and devastating to an already reeling OPM. It also underscored the sharp contrast between a policy based on the public's right to know the facts and the view of the military and most government agencies that the flow of information had to be strictly controlled. The military was adamant that it ought to be the sole judge of what news concerning its activities got released, and when, and what it should contain or omit.[31]

"The Government Needs a New News Policy," proclaimed columnist Ernest Lindley, adding that "a line should be drawn between news and the various devices for improving morale." During that confused winter the demands for a reorganization of handling war information came from all sides. On March 7 Harold Smith submitted a detailed plan that left individual agencies in charge of disseminating information about their own activities but created a new agency "responsible for policy coordination and for providing centralized control over Government use of such media as the radio, motion pictures, and posters." He and Rosenman discussed the plan with Roosevelt, who raised a number of questions. Rosenman again got the assignment of thrashing out the differences and coming up with a final version. Two months passed in wrangling over final details of what the new agency should and should not be. Finally, on June 13, Roosevelt signed an executive order creating the new Office of War Information (OWI).[32]

The OWI absorbed both the OFF and OGR as well as the Division of Information and the coordinator of information. Composed of three branches, it was housed within OEM and reported directly to the president. A Committee on War Information Policy would formulate basic policy and advise the director, whose job was to "facilitate the development of an informed and intelligent understanding, at home and abroad, of the status and progress of the war effort and of the war policies, activities, and aims of the Government." The new agency did not include the Office of Censorship or some of Donovan's duties as coordinator of information. It took over Donovan's chores of creating overseas propaganda. On that same June 13 another executive order changed the office of the coordinator of information to a new agency, the Office of Strategic Services (OSS), the forerunner of the modern CIA, with Donovan still in charge.[33]

For director Roosevelt chose Elmer Davis, a veteran newsman at CBS with a strong reputation for integrity but little experience as an administrator. Told to call on the cabinet members as one of equal rank, he went first to Stimson. "He sat under a portrait of Elihu Root looking very much like him (apparently intentional)," Davis wrote his wife. Stimson lectured him on the need for military secrecy and the difficulties of getting news from a modern naval battle. Davis went next to visit Knox, who talked to him as one newspaperman to another and also stressed the importance of military secrecy. Knox said he would be glad to help but knew only what they told him. Evidently the big obstacle to information was Admiral King.[34]

Stimson came away from the meeting disappointed. "He is a typical newspaper man," he observed, "and started off with the idea that the Army and Navy were holding back information from them that the people were entitled to know." Davis was hardly alone in that belief, and he chafed at the conflicting reports coming from different bureaus. In a radio broadcast before his selection Davis said in his flat midwestern voice, "The whole government publicity situation has everybody in the news business almost in despair, with half a dozen different agencies following different lines ... Under one head, with real power, they might get somewhere."[35]

He did not expect to be the one head, and he was soon to discover that he too lacked real power. Nothing in the executive order clarified whether Davis's primary mission was to produce information or propaganda. Obviously the new agency, with its reach across all available media, would be involved in both, but which had priority? Men like MacLeish and Horton wanted simply to let the facts tell the story, confident that the American people could handle the seemingly endless parade of bad news that bleak winter. It was the honest thing to do, and truth was supposed to be the cornerstone of a well-informed republic.

However, many prominent voices urged a more aggressive approach. "Public relations, advertising and public opinion are war industries," insisted Harvard psychologist Gordon Alport, "and ought to be mobilized." Harold Lasswell, an expert in propaganda and major influence in OFF, said candidly that propaganda required "a large element of fake in it ... That only truthful statements should be used ... seems an impractical maxim." Sherman Dryer of the University of Chicago, a well-known critic of radio, went even further. "The strategy of truth," he wrote, "... is a handicap. It might enhance the integrity of our officialdom, but it is a moot question whether it will enhance the efficiency or the effectiveness of our efforts to elicit concerned action from the public."[36]

To his dismay MacLeish saw OFF moving in this latter direction. Truth in communication, Lasswell emphasized, required "the *tactics* of clarity and vividness." No story could be told literally; it needed shaping and purpose, which was precisely what public relations men, advertising men, and radio dramatists excelled at. They knew how to put the best spin on any subject, and how to sell everything from mouthwash to soap powder. A series of radio shows called *This Is War* began in February and was hooted down by many critics. "We Americans are affable enough," went the speech of one actor. "We've never made killing a career, although we happen to be pretty good with a gun . . . A sentimental people, a sympathetic people . . . We show it and we act it." Raymond Moley dismissed the show as drivel. "It was," he wrote, "as if Mr. MacLeish . . . had handed a man who wanted 'accurate' information about Denmark a copy of Hamlet."[37]

MacLeish was hardly to blame. Another series, *Your Army,* better suited his notion of what such material about the war's aims should be. However, its stronger, more forthright approach prompted a friend of Roosevelt's to complain that the message "would depress people to the point of suicide." MacLeish could not swallow the Lasswell approach. On the only occasion they met, he recalled, Lasswell had "talked to me for an hour in my office . . . and left me glassy-eyed." In trying to please the president he found himself squeezed between the advocates of fables and the clash of competing bureaucracies anxious to tell their own story in their own way. Aware that a new agency was on the way, MacLeish urged Roosevelt to make it "the occasion of my elimination." The selling of the war would take place within the time-honored traditions of Madison Avenue and the rose-colored lenses of American culture by the people who knew best how to manufacture the stuff of dreams.[38]

AS ALWAYS, THE challenge of conversion began with the automobile industry. Everyone knew what was coming; it was only a matter of when. Leon Henderson delivered the answer: The manufacture of all cars and trucks for civilians would cease on February 1. The factories would then begin full conversion to war goods. While the plants retooled, an estimated 300,000 workers would collect their newfangled $16 a week in unemployment benefits. However, no such help was available for the 44,000 car dealers and their half-million employees. Thus did the world's largest industry, which had turned out nearly 86 million cars and trucks since 1900 and changed the face of the world, go into hibernation. No other nation had ever wiped out its major industry in wartime. Altogether the automobile industry provided jobs for more than 6.7 million people, ten times as many as any other industry.[39]

Every step on the road to its demise had been pocked with controversy and bitterness. Management had resisted not only the government's attempts to curtail output in favor of war materials but also what it deemed threats to its own control over policy and decision-making. The core of the dispute involved a plan introduced in December 1940 by Walter Reuther, a bright, dynamic organizer for the UAW. Short, red-haired, and barrel-chested, Reuther was trained as a toolmaker but moved early into labor organizing. After being blacklisted by the industry early in the depression, he traveled around the world with his brother, stopping in Germany, Russia, and Japan among other places. The tour convinced him that the old order was dissolving, and the onset of war told him that Hitler had become the main enemy.[40]

To many labor officials Reuther was a young, overly ambitious intellectual, but Knudsen took his measure early. During a negotiating session between GM and the UAW, Knudsen said, "Young man, I wish you were selling used cars for us." Reuther gave him a puzzled look. "Used cars?" he asked. Knudsen nodded. "Yes, used cars. Anybody can sell new cars."[41]

Reuther had the intellect to look beyond short-term labor gains to broader ideas of general welfare. He saw in the auto industry resistance not only to unions but also to conversion despite what he viewed as idle capacity. The plan he devised was designed to utilize that capacity as well as give labor a voice in how it was done. It had three basic elements: conversion of unused capacity—*not* the entire industry—to wartime production; pooling of unused equipment and manpower of the entire industry into a single organization, a sort of "Detroit Incorporated"; and a joint board composed of management, labor, and government representatives to make decisions and conduct planning. This last provision, by far the most controversial, Reuther borrowed from Phil Murray, who had a plan for industry-wide production councils composed of the same three groups. Management loathed and feared the plan because it admitted labor into the realm of decision-making that had always been reserved for those in charge of companies.[42]

Joint committees were hardly new. They were commonplace in England, were widely used in Canada, and had proven successful on the Baltimore & Ohio Railroad. The key to their success lay in keeping them rigidly apart from any collective bargaining or grievance activities. Their purpose was to bring together in a neutral atmosphere representatives of all sides to bat around ideas on how best to improve production. The presence of a national emergency lent special urgency to the need. Along the way there would ideally develop a sense of teamwork that would make production a collaborative process without stepping on anyone's toes. For that to happen, however, the plan had to overcome a formidable obstacle: decades of embittered distrust between management and labor.[43]

Early on Reuther outlined the plan to Hillman, who liked it and showed it to Knudsen, who didn't like it. Encouragement from Bob Patterson, Bob Lovett, and the press helped keep the plan alive. After it went public on December 22, 1940, Murray and R. J. Thomas, head of the UAW, forwarded it to Roosevelt, who praised it and sent it along to OPM. There, Reuther claimed later, it languished for months until Knudsen finally sat down with him, Thomas, and some other labor leaders. Nothing came of the talks, and the UAW accused the auto industry of mounting a campaign against the plan. On January 1 an AP dispatch from Washington quoted "OPM experts" as saying the plan had been reluctantly turned down as impractical. Throughout the next year efforts were made to bury the plan in silence, but enough prominent commentators favored it to keep it in circulation. Henderson liked it, as did other New Dealers. One of Morgenthau's aides arranged a meeting between his boss and Reuther.[44]

Morgenthau warmed to the plan at once. "There is only one thing wrong with the program," he warned Reuther. "It comes from the 'wrong' source." A conference with Knudsen and Reuther resulted in a standoff about which both sides held contradictory views. "Mr. Knudsen and I had previously met on opposite sides of the table," Reuther recalled. "I thought on this matter of national defense we might sit on the same side. I was mistaken." For his part Knudsen called the plan "a good toolmaker's version," akin to one he was trying to work out with auto and airplane manufacturers.[45]

Nelson did not meet Reuther personally until a few days after becoming head of the WPB. One of his assistants brought Reuther to Nelson's office, and the two men chatted for half an hour. After Reuther left, Bruce Catton, who was present, asked Nelson what he thought of him. "He's quite a fellow," Nelson said, grinning. "We had a nice talk." He paused, then chuckled. "Three-fourths of the dollar-a-year men around this place are scared to death of that little fellow," he said. "And, you know, they ought to be scared of him—because he's smarter than they are."[46]

By then the controversy over Reuther's plan had mutated into a new form. After Pearl Harbor the OPM staged a large conference for automotive, labor, and government experts. Reuther presented an updated version of his retooling plan; no one challenged it. Later, however, five industry spokesmen met with their labor counterparts and disputed Reuther's right to participate in a discussion of production methods. "If you are interested in production," said one, "I'll give you a job." Reuther said no thanks. The meaning of Morgenthau's warning had become clear: Management wanted no part of any plan, however sound, that meant sharing their responsibilities with labor. While many in OPM waffled, Charles Wilson of General Motors said outright what many businessmen thought but hesitated to say. "To divide the responsibility for management," he declared, "would be to destroy the very foundation upon which America's unparalleled record of industrial accomplishment is built."[47]

Management had no plan, but it did not want one coming from labor, especially one that impinged on its own authority. On January 5 the military handed the auto companies a shopping list of their needs and asked them to produce as much of it as possible as fast as possible. Knudsen presided over a meeting of automobile leaders that devolved into an auctionlike session of who could make what items on the list. "We want more machine guns," he said at one point. "Who wants to make machine guns?" Some firms that had done war work the last time around expressed a willingness to do so again. Others suggested making parts for the hard-pressed machine tool industry on which the auto manufacturers were so dependent.[48]

The spectacle appalled Bruce Catton, who saw in it the bankruptcy of conservatism and liberalism alike. Eighteen months had passed since the beginning of the defense program, a month since Pearl Harbor, and OPM found itself desperately asking the nation's largest industry who could make what. At this late date companies that once made war materials suggested that possibly they might be willing to do so again. And the industry that used over half the nation's machine tools thought that perhaps, if it had nothing better to do, it might help relieve the bottleneck in machine tools. The industrial leaders of OPM could not even mobilize Detroit to the war effort and vetoed the only plan on the floor because it threatened their prerogatives. But liberals also lacked any sort of plan beyond a fallback to the threat of antitrust action. With this failure OPM breathed its last pitiful gasp.[49]

Throughout 1941 another powerful influence had been at work behind the scenes. John Lord O'Brian, the general counsel for OPM and later WPB, had spent the year working out a guiding policy for the relationship between OPM and industry. Determined to avoid the Baruch plan, he rejected the idea that industry committees should be set up as agencies of government using the latter's powers to regulate industry. When the dollar-a-year men asked how they could get around the antitrust laws, O'Brian said flatly that it couldn't be done. In March 1941 the War Department asked that the antitrust laws be suspended for the duration; O'Brian rejected the request outright. Working closely with his good friend Bob Jackson, he formulated the policy that was to prevail throughout the war.[50]

The policy was rooted in the dictum that government delegated no powers to private agents. Industry committees would be used but would remain strictly advisory; they would make no policies, issue no orders, and have no power to police any regulations issued. The distinction between government and private interests would remain clear-cut. If government wanted concerted action from any industry, it had to get advance approval from the Justice Department in writing. No industry committee could even propose such a plan, and in return the government guaranteed its members protection from anti-trust actions. Having worked out this policy with Jackson, O'Brian then created the machinery to make it work. By the end of 1941, despite grumbling and complaints, the policy was firmly established and operating. It proved to be an invaluable contribution from a man whose importance to the defense and war effort went unnoticed except by those who worked with him.[51]

As Eliot Janeway observed, "In the end it was not reason which converted the auto plants but Pearl Harbor." Still, debate continued on the Reuther plan until by early 1942 it had become distorted into many things it was not. Columnists bloated it into what Ralph Robey derided as a blueprint for converting "the automobile industry into one vast airplane production plant." The prewar version had been far more limited and fragmentary than it appeared after Pearl Harbor. Critics and supporters alike focused on different elements of the plan: the joint management-labor committees, the conversion program, and the pooling of resources. Catton thought that in the end O'Brian's policy, designed to keep big business from gaining complete, perhaps permanent control over the economy, also worked against the Reuther plan. It was, he wrote, "a gun aimed at the philosophy of Bernard Baruch, which finally brought down that of Walter Reuther."[52]

When Nelson took charge of the WPB and put Ernest Kanzler in charge of converting the automobile industry, he announced that there would be no joint management-labor committee to offer counsel. Privately he declared that "my experience in NRA was that whenever you set up a joint committee of government, industry, and labor to handle something, the first thing you know industry and labor representatives get together to see how they can screw the public." Yet he did not drop the idea entirely. In March he went on nationwide radio and called for management-labor committees to be created in all war plants to speed up production. These were not to be grievance or collective bargaining committees; their mission was limited to finding better ways of getting things done and removing bottlenecks. Nelson followed this broadcast with two more in succeeding weeks.[53]

The response astonished him. After the first broadcast more than a hundred telegrams arrived the next morning, and more continued to pour in over the next few days. They came from bankers and foundry hands, housewives and local officials, from all over the country. Most welcomed the idea of joint committees, but protests came from two groups. A small group of businessmen accused Nelson of trying to sovietize American industry and creating a vehicle for labor to take over plants. An equally small number of labor people charged that the committees were mere ploys to install speed-up techniques in plants, that they would destroy collective bargaining and put the unions under the thumb of management.[54]

Although both sides were dubious that anything could come of it, a large steel mill near Lake Michigan formed a joint committee about a month after Nelson's first broadcast. The first few months passed in mutual suspicion with each group anchored on its own side of the table. Finally, the representatives agreed, because of the plant's size, to form two-man subcommittees composed of a management and union man to look into a host of different problems. The teams surveyed their departments and reported back to the main committee. A key breakthrough came when the main committee agreed to install more than sixty suggestion boxes throughout the plant along with a system that preserved the anonymity of the contributors. Suggestions began pouring in at a rate of 160 a week, and about 15 percent were adopted.[55]

Here as elsewhere, it turned out that workers had something valuable to contribute besides their labor. In the process they came to realize that qualitative improvements could increase output without the dreaded speed-up techniques. The changes did not have to be drastic or threatening; in many cases they involved the smallest of details that, once corrected or improved, removed bottlenecks or eliminated other problems. And who knew those problems better than the people actually doing the work? A truck driver pointed out that more explicit hauling orders could reduce delivery times; a repairman showed how moving petcocks on heavy tanks to a more accessible position could save hours of repair time. These and other suggestions amounted to small changes that could add up to big improvements over time. However, as Nelson discovered, the biggest obstacle of all remained that of getting both sides to overcome their prejudices and give the joint committees a try.[56]

FOR MORE THAN two years the conversion process had been an endless battle between the all-outers and the conservatives who argued for a gradual pace to soften the dislocations involved. Pearl Harbor settled the debate, leaving only the question of how rapidly to expand existing facilities and build new ones. Early in 1942 WPB stopped all nonessential construction to husband resources for wartime facilities. The brunt of conversion work fell to Knowlson's Division of Operations, which oversaw the Bureau of Industry Branches, the Bureau of Priorities, and the Bureau of Industry Advisory Committees. The basic working units of WPB were the industry branches, forty-two in number by March. Under the direction of Philip D. Reed, chairman of the board at General Electric, they handled the day-to-day work and grew steadily in significance.[57]

The chief of each branch, who wielded authority over it, could not be from the industry he controlled, an arrangement that avoided conflict of interest but left the branch in the hands of someone unfamiliar with it. However, those beneath him could and often did come from the industry, and most branches had industry advisory committees to assist them. For these committees Knowlson and Reed recruited hundreds of executives, most of them dollar-a-year men, and thereby aroused the wrath of the Truman Committee and other critics. What they lacked was any kind of master plan for converting the economy or curtailing nonessential production. The lack even of guidelines forced them to improvise on the premise of matching conversion with available war contracts to keep plants humming and employees from drifting to other jobs. As a result the conversion process got off to a slow and uneven start that drew fire from all sides.[58]

Nelson viewed the conversion process as having three stages. First, the requirements for men, materials, and machinery for every part of the war economy, both military and civilian, had to be charted to calculate the total demand. Once WPB knew how much of what was needed, it had to determine accurately what resources were available, how much of each one could be had, what shape they were in, and how readily they could be adapted to the demands for them. Finally, the requirements had to be matched against the resources and some sort of balance struck between them. Where gaps existed, efforts had to be made to find new sources of production. If it became clear that available resources could not possibly meet the demand for them, then the requirements had to be reduced to more realistic levels. All of this was difficult enough, but since the war picture changed constantly, the productive machinery had to be flexible enough to adjust to whatever modifications were needed.[59]

The task was not only huge but had to be accomplished on the run under the drumbeat of constant criticism from all sides. Of necessity much had to be improvised. "Industry—in fact, the entire economy—shivered under the impact of conversion throughout the first six months of 1942," Nelson recalled. "It was like nothing else the nation had ever felt or witnessed." Designs were changing, new technologies were emerging, some of them scarcely off the drafting board, new plants had to be built and existing ones overhauled, and the clamor for key materials grew ever more incessant. There arose what Nelson called "some hysterical argument for the type of conversion which would have closed down almost every plant in the country able to produce for war." Some came from WPB personnel who wanted civilian production halted even though it was not yet clear what the idled plants would manufacture instead.[60]

Nelson found it amusing that WPB was being criticized for being too slow in cutting off civilian production. "Actually, the job was done with tremendous speed," he insisted. His only misgivings later concerned "the possibility that in some cases we cut too fast and too far." By the end of June the production of consumer durable goods had been cut 29 percent. Although critics carped that some firms and industries continued to resist conversion, the process was not easy and in many cases not even possible. Of the nation's 184,000 manufacturing firms, some 78,400, or 43 percent, could not be used for war production and found it virtually impossible to obtain critical materials for nonessential production even at reduced outputs. The plight of these mostly small- to medium-sized plants was genuine and not easily fixed. The Office of Civilian Supply (OCS) tried to help them but lost much of its clout in the transition of agencies. In OPM it had overseen those industry branches not directly involved in war production, but it had no such control in the WPB.[61]

Nelson sympathized deeply with these firms and recognized the need for a continued flow of civilian goods, but his primary task was to convert industry to the production of munitions. "We are now going through a period of basic economic transition," he wrote early in 1942. "Ours is consequently the problem of converting civilian establishments to the production of war materials. It is an unwelcome job of vast proportions, full of heartaches and risks." In March WPB launched a major production campaign entitled "Taking the Fighting Fronts into the Factories" with the goal of instilling "a missionary-like zeal along the assembly lines and work benches." Nelson asked plants to form management-labor committees to oversee the campaign and help spread the gospel. The expected protests arose at once, especially over one suggestion that the committees consider ways of improving plant efficiency. Management complained that such committees were an entering wedge to socialize plants; unions registered their own fears.[62]

Although the campaign floundered, the pace of conversion quickened. Production of numerous civilian products ranging from refrigerators to gaming machines to metal office furniture was shut down. Knowlson favored a gradual approach that kept a factory and its workers intact rather than an abrupt stoppage before management could obtain war orders to replace its lost output. However, he admitted that his effort at synchronizing conversion with war contracts was not entirely successful. The most obvious and direct method of forcing conversion on a company was to deny it raw materials needed for any nonessential products, but WPB proved lax in resorting to this weapon.[63]

In practice most conversion took place through L (limitation) orders, which banned in part or whole the production of certain items, most notably consumer goods, or M (material) orders, which limited how a scarce material could be used. Created on August 30, 1941, by OPM, the L order was used at first to reduce the output of the automobile industry, and was gradually extended to refrigerators and other products. After Pearl Harbor such orders were applied more freely and in some cases with insufficient information on the industry in question. By March 14 WPB had issued forty-eight curtailment or shutdown orders and ninety-one conservation orders curbing or prohibiting the use of critical or scarce materials. During the next three weeks twenty-five major L orders went out, stopping the manufacture of products ranging from lawn mowers to vacuum cleaners to vending machines, while a host of other goods received curtailment orders.[64]

For all the angst shed over its performance, the automobile industry moved smartly toward full war production. Whole rows of giant machine tools sat in outside yards wrapped in brown paper or merely coated with grease, awaiting the day when they would return to making cars. Nearby vacant lots overflowed with the last new cars sitting locked until the government churned out rationing tickets for their release. "Business-as-usual in Detroit is not dead; it is forgotten," proclaimed *Newsweek* in March. On every side could be seen new plants opening or going up even as existing ones pushed toward record outputs. Ford's River Rouge spewed out airplane engines along with Packard's big plant for Rolls-Royce engines. Chrysler's three assembly lines bristled with tanks in the making. Hudson Motor Car's plant at Center Line had tripled its production of antiaircraft guns and other naval ordnance since December 1.[65]

Girders were in place for a Fisher plant that would make all-welded tanks. A Briggs factory was ready for brickwork, and Ford's enormous Willow Run seemed near completion. "Breathtaking in its hugeness," marveled a reporter of the cavernous building, but even smaller, older plants impressed. A former AC Spark Plug factory in Flint set weekly output records for machine guns. A series of clever shortcuts expedited the conversion of many facilities. Plymouth managed to replace what it called "the world's longest assembly line" with dozens of new machines in only a month. DeSoto ripped a machine out of its tank arsenal to squeeze in three new assembly lines, then put the machine back in three days later. Chrysler salvaged fifty old machines destined for the scrap heap and used them to help produce antiaircraft guns. It also had a $100 million contract to build a bomber plant at Chicago.[66]

Improvisation became a crucial technique in the process. Told that they could not get a machine to make a new type of universal joint, Dodge engineers altered some old passenger-car equipment and went into production in only two months. Ford engineers adopted castings in place of forgings on air-cooled airplane engines, thereby saving time, machining, and thirty-five pounds of steel among other materials. They also managed to convert a four-spindle boring machine for V-8 engines into a three-spindle unit for tank-gun mounts. At Flint, Fisher Body's engineers built their own huge vertical boring mill in less than two months after learning they could not get one until fall, and offered to supply other tank producers as well. Across town at the Buick works, employees in a former warehouse were increasing production of plane-engine parts machined to tolerances finer than those required by watches.[67]

By June the auto industry could report that conversion was complete and war goods of all kinds were rolling out of its factories ahead of schedule. Detroit was building 75 percent of the nation's aircraft engines, more than half the navy's diesel engines, more than a third of all machine guns, and nearly half of all tanks, along with thousands of motorized vehicles, weapons, parts, and accessories. One company agreed to produce shells, substituted forging for the usual tooling method, used equipment originally designed to make wheel hubs, and turned out a million shells in thirty-five days. A producer of an antiaircraft gun cut eighty days from the British production schedule for it. A parts firm devised equipment that produced machine-gun parts thirty times faster than the regular arsenal machinery could assemble them. One company boasted that it would soon handle in one day the materials it handled in thirty days a year earlier.[68]

When battle experience in North Africa showed glaring defects in riveted tanks, manufacturers moved quickly to a new, all-welded version with a revolving turret; to the surprise of many, the switch went more smoothly than the old annual model change. Nearly all military vehicles were equipped with all-wheel drive that enabled cars to climb grades of 40 to 50 percent. On a contract for a small combat vehicle, one company saved 41,000 pounds of nickel. Another developed a new solder of silver, antimony, and lead to replace the usual tin and lead. New methods of controlling carbon steels saved large quantities of alloys. More than a hundred companies were engaged in aircraft production. One of them, with fifteen contracts, announced that it was 15 to 39 percent ahead on every one of them. Some parts, once ground by hand, were grouped into special jigs and automatically ground out fourteen at a time.[69]

In the process of refining their production methods, companies often succeeded in lowering the cost of items as well. One firm devised efficiencies that reduced the price of a naval component six times from $30,000 to $20,000. Another plant used automotive-type machinery to cut the time required for a wing-panel operation by 75 percent and the cost by $1,000. Bruce Catton attributed this remarkable turnaround to "the industry having at last discovered that all but a fraction of its tools could be used to make munitions, and government having finally discovered that the way to convert the auto industry was (a) to keep the industry from making autos, and (b) hand out profitable contracts."[70]

As the conversion process ramped up production, however, its very success amplified another problem area, that of shortages. With more and more companies going all out to increase their output, with construction of both military and war production facilities climbing sharply, and with the demand for skilled workers growing more intense, collisions were bound to occur in the competition for men and materials. Someone had to orchestrate the flow and distribution, weigh the urgency of one claim versus another, and balance the process in a way that did not allow one element of it to short-circuit the others. The key concept in approaching this fiendishly difficult task was one little known and much despised by most businessmen and the military: feasibility. With it came another round in the seemingly endless intramural wars.

AT THE JUNCTION of two country roads near Rockford, Illinois, far off the beaten path, stood an emblem of conversion in its most basic form. The white clapboard farmhouse with its old-fashioned gambrel roof, dormer windows, and neat flower boxes on the windowsills looked like any other, but it had become the Harrington Bros. Machine Tool & Fixture Co., which turned out a thousand dollars' worth of machine tools a month for making shells and tank turrets. At sixty-eight John Harrington still had the energy to work long hours at a grinder while his wife, ten years younger, manned the lathe. Their thirty-four-year-old twin sons, Richard and Russell, rounded up orders, swept out at night, and often spent sixteen hours on the job. Richard's wife kept the books, Russell's did all the cooking. So good was their work that the big companies who gave them subcontracts no longer bothered sending inspectors to the shop. "I used to get a laugh out of those guys," said Richard. "When they spotted this place, they went nuts."[71]

   The boys had actually started the company during the depression, borrowing money to build the house and machine shop. They ran it as a spare-time operation until the war came, when they set up to get some bigger contracts. Their first offer required a new $4,000 machine, a sum they had never seen. Instead they rigged up their own version from a junked lathe, the motor from an old washing machine, an oil pump from a 1926 car, and one of Mom's old washtubs to catch the oil that leaked. It got the job done. The twins got four more contracts, providing work for two brothers-in-law and five others, all of whom kept the same hectic hours for a share of the profits. "They're doing a swell job," said Rockford's local WPB director. "I don't think they knew what they were getting into when they started, but they had the nerve to make a success of it." Old John Harrington shrugged off the long hours, saying, "I have more fun than a kid in this place."

CHAPTER 17

THE FEASIBILITY FOLLIES

As money began to pour into the treasury, contracts began to flood out of the military purchasing bureaus—over $100 billion worth in the first six months of 1942, a stupefying sum that exceeded the value of the entire nation's output in 1941 . . . Military orders became hunting licenses, unleashing a jostling frenzy of competition for materials and labor in the jungle of the marketplace. Contractors ran riot in a cutthroat scramble for scarce resources.

—DAVID KENNEDY[1]

This critical review of material demands . . . revealed the all too-human propensity of energetic supply officers . . . to overlook completely the needs of other services and other needs of the total economy . . . Many supply officers were caught trying to complete in 1942 end products which would have been stored for 2 years . . . It was surprising to discover how passionate, tricky, and ill-balanced men can become because of short-sighted over-loyalty to their own program.

—BUREAU OF THE BUDGET[2]

Amid the cheers one great fact remained largely obscured: no matter how ably Boss Nelson and his War Production Board . . . perform their functions, all of them collectively will not produce so much as a single screw for a plane or tank or gun or ship.

—FORTUNE[3]

"GIVE US THE ORDERS!" CRIED the industrialists, large and small, "and we'll solve production." But the problem was much more complicated than simply increasing output. The war production machine was a giant engine with an enormous number of parts that had to be synchronized to work properly. This proved to be the most fundamental task facing the WPB, and the most difficult as well.[4]

Early in 1942 feasibility emerged as the central issue confronting WPB. It involved determining the maximum demand for goods, both immediate and long-term, that mobilization could handle without becoming unstable. Until this was known, there was no way to create balanced programs, schedule production, or impose priority and allocation controls. The problem was that few businessmen even knew about the concept of feasibility, fewer still gave a damn about it, and the military ignored it almost entirely. Feasibility was an analytical tool, the brainchild of academics and statisticians who were resented by the military and most businessmen for meddling in matters where they did not belong. Acceptance of the concept, after all, would impose limits on their power to make decisions and would elevate the role of impractical outsiders. The task of figuring out maximum demand was difficult enough; getting it accepted by so many nonbelievers in positions of authority made it almost impossible.[5]

The typical procurement officer, military or civilian, thought only in terms of what he needed and simply had to obtain by a certain date, be it tanks, shoes, beef, or packing boxes. The nature of the job compelled him to believe that no one else's order could possibly be as important or urgent. He labored tirelessly to place his orders wherever possible. The supplier accepting his order then hired more workers, ordered more machinery, and placed orders for steel, wool, lumber, ball bearings, or whatever he needed to fill the order. By this random process thousands of orders accumulated until they began to exceed the capacity of machine-tool manufacturers, mines, and sources of raw materials to meet their demands. They too needed to expand, which required still more raw materials and workmen. As the inevitable shortages developed, no mechanism existed to determine a hierarchy of needs.[6]

Roosevelt aggravated the problem with his inflated production demands in January, forcing military and civilian agencies alike to scramble madly in an effort to meet them. He asked for an expenditure of $52–55 billion for munitions and construction in 1942 and $60–65 billion in 1943, staggering amounts given that total defense outlays in 1941 totaled only about $18.5 billion and the sum value of construction and goods actually delivered was only $14.7 billion. In part Roosevelt drew on SPAB's Victory Program of December 1941, which called for spending $110–115 billion by September 1943. By contrast OPM had projected peak production goals of $27 billion for 1942 and $34 billion for 1943. For its part the ASP submitted a program calling for expenditures of $63 billion for 1942 and $110 billion in 1943, far beyond what was considered feasible for the economy to produce. Even the rosiest estimates of the economy's ability projected shortfalls against these demands of $20 billion in 1942 and $45 billion in 1943.[7]

Nor was that the only problem. The flow of materials desperately needed better orchestration, as did the balance between military and civilian needs. As shortages mounted, bottlenecks proliferated, deranging schedules and clogging plants with unfinished goods—planes needing propellers, tanks needing guns. The priorities system helped only slightly because, among other defects, it lacked any form of quantitative control. By the time the WPB appeared, the priorities system was bankrupt, a victim of bloated categories and rankings. The scramble for raw materials took place on several levels. Military needs competed first with those of civilians and then with each other. The military's voracious appetite prompted Leon Henderson to remark ruefully that, having fought for a year to keep a boom in civilian goods from devouring war materials, now he had to turn around and fight to save civilian goods from being wiped out.[8]

Part of the problem involved the huge construction programs proposed by both the military and the government. Together they accounted for a major portion of the total munitions budget and posed the threat of becoming white elephants. The building of new plants or bases could swallow large amounts of increasingly scarce raw materials only to find that, once ready, they could not obtain needed machinery, equipment, and supplies. They would be as useless as tanks without guns or planes without propellers. The object of feasibility studies was to prevent this kind of imbalance and waste of resources.[9]

The thankless task of grappling with the feasibility issue fell to Bob Nathan's Planning Committee, which had close ties to the two agencies headed by Stacy May. When Nelson created the committee in February, he told reporters, "I want a group of . . . the best people I can get, to do a lot of thinking about how the job might be done better . . . Its job is to look ahead and spot problems that we will be running into six months from now, and develop proposals to solve those problems." Nathan and Fred Searls doubted the accuracy of the figures underlying the Victory Program and therefore distrusted its feasibility conclusions as well. They agreed that a new, larger study had to be made, one that embodied less guesswork and embraced the entire economy.[10]

To conduct the feasibility analysis Nathan chose economist Simon Kuznets, a pioneering authority on national income who toiled in May's Statistics Division. Kuznets had been Nathan's mentor and boss; when Nathan took over OPM's Bureau of Planning and Statistics he went to work for his former student. A native of Pinsk, Russia, he became the third winner of the Nobel Prize in economics. Since 1927 he had worked for the National Bureau of

Economic Research except for brief periods of government service. The call from Nathan was one such assignment, and one eminently suited to Kuznets. No one knew more about the relatively new concept of national accounts and their value for taking the measure of a national economy. During the 1930s Kuznets had taken charge of a belated project by the Commerce Department to gather such data for coping with the depression. In that project a young Bob Nathan had served as one of his assistants.[11]

All three men had worked closely with Henderson as fellow all-outers; once into the war, they struggled to keep unharnessed military spending from sinking the overall economy. By mid-March Kuznets completed a preliminary analysis showing that $48 billion was the maximum amount in munitions and construction that the economy could manage in 1942. Nathan and May alerted Nelson that immediate action was needed to curb the military's demands. "Any attempt to attain objectives which are far out of line with what is feasible," they warned, "will result in the construction of new plants without materials to keep them operating; vast quantities of semi-fabricated items which cannot be completed; production without adequate storage facilities; idle existing plants due to lack of materials; and similar disrupting situations."[12]

Nelson accepted these conclusions and asked the armed services to help him lower the requirements to more reachable levels. The navy refused, but Patterson agreed to try. Roosevelt approved a reduction from $63 billion to $45 billion for 1942 but neglected to do so in writing or notify the military of his decision. By the end of April the munitions total had been cut by $4.5 billion but construction and facilities increased $1.6 billion, for a paltry $2.9 billion net reduction. To Nelson fell the dreary task of trying to persuade the military to cut its requests to more reasonable levels. Patterson tried to be cooperative but strong resistance came from elsewhere, especially from the strong-willed Somervell, who had just taken charge of ASF in March. Somervell insisted that production could be increased sharply if WPB would only be more forceful in providing raw materials. He wanted no limits placed on his supply goals, especially by a civilian agency that in his view had no business meddling in military requirements. He admitted freely that his want list did not include "any consideration for the practical limitations of available raw material and other industrial resources." Stimson, Patterson, and Marshall all supported or at least tolerated Somervell's stand, as did those WPB officials who agreed that the military should have direct control over its supply operation.[13]

To Nelson's dismay, Roosevelt changed his position. On May 1 he wrote Nelson, "I am apprehensive that the schedules established . . . are not being met, and I am convinced that a more determined effort must be made at once." The letter reiterated and even expanded his earlier want list; it also included ASF's entire shopping list. Another letter followed three days later, both of them couched in an uncharacteristically formal tone. Dumbfounded by the president's stance, Nelson could only reaffirm his loyalty and dedication. "Please know that I appreciate fully the helpfulness of your directives," he replied meekly, "and that my complete energy and devotion will be focused on carrying them out." For the moment the feasibility program dangled in limbo, but its authors had no intention of leaving it there. Within a few months it would return in a blaze of controversy.[14]

WHILE THE FEASIBILITY fight dragged on, a related battle developed over how to fix the broken priorities system. Nearly everyone agreed that the major bar to high production goals remained the lack of effective controls over the flow of materials. The problem grew steadily more acute as the defense program expanded and shortages of key materials began to appear. Some rational way had to be found to prioritize the process of who got how much of what. After a decade of depression in which surpluses tormented the economy, the adjustment to the reverse condition of growing scarcities proved difficult and fiendishly complex.[15]

The quest for a system began on August 12, 1940, when the ANMB received authority to issue priority ratings on critical and essential items for all army and navy contracts. Two days later it released the first Priorities Critical List of items to which preference ratings might be assigned. From this arose the preference rating system that encountered operational problems from the start. Apart from generating a blizzard of paperwork, the system foundered as the war production program expanded. When the use of M and P (General Preference) orders proved inadequate as control instruments, OPM added the limitation (L) order in August 1941 to cope with the growing shortage of key materials. Still the overall organization of American industry lacked any cohesive plan or quantitative controls.[16]

A first step toward forging a more effective system came in May 1941 with the introduction of the Defense Supplies Rating Plan (DSRP). It streamlined the cumbersome individual preference ratings system and allowed manufacturers to apply to OPM in advance for a rating to cover supplies of scarce materials for an entire quarter. Although DSRP greatly improved the process, it could not handle the accelerating demand for so many goods and products that undermined the preference system. No machinery existed to measure the magnitude of the overall priority load, which kept expanding. By November 1941 more than 5,000 firms were operating voluntarily under DSRP, but priorities inflation had already eroded its effectiveness. An amended

version of DSRP was introduced under the name of Production Requirements Plan (PRP or "Purp"), which provided a mechanism for quantitative
control of both input of materials and output of finished products.[17]

PRP had several advantages over its predecessor. It was more flexible and
offered a broader range of classifications, but it remained voluntary, and a
large number of manufacturers continued to work outside it as they had with
DSRP. With so many firms outside PRP, WPB officials had no way to develop
a complete statement of the material requirements needed for the wartime
economy. By the time of the attack on Pearl Harbor they were still groping for
a viable integrated control system, which seemed as far away as ever. Under
the urgency of war, two key problems had to be solved as quickly as possible.
A satisfactory method for estimating material requirements had to be developed, and the existing system had to be replaced with one that could guarantee that every claim to scarce materials would be honored once it had been
validated. The latter could only be done by limiting allotments to the total
available supplies, which in turn required a reliable estimate of how much of
any given material could be had.[18]

By March the ratings system was in such disarray that 56 percent of the
huge munitions program had been stuffed into the A-1-a subcategory, making it all but useless. Military orders had overwhelmed civilian needs and
were competing with each other for priority. Even worse, three separate entities were struggling to gain control of the process: WPB, the army, and
ANMB. Nelson was determined to keep the reins in civilian hands but faced
heavy opposition. Once installed as head of ASF, Somervell waged an aggressive campaign to get priorities, if not the entire economy, out of civilian
hands. ANMB also had a new head in Ferdinand Eberstadt, who took charge
on Pearl Harbor day. The executive order creating WPB stipulated that the
ANMB report to the president through the head of WPB. Since the civilian
agency served as the meeting ground where all sides asserted their claims for
resources, Eberstadt defined his role as one of advocating the military's needs
"in this contest of conflicting demands." The army, in the person of Somervell,
was its own advocate.[19]

Late in February Eberstadt, with Nelson's approval, got the president to
approve a revision of ANMB's authority. Among other things it was directed
to translate military requirements into materials, productive capacity, and
equipment and develop plans to meet them. It was also to ascertain potential
bottlenecks in the procurement and production process and suggest measures to resolve them. In all its work, however, ANMB remained subject to
orders, directives, and instructions from WPB. It had duties but no powers.
Nelson remedied that shortcoming by delegating to ANMB the authority to
establish preference ratings for army, navy, Maritime Commission, and for-

eign government orders under the Lend-Lease Act. Knowlson persuaded Nelson to extend ANMB's reach to priority ratings on military contracts, machine tools, and military construction on the grounds that WPB lacked the organization and expertise to do the job.[20]

From that point on, ANMB became a major player in the battle over priorities. Eberstadt arranged to get ANMB representation in both Knowlson's industry branches and Batt's commodity branches. On May 20 ANMB handed WPB a proposed new priority directive in which military production and the facilities needed for it were ranked in five categories that were to take precedence over all other priorities, and no items were to be added to the categories without ANMB consent. No provision was made for indirect military, civilian, or Lend-Lease requirements. In effect the proposal gave ANMB the right to prevent WPB from extending military priorities to cover these other areas. Nelson understood the military's need to "determine which weapon was needed first," but leaving out all the other categories would in effect deliver control of the economy to the military.[21]

Both the Planning Committee and WPB's operations staff vigorously attacked the proposal, citing two major weaknesses: the lack of provision for civilian and other needs, and its failure to translate end-use items into the raw materials needed to produce them. But ANMB had no responsibility for civilian needs; its duties were confined solely to the production of military goods. Joe Weiner of OCS went to see Eberstadt and pointed out the lack of any provision for repair parts needed when factory equipment broke down or trains and buses needed replacement parts. Eberstadt agreed and inserted a new priority rating into the proposed scheme. Still Knowlson and Nathan urged Nelson not to approve the new rankings. The Planning Committee wanted a top-level production and strategy group to determine the size, composition, and timing of the entire production program, and it did not want ANMB as an intermediary in the process.[22]

Under pressure from all sides, Nelson had few options. Roosevelt's May 1 letter had emphasized the necessity for pushing "must" programs without delay and supported ANMB in other ways. ANMB had submitted its proposal as an emergency measure, and Nelson had no clearly formulated civilian program to offer as an alternative. Against the advice of his own agency people he reluctantly decided to approve the new ratings with the included provision for urgent civilian needs. At almost the same time he also decided to put in place a revised version of PRP on a basis that hoped to fix its earlier weaknesses. By making it mandatory rather than voluntary, WPB could acquire the data to tabulate the total material requests from all industry for a quarter or more in advance. Using this information and knowledge of available supplies from its material branches, WPB could then make allocations of material on a plant-by-plant basis within the limits of available supplies. For the first time WPB would gain nearly complete information on the overall wartime industrial load, and with it a tool for maintaining economic stability.[23]

PRP was a horizontal control system in that it relied on direct dealings between WPB and individual firms. By contrast a vertical system channeled requirements estimates and material allotments vertically through the procuring agencies and the contractual chain associated with each contract. The military, WPB's materials branches (staffed largely by industrialists), and other WPB officials strongly preferred a vertical system, partly because it kept control of the priorities process in their hands. Patterson and others regarded PRP as a utopian fantasy. Its complexity presented herculean administrative challenges as well as a mountain of paperwork. Eberstadt also complained that PRP departed from standard industrial practice. "The most important factor," he emphasized, ". . . is fully balanced timing [of materials flows] aimed at steady and uninterrupted flow of end products." How could such crucial timing be performed by a central agency rather than at the relevant operating levels?[24]

Everyone conceded that PRP was an ambitious reach. It hoped to track and orchestrate the flow of at least 90 percent of thirty-six metals basic to manufacturing. The paperwork was enormous and the task of tabulating, classifying, and analyzing the blizzard of reports monumental. Months were needed to acquire and train enough staff as well as set up procedures, but WPB did not have the luxury of time. Months had passed not in doing this work but in fighting to get PRP accepted. On May 13 Nelson notified the War and Navy departments that he had tentatively decided to place PRP on a mandatory nationwide basis as of July 1. The implementing order finally appeared on June 10, only three weeks before the plan was to take effect. It promptly touched off another round of intramural warfare.[25]

More than two years had passed since the start of defense mobilization, and six months since Pearl Harbor, yet the need for an overall grasp of the production process and its basic components was still being debated and the techniques crucial to acquiring the needed data and implementing a program still languished on the drawing board. Without this basic information, how could policy decisions on the organization of industry for maximum output be made? In April a special committee appointed by Nelson confirmed the lack of effective controls over the flow of materials as the primary weakness. Nelson hoped that a strengthened version of PRP would remedy the problem, but the opposition to it ensured that it would not succeed. The first quarter of its operation became an exercise in improvisation and dissolved into administrative chaos, reaffirming to its critics that they had been right all along.[26]

No one objected to PRP more strongly than the military, especially the army. During the months of its planning and operation, the services kept placing contracts for all types of war materials with absolutely no concern over whether the level of deliveries could be met by the quantities of scarce raw materials allocated for them. Despite repeated efforts, Nelson and WPB had found no way to compel the military to limit their orders within the boundaries of available raw material supplies. As Allied forces endured one defeat after another, Patterson insisted that nothing stand in the way of getting materials for what he called "a limited balanced program" of munitions. But the military's own strategists could not define such a program or compute requirements for a global war, the future course of which they could only guess. "We have been waiting for over a month now," Patterson complained on April 7, "for a list of objectives from the Combined Chiefs of Staff . . . which will furnish a firm basis for sensible priority ratings. But I do not believe we can wait any longer." He told the ANMB to prepare a tentative program and set of super-ratings to achieve it, thereby setting in motion the May proposal that directly challenged the WPB's authority over priorities. When Nelson responded by instituting the PRP, the stage was set for overlapping jurisdictions and inevitable conflict between the two agencies.[27]

Like the fight over feasibility, the battle over priorities raged on through the summer. The military came to view Nelson and WPB as advocates of a comfortable civilian economy and therefore an obstacle to expanding munitions production. He in turn saw their demands as attempts to gain military control of the economy, which he staunchly resisted. A distracted Nelson found himself putting out fires on several fronts even while he presided over a reorganization of the WPB itself. By midyear he had gained enough experience to see the need for refining the structure that had been thrown together so hastily.[28]

ALTHOUGH NELSON DECLARED on April 21 that conversion would be completed by the end of May, criticism of WPB continued to pour in from many sources. Congress bemoaned the slow pace of conversion, and the army complained of weak management. Every muddle over procurement or delay in production led it to insist yet again that the military's needs were being sacrificed to "soft civilian desires." Moreover, WPB continued to grow as its workload swelled; by July 1 the original staff of 6,600 inherited from OPM had nearly tripled to 18,000. In many other respects as well, WPB had outgrown the organization it inherited. On July 4 Nelson showed Roosevelt a proposal to revamp the organization and won his approval.[29]

In preparing the new plan, Nelson recognized that the strategic landscape had evolved. With conversion well in hand and the output of munitions soaring, the main task revolved around the meeting of production goals some thought to be all but impossible. To accomplish this required more attention to the integration of military strategy and production programs, scheduling and control issues, and more efficient distribution of materials to the proper military and civilian users. The collapse of the preference rating system made this job even more urgent. Nelson envisioned six primary tasks for the reorganized WPB: control the flow of materials; coordinate economic and military strategy and military plans with economic possibilities; balance the whole production program; stimulate the production of raw materials and components; track production progress, assess its results, and anticipate bottlenecks; and fully utilize the potential of smaller plants.[30]

It was not a reorganization but a "realignment," Nelson told the press. "Whatever the name," concluded *Newsweek*, "he intended it chiefly to strengthen his control over the flow of materials." With conversion completed, the prime challenges became materials and their allocation. The realignment sought to address those issues, but, as *Newsweek* observed, "it falls short in its failure to clarify relations between WPB and the military services on material control." Nelson seemed to have the upper hand; after a meeting with Somervell, reporters noticed, Nelson emerged smiling while the general left angry. But those acquainted with Somervell knew better than to sell him short.[31]

The changes were far reaching. Bill Batt became Nelson's deputy as vice chair. Jim Knowlson moved to the position of vice chairman for program determination, which made him chair of the key Requirements Committee. His chief task was to match output with the requirements of claimant agencies and maintain a balance between them. The Division of Industry Operations was replaced by a director general for operations, who presided over the former Materials and Production divisions, all commodity and industry branches, and several bureaus, including those for priorities and industry advisory committees. This arrangement swept together all the operating units under central direction for the first time. In September Ernest Kanzler, the Ford official who had overseen conversion of the industry, took this post. Special emphasis was given to strengthening WPB's field staff, which had been a major weakness. Knowlson took charge of this task, creating an Office of Field Operations that gradually consolidated its power over the agency's decentralized system based on a dozen regional centers and seventy local offices.[32]

The new structure reduced the number of executives reporting directly to Nelson from eight to three. It released him from overseeing day-to-day activities and allowed him to concentrate on "essential policy problems and . . . the increasing important relations of WPB with other agencies." The Planning Committee still reported directly to him, as did the Division of Civilian Supply, which became OCS. However, Henderson's unit continued to lose power and prestige under the new setup, which reduced it to a weak claimant struggling to protect output for civilian use at a time when policymakers were pushing intensely for more military production. Labor gained some clout by the creation of a Labor Advisory Commission attached to the Labor Production Division. But the plan also created two potential centers of power rather than one, which would require Knowlson and Kanzler to coordinate their efforts.[33]

Although the new organization greatly improved WPB's effectiveness, it still could not bridge the gap between economic output and military demand based on strategy. For that to happen Nelson needed accurate data on the military's long-range plans. He could not get it because neither Patterson nor Forrestal, who sat on WPB, could get it. They dealt in matters of procurement and supply, not strategy. The Joint Chiefs of Staff (JCS) were responsible for strategy, but the statements on military needs didn't come from them. The Planning Committee had proposed a top-level war production council to integrate all these factors, but the military would have none of it. Nelson tried to get Roosevelt to approve a process whereby WPB would collaborate with the JCS in coming up with a balanced, feasible program of requirements ranked by urgency, but the effort failed. In October the JCS finally agreed to delegate a group of officers to advise the WPB on the production requirements necessary to implement strategic plans.[34]

It was barely half a loaf, and a poor half at that. No joint mechanism for collaboration ever got beyond the drawing board, leaving WPB to struggle along trying to meet demands over which it had no control.

WHILE THE INTRAMURAL wars raged, individual towns and manufacturers scrambled as best they could to find their place in the radically altered landscape of wartime, eager to do their part while protecting their own futures. Evansville, an industrial town of 111,000 people perched on the Ohio River in southwestern Indiana, was typical in many respects. Located only seventy-five miles from the nation's center of population, it had more than 200 factories dominated by a Big Four: Servel and Sunbeam, both of which made refrigerators, and Briggs, which produced auto bodies for the fourth member, a Plymouth assembly plant. At their peaks in 1941 Servel finished an Electrolux refrigerator every twenty-three seconds of the working day, Sunbeam turned out 1,800 Coldspot refrigerators for Sears, Roebuck every day, and forty Plymouths with Briggs bodies rolled off the Chrysler assembly line every hour.[35]

But defense priorities had thrown 3,800 people out of work, and USES had found only 112 new jobs in three months. Unemployment insurance kept most of the skilled workers in Evansville, at least for its sixteen-week duration, and the Mechanic Arts School ran around the clock training 1,800 people in the skills needed for war work. Here, as elsewhere, conversion foundered on the plethora of single-purpose machines used by the plants. Studebaker, for example, undertook to manufacture Wright airplane engines only to find that only 414 of its 3,000 machines could be adapted to the new product, and all but 64 of them were simple drill presses. In terms of layout, organization, and labor skills, large American factories were themselves huge single-purpose machines designed to turn out one special product in enormous quantities. That is one reason why so many new facilities had to be built from scratch to produce planes, tanks, and other specialized war implements.

When conversion threatened to throw 21,000 Evansville factory workers onto the streets in July 1941, Mayor William H. Dress led a delegation to Washington, where they spent two hours with Sidney Hillman. They returned home with Evansville as one of the first cities to be certified by OPM as "distressed," meaning they could negotiate defense contracts at up to 15 percent over competitive prices. When this proved of little help, Dress called a meeting of more than a thousand representatives from towns in eleven midwestern states. Two OPM engineers came to town to survey its manufacturing facilities and were followed by a swarm of military engineers. The local Manufacturers and Employers Association had compiled a list of every machine tool within a fifty-mile radius of Evansville and sent it off to all the relevant agencies. In December one of Floyd Odlum's defense trains chugged into town to display a variety of parts and goods that local manufacturers might like to make on subcontracts.

Meanwhile, the manufacturers did some hustling on their own. Servel studied 169 sets of military specifications and issued a brochure listing all of its facilities that might be used in arms production. Work began to trickle in; when a sizable order for 37 mm shell cases arrived, Servel threw up a new building. A $3 million subcontract for navy parts soon followed. After Pearl Harbor a flood of new offers took the place of refrigerators that could no longer be made under conversion. Sunbeam did not fare as well. By early 1942 it had only half as many employees on the payroll as during the previous June. Many of its skilled employees had drifted off to other cities offering war work at higher pay with longer hours. "Conversion is a painful process," admitted one Sunbeam executive. "It's like having a tooth pulled. You keep putting it off." Still the company continued to scour the horizon for war contracts.

In January Briggs received a contract for assembling airplane wings and tail surfaces that meant adding several thousand employees to its Evansville plant. Chrysler followed with a contract for small-arms ammunition that would increase its workforce over 1,000 percent. Both manufacturers would have to retool their factories almost entirely, but the work was there. Some of the town's smaller manufacturers got into the defense business early. Hoosier Lamp & Stamping had always been a subcontractor with a plant full of general machine tools that turned out large quantities of small parts, mostly for refrigerators. When the defense program started in 1940, Hoosier's managers went looking for defense work. Normally about 70 percent of the sales price for a stamping went for material, but Hoosier had what it deemed "a pretty fair engineering staff and machine shop." It charged only 20 percent for material, the rest for finishing, and brought this approach to the navy's attention.

By 1942 a quarter of its work was for the navy, with half the parts designed by Hoosier's men. Another 60 percent went to producing airplane parts as a subcontractor for Vultee, Republic, and Curtiss-Wright, and it expected the last 15 percent to be headed soon for war work. An in-house training program graduated twenty men and ten women every ten days, with those numbers expected to be reversed within a short time. The plant ran two ten-hour shifts a day, seven days a week, and planned to go to three seven-and-a-half hour shifts every day once enough workers joined the force. An even smaller firm than Hoosier, George Koch Sons, an old family business that made metal gadgets and objects, scoured two private publications, the *Bidvertiser* and the *U. S. Government Advertiser*, for subcontracts to bid on and managed to submit low bids on fourteen of twenty-one items.

In Kansas City thirty-one machine shops led by engraving company executive Lou Holland used the York, Pennsylvania, model to form a pool for bidding. In September 1941 Holland landed a $250,000 navy contract for precision instruments and parceled it out to sixteen of the members. A staunch conservative, Holland distrusted Washington and avoided seeking another contract until the members proved their worth on the first one. The association hired an expert engineer who went to each shop to help adjust the tools and train the workers. "Suppose a contract is given to General Electric or Westinghouse," Holland observed. "Well, they have their bond up and they have to get the work done and are responsible for having it right. They don't want to farm it out to some fellow out in Atchison, Kansas, they never heard of and who has been making nothing more exact than farm machinery for thirty years."

But if the government insisted they subcontract, Holland added, they'd do it. "They'll assign the work to the little shop. The little manufacturer has never seen anything like it. He tries to make it and can't. So the prime contractor turns it down and goes to the government and says, 'See, we told you these little guys couldn't do the work and we haven't got time to wet-nurse them.'" For his work Holland compiled a comprehensive list of Kansas and Missouri machine tools, which he kept locked in his desk lest the government find out about it and requisition some of the machines for use in eastern plants.

Contrary to Holland's belief, several large companies thrived on subcontracting, including Sperry, maker of precision war instruments, Curtiss-Wright, and the Timken-Detroit Axle Company. Colonel Willard Rockwell, chairman of Timken's board, had seen his company's production soar 580 percent since 1938 even though its floor space increased by only 32 percent. His formula for success consisted of three points. The company increased the number of its own employees by 217 percent and shifted the workweek from 40 to 168 hours; it standardized models by reducing their number from 200 to 20. "If a machine must be shut down to change over tools several times in a week," he explained, "it usually requires a skilled operator and considerable supervision. If, through standardization, the same machine can run continuously on one part, it may be possible to train an unskilled operator in a few hours."

The third point was subcontracting, which Timken had refined into an art. Before the war it utilized about a hundred other manufacturers; after Pearl Harbor it doubled that number. "You find subcontractors by going out and looking for them," said Rockwell, "the way you find any business . . . Under present circumstances, the prime contractor does not want to expand his own facilities to such an extent that he will have a large part of his fixed assets standing idle and absorbing all the profits from his normal business after the war. For this reason the prime contractor is anxious to sublet as much business as possible."

A. W. S. Herrington, president of Marmon-Herrington Co. of Indianapolis, shared these views. Deluged with orders for heavy trucks, tanks, and armored cars, Marmon-Herrington kept expanding its own facilities but still could not handle the backlog of orders even with production nearly twenty-five times that of 1939. "Our company subcontracts 73 per cent of its work," Herrington declared. "We have 1,200 subcontractors. To do this we had to work with the little five- ten- and twenty-five tool shops." But 95 percent of those shops couldn't comply with the government's minimum financial requirements. Their owners, who often worked a machine as well, were baffled by the blizzard of priority reports and other government paperwork.

To enlist their help, Herrington set up a subcontracting department, which surveyed a small shop's tools to see what they could make and whether they could do accurate work. If so, Herrington supplied them with materials and operating sheets to show how to do the job required, then inspected the finished product to see if they matched specifications. If they passed, Herrington bought the goods. On one point he remained adamant. "The responsibility for spreading work to the little outside shops is not that of the army or navy or WPB," he said. "It is our responsibility."

THROUGH THE SWELTERING summer the Planning Committee continued to revise the proposed production figures for 1942 and 1943. Earlier the president had reluctantly agreed to recast the figures to $45 billion for 1942 and $75 billion for 1943 by whittling down the army's ordnance and munitions requirements. At Nathan's suggestion Nelson set up a Committee on Feasibility, which called for a complete feasibility report. While Simon Kuznets worked on the report, Nathan made the political rounds, impressing on a variety of influential people the importance of getting feasibility right. His intense, engaging manner won some converts, giving him hope for more support in the next round of the struggle. On August 8 Nelson, mindful of the shortfalls in key raw materials, warned Patterson, Forrestal, and Eberstadt that "I am convinced and have been convinced for some time that the total objectives for 1942 and 1943 are beyond attainment." However, he proposed no solution.[36]

Four days later Kuznets handed the Planning Committee a lengthy feasibility report that estimated 1942 output would fall $15 billion short of the revised $60 billion goal. He proved to be close; actual production totaled $44 billion. His main focus was on the figures for 1943, which had climbed to $93 billion. Kuznets estimated this amount as too high by 20 percent, calculating real output as no more than $75 billion. Another $18 billion was projected for nonmunitions spending such as pay and food, and $4 billion for 1942 shortfalls, swelling the total to $115 billion. This would require monthly expenditures of nearly $9.6 billion by the end of 1943, or about 75 percent of all national product, compared to 27 percent in the first half of 1942. Nathan doubted whether any economy could devote more than half its output to war production, let alone 75 percent. Kuznets reiterated his warning that the military's production objectives were so huge that attempts to realize them would result in fewer rather than more finished products.[37]

The inflated goal of $115 billion might be obtainable, Kuznets added, if some system existed of scheduling and production controls that allowed sensitive adjustments in the flow of materials, components, and end products, but no such system had yet been devised. As the Planning Committee told Nelson in September, "We do not now have a program with reference to whose scope, contents and levels of urgency there is complete agreement." Without such a program in place, the only choice was whether or not to cut the estimates. Nathan urged WPB to reduce the projections to more feasible levels. An inflated figure, he argued, might provide incentives but also had a host of disadvantages, which he outlined. What was needed, he stressed, was a mechanism for integrating the three key areas currently treated separately: production factors, military strategy, and social policy. To that end Nathan urged creation of a supreme war production council with complete authority over all the agencies, including the military.[38]

Nelson praised the report as "a magnificent analysis of our production program" but found himself in a quandary. He had already tried several approaches to getting the military to work more closely with the WPB without success. He had to accept the constraint that the civilians could deal only with aggregates and that specific cuts were the province of military judgment. However, he did not know that the army was tangled in its own intramural squabbles between the ASF and the Operations Division of the General Staff. The supply services of the army and navy were crucial to material operations, yet their statistical and reporting systems were crude, uncollated, fragmented, and often filled with errors. They would hardly welcome the Kuznets report, and Nelson himself doubted the propriety or feasibility of a supreme war council.[39]

Faced with the dilemma of how to get the army to accept the cuts recommended by Kuznets, Nelson resorted to an uncharacteristic maneuver. To protect his own position in case of failure, he sent on September 8 copies of the report to Somervell, Admiral Samuel Robinson, and Harry Hopkins not as an official WPB document but with a letter signed by Nathan, giving it a status well beneath that of the recipients. In this way Nelson could avoid responsibility for it should anything go wrong. Neither Hopkins nor the Navy Department even acknowledged Nathan's letter or the report. However, Somervell, of whom Nelson was already wary, exploded when he read the report and countered with a handwritten reply four days later. Pouncing on Kuznets's admission that his analysis might have a wide margin of error, he categorically rejected the report's figures and insisted that any problems in production could be solved through proper scheduling of orders.[40]

Somervell saved his harshest scorn for the notion of a supreme war production council, calling it "an inchoate mass of words." In conclusion he said, "I am not impressed with either the character or basis of the judgments expressed in the report, and recommend that they be carefully hidden from the eyes of thoughtful men." Kuznets he had already dismissed as "too academic and impractical to help us very much on the problem which he attacked." In his view the issue was not the size of the war program but inefficiency and lack of drive on the part of the WPB. Infuriated by the letter, Kuznets got Nathan's permission to draft a reply under the latter's name. In it he dismantled Somervell's assertions with barely disguised contempt, opening his rejoinder with the statement, "In view of the gravity of the problem discussed in these Documents . . . I hesitate to take your memorandum seriously."[41]

Aware that a showdown on feasibility could no longer be avoided, Nelson placed it on the WPB's agenda for October 6. As the meeting approached, the Washington gossip circuit buzzed with anticipation over what was billed as a showdown between the civilian and military authorities. Roosevelt let it be known that he wanted no postponements of the meeting. Nathan secured Henderson's endorsement of the Kuznets report and spent an hour going over it with Hopkins and his aide, Isador Lubin. Somervell drafted a letter that General Marshall signed, designating him as the army's spokesman on strategy before the WPB and opposing the creation of a supreme war council. He also enlisted the support of Patterson and Robinson. The meeting drew an unusually full house. Besides the board members and staff, seventeen other people were invited, including the Planning Committee members, Kuznets, Stacy May, Somervell, Robinson, representatives of the Maritime Commission, and Paul McNutt.[42]

The meeting lasted three hours, twice as long as usual. Nathan opened by reviewing the Kuznets report and urging the creation of "an administrative mechanism to combine strategy and production." Nelson and McNutt emphasized the problems inherent in the military's flawed statistical reports, after which Henderson complained about the army and navy's continuing inability to schedule their production. Somervell then challenged Nathan's figures. The 1942 war program, he asserted, would probably fall 10 percent short, not the 19 percent Kuznets estimated, and the shortage could be eased by more effective control over the distribution of raw materials. Dollar figures, he added, could not be relied on to measure productive capacity. What the WPB should be doing was finding ways to increase supply rather than reducing demand. As for the proposed supreme council, Somervell said, "We already have the Combined Chiefs, the Joint Chiefs, the Combined Production and Resources Board, the Munitions Board, the Army and Navy Munitions Board, and the War Production Board. What good would be a board composed of an economist, a politician, and a soldier who does not know production?"[43]

Henry Wallace pointed out that the war program Somervell envisioned would require cuts in output for civilians to a level 40 percent below that of the depression year of 1932. Civilians were asked to sacrifice for a military budget that, in his view, was "larded with fat." Others criticized the military's program, releasing frustrations that had long been mounting, but Somervell would make no concessions to the Planning Committee's findings. As the meeting neared its end with no decision in sight, Henderson could stand it no longer. He was the only one in the room whose pugnacity rivaled that of Somervell. "Maybe if we can't wage a war on 90 billion," he said abruptly, "we ought to get rid of our present Joint Chiefs and find some who can."

Dead silence greeted this observation. Before anyone could speak, Henderson turned on Somervell and delivered what one observer called "the most violent personal attack ever heard in a meeting of the War Production Board." He was disgusted with Somervell's constant obstinacy, his overbearing manner, and his ignorance of production problems. He was certain that Somervell had always padded his requirements and had no concept of the disastrous implications of infeasible goals. The tirade went on while everyone sat slack-jawed. Even Somervell, who was not used to being challenged, offered no reply. Finally Bill Batt attempted the role of peacemaker by pointing out that Somervell did not make strategy. Henderson waved the remark aside by saying scornfully, "Ain't he got a letter?"

After some embarrassed and ineffectual attempts at further discussion, the meeting adjourned without a decision. But a turning point had been reached. Patterson recognized that a resolution of the dispute was essential and that the WPB argument had some validity. On the day after the meeting he wrote Somervell, "The WPB position, that production objectives ought not to be far in front of estimated maximum production, is believed to be sound as a general rule. Otherwise our scheduling of production cannot represent reality, and it is generally agreed that without realistic scheduling we will continue to suffer from maldistribution of materials, thus cutting down the actual output of finished weapons." At the next WPB meeting on October 13, Patterson and Somervell surprised the civilian representatives by not objecting to proposed cuts. Patterson suggested that the board communicate with the Joint Chiefs on the matter of reductions.[44]

The proposal for a supreme council was quietly dropped, but a new channel had been opened. By late November the WPB and Joint Chiefs reached agreement on a figure of $80.5 billion instead of $93 billion for 1943. It exceeded the Planning Committee's ceiling by $5 billion, but Nathan and Kuznets agreed it was within acceptable limits. The feasibility fight ended with an uneasy agreement that had at least averted a major crisis between the civilian and military authorities. If the civilians in the WPB regarded the outcome as a victory, they had little reason to cheer. Unfortunately for Nelson, an equally savage fight was brewing within the WPB and between it and other agencies during these same turbulent months.[45]

THE FEASIBILITY FIGHT was far from the only intramural war in town. The squabbling reached a point where on August 21 Roosevelt felt obliged to release a public statement ordering government officials to stop their bickering in public. "The object," he explained to reporters, "is to prevent the people, from the top to the bottom, in these different agencies from talking too much, thereby creating false impressions, and in many cases taking opposite sides of a policy argument out in public which hasn't been passed on in any way, trying to make you good people decide that this is going to be the policy of the Government, and then citing somebody who has talked too much." No one wanted to suppress honest differences of opinion, he stressed. "But it is no solution to a controverted question to argue it out in public. If the agencies would refrain from resorting to public debate of this kind they would have a good deal more time to attend to their business."[46]

His admonition fell largely on deaf ears. Nothing could stop the sniping in private or the clashes over policy or procedure by earnest men convinced that they were right and others were wrong. The national mood was particularly sour that August. The war was still going badly. Japanese expansion had reached its zenith and was threatening Australia. The Germans were hammering away at Stalingrad, where a breakthrough could prove disastrous to the Russians, while in North Africa Rommel had swept through Egypt and was stalled at El Alamein. Public sentiment had not yet recovered from the fall of Bataan in April or the surrender of Corregidor in May. Only the stunning naval and air victory at Midway early in June revived hope of reversing the tide of battle. A week later, however, the Germans launched an offensive in the Ukraine. Those Americans trying earnestly to follow the course of war could barely keep up with the rapid sweep of events around the globe.

The mood at WPB and within the military was no less somber. At the end of August, eight months into the year, the production of munitions totaled less than half the amount forecast for the year. Production was still advancing but at a slower rate. When the shortage of raw materials grew worse in July, Stimson asked Patterson, McCloy, Somervell, and Knudsen for an explanation and did not like what he heard. "The real trouble is that Nelson has not got an efficient organization," he wrote privately. "He is not taking the steps which the War Department thinks should be taken to allocate raw materials so as to minimize shortages. The time has come when this must be done. Nelson has a lot of weak men around him, none of whom is competent to face and handle this vital problem of allocation, particularly between war activities and civilian activities. The difficulty is enhanced by the fact that Nelson has a big reputation which thus apparently is fictitious." Forrestal gave Stimson the same message on behalf of the navy.[47]

The heart of the matter was again the conflict between military and civilian demands. At a meeting two days later Nelson said the country was "at the bottom of the can" in raw materials and could not increase supplies in one area without taking them from another. Stimson emphasized that work stop-pages in aircraft plants, shipyards, and other facilities loomed if the flow of materials slowed and that civilian needs had to be sacrificed to military ne-cessity. The diversion of key materials and facilities into what he called "un-necessary civilian channels" had to be halted. Stimson also talked frankly about the shortcomings of the WPB and some of Nelson's assistants and sug-gested some names of men who might be brought in to improve the organiza-tion. Nelson listened patiently and said he welcomed the suggestions. The July reorganization of the WPB resulted partly from this session, but it eased the tension between WPB and the War Department only temporarily.[48]

Late in August Ralph Robey reported, "It is now clear beyond any question that we are on the verge of a major campaign to discredit Donald Nelson . . . Rumors of the impending attack have been going the rounds for more than a month. Last week the charges began to break into print in increasing vol-ume." It was, Robey added, a repeat of the campaign against Knudsen with the same complaints: Nelson couldn't get anything done, was short-sighted, was unwilling to force recalcitrant businessmen into line, and failed to cre-ate an efficient organization. Robey offered a vigorous defense of Nelson, citing the political and other obstacles in his path. "The amazing thing," he concluded, "is not that Nelson has not done better but that he has been able to do as well as he has." Raymond Moley also rose to Nelson's defense, observ-ing that "there never will be exactly enough raw materials at exactly the right places. If raw materials piled up, it would be a sign that production is lagging."[49]

A few days after Moley's column appeared, Nelson underwent a new trial when Reese Taylor, the hulking chief of WPB's iron and steel branch, quit in disgust over the obstacles preventing him from sorting out the mess in steel allocation. A widely admired young businessman, he railed against having to push decisions that already had Nelson's approval through what *Time* called "the crew of second-rate dollar-a-year men . . . which had grown so big that Washington called it WPB's 'flim-flam layer.'" The last straw was an unau-thorized report by a hireling that criticized Taylor's proposed steel quota plan. After losing Taylor, Nelson summoned a hundred of his top men and told them to stop bickering, adopt a tough, realistic attitude, and forget their concern for the niceties of the civilian economy. "It just takes too damned long to get things done around here," he admitted.[50]

By August it was also woefully clear that PRP was foundering badly, thanks in part to its hasty implementation. "Don Nelson's 'Purp' is a very sick dog," reported *Time*, "and if it does not soon recover to perform the miracles its master hopes for, it is apt to be a dead dog this autumn." The reporter thought he knew the main reason for its difficulties: "Every contractor has been so anxious to be well-heeled with materials (and so sure of being short-changed) that he has been inclined to ask for more than he needed at any one moment. There is no reason to believe Purp can stop this overestimating, since contractors can always alibi later that it was impossible to forecast accurately five months ahead and anyhow they were expecting a contract they did not get."[51]

So many problems cropped up during PRP's first use in the third quarter of 1942 that full operation was postponed until the fourth quarter. Its sheer complexity, along with the preference of many officials for a vertical rather than horizontal system, doomed any chance it might have had of succeeding. The military despised it, and while the War Department made adjustments to accommodate it, Somervell tended simply to ignore it and threatened to have the army take it over. Nor was he alone. During one WPB Requirements Committee meeting, Jerry Land said curtly, "Gentlemen, you have my requirements for steel plate; it's up to you to split the rest," and walked out. In August Nelson declared that because of the shortages in raw materials he was restoring to the WPB the priority powers he had earlier given to the ANMB. At the same time, sentiment was growing to implement a vertical system of material controls even before PRP got off the ground. Nelson encouraged this belief with surprise moves that brought two key new faces into the WPB.[52]

Nelson had known Charles E. Wilson, president of General Electric, for a long time and regarded him as fair, capable, and forceful. He had tried in vain to recruit him for the WPB, but Wilson considered his work at GE more useful to the war effort. Under the duress of that summer he made a concerted effort to recruit Wilson. He approached Owen D. Young, the retired chairman and president of GE, for assistance and asked Stimson and Knox for help as well. They were eager to assist, but an unexpected snag developed. Young told them and Roosevelt frankly that Thurman Arnold was preparing a series of indictments against GE for antitrust violations not covered in his earlier agreement to defer such suits until the war's end. Young did not want Wilson leaving GE or coming into the government under this cloud.[53]

Stimson emphasized to Young that they wanted Wilson regardless of the charges. He called Roosevelt and asked that Arnold's suits be deferred until the war's end because Wilson was badly needed. Roosevelt referred him to Biddle, who seemed lukewarm about the request. For once Nelson, Stimson, Knox, and Patterson were working together to get something done. Ironically, the evidence for the fraud charge against GE had been supplied by the navy, although Knox lamely denied it at first. Biddle relented enough to provide some help, and the cases were postponed. The GE board finally agreed to let Wilson go, and on September 17 he surrendered his six-figure salary for a position as a vice chairman of WPB and chair of the newly created Production Executive Committee (PEC).[54]

"Mr. Wilson will be the top production authority in the war program," Nelson announced, "and will have the responsibility of seeing to it that programs and schedules for all phases of our war effort are met." But no indication was given as to how this would be done. That same day Nelson also announced that Eberstadt had agreed to become a vice chairman of the WPB. The move delighted the military; Eberstadt was close to Somervell and known to be a strong advocate for the military's needs even though he was a civilian. The services were less than enthusiastic about Wilson, though he was considered one of the top production men in the nation. Possibly Nelson hoped that the presence of the two men as his chief lieutenants would balance the civilian-versus-military conflict. *Time* labeled the appointments as "the installation of a new top management in WPB."[55]

The new setup amounted to a major reorganization of the WPB. The new PEC looked to be an effort to centralize authority over the process and cut through the bureaucratic layers that had slowed production. Nelson regarded Wilson as the production man and Eberstadt as the materials man. Their presence also removed Nelson even more from day-to-day oversight. Much depended on how well the two men worked together and defined their roles, and how well the military worked with them. No one doubted Eberstadt's ability to do so, but Wilson remained a wild card. A ramrod-straight, muscular six-footer, he had an impressive background. Born in Manhattan's Hell's Kitchen, he lost his father at age three and went to work at twelve as an office boy at a GE subsidiary. Through the years he rose through the ranks as factory hand, clerk, accountant (which he learned in night school), and vice president of the company's appliance business. In 1940 he replaced Gerard Swope as president; now Swope was leaving retirement to replace Wilson at GE.[56]

As a young man Wilson boosted his income by playing semipro basketball, changing shirts every night to play for different teams. Now he was about to change shirts for the first time in decades. "It took me 40 years to climb to the presidency," Wilson told reporters after his appointment, "and 40 seconds to step out . . . [But] I keep reminding myself that there's a war on. Hell's broke loose and I've got to do something about it."[57]

He had every intention of doing just that, and so did Eberstadt. As head of the ANMB he had developed the germ of a plan that he thought might supersede the despised PRP. This too endeared him to the military.

CHAPTER 18

OLD FRANK COMES
TO CALL

*The Government has an effective poster to illustrate the slogan,
Loose Talk May Cost Lives . . . Some of the most damaging loose
talk has come from officials of the Government itself . . . The way
to get co-operation from the American people is . . . to tell the
whole truth, reveal what sacrifices must be made and why they
are necessary, and reduce irresponsible talk to a minimum.*

—SATURDAY EVENING POST[1]

*The most sensitive single nerve in American life had been
touched with an iron finger, violently, and the administration
reacted with unco-ordinated vigor. It was bad enough, in all
conscience, to reflect that the war might be lost for lack of rubber; it was even worse to consider how the average American
might feel if, through official bungling or the contrariness of fate,
he was prevented from making free use of his own auto.*

—BRUCE CATTON[2]

*It looks as if we are going to have plenty of transportation trou-
bles, not only for coal and oil but generally during these next
months just because we could not look ahead and prepare for
the emergency that everyone knew was coming.*

—HAROLD ICKES[3]

ON THE EVENING OF SEPTEMBER 17, the same day that Charlie Wilson
agreed to come to WPB, Franklin and Eleanor Roosevelt boarded the ten-car
presidential train along with two of Franklin's spinster cousins, Laura Delano and Margaret Suckley. They were invited, he told them, because "you are
the only people I know that I don't have to entertain." The other passengers

included lawyer Harry Hooker, Dr. McIntire, Steve Early, Navy Captain John McCrea, three newsmen, and Fala, Roosevelt's beloved Scottie, who was entrusted to Suckley during the journey. The trip was supposed to be a secret, but every day Fala got walked outside the train, and he was the most famous dog in America. The three reporters represented the three wire services that provided news to nearly every newspaper and radio station in the country.[4]

Roosevelt had planned a two-week trip across the nation to inspect factories, army camps and shipyards and, incidentally, to get away from Washington for a time. It was for him a rare opportunity to witness the war effort up close, and one he could do comfortably only by train. He informed Mike Reilly, his Secret Service aide, that the trip was to be strictly off the record. No parades or tedious receptions or anything that would get in the way of actually seeing what went on in the facilities. Plant owners and state governors would not be informed until 3:00 A.M. of the day he planned to arrive, and the disgruntled reporters were forbidden to write about the trip until it was over. Even more, Roosevelt insisted on personally reviewing everything they wrote during the journey for later publication.

In all the train traveled through twenty-four states, stopping in eleven of them at twenty-six industrial and military facilities in twenty cities. The first visit was to the huge new Chrysler tank plant in Detroit. The president rolled into the factory aboard his special open-top car in the company of Eleanor, Governor Murray Van Waggoner of Michigan, and K. T. Keller, Chrysler's president. Startled by his appearance, workers whooped and whistled their delight. One smudged-face mill worker shouted, "By God if it ain't old Frank!" Old Frank laughed and waved his hat at the man. The party observed every phase of production from materials to final assembly, then moved on to a testing ground where the new Sherman M-4 tank was put through its paces before rumbling at top speed toward the presidential car. Roosevelt's eyes widened as the tank screeched to a halt barely ten feet short of his car. "A good drive!" he laughed. He was deeply impressed by the plant's ability to shift from manufacturing M-3 tanks to M-4s without losing a single hour of production.

From there they went on to tour the massive $86 million Willow Run bomber plant, which so far had turned out only one plane. Henry Ford was not among the officials who greeted the presidential party; he stood in a far corner of the plant fiddling with a new machine and only reluctantly joined the guests. Never a Roosevelt admirer, he sat stone-faced as his workers cheered the president. Charles Sorensen, who had never seen Roosevelt before, was astonished to see how helpless he was as he was lifted into the car. He thought the president was in pain, but once in the car Roosevelt was unfailingly jovial, calling him Charlie, stopping the car often to ask questions, and talking constantly. They stopped for five minutes at the mammoth metal presses while some workers demonstrated how they worked.[5]

Sorensen explained the operation to the president while Edsel did the same for Eleanor, who was no less enthusiastic about what she saw. Roosevelt noticed two midgets working atop the tail section of a B-24 and asked to meet them. They hurried down to shake his hand. Eleanor noted with pleasure the hundreds of women working as riveters, welders, blueprint readers, and inspectors, the first in Ford's history. The tour lasted seventy-five minutes, twice as long as originally planned. Through it all Henry Ford sat in silence wedged between the two Roosevelts, burning with resentment at the attention showered on them. Sorensen called it "one of the worst days . . . that I had ever spent with Henry Ford."[6]

That night the train journeyed to Chicago, where Roosevelt toured the Great Lakes Naval Training Station, the nation's largest. Thousands cheered him despite a pouring rain. Eleanor asked to visit Camp Robert Smalls, a segregated school where the Navy was training its first black recruits. Then came a midnight visit to the Allis-Chalmers plant in Milwaukee. Eleanor flew back to Washington that evening while the train headed to the Twin Cities, where the president greeted the night shift of a cartridge plant. Somervell had joined the party and beamed when Roosevelt said afterward, "Brehon, that was grand!" The president too was struck by the large number of women operating machines of all sizes, and their skill and accuracy in performing work.

They pushed on to Camp Farragut, a giant naval station located improbably in the Idaho panhandle alongside the very deep Lake Pend Oreille. It had just gone into service five days before his arrival and already had a thousand trainees, with more coming in a steady stream. As the train chugged toward the West Coast, the trip began to wear on the three reporters. "The porters burned incense in the Pullmans as the dirty laundry piled up," noted Merriman Smith, the UPI correspondent. At Fort Lewis, Washington, outside Tacoma, Roosevelt reviewed the 33rd Division, then headed to the naval yard at Bremerton, where he saw wounded men and crippled ships. There he grabbed a microphone and from his car told about 5,000 assembled workers, "I can only say a word or two to you. The first is that I am not really here . . . so just remember that for about ten days, you haven't seen me." He then drove through downtown Seattle, waving to thousands of cheering people. "An entire city off the record," noted Smith wryly.

They took the ferry and went to the Boeing plant, where women comprised 47 percent of the workforce. That night Roosevelt dined with his daughter, Anna, and her husband and took her with him on the train to Vancouver, where he toured the Alcoa plant and came away still baffled over how aluminum got made. Afterward they crossed to Portland, where Henry Kaiser hosted a tour of his shipyard. Roosevelt reminded a surprised Clay Bedford that they had met before, and Anna cracked a bottle of champagne across the bow of a new Liberty ship in full view of photographers. Thousands of people swarmed below his automobile, which sat on a high platform. Over a loud-speaker Roosevelt cried, "You know I am not supposed to be here today," and joined them in laughter. The steaming reporters found nothing funny in the performance. Here was the president making an appearance in front of a huge crowd, yet the newspapers and radio stations had to pretend it wasn't happening. Roosevelt even rubbed it into the reporters. "You are the possessors of a secret which even the newspapers . . . don't know," he told the cheering crowd.

A smiling Henry Kaiser had a very different reaction. "Just look at those assembly lines," he crowed.

The next day passed in whirlwind visits to the Mare Island Navy Yard and an Army Port of Embarkation and Naval Supply Depot in Oakland that had tripled in size. At Mare Island Roosevelt saw a Japanese two-man submarine captured at Pearl Harbor, along with an American sub with nine Japanese flags painted on its conning tower. Afterward Anna returned to Seattle while the presidential train chugged down the coast to the Douglas Aircraft plant in Long Beach, where unsuspecting executives gaped in amazement when his car rolled inside the air-conditioned, windowless building. Margaret Suckley cringed at the effect of the "blue lighting" that created "a horrible effect on the looks of the workers" and, in her view, lowered their morale. A woman work-ing on a fuselage high off the floor got so excited by his presence that she pointed her riveting gun at the president's car until a Secret Service man barked, "Put that thing down."

Roosevelt went on to dedicate Camp Pendleton, the largest marine train-ing center in the country. It stood on the site of what had been Rancho Santa Margarita, the graceful old ranch house of which remained intact. The presi-dent devoted nearly an hour to going through the house and said, "If anyone touches this, they get court-martialed." The base commandant suggested shooting instead, to which a laughing Roosevelt replied, "That's better yet." He moved on to San Diego for a tour of the Consolidated Aircraft plant, the marine base, and a naval hospital filled with men wounded in the Pacific. The train traveled to Uvalde, Texas, where Roosevelt enjoyed a brief visit with his first vice president, John Nance Garner. They had parted bitterly and not met since Garner declared he was not voting in 1940 because no true Democrat was on the ticket, but the rancor was forgotten as they chatted amiably like old friends. As Garner left the train, he told Ross McIntire, "Keep that man in good health and all the rest will take care of itself."

The president ventured deeper into Texas, visiting Kelly and Randolph air bases, where pilots were being trained, and then Fort Sam Houston, an army base. Then on to Fort Worth, where Eleanor rejoined him and they inspected the Consolidated bomber plant. It had the world's longest assembly line and was preparing to turn out an endless stream of B-24 bombers. It was at this plant that executives experienced a revelation at the proficiency and dedication of women workers, black and white, which pleased Eleanor no end. Throughout her visits to the South she had been harassed by angry charges from whites that black servants were forming "Eleanor Clubs" in her honor and demanding higher wages, more privileges, and fewer hours. Finally she asked the FBI to investigate whether such clubs existed. The FBI did so and reported no evidence of any such thing. The real problem, it added, was that southern women had trouble keeping servants, who flocked to higher-paying defense jobs.

From Texas the train pushed on to New Orleans, where Roosevelt met Andrew Jackson Higgins for the first time. The voluble Higgins and his four sons met the presidential car on a special platform at the company's spur track and formed a three-car procession for an unannounced drive through the plant. The night before, workers had widened a door opening and shifted machinery without being given an explanation. Roosevelt inspected the assembly bay where four production lines put together 36-foot LCVPs, and the production bay where another two lines fabricated PT boats. Alerted to his presence, workers began piling into the building to catch a glimpse of him. Members of the Higgins band, who had been told to bring their instruments to work, struck up "Hail to the Chief," "Anchors Aweigh," and the "Higgins Victory March" as the tour neared its end. A pleased Roosevelt kept time by drumming his fingers on the side of the car.[7]

When the music ended, Higgins stood up in the car and yelled, "All right, everybody! For the world's greatest man, three cheers!" The workers responded loudly. Higgins led the ovation, then cried, "And now, the President would like to see how quickly you can get back to work." Roosevelt huddled with Higgins and late-arriving Governor Sam Jones for a lengthy discussion before boarding the train and heading for Camp Shelby in Mississippi. Margaret Suckley came away unimpressed by Higgins. "His trouble is that he is too blunt & fights with everybody," she observed, "so that the maritime commission hates him & won't play ball with him." But Higgins did good work, and he was needed.[8]

After Camp Shelby Roosevelt stopped at Fort Jackson outside Columbia, South Carolina, before heading back to Washington. Despite all the activity, the trip both rested and refreshed him. For two weeks he had been free of Washington's stifling atmosphere, free of political and bureaucratic infighting, and able to mingle directly with the American people. Such opportunities were rare for a president, especially in wartime. "During the war Roosevelt was cut off from people more than usual," noted Frances Perkins. ". . . He suffered actively from separation from the life of the people during the war."[9]

But not during these two weeks. For this brief time he could directly breathe that heady but elusive air called democracy at its very core, which was for him a great psychological tonic. He had also seen firsthand so many activities that had heretofore been only abstractions to him: planes, tanks, and ships actually being built, men undergoing the rigors of training, troops wounded in battle, the nuts and bolts of production lines for everything from giant aircraft to cartridges. What a contrast it all was to the stuffy, insulated corridors of government!

On October 1, the day of his return, he held a press conference to confront more than a hundred newsmen rankled at being silenced on "one of the biggest stories of this or any other year." Skipping his usual banter, Roosevelt gave them a detailed rundown of his trip and told them how much he liked nearly everything he saw. Production was "nearly up to the goal"; labor and management were working together; the people had "the finest kind of morale." The only politicians he talked to during the trip were the eleven governors. He had been deeply impressed by stories he heard of how small farming communities managed to harvest their crops despite a shortage of laborers. "They then decide on three days, or four days," he said, "and the editor of the paper, and the drugstore fellow, and the garage man, and the children, they all give up what they are doing and go into the fields for three or four days, and—by gosh!—get the crops in."[10]

Then his voice turned sharper as he noted three things in Washington that did not please him, especially in contrast to what he had just seen. Too many people were trying to justify their role in the war effort; the press lacked real touch with the country and gave out sententious views based on partial truths; and too many people in the administration were rushing into speech or print over issues without knowledge of the bigger picture beyond "their own version of the little individual piece of work which they themselves are doing." The reporters, already surly over the blackout of the trip and censorship in general, pressed him for specifics, got little of what they wanted, and began walking out even though he was still talking. It was an ugly scene between two parties that normally got along splendidly, and no one knew what it portended.

ON SEPTEMBER 17, the same day that Roosevelt left on his tour, he issued an executive order giving Nelson full authority over the nation's rubber program and authorizing him to appoint a rubber director who would serve under him. Pearl Harbor confirmed the worst fears about the rubber supply;

the Japanese conquest of Singapore and the Dutch East Indies cut off 95 percent of it. By July 1, 1942, the nation had only 578,000 long tons on hand; projections indicated that the supply would be exhausted by mid-1943 at the latest. The country would have to depend on synthetic rubber, but that program, after long delays, was bogged down in a maze of contradictory stories, rumors, and warnings. Having failed to give synthetic production his support earlier, Roosevelt compounded the crisis by failing to grasp its gravity for most of 1942.[11]

Before its demise SPAB created a rubber allocations committee that issued guidelines for parceling out rubber to make the existing supply last until March 1943. Once installed as chief of WPB, Nelson made rubber a top priority. He appointed Arthur Newhall, a rubber manufacturer, as head of the rubber branch and asked him to produce a balance sheet on supplies. A quiet, capable executive, Newhall collected enough data to make some startling predictions. Between April 1, 1942, and December 1, 1943, the Allies altogether would have an estimated 1.1 million tons of crude and synthetic rubber. Of that amount the United States would get 736,000 tons, of which the army and navy alone needed a bare minimum of 734,000 tons. Essential civilian needs, not including any allowance for passenger car tires, came to 226,000 tons, making a net shortfall of 224,000 tons. A vigorous scrap rubber program could reduce but not cover this deficit, and more tires would most certainly be needed.[12]

"No material in the entire category of stringent materials is more critical than rubber," warned the ANMB's Eberstadt on February 16. Clearly the long-delayed synthetic rubber program had to be pushed as vigorously as possible. Bill Batt of WPB's Materials Division gave quick approval to construction materials for building synthetic plants. Newhall urged that the program raise its production goal from 300,000 to 350,000 tons for 1943 and its total capacity of new plants from 600,000 to 800,000 tons. Jesse Jones, under siege by critics for his earlier hesitations, approved the contracts needed for construction. The estimated cost of $700 million dwarfed the previous protests over a $30 million experimental program. By spring the synthetic program was actually well under way, but it would take months before a meaningful supply of rubber could be turned out. In the meantime stringent conservation was needed to curtail usage and extend the life of existing supplies.[13]

The most obvious target was the automobile and, as Knudsen liked to say, the American urge to go from one place to another sitting down. Tires were by far the largest consumer of rubber, and they were about to be in very short supply. As a first step the sale of new tires was banned on December 26, 1941, and a certificate program devised to determine eligibility for purchases. On

March 5, testifying before the Truman Committee, Leon Henderson brushed aside earlier reassurances from Jones and asserted bluntly that car owners would have to get along for the next three years without "a single pound of crude rubber for new tires or for recapping," that the government might even have to requisition tires from private cars to keep essential vehicles operating, and that cabs and general utility trucks had "very little prospect of getting any more tires." Less than three weeks later Bill Batt gave the committee much the same message. "You and I are not going to get any automobile tires for the length of this emergency," he said, and went on to explain why. He reminded the committee of how Jones had thwarted NDAC's efforts to get synthetic factories up and running.[14]

Patterson insisted that strict measures be imposed, arguing that Americans would willingly sacrifice their pleasure driving in the national interest. The facts that winter repudiated his belief. Normal driving continued through the winter and spring, consuming an estimated 800 pounds of rubber a day. Patterson offered a long and ruthless list of restrictions to curb this excess, such as reducing average speed from 60 to 40 miles an hour, which would increase tire life by 73 percent. The sight of Washington's bumper-to-bumper traffic infuriated him, especially large trucks hauling what he considered nonessentials like soft drinks. Reporters who got an earful on the subject from Patterson began referring to him as "Judge Seven-Up." Nelson cautioned against what he deemed "unnecessary" restraints on civilian driving. Early in April the WPB allotted 15,000 tons of new rubber for truck and bus tires.[15]

Changing the driving habits of Americans proved to be both a political bombshell and a bureaucratic nightmare. Walter Lippmann identified no less than seven major agencies with responsibility for some aspect of the rubber issue, none of which coordinated their efforts with any of the others. Another problem, seemingly unrelated, placed added pressure on the government. German submarines were having their way with coastal tanker traffic, severely reducing the flow of oil to refineries and the supply of gasoline to the Northeast. The navy, struggling with huge commitments across the globe and embarked on the largest construction program in its history, was helpless to stop the carnage. In desperation it was converting yachts into patrol vessels and using sailing ships for scouting. Nearly 95 percent of all gasoline and fuel oil used in the Northeast came up the coast; as the supply slowed to a trickle severe shortages loomed.[16]

The connection between the two problems was obvious: a shortage of gasoline meant less driving, which would save tire wear. Since gasoline would have to be rationed, it seemed logical to attack both issues there. On April 22 Henderson announced that rationing would begin on May 15. Two days later he told WPB that rationing gas was the best way to conserve tires. A short time later an anonymous WPB official let slip that motorists in the sixteen-state northeastern region would soon have to get along on 2½ to 5 gallons a week when rationing began on May 15. The rumor touched off panicky protests and launched a parade of confusing and contradictory statements by government officials and others that thoroughly muddied the basic message. The oil industry dismissed Henderson's plan as "half-baked, ill advised, hit or miss," and "indicative of the lack of intelligent understanding which that government agency has shown in dealing with a problem so vital to the people."[17]

Unperturbed, Henderson and Harold Ickes declared on May 9 that the allowance for nonessential motorists would be three gallons a week. Only about a third of drivers fit this category; others would get extra rations awarded by local rationing boards. Trucks, taxis, buses, and commercial vehicles were not affected, and those like doctors, police, and ambulance drivers, who depended on driving, could obtain X cards for unlimited amounts. A Brookings Institution report concluded that the time had come to transform American driving habits "quickly and severely." A Truman Committee report countered that "*there is no virtue* in sacrifice for sacrifice's sake." Patterson and others badgered Nelson to impose nationwide gasoline rationing. Gradually the uproar over the stopgap gasoline rationing system to alleviate the crisis in the Northeast overshadowed the larger and more serious rubber problem.[18]

The confusion of messages grew steadily worse. Nelson believed that the drumbeat of protests against gas rationing came from "interests that stood to lose money and markets" and from "politicians who wanted to protect their constituents from the 'hardship' which such controls would impose." This indirect way of conserving rubber backfired. The idea of rationing gasoline nationwide, for example, made no sense to people who argued correctly that the shortages were only in the Northeast and due entirely to a lack of transportation. Tire wear was another matter, and one few public figures cared to face. Wholly apart from joyriding, the America of 1942 depended heavily on automobiles to get people to work. Many places, especially newly built defense and war facilities, lacked alternative public transportation, and their living conditions were so inadequate and overwhelmed by the influx of newcomers that workers had of necessity to live miles from the plant. Tires would be needed, but for a time they could only come from strict conservation measures.[19]

Through these early months Roosevelt remained strangely indifferent to the problem. At one point he deplored the "overexcitement" about the future of motorists and mentioned the experiments being done on rubber substitutes that should ease the problem. Reporters asked Nelson and Newhall what this meant, forcing Nelson to mumble platitudes about the possibility of substitutes while reaffirming the very real crisis. Henderson decided that a meeting with the president was needed to brief him on the necessity of an overall gasoline rationing program. It was held June 5 with Nelson, Newhall, Henderson, Ickes, Joseph Eastman, and Archibald MacLeish present. Roosevelt opened the meeting by saying, "Personally, I'm not at all worried about the rubber situation." Henderson outlined the case for gas rationing but found Roosevelt unreceptive.[20]

One possible solution, suggested Ickes, who denied there was a serious rubber shortage, was to launch a vigorous drive to collect scrap rubber. He had heard that the right sort of campaign might fetch as much as a million tons. Newhall dismissed the figure as absurdly high, but Roosevelt pounced on the idea as much more desirable than gasoline rationing. No one knew how much scrap actually existed. Some senators talked grandly of 10 million tons just waiting to be salvaged; more informed estimates put the figure at well under a million tons. Nevertheless, Roosevelt held a news conference on June 9 at which he announced the start of a two-week "Pick-Up-the-Rubber" campaign. Three days later, in a fireside chat, he designated June 15–30 as the dates for the campaign. "We don't know how much used rubber there is in *your* cellar—*your* barn—*your* stock room—*your* garage," he told the people. ". . . The only way to find out is to get the used rubber in where it can stand up and be counted."[21]

The public responded well to the campaign, bringing their scrap to 400,000 gas stations around the country. In rural areas oil delivery trucks collected it. In Coatsville, Pennsylvania, 14,582 citizens turned up 680,761 pounds of scrap, an average of 50 pounds each. The White House did its conspicuous share by donating floor mats from its automobiles, two of Fala's rubber bones, and a basket of rubber toys belonging to Hopkins's daughter Diana. At the White House Ickes rolled up a door mat leading to the executive offices and told his chauffeur to take it to the nearest collection site. Newhall stewed over the futile gesture; the mat was made of reclaimed rubber and good only for making more door mats. By June 30 only about 300,000 tons had been gathered. Without consulting Nelson or anyone else, Ickes persuaded Roosevelt to extend the drive for ten more days. The final tally neared 450,000 tons, not all of it usable. Meanwhile, a decision on rationing gasoline nationwide went begging.[22]

"In summary," concluded a War Department consultant gloomily, "the scrap collection campaign, the progress of the synthetic program, and the possibilities of other tire substitutes do not materially alter the situation as it stood six months ago. The need for getting along for the most part with the tires now on the road is still the only sensible approach . . . Yet at this late date we not only have no effective conservation plans in operation, but we even lack the machinery and the will to do the job."[23]

By July the rubber riddle had become a Tower of Babel with so many officials from so many agencies saying so many different things at a time when the war was still going badly. The Russians had evacuated Sevastopol, and the Germans seemed poised for a run at the rich oil fields of the Caucasus. Rommel was within eighty miles of the Nile delta, and the Japanese had invaded the Aleutians. Roosevelt compounded the confusion by saying first that the time might come when the government would have to requisition everyone's tires, then adding that if he owned a car with four good tires he could see no good reason why he should not drive it freely on his own business. Those who read his remarks in the newspapers hardly knew what to think.[24]

Meanwhile, the transportation system got increasingly snarled as Eastman tried to revamp urban traffic systems to save tires. He banned sightseeing buses and drastically curtailed charters to beaches, ballparks, and amusement centers. Another order reduced retail store deliveries by 25 percent. New York City's milk trucks shortened their delivery schedules despite a strike threat from drivers. Cabbies in Washington, upset over a new zoning system that threatened their earnings, also threatened a walkout. The railroads and urban public transport systems alike groaned under the weight of heavily increased traffic. In Detroit the volume soared 32 percent, with buses hauling 800,000 people daily and streetcars another 500,000. The mayor of Los Angeles appealed to drivers to put four passengers in every car. Several cities went to staggered shifts to ease the traffic bottleneck.[25]

As the debate over gas rationing continued, the need to elevate the synthetic program grew more urgent. But politics infected the effort that dismal summer. Newhall's program relied on petroleum to make butadiene. Senator Guy Gillette of Iowa stressed that butadiene could also be made from alcohol and accused Newhall and WPB of favoring the oil industry. Alcohol could be made from corn, of which the nation and Iowa had an enormous surplus. Rubber made from alcohol cost about 25 cents a pound compared with 10 to 15 cents a pound from petroleum. However, the critical need for expanding synthetic rubber as fast as possible outweighed cost factors, and the large farm interests very much wanted to see rubber made from alcohol. Nelson was obliged to explain the rubber situation before seventeen congressional committees—including the Coinage Committee, for reasons never made clear to him.[26]

Between March and June the RRC contracted for 646,000 tons of butadiene. Of that total 526,200 tons (81 percent) would come from petroleum, 80,000 tons from alcohol, and 40,000 tons from benzene. However, the alcohol-based butadiene would be made by a company using synthetic alcohol derived from petroleum, shutting out the agricultural interests entirely. After holding hearings, Gillette concluded that Jersey Standard had used its influence to block the use of alcohol. In May the RRC increased the alcohol-based proportion to 220,000 tons (35 percent), but the farm interests were not appeased. On July 18 Gillette introduced Senate Bill 2600, which sailed through both houses in four days. The bill created a new, independent agency to oversee the production of synthetic rubber with butadiene derived from agricultural commodities and gave its work priority for materials over any other agency. Nelson called it "probably the most unwise and unwarranted piece of legislation passed by Congress during the war."[27]

Passage of the bill finally galvanized Roosevelt to action. On August 6 he issued a ringing veto dissecting all the flaws in a bill that, he declared, would "block the progress of the war production program, and therefore of the war itself." But he could not leave the synthetic rubber program in the air any longer. Some more positive step was needed to assure the public that progress would not be delayed. To that end he turned once again to Bernie Baruch, who in June had urged him to appoint someone of high caliber to investigate the rubber-gas rationing conundrum and submit recommendations. Two months later Roosevelt accepted the suggestion and asked Baruch to head a committee of three for that purpose in a "Dear Bernie" note saying, "Because you are 'an ever present help in time of trouble' will you 'do it again'? You would be better than all the Supreme Court put together!" Baruch picked two outstanding men to join him: James B. Conant, president of Harvard, and Karl Compton, president of MIT.[28]

The president wanted the task done quickly, and Baruch obliged. A staff of twenty-five engineers and technicians was put together while the committee, lacking office space, met on a bench in Baruch's favorite haunt, Lafayette Park. Baruch did not pretend to understand the complexities of synthetic rubber production and left it to his colleagues to evaluate the conflicting claims from the oil and alcohol interests. "All I want to know," he told Conant, "is what process will produce rubber the quickest." Conant, Compton, and other scientists agreed that the best source was butadiene from oil. Conant unfolded a large chart to explain why to Baruch, who said, "All I want to know is, does it work?" Conant assured him that it would. "Well," said Baruch, "fold it up. That's what we're going to do."[29]

After five weeks of hearings and deliberation, the committee issued its report on September 10. It concluded that the rubber crisis was real and that rubber should be conserved by rationing gasoline nationwide, reducing speed limits, and other measures. All obstacles for the production of butadiene should be removed, including priority restrictions on materials, and a rubber administrator should be appointed with complete authority to oversee all aspects of the program. Idle gasoline refining equipment should be used for "quick butadiene" production and plants built in grain areas to speed production by use of alcohol. The WPB's existing production goal of 705,000 tons by the end of 1943 should be increased to 845,000 tons.[30]

Here at last was the voice of authority clearing the air on what had been a befogged controversy. No one was more respected than Baruch or carried more credibility. "He had reached the kind of apotheosis which all public men desire but which only a very few ever attain," observed Bruce Catton. "He had become a great name, a sage, an elder statesman, a Sacred Cow (using the expression with all reverence) for publishers and for editorial writers, an oracle whose word it was sheer impiety to doubt." For Roosevelt the committee's report proved a godsend. One week after the report appeared, he issued an executive order creating a rubber administrator answerable only to the head of the WPB. Conant and Compton had wanted him to be entirely independent, but Baruch argued strongly against dividing authority. Even so, the new position was viewed as a czar and a further weakening of Nelson's authority.[31]

The report became the blueprint for the nation's rubber program. On September 15, Nelson named William M. Jeffers, president of the Union Pacific Railroad, as the new rubber director. The Baruch committee had urged appointment of an administrator "to bull the present program through." Newhall had done a capable job, but he was not the tough guy needed for this job. Bill Jeffers looked to be an ideal choice. A burly, thick-necked, cigar-smoking Irishman, he had no interest in and less patience for political niceties or bureaucratic gamesmanship. He was the product of a railroad culture in which the boss reigned supreme, his word was law, and his style was as subtle as a bulldozer. Washington's finely layered world of bureaucrats rarely saw the likes of men like Jeffers and were dumbfounded over how to deal with them.[32]

Nelson had never found a way to control the War Department. One of his associates described his style in harsh terms. "One of these War Department generals will stick a knife into Nelson," he said, "and all Nelson does is pull the knife out and hand it back and say, 'General, I believe you dropped something.' And the general will say, 'Why, Don, thanks, I believe I did.' And right away he sticks it back in again." Jeffers was quite another species.[33]

For the moment the rubber crisis had been settled, but it was far from finished. Much depended on whether Jeffers could carry out his clear but difficult mandate to sweep all obstacles aside and get synthetic rubber produced. To some observers the uproar over rubber was one that should never have occurred. "The administration turned the rubber problem into a public relations problem and then resorted to an elegant variety of hocus-pocus to solve it," concluded Bruce Catton. ". . . The mess had come into being because . . . Congress and the President had spent their time worrying about what people were going to think, rather than about the action the facts in the situation demanded. Because of that mental attitude at the top, the rubber problem became the rubber mess; because of this desperate, overpowering fear that the people might think the rubber situation was in a mess, the people finally did think so—with, by that time, abundant justification. Because they did think so it was at all costs necessary to get them to think something else."[34]

PRODUCTION WAS ONLY one half of the victory formula; transportation, the other half, was no less important and equally plagued with problems. German submarines still terrorized the North Atlantic and the waters off the East Coast. In June, sinkings reached a new high of nearly 900,000 tons, and the flow of crude oil up the coast slowed to a trickle. For the entire year losses averaged a million tons a month, 75 percent of it from submarine attacks, and exceeded new construction by almost 1.5 million tons. During the first half of the year sixty-one ships went down along the East Coast; during February and March alone forty-two were lost in the Caribbean and eight in the Gulf of Mexico. As late as June 15 bathers at Virginia Beach watched in horror as submarines sank two vessels. The losses on the East Coast created a steady decline in petroleum inventories that never fully recovered during the war.[35]

With the coastal tankers under constant attack, other ways had to be found to get oil to the East Coast refineries. For nearly two years Ickes had battled in vain to gain approval for a pipeline that would connect the Texas oil fields to the eastern refineries. Time and again his pleas had been rejected on the grounds that precious steel for so grand a project could not be spared. The sudden acute shortage of oil on the Eastern Seaboard finally led administration officials to realize their mistake. In June the western half of the project was approved and work started on construction of the largest pipeline ever built in the country. However, it would be months before oil began flowing eastward; in the meantime other expedients had to be devised. The most obvious alternative was to use railroad tanker cars.[36]

To many people the railroads were yesterday's industry, once the largest and most powerful in the nation but now a shrinking relic. They had an especially bitter legacy from World War I, when a colossal traffic jam on the East Coast forced President Wilson to nationalize the industry for the duration of the war. They did not return to private ownership until 1920 and then had to face more stringent government regulation and fierce new competition in the form of automobiles, trucks, and eventually airplanes as well as ships, pipelines, and barges. The prosperity of the 1920s boosted their earnings but did not solve their basic problems. Railroads were the most heavily regulated and fully unionized industry in the nation. Their managements tended to be prisoners of tradition presiding over a proud but insular, often hidebound culture that viewed outsiders and new ideas alike with suspicion.

American railroads entered the war in poor shape, ravaged by years of depression that threw many companies into receivership and left many more unable to maintain their physical plant on meager earnings. When the defense program started up, a third of the nation's railroad mileage was still in or just emerging from receivership. In July 1940 several leading roads announced plans to spend $70 million for new equipment to meet the expected load of the armament program. Nevertheless, a survey by Robert Janeway noted in January 1941 that the supply of serviceable freight cars had declined 30 percent since 1929, largely as a result of company adjustments to falling demand. The surge of business caused by the defense program had already absorbed the surplus of cars and overtaxed the reserve fleet of unserviceable ones. Most of the serviceable cars were old, he warned, and of obsolete construction. Janeway doubted whether the existing fleet could handle upcoming demands or that new cars could be built fast enough and in sufficient quantity to do so.[37]

To these charges the industry's trade group, the Association of American Railroads (AAR), countered that it foresaw no transportation problems in wartime. Like other industries, its members still bore financial scars from the depression and feared the specter of overinvestment. "Everything will be all right if private transportation is left alone," insisted its spokesman. Railroads stepped up their orders for new locomotives and freight cars in 1940, having already launched a major repair program to return unserviceable cars to active duty. Ralph Budd, one of the most prominent railroad executives in the nation and the transportation commissioner since NDAC, insisted repeatedly that the railroads could handle any amount of traffic thrown at them, as did officials of the AAR. During the summer of 1939 Lauchlin Currie, one of Roosevelt's aides, worked out an intricate plan allowing railroads to modernize their equipment at virtually no interest cost; the AAR managed to get it defeated. Currie then ordered the Janeway study that revealed a need for building 100,000 cars at once as part of an overall 500,000-car program, warning that delays would make such orders impossible once defense orders overwhelmed steel mills. Budd dismissed the report as "astronomical statistics."[38]

By the spring of 1941 Budd and the AAR had to change their tune and admit that 100,000 more cars were needed. But manufacturers were already fighting for steel, plant space, new machinery, and high priorities, making it hard for railway car shops to fill even minimum orders. Budd was forced to admit that car orders had fallen down because of materials shortages, but the AAR continued to maintain that "there is no question of a car shortage ... We'll keep ahead. We don't care how fast it [defense expansion] goes." When ICC chairman Joseph Eastman suggested that trucks be enlisted to relieve part of the railroads' load, the AAR bristled. The railroads, huffed a spokesman, "are still in the game of looking for more business." Budd managed to gather a laudable set of statistics on the overall transportation picture and pushed railroads to reduce their "bad order" inventory of cars, but he did little else as the controversy over the car shortage heated up.[39]

Critics demanded Budd's scalp. "His mischievous failure as Transportation Commissioner," wrote Eliot Janeway, "was due to his insistence on catering to the prejudices and the ignorance of the railroad presidents whose performance contrasted with his own. They viewed the emergency as a New Deal plot to have the Government take over the railroads." As commissioner, Janeway complained, "he acted not like the Government official responsible for telling the railroads what to do, but like the railroad spokesman telling the Government what the railroads would not do."[40]

October was the peak season for the carriers, the crucial month when crops and coal moved in volume even without the added burden of defense business. To the surprise of many and relief of others, the railroads handled weekly carloadings of more than 900,000 cars for seven straight weeks with little strain. But shortages kept the shops backlogged, and the supply of new cars trickled in slowly. Pearl Harbor radically altered the transportation landscape, as it did so much else. Normal patterns of railway movement were disrupted as new industries and military facilities sprang up in locations that had never been rail centers. A global war meant that troops, equipment, and supplies had to flow to both coasts. The traditional pattern of rail traffic had always been west to east, but the growth of new industries and the Pacific War meant a steady flow of traffic westward as well. The six major transcontinental railroads were all long, mostly single-track lines accustomed to hauling freight eastward and returning with strings of empty cars. Suddenly they found themselves at the epicenter of an enormous expansion in the amount of traffic.[41]

The challenge facing them—and other roads as well—was formidable. Men had to be moved in large numbers to and from camps and embarkation points along with their equipment and supplies. Raw materials had to reach plants, and their products be carried to wherever they were needed. The growing shortage of ships thrust an even greater burden on the railroads. The submarine menace aggravated the problem even more, especially for oil shipments. Much of the traffic that normally moved from the West to the Atlantic states via the Panama Canal got pushed onto the railroads when ships ran short. Where eastern railroads ran shorter distances and encountered only a few mountain ranges, western roads crossed not only prairie but deserts and mountain ranges that were more numerous and far more formidable.[42]

Few people believed the railroads could handle the greatly enlarged load thrust on them so suddenly by the war. They had 20 percent fewer employees, freight cars, and locomotive tractive or pulling power than in 1929—a good year for them—and 27 percent fewer passenger cars than in 1920. They were asked to do more with less, always with the threat of possible nationalization hanging over them. The Transportation Division, lacking any real authority, had already demonstrated its inability to cope with the growing flow of freight and people in all directions. Convinced that inland transportation needed an independent agency with real power, presidential advisers thrashed out a plan for one and presented it to Roosevelt on December 5, 1941. The attack on Pearl Harbor only made the need more imperative. On December 18 Roosevelt signed an executive order creating the Office of Defense Transportation (ODT). Two weeks later Joseph Eastman was made director, reporting directly to the president.[43]

Nearly everyone, including Ralph Budd, agreed that Eastman was the best man for the job. He did not come from the industry, but his ICC experience made him thoroughly familiar with it. Like railroad executives, he wanted to keep the carriers in private hands and avoid the specter of 1917. That debacle occurred when huge quantities of war goods flowed to Atlantic seaboard ports faster than ships could be provided to load them. As warehouses filled up with munitions, arriving freight cars turned into portable warehouses and piled up on sidings until virtually every major rail yard on the East Coast was clogged and nothing could move. This war was being fought on a far greater scale with numbers of men and amounts of supplies that dwarfed its predecessor. The dismal prospect loomed that the mess of World War I could be repeated on both coasts at the same time.

Eastman was determined not to let that happen. He worked closely with AAR to monitor congestion at key ports and organized a Transportation Control Committee to orchestrate the flow of freight to ports tied to ship schedules. To maximize the use of freight cars, he issued a long-overdue order restricting the movement of less-than-carload freight unless loaded with minimum weights. In normal times less-than-carload freight accounted for less than 2 percent of all ton-miles traveled but used 14 percent of available boxcars. Since production outran the capacity to transport, Eastman persuaded manufacturers to build and pool federal warehouses. By getting railroads to alter other traditional practices and coordinate their efforts more closely, he helped generate a stunning improvement in performance. Trains ran heavier and faster, and their turnaround time improved steadily. Shippers cooperated by loading and unloading cargoes faster. If a terminal looked in danger of becoming clogged, ODT—with AAR's approval—disregarded one of railroading's most sacred tenets and arbitrarily rerouted cars regardless of the shippers' directions.[44]

Nothing taxed the railroads more severely than the oil shortage on the East Coast. The shortage of tankers and submarine sinkings led the carriers to haul out of retirement every workable tank car in their inventory. On January 1 their number totaled 153,662, of which only 9,764 belonged to railroads; the rest were owned by private companies. Of that number only about 120,000 were in shape to carry petroleum. During January a weekly average of 2,955 tank cars carried an average of 94,995 barrels of oil to the Eastern Seaboard every day. During the next eight months, as the submarines took their toll, more and more tank cars were diverted to the task of getting petroleum to the East Coast. By September a weekly average of 27,963 tank cars were delivering an astounding 838,883 barrels of oil to the Eastern Seaboard every day. The railroads were also setting similar records on other war freight as well as passenger service, much of which had become military personnel. On August 1 ODT helped create sixty through routes for unit trains to move on fast schedules over uncongested lines to improve turnaround times by 20 percent.[45]

Few people outside the industry believed the stodgy railroads capable of performing such a feat. "Two years ago the prophets and men in transportation said the railroads could not carry the burden," declared an ICC commissioner in July. "Today, with 600,000 less cars than in 1929, railroads are carrying the greatest burden in history." Under Eastman's guidance they were working together and changing long-encrusted habits. Empty cars, instead of being returned as usual to their owning line, were put back into use on the basis of more timely information as to when and where they were needed. Since Pearl Harbor the railroads had carried 30 percent more freight and 40 percent more passengers with less equipment, and an amazing 80 percent more of both categories compared to 1939. They were also earning profits again, enabling many roads to pay down their crushing debt load.[46]

Still, like many other industries, the railroads could not help worrying about what their future held. "Goddam it all anyway," growled one operating officer. "Whenever I get time to talk to myself, I always wonder what the *hell* we're going to do when the shooting is over." The carriers were hauling the largest volume of traffic with the lowest operating ratios—a measure of efficiency—in their history. But after the war the ships would return, more and larger trucks would appear, automobiles would be produced again, and new, larger, and faster aircraft would fill the skies. Where would all this competition leave the railroads?[47]

No railroad occupied a more strategic location or faced greater challenges than the Southern Pacific. Its lines embraced two of the major transcontinental routes to the West Coast: the original line, shared with the Union Pacific, from Omaha through Utah to Sacramento, and a southern route stretching down from San Francisco through Southern California to New Orleans. The war escalated these lines to strategic importance, not only because men and munitions for the Pacific theater embarked from West Coast ports but also because so many major wartime industries—everything from ships to aircraft to steel to mines—sprang up in its territory. The West, which contained half the area of the United States but only 14 percent of its population, was undergoing a vast transformation.[48]

The Southern Pacific had to surmount some of the most formidable physical barriers in the country. Along with the deserts of the Southwest, it penetrated mountain ranges everywhere. Travelers could ride across the entire continent and encounter only two or three mountain ranges; on the 2,700 miles between Portland, Oregon, and San Antonio, Texas, they would climb over at least eight summits. Going from any major terminal to another on the road meant crossing a chain of mountains. Track through mountain regions meant slower speeds, heavier fuel consumption, and much more power—to say nothing of fickle weather. Climbing a one-foot grade (one foot rise in a hundred) required four times the motive power, a two-foot grade twice that amount, and trains had to descend as carefully as they ascended. The line had more curvature as well as switchbacks at especially difficult points. To complicate matters, only the original main line from Sacramento through the Sierras was double-tracked.[49]

The physical obstacles became even more of a challenge as wartime traffic began clogging the Southern Pacific. Trains ran heavier and slower, especially through mountain country, and there were more of them. The Los Angeles division alone accommodated over fifty a day on its single-track line. "We don't classify any of these spots as bottlenecks," said a Southern Pacific operating man as congestion grew worse, "but merely as places where we got to have hard work, top-notch operation, and perfect dispatching." In this demanding work the dispatcher was king. He had to know not only every mile of his territory but also the condition and capability of every locomotive and engineer, the location of every signal, siding, and spur, and what problems weather might cause.

Running trains in opposite directions on a single line was a ticklish business. Passenger trains alone ran on fixed schedules; regular freights used a hypothetical schedule and special trains none at all. The dispatcher had to know which trains must be put in the hole (moved to a siding) to let another one pass while losing as little time as possible. Any mistake could result in an accident, and the dispatcher never knew what was happening to a train between telegraph stations. Plans were under way to equip dispatchers and train crews with shortwave transmitters and receivers to allow constant communication. Even more promising, a system known as Centralized Traffic Control (CTC) had made its debut on the Southern Pacific in 1931 and was being installed in key stretches throughout the system. CTC gave the dispatcher direct control over block signals and switches at all passing sidings and told him the exact location of each train via an electric signal. It could increase a track's capacity by as much as 50 percent, but it cost $15,000 a mile to install.

Yard congestion posed another problem. As trains arrived at a classification yard, they had to be broken up and the cars attached to other trains bound for their destination. Unlike the major eastern railroads, the Southern Pacific lacked modern yards with mechanical systems that did this work automatically. For the first time in years, the Southern Pacific and other roads needed more workers just as manpower was growing tight. Youngsters were being hired and older heads who had retired brought back. "There is a job for anybody not absolutely decrepit who can show experience as engineman, brakeman, switchman, operator, dispatcher, boilermaker, or mechanic," noted a reporter. The work was hard and the hours long, but the pay was good. However, the Southern Pacific had a serious blind spot in this area. Although a major employer in the Southwest, it refused to hire Hispanics or Indians as firemen or brakemen. This longtime prejudice soon gave way to wartime necessity.[50]

In every respect the Southern Pacific was learning to do more with less. It managed to squeeze an average of nearly 700 miles a day out of overworked passenger locomotives and 6,000 miles a month out of freight engines. In April less than 5 percent of its fleet was laid up for repairs, a company record. Every roundhouse operated on a three-shift basis for repairs, and the shop force worked forty-eight-hour weeks and looked to reach three shifts with more hires. The company desperately needed new, more powerful locomotives as well as freight cars, but few would be forthcoming. Meanwhile, it continued to haul record loads of people and freight while it searched for ways to make the process even more efficient. Like so many of its peers, the Southern Pacific was an old dog trying to learn enough new tricks to accomplish two things: contribute mightily to the war effort and keep the railroads out of the government's hands.

CHAPTER 19

GENERAL MAX
TAKES COMMAND

*All of this deals with, perhaps, the most important phase of the
war since Pearl Harbor. If the fight against inflation at home is
not won, the global war is as good as lost and the President fully
realizes it.*

—WILLIAM HASSETT [1]

*I do not believe in piecemeal price fixing. I think you have first to
put a ceiling over the whole price structure including wages,
rents, and farm prices up to the parity level—and no higher—
and then adjust separate price schedules upward or downward if
necessary, where justice or governmental policy so requires.*

—BERNARD BARUCH [2]

*General Max (the General Maximum Price Regulation) is with
us for the duration to the expansion of OPA, the bewilderment
of wholesaler and retailer, and the good fortune of the legal pro-
fession. Basically the ceilings were the inevitable improvisation
of an Administration that, on the one hand, has promised the
American people it will curb inflation, and, on the other hand,
has so far failed to begin to get at its root cause through taxation.*

—FORTUNE [3]

EARLY IN 1942 IT BECAME CLEAR that this would be the most expensive war in American history. Two major problems stood out even before
Pearl Harbor and grew more critical after it: how to pay for the war and how
to prevent a runaway inflation from wrecking the economy. No one wanted a
repeat of the World War I experience in which, by Baruch's estimate, inflation
increased its cost by about 40 percent. "All wars in this country," Henderson

told a Senate committee, "have produced an inflationary period followed by a deflation which paralyzed recovery." The collapse after World War I had been particularly severe, causing widespread business failures, farm foreclosures, and a stalled economy. Henderson warned that some $13 billion of the $67 billion already authorized for armaments and munitions as of December 1941 would be swallowed by price increases. A strong price control law, he insisted, was as essential as manpower for the military or materials for war production.[4]

Everyone agreed that inflation had to be curbed but disagreed wildly over how it should be done. Two broad approaches could be used. The government could directly impose controls over prices or it could try to curb purchasing power indirectly through broad fiscal policies such as taxation. Both approaches had their champions within the government, which led to rousing and often bitter debates over which course to follow. Morgenthau strongly favored taxation and other broad policies, as did Marriner Eccles, chairman of the Federal Reserve's board of governors. "The job of trying to control many consumer prices by direct action is more difficult than is often supposed," argued Eccles. "Who is to set the price of lingerie, and women's stockings, and boys' hats, and golf balls, and a million other items that indirectly affect the cost of living? And how are we going to distribute the products equitably once the price is set? For when you fix a price you are just at the beginning of your troubles."[5]

But taxation had its controversies as well. Although polls showed a willingness by Americans to pay higher taxes, deep divisions existed over who should be taxed how much. The administration wanted to spare low-income groups from paying taxes, arguing that the burden should fall on the well-to-do and companies that benefited most from the huge outlays for munitions. Opponents countered that defense and war expenditures had put more money in the pockets of working Americans, giving them more ability to consume goods than they had enjoyed in years if ever. Since they formed the bulk of the consuming public, taxing them was crucial to slowing inflation. Politics bound the inflation and taxation debates tightly together, especially in an election year; this constant of American life the war left unchanged. It also ensured that Congress would move at a glacial pace on the issues despite the pressing need for action.

Roosevelt first asked Congress for price control legislation on July 30, 1941, but did not get a bill to sign until January 30, 1942. The Emergency Price Control Act strengthened OPA somewhat but left Henderson unable to control wages or agricultural prices. These two political footballs thwarted every attempt to devise a coherent anti-inflation policy, partly because they occupied different centers of power. No other pressure group rivaled the power of the farm bloc in Congress, which insisted that agricultural prices be sustained at a level no lower than 110 percent of parity. On the other side, the administration sided with labor in resisting controls over wages. Henderson himself admitted to a Senate committee that "personally I have particularly tried to avoid having it in a price bill, lest it complicate an already difficult job."[6]

Parity was a system devised to give select commodities the same purchasing power they enjoyed in an age of relative prosperity. The parity price for each commodity was its average during the years 1910–14, considered a good period for farm prices. The sharp fall in farm prices relative to other prices after World War I never recovered, leaving agriculture a troubled sector even during the prosperous 1920s and a disaster area during the depression years. Many farmers were hopelessly in debt, having bought more land, machinery, and livestock at the high prices prevailing during the war. New Deal programs had established parity prices for major commodities as a floor to help farmers survive. If the market price for the commodity fell below parity, which it nearly always did prior to 1940, the government bought the farmer's crop and stored it as surplus. After 1940, however, farm prices began at last to climb above parity, creating a very different set of problems and triggering a debate over whether farm subsidies were needed at all.[7]

Henderson grudgingly acquiesced in the 110 percent provision, but after Pearl Harbor he urged Congress to restore the original version fixing prices at parity. A November poll showed that 52 percent of farmers were satisfied with the prevailing price levels, but the average farmer did not drive the farm bloc in Congress. The demand for 110 percent came from the powerful American Farm Bureau Federation, which represented large commercial farmers, the top 10 percent who sold half of all agricultural products and had the most influence on Capitol Hill. When OPA placed price ceilings on nearly all types of fats and oils, many of which were imported from the Pacific region, the Farm Bureau's president protested and prompted a Senate resolution to rescind the order. Through lobbying it also got a provision inserted into the Emergency Price Control Act requiring Henderson as price administrator to get prior approval from the secretary of agriculture on any action affecting agricultural commodities.[8]

Although the Price Control Act was serviceable, it lacked the teeth to hold down the cost of living, which continued to rise at a rate of more than 1 percent a month. Wages and farm prices remained unharnessed despite a growing clamor to check them. Roosevelt made a stab at reining in agricultural inflation. "I feel that most farmers realize that when farm prices go much above parity, danger is ahead," he declared. His plan was to stabilize the price of basic staples like wheat, corn, and cotton by having the government sell part of its huge surplus of these commodities, but the Farm Bureau fought these efforts. As for wage disputes, it was hoped the newly created WLB would help devise reasonable settlements. But cases piled up faster than the board could create an organization to handle them, and workers chafed at being stalled in their demands while the cost of living continued to increase. Wildcat strikes began to shred the no-strike pledge despite efforts by union leaders to restrain them.[9]

By March food costs had risen 4.9 percent and clothing prices 7.7 percent since Pearl Harbor. As the wage-price spiral continued its upward climb, Roosevelt asked Harold Smith of the Bureau of the Budget to oversee development of an integrated anti-inflation program. Treasury, Agriculture, the Fed, and OPA all took part but disagreed over several issues. Roosevelt then turned again to Sam Rosenman, who hosted a meeting of Henry Wallace, Morgenthau, Eccles, Smith, and Henderson in the Cabinet Room on April 10. Using a twenty-five-page memorandum submitted by the Budget Bureau, they haggled over a lengthy agenda of issues, two of which split them badly: whether to freeze wages, and whether there should be voluntary or compulsory savings through bond purchases. More meetings followed while Rosenman and Bob Sherwood worked on drafting a speech for the president. Morgenthau became the most stubborn holdout, concerned about what effect any request for more taxes would have on pending tax legislation. In the end he refused to sign the memorandum submitted to Roosevelt on April 18.[10]

"We have come to the conclusion," read the memo, "that partial programs will not work and that only a simultaneous attack on prices, rents, wages, profits, and mass purchasing power will suffice." The group submitted a list of strong recommendations, saying that "only a program as drastic and broad as that here outlined can stop inflation. Any lesser program must fail. Such failure will be a major defeat." More drafts of the speech followed with input from Baruch, Hopkins, Henderson, and others. Rosenman found Baruch especially helpful. "He could always be counted on for brutal frankness in criticizing speeches," he recalled, "and for keen wisdom in suggesting ideas ... He was shrewd and farsighted about political matters and public reaction, more so than anyone but Roosevelt." Henderson implored the president to ask Congress to rescind the 110-percent-of-parity provision. Morgenthau opposed just as strongly any form of compulsory savings, a heavier tax program, and a wage freeze.[11]

On April 27 Roosevelt sent Congress a seven-point program to stabilize the cost of living. It called for imposing heavier taxes to keep personal income and corporate profits at a reasonable (i.e., low) level, placing price ceilings on most products and rents, rationing essential commodities, discouraging credit and installment buying while encouraging the paying off of mortgages and other debts, and purchasing war bonds instead of consumer items. On the two key areas he wavered, urging only that "we must stabilize wages and farm prices" without including any mechanism for doing so. He had accepted Morgenthau's argument against a wage freeze and compulsory savings. Wages could be stabilized, he declared, only after the cost of living had been stabilized. The boards and agencies dealing with labor relations were invited to work out methods for stabilizing wages. Only two of the seven points required congressional action: tax legislation and elimination of the 110-percent-of-parity provision. OPA already had authority to carry out the other five points.[12]

The next evening Roosevelt held a fireside chat to explain the new program. "We are now spending, solely for war purposes, the sum of about $100,000,000 every day in the week," he said. "But, before this year is over, that almost unbelievable rate of expenditure will be doubled ... The spending of these tremendous sums presents grave danger of disaster to our national economy ... The blunt fact is that every single person in the United States is going to be affected by this program ... The price for civilization must be paid in hard work and sorrow and blood. The price is not too high. If you doubt it, ask those millions who live today under the tyranny of Hitlerism ... This great war effort ... must not be impeded by the faint of heart. It must not be impeded by those who put their own selfish interests above the interests of the nation."[13]

Sam Rosenman thought that the talk "shocked a good many Americans" and that the program "was extraordinarily successful in checking inflation." On that point he missed the mark.[14]

THUS WAS BORN General Max.

On April 28 OPA issued the General Maximum Price Regulation, which used the highest price charged by each of the nation's 2.45 million retailers in March 1942 as a ceiling for almost every ordinary commodity. John Kenneth Galbraith called it "the most important date in the history of wartime economic policy." General Max, as the press quickly dubbed it, was supplemented that same day by eighteen price regulations on specific commodities such as solid fuels, farm equipment, paper and paper products, and construction equipment. Another order covered 302 defense rental areas that joined 21 others already designated under the Price Control Act. The average consumer, intoned *Newsweek*, was "about to find totalitarian economic control has entered their democratic way of life ... Long preached by Bernard M. Baruch, over-all freezing of wholesale and retail prices to halt the upshooting cost of living is finally on the way."[15]

But not entirely. Although Roosevelt had called for "a drastic reduction in our standard of living" and "rigid self-denial," he stopped short of embracing the Baruch plan by omitting wage controls and compulsory savings. Baruch had stressed that price-freezing alone would fail unless accompanied by soaking up excess consumer purchasing power through taxes or other means. "The chief criticism of the President's sweeping anti-inflation program, drastic though it is, is inadequacy," concluded *Newsweek*. Ralph Robey was even more blunt, saying that the program fell "so far short of what is needed that it scarcely deserves to be called an anti-inflation program . . . You can't stop a pot from boiling by putting a lid on it. You must put out the fire." *Fortune* projected the "inflation gap"—the difference between disposable income and available goods—as $17 billion and labeled the price ceilings as "a thin and none too stable line flung across this excess of consumer incomes."[16]

Henderson did his part. He held weekly "lessons in economics" for Washington reporters to explain what was happening and its underlying causes. He traveled an exhausting circuit of meetings, banquets, luncheons, and conventions to preach the gospel of price stabilization, becoming what one writer dubbed "the Billy Sunday of economics." Even with General Max his overall authority remained limited and every action charged with controversy. A shrewd elderly Washington lady described the job of price control as one that required "a good bluffer with a big bazoo." Henderson fit the job description, but he got precious little help from other agencies and departments or Congress.[17]

General Max struggled from the start. Two days after it was issued, 700 Chicago landlords quashed hopes for voluntary rent stabilization by voting to withhold approval of rent freezes unless taxes, wages, and other costs were frozen first. New York State food merchants and others protested the March date and demanded different dates to suit their particular situation. Ten Illinois coal mines shut down, throwing 2,000 miners out of work, when operators claimed that the ceilings made it impossible to earn a profit. More than 10,000 tailors faced layoffs because manufacturers contended that they had already contracted to deliver fall clothing at April prices and could not meet expenses at their highest March prices. Grocers moaned that thousands of small food stores would go bankrupt. Shoppers found different prices for the same goods at various stores because their highest price in March had been different.[18]

"What we face," observed *Fortune*, "is an economy where the forces of the market have been turned against rather than for the war effort." The combination of frozen prices and rising costs, especially labor, could impede production. On the distribution side, price ceilings coupled with uninhibited consumer purchasing power could exhaust the nation's stocks of goods rapidly. This had to be met with inventory controls and rationing. The relationship of wholesale and retail prices posed another knotty problem. To drain consumer purchasing power, some mixture of new taxes and forced savings was essential, but that was a job for Congress. "The place where we have failed to tax really severely is the great middle-income groups ranging from $1,500 to $10,000," emphasized *Fortune*. "Yet it is here that almost 60 per cent of consumer income lies."[19]

The heart of the matter, added *Fortune*, lay in one key question: "whether we wish to use the taxing power to bring about an efficient war economy using the natural forces of the market (as well as some direct controls) to this end, or whether we wish to rely on an ever more complicated system of total controls which waste administrative personnel and in the end defeat themselves." Henderson soon discovered that enforcing General Max was an organizational nightmare. OPA had a staff of 6,500 employees and 20,000 volunteer workers; one prediction had it expanding to as many as 50,000 paid workers. It had a nationwide network of 8,000 local rationing boards as well as twenty-five district offices that were to administer price controls in the field under the supervision of eight regional offices. The program required vast quantities of paperwork that had to be printed and distributed: regulations, registration forms, coupon books, and information bulletins. Like other agencies, the Government Printing Office was wholly unprepared to deal with the avalanche of demands piled on it.[20]

OPA's loosely constructed organization foundered under weak supervision and overlapping jurisdictions. The agency lacked capable leadership below Henderson, who was preoccupied with larger questions of policy along with relations with Congress, the public, and other agencies. Pressing problems went unresolved as the national office, swamped with work, struggled to keep up with the demands on it. Field offices were even less prepared to handle the immense workload that confronted them. Under pressure from all sides, Henderson had little choice but to improvise. The price of raw fruits, still protected by Congress, rose sharply, while the ceiling price of canned fruit did not, forcing OPA to raise the ceiling 15 percent. Henderson asked Congress for $161 million to run his agency and enforce General Max. When Congress gave him only $75 million, he warned that lack of enforcement could trigger a runaway price spiral that would cost the country $62 million in extra war expenditures.[21]

Meanwhile, Congress dawdled over a $5.9 billion tax bill, which was $2.8 billion less than Morgenthau had requested and nowhere near what was required to drain consumer spending power. Nor did it move on reducing the 110 percent provision despite a rebuke from Roosevelt. War bond sales lagged behind quotas despite Morgenthau's dogged insistence that voluntary purchases would be sufficient to curb inflation. Wages continued to rise along with farm prices. When the administration tried to sell for fodder 125 million of its 260 million surplus bushels of wheat at 83 cents a bushel to increase the meat supply and help keep wheat prices in line, the House farm bloc—led by Clarence Cannon of Missouri and Everett Dirksen of Illinois—insisted on a sliding scale price that amounted to about $1.34 a bushel and attached it to the Agriculture Department's appropriation so that Roosevelt could not veto it.[22]

The so-called farm bloc in Congress responded to an army of agricultural lobbyists dominated by the American Farm Bureau Federation. Half of its 690,000 members and most of its leadership came from six states, three in the corn belt and three in the cotton belt. A private lobby, it was ironically the offspring of the government it sought to influence. In 1914 Washington began matching funds spent by states and localities for extension work, thereby underwriting the tie between local farm bureaus and county agents. Within a few years the local bureaus banded into state federations and then a national bureau. Gradually the national Farm Bureau emerged as a powerful lobby dominated by a few key state bureaus.[23]

Two men dominated the Farm Bureau. Alabaman Edward O'Neal, its president, had lobbied for higher farm prices since 1931 and once said, "If we, the farmer majority, vote for the good of agriculture, the minority, damn 'em, have got to get into line." His formula for harnessing House votes was deceptively simple: adding the 137 votes of the corn belt to the 120 of the South totaled 39 above a majority. Earl C. Smith of Illinois, whom some called the most powerful farm lobbyist in the nation, was vice president of the Farm Bureau but also president of the 75,000-member Illinois Agricultural Association, the largest single farm group in the country. His supporters boasted that Smith could outwit any broker on LaSalle Street. Once a year he wined and dined the state's congressional delegation to offer them pointed advice. Both O'Neal and Smith liked to assert that farmers were making a greater relative contribution to the war effort than any other economic group, while the administration did nothing to control wages or the costs of manufacturing and distribution.[24]

The WLB was no less overwhelmed by the number and complexity of cases heaped on it during the first half of 1942. While it struggled to establish standards for settling wage disputes, other agencies attacked the problem in their own areas. In May the Department of Labor negotiated an agreement with the building trades for stabilizing wages on government war construction. The WPB sponsored its own wage stabilization agreement in the shipbuilding industry and looked to extend it to other areas. Different agencies had different goals that overlapped and often conflicted. WPB sought to increase production, WMC concerned itself with the nuances of labor supply, OPA wanted to keep the lid on wage hikes, and WLB had the thankless task of devising the specifics to resolve wage disputes. Union officials were adamant not only in protecting their hard-won gains but also in getting wage raises to match increases in cost of living. The result of these often incompatible goals was constant turmoil and frequent sniping among the agencies involved.[25]

WLB began life with no clear mandate or instructions on wage policy from either Roosevelt or Congress. Henderson badgered it to adopt a firm policy to help control prices, while the unions just as adamantly opposed such an approach. Without a clear guide, the board chose to operate on a case-by-case basis as its predecessor had done even as the general level of wages rose at an accelerating rate. Roosevelt's seven-point program in April touched off a spirited debate within WLB as to how best to realize its goals. Gradually the board formulated a set of criteria for handling wage increases. The first of these was a "standard wage," which amounted to an arbitrary base date that became January 1, 1941; some called it a "parity wage." Between that date and May 1, 1942, the cost of living index had risen 15 percent. Should wages be allowed to increase that amount to keep pace? OPA argued vigorously against fully offsetting inflation, but WLB chose a modulated course embodied in what became known as the Little Steel cases decided on July 16.[26]

WLB was itself divided over whether workers should receive full compensation for increases in the cost of living. Chairman William H. Davis originally opposed a full offset but changed his thinking to support it. In one early case Wayne L. Morse, a public member writing for the board's majority opinion, declared that "labor, especially workers in the high paid brackets, have no right to expect that they should receive wage increases during this war period which will enable them to keep day for day pace with upward changes in the cost of living. Labor, too, must take financial sacrifices in the interests of checking the menace of inflation." But in the Little Steel cases the WLB applied the full 15 percent in its decision and came up with a yardstick for future cases in the process. Known as the Little Steel formula, it remained in place for the rest of the war despite unleashing nonstop controversy.[27]

The steelworkers union had demanded a raise of 12.5 percent above the existing average of a dollar an hour. WLB calculated that they had already received wage hikes of 11.8 percent since January 1, 1941, and awarded them a 3.2 percent increase plus another 2.3 percent because the case predated the president's seven-point program and the cost of living in steel towns had jumped more than the national average—making a total increase of 5.5 percent. In reaching this conclusion a WLB panel spent nearly five months taking 2,500 pages of testimony for its 67-page report recommending the full 12.5 percent increase. However, WLB had already rejected or amended fifteen of the forty-five recommendations of its fact-finding panels, and did so again.

The Little Steel formula of allowing raises to match the 15 percent increase in cost of living was set, though nothing was said about any future jumps in the cost of living.[28]

Predictably the decision pleased no one. Davis knew that automobile, aluminum, textile, and rubber workers were waiting in the wings with dollar-a-day demands. Henderson fretted over the impact the decision would have on inflation, while Phil Murray of the steelworkers and CIO recognized the danger posed to workers by inflation but had to cope with the specter of John L. Lewis should he falter in defending labor's interests. In uncharacteristic language Murray lashed out at "the crazy quilt of OPA" and denounced the whole effort to keep wages in check as "unfair . . . intolerant . . . a victory for Hitler." Others protested the growing power of labor in the administration. If the dollar-an-hour steelworkers deserved a pay raise, asked *Time*, "why shouldn't practically every other worker in the country get a raise too? And then where will price control be short of Kingdom come?" The *New York Times* warned that "if adhered to, the new formula can only lead to economic disruption and a disastrous inflation. Mr. Davis calls it a 'terminal' for the tragic race between wages and prices. It sounds much more like the starting pistol."[29]

But WLB's scope was limited. It dealt only with disputed cases brought before it and had no influence on other wage negotiations. Despite the no-strike pledge given when Roosevelt created WLB, wildcat walkouts escalated as more workers demanded wage hikes to meet the rising cost of living. The number of strikes jumped from 27 in January to 192 in June and showed no signs of slowing down. Union leaders did not call the strikes but struggled to control their locals. When a thousand workers at a tank plant in Berwick, Pennsylvania, walked out, an annoyed Roosevelt said, "This strike is a serious threat to the nation's tank production . . . I *insist* there be an immediate resumption of production." The workers complied, but jawboning even by the president could only go so far. Controls were needed to handle wage increases not in dispute.[30]

BY AUGUST THE fight against inflation seemed as forlorn as the flow of news from overseas battlefields. The seesaw relationship between agricultural prices and wages escalated another notch as the farm bloc saw in the Little Steel formula a reason to seek even higher prices. Congress wanted out of Washington to mend its fences at home during an election year, and many of its members were gone by the end of July, having fumbled or stalled most of the key issues before them. "What's the Matter with Congress?" asked columnist Ernest Lindley, who recited its inept handling of gasoline rationing, the inflation program, and the tax bill for openers. Raymond Clapper was even more unsparing. "Congress has remained a collection of 2-cent politicians who could serve well enough in simpler days," he wrote. "But the ignorance and provincialism of Congress render it incapable of meeting the needs of modern government. Consequently the center of gravity has shifted toward the executive branch."[31]

Congressional leaders warned Roosevelt not to try to get a tighter grip on wages and farm prices, but a group in New York City called Citizens for Victory published an ad with the glaring banner "WHAT'S THE MATTER WITH THIS COUNTRY?" While American, Russian, British, and Chinese boys were dying in battle, it declared, the disgusting spectacle of pork-barrel politics went on as usual in Washington. It denounced the farm bloc as "those to whom V means Votes in November" while also rebuking the labor lobby, the antilabor bloc, and several other groups. Henderson, struggling to maintain General Max's price ceilings, was forced to make one concession after another, especially on food prices. The March date for ceilings hurt grocers whose prices that month were based on foods bought months earlier. Wholesale prices had increased, making it impossible for them to restock except at a loss. Supermarkets, chain stores, and other low-margin operators also pleaded for adjustments on the same grounds.[32]

Two problems plagued efforts to control food prices. The restrictions in the Price Control Act kept several key commodities—poultry, eggs, sheep and lambs, milk and milk products, and wheat products, including flour—from price controls under General Max. A second issue involved the "squeeze" created by pegging prices to March levels. When retailers began replenishing stocks of canned goods, they found that the ceiling prices on their supplies tended to be higher than their retail price ceilings. Farm prices and labor costs rose about 10 percent during the year and transportation costs about 5 percent. No solution to this problem existed that did not involve either raising prices, removing controls (which had the same effect), or using government subsidies to cushion the squeeze. Roosevelt urged both Claude Wickard and Henderson to maintain price ceilings while keeping agricultural production high, but the dilemma of how to do both things at once remained.[33]

The executive branch had already concluded that more than General Max was needed to fight inflation. OPA sent Rosenman a proposal for tightening wage and farm price controls, arguing that the cost of living could not be stabilized unless *all* factors were subject to restraint. It urged the creation of a new board to regulate wages, but the request was rejected as unworkable. However, the idea of a new board to coordinate all stabilization efforts took wing in discussions among White House and Budget Bureau staff. A Gallup poll in August revealed that 70 percent of respondents thought every family not on relief should pay much higher taxes to support the war, while 71 percent approved the freezing of wages, salaries, and food costs. Some advisers pushed Roosevelt to act on his own without waiting for Congress, arguing that the Second War Powers Act, passed in March, gave him all the authority he needed.[34]

Roosevelt was ready to act but hesitant to ignore Congress. On September 7 he sent a stern message to Congress and delivered a fireside chat explaining what was needed to control inflation. In crisp language he recalled for Congress the seven points of his anti-inflation program and noted that it had not provided the legislation he asked for to reduce parity to 100 percent, curb wages, and absorb consumer spending power through new taxes. His message amounted to an ultimatum: If Congress did not reduce the 110 percent and pass a new tax bill by October 1, the president would take powers into his own hands. He also promised to stabilize wages but did not say how he would do so. Reporters thought they sniffed an implicit bargain that if Congress took care of farm prices Roosevelt would handle wages, but no details were forthcoming. "Never before," said *Newsweek*, "had the opposing interests of labor and agriculture been so sharply focused in public attention."[35]

To the people Roosevelt conveyed the same information and determination to do the job if Congress did not. He opened with three stirring stories of American heroic deeds in combat and urged everyone to make the same full commitment to the war effort. After explaining what parity was and how it worked, he emphasized the importance of the fight against inflation. "I realize it may seem out of proportion to you to be overstressing these economic problems at a time like this, when we are all deeply concerned about the news from far distant fields of battle," he said. "But I give you my solemn assurance that failure to solve this problem here at home—and to solve it now—will make more difficult the winning of this war. If the vicious spiral of inflation ever gets under way, the whole economic system will stagger. Prices and wages will go up so rapidly that the entire production program will be endangered. The cost of the war, paid by taxpayers, will jump beyond all present calculations."[36]

He repeated the October 1 deadline and added that "at the same time that farm prices are stabilized, I will stabilize wages," but gave no details. In stressing the need for higher taxes, he said, "The Nation must have more money to run the war. People must stop spending for luxuries. Our country needs a far greater share of our incomes." The war, he added, would cost about $100 billion in 1943 alone. "Battles are not won by soldiers or sailors who think first of their own personal safety," he stressed. "And wars are not won by people who are concerned primarily with their own comfort, their own convenience, their own pocketbooks." This was, he concluded, "the toughest war of all time," one the American people dared not lose or they would lose everything.[37]

Congressmen grumbled over the president's tough tone but got the message. New bills were introduced and hearings opened, only to bog down in clashes over the parity and tax issues. A convoluted tax proposal advocated by Morgenthau so befuddled the Senate Finance Committee that the presentation was interrupted and not allowed to finish. The farm bloc agreed to surrender the 110 percent provision if the parity formula was changed to include farm labor costs as well. The Department of Agriculture calculated that such a change would actually raise the parity to 112 percent. The usual barrage of telegrams and letters inspired by the farm bloc poured into the House, which passed the change despite loud protests. Frantic efforts at compromise produced a bill that gave Roosevelt what he wanted—a return to 100 percent parity—and directed him to issue an order stabilizing wages by November 1. The president signed it on October 2, only one day after his stated deadline. *Time* called it a "soul-satisfying happy ending."[38]

One day later Roosevelt issued an executive order creating the Office of Economic Stabilization (OES) composed of eight top administration officials and two members each from labor, management, and agriculture. To head the new board Roosevelt persuaded James F. Byrnes of South Carolina to resign from the Supreme Court and take the job. In the same edict the president included a number of long-awaited steps. He ordered all wages and farm prices stabilized at their levels on September 15 and extended to WLB the power to approve or cut all wages, not just those in dispute. The farm order covered about 90 percent of all foodstuffs; fresh fruits and vegetables were almost impossible to regulate. Ceilings on rent were extended beyond the original specific group to the entire country. All salaries over $5,000 were to be frozen except in exceptional circumstances, and where practicable salaries were not to exceed $25,000 a year after payment of taxes, insurance premiums, and fixed obligations already incurred.[39]

"This Government is determined to use all of its powers to prevent any avoidable rise in the cost of living," Roosevelt wrote Henderson. However, as Ralph Robey never tired of pointing out, he had merely put a tighter lid on a pot that would not stop boiling until more consumer spending power was drained away through higher taxes or other means. The effectiveness of the order depended on how well Byrnes managed to enforce it. He had long been regarded as one of the smoothest politicians on Capitol Hill before going to the Supreme Court. *Time* described him as "a middle-of-the-roader who can get along with men of all beliefs; he knows when to hold his tongue; he is an expert at finding the common denominator." Bruce Catton referred to him as "the super-umpire." Byrnes himself had no illusions. "I know it is a tough task," he said. "It will require the proper appreciation of the frequent use of the word *no*. You are bound to be unpopular when you say *no*."[40]

FEW THINGS POSED more problems or aroused more controversy than rationing. The image of Americans cheerfully accepting the need for it and patriotically abiding by its strictures is largely a fantasy spawned by the "Greatest Generation" myth. In reality it was violated almost as much as it was obeyed, and its complexities and logistical nightmares drove officials and citizens alike to despair. While many if not most people were willing to make sacrifices for the war effort, they differed radically on what to give up and how far they were willing to go. Inevitably rationing, apart from being difficult to enforce, gave rise to "Mr. Black," the black market operations that recalled the unsavory days of prohibition and the rise of the mobs. Americans had avoided rationing in World War I, but Roosevelt warned repeatedly that it would be needed in 1942. In the end Mr. Black trumped General Max.

Rationing served two main purposes. Most obviously it tried to allocate on an equitable basis goods and materials in short supply. On another level it joined with price controls to help limit what Americans could buy at a time when they had more money in their pockets than anytime since the 1920s if ever. But a fair and effective rationing program was even more cumbersome to impose than price ceilings. The public squawked loudly over having to deal with the system, its wrath heightened by the fact that many of the items rationed were among the most important to their daily routines. To some it smacked too much of the totalitarian methods against which the war was being fought. No one wanted to fight Germany by emulating Germany.

Rubber was the obvious first target. Four days after Pearl Harbor OPM halted the sale, transfer, and delivery of new tires. Rationing began on January 5 after an organization had been set up for the task. Gasoline followed on May 15, using a sticker system. Holders of "A" stickers, nonessential drivers, got only three gallons a week; "B" holders, such as workers who drove to war plants, got a supplementary allowance; "C" stickers went to essential drivers like doctors, while "X" cards for unlimited amounts were given to a select group of people. Congress raised a storm of protest when more than 200 of its members asked for and received X stickers, and the Senate embarrassed itself further by voting overwhelmingly not to return them—although a handful of congressmen did so. Truckers got a special "T" sticker allowing them all the gas they needed.[41]

The system never worked well. An OPA survey estimated that nearly half of all Americans had B or C stickers, while a Gallup poll revealed that three fourths of the 45 percent of Americans who drove to work said they could get there some other way if necessary. Inevitably a black market sprang up for both tires and gasoline, the latter mostly in the form of counterfeit coupons. Professional criminals moved into the racket and sold the phony coupons largely to filling station operators. When a filling station did not cooperate, the mob resorted to violence. One woman in New Jersey was tortured with a burning paper torch when she refused to play ball with the counterfeiters. Truck drivers also sold their excess to filling station operators who in turn sold extra gas to favored customers without coupons.[42]

However, rationing did reduce driving, and with it deaths on the highway. Labor Day 1942 recorded 169 automobile deaths compared to 423 in 1941. Most states reported a drop of 50 percent in traffic and cringed at their loss of gasoline taxes, bridge and tunnel tolls, and canceled license fees. Service station operators saw their profits plummet along with those of garages, parking lots, and the cluster of roadside businesses devoted to travel. Eastern filling stations ran dry of gas, and motorists took to stalking gasoline trucks and lining up quickly whenever they stopped at filling station pumps. "Hell had seen no furies," reported *Time*, "like the motorists who did not have enough gas left to drive around to a service station for gas that was not there."[43]

"*Gasoline rationing is not a phony,*" Kiplinger's assured its readers in April. "Neither is rubber shortage." Neither was the shortfall of sugar, which underwent rationing that same month. Nearly everyone knew rationing was inevitable and aggravated the shortage by buying and hoarding shortly after Pearl Harbor. Businesses, bootleggers, and people who remembered the sugar crunch during World War I loaded up on hundred-pound bags before the loss of the Philippines turned an artificial crisis into a real one. Sugar was also imported from Cuba and Puerto Rico, but the lack of ships curtailed those imports. Beginning in May, citizens made their way to local schools, where volunteers under OPA supervision distributed one War Ration Book for each member of the family after deposing them on how much sugar they had at home. Some 6.4 million people were denied cards because they admitted to holding more than six pounds of sugar; one New Jersey man confessed to a hoard of 15,000 pounds, saying he had planned to go into the sugar-jobbing business.[44]

Sugar mattered because it was far more than a sweetener. From sugarcane came sugar molasses, a major source of ethyl alcohol used in the motive power for torpedoes, a solvent in gelatin dynamites and smokeless powder, and a dehydrating agent in manufacturing nitrocellulose. As a raw material it found uses in thousands of chemicals, everything from paints to cosmetics to medicines to embalming fluid. Americans consumed far more sugar than any other people, about a hundred pounds per capita every year, and no relief was in sight. Sugar rationing lasted even beyond the war's end. "Roses are red, Violets are blue," chanted columnist Walter Winchell, "Sugar is sweet. Remember?"[45]

By fall it was clear that a broader range of rationing would be needed. During 1942 OPA instituted ten major rationing programs, with more to come. Coffee joined the list, as did some canned goods and shoes, each one for a different reason. Coffee, like sugar, had ample supplies but too few ships to carry it to the United States; canned goods suffered from a shortage of tin, and military needs swallowed a giant portion of shoes. Warned that coffee would be rationed in a few weeks, housewives responded by emptying the shelves of it. OPA countered by freezing sales of coffee a week before rationing began (one pound every five weeks for every person over age fifteen) and announcing the freeze on a Sunday when stores were closed. Later it used this same approach on other commodities.[46]

Meat posed a special problem. The shortage especially of steaks and chops arose because Americans, flush with war industry jobs, were eating more meat—and better cuts—than ever before. Roosevelt suggested at a news conference that maybe the nation needed one meatless day a week, a notion that WPB's Food Requirements Committee had rejected as useless only three hours earlier, saying, "If there isn't enough meat for everyone to eat all he wants, it doesn't make much difference on what day he eats it." The allotment for the army and Lend-Lease was raised from 2.2 billion pounds in 1941–42 to 6 billion pounds for 1942–43. With an extra billion pounds earmarked for Great Britain, American consumers would be left with 10 billion pounds compared with 12.3 billion pounds the previous year. "With the new rich buying as never before," observed *Time*, "the public will probably try to buy 14 billion pounds this year," making rationing necessary.[47]

However, unlike sugar, which rich and poor alike consumed in almost the same amounts, the well-to-do ate three times as much meat as the poor. Imposing a ration of two and a half pounds per person, as Claude Wickard proposed, meant that more than half the American people would actually get more meat than they currently bought, while those with higher incomes would incur a 40 percent reduction. OPA also concluded that most of the big packers were upgrading meat and short-weighing butchers to evade price ceilings. To curb these abuses it extended licensing from retailers to packers and wholesalers as well, but the process remained muddled in controversy. WPB urged restaurants across the country to cooperate in a voluntary meat-rationing program. Kiplinger's reminded its readers, "*There must and will be a lot of food rationing.*"[48]

Food supplies remained the most complex and thorny problem. Although the fall harvest proved to be the greatest crop in history, exceeding the previous year's record by 10 percent, empty spaces loomed on grocers' shelves. The actual amount of food available was the largest in American history, but shortages occurred because of heavy demand for certain types at home and abroad as well as the voracious demands of a growing military. In future years the supply might well decline because of a shortage of manpower. Taken together, these factors pointed to the inevitability of rationing and the urgent need for strong leadership free of political bickering. "The major responsibility for the supply and distribution of food," said Ernest Lindley, "needs to be centralized in a man or an agency endowed with power and the courage and imagination to use it."[49]

In his September 7 message to Congress Roosevelt admitted that "the movement of uncontrolled food prices since May 18 . . . has been so drastic as to constitute an immediate threat to the whole price structure, to the entire cost of living, and to any attempt to stabilize wages." As Ralph Robey observed, rationing performed two distinct functions. The first dealt with shortages of a given commodity, while the second sought to prevent a rise in prices and hold down inflation. Both were handicapped by the enormous excess of buying power in the hands of the public compared to the dwindling volume of goods available as the military and Lend-Lease siphoned off increasing amounts of supplies of all kinds. Trying to solve this riddle resembled attempts to square a circle.[50]

The furor over gasoline exemplified these difficulties. The submarine depredations had created a genuine shortage of gasoline and fuel oil in the East but not in the rest of the country. However, the rubber shortage existed everywhere and had to be met primarily by reduced driving. The logical way to do this was to ration gasoline across the nation, but people outside the East protested that they had ample supplies of gasoline. Senator Edwin C. Johnson of Colorado observed that it would be hard to "convince people in oil-producing states that they can't have gasoline." Despite some delays, gas rationing was extended to the entire nation as of December 1 along with a speed limit of 35 miles per hour on all but emergency vehicles.[51]

Opposition mounted at once. A bloc of seventy-five western congressmen demanded a ninety-day deferment of what they denounced as a wholly unnecessary act. A flood of postcards asking for the same delay, orchestrated by the director of the Hoosier Motor Club in Indianapolis, descended on Congress. Louisiana's governor reported "almost universal" opposition to rationing in his state, Texans were furious, and Oklahomans refused to register for coupon books, as did 166,000 war workers in Detroit. New England had a still larger problem; its six governors predicted a "completely ruinous fuel oil shortage" as winter loomed. OPA investigated 500 eastern filling stations and found that 70 percent were bootlegging gasoline and violating rationing rules. Henderson denounced the protesters as "men who gamble America's future not for a mess of pottage but for a gallon of gasoline."[52]

Already easterners had put into circulation 150 million gasoline ration coupons every month, to which the nation added another 130 million sugar ration stamps. As the rationing system grew, the paperwork threatened to overwhelm it. Ration boards were set up in every county of every state, manned by more than 30,000 volunteers to process the mountain of paper. The government printed 200 million comprehensive coupon books for distribution that fall. Buying any rationed product required not only cash but the proper coupon or stamp, which had to be used within a given period of time, usually a month. The process was not only cumbersome but imposed an unprecedented degree of regimentation on Americans unaccustomed to it.[53]

Fresh off the most bountiful harvest since the Pilgrims landed at Plymouth Rock, Americans found it hard to believe that a food crisis was approaching. Paul Willis, the head of the Grocery Manufacturers of America, believed it and said so. "A scandal far greater than the rubber situation looms in the near future," he warned late in October. "Unless immediate steps are taken to coordinate this country's system of food production and distribution, a major food shortage is a certainty." About 570,000 hands left American farms in 1940, another million in 1941, and an estimated 1.3 million were likely to be gone by seeding time next spring. In New York 1,400 farms had already gone out of production, and northeastern dairy farmers were expected to sell off 35,000 cows, reducing the milk supply by 64 million quarts. Arthur H. Lauterbach, manager of the Pure Milk Association, predicted that at the present rate 20 percent of the nation's dairy cows would be sent to slaughterhouses by next summer.[54]

"In the twelve months since Pearl Harbor," concluded *Newsweek* in December, "the American family has *begun* to experience war on the home front." Nearly a year had passed before people outside the East had to endure gas rationing, the sugar pinch was gentle so far, meat rationing would not begin for another month, and the effects of the fuel oil shortage remained an unknown. Although the family food bill had gone up 16 percent in a year, daily fare had hardly changed except for a limit of one cup of coffee. Thanksgiving dinner seemed as full a feast as ever, marred only by the absence of loved ones serving in the military. Travel had become an ordeal. The gas crunch limited the range of driving, and trains were jammed with soldiers as well as civilian travelers. To save fuel, the government wanted those with oil burners to switch to coal if possible and asked everyone to keep the thermostat no higher than 65 degrees. A Gallup poll revealed that 68 percent of those with oil and 72 percent of those with coal ignored the request.[55]

"The real hard truth," predicted *Newsweek*, "is that Americans not only are going to have their standard of living reduced all along the line, but will have to sacrifice for the duration the traditional American way of life." Yet how much was really being sacrificed? More Americans were earning more money and living better than they had in years. Many kinds of consumer goods could no longer be had, but enough remained to make daily life more comfortable than many people had experienced recently if at all. Looking back on these years, John Kenneth Galbraith concluded that "never in the long history of human combat have so many talked so much about sacrifice with so little deprivation as in the United States in World War II."[56]

CHAPTER 20

MIXED SIGNALS

We have no other dependable source of leadership except in Roosevelt and some of the men around him. That is a terrible thing to say about a democracy but I believe it to be true . . . The Republican party? What a pitiful thing it is. What has it offered us during the last nine years except stupidity, five-cent criticism, and complete misunderstanding of our main problems, domestic and foreign?

—RAYMOND CLAPPER[1]

A single year could change our food position from abundance to scarcity.

—CLAUDE WICKARD[2]

Once the planning is done, once you get the production rolling—then it's only a matter of constant operational headaches, design changes, and the like. That's where we are today. We're past the beginning . . . It means only one thing: that from now on our war needs are limited only by materials and manpower.

—NEWSWEEK[3]

THE WAR WAS GOING WELL AND YET it wasn't. Production was surging but plagued with shortages. Inflation was under control and yet it wasn't. The administration had a firmer grip on the war effort and yet it didn't. The nation strongly supported Roosevelt's leadership but the Republicans made sizable gains in the off-year election. Americans were resigned to increased austerity for the duration of the war and yet they weren't. Many people were living better than they had in years, yet thousands who flocked to jobs at war plants endured ghastly living conditions in overwhelmed communities. As the year drew down, mixed signals poured in from all sides, leaving the

American people confused on nearly everything but the realization that the war would not end anytime soon.

Early in November British forces won a crucial victory at El Alamein and Allied forces, mostly American, landed in North Africa to join the seesaw fight against Rommel's Afrika Corps. In the Pacific the Japanese island-by-island march southward had finally been halted, but the United States remained on the defensive. Starting an advance northward, Roosevelt admitted, "will take a long, long time, because ... it takes months to get a ship with men or munitions from the United States down there and back again." In both theaters the task of seizing the initiative seemed distant, especially when German submarines continued to inflict heavy losses on Allied shipping. Americans had been at war for almost a year, while Europeans entered their fourth year of fighting with no end in sight and most of the continent under the Nazi heel. The Russians were making a heroic stand against the German onslaught at a terrible cost in lives and destruction.[4]

At home the fall elections inflicted a rare setback on Roosevelt as Republicans gained forty-four seats in the House and nine in the Senate, mostly at the expense of northern liberals. This victory strengthened the conservatives in Congress and encouraged the coalition of northern Republicans and conservative southern Democrats who found common cause in a number of issues ranging from white supremacy to cutting federal spending except on the war. Together they could make or break nearly any legislation. Southerners occupied more than half of all Democratic seats in the House and beat down every attempt at racial reform, such as repeal of the poll tax. The political landscape was undergoing a radical shift, one that made relations on the Hill more divisive than ever. Liberals saw their long-dominant influence slipping away and despaired that the war was delivering power into the hands of business and the military. Conservatives, intent on rolling back what they deemed the excesses of the New Deal, labeled any piece of legislation they disliked as an attempt at social reform disguised as a war measure.[5]

A major reason for the poor showing of Democratic candidates appeared to be the shockingly low turnout at the polls—barely half the number who voted in 1940. Industrial regions, whose workers formed a key element of Democratic support, suffered from low registration and poor voter turnout, partly because so many people had moved around the country in search of war jobs. The solidly Democratic South had always been split between its arch conservatives and more liberal New Dealers, and the midwestern rural vote had largely returned to the Republican Party despite all that Roosevelt had done for farmers. Soldiers and sailors serving overseas could not vote because absentee ballots could not be submitted from abroad. Eleanor Roosevelt could not vote in the election because she happened to be in London on election day.[6]

It galled Roosevelt that not only were Democratic seats lost in Congress but that two of his arch enemies, Thomas A. Dewey and Hamilton Fish, won election as governor of his home state and representative from his home district. "Mr. Roosevelt was a politician before he was a statesman," wrote Raymond Clapper, "and the love of the game of politics still remains. He turns back to dabble in it at times as a famous engineer might go back to playing with electric trains in his basement on a rainy Sunday." But politics had taken an ugly and unpredictable turn in wartime, one that often baffled and frustrated even FDR. The dilemma that haunted his liberal supporters bothered him as well: how to win the war without losing the New Deal. The Republicans, aside from Willkie, seemed to offer nothing but negativity and righteous slogans.[7]

"We have been drifting into dead waters in this country," observed Clapper in October. "Except for Roosevelt, we have had little leadership of national stature. We had some synthetic personalities, some who tried to get there by hiring press agents. But mostly it's been second-string stuff . . . If we ever needed not one big man but many big men in America it is now."[8]

"WE HAVE TO change our way of looking at taxes during the war," wrote Clapper in March. "A lot of people want to help the Government win the war . . . They can at least pay taxes. More than that, they can give their support to every proposal to increase taxes. They can help club down special-interest groups that will try to chisel away the heavy taxes just proposed." Seven months later, after months of bitter and confused wrangling, Congress finally passed and Roosevelt signed the Revenue Act of 1942. One provision did away with the requirement to have returns sworn before a notary public. A Treasury official noted wryly that "the taxpayers probably will do enough swearing anyway when they add it up."[9]

The new law nearly doubled federal taxes and in the process transformed the American way of taxation. It increased the normal and surtax rates on all incomes, with the latter reaching a high of 82 percent on incomes above $200,000. In all, the two rates totaled 19 percent of the first $2,000 in income and increased at higher income levels. More significantly, the new act lowered personal exemptions, which had been dropping steadily since 1931. In that year a married couple with income below $3,500 paid no tax; the new law lowered the exemption from $1,500 to $1,200 for married couples and $624 for single persons, bringing into the system more than 13 million lower-income taxpayers for the first time. Those who argued for the need to spread the tax load across lower incomes to reduce consumer spending got their wish, but so did those who wanted higher taxes on corporations and the wealthy. The corporate rate increased from 31 to 40 percent, and the graduated excess profits tax of 35 to 60 percent was replaced by a flat rate of 90 percent.[10]

Another innovation caused the biggest stir. On top of their regular taxes citizens with incomes above $624 would also pay a special 5 percent Victory Tax but would receive a credit—25 percent for single people, 40 percent for couples, and another 2 percent for each dependent—that could be used as an offset in some cases on 1943 income taxes or reclaimed as a non-interest-bearing bond after the war. The Victory Tax would be withheld from individual paychecks. Corporations could reclaim 10 percent of their excess profits payments after the war as well. Under the new system income taxes became for the first time a way of life for most Americans. In 1940 about 7 percent of the population paid income taxes; by 1944 the figure would top 64 percent. The Victory Tax was an obvious attempt to curb excess consumer spending. Hardly anyone liked the new tax system, but for very different reasons.[11]

"The tremendous new tax load has a dual purpose," said *Newsweek*: "to control inflation and to pay for the cost of the war. It falls far short of both." The projected revenues amounted to only a third of the war's annual outlays and only half of what Roosevelt sought. They also fell an estimated $50 billion short of what was needed to close the inflation gap. For months Ralph Robey railed against the proposed tax bill as inadequate and argued for a national sales tax that would bite more directly into consumer spending at every income level. It was, he conceded, "one of the most regressive known" taxes, but it fought inflation directly and, since end users paid it, the tax could not be passed along to someone else. The cost of the war had barely been touched, inflation remained a threat, and the new system pretty much ended the usefulness of income taxes as a source of more revenue.[12]

One other flaw in the tax system ultimately led to an innovation that proved enduring. Income taxes were due at the end of each year, which put the burden on taxpayers to save enough money during the year to meet their obligation. This arrangement deprived the government of the revenue until year's end, and major shortfalls were likely with the new act bringing into the system so many new taxpayers unfamiliar with it. Beardsley Ruml thought he had a solution to the problem. The treasurer of R. H. Macy & Co. and chairman of the Federal Reserve Bank of New York, he advanced the novel idea of having citizens pay their taxes in installments throughout the year, either directly or through their payroll at work. This pay-as-you-go plan would regularize income to the government and relieve taxpayers of having to meet the total bill at year's end. It had only one serious flaw: If the plan commenced at the beginning of 1943, taxpayers would owe their entire tax bill for 1942 while making payments toward their 1943 taxes at the same time.[13]

The flaw already existed. The first time any taxpayer tried to save enough money during the year to pay his current taxes, he also had to pay the previous year's taxes that same year. "Nothing is to be gained by arguing that people ought to save the tax on this year's income out of this year's income," Ruml argued. "The fact is that they did not do it, and now they cannot do it. We need, therefore, to find and adopt a plan that automatically shifts taxpayers to a current basis." Ruml's idea was disarmingly simple: forget paying taxes on 1941 income and start making periodic payments for 1942. The Treasury would continue to receive income every year based on the income of that year; thereafter payments would be on a current basis of paying estimated installments on that year's taxes. The plan, said Ruml, would move the "tax clock forward, and cost the Treasury nothing until Judgment Day."[14]

Ruml's plan found favor among the public and some congressmen but not in the administration. Morgenthau called it "rather disgusting" because it would allow those who amassed windfall earnings or profits in 1941 to avoid having to pay taxes on them. His influence managed to kill the plan in 1942, but support for it continued. "Nobody wanted Mr. Beardsley Ruml's pay-as-you-earn income-tax plan except the people," declared the *Saturday Evening Post*. "The Treasury opposed it on the ground that people who had bigger incomes in 1941 than they had in 1942 would get away with something." Roosevelt was equally unhappy with the huge revenue bill dumped on his desk along with a lengthy report on it from Treasury. It might as well have been in a foreign language, he complained. He didn't understand it and thought Treasury didn't either, so he made a joke of it. But he was told that it had to be signed that day to save some $60 million in revenue, so he signed it.[15]

The president also felt the sting of the new law personally. Two weeks before signing the bill he wrote a memo to Eleanor warning that the new law would "result in such a cut in the net I receive from the Government that we shall have to take some steps to reduce the White House food bill, to which I pay $2,000 a month ... Next year the taxes on $75,000 will leave me only about $30,000 net and SOMETHING HAS TO BE DONE! ... The only thing I can think of is to reduce the number of servants we feed ... I would suggest that something drastic be done about the size of the portions served."[16]

For all its radical changes to the tax system, the act omitted the Ruml plan, a sales tax, and some important reforms advocated by Treasury. Half of its several hundred pages provided tax loopholes at a time when American troops were about to land in North Africa and launch a counteroffensive against the Japanese at Guadalcanal. And it raised a paltry $7 billion in new revenue by Treasury estimates. "I am 'plumb disgusted' with the favoritism and privilege," wrote editor Josephus Daniels, a staunch liberal and longtime supporter of Roosevelt. Morgenthau agreed and admitted that "I do not know when we are going to get total war on taxes."[17]

LABOR EMERGED AS the major problem on most farms. Too many boys and hired hands had joined the military or gone off to factory jobs that paid much better. On the Pacific Coast the abrupt removal of Japanese Americans left a huge hole in the farm labor and grower force as white growers took over their land without having experienced men to work and harvest it. Small farms too struggled to increase their yields with fewer hands. In Madison, Missouri, Fred Forsyth and his wife, Ruby, who had worked the land all their lives, put in even more hours than usual to coax higher yields from their 218 acres. The government wanted more meat, milk, eggs, and especially soybeans to replace the lost vegetable oils from the Far East. "Now," said Forsyth proudly, "we work an eight-hour day—twice."[18]

Like a factory, Forsyth's farm had war production goals, set in collaboration with Stanley Crow of the Monroe County War Board and the Department of Agriculture. For a labor force, however, Forsyth had only his three children—Eugene, eleven; Dorothy, nine; and Jack, five. They too were putting in longer hours. Already Eugene could drive the family tractor, helping to cultivate the soybeans that had quadrupled in acreage this year. Dorothy helped with the milking, which Fred had increased by 50 percent. Dorothy and Jack hauled buckets of corn to the chickens and helped in their mother's vegetable garden, while Eugene fed the fifty lambs. Fred also had 50 percent more poultry to increase egg output and thirty more hogs for pork supply. They were doing their part to help the war effort and, despite the long hours and hard work, relishing the closest thing to good times that they had known in a long while.[19]

Across the continent on the Pacific Coast, a comparable battle was being waged on a much larger scale to save the region's $1.35 billion worth of crops from rotting in the fields. At stake were 200 million pounds of vegetables needed by the military to dehydrate for expeditionary forces, millions of gallons of citrus juices, tons of berries, huge tracts of sugar beets, and nearly all the dried fruits needed to feed not only Americans but the Allied nations as well. Here too the Department of Agriculture's "food will win the war" drive had increased crops by 10 to 50 percent, but who would harvest them? Farm boys and whole rural families had departed for high-paying city jobs, the hardworking and savvy Japanese American farmers were gone, and the annual flood of migratory workers had slowed to a trickle.[20]

Ray Wiser, head of the California Farm Bureau Federation, offered a possible solution. "We've got a billion-dollar crop on our hands," he said. "Our only chance to save it is by mobilizing the city people for farm work." It seemed a dubious proposition. Hadn't many people gone to the city to get away from farms in the first place? Didn't they also have good-paying war work? But Wiser persisted and found willing hands in the unlikeliest of places: high school students, housewives, and professional people willing to give up their vacations and weekends to help save the harvest.

In Placer County, nestled in the foothills of the Sierra Nevada, the Loomis District Union High School reluctantly agreed to open its doors for the summer to a hundred boys from Oakland High School as a camp run by the YMCA with Oakland's track coach, Alvin Eustis, and his wife in charge. Every morning farmers arrived in their trucks to fetch work crews, returning them at night, when the boys could enjoy movies, sports, and a nearby swimming hole. A third of the boys dropped out the first week, done in by the long hours and hard work, but the YMCA's ample waiting list replaced them. Most of the boys had never seen a farm before and did some weird things, but they soon learned the ropes. The YMCA set up a score of camps in California on a similar basis. The boys earned 50 cents an hour and paid $1.20 a day for their meals.

"You'd be surprised how many farmers didn't want these kids at first," said Bill Bethell, chairman of the county farm labor committee. "Now they wouldn't swap them for the more experienced migrants if they could. I know I wouldn't." Besides learning the art of picking fruit, they could be counted on to show up on the Monday after Saturday payday. But they were not alone. Using the same general plan as the YMCA, the American Women's Volunteer Service set up camps using women over seventeen, mostly from the Los Angeles and San Francisco areas. One such unit, seventy women strong, set up cots in a high school gym at Vacaville to pick the fast-ripening apricot crop. Normally the townspeople handled the harvest, but most of them had gone off to jobs in shipyards. "The women were tops," marveled one grower. "I've never seen better pickers or cutters."

North Dakota took a different tack. When the governor broadcast a desperate appeal for harvest hands, a thousand University of North Dakota students gathered at a mass meeting where the dean told them, "Field work is not beneath any of us, and any one of you who thinks so is a slacker in every sense of the word." The university shut down for two weeks and sent the students into the fields, as did the state teachers college. The football teams canceled their games and piled into the trucks along with high schoolers to thresh wheat, pick potatoes, top beets, and get a different form of education. The president of the teachers college called it "the finest community spirit I have ever seen displayed by any student body anywhere." Once the crops were in, everyone went back to school.[21]

In Oregon's Willamette Valley the business and professional men of Salem closed the town and joined their employees, housewives, and children in the fields to save the bean and hops crops. To prepare in advance for the next season's crop, state and local officials created an organization of twenty-four permanent and thirty seasonal offices to survey and recruit women and school children for harvest work. The growers agreed to stabilize wages for each crop so that workers would not lose valuable time shopping around for higher pay. In Washington State high school boys from eastern towns saved the asparagus crop and thinned the sugar beets. A few weeks later hundreds of business and professional men put their offices on a half-day basis and devoted the other half to harvesting the fresh pea crop.

The "dude harvests" proved a learning experience for both sides. "A lot of farmers have been surprised to see how city people can work," observed one USES official, "and a lot of city people have discovered how hard it is to earn a dollar down on the farm."

FOR ALL THE emphasis given to industrial expansion, victory depended greatly on rural America. More food was needed than ever before to feed not only the population but also a rapidly growing military and Allies who were in some cases on the brink of starvation. Russia and China desperately needed food, but so did Great Britain. Producing more food became an urgent goal, but agriculture could not be harnessed to the war effort as easily or efficiently as industry. By 1940 farmers had endured twenty years of hard times that drove many from the land and left many more barely surviving. They suffered from the long-standing problems of excess capacity, surpluses, and too many marginal producers that created a rural version of unemployment.[22]

But farming had also undergone a transformation that enabled fewer farmers to produce much more food. Mechanization continued to exert a profound effect. The number of tractors on farms almost doubled between 1929 and 1940, while horses and mules declined by 25 percent. Their absence released more than 22 million acres of crop and pasture land for production. More extensive use of fertilizer and lime increased output, as did the use of hybrid seed to withstand drought, disease, and parasites. But the 1930s had been brutal on farmers and their land. The prolonged drought of that decade on the Great Plains, which gave rise to the Dust Bowl and devastated cropland and range alike, was only the most spectacular example of soil erosion. A government report in 1940 estimated that 50 million acres of once-productive cropland had been ruined and a like amount almost ruined, with half the topsoil gone from another million acres. Soil conservation gained momentum under the New Deal but could not offset losses on so grand a scale.[23]

Like their industrial counterparts, farmers entered the war years in a depressed state. The census of 1940 counted over 6 million farms, 99 percent of which reported incomes below $10,000. More than 1.8 million farmers rented the farms they worked; another 540,000 were southern sharecroppers. Only 30 percent of their houses had indoor plumbing, and a mere 25 percent enjoyed electricity. The number of farms dropped steadily during the 1930s, while their average size grew larger. Half of them had become commercialized and produced 90 percent of the crops that went to market. Many farmers had of necessity embraced conservation practices, but some 3.6 million families still worked erodible land. As a group they had somehow survived hard times, had learned new techniques, and saw hope in improving their lot if they could find a way to afford the machines that eased their work and increased their yields.[24]

The war brought farmers unexpected opportunities that amounted almost to a new golden age. Instead of coping with surpluses of staple crops they were asked to produce even more, forcing them to shake the fear they shared with industrialists of finding themselves saddled with excess capacity when the war ended. By the fall of 1942 shortages already existed of meat, fats and oils, dairy products, sugar, and canned foods. To meet the soaring demand from civilians, the military, and the Allies, they had to adjust their habits and practices to a new reality. Most of them were accustomed to growing certain crops and had learned the best ways of doing so while minimizing their risks. They were reluctant to change to some other crop more urgently needed by the war effort, and trying to persuade millions of small producers to change their ways was worse than trying to herd cats.[25]

Increased yields depended first, as always, on the weather, but also on overcoming problems familiar to industrialists as well. Farmers needed more machines, especially tractors, and phosphate fertilizers, both of which required priorities for materials and production. They needed an efficient distribution system and a market that did not squeeze their profit margins. Above all, they needed more labor and a clear organizing voice in Washington to oversee the whole process of food production and distribution. Despite the promise of better times, more farmers were going out of business. Some were being drafted; others left for factory jobs, and still others simply couldn't afford to keep going. Between January 1940 and July 1941 some 1.8 million workers left the farm for greener pastures in war plants. A careful survey in the fall of 1942 revealed that 3,600 farms in Kansas would go entirely out of production and another 10,200 partially so during the next year.[26]

For 1942 WPB had allotted enough materials to manufacture 83 percent of the farm implements produced in 1940; the projection for 1943 sliced that amount to 33 percent. The shortage of both labor and equipment did not bode well for plans to increase yields. Dealing with these problems demanded stronger, more centralized leadership in Washington, but so far Roosevelt had resisted all suggestions for creating a food czar. Most of the burden fell on the Department of Agriculture, which Claude Wickard had reorganized in December 1941 to handle his increased load. The creation of WPB a month later, however, scattered responsibility for management of the food supply across several war agencies, thereby limiting Wickard's power. No one had clear-cut authority to oversee the whole process or plan for future emergencies. The onset of shortages made this need more evident, but a solution was not easy to formulate.[27]

The dispute over the handling of fats and oils illustrated the difficulties involved. Early in the year Harry Hopkins recommended that food management be centralized in the hands of Agriculture. His interest lay in finding more effective ways of dealing with Lend-Lease purchases. A few weeks later Nelson suggested that Agriculture assume the job of overseeing a fats and oils program to control their production and distribution. Wickard declined to do so unless he also had control of foreign purchases of fats and oils. Too many other elements were involved. A single agency could not oversee food management because some of its work would impact military issues as well. Fats and oils were vital not only for cooking but for soap and other military and industrial uses. Numerous farm products—grain used to make alcohol, for example—played roles that went beyond the reach of Agriculture. Months of debate passed without action on the fats and oils problem.[28]

In June Nelson tried another tack. He created a Food Requirements Committee headed by Wickard but reporting to himself. It proved ineffective as the shortages mounted. During the summer Agriculture and OPA fell into protracted squabbles over food prices, which neither Wickard nor Henderson had authority to resolve. Roosevelt created OES in part to give its head authority to settle differences between OPA and Agriculture, but Nelson sought something more. He urged the creation within WPB of a food director with powers comparable to those of the rubber director. "Without such central direction," he wrote, "there is sure to be lost motion and disastrous delay in solving this vital problem." Wickard opposed this idea and urged instead that the Food Requirements Committee be transferred from WPB to Agriculture and given more authority.[29]

Sentiment grew within and without Congress for appointment of a food czar to take charge of the food program as had been done with rubber. While influential voices lined up on one side or the other of the debate, Roosevelt came to his own conclusion. A food czar would solve some problems but create others. Conflicts would arise with the manpower, transportation, and other agencies. He might deem a carload of food crucial only to interfere with the use of the car for steel considered equally or even more crucial. Such conflicts, and they would be many, would have to be mediated, wasting even more time. "I agree that food as a general problem should be coordinated," Roosevelt wrote Jimmy Byrnes on October 22, ". . . and the people most concerned with food are you, Henderson, and Wickard. The War Production Board has plenty to do without taking on the responsibility of running all the problems of food."[30]

Having eliminated WPB in his thinking, the president chose Agriculture. On December 5 he issued an executive order centralizing war food policies in that department. The Food Requirements Committee was abolished and replaced by a Food Advisory Committee reporting to Wickard. The order was an important first step in rationalizing the food problem along lines similar to what had been done with industrial production. Wickard was authorized to perform four major tasks: determine the total national and foreign food requirements; develop and execute a production program to meet those requirements; establish allocation and priority controls to ensure proper distribution of available food supplies; and procure food for the military and other government agencies. It was a tall order, one that would require yet another reshuffling of Agriculture.[31]

BRYANT FRIEND SHARED a 20-by-20-foot shack in Richwood, West Virginia, with his wife, Hazel, three-year-old son, and father. To eke out a slim living he farmed a small corn patch and did odd jobs at mines and a nearby lumber mill. The family barely scraped along and had little hope of anything better until an agent from USES happened by one day looking for workers to harvest crops in upstate New York. Bryant signed up, then came home to inform the family that they were moving 529 miles to Albion, New York. The FSA arranged their transportation and took care of their meals and medical needs during the trip. They boarded a train and slept as best they could in a day coach along with 300 other workers making the same journey. Once in Albion, Bryant and his father contracted to work for a local farmer at a minimum of 30 cents an hour and went right into the fields that same day. After the day's work they moved into a house much larger than their shack in West Virginia. It had stood vacant for years, but they got it rent free and planned eagerly to renovate it into a real home.[32]

For Bryant and others like him, the farm work offered an opportunity for a fresh start in what had been a dead-end life. In return, their employers got hands for a harvest that might otherwise have rotted in the fields. Elsewhere the locals had no such luck and had to make do on their own. The red-clay fields of Walthall County, Mississippi, had already sent 750 of its sons into the armed forces and dozens more to war plants in New Orleans, Mobile, and Baton Rouge. Undaunted by their losses, the farmers who stayed behind, black and white, redoubled their efforts and turned in what one impressed observer called "barn-bursting harvests," including 23 percent more cotton, 146 percent more hay, 110 percent more eggs, and a whopping 619 percent more truck crops. To celebrate, they decided to hold a "Food for Freedom Thanksgiving" early in October in Tylertown (population 1,100), the county seat and only post office.[33]

They streamed into town in old Model T Fords, school buses, mule-drawn wagons, and on foot, bearing 5,000 fried chickens, 350 turkeys, and enough potato salad, salads, breads, pies, and cakes to overflow pine tables a thousand feet long and feed 5,000 people. The town's few streets bristled with bunting, flags, and welcome signs beneath a hot October sun. Dressed in their Sunday best, blacks and whites alike formed a procession of Future Farmers, 4-H Clubbers, school classes, cotton trucks, wagons crammed with farm families, no less than seven bands, and an infantry company packed with local boys for the march from the school grounds to the ballpark. A special guest, Claude Wickard himself, arrived to speak to the crowd and share in the fun. "This is a great idea," he beamed as the wife of a local merchant handed him a paper plate stuffed with fried chicken, chicken pie, potato salad, warm spice cake, and two kinds of pie.

"At this season," Wickard told them in his speech, "we have much to be thankful for—and much need for future courage and endurance. All of the nation's farmers . . . join you in the resolve never to let up in the battle of production. The road ahead for farmers is long and difficult, but it is the only road that leads to victory."

DESPITE ALL EFFORTS, the steel shortage would not go away. In August shipbuilding fell behind after the WPB slashed the allotment of plate steel to shipyards by 50,000 tons. The steel industry's salvage committee warned that lack of scrap would curtail output of steel within months. Stimson got a dose of it in October when he talked with Ickes about the steel needed for the pipeline from Texas to the East Coast, which Ickes regarded as crucial to winning the war. Three days later, at a White House meeting, he listened to the navy and Maritime Commission argue for pinching enough steel from other claimants to build seventy more escort vessels and some merchant ships. Only about 1.5 percent of the annual output was needed, the argument went, but Nelson proceeded to outline how much of that output was already under "must" allotments, earmarked for Britain and Russia, the navy for other ships, the army for tanks and planes, and Lend-Lease, leaving a pittance for civilian needs. It could only be done, Nelson concluded, by cutting some of the other "musts."[34]

More steel than ever was being produced, yet it still was not enough. Some thought the problem lay not in production but with the military, which hoarded steel as it did so many other crucial materials. "The Army is the worst offender of all the agencies," charged *Fortune*, "month after month allowing orders to pile up to double and triple the amount of steel allocated to it, and stubbornly refusing to scale them down, the first requisite of any sensible plan for scheduling production." The army continued to insist that it should have even more than it got, and no one knew exactly how much it actually had. Companies too stockpiled steel far in advance of use, and no overall inventory existed to reveal their total stocks on hand. PRP hoped to rectify this imbalance but received too little cooperation. *Fortune* also had harsh words for WPB, charging that its planning "has been almost as extravagantly unconnected with the raw-material realities as the military."[35]

The pattern was a familiar one. Zealous procurement officers prodded manufacturers to exceed their schedules and load up on materials as fast as possible to fill even long-term contracts, and to raise their priority ratings to force more steel out of the steadily tightening supply. As a result, big inventories of steel plate piled up in some shipyards while others went begging. Aircraft manufacturers waited incessantly for crucial parts to finish planes while the steel they needed languished in other yards. Unfinished planes, tanks, vehicles, and ships clogged production lines, delaying production. Steel plate grew especially hard to get. When the year opened, producers already had a 4.5-million-ton backlog of unfilled orders, more than 75 percent of the entire capacity in 1941. Plate was put under complete allocation on December 1, 1941, and new facilities were rushed through conversion or construction. By May production increased to a million tons compared to 650,000 the previous December, but the demand kept growing.[36]

Roosevelt had wanted steel capacity expanded by 15 million tons and new facilities operating by early 1942. Tough bargaining by steel executives pushed the figure down to 13 million tons, no new facilities opened until later in the year, and the entire program was not completed until mid-1944. Meanwhile, manufacturers screamed for steel as well as other critically short materials such as copper. The United States produced about half the world's entire output of steel and had twelve times the capacity of Japan and far more than all of Nazi-controlled Europe, yet it still did not have enough. By midsummer the steel crisis was full-blown. In May WPB banned the use of steel on 400 civilian products. Already it had tried several devices to alleviate the shortage of scrap, a crucial ingredient in the manufacture of steel.[37]

Steel was normally made by melting together equal parts of pig iron and scrap. It could be produced by using 100 percent of either one, but using a ton of scrap in place of the same amount of pig iron saved the two tons of ore, 1.2 tons of coal, and half a ton of limestone needed to make the ton of pig iron. In 1941 the industry used 42 million tons of scrap to produce 83 million tons of steel, which meant it required a steady flow to keep production humming. Some scrap came from the mill itself—trimmings from ingots, semifinished billets, and other sources. Most came from factories that made steel products, automobile graveyards, and junk dealers. Every pound of scrap had to be processed. Light amounts had to be baled into compact two-foot cubes to resist heat oxidation in the furnaces; larger pieces had to be cut up and all of it sorted according to alloy content.[38]

After Pearl Harbor, scrap dealers were hit hard as thousands of junk dealers went into war plants for better pay. An enormous amount of American semifinished steel went to the Allies, giving them and not us the scrap from trimmings. WPB did not recognize the scrap yards that remained open as a war industry and handed them the lowest priority rating, which forced some yards to close because they couldn't get even nails for upkeep and repairs. To ease the shortage, WPB launched a nationwide campaign to gather scrap from all sources. International Harvester mobilized its chain of 10,000 dealers and large publicity department to beat the bushes in rural America, telling farmers, "There's a Bomb in Your Barnyard." Nelson published a plea to industrial executives that "all unusable material, equipment and stocks should be scrapped at once and put back into war production."[39]

Individuals got a similar message. Surveys indicated that about 700 pounds of scrap could be got from an average farm and 100 pounds from an average home. Theaters offered free admission for scrap, churches and civic clubs organized drives, and the Brooklyn Dodgers offered kids a free ticket for every ten pounds of scrap. The offer produced 60 tons of scrap and got 60,000 diligent kids a free visit to Ebbets Field. The old cruiser *Olympia*, once the flagship of Admiral Dewey at Manila, had her 5,865 tons reduced to scrap. The Union Pacific Railroad pulled up the historic rails of its original transcontinental line across Utah for scrap. Every town had its odd scrap story, like the widow of a Spanish-American War veteran who donated the iron bench she used to sit by her husband's grave. The steel industry conducted its own drive, reversing the role of its 2,000 salesmen by sending them on the road to buy scrap from their former peacetime customers. Yet *Fortune* called WPB's scrap drives "flaccid and disappointing."[40]

Some experts predicted that the scrap shortage and the slowed production it caused could cut steel production for 1943 by 20 percent, more than wiping out any gains from expanded facilities. In October WPB approved funds for Republic Steel to build a plant for producing sponge iron, a long-controversial substitute for pig iron, in hopes of proving its value one way or the other. The shortage had already produced casualties, most notably the abrupt cancellation in July of Andrew Jackson Higgins's record contract for 200 Liberty ships for lack of steel to complete the huge new yard he was building for the work. The volatile Higgins protested loudly, insisting that the problem had more to do with politics than with the steel shortage. Outraged that he had been persuaded to take the contract only to be stopped in midstride, he rushed to Washington and demanded an investigation. One reporter called the episode "the most colossal, $20 million blunder of this whole cockeyed war."[41]

Over $9 million had already been spent on the yard's construction, and people had moved to New Orleans expecting to get jobs there. The AFL tried to use its influence, and black leaders protested the loss of opportunity, but to no avail. Congress investigated, but the decision held. The yard, said Jerry Land of the Maritime Commission, was the last to start construction and the easiest to cancel. Halting work would allow tons of steel to be redeployed at other yards for building ships. Vickery assumed full blame for the uproar. "I proposed the contract, I proposed it be canceled, and I am responsible for the action," he said publicly in New Orleans. It happened because other yards had shortened their time for completing Liberty ships so well that they burned through the allotment of steel twice as fast, leaving none for a large new project like Higgins's. As the shortages and subsequent delays continued to mount, it became clear that expansion of facilities alone would not solve the problem.[42]

A more pressing issue was finding a better system of distribution and allocation to make the best use of the existing supply. PRP had not done the job—had not even been allowed to try, in the opinion of some supporters. Neither the army nor the navy cooperated, relegating PRP to "a handsome set of statistics with no place to go." By September even the advocates of PRP conceded that it had no chance of succeeding. David Novick of WPB, a strong supporter of PRP, later outlined the dilemma. "The selection of operating methods—*the problem of how to do it*—is the fundamental administrative assignment," he wrote. "Neither the wartime economy as a whole, nor any part of it, can be governed by a czar who from his Washington desk decides all things . . . No man, no organization, and no system could possibly handle such an assignment. And yet a way must be found to accomplish the necessary objectives of wartime control." The only hope for success was to determine centrally the policies required and then figure out the best methods for turning existing industrial procedures toward war ends.[43]

The role, in short, was that of a go-between, and it had to be handled delicately. "If they disturb industrial practices too much," Novick warned, "there is grave danger that manufacturing activity may be impeded so that it will not reach maximum production goals. If they do not interfere enough, there is equally grave danger that materials, labor, and industrial plant and machinery urgently required for war production will be diverted to other uses." Put another way, finding the best means of balancing the flow of materials in a wartime economy required finding the best method of balancing controls over the process. The old priority systems had not gone far enough, but PRP had gone too far. Some other approach was needed that undercut the resistance to controls of both industry and the military.[44]

So widespread was opposition to PRP that Nelson saw no choice but to seek an alternative method. In September he took back priority authority from ANMB and appointed Ferdinand Eberstadt as vice chairman of program determination for WPB. Eberstadt, a leading advocate of vertical allocation, set about designing a new system for controlling materials. Half a dozen other proposals for vertical systems also competed for attention. Nathan's Planning Committee had turned its attention to the allocation problem in August and a month later officially endorsed a vertical approach. However, it was the talented and hard-driving Eberstadt who seized the leadership role that WPB had so often lacked. The vigorous debate over philosophies, policies, and techniques of control, which had been ongoing since May, culminated in October with the decision to adopt a plan that embodied elements from several other proposals. Announced publicly on November 2, it was called the Controlled Materials Plan (CMP) and proved ultimately to be a turning point in the constant battle over production and priorities.[45]

In designing and appraising a control mechanism, six points emerged as fundamental. How rapidly could it be put into operation? How useful was it as a device for gathering essential statistical data? How feasible was it to administer? How effective was it as a device for carrying out broad policy decisions? How flexible was it in meeting the demands of constantly shifting military requirements? How much paperwork was involved in making it function?[46]

The last point was far more important than many people realized. The sheer volume of paperwork had overwhelmed more than one approach to controls and did much to sink PRP. During a manpower squeeze clerks were in as short supply as other workers. "In dealing with an operation as complex and large as the American industrial system," observed Novick, ". . . it is not difficult to develop a control system which will break down of its own weight." The early priorities system had done just that. Novick concluded that "in retrospect, it is difficult to name a factor more important than paper work in delaying the appearance of a real vertical system of control until 1943." The trick lay in finding a way to minimize the flow of paper and reports while still providing WPB with the essential tools to push the production effort.[47]

For CMP to be effective, it had to be introduced slowly and with careful preparations. PRP had foundered in large part because it had first been delayed and then rushed into service before necessary preparations had been made. It suffered from lack of staff, inadequate training for those it had, and incomplete processing procedures among other things. Nelson determined not to make the same mistake again. The thrashing out of the plan remained internal until the November 2 bulletin to avoid criticism from special interests and politicizing the process. The bulletin outlined how CMP would work and included a chronology of the steps to be taken to implement it. The process would take place gradually over an eight-month period, go into partial effect in March, and finally take full effect on July 1, 1943. During those months staff would be carefully trained, criticism absorbed, adjustments made, and procedures refined to accommodate any problems not foreseen by the plan.[48]

WPB created a new Controlled Materials Plan Division to train and educate both government and industry personnel. Other boards were set up and three manuals issued to cover every aspect of the program. The original plan would be subjected to painstaking review and to test runs and modified on the basis of this experience. CMP promised to be a major step forward, but it would not take effect for months. Meanwhile, the problem of production scheduling and allocation still had to be met. Since summer Stacy May had warned that production rates were slipping. Through July munitions output had grown at an average monthly rate of 13 percent, but since August the rate had dropped to 4 percent—too low to meet supposedly even feasible goals. May, Nathan, the Truman Committee, and others all pointed to flawed scheduling by the military as the main problem.[49]

The issues were many and familiar. Some shipyards hoarded an eighteen-month supply of steel while the building of escort vessels to defend against submarines was delayed for lack of steel. Critical machine tools went to the wrong firms, depriving those who needed them urgently. Some components were underordered, others overordered, causing bottlenecks. No agency tried to coordinate and reconcile the competing demands for materials, parts, tools, and other components. May and Nathan urged WPB to take on production scheduling but warned that in doing so it needed to get past annual projections and deal in quarters, months, or even weeks to work through bottlenecks. Nelson agreed and brought in Charles Wilson to do the job. He was the production guru with a reputation rivaling that of Knudsen, and great things were expected of him. Meanwhile, the tension between WPB and the military, born of simultaneous clashes over feasibility, priorities and allocations, and production scheduling, continued to intensify as the year wound down.

No ONE WAS surprised to see Tom Girdler sitting behind a big desk holding conferences, issuing orders, and scanning papers, his eyes darting restlessly behind owlish horned-rim glasses. The shock came from the desk being located not at Republic Steel but at Consolidated Aircraft in San Diego. Executives who had been in the aircraft business all their careers wondered what the hell he was doing in their plant. He told them that he had come to take charge of the company and improve its output. One vice president rudely called him an "interloper" who had bought his way into a business of craftsmen and pioneers and said that the best thing he could do was go back to where he had come from. Girdler eyed the man coldly but said nothing. "You straighten this out," he told another executive and stalked out of the room into an office marked VISITING EXECUTIVES. He was a visitor, but he had come to stay awhile.[50]

Girdler denied that he had made a career change at sixty-five. "Republic is the best-hitched-up outfit in the country—it can get along without me," he said. "There was a job to be done here, and because I'm crazy about flying, I came." He still kept a close eye on the steel company, but his main energy went to shoring up Consolidated's production, especially of its B-24 Liberator, the nation's major long-range bomber along with the B-17. When Girdler arrived on the job in January, output had dropped by 80 percent since December, Willow Run was still under construction, other new facilities were months away from opening, and only Boeing's bomber program was ramping up production. Girdler arrived just as Consolidated was about to make a model change on the bomber, which meant still more delays. Girdler studied the plans for the changeover and said, "They stink." Since the changeover meant delays anyway, he decided to risk even more lost time by revising the production setup as well—this only a month after Pearl Harbor.

Consolidated was not a bad company; it had simply been overwhelmed by the rush of defense orders. Between 1939 and the summer of 1941 its workforce soared from 1,500 to more than 30,000 and its floor space increased several times. Reuben Fleet, its founder, had nursed the company through hard times, supplying the Air Corps with trainers and fighters before heeding the president's call for heavy bombers. But he tangled constantly with labor and insisted on running a one-man show even as the demand for more planes swamped the factory. He had married a young wife and was willing to sell out. From the army's point of view the difficulty was not in finding a buyer with money but rather in finding one with production experience who could improve the operation. Several firms looked into it but walked away. Then a utilities operator and financial man named Victor Emanuel quietly entered negotiations.

In 1937 Emanuel had headed a syndicate that bought up the scattered holdings of E. L. Cord and reorganized them into the Aviation Corporation. Its holdings included Vultee, which had impressed army procurement officers with a line of good planes and the first moving assembly line in the industry. One member of the Aviation syndicate was Tom Girdler, whose management of Republic Steel the army also admired. In December 1941 Vultee (76 percent owned by Aviation) bought Consolidated from Fleet. "When we finally took Consolidated over," said Emanuel, "I was deeply worried, since we knew nothing about big airplanes and the situation was a danger to the country." He asked Girdler to "loan himself to Consolidated" and got Republic's board to approve the move. Suddenly Girdler found himself chairman and CEO of both Consolidated and Vultee while still chairman of Republic. Through Aviation his influence also extended to a handful of other companies making important war products.

After a lifetime spent amid smoking steel mills, the former Indiana farmboy landed deep inside the war effort. "Now I'm beginning to see what war means," he told a friend. To his new prominence he brought an unsavory reputation as a tough guy, especially with labor because of his dogged resistance to unions. John L. Lewis once referred to him as a "monomaniac with murderous tendencies," while Harold Ickes called him the "hero of the Memorial Day massacre in Chicago." Girdler also despised Roosevelt and the New Deal, but in this new role his demeanor softened. Both Consolidated and Vultee had union contracts, and Republic was in the midst of negotiations. At the aircraft plants he surprised the unions with his cooperative style, leading one union man to admit, "I hate like hell to put any feathers in old Girdler's hat, but so far the changes are beneficial to labor. We know who to go to when we want one thing or another now, and that's a very good business procedure."

Girdler also seemed to have laid aside his feud with the New Deal, at least during the war, but his blunt style remained intact. The directives to his officers were short and to the point: "Get the airplanes out. Be absolutely sure they are mechanically all they ought to be. Fight like hell for the proper guns and armor. Keep costs down and forget about profits. We'll work that out at the proper time with the government." He insisted that he was an executive rather than a production man, "and there is a hell of a difference." The trick, he once told Emanuel, "is in putting a man in a job, giving him complete responsibility, not bothering him, and not letting anyone else bother him."

For years aviation had been enshrouded in romantic legends, one of them being that to manufacture planes you had to be a pilot. "This is the craziest goddamned business in the world," said Monte Williams, an executive brought in by Girdler who had been out of the aviation industry for two decades. ". . . Making airplanes is a manufacturing process. Whether the product flies at the end, or is driven away like an automobile, or carted off like a refrigerator, is of no consequence on the factory floor, assuming the manufacturing process is sound." Another executive, listening to an engineer speak reverently of how a propeller blade had to be perfect because a pilot's life depended on it, said bluntly, "To me this is just another pressed-steel job. If the halo you've thrown around this piece of steel has got you all befuddled, we'd better give it a different name. Then we'll get on with the manufacturing."

Consolidated did exactly that. By March Girdler could proudly show visiting newsmen the company's new 3,000-foot assembly line, modeled after Vultee's, along which the big B-24s moved slowly from one station to the next until a finished plane emerged. A new subassembly plant furnished wings and fuselages, and a new method of installing instruments created sections with instruments already in place. Consolidated boosted its production schedule to three eight-hour shifts a day, six days a week. It could not work seven days because subcontractors could not supply parts fast enough. Along with the B-24 the company also built two flying boats for the navy, the Catalina and the Coronado. Newsmen also could not help but notice the 2,500 women, all dressed in blue slacks, who worked alongside men on the same jobs. Tom Girdler was, as he admitted, deep into the war, and with a labor force unlike any he saw in a steel mill.[51]

ACROSS THE CONTINENT, in a field twenty-one miles west of Ford's huge River Rouge plant, Charles Sorensen struggled to complete his vision of the world's largest bomber plant. Willow Run sprawled a mile long and a quarter-mile across, enclosing more floor space than the prewar plants of Consolidated, Boeing, and Douglas combined. On its vast floor stood 1,600 machine tools and 7,000 fixtures and jigs, some of them sixty feet long. Overhead ran a conveyer system that would carry nose and tail assemblies for the stream of B-24 bombers that would flow out of the plant's doors once it became operational. The talk was of possibly a thousand planes a month, but production would not likely start until late 1942 or early 1943. "We did not know," admitted Sorensen, "until this war job came along what it meant to be really busy again, really making things again." And now he was itching to get started making what many believed was the most important weapon in the new kind of war being fought.[52]

At sixty Sorensen, who had known Henry Ford since 1903, was already a legend in automobile production. A former patternmaker in his father's stove shop, he still insisted on taking the design of anything he made and mocking it up into three dimensions so that it could be studied and prodded to find its flaws. He had made models down to the last detail of a tank, an aircraft engine, and even both the River Rouge and Willow Run plants. His production planning philosophy came from Henry Ford and remained inviolable. "Unless you can see a thing," he said, "you cannot simplify it. And unless you can simplify it, it's a good sign you cannot make it." But Sorensen had also acquired a mastery of metals through experiments on his own. Above all, he demanded a full effort at production. Once at the Rouge he wanted to boost engine output to 2,000 units a day. The foundryman said flatly it could not be done. "Then," said Sorensen, "I'm afraid you are fired." His successor struggled in vain to reach the goal, but at least he tried, which was all Sorensen asked. Eventually production reached 9,000 units a day.[53]

When Ford agreed in 1940 to make airplane engines for Pratt & Whitney, Sorensen learned the vast difference between them and automobile engines. An eighteen-cylinder Pratt & Whitney 2,000-horsepower engine packed the same power as one and a quarter Ford V-8 engines, yet weighed only one pound per horsepower compared to the V-8's seven pounds. The machining required much higher tolerances, and expensive new tools were required along with a new plant to house them. Sorensen got it done so vigorously that the first engines rolled off the line in August 1941, eleven months after ground was broken for the new factory. He managed it by using the aircraft company as a classroom to learn new skills, and he did the same when Knudsen asked the auto manufacturers to make bomber parts. Willow Run was the outcome of that education; some thought it might well turn out to be a white elephant that swallowed some 7 million man-hours of work in tooling alone.

The B-24 posed an even more formidable challenge. Sorensen had one flown to Dearborn, where his engineers tore it down piece by piece and then put it back together again. Where an automobile averaged 15,000 parts, the B-24 had 30,000 different kinds of parts and more than 100,000 in all. Each kind required its own blueprint, which meant miles of paper, and precise machining on tools foreign to automobile makers. Henry Ford gave tacit consent to the project but told Sorensen, "Those planes will never be used for fighting. Before you can build them, the war will be over."[54]

Sorensen never doubted that the Run would produce as he said it would, but the question still haunted him: When would it finally go into full activity?

*   *   *

A GROUP OF seven California companies plus Boeing in Seattle made the bulk of American warplanes, and they faced a backlog of $9 billion in orders. They had always been fiercely competitive and individualistic, but the war had put them in an unprecedented situation. More planes than they had ever built were demanded faster than they had ever built them. Everyone was fighting labor shortages, pinching workers from one another, crying for materials, and fearful of a recommendation by the Truman Committee that the president appoint an aircraft czar to organize and drive the production effort. In April Donald Douglas called his peers together in a series of meetings to ponder the problem. "We looked at each other and realized that any one of us might be picked for the czar," he said later. "Nobody wanted to be czar, and we didn't want anybody else as czar. So we decided to offer the President an eight-president soviet to regiment our part of the industry."[55]

The result was the Aircraft War Production Council (AWPC), which Douglas waggishly called "an outstanding example of capitalistic collectivism, which spells democracy." Members referred to it simply as "the Western pot." The premise was disarmingly simple: The companies would share everything from technology to techniques to parts to keep production moving. J. H. "Dutch" Kindelberger of North American became AWPC's first president and set the tone by calling together his department heads and telling them, "From now on, we're going to give our competitors anything we've got, with no hedging or holding back. They're going to do the same for us." By the following week subcommittees were meeting to deal with special problems. Some officers went away dazed at the transformation. "I've worked on airplanes for thirteen years," said a Lockheed official, "but I'd never seen the inside of another factory until the subcommittee I'm on visited North American."[56]

He made the tour with a man from Consolidated. "Boy," he said, "the minute we got into the tubing department, Kelly, of Consolidated, and I began getting ideas. They were cutting tubing with a speed we couldn't touch. Then I noticed all their jigs were painted light color, so that plane parts were easy to see. Ours were dull gray. They had girls doing work that our gals never attempted." For his part Kindelberger reported that Vultee had given him engineering data that had cost it $250,000 and several months' time. Vultee also loaned thirty of its best engineers to Vega to speed up its production line of B-17s. If one company was short of parts or material, it called around to see who had extras. Consolidated sent sixteen engine-mount forgings to North American, Lockheed 1,000 stop nuts to Vultee, North American 150 sheets of aluminum to Vultee, Consolidated a half ton of flathead Monel rivets to Ryan, Vultee 1,000 cotter pins to Douglas. "It's hard to think of cotter pins keeping planes on the ground," said a Douglas official, "but that is what lack of them did one day."

The Navy dive-bombers built by Douglas at El Segundo were stalled for lack of binding-braid wire used to eliminate static electricity. North American located some in its stockroom, and the dive-bombers went off to play a key role in the Battles of the Coral Sea and Midway. North American had a delivery of P-51 Mustangs and Apache fighters ready for the British but needed engine-cooling fluid for their motors. Lockheed happened to have a good supply and sent it over. "Even if we had only a little, we'd have divvied up," said a Lockheed official. A week earlier they had been stymied by a lack of two-inch chrome molybdenum for their P-38s. North American had only a small supply but divided it with Lockheed to get the planes moving. By one count such borrowings totaled 1,800 in a single month. Everything got traded at cost with AWPC serving as clearinghouse, but no one waited on paperwork to move the parts from one company to another.

Engineering data got swapped as easily as parts, and so did machine time. When a hydro press that shaped fuselage and tail parts broke down, Northrop avoided a two-week delay by moving the work to North American. Once the Northrop machines were back online, Douglas sent some of its work there. A few weeks later Consolidated's hydro press quit working, and Douglas offered one of its machines that stood idle at night. Consolidated piled its dies and materials into trucks and did its work at Douglas overnight. One pool subcommittee discovered that some plants had machines capable of doing their work faster than assembly lines could absorb the output. It made an inventory of machines with excess capacity that other companies could use. Studies of new war-induced problems were also pooled. Boeing agreed to research more use of plastics in planes because it already had a head start in the work, thereby freeing the research staffs of other companies to focus on other problems.

Lockheed had studied the problem of getting workers to and from the plant. Its expert juggled jobs to enable more workers to carpool, taking more than 5,000 cars out of use. He also promoted bicycle brigades, bought 4,000 bikes to lease to workers, and arranged for special employee bus routes. All these arrangements he turned over to the other companies for their use. For all the benefits, the production men agreed that "the best part of the deal is the know-how you pick up visiting other factories." Faster output was the most immediate and important result. Every borrowing eliminated a bottleneck. As Kindelberger observed, "A lot of these planes were delivered ahead of schedule because we threw everything we had into the pot."

The basic rule was that no one asked for anything unless he absolutely needed it, and the rule was honored. Once the war ended, the pot would dissolve and the companies would go back to being rivals. "It's going to make some tough competition," predicted Douglas, "because nobody has an advantage over anybody else any more."

1943: THE YEAR OF PRODUCTION

CHAPTER 21

CITY OF PAPER

Washington's a funny town. It's got scores of hotels, and you can't get a room. It's got 5,000 restaurants, and you can't get a meal. It's got 50,000 politicians, and nobody will do anything for you. I'm going home.

—SMALL BUSINESSMAN[1]

The administration of wartime industrial mobilization is not a production job . . . Neither is [it] . . . a sales job . . . The critical functions in the administration of the war economy might be freely described as those concerned with "paper-pushing." The term . . . has disparaging overtones which cheapen it. In the giant organization "paper pushing" is the motor impulse of administrative action . . . the technique by means of which policy decisions are translated into action.

—DAVID NOVICK[2]

I wish the job could be accomplished without these head-on collisions . . . It is my experience with businessmen in government that they always get into these battles, not alone with one another but with the heads of other government agencies. They do not know how to administer the things they must administer as well as the politicians know how.

—FRANKLIN D. ROOSEVELT[3]

No battle of the Second World War was fought more furiously than the battle for controls.

—MARGARET COIT[4]

THE NATION'S CAPITAL WAS A CITY of strangers. John Dos Passos called it "essentially a town of lonely people." A reporter dubbed it "the city of lonely hearts." So many girls from small towns who knew nobody and nobody knew or cared about them. Boys away from their families. Wives with husbands overseas. Nearly everyone seemed to be a transient, come to do business of some kind for however long it took or in search of opportunities not available at home or simply a tourist admiring the sights while cursing the prices and the weather. Those residents closest to being a native elite were called "Cave Dwellers" because so few people ever actually saw them. They belonged to families who had been there forever and shunned anyone with roots going back less than half a century or so. The Cave Dwellers tended to mingle only with each other in their secluded mansions on Massachusetts Avenue and in the Kalorama neighborhood. They despised Roosevelt and the New Deal for being not only radical but boorish and ill-mannered.[5]

One self-confessed bureaucrat called it "a city without guts . . . A lot of real people live in Washington but they don't make a real community . . . Washington is politically castrated—nobody here can vote. The population is transient . . . Washington is a one-industry town . . . just the company town for Uncle Sam's bureaucracy." Its people lived under the spell of a "dull gray psychosis" that he considered an occupational hazard of government work. He bemoaned the absurdity of a city run by congressmen who knew nothing about it; whose ears were finely attuned to a voter's voice half a continent away but deaf to the needs of half a million inhabitants surrounding them. What other great world capital was hemmed in by horrible slums overseen by an agency called the Alley Dwelling Authority?[6]

"Since the days of Henry Adams . . . newcomers had found Washington hard to understand," wrote David Brinkley, himself a newcomer in 1943 when he started his career as a correspondent after two years in the army. ". . . It was a city conceived and built as a national government factory and nothing else—producing nothing but paper."[7]

At heart and by location, Washington was a southern town in manner, style, culture, cuisine, and weather. Most of its restaurants specialized in dishes fried in deep fat. At night locals sat on screened porches, if they were fortunate enough to have one, and read, chatted, or played bridge while fanning themselves. Since the Civil War the pace of life, interrupted only by World War I, had moved as slowly as the federal bureaucracy until the New Deal came to town. As newcomers liked to joke, the city combined the charm of the North with the efficiency of the South.[8]

Like the South, too, Washington had a large black population. Nearly a third of its people were black, most of them conveniently tucked away in ghastly alley slums that ringed the downtown area. The squalor in which they lived was stultifying and a constant health hazard. Plumbing scarcely existed; a single faucet often supplied water to several families, and open-topped barrels set over holes in the ground served as privies. The city health department counted 15,000 of these barrels, some of them used by thirty people. Outside their crumbling shacks black people had to deal with a city that was rigidly segregated. White residential neighborhoods had covenants that forbade homeowners from selling to blacks and often to Jews as well. As a final insult, the district was governed not by its people but by two congressional committees. On the Senate committee sat the most virulent racist in Congress, Theodore Bilbo of Mississippi. Congress had a dubious consistency in things both large and small; it managed Washington as poorly as it did the nation.[9]

Discomfort was a way of life in Washington. In summer many business and professional men headed to work dressed in white linen suits with Panama hats and black-and-white wingtip shoes. Their crisp look lasted perhaps an hour before the linen wilted in the heat and humidity. The slow, small-town atmosphere they preferred was already in retreat before Pearl Harbor. The quickened pace of mobilization brought thousands of newcomers into the city, seeking jobs, contracts, offices—everything from favors to a better life. The once-placid southern town began evolving into a big city with its noise, crowding, spiraling costs, and traffic jams. After Pearl Harbor many residents sensed what was coming. By nightfall on December 8 they had cleaned out local markets, stockpiling for shortages to come.[10]

The physical landscape changed as well. As the number of government agencies mushroomed, twenty-seven prefabricated buildings known as "tempos" were thrown up to join the still-present temporary structures erected during World War I. An army of 500 workmen would arrive at a vacant lot and hoist posts, crossbeams, and gray asbestos board like a movie set. The fastest completion took thirty-eight days. The tempos cost $835,000 each and were as hideous as their predecessors. Every vacant building in the city soon filled as well, yet square footage could barely keep pace with the flood of people pouring into the city. New federal workers arrived at the rate of 5,000 a month, some with families but mostly women, coming in response to recruiting advertisements in local papers across the country. War did not permit the luxury of civil service exams; anyone who could type and had a high school diploma could get a job paying $1,440 a year.[11]

Not all of them stayed. Like other wartime boom towns, Washington endured miserable living conditions as the crush of arrivees overwhelmed facilities. Newcomers worked mostly in drab, unappealing offices and paid anywhere from $24 to $35 a month for a room in a shabby boardinghouse where they competed with fellow roomers for access to a bathroom. Families despaired of finding enough space, let alone at a price they could afford. Buses were always jammed, their schedules irregular and uncoordinated, making the trip to and from work an ordeal. To provide more space, the bus companies removed seats and replaced them with "stand-sits" to accommodate more riders. Hotels began limiting guests to a three-day stay, and laundries were so overwhelmed that many began refusing new customers or anything besides uniforms.[12]

Salaries that looked so generous at first soon proved inadequate for the city's cost of living. The thousands of greenhorns arriving on trains and buses passed thousands more who had given up and were heading back home. One report estimated that within six months of Pearl Harbor, more than half the young women hired as stenographers and typists had quit and left town. During the first year of the war patriotism steeled them to work long hours and endure lousy living conditions, but gradually a sense of apathy and fatigue set in, a feeling of "living in a fog." The strain of wartime living exacted its own version of combat fatigue, especially in the city that was the nerve center of the war effort. When writer John Dos Passos hopped into a cab and said he was in a hurry, the driver snorted, "Hurry? Nobody ever used to be in a hurry in Washington."[13]

Nothing defined the city of paper more than its bureaucratic fog. On one memorable occasion the vice president of a New York City bank applied for a job in Washington at the Office of Economic Warfare. While he awaited a reply, the agency's head, Leo Crowley, happened to drop into the same bank and asked its president to recommend somebody for the same job. The president suggested the very same vice president who had applied. Crowley hired him on the spot, and the banker moved to Washington. Weeks later he received a letter forwarded to him from New York. It was from the agency, which rejected his original application on the grounds that he was not qualified for the job. That was painful enough, but on closer inspection the man discovered that he had signed the letter himself.[14]

WITHIN THE AGENCIES the strain was no less palpable. The frantic pressure to boost production, rationalize the flow of materials, and reconcile overlapping authorities kept everyone on edge. The clashes and backbiting continued and drew at least emotional blood. Inevitably the bureaucratic casualties mounted at all levels, sparing neither incompetents nor the most talented. OPA took more heat than most agencies because of the sensitive nature of its work and the gross unpopularity of price controls and rationing. "I collided regularly with commodity groups," recalled Galbraith, "the cattlemen, the dairymen and the wool growers, people that Ed O'Neal himself had once told me were too single-mindedly selfish to be tolerable companions in the farm movement." One meeting on cattle prices turned into a three-day shouting match joined freely by congressmen and senators from the range country.[15]

Galbraith admitted to being "unduly self-righteous" in his defense of price controls, but he could not conceal his disdain for "the lobbyists, trade association representatives, professional business spokesmen and hireling Establishment lawyers who sought to associate patriotism with the need for even more money than they were already making." The heavy Democratic losses in the November elections, especially in the Midwest, intensified the attack on OPA. Lower-level personnel began leaving the agency, prompting Henderson to quip, "It's now the mice who are leaving the ship." Then it was the captain's turn. On December 18, 1942, Henderson resigned from OPA, pleading ill health. More attacks were coming, he told his staff, and he could best help the agency by leaving it.[16]

"Henderson did not fall," concluded *Time*. "He was pushed: by the farm bloc, by Midwestern congressmen who loathe gasoline rationing, by Democrats who thought that his restrictions had been the biggest factor in November's election returns." Henderson had also deeply offended Congress by refusing to play its patronage game in making appointments, and the strengthened Republicans seemed poised for another assault on OPA's budget. "I predicted when I took this job that I would soon become the most unpopular man in this country," said Henderson, "and I seem to be making progress." Few believed that his eyesight difficulties and recurring back ailment were the real reasons for his departure. Fewer still appreciated the quality of the job he had done with so few tools in the fight against inflation. In his place Roosevelt appointed Prentiss Brown, a liberal senator from Michigan who had just lost his seat in the election. He was much more low-key and agreeable than Henderson, and far less dynamic in heading the agency. The attacks paused only a few days before resuming. Despite much speculation over his next post, Henderson did not take another government job. Galbraith thought he was never again a happy man, that "divorced from public concerns, he did not wholly exist." I. F. Stone mourned his departure as "part of the general movement away from liberalism."[17]

Through the last half of 1942 manpower raised nearly as many hackles as rationing and price controls. It threatened to replace the allocation of raw materials as the chief bottleneck in war production. In his October fireside chat after returning from his tour, Roosevelt emphasized two main objectives for manpower: finding and training enough men for the military, and finding enough workers to man the factories already in production and those coming online, as well as providing farms with enough laborers to assure an ample food supply. The difficulty was not lack of people, he stressed. "The problem is to have the right numbers of the right people in the right places at the right time. We are learning to ration materials; and we must now learn to ration manpower." For that to happen workers had to stop moving from job to job;

companies had to stop stealing labor from one another; and more women and grown children had to be employed along with older men and disabled people to free more fit men for military service.[18]

Like rationing and price controls, manpower had become a political bombshell. "Scamping"—the pirating of workers—continued to haunt many plants despite all attempts to curb it. Desperate foremen made the rounds of workmen's homes at night trying to lure them to new jobs. One factory even sent telegrams to a rival's workmen offering them good jobs, sight unseen, if they showed up the next morning. Personnel managers had a new mantra: "The way to get one good man is to hire four because three will quit." Pittsburgh Coal Co. suffered a 35 percent turnover and lamented that it took longer (two years) to train a miner than it did a soldier. At one Los Angeles steel-castings company 10 percent of the workforce was absent every day, most of them looking for better jobs. "Well, another of our old employes [sic] just left us," said the personnel manager. "He was with us three and a half days."[19]

In recruitment the military, WPB, and Selective Service all operated independently of each other. The military insisted that it had first claim on all able men regardless of their occupation or expertise; the navy continued its policy of ignoring all restrictions to enlist whomever it wanted; the farm bloc protested the drain of laborers that turned harvests into nightmares; industrialists pointed out the absurdity of drafting men whose skills were irreplaceable; and educators warned that emptying college classrooms and laboratories of students would cripple the nation's need for more scientists and other specialists. Debate still raged over whether to draft eighteen-year-olds for combat duty and what criteria should be used for occupational deferments. The idea of a national service bill on the British model commanded attention, as did the inevitable clamor for the appointment of one person—a manpower czar—to coordinate and rationalize manpower.[20]

Paul McNutt wanted very much to be that czar. Since taking charge of WMC he had pursued a cautious, go-slow approach based on voluntarism. Here, as elsewhere, the ceaseless battle over compulsion versus voluntarism complicated attempts to formulate policy. Within WMC McNutt had antagonized the military by reducing its influence, but his approach, which pleased those groups like labor demanding a voluntary policy, had proved ineffective. An attempt in September to freeze 200,000 workers, including lumberjacks and copper miners, in their jobs flopped for lack of enforcement mechanisms. Early in November *Business Week* complained that attempts to control manpower "have been so haphazard, so unintegrated and so irresolute that, instead of simplifying the problem, they have served to add to its seriousness and to multiply its complexities." *Time* warned that "the day is not far distant when men may say: All troubles lead to Paul McNutt . . . For every manpower problem that has arrived, 100 or 1,000 are on their way."[21]

Like Nelson, McNutt had become a target for New Dealers and the military alike, both of whom regarded him as ineffective for different reasons. Unlike Nelson, McNutt had sensitive political antennae that alerted him to the growing discontent with his leadership or lack thereof. In September he began to reverse course by declaring in a speech, "It is my considered judgment, based on the best available knowledge of the manpower situation, that some type of national-service legislation is inevitable." A month later, besieged by lobbyists from the dairy industry, which had lost thousands of hands to war industries, he proposed the mass deferment of 50,000 dairymen. Congress resolved that issue on November 20 by passing the controversial Tydings Amendment barring the drafting of farmers, dairymen, and other agricultural workers unless replacements for them were available. It also argued strongly for placing the manpower muddle in the hands of one man. Aware that he had failed to build rapport with Congress, McNutt cleverly endorsed this suggestion and advanced a plan to carry it out.[22]

The plan was simple: transfer control of Selective Service to WMC, end all voluntary military enlistments, and put USES in charge of all hiring for war industries. On October 30 Oscar Cox, a New Deal lawyer in the Justice Department, submitted to Hopkins a report Sam Rosenman had asked him to prepare on the manpower mess. It recommended a single administrator trusted by both the public and organized labor. Early in November McNutt showed his own plan to Roosevelt, who seemed receptive to it. At the War Department Stimson, already engaged in controversies over drafting eighteen-year-olds and how large the army needed to be, heard rumors as early as September that McNutt was "seeking to coordinate under one head in his department the functions which are now performed by the Selective Service and also the production of sufficient manpower for industrial work." Stimson labeled the idea a "calamity," especially the control of Selective Service by McNutt.[23]

Stimson welcomed the idea of centralization but not under McNutt. Jim Forrestal suggested that the man best suited for the job was Baruch, but Stimson, himself now seventy-five, feared that "Baruch was a little too old to give the supervising efficiency that would be necessary to preserve the situation from McNutt's encroachments." Yet Baruch was far superior to McNutt or Nelson, both of whom Patterson dismissed as "only second line men." They took the idea to Byrnes, newly installed as director of OES, who seemed to like it and agreed to approach Roosevelt on the subject but warned that McNutt was already at work on the president. After a cabinet meeting on October 22 Stimson asked Roosevelt not to decide the issue until they had talked.

The president admitted to being perplexed on how to resolve the conflicting needs of the military, industry, and agriculture. He didn't want to create two sets of local boards to decide such matters, but Stimson countered that dumping the whole problem on the existing draft boards might well politicize them.[24]

Stimson embodied his views in a memorandum for Roosevelt arguing that Selective Service and any system for regulating civil manpower were so incompatible that they must be kept separate with an arbitrator to adjust any differences between them. Although independent in theory, Selective Service had always been dominated by the War Department, and Stimson did not want that relationship disturbed. By November McNutt's proposal had gone public along with two others from Congress. One from the Truman Committee branded WMC a failure, omitted mention of McNutt, and called for a director to oversee the entire manpower program. The second proposal came from five Democratic congressmen and was far more radical. It called for creation of an entirely new agency, the Office of War Mobilization, to absorb WPB, Selective Service, OES, and both military procurement divisions to centralize the entire war effort. Selective Service would be merged into WMC as a single manpower division.[25]

Baruch himself let Roosevelt know that he favored the McNutt plan but without McNutt in charge. Rumors flew that the president would turn the job over to the Labor Department; Frances Perkins would retire, Ickes would take her place, and McNutt would move to Interior. Ickes balked, as did most of Interior's constituency. Even the oilmen lobbied to keep Ickes at Interior. Budget director Harold Smith went to see McNutt and, after a long conversation, wrote a lengthy memo to Roosevelt stating that McNutt should stay in the manpower job. When Roosevelt agreed, Smith and Sam Rosenman urged him to give McNutt control of Selective Service as well despite Stimson's objections. On December 5 an executive order drafted by Smith and signed by Roosevelt transferred Selective Service to WMC and required the army and navy secretaries to consult with McNutt before determining their monthly manpower needs.[26]

Stimson was away enjoying a brief rest when Roosevelt made the decision. When he returned, the president welcomed him back at a cabinet meeting and said jovially, "Harry, I've been robbing your henroost while you were away." Unamused, Stimson snapped, "I won't go away again."[27]

Stimson was furious at the decision but reconciled himself to working with McNutt as best he could. After talking with McNutt for ninety minutes, he came away believing that Selective Service would not be gutted by being in WMC. Frank Knox had a more parochial concern. The navy had relied entirely on volunteers. When the provision eliminating voluntary enlistments was announced, he said to McNutt, "Paul, give me just three more months for naval enlistments." To that McNutt replied, "Frank, when the President signs that order, I won't give you three minutes."[28]

While this fight continued, Congress moved at last to resolve another conflict. The army needed not only more men but younger ones as well. By the end of the Civil War the average age of federal soldiers was 19.5 years; in World War I the average age climbed to just under 25. The current army's average age exceeded 28 by August 1942. "That's too old!" complained Stimson in October. "Our Army is getting too old." Stimson and Patterson believed fervently that war was a young man's game. The pool of younger single men for the draft was running dry, leaving only married men, fathers, and older men unless the draft age was lowered to eighteen. "The nation's 6,443 draft boards are scraping the bottoms of their 1-A barrels," reported *Time* in December. Polls showed that drafting teenagers had solid approval from both that age group and the general public. After beating back several amendments, Congress finally approved a bill to draft the younger men in late November.[29]

The ongoing dispute over the size of the army resisted easy resolution. It required a calculus that no one could devise accurately. The number of useful troops depended on the amount of weapons, munitions, and ships available for support and on how many workers were needed to supply them, as well as how rapidly casualties depleted the ranks. Strong emotions colored every estimate. Stimson, Patterson, and Marshall were adamant that the army should have all the men it wanted without exception. They were cold to the idea that some men were far more valuable for the work they did than as cannon fodder. As a result the debate grew even more contentious than that over manpower, the more so because no clear yardstick existed to resolve it.

Late in the summer of 1942 the army projected a manpower budget for 1943 of 7.5 million enlisted men, which together with the other services created an aggregate military of nearly 10.9 million men. WMC and WPB objected at once, saying that figure would unbalance the national economy. McNutt estimated that no more than 9 million men would be available by the end of 1943, and WPB had geared its production studies to a military of 7.6 million. A study by Nathan's Planning Committee concluded that lack of shipping space would prevent the army from deploying in combat zones anywhere near its projected numbers. Every man drafted but not used amounted to one less factory worker, miner, or field hand. The Joint Chiefs endorsed the higher figure but agreed to meetings on the subject. At a meeting on November 3 Marshall asserted that "we cannot make any cuts in our requirements for combat units if we expect to win the war."[30]

Roosevelt at first approved the figure of 7.3 million, then backtracked under pressure from Marshall and the War Department. Several congressmen and committees jumped into the fray as the debate dragged on through the winter. Despite McNutt's victory in gaining control of Selective Service, neither Marshall nor Stimson would budge on their projected needs. Stimson went so far as to deliver a radio speech on the subject, at the end of which he went public for the first time in support of a national service law. Roosevelt finally agreed to the military's figures, and by doing so implied its right to determine its size. In March he appointed a special committee to review his decision and the manpower problem. The committee concluded that with proper conservation measures and the utilization of more women in industry the country could sustain a military of nearly 11.2 million.[31]

The committee also decided that a prolonged war would make a national service law inevitable but that the nation was not yet ready to accept one. This debate, like so many others, was far from over, and the manpower muddle remained unresolved. William Hassett noted in March that Hopkins was "deeply concerned about manpower—said the problem is to find 12,000,000 more workers to produce for the war either by deferment of military service or by shifting workers from nonessential to essential jobs. Demands for Paul McNutt's head increase in and out of Congress."[32]

"WHEN SAM ROSENMAN is in town," observed *Newsweek*, "almost certainly there will be some changes made." For more than thirteen years, going back to Roosevelt's stint as governor of New York, Sammy the Rose had been his Mr. Fix-It, handling the most delicate political problems and helping to assemble the team that got Roosevelt elected in 1932 and became known as the Brain Trust. A quiet, modest man with what he called a "passion for anonymity," Rosenman continued his work after being made a judge. Since the war began he had become expert in untangling the endless administrative snarls that erupted. But there were tangles that even he couldn't fix. The worst of these continued to be in the strife-torn WPB, where every step forward seemed to be followed by two steps backward.[33]

On paper the new arrangement seemed ideal. Ferdinand Eberstadt took charge of materials and Charles Wilson of production. Both were expert at their new assignments. "In Eberstadt I have an intellectually tough fellow," said a pleased Nelson, "with substantial experience in control of materials. He has been enforcing some discipline which I admit was badly needed around here. In Wilson I have the country's top production man. With control over the flow of materials in Eberstadt's hands and control over production in Wilson's, I will be in a position to do the job I can do best, which is to referee, to coordinate." WPB seemed at last to be springing loose from its notorious lethargy. Even Baruch remarked with satisfaction, "It looks as if Nelson was cleaning out that Museum of Tired Old Men."[34]

The complaints about WPB had been there since its inception. It had too many layers, too much organizational deadwood that Nelson was reluctant to prune. It lacked pride and confidence and worked under a pall of complaint; too many of its people kept threatening to resign but never did. It had too much animosity toward the military, with whom it seemed in constant conflict. The infighting was incessant, and the constant tinkering with its structure and authority left executives afraid that the rug might be pulled out from under them at any moment. As one man complained, "Nothing is ever allowed to stay put." Eberstadt and Wilson took on the task of changing this culture. Eberstadt in particular plunged into the challenge with gusto. Working seven days a week from 8:30 A.M. to 7:30 P.M. behind a desk perpetually swept clean, talking in clipped sentences with an unmistakable air of authority, he imposed an unaccustomed air of order and drive to the agency. His style was coldly efficient; as one employee said, "He looks at you like an icicle."[35]

But he impressed many with his ability to get things done. "Until Eberstadt arrived," said one admirer, "no one was willing to make decisions. When Eberstadt came in, the change was immediately perceptible. Men suddenly realized that they had a boss who was going to make decisions and who was going to demand that they make them in accordance with policy and within their appropriate areas."[36]

Unlike many other government officials, Eberstadt made a fetish of avoiding publicity and kept his personal life intensely private. "My job is to work," he said. "It's not to talk to the press and not to make speeches." He and his wife seldom entertained or went out; Eliot Janeway called him "a fish out of water in Washington." He remained aloof from the city's cocktail party circuit and went so far as to give up drinking to avoid any interference with his work. A short, square-shouldered man who had risen to captain in the last war and still enjoyed the company of his veteran buddies, he took pride in his toughness and ability to say no to people, including the president. He was close to Patterson and considered a protégé of Baruch. To those who complained that he was too close to the military, Eberstadt growled, "What are we here for if not to favor the services? This is a *War* Production Board."[37]

Apart from his impact on WPB, Eberstadt impressed everyone with his CMP, the implementation of which went forward smoothly. Borrowing from various plans already in the air, he fashioned a composite vertical materials allocation plan that was deceptively simple. "On one side of the table, you put the people who make steel," he said later in describing it, "and on the other those who need it, with the government in between." Unlike PRP, it revolved around control of only three key materials—carbon and alloy steel, aluminum, and copper—that were basic to virtually all munitions and war products. Sixteen other materials were monitored but not included formally in the plan, which assumed that proper allocation of the big three materials would force the others into appropriate channels as well. What David Novick called the "truly revolutionary step in CMP" lay in one simple statement: "The delivery of controlled materials . . . shall not be affected by preference ratings." It meant the adoption of a total allocation system for the most basic war production materials. *Newsweek* hailed it as "a switch from theory to realistic business practice."[38]

In simple terms CMP worked this way. The designated key materials would be allocated to seven claimants—army, navy, Maritime Commission, Lend-Lease, Board of Economic Warfare (BEW), OCS, and a new aircraft scheduling unit in WPB headed by Wilson—who stated their needs, broken down by major programs, for the coming eighteen months. The WPB's divisions for steel, aluminum, and copper balanced the total needs of claimants against the estimated supply of each material and apportioned the available supply among them. Problems and disputes were referred first to the Requirements Committee and ultimately to Nelson. Once told the amount it would get, each agency parceled it out among its prime contractors, which had earlier given WPB their needs as well. They in turn were responsible for doling out whatever portion of their share was needed by subcontractors.[39]

In theory this system would produce a balance of supply and demand for the three essential materials, and hopefully others as well. Uncontrolled parts and materials still received priority ratings from WPB industry divisions or claimant agencies, but nearly all such ratings were inferior to allotment numbers, which became central to the entire operation. They identified the claimant agency, production program and schedule, and the month authorized for shipment of the controlled material. Every stage and input of production, as well as all orders and other paperwork, carried allotment numbers. Among other things they provided a guarantee of delivery.[40]

To implement CMP, Eberstadt got Nelson's approval to reorganize WPB in a way that enabled him to oversee its entire operating structure. The industry branches were elevated to divisions and staffed with new executives. They became the board's basic operating units, functioning in effect as mini-WPBs that spoke for the industries they represented. Eberstadt became program vice chair and headed the Requirements Committee. Ernest Kanzler served directly beneath him with Julius A. Krug as deputy director general for distribution and head of the Controlled Materials Plan Division, which thrashed out the details for implementing the new system. The gradual implementation went smoothly enough, partly because it relied more on existing practices and agencies. It seemed relatively simple in concept, yet Novick called it "the most complex piece of administrative machinery created during the . . . war emergency."[41]

While Eberstadt worked at orchestrating the flow of materials, Charlie Wilson struggled to unravel the production conundrum. Scheduling lay at the heart of the problem. "The administrative key to mass production," wrote David Novick, "is the painstaking planning, timing, and direction of the flow of materials and parts through the manufacturing process so that each item arrives at the final assembly line where and when it is needed." Early arrival cluttered up the production line; late arrival interrupted its operation and slowed output. This model held equally true for an individual plant or for the nation's overall economy. Integrating this process was an immensely difficult task, and Wilson was reputed to be expert at it. He was the first executive at the agency since Knudsen renowned for his mastery of mass production.[42]

Charlie Wilson had literally always been a fighter. As a young man he had been a semipro boxer and liked to spar at smokers. Recently, while touring a war factory in Connecticut, he had been stopped by the watchman at the gate who said, "I knocked you out once." Wilson looked at him, then said with a grin, "Then you're Joe So-and-so. He's the only man who ever knocked me out." His fighting instincts carried over into business, where he aroused mixed feelings even among some who conceded his ability. "Massive, powerful, abrupt, with a rasp to his voice like a top sergeant's," wrote Bruce Catton, "Wilson rather looked as if he had been hewn from a block of weathered hardwood with an adz . . . He had drive and he knew how to impart it . . . When he sought the solution to a problem his instinct was to put his head down and slug his way through; never mind weighing all of the subtleties and abstractions, make a decision and stick to it."[43]

Known as a liberal businessman, he also had a curiously parochial streak. "Narrow, cautious, and conservative," wrote Paul Koistinen, "Wilson was a capable industrialist but an ineffective public leader. Having risen from the bottom to the top of GE, he functioned well only within the GE environment . . . While powerful and shrewd, Wilson was insecure, petty, and ruthless. He surrounded himself with yes-men." He also had one of the toughest jobs in the wartime bureaucracy, and he determined to make the most of it. Rationalizing the flow of materials meant little unless they were synchronized with the facilities using them. Unfortunately, these two functions, production and control of materials, could not be cleanly divided, which meant overlapping jurisdictions. Eberstadt and Wilson were both talented, strong-willed men determined to let nothing stand in the way of getting their job done.[44]

The basic challenge was to relate the controls over the manufacture of end products through distribution of component parts to the controls used to allocate materials for these products. Serious shortages existed of both materials and components. Production schedules performed this job and directed both to the specific plants that would use them promptly and effectively. Nelson realized that the responsibilities of Eberstadt and Wilson were "closely interwoven" and that "each official must consult the other in many cases." But his hopes were blighted by three forces: the strong wills of the two men, the influence of "palace politics," and another chapter in the ongoing clash between WPB and the military procurement agencies. In the latter fight Eberstadt was championed by the military and Wilson by the New Dealers and others who believed ardently in keeping the economy in civilian hands, even though Stimson and Patterson had worked hard to bring Wilson on board.[45]

The two men sat together on PEC along with the military representatives. After two months of relative quiescence, Wilson unveiled his hand on November 11—the same day Eberstadt issued the order reorganizing WPB—by presenting PEC with his plan for solving the scheduling mess. It had the effect of placing full responsibility for scheduling as well as allocation of materials in the hands of WPB. The committee unanimously endorsed the proposal, but Somervell was not at the meeting, having sent General Lucius D. Clay in his place. As soon as he learned of the proposal, Somervell rejected it outright and enlisted Patterson and the navy to oppose it on the grounds that WPB should exercise control only over allocation of materials. On November 21, Nelson sent Patterson a draft memorandum formally creating the office of vice chairman of production and defining its powers in provocative terms that, among other things, terminated the military's powers over production. Thus began what Nelson called "the bitterest fight I ever had with the War Department people."[46]

Stimson had gone to Highhold, his estate on Long Island, for the weekend of November 20–22, trying in vain to replenish his energy, only to have Patterson and Somervell descend on him when he walked into the office Monday morning. "Every time I come back from a little bit of rest I find a new bad trouble," he sighed, "and this was one of the worst. It turns out that Nelson has apparently gone completely off his head and is trying to make an order taking over all production work of the two services. That is one of the most violent breaches of precedent and tradition of anything that has happened. The man must be crazy to do it. He has made a bad flop on his own work . . . of securing raw materials and how he should think that the President would turn over to him the work which we, the Army and Navy, are doing pretty well after he has shown such a failure in his own work, I cannot see."[47]

Patterson too was infuriated and called Nelson a liar whose word couldn't be trusted. In a sharp memo to Stimson, he argued that Nelson's proposal would remove entire control of weapons production from the hands of the military and set production schedules for both services: "This proposal would take from the Army and the Navy the power to decide what weapons they need, how many they need, when they need them and where they needed them. The loss of such control would cripple the armed services in supplying the needs of their forces." The best way to ensure victory, he declared, was to keep the existing system in which the responsibility for military goods "from drafting board to scrap pile" remained in the hands of the services. WPB insisted that Wilson had to exercise "central review and control of scheduling" to avoid conflicts among war programs and end "the confused scramble for facilities, materials, and labor."[48]

Stimson was convinced that WPB people were behind "provocative articles" in the papers claiming that Nelson was going to take over much of the military's work and teach them a lesson. In Stimson's view the army and navy had done an outstanding job in turning the nation into an arsenal. Patterson had been magnificent, Somervell had injected new life into ASF, new factories were springing up everywhere, the tool shortage had been surmounted, and labor was ample. The only problem was shortage of raw materials, which was Nelson's department. The War Department had warned Nelson of the problem two months earlier, but to no avail. "It isn't wholly his fault," Stimson conceded. "It is largely the lack of system in the WPB and that primarily began with the President's lack of organizing ability." The War Department had lobbied hard for Wilson, who, Stimson feared, "isn't quite as good a man as we thought." He talked the whole business over with Baruch, who agreed that a talk with Wilson might help the situation.[49]

Stimson refused adamantly to see that the army bore any responsibility for the shortages of raw materials and bottlenecks in production schedules. The interconnections between all these processes interested him little; the important thing for him was to keep control of them in the right hands—namely, those of the War Department. Wilson went to see him the next morning, November 26, but to Stimson's chagrin Nelson came along with him. Stimson thought that Nelson "appeared very badly . . . as if his troubles were upsetting him. And then he was not frank; he was not ingenuous; he wrung his hands and said he wished he could get out; that the job was a very unhappy one for him. And all the time I knew that he was inspiring the unpleasant press campaign against the Army which he denied knowing anything about the source of. He is a weak man who can't face the troubled situation that he has."[50]

What Stimson did not know was that Nelson suspected the army of being behind a press campaign against *him*. "I found out one thing about the Army," he wrote later. "The minute you start making decisions which they don't like they complain that you are indecisive, and that the big trouble with you is that you can't make decisions."[51]

Stimson had also appealed to Roosevelt via Harry Hopkins. The president summoned Nelson and said, "I understand you are in a fight with the Army again." Nelson admitted that he was, adding that it was a life-or-death struggle over the scheduling of components that had to be won if production goals were to be met. When Roosevelt offered to help, Nelson said he would fight the battle himself. "All I ask of you," he said, "is, don't help the other fellow." Roosevelt laughed and replied, "Well, if you need me, come to Poppa." As the controversy grew more heated, the president threatened to lock all parties in a "foodless room" until they came to terms. Yet years later Eberstadt claimed that, although he read about the fight with Wilson in the papers every day, he had in fact never even met him.[52]

Nelson and Wilson talked with Stimson that morning of November 26 and again the next day, joined this time by Patterson and John McCloy. Stimson made clear his belief that the problems had nothing to be do with the army's responsibilities but with the shortage of raw materials, which was WPB's job. Wilson said he was a production man, not a raw materials man, and that he wanted to go home. Stimson didn't want him to leave because he thought Wilson could do a better job than anyone else in WPB. Between the meetings Nelson sent Stimson two letters couched in conciliatory language. At the second meeting everyone agreed to a memorandum that seemed a reasonable compromise. Nelson put out his own statement as well, which Stimson dismissed as "more for the purposes of publicity than for the solution of the problem." Patterson drafted a letter that Stimson considered "too much of a red flag to be conducive towards getting Nelson to our terms." He and McCloy proceeded to rewrite it in more conciliatory language.[53]

The compromise agreement mollified but did not resolve the larger conflict between WPB and the military. Asked how it was settled, Somervell admitted, "I don't know exactly." An administrative order issued by Nelson on December 9 emphasized Wilson's authority more than the limitations imposed on it. No sooner did this controversy simmer down than another even more explosive one erupted. The overlapping of authority between Wilson and Eberstadt remained unsettled, partly because of a shift in needs. As CMP gradually came online, the shortage of materials eased and components emerged as the primary obstacle to scheduling. These ranged from the smallest bearings to heat exchangers, blowers, turbines, pumps, and thousands of parts essential to the larger end products such as ships, planes, tanks, trucks, and synthetic rubber. By late 1942 the shortage of key components had forced WPB to orchestrate carefully their production and distribution among claimants.[54]

Within WPB Eberstadt had control of all the industry divisions except aircraft, shipbuilding, and radio and radar. These had been given to Wilson, who did an impressive job with the floundering airplane production. The December agreement also gave Wilson complete authority over the scheduling of thirty-four critical components. Wilson insisted that to orchestrate production properly, he needed more control over the industry divisions. It did not help that their personalities clashed as well. Wilson was the jovial, outgoing bear, Eberstadt the tight-lipped, precise introvert. A major difference between them arose over the scheduling of components for key programs—airplanes, shipbuilding, rubber, and 100-octane gasoline. Eberstadt resisted demands for what he deemed extravagant rush orders for scarce materials used in these special projects. Wilson complained that this slowed production and complicated his job.[55]

Roosevelt had done much to create this problem by placing the production of airplanes, 100-octane gas, escort vessels, merchant ships, and the construction of rubber facilities on a "must" list with priority over everything else. Since they required many of the same scarce materials, it was impossible to fulfill all of them at once. Nevertheless, the head of each affected department was ordered to fight for his special product over anyone else. The result was a constant battle among the claimants for materials and components. No one took his charge more seriously than Bill Jeffers, the rubber czar. Taking the Baruch report as his bible, he determined to bull through its recommendations at all costs. The construction of new rubber factories required large amounts of critical materials and components needed elsewhere. The services complained that the rubber program impinged on 100-octane gas and escort vessel production and insisted that it be reduced. Jeffers refused to budge.[56]

Bill Jeffers was a bull of a man, a dictator on his railroad, where he ruled by force of personality. Disdain came naturally to him, especially of college men and know-it-alls and bureaucrats, who in his mind never did a real day's work in their life. He did not reason to get his point across; he pounded the table and swore like the railroader he was, and he terrified Nelson as he did many people. "The country will expect of Mr. Jeffers," said the New York Times after his appointment, "only that he do a thorough, competent job without worrying about 'public reaction,' the elections or any political considerations." Little did the Times suspect how ruthlessly Jeffers would fulfill these criteria. As a first step Jeffers thanked and fired everyone associated with the program so he could replace them with industry experts. Stimson found him a "very forceful man," but he and Patterson stood their ground. Patterson was adamant that 100-octane gasoline was the most urgent immediate need, and Nelson tried in vain to broker a compromise. The dispute moved up to Jimmy Byrnes for resolution.[57]

On January 9 Stimson and Patterson, Knox and Forrestal, Nelson and Fred Searls, Jeffers and an associate, and Ickes gathered in Byrnes's White House office to thrash out the issue. Jeffers came on in his forceful way, arguing that Americans could not be expected to produce food on their farms or weapons in factories if their needs were ignored. He knew them firsthand, Jeffers insisted. He carried a union card, and he knew farmers from having eaten in their kitchens during inspection trips on the Union Pacific. Stimson met his argument in kind. "I do not carry a union card," he said wryly, "and I prefer to eat in the dining room. But I still think I know something of the willingness of the civilians to make sacrifices for the war effort." During the heated exchange Searls sat quietly not at the table but in a corner, saying nothing until Forrestal asked him a question.[58]

"It was a pathetic spectacle to me," admitted Stimson. ". . . It was like four hungry dogs quarreling over a very inadequate bone." The more Stimson listened, the more contemptuous he grew of Nelson. "Practically all of us representing the Army and Navy and I think Ickes believes that the President ought to appoint Barney Baruch. The whole country is clamoring for it but nothing has been done." Byrnes listened in his patient way and agreed to make a recommendation to Roosevelt. He decided that Jeffers would get enough equipment and materials to produce 452,000 tons of synthetic rubber, only 43.6 percent of what the Baruch report had recommended. Fred Searls came up with the number at Byrne's request, the military agreed with it, and Byrnes promptly drafted Searls as "an ever present help."[59]

Jeffers accepted the ruling but vented his unhappiness in some remarks before the Council of State Governments. "In our failure to get what I would call even adequate [rubber] production," he barked, "we have too many so-called expediters . . . Army and Navy men, commissioned officers . . . If we can keep the Army and the Navy and these loafers out of these plants . . . we will get the production." Later reporters learned that in railroad parlance a "loafer" was someone with an unnecessary job, but the comments infuriated the War Department and threw Washington into a dither. Patterson, who didn't want to make *any* concession to the rubber program, was beside himself and had to be soothed by Stimson. At his weekly press conference Stimson did not rise to the bait and said he had no intention of waging verbal combat with other departments.[60]

Just as this controversy simmered down, the clash between Wilson and Eberstadt escalated. The Jeffers firefight highlighted the need for more decisive lines of authority over scheduling of key materials and components. Among other things, Wilson did not like CMP. On January 20 he issued an order requiring war contractors to file half-year requests for thirty-four major components by February 6, but the order was delayed and Eberstadt did not even know about it for several days. Nelson took responsibility for the confusion, then on February 4 transferred to Wilson several industry divisions formerly under Eberstadt. It was a compromise that pleased no one and promised to create more strife. Stimson and Patterson were furious and fearful that Eberstadt would resign. Patterson decided that the time had come to urge Roosevelt forcefully to replace Nelson with Baruch. He did not know that the president had already taken steps in that direction.[61]

Sometime in January Wilson had gone to Roosevelt and handed him his resignation. The president refused to accept it and asked Byrnes to resolve the quarrel. Roosevelt harbored a resentment against Eberstadt for flatly refusing to fire a man the president wanted discharged. Eberstadt said he would leave if he had to fire the man, and Roosevelt had backed down but did not forget the slight. A corps of hard-core New Dealers were rumored to have lined up behind Wilson because of Eberstadt's closeness to the military. The press was having a field day with the fight, taking sides freely and using it as a prime example of a dysfunctional WPB. Byrne's first task was to persuade Wilson not to quit. Wilson gave him a second letter of resignation and asked that it be passed on to Roosevelt. Instead he brought Nelson and Wilson together and arranged an uneasy truce between them. Meanwhile, rumors of Wilson's impending resignation filled the papers.[62]

The pressure on WPB had become intolerable. The Truman Committee continued to criticize Nelson, and support was growing for a bill introduced by Senator Claude Pepper in January to replace WPB with a new agency. At one point Nelson had urged Baruch to persuade Wilson to remain, then a week later complained to him that Wilson was unacceptable and could no longer stay. On February 3 Eberstadt called on Baruch and showed him a proposed letter of resignation. "Don't send it," Baruch said at once. "There are developments you don't know about." Five days later Baruch's wife in Boston opened a newspaper and read, "Eberstadt fired." Eberstadt himself knew nothing about it.[63]

To end the infighting, a disturbed Roosevelt floated the idea of replacing Nelson with Wilson. On February 5 Byrnes responded with a letter arguing persuasively why Wilson should not be appointed and suggesting instead that Baruch be made head of WPB. His appointment would likely kill the Pepper bill and restore confidence in the agency. Stimson had, at Patterson's urging, asked both Byrnes and Hopkins to get behind Baruch even though he knew Roosevelt wouldn't like the idea. "He has dodged away from Baruch," he mused, "although Baruch has long been the outstanding man for the position."[64]

For his part Baruch had been working both sides of the controversy. On February 3 he had dinner with Nelson and went over the whole affair with him. While pledging full support for his authority, Baruch told Nelson that his quarrel with the army was harmful to the country and had to end. At the same time, he also met with Stimson and Patterson and dismissed the WPB's fears of militarism as nonsense. "My philosophy in the Army-WPB dispute was simple enough," he wrote later. "I believed that the armed forces must have what they wanted, when they wanted it, with the least possible dislocation to the civilian economy. In any conflict between civilian and military needs, the military would have to have priority . . . Guns had always to come *before* butter."[65]

On one occasion Walker Stone of the Scripps Howard news chain strolled into Baruch's rooms at the Carlton Hotel and heard him talking to Nelson on the phone. "You're dead wrong," Stone heard him tell Nelson. "You can't dictate to the military what its requirements should be; it's your job to get out what they need." Baruch then picked up another phone and told an army representative, "The military does not know what industry can produce." Stone concluded that Baruch was "trying to prop everyone up, rather than pull the rug out."[66]

Baruch professed to have no sympathy for "groaners who complained of small deprivations, and who . . . could not understand why they could not eat as much, wear as much, drive their cars as much, or carry on as though the war did not exist. Yet, there were people like this, and I am sorry to say that some of them were in official Washington." Neither did he have patience with "the shabby evasions of wartime restrictions I could see going on around me," and he felt nothing but contempt for "those who, under the guise of free enterprise, profiteered during the war." But on the subject of direct service Baruch remained as coy as ever. He went away from the dinner with Nelson believing that he would try to heal the breach with the army. Two nights later Byrnes appeared at his hotel with a letter from the president.[67]

Earlier that day Roosevelt had read Byrnes's letter and told him he was very fond of Baruch and respected his ability, but he feared that if appointed to WPB Baruch would talk to the press about other issues as well, and Roosevelt did not want advice in public. He had resisted putting Baruch in charge for two years, but now he reluctantly agreed to the move. Byrnes hurried to his office, where he kept a supply of the president's green letterhead used for more personal correspondence, and drafted a letter to Baruch. He composed it hastily in the inner office with orders to place the only copy in the locked files, then carried the original and copy to Roosevelt for his signature. He did not want the president to consult Hopkins, who Baruch thought was unfriendly to him. Roosevelt signed the letter, and that evening Byrnes personally handed it to Baruch at his hotel.[68]

Shocked but pleased by the offer, Baruch hesitated. He was leaving for New

York that night and promised Byrnes an answer the next day. Byrnes urged him to accept at once, but Baruch said he had to consult his doctor and wanted to talk with John Hancock, whose help would be essential if he took the job. The bluff, hearty Hancock looked more like a rancher from his native North Dakota than an investment banker and specialist in corporate reorganization. He had both an independent mind and a remarkable ability to master detail, and Baruch regarded him as indispensable. When asked once how he managed to do so many things, he replied, "John Hancock is the answer." But on his way to New York Baruch fell ill in Philadelphia and was put to bed by the doctor. He remained in bed for several days while the doctors disagreed over what ailed him and did not return to Washington for a week. By then Hancock had agreed to assist him and Baruch had decided to take the job.[69]

By then, too, some bizarre happenings had taken place. On February 15, Stimson moaned that "nothing yet has been done apparently about getting Nelson out and Barney Baruch in to WPB." The next day Knox told him that Roosevelt had made the decision to replace Nelson with Baruch. Sometime earlier that week, however, Nelson received a call in the middle of the night from one of his assistants, saying he had urgent news to report. They met over breakfast, and Nelson was told the army had arranged to have him fired. With uncharacteristic haste Nelson summoned reporters and told them that he had decided to fire Eberstadt, who learned of his fate through a press release. This unexpected move put Roosevelt in a not entirely unpleasant quandary. On one hand, he could hardly fire Nelson without it appearing to be support for Eberstadt. On the other hand, it freed him from having to appoint Baruch.[70]

Nelson offered a reasonable explanation for his action. "Because our entire effort must now center about the production lines," he said, "and because this involves the closest control over scheduling, it is essential that . . . a production man be in full charge . . . [and] that all related problems be within the jurisdiction of that production man . . . Materials control and production control today are all one integrated job. They cannot be considered separately. They must be directed as one job, not two."[71]

Unaware of these developments, Baruch arrived at the White House to inform Roosevelt of his acceptance. In the hall outside the oval office he met Sam Rosenman and Pa Watson, who said, "The President has changed his mind," but could not elaborate before Baruch was summoned inside. Leaning back in his chair, a cigarette in his uptilted holder, Roosevelt greeted him as cordially as ever. "Mr. President," said Baruch, "I'm here to report for duty." Without acknowledging this greeting, Roosevelt said, "Let me tell you about Ibn Saud, Bernie," and launched into a monologue on the subject before excusing himself to go off to a cabinet meeting. The WPB chairmanship was never mentioned then or afterward. Later Baruch concluded that Nelson had appealed to Hopkins for help in persuading Roosevelt to make no change. Bob Sherwood thought Hopkins might well have played a part. Eberstadt was the primary casualty; some expected him to be Baruch's deputy at WPB, but the firing rendered him persona non grata in both public and political eyes.[72]

For the moment an uneasy peace descended on WPB, but no one came away pleased by the outcome. Stimson and Patterson lost none of their desire to oust Nelson but had to bide their time. Nelson had kept his job but still had to deal with dissension in the ranks. Wilson got the added authority he craved and now had to deliver on it. While firing Eberstadt, Nelson also elevated Wilson to executive vice chairman of WPB and turned over operating control to him. In March Wilson put into effect one final reorganization of the board. He kept under his own control the board's production-scheduling apparatus, the CMP units, and some other key offices, leaving the rest to the care of four vice chairs that all reported to him. Of these, the program vice chair, Julius Krug, proved the most important and enduring. However, CMP endured, and Wilson soon conceded its value. Eberstadt lost the battle but won the war in that respect.[73]

Strangest of all, Nelson also turned the Planning Committee over to Wilson, who neither liked it nor appreciated its value. Aware of the military's hostility toward the committee, Wilson downgraded its stature until Nathan and the other members resigned before the month's end. The ambitious Krug declined to have either the Planning Committee or the Statistics Division under his wing because of their reputation as being dominated by academics and New Deal theorists. The talented Stacy May drifted to a Bureau of Planning and Statistics that was a mere shadow of the former entities. By March WPB seemed at last to have achieved enough stability to press production forward despite its continued inner tensions. Its record during the remainder of the year would be impressive even though yet another change in its status loomed in the near future.[74]

The seemingly endless struggle within WPB struck many observers as simply one more case of bureaucratic infighting in the City of Paper, but I. F. Stone warned that it was "only superficially a military-civilian struggle. Only 9 percent of the men in the War Department's services of supply are regular army officers; the rest are businessmen in uniform. It is a clash between two groups of big-business men, one linked with the military bureaucracy, the other somewhat tenuously allied with New Dealers and labor."[75]

Stone was right; much more was at stake. The clash also reflected the continuing struggle between the military and civilian authorities over who was to direct the economic foundation of the war effort. Indirectly it also illuminated the issue of who was in charge of that process. Roosevelt remained determined to keep control of it in his own hands because of his distrust of both business and the military, but the endless struggles made clear the weaknesses of this goal. By the spring of 1943 it had become obvious that some new and better arrangement was needed. For many analysts, too, there remained the difficult question of how far a democracy could venture in wartime without becoming in large measure the sort of totalitarian state that was its enemy.

CHAPTER 22

THE STUFF OF VICTORY

If, therefore, oil has set the pace of this war, oil must see it through, and the side that can throw the most oil into the fray over the longest sustained period of time will win.

—HAROLD ICKES[1]

Oil has become the most critical of munitions.

—RALPH K. DAVIES[2]

Being an oil driller since the last war hasn't blinded me to the fact that this war is going to be won with five essential things: guts, steel, oil, groceries, and a lot of faith.

—NEW MEXICO OIL DRILLER[3]

IT WAS A LOVE AFFAIR THAT NO one expected, and it could not have come at a better time. While other government agencies, business, and the military clawed and scratched at each other, Harold Ickes and the oil industry settled into a smooth, cooperative relationship grounded in mutual trust and respect that resulted in efficient production of the most critical products needed for military and civilian use alike. "We have issued no fiat or ukase," boasted Ickes. "No dictatorship exists or impends. We . . . had been working in close harmony for many months, but on that memorable morning of December 8, 1941, we really became full-fledged partners in a total war on a common enemy." Much of that cooperative attitude stemmed from Ickes's wise choice of Ralph Davies as his deputy. Of him the often harshly critical Ickes said, "I have never encountered greater loyalty or more unselfish devotion to job, or more intelligent cooperation than I have found in . . . Ralph K. Davies." Their leadership did much to forge a unique bond between the government and an industry that had long been at loggerheads with it.[4]

On the eve of the war the petroleum industry was a $15 billion colossus that employed a million people directly and provided jobs for another 200,000 indirectly through the billion dollars it spent for services and supplies. Its products and by-products comprised 40 percent of the nation's total mineral output. The military alone routinely used more than 500 different petroleum products, many of them indispensable. In wartime the drain on oil supplies grew exponentially. "The real challenge," declared Ickes, "is to deliver oil of specified grades, in sufficient quantities, over stretches of land and sea that vary in length from 3,000 to 10,000 miles, and to deliver it on time to do the job, the doing of which depends upon oil, and ever more oil, up to our capacity to supply, refine, and transport it."[5]

Everyone recognized the primary role played by oil in the industrial system as well as the war effort, but harnessing it posed a difficult and frustrating challenge because of the complexity of its operation and the bitter, long-standing feuds among the major oil companies and independents, who fought each other as tirelessly as they did foreign competitors and the government. As petroleum coordinator Ickes found himself in the familiar position of having no real power; the office had been created by a presidential letter and had no statutory standing or clout. More than thirty agencies were involved in some aspect of oil and would be difficult to coordinate. Nor did it help that most of the public and government alike indulged in the misconception that the nation had all the oil it needed and had only to open the tap. Since the 1920s the industry had been saddled with excess capacity to produce, refine, and distribute petroleum, and few people realized what huge quantities were being sucked up by the war effort. America was supplying not only its own needs but the Allies as well under Lend-Lease.[6]

The pressure arose even before Pearl Harbor. Between 1939 and 1943 American consumption rose 28 percent while its proven reserves increased less than 16 percent. Before most people realized it, the industry's central challenge reversed from trying to control excess production to maximizing output. For this to happen, government and the industry had to reshape their longtime adversarial relationship, and new sources of petroleum had to be found at home and abroad. Ickes and Davies understood this earlier than most, but most of Ickes's attempts at easing the crisis had been blocked. To make his office effective, Ickes surprised many observers by organizing it along lines that paralleled the main functions of the industry and then staffing it with men from the industry. This approach departed from the usual government way of doing things, and it had to overcome the dark suspicions and distrust of men in the industry toward the government. In this work Davies proved invaluable.[7]

To bring the industry together and coordinate its efforts, Ickes divided the country into five districts, each of which contained committees for production, refining, transportation, natural gas and gasoline, and distribution.

He then created a Petroleum Industry Council for National Defense composed of seventy-eight industry leaders from both the big companies and the independents. The latter dominated the council but chose as president William R. Boyd Jr., head of the American Petroleum Institute and considered as "belonging lock, stock, and barrel to the major companies." Ickes had the final say on any decision but took care to run everything through the Council for their input. Boyd could not have been more pleased at the approach of his old adversary. "It is the luckiest thing that ever happened to the oil industry," he said, "that it fell into the hands of its archenemy."[8]

However, Ickes recognized that no amount of effort or goodwill would get the job done as long as his office remained toothless. The big companies hesitated to do much on a cooperative basis lest their old enemy, Thurman Arnold's Justice Department, charge them with collusion. During 1941 and 1942 Standard Oil of New Jersey (Jersey Standard) was already entangled in an ugly dispute with Justice over its prewar relations with the giant German chemical trust IG Farbenindustrie, which generated a huge outpouring of negative publicity. In one heated committee meeting Harry Truman sat tight-lipped while listening to a letter written by Frank Howard of Jersey Standard, then blurted out, "I think this approaches treason." In his vigorous defense of the agreement, William S. Farish of Jersey Standard argued that "the U.S. got far more from Germany than Germany ever received from us." He may well have been right, but the political outcry against his company was hardly conducive for a smooth working relationship with the government.[9]

Exasperated by his losing battles over gasoline rationing and pipeline construction, Ickes in August 1942 drafted a memo to Roosevelt arguing that a central authority should be established over oil. Roosevelt agreed and referred Ickes's draft proposal to the Budget Bureau, which spent four months toning it down and reconciling it to the views of affected agencies. Finally, on December 2, Roosevelt issued an executive order creating the Petroleum Administration for War (PAW) with Ickes as its administrator. Although the new agency had only slightly more power, it stood apart from other agencies and reported directly to the president. A skilled bureaucratic infighter, Ickes knew how to maximize and extend what power he had. The irony was that in this field, where more harmony prevailed than in others, he needed it far less often than men like Nelson, Wilson, and Jeffers in agencies torn by perpetual conflict.[10]

IN THEIR WRATH over gasoline rationing most Americans associated oil companies chiefly with the production of fuel. They would have been shocked to learn how large a menu of products for wartime, let alone civilian use, flowed from the refineries. Besides gasoline the most critical of these included fuel oil for heating and powering ships, lubricating oils of all kinds, hydraulic oils, greases of many types, waxes, synthetic toluene for explosives, industrial alcohols, asphalt, insecticides, kerosene, rust preventatives, naphthenic acid (used in napalm), and several key ingredients for making synthetic rubber, especially butadiene. The demand for these products shifted constantly with the theaters of war but kept growing in quantity. Throughout the war the oil industry was pressed to produce and refine ever more product and to maximize the output from every barrel (forty-two gallons) of crude oil. For nearly four years refineries ran straight out to keep up with demand, and new facilities came online to increase production.[11]

Technology played a vital role in this performance. While all the major oil companies had research facilities, none matched those of the industry's giant, Jersey Standard. For decades Jersey Standard had been the whipping boy for Americans who despised giant corporations. After the dissolution of Rockefeller's empire in 1911—a move that "punished" him by doubling his fortune—it remained the largest entity and never lost that title. To reformers and antitrust advocates it was the biggest baddest wolf of a beastly industry that they loved to hate. While there may have been much to hate, there was also much to admire if one bothered to look closely enough. During the interwar years Jersey Standard and its affiliates emerged as a leader in research that was to prove crucial if not decisive in the war effort. Ironically, much of the impetus for these developments derived from its relationship with IG Farben that had drawn the wrath of the Justice Department down upon its corporate head.

In 1922 the company created a new affiliate, Standard Oil Development Company, to conduct a broad program of research. Frank Howard, a patent lawyer and engineer, took charge of the new operation and was quick to put a corps of outstanding scientists on retainer to keep Jersey Standard abreast of the latest scientific developments and work on solving specific problems. Petroleum technology was in a state of rapid flux and change. In 1913 Dr. William Burton patented a thermal cracking process that greatly increased the yield of gasoline from some low-value oils. During the 1930s a French engineer, Eugene Houdry, introduced a new catalytic cracking process that produced gasoline with a higher octane rating and yield than thermal cracking did. Jersey Standard looked into licensing the Houdry process but decided instead to redouble its own efforts for an even better method.[12]

The decision proved a wise one. Jersey Standard scientists developed an alternate approach called the fluid catalytic process that solved a major problem with the Houdry process. In 1940 a small pilot plant was built in Baton Rouge to test the new process, which exceeded all expectations. The fluid method not only increased the amount of high-octane gasoline produced from a given amount of crude oil, it also generated a large volume of light hydrocarbon gases useful as raw material for aviation gasoline components and synthetic rubbers. Work began at once on designing equipment for production on a commercial scale. The fluid process became one of the most crucial elements in expanding wartime production.[13]

Hydrogenation also attracted Development's attention during the interwar years. German progress in converting coal into oil initiated Jersey Standard's relationship with IG Farben. In 1926 Howard journeyed to Ludwigshafen to visit a German company's research facilities. The sight astounded him. "I was plunged into a world of research and development on a gigantic scale such as I had never seen," he wrote later. Although Howard found the methods used too costly for commercial development, Jersey Standard decided, as a hedge against future shortages of crude oil, to enter into a twenty-five-year agreement with Farben. The company was especially interested in the more immediate possibility of using hydrogenation to convert the worst types of crude oil and even tar into gasoline. By 1928 its researchers were convinced that hydrogenation could convert heavy oil into light oil and even into gasoline. Even more, a barrel of heavy crude would yield more than a barrel of high-grade gasoline and better lubricants, eliminating unwanted byproducts.[14]

Jersey Standard promptly bought from Farben the hydrogenation process, as well as some others relating to the petroleum industry, and Farben patents for all of them to use throughout the entire world except Germany. Further research revealed that it was possible to produce any desired percentage of high-grade gasoline from a barrel of petroleum but that the process was inherently more costly than ordinary refining. However, a modified version of hydrogenation known as hydroforming enabled the company's researchers to develop a method for producing toluene in quantity. Trinitrotoluene, or TNT, had long been the dominant high-grade explosive because it could be burned without exploding and was relatively immune to shock, yet could be easily detonated with fulminate of mercury. It was produced through nitration of toluene, a by-product of coke, but it required a ton of coke to make only about two quarts of toluene.[15]

During World War I Germany, with its large coal supply and well-developed coke industry, enjoyed a lead over the Allies, who remained short of toluene throughout the war. Petroleum chemists had known for a long time that some types of petroleum contained small amounts of toluene. The experiments with hydrogenation led unexpectedly to discoveries that made it possible to produce toluene synthetically. During the mid-1930s Jersey Standard scientists worked with the Ordnance Department to create a higher-grade toluene from oil that could be produced commercially. The hydroforming process, which had been devised chiefly to improve the octane rating of gasoline, proved to be the key for producing high-grade toluene in quantity as well.[16]

After the outbreak of war in September 1939, the army realized that existing methods of producing toluene could not begin to supply the demand for it. In June 1940 Jersey Standard agreed to provide the army with 20,000 gallons of toluene made in existing commercial facilities. The order cost Jersey Standard a financial loss but demonstrated that high-grade toluene could be made in commercial quantities. After protracted negotiations a large plant was built in Houston by Humble Oil, a Jersey Standard affiliate, to produce 2,000 barrels of toluene a day. The plant opened in September 1941, and the first tank car of toluene rolled out on October 21, six weeks before Pearl Harbor. During the last quarter of 1941 the Baytown Ordnance Works, as it was known, produced 2.4 million gallons of toluene, or nearly 60 percent of the nation's total supply derived from petroleum; the remaining 40 percent came from a Shell affiliate that used a different process. This figure paled once the United States went into the war. During 1942 the works, which had contracted to make 30 million gallons, produced more than 49.7 million gallons, then dwarfed this figure by churning out nearly 66.8 million gallons in 1943.[17]

Although the demand for toluene kept soaring as the war intensified, it never joined the list of shortages. The ability of American refineries to make as much toluene as was needed ensured a nonstop flow of explosives for the military even as supplies of other key materials ran short. The same could not be said for another product deemed even more vital: 100-octane aviation fuel. Despite impressive innovations and production techniques by Jersey Standard and other oil companies to ramp up their output, they never satisfied the insatiable appetite of the fast-growing Allied air forces.

HIGH-OCTANE GASOLINE WAS nothing new. Its origins traced back to 1921, when a young mechanical engineer named Thomas Midgley tried to solve the problem of engine knock in both automobiles and small engines that ran on kerosene. For years it was assumed that the problem was a mechanical one, but Midgley was convinced it had to do with the fuel. A lucky accident revealed to him that adding iodine to the kerosene made the engine run smoothly. Since iodine was too expensive to be used commercially, Midgley waded into what became thousands of experiments to find a cheap, effective additive. He finally discovered one in a mixture of lead and alcohol called tetraethyl lead, and thereby changed the history of transportation. Jersey Standard picked up the research to develop a cheaper process for making tetraethyl lead, and in 1924 a new company, Ethyl Gasoline Corporation, was formed jointly by Jersey and General Motors to produce it.[18]

Engineers had long known that engines could be made more powerful by increasing the compression ratio, but even the best fuels caused them to knock at a certain level. Adding a few drops of tetraethyl lead raised the octane level of the gasoline, which in turn allowed the production of engines with higher compression ratios. Raising the octane from 70 to 95, for example, increased the compression ratio 65 percent, raised horsepower 40 percent, and lowered fuel consumption by 25 percent. Automobile manufacturers were ecstatic. "These cars have wings," exulted Walter Chrysler. Other inventors, Eugene Houdry among them, came up with alternative methods of obtaining higher-octane fuel in the refining process without adding lead. In 1926 an Ethyl scientist, Dr. Graham Edgar, discovered a fuel that burned perfectly, a pure hydrocarbon; it came to be known popularly as "iso-octane" and served as the standard for a perfect fuel. As commercial gasolines improved in performance, they were assigned octane numbers approaching 100.[19]

No established method existed for measuring the tendency of an engine to knock. Edgar tested the knocking tendency of every pure compound he could find that had the general characteristics of gasoline. Iso-octane prevented knocking in any engine then in use. At the opposite end of the scale, a compound called normal heptane did so poorly that it knocked violently in any engine. Mixing the two in varying proportions produced fuels of intermediate qualities, and the amount of iso-octane in any given mixture became known as its octane. Commercial gasoline at the time had octane ratings from 40 to 75; the addition of tetraethyl lead increased the best of them to a maximum of 87. But every increased octane level spurred engine makers to increase their compression pressure, which could only be met by improving the quality of gasoline or increasing the amount of lead used.[20]

Aviation fuel posed an even greater challenge. A knock that limited power in a car engine could prove disastrous for a plane in flight. In 1930 the Army Air Corps adopted the octane scale and chose 87 octane as the grade for combat planes. A year earlier Jersey Standard had developed a method for producing iso-octane in quantity. The process was too expensive for commercial production, but the company made small amounts and sold it to the Air Corps for testing. Other companies intensified their own research for better and cheaper methods. In 1934 the Air Corps bought a thousand gallons of iso-octane from Shell, which used a different method, then blended it with high-quality aviation gasoline and enough tetraethyl lead to bring the octane rating to 100. Jersey Standard then decided to build facilities devoted to making iso-octane at refineries in New Jersey and Texas. In June 1935 it sold the first batch of 100-octane gasoline for commercial use.[21]

That same year the Air Corps issued requests for a million gallons of 100-octane gas and two years later adopted it as a standard for all combat planes. The reasons were obvious. Higher octanes meant engines with higher compression ratios that gave planes more power, higher speeds, faster take-offs on shorter runways, longer range, and greater maneuverability. Planes could travel farther, wear heavier armor, and/or carry heavier loads, all of which gave them an enormous advantage in combat. The problem was finding techniques that made commercial production cheap enough to be feasible. Jersey Standard developed a process using sulfuric acid as a catalyst that nearly doubled the yield of iso-octane. Then, in 1937–38, Humble introduced an improved process called alkylation, which made possible the production of iso-octanes in virtually unlimited quantities at far less cost than earlier methods. Catalytic-cracked gasoline had made its appearance two years earlier with the Houdry units. In essence, "cat cracking" made possible the production of better aviation fuels in large volume, while alkylation made it possible to improve their quality more cheaply.[22]

None of these developments were secret. The French and British both experimented with 100-octane fuel and appreciated its superiority. The French floundered in their attempts to build facilities or buy the gasoline from abroad. The British decided to make the fuel its fighting-grade standard but had no local production and had to purchase it from the United States and elsewhere. Germany had neither a native oil supply nor the highly developed refining industry needed to produce 100-octane gasoline in quantity. Instead it chose to rely on high-performance planes using aromatic types of synthetic fuel. This decision cost the Nazis dearly in the Battle of Britain, where outnumbered RAF fighters using 100-octane fuel outmaneuvered and outfought them to inflict heavy losses. Between August 8 and September 30, 1940, the Germans lost 2,152 planes compared to 620 for the British, forcing them to discontinue daytime raids and reduce their attacks.[23]

Isolationist sentiment and the Neutrality Acts made it difficult for the British to buy 100-octane gas from continental American refineries. To skirt this obstacle, Jersey Standard in 1938 built a new plant at its Aruba refinery to provide the fuel for British orders. Still the supply ran so short that during the Battle of Britain a race developed to get enough tankers through the packs of German submarines to keep the RAF flying. During the first year of the war, however, Washington showed surprisingly little interest in developing a larger supply of 100-octane gasoline. The fuel had three basic components: a base stock of 70 to 80 octane, a blending agent that raised it to about 85, and tetraethyl lead that boosted it to 100 octane. About 70 percent of the base stock came from natural naphthas, 20 percent was derived from cat cracking, and the rest from hydrogenation. Alkylation produced 95 percent of the blending agent, hydrogenation the other 5 percent. Refineries were not constructed in cookie-cutter fashion; every one was somewhat different and built to turn out certain products. Only fifteen companies had the capacity to produce the fuel.[24]

Roosevelt's call for 50,000 planes in May 1940 spurred concern over the nation's capacity for producing 100-octane gas. In December the head of Jersey Standard's economics department alerted William Farish that estimates indicated a surplus of the gasoline during 1941 but a major shortfall the next year, so plans should be made for constructing more blending-agent plants on short notice. Farish then wrote the presidents of the fourteen other oil companies that produced 100-octane gas suggesting that the industry invest $30 million in new refining equipment even though the supply of 100 octane seemed ample for 1941. New plants took twelve to fourteen months for completion. Meanwhile, yields could be raised 30 percent by increasing the dose of tetraethyl lead from the usual 3 cc to 4.5 cc, hiking the industry's output from 30,000 to 45,000 barrels a day, storing the excess to meet the next year's anticipated shortfall.[25]

That winter the army and navy made commitments for a million barrels of 100 octane as a reserve. Originally the storage program called for 7.5 million barrels, but the figure was reduced to 3 million at the end of 1941. The oilmen hesitated to expand capacity until tax and other financial arrangements had been made with the government, for the usual reason that they did not want to get stuck with excess facilities once the emergency ended. However, the soaring demands of the Allies and Lend-Lease compelled Ickes in July 1941 to warn the oil companies that "the shortage of aviation gasoline is increasingly critical" and to urge them to "achieve and maintain an absolute maximum production" even if it required "uneconomic operations." It was to take precedence over all other products. A month later Davies suggested that the supply of tetraethyl lead might shrink by as much as 40 percent. That same month he also issued a recommendation confining the use of blending agents to 100-octane gasoline.[26]

Davies had figures showing that by 1942 estimated production of 100 octane would total just under 50,000 barrels a day to meet a projected demand of more than 106,000 barrels a day. Some forty to fifty new plants would be needed to close the gap. The problem, he wrote Frank Knox, was that "we are calling upon the industry to build this equipment, yet no assurance can be given as to the purchase of product over a period of time." By October the drain on reserves alarmed Davies. He warned Nelson that a total output of at least 80,000 barrels a day, or twice the current capacity, would be needed by July 1942. Even with high priorities for construction materials he doubted that figure could be reached before the end of 1942; meanwhile, reserves were shrinking fast because of the imbalance. Jersey Standard was building a commercial-sized cat-cracking unit at its Bayway refinery in New Jersey, but it was not expected to go into operation until the last half of 1942.[27]

In mid-November Ickes and Davies, in a detailed report to SPAB, urged that construction of new facilities receive top priority and that the Defense Supplies Corporation (DSC) negotiate contracts to buy the industry's output for at least three years. Nineteen days later Pearl Harbor reinforced the urgency of the need. On December 9 Patterson recommended an increase in production to 150,000 barrels a day by July 1943. Meanwhile, more 100 octane was needed at once. Jersey Standard and some other refiners had a few tricks that allowed them to increase output immediately at greater cost, but economy was no longer a primary concern. One obvious move was to raise the specification for tetraethyl lead to 4 cc, although the increased amount of 100 octane came at the expense of other needed products and the military worried that the increase might result in increased engine maintenance from lead deposits. As the aviation program expanded, the supply of tetraethyl lead became a problem. The compound had only one use, and only the Ethyl company made it. To increase the supply, more of it was withdrawn from civilian gasoline.[28]

The larger oil companies moved ahead with plant expansion before contracts with the government had been arranged so as not to lose time, even though they believed the new facilities would be useless once the emergency ended. While other firms haggled over terms, Jersey Standard did not ask for a three-year commitment from the government. Instead it signed a one-year contract and relied on the government to treat it fairly in later years. New facilities, ranging from those already under construction to those still in the initial development stage, were estimated to add more than 123,000 barrels a day to the mix. By January the official figure had been raised to 150,000 barrels, then 180,000 barrels a month later. Jersey and its affiliates began 1942 with a production capacity of 13,000 barrels a day; by the year's end its output reached 42,790 barrels a day, or more than the entire nation's capacity in 1941.[29]

To hike output quickly, the industry borrowed a page from the aircraft manufacturers. Components were shared by moving them to the refinery best suited to maximize their use for production of 100 octane and nothing else. If one company's blending agents would produce more 100 octane with another firm's base stock than with its own, it was sent there. This sharing cost money, violated contracts, and reduced the output of other petroleum products, but it produced more 100 octane. The Justice Department signed off on the practice as it did on other joint arrangements on patents, processes, and licensing. Jersey Standard opened its fluid cat-cracking process to other companies and invited them to send technicians to study the method in operation. Hardly anyone had expected so much cooperation among companies accustomed to fighting each other. As Ickes noted wryly, the early meetings "were not love feasts," but gradually the cooperative spirit took hold, especially after Pearl Harbor.[30]

Still the pressure mounted. In March WPB bumped the daily capacity goal to 200,000 barrels. Davies assured an anxious Patterson that "everything else will have to be regarded as decidedly secondary and adjustments, regardless of severity, must be made to accomplish the military purpose . . . Whatever is necessary to keep the production of these critical products at maximum will be done, even though this mean [sic] as an extremity that products normally marketed be considered as waste if there is no possible way of storing them." The search for new components to improve fuel performance turned up a benzene derivative called cumene, which proved extremely potent in enhancing rich mixture. By July an Ickes assistant could report that "5 months ago cumene was a laboratory curiosity, whereas it is today being produced in commercial quantities." Its use allowed refiners to include larger quantities of base stock and thereby increase the capacity of some producing units.[31]

By September 1942 sixteen refineries were producing 100 octane, and the number was expected to double within a year. Nearly all existing refinery equipment had been converted to producing only catalytic-cracked base stock, cumene, and codimer, another superior blending agent. Production still lagged behind requirements by 25,000 barrels a day. Inability to get needed materials slowed construction of new facilities, and the rubber program was draining away feed stock. It was this situation that sparked the clash between Jeffers and Patterson. "If the matter is permitted to stand as it is today," a PAW official warned Eberstadt, "it will be necessary for those in authority to definitely say that the completion of the synthetic rubber plants is of greater importance than is the production of aviation gasoline." A week later Davies asked Eberstadt for priority ratings, arguing that "because our petroleum refinery construction program needed for the production of 100 octane gasoline, toluene, and aviation lubricating oil has bogged down almost completely, it is apparent that something of a drastic nature will have to be done if we are to supply the end products in the quantity in which they are required."[32]

Ickes added to the pressure by asking WPB to authorize production of an additional 100,000 barrels a day of 100 octane, but Nelson hesitated until the conflict with the rubber program could be resolved. Concentration on 100-octane production also cut into the output of other needs such as 91-octane gasoline. The marginal base stock used for 100 octane was 91 octane; the use of cumene boosted more of it to 100 octane. The result amounted to 19,500 barrels a day less 91-octane gasoline than would normally be the case. Degrading one barrel of 100 octane could produce five barrels of 91 octane, but PAW looked for other ways to increase the supply of 91 octane. Through much of 1943 delays in obtaining construction materials and turnover of labor on construction crews continued to slow completion of new facilities even as expanded military operations increased the demand for 100 octane. During the spring the shortfall ran between 1.5 million and 2 million barrels, forcing a cut in allocations to the military and Allied nations. An even heavier demand for blending stocks was expected during the second half of the year. The game of catch-up continued with no end in sight.[33]

FOR ALL THE emphasis on the refineries, everything depended on transportation—getting crude to the plants and finished products to the sites where they were needed. The peacetime industry already had an odd pattern. The East Coast contained nearly half the nation's population, 40 percent of its motor vehicles, and a third of all oil burners. It consumed more than 40 percent of the nation's petroleum goods, nearly all of it brought there by tankers. For many years the United States had been an exporter of oil except for residual fuel oil, which it imported from the Caribbean. The Pacific Coast and Rocky Mountain states, which consumed about 18 percent of the nation's petroleum products, had enough crude and refinery capacity to be self-supporting. The Midwest had enough refining capacity but not enough crude oil, and its supply was declining. The East had some refineries and only minimal crude supply, making it dependent on the enormous Southwest and Gulf Coast complex of oil fields and refineries for about half of its refined product and most of its crude. Another supply of crude came from foreign sources.[34]

This system depended entirely on the smooth functioning of transportation, especially the tanker fleet. Submarine attacks utterly disrupted this arrangement. Their toll was appalling. One Jersey Standard tanker suffered two torpedo hits on January 18, 1942, broke in two, and sank within ten minutes. As blazing oil from shattered cargo tanks swept over the decks, only one lifeboat with eight men managed to get into the water. Several others who jumped or were thrown overboard by the explosion managed to survive by clinging to boards. One was picked up by the lifeboat; four others survived seven hours until an American destroyer found them, as well as the lifeboat. Another twenty-two men died in the attack. All year long bodies, body parts, charred lifeboats, dead fish and waterfowl, and oil-slicked debris washed ashore along the East Coast as the submarines hunted down tankers. Another Jersey tanker, bound in winter for Fall River, Massachusetts, with a cargo of fuel oil, lost forty-eight of fifty men when sunk.[35]

The submarine attacks forced a radical reorganization of transportation until the sea lanes could be protected. The two available overland sources were railroad tank cars and pipelines. The latter would take time to expand, while the rail tank car fleet was old and largely rusting away in storage. To a limited extent barges could also be used, but steel, plants, and labor lacked priorities to build any of them, as Ickes learned to his dismay. Rail cars offered the most immediate relief. Most of them belonged not to railroads or oil companies but to firms that built and leased them. About 125,337 were in service, but Ickes had to combat the myth that some 20,000 of them stood idle. To cope with the looming oil famine on the East Coast, Ickes called executives from eleven major oil companies together and got them to agree to use all their influence to utilize as many tank cars as possible for movement of oil eastward.[36]

The average tank car held 8,000 to 10,000 gallons, or about 215 barrels. Their use was much more costly than tankers. Over the years the oil companies had moved away from rail to tanker deliveries; their facilities were organized to receive oil by sea rather than land. To increase tank car use they had to build new or enlarged loading and unloading racks, new tracks, pumps, storage tanks, and short pipelines to accommodate more rail deliveries. Some like Jersey Standard resorted to using reclaimed pipe, valves, and other scrap from their plants for the work. To increase the fleet, tank cars normally used for other liquids were drafted and other methods found to handle the displaced cargoes. Unit trains of tanker cars were put together and special schedules designed for their movement. In May 1942 ODT shifted the movement of oil from tank cars to tank trucks for any distance under a hundred miles, releasing more cars for longer hauls.[37]

Before Pearl Harbor tank cars moved 70,000 barrels of oil a day; by July 1942 an estimated 70,000 of them hauled an astounding 850,000 barrels a day. Before the war a fleet of 1,400 barges carried petroleum, about 950 of them on the Gulf Coast and Mississippi River and another 300 on the Atlantic Coast. Only about 100 large oceangoing barges with a capacity of about 15,000 barrels were in service, along with 1,300 inland barges that averaged about 5,000 barrels. Their increased service in the Midwest released tank cars for use in eastern deliveries, but most of their work consisted of short hauls and did little to relieve the critical need for longer hauls. Tank trucks, operating on a 24/7 schedule, also did much of the short-haul work.[38]

The most promising solution lay in pipelines. Two new units had already gone into service—the one from Portland, Maine, to Montreal in November 1941 and the controversial, long-delayed Plantation pipeline from Baton Rouge to Greensboro, North Carolina—but the most ambitious project still dangled in limbo. For two years Ickes had pleaded in vain for enough steel to build a major pipeline from the Southwest to the East. A consortium of eight oil companies led by Jersey Standard had proposed the project in the spring of 1941 only to be turned down for the materials needed. The Cole Bill, signed by the president that July, authorized him to designate any proposed pipeline as necessary to national defense and confer on it the right of eminent domain, yet the project made no headway. Three times Ickes pushed the project only to be rejected even though the advantages were obvious. A pipeline would send crude flowing northward 24/7 in all kinds of weather with little manpower and could not be touched by submarines.[39]

Ickes kept pounding away at WPB until his arguments gained traction after Pearl Harbor. In the spring of 1942 he observed trenchantly that more steel had been lost in the tanker sinkings than the pipeline would have consumed and that it would have been ready in a month if it had been accepted earlier. Finally, in June the WPB approved enough steel to build the 550-mile first half of a 24-inch pipeline from Longview, Texas, to Norris City, Illinois. By then Ickes and the oilmen had formulated an even more ambitious program. At a conference in Tulsa, Oklahoma, in March, they agreed on four major projects: construct a 24-inch pipeline from Texas to New York; construct a 20-inch pipeline from East Texas to New York; extend and increase the capacity of the Plantations pipeline; and reverse the flow of Jersey's Tuscarora pipeline. The latter moved finished product westward from Standard Oil's Bayway refinery at Linden, New Jersey, to Negley, Ohio; reversing the flow would enable it to move crude from Ohio to Bayway.[40]

The Tulsa meeting thrashed out a comprehensive pipeline program, most of which gained approval. Nine of ten specific proposals, all of them designed to relieve the East Coast shortage, won immediate acceptance and were started. None drew more attention than the two pipelines from Texas to New York. The 24-inch project would be the largest pipeline in the world, the 20-inch the longest. Workers soon dubbed them "Big Inch" and "Little Inch." Several leading oil companies would operate them, the RFC would finance them, and the DPC would own them. Once under way, the projects encountered no more refusals in getting materials. In October 1942 WPB approved the second half of Big Inch running from Norris City to Phoenixville, Pennsylvania, where feeder lines carried oil to the New York area. Work began in August 1942 and reached New York in October 1943. Little Inch extended from Beaumont, Texas, to Norris City and from there to Phoenixville. Construction got under way in April 1943 and was completed in February 1944.[41]

Nothing like the two massive projects had ever been attempted. Big Inch was designed to move halfway across the continent five times as much oil as had ever been moved before. It had to traverse 1,400 miles across eight states and twenty rivers as well as climb the Allegheny Mountains. The pumping stations had to be more powerful than any used before and required huge electric motors for which power sources had to be found. Harsh weather, delays in getting pumps and other equipment, and other obstacles slowed but did not stall progress. Early in the work the pipe across the Arkansas River was welded and suspended by cables from barges when a flash flood snapped all the lines and the pipeline collapsed. At the Mississippi River in late December another flood broke the lines and dropped the pipe into the river mud. At the Delaware and Susquehanna rivers crews had to fire tons of explosives into bedrock to dig trenches for the two lines. *Time* called Big Inch "an engineering and construction monument."[42]

Big Inch covered 1,254 miles with another 222 miles of feeder and distribution lines. Little Inch extended 1,475 miles with 239 miles of feeder and distribution lines. Networks of branch lines fed the two pipelines at the Texas end. At its peak Big Inch moved 334,456 barrels of oil daily, while Little Inch carried 239,844 barrels of gasoline. To do its job Big Inch consumed more than 2 million kilowatt-hours of electricity daily compared to 1.89 million kilowatt-hours for Little Inch. The Tuscarora, once reversed, brought another 20,000 barrels of crude daily to Bayway. Together they were expected to relieve the Northeast's oil shortage, but they could do nothing to overcome the shortages plaguing the region well before construction began on either major pipeline. However, in July 1943, three weeks after Big Inch opened, the unit trains of tank cars set a new record by delivering more than a million barrels of oil daily to the East Coast.[43]

By the fall of 1944 the two pipelines, operating at capacity, were earning the DPC nearly $100,000 a day in profits and supplying a fourth of the Northeast's petroleum requirements. Big Inch carried oil at a cost of 38 cents a barrel compared to 61 cents via tanker and $1.60 by railroad tank car. Little Inch moved oil at an impressive 24 cents a barrel versus 40 cents for tankers and $1.74 for tank cars. They were fast paying for themselves, not only in cost of construction but in the money the government saved by not having to subsidize movement by rail and tanker.[44]

Yet it was never enough. Despite heroic efforts, shortages continued to plague both military and civilian use. During the harsh winter of 1942–43 northeasterners endured rationing of both gasoline and fuel oil. Amid subzero weather Ickes ordered tank cars to haul only fuel oil instead of gasoline to the shivering East and cut the ration of fuel oil for nonheating use by 40 percent. By spring eastern reserves hit a record low of 25.5 percent of normal. Prentiss Brown, who had adopted his own version of the honor system against pleasure driving, yielded reluctantly to the pressures and resorted to enforcing a mandatory ban on nonessential driving in twelve eastern states. A major reason for the shortages lay in the expanding war effort and the voracious appetite of planes, ships, tanks, trucks, and other vehicles for fuel. Bombers consumed up to 400 gallons of gasoline an hour, while destroyers on convoy burned up to 3,000 gallons of fuel oil an hour.[45]

As early as the summer of 1942 concern arose over not only the prospects for the coming winter but also the larger issue of America's dwindling oil reserves. For five years the rate of discovery of new oil in the nation had been falling. A Sun Oil geologist estimated that in 1941 only 622,000 barrels of oil were discovered for every wildcat hole drilled compared to nearly 1.7 million barrels in 1937. If Hitler succeeded in grabbing the Iraq-Iran-Caucasian oilfields, the Allies would be totally dependent on the western hemisphere for their petroleum. More drilling was needed, especially by wildcatters, who were responsible for finding three fourths of all known American oil. But, as *Time* quipped, wildcatting was "a bigger speculation than play producing." The costs of drilling had soared, machinery was hard to get, and dry holes were becoming more frequent. New discoveries in 1942 dropped to 317 million barrels, less than a quarter of needed replacements.[46]

Since the fall of 1941 Ickes had warned of shrinking reserves and low replacement rates. During 1943 America's declining reserves above and below ground became hot topics. Frank Knox predicted a major shortage of crude oil within a year at the current rate of consumption. Ickes stressed that the completion of Big Inch would increase the supply for the military but "give no more gasoline for pleasure driving." He promptly fell into a dispute with Brown, who insisted that motorists would get more gas. Hurricane damage to Gulf Coast refineries cut their production by half a million barrels for several weeks. The switchover of refineries to 100-octane production reduced the yield of regular gasoline by another half-million barrels daily. "For a nation with about half of the known crude-oil reserves of the world and two-thirds of the total production," admitted Humble Oil president Harry C. Weiss, "it seems almost incredible to the layman that any shortage [of gasoline] could exist." But it did, and it would get worse. The nation was fast approaching the point, Weiss added, "where it is, or will be, producing crude oil at the maximum efficient rate."[47]

Discussions arose as to whether the government should go partners with Standard Oil of California and the Texas Company in a firm developing the 160-million-acre oil concession in Saudi Arabia that Standard had acquired in 1933 and shared with the Texas Company three years later. As one writer emphasized, the nation "has arrived at a point where it consumes immediately every barrel that comes out of the well, and a little more, and in a general way the wells are giving about all they can." Demand showed only signs of increasing as new weapons came online and American forces seized the initiative on both fronts. Ickes did what he could to push policies that would increase wildcatting as well as conservation. In the meantime little could be done to balance the outflow against supply except follow the admonition of the oil industry: "Oil is ammunition. Use it wisely."[48]

ALONG WITH 100 octane and its many other products, the petroleum industry also made ingredients for the government's other crucial program, rubber. The clash between Patterson and Jeffers showcased the extent to which rubber competed with 100 octane as the most urgent stuff needed for the war effort. That both depended on the same industry for their production underscored the importance of oil in the Victory Program. There was more than a little irony in the fact that the giant corporations Americans loved to hate became the most significant players in the mobilization for war and the war itself. If the big oil companies had not gone to extraordinary lengths in their performance, the war might well have been lost. Of these companies Jersey Standard emerged as the most conspicuous and controversial, not only because of its history but also because of its relationship with IG Farben—a connection that contributed more to the war effort than anyone realized.

Buna-S emerged as the primary synthetic rubber for making tires. It consisted roughly of three parts butadiene and one part styrene. Butadiene was a relatively simple hydrocarbon familiar to most chemistry students, composed of four atoms of carbon and six of hydrogen. The fact that it could be made from either petroleum or alcohol—which itself could be made from petroleum—had the ironic twist of injecting a political dimension into the problem of how best to produce a lot of it in the shortest possible time.[49]

Shortly after his rubber report was issued in September 1942, Baruch told Frank Howard, who had not been involved in the research or testimony, that the rubber program was industry's job, not the government's, and that he should raise hell with anybody in Washington who wasn't moving fast enough on it. He also thought that butadiene production would likely be the bottleneck of the whole program and that it was up to Jersey Standard and an affiliate of Union Carbide to get their new plants up and running on schedule with their new processes. They were the linchpins on which everything else depended. "I know you can do it," Baruch added, "and if you don't, I'll take your hides off." Not until the following May did Howard feel confident that his hide was secure.[50]

Getting industry-wide agreement on butadiene production became an ordeal in itself. It could be made by several different processes involving many different industries and so lacked a common production denominator. The RRC, having labored long and hard to get a cross-licensing and information exchange agreement on synthetic rubber in December 1941, brought together the four companies of the Standard Oil group along with fifteen other oil, rubber, chemical, and engineering firms to do the same on butadiene. The chemical and rubber companies had always depended on secret data and special techniques to maintain their competitive positions and didn't care to share anything with anybody else, least of all their rivals. But everyone involved needed as much pertinent information as possible in pursuing their programs. A makeshift solution was worked out whereby the oil companies alone would exchange information fully and directly via a special subcommittee while the other parties made their exchanges only through the RRC. The final agreement was signed on February 5, 1942. A separate agreement on the manufacture of styrene, the other ingredient in making Buna-S, followed a month later.[51]

The goal given the oil industry was expanded from its original 40,000 tons to 400,000 tons in January 1942 and then, after the fall of Singapore in February, to 805,000 tons of Buna-type rubber with butadiene as its main raw material. The butadiene could be made in several ways, but two stood out as the most feasible: convert butane into butylene and the latter into butadiene, or start with butylene—a by-product of the refining process—and go directly to butadiene. Everyone agreed that there was more than enough butane to make all the butadiene needed, but the two-step process required was obviously longer and more cumbersome than starting with butylene. The question was whether enough butylene could be obtained as a by-product without cutting into the production of 100 octane, which also required it. Jersey Standard had studied the issue for two years and concluded that its refineries had enough butylene to make both products. Shell came to the same conclusion, but the rest of the oil industry disagreed and based their plans on butane even though it meant expensive plants and serious operating difficulties.[52]

A technical discovery by Jersey Standard resolved this impasse. The fluid cat-cracking process had already become critical to the production of 100 octane. At first Jersey Standard's technicians thought that maximum efficiency depended on running it at low temperatures. Early in 1942 they learned how to operate it at very high temperatures, which produced even more and better aviation gasoline base stock and also multiplied the yield of butylene. Once apprised of this major innovation, all the other oil companies in the program except one dropped their plans for butane production and adopted the Jersey Standard process. However, it would take months for the oil companies to expand their facilities and build new ones. The first two plants with a combined butadiene capacity of 165,000 tons annually were not scheduled to come online until March 1943. Until then the industry's best option was to convert idle or makeshift machinery for the job. Fortunately there existed a large amount of older thermal cracking equipment that had been displaced by the catalytic process and could be adapted for temporary production.[53]

The use of grain alcohol to produce butadiene had its own complications. American grain elevators bulged with 810 million bushels of stored wheat, the price of which was maintained at $1.20 by the government. As a result, most industrial alcohol was made by fermenting molasses instead of grain because it was cheaper. In particular it used blackstrap molasses, an otherwise worthless residue from the refining of cane sugar that could be obtained cheaply from Cuba. The outbreak of war accelerated the demand for industrial alcohol for the production of explosives, but the shipping shortage and the submarine coastal raids after American entry into the war slashed the importation of molasses from Cuba. Some major oil companies also produced industrial alcohol as a by-product. In May Jersey Standard offered to the Department of Agriculture free of charge any of its processes and technical assistance that might be useful in the production of butadiene from grain alcohol. The company worked with the Gillette Committee in trying to sort out the most efficient means of getting as much butadiene as fast as possible. For that to happen, all sources had to be developed.[54]

During 1942 the alcohol situation reversed itself from a deficit caused by the loss of Cuban molasses to a surplus triggered by the major liquor distillers, who offered to convert their plants to the manufacture of industrial alcohol. After much delay and a congressional hearing the offer was accepted, and the government went even further by enlisting the straight whiskey or so-called high wine distillers as well. The production of blended whiskey and gin ceased—a large reserve already existed—and was replaced by an outpouring of industrial alcohol that promised to double or even triple its output by 1943. The cost was higher than alcohol made from blackstrap molasses, but cost became less of a relevant factor in the emergency. A more difficult problem involved the familiar one of allocating raw materials between plants using alcohol and the refineries using petroleum.[55]

The furor over oil versus grain as a source of alcohol reached its peak during the summer of 1942 with the Gillette bill and Roosevelt's veto of it, which led to his appointing the Baruch Committee. Between March and June the RRC contracted for 646,000 tons of butadiene, 526,200 tons of it from petroleum, 80,000 tons from alcohol, and the remaining 40,000 tons from benzene. However, all the alcohol-based butadiene was to be made by a Union Carbide affiliate that used synthetic alcohol made from petroleum. The farm bloc protested that grain alcohol could make butadiene faster and more cheaply with simpler facilities. The RRC promptly shifted 140,000 tons from petroleum to alcohol base, but the controversy continued. In their report the

Baruch Committee took no stand on the issue. When Bill Jeffers was appointed rubber director in September, his marching orders were simple and direct: take the muddled synthetic rubber program with all its controversies and bull it through.[56]

But Jeffers was appreciative of the work Jersey Standard had done. "Had it not been for the research and engineering development work carried on by Standard Oil of New Jersey prior to Pearl Harbor," he told a reporter, "the synthetic rubber program would be one and a half to two years behind what it is now."[57]

BY WASHINGTON STANDARDS Bill Jeffers was a monk. He harbored no political ambitions, took no part in its social life, curried no favors, and showed no interest in anything except doing the job he had been summoned to do. In taking the post he told Roosevelt he would stay for one year; he expected to get the job done in that time and go back home to the railroad he loved. During that time he utterly ignored the Washington way of doing things and emerged as something of a folk hero in the process. "Here at last," declared the *New York Herald Tribune,* "is a man in high position who says in blunt words what every American has longed to hear said by those in charge of our war program in Washington."[58]

Doc Churchill, his long-suffering secretary, knew painfully well his boss's monastic regimen. Instead of cells they shared a pleasant suite at the Mayflower Hotel, but it might as well have been a monastery. During their entire stay they ate nearly every breakfast and dinner in the suite. Only twice did they venture out, once to a performance of *Blossom Time* and once to see a Washington Senators baseball game. Jeffers enjoyed the game, especially when an Irish catcher got into a fight at home plate, but he never went to another one. Their evening regimen seldom varied. Depending on Jeffers's mood, they would read, talk, or work until seven o'clock, listen to the radio news of Fulton Lewis Jr., and then order dinner from room service. At eight o'clock the radio came back on to catch H. V. Kaltenborn, then off again at 8:15 for another round of reading, talking, or work. Around nine o'clock Jeffers would glance at his watch and say, "Let's go for a walk, Doc."

Every night they followed the same route, turning left outside the hotel door and tracing a large circle around several blocks, always getting back by around 9:30. On their way through the lobby Churchill would grab the morning papers, and they would read, talk, or work until Jeffers turned in around midnight. "Anything special for breakfast?" Churchill would ask. "No, you order it," came the unvarying reply. Next morning the routine would begin again. Breakfast arrived at 7:30, after which a Union Pacific man drove them to the office for another day's work. Except for an occasional trip on WPB or railroad business, Jeffers stuck to this Spartan routine during his entire stay in Washington.

William Martin Jeffers had railroading in his blood. Born in a tough, Dutch-Irish section of North Platte, Nebraska, the son of a Union Pacific shopman who married the daughter of a Union Pacific shopman, he never worked for any other railroad. He started early as a janitor and then call boy, having left school at fourteen after getting into a fistfight with a teacher. "I can't remember when I was a boy," he said later. "It seems I've always been a man, a working man." He learned telegraphy, became an operator and then a dispatcher, and proudly carried his telegrapher's union card throughout his career. After winning promotion to chief dispatcher in 1900, he celebrated by marrying the daughter of a company blacksmith and taking her on a honeymoon. It was the only vacation he allowed himself in forty years.

His dedication and toughness pushed him steadily up the railroad's ladder through the ranks of trainmaster, assistant superintendent, division superintendent, and general superintendent. Shortly after taking charge of the Wyoming division, the toughest on the railroad to run, he asked a conductor at Rawlins where he was going. "You may not believe it," came the insolent reply, "but I'm going to leave here on a train."

"That's what you think," said Jeffers, who proceeded to knock him out cold on the station floor. In October 1937 he realized his lifelong dream of becoming the railroad's president. "I'd rather be president of the Union Pacific than president of the United States," he once said. In that role he ruled as a czar long before receiving that title in Washington. "He was rough and tough," said Churchill, "and I think he absolutely ruled by intimidation." Although Jeffers liked to boast of his popularity among the men, one old-timer offered a succinct dissent. "No, he wasn't liked," he said. "Feared. Very much." He ruled by terror, firing men as freely as actual czars imprisoned or tortured them, the difference being that Jeffers usually took his victims back into the fold. Officers summoned by him never knew whether they were about to be promoted or fired. "Jeffers would not accept failure, period," said a shop veteran. "Somebody paid with his scalp."

At sixty-six he resembled an Irish ward politician more than a railroader. He carried a still-solid 220 pounds on his five-foot eleven-inch frame. His round, balding head housed a ruddy, clean-shaven face with steely eyes beneath thick brows. Its expression shifted easily from a genial smile to a bone-chilling scowl. A high-pitched voice alone marred the image he cherished as a gruff, two-fisted railroader. In part he fit the stereotype of the "Irisher." He loved Irish music and grew maudlin over anything to do with mothers, but he rarely drank and had a prim, puritanical streak more befitting a Calvinist than an Irish Catholic. He had no hobbies or outside interests; work was his life, and for the first time that work was something other than the Union Pacific Railroad.

"Big Bill Jeffers tackled the chaotic Rubber Scandal this week in the hell-bent, direct-action way he has run the Union Pacific Railroad," wrote an approving *Time* reporter after his appointment. "What we need is action and we need it quickly," Jeffers said. "And we are going to get just that . . . I have all the authority I need. I am perfectly willing to assume all the responsibility to see that this work is done." True to his word and his reputation, he took on all comers. "His conception of his job was so simple and direct," wrote Frank Howard, "that no amount of bureaucratic complication or opposition had any effect on him." Jeffers simply took the Baruch report as gospel and assailed any deviation from its recommendations. Less than a month into the job the Senate Agriculture Committee, dominated by cotton-state solons, summoned him to explain why he planned to expand rayon production to get enough fabric for military tires instead of using cotton, which army tests showed had a tendency to overheat.[59]

Why not delay the program until more experiments could be made with cotton, asked a scowling Cotton Ed Smith of South Carolina, seconded by Kenneth McKellar of Tennessee. Jeffers brushed the request aside. "We have gambled too damn long already on the rubber situation," barked Jeffers. ". . . The trouble with this whole situation is that it has been a muddle of men who were afraid that some Congressional committee or pressure group wouldn't like their decisions. I am going to make my decisions and I'll stand by them." During the winter of 1942–43 he took on the War Department with gusto and crossed swords with the equally hard-nosed Patterson. Their clash took place at a time when the air war had intensified, submarines still ravaged shipping, and the need for more 100 octane was soaring. Patterson acknowledged the importance of the rubber program but stressed the need for more high-grade aviation fuel. "I know that the men flying these planes must be furnished with the best gas available," Jeffers told the Truman Committee, "but at the same time I am still convinced that the most important thing in America today is the rubber program."[60]

Jeffers also antagonized Patterson by his insistence that civilians needed tires as badly as the military. "A man who works in a grocery store," he said to the Truman Committee, "is just as important in the war effort as a man who works in a war factory." This attitude infuriated Patterson, who saw any allocation to civilians as unnecessary. "Which will do most to win the war," he chided, "continue to deplete our rubber resources in unessential automobile travel, or produce the 100-octane gasoline that will be needed for Army and Navy combat planes?" After Nelson's attempt at a compromise failed, Jimmy

Byrnes settled the immediate dispute, but the struggle continued afterward, inflamed by Jeffers's off-hand reference to army loafers that the press seized on as one more example of the disunity in Washington bureaus. Misunderstandings multiplied by the papers muddied the dispute between them, leading Jeffers at one point to tell reporters, "If other officials would copy my methods" instead of "sitting around desks and issuing orders and grousing," they would get more done.[61]

The press whooped with delight at the fireworks, and at the fact that Jeffers seemed immune to what *Time* called "Going Washington," a disease peculiar to czars who caught Potomac fever and clung desperately to the spotlight. "Operating day & night on a devil-take-the-hindmost policy," chortled the magazine, "'Bull Bill' Jeffers has butted his brow through so many walls, bellowed down so many other czars that he finally got a super-duper WPB priority overriding most other priorities." Patterson and Ickes both lambasted Jeffers for what the latter claimed was "a sock in the jaw for the 100-octane program" that had "already cost us 7,000,000 barrels that are gone forever." Jeffers responded by demanding an investigation of their charges. When OWI's Elmer Davis predicted that the nation was overly optimistic about synthetic rubber, Jeffers roared that he didn't know what he was talking about.[62]

That spring the Truman Committee held hearings on the matter and summoned both contestants. On the weekend before they were to testify, Ferdinand Eberstadt, who was friendly to both men, invited Jeffers and Patterson to his home. Jeffers made a rare pilgrimage from his Mayflower suite to hear Eberstadt impress on them their mutual dedication to the work at hand, the importance of their tasks, and the need for them to cooperate rather than fight. Eberstadt's intervention succeeded; in their testimony both men tempered their views with expressions of mutual respect and esteem. Jeffers, said Patterson, "has performed his duty in pressing the synthetic-rubber program vigorously, and I don't resent it." He had done the same for the 100-octane program and asked that Jeffers respect that, which he did. Although Patterson was more convinced than ever that Nelson had to go, his animosity toward Jeffers melted away.[63]

Despite all the furor, the bull got his way. The rubber program moved forward at an impressive pace. Early in April the first two plants producing synthetic rubber went into operation, one using oil-based butadiene and the other alcohol-based butadiene. Other plants were about to come online. "The country is not yet out of the critical stage," Jeffers warned, but he celebrated by bouncing a synthetic tire in front of the Senate Agricultural Committee. In getting critical components for his plants, Jeffers mined his railroad network of contacts. On one occasion he called Charlie Hardy of American

Car & Foundry and asked if he could make heat exchangers. "I don't know," answered Hardy. "What are they?"[64]

"I don't know," said Jeffers, "but I'll put a man on a plane today to come up to Boston to explain it to you." A day or two later Hardy called back and said he could make them. That to Jeffers exemplified how to eliminate bottlenecks: "Just tell American industry you need 10,000 heat exchangers, and then get out of their way and they will make them for you." Of course, it was not that simple. To get what he wanted Jeffers fought with everybody, including Nelson. One of the dustups grew so heated that Roosevelt took them aside to mediate, saying in his best "Poppa" voice, "Well, you fellows are just going to have to get together." Jeffers glared at him and said, "Well, we're not going to get together on the basis of anything I heard here today." And walked out.[65]

By the end of May Jeffers could report that "while the Rubber Program is not yet solved, it is in the best shape it has ever been." Some 30 percent of the entire program was finished, and the rest was expected to be in production by the year's end. Much of the credit for its progress belonged to Bradley Dewey, the head of a Boston chemical firm who served as Jeffers's assistant. Most of the early plants coming online used alcohol as a base for their butadiene because the distilleries could convert faster than petroleum-based units could be built. Jersey Standard already had one large plant in production and, as others were completed, churned out nearly a third of all the oil-based butadiene used in the war. Of the 204,130 tons of Buna-S produced in 1943, however, 83 percent came from alcohol-based butadiene. Unlike the 100-octane program, synthetic rubber output eventually caught up with demand; by July 1944 more butadiene was being produced than the rubber-fabricating factories could consume.[66]

Altogether the government spent $700 million to build fifty-one synthetic rubber plants. Overall production soared from 22,434 tons in 1942 to 231,722 tons in 1943 and 753,111 tons in 1944. Later the program would be hailed as one more "miracle of production," but it was far from that. Robert A. Solo, who had worked in OPM and elsewhere during the war, wrote after the war that "stripped of its mythology, the planning of the synthetic rubber industry was a scandalous, a complete, a nearly catastrophic foul up." The Baruch report finally brought some order to the chaos it had been, and Jeffers did his part in belatedly hammering it into existence against all obstacles. True to his word, satisfied that his work was done, Jeffers turned his post over to Bradley Dewey and went back to Omaha to reacquaint the railroad with his special brand of intimidation.[67]

Before leaving Washington, Jeffers made his peace with Patterson and Jim Forrestal. To both men he sent a copy of what he called a "touching" poem penned by a woman furious at not being able to get rubber for her girdles and garters. Surely, he joked, this was clear evidence that he had not coddled ci-vilians. He lauded Patterson for being open-minded and thanked him for his help with the rubber program. "You are a great fellow," he added, "and I like you!" Patterson responded in kind. "If we had a dozen Jeffers," he wrote, "we would beat the Union Pacific for speed. You have done a grand job."[68]

CHAPTER 23

WEAPONS OF MASS PRODUCTION

Here was the beginning of perhaps the most important industrial innovation in the whole war, the use of average skills and mentalities, without previous experience, in super-accurate jobs by segregation on a single operation and then high-pressure training in it . . . A new principle was demonstrated: let a single highly organized machine replace human skill at tens or hundreds of times the human operating speed; end up with a highly accurate and uniform product turned out by the hundreds of thousands.
—DAVID O. WOODBURY[1]

The Germans always—save for a brief period in North Africa when the enemy sent the first of their Tigers to Russia—have been ahead of us on the battlefield. And it is battlefield service that counts . . . In anti-tank guns, mines and mining technique, and self-propelled guns, the Germans have been consistently ahead of us on the battlefield. The Germans beat us to the battlefield with rockets. They were the first to use robot bombs, giant rockets, and jet-propelled planes.
—NEWSWEEK[2]

In the inescapable trade-off between quality and quantity, the Germans characteristically chose the former, the Americans the latter . . . If Germany aimed at the perfection of many things, America aspired to the commodification of virtually everything.
—DAVID M. KENNEDY[3]

MASS PRODUCTION WAS THE ULTIMATE weapon in the American arsenal. The American way of war was of necessity shaped by the American way of production. The goal was to smother the enemy in weaponry; the method was to devise an organization, a system, and a plant layout that would produce as much as possible as fast as possible. A month after Pearl Harbor Roosevelt said as much in his State of the Union address. "The superiority of the United Nations in munitions and ships must be overwhelming," he stressed, "so overwhelming that the Axis Nations can never hope to catch up with it." The finished product did not have to be perfect—the cost of perfection in both time and money was too high—it just had to be somewhere between good and really good. As historian Alan S. Milward observed, everyone understood that "the gain in output was far greater than 10 percent if an armament was produced to only 90 percent rather than to 100 percent, of the specifications . . . It was open to the United States to sacrifice some quality in production for quantity, but Germany could not compete in quantity production and opted to produce armaments nearer to perfect specifications in the hope that this might give some tactical advantage."[4]

The emphasis on machines over men had many advantages. "Expending motors and metal," wrote David Kennedy, "rather than flesh and blood was the least-cost pathway that the Americans could take toward victory." It was also the pathway most familiar to them. Production could not only win the war but also lead them out of the morass of the depression and position the nation as an economic powerhouse after the war. The Germans excelled at advanced technologies, research, and high-precision weaponry that performed flawlessly, but they were slow to standardize and maximize production. At one point their factories were turning out 425 different kinds of airplanes, 151 types of trucks, and 150 different motorcycles. For all their breathtaking scientific and industrial achievements, they were at heart craftsmen.[5]

"With such a variety," wrote Richard Overy, "it was difficult to produce in mass." Within the German system the military dictated what weapons would be produced. Hitler himself remarked in 1942 how industrialists "were always complaining about this niggardly procedure—today an order for ten howitzers, tomorrow for two mortars and so on." The military had only contempt for American mass-production methods that, in Hermann Goering's sneer, produced only razor blades. Overy concluded that "as long as the military tail wagged the industrial dog, German war production remained inflexible, unrationalised and excessively bureaucratic."[6]

Albert Speer, the armaments minister who oversaw Germany's brand of converting piecemeal armament output to industrial mass production, understood the problem well. But he could only go so far. "The longer I fought the typically German bureaucracy, whose tendencies were aggravated by the authoritarian system," he admitted, "the more my criticism assumed a political cast." Nevertheless, in a memorandum to Hitler he described the war as a "contest between two systems of organization." The Americans "knew how to act with organizationally simple methods and therefore achieved greater results, whereas we were hampered by superannuated forms of organization and therefore could not match the others' feats . . . If we did not arrive at a different system of organization . . . it would be evident to posterity that our outmoded, tradition-bound, and arthritic organizational system had lost the struggle."[7]

The Germans introduced the world to blitzkrieg warfare but never fully mechanized their ground forces. For all their sophisticated weaponry, horses remained a staple of their transportation, increasingly so as the war took its toll. By one estimate 75 percent of their field artillery still relied on horses. Once determined to do so, no nation was better prepared to mechanize its ground forces than the United States. It was, after all, a nation of cars and drivers, having introduced mass production to the world in the very industry that put the country on wheels. In 1937 there existed 200 automobiles for every 1,000 Americans compared to only sixteen for every German and less than one for every Japanese. The heartland of America boasted the largest industry on the planet, one dedicated to putting the American people on the road. No one was better suited to converting production to the goods needed for mechanized warfare.[8]

During 1943 the leviathan that was American industry was at last roused from its slumber and pushed toward maximum output. Old and new weapons poured forth from old and new factories in unprecedented quantities. One estimate measured American output per worker-hour as double that of Germany and five times that of Japan, and the United States had many more workers. By year's end the United States boasted an arsenal that gave it three times the munitions of the Axis. Roosevelt's call for overwhelming superiority in arms had been realized. During that decisive year the tide of production turned the tide of battle. Amid the pride over the sheer quantity of goods rolling off the assembly lines, however, some nagging questions remained. Was the right stuff being made? Was it good enough to compete with the known superiority of many German weapons? Were the weapons suitable for two theaters of war—Europe and the Pacific—that could not have been more different from each other?[9]

AFTER SO MUCH had gone wrong for so long, it was a refreshing turn of events when some things began at last to go right. First and foremost, news from the fronts grew more encouraging as the Allies shifted gradually to the offensive. After nearly six months of bitter, bloody fighting, the Russians finally won a decisive victory at Stalingrad. In North Africa American troops got their first taste of offensive combat after landing there in November 1942. By May the Allied forces had pushed the Germans out of North Africa; they invaded Sicily two months later and took control of the island in August. By then a coup had overthrown Mussolini, and the Allies prepared to invade Italy. In the Pacific a brutal six-month struggle for Guadalcanal finally ended victoriously in February, and American marines began their long and costly offensive against the seemingly endless chain of Japanese island strongholds. Even the North Atlantic brought good news as fresh "hunter-kill" tactics inflicted heavy losses on the German submarine fleet, opening vital sea lanes to more traffic.

During the first twenty days of March 1943 U-boats sank ninety-seven Allied merchant ships with tonnage totaling more than 500,000. This was twice the rate of new ships being built; the Germans lost only seven submarines, half the number of new boats coming out of shipyards. Then the tide began to turn as the Allies relied increasingly on a long-range version of the B-24 Liberator, escort destroyers, and escort or baby carriers to protect the sea lanes. In May the Germans lost forty-one U-boats while sinking only fifty merchant ships, a devastating turnabout. By July the launching of new ships from American shipyards finally exceeded the tonnage lost since 1939.[10]

The tide of battle had turned, and so had the tide of production, although it did not seem so at first. Despite all the intramural turmoil during the winter of 1942–43, real progress was made in production scheduling and the allocation of materials. PEC eased one major bottleneck by devising a new approach to the production and allocation of thirty-four common components that ultimately tabulated, verified, and tracked them much as the three key materials were under CMP. By winter the component crisis had replaced the materials shortage as the major threat to production gains. More than 5,000 manufacturers made critical components, but no one coordinated the scheduling and allocation of their output. Instruments rolled off the assembly lines only to stack up in warehouses because the claimant did not need them at once while other claimants screamed for them. In one typical case 200 instruments went to a plant that was not scheduled to open for several months.[11]

"Examples of plants being held up for lack of components ran into the hundreds and were almost routine," admitted a WPB engineer. WPB attacked the problem by freezing orders so they could be scheduled according to when and where they were actually needed. At one plant output increased by 20 percent simply by eliminating the interruptions of production when an order in progress was set aside to produce one with a more urgent priority. More subcontractors were recruited, and Charlie Wilson brought in an associate from GE, Ralph Cordiner, to take charge of component scheduling. After surveying manufacturers for statements of unfilled orders, capacity, and material needs, Wilson and Cordiner issued General Scheduling Order M-293 imposing controls on eighty-six products and classifying critical items into three groups based on relative scarcity. Although this ambitious and complex scheme helped, it did not solve the larger problem.[12]

Fred Lucker, a veteran production man at Ingersoll-Rand, who had been scheduling compressors since May 1942, despaired over the crisis facing him. His desk overflowed with demands of a million horsepower for the coming year; the industry's capacity was only 600,000 horsepower. When he started looking more closely at the orders, however, "the smoke blew away." One plant, for example, ordered 45,000 horsepower for October 1942 delivery even though it was not due to open until late 1943. Lucker began insisting on true needed dates and remained flexible in his allocations. When the Boston Navy Yard needed a compressor in three weeks to put a damaged ship back into service, Lucker diverted one from a new steel foundry that was running behind its intended completion date. "In general," said Lucker, "we find that 10 per cent of an industry represents 90 per cent of our problems."[13]

Expanded capacity helped ease the crunch, and so did subcontracting, even though it increased costs. Industrial pump output soared six times above normal in 1942 yet still ran behind demand. Fisher Governor of Marshalltown, Iowa, which made control valves, thought it could go no further in subcontracting until it sent two men to scout neighboring rural areas for machine shops. In short order its subcontracted machine-tool hours jumped from 200 per week to 3,000. For the control-valve industry as a whole, the hours per week rose from 6,400 in February 1943 to 10,500 in March. "We are confident," said Cordiner, "we can lick all but a half-dozen of the eighty-six critical components by July."[14]

THE WEAPONS POURED forth in incredible quantities. During the first year after Pearl Harbor American plants built 47,826 planes; in 1943 they produced 85,898. Those rolling off the assembly lines at the end, especially the flood of bombers, were much larger than their predecessors at the start of the war, averaging 11,000 pounds compared to 4,000 pounds. The number of major ships jumped from 1,854 in 1942 to 2,654 in 1943 and tanks from 24,997 to 29,497.[15]

After hitting its stride in 1943, the industrial leviathan buried the Axis powers in output. Between 1939 and August 1945 American manufacturers produced a total of 303,713 military aircraft compared to 111,787 for Germany, 131,549 for Great Britain, and 76,320 for Japan. These figures included 99,950

American fighters as opposed to 55,727 for Germany and 30,447 for Japan; 97,810 American bombers compared to 15,117 for Japan and 12,539 attack aircraft for Germany; and 23,929 American transports, dwarfing Germany's 3,079 and Japan's 2,110. In training aircraft the United States had an overwhelming edge of 57,623 to Germany's 11,546 and Japan's 15,201. Between 1940 and 1945 the military accepted 802,161 aircraft engines from American manufacturers.[16]

For ground warfare, American factories produced 88,410 tanks, Germany only 46,857, and Japan a meager 2,515. Of artillery, including antitank and antiaircraft weapons, the United States turned out 257,390 to 159,147 for Germany and 13,350 for Japan. American machine guns totaled nearly 2.68 million as against 674,280 for Germany and 380,000 for Japan. Some 2.38 million military trucks rolled off American assembly lines compared to 345,914 for Germany and 165,945 for Japan. The United States also manufactured 6.5 million rifles and 40 billion bullets.[17]

For its navy the United States produced 10 battleships, 18 large aircraft carriers, 9 small carriers, 110 escort carriers, 2 large cruisers, 10 heavy cruisers, 33 light cruisers, 358 destroyers, 504 destroyer escorts, and 82,028 land craft of various types. Japan could counter with only 16 carriers, 2 battleships, 9 cruisers, and 63 destroyers. Germany manufactured no carriers or cruisers, 2 battleships, 17 destroyers, and 23 convoy escorts. Only in the output of submarines did Germany excel, turning out 1,337 compared to 211 for the United States and 167 for Japan. As for merchant vessels, including the ubiquitous Liberty ship, American shipyards put 5,777 of them into the water. This crushing superiority ensured ultimate American control of the seas as well as the air.[18]

Planes, ships, and tanks got the most public attention, but other munitions were no less impressive: jeeps, armored cars, rifles, machine guns, artillery, antiaircraft guns, bazookas, rockets, torpedoes, ammunition of all kinds, bombs, radios, electronic equipment, searchlights, plastic fuses, and thousands of other items. New devices for the battlefield were invented as the need arose. The demand for emergency repair tools led to the creation by General Electric of the welder-jeep, which had a generator and electric arc-welder installed in the passenger seat with a belt connected to the jeep's engine. In the field it went into operation as soon as the jeep stopped and could cross terrain that stymied larger, heavier repair units. GE also developed a special fire-resistant plastic for rocket launchers that attached under the wings of a plane. Tanks were also fitted with special racks that fired sixty rockets, then detached themselves so that the tank could use its regular gun.[19]

Ships poured forth in such quantity that by the end of 1943 the nation had replaced all its maritime losses and seized first place among the merchant fleets of the world. Seven freighters were sliding into the water every twenty-four hours, yet so routine had the output become that the media hardly noticed it. In eighteen months more new tonnage had been built than during the five years of the last war. If, as expected, another 15 million to 20 million tons floated into action during 1944, the United States, having started the war with a fleet half the size of Great Britain's, would possess one two to three times larger. In July 1944 Kaiser's Richmond Yard No. 2 completed its 1,147th and last Liberty ship, leaving only a scattered handful in eastern yards to be finished. By then the navy's fleet was larger than the combined fleets of all the world five years earlier.[20]

Quantity mattered in the American way of production. Early in the defense mobilization effort Patterson discovered that it was difficult to get the production rates he wanted from manufacturers for any complex item such as trucks unless he projected the order on a massive scale with plenty of lead time for them to organize the needed resources. Once the United States entered the war and weapons took priority, conversion caused delays but ultimately shortened the lead time and increased output. It was in fact the rapid expansion of facilities that caused many of the shortages in materials. The weapons produced at first were often inferior and sometimes already obsolete, but they were birds in hand that had to suffice until something better could replace them. The challenge of so far-flung a war with such rapidly changing demands also bedeviled production. Not only did hundreds, sometimes thousands of design changes get imposed in midmanufacture, but some items were abruptly terminated altogether when improved versions appeared or needs at the fronts changed.[21]

At first many American weapons were an embarrassment. Although General Hugh S. Johnson boasted in 1940 that the United States had "the best guns in the world on paper," they were inferior in almost every category. American tanks were little more than toys compared to the best German models. It took more than five years and a major controversy to replace the World War I Springfield bolt-action rifle with the semiautomatic Garand. The tommy gun and machine gun of that era were also in urgent need of updating. American artillery could not compete with German field guns, and the army utterly lacked the mobility to fight in the age of blitzkrieg. It did have some first-rate aircraft, most notably the B-17 (which by 1941 had already evolved into its fifth, or "E," version) and B-24 bombers, and the P-38 and P-47 fighters, yet as late as October 1941 an authority on military aviation published an article entitled "We Have No Air Power" explaining why American fighters were inferior to their British and German counterparts.[22]

In design even more than quantity, Americans had to play catch-up in weaponry. Despite the inevitable false starts and missteps, they did so in some categories. They created the world's best fighter, the P-51 Mustang, and the first superbomber in the B-29. Their 105 mm and 155 mm artillery pieces were superb, but Americans never developed a good antitank gun and had nothing to equal the German 88, the deadliest antitank gun of the war, which was also mounted on their giant Tiger tanks. M-4 Sherman tanks proved no match for German panzers, let alone Tigers, and a newer model, the Pershing, arrived too late in the war. The Tigers and panzers could penetrate American tank armor at 2,500 yards; the Shermans had to approach within 400 yards to breach enemy armor. When hit, the Sherman was so prone to burst into flames that it received the nicknames "Ronson" and "Tommy cooker." A rule of thumb held that it took five Shermans to kill one panzer.[23]

The Garand rifle outperformed the German Mauser, but German machine guns, especially the MG-42, fired at twice the rate of any American or British versions. To fight tanks the Americans came up with the bazooka, an ingenious rocket tube that was light and portable and required only two men. But it could disable a tank only from the side and proved more effective against field targets. Although one writer called it "the most important ordnance development of the war," the Germans had a greatly superior version called the panzer faust, which they distributed in great numbers and used to devastating effect. As for the American version, one commander rendered this verdict: "Numerous cases have been reported where bazooka teams have succeeded in immobilizing tanks, but since they are unable to destroy them, they themselves have been killed by retaliating fire from the tank."[24]

The American strength in weaponry lay far more in quantity than in quality, and the military determined to exploit that advantage to the fullest. In the case of air power, where it achieved an edge in both categories, the army used it to full effect and ultimately fell too much in love with it. The worst devastation of the war in both theaters came from strategic bombing that rarely achieved any other goal beyond the horror of wholesale slaughter and destruction. In the end the most decisive use of air power proved to be tactical sorties that helped neutralize superior enemy numbers or weaponry, and in this effort quantity provided a decisive superiority. But that was the military's business. For American workers and their bosses, the job was to keep the flow of munitions coming nonstop.

BESIDES ITS INCREASING flow of gasoline, fuel oil, distillates, lubricating oils, and other products, the oil industry contributed another vital material in the form of toluene, the primary ingredient in TNT. After the trial order from the military for 20,000 gallons proved successful in 1940, Humble Oil on its own initiative built a plant near its Baytown refinery in Houston capable of producing 2,000 barrels a day. Under a contract the government owned what was named the Baytown Ordnance Works, and Humble ran it for cost plus a fixed fee. The first tank car of toluene left the works six weeks before Pearl Harbor. Once into the war, Jersey Standard constructed a second plant at Baton Rouge. During 1943 output soared to nearly 66.8 million gallons. So effectively did Baytown increase production that the Baton Rouge plant was converted to making components for aviation gasoline. Altogether American refineries turned out nearly 151.5 million gallons of toluene in 1943 compared to 85.4 million gallons in 1942. Baytown alone produced nearly half of all the toluene made from petroleum. What had been a critical shortage in World War I became an abundant material for the American military's explosives.[25]

Toluene offered one more example of a war material provided by the organizations many Americans, especially New Dealers, loved to hate: the major corporations. Their domination of the production effort was as obvious as it was necessary. The Truman Committee found that the 100 corporations having the largest contracts for war materials owned about 70 percent of the total prime contracts for the period June 1940 to September 1943 compared to their having only 30 percent of prewar civilian business. Put another way, when the defense program began in 1940, about 175,000 companies produced 70 percent of the manufacturing output, with the top 100 firms providing the other 30 percent. By March 1943 this ratio had been reversed. Not surprisingly, the big companies grew even bigger. By December 1944 firms with more than 10,000 workers employed over 30 percent of all manufacturing workers compared to only 13 percent in December 1939. During this same period the share of workers employed by small manufacturing firms with fewer than 100 employees dropped from 26 percent in 1939 to 19 percent in 1944.[26]

It was inevitable that the big corporations would dominate the production process and fanciful for anyone to imagine otherwise. Like it or not, they alone had the resources necessary to tackle immense undertakings as well as a plethora of assignments large and small. Who but Jersey Standard and its peers had the capability to turn out the ocean of petroleum products needed for the war effort? Who but the automobile manufacturers had the capacity and the expertise to mechanize the military, or General Electric and Westinghouse the tens of thousands of electrical products and components required? In terms of sheer dimensions and quantities, this was by far the nation's largest war and one that demanded almost everything on a colossal scale. The marvel is not that the giant corporations played so overarching a role; it is rather that so many smaller companies played as many varied and invaluable roles as they did. Nor should it be overlooked that the big corporations relied heavily on platoons of subcontractors in most of their projects.

General Motors, the giant among giants, poured out of its factories and subsidiaries more than 2,000 different items ranging from ball bearings so small that 3,000 of them would fit in a thimble to 30-ton tanks, airplanes, engines, trucks, guns, and shells at the rate of $10 million worth a day.[27]

When the war began, General Electric had thirty-four plants housing 29 million square feet of floor space. During the war it built eleven major new plants as well as additions to existing facilities. By 1945 it owned a total of sixty-eight plants with 41 million square feet of floor space. Its workforce increased from about 76,000 to approximately 170,000; along the way it also had to replace about 50,000 employees who entered the military and thousands of others lost through death, injuries, retirement, or other causes. Altogether it recruited, trained, and put to work more than 200,000 men and women during the war. Some worked part-time, putting in a shift after their regular duties as lawyers, real estate agents, insurance salesmen, clerks, teachers, even students, and, in at least one case, a minister who took Saturday as his day off so he would be fresh for preaching on Sunday. Their ranks included some GE employees who worked in an office during the day and pulled a shift on the lines in the evening.[28]

Tempting as it was, their training could not be rushed. "You can't train more than so many people at once," said a plant manager, "any more than you can eat a whole week's meals at once." Here too women proved a godsend. One GE manager got the bright idea of hiring unemployed watchmakers to assemble delicate aircraft instruments only to find that they were "the crudest mechanics in existence." If a part didn't fit, they filed it to fit, and they were utterly helpless in dealing with interchangeable parts. Women sailed through tests for finger dexterity and did the work easily. But it took a month or six weeks to train anyone for even a simple repetitive operation, and eight months or more for turbine work requiring ten-thousandths-of-an-inch tolerances. Foremen were especially hard to get and keep in the numbers needed, and they were the heart of production. "Without competent foremen," observed one writer, "greenhorns would stay green, spoilage would soar, quality would slide, and production would evaporate."[29]

The big corporations also owned many of the nation's research laboratories and much of its personnel. At General Electric researchers and engineers were the elite corps. Some 350 scientists and inventors toiled on new products in its laboratories, and a much larger number of engineers learned the art of versatility. In converting its output to war goods, the company had to adapt or redesign nearly every one of its standard motors and take on projects at which they had no experience. In this challenge GE reaped a dividend on its investment in three-year courses that educated engineers to meet all kinds of problems. As demand shifted and new projects arrived, engineers were shifted from one department to another. Radio engineers moved to aircraft instruments and refrigerator engineers to ordnance control.[30]

Along with its own large force GE also utilized more than 2,000 subcontractors that supplied everything from one-ounce taper pins to 40-ton castings. They too knew how to adapt out of necessity; in one case a gravestone maker used his facilities to sandblast castings for electrical apparatus. In another a small company of ten skilled workmen that made model airplane engines did some machining work for GE with a precision that larger firms couldn't match. In other cases GE turned over its designs and drawings to other companies working on some aspect of the same product. Wilson had in 1942 offered to the military all GE designs and techniques, patented or otherwise, for use by other concerns for the duration of the war. To save scarce materials, the company used substitutes where possible and worked out designs based more on availability of materials than ease or economy of production. Cutting techniques were devised to reduce the amount of scrap left over.[31]

These things mattered because GE operated on so gigantic a scale. The roster of finished goods, components, and parts it made was enormous. Altogether it produced about $4 billion worth of war equipment, including 75 percent of the navy's total propulsion and auxiliary turbine power that came from its own or other factories using GE's design. Some factories specialized in one primary product; others turned out a smorgasbord of goods. Where the Fitchburg, Massachusetts, plant produced naval auxiliary turbines, the Edison General Electric Appliance factory in Chicago turned out ammunition boxes, antiaircraft direction finders, bombs, cartridge cases, machine-gun trainers, shell cores, and shipboard electric cooking equipment, among other things.[32]

The other electrical giant, Westinghouse, followed a similar pattern, making a broad range of products from turbines to guns to radar and radio equipment to lighting equipment and hundreds more. When its South Philadelphia plant proved unable to handle a huge increase in steam turbine orders for C class merchant ships, the company broke ground in August 1941 for a new facility nearby. Completed in fourteen months, it became the largest in the world devoted to this one product. The roof was finished in January 1942, but the building had no heat. Undaunted, the company rented a Pennsylvania Railroad locomotive and its crew for $330 a day and backed it up against the plant to make steam enough for warming the building until the heating unit was installed.[33]

Within a year the plant had nearly 2,700 employees, nearly all of them without experience or the slightest acquaintance with the mechanical arts. They were the raw material for a pioneering effort at the straight-line manufacture of giant-size precision machinery. A veteran Westinghouse manager,

Ellis Spray, scrounged instructors from every company plant, recruited boys from local high schools and vocational training centers, and brought in large groups of women. One girl, a refugee from the ribbon counter at a Philadelphia dime store, became expert at the tricky task of pouring molten metal onto turbine valve seats, doing it faster than the skilled mechanic who had taught her. Automatic machinery along with $2 million in jigs and fixtures, some of them clever improvisations, were installed to simplify tasks. This combination of greenhorns and shortcut engineering techniques enabled the plant to produce 385 complete ship-propulsion units during the war at the rate of more than a million horsepower a year, three times the scheduled capacity.[34]

A similar pattern unfolded at the Louisville, Kentucky, plant, which made single and twin 5-inch naval antiaircraft guns. A series of improvised shortcuts, coupled with solid training, enabled greenhorns to perform jobs normally reserved for seasoned workers. At peak production the plant turned out seventy-five singles and twenty-eight twins a month; the navy had reckoned on fifteen and five because the machining required had to be so precise. To eliminate the possibility of any backlash, gear teeth had to be scraped in by women with deft hands while being monitored by a complex electronic device that spotted the tiniest errors. The guns then underwent numerous inspections, tests, and finally test firings on a special range carved out of some hills at nearby Fort Knox. The firing test itself was risky because it used a powder charge twice that employed in combat. Afterward the interior of every barrel was inspected for flaws with a telescopic probe. If any appeared, the whole bore had to be rehoned and replated with chromium.[35]

The people who built these guns came from 257 different vocations ranging from dentist to salesgirl to cartoonist. At first the company hired a nucleus of skilled men from the Louisville & Nashville Railroad and a local cigarette company and sent them for training to the Naval Gun Factory. They became the core foremen and inspectors for a workforce that brought only average strength and intelligence to the job. The key, as always, was careful specialization. Every worker did one job only, day in and day out, and those jobs were carefully planned by the engineers and supervisors, who devised hundreds of special tools, jigs, gages, routines, and inspection systems. Black workers were recruited, along with deaf people, who received special bright red caps so fellow workers knew to warn them of steel swinging overhead or other perils. At least the Louisville workers got to see their finished product. At the Westinghouse factory in Canton, Ohio, the employees toiled endlessly on millions of component parts for weapons they never saw.[36]

The key to this system lay in rigid quality control. No finished product left the factory until it was approved by the military's own inspectors. To eliminate the waste of rejects, the company's inspectors hovered over every step of production. Catching flaws early minimized the loss of further time and resources later. The raw-materials inspectors scrutinized every form of incoming supplies, not only visually but with magnetic and X-ray tests before they reached the floor. The pressure on the inspectors, especially the navy's own men, was terrific. Sometimes they held up production because they didn't know enough and had to consult the Naval Gun Factory; sometimes the drawings given them had not been updated with the latest changes. Under the duress of mass production, speed and quality made strange bedfellows.[37]

Nor did Westinghouse and General Electric neglect the most familiar of their products, lights. In 1944 alone Westinghouse manufactured 190 million lamps in more than 1,021 wattages, including more than 65 million miniature lamps in 100 styles for the army and 60 for the navy, ranging from lights on small boats to emergency lights on large ships. Military vehicles required 50 types of bulbs, and naval vessels 75 types, mostly shock-resistant to stand the constant pounding of battle and rough seas. Ten different types of searchlights were made, including tiny but efficient lamps operating on batteries that were used to help rescue pilots lost at sea. The company also made electronic tubes for use in radar, amplifiers, rectifiers, Sterilamps, and X-ray machines. The Sterilamp used extremely short wavelengths to sterilize surfaces in hospitals and manufacturing laboratories.[38]

One Westinghouse engineer, W. H. Kahler, solved a major but more mundane problem of how to light huge working areas in factories cheaply and efficiently. Conventional lighting used too much copper, which was so scarce that silver was being used as a substitute, and didn't provide enough illumination. The mercury lamp offered a possible solution but had never been made in sizes above 400 watts. Kahler devised a 3,000-watt version that was easy to manufacture but tricky to install and usable only in inside spaces. Later Westinghouse developed a 10,000-watt version and a smaller but innovative 1,000-watt type that gave off as much light as three 1,000-watt incandescent bulbs. In more ways than could be counted, improved lighting contributed to the war effort both in factories and at the front, and the stuff of lighting lent itself superbly to mass production.[39]

NO ONE LOOKING at the grounds of Cutler-Hammer, Inc., would have given it a second glance or suspected it had any importance. Its plant in Milwaukee was a motley assortment of unpainted brick buildings that showed no signs of growth. This lack of show was company policy. "Costly buildings don't make business," said president Frank R. Bacon, who first invested in the company in 1896 and whose family owned nearly 19 percent of its stock. "You make money with old buildings, not new ones." Cutler-Hammer had always made its money from one product that grew increasingly important over the years: motor controls. Half a century earlier it made magnetic starters for streetcars and later automatic push-button controls for elevators; now it was creating the brains for battleships and other vessels along with switches and magnetic clutches and brakes. In its field Cutler-Hammer ranked above every other electrical firm except GE, with whom it stood about even.[40]

Motor controls regulated and protected all sorts of motors, smoothing out and speeding up their operation. They were more than mere convenience. The ability to set in motion a sequence of processes by pressing a button was invaluable in everything from running a steel mill to operating mines and oil refineries to sending a warship into battle. The machine efficiency and productive power of entire industries depended entirely on reliable motor control, as did the functioning of many weapons. Cutler-Hammer also designed most of the switches used in such items as appliances as well as airplanes, tanks, and other ordnance. Like the giant corporations, Cutler-Hammer had its own research staff that kept it competitive with them. The war severely tested their ability to come up with new and improved designs for devices operating in the extremes of combat conditions and global weather.

Manufacturers liked to joke that the navy always wanted its stuff half as large, half as heavy, half as expensive, and twice as good. For Cutler-Hammer the joke became of necessity a mantra. Switches kept getting smaller, and tolerances kept shrinking. "The war plane," said the head of the company's development department, "is getting us into the whole field of motor control all over again." Along with new designs the engineers had to come up with good substitute materials to replace scarce ones. Before the war only 30 percent of the company's products had to be specially engineered or assembled; by 1942 the figure had reached 85 percent. The business threatened to overwhelm Cutler-Hammer. "A couple of years ago," said a vice president, "we felt our limit was $18 million, but that we might go to $20 million. Now we're getting $50 million, and we aren't done yet." Billings for the entire grim year of 1932 totaled $3 million; they reached $2 million for one day, June 8, 1942, alone.

But Frank Bacon didn't believe in undue expansion. Total employment jumped from 3,000 to 7,000 in two years, but the number of salaried supervisors nudged up only from eighty-four to eighty-six. As one of them observed, "All key men are averaging 50 per cent more hours and 100 per cent more effectiveness." Instead of building new plants or additions, the company scrounged for space elsewhere. About 10 percent of its work was subcontracted out to sixty other companies.

Like many other companies, Cutler-Hammer discovered early that both their attitude and aptitude made women better assemblers of instruments and small machines. It also learned that even highly educated and intelligent women, long thought to be bored with assembly work, took to it well. Once having mastered an operation, they could do it flawlessly while being free to think about other things. Cutler-Hammer was not known for being overly generous with employee benefits, but it did provide one curious amenity. Every Friday at noon an employee band assembled in the north parking lot to play a short concert for lunching workers.

At the far opposite end of the benefits spectrum stood one of the nation's most remarkable and controversial companies, Jack & Heintz, or "Jahco" as it was called. The Cleveland manufacturer of airplane starters, automatic pilots, and precision flight instruments aroused a storm of mixed feelings over its approach to business, as well as a congressional investigation over alleged excess profits. From every standpoint Bill Jack, a stocky, graying man of fifty-five, was a maverick. His employees had a closed-shop union agreement but worked twelve hours a day, seven days a week. Yet in a tight labor market where skilled employees were coveted like precious jewels, Jack had on file the names of 40,000 people eager to work for him. A House Naval Affairs Investigating Committee was all over him for reporting profits of only 11 percent on $58 million worth of government business because he had charged off huge sums for salaries, bonuses totaling more than $600,000, and other expenses deemed illegitimate.[41]

What were his crimes besides working his people hard? Jack pleaded guilty to being more than generous to them. He gave $39,000 in compensation to the woman who had been his trusted assistant for a quarter century, and large bonuses to other key officers. As for the other employees, all they got was hot coffee anytime they wanted it; hot soup in winter or cold drinks in summer and fresh doughnuts once a shift; dispensaries for first aid; free dental exams and emergency treatment; uniforms; specially designed shoes of the same type Jack himself wore; free life, sickness, accident, and hospital insurance; two weeks' paid vacation every year at company-leased cottages in Florida; a welfare fund for flowers for the sick; and free health centers equipped with steam rooms, ultraviolet lamps, infrared lamps, foot treatment, an expert masseur, shortwave diathermy, and other amenities.

Jack admitted freely that he was generous to his associates, as he preferred to call them, "from the floor sweeper to the top, because we believe that this is the only way for an all-out war production, to get the job done and get it done quickly." That they did. Jack insisted that his company produced more per person and square foot of plant than anyone else in the country. At the end of 1942 he had $240 million in government contracts and had increased his workforce from 1,400 to 4,000. By February the roster reached 6,000, and newcomers were being hired at the rate of 200 a week. Unlike in nearly every other plant, absenteeism did not exist as a problem. In February 1943 Jack's plant had zero absences; thrilled by the record, he offered $6,500 in war bonds to the workers of any other plant that could match it.

Where other plants had huge back-order lists, Jack & Heintz was two years ahead of schedule on airplane starters and had contracted to produce automatic pilots that were 25 percent lighter and 30 percent cheaper than those of its only rival firm. The finished products were so good that in November 1942 the air force discontinued its own separate inspections of them. At one of the monthly banquets Jack hosted for his associates at Cleveland's public auditorium (the only place big enough to hold them all), a brigadier general gushed to the crowd, "I can't tell you what a job you did for the Army Air Forces when you took this little gimmick and produced it . . . You people have done a marvelous job here."

Chastised for his sins by the committee, Jack did take action. He renegotiated contracts that saved the army $9.5 million, slashed the salaries of himself, his son, and Ralph Heintz from $100,000 to $15,000, reduced the pay of his secretary (at her request) from $25,000 to $6,000, and agreed to stop all bonuses and dividends to company officers for the duration of the war. But the associates kept their perks. Most of Cleveland's businessmen disliked Jack intensely and resented his indifference to Cleveland society and business organizations. "He never co-operates with any of us," said one. "Why, if we had serious labor trouble in Cleveland . . . he'd do nothing to help us." James F. Lincoln's electrical company also got spanked by the committee for its bonuses and high rate of pay, but Lincoln belonged to the chamber of commerce and, like many of his peers, despised both closed shops and the New Deal. Employers complained that Jack cornered all the best workmen, leaving them with leftovers. "Lincoln Electric's plant is a factory," sneered one. "Jack & Heintz's plant is a club."

Time took a different view of the five plants, calling them "a nifty combination of a college campus, a workman's paradise and zooming production. J. & H. has a band to rival Ohio State's, victory song and cheerleaders, boisterous parties to celebrate production records." Nine months after the committee's investigation the company was prospering as the largest maker of aviation starters and automatic pilots. To his critics Jack repeated loudly, "We're turning out more per man than anybody . . . and more stuff per square foot of plant than any other plant in the country."[42]

A lone wolf, Jack did things differently. He was always on the job—literally. For weeks at a time he seldom left the plants; all five of them had a cot in his office where he could snatch an hour or two of sleep. Coatless, in a brown work shirt, he roamed the floor talking to the associates, looking for problems to solve, calling them by name and insisting that they call him Bill. He ate in the cafeterias with the associates. The plants had no time clocks, but everyone showed up on time, even those with a long commute, because they cherished their job with all its privileges and knew they would never have another one like it. "It's a great place to work, just like they say it is," said a machinist. "That fellow Jack is a wonder. People *work* for him." The twelve-hour shift was long, admitted another worker, especially the first part of the night, but the coffee and doughnuts broke it up, and often Jack came around to sit and chat with one group of associates or another. Popular music drifted across plant floors from loudspeakers, interrupted only by occasional announcements from Jack.

Bill Jack was a native of Cleveland's South Side. A musician and a baseball player, he quit school to become a toolmaker and got involved early in union work. In May 1917 he started a small machine company and did well enough to buy and sell a number of manufacturing concerns. From the first he paid his employees well and introduced a profit-sharing plan. In 1933 he started the Pump Engineering Service Corporation (Pesco) in an old garage and turned it into a $2 million factory employing 265 men. Eager to expand, he sold out in 1939 to Borg-Warner with the understanding that he would remain in charge. In seeking someone to head up his experimental research work he happened on a tall, quiet engineer named Ralph M. Heintz, whom he later called "the greatest electrical and mechanical mind in the world."

Four years younger than Jack, Heintz hailed from St. Louis. After a stint in the Signal Corps during the war, he started a small chemical laboratory with his father and devised a system of ionization in fusion that he sold for $5,000 to a company that hired him as chief chemist. While working as head of a small company he renewed an old interest in radio and began designing vacuum tubes just at the dawn of broadcasting. He formed a company to make radio equipment and did pioneering work in developing shortwave equipment. By the 1930s his résumé was impressive enough to earn an army contract to develop a power system for aircraft. In 1937 Heintz sold his company to Bendix and went to work for them. However, his dislike of a salaried position made him receptive to Jack's offer.

No sooner had they set up shop than Borg-Warner told Jack they wanted no further expansion of Pesco and asked for his resignation. Jack said no and was promptly fired. Borg-Warner summoned Heintz to Chicago and paid him $5,000 to stop all developmental work for Pesco. Since both men were out of a job, they decided to form Jahco and produce something, which turned out to be an airplane starter on which Heintz had already done some work. Jack persuaded twenty-five of his former Cleveland employees to come to California and work for the new company. The starter proved a success, and Jack got a contract, only to have the local machinists' union in San Francisco go on strike in October 1940. They did not want outsiders from Cleveland and insisted on the right to say who could be hired. Jack had no qualms about the union but said he had to be able to pick his own men. When the union refused, Jack sold the Palo Alto plant and packed his operation off to Cleveland. The men who had moved to California and had to move back again became known in the company as the "covered wagon group."

With millions of dollars' worth of machinery heading east on freight cars, Jack located a rat-infested old building in Bedford that became Plant No. 1 and gave it a face-lift. It was Heintz who designed and perfected the starter and automatic pilot, but all he would say was that Jack came up with the pilot idea. An unassuming man who relished staying in the background, he was known as one who "eats, sleeps, and dreams work." Heintz had seen an article describing the automatic pilot made by Sperry Gyroscope Company, the only one in existence, and declaring that the complexity of the instrument made it impossible for anyone to compete with Sperry. "That was really kind of a silly claim to make," said Heintz. He proceeded to design and build a model that enabled them to underbid Sperry because, as Jack put it, "We are making a production problem and a production article out of something everybody had made a laboratory article out of before."

One innovation exemplified Jack's approach to production. His rival, Bendix Aviation, made airplane starters by sand-casting its shells, gear cases, and other bulky parts. When Jack learned that Cleveland foundries could provide him with only twenty-five sets of castings a day, he went to Doehler Die Casting to see whether that method could be employed. Doehler sent one of its top engineers to Cleveland, where, after poring over the blueprints for a few weeks, he found ways to adapt every part in the job to die casting. The shell that covered the starter's motor, for example, weighed 3.08 pounds before machining when sand-cast but only 2.03 pounds die cast, a savings in aluminum of nearly one third. Overall the die casting cost about half as much as sand-casting while reducing man-hours by 65 percent and machine-hours by 70 percent. A year's production of starter motors saved in all about 27 tons of aluminum.[43]

No one in Cleveland or the larger business world knew quite what to make of Jack & Heintz. Were they a model for labor-management relations or a fluke made possible by the unique personality of Bill Jack? Opinions divided deeply on the subject. "Of course Jack's men like him," said one detractor. "But you can't have that kind of relations with your men without being in the shop all the time. I could get that kind of loyalty—and the Lord knows I could do with more of it—if I were at the plant more, with the men. But if you do that you haven't time for more important things." He paused, then added,

"By God, what would this town be like if everyone treated labor the way Jack does?"

THE MOST VERSATILE weapon in the army was also its most unassuming one. The midget combat car was called many names but most often "jeep," an all-inclusive label pinned on anything insignificant from a raw draftee to a tiny observation plane. This jeep was anything but insignificant. "The jeep positively will not fly," reported *Time*, "but there is a widespread notion in the Army that it can do anything else." A crossbreed between the half-ton command car and the motor tricycle, it had only an 80-inch wheelbase and a four-wheel drive that gave great traction to its 42-horsepower engine. It could bounce along at 60 miles an hour carrying men, weapons, radio gear, or cargo while pulling a light fieldpiece. If it turned over, a few men could easily set it right again. Stimson loved the little car and was particularly impressed by an amphibious version that took him down to the Potomac, halfway across the river, and then back up the bank. "The car ran just as easily as a limousine car," he observed, ". . . through the woods over as rough a country as any ordinary jeep ever went and up and down hills in a way that was simply marvelous."[44]

The original order for 4,500 jeeps was soon followed by one for 16,000 more from Willys-Overland, Ford, and American Bantam at a cost of $900 apiece. The automobile industry knew how to mass-produce jeeps; airplanes were another matter. Visitors to a General Motors plant in New Jersey that made navy torpedo bombers were disappointed to see the assembly line crawl along only inches at a time. "You can't make fighting airplanes like automobiles," said the manager, with supporting nods from Charles Wilson and Alfred P. Sloan Jr., the company's top two men. "They can't come off of production lines one a minute . . . Until the time comes when we can standardize design and reduce the importance of weight, we cannot hope to produce planes by the manufacturing methods employed in the production of automobiles."[45]

To many people in both industries the marriage of airplanes and automobile manufacturers was a shotgun wedding. Yet by the winter of 1943 it seemed to be working. With a backlog of orders amounting to $22 billion, new and expanded plants expected to churn out record numbers of planes, most of them superior to existing models and ready to swallow more 100 octane than ever before. Debate still raged over whether the endless changes in specifications imposed by the military were worth the losses in production time, and a handful of companies still struggled to produce. When Brewster Aeronautical of Long Island, contracted to make the Vought Corsair fighter, became what *Time* called "among the most substantial U. S. production fizzles" of the war, the navy asked Henry Kaiser to take over the management. Only two weeks earlier Kaiser had acquired plane builder Fleetwings, Inc., of Bristol, Pennsylvania. Rumors surfaced at once that it would be merged with Brewster.[46]

No such thing happened. Brewster's management was in shambles. It had a $275 million order from the navy and 20,000 employees yet in February produced only eight planes. Five different managers had come and gone since 1942 amid curdled relations with labor and a rancorous stockholders' suit over finances. That year the company lost more than $1.4 million, and its production sagged so badly that draft boards, asked to defer Brewster workers, said flippantly, "Brewster's not in war work." Kaiser appointed a new manager and reportedly spent only days at the plant, which made a congressional committee unhappy, but the new president gained support from the workers and increased output through the spring. Then another labor squabble led to a four-day strike that slowed production during the summer; in August not a single plane was delivered. The Truman Committee gave Kaiser an ultimatum: take over the management personally or resign from the board.[47]

"It's not an alluring prospect to take over what's reputed to be the worst situation in the country," Kaiser said, but he agreed to do so. The president was let go and Henry Kaiser Jr. installed as administrative assistant to oversee the company. The elder Kaiser also brought in Henry Morton, his labor troubleshooter, as vice president of labor. The major problem continued to be Thomas De Lorenzo, a hard-nosed union chief who had tied Brewster's management in knots with labor rules that forbade the company from firing, shifting, or disciplining workers without union permission. "Every time I got in bed with Tom De Lorenzo," testified the former president, "I got out with less than I went in with." Materials scheduling also remained a problem, often leaving workers idle for want of parts. The WLB helped out by intervening in two labor issues that had stalled production. Nevertheless, *Time* referred to Brewster as "the nation's weirdest war plant," and James Forrestal threatened to move the navy's contracts to other companies if production did not ramp up. Production did improve as the year wound down, but the company's future remained uncertain.[48]

DISAPPOINTMENT OVER BREWSTER'S performance, however intense, paled before that expressed about Willow Run. Here was the largest factory ever built, with more than 2.5 million square feet of floor space, a monument to the American genius for mass production, called by Charles A. Lindbergh "a sort of a Grand Canyon of the mechanized world," yet by August 1942 it had not turned out a single B-24 bomber for the war effort. For all the hype heaped upon it, much of which came from Ford's own public relations people, the plant had produced only a single hand-produced plane that was used as a trainer. Critics soon took to deriding the place as "Willit Run." Airplane manufacturers, who loathed the idea of the automobile industry venturing into their turf, cackled with glee at the fiasco. North American's Dutch Kindelberger sneered, "You cannot expect blacksmiths to learn how to make watches overnight."[49]

Nearly everything had gone wrong for Ford, most of it because of Henry Ford. Nearing eighty, the old man basked ever more in his reputation as one of America's great inventors and production geniuses even though his considerable talents had long since been soured by rigidity of beliefs, a crabbed mind that shunned realities, and a fatal inability to judge ability. He had long since lost touch with the world evolving around him, preferring instead to dwell in the comfort of simplistic homilies he had long cherished. His ways had deeply damaged his only son, Edsel, whom he loved dearly, and ultimately would kill him. He continued his long-standing policy of driving away his most talented executives, all of whom found welcome mats at rival companies, while relying ever more on the thuggish Harry Bennett to carry out his warped and outmoded policies in a company ruled more by terror than anything else.

The two pillars of sanity at Ford remained Edsel, who did what he could to ameliorate his father's aberrations, and Charles Sorensen, who had done most of the work on Willow Run, but they could only do so much. Some said the old man was senile, others that his rigid, narrow-minded approach had simply grown worse. He had built Willow Run not in a straight line, as the original plans called for, but in an L shape with two special turntables at the bend to turn the assembly lines. Why? The land beneath Willow Run lay in Washtenaw County, a solidly Republican enclave. Extending the plant straight ahead would carry it across the line into Wayne County, the home of liberal Democratic administrations with their prolabor sympathies and tax assessors. Henry Ford wanted no part of them.[50]

Neither would he listen to advice from others. He had, after all, built airplanes before, the Ford trimotor transport in the mid-1920s. Like his celebrated Model T it was innovative but eclipsed by others whose designs marched forward while Ford's remained unchanged. He stopped making the plane in 1931, and the design of Willow Run owed far more to his automobile than airplane experience. He decided on extensive use of hard steel dies, which were durable and ideal for big production runs but harder to change out than soft, cheaper dies. People experienced in building planes tried to warn him that design changes were too frequent to invest in hard dies, but Ford

ignored their advice. Later the Truman Committee found that he did not listen to the few outside experts; neither did he send many layout and production men to see how planes were made on the West Coast. Ford knew better.
He ridiculed the airplane builders as "antiquated" and declared that "the
bomber job" differed little from "making auto bodies." Jeeps were rolling off
the assembly lines at River Rouge "like cookies out of a cutter," and so would
bombers at the Run.[51]

But they did not. When the army presented Ford with hundreds of modifications to the B-24 born of combat experience, the changeover in tooling
became slow, cumbersome, and expensive. The changes drove Sorensen
to despair. "We would agree upon freezing a design, then be ready to go
ahead," he recalled. "Back from the fighting fronts would come complaints
or suggestions . . . and the plane designers came through with alterations in
design with no consideration for the production program." The latter
slowed or stopped while the air force decided which changes if any to require. Every change meant junking one of the expensive steel dies and the
machine tool fitted to it.[52]

In July 1942 General Bill Knudsen arrived at Willow Run to examine the
problem. Charles A. Lindbergh was there as well in the role of consultant to
men he found unreceptive. "There are many things the Ford Company could
be shown about operating an aircraft factory," he confided to his diary. "Unfortunately, Sorensen is typical of many Ford officers who *don't want to be
shown*." Knudsen thought he had the answer to the design change dilemma.
Earlier he had urged Patterson to "freeze the designs for a while so we can get
some airplanes . . . If we try to keep up to the minute on every airplane we
make, we will end up by being late on every airplane made." Build the planes,
he urged, and then add improvements at some place especially equipped for
that work.[53]

The answer lay in the creation of special modification centers. Beginning
in January 1942, the air force began opening such centers, relying at first on
the maintenance shops of commercial airlines for facilities. By July, when
Knudsen arrived at Willow Run, twelve centers were in operation; ultimately
the number reached twenty-eight, although all of them never operated at the
same time. In all the government spent $100 million on twenty-one of the
centers, eighteen of which worked exclusively on air force planes as opposed
to navy or foreign aircraft. But it took time to get the centers up and running,
and other problems continued to plague Willow Run.[54]

Nothing sabotaged Henry Ford's hopes more than his disastrous labor
policies at the Run. To man the nearly seventy subassembly lines, he needed
nearly 100,000 workers for a plant thirty-five miles from downtown Detroit.
They would all have to live somewhere. Neither Detroit nor the surrounding

communities had even remotely adequate facilities for this flood of newcomers. One survey showed that it was nearly impossible to rent a room within fifty miles of Detroit. New housing was needed on a massive scale. Ford owned considerable land around the plant but showed no interest in the problem. Neither did the government until the spring of 1942, a year and a half after construction began.[55]

The Detroit office of the Federal Public Housing Administration sent engineers to survey the land around the plant. At the same time, the UAW in Washington asked the government to build a model city of permanent homes for the workers. Ford responded by having Harry Bennett evict the engineers from Ford property and pull up 700 stakes that had been laid out. Local farmers, who owned the land Ford did not, promptly followed suit as Ford launched a statewide campaign against public housing in general. His reasoning was simple: He did not want solidly Republican Washtenaw County infested with thousands of prounion, potentially Democratic voters. A Ford spokesman assured the government that the Run had no housing problem, that nearby areas had plenty of homes and apartments. Finally, in October 1942, Ford relented enough to sell the government 295 acres of his land to build emergency war housing only.

Meanwhile, people eager for jobs at the Run streamed into the area. By the spring of 1943 the plant had 35,000 employees living in shacks or trailer camps or sleeping in cars, with no stores or schools or other facilities. One group paid $250 a month for some unheated cubicles in a converted chicken coop. Whole areas had neither safe water, sewage, nor drainage, raising fears of an epidemic. When a citizens committee from nearby Ypsilanti asked a Ford official for help in dealing with the social needs of the workers, he replied, "Gentlemen, we are concerned with building the best bombers in the world. What our workers do outside the plant, or how they live, is no concern of ours. The community will have to take care of that." The task fell to county and UAW Local 50 officials, who tried to organize the community on a self-help basis.

Despite these difficulties, Ford continued to solicit workers from the South and elsewhere. Thousands of people migrated north in hopes of good jobs, utterly misled as to what they would find for housing and other conditions. Many, especially those with families, experienced the shock of reality and headed back home again. In the end, half of the Run's workers never found housing close to the plant and had to commute long distances. The *Wall Street Journal* reported in the spring of 1943 that the average worker endured a daily round trip of forty to seventy miles. Two railroads reached the plant but carried only war freight and had no passenger cars. Two bus lines, one private, hauled commuters from Detroit but took over an hour for the trip at best and cost at least 70 cents round-trip. The company did nothing to help. One day in March, it imposed a change in shift schedules without informing the workers, completely fouling up the transportation arrangements for two shifts.

It soon became evident that at the Run Bennett would honor recognition of the union while doing everything he could to thwart it. For months he stripped foremen of the power to settle grievances, referring all the complaints of 35,000 workers to one man's office. Men and women were required to eat at separate cafeterias for no apparent reason, which rankled both single and married workers. The company had no mechanism for soliciting suggestions from workers and wanted none. When prodded by WPB and the military to create some version of management-labor committees, Ford dismissed the idea as impossible because "in the way of experience or ability along management lines, labor has nothing to offer." Small wonder that the Run had horrible labor relations and soaring absentee rates. Turnover at the plant ran as high as 50 percent a month.

Willow Run was also cursed by personal misfortune. Ford's top production vice president suffered a heart attack in 1941 and was unable to play any role at the plant. Edsel Ford, who had fought uphill battles for years against both his father and Bennett, did much to improve the factory, but his health failed rapidly. Told to slow down, he said, "The war won't wait," and pushed even harder. He contracted undulant fever after drinking milk from his father's cows that Henry insisted remain unpasteurized, yet he continued to work. Henry Ford showed no sympathy for his son's decline, calling it the product of a lifestyle grounded in cocktails and other decadent habits. "If there is anything the matter with Edsel's health," he told a concerned Sorensen, "he can correct it himself." On May 26, 1943, Edsel died of stomach cancer as well as undulant fever at the age of forty-nine. His unbelieving father was crushed by the loss and never fully recovered from it.[56]

Edsel's death spurred the rise of Bennett's influence at the Run. In June he received a seat on the board of Ford Motor and a new title, director of administrative affairs. His first order of business had less to do with production than with ousting his old rival, Sorensen. Other capable Ford officials saw the handwriting on the wall and either left the company or were purged; all found homes at other automobile companies. Sorensen hung on until March 1944, when he departed and went to Willys-Overland. In July 1943 the Truman Committee issued its findings on the Run that damned far more than it praised. As of that date the plant had yet to complete a single B-24 fit for duty at the front. The workforce was demoralized by their lack of output. One senator labeled them "aircraft workers who have never produced a plane."

Absenteeism averaged about 17 percent of the total workforce, the highest of any war production plant in the country.[57]

Despite all its troubles, Willow Run was destined for better days. Before his departure Sorensen had completed tooling the plant and making test production runs. The engineers and workers had finally come to grips with their toughest task of making changeovers quickly and efficiently. Ford had relented in his refusal to farm out the making of parts or subassembly work to other Ford plants, simplifying the Run's operation. Edsel had persuaded his father to do this shortly before his death. The company eased its shortage of workers by hiring more women, and Bennett found it necessary to grant some concessions to the union. He acceded to demands from the union and the military to replace his director of labor relations by hiring in November Colonel August M. Krech, who promptly went to the West Coast to see how aircraft plants there handled their labor force. And in August it had a new executive to duel with Bennett in the form of Edsel's eldest son, Henry Ford II. After more than two years of turmoil, frustration, and disappointment, the Run seemed poised at last to fulfill its promise of mass production.[58]

But the promise did not come easily. In mid-April Charlie Wilson paid his first visit to Willow Run. He inspected the long assembly line, checked the production schedule, talked to the production men, and said confidently, "The Willow Run plant is on the beam . . . Willow Run will be in full production, turning out 500 planes a month, by the time the next snow flies."[59]

Next day it snowed in Detroit.

CHAPTER 24

THE NEW WEST

Out here, you've not only got space, you've got space that can be used by human beings—a land of opportunity.
—FRANKLIN D. ROOSEVELT[1]

Some of us honestly believe that if the Japs invade and conquer the West Coast, the rest of the country won't do a thing to get it back until they've taken care of Hitler. It ought to be fairly easy to hold the Japs behind the mountains here. It's not that we think the rest of the country wouldn't want to help us, and it's not that we think we're not important to the nation's war effort. But we do think we're not absolutely vital to the war effort; the country could go on fighting without us and we can easily understand how they might consider it more important to beat Hitler first before they set about recapturing the Coast.
—LOS ANGELES BANKER[2]

How the hell can I make my plans? One day I'm going to be drafted, next day I'm going to be froze to my job. I don't know what to expect.
—SHIPYARD WORKER[3]

THROUGHOUT ITS CHECKERED HISTORY the West had harbored an inferiority complex in its relationship to the East. It was the land of beauty and barrenness, of myth and make-believe, of glamour and ghost towns, the home of Hollywood and wide-open spaces drenched in equal parts of dreams and disappointments. In the light of harsh reality it was an economic stepchild of the East. Manufacturing provided less than 5 percent of its income in 1940. To its chagrin a host of advertisements included the line "Slightly higher price west of the Rockies" for the simple reason that so few goods were manufactured there. Westerners had a colonial complex and a resentment that "Eastern Seaboard thinking" dominated Washington. "What we need out here," went the lament, "is an ambassador to Washington." In 1937 Western historian Walter Prescott Webb charged that "Back of the North's present might and behind its increasing control of . . . the West is its undisputed command of the mighty forces of the industrial revolution in America."[4]

The war changed all this in an incredibly short time. Some called it "the second winning of the West," the driving force this time around being not settlers but industry. An economy long dependent on agriculture, mining, lumber, and resorts was blossoming into a new industrial empire that promised to replace the region's colonial status with self-sufficiency. With this growth came an influx of migrants. In the first two months of 1942 alone a million people flooded into the three West Coast states, most of them into cities and towns. Los Angeles added half a million and once-sleepy San Diego 100,000, an increase of 50 percent. Unlike the Okie and Arkie migration of the 1930s, these newcomers tended to be young, urban, and ethnically mixed. Whatever their background, nearly all of them came for the same reason: the promise of defense jobs and a better life.[5]

The opportunities were there. The West had space, resources, and a fresh supply of hydroelectric power to propel plants. Although not yet fully online, the three great western dams alone—Grand Coulee, Bonneville, and Shasta— could provide 39 percent of the nation's potential hydroelectric power. "These dams," admitted the administrator of the Grand Coulee and Bonneville, "are a frank subsidy." The government built them to help develop thinly settled regions, and they were about to pay enormous dividends because of the war. Two new integrated steel plants, the first in the West, arrived by different routes. The government financed the Geneva Works of a U.S. Steel subsidiary in Utah, while Henry Kaiser, after a dogged fight to gain approval for his plans, had to borrow more than $100 million to build his steel mill at Fontana, fifty miles from Los Angeles.[6]

Portland led the West in aluminum output, thanks to an Alcoa facility. A new plant in Nevada extracted magnesium from local ore, while another new facility in California produced it. Where the nation imported 97 percent of its magnesium before the war, eight western states were on track to process 60 percent of a new domestic supply. A chemical industry was springing up in Los Angeles, Seattle, and Oregon. The crown jewels of industry remained the aircraft plants and shipyards, which kept growing and improving their output. The West Coast shipbuilders employed 200,000 workers; Kaiser's Richmond yard alone worked three shifts of 16,000 workers each, while his three Portland yards had 30,000 employees. The aircraft plants loomed even larger with a workforce exceeding 300,000. The eight companies based in Southern

California had transformed the Los Angeles and San Diego areas just as Boeing had done to Seattle. At their peak in 1943 the Southern California aircraft plants employed 243,000 people.[7]

The military brought another major wave of migration to the West. Altogether the government invested some $40 billion in western facilities during the war. By 1942 the government had established ten major military bases in Utah alone; they contained some 60,000 personnel and employed another 60,000 civilians. A supply depot at Ogden, first built in 1935, expanded steadily into the largest quartermaster depot in the nation. A prime supplier for the Pacific theater, it employed 6,000 people and turned into a small city. Nearby Hill Air Force Base had as many as 22,000 people on its payrolls, while Tooele Army Depot, farther south, generated 8 percent of all the income in Utah. Within its 44,000 acres could be found 902 igloos used to store explosives, thirty-one large warehouses, and a tank repair shop. The huge Wendover military reserve, the world's largest, straddled the Utah-Nevada border on the salt flats and served as both a bombing range and training school for pilots and bombardiers.[8]

The remoteness and isolation of the West made it an ideal location for military bases, training camps, storage depots, test ranges, and a super-secret facility like Los Alamos. The barren wastes of southern Utah held the military's special centers for chemical warfare needs. The Dugway Proving Ground, only eighty-five miles southwest of Salt Lake City, embraced 850,000 acres and was used for toxic chemicals testing as well as producing flame-throwers and incendiary bombs. Federal money supplied 90 percent of the capital that flowed into the West for wartime mobilization and production. The new plants and facilities that sprang up required housing, banking, retail outlets, and other services, creating what an earlier generation called "mushroom cities." They also needed a network of subcontractors and suppliers of all kinds. California alone attracted more than $70 billion in federal funds between 1941 and 1945, creating a boom mentality not seen since the gold rush.[9]

With the war boom came drastic cultural upheavals. Apart from the immediate problems of housing, sewage, transportation, water, and other needs, cities and towns underwent profound adjustments to the waves of men—and women—filling their streets at all hours, some in uniforms, others in workclothes. California's birth rate soared to record heights; in San Francisco venereal disease and pregnancy rates doubled among schoolgirls; overall venereal disease shot up 75 percent in 1942 and 1943. Uniform-struck teenaged girls, known as "V-girls" or "khaki-whackies," clustered around train depots, bus stations, drugstores, or anywhere else they might encounter soldiers or sailors, offering themselves in exchange for a date as simple as a movie or a dance. "I'm off to Walgreens to meet a girl," said the sailor in a standing joke. "What's her name?" he was asked. "How should I know?" he replied.[10]

This too, and much more, was part of the new West.

ALTHOUGH HENRY KAISER did his best work in Washington navigating the shoals of obtaining government contracts, he seemed to be everywhere in the West. The shipyards drew the most publicity but comprised only a small part of his overall activity. He had at one stage or another the Fontana steel mill, the magnesium project, the Permanente cement plant, coal mines, a proposal to ease the shipping shortage by building a fleet of giant air freighters, and plans for constructing a fleet of baby aircraft carriers. All of his developmental work was centered in the West, which he wanted to make self-sufficient in basic industries. He had long since tied his destiny to the region, and it was paying off handsomely. In the process he had become famous and a national symbol for getting things done. *Time* hailed him as the most publicized businessman of 1942, an honor the Luce publishing empire did much to bestow. Henry Luce had early taken a shine to Kaiser as the very model of an enlightened industrialist and a man who defied the stifling strictures of bureaucracy and convention.[11]

Fontana repeated the pattern of Kaiser's shipyards. Despite the hostility of the steel industry, his men managed to get some valuable technical information and equipment from experienced steelmen. "We rushed drawings from Oakland to Fontana," recalled an engineer, "but parts of the plant were built before there were any designs." Despite all obstacles, the first blast furnace was fired on December 30, 1942, and produced steel plate three months ahead of the Geneva plant. At the dedication Kaiser thanked Big Steel for its help and portrayed the mill as part of a new era that promised to end or at least minimize the West's long dependence on eastern manufacturing. Ultimately he also became one of the RFC's top ten wartime borrowers with a total of about $300 million, including $97.2 million for the Fontana mill and $26.2 million for his Permanente magnesium plant.[12]

The finished steel mill complex was impressive. Its ninety coke ovens handled 1,740 tons of coal a day, and its 1,200-ton blast furnace could smelt 438,000 tons of raw pig iron. Six 185-ton open hearth furnaces had a capacity of 675,000 tons of ingot a year, while the rolling mills could turn out 472,000 tons of alloy-finished steel products. The engineer who designed it, Hungarian-born George Havas, knew no more about steel mills than Clay Bedford did shipyards when he started, but he had been with Kaiser since

1928 and knew how his boss worked. Most of the men hired to do the building also knew the Kaiser style, having cut their teeth on Boulder Dam. Kaiser
named the blast furnace "the Bess," after his wife, and proclaimed that "for
the first time on this side of the Rockies we begin the manufacture of iron . . .
from ore mined in our own mountains . . . The westward movement which
began so long ago has not come to an end on the Pacific Slope. It is poised
now for the next great thrust."[3]

When the RFC asked Kaiser what his parent company was, he laughed and
said, "We don't have one. We're just a bunch of amoebae dividing into new
cells." In Washington he had earned a reputation among New Dealers as "the
great contractor from the West who can do any job," but he had critics as
well. A tireless worker with no hobbies to distract him, he surrounded himself with bright young men who oversaw the projects he thrust on them or
provided expertise. He ran up enormous long-distance telephone bills holding conference calls with his key men on every project, taking care that everyone's views got aired. His interest in a project tended to wane once its
problems were resolved, at which point he liked to say, "We've got to look for
more work."[4]

The setbacks with the magnesium plant had discouraged even Kaiser.
Jesse Jones, who had taken a dislike to Kaiser, recalled that "Kaiser knew
nothing about manufacturing magnesium, so I was a little skeptical . . . The
whole set-up looked a little screwy to me, one that would be of doubtful outcome." He regarded Kaiser as someone "who was ready to try anything if the
government would put up the money." But Kaiser persisted in his quest to
develop production. Besides the Permanente facility his lieutenants also
managed a seawater magnesium oxide plant at Moss Landing, a dolomite
quarry near Salinas, and a magnesium reduction plant at Manteca. During
the summer of 1943 his engineers finally solved the flaws in the carbothermic
process used at Permanente, and production of magnesium ingots soared.
Then, late in the year, the engineers helped the Chemical Warfare Service
develop a mixture of powdered magnesium, asphalt, and a distillate that
proved to be a devastating incendiary material called "goop." The military
was so enamored of the stuff that early in 1944 it ordered Permanente to produce only goop. By the war's end the plant had turned out 41,000 tons of the
lethal mixture.[5]

Few projects attracted more public attention than one that didn't pan
out—the giant cargo plane. Kaiser's solution to the submarine menace was
audacious: He proposed building a fleet of 5,000 transport planes. In July
Glenn L. Martin's company produced a 70-ton transport that did well in
tests. That Kaiser had no experience in the aircraft industry did not deter
him. He launched a whirlwind nine-day tour of Washington, seeing everyone

from Roosevelt to the military. Arnold and Somervell voiced their doubts that Kaiser could deliver, and the military did not want to give up any precious materials for such a scheme. He managed to convince Nelson and his advisers, as well as two congressional committees, and walked away with authority to build a hundred of the planes. The airplane manufacturers fought the project, not wanting Kaiser to horn in on their turf. When they did not cooperate with his plans, Kaiser went hunting for a different partner and found one in the brilliant but eccentric Howard Hughes.[16]

Controversy arose at once over the project, fueled by pundits dueling over Washington's treatment of the two men. When it became clear that the 70-ton contract would not be forthcoming, they received one in September 1942 to build three prototype cargo planes in the 100-ton range—but only if they did not use much critical material. Hughes was to design and build the prototypes, which Kaiser would then produce, but their relationship soured early. Hughes was secretive, hard to reach, and sparing of information. Late in August 1943 the project manager warned Donald Nelson, "We have a terribly chaotic situation out here. It is going to blow up in your face." Nelson canceled the project in February 1944, and Kaiser dropped out. But Hughes persisted, using his own rather than government funds, and ultimately produced the infamous "Spruce Goose" made of wood.[17]

Although the planes never materialized, Kaiser's reputation as a man for all seasons and all tasks only grew. Outsiders loved his disdain for bureaucracy and plodding through channels. His early experience in Washington taught him how to get things done there. He became one of the first to hire a new breed of lawyer/lobbyists who specialized in leading clients through the bureaucracy's maze of red tape. As early as 1940 he opened an office in Washington, where his man Charles F. "Chad" Calhoun cultivated contacts, gathered information, and reported on the state of things. For all his reputation as a brash outsider, Kaiser mastered the art of being an insider as well. Gradually he insinuated himself into Roosevelt's inner circle even as his public image began to loom larger than life, thanks in large part to the Luce media that lionized him. He acquired the label of "fabulous" Henry Kaiser, "around whom news and fables now collect as about a Paul Bunyan."[18]

The combination of inside influence and publicity worked wonders. Kaiser became too important to ignore his proposals. His plan to convert a hundred cargo ships into baby flattops got rejected by several admirals before Roosevelt intervened and Kaiser got a contract for fifty of the ships. "Kaiser does things in ways and quantities and speed that have never been done before," burbled Frazier Hunt in a newscast. "He's a sort of Henry Ford, and Boss Kettering and Charlie Wilson all rolled into one. He's terrific; he's colossal; he's completely unbelievable . . . He's the Master Doer of the world." He had become a public hero and a reigning symbol of the new West with his energy, driving spirit, and staunch individualism.[19]

THREE BROAD CRISES beset the war mobilization effort, each one fueling the next. The first was the conversion of industry to wartime production. Once this was accomplished, its soaring output led directly to the second crisis, the shortage of raw materials. As that crisis eased during 1943, it aggravated a third one already under way: the manpower muddle. The first problem was chiefly one of machines, the second of materials. The third proved more intractable because it involved people and therefore became a political hot potato. "It calls for decisions from which the people and government have hitherto shrunk," observed *Fortune*. "It requires voluntary and involuntary sacrifices that the people have never contemplated. The issues go beyond mere numbers. They will cut across the citizen's social prejudices and prerogatives at every turn."[20]

Everyone agreed that the overall supply of people was ample. The difficulty, as Roosevelt had stressed, was having the right number of them in the right place at the right time. "What we had," said Nelson, "was a series of acutely localized manpower shortages, in some city, or in some industry; shortages of certain skills [or] . . . trades—but never an actual over-all shortage of manpower." Too many claimants tugged insistently at the available supply: the draft, the military, the war plants, shipyards, lumber camps, farms, mines, and a host of other, more specialized needs. Meat grew scarce in part because western ranchers could not keep their cowpunchers, fence riders, and cooks from wandering off to war plant jobs that paid $80 to $100 a week. One copper producer fell 3 million pounds behind monthly capacity because he lacked 500 miners and 300 smelter workers. Since it needed the copper for ammunition and other uses, the army found itself in the distasteful position of furloughing men back to the mines.[21]

"Manpower is like gasoline," concluded one observer. "There's plenty but not where you want it." Paul McNutt saw it differently. "It is not like dealing with money in the bank," he told a Senate committee. "You can draw all your money out, and if your credit is good you may borrow more. But when you are dealing with manpower, when it is gone that is all there is. There isn't any more."[22]

Several factors fed into the issue. Absenteeism remained a serious problem despite dogged efforts to curb it. *Fortune* called it "The New National Malady." The aircraft industry seemed especially prone to it. On the day after Christmas 26 percent of all Boeing employees failed to show up for work, as did 11,000 workers at Douglas. The following month the Bureau of Labor Statistics estimated absenteeism for all industries at about 7 percent, many times the normal rate in peacetime. By contrast, Edward R. Murrow reported from London, unauthorized absences among British workers averaged an astounding thirty minutes per worker per year. No one reason accounted for the sorry American record. Some workers suffered from Monday Morning Disease (hangovers), but in most other cases the causes ranged from illness to transportation problems to living conditions to job hunting to family needs, especially for women workers.[23]

The WMC attributed much of absenteeism to these personal and environmental issues, which made Bob Patterson furious. To him it was one more example of soft civilians being coddled. "The men at the fighting fronts *have* to get there," he told a House committee. "If there is no transportation, they march, and if the weather is bad, they go just the same ... There is no excuse for absenteeism in the fact that transportation is difficult and that it is a long distance to work." Another harsh truth accounted for the absences. Like it or not, employers were dealing with a sellers' market in labor. Workers could earn in four days what they used to make in six, and absenteeism soared right after payday. Nevertheless, after analyzing the different reasons for the malady, *Fortune* concluded that "it is this failure of the worker to appreciate the momentous character of what he is doing that remains, in moral terms, the most significant cause of absenteeism."[24]

Turnover also plagued the war plants. One aircraft plant with 60,000 workers had an annual turnover rate approaching 100 percent. It hired 5,000 new workers a month only to see a like number leave for other jobs or to enlist. In one twelve-month period the builders of cargo ships suffered a turnover rate of 133 percent. The same army that complained about lagging production sent recruiting officers into plants and shipyards to sign up workers. Farm labor occupied a special niche in the controversy, if only because the powerful farm bloc and special interests stood ready to protect the rural workforce with legislation even more far-reaching than the Tydings Amendment. One bill proposed to defer anyone regularly engaged in an agricultural pursuit. "This measure would excuse from military service anyone who raises a few vegetables or has a few apple trees," snapped Patterson. Fortunately, the bill died.[25]

California senator Sheridan Downey offered a more sympathetic explanation: "We have hundreds of thousands of women who are working in our war factories, who are also keeping homes for their husbands and children ... They may be able to stand the gaff for 60 days or 6 months, but then they are exhausted and quit ... Many of the workers are living in such deplorable conditions that they do not have the proper school facilities . . . shopping facilities, or recreational facilities and they just move around attempting to better their conditions."[26]

When Roosevelt acceded to Paul McNutt's wishes and placed Selective Service under the WMC, he hoped that the move would ease if not resolve the persistent manpower question. It proved a vain hope. The issue was too complex and too politically explosive for McNutt or anyone else to tame. It was also an issue with deep roots in the West even though it affected every section of the country. The plethora of new war facilities there acted as magnets drawing thousands of workers westward in search of jobs, creating the hellish living conditions at nearly all the major shipyards and aircraft plants. The West also had most of the mines and a large portion of the farms and ranches sorely in need of labor lost to the military or factory jobs. During the war more than 8 million people moved west of the Mississippi River along with another 3 million transients in the form of servicemen and women. Nearly half of them went to the West Coast. Before the war old people went to the West Coast to retire and die; during the war young people flocked there to live and do better than they had at home.[27]

Farm workers posed a special and hotly controversial problem. To help draft boards determine whether a farm worker was essential to the war effort, the Department of Agriculture created a table converting every type of crop and livestock care into war units. The care of one milk or three beef cows or five yearling steers or heifers, for example, comprised one war unit. To be deferred, a worker had to be responsible for only eight war units, a figure that was raised to ten in February 1943, twelve in May, and sixteen later. The Tydings Amendment, attached to the bill that lowered the draft age from twenty-one to eighteen in November 1942, added a unique layer of statutory protection to agricultural workers that no other occupation received. If nothing else, the amendment curbed the drift of farmboys to the city in search of jobs. By midsummer 1943 about 1.8 million men were on the deferred rolls for agriculture.[28]

As early as mid-1942 the West had virtually exhausted its local labor supply. By year's end the shortages threatened to disrupt production. Downey investigated in January 1943 and concluded that California alone needed 123,000 more shipyard and 55,000 more aircraft plant workers. To alleviate localized shortfalls, McNutt tried every voluntary trick he could devise. An experimental program in Baltimore did well enough to launch similar ones in fifty other cities, but they did not solve the basic problems. At the heart of the difficulty lay an old and familiar issue: a voluntary versus compulsory policy. The American way had always been to persuade rather than coerce people to do what was needed, but it did not always work. Compulsion was inevitably associated with the dictatorships that were the enemy, yet the British had legalized absolute state control over labor early in the war and it seemed to work well for them.[29]

The British Ministry of Labor and National Service had power to allocate manpower for both industry and the armed forces. Its decisions were based on essential needs rather than number or type of dependents and were final. Its head, Ernest Bevin, presided over all the crossroads where manpower issues converged, including agencies for mediation, arbitration, conciliation, and wages. The United States had resorted to compulsory service in only one area, the military draft, which had precedents reaching back to the Civil War. Nothing like a draft for civilian labor had been attempted, although one plan had floated about in the 1920s for what was called "universal service" and later refined to "national service." Groups ranging from the Republican Party to the American Legion to industrial mobilization planners in the War Department favored conscripting workers when necessary, but sentiments changed entirely during the depressed 1930s in favor of a voluntary distribution of labor.[30]

The most forceful voice for national service remained that of Grenville Clark, one of the founders before World War I of the so-called Plattsburg Idea of creating military camps to train civilians. The aristocratic Clark, a partner in the prestigious law firm that included Elihu Root, had played an instrumental role in getting the Selective Service Act of 1940 passed, after which he devoted his energies to advocating a mandatory national service system to register and inventory men and women between the ages of eighteen and sixty-five and direct them into the most essential wartime production work. As early as April 1942 he urged this program on Roosevelt. Although he was mostly ignored at first, the growing manpower crisis prompted Senator Warren R. Austin and Representative James Wadsworth to introduce a bill in February 1943 calling for national service.[31]

The issue divided Congress and the cabinet as well as the public. Stimson and Patterson strongly favored it, Byrnes opposed it, and Baruch reiterated his longtime view that "one man should not be required to work for another." McNutt and Nelson had long defended voluntarism as the proper policy, although McNutt had in recent months sidled toward national service. Roosevelt lent Clark and Stimson support in private but remained politically aloof in public because the issue was so volatile. Then Clark fell seriously ill, and the task of developing the plan fell to Goldthwaite Dorr, who had helped Stimson reorganize the War Department. The Wadsworth-Austin bill was vague enough to spark controversy once hearings began. Labor leaders displayed rare unity in denouncing it as an "unconstitutional resort to slave labor," a view seconded by Baruch. Roosevelt responded in typical fashion by asking Sam Rosenman to ponder the problem with an informal group of the usual suspects: Hopkins, Baruch, Byrnes, and Admiral William D. Leahy.[32]

The group decided that compulsory measures were not yet needed, though they probably would be later. Stimson was not pleased. "It was evident that the only remedy is passage of a General Service Law," he wrote, "and that anything that we can do short of that will be inadequate and chicken-feed." The bill died in committee without a vote in both houses, but the issue persisted. McNutt was struggling to overhaul USES, especially the glaring weaknesses in its field personnel. It had long been manned by political hacks at the state level, where the salaries fixed by state law made it all but impossible to recruit competent people. In February he tried to get tough by issuing a "work or fight" order and imposing hiring controls on thirty-two work centers with shortages of essential workers. When he asked a House committee for $2.5 million to give USES employees raises that would bring them in line with federal workers, however, he was turned down cold. *Time* concluded that "a concerted Congressional move to 'get' McNutt" was on.[33]

Roosevelt entered the fray in February on a tangential angle with an executive order establishing a minimum forty-eight-hour workweek. Later Rosenman claimed that it operated as a check on inflation and "helped to solve serious manpower shortages in critical areas." Although the order extended the forty-eight-hour week to all metal mining and all phases of the lumber industry, most workers remained unaffected by it. The vast majority of war industry employees already worked that many hours, and a large portion of the remaining workforce fell under a series of exemptions and exceptions contained in the regulations issued by WMC. Overall the order had little impact on the labor situation.[34]

Given the worsening labor shortage, Senator John H. Bankhead of Alabama wondered whether the military's quotas for a total force of 10.5 million were still realistic. "In view of the absolute necessity of at least continuing, and if possible increasing the production of war materials," he declared, "... it will be too dangerous to withdraw from war production many more men for service in the armed forces. We should not shrink from the adoption of any program which endangers in the slightest way the production of all of the things that our armed forces and our allies need." The War Department and General Marshall insisted that their quotas were essential to gaining superiority over the Axis powers.[35]

At a more parochial level the boss of the National Maritime Union asked the U.S. Merchant Service to decrease its merchant marine sailor training program, claiming it was graduating 50,000 new seamen when only 20,000 were needed. He also wanted the navy to remove its gun crews from merchant ships in favor of ordinary sailors. The graduates pouring out of an experimental training school on Long Island at the rate of 10,000 every ninety days were not flocking to the union, which saw its power threatened. But with three to five new Liberty ships sliding off the ways every day, the government wanted an ample supply of seamen. Replacements were also needed. Figures released by Jerry Land in February revealed that the number of merchant sailors killed or missing totaled 3,200, or 3.8 percent of the full force. By contrast armed service casualties reached only three fourths of 1 percent. Despite these high losses, Land emphasized, large numbers "voluntarily sign on for another voyage and keep delivering the goods."[36]

By spring the pinch affected all the major claimants. The backlog of unemployed women had vanished except for blacks, who still faced resistance from employers. WMC launched special advertisements and recruiting programs to lure more females into the workforce at the very time the army plunged into a vigorous campaign to recruit them for the WAACs. Attempts to tap the large pool of available black workers ran headlong into the familiar dogged resistance from workers and unions. The West, having foolishly incarcerated its Japanese Americans, looked to import workers from elsewhere, as did other sections of the country. Congress appropriated $26.1 million to create a "land army" of 3.5 million called the United States Crop Corps. As a start arrangements were made to import 50,000 farm workers from Mexico, 10,000 from Jamaica, and 5,000 from the Bahamas. It also planned to recruit 360,000 women as part of the army. Roosevelt told farm leaders that the army would transfer soldiers over the age of thirty-eight to inactive status if they agreed to go to work on farms.[37]

Selective Service also struggled to make its quotas. A report showed that the military's program called for 8 percent of the nation's population to be under arms compared to 12 percent for Germany and 10 percent for Britain. Even so, the bodies remained elusive. Part of the problem lay at the army's own doorstep; it had 800,000 civilian employees, an estimated 480,000 of whom were eligible for the draft. Nor did it help that a quarter of the first million teenagers drafted under the new law flunked their physicals. The pool of single men was gone, and that of married men with no children was about to vanish, leaving only the distasteful and highly unpopular alternative of drafting fathers. A WMC proposal to leave fathers on farms untouched and pluck more single men from war factories raised a storm of protest. "The time has come," declared McNutt, "when every worker must justify himself in terms of contribution to the war effort ... Fatherhood does not excuse any man from making his contribution to victory."[38]

The WMC's goals were clear: keep all workers in critical war industries on their jobs; find ways to transfer noncritical workers to war industries desperate for people; and supply men to the military without cutting into production.

Unfortunately, they proved impossible to achieve. By August the manpower muddle had only worsened, and a crisis was surfacing on the West Coast. As early as February the head of Boeing had warned Roosevelt that the company would fall behind production schedules by June unless its acute shortage of workers could be met. In June Boeing fell behind by thirty planes, and other aircraft manufacturers echoed the same complaint. A month later the total shortfall of the industry reached 800. Boeing drew special attention because it was the primary manufacturer of B-17 bombers. In August 1942 the Army Air Forces had launched their first major bombing raid on Europe; increased use of this tactic demanded a constant supply of new planes.[39]

McNutt insisted that Boeing's problems had less to do with labor shortages than with management's personnel policies. Sending it more workers, said a WMC official, would amount to "pouring water down a rat hole." When a War Department investigation came to the opposite conclusion, Patterson decided on direct action. He had long since lost faith in McNutt, as he had in Nelson, and appealed to James Byrnes for help. Byrnes obliged by summoning the familiar team of Baruch and Hancock to study the matter and make a report. Patterson sent a trusted and experienced lieutenant, John Hertz, to make an independent evaluation of the West Coast situation. He confirmed the depths of the crisis and warned that the manufacturers were likely to fall even more behind schedule during the second half of the year.[40]

In preparing their report Baruch and Hancock were particularly impressed by an approach that was working well in Buffalo. It had been devised by Anna Rosenberg, a small, Budapest-born bundle of brains and energy whose labor expertise had been invaluable to Roosevelt since 1934. Forever at the doorstep of controversy, wielding the vocabulary of a longshoreman when needed, Rosenberg was called "Mrs. Fix-It" by one writer. Her scheme, known as the Buffalo or "controlled referral" plan, applied to labor an approach borrowed from the CMP. It funneled men into plants where they were most needed on the basis of two principles: unemployed men could get jobs only at plants designated by USES, which issued them a certificate of availability, and those with jobs could change only with permission of their employers or WMC. Union leaders promptly denounced it as "labor servitude," but Rosenberg stood her ground and ordered the plan into effect in June. Since then the labor crisis in Buffalo plants had eased.[41]

Neither management nor labor liked the plan's strictures, but it seemed to be working as nothing else had. Baruch and Hancock incorporated its essential features in their report, which they presented to Byrnes on August 19. In typical Baruch manner the report offered a magisterial canvass of the major problems, sounded familiar alarms, couched its observations with cautionary reminders, appealed to civic duty, and offered several commonsense recommendations. The measures needed had to be coordinated into an overall, efficiently administered plan, he stressed, adding that "the only alternative to some plan of this sort is a national service act for the drafting of labor." Using the report as a guide, WMC drafted what became known as the West Coast Manpower Plan, which went public on September 4. *Newsweek* described its set of controls as "the most drastic ever invoked in this country."[42]

The War Department thought otherwise. The plan contained no heroic or radical proposals to solve the immediate crisis. Instead of providing specific relief, it looked to devise more effective long-range methods of improving local labor mobilization. Patterson was convinced that the plan bore the imprint of McNutt with its reliance on the WMC to implement solutions that might in fact worsen the problem. His fears were confirmed when airplane production in August dropped nearly a thousand units below schedule. Patterson appealed to his old mentor Baruch to soften his opposition to national service but got nowhere. A series of stormy meetings followed in which everyone accepted the West Coast Plan in principle but rejected WMC's proposed implementation of it. Baruch and Hancock alone supported the WMC version. Byrnes accepted most of the WMC version as the basis for what he announced on September 4.[43]

The West Coast Plan did little to solve the immediate crisis and, despite Byrnes's efforts, ultimately reduced WMC's influence. However, its inability to solve the labor shortage led to changes that improved the situation. Controlled referral channeled a larger proportion of the manpower flow through USES, which in turn steered hirees to where the need was greatest. The plan also led officials in Washington to pay closer attention to the labor supply in placing contracts, canceling some and redirecting others to different sections of the country. The apparent labor shortage was also in part a statistical illusion born of highly inflated requirements that limited supplies of people and materials—as well as threatening the loss of contracts—and induced manufacturers to cut their requirements. The plan provided an administrative framework that, while ineffective at first, proved useful later.[44]

"Last week the nation was in its 22nd month of war," declared *Newsweek* in late September, "and not yet had the Administration evolved a policy for manpower . . . Now that the crisis had arrived, the Administration was struggling, through the Baruch plan, to avoid compulsory national service." Writer Henry F. Pringle thought he knew the underlying reason for the muddle: "Behind it lies the obvious truth that this is the first total war in American history. The demands for soldiers, sailors and workers in the last World War were but a fraction of the needs today." Total war required a degree of commitment that intruded deeply on the American love of independence and personal freedom. No one expected that issue to be resolved anytime soon.[45]

That same month Frank Roney of the WMC conceded that the West Coast remained the flash point of the problem. "The entire West Coast economy is completely dominated by critical war industries," he said. "The economy of the West Coast centers around . . . aircraft, shipbuilding and repair, military installations of all types, non-ferrous mining, logging and lumbering, high value agriculture, and fishing . . . That means that all major production areas on the West Coast today are . . . now facing a serious labor shortage."[46]

Manufacturers did what they could to get and keep the workers they needed. One company, the Albina Engine & Machine Works in Portland, came up with several original schemes to keep its 4,500 workers happy and on the job even though they dwelled in the shadow of three Kaiser shipyards. The company persuaded 350 female employees, called the "vow" girls, to sign a pledge refusing to date any Albina man lacking a perfect attendance record. When workers complained about high vegetable prices, Albina got local farmers to bring their produce to the company gate at shift time with prices lower than downtown stores. A company cobbler offered three-day shoe service compared with three weeks downtown. Local barbers were asked to shorten wait time for its workers with signs that said AN ALBINA MAN IS ALWAYS NEXT. The company also bought up a supply of old washing machines and alarm clocks from far and wide, repaired them, and sold them to workers at cost. These and other ploys lowered absenteeism at the plant from 11 percent to less than 3 percent.[47]

In December Congress gave the manpower issue a parting shot for the year by passing a bill that was called "well-intentioned and toothless." It provided halfhearted protection for fathers in the draft and, to McNutt's chagrin, removed Selective Service from his command and restored its independence. Where McNutt and Lewis Hershey had warned that half a million fathers might have to be drafted during the last quarter of the year, only about 100,000 were actually called up. A few contract cancellations and cutbacks in the East and Midwest released some 30,000 workers for other jobs, but overall unemployment had dropped to 700,000, lower than anyone thought possible. In Lake Charles, Louisiana, a new 100-octane plant needed a thousand more men, and an oil industry leader warned of "a creeping manpower crisis" in his field.[48]

UP AND DOWN the West Coast the major cities recoiled from the impact of what the *San Francisco Chronicle* called "The Second Gold Rush." Instead of mining camps, this flood of newcomers flocked to urban areas, overwhelming local resources of every kind. Between April 1940 and March 1943 the civilian population in metropolitan areas of the three Pacific Coast states jumped 847,000 or nearly 13 percent. People went where the jobs were, mostly aircraft plants and shipyards, creating what historian Marilynn S. Johnson called "migrant ghettos" that varied in nature but not in hardship from city to city. Inland western cities, which had endured earlier mining and railroad booms that in some cases literally created them, experienced a similar inrush of newcomers in search of jobs, a fresh start in life, or simply adventure. Like the Great Depression, the war inflamed the rootlessness and restlessness that had always been an American trait. "One-sixth of our population are in a state of flux, physically and psychologically," noted a federal housing consultant. "If you ask them where they expect to be five years from now, they shrug their shoulders."[49]

The great migration of the war years exceeded all its predecessors in both size and diversity. It transformed all five major coastal cities—Seattle, Portland, the San Francisco Bay Area, Los Angeles, and San Diego—as well as inland cities such as Denver, Las Vegas, Phoenix, Tucson, El Paso, Tulsa, and Salt Lake City. Housing was an obvious problem that no city succeeded in solving well. San Diego, its economy revolutionized by the war, morphed from a sleepy navy town into a major metropolitan region. By 1943 it had built more new housing than during the past thirty years, most of it with federal money, and still it was not enough. "People have been compelled to live in crowded quarters under conditions which seriously impair health and morale with the consequent adverse effect on working efficiency," said a labor official, who dubbed housing "the most pressing problem facing the war workers in this area."[50]

Los Angeles did better at absorbing newcomers, thanks in part to a housing slump before the war due to overbuilding. By mid-1943, however, its vacancy rate had dwindled to nearly nothing. Private and public housing added 160,500 new units during the war to ease the strain. Farther north, San Francisco felt the impact of sudden growth most severely in the East Bay Area, which had several major shipyards including Kaiser's Richmond complex. More than half a million people swarmed into the region, reducing it to near chaos by 1943. Using federal funds, the San Francisco Housing Authority threw up temporary housing in two locales near shipyards, creating instant slums. "The impact of war activity has revolutionized the economy of the entire east bay area," moaned Oakland's city manager. His litany of complaints echoed those of other coastal cities: lack of housing, schools, and recreational facilities, breakdown of local services under the load, health and sanitation problems, and increased crime.[51]

At Vallejo, near the navy's Mare Island shipyard, the population had increased fivefold since 1940. People lived in shacks, stores, trailer camps, or temporary housing units thrown up by the Maritime Commission, or simply camped out. Some 14,000 workers could not find any place to live and traveled more than five hours a day to and from their jobs. The situation at Richmond was so hellacious that an investigating congressman admitted it to be "the worst that we have run across in the entire country in these congested areas." By 1943 Richmond contained four major Kaiser-managed shipyards along with fifty-five other war industries. A former sheriff found people living in "trailers, tents, tin houses, cardboard shacks, greenhouses, barns, garages, in automobiles, in theaters, or just fenced-off corners with the stars for a roof." It was the Depression all over again but for very different reasons. One landlord stuffed sixty-five people into his house until the fire department forced him to vacate it. Local residents did what they could in providing rooms with "hot beds" in which people working different shifts took turns sleeping.[52]

The Portland-Vancouver area fared somewhat better, but the Kaiser yards still hired people faster than housing could be provided for them. During 1943 more than 175 new trailer camps appeared around the fringes of the city. Public housing was built, including some dormitory and barracks units for 21,700 single workers. The most ambitious project created Vanport, or "Kaiserville" as the *Portland Oregonian* called it, just north of Portland, which in three years turned a barren stretch of mudflats into a city of 10,000 housing units occupied by 40,000 people, most of them Kaiser employees. In one stroke it became Oregon's second largest city, but no one liked living there. The cold, damp region had poor drainage, and the homes had concrete floors because the contractor could not get priority for lumber. The cooking stoves consisted of two-burner hot plates, iceboxes provided the only refrigeration, and coal burners the only heat. The hot plates burned out so regularly that the housing authority kept twenty-two electricians on the payroll around the clock chiefly to fix them.[53]

"No community can expand as this one has done, without it being a strain on the entire population," admitted Edgar Kaiser, but his father did what he could to improve things. Health care having always been a major issue to him, Henry Kaiser organized Portland's doctors into the Portland Physicians Service to provide medical care. In the Vancouver area the Kaisers formed a nonprofit foundation to build a new hospital and also gave their workers prepaid medical coverage. Conditions in the Portland-Vancouver area were less horrible than elsewhere partly because of the Kaisers and partly because there, unlike in other coastal urban areas, federal, state, and local officials met and thrashed out problems together with at least some success.[54]

Seattle and the Puget Sound region floundered badly in trying to cope with the boom. Shipyards lined the Sound at Bremerton, Seattle, Tacoma, Everett, Kirkland, and Bainbridge Island. Kaiser's yards alone employed between 70,000 and 100,000 workers, and Boeing's huge complex turned Seattle into a company town with 50,000 workers there and almost the same number working in branch plants and with subcontractors throughout the region. In 1939 the value of Seattle's manufactures totaled only $70 million, with $10 million of it coming from Boeing. By 1944 Boeing alone was producing $600 million worth of planes, and the city had some of the worst housing conditions in the nation as shortages of lumber and sheeting materials delayed the construction of new housing. What was thrown up helped sow the seeds for later inner-city decay.[55]

"Clothing must be washed by hand in the kitchen sink and dried above the kitchen stove," recalled one tenant who lived in a public housing project near the Puget Sound Navy Yard. ". . . Remember the kitchen and living room are actually one small unit . . . Due to poor design adequate chimneys are not provided on buildings, causing stoves to fill the homes with smoke . . . Refrigerators in the apartments consist of a small built-in cupboard with a metal pan for holding the ice. Food will not keep overnight . . . and the danger of eating contaminated food is always present. No playgrounds or recreational facilities available, and the area even lacked a school. Only one doctor is provided for a community of approximately 4,000 people."[56]

Smaller-scale versions of this same pattern unfolded in all the major interior cities of the West as well, including one obscure town that hardly anyone had heard of until recently. The building of a railroad between Los Angeles and Salt Lake City in the 1900s had created several new towns. One of them, Las Vegas, attracted little attention until the construction of Boulder Dam and Lake Mead nearby created a recreational area that drew some tourists. Power from the dam and deposits of brucite and magnesite helped state officials get a magnesium plant that opened in January 1942. The air force and navy moved in with air bases and ammunition depots. The town's proximity to several western cities, especially Los Angeles, made it a convenient divorce mill and playground, not only for celebrities but for workers and servicemen as well. The climate was pleasant, and gambling had been legal since 1931. The first large tourist hotel opened for business in November 1941, and entertainment soon emerged as the city's chief business.[57]

Here again was a formula that, in playing itself out all over the West, did not bode well for the future. Thanks to the war, the New West was faster, richer, more crowded, more diverse, and a far less pleasant place to live. It was no longer a mere colony of the East, but neither was it free. For all its mythology about self-reliance and rugged individualism, it had become largely a creature of the federal government. The huge influx of newcomers brought to the West a cultural richness that did not always square with native temperaments. Increasingly the Old West belonged to the novels and movies, where it would endure forever even as the war obliterated many of its roots.

CHAPTER 25

IRONING OUT THE WRINKLES

It was this sharing of power between the White House and the War Department which prevented the War Production Board from exercising its control on the home front.

—ELIOT JANEWAY[1]

The President uses those who suit his purposes. He makes up his own mind and discards people when they no longer fulfill a purpose of his.

—ELEANOR ROOSEVELT[2]

Scarcely six months have ever gone by since I have been in office . . . without a "labor crisis." This time it is very much involved with the cost of living and inflation difficulties. I am definitely on the minority side and it will be quite clear that if they force my hand on inflation, wages and food prices will have to go up too . . . The general attitude seems to be that a little inflation would not do any harm, in spite of the fact that I am telling them that a pill or two of opium would not do much harm except for the fact that in most cases it leads to addiction.

—FRANKLIN ROOSEVELT[3]

THE MACHINERY WAS FINALLY IN place. After seemingly interminable false starts and missteps a workable administrative structure needed only some fine-tuning to run the war's production. Few people appreciated the staggering complexity of the overall task of running it. No one understood its intricacies better than the man at the center of the whole structure. Franklin Roosevelt had been roundly criticized for trying to do too much and for trying to keep all the reins in his own hands. It was a natural mistake for one who believed he knew the larger picture better than anyone else, which happened to be true. As he had during the depression years, he fussed and tinkered with one approach after another until he found something that seemed to work. This pragmatic course had not solved the riddle of the depression, but it had improved things greatly and changed American life profoundly.

The war posed a similar problem in that it was a temporary condition that required extraordinary but not necessarily permanent measures to meet its demands. It was this thinking that lay behind the proliferation of new agencies, much as it had with the New Deal. "It seems to me it is easier to use a new agency which is not a permanent part of the structure of government," Roosevelt told Frances Perkins. "If it is not permanent, we don't get bad precedents that will carry over into the days of peace. We can do anything that needs to be done and then discard the agency when the emergency is over." His tactic was to divide responsibility among several people so as to leave himself in position to decide the main questions. For this to happen, he needed a suitable administrative structure to make the temporary agencies function efficiently. No useful models or precedents existed for what this structure should be.[4]

The machinery was still far from perfect, but each stage of its evolution had improved the situation. "Examined closely, by the myopic eye of the perfectionist," wrote I. F. Stone in 1942, "Mr. Roosevelt's performance in every sphere has been faulty. Regarded in the perspective of his limited freedom of choice and the temper of the country, which has never really been warlike, the year's achievements have been extraordinary." For all the clamor and chatter about czars, only a few had been created and only in areas tied to specific needs. They in turn reported either to WPB or to Roosevelt himself. By 1943, however, Roosevelt had reluctantly come to realize that one more step was needed—one that had been urged on him from the beginning. He had to deal with not only production and domestic affairs but also foreign policy and the conduct of the war, which made it impossible for him to keep all the reins in his hands. Whatever the merits of WPB—and they were many—it had failed utterly to coordinate the efforts of all the agencies and reduce the infighting among them. Something more was needed to relieve the president of this part of his burden.[5]

The intramural warfare continued, as did the controversy among claimants for labor and materials. If anything, these clashes had grown more urgent as the United States shifted from the defensive and seized the offensive in both Europe and the Pacific. Once past conversion, the demand for new and better weapons, and more of them, rose sharply, as did the need to rethink overall strategy and the balance of forces between the two theaters of war. More and more, questions of military strategy and relations with the other Allies occupied Roosevelt's attention, leaving him less time and energy to deal with domestic issues. He needed someone or something to relieve him of those concerns as much as possible, while still keeping him involved in them at a greater distance.

"Roosevelt had recognized for some time that the home front had grown too big, too complicated, too controversial to be administered personally by him," wrote Eliot Janeway. ". . . The problem was a standard one in the business world, and it called for a standard solution—the principal must recognize that the time has come to promote himself to the Chairmanship of the Board, and to find a successor qualified to represent him as deputy without and executive within."[6]

Roosevelt's solution was yet another agency, but of a different kind. Already he had created OES to oversee prices and wages as "a sort of holding company for most of the non-legislated war agencies." Jimmy Byrnes had shown impressive ability to arbitrate and mediate, but the agency's authority extended only to its limited sphere of economic stabilization. Oversight over all the war agencies involved in the national economy still did not exist except in the hands of an overworked president. Bills had been introduced in Congress to create a super-agency to perform this role, but Roosevelt feared the result would only be another top-heavy layer of bureaucracy that would curb the flexibility he needed to meet constantly changing situations at home and on the battlefields. Any such agency had to be created by executive order to preserve that flexibility. It also had to be small but powerful and nimble—tall orders for any government body.[7]

On May 27, 1943, Roosevelt took the plunge by issuing an executive order creating the Office of War Mobilization (OWM). Jimmy Byrnes, who had done a good job at OES, was made its director and presided over a War Mobilization Committee consisting of the secretaries of War and Navy and heads of WPB, OES, and the Munitions Assignment Board headed by Hopkins, all of whom were to supply any data requested by him. OWM had two missions. The first was to "develop unified programs and to establish policies for the maximum use of the Nation's natural and industrial resources for military and civilian needs, for the effective use of the national manpower not in the armed forces, for the maintenance and stabilization of the civilian economy, and for the adjustment of such economy to war needs and conditions."[8]

This in itself was a tall order, but the second mission was equally sweeping and important. OWM was to "unify the activities of Federal agencies and departments engaged in or concerned with production, procurement, distribution, or transportation of military or civilian supplies, materials, and products and to resolve and determine controversies between such agencies or departments." Within these two directives could be found the entire scope and shortcomings of the defense and war mobilization effort. The order was sweeping and the authority conferred was vast; one OWM staff member who later wrote the agency's history called it "an unprecedented delegation of executive authority." Jimmy Byrnes was to be super-referee, the head of a holding company presiding over a huge economic empire. The press quickly labeled him the "assistant president," a title that Roosevelt despised. *Time* called him "the best politician . . . outside the President."[9]

Congress and the public alike hailed the Byrnes appointment as a good one and sensed that the new agency was more than just the latest ingredient in the endless alphabet soup. The president, observed *Newsweek*, "explicitly told Byrnes to issue orders to all other czars and department heads, and told the czars to obey. The order left no room for the short-circuiting that has left many a czar uncertain whether he had to take orders from Nelson or only from the President." Roosevelt also told Byrnes to make decisions with "dispatch," a less than subtle slam at Nelson. Unlike Nelson, Byrnes was a smooth, skilled politician adept at compromise as well as putting his foot down.[10]

Presidential aide Bill Hassett regarded the Byrnes appointment as a good choice. "He must also 'resolve and determine controversies'; i.e., make Harold Ickes cease sniping at fellow Cabinet members, in itself a full day's work," he observed. ". . . This intergovernmental sniping threatens our home front . . . If Byrnes can do half this, he will qualify for President of the Solar System."[11]

WHETHER ROOSEVELT LIKED the epithet or not, he had in effect made Byrnes assistant president. OWM had no operational responsibilities, and a year after its creation the staff numbered only ten. It never became a lumbering giant, but it wielded great power and Byrnes knew how to use it. He did not hesitate to issue directives for WMC or WPB or other agencies to implement, and he was careful not to get involved in their execution. Judge Fred Vinson replaced Byrnes at OES, which remained independent of OWM. No clear line separated their jurisdictions, but Byrnes worked well with Vinson, as he did with most of the agency heads, virtually all of whom liked and trusted him. It was in his capacity as OWM head that Byrnes presided over the stormy meetings that led to his announcing in September the West Coast Manpower Plan.[12]

"The modest size of our staff and quarters," said Byrnes, "effectively demonstrated our resolve not to compete with other agencies." At the same time, he was determined to establish his authority by making it clear that his decisions carried the full weight of the president. He instructed his staff never to go to other offices for consultation, saying that the operating agencies had to bring their problems to OWM. As a first step he asked all agencies to review their procurement programs realistically and objectively. As always, the stiffest resistance came from the military, which continued its reluctance to share sensitive strategic materials with civilians. Stimson took the new structure to mean "a new heavy burden for me." Byrnes assured him that the problem of inflation would remain with OES and not the new committee. At the first meeting on June 8 Roosevelt presided over a free-ranging discussion of both the OWM's main charges and the issues involved in them. Stimson came away impressed.[13]

After nearly a month of working with OWM, Stimson concluded that it brought him "a lot of opportunities and work on my shoulders. Byrnes is becoming virtually a deputy President in trying to iron out all the troubles which the President has brought on himself by faulty organization which places on him the decision in too many things." The War Department gave Byrnes reasonable cooperation, and he was careful not to intrude in matters of strategy. For the navy Knox and Forrestal were helpful, but the admirals led by Ernest J. King continued to fight civilian interference in their affairs. When Byrnes appointed William Gibbs, the celebrated ship designer, as OWM's man on the naval procurement board, the admirals argued that this would reveal military secrets to a civilian. Only after Byrnes threatened to take the issue to Roosevelt did the admirals relent.[14]

Gibbs did not like what he found. He reported that the navy was building too many escort vessels, patrol craft, and minesweepers, that its airplane program was badly unbalanced, and that its inventory control was extremely weak, among other problems. Its construction schedules would require a 22 percent increase in shipyard workers by July 1944, mostly on the West Coast, where labor was scarce. Cutbacks were needed to save huge amounts of manpower and materials. Fred Searls, now on the OWM staff, reminded Byrnes in September that to succeed he had to get tough with the military, that Nelson had squandered his chance to oversee military requirements and paid dearly for it. "The people in uniform have successfully reduced [Nelson's] authority," he added. "I am very much afraid that, within the next 30 days, they will accomplish much the same end with respect to yours."[15]

Byrnes took the matter to Roosevelt, who responded on September 24 by creating within the JCS a new body, the Joint Production Survey Committee (JPSC). Composed of senior officers, the new committee was to coordinate civilian and military mobilization efforts, inform the JCS of concerns raised by OWM, and reduce military requirements where possible. Byrnes attended both JCS and JPSC meetings and appointed Searls as OWM's observer on the latter. JPSC was the closest the nation came to a body charged with coordinating strategy with production, and the nearest thing to the supreme war council urged earlier by the Planning Committee. For Byrnes it became a way of scrutinizing military procurement and the critical factors shaping it. But the services still managed to stonewall his efforts to gather reliable data for evaluating their needs and requests.[16]

FOR BYRNES THE summer of 1943 proved long and hot in part because of the internal feuds that continued to plague the administration. The internecine warfare took place on two broad levels: the occasional clash of titans between top executives of warring agencies and the endless petty sniping by troops of lower rank who made up in malice what they lacked in stature. One disenchanted minor official described the setup of the agencies as "essentially absolutely feudal. There is a big boss at the top, a lot of sub-bosses, and a legion of sub-sub-bosses. Each agency unit, section and subsection is . . . simply a glorified form of the lord and his manorial underlings." The base cause, he thought, lay in "the desire of the little officials to be more important than those working with them, to monopolize credit, and to belittle others who are getting credit." In citing this complaint Raymond Moley added that "the fear of being wrong in the few government agencies I know anything about is almost pathological. And that means considerable time is spent covering up and buck-passing."[17]

For all the backbiting in the ranks, explosions at the top inevitably drew the most attention from the press and the chattering classes. Excitement over the Jeffers-Patterson row had scarcely subsided when others took its place. In March Roosevelt created a new organization that became the War Food Administration (WFA) and named Chester C. Davis to head it. Davis found that his approach to food policy clashed with that of OPA. On June 16 he wrote Roosevelt that to do his job he needed the OPA's authority over food distribution and prices. Twelve days later the president invited his resignation, which was given. Gossip swirled on the Hill that someone had sabotaged Davis in Roosevelt's eyes. That controversy quickly paled when an even more serious row erupted seemingly out of nowhere between two heavyweights: Vice President Henry Wallace and Jesse Jones.[18]

The enmity between Jones and Wallace was long-standing, a clash between the emblem of hard-core southern conservatism and the quintessential New Dealer and unabashed advocate of social reform. In particular they came to blows over the relationship between the Board of Economic Warfare, which Wallace headed, and the RFC. Created in July 1941, the board oversaw export controls and purchases of foreign raw materials and other wartime necessities. In Jones's cynical view Roosevelt had devised it "to provide Vice President Wallace with important war work so that he would remain the logical successor to the Presidency." Most of its work involved South America, where the objective was not only to procure raw materials but keep the Axis powers from doing so. Some of this work duplicated the stockpiling RFC did or was supposed to be doing.[19]

Aided by his executive director, the intense, tireless Milo Perkins, Wallace steered BEW onto an innovative and aggressive course that soon collided with other agencies. The State Department zealously guarded its prerogatives in licensing exports and imports, and Lend-Lease had its own arrangements for shipping vital materials to America's allies. The RFC and its related lending agencies were especially determined to dictate terms for import purchasing, and the Department of Agriculture had its own procurement authority for foreign purchases. Even some WPB officials considered themselves the final word on foreign purchases. In March 1942 Wallace protested this tangle of overlapping authority in a strongly worded memo to Roosevelt in which he emphasized in capital letters, "THERE CANNOT BE ANYTHING BUT FRUSTRATION AND CONFUSION" if the president did not give someone, preferably himself, the power to let BEW do the job. Roosevelt complied in April with an order directing the RFC to finance the purchases of BEW and pay for anything contracted by it outside the United States. The order also allowed BEW to send technical and economic representatives abroad.[20]

In policy terms Jones believed that the order overstepped the purchasing authority given him by Congress in 1940. He also ridiculed Wallace's ambitious efforts to introduce what he considered social reform programs for South American workers. He lampooned what he described as "Mr. Wallace's desire to provide free food for everybody in the Amazon Basin and of his dream of strengthening them with vitamin pills and vitaminized flour . . . Mr. Wallace had a notion it would make for a happier world to teach the Indians in the jungles of the Amazon to grow vegetables in the North American manner." The State Department asked Roosevelt to reconsider the order. After several meetings the president issued another order in May restoring some of State's authority.[21]

Jones was not satisfied. On a more personal level he resented even the smallest nibble at his power, and BEW amounted to a large bite. He still smarted from criticism that he had moved too slowly in buying raw materials before Pearl Harbor and that his slow, cautious manner remained an obstacle to getting things done fast. He deeply resented Wallace and Perkins, a longtime liberal reformer who had devised the New Deal's food stamp program. Later he sneered that as BEW chairman Wallace "could sit in the big chair once a week and 'play like' he was already Mister President." Perkins he dismissed as "a former bag salesman and self-ordained cultist 'priest' from Texas," where he was a nobody compared to Jones. Politically speaking, Jones had the support of his extended network of southern friends in Congress, who disliked Wallace intensely and had grown far more powerful than the New Dealers.[22]

Jones responded to the order with one of his most effective and annoying traits: inertia. Told by a jaded New Dealer that "nothing in this town is so easily ignored as a White House directive," I. F. Stone watched Jones practice this maxim relentlessly. "No one else in Washington except the accomplished bureaucrats of the State Department has gone so far in perfecting the art of governing by *not* doing things," he said, "by mislaying documents, overlooking directives, and forgetting to sign checks. This last has been Jones's forte since the President on April 13, 1942, placed the acquisition of strategic materials in the hands of the BEW, with full power—on paper—to direct the RFC to make the necessary expenditures." Since that date, Stone charged, Jones had continued to be "the biggest single bottleneck of the war program." Jones also worked the Hill, cajoling and calling in chits, hinting that BEW was an irresponsible one-man show and that it was giving away American money to build postwar industries in Russia and South America.[23]

For months Wallace stewed over Jones's obstructionism and his whispering campaign. Then, on May 29, 1943, Jones went with his aide W. L. Clayton to Wallace's office in what he called "a final exasperated effort to try to please Mr. Wallace and get his long-haired, incompetent, meddlesome disciples out of our hair." They came to an apparent agreement, but the draft of it displeased Jones, who thought that "the boys of the BEW were trying to grab more than we had agreed to." Letters to the president followed, dumping the conflict on his desk. Then Wallace learned that the Senate Appropriations Committee was about to cut BEW's travel funds and give Jones veto power over its foreign purchases. Bristling with anger, Wallace decided on a bold and dangerous move. On June 29 he sent the committee a two-page letter attached to a twenty-eight-page report that baldly denounced Jones's conniving and obstructionism. He called Jones a liar, accused him of harassing BEW employees, and dredged up all the past examples of Jones's failure to buy strategic materials. "We are helpless when Jesse Jones refuses to sign our checks in accordance with our directives," he said. ". . . All this, and I want to emphasize it, is bureaucracy at its worst; it is utterly inexcusable in a nation at war."[24]

Wallace claimed he was merely correcting testimony given by Jones before the committee, and he added that the best remedy was for Congress to fund BEW independently of the RFC. But Wallace had gone public with his charges, which violated Roosevelt's decree of the previous August that all intramural disputes be brought to his office and not aired publicly. For several days Jones alternately blustered and brooded. He called friendly senators and demanded an investigation, telling them, "That damned liar has called me a liar three times. I'm going to call him one ten times." To one sympathizer he said, "I'm 69 now, but if I can't handle that little ____ from Des Moines I'm older than I think and maybe I ought to go back to Houston." He had no intention of going back to Houston. Instead Jones assembled a thirty-page rejoinder with a five-page cover letter of his own and dispatched it to the committee.[25]

Caught by surprise, Roosevelt was furious at having his decree against intramural squabbling in public so blatantly defied. He shoved the problem into Byrnes's waiting lap. A few days earlier Congress had overridden the president's veto of the Smith-Connally antistrike bill, the worst setback it had ever handed him, and it left the impression that the president no longer controlled his own party, at least on domestic issues. The public brawl between Wallace and Jones added to this image. As Robert Sherwood observed, "It gave to the American people—not to mention the people of other United Nations—an alarming sense of disunity and blundering incompetence in very high places."[26]

Byrnes summoned the two men to his office on the afternoon of June 30 to thrash out a solution. Jones deliberately arrived fifteen minutes late, ignored greetings from both Byrnes and Wallace, and sat down without saying a word. For nearly an hour Byrnes and Wallace did most of the talking; Jones merely said that Wallace had called him a liar and demanded that he prove it. Byrnes said they owed it to the president to settle their quarrel. Jones said he had heard that Wallace was a praying man and advised him to ask God that night to stop him from lying. Then he excused himself, ostensibly to make a phone call but actually to give Wallace more time to talk with Byrnes. When he returned, nothing got accomplished. Less than an hour after the meeting broke up, Wallace issued another statement, to which Jones took exception and replied with one of his own calling it a "dastardly attack."[27]

Next day Byrnes wrote Roosevelt that he saw no hope of reconciling their differences. He recommended that the president move at once to strip both men of their authority over foreign economic affairs and vest it in a new agency with Leo T. Crowley as its head. The new agency would also take on some other functions currently performed by the RFC. Roosevelt talked it over with Byrnes and on July 15 issued an executive order abolishing the BEW and creating the Office of Economic Warfare. At the same time, he sent the same letter prepared for him by Byrnes to both Jones and Wallace, spanking them for their behavior. "In the midst of waging a war so critical to our national security and to the future of all civilization," he said, "there is not sufficient time to investigate and determine where the truth lies in your conflicting versions as to transactions which took place over a year and a half ago . . . We must go forward without any further public debate as to matters which are now academic so far as winning the war is presently concerned."[28]

"His swift and drastic action," observed Hassett, "should be a lesson to plenty of others—Honest Harold Ickes among them—to quit fighting each other and concentrate on the enemy." Byrnes also drafted a second letter that Roosevelt sent to the heads of all agencies and departments. He reminded them that "disagreements either as to fact or policy should not be publicly aired, but are to be submitted to me by the appropriate heads of the conflicting agencies" and warned that he would not overlook any future violations. Any subordinate official who ignored these instructions should be asked for his immediate resignation. Roosevelt was determined to end the intramural wars once and for all. There was a war to win, and it would not be won by fighting each other in public at home. Privately the president thanked Byrnes for doing what he could to end feuds and, during the last week of July, took him and the rest of the presidential staff off to Canada on a fishing trip.[29]

Although seemingly just one more intramural spat, the dispute had serious repercussions. Jones thought he had won the fight. Roosevelt did appoint Crowley, whom Jones considered a friend, and they worked together smoothly afterward. "Mr. Wallace was out of a war job," Jones wrote gleefully later. "He was once more just the Vice President with little to do but wait for the President to die, which fortunately did not occur while Henry was Vice President." The press agreed with him. *Newsweek* pronounced Wallace "the big loser" in the shakeup, losing his top war job while Jones remained head of RFC and secretary of commerce. "Ably and well he had fought against the dollars-as-usual policies of the most conservative man in the Administration," reported *Time*, but Wallace had committed the cardinal sin of violating the president's dictum that disputes not be thrashed out for all the world to see.[30]

"There was not a semblance of visible justification for Wallace's outburst," concluded Ernest Lindley. ". . . No fundamental issue was involved in their feud. It grew out of a faulty administrative setup and was aggravated by differences of temperament and method and personal animosities." Lindley blamed the incident on Milo Perkins, "the man who organized and ran the BEW. He is dynamic, a zealot who brooks no obstacles." Whoever was at fault, nearly everyone agreed that the most serious consequence was the damage it did to Wallace's standing as the potential successor to Roosevelt in 1944. If, as expected, Roosevelt ran again that year, Wallace would almost certainly be dropped from the ticket. As one Washington wag put it, "They have just buried the last New Dealer." Few observers believed it was mere coincidence that more and more businessmen and southern conservatives were occupying positions of power formerly held by a corps of ardent New Dealers. In that political war Wallace had become simply the latest casualty.[31]

*   *   *

Few members of the administration absorbed more abuse than Henry Morgenthau. Once, while discussing one of his many tax proposals with the president, Roosevelt laughed and said, "Well, you know, Henry, I always have to have a couple of whipping boys."

"Yes," replied Morgenthau, "I realize that I am one of them and right now I am getting plenty of whippings."[32]

Especially did he get them from Congress, that den of hostiles to whom he had to present his tax plans. The long, harsh fight over the Revenue Act of 1942 had transformed the tax system and doubled federal tax revenue, but it left unresolved the inflation gap and the Ruml plan for a pay-as-you-go approach. During the year the inflation gap had widened, and the Victory Tax grew even more unpopular. Morgenthau could expect nothing but more punishment as he reopened all these wounds in 1943.

Tall and stooped, painfully shy, his expensive ties carelessly knotted, he struck most people as an autocratic cold fish. The son of a Jewish New York lawyer who made a fortune in real estate, Morgenthau never graduated from college and floundered at several early career tries before buying at twenty-two a farm in Dutchess County. There he became fast friends with a fellow gentleman farmer named Franklin Roosevelt, who lived only twenty-five miles away. Morgenthau got involved in Roosevelt's gubernatorial campaign, went to Albany with him, and moved on to Washington as treasury secretary, where he revealed an unhappy talent for making enemies. New Dealers and conservatives alike distrusted him, and many of the people at Treasury disliked him as well. Those who took the trouble to know him found a reservoir of warmth and intelligence, but they were few in number.[33]

Going before congressional committees to present his tax proposals became an excruciating ordeal for Morgenthau, who hesitated to express his views strongly. In 1942 alone he presented a dozen major tax recommendations only to see every one of them rejected. In one last bill Congress inserted a clause authorizing it to circumvent the secretary in seeking advice from Treasury experts. Although majority leader Alben Barkley pleaded with his colleagues not to "slap the Secretary of the Treasury in the face," the Senate adopted the clause 74–10. Morgenthau flinched but never wavered; courage and loyalty were his strongest suits. He understood that none of his predecessors had ever faced the demands thrust on his slender shoulders.[34]

In his annual budget message the president said that the United States planned to spend or lend about $109 billion in the coming year, of which he wanted $51 billion raised without borrowing. The Civil War had cost the nation $3.35 billion and World War I $35.4 billion. Obviously more money had to be raised through taxes and other sources. Inflation remained a major problem and one closely tied to taxation. On both issues members of the administration agreed strongly that they had to be dealt with but divided sharply over how best to handle them. Congress, ever more conservative in its temperament, showed little inclination to confront these issues directly. A solid wall of special interests stood ready to block any bill they deemed unfavorable, let alone one that even hinted of social reform as well. Prospects for quick action of any sort looked grim.[35]

"Inflation is here now—we are in the foothills of inflation," declared Raymond Clapper. ". . . The best way to hold back inflation is to levy higher taxes." Nearly everyone agreed that new taxes offered the best way to soak up excess spending power, yet Congress remained fearful of the political repercussions or, in some cases, simply opposed anything the administration wanted. Any tax bill had first to run the gauntlet of Muley Doughton's committee in the House and Walter George's in the Senate. Both were sympathetic to the administration but could not always carry their members with them. Then there was the army of lobbyists. "All over Washington the pressure groups are out in hobnailed shoes trying to break through the controls and get foot-loose for an inflation orgy," said Clapper. ". . . Everyone is represented in the big push except the little fellow in the middle, the white-collar salaried worker, his salary frozen. He is unorganized . . . There's somebody else not represented. That's the American soldier."[36]

Treasury studies projected the inflation gap—the estimated excess of consumer income over the value of available goods—at $16 billion for 1943. To keep inflation in check, this amount had to be absorbed by taxes and savings. New sources of revenue had to be devised and old ones strengthened. Roosevelt was equivocal about taxes. "I could tell by the look on his face," Morgenthau told his staff after meeting with the president in December 1942, "that he hadn't seen the budget, and didn't know and didn't care." Morgenthau favored a package that included a stiff withholding tax, increases in the corporate, individual, and Social Security taxes, strict rationing on all scarce articles, and no compulsory savings provision. Harold Smith of the Budget Bureau advocated compulsory savings and a national sales tax. The two men locked horns not only over policy but also over who should be formulating tax policy in the first place.[37]

One key issue remained: not only getting more revenue but getting it quicker. In this debate the Ruml pay-as-you-go plan, having survived four months of bitter debate, still held center stage. The sticking point continued to be fierce disagreement over the idea of forgiving the payment of income taxes for 1942 and withholding tax at once on 1943 income. Otherwise, the implementation of a withholding system at any time would require the collection of taxes for two years at the same time, which few people were willing or prepared to pay. This would provide an obvious windfall to people, especially war industrialists, who made more money—in some cases much more—in 1942 than in 1943. Morgenthau adamantly opposed the plan, arguing that it would reward sixty taxpayers who earned over a million dollars in 1942 with a windfall of $854,000 each. Those with net income over $100,000 would get about $64,000 compared to $2,150 for a man earning $10,000 and only $140 for one earning $2,000.[38]

Ruml admitted privately that his plan benefited wealthy taxpayers more than others, but he saw nothing wrong with that. The plan had a host of influential supporters. Ralph Robey argued that it would bring the government more revenue at a faster rate, provided greater protection against inflation, would make it easier for taxpayers to meet their obligations, and was favored by a majority of the public. Admitting that some wealthy taxpayers would reap a windfall, he asked, "Why should 25,000,000 others of us have to suffer because of these few?" *Look* declared that "the greatest single contribution Congress can make to our national morale is to stabilize income tax rates and place future tax-paying on a sane, pay-as-you-go footing." Collections for income taxes due March 15 came in glacially as taxpayers waited to see what the outcome of the debate over Ruml would be. The slow volume of returns occurred even though the Revenue Act of 1942 had increased the number of people with taxable income from 26 million to more than 40 million.[39]

The burden of steering a viable tax bill through the House fell on Muley Doughton of North Carolina, who got his nickname from a tendency to cling stubbornly to an idea once he got it. The son of a Confederate Army captain, he had been in Congress for thirty-two years and chairman of the Ways and Means Committee since 1933. He still struggled to absorb the complexities of tax proposals and described his own tax philosophy as one "to get the most feathers with the fewest squawks from the goose." At seventy-nine he still worked hard and was hard-nosed about smoking, drinking, and partying. Once he congratulated a young female assistant who arrived on the Capitol grounds at 6 A.M. for coming to work early, unaware that she was just coming home from a party. He could be gruff and impatient, but those who worked for him found him thoughtful and pleasant.[40]

An administration loyalist, Doughton agreed with Morgenthau that any tax plan adopted should not forgive 1942 taxes, but the pressure for Ruml kept mounting. For four days the House argued over three versions of pay-as-you-go, then tossed the whole problem back into the lap of Ways and Means when none of them could muster a majority vote. At one point the House voted 199–188 to approve Ruml, only to have a roll call vote reverse the decision 215–198. The administration continued to denounce Ruml as a boon to the rich, while an alternative plan submitted by Aime J. Forand of Rhode Island was labeled socialistic because it discriminated in favor of the small taxpayer. "Sixteen months after Pearl Harbor we still lack an adequate system of war taxes and compulsory savings," complained Ernest Lindley. He blamed Treasury's leaders, whose "tax recommendations were pretty consistently a year out of date when they were made," but also faulted Congress for its lack of leadership.[41]

After four months of wrangling, Doughton brought forth a compromise bill only to have it rejected 230–120. A modified version of Ruml then barely missed passage, after which the House passed a version of Forand's compromise bill 313–95 and sent it on to the Senate. Forand's bill wiped out 1942 liabilities for 90 percent of taxpayers and 75 percent of the total taxes due. The Senate Finance Committee promptly voted 13–6 in favor of total forgiveness. On May 17 Roosevelt entered the fray with a letter to Doughton and Senator Walter George saying he was eager to see taxes put on a pay-as-you-go basis as soon as possible but opposing the Senate bill because it enriched wealthy taxpayers. Five alternative versions surfaced in the Senate before a modified version of Ruml passed 49–30.[42]

By June the struggle had left everyone exhausted and eager for some resolution. Asked to provide another letter, Roosevelt snapped, "The people aren't interested in letters. What they want is to see a bill get through." Five days of joint committee haggling finally produced a bill that passed. It amounted to a Ruml victory of sorts in commencing pay-as-you-go and providing for 75 percent tax forgiveness with total cancellation for obligations of $50 or less. Taxpayers could take the 75 percent forgiveness for whichever was lower of their 1942 and 1943 obligations. "It's been one of the most bitter experiences of my life," said Doughton. ". . . We just got to where we had to take this or go back and get something worse or take nothing."[43]

As the fight wound down, Morgenthau conceded that he could manage with $12 billion in new taxes instead of $16 billion originally requested. The new tax law transformed the way Americans paid their taxes, but it came nowhere near raising that sum. Other taxes would be needed, possibly increased levies on cigarettes, beer, and liquor. A national sales tax remained an option, as did a "spending tax" on nonessential outlays. Congress would have only a brief respite from the odious subject. Meanwhile, an even greater menace continued to hound the government. Like taxes, the problem of inflation desperately needed a solution, and none was in sight.[44]

IT BECAME CLEAR early that Prentiss Brown was no Leon Henderson. The genial ex-senator was much less abrasive and more tactful. From the start he emphasized that he would replace Henderson's "get tough" policy with his own "be nice" version. At his first news conference he conceded that prices would probably continue "an inevitable, slow, well-ordered rise" at their current rate of half a percent a month, but he stopped short of declaring how much of a rise the government would permit. The twin terrors of the inflation war, organized labor and the farm bloc, intensified their tag-team ritual of using the other's demands as an excuse to increase their own. It did not help that labor had the most influence with the president and the farm bloc with Congress at a time when tension between Roosevelt and the Hill continued to worsen.[45]

By appointing Brown the president had hoped to improve relations with Congress on curbing inflation. Instead the move was interpreted as a softening of Henderson's tough policy on prices. Outside interests of many kinds took it as a signal to increase their pressure on OPA to ease price controls and raise price ceilings.[46]

Scarcely had Henderson cleared the door of OPA when both labor and the farm bloc opened yet another round of demands. UAW president R. J. Thomas wanted a 30 percent raise for his people, arguing that "the Little Steel formula has never been a fair means of deciding what are proper wage increases." John L. Lewis warned that negotiations for his coal miners would begin in March. "The men who mine the nation's coal will ask for bread," he intoned. "They will hope that a government bureaucrat will not hand them a stone." Lewis's idea of bread amounted to a raise of two dollars a day for his 450,000 bituminous miners. Nonoperating railroad employees numbering 900,000 asked for increases of up to 30 percent an hour in their wage rates. The House Agricultural Committee quietly approved without hearings the Pace bill to include the cost of farm labor in the farm parity formula even though similar efforts had been defeated three times in the last Congress and the measure would increase food costs by $3.5 billion. Businesses also demanded price hikes to compensate for growing labor and materials costs.[47]

The Economic Stabilization Order of October 1942 had been issued to stop the rise in the cost of living. But by the following April prices had jumped another 6.2 percent; food prices rose 13 percent and those of fresh fruits and vegetables a whopping 58 percent. Roosevelt's call for a national wartime forty-eight-hour workweek in February added to the inflationary pressure even though he and Byrnes insisted that increased production would offset any such influence. In this manner income rose even when base wages did not. Those working more than forty hours received time-and-a-half for the extra hours. The extra hours fattened their paychecks, giving them more disposable income to chase a dwindling supply of consumer goods and driving up prices. The nation's war plants were already working forty-eight hours a week or more, but industry overall averaged only forty-four hours a week. At the same time, the sharp increase in munitions output reduced the supply of consumer goods, thereby adding fuel to the inflationary fires.[48]

Ralph Robey was not alone in offering a formula to fight inflation: impose more taxes to siphon off disposable income; hold down costs, especially wage increases; maximize production of civilian goods to ease the pressure on prices; and limit price fixing to raw materials and necessities, letting the price of luxuries rise to help absorb excess buying power. On paper the plan seemed elegant; getting it accomplished was quite another matter. The tax issue was a political minefield, the clamor for higher wages grew steadily louder, and the farm bloc was relentless in seeking more concessions for its preferred farmers. The root cause of inflation remained the excess of purchasing power over the total volume of available goods, which increases in income or wages only aggravated.[49]

Robey also regarded Henderson's departure from OPA as the perfect time to overhaul the agency. "Although the OPA is less than two years old," he wrote, "it has issued a series of rules, regulations, and instructions, which from the point of view of both volume and wording are hopeless to the ordinary individual." The impression prevailed, especially among businessmen, that Henderson's leaving meant a general relaxing of OPA strictures would be forthcoming. Brown recognized that to many Americans OPA seemed "a bully, an irritant, a source of confusion." He set out to induce citizens to like the agency, and as a first step promised to prune deadwood from its ranks. He brought in as a major deputy Lou Maxon, head of a Detroit advertising agency, to help sell OPA to the public and ordered that all future plans, orders, and regulations be cleared through Maxon. One writer described Maxon as "a walking, talking version of the deep-dyed conservative."[50]

Old-line OPA employees were appalled by Brown's "sugar-coating policy." They protested Maxon's presence and the new order at once, forcing Brown to amend it by giving them a right of appeal to himself in any dispute with Maxon. Within days Maxon stirred up another uproar by reviving an old issue, canned goods. Shortly before his departure, Henderson had issued an order for compulsory grading of canned food as a precaution against canners meeting price ceilings by cutting quality. Grade would determine price and help those families, according to John Kenneth Galbraith, who used a week's ration stamps "for some thickened water and a few isolated vegetables." The National Canners Association promptly unleashed a major law firm to attack the order, insisting that grade-labeling was a needless "social reform in wartime." Brown, who had earlier endorsed the order, agreed to reconsider it. Maxon, whose clients included a major canning company, infuriated OPA men by urging repeal of the order.[51]

The main opposition to Maxon came from former Henderson men who still believed in a "get tough" policy. The order was rescinded, and that spring several of Henderson's young Turks—what *Time* called OPA's "slide-rule boys"—left the agency. Some were drafted, others simply let go, including Galbraith after he fell into an acrimonious dispute with Maxon. "The applause on my departure was brief but intense," recalled Galbraith; "not often have I so succeeded in pleasing conservatives." He was, conceded his friends, often tactless and "unintentionally irritating in his mannerisms." The departures spurred talk of yet another agency beset with inner turmoil. Brown tried to calm the storm, saying that OPA could stand six or seven resignations without damage. An observer sneered that the agency had become "the world's greatest jellyfish, formless, sexless, and characterless."[52]

The disputes within OPA reflected the growing concern over how to cope with the rising tide of demands for increases in prices and wages. On February 25 the Senate had passed by overwhelming vote the Bankhead bill, which prohibited the deduction of subsidies paid to farmers from being part of the computation of parity prices. The bill was a blatant end run around an Economic Stabilization Order's provision that included subsidy payments as part of the computation. A similar bill passed the House on March 24, and a final version landed on Roosevelt's desk a week later. On April 2 he vetoed it as inflationary, not only raising food prices but inviting the UMW and other unions to press their demands for wage increases. The Senate returned the vetoed bill to committee, where, explained Senator John Bankhead, it would sit as a "club" to be used if Lewis got higher wages for his miners.[53]

Bedeviled by the threat of an inflationary spiral, Roosevelt resorted on April 8 to issuing an executive order to "Hold the Line" on prices and wages. On prices it stipulated that "all items affecting the cost of living are to be brought under control. No further price increases are to be sanctioned unless imperatively required by law." Adjustments in price relationships between different commodities would be allowed if they didn't raise the general cost of living. As to wages, no further increases in wage rates or salary scales would be permitted beyond the Little Steel formula "except where clearly necessary to correct substandards of living." McNutt received the authority to prevent any worker from changing jobs for higher pay unless the change aided in prosecution of the war. Brown's theory of a gradual rise in prices was sent packing.[54]

Still the pressures on prices and wages mounted. The St. Louis CIO industrial council, representing 60,000 workers, called flatly for an upward revision of WLB's cost-of-living formula. David Dubinsky's garment workers struck until he summoned them back, saying that Little Steel's 15 percent formula had "outlived its usefulness" and could not apply to his industry. The farm bloc continued to push the Pace bill, and food prices remained the most frustrating area of all. WLB ordered its regional offices to make no exceptions to the Little Steel formula, but several areas lay outside its jurisdiction. All firms with eight or fewer employees were exempt along with farm wages, which Byrnes had shifted to the Agriculture Department in November 1942. The Labor Department's Wage Adjustment Board oversaw building-trades workers on federal projects, and WPB's Shipbuilding Stabilization Committee handled wages for 1.25 million shipyard employees. In February an executive order assigned 1.4 million railroad and airline workers to the National Railway Labor Panel.[55]

In its struggle to maintain the Little Steel formula, WLB had done better than most people suspected. Some 70 percent of its findings were unanimous, yet the other 30 percent often grew so contentious as to leave the impression that the board was falling apart. That spring both the AFL and CIO wanted Little Steel scrapped but not the board itself, while John L. Lewis wanted the board emasculated and yanked his representative from it. Portraying himself as the one labor leader who had not sold out to the administration, he pursued his quest for a $2 raise through lengthy negotiations. In April he sent his men out of the mines. Roosevelt issued an ultimatum for them to return and made preparations for the army to take over the mines.[56]

By May 1 some 400,000 miners were out. Roosevelt ordered Ickes to take control of the mines, and within a short time the government had charge of 3,400 bituminous mines. The men returned to work, but Lewis pulled them out again on June 1 for six days, making clear his determination to get the increase at any cost. Ever the opportunist, he recognized the strategic role of coal in the war effort and was determined to exploit it. Rising public wrath and threats of antilabor legislation did not faze him. He had organized workers whose mines were scattered across twenty-six states, which made it difficult for the operators to get together on a common policy. He had a genius for creating uncertainty and dismissed William Davis of the WLB as a "rapacious, predatory, Park Avenue patent attorney." Whatever their feelings about Lewis, most people conceded his prodigious gifts. "When he goes into action," wrote an admiring John Chamberlain, "he makes the men around him seem like dull, creeping clodhoppers. Clever at negotiation, he is equally able at handling a bludgeon, a rapier, a derringer, or a sawed-off shotgun." Nor did anyone doubt the genuineness of his concern for the miners.[57]

"The coal miners will get more money, one way or another," observed *Newsweek*, ". . . and John L. Lewis has outsmarted the Administration again . . . He still rates as a man who goes after something and comes back with it no matter how dangerous the gamble to himself or to his country."[58]

The mine owners had a healthy respect for Lewis, as did some government officials. "Lewis keeps his word, even in little things," admitted one government negotiator, "and that's a rare thing in Washington." But the backlash against his demands escalated. Thirteen states were drawing up their own labor legislation to prevent strikes. In June Congress passed the Smith-Connally bill that authorized government takeover of war plants threatened by strikes, barred strikes in federally operated facilities, required a thirty-day waiting period between a strike vote and a walkout, and banned political contributions by unions for the duration of the war. Roosevelt vetoed the bill, saying he agreed with some but not all of its provisions, and Congress promptly passed it over his veto.[59]

While negotiations between the mine operators and the UMW proceeded through the spring, Lewis announced that his men would walk out again on June 20 if agreement had not been reached. At one point he walked into a meeting of the operators, slammed down his briefcase, and said, "Gentlemen, you have had plenty of time to confer, and I suppose you are ready to sign a contract. You are familiar with the War Labor Board's proposal, which we accept, but we want $2 a day additional, as we originally requested. And I do not want any one-legged counter proposals from you!" The sticking point remained portal-to-portal pay. At present workers got paid only for the time spent actually digging in the mines; Lewis wanted them paid a flat rate for the time spent going to and from the mine and demanded the same even for clerks and checkers in offices aboveground. This had become virtually the only point under dispute.[60]

In June Lewis agreed to a contract extension that would keep the miners at work until November, but the threat of a strike then still loomed if a settlement was not reached. By then an even more serious labor problem had arisen in the form of a threatened strike by railroad workers.[61]

WHILE THE COAL miners' saga played itself out, Prentiss Brown groped for ways to enact the president's Hold-the-Line order. Food prices especially had frustrated attempts to keep prices down; since September 1942 they had risen by 11 percent, twice the rate of the cost of living increase. Some labor leaders had come around to sharing the belief that higher wages offered no real protection against the menace of inflation. On April 1 Phillip Murray, speaking for a committee of AFL and CIO leaders, asked Roosevelt to lower food prices back to September 15, 1942, levels and keep them there. Originally the labor men had scheduled the meeting to seek a raise in the Little Steel formula from 15 percent to 23 percent. Agnes Meyer of the *Washington Post* spent four days touring the bituminous region of southeast Pennsylvania and heard the same message everywhere: "Tell those folks in Washington to give us enough to eat at the right prices and we'll go along. But if they can't make good, we've got to have more money."[62]

Brown had already decided on an uncharacteristically bold frontal attack.

On April 30 he announced a new four-point program: price controls would be extended across the board to every important commodity; retail fruit, vegetable, meat, butter, and coffee prices would be rolled back; specific food prices would be established community by community as quickly as possible so that housewives and retailers alike would know the ceilings; and enforcement would be tightened to "bring the chiseler, the racketeer, the black market operator to justice." The goal would be "to roll back the cost of living and then to hold it." The confused jumble of prices that haunted earlier freezing orders would be replaced by one maximum price for each commodity on the most important foods in 150 major cities. The most sweeping action reduced the price of meats, butter, and coffee by 10 percent. By the end of June maximum prices covered about a thousand grocery items in nearly 200 cities. Ceiling prices had also been placed on twenty-two commodities and rolled back on thirty-nine others. Restaurant fare also received ceiling prices.[63]

The most obvious and difficult problem with any such approach was squaring inflexible prices with variable and rising costs. Lower prices for consumers put the squeeze on retailers, suppliers, and other middlemen. To offset this pain, Roosevelt, Byrnes, and Brown agreed to introduce a new subsidy program that paid processors and others hurt by the rollbacks. To get around Congress, the administration simply used funds available from RFC. One early estimate placed the cost at $2 billion a year with $400 million of it going to the processors of seven key foodstuffs. By the war's end the program was paying about $1.6 billion a year on eighteen different foods and agricultural products, nearly a third of it to maintain the rollback in meat prices alone. In 1943 the government was already paying $500 million a year in subsidies for marginal copper mines, sugar, and coal and petroleum transportation.[64]

A storm of protest over the new program arose immediately. "I've had three letters favoring subsidies," drawled Texas representative and cattle rancher Richard M. Kleberg. "One from a no-account cowhand who used to work for me; one from a man in Brooklyn whose name I can't pronounce, and one from Phillip Murray, president of the CIO." Trying to run the economy with a frozen price system, sneered Walter Lippmann, was like trying to drive a car without a steering wheel. Congress—i.e., the farm bloc—despised subsidies, even though its members had been bolstered by a form of them for years, and threatened legislation to do away with them. The House actually voted 160–106 to terminate the rollback subsidy program and prohibit future ones. Retail distributors feared "complete demoralization if not annihilation." The big grocery chains, which operated on slim profit margins, predicted bankruptcy, while the association representing 360,000 independent stores took their complaints straight to the president. "The anti-inflation measures taken so far," proclaimed *Fortune*, "are a sorry patchwork of hasty improvisations that only succeeded in making everyone hopping mad at someone."[65]

From far and wide came reports that rigid prices hampered production. In Gonzales County, Texas, one of the largest chicken-raising areas in the nation, many growers were boarding up the coops and taking jobs in shipyards because the 27.1-cent ceiling on broilers couldn't cover higher feed and labor costs. Potato farmers in Bexar County, Texas, warned that they would not plant a fall crop, while growers in the Houston area vowed to let their potatoes rot in the ground rather than market them under a ceiling of $2.50 a hundred pounds. Chicago meatpackers moaned that they were losing $2.30 for every hog slaughtered. New Jersey fishermen released hundreds of thousands of whiting from their traps, complaining that the ceiling of 4 cents per pound was a penny less than the cost of freezing them. Congressmen listened willingly as a parade of businessmen, farmers, and labor bosses complained about the "foolish fumblers" and "Malice in OPAland."[66]

The clash between Galbraith and Maxon added more fuel to the growing impression of OPA as an agency in shambles. The press portrayed it as another episode in the continuing fight between the professors and the practical businessmen. "All week long," reported *Time* early in June, "there came hints and headlines about the 'collapse' of the Office of Price Administration." Brown assured reporters that the agency was not "coming apart at the seams," but few believed him. Ralph Robey offered his own autopsy of OPA as an agency plagued throughout its life by four basic faults: bad personnel, lack of foresight, failure to grasp simple economic processes, and needlessly complicated orders and controls. In July Maxon, who had vowed to improve OPA by ridding it of "slide-rule boys" and theorists, abruptly resigned after five months in office, prefacing his remarks with what *Time* called "commuter-train anti-New Deal invective" trashing the agency's "internal weakness—confusion, indecision, compromise, miles of legalistic red tape, and the presence of theorists in policymaking positions." In his place Brown appointed yet another advertising man but of a very different stripe, Chester Bowles.[67]

Bowles and his partner, William B. Benton, had launched their advertising agency in the fateful year of 1929 and maneuvered it brilliantly through the depression years into a profitable enterprise. In 1936 Bowles retired and took a job as vice president of the University of Chicago. Six years later he set up and oversaw the OPA's office in Connecticut, where he resided, and made a striking success of it. He knew something of businessmen and professors and promised that OPA would not be "a walking door mat." In June Congress had decreed that all OPA price controllers must have actual business experience, thereby reducing the professors to advisers. In their place Bowles recruited businessmen with broad views, one of whom said cheerfully that the professors he met at OPA were "nice guys and pretty damned smart." A staunch liberal, Bowles gave the agency a decidedly different tone. In October Brown left OPA and Bowles moved up to the top job, which he held for the remainder of the war.[68]

Although inflation remained a serious threat and Congress along with other critics continued to heap abuse on OPA, enforcement of the Hold-the-Line order worked surprisingly well through the rest of the war. Between April 1943 and August 1945, average monthly consumer prices rose only 0.15 percent. For all its continuing pressure for raises, labor bruised but did not break the Hold-the-Line order on wages. Strike threats and labor disputes continued to plague the administration, as did the never-ending struggle with Congress over taxes. Fear of inflation could be seen in the booming real estate market, especially in the Midwest. Farms were being sold mostly to city folk, who paid cash or down payments of nearly half the price. Unlike in World War I, farmers were not using their record income to buy more land but rather to pay off their mortgages. Nevertheless, the *Saturday Evening Post* was not alone in asking whether the nation was heading for "another tragic land boom."[69]

As December came on, prospects for curbing inflation seemed as gloomy as ever. An antisubsidy bill sailed through the House 278–117 and was expected to pass the Senate just as easily. Morgenthau's plea for $10.5 billion in new taxes got whittled down to $2.14 billion in Muley Doughton's Ways and Means Committee and passed the House unchanged. Lewis's miners were poised for another strike, as were the railroad operating unions, which would shut down the nation's vital transportation arteries. For the administration, Christmas looked to be anything but merry.[70]

Near the month's end, Raymond Clapper offered a different perspective, one shared by many Americans. "In the coming year American industry probably will produce more war goods than any nation ever produced before," he wrote. "To do that, some very uneconomical expenditures must be made by our Federal Government . . . You can't be economical in running a war. War is the most wasteful enterprise of the human species . . . Any cost is cheap if you win." But not the cost of runaway inflation. "Inflation," warned *Saturday Evening Post*, "is of all taxes the one which discriminates most against people with small incomes." Labor had no stauncher friend than I. F. Stone, but he joined other voices in saying that "never before was it so necessary for the leaders of each group to forget the coming elections—political and trade union—and tell a few unpleasant economic truths to their own people . . . Ultimately none will suffer more than labor if wages and prices begin chasing themselves around and up the inflationary Maypole."[71]

CHAPTER 26

FEEDING FRENZIES

We are witnessing an extraordinary spectacle—that of the richest nation in the world facing a catastrophic food shortage . . . Very nearly every possible handicap has been placed on the production of more food and even of maintaining the normal supply.
—LOUIS BROMFIELD [1]

When a government runs around like a chicken with its head cut off and doesn't know what it wants to do, then the farmers will get disgusted and quit. They want you to produce more and they won't give you anything to handle the crop with.
—CORN BELT FARMER [2]

Meat rationing is a chiseler's paradise. Everyone can chisel— everyone from the farmer to the consumer. You don't even need to own the meat.
—SATURDAY EVENING POST [3]

OF ALL THE PROBLEMS SPAWNED by wartime mobilization, none was more steeped in ironies than that of food. A nation that produced more food than any other, that for years had found itself drowning in surpluses, suddenly encountered shortages amid debates over whether the shortfalls were real or apparent. The best-fed people on earth, many of whom had gone hungry during the lean depression years, could at last afford to eat well, thanks to wartime jobs, only to find that many of the foods they craved were unavailable. Prosperity in the land of plenty proved almost as frustrating as deprivation in the depression years. Inevitably the question arose and demanded an answer: Who or what was to blame?

By most reckonings the United States never ran literally short of food. As the war progressed it had to feed more and more people: first the mushrooming military, then its hard-pressed Allies, and finally the peoples liberated from Axis rule by military victories. Unlike munitions production, the supply could not be increased simply by ramping up output, which depended as always on a host of variables ranging from the weather to the availability of equipment and labor. Even the biggest farms were not factories that could retool or convert to increase or speed up production. Nor were they as big or concentrated as the giant corporations that dominated munitions output. They constituted a vastly enlarged version of the difficulties in trying to harness thousands of small businesses to the war effort. To make matters worse, the greatest complexities arose more from the distribution rather than the production of food.

Once the defense mobilization effort began in 1940, agriculture recovered more slowly from the depression than did industry. When the year opened, Glenn E. Rogers held the dubious title of "America's Biggest Farmer." A third vice president of Metropolitan Life Insurance Company, he presided over a portfolio of nearly 2 million acres of defaulted prime farmland valued at $120 million, most of it accumulated during the dismal 1930s. After Pearl Harbor, however, the inventory gradually worked off until by December 1943 only about $25 million remained on the books, and Rogers expected it to be sold within the next year. Most of the land was going back into production. Of the 7,427 farms sold by Met Life, 3,873 went to former tenant farmers, 2,400 to former farm owners, 736 to investors, 168 to city folk returning to the farm, and only a dozen to known speculators. Farm real estate values were rising and more farmers were paying down their mortgages, a far cry from the speculative debacle during World War I when farm mortgage debt soared from $1.7 billion to more than $6.5 billion.[4]

LIKE OTHER SMALL businessmen, small farmers found the going rough. "At present," said Ed Will, a farmer living near Onessa, New York, "the lot of the farmer is not a particularly happy one." He could not keep help because the ceiling on farm prices did not allow him to pay wages high enough to compete with factories. He worked longer hours than anyone in industry—about sixty per week—but received no overtime pay even though food was as crucial a war material as any munition. Nor did he get Social Security, and seldom could he afford accident insurance. The criteria for deferring small farmers from the draft were set far too high, especially for the Northeast. And even though farming was a skilled occupation, his return on investment produced less income than an unskilled laborer in industry.[5]

"The bathroom, the great symbol of the American standard of living," added Will, "is practically nonexistent in this community, although farm bathrooms can be installed in peacetime for a couple of hundred dollars." The lack of help forced farm women to carry an onerous burden of extra work, usually without most labor-saving devices like washing machines. Will blamed the administration for most of his woes and reluctantly saw the farmer's only hope in organization. "I regret the necessity of farmers to organize," he admitted, "as I have a fear that after such organizations achieve . . . fair treatment for the farmer they will run away with their power, as labor organizations have done." The *Saturday Evening Post* took up Will's lament, declaring, "It's time to recognize agriculture as a war industry." Farming had become a highly mechanized industry, yet farm machinery had a low priority. Deprived of equipment and labor, the farmer was still expected to produce more. In effect the farmer's production problems had been relegated to a backseat position in the war effort.[6]

Ample statistics existed to show how well farmers were doing, and how well off they were compared to past years and even the last war. But the numbers were no consolation to those not sharing the good times. "Agriculture to date has been the runt pig in the litter of war production when it came to men, machinery, and material," observed *Newsweek* as 1943 opened. Farm machinery had been cut 80 percent, and 1.5 million farm hands had left for the military or jobs in war plants. Yet Claude Wickard exhorted farmers to exceed the record crops of 1942, which owed much to almost perfect growing weather. Hopefully he ordered shifts in output, cutting less essential crops in favor of more plantings for more needed foods. Whether farmers would pay any attention to the order was quite another matter.[7]

HARRY SCHNEITER HAD every reason to be discouraged as the last of a string of hired hands departed his 200-acre dairy farm for a factory job in Minneapolis, leaving him alone with his wife and five children to tend twenty-one purebred Holstein-Friesian cows and other livestock. But not even the brutal cold of a Minnesota winter could chill his determination to keep producing milk, which Wickard pronounced "probably the most important food going to war overseas." Schneiter intended to do his part in the war effort. Besides the cows, he owned 350 White Leghorn chickens and two draft horses to work the farm. Harry separated the skim milk in his own barn and fed it to the chickens; the whole milk went to a nearby creamery. His seventeen-year-old son, Harry Jr., tended hogs that had earned him a 4-H award, and put in hours of work in the morning before heading off to school. So did three of his daughters, ranging in age from nine to fifteen; a fourth girl was only a year old, and a fifth daughter was away at college.[8]

The Schneiters lived in a seven-room house in a box elder windbreak on the plains of Meeker County. Across from the house stood an empty bunga-low once occupied by the hired help. Behind the bungalow sat the barn, feeder crib, and brooder house along with an old windmill, idled since the coming of the Rural Electrification Administration in 1936. Harry was secretary-treasurer of the local Farm Bureau, which sometimes met in his liv-ing room over cake and cocoa to discuss mutual problems and solutions for them. The meetings were a pleasant diversion, especially in winter when sub-zero weather taxed everyone's heart for outdoor work. When the day's work was done, there was still paperwork to go over at the oversized desk housed in the small addition he had built for it. Every month it seemed the stack of pa-perwork grew higher.

They lived a quiet but busy life. Along with all her work at home, Mrs. Schneiter belonged to the Litchfield Presbyterian Church and the League of Women Voters and lent a hand to Farm Bureau social affairs. Daughter Mar-garet at fifteen made her own clothes, helped her mother with the cooking, played basketball for her high school, and proudly earned the title of style queen at the 1942 4-H County Fair. Janice, twelve, and Roberta, nine, packed the cookies their mother baked to send overseas, along with their other chores. Roberta's list included helping Dad with the outside chores, especially carrying wood and gathering eggs. Alongside his father, Harry Jr. did what-ever tasks needed to be done. Come fall, he would be heading off to study agriculture at the University of Minnesota unless the draft board claimed him first. In either case his father fretted over how he would make do with yet another set of hands gone.

"You want to know why we aren't producin' more food?" said the small southern backwoods farmer with gray hair and untidy eyebrows. He lounged in a rocking chair on the porch of a shabby hotel alongside writer John Dos Passos, a spittoon separating their chairs. ". . . I have a boy in the service an' a girl who's enlisted as an army nurse an' even if we hadn't, the old woman an' I would have wanted to do the best we could for the country . . . Well, I fig-ured that I raised thirty acres of beans last year an' I could raise a hundred this year with my tractor an' one extry hand. Well, I got my land plowed up all right but my new hand was so no account—he stripped me a gear on the tractor, an' I was drivin' all over the country like a crazy man tryin' to get me that extry part. Couldn't go no satisfaction nowhere."[9]

Undaunted, the farmer got tired of waiting and boldly plunked down $1,350 for six head of mules. It was a big risk and hiked his labor costs, but he was a stubborn man and "all hell an' high-water wasn't goin' to keep me from gettin' those beans planted." He got them in the ground only to have a late frost come along and freeze them down. Sick with worry, he took to his bed and sent his wife to town to buy some more seed for replanting. She came back empty-handed. "Damn if some bureau in Washington hadn't frozen the seed," he said in disgust. "They unfroze it later on but it was too late for our season out here." All he could do then was plant corn. He would never get his money back, but that wasn't the worst of it to him. "We've lost a whole early season crop that might have produced food folks could eat. I swear if they don't quit hogtyin' us with priorities an' restrictions an' regulations the only thing us truck-farmers'll be able to do is close up an' go to work at somethin' else. How are we goin' to produce crops if we can't get spare parts for machinery?"

IN MARCH FORMER president Herbert Hoover returned to the rich black soil of Iowa from which he sprang and preached to the choir of the Midwest Governors Conference. "Of the different sectors of the home front, food is the greatest," he told them. "It stands next to the military effort in importance. [Yet] there are symptoms of a dangerously degenerating agriculture that must be stopped . . . We have drawn undue manpower from our farms . . . Our farm machinery is wearing out faster than the replacement . . . Our protein feed for animals is very short. We are compelled to divert our nitrate fertilizers to explosives . . . We have a price system in force that often strangles production and distribution. And prices are often below the farmer's cost and just wages."[10]

Four days later the Department of Agriculture released its annual spring planting forecast with figures that astounded Claude Wickard. Despite all their woes, farmers planned to plant some 279 million acres, 10 million more than the past year. Not all would come to harvest; fickle weather, pests, disease, and lack of harvest hands would take their toll. But the starting point was something to crow about. The lack of hands grew steadily worse as the draft took younger men. On the plains of Colorado's Delta County, filled with beets, potatoes, and livestock, farmers watched their sons and hired hands march off to war, most of them too proud to ask for a deferment. One departing Denver & Rio Grande Western train carried forty-four men bound for the army, half of them born and raised on Delta County farms. Talk everywhere around the county centered on how they would be replaced come harvest time. "A green man is helpless on a ranch," grumbled one farmer. ". . . My crops are shot to hell."[11]

One Minnesota farmer provided his own labor force. Peter Krump, having lost his wife, operated a farm on 1,120-acres near Kent on the North Dakota border with the help of his seventeen children, only six of them boys, ranging in age from two to twenty-five. Everyone had assigned tasks. Two of the sisters did the cooking and took care of the twenty-two-room house; other older girls looked after the six children under ten. Somehow the family managed to grow 260 acres of oats, 160 of corn, 90 of flax, 80 of barley, and 160 of alfalfa while also tending 35 dairy cows, 700 chickens, 160 sheep, 220 hogs, and 160 steers. The Krump farm was a big operation, and only one of the boys, Lester, was old enough for the draft; the next in line was only fifteen. The young women did yeoman work alongside their father, whose response to complaints about the shortage of labor was "We will start before daylight and continue till after dark to do our part."[12]

RELOCATION AGENTS STAYED busy all over southern counties where the war brought change. Bulldozers plowed through houses and barns, grinding their innards and whatever dreams their occupants once held into the clay. Behind them came the cement mixers to bury them with finality. Other bulldozers chewed up hills while roadscrapers leveled off pastures to make way for a runway or new factory or the scattered buildings of a powder plant. Families who had worked the land for generations had to move off it, sometimes with only two weeks' notice. Some watched their crops destroyed in the fields before they could be harvested, yet only a few protested or resisted. The complete uprooting of their lives was, most thought, a small price to pay for defense of their country. Only a handful went to court to challenge the price paid in condemnation.[13]

One white-haired man with a creased round face sat rocking gently in the back of his brother's country store. He once owned a thousand acres worked by about a hundred black folk who had been there since slavery days. His great-grandfather had moved there from South Carolina with all his stock and slaves and worked the land ever since. Now the land went for a powder plant and the government hadn't paid him for it yet, but he reckoned he would be all right. He planned to buy a couple hundred acres from some kinfolk and figured to be better off. It was the blacks that worried him most. They had never been farther than the county seat in their lives. Most of the men were making $4 a day as laborers on construction jobs. "But what in the world are they goin' to do when they get turned off?" the man asked with a frown. "I'm not goin' to be in a position to look after 'em."

THE WEATHER DID not help farmers that spring as it had in 1942. Record floods raged through the Midwest in May, drowning half a million acres of wheat and oats, truck farms, and orchards, bringing field work to a halt and throwing corn planting a month behind schedule. Late frosts crippled southern fruit crops, early vegetables, and cotton, while the Pacific Northwest's winter forced the abandonment of winter wheat. On the Plains a late spring meant slow growth for pasture and hay crops, threatening the supply of livestock feed and milk production. Drought and dust storms hounded the Southwest, triggering unpleasant memories of the 1930s. For farmers around Omaha, Nebraska, the floods were quite a comedown from 1942, "the Beulah Land, when rains came at just the right time," that led one old-timer to chortle, "I've waited fifty years for this."[14]

Beulah Land was long gone. In June Agriculture admitted that its earlier crop forecast was but a scrap of useless paper, replaced by the poorest outlook in three years that boded ill for the winter of 1943–44. Wheat looked to be down 26 percent, feed grains excluding corn 15 percent, fruits 25 percent, early vegetables 13 percent, cheese 21 percent, and evaporated milk 30 percent. The corn forecast was not yet complete. Chester Davis stressed that "everyone should conserve every scrap of food and waste nothing." Another official warned that "we as civilians cannot have as much food as we have had or might want." Two foods in particular seemed to cause endless perplexities in their supply and distribution: milk and meat.[15]

The quantity of milk going overseas to troops and civilians increased dramatically thanks to spray-drying techniques that reduced the liquid to a fine powder the texture of flour. *Look* hailed the process as "one of the most dramatic transformations in food since the miracle of the loaves and the fishes." A 200-pound barrel of dehydrated milk traveled easily and could be reconstituted into 1,068 quarts of skim milk used mostly for cooking and baking. Milk from the Schneiters' farm went to a cooperative creamery next to the plant where it was separated and pasteurized before heading into a large tank. There a tiny nozzle, blasting air at a temperature of 300 degrees under 5,000 pounds of pressure, sprayed the milk about the chamber until it dried. During a twenty-hour day 22,000 pounds of fluid milk entered the cone-shaped chamber to be dried. Overall the nation expected to produce 650 million pounds of dehydrated milk in 1943.[16]

Dehydration increased the demand for a product that was already under stress. Milk and dairy products required more labor than most other farm products and on a year-round basis. Cows needed high-protein feed such as fish meal, which hogs and poultry also used. Balancing the price of milk and dairy products against their costs frustrated farmers and bureaucrats alike, causing many small dairy farmers to sell their cows and take a factory job. Although most farmers had ample feed on hand in 1940, the supply was running short by the spring of 1943. As early as 1940 the government buttressed dairy and poultry products with support prices. In response the output of dairy products jumped 9 percent between 1940 and 1942 and that of poultry 20 percent, the largest increases ever recorded. In 1942 production reached an all-time high of 119 million pounds but was expected to fall well short of the 1943 goal of 122 million pounds.[17]

Beginning in April, milk production fell steadily below the 1942 level every month. A variety of forces threw it out of balance. Canned milk output fell 25 percent short of projections because huge quantities of fluid milk had been diverted instead to making butter, cheese, and dried milk for the military and Lend-Lease. Thousands of gallons were wasted because some processing plants lacked enough help or had more milk than they could handle. Civilians were buying more milk and cheese than ever before because they had the money and couldn't get other sources of protein. Feed ran short despite government efforts to provide extra supplies, and a rigid price ceiling left many farmers struggling to turn a profit. A dairy feed payment program devised in October eased the downturn in production, but not until May 1944 did output in any month equal that of the previous year.[18]

The severity of the milk crisis paled before the mess in meat. No single food posed more complexities or caused more frustration than the meat supply, which consisted of three very different types: beef, pork, and poultry. Beef had always been America's favorite meat and the most complicated in its supply. The old distinction between dairy cows and meat cattle had broken down; the milk breeds provided about a third of the beef supply in the form of cows that were no longer useful milkers and were used mostly for lower-quality beef. The cattle bred for meat divided into those fed on the range and those sold to farmers who fattened them with corn before selling them to slaughterhouses. The latter produced more than half the beef poundage but divided their attention among fattening cattle, raising hogs, or growing other crops. The rancher could do little else but raise cattle or sheep, yet he ultimately controlled the supply of meat.[19]

The rancher could do several things with a calf: slaughter it for veal; hold it for breeding stock; castrate it and feed it on the range as a steer; send it to a feed lot for fattening; or sell it to market as one of many grades of meat. Circumstances had always dictated the rancher's decision, and until recently they did not include artificial controls. Ranchers were tough people in a tough business and never shy about telling government personally what they did or did not want. When OPA tried freezing beef prices in March 1942, the unintended result was to make old cows and lean cattle more profitable to sell than corn-fed steers, which cost more to feed. Some years before the war Henry Wallace had asked the president of the American National Livestock Association to devise a rational plan for the cattle industry. The president mulled the matter over and consulted other cowmen, then concluded that "if anyone is going to try to write a national cattle plan it had better be some idiot who doesn't know a God damned thing about the business."[20]

The ranchers wanted nothing from the government except to be left alone, but the war made that impossible. One rancher, sent a questionnaire on gasoline use, replied, "No one but a damned fool could have written this, and no one but a damned liar could fill it out." Cowmen really did, as the song said, "ride the range in a Ford V-8," and there was nothing romantic about it. Loss of helpers, shortage of gas and equipment, forms to fill out—all these aggravated ranchers, but price ceilings infuriated them the most because they squeezed everyone along the line, especially the farmers who fattened cattle and the packers. For all of them the key number became the cost of corn. If it cost more to fatten cattle than the ceiling price for beef allowed, it meant losses for the farmer and packer alike and loss of business for the rancher. The result was not only confusion but the rise of a strong black market for beef that in New York and Chicago alone was reputed to gross more than $1 million a week.[21]

The government bought only federally inspected meat, mostly from packers in big cities. In the fall of 1942 it had trouble finding enough meat for the military and Lend-Lease. It ordered packing houses to sell for civilian use only 70 percent of the beef they sold a year earlier but exempted small outfits that handled less than 500,000 pounds a quarter. Civilian buyers thus found themselves with less available meat at a time when they had the money and appetite to buy even more than usual. Most beef moved toward the large packers, leaving thousands of smaller houses without a supply to meet even their quota, let alone soaring demand. To avoid going out of business they patronized the "meatlegger," buying cattle of dubious weight or grade and not inspected. Slaughterhouses in turn sold their customers carloads of carcasses shortweight, and butchers in turn passed them on at premium prices to customers grateful to get any kind of roast or steak.[22]

"I gotta make a living," explained a California butcher, "and I gotta keep my customers satisfied. Every morning I make the rounds of four black-market outfits. In one I say to the guy, 'I'll bet you $25 you can't get me a side of beef. I lay the cash on the table, and I always lose the bet. What the hell would you do?" One government official guessed that as much as 20 percent of all livestock slaughtered was finding its way to Mr. Black.[23]

During a three-month meat famine in Los Angeles, Northrop willingly patronized the black market to get meat for its cafeteria. "I can't tell you where we get our meat," said one official. "If I did, we wouldn't get any more. It is more important to pay higher-than-ceiling prices and keep quiet." Douglas complained that its 75,000 employees who ate at the company cafeteria were being "starched to death." A CIO representative added that "our absenteeism is going to increase unless we can get meat." One packer warned that under current regulations Southern Californians would be lucky to get twenty-four ounces of meat each per week. California state prison officials got permission to graze cattle in a state park to supply meat for the inmates. "How to obtain plenty of meat—become a convict," quipped the *Los Angeles Times.*[24]

Not even a thousand OPA inspectors could put a dent in the operation of Mr. Black, so diffuse was the business. Nor could federal inspectors possibly examine every steer marked for slaughter. Even worse, the war with its huge demands deranged the normal supply chain. When large orders emptied the large packing houses, small clients went begging. Gradually local butchers began slaughtering their own animals, and small packers set up shop where there were cattle to be had. Small operators who once killed twenty head a week now killed fifty. Much of the cattle arriving at stockyards were bought by smaller interests willing to pay more than the big packers supplying the government. Customers in midwestern rural areas got plenty of meat, as did nearby cities, while shortages grew worse on both coasts. By the end of April 1943 the shortfall at major packing houses amounted to 332,000 head.[25]

"Never see so many folks want meat," said a rancher that summer, "and they pay most any price we ask." By one estimate half the nation's retail meat dealers relied on ration-point-free or above-ceiling-price meat for their supply. To get the cuts he needed, he took by-products he didn't want and sometimes added a bribe as well for the salesman. "It's making thieves of us all," admitted a salesman. OPA was helpless to deflect Mr. Black with only 2,500 investigators to oversee a nation of suppliers that in the seven-state jurisdiction of its Chicago office alone numbered 300,000. The best cuts of beef from corn-fed cattle depended entirely on the price of corn and what use was made of it. Corn could be used to feed dairy cattle, steers, hogs, chickens, or people directly, and it was also wanted in large quantities for making alcohol. Most people assumed that the country had all the corn it would ever need or want. In this they were mistaken.[26]

The shortage of feed grain that spring caught nearly everyone by surprise. A survey by the Agriculture Department showed that feed grain production in 1943 would be 11 percent lower than in 1942 while the number of livestock being fed had increased 11 percent. *Prairie Farmer* magazine discovered that for every five bushels of corn being produced, seven were being used for feed, food, or alcohol. The great corn surplus was drying up faster than anyone thought possible, and some farmers were holding back their surplus grain in hopes of higher prices. Agriculture officials warned that feed grain reserves could be virtually depleted within eighteen months. Grain could be imported from Canada, which had a large surplus, but would have to compete for boats on the Great Lakes with iron ore vitally needed for war production.[27]

By July an absurd paradox had emerged. Packing plants were closing for lack of cattle to kill, retail butcher shops for lack of beef to sell, and corn-processing plants for want of corn to grind. At the same time, American farms and ranches had more cattle, hogs, and bushels of corn than ever before: 70 million head of cattle, 3 million above normal; and 128 million hogs, or 23.1 million more than the record-breaking number of 1942. Corn supplies were at an all-time high of nearly 2.7 billion bushels but dwindling fast, partly because of the large cattle and hog population that led farmers to hold some 950 million bushels in storage. The pinch in feed grain also worsened things; farmers balked at selling corn for table consumption at the ceiling price of $1.07 when they could get anywhere from $1.24 to $1.50 for it as hog feed. Cattlemen refused to send their stock to market at prices below what they thought they should get, and packers hesitated to bid because they did not yet know whether Washington would subsidize them for the rollback in meat prices.[28]

"The situation would solve itself if only government officials would let the unrepealable law of supply and demand work without regulatory interference," declared a spokesman for the Texas and Southwestern Cattle Raisers. "Everybody would have meat. There would be so much meat that in our opinion, prices would be forced below present ceilings."[29]

In Columbus, Ohio, W. C. Denison Jr., president of the Denison Engineering Co., attacked the food problem in his own creative way. Twelve miles from the plant, just behind the company's research laboratory, fourteen farmers hired by Denison worked 650 acres of prime farmland that housed 75 head of beef, 120 sheep and lambs, 100 hogs, 2,500 chickens, and 40 registered Guernsey cows along with fields of vegetables. All of the farm's output was destined for the company's cafeteria, with fruits and vegetables canned for the commissary. Any surplus would be offered to employees at slightly under market prices. Both the commissary and cafeteria, Denison said cheerfully, would operate under the regular ration coupon system, but his employees would eat well.[30]

WHILE CRITICS LIKE Ralph Robey lambasted what he called "The Growing Distribution Debacle," Roosevelt struggled to bring some semblance of order to the mess. So far everything he tried had turned out badly, especially his efforts to find the right man to head the right organization. In December 1942 he had shifted all responsibility for finding food needs, formulating programs to meet them, making allocations, and assigning food priorities to Claude Wickard at his request, relieving WPB of any duties in that sphere.

Under the new arrangement all major food activities were swept into two agencies, the Food Production Administration and the Food Distribution Administration, both of which reported to Wickard. It was a rare instance of the president entrusting a major war program to an existing cabinet department, and it lasted barely three months.[31]

During the winter of 1942–43 the food supply deteriorated rapidly. "The American people have been caught short on food," admitted Wickard in February. "The food situation is going to become very critical so far as production is concerned." The reasons he gave to a Senate subcommittee sounded drearily familiar: lack of labor and farm machinery. Mr. Black was flourishing, and butter stocks had dipped to their lowest level in eighteen years. Rumors insisted that sudden huge shipments to Russia accounted for the shortage of butter; the real reason was increased demand by civilians and the military. Civilians were told they would receive only half the amount of canned goods as the previous year. "Everywhere," declared *Time*, "the people could see that a year's indecision and vacillation had finally caught up with Claude Wickard and the Administration."[32]

Faced with still another crisis, Roosevelt moved with uncharacteristic speed to undo his previous action. On March 26 he combined the two new agencies along with the Commodity Credit Corporation and Agriculture's Extension Service into yet another new one that became known as the War Food Administration (WFA) with Chester Davis as its head. The WFA resembled the World War I model of a separate Food Administration set up under Herbert Hoover unrelated to Agriculture; it was abolished immediately after the war. The move eased the political clamor for a "food czar" by placing war-related activities in one set of hands reporting directly to Roosevelt while leaving Wickard free to run his department. However, one peculiar section of the executive order posed potential problems by giving both Wickard and Davis "authority to exercise any and all of the powers vested in the other by statute or otherwise."[33]

Davis seemed a sound choice. The president of the Federal Reserve Bank in St. Louis, he was an Iowa farmboy who had spent four years as Montana's commissioner of agriculture, where his "fairway farms" program attracted the attention of Henry Wallace, and developed a reputation as an excellent administrator with the New Deal's ill-fated Agricultural Adjustment Administration. When the war broke out, Roosevelt appointed him to the NDAC to represent agriculture. Wickard, denying rumors that he would resign, declared that the new arrangement should work out all right, saying, "I had a nice wire from Mr. Davis." For his part Davis insisted that "the main thing is team work." A veteran of Washington power politics, he had already turned down Roosevelt's invitation to become director of civilian supply and accepted the new post only with assurances that he would be free of the dreaded curse of divided authority.[34]

Like Wickard, Davis lasted only three unhappy months in his role as food czar. He resented OPA's power over food pricing and rationing and adamantly opposed subsidies as a means of fighting inflation. When Roosevelt announced a limited subsidy program on June 15, Davis submitted his resignation on the grounds that he could not defend subsidies and lacked sufficient authority over food policy. The president then tapped Judge Marvin Jones, a former chairman of the House Agricultural Committee, for the job. A quiet, modest Texan who insisted that he never wanted to be an executive, Jones held the job until June 1945 and did well at it. The potential conflict with Wickard never flared up because the two men worked well together.[35]

However, the shuffle in March confirmed for some observers that the cabinet had become virtually irrelevant in wartime. Declaring that "all the real work was now done by Czars, of which the U.S. has ten," *Time* lampooned the cabinet as "a little group of aging men and women, busying themselves with routine little duties, junkets, paper-shuffling, the general hobbling of bureaucracy." Of their number Harold Ickes alone had a real job; he was also the petroleum czar and fisheries coordinator.[36]

FISH SEEMED ONE logical solution to the meat muddle. Americans had never been a nation of fish eaters, but the war was changing that somewhat, to the delight of those who had devoted their lives to earning a living from the sea. One of them, Captain Leonard Guptill, was steering his 50-footer, *Ruth and Kathleen*, through the pitch black of a foggy night laden with thirty-five hogsheads of sardine herrings with more than the usual difficulty because of the blackouts necessitated by submarines lurking off the outer channel that closed the steamer lane to St. John. Lighthouses, village streetlights, and the boat's own lights were doused except for a shielded binnacle lamp, forcing Guptill to grope his way gingerly into the channel leading out of the Bay of Fundy through Passamaquoddy tidal rips between Quoddy Head and Campobello Island toward the canneries at Eastport and Lubec, Maine, all the while straining to hear the clang of the bell buoys on Iron Light shoal.[37]

The radio beacon on West Quoddy Head was off the air, and the boat's own compass had somehow gone haywire as well. But the packers were crying for canned fish to feed the insatiable demands of Lend-Lease, and the haul was a good one. Guptill swore that if he couldn't see or hear, he'd smell his way to the canneries by morning. His was a clean, comfortable craft with fresh running water, toilets, and electric lights as well as ship-to-shore radio and radio direction finders, neither of which could be used while the submarines preyed. At midnight, after a tense ride, the crew started suddenly at the shriek of the cannery whistle "blowing for fish," five blasts that summoned the picklers. The captain had found his way blind to Lubec. The crew turned in while the fish were hoisted to the pickling vats. Later two more siren blasts called the "flakers" in to precook the sardines.

After many lean years, times were good at Lubec's six, Eastport's six, and thirty-some other canneries up and down the Maine coast. The war had ended competition from Norwegian and Portuguese sardines and cleaned out the last stocks of tinned fish. The military and Lend-Lease demanded 3 million 100-can cases, which required Maine fishermen to break all previous records by a million cases. The finished product went hot from the cookers with no carryover for storage or reserve. California sardine fishermen were under the same pressure; the lowly sardine had become a luxury item. The goal for 1943 was no less than 4 million cases, which figured out to about 3 billion sardines. To make it would require some 20,000 men and women toiling at the task. Some 1,500 fishermen, twice the usual number, were at sea despite the lack of boats and equipment, while thousands of men and women had been trained at packing.

Jay Lakeman had just come in from a three-day run up the New Brunswick shore with thirty hogsheads of sardines that fetched $105. Of that sum $35 went to the boat owner, who provided everything except food for the two-man crew, $42 to Jay as skipper, and $28 to the engineer. "They're runnin' plenty out on the Grand Manan," he said, watching his boat being unloaded. "Want to hustle out there and get me some turns." Fishermen lived by their turns at the big fish traps known as weirs. Setting up a weir was a major piece of construction costing anywhere from $1,500 to $5,000 for what amounted to a crapshoot in which the giant nets might come up empty or haul in $30,000 worth of sardines over a season. In this hit-or-miss business Lubec was the only one of fifteen canning towns between Eastport and South Portland that had no other industry to help sustain it.

The sardine herring cooperated by gathering in huge schools and by shaking off their own scales. Dumped into the fish tank with seawater and some added salt, they obligingly stirred up their own pickling brine. Scalers loaded the fish and took their pay in scales that were used in artificial pearls, costume jewelry, and replacing chromium plate on household gadgets. The shriek of the cannery whistle signaled 400 to 500 women to drop their household chores and hurry to the packing rooms, where they took their places along the conveyor belts to grade the sardines, snip off heads and tails, and arrange them neatly in cans with hands that moved almost too fast for the eye to follow. One woman, who deemed herself an average packer, earned $547 by packing 2,188 cases working four hours a day. The job had another fringe benefit. "Working so much in pure oil keeps our hands soft and white," she admitted.

The dean of packers was eighty-three-year-old Aunt Lizzie Thayer, who had worked at the cannery since it opened in 1880. As the pace quickened during the war, her boss, himself a second-generation leader, came to her and asked, "Don't you think the older women should lay off the night work?" Lizzie nodded. "Yes, Carroll," she said, "I think those older women should."

Fishing had to endure the same difficulties as other forms of food production. The total catch in 1942 dropped 22 percent below the previous year for familiar reasons: lack of manpower, shortage of engine parts and other gear, and the loss of hundreds of the biggest, most efficient boats taken over by the government for coastal patrol, antisubmarine, and overseas duties. McNutt was asked to grant commercial fishermen ninety-day draft deferments, but nothing got done. Despite these handicaps, a fishing boom was on as the remaining boats and crews braved repeated trips to bring in record hauls. Sardines still dominated, accounting for a fourth of the total American fish catch. Because they had to be caught in the dark of the moon, when their phosphorescent glow revealed their location, the navy began escorting the boats out in the afternoon and staying with them until their return journey in the morning.[38]

German submarines sank more than a few fishing boats, but still the fishermen went out because the money was good and getting better. Iver Carlson, a Boston skipper, took his trawler *Cormorant* out as fast as he could sign up crews, lay in supplies, and get union clearance. He managed to bring in 653,000 pounds of fish in five trips and earn $10,960 in sixty days of fishing. The story was the same on the West Coast, where every vessel from the sardine boats to the tuna clippers to the blue crab boats seemed to be prospering. Andrew Vilicich, master of the sleek 77-foot *Gallant*, worked year-round and took in $112,000 during 1942, of which his crew got $61,000. Vilicich owned his boat, a share in a San Francisco sardine plant, and a comfortable two-story house. For fishermen times were good; they were not only prospering but recognized for the first time as vital to the nation's food supply.[39]

EVERY SUMMER A ragtag civilian army assembled for the long hot march through Oklahoma, Kansas, Nebraska, the Dakotas, and Montana, the breadbasket of America, to harvest the wheat crop. In 1943 it was a decimated band of farmers and townfolk, mostly dressed in patched overalls and hickory shirts with bandannas wrapped around their necks to keep out the dust and chaff. Gathering reinforcements wherever they could, they tramped steadily northward, toiling fifteen long, sweaty hours or more a day in temperatures bracketing a hundred degrees while the women cooked huge meals for them in even hotter kitchens. More than ever before they lacked men and machines, with 2 million men having left the farms and nearly all the itinerant hands that once filled the ranks having gone elsewhere to work or fight. In their place came a motley assortment of local merchants, businessmen, schoolchildren, and citizen groups who volunteered because so much depended on reaping the harvest.[40]

Tractor-drawn combines did as much of the work as possible, but new machines could not be had and older ones sometimes broke down. Every available horse and mule was pressed into service, and harness, rigs, and old-style threshers reclaimed from the scrap heap, to do the work. Normally when a machine broke down, the farmer's sons or younger hands had the skill to fix it. But they were mostly gone now, and the farmer himself often did not know how to do the job. Throughout the wheat belt automobile mechanics took time to come out and mend the machines. Once cut and threshed, the wheat sat on the ground or went into local storage until the railroad could find enough cars for it. The major roads in the wheat belt had only about 40 percent of their normal fleet of grain cars on their own tracks.[41]

The only good news was bad news in its own way. Storage room would be available once the wheat got to it. This year's crop ran about 25 percent below that of 1942, and wheat had been disappearing from storage at the fastest rate in recent times, going for livestock feed and alcohol for munitions. During the past year the Commodity Credit Corporation alone sold 225 million surplus bushels for feed. The Agriculture Department also contributed by ordering a reduction of 2 percent, or 927,000 acres, planted in wheat compared to 1942. At least the United States would not have to do as much in feeding the rest of the world. Both India and Egypt reported record harvests, and Australia and Argentina had huge stores.[42]

"Everywhere Americans saw the specters of food shortages," declared *Time* at June's end, "in meat, in milk, in other foods. The food front was in real danger . . . There was still food aplenty. But it was at the wrong places, it was going to waste, it was being badly mismanaged." As if to emphasize the point, a large corn refinery in Clinton, Iowa, the third largest in the world, shut down for lack of corn. Nearly everyone pointed the finger of blame at "a fantastically mixed-up Government food policy, pulled and hauled among nine agencies." Corn was being hoarded to feed to pigs and cattle, and pigs were being withheld from the market because the price was too low. A bipartisan congressional delegation descended on Roosevelt and demanded an end to subsidies and the appointment of a food czar to sort things out. Behind them came the House Agriculture Committee with the same message.[43]

Roosevelt defended the subsidies and dismissed the idea of a czar as absurd. Suppose, he asked in a news conference, such a man had the authority to order a carload of foodstuffs shipped ahead of anything else. The order might well delay a vital shipment of munitions to the war fronts. As for the price rollbacks and subsidies, he intended to pursue them until someone showed him a better way. Then the disgruntled Chester Davis was out the door, replaced by the smooth, bland Marvin Jones. Congress threatened legislation to kill the rollbacks and subsidies. "The main Congressional feeling, beneath all these," suspected *Time*, "was a deep suspicion of Federal controls." While the bureaucrats raged, nature did what it could to ease the strain. Good June weather did much to repair the spring damage from floods and frosts. By July hogs were going to market in record numbers, and drying grass on the range meant that ranchers would either have to start feeding their cattle corn or send them to market. Dairy cows produced a record amount of milk in June.[44]

A few states improvised to lend farmers a helping hand. Ohio sent 175 state-owned tractors manned by state employees to plow fields where needed. Indiana made eight tractors but no men available to farmers. Nevada rented some of its state equipment to ranchers, and three states offered leaves of absence to highway employees willing to work on farms. Officials in twenty-eight states declined to follow Ohio's lead because state laws prevented the use of equipment on other than state projects. In St. Louis Anheuser-Busch, the beer makers, experimented hopefully with a mixture of molasses, ammonia, water, yeast, and air that would produce a ton of "good rich meat" every twelve hours and taste as good as sirloin steak but with more proteins and vitamins.[45]

No such spirit of innovation penetrated Iowa. A research associate at Iowa State College committed heresy by daring to suggest in a pamphlet that the milk shortage could be alleviated by making oleomargarine instead of butter, replacing the entire crop of the latter with half the land and an eighth of the labor. The state's dairymen protested that his pamphlet had jeopardized the nation's entire food program and wrought "untold injury" to the state's $100 million dairy industry. "The farmers are alarmed over this tendency to make Iowa State College a tax-supported Harvard," said the president of the state's Farm Bureau. "They're not ashamed of the 'cow college' label." The hapless researcher was forced to recant and revise his pamphlet.[46]

The brightened mood of farmers dimmed in August when drought settled onto the East Coast and Southwest, causing an estimated $50 million loss in the East and heavy losses in Texas and Oklahoma. Outside the Campbell Soup plant in Camden, New Jersey, 100 freight cars and 800 trucks bulging with tomatoes sat waiting to be unloaded. To avoid losing half a million bushels of tomatoes, some 2,000 volunteer servicemen and citizens spent a weekend emptying the cars and trucks. Beef and hog raisers hurried their animals to stockyards as range grass grew scarce and the pig glut grew worse. To ease the crunch in stockyard pens, the government lifted quotas on live-stock slaughter and lowered ration points on several meat items. Despite the fresh flow of meat, the Agriculture Department warned Americans that the coming year would see more beans and other meat substitutes in their diet. Even tobacco was running short as Americans smoked more than ever and large quantities of cigarettes went to the military.[47]

As the year wound down, the fights over food continued with little relief in sight. Agriculture tried to ease the vegetable shortage by promoting victory gardens among city, town, and suburban dwellers. An estimated 10 million gardens were planted along with the 5 million to 6 million vegetable gardens found on farms. The hope was that every urban garden might produce $10 worth of vegetables and every farm version $50 worth, easing the demand for many basic vegetables. Amateur gardeners took up the challenge with enthu-siasm and provided a few laughs along the way. Seed companies reported getting dozens of requests for coffee seeds as well as one for succotash seed.[48]

In the spring Agriculture had issued a list of nonessential vegetable crops and asked growers to plant other, more nutritious vegetables in their place. The nonessential list included watermelons. Growers obligingly dropped their watermelon acreage considerably only to discover at harvest that the price of melons had risen sharply. They proceeded to double their acreage for the coming year. When most cities nearly exhausted their supply of potatoes in the spring, growers expanded their plantings and produced a near glut by fall. The combined early and late crop was the largest on record. Cotton was a major source of trouble in that even with a decline in acreage of 17 percent more was being grown than was needed. But many farmers would not budge from planting the crop they knew best instead of one more needed but unfa-miliar to them. The nation's most important cash crop, cotton occupied a quarter of the farm population.[49]

By November the stockyards were glutted with hogs and the WFA was fighting with OES director Fred Vinson over a price ceiling recently imposed on live cattle. "It would take a Philadelphia lawyer to figure out just what the program is," snapped a WFA official. "It gets into metaphysics." Lack of work-ers kept the yards from slaughtering hogs as fast as they arrived. To ease the labor shortage, the government resorted to using prisoners of war, paying them a pittance for their work. For some emergencies the army had released men to help save crops that might otherwise be lost. Still deeply concerned, Roosevelt asked Sam Rosenman to start collecting material for a radio speech he planned to deliver.[50]

*   *   *

THE ROOM WHERE the president met with his cabinet had few trappings of power or majesty. During the war years its white walls were unadorned except for portraits of Jefferson and Jackson on the west wall and one of Woodrow Wilson above the plain fireplace at the north end of the room. The east wall consisted of French windows draped in red damask that had been swallowed by the addition of blackout curtains. Two doors on the opposite wall provided entrance from a main hall running through the White House office wing. Cabinet members and any other participants in meetings entered through them, and if the president was attending, a Secret Service man stood guard at each door. The president had his own entrance through a tiny secretary's office that separated the room from his own private office. Sam Rosenman thought it "the simplest and least ornate room in the world used for any similar purpose."[51]

A gigantic mahogany table dominated the room. It had eight unequal sides and was four or five times as long as it was wide, giving it the appearance of a misshapen rectangle, and was so designed to give the president a clear view of every cabinet member on either side and in front of him. On its highly polished surface sat only a telephone with a long wire and a few reference books in front of the president's place. Before a cabinet meeting large yellow pads and a few pencils were placed in front of each chair. Some chairs and small tables sat along the wall and a large globe near the fireplace. A clock chimed every quarter hour, reminding those present that time was passing all too quickly. The carpet was plain and serviceable, nothing more. The windows offered a gorgeous slice of Washington to the viewer. Above the Rose Garden with its enclosing green hedge one could see the south entrance of the White House with its magnificent curved balcony and winding staircase leading up to it, the white walls embellished by the large magnolia tree planted by Andrew Jackson that now soared above the balcony itself. To the right the South Lawn of the White House stretched luxuriously down toward the Washington Monument, lined with the stately old elms and oaks that so enchanted tourists. Through the windows, too, could be seen the president scooting along the covered walk in his armless little wheelchair at a speed that seemed to bode impending disaster, the familiar cigarette holder tilted in his mouth and his hand clutching whatever document he had been perusing. Fala scampered alongside the chair, as did a Secret Service agent. Behind them trailed a messenger carrying a large wire basket with the mail and memoranda on which the president had worked that morning or the night before.

A bell clanged three times to alert the White House police that the president was on his way so that officers could scramble to their posts along the path. Sammy the Rose liked to stand at the window after the bell rang to wave to the president, who would smile and wave back unless he was engrossed in reading whatever document he clutched. In September, exhausted from his dual role, Rosenman had finally surrendered his place on the New York State Supreme Court to become special counsel to the president at less than half his old salary. His duties still included working on presidential speeches, which was what brought him to the cabinet room that fall. The speechwriters—himself, Sherwood, Hopkins, and whoever else might be involved—liked to spread out in the cabinet room, one of the quietest places in the White House when the cabinet was not meeting, and work to all hours without interruption. If the president needed to see them, he had easy access from his office.[52]

The president regarded his speech on food as extremely important and set Rosenman to work on it a month in advance. He had said nothing publicly on the subject since his press and radio conference on June 15 except for a letter he wrote in response to Chester Davis's resignation on June 28. He had hoped to do a radio broadcast on the subject, but the material Rosenman gathered grew so extensive that doing the subject justice would exceed the half-hour limit Roosevelt imposed on radio speeches. The president decided instead to prepare a full report and deliver it to Congress as a message. As always he wheeled into the cabinet room to scan each draft, looking first at the number on the last page to see how long it had grown. Before long he began ribbing Rosenman on the ever-expanding length of the message, but he could find nothing that he wanted to cut out.[53]

"Go ahead, put it all in," he said finally. "Maybe nobody will ever read the whole thing, but the whole story will be there. You'd better put in a table of contents—and an index too." By the time the message went to Congress on November 1, it was 10,000 words long, the lengthiest message the president had yet sent to the Hill. Almost from the start of the war Roosevelt had taken flak on the food, pricing, and rationing programs; the message became his long-delayed answer to the critics who had found fault with nearly everything he had attempted. "Food is as important as any other weapon in the successful prosecution of the war," it began. "It will be equally important in rehabilitation and relief in the liberated areas, and in the shaping of the peace that is to come."[54]

The first major objective, he explained, was to "raise in the most efficient manner enough food and the right kinds of foods to meet our needs," both at home and abroad. The second goal was to see that the food available for civilians at home was divided fairly among them and obtainable at fair prices. Problems arose because the steps needed to accomplish these objectives sometimes conflicted with each other. Helping farmers get a good price for their wares often sent the price of food to the consumer too high, for example, which meant rising wages and prices. The whole point of price controls, rationing, and subsidy programs was to resolve these conflicts and achieve some sort of balance. He praised the heroic efforts of farmers, volunteers, and others in keeping food production at record levels despite all the handicaps they faced.[55]

The shortages that emerged during the year, he emphasized, came from rising demand at home as well as supplying the troops and Lend-Lease. "Many of our workers in war factories, in the mines, on the farms, and in other essential pursuits are eating more and better food than they ate before the war," he said. "Many of them for the first time are approaching an adequate diet." Feed grains seemed short only because an increased supply still didn't match the growth in number of animals to be fed. On the controversial topics of price controls, price supports, and subsidies, Roosevelt was adamant that they were crucial to preventing runaway inflation as well as ensuring that farmers got paid a fair price for their efforts. The subsidies had worked well for copper and transportation of coal and oil, and they would do the same for food.

"The subsidies that are used cannot properly be called producer subsidies or consumer subsidies," he stressed. "They are war subsidies. The costs which they cover are war costs . . . It is entirely appropriate that they should be met out of the public treasury, just as are the costs of producing tanks and planes and ships and guns." The programs had also kept severe wartime inflation at bay. Since August 1939 the cost of living in the United States had risen just under 26 percent compared to a rise of 53 percent for the same forty-two-month period during World War I. As for rationing, he expressed confidence that the American people were "ready to give up certain eating habits and accept certain shortages. They know that they must, if the war is to be won. A sharp line will have to be drawn between the luxuries of life and the necessities of life. A shortage in sirloin steaks or in choice fruits does not mean that the war food program has failed."[56]

The message was well received but changed few minds in Congress, which stood poised to pass a bill renewing the Commodity Credit Corporation but stripping it of the power to pay out subsidies designed to reduce food prices. Roosevelt promised a veto if it passed, but the farm bloc claimed to have enough votes for overriding a veto as well. Still, how many congressmen were willing to shoulder the responsibility for failing to hold the line on prices? By the end of 1943 the food wars had abated but not died out entirely.[57]

CHAPTER 27

THE SLIDING SCALE OF SACRIFICE

There were no sunbonnets and calico, no covered wagons wending their way across the untracked prairies of the West. But just as surely as their ancestors a century ago, American families this week were blazing the trails of a new and unfamiliar world—pioneers not of the forest but of a wilderness of ration coupons.

—NEWSWEEK[1]

With the exception of some low-paid workers . . . and a stratum of white-collar workers with fixed incomes, there is not a class or a group in this country which has not benefited by the war, which is not eating better—yes, eating better—and living better than it did before. Anyone who spends a few days covering the present price-control fight comes away with the impression that we are the world's greatest nation of cry-babies . . . This is no reflection on our good men at the front, but only upon the snivelers at home, where everybody wants the cost of living held down, but everybody also wants his own income pushed up.

—I. F. STONE[2]

Anybody who mentions "sacrifice" or "hardship" ought to think about being sent to charge up a hill at night with a bayonet for your only weapon. No ammunition, because a rifleman can't hit what he can't see, and .30-caliber bullets are very heavy. These are the men who can legitimately talk about their parts in the war . . . The next time anybody is overheard to say in the bar of the Mayflower, "I sacrificed thirty-six thousand dollars a year to come down to this sink," we hope somebody remembers out loud

that infantryman charging up a hill at night with his knees shak-
ing under him. Sacrifice!
                                        —SATURDAY EVENING POST[3]

Spam fried in butter makes a very tasty Easter dinner.
                                        —A MOTHER[4]

MAXIM LITVINOV, THE NEW AMBASSADOR of the Soviet Union, arrived with his wife in San Francisco on the day before Pearl Harbor. They had come from Moscow, where life had been stripped down to its bare essentials amid a formidable military presence that included antiaircraft batteries ringing the city. Life in Washington utterly bewildered them. The nation had just gone to war and was frantically trying to mobilize and organize its resources, yet life seemed to go on as usual. Sleek, shiny cars purred impatiently in traffic jams, the hotels were jammed with people dancing and drinking the nights away, and the party circuit spun merrily without pause. Madam Litvinov was no peasant woman; she was in fact the former Ivy Low, daughter of a noted British philologist, but she had little patience or taste for life's trivia. She bridled when reporters wanted to know about her clothes and whether Russian women had permanent waves, and she asked crossly why it mattered which dress she wore to a party.[5]

At the huge, pretentious Russian embassy, originally the home of Mrs. George Pullman, the Litvinovs confined themselves to living simply in three or four rooms. The lavish parties given by their predecessor gave way to fewer, smaller affairs with far less outlay of caviar and champagne. Not for them the spectacle of grand living in grim times. Americans were very strange, they concluded from their small sample. They did not live in perpetual fear of attack as the other Allies did, but couldn't they at least realize there was a war on?

To many observers at home and abroad it was a question worth asking. The Russians, the British, the Chinese, and the captive peoples under Nazi or Japanese rule were all paying a steep price in brutality and destruction. Americans on far-flung battlefields were giving what Lincoln so aptly called the last full measure of devotion. Plenty of people at home were doing everything they knew how to aid the war effort, giving freely of their time and energy—to say nothing of their sons, daughters, and husbands—for whatever was asked of them. Yet what was being asked of them that fell outside the category of inconvenience? To the generation that had endured a decade of the worst depression in American history, the war years seemed a strange and ghastly mixture of the best and worst of times.

An English visitor on wartime duties in the United States in the spring of 1943, flying over the Nebraska plains, marveled at the sight below him. "Here, if anywhere," he reflected, "was normality—hundreds of miles of it and not a sight or sound to remind one that this was a country at war. And then my . . . stewardess deposited my lunch tray in front of me . . . As I reached avidly to attack my butter pat there, neatly inscribed on it, was the injunction, RE-MEMBER PEARL HARBOR. It needed the butter to remind one of guns." The contrast was all too easy to grasp for someone from war-torn London, as it would have been for someone from Leningrad or Manila or Chungking. For Americans it was not so obvious. As one who did see it observed, the United States was "fighting this war on imagination alone."[6]

A MIXTURE OF IRONY and paradox encrusted every layer of the war effort. Officials, especially in the War Department, fretted and politicians preened over the fact that, as Julius Krug noted, "people were subjected to inconvenience rather than sacrifice." Even the hard-nosed Truman Committee declared that "*there is no virtue* in sacrifice for sacrifice's sake." After the fall of Singapore Eleanor Roosevelt wrote hopefully, "Perhaps it is good for us to have to face disaster, because we have been so optimistic and almost arrogant in our expectation of constant success. Now we shall have to find within us the courage to meet defeat and fight right on to victory. That means a steadiness of purpose and of will, which is not one of our strong points."[7]

Instead, Americans pocketed record earnings, paid off their debts, amused themselves, and spent freely on whatever they could find. Restaurants and nightclubs flourished despite shortages of food and liquor. The price of musical instruments soared, and Mr. Black enjoyed a boom in grand pianos. Books, records, and sheet music sold at unprecedented volumes. Spectator sports enjoyed record crowds, as did resorts when people could get to them. Jewelry flew out of stores, especially items like cigarette cases, lighters, rings, watches, and silverware. "People are crazy with money," said one Philadelphia merchant. "They don't care what they buy. They purchase things . . . just for the fun of spending." For many people it had been a long time if ever.[8]

Midway through the war seven out of ten Americans admitted that it had not required them to make any "real sacrifices." Total civilian consumption of goods was higher in 1943 than it had been in 1940, and total personal consumption expenditures by civilians drifted upward during the war years. Once the outrage and apprehension following Pearl Harbor subsided, the war became a distant thing fought sometimes by friends and/or family members but not seen or heard personally. Americans endured inconveniences rather than deprivations, and at a time when the economic boom lifted their standard of living from the long dreary doldrums of the depression. Sharp, agonizing pain came only with the loss or maiming of a loved one.[9]

Raymond Clapper saw what was happening. "People are affected by this war in a strange way," he wrote. "It is an offshore war and so much is secret that its magnitude is difficult to grasp. So it reaches out like an unseen hand to clutch people by the throat, with rationing, goods disappearing completely, with sons and husbands disappearing into the unknown where they may be either alive or dead." Later he added, "War is not only deep personal loss. It is also a mass of trivial irritations. The small irritations of today are the big antiadministration votes of tomorrow." Walking in the woods by his house one day, he sat down on his favorite rock and saw in it a metaphor for what bothered him. "My particular rock is like America," he observed. "It is big and inert and does not know its own strength . . . If Americans could only believe in America."[10]

MR. BLACK CAME early to the war and stayed late. He was as resourceful as he was ubiquitous, and he dealt in anything that was lacking and promised a profit. His most common specialties were gasoline, meat, cigarettes, tires, and stolen or phony coupons, but nothing escaped his ambitious eye. Somehow he always had what you wanted if you were willing to pay his price. "Don't be a bootlegger," exhorted *Look*, adding, "The boys at the front aren't chiseling!"[11]

In Los Angeles Gus "Tryin'" Bryan ignored the plea and stockpiled tires to sell at inflated prices before the police caught up with him. A Chicago grocer amassed 22,000 pounds of sugar but registered only 2,500 pounds, saving the rest for the black market. Another practitioner sold a bundle of iron and steel grade scrap with an outer layer of high-grade material covering a mass of brick, ash, junk, clay, refuse, and other useless items. When silk went on the rationed list, a Brooklyn textile company kept spinning it for customers willing to pay double the ceiling price. In Washington itself two large stores were charged with ceiling violations. An OPA investigation revealed that 40 percent of 12,000 grocers and butchers were ceiling violators and that 70 percent of 500 East Coast gas stations disobeyed OPA regulations.[12]

Meat posed an especially thorny problem because the demand was so widespread, the dealers so numerous, and the rules so easily evaded. "Meatleggers" bought cattle from individual farmers at prices slightly over market, rented a farmer's barn for a slaughterhouse, worked at night, and sold the meat to dishonest dealers at a few pennies above the legal prices. In Chicago, Peter Golas netted a profit of $650,000 on $3 million worth of meat before being nabbed. "We're just working people," pleaded his wife. "I used to drive a truck." Tires that once sold for $11 to $15 brought anywhere from $30 to $60. Even chickens got into the act when illegal dealers bought so many of them from the Delmarva area that the army was forced to join the OPA in cracking down to secure its quota of the meat.[13]

A federal judge hearing the case of a man trying to compel delivery of 150 tires he had bought before the freeze said wearily, "These are times of great emergencies. I am not sleeping any too well, realizing, as we all must, the dangers our country is in."

"I am sleeping perfectly," countered the defense attorney.[14]

A CARTOON IN *Look* featured the "Pillory of Shame" with the hoarder, black market operator, and profiteer clamped in stocks. "A greedy few are trying to capitalize on the war for personal gain," said the magazine. "It is our duty to expose them . . . The self-seeking few cannot be allowed to fatten at the expense of the self-sacrificing many."[15]

Americans had always liked to stock up on canned goods, but the rationing of them provided incentive as never before. After OPA announced a freeze on sales of canned fish and meats beginning February 2, housewives and others swarmed into stores with wagons, perambulators, anything with wheels, to pile them as high as possible with "whatever looked shiny and had a label on it." One California lady deposed later admitted to having 8,400 cans in her private cache. Other kinds of canned foods were added to the list on March 1. During February War Ration Book Two was issued with its rows of blue and red stamps marked A, B, C, and beyond. Blue stamps or points went for processed foods, red ones for meats, cheese, and fats. At the same time, the rules for the coupons got more flexible and more complicated.[16]

The earlier version of rationing utilized a single-item basis in which a coupon was good for so many pounds of sugar or a pair of shoes or whatever item it covered. Distinctions of quality, grade, or type did not matter; the same coupon covered a pair of shoes worth $5 or $50. The new system tried to balance supply and demand by using a point system that could be adjusted as items grew more scarce or plentiful. Point values were adjusted each month to accommodate changes in the available supply. Meats, for example, used Department of Agriculture grades as well as scarcity to fix their point value, with organs and tripe costing few points compared to steaks and chops. Every man, woman, and child received forty-eight blue points a month, which would buy twenty to twenty-five pounds of canned vegetables a year. In 1943 a one-pound can of beans cost eight points, a pound can of fish seven points. Fresh fruits and vegetables remained unrationed.[17]

For housewives and others the new system offered greater flexibility of choice but required them to budget both money and points each month. The coupons were valid only for select periods of time to prevent hoarding at first issue. The new February rules covered 200 processed foods, and on March 29 the point system was extended to meat, butter, cheese, canned fish, lard, shortening, margarine, cooking oil, and salad oil. By then rationing covered more than 95 percent of the nation's foodstuffs as well as shoes, tires, gasoline, and other items. A list of items including most fish, poultry, pure olive oil, salad dressing, mayonnaise, soft and perishable cheese, and cheese spreads remained off the ration list, and some items received periodic adjustments. Dried beans, peas, and lentils had their point value cut from eight to four when imports from Mexico improved the supply, and a pound of prunes or raisins was reduced from twenty to twelve points because they had to be sold before the hot weather spoiled them.[18]

By summer even soap was running short of supply. Scare buying, fueled by persistent rumors that it would be rationed, emptied shelves, and manufacturers could not keep up with demand in part because they lacked raw materials. Normally soapmakers used a pound of imported tropical oils for every two pounds of domestic fats or oils, but the war had cut off their overseas supply of coconut oil, palm oils, and babassu oil. Meat rationing encouraged butchers to trim less fat from their cuts, reducing that usually reliable source. Even worse, the large amount of fat trimmed by slaughterers of black market meat simply went to waste. Attempts to salvage waste fats and grease from home and restaurant kitchens helped but could not begin to cover the loss. Not surprisingly, the soap being made scarcely resembled the prewar product. Even glycerin, a normal by-product of soapmaking, was removed for use in making explosives.[19]

Meat rationing in particular annoyed everybody because of the sheer impossibility of devising a fair and rational system. OPA drove butchers to despair in its attempt to do so. Its pamphlet on the rules and regulations of meat cutting ran twenty-four pages, the first twenty of them with three columns of fine print—a 40,000-word treatise guiding the butcher's every stroke. Housewives poring over beef charts explaining point values gazed blankly at such criteria as "yoke, rattle, or triangle bone in." Lawyers, not butchers, had written it. "The whole thing is nutty," complained Senator Hugh Butler of Nebraska. "It just shows what a bunch of young lawyers do when they meet up with a beef chart." The meat shortage that began during the winter of 1942–43 and grew steadily worse led to the appearance in March of horsemeat in several cities. The Man O'War Meat Market in Milwaukee sold 8,000 pounds of it in less than two days.[20]

The rationing of meat imposed on March 29 slowed the panic that had engulfed butcher shops across the country. Gradually Americans learned how to live with rationing and how to get around it, but uproars still occurred over the most unlikely actions. A storm of protest arose when Claude Wickard announced a ban on sliced bread as a measure to hold the price down. Housewives flooded hardware stores in search of bread knives and dutifully absorbed advice on how to slice a loaf of bread. An old cliché, "the greatest thing since sliced bread," reentered the vernacular. Bakers protested that the order cost them business and offered to provide sliced bread without raising the price. The order was rescinded and bread knives promptly went into storage.[21]

On the West Coast, a shortage of fresh vegetables rammed home to many how sorely the exiled Japanese Americans were missed. Labor and transportation both were in short supply, and unpicked crops rotted in the fields. Officials and other witnesses had sworn confidently before the removal that no labor shortage would result; by 1943 they were feasting on crow. "You'll never get a white farmer to work from sunup to sundown as the Japanese did, with his whole family helping him in the fields," admitted the most candid among them.

Special cases complicated the rationing process as well. The shortage of butter could be eased by supplementing it with margarine. Several butter-producing states such as Wisconsin, North Dakota, and Pennsylvania, however, had tax and packaging restrictions that blocked the sale of margarine. If butter and margarine rationing were coupled, citizens in those states would be handicapped. However, if they received an extra ration of butter to compensate, people elsewhere would howl in protest. Rationing intensified an ongoing campaign to remove the stranglehold of the butter interests in those states.[22]

Miners, lumberjacks, and other workers in heavy industries demanded more meat. Wyoming sheepherders depended almost entirely on canned goods because they were nowhere near stores to get fresh vegetables; they managed to get their basic blue ration hiked from 48 to 288 points. It soon became clear that rationing prompted people to hoard or to patronize Mr. Black to get what they wanted. "Sooner or later the hoarder is going to have to face the shortage," exhorted Eleanor Roosevelt, "and it is a lot more chummy to get into the boat with the rest of the citizenry from the start." However, many people preferred the company of Mr. Black to that of everyone else. "It never crossed my mind," admitted Eleanor forlornly, "that you couldn't tell the American people the truth and count on them to behave themselves accordingly."[23]

Shortages popped up in a wide variety of areas. Furniture making, the nation's second-largest industry, dropped 20 percent as half the nation's manufacturers, unable to get raw materials, turned to war work, producing over a thousand different items. Sixteen manufacturers in Grand Rapids, Michigan, pooled their woodworking facilities to make airplane and glider parts. A government directive limited patterns to one third their former number, forcing simplified designs. Civilians got half the supply of beds manufactured, but the industry's usual 300,000 tons of steel was reduced to 50,000 tons. WPB banned metal springs in beds and living-room furniture; a new wooden spring helped fill the gap. Despite its difficulties, no one expected the industry to be reduced to the British model in which 175 licensed companies turned out Spartan utility furniture while the rest of the industry was engaged in war work.[24]

Fuel oil remained in desperately short supply that winter. Boston endured fifty consecutive days of below-freezing weather and at one point had only enough oil for one more day. Ickes managed to rush fresh supplies in, thanks in part to the release of oil by the navy. Thousands of homes also depended on kerosene, which was also in short supply. New York closed its schools for a week at the start of February when 20 percent of the city's oil dealers reported empty tanks. Providence and Washington had similar emergencies. Gasoline remained short as well, and in New York automobile traffic declined an estimated 75 percent. Plants, stores, offices, hotels, and laundries scrambled to stay open amid the shortage.[25]

One shortage, that of paper, could easily be blamed on the bureaucrats, but there were other causes. Lack of manpower and electric power lowered the output of paper mills, transportation difficulties slowed delivery from mill to publisher, and the military planned to use a million more tons of paper in 1943 than the previous year. WPB imposed what amounted to a 10 percent cut in paper supply. The squeeze led newspapers to do what they hated most, turn away business. The *New York Times* rejected fifty-one columns of advertising in a single day, the *Louisville Times* seventy-four columns of ads in three days. The *Milwaukee Journal* reduced its Saturday edition from eighteen to eight pages, while a Norfolk paper froze its circulation and refused to accept any new customers. Papers and magazines alike reduced their page size and margins, cut out extraneous features to save space, and tightened up their content. Some magazines went to lighter paper to meet the strictures of paper rationing. Later in the year WPB hiked the reduction to 15 percent; when many publications failed to meet it, the agency ordered an 18 percent reduction for the first quarter of 1944.[26]

A shortage of sole leather along with panic buying over several months forced shoes onto the rationed list in February. The order also eliminated several styles, reduced colors, and shortened heels. The decree was imposed on a Sunday without warning to prevent more hoarding. It promptly triggered a frantic orgy of clothes buying on fears that they would be rationed next. Department stores reported twice their usual sales. A Cleveland shopper bought 75 pairs of stockings; another got four coats in different sizes for her growing daughter. One Pittsburgh shop sold $30,000 worth of coats in a single day. A Los Angeles matron took home sixteen dresses, four suits, and three coats. No amount of denials from Washington could stem the rush. "The American public has not yet decided to do without things during the war," said one embittered department store executive. Another added, "Patriotism? Sense? Everywhere it's me—me I'll take care of."[27]

The targets of panic buying varied widely from city to city. New Orleans endured runs on matches, soap, and even salt, which Louisiana produced in abundance. In Los Angeles it was cleansing tissues and cosmetics, in Washington lipstick, light bulbs, matches, macaroni, eyeglasses, toilet paper, razor blades, pepper, and sanitary napkins. "Nobody seemed able to convince the people that buying runs were the best way to bring on rationing," noted *Newsweek*. Some of the targets made no sense. Lipstick, for example, was deemed essential to the morale of women war workers and would never be rationed. The British even distributed lipstick and face powder free to its female workers. To counter the persistent rumor on clothing, several stores bought newspaper ads assuring customers that clothes would not be rationed. Lord & Taylor's ad read, "We wager $5,000 that clothes will NOT be rationed this year."[28]

The citizens who sat on ration boards conceded that they were "about as popular as tax collectors." One Manhattan member was confronted by a large and angry woman reeking of perfume. She had already been to the board four times for more gasoline and been denied each time. "I'm an American citizen," she proclaimed, waving a finger under his nose. "You can't do this to me. I've written to that man Henderson; I've written to the President. If you don't give me my gasoline, I'll write to Uncle Sam!"[29]

UNLIKE AMERICANS, RUSSIAN citizens endured the most desperate forms of sacrifice. Rationing to them meant something quite different than not being able to get a good steak or as much sugar or gasoline as they wanted. They had endured chronic shortages of food during World War I and the revolution, followed by the relentless drive for industrialization and the brutal collectivization of agriculture in which millions of peasants died of famine. Rationing had been introduced in 1929 and lasted until 1935; the standard of living fell again during the intense drive for rearmament from 1937 until 1940. Not even these sufferings matched those that arose after the German invasion of the Soviet Union, when the advancing Nazi army swallowed huge tracts of agricultural land and major industrial facilities. The supply of food diminished sharply even as the needs for the huge Russian army grew ever more demanding.[30]

Introduced in stages between July and November 1941, rationing was extended to all urban areas but covered only a small portion of the rural population. Bread was the staple food and rationed to about 62 million people in 1942 according to five categories: manual workers, white-collar workers, dependents, children under thirteen, and people employed in important war industries, including scientists and technicians. Able-bodied, unemployed adults received no rations. Workers in demanding occupations such as miners, steelworkers, and oil industry workers got extra rations and free meals at work. Rations also varied by region, depending on the availability of local food supplies.

Official rations bore little resemblance to what was actually distributed because of shortages, the changing war front, and sometimes extreme circumstances like the siege of Leningrad. Over half the people, mostly those in rural areas, received no rations and had to depend on local supplies or their own gardens or other sources. For them inflation and the black market became an integral part of their struggle to survive. The price of the two staples in their diet, bread and potatoes, rose to twenty-six and twenty-three times their July 1941 level respectively. Peasants depended on their private plots, where the main crop was potatoes, just as urbanites relied on bread. Malnutrition became a way of life for millions of Russians. Thousands died of starvation. According to one Soviet source, by 1942 "the sight of men and women falling dead of starvation on Moscow streets became too commonplace to attract crowds."

Malnutrition also fostered the spread of diseases. During 1942 cases of typhus, typhoid fever, and tuberculosis rose sharply, aggravated by the lack of adequate medical personnel caused in part by their draft into the army. The government tried feverishly to halt the march of diseases through sanitation measures and an immunization program. Crime also grew rampant as desperate people did anything to get food. Reports of cannibalism trickled out of Leningrad as corpses gathered for burial routinely had fleshy parts of their bodies missing. Murderers butchered their victims and sold their flesh cloaked as something else on the black market. Given the conditions that existed elsewhere, some thought that cannibalism was by no means confined to the luckless inhabitants of Leningrad.

NO ONE SACRIFICED more for the war effort than the soldiers who fought and died in the mud and filth of distant battlefields, but their story seldom got told except in the form of fables. Elmer Davis wanted to tell it straight.

"Our job at home," he said in December 1942, "is to give the American people the fullest possible understanding of what this war is about . . . not only to tell the American people how the war is going, but where it is going and where it came from." But the war was so remote as to seem almost abstract, and pressures to simplify and sanitize news about it were unrelenting, especially from the military. As head of OWI Davis, despite his reputation for integrity, was looked upon by many critics not as a newsman but as a shill for an administration they despised. To others he embodied the belief that good newsmen made lousy administrators. More to the point, he held a thankless position guaranteed to please no one.[31]

Davis seemed an ideal man to tell the war's story straight. After graduating from Franklin College in Indiana, he became a Rhodes scholar but returned from Oxford still the quintessential Hoosier with a midwestern twang that became his trademark as a newscaster. He spent ten years on the *New York Times* and wrote on the side several novels along with everything from adventure stories to essays on literature and politics. Having become a successful author, he moved almost accidentally to radio as a commentator. By the time of Pearl Harbor his five-minute summary had attracted some 12.5 million listeners and a $53,000-a-year contract from CBS. His studio estimated that half the families in the country heard him at least once a week. The calm, folksy voice became for many people an oasis of reassurance and common sense in troubled times.[32]

After Davis's appointment in June 1942, *Newsweek* viewed him as having "almost complete control over all official news and propaganda issued at home" in all forms of media. But censorship, foreign propaganda, and news to Latin America remained in other hands. The organization he shaped looked to be a strong one. Robert Horton and Lowell Mellett agreed to take subordinate positions, and Archibald MacLeish stayed on as an adviser and assistant director. Milton Eisenhower came aboard to handle the administrative end, and Robert Sherwood took charge of the overseas operations left to OWI, mostly radio propaganda, posters, and pamphlets. A fourth assistant director, Gardner Cowles Jr., president of *Look* magazine, oversaw the six bureaus through which most of the information reaching the public flowed. Mellett and Horton worked under Cowles.[33]

The military remained Davis's major obstacle in its determination to dictate what information would or would not be released about its activities. Soon after his appointment Ernest Lindley, himself a fellow Rhodes scholar, author, and reporter, warned in his column that "it is doubtful whether any war information service can win confidence in this country until it gets more authority over the information services of the Army and Navy." A few days later a reporter asked Stimson in his news conference whether Davis would have such authority. Stimson looked at him in surprise. "Is Mr. Davis an educated military officer?" he asked pointedly. Nothing more was said on the subject.[34]

Gradually Davis came to an understanding with the army and navy, largely on their terms. After one early clash he admitted that he saw "perfectly clearly the point about military secrecy, which I did not see when I was on the other side of the fence." To the House Appropriations Committee he declared, "We are in a sense an auxiliary to the armed forces—an organization whose operations can pave the way for their operations and make their success easier." But he continued to lock horns with them over how much and what information should be released or withheld, and with the committee over funding for his agency. He never succeeded in acquiring operational jurisdiction over the output of information either of the military or OSS.[35]

Other agencies demanded independence from OWI as well. Bill Jeffers got into a dustup with Davis when he tried to kill a story about the ongoing shortage of tires. The irascible Ickes defied OWI by publishing over its objections a story in *Collier's* about the UMW strike in the bituminous fields in which he characterized the walkouts as "a black—and stupid—chapter in the history of the home front." Davis wanted the phrase deleted, but it got published, Ickes explained, because OWI was too slow in voicing its objections. In these and other conflicts Davis had the difficult task of trying to get agencies to tell the truth about what was going on while at the same time not undercutting official policy. Yet as a coordinator he lacked the authority to impose his will.[36]

Within OWI Davis had to preside over conflicting views of what its role should be. MacLeish and other liberals argued that it should put before the people "the principal issues which must be decided, in a form which will excite and encourage discussion." Eisenhower disagreed, saying the agency should have no blueprint of its own but simply disseminate the relevant facts that would encourage public debate. "Our job is to promote an understanding of policy, not to make policy," he emphasized. Two early one-reel shorts produced by the film unit under Mellett exemplified the best of this approach. "Salvage," narrated by Donald Nelson, forcibly revealed the urgency of the need for scrap by showing the crucial weapons created from waste materials. Paul McNutt narrated a second short, "Manpower," which dramatized the seriousness of that problem and what was being done to solve it. In contrast to the fictionalized "America Speaks" series, *Newsweek* found the shorts to be "straightforward, timely reports from your government to you" that utilized "the screen's potentialities in educating and informing a nation that can take its news straight."[37]

During the spring of 1943, however, the ongoing clash over reporting the news versus sanitizing it erupted again. OWI's core of liberal writers, headed by Henry F. Pringle, a Pulitzer Prize winner for his biography of Theodore Roosevelt, resented the Madison Avenue influence and took pride in preparing pamphlets and other copy that went beyond and often contradicted the usual accounts in the media. One pamphlet tried to explain why the war was being fought, citing the Four Freedoms, the Atlantic Charter, and the Declaration of the United Nations. Others told the story of the European underground, the impact of inflation, and the shortage of doctors for civilians; controversial publications included a picture book entitled *Negroes and the War*, a cartoon biography of the president, and *Battle Stations All: The Story of the Fight to Control Living Costs*.[38]

Critics of all stripes pounced on some of the publications. New Deal and Roosevelt haters denounced the cartoon biography as political propaganda, southern congressmen were outraged by the sympathetic treatment of blacks, and an acerbic Ralph Robey lambasted *Battle Stations* as "one of the most barefaced pieces of prejudiced propaganda that has ever been directed at the American public by a presumably nonpartisan government bureau . . . On almost every subject which is controversial the discussion is one-sided, incomplete, and prejudiced . . . on the side of the Administration and the bureaucrats." Roosevelt haters were not appeased by the fact that the pamphlet on him had been produced not by the Domestic but the Overseas Branch and was intended strictly for foreign distribution. As congressional protests mounted, Cowles recruited two new assistants, William B. Lewis, a former vice president of CBS, and Price Gilbert, onetime advertising manager for Coca-Cola, along with some other admen and public relations specialists.[39]

Pringle and the other writers respected Cowles but deeply resented the newcomers, whose approach they saw as deodorizing content and replacing it with advertising gimmicks. The writers went to Davis, who listened to them over dinner and drinks and sympathized with their complaints—or so they thought. A few days later Davis gave Lewis permission to abolish the writers' division and regroup several desks around a new Bureau of Graphics headed by Gilbert. Outraged, Pringle and thirteen others placed their resignations on Davis's desk. Deeply distressed because many of them were his personal friends, Davis called them in and asked them to reconsider. They agreed to do so only if they worked directly under Davis and were responsible only to him. But that posed a problem, replied Davis. In resigning they had gone over Cowles's head directly to him; he could not do the same thing by transferring them without undermining all loyalty in the organization.[40]

Out the door went Pringle and some of OWI's best talent, including Harold Guinzberg, president of Viking Press; Edward Dodd, vice president of

Dodd, Mead; Henry Brennan, former art editor of *Fortune*; and a young Arthur Schlesinger Jr. At a press conference Davis said the rebels were sincere but wrong in their premises. For the moment OWI belonged to Madison Avenue. Pringle and his friends showed their contempt by a mock poster of a smiling girl with the message "The Four Delicious Freedoms—the War that Refreshes."[41]

Although some regarded the clash as just one more intramural dispute, *Time* castigated the outcome in unsparing terms. "From now on U.S. citizens will get their war news well washed and perfumed . . . The men who had tried to be realists about the war were unhorsed, while the so-called soap salesmen were in the saddle." The victory of the admen was short-lived. The House showed its wrath by abolishing the Domestic Branch but concurred reluctantly when the Senate restored it. However, the OWI's appropriation bill banned the production of pamphlets, abolished OWI field offices, and cut funding severely enough to limit its coordinating activities. The reduced funding forced the Domestic Branch to drop its production of motion-picture documentaries, posters, and pamphlets, and discontinue its news services in field offices. Other agencies, especially OPA, took up some of the slack, but the Domestic Branch of OWI had been effectively neutered. That summer Cowles left the agency and was replaced by Edwin Palmer "Ep" Hoyt, a self-described "Lifelong Republican" who vowed to produce news and not propaganda.[42]

In September, however, Davis managed to win one important victory for truth telling. At a White House press conference, while Roosevelt and representatives from the War, Navy, and State departments listened, Davis told reporters that the public had grown complacent because it got only the rosier side of the war. Nearly everything that had to do with American losses was suppressed, and no pictures of American dead could be published. The campaign in Sicily cost the Allies 25,000 casualties, yet Americans saw only pictures of locals tossing flowers at American troops or hurling fruit at posters of Mussolini. Let OWI show the people the real face of war, Davis said, or do away with it.[43]

Afterward Roosevelt issued a directive to the departments stating that Davis would hereafter decide when, where, and how to issue war news. They did not always honor the directive, but stories on engagements and losses grew more timely and detailed, and photos from the front more graphic. One of the first to be published showed the corpses of American paratroopers in Sicily. The true face of war, the most awful dimension of sacrifice, was at last coming home from the distant battlefields.

*   *   *

AMERICA'S OLDEST AND deepest social wound never really went away. Most of the time it simply festered in the background, but in 1943 it burst forth in all its ugliness. Racial prejudice was as American as apple pie. "We won't wrap the apple pie in red, white, and blue," noted an officer trainee. "But most people do. That's what their war's about—and to keep the blacks and the Jews out of the neighborhood when it's over, too." As the largest minority group blacks bore the brunt of hometown prejudice, but in the West, especially after removal of the Japanese Americans, Hispanics became the primary target. The war itself fed the ongoing national prejudice against Japanese; in 1943 the WPB approved an advertisement calling for extermination of the "Japanese rats."[44]

Southern blacks who managed to join the army encountered discrimination there as well as the same old prejudices upon returning home. In August 1942 a black private was shot to death in Mobile for the crime of asking a bus driver to lift his suitcase off the bus. During a quarrel between white soldiers and black civilians in Macon, a black soldier grabbed a pistol and killed a policeman. Two Beaumont, Texas, policemen beat and shot a black private who dared take a bus seat reserved for whites. The head of Georgia's state guard ordered it on alert because of "reported efforts on the part of Negro men and women to demand certain privileges which are not granted in Georgia and which never will be." At a Mississippi camp, after a sheriff shot a black soldier fleeing arrest, other blacks stole rifles from a stockade and exchanged fire with a riot squad. These incidents, which kept piling up, contrasted sharply with news from the Pacific that three black privates had been awarded the Soldier's Medal for dashing through gasoline flames to rescue a pilot from a burning plane.[45]

By 1943 the marines had finally admitted blacks and planned to recruit more, but none could receive a commission. The army went so far as to segregate the blood plasma of blacks and whites—a decision endorsed by the Red Cross—even though a black doctor, Charles R. Drew, pioneered in the creation of blood banks. Prejudice in the military was bad enough, but it was even worse at home. The pervasiveness of Jim Crow segregation persisted across the land. Years afterward one soldier could not shed his memory of one cruel irony. He and some fellow black soldiers were refused service at a lunchroom in Salina, Kansas. On the way out they noticed a group of German prisoners of war having lunch at the counter. So much for the Four Freedoms. "Freedom," said a black Georgia soldier that winter. "They say they's fightin' for Freedom ... Whose Freedom? ... There ought to be Freedom for everybody."[46]

The freedom did exist to go north or west in search of jobs, and some 400,000 southern blacks did so, most of the them in 1943. The proportion of blacks employed in war industries jumped from 4.2 percent of all employees in 1940 to 8.6 percent by the war's end. Their arrival, especially in industrial cities, exacerbated already existing shortages of housing and other facilities. Most of the other workers were recently arrived white migrants from the South or members of European ethnic groups, neither of which wanted anything to do with blacks and deeply resented their presence as competitors for housing and other needs. Tensions mounted steadily during the year, especially in the worst tinderbox of all, Detroit, a city long plagued by its inability to catch up to its explosive growth. One critic described it as "a city of transplanted Southerners . . . a great ant heap of newcomers and strangers, to which more newcomers and strangers are forever being added."[47]

No other city in the country did more war work than Detroit. The state of Michigan received more than 10 percent of the $200 billion in major contracts awarded by the federal government and foreign buyers during the war, and the four-county Detroit metropolitan area got more than 70 percent of them. The city's labor force soared from 396,000 in 1940 to a peak of 867,000 in November 1943. As late as December 1944 some 20 percent of Michigan's people were directly engaged in war production. So many of them had migrated from the South that a local joke said the nation now had only forty-six states because "Tennessee and Kentucky are now in Michigan." They were not well received. Detroit folklore condemned the typical southerner as "clannish, dirty, careless, gregarious in his living habits. He lives on biscuits and beans, never buys more than the most basic necessities of life, saves his money, is illiterate and yokelish." And he did much to worsen racial tensions in the city.[48]

Detroit's population of 465,766 in 1910 shot up to 1,623,452 by 1940 and an estimated 2.5 million in 1943. Of the UAW's 450,000 members in Detroit, about 55,000 were black. Housing, transportation, recreational facilities, and other necessities were in short supply for everybody and pitifully inadequate for the growing black population. A mixed bag of ethnic and racial groups rubbed elbows uneasily in the plants. The city and the unions became fertile ground for agencies of intolerance such as the Ku Klux Klan, the Black Legion, the Dixie Voters League, and the National Workers League, all of which made blacks their primary target as more of them worked alongside white workers and tried to move into or near white neighborhoods. One of every seven white and one of every two black families lived in substandard housing. One investigator discovered a converted one-family residence housing "150 Negroes, often one family to a room."[49]

To ease this crunch, Roosevelt in May 1941 approved federal funds to build a thousand housing units in Detroit, 200 of them for blacks. The United States Housing Authority designated the Detroit Housing Commission to build and manage the project. The site lay between major factories and a black neighborhood; it also sat near a Polish American community, whose representatives promptly protested the presence of black housing. Both federal and city agencies brushed aside the complaints and pushed ahead. The USHA named the project "Sojourner Truth Homes" in honor of a former slave woman and gifted poet. The Poles appealed to their congressman, who accused Detroit blacks of following Communist leaders. Members of a House committee visited the site; their report, coupled with rising racial tensions, led the government to change the project to all-white occupancy and develop another site for blacks.[50]

Detroit blacks and other black leaders promptly protested the decision. Edward Jeffries, Detroit's mayor, and the UAW favored the original plan, as did Eleanor Roosevelt, who had long battled for equal rights. With Eleanor urging the president not to surrender the original plan, the decision was reversed. When the first black families arrived on February 28, 1942, to move into their new homes, they were greeted by 700 white pickets armed with guns, knives, and clubs along with a burning cross. City officials postponed occupancy until adequate protection could be arranged. Fights broke out between black and white groups in the area, and a small group of whites led by the KKK picketed the area for several weeks. Mayor Jeffries remained a staunch supporter of the black settlers, saying, "If we are one people, the Negroes should go into the project." Finally, after several failed compromise efforts, the new residents moved in under protection of state militia and police.[51]

Race relations in Detroit went steadily downhill from the Sojourner Truth confrontation. When *Life* warned in August 1942 that the city was dynamite, officials issued outraged denials. A Justice Department report noted that interracial conflict had exploded within the city's high schools. Blacks feared the police force, which was inefficient at best and depleted by the draft. "Police seem bent on suppressing Negroes . . . to keep the peace," said another government report, "and . . . the choice is . . . made from the fact that the Negro group is smaller." The Justice Department took a dim view of the city's people. "Detroit is a swashbuckling community, not conspicuous for its social maturity," declared its report. "Negro equality . . . is an issue which . . . very considerable elements of the white community resist . . . White Detroit seems to be a particularly hospitable climate for native fascist type movements . . . Large segments of the Negro community hate the police, probably not without reason." Of the city's 3,600 policemen, only 40 were black.[52]

On a torrid Sunday in June the pot of racial hatred boiled over. Somewhere between 50,000 and 100,000 people of both races spent the day at the city park on Belle Isle, an island in the Detroit River not far from a black ghetto

with the ironic name of Paradise Valley, described as "one of the most intensely crowded urban districts in the United States. Filthy, smelly, dive-
ridden, whore-infested Hastings Street is as crowded as Coney Island on a hot
Sunday." The sardinelike living was especially bad in the dirty houses and
apartment buildings of Paradise Valley, where four or five families were
crammed into space that once barely accommodated one or two. Belle Isle
was a welcome relief from its sweltering congestion, but whites resented its
domination by so many blacks.[53]

Sporadic incidents and fights broke out on the evening of June 20 and
drew in some white sailors from the naval armory near Belle Isle. By 10:30 a
series of fights was raging, fueled by rumors that all proved false. One claimed
that whites had thrown a black woman and her baby off a bridge, another that
a gang of blacks had raped and killed a white woman on the bridge. A mob of
blacks formed and began wrecking white-owned stores in the vicinity; another stopped a streetcar carrying fifty white factory workers and beat them.
Whites waited for blacks to emerge from two all-night theaters and pounded
them while police in two squad cars watched. Cars were overturned and set
ablaze. Police towed nineteen wrecks from one six-block area.[54]

By the wee hours a full-scale riot was in progress and deaths began to
mount—a white doctor and milkman beaten to death, blacks who unwit-
tingly strayed into the paths of white mobs. In all twenty-five blacks and nine
whites died, four blacks and one white by police bullets. People of both races
began shooting at each other. Women stood near the brutalities, urging on
the men "with a savagery that exceeded that of the men," according to the
Detroit News. Most of the rioters were young people with plenty of elders to
egg them on. "Jesus, but it was a show!" boasted one nineteen-year-old afterward. "We dragged niggers from cars, beat the hell out of them, and lit the
sons of bitches' autos. I'm glad I was in it! And those black bastards well deserved it." A sixteen-year-old who admitted being too scared to kill anyone
said excitedly that "I saw knives being stuck through their throats and heads
being shot through, and a lot of stuff like that. It was really some riot. They
were turning over cars with niggers in them, you should have seen it. It was
some riot."[55]

A white college girl thought the "whites were raving with hate." A reporter
believed "the Negroes were berserk. They were smashing up everything that
didn't have a colored sign on it." He ventured uptown and saw a seventeen-
year-old white girl standing on the corner and yelling to the boys, "I haven't
seen any blood yet. What's the matter with you guys?" The rioting went on all
day Monday and into the night. Driven back into Paradise Valley, blacks began looting what a white Detroit civic leader called "stores of decidedly ex-
ploitive character." Helpless to stop the violence, Jeffries appealed to Governor

Harry F. Kelly, who hurried home from a governors conference in Columbus, Ohio, and proclaimed a state of emergency. Kelly ordered a curfew, barred the sale of liquor, closed all places of amusement, canceled a Tigers baseball game and racing, and sent state police into the city.[56]

Still it was not enough. Despite his stubborn determination to handle the situation on his own, Kelly was obliged on Monday night to ask Roosevelt, who was at Hyde Park, for federal troops. Stimson was ready for the president's call, having alerted three battalions near Detroit and ordered units of the Second Divison at Fort McCoy, 400 miles away, to head for Detroit. The necessary papers were already drawn up for Roosevelt to sign. Some 3,800 troops rolled into the city in full battle dress, followed later by others. The riot ended without a shot being fired, and order was restored. A white paper issued by a panel appointed by Kelly proved to be just that: It blamed the riot on the blacks, their newspapers, and the NAACP. Others north and south blamed Eleanor Roosevelt for her constant harping on equal rights. One Detroit resident held Eleanor and Jeffries responsible "due to their coddling of negroes."[57]

The toll besides the dead included 700 people injured, 1,300 arrested, a million dollars in property damage, and a 40 percent drop in the city's war production. German and Japanese propagandists seized on the riot as choice material, as they did every racial disturbance. Even Governor Kelly understood that the problem went far beyond Detroit's miseries. "Whatever the cause," he said, "it is not a local problem. It is America's problem." The patrician Stimson listened to a report on the twenty-fourth that confirmed "this trouble in Detroit is merely an omen of what may come anywhere . . . a very somber situation throughout the country in regard to the relations of the two races." The report blamed the efforts of certain radical black leaders "to use the war for obtaining the ends which they were seeking . . . race equality and interracial marriages, if necessary; the equality to be social as well as economic and military; and they are trying to demand that there will be this complete inter-mixing in the Army."[58]

DETROIT WAS HARDLY an isolated event. Three weeks earlier the upgrading of a dozen skilled black welders in Mobile, Alabama, led to their being attacked by white workers who refused to work alongside them. "No nigger is goin' to join iron in these yards," yelled one worker as the fighting spread across the yard. Eleven blacks ended up in the hospital. In August fighting and looting broke out in Harlem after a white policeman arrested a black woman for disorderly conduct and a black soldier tried to intervene. Two British seamen leaving the Apollo Theater were beaten up, six black rioters died, and 543 rioters and police were injured. Mayor Fiorello La Guardia denounced the outburst as "the thoughtless, criminal acts of hoodlums, reckless, irresponsible people. Shame has come to our city, and sorrow."[59]

Nor were the clashes confined to blacks. In the West discrimination against Spanish-speaking peoples rivaled that against blacks and produced occasional outbursts of violence. The worst incident occurred in Los Angeles, where ethnic tensions had long been brewing. By 1943 the zoot suit had become popular among young men in slum areas, especially blacks and those Chicanos known as pachucos. The outfit featured loosely cut coats that reached midthigh with wide padded shoulders, and pants that ballooned out below the waist but were pegged around the ankles, accesssorized with thick shoes, a wide-brimmed hat, a long watch chain, a tee or a sport shirt with long collar points, and a ducktail haircut. A popular song, "I Wanna Zoot Suit," celebrated the costume.[60]

In some cities like Detroit the outfit became a badge of organized gangs; in others it was more a cultural fad. "I wouldn't say the zoot suiters were mother's angels," concluded writer Carey McWilliams, one of their champions, "but they weren't devils either. The papers were dreadful. The officials were no better." Although by one estimate two thirds of Mexican American boys in Los Angeles wore zoot suits, only about 5 percent of them belonged to pachuco gangs who committed criminal acts. However, the popular mind soon stereotyped zoot suiters as pachucos and therefore potentially dangerous. The police began to harass zoot suiters, while pachuco gangs vented their frustrations on men in uniform. Clashes between zoot suiters and servicemen mounted during the spring; the last week in May saw eighty-three incidents involving navy men alone.[61]

Some said the zoot suiters attacked servicemen because they viewed them as rivals for their girlfriends. "A sailor with a pocketful of money has always been fair game for loose women," said Newsweek, "and the girls of the Los Angeles Mexican quarter were no exception." Many of the confrontations did not go beyond name-calling and some shoving. By mid-May they had grown more violent, and in a few cases zoot suiters harassed the families of workmen. Fed up with the attacks, some servicemen piled into taxis and cruised the barrio of East Los Angeles seeking out zoot suiters. On May 30 eleven soldiers and sailors, walking in the worst slum area of Los Angeles, were set on by thirty-five zoot suiters but managed to fight them off. Infuriated when the police did little because of their limited authority over military personnel, the sailors vowed to clean up the situation. "If the police can't handle the little gangsters," said one, "then we will."[62]

On the evening of June 3 several hundred servicemen armed with rocks and sticks roamed the barrio attacking anyone in a zoot suit. Some of their first victims happened to be members of a Mexican American club dedicated to crime prevention, but no distinctions were made. The servicemen stopped streetcars and went into theaters, bars, arcades, and restaurants, dragging out zoot suiters and some blacks as well for beatings. For two more nights the fighting raged as servicemen returned to the barrio to confront growing gangs of zoot suiters. The police were content to watch the fighting, and the naval commandant said in a memo that "the enforcement of laws rests in the hands of the civilian police and is not a matter which should be undertaken by any unauthorized groups of Navy personnel." He did urge officers to restrain their men. The army commander was more forthright, saying that "military personnel of all ranks must understand that no form of mob violence or rioting will be tolerated."[63]

The police did little to douse the fires of outrage by arresting zoot suiters and letting the sailors who started the riot go free. The city fathers demonstrated their grasp of the underlying causes by passing an ordinance banning the wearing of zoot suits within the city limits. Along with the ancient poisonous stew of racial and ethnic prejudice there existed deep social dislocations, poverty, and the bewilderment inherent in life within a strange new environment like the big city in wartime. These adjustments unsettled nearly everyone regardless of race, creed, or color. A few cities made an effort to ameliorate tensions. In Atlanta twenty-nine southern leaders, sixteen white and thirteen black, formed the Southern Regional Council to advance the cause of equal opportunity for blacks. Elsewhere Joseph C. Grew, who had spent ten years as ambassador to Japan, spoke out on behalf of rights for Japanese Americans. "I do know," he stressed, "that like the Americans of German descent, the overwhelming majority of Americans of Japanese origin are wholly loyal to the United States."[64]

Grew spoke out in the wake of an outbreak at Tule Lake, the camp where Japanese Americans considered to be troublemakers had been confined. A large group of inmates refused to harvest vegetables, penned up the camp's director and nearly a hundred whites in the administration building, and beat up the camp doctor, who had openly displayed his contempt for them. The army rushed a thousand men along with tanks and tear gas to the camp and quickly restored order. The incident, fumbled badly by the WRA, triggered another round of hate-mongering in the West. The mayor of Kent, Washington, near Seattle, had signs printed up saying, "WE DON'T WANT THE JAPS BACK HERE EVER." The mother lodge of the Fraternal Order of Eagles in Seattle voted unanimously to deport all Japanese Americans after the war, as did the Portland Progressive Business Men's Club and the Oregon State Legion.[65]

"We have been told," said a California legislator and Legionnaire, "it would be unhealthy for Japanese—even American born—to be seen on California streets, and that returning Marines and soldiers would slit their throats." Not all marines agreed. One young Chicago leatherneck, recovering from malaria in a California camp after fighting on Guadalcanal, sent his views to an unreceptive American Legion. "We find . . . a condition behind our backs that stuns us," he wrote. "We find that our American citizens, those of Japanese ancestry, are being persecuted, yes, persecuted as though Adolf Hitler himself were in charge. We find that the California American Legion is promoting a racial purge. I'm putting it mildly when I say it makes our blood boil . . . We shall fight this injustice, intolerance and un-Americanism at home! We will not break faith with those who died . . . We can endure the hell of battle, but we are resolved not to be sold out at home."[66]

WHILE IN RECESS, the members of Congress indulged in their usual ritual of sounding the home front on its attitudes. As expected, many of their constituents objected to the drafting of fathers and wanted legislation prohibiting it. The members found considerable uneasiness over the price and availability of food and much dissatisfaction with strikes and what they deemed union excesses. But local sentiment overwhelmingly opposed a national service law to draft labor. The public was resigned to paying higher taxes and thought they should do so; some said the war should be paid for while it was being fought. What surprised the congressmen the most was the nature of the complaints they heard. "It's amazing," said one, "how willing people are to have somebody else sacrifice for the war." Another admitted that "Voters say they're willing to make more sacrifices but they bellyache if any of their gas or food is taken away."[67]

Ernest Lindley found what he called a "Psychological Deadlock in the Nation." He saw no lack of patriotism but "clearly a fear on the part of nearly every economic group that its patriotism is being or may be exploited for the private economic gain of another group. The seat of the trouble is a sense of unequal sacrifice." Asked to make some concession, every group pointed to the gains of other groups. "Absolute equality of sacrifice cannot be achieved," Lindley emphasized. Where administration spokesmen complained of public complacency, Lindley found "less evidence of complacency than of discontent. The main ingredient of this discontent cannot be the hardships imposed by the war because only a few have felt them and they are not complaining." What then? Lindley thought the root of the problem lay in the administration "treating American civilians as if they were soft and selfish when they want to live like heroes." The way to break the psychological deadlock, he concluded, was through "inspiring leadership which assumes that the great majority are eager to sacrifice until it hurts."[68]

Concern over the nation's morale arose within weeks of Pearl Harbor. In May 1942 writer Vincent Sheean urged Americans to "stop kidding ourselves, admit our defeats, realize that our very lives are at stake." The attack on Pearl Harbor had left Americans numb with disbelief, especially since—unlike the British with Dunkirk and the German bombing raids—it was all too far away to experience firsthand. "The war came to us in a form for which we were psychologically unprepared," he noted. ". . . Generations of Americans have grown up believing that nobody would dare offend us: how can we suddenly be brought to the stark realization that our enemies not only dare attack us, but are actually threatening our national existence? We do not realize this; we are 'complacent.' We are worse than that—we are apathetic . . . We allow our representatives in Congress to behave like vaudeville performers, with no sense of the gravity of the hour."[69]

Nearly a year later Marquis Childs asked, "What's Wrong with the Home Front?" and declared it to be "in a muddle . . . Hoarding and black market are on the increase; essential civilian services languish." He found the American people "reluctant to give up our normal prerogatives of leisure and a little luxury now and then. We cling to old habits and familiar ways. But mostly, we are not sure where our duty lies." For this he blamed the government for failing to take the hard steps necessary to get things done. Claude Wickard had tried to recruit a volunteer agricultural army instead of stepping on political toes to create one. Henry Morgenthau blundered by insisting on voluntary rather than compulsory savings. Congress had been Congress in its perpetual dawdling over one crucial issue after another rather than showing the political will to get things done. "The hard fact is," concluded Childs, "that total war cannot be fought with voluntary methods."[70]

Five editors, all Pulitzer Prize winners, were asked the same question. One concluded, "What's wrong with the home front is simply this: It isn't a front." It lacked cohesion, coordination, order, and teamwork. Another found "too much of too-narrow groupism. Political groupism and economic groupism." A third blamed Congress for "wasting time over relatively insignificant matters and delaying for weeks and months vital decisions," and the president for playing politics for 1944. Still another saw "poor administration" as the culprit, while the fifth castigated the political game-playing, the "manpower morass," and the fact that "we are spatially too far removed from bombed bedrooms and our own and neighbors' children slain from the air." All agreed that the war could not be won without a deeper public commitment to its demands.[71]

As the year wound down, talk turned to a different facet of morale. The war fronts had improved. In November the Russians took Kiev, and the marines won Tarawa after yet another bloody battle. Production hit its peak at $5 billion worth in a single month. As early as August concerned voices began warning against complacency. "All talk about an early ending of the war is wishful thinking," said Frank Knox. "It has caused a letup in production and we're already feeling the effects . . . It's just criminal." Two months later *Newsweek* pronounced complacency as "the No. 1 foe on the American home front last week." To ram home the point, the army and navy announced their total casualties to date as 115,201 with 21,900 deaths; a much higher toll was expected in the coming year. On October 1, Selective Service finally began drafting fathers despite heavy opposition.[72]

The War Department hosted a conference for business and labor leaders as well as reporters to spell out some ominous facts. The German Luftwaffe was larger than it had been in 1939 and building more fighters than bombers, indicating a shift from offense to defense. Hitler still had 300 well-equipped divisions, three times the number when he attacked Poland. Japan's air strength was also increasing despite heavy losses, and two million of its men had not yet been called to arms. The Nazis had 35 million factory workers compared to 23 million in 1939, and a food ration higher in caloric content than four years earlier. To military leaders this meant that American munitions production, high as it was, would have to be boosted 21 percent in 1944, which meant more skimping on civilian goods and longer work hours. The war, in short, was far from over, and the toughest work lay ahead.[73]

1944: THE YEAR OF HOPE

CHAPTER 28

THE WINTER OF DISCONNECT

Week by week the gulf is widening between the war fronts and the home front—between those who are primarily concerned, in action or thought, with benefits during the war or securing a head start when the peace comes. The breach is possibly most noticeable in Washington.

—ERNEST K. LINDLEY [1]

It is curious how everybody is showing the effect of the war strain now. I never knew the atmosphere of Washington to be so sore and disgruntled even among people you are accustomed to rely on, and even the commentators and publicists are snarling around like a pack of Indian wild dogs.

—HENRY L. STIMSON [2]

Politically the war is changing everything. It is changing the New Deal almost beyond recognition. I think the term itself is ceasing to have much significance ... I have never thought there was anything very revolutionary about Mr. Roosevelt. The New Deal to me has always been a mild affair. It has been improvised and usually played by ear ... Relief and reemployment came first. Then there were several reform measures ... A third line of activity was in behalf of organized labor ... That's about all there ever has been to the New Deal.

—RAYMOND CLAPPER [3]

As 1944 OPENED, THE PRESIDENT was in a fighting mood. The last weeks of the old year had been marked by yet another round of labor crises dominated by John L. Lewis. As the clock ticked down to the November deadline for a coal settlement, Lewis again undermined the WLB and the Little Steel formula by reaching an agreement for 30,500 Illinois miners even as he testified before the board with unexpected gentleness of manner. In September he came up with a new formula that gave miners portal-to-portal pay without calling it such; the operators rejected it as too expensive. Reports began circulating that a shortage of coal loomed for the winter season. "Coal production has been unable to keep pace with the expansion of war requirements," said Harold Ickes in his role as solid fuel administrator. "The situation is bad and getting worse."[4]

Wildcat strikes broke out over the ongoing lack of a contract. Lewis blandly labeled them unauthorized but reiterated his position: His men would work for the government without a contract but not for the operators. When the deadline arrived, the miners walked out for the fourth time in 1943. Wearily Roosevelt ordered Ickes to seize the mines again while the WLB toiled furiously to come up with a suitable formula for a contract. It devised one that *Time* called "so tortured in its reasoning, so filled with economic Greek, that it took WLB's own statisticians 48 hours to decipher it, and put them through Einsteinian mathematics to justify it." In essence it gave the miners $55.50 a week of the $57 Lewis had sought with his $2 raise demand. By one reckoning the miners actually got $58.87 for a full week's work.[5]

Technically the new agreement, with all its sophistry, did not violate the Little Steel formula, but most observers agreed that it amounted to an epitaph. *Newsweek* proclaimed Lewis "The Winner and Undefeated Champion." The two-year contract meant peace with the miners, but everyone braced for the demands sure to follow from other unions. For months the fifteen nonoperating railway unions had been demanding a blanket raise of 20 cents an hour. In May a special board set up by Roosevelt recommended 8 cents only to have OES reject it as inflationary even though the railroads accepted it. A second board in October came up with 4 cents; the unions angrily dismissed it and called a strike for December 30. The five operating brotherhoods supported the move as well. "If we strike," said one leader in a twist on Lewis's approach, "we aren't striking against the carriers, we are striking against the Government."[6]

Roosevelt took this assertion at face value. Just returned from his trip to Cairo and Tehran, he was tired and ill. "To what a mess the President returned this morning," sympathized Bill Hassett. "In seven states Phil Murray's steel workers remained away from their jobs despite the President's appeal . . . Thus his enemies, who also are the enemies of labor, can now gloat . . . that organized labor . . . has let them down."[7]

On December 23 Roosevelt stunned Stimson and Marshall by telling them he planned to take over the railroads before the strike date so that a strike would have to be against the government. Since the nineteenth a series of meetings held at the White House had failed to produce a settlement. At a final meeting on the afternoon of the twenty-third, the carriers and two of the five brotherhoods agreed to accept Roosevelt as arbitrator but the other three refused. The nonoperating unions did not decline the offer of arbitration but instead put a new proposal on the table that Roosevelt could not accept. Almost as an aside, Roosevelt stroked Stimson by saying he would probably have to ask for a national service law and giving him leave to prepare the paperwork for that as well.[8]

The threat posed what Stimson considered "a crisis of major order." A despairing George Marshall warned that a rail strike would set the war effort back six months, galvanize German propaganda, stiffen their resistance, and dash all hopes of ending the Europe war in 1944. The threat was, he said with uncharacteristic bluntness, "the damnedest crime ever committed against America." In his frustration he even talked of going on radio and then resigning as chief of staff. Patterson and other civilian heads in the military establishment joined in a letter to Roosevelt that said, "The war has now progressed to a point where maximum production at the highest possible speed is a vital necessity. The lives of millions of men in the Armed Services depend upon the uninterrupted supply of material, ammunition, and equipment."[9]

A statute passed in 1916, which Wilson had used to take over the railroads, was still on the books. Stimson spent some time boning up on its provisions and concluded that it was a good law, but a lot of paperwork had to be done in a few days. Wilson had nationalized the railroads for the duration of the war; Roosevelt wanted only to avert a strike by having the government operate them until a settlement could be reached. Stimson put Somervell to work on contingency plans and braced himself to work with the Justice Department on the legal plan. In the past he had found cooperation with its people difficult. This time they worked smoothly together. Shortly before noon on the twenty-seventh Somervell handed him plans that Stimson found, "beautifully and completely prepared in a volume of orders and papers all clipped together in very perfect shape—one of the best jobs I have ever seen."[10]

Stimson went with Somervell to the White House, where Byrnes said they would take over the roads that evening. At 5:00 P.M. the nonoperating unions backed down and agreed to arbitration, but the three brotherhoods continued to hold out. Their arrogance and stubbornness rankled both Roosevelt and Byrnes. That evening Roosevelt issued his executive order to seize and operate the railroads. The chief of transportation for ASF took charge, assisted by railroad officials and representatives from the cooperating brotherhoods. The next evening Stimson gave a short radio talk explaining what had happened. "It is unthinkable," he said in closing, "that the complex demands of modern war can be met without railroads. It is unthinkable that the

Nation can meet its own responsibilities in the coming offensive in Europe, in Asia and in the Pacific without their full assistance, working at the peak of their great operating capacity. The successful outcome of all our strategic plans depends upon this continued service."[11]

The transition went smoothly, and actual operation of the railroads remained in the hands of railroad men. On January 14 the three recalcitrant brotherhoods agreed to a settlement, and the nonoperating unions followed suit three days later. At midnight on January 18 the railroads returned to private hands. However, as 1943 closed, 170,000 of the nation's 750,000 steelworkers went out on strike. To both groups Roosevelt had said he would offer any reasonable concession within the bounds of the Little Steel formula. The USWA wanted a straight raise of 17 cents an hour plus a guaranteed annual wage for members laid off during the life of the contract. Negotiations soon reached an impasse and moved to the WLB. The railroad unions walked away with raises that many observers thought exceeded the 8 cents that Fred Vinson of OES had vetoed earlier. Administration spokesmen were quoted as privately admitting that the settlement was "built upon technicalities which in name only preserve the Little Steel formula."[12]

Time's assessment was more blunt. "Once more," it said, "as in the coal crisis, the Administration had honored the letter of Little Steel, while doing violence to its spirit." Phil Murray of USWA was equally candid. "Frankly," he said, "we are trying to change the stabilization policy." But amid the swelling chorus of threats and strikes, one small hopeful note emerged. When seventy-two rubber workers in Akron staged an unauthorized strike, their union ruled that they had broken its agreement with management and revoked their memberships. Nevertheless, the sense of disconnect between management, labor, and the government, seemed worse than ever.[13]

THE NATIONAL SERVICE issue resurfaced early in the winter because manpower continued to be the most pressing problem. In both Europe and the Pacific the Allies had seized the offensive, fighting had intensified, and casualties were mounting ever faster. Projections indicated that by July the nation would need a labor force of 66.3 million, an increase of 1.5 million over July 1943. The military already had 10.1 million men on December 1, 1943, and wanted another 1.2 million by midyear. To get them, some 300,000 would have to be plucked from deferred occupations, and 100,000 to 200,000 rehabilitated from the unfit in 4-F. The rest would have to come from that most politically touchy of categories, fathers. If the estimates held, nearly every pre–Pearl Harbor father would be in the military by July unless he was unfit or in an essential job.[14]

THE PRESIDENT'S MEN:
(Top left) Franklin Roosevelt
and his treasury secretary, the
much-maligned Henry Morgenthau (*FDR Library*) (Top right)
Harry Hopkins, the man closest
to the president. (*Library of Congress*) (Bottom) Harry Truman,
his old friend Charlie Ross, and
Sam Rosenman, one of Roosevelt's closest advisors. (*Truman
Library*)

RUBBER RELIEF: (Top) A political cartoon from the Washington *Evening Star*, September 6, 1943, praises the efforts of William Jeffers as rubber czar. (*Union Pacific Museum*) (Bottom) Harold Ickes poses with the White House doormat he snatched for the rubber drive. (*Truman Library*)

"Daddy, ain't *you* got a uniform?"
"Yes, son, *this* is my uniform"

THE RAILROADS ARE THE FIRST LINE OF DEFENSE
"KEEP 'EM ROLLING"

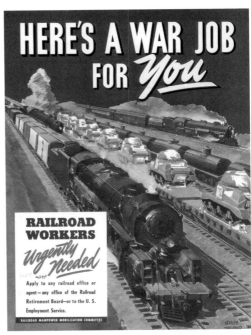

HERE'S A WAR JOB
FOR *You*

RAILROAD WORKERS
Urgently Needed

Apply to any railroad office or
agent — any office of the Railroad
Retirement Board—or to the U. S.
Employment Service.

RAILROAD MANPOWER MOBILIZATION COMMITTEE

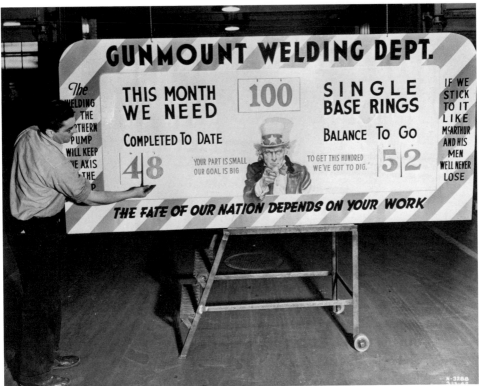

SIGNS OF THE TIMES: (Top left) William Jeffers makes his views clear on the importance of railroad men to the war effort. (*Union Pacific Museum*) (Top right) As this poster indicates, the need had grown critical by 1944. (*University of North Texas Digital Library*) (Bottom) This scoreboard at the Northern Pump Company in Minnesota, created by the labor-management committee, records progress in production. (*FDR Library*)

INSTANT CITY: An aerial view in 1943 of Vanport, the sprawling city that arose from the feverish effort to house shipyard workers in the Portland-Vancouver area. It became the nation's largest housing development. (*City of Portland Archives*)

LONG OVERDUE: (Top) B-24 Liberator bombers roll down one of the assembly lines at the much maligned Willow Run plant. (*National Archives*) (Bottom) Men and women work a row of machines turning out parts at Willow Run. (*FDR Library*)

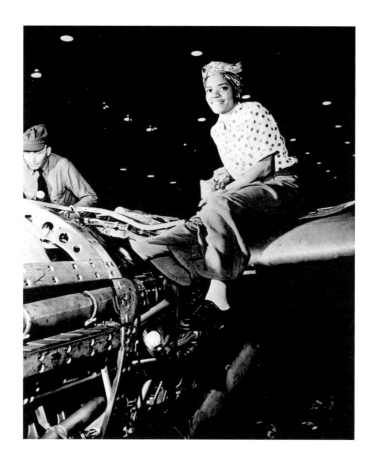

A NEW KIND OF WORKDAY: (Top) A black woman riveter pauses in her work to smile for the camera. (*National Archives*) (Bottom) At the Richmond shipyard, former waitress Estine Cowner plies her new trade as a scaler on the Liberty ship *George Washington Carver*, launched May 7, 1943. (*National Archives*)

WATER POWER: (Top) This poster emphasizes the critical role of TVA's water power in war production. (*National Archives*) (Bottom) Workers check the alignment of a turbine shaft at the top of the guide bearing in TVA's Watts Bar Dam, 530 miles above the Tennessee River. (*Library of Congress*)

FIGHTER: (Top) The pugilistic Charles E. Wilson of General Electric and WPB. (*General Electric*) (Bottom) THE NEW PARTNERS: Franklin Roosevelt and Harry Truman meet the public shortly after their victory in 1944. (*Truman Library*)

BRAIN TRUST: E. L. Lawrence, Arthur Compton, Vannevar Bush, James B. Conant, Karl Compton, and Alfred Loomis share a laugh at the Radiation Laboratory, University of California at Berkeley, in August 1940. (*Courtesy Lawrence Berkeley National Laboratory*)

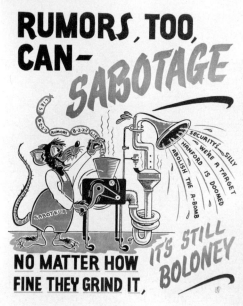

TWO LEADERSHIP STYLES: (Top left) J. Robert Oppenheimer and General Leslie Groves talk things over at Los Alamos. (*Los Alamos National Laboratory*) (Top right) SEAL LOOSE LIPS: A security poster at the Hanford facility for producing plutonium. (*Hanford.gov*) (Bottom) FRESH HANDS: A shift change of women workers at Oak Ridge's Y-12 facility. (*Ed Westcott*)

PRIMING THE BIG BOX: (Top left) Workers insert uranium slugs into the X-10 graphite reactor at Oak Ridge. (Top right) A worker secures slugs from a bucket. (Bottom left) Two men prepare the reactor slots. (Bottom right) A worker inserts the slugs by hand. (*All photos by Ed Westcott*)

THE RACETRACKS AND THEIR HOUSE: (Top) The Y-12 Alpha calutrons. (*Ed Westcott*) (Bottom) The Y-12 building at Oak Ridge for work on electromagnetic separation. (*Ed Westcott*)

OPERATORS STANDING BY: (Top left) The young women operating the Beta calutron controls. (*Ed Westcott*) (Top right) One young operator and her complex board. (*Ed Westcott*) (Bottom) TAMING THE BEAST: The Beta track unit at Y-12. (*Ed Westcott*)

SECRET FACILITIES: (Top) An aerial view of the X-10 reactor building at Oak Ridge. (*Ed Westcott*) (Bottom) The huge K-25 building at Oak Ridge for work on gaseous diffusion. (*Ed Westcott*)

FINAL CEREMONY: (Top) The stripped-down inauguration of Franklin Roosevelt for his fourth term in January 1945. (*FDR Library*) (Bottom) WEARY WARRIOR: An obviously tired and ailing president gives Congress his somewhat rambling report on the Yalta Conference, March 1, 1945. (*FDR Library*)

FAREWELLS: (Top) James Byrnes, Harry Truman, and Henry Wallace huddle at the funeral for Franklin Roosevelt in Washington. (*FDR Library*) (Bottom) Mourners crowded Pennsylvania Avenue to watch the president's funeral procession. (*Library of Congress*)

War industries, transportation, fuel, utilities, and federal agencies needed a total of 16.8 million people, 2.7 million more than a year earlier. Other industries required 7.6 million, or 800,000 fewer than 1943, while nonindustrial employment was calculated at 29.6 million (17.6 million of them in agriculture), or 700,000 fewer than the year before. The remaining million consisted of the unemployed, the number of which had actually fallen to 700,000. The wild card for manpower remained the forthcoming invasion of Europe, which some gloomy estimates predicted might cause as many as half a million casualties. A quick end to the European war could ease the manpower pinch; a prolonged conflict would impose serious strains for which no answer yet existed.[15]

The manpower issue was no longer as muddled as it had been in 1943. The extension of the West Coast Plan to ninety-six labor areas, which channeled all workers through USES and forbade an employer from hiring a worker who did not have a USES certificate, had reduced turnover significantly. During the year ending February 1, 1944, USES placed over 9.5 million workers. Since Pearl Harbor some 200,000 of the 635,000 men discharged honorably by the army had been released specifically to go into some area of essential production like mining or agriculture. But the pool of labor was running dry, which meant an even more fierce tug-of-war for the available supply between the military and other claimants. Severe and often sudden shortages plagued one industry after another in 1944, including the critical foundry and forge operations on which nearly every other key production item depended.[16]

A national service law could relieve the pressure but still faced heavy opposition. Some denounced it as totalitarian, others as un-American. Harold Smith argued that its time had passed; Byrnes, Nelson, and Baruch also remained opposed. One editor saw it as tainted by the widespread belief that "there is widespread slacking among war workers . . . due to the capricious and inconsistent too-much-and-too-late labor policies of the Roosevelt Administration." However, the United States remained the only major power in the war without such a law. Stimson, Knox, and Jerry Land continued pressing Roosevelt to come out in favor of it, but no one else in the cabinet supported the idea. After the special committee he set up concluded that the time was not yet ripe, Roosevelt waffled over the issue through the fall of 1943. But the trip to Tehran, with its exposure to some of the fighting men and what Sam Rosenman called "those neat but crowded American cemeteries," changed his mind.[17]

After his return Roosevelt decided to ask for a national service law in his State of the Union address on January 11. "I have just dictated an insert, asking for a national service act," he told Rosenman, who was working on the speech with Robert Sherwood. "I have made up my mind on it, and I don't want to argue about it any more with anybody. Therefore I want you both to keep it a complete and absolute secret—tell nobody about it. I don't want to be talked out of it again." He meant nobody, not even Jimmy Byrnes. Rosenman and Sherwood did his bidding, giving the insert the whimsical label "Project Q 38" and having Grace Tully, who had typed the original insert, handle it separately. The message went through eight drafts before Roosevelt, who worked hard on them, was satisfied. He had hoped to deliver it personally to Congress, but a bout with the flu forced him to send it to the Hill. However, that same evening he read it to a radio audience as a fireside chat because he deemed it that important.[18]

Rosenman called it "the most drastic recommendation he ever made with respect to American labor." Although the chat touched on several important issues, the section on labor stole most of the headlines and triggered a heated debate. The president spoke of suffering a "let-down" upon returning home from his visit with fighting men as well as Churchill and Stalin. "The overwhelming majority of our people have met the demands of this war with magnificent courage and understanding," he acknowledged. "They have accepted inconveniences; they have accepted hardships; they have accepted tragic sacrifices." But he condemned in harsh language a "noisy minority" that demanded "special favors for special groups" and denounced the "pests who swarm through the lobbies of Congress and the cocktail bars of Washington, representing these special groups . . . They have come to look upon the war primarily as a chance to make profits for themselves at the expense of their neighbors."[19]

The time had long since come to "subordinate individual or group selfishness to the national good . . . Disunity at home—bickerings, self-seeking partisanship, stoppages of work, inflation, business as usual, politics as usual, luxury as usual"—all threatened the morale of the men fighting overseas. As part of this effort Roosevelt listed five measures he wished Congress to adopt, the last of which was a national service law. For three years he had hesitated to recommend such a law. "Today, however, I am convinced of its necessity." It was, he said, "the most democratic way to wage a war. Like selective service for the armed forces, it rests on the obligation of each citizen to serve his Nation to his utmost where he is best qualified."[20]

Near the end of his message Roosevelt spelled out what he called an "economic bill of rights," the importance of which got buried in the furor over national service. Rosenman and Sherwood had kept the secret well. Stimson, the measure's most persistent advocate, was stunned and delighted to hear the president's endorsement. On the same day as the message an amended version of the Austin-Wadsworth bill reappeared in Congress and was shunted to committee. Summoned at last to testify before a Senate committee, Stimson, Patterson, and their staffs put together a formidable case for national service and lobbied labor and industrial leaders as well as congressmen. Stimson delivered a radio appeal for the cause, but it was all in vain. William Green, Philip Murray, and other leaders dismissed it as what Murray called "quack medicine" and a threat to the American way of life. Most industrialists remained opposed, along with the National Association of Manufacturers and the chamber of commerce.[21]

The Senate Committee on Military Affairs turned a deaf ear to the testimony from Stimson and Patterson. Stimson struck reporter Allen Drury as "an obviously old man, with a little mustache over a little mouth, pink cheeks, infinitely tired eyes, and a lifeless old man's voice, muffled and hard to hear." Some agreed with Chan Gurney of South Dakota, who actually supported the bill, that the real problem was not shortage of labor but inefficiency, waste, and slacking. The chairman, Robert R. Reynolds of North Carolina, said bluntly afterward that "Stimson didn't sell me a thing." Gurney's attempt to bring the bill to the floor failed, and Austin-Wadsworth lingered in committee for another long hibernation. If anything, the growing disconnect over manpower exceeded even that over labor.[22]

THE MANPOWER ISSUE permeated nearly every dimension of American life, often in unexpected ways. For a time it utterly dominated education at all levels. Public schools lost teachers to war industries or the draft and high school students to the workforce. Colleges and universities were transformed by the draft and by the military's need to train large numbers of men for specialized wartime duties. Illiteracy in draftees remained a serious problem for the army. For small liberal arts colleges, and even for some larger institutions, the war became a struggle for survival. Everywhere the pampered, secluded environment of the college campus gave way to harsher conditions. Change came hard to higher education. As one professor admitted, "The education of the educated is notoriously difficult. Few humans are as averse to facing reality as a college professor."[23]

In July 1942 the National Education Association, meeting for the first time since Pearl Harbor, estimated that the draft and lure of higher-paying industry jobs had left the country short 50,000 teachers, especially in the critical areas of science and mathematics. Instructors were also needed for an estimated 10 million adult illiterates. Some states had lost more than half their teachers, and twenty-nine states were already giving emergency certificates to untrained teachers, some of them recent high school graduates. Poor pay was an obvious cause for the shortage. A Utah schoolmarm, paid $75 a month at a rural school, left to take a plant job paying her $75 a week. A teacher in the nation's capital earned only $899 a year compared to the $1,440 paid a seventeen-year-old stenographer who lacked even a high school diploma.[24]

Teacher turnover doubled during the next year, and the shortfall rose to 75,000. A thousand rural schools in Illinois closed. Some Minnesota towns lost all their teachers and then their replacements as well. Nearly 40 percent of the classrooms in Mississippi were on track to be empty; forty-three schools closed in Oklahoma and fifty in California. The state superintendent in Idaho warned that within a year hundreds of schools would be "crippled and wrecked." Attempts to create a federal fund to raise the pitiful level of teachers' salaries ran into heavy opposition from several directions. One superintendent in Sioux County, Iowa, resorted to an original if desperate appeal. "If any teachers find it hard to get dates or land a man," he declared, "and they have what it takes—personality and brains—just come to Sioux County and I will get them a good job and a man within a year if they are in that big a hurry. We need both teachers and wives up here. We have the jobs and we have the men."[25]

Even as the teacher shortage mounted, more and more high school students left school to take jobs, posing a cruel dilemma. During the summer of 1943 some 3 million students went into factories, easing the manpower shortage. If they all returned to school in the fall, the already serious manpower problem would get much worse. If they stayed on the job, they would most likely never return to finish their education. In September Paul McNutt approved a new WMC "Work-Study Plan" allowing students to split time between job and classroom. Some cities had already implemented similar plans, but for many employers—shipyards being one—the split was not feasible. For them the issue loomed large; one California shipyard alone had 5,000 high school workers.[26]

Many states had induced this crisis by suspending or relaxing their child labor laws, but even those still operative proved ineffective. By one estimate 900,000 children between twelve and eighteen were working in defiance of the law in their state. Philadelphia saw a decline of 13 percent in high school attendance, while in Oakland 15 percent of the children under sixteen had gone to work. Nothing demonstrated the failings of the educational system more than the irony that many of these kids earned more than their teachers did. Employers hard-pressed for workers were reluctant to let them leave; a few offered to set up part-time schools in their plants, but these were lame stopgaps at best. Military and other leaders urged students to ignore the lure of wages and remain in school lest the illiteracy problem grow even worse.[27]

By one estimate illiteracy among draftees had cost the army the equivalent of fifteen divisions. Of necessity the army went into the education business. In February 1942 it began accepting some illiterates into special training battalions where they received three hours of military and educational schooling every day, mostly from ex-schoolteachers. They used a special "Soldier's Reader" that combined a simplified version of the army manual with a section designed to teach them the alphabet, counting, reading, and writing. By January 1944 more than 100,000 men had acquired the equivalent of a fourth-grade education in only seven to twelve weeks. "I appreciate what you done for me," one wrote his captain. "I take a shoar every day and shave every day. I am proud of my uniform so I am changing my ways. I am not a messup any more. I like the army it is a great life I wood turn a discharge down now."[28]

Higher education endured a severe disconnect from its past during the war. Many schools were already struggling financially after a decade of depression; the war brought not prosperity but yet another crisis of enrollment, especially when the draft began scooping eighteen-year-olds. Aware that most male students entered college on borrowed time, some schools began summer and accelerated course programs to shorten graduation time. At Yale 97 percent of the upperclassmen and 85 percent of the freshmen did summer course work. Three fourths of the seniors were in ROTC or the Enlisted Reserves. The curriculum underwent a major shift as well. The liberal arts, which had long reigned supreme, gave way to emphasis on science, mathematics, and engineering, the most pressing subjects for a nation at war.[29]

Enrollments fell 10 percent in the fall of 1941 and another 20 percent the following autumn. The War Department compounded the difficulties by sending mixed signals to the campuses. At first reservists were excused from active duty to continue their studies; then, in September 1942, Stimson announced that the army would be taking every able-bodied man. Brown president Henry Wriston denounced the reversal in blunt language. "Ever since the advent of the crisis," he said, "public officials and military officers have directed at the colleges and their students a series of conflicting statements, warnings, threats." Stimson replied lamely that he hoped colleges would "maintain their training of students in engineering, medicine and other sciences," which succeeded in alarming the liberal arts institutions.[30]

The military's dilemma was inescapable. It needed bodies, but college graduates provided its best pool of officer candidates on a large scale. It also needed specialists of all kinds and lacked the facilities or personnel to train them in quantity. Here too the last war bestowed a legacy, in the Student Army Training Corps program in which the government virtually took over colleges, paying a subsidy of $3 per man a day for instruction, room, and board, and set the "students" to drilling. If the military took over the colleges, it would likely choose both the students and their curriculum, dumping everything but technical and needed professional courses. To ward off such control, Harvard's James B. Conant and MIT's Karl Compton advanced a plan that trained men but kept the institutions in civilian hands. Compton warned that "cutting off the continued supply of technically competent men would be a national calamity."[31]

Women's colleges also faced dramatic changes. A leading educator predicted that "courses for women are going to be shortened and they are going to be directed toward preparation for specific types of war service." In November 1942 representatives of 110 women's and coeducational colleges met with leading businessmen, industrialists, and officers from the WAACS and WAVES in a first-ever conference to determine what the schools should do. The services wanted women to stay in school but take more science, math, and technical courses as well as get more physically fit to work long hours. The need for nurses in and out of the military was already acute, as was the need for dentists, doctors, teachers, and welfare workers. Engine maker Curtiss-Wright introduced its own program to recruit a thousand college women for training as engineers in eight universities at company expense.[32]

Still the colleges awaited some clear policy or plan as to their fate and the use of their resources. Already some 600 schools offered Civilian Pilot Training courses modified for military flying. One small liberal arts institution, Knox College in Illinois, had the second-largest program in the state and produced a hundred licensed pilots in three years. In November 1942 Roosevelt signed the bill to draft eighteen-year-olds. A month later the army and navy finally announced their new training program to send about 250,000 men to 250 or 300 colleges for training as technical specialists and officers. The War and Navy departments would control the entire program and dictate choice of schools, trainees, courses, and academic standards. The trainees would be in uniform and on active duty; the schools would be paid roughly the same amount they would get from regular students.[33]

The plan capped what both major newsmagazines called "the greatest upheaval in U.S. collegiate history." At Yale the class of 1943 graduated six months ahead of schedule without ceremony. Half its dormitories and a third of its classrooms were leased to the Army Air Forces. All the students then in the army's Enlisted Reserve, some 1,400, or 58 percent of the total enrollment, would be called into active service within a month, contrary to their belief that they would be allowed to graduate. In their place, at Yale and elsewhere, came 500 privates for a year's training under the new program. The army also introduced five "pre-induction" courses in electricity, radio, machines, automotive mechanics, and shop work into 50,000 American high schools. Electricity alone was a ninety-hour course designed to prepare students for 151 specialized army jobs. Some of the high school students found their way into the college program. Altogether the programs cost $500 million, making them by far the largest scholarship fund ever created.[34]

Stimson conceded that the program ignored the liberal arts education of men, but neither the army nor navy wished to take over the colleges. To help shape the Army Specialized Training Program (ASTP), Stimson welcomed a committee of college presidents. One key difference, he explained, lay in the tempo of education; the troops on campus had to learn on an accelerated schedule. They would be under military discipline but take prescribed courses from regular college faculty. A group of presidents and deans from technical schools visited the Army's Ordnance Training Center at Aberdeen Proving Ground and absorbed a very different way of teaching to turn out large numbers of technicians in a short time. For the duration the colleges would become to a large extent vocational schools.[35]

Along with ASTP, which began in April 1943, the U.S. Department of Education launched its own program, the Engineering, Science, and Management War Training Program, at 200 colleges to give short, tuition-free courses in hundreds of subjects ranging from toolmaking to metals inspecting. College instructors taught the courses, but classes often met in factories as well as classrooms. The ASTP program got under way at 332 schools for 150,000 soldiers chosen through a screening process. After thirteen weeks of basic training they were sent to smaller liberal arts colleges for twelve weeks of what amounted to freshman courses in math, physics, chemistry, geography, and English. Then they were screened again for their ability to specialize in one of four areas of study. Their course load far exceeded that of ordinary students.[36]

On campus they lived under strict military discipline with little time for normal college activities. Athletic programs took an especially hard hit from the new order of things. Profound changes took place at every level of institution, including the Ivy League schools. Columbia became the world's largest producer of naval officers and for the first time began its academic year in July. Princeton's civilian enrollment was cut in half, reduced to 4-F students and those under eighteen or deferred for essential work in medicine or war industries. The military took over 90 percent of the college's facilities for ASTP and the navy's training program, known as V-12. Several major student activities, such as the *Daily Princetonian*, were discontinued. The military students were segregated into four dormitories but attended classes with civilian students. The mixture was hailed as "the most democratic student body any American college has seen," and at an elite school no less.[37]

At the end of each twelve-week term (sixteen for the navy), the students might be invited to take a second term, dispatched to officer-candidate schools, or sent back to their units. Those who completed an entire thirty-six-week course took away a transcript that could be applied to any accredited college after the war. So tight was their schedule that one said with a wry grin,

"Princeton's the most G. I. camp I've ever been in." But most of them took to the grind eagerly. "Their enthusiasm is incredible," said a dean. "Almost every member of the faculty has told me they have never before experienced such rapt attention from their classes."[38]

The liberal arts colleges participating in the programs underwent major changes as well but managed to survive financially. The navy, convinced that its best officers came from college graduates, stressed a general education in its V-12 program. Schools not included in these programs struggled to survive the loss of so many students. Nursing schools found it harder than ever to attract women despite the urgency of the need. Rather than spend three years with no pay as a student nurse, women preferred jobs in war industries even though nursing offered them a permanent career. Law schools took a hard hit as enrollments dropped an average of 36 percent since 1940. Small private colleges that depended on student fees for their income also worried about folding up as their enrollments declined. "That's what makes our hair grey and our sleep light," said Carter Davidson, the president of Knox College. "I guess we'll all just have to enlist." Elite prep schools felt the same pressure as enrollments declined, faculty departed, and academic requirements drooped. Some schools simply closed.[39]

Just as the colleges settled into their new routine, a fresh crisis arose. Stimson regarded ASTP as a neat solution to several problems. It would provide a fuller education for select army men while easing the impact on colleges caused by the loss of so many of their male students. However, in November 1943 the army experienced its own manpower crunch, especially in officers, and some influential staff asked Stimson to discontinue ASTP and put the 145,000 men enrolled in it back into the ranks at once. Stimson was appalled by the idea but admitted it was a "tough and difficult issue." The staff split into two camps. Those seeking an end to the program argued that not doing so would cost the army three divisions by 1945; those opposed said it would disrupt the education of the army's most promising officers, create a scandal, and alienate the nation's leading educators.[40]

Stimson tried to impress the importance of ASTP on the president only to be diverted by one of his inevitable stories. Through the month he tried in vain to find a compromise solution. On January 27 Stimson set off alarms by announcing that the program would be tapered off in all categories except medicine and dentistry. Two days later reports said that seventy colleges in the Army Air Forces training program were being returned to civilian use. Then the army announced abruptly that it would recall 110,000 of the ASTP students to immediate duty. After more negotiating behind the scenes, the Army said that its Army Specialized Training Reserve for seventeen-year-olds would be expanded well beyond its current limit of 5,000. College presidents urged that the new limit be 100,000, replacing most of the men withdrawn from ASTP. For starters the limit was increased to 25,000, with qualifying exams scheduled for March 15. "It is of the greatest importance," declared Roosevelt, ". . . that as many as possible take the March 15 examination."[41]

When classes started up in September 1944, most campuses bore a distinctly different look. Many if not most of the students in uniform were gone, and few replacements appeared. Men's colleges felt the pinch. Harvard's normal undergraduate population of 3,500–4,500 dwindled to 730. At Hamilton College in Clinton, New York, the previous spring, twenty-eight faculty members had taught thirty students. "It's ideal," enthused one student. "You may find yourself all alone in a class. It won't be with one of the instructors either. It will be with the head of the department." The story was different at many large coeducational schools. At both Wisconsin and Carlton College women outnumbered men nine to one. The ratio at Ohio State was four to one, making its freshman class 65 percent larger than a year earlier. Other schools, both coed and women's colleges, reported larger numbers of women enrolled than ever before.[42]

Black colleges also saw climbing enrollments. The registrar at Howard University, where registration had doubled since Pearl Harbor, saw two reasons for the increase: More blacks had enough money to seek an education, and they feared discrimination in the competition for jobs once the war ended. For them victory did not necessarily mean the return of good times.[43]

THE NEW DEAL had come to resemble modern art or pornography. Nobody could say exactly what it was but everybody was certain they knew it when they saw it. A former Canadian minister described it as "a generous and progressive thought emotionally developed by amateur economists and cynically exploited by professional politicians." Stuart Chase wrote that the war had managed to accomplish most of what the New Deal had hoped to do. It took the unemployed off the dole, gave them jobs at high wages, and restored their self-respect. Diehard conservatives viewed it as evil incarnate and a threat to the American way of life. They alone seemed oblivious to the fact that the war had of necessity pushed the New Deal—whatever it was— increasingly toward irrelevance if not extinction. "The pallid remnant of what had originally been elected and operated as the New Deal," observed Bruce Catton, "was being kept alive, in those days, almost solely by the bitter attacks on it . . . made by people who supposed that it was still healthy."[44]

The disconnect over the New Deal seemed almost surreal. To some the attacks would have been comical had they not been so ugly and insistent. "The trained hounds of Congress," wrote Richard Lingeman, "sniffed each and every wartime innovation carefully for the forbidden New Deal scent (however they might define it at the moment), and when their keen noses flashed a warning, they raised a baying in committees and on the floor and in the press." As a result, he concluded, "almost nothing that be described as reform took place during the war." In November 1942 Kiplinger's thought the elections revealed "the passing of the crest of the high tide of the social and economic reforms commonly characterized as 'New Deal.'" Five months later it reported that *no one expects a swing back to 'the old days,'* back to the 20's. Many of the basic reforms of the New Deal will stick and be permanent . . . but the GENERAL veering is toward what might be called 'orthodoxy.'"[45]

Already the war had taken its toll on New Deal programs. Congress terminated the CCC in 1942, and Roosevelt himself gave an "honorary discharge" to the WPA in December of that year, although it did not die until June 1944. During 1943 Congress ended funding for the NYA and drastically sliced it for the FSA and Rural Electrification Administration. It also terminated the National Resources Planning Board, headed by the president's uncle Frederic A. Delano, which had offended conservatives by issuing reports and pamphlets culminating in a massive 1943 study outlining what it deemed as needed social welfare programs after the war. New Dealers were also disappearing from the administration, replaced in many cases by businessmen. In October 1943 Raymond Clapper noted that "we are more and more referring to the Roosevelt Administration rather than to the New Deal."[46]

Roosevelt was well aware of the grumbling and discontent among long-time New Dealers within and outside the administration. They had watched in dismay as he appointed two Republicans to the cabinet, turned the economy more and more over to businessmen, allowed the military an ever larger role, elevated conservatives like Jimmy Byrnes and Fred Vinson to key positions, and ignored or downplayed the agenda of social reform that liberals considered the heart and soul of the New Deal. Repeated attacks on the forty-hour workweek especially infuriated them, if only because it was, as Catton said, "as completely phony a campaign as the country ever saw." The law did not prevent people from working more than forty hours; it only required them to be paid time-and-a-half for any time over that amount. Nor was it relevant to most munitions production since most plants had union agreements covering overtime work.[47]

If liberals needed more fuel for their fears, it came at a press conference on December 28, 1943, when Roosevelt appeared to lay the New Deal formally to rest. Word had got out that the president no longer cared for the term "New Deal," and a reporter asked why. In response Roosevelt launched into one of his homey metaphors about old Dr. New Deal, who had been called into existence to treat the nation's grave internal disorder caused by the depression. The doctor had done a decent job treating those ailments, but then on December 7, 1941, the patient got into "a pretty bad smashup" and broke a number of bones. Dr. New Deal dealt in internal medicine and didn't know much about shattered limbs, so he summoned his partner and surgeon, Dr. Win-the-War, to bring the patient back to health.[48]

After ticking off a long list of ailments treated by Dr. New Deal, the president was asked whether the social programs would be taken up again once Dr. Win-the-War had done his job. In vintage Roosevelt fashion the president reminded the reporters that "the 1933 program . . . was a program to meet the problems of 1933. Now, in time, there will have to be a new program, whoever runs the Government. We are not talking in terms of 1933's program. We have done nearly all that, but that doesn't avoid or make impossible or unneedful another program, when the time comes. When the time comes."[49]

No one missed the significance of Dr. Win-the-War being in charge of the patient. Liberal spirits sank like a stone, yet only two weeks later those who mourned or celebrated the demise of the New Deal got a lift when Roosevelt delivered his State of the Union message to Congress. In addition to his call for unity and a national service law, the president outlined the need for what he called an "economic bill of rights" to establish "a new basis of security and prosperity" for all Americans regardless of race, color, or creed. His list included the right to a decent job, sufficient income, decent home, adequate medical care, a good education, and protection from the worries of old age, accident, and unemployment. "For unless there is security here at home," he stressed, "there cannot be lasting peace in the world."[50]

The message thrilled liberals, including his own wife, and gave rise to the hope that Dr. New Deal had not retired from practice after all. One biographer called it "the most radical speech of his life." The burning question was how Congress would respond to Roosevelt's plea for action. The answer was not long in coming.[51]

THE REVENUE ACT OF 1943 did not take long to frustrate and infuriate taxpayers. A Philadelphia carpenter named John Harl decided to be a good citizen and submit his return ahead of the March 15 deadline. He figured his tax as $40 and handed it to a clerk at a branch office of the Bureau of Internal Revenue to check. The clerk arrived at a tax of $60.47. Harl took his return to the main office, where a clerk came up with a figure of $222.38. Puzzled, the clerk went over the return again and this time came up with a refund of $30.16. A thoroughly confused Harl asked three newsmen to do the math and received three different answers. The chief of the city's tax bureau tried his hand and figured a tax of $23.16, as did Philadelphia's collector of internal revenue. The form then went to no less than the federal bureau's chief statistician in Washington, who declared that Harl owed the government $44.05. At that point the befuddled carpenter just paid the tax.[52]

Complaints that the new tax forms were too complicated swelled into an angry chorus, especially from the millions of first-time payers. Oregon's collector of internal revenue confessed that he could not compute his own tax. Already an instant new industry had sprung up in the form of self-styled tax experts who hung up TAX RETURNS PREPARED HERE signs in real estate offices, barbershops, hardware stores, private homes, delicatessens, hot dog stands, currency exchanges, and garages. For a fee ranging from $1 to half the amount they "saved" the client, thousands of "consultants" took advantage of what *Newsweek* called "the most confusing and complex tax legislation ever to enter national law books." Few actually knew what they were doing, but the hapless client did not learn this for months, when his return got bounced back for additional payment. By then the consultant had long since closed up shop.[53]

The revenue from individual income taxes rose sharply from $1.4 billion in 1941 to $3.3 billion in 1942 and twice that in 1943, but it barely touched the inflationary gap. In October 1943 a battered but unbowed Henry Morgenthau returned to Congress with a request for $10.56 billion in new taxes instead of the $12 billion he had earlier thought would be needed. After the first day's hearings Muley Doughton brushed the plan aside as "utterly indefensible," and several committee members along with a Democratic leader urged privately that Morgenthau be fired. Some congressmen suspected that "the New Deal—come war or inflation—has not given up attempts at social-economic reform via the tax route" because of its emphasis on wiping out incomes above $25,000 while sparing lower incomes. "The Morgenthau answer to inflation," observed *Time*, "was not to tax the income groups that hold most of the new inflation money."[54]

Having dismissed Morgenthau's plan, Congress had to craft its own tax bill amid a welter of different suggestions on how to simplify the system as well as raise new revenue. Taxpayers currently had to calculate and pay three separate federal income taxes, the normal, surtax, and Victory, each of which had different sets of exemptions and deductions. In addition, thirty-three states also had income taxes that the Treasury Department did not include in its calculations. Sentiment was widespread to dump the Victory Tax, and a *Fortune* poll showed surprising public opinion in favor of a national sales tax, which Morgenthau and the administration opposed. His plan had also asked for a $2.5 billion hike in excise taxes on liquor, cigarettes, candy, and other products. Clearly another battle loomed, especially with an election year on the horizon.[55]

"It has become apparent," said the *Saturday Evening Post*, "even to politicians and Treasury mystics, that the people want an intelligible income-tax law and returns that can be filled out without the aid of a certified public accountant." By early November Doughton's committee had produced a kinder, gentler bill with no increase in personal or corporate income taxes and no sales tax. Instead it included higher excise taxes, raised the tax on excess profits from 90 to 95 percent, and increased postal rates, producing $2 billion in new revenue instead of the $10.5 billion requested by the administration. It moved smoothly through both houses with minor changes and reached Roosevelt's desk in February. The president bristled at its provisions. Apart from raising a paltry $2 billion—actually only $1 billion by his calculations—the bill canceled the automatic increase in the Social Security tax, granted relief from some existing taxes, and was laced with special privileges for the lumber industry, corporations in bankruptcy, and other special interests.[56]

Having put forward an ambitious agenda of proposed legislation in his January 11 message, the last thing Roosevelt needed was another fight with Congress. A glum Morgenthau recommended that he accept it as better than nothing, but the president could not let this one pass. Jimmy Byrnes at first urged Roosevelt to let the tax bill become law unsigned, saying, "If you ask your mother for a dollar, and she gives you . . . a dime, you're not going to turn the dime down. You go back for ninety cents this afternoon." But Fred Vinson and others persuaded him to change his mind and veto it. Vinson helped draft the message along with Byrnes and Ben Cohen.[57]

On February 22 Roosevelt issued a ringing veto of what he called "not a tax bill but a tax relief bill providing relief not for the needy but for the greedy." It was, he said bluntly, "wholly ineffective" in dealing with the fiscal issues involved. Some had suggested that he accept the bill as at least part of a loaf, but the president would not hear of it. "I might have done so," he said, "if I had not noted that the small piece of crust contained so many extraneous and inedible materials." Having vented his spleen, he left that evening for Hyde Park, fully expecting a wrathful Congress to override his veto. He was not disappointed. "The effect," observed Allen Drury, "has been to create . . . a really grave crisis in the relations between the Executive and the Legislature." The next afternoon, reported Bill Hassett, "hell broke out in the Senate."[58]

Years earlier, during the early New Deal, the acerbic Senator Wheeler had said of Roosevelt, "He's like a king trying to reduce the barons." The barons in the Senate were mostly ancient but still defiant and reinforced by many defectors among southern Democrats. They ranged from Wheeler to Gerald Nye to the doddering Carter Glass of Virginia and his protégé, Harry Byrd, to southerners like Theodore Bilbo, Kenneth McKellar, William Bankhead, and Cotton Ed Smith, whose long tenure enabled them to dominate so many committees. Opposition also came from leading Republicans such as Robert A. Taft and Arthur Vandenberg. Like all good feudal barons they guarded their privileges and those of the Senate fiercely and kept their knives sharpened for Roosevelt and/or anything that smacked of New Deal reform.[59]

The president also had loyal Senate supporters, most notably Alben Barkley and Walter George. In 1944 Barkley, Nye, Taft, and numerous other senators were up for reelection along with the entire House, rendering them more sensitive than ever. Already Roosevelt had engaged the barons in a bitter battle over his demands for a bill that would enable distant soldiers to vote more easily. Republicans and southern Democrats rose in violent opposition, charging that the president was lining up votes for a fourth term. Southerners feared that such a bill would allow black soldiers to skirt the poll tax and vote. The bill that finally passed was a hollow shell of what Roosevelt wanted, and he let it become law without his signature while calling it "wholly inadequate." The national service bill was also on the floor along with the tax bill.[60]

Barkley, as majority leader, had long endured taunts and derision in the press for being a loyal lieutenant of the administration. Reporter Allen Drury thought he "acts like a man who is working awfully hard and awfully earnestly at a job he doesn't particularly like." *Time* habitually referred to him as a bumbling flunky even though his liberalism went back to the days of Woodrow Wilson. No senator had shown more devotion to the New Deal or to Roosevelt over the years, but he was up for reelection and the sarcastic tone of the president's veto message struck him as a slap in the face. On February 23, before packed galleries that sensed fireworks, Barkley rebutted the veto point by point and denounced it as a "calculated and deliberate assault upon the legislative integrity of every member of Congress." Then he shocked the Senate by resigning as majority leader. Two days later the Senate overrode the veto by a lopsided vote of 72–14; a day earlier the House had done the same by an equally overwhelming margin, 299–98. For the first time in history Congress had passed a revenue act over a presidential veto.[61]

Told of Barkley's defection, Roosevelt said only that "Alben must be suffering from shell shock." However, Byrnes persuaded him to send a conciliatory telegram to Barkley urging him to remain as majority leader and expressing the hope that he would be unanimously reelected if he did resign. The Senate did exactly that, and for a time Barkley was freed from the stigma of spineless loyalist as senators and the press alike cheered his turning on the master in the White House. The president made his peace with Barkley, who sent him a gracious note and resumed his role as administration loyalist, but a bitter aftertaste lingered, and there remained the missing $8 billion in needed revenue. Already a handful of senators were venting their true fear by coming out against a fourth term for the president.[62]

Pundits debated why Roosevelt had taken on a fight he knew could not be won, and why he had put so much sting in a veto message that was certain to antagonize the barons. He had personally inserted the most biting phrases into the message. In speechwriting sessions he often made vitriolic remarks about his enemies, aware that they would not be used, but this time he let them stand. Most likely he had simply grown weary of the parochialism and backbiting of the capital that greeted him on his return from Tehran and a mission of global significance. Whatever the reason, he was becoming less tolerant of the selfishness, greed, and pettiness that undermined the war effort. If nothing else, the veto confirmed the degree of disconnect between the White House and Congress, which could only worsen in an election year when everyone wondered what Roosevelt would do. For himself, the president enjoyed the mystery as he always did. At the White House correspondents' dinner, he roared with laughter when Bob Hope quipped, "I've always voted for Roosevelt as President. My father always voted for Roosevelt as President."[63]

Congress and the press heaped much of their generous criticism on Morgenthau and his lieutenant, Randolph Paul, blaming them for the veto as well as a defective tax bill. Some of Morgenthau's advisers urged him to tell Doughton that Treasury had opposed the veto, but he refused. He told his staff, "Somebody would have to be the ham in the sandwich between the President and the Congress, and I was expecting to be it. He got himself out of it nicely by some very fast footwork, and naturally they would like to throw somebody. And I am the natural candidate for that." Nor would he throw Paul or any other staff member to the wolves. "Somebody has to take it," he emphasized. "I am perfectly willing to take it, but it does give you a gripe when a man like Byrnes will run to cover just as soon as it gets hot . . . Anybody who is loyal to the President is going to get it."[64]

To relieve the incredible strains of wartime the president relied, as he always had, on a variety of minor pleasures and rituals. He loved to read, especially history, spent hours poring over his stamp collection, played poker, watched movies, and enjoyed the company of his inner circle of friends. The presidential study on the second floor was his refuge in the White House. It overflowed with stacks of paper, model ships, maritime pictures, and books stuffed into tall mahogany bookcases that towered over the leather chairs and sofa. "Any room that he used invariably got that lived-in and overcrowded look," said Frances Perkins, "which indicated the complexity and variety of his interests and intentions."[65]

His favorite time of all was the cocktail hour, a ritual indulged in since his days in Albany. The staff and invited guests gathered in the study to enjoy—some said endure—drinks mixed by Roosevelt himself, who liked to tinker with mixtures of gin or rum and vermouth or fruit juice and never bothered to measure the doses he poured. "The President makes a perfectly terrible dry martini," groaned Harold Ickes. "He isn't much better with his rum cocktails either." But the group grinned and swallowed, and braced for seconds when the host said, "How about another little sippy?" Sam Rosenman disliked liquor and began pouring his drinks into nearby plants until his tactic was discovered, after which Roosevelt stopped pressing him for seconds. Rosenman never saw the boss drink more than two cocktails, sipping them slowly while dominating the conversation as always.[66]

Cocktail hour was a time in which official talk was banned in favor of stories, gossip, reminiscences, and banter. For years Missy LeHand had presided as hostess, and her absence was deeply felt. Harry Hopkins was a favorite with his endless store of jokes, wisecracks, and stories laced with slang and profanity. "I didn't realize how smart Harry was," recalled a White House secretary, "because he was such a tease and would make a joke of everything." Eleanor seldom appeared and was never at ease when she did. Her dislike of alcohol, born of her drunken father, and her chronic inability to relax, left her perpetually uncomfortable in the presence of those who knew how to enjoy themselves. "She could be a crashing bore," admitted a granddaughter. "She was very judgmental even when she tried not to be. The human irregularities, the off-color jokes he loved, she couldn't take it." That was one reason why the devoted Missy presided and became the companion that Eleanor could never be.[67]

"He is protected by an unusual ability to relax at moments of hardest strain," wrote Raymond Clapper in October 1942. "Throughout the working day he snatches relaxation by exchanging stories with callers. Having finished talking business, Mr. Roosevelt is apt to put away the papers on his desk, lean back in his chair, and tell the visitor a story or some bit of gossip . . . Over the years Mr. Roosevelt has become tired at times, somewhat irritable during exceptionally difficult days, but on the whole I don't think anybody around Washington who has known him over these 10 years feels that he has changed to any degree." Yet five months before Pearl Harbor Harold Ickes, who hadn't seen Roosevelt for six weeks, observed that "he is certainly showing the wear and tear that he has been taking since March of 1933. He is a much older and changed man . . . Those of us who have known him best noticed how changed he seemed to be."[68]

To escape the burdens of Washington, Roosevelt usually fled to one of two retreats: the family home in Hyde Park, New York, or the rustic cabin at a former CCC camp for children in the woods of Maryland that he dubbed

"Shangri-La." Later it would be transformed into Camp David. To reach Hyde Park Roosevelt boarded his special train for an overnight ten-hour journey that required immense advance preparations. All rail traffic was diverted from the tracks so that railroad workers could inspect every yard of them. Parked cars were removed from the vicinity of the tracks, and security agents tested all food and drink loaded onto the train. The Pullman car in front of Roosevelt's specially built private car was loaded with typewriters and mimeograph machines for staff use.[69]

Once at home, Roosevelt basked in the sweet familiarity of sights and smells that never grew old to him. In his specially rigged automobile he loved driving about the countryside alone or with whatever company happened to be there, showing them the sights, identifying trees and plantings, talking to the locals. Other times he was content to sit in his chair relishing the view and the woods. On one trip he hauled a sleepy Bill Hassett out to a pond at 4:00 A.M. to listen to birds and identified twenty-two different species for him. Once the war started, it became increasingly difficult for Roosevelt to get away to Hyde Park. Instead he turned to the Maryland camp, which was only a two-hour drive from Washington. Although the president nearly always brought guests, he relished the time spent on a stone screened-in porch at the edge of the woods overlooking a valley. There he chatted with guests or read, examined his stamps, looked over papers, played solitaire, or just enjoyed the view.[70]

Life at Shangri-La was casual and informal, the facilities rustic. "Everyone did more or less as he pleased, as if he were off by himself," recalled Rosenman. "There was no effort to entertain anybody, and the spirit and tempo were of complete relaxation and detachment." The staff consisted of the Filipinos who served him on the presidential yacht, the *Potomac*, which in wartime was deemed too dangerous for him to use. Roosevelt loved to tease guests, especially those unused to rustic facilities, and delighted in telling them that they would have to share one bathroom. One weekend he arranged a surprise birthday party for Grace Tully complete with a cake, ice cream, and cocktails. The marine guards sang "Happy Birthday," and Roosevelt regaled them with an old marine song. "The President was able to relax completely," concluded Rosenman, who was present with his wife that weekend, "or the job would have killed him earlier."[71]

By 1944 it was in fact killing him.

The president's health had been deteriorating for some time. He still followed his familiar routine of working and reading in bed until late morning, then wheeling off to the Oval Office, stopping first at the map room with Admiral Leahy to survey military movements represented by little flags and pins. Through the afternoon he saw callers and dictated letters before returning to his study for cocktail hour and dinner. But his pace had slowed somewhat, the evenings grew shorter, and the number of guests fewer. At sixty-two he had endured an incredible eleven years in the White House, presiding over two of the worst calamities in American history. That winter he lost Harry Hopkins, who had remarried and finally moved out of the White House in December. In his place came Roosevelt's daughter, Anna Boettiger, who came to spend Christmas with him and stayed on to keep her father company.[72]

Few people gave Roosevelt more pleasure than Anna. Apart from being a tall, beautiful blonde with blue eyes and a radiant smile, she shared his ribald sense of humor and fondness for stories and gossip. Laughter always punctuated their time together. One of Eleanor's friends recalled being with Roosevelt in his study one morning when Anna walked in. "His whole face lighted up," she said; "the world's problems stopped for a few minutes. He just adored her." But Anna was disturbed by what she saw in her father. His face had lost color, he had a soft but persistent cough, and the hollows under his eyes had darkened even more. He complained of being tired and of headaches, and he slept poorly. His hands shook more than they ever had. Others noticed his fatigue even in the mornings, and his occasional nodding off in the middle of dictation or a conversation. Once he blanked out while signing a letter.[73]

That winter Roosevelt had his usual bouts of flu and sinusitis but did not bounce back from them with his usual vigor. In February he went to the hospital to have a wen removed from the back of his head. Rumors that he was seriously ill, perhaps dying, swept through Washington just as speculation over whether he would seek a fourth term began heating up. "The President not looking so well in his bedroom this morning," noted Hassett on March 24. ". . . This latest cold has taken lots out of him." Asked how he felt, Roosevelt said only "Rotten" or "Like hell." Two days later he canceled all appointments and went to bed with a fever of 104. Anna summoned Dr. McIntire, who assured her that it was only another bout of bronchitis and flu and that a week or two in the sun would restore his vigor. Unconvinced, she implored McIntire to send her father for a checkup but not tell him that she suggested it. Reluctantly McIntire agreed.[74]

On March 28 Roosevelt arrived at Bethesda Naval Hospital and submitted to a full examination. A young cardiologist named Howard Bruenn waited to examine him. He had never met the president and was told only that his recovery from the flu and bronchitis had been slow. Strangely, McIntire, a nose and throat specialist, had never probed deeply into Roosevelt's condition. Asked to provide Bruenn with results of earlier heart and chest examinations, he wasn't sure he could find them. Bruenn went into the exam with no previous history, but one glance told him something was wrong. "His face was pallid and there was a bluish discoloration of his skin, lips, and nail beds," he recalled, signs that the tissues were not receiving enough oxygen. Listening to the president's heart worsened his impression. The heart was greatly increased in size, as happens when blood pressure increases. He heard rales in Roosevelt's lungs, an abnormal rattling sound that indicated a buildup of fluids. His blood pressure was 186/108.[75]

During the exam the medical records finally arrived, and Bruenn excused himself to scan them. He saw that high blood pressure had been found as early as 1941, yet McIntire had never called in a heart specialist. Since then the damage had grown worse, leaving Roosevelt with a heart unable to pump effectively and suffering from congestive heart failure. He revealed none of this to his patient, having been ordered by McIntire to say nothing to Roosevelt. Nor did the president ask him any questions. He chatted through the exam in his easy manner about all sorts of topics other than his health and at its conclusion said only, "Thanks, Doc." To inquiries about his health at his regular press conference that afternoon he said that he was still recovering from his illness and would soon be fine. The *New York Times* reported that his color, voice, and spirits seemed much improved. But that evening he retired at 7:30.[76]

Bruenn reported his findings to McIntire along with a list of suggested treatments that included digitalis, a change in diet, and seven weeks of complete bedrest. McIntire dismissed them, saying, "The president can't take time off to go to bed. You can't simply say to him, do this or do that. This is the president of the United States." Next morning a team of senior consultants gathered secretly to review the test results and data. They refused to believe that a young lieutenant commander had found so serious an illness that McIntire had somehow missed, but Bruenn stood his ground until the doctors agreed to examine the president. Afterward they differed in views but agreed on a more modest version of Bruenn's recommendations: digitalis, a low-fat diet, reduced consumption of cigarettes from twenty to five or six a day, one and a half cocktails only, fewer callers at mealtimes, and use of a Gatch bed to ease his breathing by elevating his head.[77]

Here was another and most unwelcome parallel between Roosevelt and Woodrow Wilson, as McIntire realized gloomily. Wilson had suffered a stroke that rendered him comatose. During his slow convalescence the seriousness of his condition was kept from the public by his physician, Admiral Cary Grayson. Now Admiral McIntire found himself in the position of having to keep his patient's condition secret from the public, his family, and himself. Roosevelt was not in nearly as bad shape as Wilson had been, but who knew what might happen? Bruenn became Roosevelt's personal physician because he was a cardiologist, although McIntire continued in that role to all outward appearances.[78]

Of all this the public knew nothing. On April 4 McIntire told reporters that the results of the checkup were excellent and that the president was recovering from bronchitis. To Bruenn's amazement, Roosevelt himself never asked the doctors about his condition. Every day he dutifully took his digitalis pills and had his blood pressure checked without asking why. Within two weeks tests showed that the digitalis had reduced the size of his heart, and his lungs had cleared significantly. The cough diminished, some color returned, and his sleep improved, but he still needed rest. The doctors urged him to get away from the White House for a significant period of rest. Bernie Baruch promptly invited him to stay at Hobcaw, his baronial estate in South Carolina. It was the perfect retreat, overlooking the Waccamaw River, surrounded by lush, intoxicating gardens and broad expanses of fields and woods.[79]

Roosevelt arrived at Hobcaw on April 19, Easter Sunday, in the company of McIntire, Bruenn, Pa Watson, and Admiral Leahy. "I want to sleep and sleep, twelve hours a night," he announced, and he did. Ensconced in a corner bedroom, he spent the days reading the papers, doing his mail, and sometimes going fishing or driving around the estate to enjoy the gardens and the wildlife. Visitors came and went, the locals cooperated happily in keeping the president's presence a secret, and the three press association reporters marked time eight miles away at the Prince George Hotel in Georgetown. "He looked ghastly and listless when we arrived," observed Merriman Smith, but perked up considerably as the days passed. However, Bill Hassett noted sourly that "the Boss paid a heavy penalty in accepting Bernie Baruch's hospitality. Bernie added himself to the household and so was there most of the month."[80]

Bruenn recalled the whole experience as delightful. "The president thrived on the simple routine," he said. "I had never known anyone so full of charm. At lunch and dinner alike, he animated the conversation, telling wonderful stories, reminiscing with Baruch, talking of current events, pulling everyone in. He was a master raconteur." He did not return to Washington until May 7, having enjoyed the longest vacation of his presidency. Hassett found him "brown as a berry, radiant and happy," with good color but thin. Roosevelt told him that at Hobcaw he had worked four hours a day and that he planned to continue that schedule. He would see no one at lunch and rest for ninety minutes before resuming the day's schedule. "This is too good to be true," wrote Hassett. "We shall see."[81]

During his absence Frank Knox had died suddenly of a heart attack, and Roosevelt had missed the funeral. In talking with the president about the loss, Merriman Smith got the impression that he "sounded more like a housewife who'd just lost a maid than a man who'd just lost a close assistant." Stimson had taken the news hard. "Frank had been a close friend," he mourned, "and we had been so similarly situated that we seemed like side partners here in Washington." James Forrestal, the logical and able successor, replaced him as secretary of the navy. At his first press conference two days after his return, Roosevelt pronounced himself healthy and deftly sidestepped all questions about a fourth term. Still rumors abounded that he was deathly ill, that three psychiatrists had gone south with him, and—most pointed of all—that he might not run for a fourth term because of his health.[82]

"*The President is overworking himself,*" observed Kiplinger's. ". . . It is more than any one man can do, and do well. Many high officials are whispering about the situation." Nelson had the same feeling. "He was a strong man," he recalled, "but obviously he was operating upon his almost superhuman reserve of strength, and the time was bound to come when there would be no reserve left."[83]

To the press McIntire pronounced himself "perfectly satisfied with his physical condition." The president, he added, was "as strong as he was a year ago." Some remained unconvinced. Many of the newsmen, reported *Time*, "were struck by the realization that Franklin Roosevelt at 62 is an old man." Anna talked with Bruenn, who impressed on her the urgency of changing Roosevelt's diet. She fretted that he would fall back into his old habits and determined to enforce the new regime. To Baruch's shrewd eyes the president looked tanned and rested but tired easily. He advised Byrnes to discuss any important business with Roosevelt in the morning and try to keep him from working much in the afternoon. "But, of course," Baruch conceded, "no one could keep Franklin Roosevelt from his man-killing task."[84]

THEY CALLED RAY Clapper the columnist for the average man. Ernest Lindley, who had known him for fifteen years, called him "a conscientious searcher for facts." He had gone to Europe and North Africa to get those facts directly from the fighting men. He admitted to knowing nothing about military affairs, but he knew plenty about ordinary soldiers. One of his classic columns concerned a soldier's first reaction to eating K rations. His chief virtue, said his wife, was that "he isn't selling anything." On December 28, 1943, Clapper tossed over a $40,000 radio contract to head for New Guinea, hoping to give his readers a closer look at what he considered a neglected theater of the war. While there he boarded a carrier to cover the invasion of the Marshalls. Aware that seven war correspondents had already died in the Pacific, he treasured a small brown bear given him by his daughter, writing that

"I never get in a plane any more without checking with the little brown bear."[85]

On February 3 the public learned that Clapper's plane had collided with another while maneuvering to get into formation. Everyone on both planes was lost, including the little brown bear. He was the sixteenth correspondent to die in the war and would not be the last. One of his last dispatches from the carrier said, "You have a sense of living in a world apart from what you knew at home, and there is almost no talk of life back in the States now. You live only minute by minute through the routine that carries you smoothly, as if drifting down a river, toward the day of battle." Ironically, during the battle for the Marshalls the navy for the first time allowed correspondents to send dispatches via ship radio directly from the scene. A spokesman, explaining the change in policy, said, "We've got so much stuff and power now we don't have to give much of a damn what we tell the Japs. What he does find out will scare him."[86]

By a sad coincidence that same week saw the death of a very different journalistic lion, William Allen White, of a heart attack twelve days short of his seventy-sixth birthday. White was the legendary editor of a small-town newspaper whose career stretched back to the depression-wracked 1890s. The author of a dozen books as well, he far outgrew but never left Kansas despite ample offers to do so, saying that death alone would take him from his native state. At first glance he and Clapper seemed to have little in common. White was a pillar of the old school of personal journalism, Clapper one of the best practitioners of a new breed that found expression in syndicated columns and chain broadcasting. White was a lifelong Republican, though freely critical of the party; Clapper was respected for his nonpartisanship.[87]

Yet during this difficult winter of disconnect the two departed journalists offered at least a thread of connection. Both were the product of small towns in Kansas, an influence that permeated all of their work. They loathed extremists of any kind and sought to be the voice of the common man who simply wanted to get on with his life. "Both knew, interpreted, exemplified, and strengthened some of the most admirable American characteristics and aspirations," wrote Ernest Lindley in tribute. Above all, both men had open minds and did not hesitate to change them in the light of new evidence. "Events are not consistent," Clapper once wrote, "so why should I be?" White was more eloquent on the subject. "Consistency," he observed, "is a paste jewel."[88]

CHAPTER 29

THE CHANGING FACE
OF WAR

In this new kind of warfare science and technology alone could win . . . Nor was the mass production of heavy equipment enough. Each new design must be engineered, built experimentally, and tested like a precision instrument, then standardized and mass-produced to the utmost degree of accuracy and uniformity. Still more, they must all be invented, developed, put into production without the usual interval of time considered vital for untried commercial goods.

—DAVID O. WOODBURY [1]

The Boeing B-29 is by far the deadliest bomber ever sent into combat. Yet, aerodynamically, it is a giant with all the grace, streamlining, and light-wingedness of a swallow.

—NEWSWEEK [2]

I see trainload after trainload of stuff come into this plant but nothing ever goes out of it. What the dickens do we make here, anyway?

—OAK RIDGE FOREMAN [3]

ALREADY THE FACE OF WAR had changed several times. The brutal, crushing onrush of blitzkrieg had stalled out in both Russia and North Africa, forcing Germany back on the defensive. The bold thrust of Japan across the Pacific had been reversed, forcing the empire to surrender island after island it had captured earlier. In both theaters of war the Allies seized the initiative, closing the circle around Germany and pushing the Japanese ever closer to their home island. In January the Russians at last relieved the siege of Leningrad, while the Americans and British landed at Anzio to launch what proved to be a bloody and dogged attempt to shorten the Italian campaign. Italy had surrendered to the Allies in September 1943, but strong German units continued the fight. In the Pacific American troops captured Kwajalein and Eniwetok atolls in the Marshall Islands, giving them forward bases for attacks on the Marianas.

On February 20 the Army Air Forces and the British launched what came to be known as "Big Week"—a period of sustained strategic bombing of German industrial facilities intended not only to cripple production but to lure the Luftwaffe into defending the targets so as to inflict crippling losses on it. Waves of American bombers with heavy fighter escort attacked by day, British bombers by night. This strategy amounted to a modern salute to that of U. S. Grant in the last year of the Civil War: victory by sheer attrition. Although losses would be heavy on both sides, the Allies could replace planes and pilots much more easily than the Germans, and their plants remained unscathed. Increasingly air warfare came to dominate both strategic and tactical thinking as the fastest, most effective route to victory.

The new and constantly evolving face of war was shaped primarily by American productivity that continued to pour forth improved weapons, and more of them than ever before. Overwhelming productive superiority remained the central goal, but the emphasis within it had changed. By 1943 strategic thinking had shifted from building a huge land army to a smaller one with maximum mobility and mechanization. Complementing it would be an air force dominated by massive numbers of long-range bombers capable of delivering huge amounts of destructive bombs under a canopy of superior fighter escorts. In Europe fighters also emerged as potent tactical weapons against ground targets. This new face of war demanded new and improved weapons in record numbers. They in turn required innovations in design and production that would transform not only the face of war but that of the world afterward.[4]

ON THE MORNING of January 12 Stimson took time out to watch a short film of a newfangled jet aircraft. "It was a wonderful sight," he enthused afterward. "You could hardly believe your eyes; to see this airplane take off without any propellers and nothing but an almost invisible jet of flame coming from the jets behind. It has tremendous speed, great maneuverability and balance." The only drawback seemed to be that it consumed three or four times the fuel of a conventional fighter plane the same size. Later that morning he met with General Dwight Eisenhower to discuss Operation Overlord, the forthcoming invasion of France. Chief of Ordnance General L. H. Campbell Jr. was there to show Eisenhower photographs of a proposed new rocket launcher that could be attached to Sherman tanks. Vannevar Bush also attended to express his deep concern about Germany's new rockets and the possible use of poison with them.[5]

All this was heady new stuff for Stimson, and one more dimension of the changing face of war. The focus was on Overlord and what could be done to ensure its success and minimize as much as possible the expected severe losses that would be incurred. Work was under way on a special armor-piercing shell to penetrate the big German tanks, but production would not start until that summer. The core would be made of cemented tungsten carbide, the hardest metal made by man. Set inside a streamlined body, the version for a 76 mm gun weighed only nine pounds, six less than a conventional steel shell, which increased its velocity. Earlier a plastic fuze had been developed for the 60 mm trench mortar, replacing an aluminum version. Every one of the 29 million plastic fuzes produced by General Electric saved a pound of aluminum and eventually cost only a quarter each compared to more than a dollar for the aluminum one.[6]

"Perhaps the most complex of all ammunition components," observed historian R. Elberton Smith, "were the marvelously intricate and sensitive fuzes, which individually or as a class had to perform some of the most difficult and versatile assignments of the war." They had to serve many different calibers of ammunition with a wide variety of settings. Some had to be sensitive, yet permit delayed detonation after the shocks of launching, impact, and penetration through their target. Others had to detonate within a certain proximity of an aerial target. They were an engineering masterpiece of design, development, and mass production, one of the most basic yet critical components of weaponry.[7]

Innovations in fuzes became a priority as the use of bombers increased. The early M-110 bomb nose fuze was complicated and poorly designed. Since millions of the units were needed, Westinghouse and other companies plunged into research on a new design. The result was the M-110A that could be made more easily and at less cost. Ultimately Westinghouse alone made nearly 5.7 million of them even as it and other manufacturers worked at designing a much more advanced device, the proximity fuze, deemed important enough to remain shrouded in almost as much secrecy as the Manhattan Project. In essence it was a tiny signaling unit, operated first by light and then by radio, and could be used in most types of missiles from bombs to rockets to artillery. One version, the Navy's VT (variable time), which used the bomb's own nose as its antenna, proved especially devastating in its accuracy and fiendishly tricky to manufacture. "Never, perhaps, in the history of assembly-line methods," wrote author James Baxter, "have the standards of performance been more difficult to meet."[8]

The use of radio waves to guide bombs was only one example of how that technology had come into its own since the last war. The stunning development of commercial radio during the 1920s brought with it the potential for a revolution in battlefield communications just as theaters of war expanded to unprecedented size. Contact had to be maintained with troops on far-flung battlefields, planes in the air, and ships at sea, each one posing different technical challenges. By 1940 radio communication had become well standardized, but an exciting new field, microwaves, was just emerging. Intensive research produced a host of new devices for communication and ever more sophisticated versions of radar, a technology that first proved its worth in the Battle of Britain. Westinghouse alone turned out some fifty major products, including nineteen different radio units, a like number of radar types, six industrial electronics items, and two radar fuzes, most of them for the navy. It also organized and trained a team of fifty engineers and technicians who came in behind the combatants to keep equipment at peak efficiency.[9]

As its orders multiplied after 1940, Westinghouse's Radio Division enlisted 600 subcontractors to supply small parts and subassemblies. The division itself started military work in 1935 with 500 employees; by 1945 it had 6,000 employees and had done $400 million worth of business. Midway through the war the navy asked for radio telephone sets of very high frequency that could be automatically controlled by multiple quartz crystals for at least ten bands of transmission, to be used in carrier-based bombers. The result was a marvel of complexity and intricacy called the AN/ARC that crammed 4,600 parts with precision into a box 29 by 19 inches and 9 inches deep. The Bell Laboratories put together the first five samples, after which the struggle to produce in quantity began. Even workers, mostly women, familiar with precision work were slow to grasp the degree of exactness required by AN/ARC. The company resorted to all sorts of inducements to upgrade the quality of work, including a play written by shop people depicting a worker who lost her boyfriend in combat because his AN/ARC failed to work.[10]

While Westinghouse served the navy, General Electric did much of its radio work for the army and its air forces. It supplied 70,000 75-watt radios known as the SCR-287, used in nearly every bomber and featuring a long-range transmitter for both voice and key operations. GE factories also turned out 40,000 SCR-506 radios, a compact and rugged new model. Designed originally for tanks, the versatile SCR-506, with its five frequencies, four pretuned and one variable, that switched from one to another almost instantly, was quickly adapted to other vehicles, command posts, airplanes, headquarters, and infantry on the move. For the marines GE devised a portable transmitting and receiving set called the TBX, which did yeoman's work in amphibious landings. It was sturdy enough to be tossed overboard and washed ashore without being damaged and could be put into operation at once. The company also developed a wire recorder capable of recording sixty-six minutes of continuous speech on 15,000 feet of thin wire wrapped around a spool. Both the army and navy used them to record reports and observations and sometimes allowed the media to use them as well.[11]

Radio transformed the face of World War II much as the telegraph did the Civil War. It enabled communications to keep up with the faster pace of war created by mechanization and the enormous distances of a global conflict. No form of radio played a more important role than radar, the mysterious "magic eye" as some called it. No one person invented or discovered radar; scientists in England, France, Germany, and the United States figured out during the 1930s that shortwave radio impulses could be bounced off distant objects and returned as an echo. As early as 1935 Britain secretly set up a cluster of five "radio location" stations along its east coast to detect the approach of enemy planes. Two years later it added fifteen more stations, extending coverage from the east coast of Scotland to the Isle of Wight. Their advance warning gave the Royal Air Force fighters precious time to scramble and meet incoming German bombers during the Battle of Britain.[12]

Both American electrical giants had been experimenting with radio waves as detection devices since the 1930s. So had the Naval Research Laboratory under Colonel Roger B. Colton, the director of research and development. Colton was almost a lone wolf in pushing the development of a radar device that could be standardized. Once he had a suitable design in 1939, he persuaded Westinghouse to make some experimental models that might later be produced in quantity. Creating a shortwave beam powerful enough to amplify the weak reflections from distant objects required an entirely new kind of transmitter tube. "Radical changes were necessary," admitted a Westinghouse engineer, "so we proceeded to violate just about every known rule of radio-tube design." The result of their work was the WL-530 tube, two of which in parallel could deliver a peak power of 500 kilowatts instead of 35 kilowatts each. It formed the core of a radar set that could detect a two-seater bomber a hundred miles away and served as the basis for the development of later radars.[13]

The first radar to be standardized, the SCR-270/271, was installed at Pearl Harbor, among other uses, and detected the incoming Japanese planes only to have the warning ignored. In the spring of 1941 the navy asked GE to build 400 radar sets for use on shipboard. As the nation inched nearer to war, the company dropped all work on commercial radio development to concentrate on government work, especially the still ultra-secret radar. The first sets went into a group of destroyers in November. Eventually the number, including improved models, reached 1,500. Westinghouse's first project for the navy was for twenty-five small (eighty-five pounds) ASB units for carrier planes except fighters. During the next three years the ASB production line, operating day and night, turned out 18,000 units despite having to incorporate more than 2,000 alterations.[14]

In 1943 radar took on a crucial new role in the fight against German submarines. Early in the year they took a deadly toll, sinking 205 ships in the North Atlantic between February 1 and March 20. Admiral Ernest King distrusted all civilians and refused obstinately to let go of naval traditions. In particular he ignored potential new weapons against the submarine and clung to the hoary, ineffective practice of convoys. "Escort is not just one way of handling the submarine menace," he insisted. "It is the only way that gives any promise of success." In vain did Stimson, who was surprisingly receptive to new ideas and innovations, try to convince King that a combination of radar, planes (especially Very Long Range B-24s), and escort destroyers could curb the submarine menace. It took a tough, concerted effort by Vannevar Bush to bring King around to trying a new approach to combating the U-boats.[15]

The new destroyer escorts had the speed and firepower to outmaneuver and sink U-boats when they could find them. The submarines, which had to recharge their batteries and take on fresh air, surfaced at night when they could not be seen. But radar installed on the destroyer escorts and in spotter planes could detect them even at night and attack before the U-boat had time to submerge. Using a captured British radar set, the Germans began equipping submarines with a listening device that let them know when the area was being swept by radar. The Americans responded by replacing older radar sets with a new type of shortwave radar for which the Germans had no counter. This change helped account for the heavy toll on German submarines during the spring and summer of 1943.[16]

Once the submarines were spotted, not only ships but planes went after them with a vengeance. The most effective aircraft proved to be B-24s flown by both American and British pilots from land bases, but they were not alone. Operating from the baby carriers Henry Kaiser had promoted to much derision from scoffers, Grumman Wildcats and Avengers sent thirty-one U-boats to the bottom in one six-month period, more than half the total sunk by the navy in that time. Together with the destroyer escorts and radar, they finally won the Battle of the Atlantic, opening the sea lanes not only across the ocean but along the American coastline as well. By the summer of 1944 Roosevelt and Churchill could declare that the U-boat had become the hunted rather than the hunter.[17]

As the war on submarines illustrated, the new face of war gave fresh dimensions to an old pattern of seeking ways to neutralize a superior weapon. In this case the task pitted dueling versions of upgrades in technology against each other. Once aware of radar's role after the Battle of Britain, the Germans devised a method of jamming Allied radar signals. Desperate for a countermeasure, the military asked NDRC's scientists to make a study of radar interference and ways to thwart it. An organization known as Division 15 was created in Schenectady, GE's headquarters, to develop counter-radar systems. The solution lay in changing to a new type of shortwave radar that proved less susceptible to interference. At the same time, the engineers and scientists worked on new ways to jam German radar.[18]

When American strategic bombing of German targets began, the Germans massed antiaircraft guns and radar around key areas. The guns took a heavy toll of American and British planes until two countermeasures were devised. The first one, with the code name "Window," consisted of dropping several thousand long strips of metal foil in the area, creating fake echoes on the radar and making it almost impossible to separate the bombers from what the air crews called "chaff." The second, more sophisticated counter, called "Carpet," involved producing a continuous electric "noise" to drown out the echoes returning to German radars. GE rushed production of the special electronic tubes needed for the jammers. First used in an American raid on Bremen in October 1943, the jammers cut plane losses significantly. By war's end nearly all heavy bombers were using both methods.[19]

A discouraged German scientist admitted that "our defense is practically blind. The awful destruction of our cities which the enemy oftentimes carries out with negligible losses is an eloquent proof of the effectiveness of these jamming means used by the enemy." Despite frantic attempts, the Germans failed to find a means of countering the jamming. When Japanese torpedo bombers equipped with radar made their appearance in the Pacific in the fall of 1944, the navy asked the General Electric Research Laboratory to create a modified electronic tube to counter them. The new version also required different antennas keyed to the new frequency and other modifications. Nine days later GE gave the navy ten sets of the new jamming device. That same afternoon a navy transport picked them up for delivery to Pacific warships, where in short order they succeeded in forcing several Japanese planes to veer away from attacking because their radars failed at the crucial moment.[20]

During 1943 both GE and Westinghouse took contracts to manufacture a special type of shortwave radar to guide antiaircraft guns defending against the new German V-1 rocket, or "buzz bomb." Allied intelligence learned that the Germans planned to use the V-1 against English cities to counter the expected forthcoming invasion of France. The rockets were expected to become operational sometime in 1944, which gave the engineers only months to come up with an effective new radar system. They responded with SCR-584, a portable unit mounted on a single trailer that could track an approaching enemy plane forty miles away. When the plane got within a few miles, the operator linked the radar to an automatic gun director that would follow the target and fire with an accuracy beyond human eyes and hands.[21]

The gun director was a marvel in itself—an electronic device that combined data on range, windage, barometric pressure, temperature, and shell characteristics to aim the gun. With production moving at top speed, the 584 made its debut in the Italian campaign along with a hundred sets rushed to England. The buzz bombs, first launched in June 1944, while causing some damage and casualties, proved too erratic to be effective, and the guns steered by SCR-584 took an impressive toll on them. In one raid only 3 of 105 rockets got through the defenses. Antiaircraft guns improved dramatically during the war, as did the planes that challenged them. American engineers took two of the best foreign versions, the Swedish Bofors and the Swiss Oerlikon, and modified them in ways that enabled them to be produced in quantity at much lower cost. At the same time, other engineers were hard at work crafting a plane that only the heaviest antiaircraft guns could touch.[22]

TWO LATE-BLOOMING WEAPONS did much to shorten the war and became emblems for its ugly new face. Both were huge, expensive projects, gambles on a grand scale that no other country could have afforded to undertake. One was a plane, by far the largest and most complex ever built; the other became its payload—the most devastating bomb ever devised and the harbinger of a terrifying new era of warfare.

The Boeing B-29 Superfortress fully deserved its name. Nearly twice as heavy as a B-17, it had a wingspan of 141 feet compared to 100 feet for the Flying Fortress. It was designed to fly at 30,000 feet, above the range of most antiaircraft guns, with a reach of 3,000 miles, well beyond the ability of fighters to escort it. Despite its size, the B-29 was designed to fly 30 percent faster than a B-17 while using only 83 percent more horsepower. To do that the 99-foot fuselage had to be streamlined as completely as possible. The plane featured a pressurized cabin, the first of its kind, and was all-electric; everything except the engines ran on electricity, including gun turrets operated by remote control. The Wright engines were the most powerful ever built, producing 2,200 horsepower compared to the B-17's 1,200. To cope with the thin air of high altitude, each engine boasted two turbochargers. The plane's ultrasleek body, streamlined to minimize drag, looked like no other plane. It was a marvel of technological innovation, and largely for that reason its development was long and costly, consuming more funds than even the Manhattan Project.[23]

The Superfortress owed its existence largely to the persistence of two men:

General Hap Arnold and Wellwood E. Beall, Boeing's chief engineer. In May 1939, before the war had even begun, Arnold formed a board to study all types of aircraft and suggest what the Air Corps should develop. The board, which included Charles A. Lindbergh, turned in a detailed report that recommended, among other things, the development of several long-range bombers. Convinced of the need, Arnold got approval in late December to let contracts. A list of requirements went out to several companies and reached Boeing on February 5, 1940. Three weeks later it submitted plans for what it called Model 341, an 85,700-pound plane. Before any decision was made, the Air Corps, learning lessons from the war in Europe, changed the requirements to include armor, defense armaments, and sealed fuel tanks.[24]

No company was better suited to the challenge. Boeing was known as a company of engineers. The president, Philip Johnson, was a former draftsman who encouraged his designers to toss ideas around. Chairman Clairmont "Claire" Egtvedt viewed himself as the link between the engineers and the front office and liked to sit in on the engineering conferences. Beall started with Boeing in 1932 and was only thirty-two years old when he rose to chief engineer in 1939 on the eve of the war. A Falstaffian figure with a large round head, an anorexic mustache, and a flair for loud bow ties, he knew bombers from having nursed the original 1935 B-17 through its D, E, F, and G series that incorporated more than 2,000 engineering changes. Pilots loved the Fortress. "This was an airplane you could trust," said one. ". . . To me the Flying Fortress was, and always will be, the Queen of the Sky. I owe my life to the Queen."[25]

The B-17 became the mainstay of the Allied air armada in Europe along with the B-24 Liberator. Altogether the Army Air Forces dumped 1.5 million tons of bombs on European targets during the war. Of that amount B-17s dropped 640,036 tons, or 43 percent, compared to 452,508 tons (30 percent) by the Liberators. But the Fortress had a combat radius of only 800 miles carrying a bomb load of 5,000 pounds and cruised at 160 miles an hour with a maximum speed of 299. While it did yeoman service in Europe, it was not suited to handle the huge distances to targets in the Pacific.[26]

During 1940 Boeing received a contract to build three prototypes of a revised version incorporating the requested changes. More than a thousand engineers spent 1.5 million man-hours and $2.8 million to produce 10,000 drawings for three versions of what became known as XB-29. Getting the plane off the ground required an entirely new wing design featuring the largest flap ever made. The fuselage consisted of five joined sections with a tunnel across the bomb-bay section to allow passage between the pressurized nose and waist sections. Unlike the B-17, it would have a "tricycle" landing gear that would be fully retracted in flight because the plane's air drag doubled when the landing gear was down. Two bomb bays were included to keep the diameter of the plane trim. Since emptying one bay before the other would disrupt the center of gravity, an intervalometer was added to alternate the release of bombs.[27]

The mighty Wright engines drove huge propellers of a special design that turned more slowly than those of any other plane. The gun turrets were sleek and sealed to reduce drag and operated remotely through GE's new fire control system consisting of a small computer that made corrections for speed, range, altitude, wind, temperature, deflection, and bullet drop. The system enabled any gunner except the tail to use more than one turret at a time through a switch box. After sighting the target and tracking it briefly to provide the computer with speed, range, and angle, the gunner pressed a switch to start the guns firing 800 rounds a minute. All the guns except the tail were sighted and fired from positions away from the actual turrets, which protected gunners from vibration or recoil. Range was increased beyond the typical 600 yards because the correct lead could be established automatically.[28]

Powering this behemoth required an entirely new type of electrical system for an airplane. To provide the amount of electricity needed, the plane used six generators with a total capacity of 54 kilowatts gear-connected to the main engines. A small gasoline engine provided power if the engines failed or were shut off. Since the engines ran at wildly varying speeds, voltage regulators were crucial. To operate all the plane's systems, GE designed an electrical system that included 170 electric motors, 26 motor-generator sets, and 15,000 feet of electric wiring. More of the company's components went into the B-29 than into any other project. To distribute power the engineers created a special new type of aircraft wire that was thin, flameproof, lightweight, flexible at extreme temperatures, and resistant to oil, solvents, and moisture. In effect every B-29 had its own electric plant.[29]

Like the crews, airplane engines needed extra oxygen at high altitudes. At 30,000 feet a normal engine lost 75 percent of its power. To offset this loss, GE developed the turbosupercharger, a device that compressed thin air to air at sea-level pressure and fed it to the engine's carburetor. GE built 162,380 of them during the war and still could not turn them out fast enough. The company loaned its designs and some of its personnel to two other companies that had the equipment to make them. Turbosuperchargers went into the B-17, B-24, P-38, P-47, and two other planes before the B-29. The Superfortress required eight turbosuperchargers, two for each engine, two of which served also to pressurize the cabin so that the crew could function most of the time without oxygen masks.[30]

"Designwise," said Beall, "the B-29 was a full step forward." It was also a step that involved tough arguments with the army at every turn. After extensive tests to measure the durability of every part of the plane, construction of the first prototype began six months before all aerodynamic work was finished and a year before drawings of all parts were ready. The army wanted XB-29 ready to fly by August 1942. Hap Arnold believed in the project and persuaded the government to place orders totaling $750 million for a thousand planes, as well as hundreds of millions more for engines and plant facilities, months before the first prototype was ready to fly. Roosevelt supported him, convinced that such a plane was the only practical way to hit the Japanese mainland. In September 1942 the first prototype roared down the runway at Boeing Field in Seattle and stayed aloft for seventy-five minutes. Then a series of engine problems plagued and delayed tests on it for the rest of the year.[31]

The first flight of the second prototype ended with an engine catching fire. After being grounded for three weeks of repairs and adjustments, test pilot Eddie Allen took the ship up again on February 18, 1943. Fire again broke out in one engine but seemed to be under control. As the plane passed over the Lake Washington Bridge en route to landing, a gasoline fire swept over one wing. With flames marching toward the cockpit, the plane skimmed downtown Seattle. Despite frantic efforts by Allen to control it, the plane nicked some high-tension wires and rammed into the fifth floor of the Frye Packing Plant with a huge explosion and raging fire. Allen and his entire crew died along with nineteen people in the building and a fireman. A stunned Arnold ordered an investigation into the engine problem, and the Truman Committee conducted its own inquiry. The committee discovered that Wright, with orders for more than 40,000 of the engines, had produced some substandard and defective ones. It also scolded the Army Air Forces for putting pressure on Wright to deliver.[32]

Despite the tragedy, Arnold pushed the program as hard as ever. He approved a proposal from Colonel Leonard "Jake" Harman to create the "B-29 Special Project that would take charge of flight tests, production, and crew training in one package." After gaining approval from General Marshall and the president, the new team took control of the testing. The Special Project received a priority exceeded only by that of the mysterious Manhattan Engineer District. Ultimately the engine-fire problem was traced to a flaw in the original Wright design, and a number of changes were incorporated. A new group of test planes, the YB-29s, was built and used to ferret out continued bugs in the engines and other problems. Meanwhile, the training of handpicked crews to fly the most complex plane ever built went forward. A crew consisted of six men—pilot, copilot, bombardier, navigator, and flight engineer—in the forward pressurized cabin and three gunners in the rear section. Despite the size of the plane, space was cramped for all of them, but it included four bunks for the crew to rest on long flights.[33]

The struggle to get serviceable planes built and crews trained to fly them dragged on for months. At the Boeing plant in Wichita a victory bell clanged every time a finished B-29 rolled off the assembly line. Air Forces officials chastised the company for giving enemy agents a way to count the number of planes but backed down when told that Bill Knudsen himself had suggested the idea. In April a special new unit, the 20th Air Force, was activated with Arnold as commander and his staff members doubling in similar roles. The new unit of B-29s reported directly not to the army but to the JCS, a small but significant step in making the Air Forces a separate wing of the military. Engine problems continued to plague the plane. "The engine-fire stories were not overdone," said one pilot, "and if anything they were underplayed. I had more two- and three-engine time on the B-29 than I had with all four engines running."[34]

After numerous missions from fields in India and China, the B-29s made their first raid against Japan on June 15, 1944. The target was the ironworks at Yawata, which the press called the "Pittsburgh of Japan." Japanese radar detected the approach of the sixty-eight bombers, and the activity grew frantic. "Signals were starting to crescendo until my earphones were whining as if a thousand devils were screaming in unison at us," reported a lieutenant monitoring the activity. "It was an eerie feeling to know that far below our every move was being carefully plotted on scopes and plotting boards." Flak damaged six bombers, and sixteen fighters were spotted, but only three fired and all missed. Four bombers were lost, one from flak fire and the others from accidents. One of the crashed planes took the life of *Newsweek* reporter Bill Shenkel as well as the crew.[35]

The damage to Yawata was minor but the public relations value of the first raid on Japan was immense. In carefully worded statements the JCS gave a surprised public not only news of the raid but their first official information on the B-29 itself. Marshall said that the raid "introduces a new type of offensive against our enemy." Arnold praised the new plane but cautioned people that "The Superfortress is not going to win the war by itself . . . It goes directly into battle from the production lines and we have a lot to learn before its full power may be developed." An overenthusiastic congressman muddied the waters by informing the House that the planes "have successfully bombed Tokyo in a very heavy raid." Despite his gaffe, the B-29 had made its public debut, and much more was expected from it.[36]

Although the plane would experience more hard times ahead, the $3 billion gamble had panned out. In March 1945 the 2,000th B-29 rolled off the assembly line. Wellwood Beall offered the last word on the subject. "The B-29 had to work," he said with a wry smile. "If it hadn't, there would be a new engineering department at Boeing, and, I imagine, a new crop of air generals in the Pentagon."[37]

WHILE WORK ON the B-29 went forward, an even larger and more ambitious project was launched to create the most destructive weapon ever made. In a time of endless secrets, it was the most secretive project under way and the most expensive except for the B-29. Although it swallowed huge sums of money that Congress had to allocate, Stimson did not inform its leaders of what the project involved until June 1944. Even then several basic questions overhung the entire effort. Would the weapon, the most novel and complex technical challenge ever attempted, prove feasible? If so, could it be completed in time to be used in the war? If so, should it even be used? If so, how and against whom? The first two issues were purely technical, the last two political and moral ones.

The project's roots went back to October 1939, when Roosevelt received through economist Alexander Sachs a letter signed by Albert Einstein warning that the Germans were developing an extremely powerful bomb. Roosevelt summoned Pa Watson and said, "Pa, this requires action." An advisory committee on uranium was set up but made little progress, and the issue remained dormant until the abrupt end of the phony war galvanized the need for action. In June 1940 Roosevelt had created NDRC, and the uranium advisory committee operated under it. Hitler's stunning conquests, and the progress their German colleagues had made in the field, filled a group of American scientists, especially the European refugees, with alarm. "Although we hardly grasped the revolutionary possibilities at the time," Vannevar Bush said later, "the threat of a possible atomic bomb was in all our minds."[38]

That same month Bush managed to eliminate the military members from the advisory committee and change it into a scientific group with its own funding. Still little progress was made, but Hitler's growing power created a need for some way to convert scientific research into practical military technologies. In June 1941 Bush persuaded Roosevelt to create a new body, the Office of Scientific Research and Development (OSRD), to oversee NDRC, which was reduced to an advisory group, and another new entity, the Committee on Medical Research. Bush helped Rosenman draft the executive order and moved from head of NDRC to director of OSRD with James Conant as his second in command and chairman of NDRC. Under the new arrangement OSRD could push projects all the way through the engineering stages. The uranium advisory committee took on the innocuous new name of S-1 and an expanded mission as an operating body. Conant served as chairman of its executive committee and did the heavy administrative lifting for Bush.[39]

The British had their own committee, which bore the quaint name of MAUD, delving into the possibilities of an atomic weapon. That summer Bush learned of its two reports, including the conclusion that "release of atomic energy on a large scale is possible and that conditions can be chosen which would make it a very powerful weapon of war." Already he had been lobbying Wallace, the one cabinet member who knew something about technology. On October 9 he met with Roosevelt and Wallace and reviewed for them the MAUD report and its conclusion that a bomb could be built before the war's end. Although Bush knew little about the German program, he talked of its progress and possibilities. Roosevelt got the message. He ordered work on a bomb "expedited . . . in every way possible" and all discussion of policy limited to a new top group of himself, Wallace, Bush, Conant, Stimson, and Marshall. Nothing definite would be done without the president's express approval. He alone would decide whether such a bomb would be built, and Congress was to know nothing of the project.[40]

On November 27 Bush delivered to Roosevelt a copy of the third report by a National Academy of Sciences committee headed by physicist Arthur Compton. In terse language it concluded that "*a fission bomb of superlative destructive power will result from bringing quickly together a sufficient mass of element U235. This seems to be as sure as any untried prediction based upon theory and experiment can be.*" Going even further, the report warned, "The possibility must be seriously considered that within a few years the use of bombs such as described here, or something similar using uranium fission, may determine military superiority." Neither Roosevelt nor the JCS nor anyone in the cabinet understood a thing about the science involved, but they got the point. The report confirmed both MAUD and the president's decision based on it.[41]

Money would be needed, lots of it. "To get this money and yet maintain secrecy was a problem which Harold Smith and the President had to solve," Wallace observed. They managed it by creating the nation's first secret weapons budget and then later by burying much of the bomb's cost in the annual budget of the Army Corps of Engineers. The army would run the project because it had the most experience with large-scale construction work. Within OSRD the revitalized S-1 would take charge of the research. No commitment was yet made to build a bomb; Bush's task was to organize the work of discovering whether it could be done. Although Bush did not know it, the Germans had a lead of about two years over the American effort.[42]

The task of S-1 was twofold. It had first to determine whether atomic bombs could be built, and if so, how quickly. If they could, the larger project of building them had to be undertaken. This work had two distinct parts: creating an adequate amount of fissionable material and then finding ways to incorporate it in bombs. At the committee's first meeting on December 6 Bush handed out assignments to some members. Each one had a free hand to choose personnel and places for his work. They agreed to meet every two weeks to compare notes on progress and firm up plans for future work.[43]

One day after the meeting Pearl Harbor cleared the air of doubt and gave the mission fresh clarity and urgency. "Gone was the confusion of objectives," wrote the project's official historians. "Gone too was the old day of leisurely research with its almost mystical faith that society could depend on the largely undirected, unplanned, and capriciously financed efforts of lonely toilers in the scientific vineyards. Gone was the hesitation, so pronounced just two short years before, to spend public money on the theories of a few research men. American science would never be the same. The United States would never be the same. The world would never be the same."[44]

Two very different projects had to be pursued. Teams of scientists had to figure out how to turn theories into a usable weapon, and a cluster of large, secret new facilities had to be built for their experimental work. Bush had already decided to turn management of the entire project over to the army. The Engineers Corps had the competence to do the construction work, and it would be far easier to secure funds through army channels. Marshall put Major General Wilhelm D. Styer in charge of the project. "I never had the pleasure of working with a more competent and broad-minded officer," said Bush afterward. On June 17, 1942, he sent Roosevelt a detailed report on the program with his belief that it was possible to make a bomb that could be used in combat and that it might be ready before the war's end. Roosevelt approved the report, and the pace of development quickened.[45]

The next day Styer ordered Colonel James C. Marshall to create a new engineer district for the project. It received the cover name Manhattan Engineer District (MED) because Marshall made his headquarters in New York City. In time it became known simply as the Manhattan Project. In his briefing Marshall was told that scientists wished to pursue four different methods for producing fissionable materials in quantity and that his job was to build facilities for them with a budget of $90 million. "I spent the night without sleep trying to figure out what this was all about," recalled Marshall. "I had never heard of atomic fission, but I did know that you could not build much of a plant, much less four of them, for $90,000,000."[46]

While Marshall got his work under way, the scientists continued work on a puzzle in which practical knowledge still lagged well behind theory.

Nuclear fission had been discovered in 1938, and insights into its nature had been rapid since then, including the concept of a chain reaction capable of unleashing tremendous power. The key element was uranium, but its natural state could not serve as the basis for a chain reaction unless it was purged of the isotope U-238 and reduced to pure U-235. In February 1941 a team headed by chemist Glenn T. Seaborg discovered a promising new element that became known as plutonium or Pu-239, but even less was known about it.[47]

Uranium consists of a mixture of U-238 and U-235 atoms that occur in nature at a 140:1 ratio. Capturing neutrons by U-235 atoms causes the fission that creates a chain reaction. The neutrons captured by U-238 atoms produce plutonium. Fission propels the emitted neutrons out at very high speed. A U-235 atom undergoing fission emits an average of 2.56 neutrons. In uranium metal most of these neutrons get captured by the U-238 and too few get caught by the U-235 to keep the reaction going. If the neutrons were slowed down, the U-235 would have a better chance of capturing them and prolonging the chain reaction. The neutrons could be slowed by embedding the uranium in some material or "moderator," the two most useful of which were graphite and heavy water.[48]

Plutonium was the wild card in the project. After the December 6 meeting Bush, Conant, and Compton went to lunch at the Cosmos Club in Washington. During the table talk Compton suggested giving more thought to producing plutonium as an alternative to separating U-235. It might be done, he added, through operation of a pile, putting its contents through chemical reactions to separate plutonium from the uranium. Bush pointed out the obvious difficulties of trying to utilize a process completely unknown to industry and which had not yet even been shown to be possible in the laboratory. Conant, himself a chemist, reminded Compton that the chemistry of plutonium itself was unknown. However, they agreed that it was worth a try. A few weeks later Bush authorized Compton to construct a pile at Chicago.[49]

Little was known about the properties of pure U-235 as well, and isotope separation was fiendishly difficult. The scientists decided to explore four possible methods: centrifuge, electromagnetic separation, gaseous diffusion, and thermal diffusion. Eger Murphree headed the centrifuge project, which did not pan out, and helped lead the gaseous diffusion work at Columbia University. Philip Abelson directed research on thermal diffusion first at the Carnegie Institution and then at the Naval Research Laboratory. Ernest O. Lawrence of the University of California at Berkeley, already renowned for his invention of the cyclotron, had his team investigate electromagnetic separation. The scientists also needed to find the most suitable moderator. Two lines of research were pursued. Harold Urey at Columbia continued his work on heavy water while Compton brought his team of scientists to the

University of Chicago to study reactors using graphite as a moderator. Bush and Conant also gave Compton another daunting task, that of devising the bomb itself.[50]

"We had, in effect, told Bush that since we could not decide on which of four horses to place our bet," said Conant, "all four should be kept in the race, though we thought they might be running neck and neck until the final lap." As it happened, only the centrifuge method dropped out early. The program chiefs met with Styer on May 23, 1942, and estimated that facilities needed would cost about $80 million with $34 million in annual operating costs. They projected July 1, 1944, as the date by which a few bombs might be produced. When Conant asked why construction could not be speeded up, Murphree, an experienced chemical engineer, replied, "Doctor, you can't spend that much money any faster." Bush took the cost and time estimates to Roosevelt, who approved them even though a huge financial commitment was involved along with scarce materials, equipment, and manpower.[51]

Shortly after the May meeting Bush dissolved S-1 and replaced it with an S-1 executive committee composed of Lawrence, Urey, Compton, Murphree, Lyman J. Briggs, who had headed the original uranium committee, and Conant as chairman. They would survey the technical progress while the army took charge of process development, engineering design, materials procurement, and site selection. Marshall had neither the time nor authority to recruit his staff from beyond his own limited circle of officers. He found one gem in balding, bespectacled Lieutenant Colonel Kenneth D. Nichols, who was only thirty-four but had already graduated from West Point, earned a doctorate in hydraulic engineering at Iowa State, studied civil engineering in American and German universities, and gained practical experience in two large-scale construction projects under Marshall. His academic background and understanding of the Engineers Corps enabled him to work smoothly with the scientists.[52]

Through the summer of 1942 Marshall and Nichols struggled in vain to push the construction project forward. At every turn they were stymied by the priority system. Despite Roosevelt's endorsement, they received only an AA-3 rating at a time when higher rankings were multiplying and materials were scarce. At the same time, no clear relationship had been established between the army and S-1 over who was to do exactly what. Some scientists resented the army's taking control, the more so as progress on building facilities lagged. A large site seventeen miles west of Knoxville, Tennessee, had been selected as suitable, but Marshall hesitated to purchase it until he had more evidence that the research was far enough advanced to justify the enormous project. He insisted on doing things in an orderly manner, however much time it took.[53]

By September Bush and his team were at their wit's end over the lack of progress. Convinced that stronger leadership was needed, Bush talked the problem over with Brehon Somervell, who offered his own solution. He wanted to place the entire operation, including the research, under the Corps of Engineers, reducing S-1 to advisers, and give it a strong leader with clear authority to get things done. Without informing Bush he chose Colonel Leslie R. Groves, who was just finishing his oversight of the construction of the Pentagon and was expert at handling large-scale projects. Groves had just been offered an attractive post overseas and was eager to accept. Somervell informed him that he had been chosen instead for a much more important position. When Groves said he didn't want to stay in Washington, Somervell replied, "If you do the job right, it will win the war."[54]

A jowly figure with blue eyes, a slender mustache, and an expanding waistline, Groves had graduated fourth in his West Point class of 1918 and served in Hawaii, Europe, and Central America. One subordinate described him as "a tremendous lone wolf." Nichols regarded him as "the biggest sonovabitch I've ever met in my life, but also one of the most capable individuals. He had an ego second to none, he had tireless energy . . . He had absolute confidence in his decisions and he was absolutely ruthless in how he approached a problem to get it done. But that was the beauty of working for him—that you never had to worry about the decisions being made or what it meant . . . I hated his guts and so did everybody else but we had our form of understanding."[55]

He was, in short, the ideal man for the job, but the surprised Bush had his doubts at first. Groves recalled that Bush "was quite mystified about just where I fitted into the picture and what right I had to be asking the questions I was asking." After this awkward start Bush soon warmed to Groves's ability. The new arrangement was confirmed at what Stimson called "a very important meeting on S-1" in his office on September 23, 1942. Bush, Groves, and Rear Admiral W. R. Purnell would serve as a Military Policy Committee (MPC) with Bush as chairman. Conant would serve as Bush's alternate, and Groves formally took charge of the entire project. That same day his promotion to brigadier general also became official. It was intended to give him more clout with the scientists. Already he suspected that "the prerogatives of rank were more important in the academic world than they are among soldiers." It was also decided to replace him on the MPC with Styer, a change that Groves did not mind.[56]

Never one to stand on ceremony, Groves got started even before his promotion arrived. On September 19 he visited Donald Nelson, stressed the importance of the project without revealing details, and laid out his case for a top priority ranking. Nelson said no. In that case, said Groves, he would have to urge the president to abandon the project because the WPB refused to co-operate in its needs. It was a bluff, but it worked; Nelson reversed himself and gave him a letter authorizing a top priority for whatever materials or equipment the project needed. After the September 23 meeting Groves boarded a train for Tennessee to inspect the site that still had not been purchased. He found it to be more ideal than anyone had suspected. It had ample water from the Clinch River, an easy connection to TVA power, adequate rail service, decent roads to Knoxville, and no towns or villages. The 56,000-acre site was isolated and would force only about a thousand people to relocate. A series of mountain ridges would help shield the spread of any damage an explosion might cause.[57]

On this barren site arose a frontier town that evolved steadily into a small city. Known first as the Clinton Engineer Works, because Clinton was the nearest town, and as "Site X," it soon took the name Oak Ridge because it lay on the slopes of Black Oak Ridge. Clearing of the land began in October 1942 for construction of a village for a projected population of 13,000. By May 1945 the wilderness town would house 75,000 people and the complex would employ a total of 82,000 workers. The entire site was fenced off, and every entrance had a guardhouse. No one except employees could enter without permission. Governor Prentice Cooper remained uninformed about the restrictions until a junior officer was unwisely dispatched to show him the presidential proclamation authorizing the action. Cooper ripped it up angrily and sent the officer packing. The government, he growled, had stolen the farmers' land and not reimbursed the counties for roads and bridges. He denounced the whole project as "an experiment in socialism" by New Dealers under the guise of a war facility.[58]

Along with building a town from scratch, the contractors started work on the reasons for it all: an electromagnetic plant, gaseous-diffusion plant, thermal-diffusion plant, and the first plutonium-producing pile with its chemical-separating buildings. No one outside the complex had the foggiest idea of what went on at Oak Ridge, nor did the army of workers who trooped through the gates every day. By the end of 1943 that army numbered 20,000 and had swamped housing both inside and outside the complex. Like other war industries, Oak Ridge suffered from a high turnover rate; by mid-1943 four people came and went for every one that stayed. The residents of Oak Ridge endured all sorts of hardships, shortages, and inconveniences as well as the hostility of people in neighboring towns, who saw a huge and constant pile of goods flow into the town and assumed the residents were immune from shortages.[59]

"Tons and tons of stuff goes in," said one local, "and nothing ever comes out." Another local, who quit at Oak Ridge in 1944 and went back to selling eggs, explained why he left. "There they were, all those thousands of people. They were all getting good money, same as I was. And there were more buildings than you can imagine, and a lot of new roads and a lot of other things, and they were costing a heap of money. I thought it over . . . long and hard. And to tell you the truth, I had in mind that whatever it was the government was making over there, it would be cheaper if they went out and bought it."[60]

OAK RIDGE WAS not the only new facility rising in the wilderness. Assuming that U-235 or plutonium could be produced in sufficient quantity, a delivery system had to be designed and tested in utmost secrecy. This task posed an enormous design, research, and engineering challenge in itself. A special weapons laboratory, located in some remote area, would be needed. To oversee the physics of bomb development, Compton chose the brilliant but controversial California physicist J. Robert Oppenheimer. As Oppenheimer defined his charge, "The first job was to make the stuff. But in the hope that it would come out all right, we had to have a place where we could learn what to do with it." Groves approved the choice, saying, "I was unable to find anyone else who was available who I felt would do as well."[61]

Oppenheimer happened to own a ranch in New Mexico and suggested some remote areas around Albuquerque. In October 1942 Major John Dudley was ordered to "make a survey for an installation of an unnamed purpose" at a site in a thinly settled region where 250 to 450 people could live and work in isolation. After a couple of false starts Dudley, Groves, and Oppenheimer settled on a 790-acre property occupied by the Los Alamos Ranch School some twenty miles northwest of Santa Fe, the nearest town of any size. The water supply was adequate, the isolation superb, the scenery magnificent, and the owners eager to sell. Since the government owned much of the surrounding land, expansion posed no problem. Adjacent canyons offered ideal space for safe testing of the weapon.[62]

Moving quickly, the army in November bought the school along with some surrounding acreage, acquired the rights to government forest and grazing lands, and hired a contractor who agreed to complete the living quarters, laboratories, and other buildings as well as fencing the entire facility by May 1943. The urgency, said Oppenheimer, "started at the beginning and never let up." In all the complex embraced 54,000 acres, almost the same size as Oak Ridge. Work at what was called "Site Y" or "the Hill" began in December 1942. Originally planned as an army facility until some of the physicists balked at being put into uniforms, Los Alamos was ultimately run by the University of California under contract with the War Department.

Even more than Oak Ridge, which had its large army of workers, it became a community shrouded in secrecy. The birth certificates of babies born there listed PO Box 1663 in Santa Fe as their place of birth. As at Oak Ridge, too, tons of supplies flowed into the place but nothing ever came out.[63]

Still another large and remote site was needed for actual production of whatever materials proved satisfactory for a bomb. Oak Ridge was too small and too close to Knoxville for safety's sake. The site required a large, reliable supply of cool water and access to a huge amount of electricity, at least 100,000 kilowatts of it. After inspecting several sites, Groves's engineers settled on a broad, flat valley in a large bend of the Columbia River near the village of Hanford, Washington. A facility there could draw power from the Bonneville and Grand Coulee dams. Beginning in February 1943, the government began acquiring land in what proved to be the largest amount ever—nearly half a million acres for what was designated as "Site W." Much larger reactors would be built there to produce plutonium even though experiments had so far turned out only tiny amounts of it and no superior method of production had been established. As late as December 1943 only two milligrams of plutonium had been made.[64]

Construction of this massive complex took place under three rules: safety against known and unknown hazards; certainty of operation; and utmost saving of time. "The complications were many," Groves recalled, "for many pieces of equipment weighing as much as 250,000 pounds each had to be assembled with tolerances more suitable for high-grade watchmaking." Ten months of design work went into the shielding for the pile before construction could even begin. Local sensitivities also had to be honored. The cooling water leaving the pile would contain radioactive materials that could harm the salmon in the Columbia River. An engineer warned Groves that "whatever you may accomplish, you will incur the everlasting enmity of the entire Northwest if you harm a single scale on a single salmon." Groves declared later that the project met this challenge. Later developments proved this to be far from the case, but in 1943 the war effort overrode all other considerations. Concerns over environmental impact, and it was severe, would belong to another generation.[65]

At Hanford, as at Oak Ridge, an instant city sprang up from virtually nothing. Even more than at Oak Ridge, its residents were walled off from the outside world behind gates, barbed-wire fences, and guard posts. To outside eyes, had there been any, Hanford and Los Alamos looked like the most ordinary of small towns, but the residents and the work they did were anything but ordinary. As Groves told his fellow officers when convening a meeting of them in 1944, "At great expense we have gathered on this mesa the largest collection of crackpots ever seen." Their job was to take good care of the crackpots, and it did not prove an easy one.[66]

THE PLUTONIUM PROJECT had its roots in a fourth facility, the Metallurgical Laboratory (Met Lab) at the University of Chicago, which had been working on it since the spring of 1942. After surveying existing facilities and talking at length with the lead scientists, Groves concluded that the project's first effort should be to develop a method of plutonium production. He had also come to appreciate the enormous scale of the undertaking and the need for one large contracting firm to handle the engineering, construction, and management of the new facilities. Having worked for years with DuPont, he decided to recruit that company for the production of plutonium. Conant and the MPC agreed, as did Compton, who headed the Met Lab, but many of his physicists and staff objected strongly to bringing in an industrial firm. "They simply did not comprehend the immensity of the engineering, construction, and operating problems that had to be overcome," said Groves.[67]

Especially was this true of the European scientists, who distrusted large industrial corporations, and DuPont was one of the largest. "We don't need this great organization," protested Enrico Fermi, one of the outstanding physicists at Met Lab. "They are just too conservative." Claiming that he could design the reactors in half the time it would take DuPont, he added, "If you people will hire for me the laborers and supply them with brick, I'll tell them where to lay it." Others expected to be given complete control of the project. "The scientists all worked their heads off," said Nichols, "but they always thought they knew how to do everything." DuPont did not even want the entire responsibility and had to be persuaded to do it in the name of patriotism. When Walter Carpenter, DuPont's president, finally agreed, he rejected the contract offered him with a fixed fee, saying the company wanted no pay or profit from the project.[68]

Fermi was a decent engineer and had the task of constructing the first small experimental pile at Met Lab. Compton stumbled on a promising site known as the Argonne Forest about twenty miles southwest of Chicago, and Nichols negotiated with the county for use of the land. When a strike stalled the contractor's progress in the fall of 1942, Fermi asked Compton to let him build the pile in a building that housed a squash court under the stands of Stagg Field at the University of Chicago. Given how little was known about chain reactions, the potential risk was enormous if an accident occurred. Compton decided the risk was minimal compared to the gain and chose not to inform the university's president of his decision. "Based on considerations of the University's welfare the only answer he could have given would have been—no," Compton wrote later. "And this answer would have been wrong."[69]

Beginning on November 16, work by improvised crews went forward in two twelve-hour shifts. A pile was literally that: layers of graphite supported by brick with slots for control rods. Shivering in the unheated building, blackened by graphite dust that also made every surface slippery, the crews completed the fifty-seventh and final layer on December 1 and trudged wearily off to bed. The new breeding ground for neutrons and plutonium held nearly 400 tons of graphite, 50 tons of uranium oxide, and 6 tons of uranium metal. It cost about $1 million, all for what amounted to an experiment to see whether a chain reaction could be produced, and it lacked both shields and a cooling system. Fermi was confident that the reaction would occur and that he could control it. Asked what he would do if he was wrong, he said simply, "I would walk away—leisurely."[70]

December 2 dawned bitterly cold and raw. It was the second day of gas rationing and the eve of Chanukah, an especially poignant time since the State Department had just announced that 2 million Jews had perished and 5 million more were in jeopardy. A review committee, on its way east from visiting Lawrence's laboratory in California, stopped between trains to meet with the Met Lab people and asked why Fermi was not present. Compton told them he was busy with an experiment. After the meeting Compton received a call saying that Fermi was ready to begin the experiment. He hurried over to observe from a balcony above the squash court. One man stood ready to handle the control rods. Three others, jokingly called the "suicide squad," prepared to toss buckets of cadmium solution over the pile if the reaction could not be stopped. Still another held an ax to cut the rope holding a safety rod if the reaction grew with sudden violence. A small group of men, following the experiment by remote control, waited behind a concrete wall to throw in "safety rods" if something happened to the people inside the building.[71]

Slowly, deliberately, the rods were withdrawn as Fermi checked the readings of his instruments. The tedious process went on until midafternoon, when only the final rod remained. Step by step it was removed until it reached a point where the next movement should allow a chain reaction to develop on an expanding scale. Fermi gave the order, the rod was drawn out another foot, and the counters registering the rays from the pile began clicking faster and faster until to Compton it sounded like a rattle. Different meters showed the same result: a rising level of radiation reaching the balcony. "The reaction is self-sustaining," said Fermi. He ordered the safety rods thrown in; the rattle died down to an infrequent click and the meters dropped back to zero.

Aware that everyone was exhausted, Fermi said calmly, "We'll call it a day. Lock the control rods in the safety position and come back tomorrow morning. Then we'll start the new series of experiments."[72]

Groves was en route to the Pacific Coast and could not be reached, but Compton hurried to his office and called Conant. "Jim," he said, "you'll be interested to know that the Italian navigator has just landed in the new world."

"Is that so," said an excited Conant. "Were the natives friendly?"

"Everyone landed safe and happy."[73]

So little had happened, and yet everything had happened. A chain reaction had occurred and been controlled. For four and a half minutes men had harnessed the release of energy from the atomic nucleus. Many more months of hard, intensive work filled with doubts, dead ends, and discouragements lay ahead, but a start had been made. A chain reaction was no longer a mere theory and the possibility of its control wishful thinking. The face of war was about to undergo the most profound change in its long and bloody history.

CHAPTER 30

DAYS OF RECKONING

The year 1944 was the great year of decision, the year of omens and portents, the year that swung like a gate to the future.

—BRUCE CATTON [1]

I am inclined to be charitable when I think of what D-Day means to Franklin D. Roosevelt, of the years since the "quarantine" speech in which he tried to awaken the American people to their danger and to gird them against enemies they so long refused to recognize. How different it would have been could we have gone into France before it fell; how much easier our task . . . How poorly prepared we were in 1941 to resist, and how poorly prepared we are even today to understand.

—I. F. STONE [2]

Many people seem to believe that this is the time for the seventh-inning stretch, and while they're stretching, the Nazis are digging in.

—BREHON SOMERVELL [3]

IT WAS THE DAY EVERYONE MOST wanted to see and awaited anxiously without knowing exactly when it would be. The day that many people thought would settle the war in Europe or at least determine whether the end was near or still farther away. The day for which the military and a huge portion of America's productive capacity had worked furiously to prepare, and for which the mightiest host ever assembled in one place had been gathered. It had been a long time coming, and it finally arrived on June 6.

For days Eleanor Roosevelt thought everyone seemed to be "suspended in space, waiting for the invasion, dreading it and yet wishing it could begin successfully." Grace Tully saw the strain in her boss. "Every movement of his face and hands," she recalled, "reflected the tightly contained state of his nerves." On the eve of the assault the president delivered a fireside chat to announce the capture of Rome after four months of savage fighting. "The first of the Axis capitals is now in our hands," he chortled. "One up and two to go!" But the other two would come much harder, and now he waited nervously to learn whether the first step on the road to Berlin had been achieved. Even as he spoke, he knew that troops were already crossing the English Channel.[4]

The armada supporting the invasion dwarfed anything that had come before. The 900 warships included 9 battleships, 23 heavy cruisers, 104 destroyers along with minesweepers, antisubmarine boats, gunboats, PT boats, and transports bearing 1,500 landing craft built by Andrew Higgins. The spectacle, coupled with the extensive marine landings in the Pacific, made a cruel joke of the old controversy over the navy's reluctance to order landing craft. In the changing face of war the unwanted boats had become the indispensable vehicle for getting at both enemies. So concerned had the Allied high command become over them that Dwight Eisenhower said of Higgins, "When he is buried, his coffin should be in the shape of a landing craft, as they are practically killing him with worry."[5]

At 4:00 A.M. on the sixth Roosevelt asked the White House operator to summon every member of the White House staff except Harry Hopkins, who was convalescing in an army hospital. Once the news went public, church bells tolled, school bells rang, factories blasted their whistles, stores closed, sporting events were canceled, and people poured into the streets as if a great victory had been won rather than a bare toehold secured on the European continent. A record 181 newsmen crowded into the president's press conference that afternoon. "Most of the President's official family, from Fala to Judge Rosenman, seemed to be with him," observed I. F. Stone, who was there, ". . . waiting in a kind of holiday mood to watch the old maestro handle the press. The President was happy and confident but tired, and he has aged."[6]

That night Roosevelt went on radio to offer not a speech but a simple prayer in which he asked all Americans to join. Anna and her husband helped him write it. Sammy the Rose, who watched the talk, thought "deep religious faith was apparent in his voice and in his countenance." Stone dismissed the prayer as "a gauche affair, addressing God in a familiar, conversational, and explanatory tone, as if it were a fireside chat beamed at heaven." Roosevelt well knew, as did most of his listeners, that the day of reckoning marked not an end but only a beginning, but they hoped fervently that it was at least the beginning of the end.[7]

As the press conference closed, Stone asked the president what his hopes for the future were on this great day. "Well, you know what it is," replied Roosevelt. "It's win the war and win it a hundred percent."[8]

Three weeks after the horrors of the landing, nearly a million men had been put ashore along with 171,532 vehicles of all kinds and 566,000 tons of supplies. "As far as you can see in every direction the ocean was infested with ships," wrote correspondent Ernie Pyle during the landing. "There must have been every type of ocean-going vessel in the world." Besides the warships Pyle saw luxury liners serving as troop transports, Liberty ships, converted yachts, river boats, tugs, and barges. He went ashore on Omaha Beach the next morning. By then only sniping, some artillery fire, and the occasional explosion of a mine jarred the air; the hard fighting had moved inland.[9]

Walking around the beach, Pyle found a far uglier picture. Bodies lay in rows and still littered the sand or floated in the water. "The wreckage was vast and startling," he noted. ". . . There were trucks tipped half over and swamped, partly sunken barges, and the angled-up corners of jeeps, and small landing craft half submerged . . . On the beach itself, high and dry, were all kinds of wrecked vehicles. There were tanks that had only just made the beach before being knocked out . . . jeeps that had burned to a dull gray . . . boats stacked on top of each other, their sides caved in." Most poignant of all to Pyle was the personal debris—cigarette packs, writing paper, Bibles, socks, sewing kits, snapshots, toothbrushes—"extended in a thin little line, just like a high-water mark, for miles along the beach." The overall scene appalled him. "On the beach lay expended sufficient men and mechanism for a small war. They were gone forever now."[10]

Ghastly as the scene was, Pyle found another message in the ruins. "And yet, we could afford it," he added. "We could afford it because we were on, we had our toehold, and behind us there were such enormous replacements for this wreckage on the beach that you could hardly conceive of the sum total. Men and equipment were flowing from England in such a gigantic stream that it made the waste on the beachhead seem like nothing at all, really nothing at all." Standing on a bluff a few hundred yards up the beach, he gazed across the water at "the greatest armada man has ever seen. You simply could not believe the gigantic collection of ships that lay out there waiting to unload."[11]

To FEED THE enormous and growing demands of the European and Pacific wars, American factories continued to pour out munitions in record amounts. Even the much-maligned Willow Run finally began producing B-24 bombers at a rate of one every sixty-three minutes. In all its 42,000 workers turned out 8,685 planes. In 1944 the 96,318 planes rolling out of factories exceeded the combined output of Britain, Germany, and Japan that year. By then America was producing 60 percent of all Allied munitions and 40 percent of the world's total arms. Lend-Lease got 15.2 percent of the planes in 1943 and 16.2

percent in 1944. Of the 34,500 planes shipped to the Allies, Russia received 13,300 and Great Britain 9,500. "By the beginning of 1945," said Don Nelson with a touch of whimsy, "planes were flying out of Uncle Sam's star-spangled costume like a plague of moths."[12]

The war had pulled the American economy out of the mud of depression and pushed it to new heights of production. Aluminum capacity had increased 700 percent, steel capacity 15 percent—this in an industry that for six out of ten prewar years had operated at half capacity or less. Machine tools were produced at three times the volume of the entire prewar decade combined. Where Britain had under much greater pressure increased output by 20 percent, the United States had by 1944 doubled its production since 1939. Despite the wartime shortages, some economists claimed that the standard of living was one sixth higher than in 1939. Crowded stores reported retail sales of $63 billion, a record dollar peak. In 1943 the nation had produced $84 billion in munitions and $90 billion in consumer goods and services, a record even allowing for inflation.[13]

The industrial landscape had been utterly transformed. Huge new plants had been thrown up—not only the behemoths like Willow Run, Chrysler's Tank Arsenal, and Chrysler's airplane engine plant but dozens of massive facilities like the aircraft factories in Wichita, Fort Wayne, and Oklahoma City, munitions plants of all kinds scattered across the continent, aluminum plants, steel works, and a host of others, including the monster facilities for the Manhattan Project. Existing factories had been enlarged and modernized. As *Time* observed, "Plants from which men used to retire at 45 because of hernia were now fit places for women to work." By 1944 some $20 billion had been invested in new industrial facilities of all kinds, $16 billion of it by the government. What would happen to all this new capacity at war's end? "It is no problem to shrink from," cautioned *Time*. "The name of that problem is Plenty."[14]

By 1944, too, a new day of reckoning seemed to be approaching. Already the military had begun canceling some contracts and cutting back orders. Workers started to fear for their jobs and grow apprehensive about what the future held for them. A new term, unthinkable only a year earlier, gained rapid currency in the national vocabulary: reconversion. How would the economy convert back to peacetime production? How soon and how fast? One business executive offered a gloomy but widely held prediction as he cleared his desk at the end of 1943: "Next month unemployment begins."[15]

The ax fell first not in January but in May, with embattled Brewster Aeronautical the first plane maker to feel the blow. Henry Kaiser had finally got the company back into reasonable production of navy Corsairs and was preparing to turn the company back to the navy, but on May 22 the navy cut

Brewster's contract in half and said it would accept no more of the company's planes after July 1. Attrition of the planes had been less than expected, a navy spokesman explained. It was cutting back production, and Brewster was first on the list because it was the last firm to produce Corsairs and had a low output rate. The 12,500 workers about to lose their jobs staged a mock sit-in at the company's two plants. The laid-off workers did not lack prospects; WMC said it had lined up more than enough jobs for all of them. But the new offers paid 60 to 70 cents an hour compared to the $1.06 they had earned at Brewster and found few takers.[16]

The workers announced that they would remain at their stations until work was given them. Labor leaders won public support in demanding that such cutbacks be planned so as to minimize their impact on employment. No one wanted a repeat of the World War I experience where contracts were abruptly canceled without warning. To alleviate the crisis, Brewster received a new contract, but the impact lingered. Many war workers could not help but wonder whether the Brewster incident was a preview of coming difficulties.[17]

A FEW VISIONARIES thought about reconversion well in advance, when others thought it unseemly if not downright unpatriotic to do so. As early as December 1942, when industry was still gearing up for wartime production, Henry Kaiser dumbfounded his listeners at a National Association of Manufacturers dinner by saying, "The problems of peace are already at hand." In April 1943 Nelson, amid all his other travails, summoned Ernest Kanzler back from Detroit and asked him to do an extensive study of reconversion. The report he completed in June amounted to an outline of the problems involved once war production began tapering off but was in no way an action program. That September Nelson ordered Stacy May to make a broad study of reconversion. Hiland Batcheller, the operations vice chairman of WPB, undertook a study of the agency's limitation and conservation orders so that they might be removed in an orderly manner once controls of scarce war materials and facilities were no longer needed.[18]

Postwar planning was by no means confined to the government. As early as March 1943 Newsweek called it "the most popular intellectual pastime in the United States today." That same month the magazine launched a new section called "Postwar Horizons" dedicated to examining the problems and prospects of the postwar world. The Twentieth Century Fund calculated that no less than 150 agencies, public and private were devoted to the subject to some degree, a figure that did not include state or regional bodies, individual companies making their own plans, or informal groups engaged in discussing postwar problems. Within the government Henry Wallace was viewed as the "intellectual leader and the spokesman for Administration postwar planning."[19]

Reconversion posed far more difficult problems than mobilization. The goal of the latter was clear, simple, and direct: convert as many resources as fast as possible to the one task of producing as many munitions of all kinds as possible. Debate arose over how many of which goods to turn out, but not over whether it should be done. Reconversion raised fiercely controversial questions over what to do, when to do it, and how to go about it. Far from being clear and direct, the goal was the most treacherous and divisive issue of all. Convert the economy back to—what? The status quo ante bellum? An improved version seeking to eliminate the weaknesses that plagued the pre-war economy? Some more powerful vision of a better society grounded in lessons learned from the war? Any one of a dozen variations on these themes?

Liberals wanted some version of the better society, conservatives and businessmen a return to the status quo. The military had its own, more immediate agenda. It insisted that any action on reconversion be kept locked in the closet and all resources devoted entirely to the war effort until victory was achieved. So powerful was its influence that the debate over reconversion shifted early from that of goals to when and how to do it. As the controversy marched to its climax during the summer of 1944, it grew progressively uglier and nastier. In the process it also brought Nelson to his own day of reckoning.

"To a large extent," Nelson wrote ruefully afterward, "the military took control over the economy, and many of the reconversion difficulties which arose later, after Germany and Japan had finally been knocked out, can be traced directly to that fact." Bruce Catton, who served as director of information in WPB and sympathized with Nelson, delivered an even harsher verdict. "We came out of the war, at last, precisely as we went into it—unready, unready in spite of the most elaborate preparations, unready because the price of getting ready was a price which the men at the top simply were unable to pay. The story of 1944 and 1945 is the story of 1940 and 1941 all over again . . . Like that bright phrase, 'all-out defense,' reconversion was a concept which brought the men of destiny squarely up against the limitations imposed by the Old Order . . . The reconversion program, in other words, was a failure . . . In the end it became a showdown between those who were afraid of the future and those who were not."[20]

Everyone agreed that reconversion required early and careful preparation to avoid repeating the disaster following the last war, but agreement ended there. Those like Nelson who showed early concern for the coming transition from war to peace, had to tread carefully. No steps could be taken that might in any way appear to undermine the emphasis on producing everything the military needed to win the war. The basic issues revolved around the extent to which resources no longer needed in the war effort could be shifted to the production of civilian goods. These in turn got embroiled in debates over manpower, materials, civilian morale, and dedication to war production. Timing posed one major problem, administrative feasibility quite another. How was one to determine what could be used to increase civilian production when the military insisted adamantly that it needed every available resource for the war effort?

Roosevelt seemed to share Nelson's concern about an orderly reconversion. In a late July 1943 radio speech he noted that discussion and planning for the transition to peace was not a matter of premature optimism and would be a prodigious task. McNutt adopted the motto that the postwar should include "jobs for all Americans who want to work." Late in August Nelson sent the president a memo giving his views on what would be involved in reconversion. On October 14 Byrnes gathered the agency heads to discuss two key issues of concern: the termination of contracts and disposal of government property once it was no longer needed. The next day Roosevelt announced that OWM would create a special unit to handle postwar adjustment problems. In November the Senate got into the act by setting up a Special Committee on Postwar Economic Policy and Planning with Walter George as chairman. On the fifth a Truman Committee report urged greater attention to reconversion, contract termination, and property disposal.[21]

Byrnes remained a step ahead by announcing on November 4 that Baruch (who else?) would head the special unit and, together with John Hancock, prepare a special report on reconversion. Eight days later he created a Joint Contract Termination Board with Hancock at its head. The unspoken but vital issue at stake involved who would control reconversion. Nelson badly wanted WPB to have the responsibility, Byrnes thought it belonged to OWM, and the military longed to gain control to orchestrate production in its direction. "Washington officialdom has hush-hushed the problem of reconversion," observed the *Saturday Evening Post*. "This is understandable. If Washington talks about making automobiles, refrigerators, passenger cars or washing machines instead of tanks and artillery, then people will get the idea that peace is just around the corner . . . But whether Washington wants to face it or not, the fact remains that reconversion is a hard, inescapable reality."[22]

The army had already begun ordering cutbacks in production of some munitions. In the spring of 1943 the production of tanks and artillery shells was reduced. At the American Car & Foundry plant in Berwick, Pennsylvania, 3,000 of 9,000 workers received layoff notices, prompting a protest from the USWA as to the army's lack of advance notice. The complaints grew shrill in the fall when the Ordnance Department closed six plants that made small-arms ammunition and slashed the workforce at several others, putting more than 35,000 people out of work. One plant at Salt Lake City built by the government in 1941 was told to close up at the year's end. During its first year of operation it had turned out more small-arms ammunition than was produced by all American ordnance plants combined in the last war.[23]

The official explanations were several. Production had far exceeded expectations; by one measure the army had stockpiled more than 2,000 bullets for every Axis soldier. Fewer ammunition ships than expected had been sunk at sea. The superior destructive power of incendiary ordnance had resulted in less use of other types, and changes in strategy had resulted in less use of small-arms ammunition than originally estimated. Tanks too were no longer needed in such large numbers, and production was sliced in half. Later the army would pay dearly for its shortsightedness, but at the time the cutbacks seemed to make sense even if poorly handled. The army assumed blithely that labor discharged in one industry would simply move to others where the need was more urgent, but people, however patriotic, did not change their lives that easily. More than half the workers displaced by the closings were women, many of whom could not just pick up and go elsewhere.[24]

The army's handling of the cutbacks reflected its hard-nosed insensitivity and that of Patterson, who believed adamantly that civilians, in support of the men fighting overseas, should just shut up and do what they were told without complaint. That people should be concerned about what if any jobs they might have and businessmen worry about their prospects and competitive position after the war was indefensible to him. That continued good news from the front should encourage them to think or hope that the war's end was near he found unspeakable. That the peak of munitions output had been reached in November 1943 was no reason to slacken effort or assume that production could simply coast from that point forward. Every fiber of every nerve should be bent toward winning the war without regard to any other consideration.

Stimson was not far behind his aide in this attitude. All Americans, he declared during the hearings on the bill for national service, should be willing "to accept the same liability which a soldier must accept for service to country." He added, his voice rising in anger, "I say we have a situation of anarchy, and this is a step to cure that situation of anarchy and to restore law and order." This statement appalled Catton. "Munitions production had just gone to its all-time high," he wrote. ". . . The people had just shown, by the most fantastic production of goods in all human history, that they could and would do anything that was asked of them—and now they were being told, on the highest authority, in a shrill voice that cracked with emotion, that they were in a state of anarchy, that their selfish irresponsibility was prolonging the war and endangering victory itself, and that the sternest of measures was needed to restore law and order."[25]

Thus were the battle lines drawn in the fight over reconversion. The administration found itself trying to look in two directions at once. "Two different tunes are being sung by official Washington," reported Kiplinger's *Washington Letter* on December 4. "One is that it is unpatriotic to think about the time of the end, for such thinking is bound to divert energies from war production, and every ounce of production lost may cost the lives of many men . . . The other is that it is high time to think about reconversion, which must be undertaken within industry as soon as Germany is beaten, that it is past time when reconversion plans should have been laid . . . What the administration is *talking* is the first view, above. What the administration is *doing* is the second."[26]

As with the rubber report, little could be done until Baruch and Hancock handed their report down from Olympus. Nevertheless, Nelson tried some preliminary moves. At a WPB board meeting on November 30, with approval from Jesse Jones and Paul McNutt, he declared that WPB's official policy, "as manpower, facilities, and materials become available," would be to authorize production of more civilian goods provided it did not "limit production for programs of higher urgency." This was his first formal step toward gaining control of reconversion even before the report appeared. In December Nelson asked an assistant, Bernard L. Gladieux, to draft an organizational plan for handling reconversion. Gladieux responded with a scheme for a subcommittee beneath PEC that would be dominated by civilians and give overall direction of reconversion to the program vice chairman, Julius Krug.[27]

Krug's Program Committee made a modest start toward implementing the November 30 guideline, but the process proved dishearteningly slow and complex. On December 28 Nelson proposed to the WPB board an easing of restrictions on construction of essential civilian facilities such as hospitals, schools, flood-control projects, and railroad equipment, which had been drastically cut since July 1942. Patterson objected at once, saying he was deeply disturbed over the amount of manpower and materials that had already gone into civilian work. When Nelson tried again in January, everyone agreed that restrictions should remain in place until after the invasion. To counter the Gladieux proposal, General Lucius Clay of ASF urged PEC to take responsibility for determining policies "to govern the character, timing, and extent of any expansions or resumption for civilian use consistent with the maintenance of the military programs at peak efficiency."[28]

Clay's proposal was that of the War Department. If carried out, it would in effect eliminate Nelson and deliver responsibility for reconversion to the military and PEC. Meanwhile, Nelson tried to cooperate fully with Baruch by meeting with his assistants and handing over WPB materials, including the reconversion studies already done. On December 29 he wrote Baruch and admitted his distress over "external forces driving a wedge into our personal relationship." In fact, events had long since strained their once-close relationship. Five days later Baruch confided to Stimson that he planned to advise the president to keep Wilson and get rid of Nelson. On January 7 he dispatched a cool reply to Nelson's letter. He had moved closer to the military, which seemed to have appreciated his genius and advice more fully in recent months.[29]

Baruch and Hancock submitted their report to Byrnes on February 15, 1944. It leaned heavily on the WPB studies and, like the rubber report, soon became the guidebook for reconversion policy. Their basic point was that contracts should be canceled as quickly as needs allowed and the cancellations coordinated with planned expansion of civilian production. Instead of a new agency, it urged that policy be centered in OWM and that the military and WPB work together to prepare plans for the transition to a one-front war once Germany collapsed. Economic stability was the primary goal. "Speed in shifting this productive capacity from war to peace," the report emphasized, "is our most effective attack against the two enemies which threaten in the transition and post-war period—unemployment and inflation." A small staff within OWM should oversee and expedite the entire process, especially the critical tasks of contract termination and disposal of surplus property. The human factor mattered as well. The report suggested creation of a "work director" in OWM to deal with providing jobs for returning service personnel.[30]

Four days later Roosevelt responded by creating within OWM the Surplus War Property Administration (SWPA) and a Retraining and Reemployment Administration. Byrnes promptly named conservatives to head both entities, explaining that he could not wait for enabling legislation from Congress because 3,769 army contracts had already been canceled, affecting at least ten times that number of subcontracts, and he expected another $2.5 billion worth to be canceled by June 30. OWM had been given the leadership in reconversion, but the roles of WPB and the military had yet to be defined clearly and Congress had not yet been heard from. On March 4 the Truman Committee urged planning "designed to remove obstacles which would otherwise render reconversion difficult or impossible." Three days later Nelson outlined his vision of WPB's policy toward reconversion in a public letter to Senator Francis T. Maloney of Connecticut, who had asked him a series of questions. Nelson's response formed the basis for a program he would unveil in June after the Normandy invasion.[31]

Nelson got support from Harry Truman and his committee. Truman had predicted in January that many communities would soon have labor surpluses as more contracts were canceled and argued that it made no sense to leave people unemployed when they could be producing civilian goods. He made no bones about charging the military with thwarting production of civilian goods under their dubious theory of "beneficial unemployment" that assumed workers would move elsewhere for work and turnover would drop because they would value their jobs more. Stimson dismissed Truman as "a nuisance and a pretty untrustworthy man. He talks smoothly but acts meanly."[32]

Spring brought a growing tension over the forthcoming invasion and a widespread sense of discouragement. "There has been a revolutionary change I think in the attitude of our people as to the war," Stimson noticed late in March. "The easy-going confidence of a short and quick victory which was so prevalent last autumn and winter has faded out and they now realize that they are in for a long war and a very hard fight for the invasion." Stimson himself admitted to being "tired and discouraged with the infernal series of errors that I have to try to patch up—all brought about by the same cause—a bad organization on the part of the President. Fortunately the War Department is free of it and everybody recognizes that, but the rest of the government is pretty bum."[33]

He was not alone. Charlie Wilson talked again of quitting and insisted that he would stay on only until the summer. "It would be a tremendous loss," moaned Stimson, "because he is the life of the W.P.B." Patterson shocked Stimson by offering his resignation, saying again that "the country was not up to the war spirit" and he wanted to lead by example and go into the infantry. Stimson had to persuade him that his work in the War Department was far more important to victory. In April a frustrated Julius Krug resigned as program vice chairman; all his responsibilities were transferred to Wilson. Nelson had been unwilling or unable to reject the Clay proposal or implement Gladieux's. Either move would launch a fight with PEC and the military with little chance of prevailing, yet he was not willing to hand reconversion over to Wilson.[34]

Instead Nelson created a Policy Committee for Civilian Production with himself as chair. Composed entirely of civilians, he hoped to use the group as a counter against the military's influence. Before the committee got under way, however, the uproar over canceled contracts at Brewster in May and the widespread public reaction to it forced Nelson's hand. Reluctantly he told Wilson to set up a body under PEC to handle munitions cutbacks on a more orderly and rational basis. Wilson set up what was called the Production Executive Committee Staff but left its role in reconversion issues vague. On

June 5 Byrnes ordered Wilson to have the new staff determine uniform policies for canceling contracts. Procurement agencies were told to clear all cutbacks and terminations with the staff. The fact that Byrnes ignored Nelson
and went directly to Wilson told Nelson that PEC would be taking charge of
reconversion.[35]

Nelson found himself in a quandary. He faced opposition from not only
the military but several of the executives in WPB as well. Their differences
arose not over reconversion itself but over when and how it should take place.
For many corporate executives the how mattered as much as the when. They
believed strongly that the war should not alter the old competitive patterns.
Most large companies were still fully engaged in munitions output; if reconversion allowed smaller rivals to start making civilian goods again, it would
give them a competitive advantage, a running start for postwar markets that
were expected to dwarf any that had come before them. As Catton noted,
"One consideration should guide all reconversion planning, as the dollar-
a-year men saw it; the old competitive patterns in industry must be preserved
intact. When the last traces of the war economy evaporated, each industrialist must be able to pick up exactly where he had left off."[36]

In surrendering so much of his authority to others, Nelson had isolated
himself to a degree that now came back to haunt him. He had divested operating responsibility in WPB to Wilson and the PEC. The arrangement had
worked well until PEC emerged as a crucial instrument in reconversion.
However important policy was, it went nowhere in any organization until
operating people translated it into action. Wilson held the operating reins
and had used PEC effectively, but the military dominated the committee.
Where the top board of WPB was an advisory board, PEC was a practical
operating group. Wilson had appointed most of its civilian staff, who were
strongly sympathetic to the military's point of view; Bernard Gladieux described the executive secretary as more military than the military. They were
all loyal to Wilson.[37]

But Nelson still held one key card. He could make decisions independently
of the WPB board. Once it became clear that the Normandy landing had
proven successful, Nelson made his move. At a WPB meeting on June 13 he
unveiled a four-point program designed to initiate reconversion on a limited
basis. Limitation orders on aluminum and magnesium, which had become
plentiful, would be revoked, making the metals available for civilian use. Any
manufacturer would be allowed to make and test a single model of any product for potential postwar production. Manufacturers could place unrated orders for tools and machinery provided no military orders stood in the way.
Finally, and most controversial, a WPB regional director could authorize a
small manufacturer to start producing civilian goods if the materials, man-

power, and plant capacity were not needed for the war effort. This became known as the "spot authorization" provision.[38]

With these moves Nelson hoped to accomplish two things: allow companies to begin advance preparations for reconversion and enable the economy to take up the slack as war orders declined. "It was hedged about with safeguards," he insisted. "It was drawn up in full recognition of the fact that the paramount responsibility upon industry, labor, and government was for war production . . . It was the minimum program that WPB could have offered . . . And it touched off what was probably the most severe fight between military and civilian elements which our government ever witnessed."[39]

Surprisingly few objections arose at the June 13 meeting. Three days later Nelson circulated among WPB's board members a press release outlining the program that was to take effect on July 1. The release went public on June 18, by which time vigorous opposition arose from both the military and corporate members. A week later Nelson was rushed to the hospital with double pneumonia and could take no active role in WPB until July 26. The army jumped on the proposal at the June 28 meeting of PEC and tried to delay its starting date, but Wilson, with Nelson unable to defend his program, refused to act. At an emergency meeting of WPB on July 4, Wilson observed that no other action of the board had received such warm approval from Congress and the press as Nelson's program. Obviously people approved the beginning of reconversion, and in fact it received wide public support. The Truman Committee threatened public hearings unless Wilson moved quickly to implement the program.[40]

After a thorough airing of the issue, it became clear that most objections were to the timing rather than to the program itself. The board voted unanimously to postpone implementation until Nelson's return, but Wilson said dutifully that he had orders from Nelson to go ahead and so could not be bound by the board's vote. The War and Navy departments asked for time to appeal to Byrnes, who reached Nelson by phone and got an agreement to issue the orders in staggered fashion, setting them back about a month. Congress signaled its interest by passing the Contract Settlement Act. All sides were making their case in the press, none more savagely than the army. Patterson wrote his objections directly to Nelson, but on June 29 the JCS said in a public announcement, "A dangerous state of mind which cuts war production by causing people to throw up their war jobs is just as harmful as desertion on the fighting front."[41]

On July 7 Admiral Leahy, the president's chief of staff, wrote Nelson a letter made public warning that "we are disturbed over the existing lag in war production, which, if it continues, may necessitate revision in strategic plans which could prolong the war . . . The issuance of orders at this time which will affect our ability to produce war materials is not consistent with the all-out prosecution of the war." The military placed heavy emphasis on the recent drop in production, which by one estimate was 3 percent below schedule. No mention was made of the fact that much of the decline came from the military's own canceling of contracts. Nelson answered Leahy's letter by saying he had reviewed all the arguments against his plan and found no substance in them. This time he was not backing down.[42]

Watching the war of words flare to ever more bitter heights, Byrnes announced on July 10 that the conflict would be resolved in his office. He got the military to accept, however sullenly, the compromise of issuing the orders on a staggered basis with the spot authorization order coming last of all on August 15. The controversy did not go away because Nelson's program, as he had insisted all along, had a tiny impact on war production, but even more because the clash had elevated the basic issue of who was to control reconversion into national prominence. The military did not retreat from its position, which was simple, direct, and unrelenting: Not an ounce of productive capacity should go toward increased civilian output until the war was won. The WPB vice chairs all vowed that they would not let competitive issues interfere with resumption of civilian production, but they remained unhappy with Nelson, who had said in his reply to Senator Maloney, "I do not believe you can have a democracy and at the same time forbid new competition."[43]

When Nelson returned to the office on July 26, he was surprised at the level of bitterness present among his staff. Many of the vice chairs, who were being assailed in the press for trying to stifle competition and protect monopoly, were convinced that Nelson's own people were feeding the stories to reporters. They launched a bitter attack on Nelson's supporters, none of whom were present at the meeting, and indirectly on Nelson himself. As the dissension within WPB spilled into the papers, the army renewed its request that Nelson be removed. Nelson himself admitted that "the situation for all of us had become well-nigh impossible, for the argument over the reconversion program had become more than a disagreement over timing . . . It had acquired vast implications touching on the whole future of the American economy."[44]

Meanwhile, the army launched its own intensive propaganda campaign to convince the public that shortages of munitions and men were hurting if not crippling the war effort. Stories reached the press, many of them orchestrated by the War Department, of tragic casualties suffered in Normandy because the advancing troops ran out of ammunition, grenades, and other supplies. Senator James M. Mead of the Truman Committee set the record straight by stressing that "insufficient production in the United States has not up to this time been the cause of shortages of weapons and ammunition at the front.

Any shortage has been due, up to now, solely to transportation problems overseas." Still the army persisted in its program of misinformation suggesting that victory hung perilously in the balance and that the reconversion program could tip it in the wrong direction.[45]

The intolerable conflict within WPB convinced Roosevelt and his advisers that Nelson had to go, but his popularity in liberal and labor circles mandated that his departure be handled delicately. However, a press leak forced the president's hand. On August 19, four days after the spot authorization went into effect, he announced that Nelson had agreed to join a presidential mission to China, about as far from Washington as one could go and still remain in friendly territory. He would be gone about five weeks, during which Wilson would serve as acting chairman of WPB. A wave of public protests flooded the White House from Congress, labor leaders, and other sources after a close Nelson associate tipped a reporter that his boss was being pushed out. Wilson had been told he would ultimately replace Nelson as chairman, but the uproar forced Byrnes to tell him that his appointment would be too controversial.[46]

On August 24 Nelson and Wilson met with the WPB executives for the last time in the bleak auditorium of the Social Security Building. Originally scheduled for 10:30 A.M., the meeting did not take place until after lunch because Nelson was at the White House. He and Wilson took seats on the stage facing the nearly 500 top-level business executives who toiled in the WPB labyrinth. While reporters waited eagerly in the press room, Nelson stepped to the small rostrum and told the men he would be leaving for China. He rehashed the reconversion dispute in conciliatory terms, emphasizing that disagreements were over matters of principle and that public criticism of the executives had been unjust. As for Wilson, he said, "Charlie has my complete confidence, there is no real quarrel between us, he's a grand person and I trust him implicitly."[47]

So far everything had gone according to script. Then Wilson stormed to the rostrum and, to the astonishment of everyone, launched into a bitter tirade against those in the audience who had undermined and denigrated him with their backbiting and false leaks to the press and radio. "It seemed almost likely," said Catton, "that he would stride down the aisle at any moment and have at his critics personally." This poisonous cloud of innuendo, Wilson added, made it impossible for him to continue at WPB. If he took over for Nelson, everything he did would be measured by this criticism and he would be constantly accused of trying to cut his chief's throat. Therefore, he was leaving WPB and government service at once, as soon as he could clear his desk and remove his personal effects. Afterward Nelson and Wilson rode the same elevator to the fifth floor without exchanging a single word.

Those present lost little time carrying the story to the equally amazed reporters in the press room. "The Board never made bigger or blacker headlines," said Nelson ruefully. Roosevelt was not pleased to read the sensational stories that filled the papers and summoned Nelson for an explanation. In defending himself Nelson argued that during his entire time at WPB he had never really fought with anyone except the army. "It must be plain to you," he asserted, "that this is only a continuation of the old fight with the Army that has existed from the very first defense agency until the present. Is the trouble really with me, or with a few, a very few, leaders of the Army who want their own way and who refuse to see anyone else's way?"[48]

Nelson recommended Julius Krug as acting chairman for WPB and thought he and the president parted on good terms. When he returned from China in late September, he resigned as chair of WPB and Krug became the permanent chairman. Nelson was gone, Wilson was gone, and the conflict over reconversion passed into the hands of "Cap" Krug, a seasoned bureaucrat. On October 3 Roosevelt signed into law an act that folded OWM into an enlarged version, the Office of War Mobilization and Reconversion (OWMR), with Byrnes still at the head. One writer called the act "probably . . . the broadest delegation of authority ever granted by Congress to an executive agency."[49]

For months after his return Nelson lingered in an obscure office parsing the plan for Chinese industrial development developed during his mission. On his return the plan was shuttled among several offices, losing more of its substance at every stop. Nothing more was heard of it or of Nelson, who finally left government service sometime after Roosevelt's death. In Chungking the Chinese who had hosted Nelson smiled at the news and, having previously welcomed Willkie and Wallace, talked of renaming their guest mansion the "House of Exile."[50]

AT THE HEART of the struggle between WPB and the military lay that seemingly unsolvable riddle, manpower. The military insisted that a shortage of workers hampered munitions production, and therefore any diversion of workers to civilian output would compound an already serious situation. Nelson, McNutt, and others countered that existing shortages, however acute, were localized in specific cities, industries, and skills and had to be attacked on that basis. In Nelson's view, "the Army was, quite openly, out to protect war production by the simple means of creating pools of unemployment. The issue was as simple as that, and I have heard it stated just so bluntly." Those left jobless by cutbacks, instead of latching onto more permanent work turning out civilian goods, would be forced to seek work in other defense plants.

As Lucius Clay declared during the War Department's drive for national service legislation, "Labor must be treated from a production standpoint along the lines of material control."[51]

However, as Nelson emphasized, workers were not robots "all cut to pattern as were the men of Frederick the Great's Prussian Guards." Shut down a war plant and its workers tended simply to drift out of the labor market. Turnover, like absenteeism, had not one but a dozen reasons of varying complexity and differed from place to place. One plant, for example, had a high turnover on its night shift because the vacant lot where employees parked had no lights, and cars were often stripped of tires and accessories. Installing floodlights solved the problem. The disappearance of workers after a plant closing also had not one but a dozen reasons that varied widely in each location. At the most basic level many women, older workers, and teenaged employees simply could not relocate to another city. Another crucial variable was that of skills, which did not automatically transfer from one job to another.[52]

Part of Nelson's reasoning behind the spot authorization order was his belief that industrial workers, when laid off, looked first for work near home. If neither munitions nor civilian jobs were available, they switched to nonindustrial work or simply left the labor market instead of migrating to more distant places where war jobs beckoned. The result was not a surplus labor pool that could be funneled to where it was most needed but rather a net loss in national production and a dissipation of the industrial workforce. Nelson argued that it was far easier to control the placement of contracts than the movement of workers and urged that more reliance be placed on contract clearance procedures to curb the inflow of work in excess of locally available manpower or resources.[53]

The Truman Committee found that a large proportion of the 1.1 million unemployed in January consisted of women who had not worked before entering a munitions plant and who simply dropped out of the labor force when the plant in their hometown shut down. In some cases 30 percent of women from a closed plant declined to look for other jobs of any kind, and very few were willing to move elsewhere for a job of uncertain duration. The growing number of canceled contracts became itself an obstacle to shifting labor from one place to another of greater need. Between January and May the number of women in manufacturing jobs dropped by 134,000.[54]

In January a WMC official reported an expected shortfall of 900,000 war workers by July 1, adding that more flexibility was needed in handling manpower utilization because local conditions governed shortages everywhere in the country. An increased flow of foreign workers helped fill some gaps. By 1944 some 63,432 Mexicans were toiling in American fields and another

50,000 on American railroads. Under the terms of agreement with Mexico none were employed in states that practiced racial discrimination. This provision excluded Texas, for example, but large numbers of Mexicans simply entered the state illegally and found work. Jamaica and the Bahamas furnished nearly 26,000 more workers scattered among a number of industries from food processing to foundries. Everyone realized that the presence of foreign workers created more problems than it solved, but the need was deemed desperate enough to risk them. By June 1944 the nation housed 196,948 German and Italian prisoners, but only some could be put to work and never in war industries.[55]

More help came from one of the most neglected groups of all: the disabled. The depression years, with their surplus of labor, had chained them to the long-familiar role of castoffs. Only a few companies would even consider, let alone hire, disabled employees. Ford was a notable exception even before the war. By 1943 the company boasted 11,163 full or partially disabled workers, all earning full pay. Of that number 1,208 were totally or partially blind, 111 deaf mutes, 135 epileptics, 91 missing one arm, 3 missing both arms, 157 missing a leg, 10 missing both legs, 260 with one crippled arm, 139 with spinal curvatures, and 322 with heart ailments. One blind man, seventy-four years old, had been with Ford for twenty-four years after losing his sight. "No one will ever know, unless he has been through it himself," he said, "what the employment manager really said to me when he told me to 'report Monday.' He told me I was still useful to this world and to myself."[56]

"No company regards such employment as charity or altruism," declared Edsel Ford, who strongly supported it. "All our handicapped workers give full value for their wages, and their tasks are carried out with absolutely no allowances or special considerations. Our real assistance to them has been merely the discovery of tasks which would develop their usefulness." Ford's list of useful workers included the elderly; it had hundreds of them over seventy and seven in their eighties. Consolidated Aircraft had 700 disabled workers and Lockheed 600, 18 of them with seeing-eye dogs. At a small tool company in Minneapolis 75 of its 85 workers were disabled. But these were exceptions. One estimate thought 75 percent of the nation's 5 million disabled and 80 percent of its 600,000 epileptics were employable, but nowhere near those figures actually held jobs.[57]

Apart from the shortage of workers, the army faced a more basic problem: It needed more men. With the pool of eligible men between eighteen and twenty-six drying up and the national service bill going nowhere, two other sources remained: fathers and previously deferred men. Popular sentiment still opposed drafting fathers, and the army did not want them anyway for the hard fighting in Europe. Both General Marshall and Admiral King made it clear that they preferred "young men with young men's stamina, who could charge a machine-gun nest without worrying about wives and children back home." Deferments seemed the logical target. After a cabinet meeting on February 18 Stimson broached the subject with Roosevelt. He mentioned the curtailing of ASTP, which Marshall insisted was necessary to keep from losing ten divisions that would be needed in the coming European campaign.[58]

The War Department then produced a memorandum that the president signed and sent to Hershey and McNutt on February 26. "The crucial campaigns of this year will determine both the length of this war and its price in men and goods," it began. Declaring that "there is a very real danger in our failure to supply trained replacements at the time and in the numbers required," it concluded by saying, "The present situation is so grave that I feel the time has come to review all occupational deferments." When the cabinet exploded in protest at the news, Stimson challenged them to produce ten divisions in some other way.[59]

As Stimson expected, howls of outrage arose from all sides. "This has made a tremendous row," he noted with grim satisfaction, "because everybody is losing his pet men." Nearly 5 million young men working in industry, agriculture, government offices, research laboratories, universities, the professions, and elsewhere shivered with alarm that they might suddenly be scooped up by the draft. Nelson, McNutt, and others argued strenuously that the work being done by these men was fully as important to the war effort, which would be seriously crippled by their absence. Some factory and other work, to say nothing of farm labor, required strong young men. Why draft a trained chemist or technician or specialist of any kind, who could not be easily replaced, and turn him into a clerk or infantryman? Nelson pointed out that half the technical personnel in many tire plants fell into the target age category.[60]

To these arguments the army turned a deaf ear. Patterson dismissed them with the cavalier observation that vigorous recruitment and training of new workers could offset any losses. Marshall admitted that production would suffer to some extent but said the sacrifice was necessary to produce the troops needed. "Selective Service has not delivered the quantity of men who were expected," Roosevelt explained. ". . . The nation's manpower pool has been dangerously depleted by liberal deferments and I am convinced that in this respect we have been overly lenient." However, the draft boards still held the authority by law to award deferments. "The draft board is the most autonomous body that I have ever known," exclaimed McNutt. "It is more autonomous than a jury." In fact, it was a jury of sorts, handing down verdicts on the thousands of cases brought before it.[61]

On one occasion Roosevelt likened the manpower situation to a jigsaw puzzle. By 1944 it had become, in *Time*'s words, "more like a vast, sticky pudding which the Administration stirred and stirred, hoping that something in the way of a solution would come to the top. None did." Lewis Hershey hesitated to act on Roosevelt's directive until Stimson called him in to stiffen him up. "We pushed him and pounded him," Stimson reported, "and I spoke pretty strongly to him and as a result he promised to do it at once." Hershey promptly sent off instructions to the local boards about canceling deferments for men between twenty-two and twenty-six. Marshall and Patterson used their persuasive force on Nelson and McNutt to good effect. Meeting with steel executives who protested losing their industry's preferred deferment status, Nelson told them that "the Army and Navy must get the men, even if it means losing production."[62]

Still no clear policy or procedure existed. With the local boards so crucial to the process and Hershey their chief adviser, much depended on who had the most influence on Hershey. Fearful that McNutt and Nelson were influencing Hershey, Stimson called the general and gave him what amounted to an ultimatum. Hershey had the responsibility for deciding deferments, Stimson said, and the War Department would act on that basis. If McNutt and Nelson tried to use an advisory committee to remove this power from Hershey, Patterson would refuse to serve on it and the department's people would leave any such organization and make their requests for deferments separately. Hershey said he would support this position. Stimson then called Byrnes and said bluntly that he would not compromise, that the matter was too serious. Byrnes agreed with him that the law putting responsibility in Hershey's hands should be followed.[63]

But McNutt got his way, at least on the surface. Lengthy haggling took place over what war programs should be listed as critical and thereby justifying deferments. In the end an interagency advisory committee was formed with McNutt, at Nelson's insistence, as chairman. Stimson was furious, the more so because Wilson, having been nudged aside, made it clear that he wanted to leave. Byrnes assured him that the president would not let Wilson leave and would first move Nelson to another post.[64]

The new Inter-Agency Committee on Occupational Deferments included as members representatives from WPB, PAW, Solid Fuels, the rubber program, ODT, WFA, WSA, and the large procurement agencies. Applying rigorous standards, it listed the production programs for which deferments might be granted. Any man seeking deferment had to be certified by his employer, a representative of the government agency with jurisdiction over the plant, and his state's director of Selective Service. The practical effect, if enforced vigorously, would be to remove decisions on occupational deferment from local boards and thereby render them much more difficult to obtain.

But Selective Service remained as independent as ever. As one staff member of OWMR observed, "The Selective Service System was too elusive to come to grips with even for its own officials."[65]

The new committee tendered its advice to Hershey, who offered his to the state Selective Service heads, who passed it along to their local boards. "Warriors win wars with weapons," Hershey exhorted (or "wapsodized," as *Time* quipped) in the agency's newsletter, "but weapons will not win wars without warriors to wield them." Hershey, Patterson, and Navy Undersecretary Ralph Bard abruptly endorsed in April a proposal put forth months earlier by Representative Clare Boothe Luce of Connecticut to replace drafted war workers with noncontributing 4-Fs. Some took it to be a nod to the "work or fight" order of World War I. A noted chemist and dean at Penn State warned that drafting technicians in training promised disaster for the country and the war effort. "Chemistry and chemical engineering are important in production," he said. "The Army and Navy are not producing units; they are consuming units." Why squander such urgently needed talent?[66]

To help local boards, Selective Service provided a guide to what it considered essential occupations: production of food, clothing, fuel, raw materials and chemicals; manufacture of machines, weapons, ships, planes, and parts (including packing boxes and paper); services such as running communications and transportation, keeping people informed by newspapers, magazines, radio and movies, heating and lighting homes, and caring for health and safety. The goal was to force all men between the ages of eighteen and thirty-eight into either military service or some occupation useful to the war effort. But local boards still made the final decision, and Hershey admitted that a twenty-six-year-old soda jerk could receive a deferment if a board concluded that he was the only one in the town. He also warned that the changing tide of war could reshuffle everything, and that the latest guidelines were "permanent—for today."[67]

As the year wore on, the manpower crunch did not ease. The West Coast Plan was extended throughout the nation, and the functions of the Area Production Urgency Committees were expanded. Asked about the sweeping extensions, McNutt replied that the nation suffered from "overoptimism [about] an early ending of the war . . . This sentiment is positively dangerous." On August 4 Byrnes issued a directive favoring the military's and WMC's argument that manpower shortfalls could be met only by reducing nonmilitary production and thereby freeing up workers to seek jobs in munitions plants. WPB strongly opposed the ruling, and the dispute dragged on into the winter of 1945.[68]

While the controversy over manpower raged on, the ranks of fighting men were depleted at an accelerating rate by severe fighting in both Europe and the Pacific. On the third anniversary of Pearl Harbor the latest toll of casualties was released to a weary public. Through November 22 the army had lost 91,625 men killed, 268,099 wounded, 58,926 missing, and 56,248 taken prisoner. The navy suffered 29,738 killed, 33,469 wounded, 9,427 missing, and 4,486 taken prisoner. Of the army's 268,099 wounded, 126,440 had returned to duty, though not all to the front lines. Patterson disclosed that the army had of necessity changed its policy and was sending eighteen-year-olds into combat. "We are in the midst of a hard struggle," he said, "not at the end of it. We have a war to win; we have not won it. We have a duty to perform; it is not finished."[69]

Scarcely had he spoken when events made it painfully and shockingly clear that more days of reckoning lay ahead.

CHAPTER 31

LIFE IN THE DAYS OF

The war changed everything except human needs and desires.
—WILLIAM L. O'NEILL[1]

Well, I'll tell you. My family means everything to me. Now that our own boy is in the Army, I want to pitch in and help lick 'em.
—CARL H. WINNEBALD[2]

American children are being affected by the war in two distinctly different ways. One is injurious. It is reflected in the disturbing increase in juvenile delinquency, especially among young girls . . . But, happily, the war is bearing different fruits for a much larger number of children . . . as beneficial as the other is hurtful. It consists of the opportunities opened to the young to do something useful and to learn responsibility early.
—SATURDAY EVENING POST[3]

BY THE END OF 1944 AMERICA had been at war for three years and Europe for more than five. Although the continental United States was not bombed or invaded and did not experience firsthand the horrors of war, the lives of its people changed in a thousand ways large and small. The most drastic impact landed on those who marched off to distant battlefields. Their absence was but the most palpable and painful of the effects on those who stayed behind and did what they could to cope with the new world wrought by the war. The daily texture of their lives underwent subtle shifts and sometimes startling upheavals. Amid it all they struggled to create what Warren Harding would have called a new normalcy. The old normalcy of the depression days was nothing to mourn, but in its place came a steady parade of uncertainty and change leading to where they did not and could not know. Like all peoples in wartime, they could only hope that each day brought them nearer its end.

EVERY MIDWESTERN TOWN had its families like the Braukmillers, modest of means but grand in size. Gaunt John Braukmiller and his plump wife had thirteen children, sixteen grandchildren, and a puppy named Snowball. They were ordinary, everyday people in every sense except one. In the middle of the war they all picked up and moved from Iowa to Portland, Oregon, where fifteen of them, male and female, took jobs in Henry Kaiser's shipyards. Together they brought home $996 a week, a sum worth enduring the inconveniences of relocation to a place sorely lacking in housing and other amenities of daily life. The *Oregon Journal* hailed them as "the shipbuildingest family in America."[4]

Carl Winnebald's family numbered only five and had no reason to leave Evansville, Indiana, where they had lived for thirty years. Quiet, conservative, middle-class, churchgoing people, the Winnebalds had already sent Carl Jr., their only boy, to the army before he finished college. Lois, seventeen, was a freshman at Evansville College and Mary Louise, fourteen, a high school freshman. Carl worked as a foreman at Servel, one of the town's more than 200 factories, most of which made war products. Like many other citizens, they devoted time to civilian defense and put much of their savings into war bonds. Holidays they spent when possible visiting Carl Jr. at his camp in Virginia. Before the war Carl worked a forty-eight-hour week; now he spent nine hours every weekday and four hours on Sunday at the plant overseeing three shifts a day. The Winnebalds considered themselves fortunate to own their home.[5]

Taxes and rising prices ate into the family's income, but Carl was never one to complain. Mrs. Winnebald practiced a host of small economies and filled her fruit cellar with preserved fruits and vegetables in summertime. "I don't care if sugar is rationed," she said, "so long as I can send cookies to Carl in camp." Her spare time went to a church group that sewed for the Red Cross. The family walked places more often, and Carl took special care of his 1941 Oldsmobile to make it last. His wife did the same with her household appliances since no one knew when new ones would be available again. Where Carl once parked his car on the street in front of the house, now he locked it in the garage to prevent theft or stripping. Under the changed curriculum Lois could graduate in two and a half years instead of four with summer school and fewer vacations. She planned to become an elementary school teacher, there being plenty of jobs available.

Mary Louise helped the war effort by picking up magazines and newspapers around the neighborhood for the Evansville Defense Council scrap drive. She was less confident than her sister about the future. "I'm afraid when I'm ready to enter college conditions will be so bad I won't be able to go," she lamented. "And, if I do, I'm afraid there'll be a depression when I graduate and I won't get a job." Her father had the opposite problem. He had hoped to retire within a short time, but that hope receded further into the future than ever. He worried, too, about his son. "We sacrificed to send our boy to college," he said, "but the Army took him. If he comes back, he probably never will finish school. But he knows the fight is worth it."

Barbara Holmes Drum of Far Hills, New Jersey, lived a very different life from that of the Winnebalds. Born on Long Island, raised in New York City, she attended Miss Nightingale's private school and a finishing school in Aiken, South Carolina. After coming out in 1930–31 she enjoyed a year abroad before marrying John Drum in 1934. They had four children, moved in the most exclusive of circles, traveled, entertained, and relished their place in the *Social Register.* Lovely, elegant, always impeccably dressed, Barbara had everything she wanted in life. Then war came and her husband decided to go into the army. For three years they had rented a sixteen-room Jacobean house in fashionable Far Hills. On the day in 1942 John decided to enter the service, they bought the place, and Barbara faced the challenge of making it into a farm. "All of a sudden I had to find out about a lot of things," she said. "I'm finding out."[6]

Farming was not in the curriculum of finishing school. Five of her six servants, including the only farmhand, soon left for war work. She bought some pigs, sheep, chickens, a cow, and a duck. On her first day as a farmer the duck somehow drowned in a water trough. "I became terribly discouraged," she admitted. The children, ranging in age from one to eight, could do little to help. "With John gone," she said, "I thought it wise to learn how to feed ourselves." She took on all the livestock chores, acquired an ancient truck, and scoured the countryside to find a boar and a ram to produce pigs and lambs. She haunted local auctions until she found a tractor. "I'll never forget the day I got one," she said. "Glorious." A double saw became "one of my precious possessions. With [sons] Jay and Sammy helping, I hope to saw enough firewood for next winter." She learned how to pitch hay for livestock bedding and how to garden.

Her elegant wardrobe gave way to a new uniform of blue jeans and a sweater. At one time her entrance to a party dazzled onlookers. "I dress now," she laughed, "only to take the boys to the dentist." No more parties adorned her well-appointed house. "We've living very simply now," she said. Much of her time went to consulting local farmers, studying pamphlets on cultivation, doing endless chores, and caring for the children. She managed to find enough time to do volunteer work as an aircraft spotter at the Peacock observation post, saying, "I owe my husband that much." Some help came from an elderly man serving as a temporary farmhand. By the spring of 1943 the farm had nine pigs, twenty-six sheep, eighty chickens, a cow, a goat, some geese, and another duck who survived.

WORK HAS ALWAYS been a way of life, but in wartime it took on a new urgency. Everyone was asked to do more; some did and some did not. Herb Weiler measured his increased contribution in miles and pounds. For twenty-three years in normal times he had toted a bag averaging fifty-five pounds of mail to deliver at 563 stops on his twelve-mile route along Portman Avenue in Cleveland, wearing out four pairs of shoes a year. The war added another pair of shoes to his casualty list, doubled his load, and piled on half the route of a younger colleague gone to the military. The mail had increased enormously in volume thanks to soldier letters and packages, and his stops grew much less cheerful and neighborly at houses dreading the arrival of an envelope stamped "Verified: Killed in Action." He shared their pain, having known the families along his route for years. In all those years Weiler boasted of never losing a letter, package, or day's pay.[7]

Help for the mail carriers came from a new and unexpected source. In New York Edna Staats became the first woman to deliver mail there, but she handled only special delivery. Upstate at Old Forge, in the Adirondacks, an eighteen-year-old blonde named Ann Gibbs, all 120 pounds of her, hoisted up to thirty mail sacks a day into her truck and drove 108 miles through one of the East's heaviest snow belts to deliver mail over a route previously served by her father. When the snow piled too high, Ann strapped a bag to her back and skied to isolated camps. Like Ann, the post office was struggling against heavy obstacles. The war had increased its load by an estimated billion pieces a year, 25,000 of its employees had gone to the military or other war services, troop trains delayed its 1,800 daily rail carloads, and it too had to grapple with local rationing boards for gasoline and tires.[8]

Women had moved into almost every imaginable job. They worked as butchers, lumberjacks, steelworkers, service station attendants, taxi drivers, truck drivers, milkmaids, firewomen, bartenders, "bellehops," repairwomen for all kinds of machinery, and railroad workers. As early as November 1942 Betty Hill Karr, a welder and toolmaker, was installed as the first female president of a steelworkers local at an Atlanta mill. "The Margin Now Is Womanpower," proclaimed *Fortune*, yet by 1944 the *Saturday Evening Post* asked, "Are Women Doing Their Share in the War?" The army hoped to recruit 150,000 women in 1943 but attracted only 60,000. Publicity campaigns flopped, and scurrilous rumors of moral conditions in WAAC camps spread by a New York columnist hurt enlistments. On a practical level many women made better money in defense jobs, and those who had a son or husband already in the service often had financial and other obligations at home. Henry Stimson offered a familiar solution for the shortfall: compulsory service.[9]

Asked why more women had not stepped forward in both industry and the military, one expert replied, "Women don't have wives." After a shift at the factory many had to go home to clean house, feed their family, and take care of children. Jumping into factory work also posed a host of problems that baffled them as well as plant foremen and managers. Work clothes became a major obstacle. Skirts, sweaters, and jewelry—even wedding rings—created hazards. In some cases Catholic women refused to remove wedding rings until local priests assured them that their sanctity would not be impaired for the duration of the war. Many women vowed never to wear slacks. Welders and burners needed leather pants, but no one made them or coveralls in sizes and shapes that fit women. Nor did anyone make work gloves or work shoes in sizes for women. Hair had to be fully enclosed and covered for safety's sake, but women found caps with bills too hot. Hairnets would not do because they offered no protection from dust, dirt, and static electricity that could pull strands of hair into machinery.[10]

Every job had its own wardrobe requirements. Many of them required goggles, which to women were ugly and heavy and got too dirty for greasy hands to clean. To solve that problem, Sperry, which had 13,000 women working alongside 17,000 men in every type of job, and some other manufacturers installed a small white wagon manned by women who made the rounds all day fitting goggles and cleaning lenses. Plant managers also discovered that women's faces, hands, and bodies were easy prey for skin diseases caused by some industrial poisons that did not affect men as badly. Protective creams recommended by cosmetics experts became a factory staple. The old type of plant washroom turned into one with fully enclosed toilets, individual wash bowls with mirrors above them, full lockers for complete changes of clothes, and vending machines for sanitary napkins.[11]

More advanced plants offered menstruating women lounges with cots, compresses, and sedatives. A few provided classes teaching women remedial exercises, diet instruction, and ways to carry themselves to correct relaxed abdominal walls and exaggerated spinal curvatures. One plant cut in half the time lost to menstrual difficulties with these methods. For domestic problems some companies hired counselors to help solve dilemmas of housing, transportation, shopping, and child care. Two states, Colorado and New York, recruited middle-aged women, who could not compete for war jobs, into a homemaker service with training to serve as troubleshooters for domestic problems when an emergency arose. Some companies also learned that it paid to feed female employees well, preferably with a hot, balanced meal. Sperry boasted a modern cafeteria seating 1,500 people with five lines operating simultaneously to get all workers to their food quickly. They also discovered that regular rest periods increased production and reduced accidents significantly.[12]

Two other problems, pregnancy and abortion, proved more difficult to handle. They were constant topics of discussion among managers and workers alike, but few companies dealt well with them. One survey found that of seventy-three plants with 273,000 employees, thirty-two fired pregnant workers, three discharged them on advice of their physician, and only one gave a leave of absence. A few companies began offering leaves of absence, but women still feared that if they asked the plant doctor for one they would be fired instead. A surprising number didn't want the baby, which gave rise to abortion rings whose activities benefited from the availability of sulfa drugs that lowered the death rate. Counselors hesitated to offer birth control information lest they antagonize workers as well as the Catholic Church. Corporations also had no guidelines for their responsibility in sicknesses and mishaps growing out of pregnancy.[13]

The presence of women in factories triggered a boom in the beauty salon industry. In 1942 alone women spent nearly $504 million for cosmetics and another $350 million for treatments in more than 40,000 beauty salons. War jobs put money in the pockets of more women than ever, many of whom had never used rouge or lipstick in their lives and knew nothing of powder or mascara. Plain-looking, poorly dressed girls from New Jersey plants streamed into nearby beauty salons, flashed a roll of bills, and blurted out that they had never been to a salon before and wanted to try some of its treatments. Some spent as much as $25 for a daylong indulgence in cream mask-facials, bubble baths in pasteurized milk, and ultraviolet lamp tans. A girl who had just learned that her boyfriend was coming home from the war could rush through a frantic morning that included a massage, leg-paint shower, shampoo and coiffure, manicure, egg-mask facial, and velvety patina of makeup.[14]

Alarmists took the splurge in beauty treatments as a sign of spiritual decadence and grumbled that women were not taking the war seriously enough. They might have taken a lesson from the English, who tried banning cosmetics as a nonessential in 1939 only to find that war production dropped 25 percent. They quickly restored cosmetic production to 50 percent of peacetime levels and set up beauty salons in the larger war plants. Some American companies, including Sperry and Lockheed, did the same. Research revealed that industrial efficiency increased 10 to 15 percent when women workers were encouraged to keep themselves well groomed. Nothing of the sort worked on men.[15]

*   *   *

THEY CALLED HIM the Henry Kaiser of Idaho, and the name was richly deserved. People labeled him "a human dynamo" and "a man who can get things done in a big way." In 1943 the Junior Chamber of Commerce picked him as one of the year's ten outstanding men even though he was only thirty-three. A later generation would know him simply as the Potato King.[16]

Born on an Iowa farm, Jack (no one called him John) Simplot moved to Burley, Idaho, before he was a month old so his father could homestead a potato farm. After knocking around California and the Northwest for several years, he returned to the family farm to help make a go of it. By 1941, after several lean years, he became one of the largest growers in the state. Part of his crop went to dehydrators in California, which got him to wondering if he couldn't do the same thing in Idaho. He built a small dehydrating plant at Caldwell, center of the onion industry, just as the nation began ramping up its defenses. After Pearl Harbor, when the quartermaster general urged food processors to outdo all previous efforts, Simplot decided, in his favorite phrase, "to do something about it." The something involved expanding his dehydrator to include potatoes and in the process make it the largest in the world even though both suitable machinery and technical knowledge were in short supply.

The war turned dehydration into a big business. With cargo space at a premium, it made possible the shipment of the largest amount of food in the smallest possible space for both military and Lend-Lease recipients. In 1941 vegetable dehydration plants numbered fewer than 20 and produced about 15 million pounds of food; three years later 141 plants operated with a capacity of 270 million pounds. Two vegetables that lent themselves best to the process were potatoes and onions, Simplot's specialty. He hired specialists and built a laboratory where they could figure out the best way to squeeze water out of vegetables at a low cost and still leave something palatable to eat. He also erected the world's largest warehouse for potatoes, one capable of holding a thousand carloads. His engineers had to design and build most of the machinery needed for the operation.[17]

"The plant," said Simplot with brutal honesty, "is me." He raised $750,000 to build it and hustled after army contracts to keep it busy. Often he spent the night there, wrestling with some problem or working out a kink in the production process. He saw early that money could be made in dehydration only if labor costs were kept low, so he devised an entirely new way for handling material. Chutes in the warehouse floor dumped the potatoes into huge flumes where the water cleaned them on the ride to the peelers. Simplot discarded the old abrasive method of removing the skins. Instead he soaked the potatoes in a hot lye solution to soften the skins, then brushed them off with high-pressure water jets in steel drums. This method proved nearly 15 percent more economical. Once peeled, the potatoes were conveyed past 225 inspectors each shift, then mechanically cut to shoestring size, cooked in steam, spread out on huge wooden trays, and dried in thirty long tunnels with blasts of hot air. Machines, not people, packed the dried product in lead foil and cardboard containers and finally steel-banded wooden cases.

This system enabled Simplot to process 640,000 pounds of raw potatoes a day by 1943. To keep them coming he created the largest buying organization in the state with nineteen warehouses at strategic locations. The operation provided 25 percent of the army's dried potatoes and onions even as Simplot continued to ship carloads of fresh potatoes as well. "I could have moved 10,000 more cars," he claimed, "if I could have got the potatoes." The army said he generated 4 more pounds of finished product per man-hour than the average of all other dehydrators. In 1943 he dried 160 million pounds of potatoes and 8 million pounds of onions to create 20 million pounds of dried potatoes and 2 million pounds of dried onions, for which the army paid him $6.5 million. His goal for 1944 was 25 million pounds of dried potatoes and 2 million pounds of dried onions with a payoff of nearly $8 million.

Simplot was an energetic, restless man. Along with the plant he tended two giant farms totaling 6,000 acres while roaming the state and the country on business. A new project took hold of him as well: building a 120,000-ton fertilizer plant at Pocatello, near Idaho's vast phosphate beds. "As we pushed our agriculture here," he explained, "we were letting our soils deteriorate. So I decided to do something about it." When Idaho farmers talked of planting a smaller potato crop in 1944, Simplot bought time on local radio stations and urged them to increase production 15 percent. He bristled at the suggestion that any other potato matched those of Idaho. "When you dehydrate one of those damn things," he said of Maine's finest, "you have nothing left."

BEES HELD THE key to the future for Harry and Marie Whitcombe. As a graduate student at the College of Agriculture at Davis, California, in 1939, Harry already owned a hundred hives and tended the college's experimental apiary. Marie, a city girl, came to Davis to study horticulture and wound up marrying Harry and joining him in apiculture. They lived in a tiny apartment under a water tower on the outskirts of town. Harry knew bees, had worked with them since the age of six in Corona, and had worked at an apiary every summer of high school. At Davis he experimented endlessly and joyously with new techniques such as a pollen trap, an inverted brush at the hive entrance that scraped pellets of pollen off the bees' knees and dropped them into a container below. The pollen was stored and fed to the bees early the next spring, which led to a booming increase in the apiary's population. Harry had no end of ideas and optimism.[18]

By 1944 Harry and Marie still lived in Davis but in one of four houses he had built around a court in town. They and their three children lived in one and rented out the others. The bees paid for the houses along with two trucks and a large warehouse down by the railroad tracks. The Whitcombes were eager to build more houses once materials became available. "If the war were over and I could sell out," said Harry, "I could retire." He was twenty-eight years old. At Davis Harry owned 100 colonies of bees. By 1944 the Whitcombes had 2,000 colonies and with them a moneymaking machine, albeit one that required hard, sometimes frantic work. "We've had good luck," he admitted, but it was much more than that.

During the summer of 1939 the owner of 500 hives in Nevada lost his keeper and leased the apiary to the Whitcombes on a share basis. After stacking their own hives with supers, the Whitcombes hurried to Nevada to catch the summer honey flow in the alfalfa fields. They had $50 in cash and a bunch of five-gallon cans they hoped to fill with honey and sell for quick cash. But the weather stayed rainy and the bees huddled in their hives, fanning their wings to keep the queen and larvae warm. By July 3 the Whitcombes were down to $10; no honey had been gathered, and the season would be over in three weeks. In desperation they spent the money on wieners and buns and, using a borrowed grill, set up a hot dog stand at the rodeo the next day. The hot dogs sold out, as did some hamburgers they hastily rounded up.

On July 5 the sun finally came out and the bees flooded into the alfalfa fields. Harry watched one hive sitting on a scale grow eleven pounds heavier in one day. By week's end the hives contained more than a hundred pounds of honey each. Harry stacked storage supers six stories high. When one was full, he slipped a small pad dosed with carbolic acid under the lid, driving the bees downward. He then unloaded the four top supers and replaced them with empties, which the bees worked to fill. Working almost around the clock, Harry and Marie uncapped combs and emptied honey from them. When the flow ended three weeks later, they dropped from exhaustion and had filled every container in sight with crystal-clear white honey—80,000 pounds worth 6 cents a pound at top prices—and they had yet to harvest their hives at Davis.

By the summer of 1941 the Whitcombes had a thousand hives, each one good for about a hundred pounds of marketable honey each season. Bees gathered nectar where the gathering was easiest and worked only one flower at a time. A scientific operator like Harry moved his bees from place to place to catch the nectar flow and thereby gleaned many kinds of honey: orange, sage, cotton, clover, alfalfa, and star thistle among them. Their queens came from eggs laid by two exceptional breeding queens, one an Italian with yellow bands, the other a gray Caucasian. A vigorous queen laid more than a thousand eggs a day and produced many daughters that laid eggs in numerous other hives. At the height of the season a strong colony jumped in population from 50,000 to 80,000. This meant that the Whitcombes had some 200 million bees working for them.

The bees produced much more than honey. They were also dispatched around the state and country to pollinate orchards and fields. In 1942 Harry began losing hives to arsenic powders used to dust nearby crops that blew into his colonies when the wind shifted. Despite repeated losses, the chemical pest control had a bright side for him as well. The poisons killed off good as well as bad insects that normally pollinated crops such as almonds, pears, plums, apples, carrots, onions, alfalfa, and clover. Harry put together two new services, package pollinators and migratory apiaries, to help beleaguered farmers. The packages included a new queen and enough bees to pollinate an orchard during a crucial week before the insecticides were sprayed again. The new round of spraying killed off the bees as well as other insects, but by then they had done their job. The migrating apiaries, used only for California farms, consisted of hives moved on cool nights from farm to farm as blossoms burst. The goal was not honey but pollination, which produced far more income than the honey ever could.

The local draft board ruled that Harry and his young 4-F helper were in an essential industry. Apart from the honey, his migratory hives pollinated an estimated $2 million worth of Pacific Coast crops. Another by-product, beeswax, was also a critical war material for compounds used to coat guns and instruments against salt sprays. The Whitcombes produced 2,000 to 3,000 pounds of beeswax every year; it fetched 41 cents a pound at market. They also turned out about 180,000 pounds of honey a season from the 2,000 hives, but the frantic work took its toll on them. Harry, said his wife, "was skin and bones except for his hands." Bee stings had swollen the joints of his fingers out of shape; Harry never minded the stings and worked with only a protective face net. At the hospital the doctors removed whole vials of pus from his fingertips and restored his normal energy.

Although Harry thought about cutting back, he believed that he was doing his part in the war effort. One thing was certain: No creature worked harder or in greater numbers for the cause than the lowly bee.

NO ONE COULD HAVE predicted that the man who would prove most annoying to the president would be the tall, gaunt board chairman of Montgomery Ward, but Sewell Avery shared that dubious honor with John L. Lewis. The son of a wealthy Michigan lumberman, he had earned a law degree before carving out a brilliant business career beginning with a small gypsum plant owned by his father. In 1901 U.S. Gypsum bought the company; four years later Avery became president of U.S. Gypsum and built it into an $81 million giant in building materials. When Montgomery Ward floundered in the depths of the depression, its directors asked Avery for help. In twelve years he turned the company of 35,000 employees from a loss of $5.7 million in 1932 to one with 78,000 employees and a profit of $20.4 million in 1943. Like Henry Ford, he ruled as an absolute dictator, driving an impressive corps of talented officers from the company. "If anybody ventures to differ with me," he once said, "of course, I throw them out of the window."[19]

Avery despised Roosevelt and the New Deal, had fought the latter since 1935, and loathed unions as well. Like John L. Lewis, he challenged not only the WLB but the very principle of federal control. But where Lewis was cast as a villain in the eyes of most Americans, Avery emerged to many as something of a hero. His fight with the government festered for nearly two years before it came to a climax that was somewhere between a comedy and a sideshow.[20]

After a bitter fight a CIO union finally gained certification as bargaining agent for the 7,000 employees of Ward's Chicago plant. But it did not get a contract until Roosevelt twice ordered Avery to sign. The WLB insisted on a maintenance-of-membership clause, which was anathema to Avery. He deemed it the wartime equivalent of a closed shop, something he vowed never to accept. When the contract came up for renewal in December 1943, Avery informed the union that he would not sign under any circumstances. The labor force had suffered 200 percent turnover, he said, and he doubted whether the union still represented a majority of employees. WLB ordered a new election but also instructed Avery to sign the contract pending the outcome. When Avery refused, the union struck the plant on April 12, and WLB appealed to the president to have the army take over the plant.[21]

Thus did the dispute wend its unwanted way to the desks of Bob Patterson and Henry Stimson in April 1944. By then the army had already made seventeen seizures of property, including the coal mines and railroads. Patterson wanted no part of this one, arguing that the Ward plant had nothing to do with war manufacture. Stimson agreed and conveyed his views to Byrnes in strong language. "The business and facilities of Montgomery Ward are devoted entirely to storage, sale, and distribution of civilian goods," he wrote. "They have no relation to the war program or to the war effort, and the taking over thereof by the Army could by no reasonable stretch of the imagination be deemed an action in furtherance of the war effort. On the contrary, it would be assumed, and I think rightly, to be a bald intrusion of the Army into civilian and economic matters with which it has no concern." A Ward executive took the same position, asking, "What power has the President over a retail store?"[22]

Byrnes agreed with this position but worried about the Chicago strike spreading to all other Ward plants, a few of which did make war goods. He suggested to the president that Jesse Jones handle the situation. Roosevelt asked Jones to take over the property and operate it until an election could be held. "If the election shows that the union does not have a majority of the employees, that will end the case," Roosevelt said at a later press conference. "On the other hand, if the election shows that the union has a majority, then the management has declared that it is willing to continue the contract, and that will end the case." But it was not so simple. Avery sent Roosevelt a telegram charging that the WLB was stacked in favor of granting special privileges to labor. On April 25 Roosevelt issued an executive order authorizing Jones to seize and operate the plant. Jones promptly asked the army to help him, and the president ordered a reluctant Stimson to do so.[23]

The sixty-nine-year-old Avery was not about to bend. He repeated his opposition to the closed shop and check-off and insisted that the president had no power over plants making civilian goods. The board and stockholders of Ward backed him up. When Jones's undersecretary, Wayne C. Taylor, demanded possession of the company, Avery refused to comply. The next day Taylor returned with a red-eyed Attorney General Biddle, who had flown in at 4:00 A.M., and some military police. Again Avery refused to leave his office. Two soldiers then picked Avery up and carried him down in the elevator and out of the building, where a bevy of photographers eagerly took what became one of the most famous pictures of the war years. As he was carted out of his office, Avery hissed at Biddle the worst epithet he could think of: "You New Dealer!"[24]

A Gallup poll showed that 61 percent of the respondents disapproved of the action. Columnist Ralph Robey was beside himself. "One more nail has been driven into the coffin of private enterprise," he raged. "If the President has the authority to make this seizure of a merchandising establishment, is there any discernible limit as to how far he can go in the way of taking over private business?" On May 9 the long-awaited election produced a vote of 2,340 to 1,565 in favor of the union. That same day the company was returned to its owners and negotiations for a new contract resumed. However, Avery pledged to continue the fight in the courts, and two weeks later Roosevelt ordered the army to seize another Ward plant, the Hummer Manufacturing Co. in Springfield, Illinois, which did in fact produce munitions.[25]

The issue there was the same refusal to sign a maintenance-of-membership contract, and similar disputes were brewing in half a dozen other Ward plants. At Hummer operations had been halted for nearly three weeks by a strike of 450 workers. When Roosevelt signed the order on May 20, Bill Hassett observed, "This will be a real test in the case of Sewell Avery versus the American people in time of war." Avery's rebellion drew enormous attention from the media and stirred dinner conversations across the nation. Before the year was out, he would be heard from again.[26]

EVERYBODY KNEW SLACKERS, the people who contributed little to the war effort and took pride in evading wartime restrictions. Pete Martin, a *Saturday Evening Post* editor, met one while traveling on *The Lark*, the overnight streamliner between San Francisco and Los Angeles. Beneath a wreath of cigar smoke in the lounge car, the man confided freely about ways to get things done. "Nothing to it," he said confidently. You just had to know all the angles. When he had to travel and tickets were tough to get, a friend steered him to a woman named Jones, who seemed able to get accommodations that no one else could. He slipped her a twenty as thanks and was told that she made as much as $150 a week for the service. In many hotels bell captains bought up reservations in advance and peddled them through bellhops. "They got to make something," he conceded, "but you can't kick if you're getting a break."[27]

Meals on many trains consisted only of breakfast and dinner. "For dinner you choose between feathers and fins," he said. But the slacker asked the dining-car steward to his compartment, told him that he and his wife were eager for a good dinner, and asked what he could do about it. He slipped a folded five-dollar bill into the steward's hands. "I'll send the waiter—the one I call my upstairs boy—in here to see you," said the steward. "We've got a roast in the icebox, and I think I can slice off a couple of nice tender steaks for you."

Thinking about food reminded the slacker of the OPA, which he considered a joke. He had a friend with an interest in a small distillery who sold carloads of case goods to customers at top dollar regardless of the ceiling price. The buyers arrived with packages of hundred-dollar bills wrapped like bread to exchange for the cases. The friend was convinced that by the time anyone got around to checking up on him, the war would be over along with the ceilings. Another friend wanted to invite him for dinner but had used up all his meat points. "Don't you know any butchers who like Scotch?" advised the slacker. "Take some of that Scotch you've got hived up in your cellar and wave it in front of that butcher's nose." They went to the friend's house for a case and took it to the meat shop. His friend emerged with bundles of roasts, steaks, chops, and bacon, and other cuts, which he lugged home and tucked away in his freezer.

His wife looked stricken at the sight. "We won't be able to have anybody in for dinner," she complained. "If we give them a roast like that, they'll know we didn't have enough points to buy it honestly." The slacker intervened. "Wise up, Mary," he said easily. "You won't lose any friends. They'll be begging for invitations. Besides, maybe they know a few little tricks themselves." Getting liquor was no problem for him even when the store clerk said it was all gone. "All you've got to do is scurry around a little, and you can find some guy on a third-floor-back someplace who was smart enough to see the shortage coming and stock up. He might make you buy a case of light wines along with your Scotch, and you'll have to pay two or three times what the wine is worth, but a man deserves some reward for being foresighted."

As for gas, two or three gas tickets along with a five-dollar bill got his tank filled to the top as long as he didn't ask for change. Asked whether his approach to Scotch didn't signal a new wave of bootlegging, he shook his head, then said, "Even if it is, why should I hold back and do without my highball? What could one man do to stop it?"

"THE SOBER TRUTH," concluded a WPB report, "patriotism has swept through our penal institutions and fired the hearts of our prisoners, perhaps to a degree exceeding that manifested in the free population."[28]

The evidence was persuasive. Prisoners, said the report, had given blood "by the gallon." Some 120,000 inmates of state prisons had bought nearly a million dollars' worth of war bonds. Between August 1942 and November 1943 state prisons produced industrial goods for war use worth nearly $9.9 million, including more than $3 million in clothing and $1.75 million in cloth and textiles. Some of their output was very new to prisons: assault boats, shell cases, bomb crates, and stretchers. When the army lifted its old ban on prisoners serving in the military, 15,000 men were paroled for voluntary induction. In Massachusetts sixty prisoners, despite warnings of possibly fatal consequences, volunteered for an experiment on the effect of injecting beef blood plasma into the human bloodstream. One of them did give his life for his country.[29]

EVERY OCCUPATION SUFFERED its losses to the military in the manpower crunch, and soda jerks were no exception. In drugstores across the country fourteen- to sixteen-year-olds were being pressed into service behind the fountain with no experience and little training. This was no small calamity; the average drugstore drew 22 percent of its income from the soda fountain compared to only 17 percent from prescriptions. A milk company in Philadelphia rose to the challenge by starting a night class for soda jerkers, male and female. The course took fifteen hours and taught its disciples how to make every known fountain dish and drink. In four months it boasted 200 graduates but could scarcely begin to meet the demand. The class had an important fringe benefit, the company added. It not only helped drugstores but built future ice cream customers among the hundreds of students being trained.[30]

SOCIAL WORKERS CALLED them the "eight-hour orphans," the huge flock of children belonging to families who worked in the war plants and struggled to find ways to take care of them. The ordeal was hard enough for families who worked in factories close to home; it became a nightmare for those who migrated to plants across the country and wound up living in some hellhole. Their children found themselves cut off from everything familiar, living in wretched housing if even that, and often left to their own devices while their parent(s) toiled at work. Every company and city recognized the desperate need for child care facilities, but they were slow in coming and never equal to the demand created by the rapid rise of the big plants. Parents worried and fretted and tried desperately to find solutions, but they had to earn a living.[31]

One mother carried her baby to work and handed it off to her husband just coming off his shift. Another on the graveyard shift resorted to driving her car as close as possible to the windows where she worked and letting her four children sleep in it. Still another simply locked her two children in the car and left them all day while she worked. A couple with three children who worked in Seattle's Boeing plant lived in one of seven nearby trailer camps. "For a while we put the children to sleep in the trailer and left them," she said. "But they didn't stay asleep. I've stopped working for a few days to try to find a place to put the children. But I have to go back to the job because of the high cost of living."

One boom town, Tacoma, had decent nurseries with competent staffs but could not begin to cope with the sheer number of women flowing into the factories. As their numbers piled up, child care became, as one social worker put it, "like a snowball rolling down a mountainside." Horror stories began to appear with numbing frequency. In one Southern California trailer camp nine children and four dogs were found chained to trailers while their parents worked. "Latchkey children" with house keys on a string around their neck abounded at nurseries. Unlicensed, uncontrolled commercial day nurseries began springing up, manned by untrained older women who sometimes slapped, choked, and beat the children. Some of them had children sleeping in damp cellars. Most were overcrowded and unsanitary.

One place featured fifteen or twenty cribs crammed into one room. "The odor was so bad I couldn't stand it," reported one mother. "I went into the back yard and found children in individual kennels; not play pens—they were more like kennels for cattle. The children looked at me through the bars and cried."

City after city reported dismal statistics on child care. A St. Louis survey showed 4,068 employed mothers with 7,764 children of whom 2,563, many of preschool age, lacked care of any kind. Detroit had fifty-five nurseries caring for 1,000 children, but its mushrooming female workforce had about 80,000 children. Smaller boom towns suffered even more because they typically lacked any kind of facilities before their population explosion. Even Connecticut, which already had a sizable female workforce, scrambled to keep up with the number of children needing care. Some mothers sent their preschool children to school with an older child and told them to wait outside until he got out of school. One eight-year-old boy picked up his three-year-old sister from nursery school at noon, made lunch for her at home, and then had to leave her alone while he returned to school.

Some parents saw precious little of their kids. Two small children, whose mother worked a 3:00 P.M. to 11:00 P.M. shift, spent the morning at nursery school and the afternoon with a relative before their father took them home and fed them supper before putting them to bed. In Naugatuck, some mothers tried working only the graveyard shift so they could be home with their children during the day. But many found they could not stand the physical strain. Some plants rotated work shifts, which complicated the lives of mothers. Others had unions that insisted day shifts go to those with seniority, who were nearly always men. Everywhere factories sprang up and expanded faster than child care facilities and schools, leaving hordes of children to shift for themselves.

Los Angeles featured one shining example of what was needed and lacking elsewhere. The Gale Manor Apartments catered only to working parents and housed fifty-two families with sixty children. The four top floors contained the apartments; the bottom floor was devoted entirely to a nursery playground for the children. Mary Ellen Dye, mother of an army lieutenant, founded the place to meet a need she had endured as a single mother. Beginning at 6:30 A.M., parents dropped off their children before heading to work. The older ones were escorted to school just across the street while the younger ones, ranging in age from eighteen months to five years, had orange juice and played in the yard or inside. At noon they had lunch in their own little restaurant, then were tucked in for naps. Play began again in the afternoon and continued until parents arrived to claim their children. The charge was $15 a month. For those working overtime or swing shifts, Dye provided supper and storytelling for an extra 25 cents a day.[32]

Predictably, Gale Manor had a lengthy waiting list and offers to expand elsewhere, but Dye resisted on the grounds that success depended on her personal care. For the lucky children in her charge Gale Manor was a utopia, one all too rare in the frantic atmosphere of wartime. For many of the children whose parents worked in the plants, childhood remained a varying shade of nightmare.

PREDICTABLY, JUVENILE DELINQUENCY became a national disease during the war. For the first time in March 1944 the seventeen-year-old boy became the number one criminal in FBI records, committing nearly 28 percent more crimes than the previous year. The number of girls under twenty-one arrested soared more than 130 percent over 1941. Most of them belonged to the "V-girl" category of amateur prostitutes, some girls as young as twelve, but the number of burglaries committed by girls jumped 30 percent. One Spartanburg, South Carolina, teenager bore an illegitimate baby, abandoned it, and proceeded to marry three soldiers in quick succession, shifting among them as each one transferred to another camp. A fourth of the senior girls in a Jacksonville, Florida, high school had illegitimate pregnancies. Hartford uncovered a ring of forty boys aged ten to fifteen who broke into cars and parking meters to steal money and goods. Juvenile crime was up in nearly every major city.[33]

Sensational headlines leaped from the newspapers. In the Bronx twelve boys were indicted for raping a seventeen-year-old girl in a crowded movie theater. Two Cleveland brothers confessed to more than forty burglaries and three house fires. At home they had twenty guns and 2,000 rounds of ammunition. When their mother protested, one of the brothers shot her in the back, wounding her seriously. An eighteen-year-old in Los Angeles resolved an argument between his father and stepmother by shooting them both, then covering the murders by slaying his grandparents as well. When his eight-year-old brother started crying, he "let him have it too," then threw two of the bodies in a well. On Manhattan's Lower East Side police uncovered a vice ring that furnished teenaged prostitutes to middle-aged men. The madam running the operation was seventeen. All these revelations occurred during a single week. A month later Seattle uncovered "wolf packs" at two federal housing projects in nearby Renton. Fifteen boys and five girls admitted that to gain membership the girls agreed to have sex with all the male members. One girl submitted to thirteen boys, another to ninety.[34]

Crime of nearly every type was on the upswing and by no means limited to juveniles. At the Camp Anza officers' club near Riverside, California, a lieutenant named Beaufort George Swancutt sat drinking beer with another lieutenant and two girls. Suddenly Swancutt leaped to his feet, pulled out his service revolver, shot both girls dead, and wounded the lieutenant and a nearby officer. Running to the officer's quarters, he called out a captain and wounded him fatally. After wounding a corporal, he jumped into a staff car and forced a sergeant to drive him down the road. Near a police substation at Arlington he ordered the car stopped and waved down an approaching car containing an aircraft worker, his wife, their eight-month-old baby, and a cousin. Two policemen approached just as he ordered the family out of the car. Swancutt fired two bullets into the aircraft worker and two more into one of the policemen. The other policeman shot Swancutt, who was hauled off to a hospital with no clear reason for his rampage. The horrors of war, it seemed, were not confined to the battlefield.[35]

"DOGGONE IT," SNAPPED Dr. Harry A. Keenan, "I've often made calls when I felt a lot sicker than my patients." At sixty-six, diabetic and asthmatic, he had hoped for a relaxed retirement. Instead he saw fifty to sixty patients a day and served an area of 150 miles around Stoughton, Wisconsin. He averaged only five hours of sleep a night and hadn't had a day off in nine months. In the spare time he didn't have, he also acted as draft board examiner, seeing 250 to 400 men a session. The town of 15,000 had five doctors, including Keenan, but one had gone to the army and another to the marines. "If anything should happen to me," he fretted, "the other two doctors remaining in town couldn't handle the added burden."[36]

West Milford, New Jersey, a town of 3,500 people that added another 11,500 during the summer, suffered a severe loss in August 1942 when its only physician, a thirty-five-year-old father of three, was called up by the army. An army spokesman sympathized with the town's plight but warned that "West Milford is an example of what is going to happen in a great many other places." A petition signed by nearly 2,000 people nudged WMC into sending a replacement doctor from East Orange. The new doctor, a veteran of the last war, was fifty and had been rejected by the navy because of his age.[37]

Staying healthy remained a challenge throughout the war. Doctors, nurses, and some medicines were in short supply. People who migrated elsewhere for jobs struggled to adapt to a new climate, unfamiliar surroundings, and usually dismal living conditions. The polio epidemic made its annual summer visit to the nation; when it departed, the flu season arrived to take its toll. Not even the ravages of war could interrupt this cycle. The rate for some diseases, such as diabetes, had soared in recent years, in some case ironically because of advances in medicine. The discovery of insulin in 1922 prolonged the life of diabetics but did not cure the affliction, allowing its victims to develop other complications later in life. By 1942 it had risen from twenty-seventh to tenth among causes of death.[38]

Staying healthy went beyond avoiding sickness and disease. As the mobilization effort increased and thousands of new workers poured into factories and other work, the already high level of fatalities and injuries on the job rose steadily. In 1941, before America even entered the war, 18,000 workers died and 1.57 million were injured in on-job accidents. Another 32,000 died and 2.4 million suffered injuries in accidents off the job, making a total loss of 50,000 dead and 3.97 million hurt or maimed. Bookkeepers figured that these totals amounted to 480 million lost man-days of production. Safety campaigns became a staple of plants across the country. So did the need for medical personnel.[39]

In 1942 the United States had 180,496 licensed physicians, including about 25,000 who had retired. The military aimed to provide 6.5 doctors for every thousand soldiers, which for an army of 8 million men meant 52,000 physicians plus another few thousand for the navy. In particular they wanted men under thirty-six, of whom there were fewer than 43,000. The overall effect would be not only fewer doctors for civilians but older ones and more coming out of retirement to serve more people than ever before. Moreover, they were concentrated heavily in cities, leaving suburban and especially rural areas desperately short. Where New York, Chicago, and other large cities had one doctor for every 500 to 600 people, some rural areas had fewer than one for 1,500 to 3,000 people. The drain to the military only worsened those ratios.[40]

The nation had two other sources of physicians in the form of 8,000 women and 6,000 alien doctors. In April 1943 Roosevelt signed a bill giving female doctors equal status with men in the military; that summer both the army and navy changed their traditional policy and launched drives for more doctors, including women. While the military conducted their recruitment, rural areas went begging for medical help. When the only doctor in Pittsford, Vermont, died, thousands of patients in the town and surrounding mountain area were left without help. A young doctor in nearby Proctor tried to include them with his own practice and found himself with nearly 7,000 people to tend. In one rural town a young boy died of acute appendicitis because no doctor was available to diagnose his ailment. The one obstetrician in San Jose, California, sometimes delivered ten babies a day, while a surgeon there saw fifty patients a day.[41]

Specialists were obliged to revert to general practice and cover other fields. Nearly 30 percent of the 108,000 physicians treating civilians in 1944 were past sixty-five years of age, and replacements were nowhere in sight. They endured shortages of nurses, office staff, and equipment as well as long working days. Some 2,955 doctors were persuaded to relocate to designated shortage areas in rural spots and boom towns. Some 146 such areas induced retired doctors to resume practice, but another 166 areas found no relief. Unlike in Sweden, where physicians were placed according to medical need, American doctors went where business was best. "Physicians behave like any group of sensible business persons," said one of them. "They do business where it is good and avoid places where it is bad."[42]

By 1944, only seventy-five women doctors had joined the army and thirty-eight the Naval Reserve. Most of the others flocked eagerly to private practice, which offered them the best opportunities ever thanks to the scarcity of male physicians. Average earnings for doctors jumped from $5,047 in 1941 to $7,900 in 1943. Enrollments of women in medical school mushroomed; even staid Harvard Medical School opened its doors to them for the first time. Training programs were accelerated, raising fears about falling standards, overburdened instructors, and under-educated students. One reason, charged Dr. Evarts A. Graham, a professor of surgery at the Washington University School of Medicine in St. Louis, was that "the Army and Navy have adopted policies which have already effectively prevented our medical schools and hospitals from continuing the supply of trained doctors for the armed services."[43]

Early in the war, said Graham, the military recognized the importance of the fifteen specialty boards that certified advanced training in all the known medical specialties such as surgery. Medical students in these programs were given special consideration until a directive in April 1943 limited the total number of resident physicians in all American hospitals to no more than half the number present on July 15, 1940. No distinction was made between good and bad training programs. Five months later another mandate decreed internships be reduced to nine months compared to at least six years of approved graduate work in surgery. Teaching hospitals were assigned strict quotas on the number of young medical officers they could train. As a result two thirds of the nation's 4,000 male interns entered the service with only a few months of experience in surgery.[44]

Instead of concern for quality, complained Graham, "there has been too blind a reliance on the magic of numbers." He offered a few of his own. The military demanded 40 percent of American doctors, nearly twice as many as the British did. Through November 1944 about 117,000 Americans died in the war compared to more than 3.2 million civilian deaths during that same period. Accidental deaths alone were 250 percent greater than those in combat, never mind the large number of seriously ill patients that did not exist among

young, physically fit soldiers. "We have been spending our capital," concluded Graham. "It would be more precise to say that we have blown it all at
once. Except for the physically disqualified, there are practically no young
men outside of the armed forces who have had the training equal to that
which those have had who are making it possible for the Surgeon General of
the Army to extol the splendid record being accomplished."[45]

Medical advances during the war did much to alleviate suffering and reduce losses at home and on the battlefield. By far the most important were
penicillin and sulfa drugs. Neither was new when the war broke out, but their
properties became better known and their uses extended. Although sulfa
drugs had been used to treat infections since 1932, no one understood how
and why they worked until 1942, when a British researcher unraveled the
mystery in a series of articles. Sulfa drugs had some negative side effects such
as producing sudden drops in body temperature; penicillin reduced it in easy
stages and had no known harmful side effects. Best administered by injection
or through a salve, powder, or solution, it was hailed as the wonder drug of
1943. Demand for it rose so sharply that nearly the entire supply (the actual
amount remained a military secret) was reserved for the military. Only a few
civilians were lucky enough to get it.[46]

Dr. Chester S. Keefer of Boston had the unenviable job of deciding who did
and who did not. He doled out the limited supply to twenty-two doctors
across the country who tried it on a handful of civilian guinea pigs. A few
civilian uses nevertheless resulted in spectacular headlines that caused demand for penicillin to soar. Keefer allotted some of the drug to victims of the
horrendous Cocoanut Grove fire in Boston. It saved the life of a dying two-
year-old girl in Queens, resulting in a newspaper story that earned a Pulitzer
Prize, and that of a seven-year-old girl dying of gangrene in California.[47]

The wonder drug curbed pus infections better than any sulfa drug even
when blood poisoning had already developed. Where sulfa drugs starved
bacteria to death, penicillin prevented them from dividing and multiplying,
allowing the body's own defenses to kill them. It also proved effective against
pneumonia, streptococcus, and gonorrhea infections, all of which resisted
sulfa drugs. But it could not be produced in quantity because its precise
chemical structure remained a mystery. Instead it had to be made through
slow-growing molds from which it was extracted in minute quantities. To
produce an ounce of penicillin required 125 gallons of culture filtrate. By 1944
twenty-one manufacturers, two of them in Canada, were busy producing
cultures enough to meet the civilian demand. One drawback was that penicillin could not be taken orally because the stomach's gastric juices destroyed
it too quickly. Not until February 1945 did Dr. Raymond L. Libby solve the
problem by suspending the drug in an indigestible oil and enclosing it in a

capsule. By then the supply had grown large enough that in March the army relinquished control over it.[48]

Other breakthroughs helped the war effort as well as the home front. Early in the war wounded soldiers received blood transfusions in the field from an amazing kit the size of a cigar box filled with two tins containing dried plasma in one and distilled, sterilized water in the other along with a needle and rubber tube. In May 1944 two Boston chemists produced the first artificial quinine, a drug indispensable for fighting the malaria that plagued American troops in the Pacific. Another old, unused compound, DDT, was used in delousing powder and credited with preventing typhus epidemics in North Africa and Italy. In June 1944 *Newsweek* hailed it as "one of the three greatest medical discoveries to come out of the war" along with penicillin and plasma. A representative of the surgeon general's office predicted that "DDT will be to preventive medicine what Lister's discovery of antiseptic was to surgery." But only two months later the Public Health Service issued a warning that DDT might be toxic to people, animals, and insects. Early in 1945 researchers in a New Jersey laboratory reported the discovery of a potentially powerful new antibiotic called streptomycin.[49]

One disease resisted all efforts to conquer it. Polio remained not the deadliest but the most dreaded of afflictions, especially for children, and its cause remained a mystery. The 2,753 cases reported for the first half of 1943 doubled the figure for the previous year and was the highest for that period since 1934. Nearly three fourths of the cases came from four states: California, Texas, Kansas, and Oklahoma. By year's end 1943 witnessed the third-worst number of cases behind only 1916 and 1931. Things grew even worse in 1944, when the flood of cases hit hardest in New York, North Carolina, and Kentucky. By the time the epidemic reached its peak in September, 6,259 cases had been reported, the highest figure since 1916. No one better appreciated the hardship and suffering it caused than the best-known of all Americans, the man in the White House who had lived with the disease for twenty-three years.[50]

CHAPTER 32

THE SWEET SCENT OF VICTORY

If that boy of mine isn't home for Christmas dinner, I'll do a double somersault right over this chair.
— KANSAS CITY LAUNDRYMAN [1]

Not since the Civil War have we had an election in wartime, and it will be a severe trial for our democracy. Never have we had such highly organized pressure groups badgering Congress for special favors. There are severe race tensions. We cannot pretend they don't exist.
— RAYMOND CLAPPER [2]

Politics is the science of how who gets what, when and why.
— PAC's *POLITICAL PRIMER FOR ALL AMERICANS* [3]

BY MIDSUMMER 1944, DESPITE all warnings, optimism reigned su-preme. The war was going well, production was going well, inflation had slowed, and it was possible not merely to hope but to anticipate victory not at some far-off time but within months. The Russians moved into Poland and Roma-nia, having inflicted severe losses on the Germans. Even high-ranking offi-cers spoke of the European war ending possibly during the fall. Early in July General Marshall told Baruch that Germany was boxed in; a month later Patterson predicted the Reich's imminent collapse. In the Pacific Saipan had been secured after a bloody battle, then Guam and Tinian. Talk at table and in the media turned increasingly to reconversion and what life would be like after the war. Despite shortages and the nuisance of rationing, times seemed good. Even the rubber shortfall had eased. On July 25 Bradley Dewey, the rubber director, told Byrnes that the total supply was adequate and produc-tion no longer required a special organization. [4]

"The United States is now being swept by a wave of prosperity that makes 1929 look like a ripple," wrote Frederick Lewis Allen, an authority on those earlier times, in June. Shelves were full, beaches like Coney Island were jammed, and people were in a festive mood. Resorts did a thriving business and had more customers than they could accommodate. "You don't tell the resort when you're coming," said one exasperated vacationer. "They tell you when you can have a room, if any." An air of prosperity hung over the land, contrasting sharply with the anxieties of war. Whatever their private sorrows, most people were doing well.[5]

One small example told the tale. An elderly lady who ran a drugstore in a small New England town had complained bitterly in 1939 when her son invested in an expensive ice-cream-freezing unit. The unit ran full blast during the war years and business hummed at the drugstore. By 1944 she had paid off the freezer, her mortgage, and all her other debts, and in the bargain laid aside enough money, in her words, "to weather the postwar depression." The war had made a prophet of her son and brought profits to them. "We're getting all the business in town," she said happily, "because none of the other stores can get any ice cream, but we can make our own."[6]

As the outlook brightened, people chafed increasingly at the straitjacket of regulations binding them. One conservative anti–New Dealer pointed to the Federal Register as evidence in asking, "Will We Save the American Form of Government?" Between its first number on March 14, 1936, and June 29, 1944, it printed 76,541 directives, grants, orders, permissions, and prohibitions requiring 62,202 printed pages and 93 million words. They were the modus operandi of a bureaucracy that had begun in 1933 and accelerated furiously during the war. Even worse, argued Stanley High, they were the product not of legislation but of a proliferation in presidential directives. From Lincoln's first presidential directive in 1862 down to 1933, presidents had averaged 85 directives a year. Roosevelt's average since 1933 was 307, which among other things had created 200 new federal boards, bureaus, commissions, and administrations.[7]

Early in the year Chester Bowles promised Americans that rationing and price controls would be a lot easier to live with in 1944. "We are doing everything in our power," he added, "to simplify the rules and eliminate red tape." In May he declared a ration holiday on all meats except beef steaks and roasts as livestock production reached an all-time peak. Food czar Marvin Jones announced that "just now there is no serious shortage of food of any kind" and said Americans would have more ice cream that spring thanks to heavy milk production. In fact, 1944 proved to be another record year of farm production, exceeding prewar averages by one third. The output of farm machinery doubled the volume of 1943 as surpluses of raw materials began piling up and manufacturers wound up their military contracts and turned back to making tractors, harvesters, and other equipment at a WPB goal of 80 percent of their 1941 production. "Well, the government said they wanted production," said one Ohio farmer, "and by gum we'll give it to 'em if it kills us."[8]

Labor remained in short supply, down 4 percent from 1943, forcing more women and girls into the fields. One Ohio woman, widowed sixteen years, ran a 300-acre farm with only one helper. She picked a boy of good character for a hired hand, brought him to her house to live, and taught him the work. By 1944 she was on her third hand, the first two having grown up and married. All were good workers. Asked how he managed to tend a farm that large, the boy replied, "Well, I let the tractor do the work." To harvest a bumper wheat crop in Oklahoma and Texas, a fleet of 500 newly built combines converged on the states as a roving brigade for beleaguered farmers. Once finished there, the fleet moved on to Nebraska and the Dakotas, reaping good profits for their owners.[9]

Three years of good weather had enabled farmers to increase output 23 percent during the war despite all obstacles, including a farm population 20 percent smaller than in 1940. During World War I crop and livestock production had risen only 5 percent over the previous five years. By October warnings began appearing in farm country of surpluses in many crops. One farm journal urged its readers to "sell all high-priced equipment, crops, and livestock not needed." The value of farmland had increased 42 percent over 1935–39 averages. Some states registered much higher gains; Kentucky and Colorado values jumped 70 percent, South Carolina, Indiana, and Tennessee more than 60 percent.[10]

For Joe Wall of Yale, Iowa, summer marked the realization of his American dream. Nine years earlier he had quit his job as a hired hand, married a girl who worked on a nearby farm, and rented 80 acres north of Panora to go it on his own. Their $300 in savings and a $300 loan from the local bank went to buy a pair of mules, a cookstove, a cream separator, two brood sows, and some old farm equipment, including a harrow picked up for one dollar. The Walls' first crop in 1936 was lost to drought, and Joe had to sell the brood sows for money to pay the doctor who delivered their first child. He went on WPA to earn enough for food and interest on the bank loan. The next year he rented a farm at Yale and, with better weather and fair crops, managed to stay afloat and pay off $100 of the bank loan. Three more years of scrimping and long hours brought enough income to pay off the loan and buy a little more equipment and stock.[11]

Then Wall heard that FSA was willing to lend money on easy terms to tenants who wanted to own their land. He jumped at the chance and bought 80 acres of good loamy land. His timing proved perfect, thanks to the war. In 1941 the Walls grossed $2,500 and kept their expenses down to $500; the rest went back into the farm, with $359 going to FSA. Good weather and more hard work increased their income to $4,200 in 1942 and $5,040 in 1943. Still they held expenses at $500 a year and poured more money into the FSA loan. Like many other farmers, they made do with old equipment and resisted the urge to buy more land. In August 1944, Joe Wall, now thirty-four, stepped into the FSA office in Guthrie Center, Iowa, and paid off the last of his $8,257 loan thirty-seven years before it came due. His farm, worth an estimated $20,000, was free of debt. He had 20 acres of oats, 42 acres of corn, hay in the barn, 46 hogs, and 8 milk cows. His wife, Carolyne, added to their income with her flock of 140 laying hens, 200 pullets, and 100 cockerels.

Thanks largely to the war, life had been good to the Walls. The house would be wired for electricity in the fall, putting an end to the smelly kerosene lamps. From her egg money Carolyne planned to buy an electric refrigerator if she could find one; Joe dreamed of a small radio for the barn to hear music and news while he milked. Later they hoped to get a tractor to spell the mules and an electric washing machine. On the long hot summer evenings, their thoughts turned not to victory or politics or rationing but to plans for remodeling their four-room, two-story house, adding two bedrooms, a new kitchen, and the most delicious luxury of all, water pumped directly into the house from the well.

As it had in 1940, speculation mounted steadily through the winter and spring over the question of whether Roosevelt would run again. This time a new wrinkle had been added: the president's health. A fourth term would be historic, as was the event itself—the first national election held in wartime since 1864. A Gallup poll concluded that the soldier vote could decide the outcome, and some sources estimated that 70 percent of it would go to the Democrats. This was why Roosevelt had supported the bill allowing servicemen overseas to vote. The regular Republicans, embittered over the loss of three straight elections but encouraged by their gains in 1942, were hungry to regain control of the White House and purge their party of the Willkie heresy. In their wrath they still harbored hopes of not only stonewalling any further social reform but rolling back the core of the New Deal.[12]

Relics of the past, they still fought against reforms like Social Security that most Americans had long since accepted as necessary components of a permanent social and political structure. They did support one major reform, the pathbreaking GI Bill of Rights that passed both wings of Congress in June by unanimous vote, but this was an exception and in many ways a political necessity. Their minds clung to the hoary image of the New Deal as radical if not socialist, Roosevelt as a dictator, labor unions as hotbeds of Communism and corruption trying to seize the prerogatives of management, intellectuals in government as wild-eyed, irresponsible idealists, and all of it un-American at heart. But the Republican Party was as splintered as the Democrats and had even fewer viable candidates to offer.[13]

In their quixotic quest to restore the past, they had the support of most conservative southern Democrats who were intent on preserving white supremacy, cutting government spending except for the war, and curbing the powers of the presidency. However, Democrats north and south also wanted to win the election and keep their own jobs. The Midwestern farm vote was already lost to the Republicans, making the other components of the New Deal success story all the more crucial: the labor vote, urban machines, racial and ethnic groups, and the soldier vote. Southern conservatives despised all these elements but needed their support. The soldier vote especially troubled them because it raised the specter of black troops evading their home-state poll tax to cast ballots. For them any federal intervention in the voting process threatened possible enfranchisement of blacks.[14]

Mississippi's John Rankin denounced the soldier vote bill as the work of radicals and Jews. Robert Taft warned that under it Roosevelt would march soldiers to the polls just as, in his mind, the president had done with workers on relief earlier. Three senators, James Eastland of Mississippi, Kenneth McKellar of Tennessee, and John McClellan of Arkansas, concocted a "state control" substitute bill that merely suggested states pass laws enabling soldiers to vote. It passed the Senate and was modified somewhat by the House but still fell far short of the original bill. Rather than lose any improvements in the existing situation, Roosevelt signed it grudgingly while calling it "wholly inadequate."[15]

The parties shared a familiar dilemma in the lack of appealing candidates. Roosevelt remained his usual coy self about a fourth term, and even loyalists worried over his health problems that winter. Willkie remained the most popular Republican, but the regulars wanted no part of him. Taft had all the charisma of a dried prune. John Bricker was eager but was, as Clapper once said, "a conservative who takes no stand on anything." The Republican poll leaders were Willkie and Thomas E. Dewey, the handsome, dynamic governor of New York, who was a cold fish lacking Roosevelt's charm and warmth. For both parties everything depended on Roosevelt's decision. If he ran, the election would in many respects be a referendum on him and his leadership.[16]

The president seemed in poor shape for another run. After the high of D-day faded he was exhausted, filled with melancholy, and still suffering from the headaches and fatigue that had been plaguing him. His new diet and reduced schedule helped only slightly; his stamina was waning. One day,

Eleanor confided to Anna, he startled her by crying out, "I cannot live out a normal life span. I can't even walk across the room to get my circulation going." Most party leaders and pundits expected him to head the ticket at the convention in July, but he seemed curiously detached and preoccupied with death. As hard as she tried, not even Anna's good cheer could lift his gloom. However, on July 11, five days before the Democratic convention, Roosevelt let it be known that he would run again. "All that is within me cries out to go back to my home on the Hudson River," he said in an acceptance letter, "but the future existence of the nation and the future existence of our chosen form of government are at stake." He was running, he emphasized, as commander in chief.[17]

When the news reached three Democratic senators in committee, Allen Drury observed, "It was as though the sun had burst from the clouds and glory surrounded the world. Relief, and I mean relief, was written on every face. The meal ticket was still the meal ticket and all was well with the party. They almost sang out loud." On the Republican side, the regulars got their wish. Support for Willkie dwindled; a Gallup poll in March showed him trailing Dewey 64 to 27 percent among the rank and file. Despite vigorous campaigning he lost the Wisconsin primary and conceded defeat. Dewey gained the nomination, but Willkie did not rush to endorse him. In June he sent Gifford Pinchot to broach a startling proposal to Roosevelt.[18]

Since his ill-fated attempt to purge the Democratic Party of its hidebound southern elements in 1938, the president had pondered how best to get out from under their influence. Willkie wanted to create a new arrangement in American politics, one that drew together the liberals of both existing parties into a new liberal party. "I agree with him one hundred per cent," Roosevelt told Sam Rosenman, "and the time is now—right after the election. We ought to have two real parties—one liberal and the other conservative." He sent Rosenman to tell Willkie secretly that he favored the idea. When some complications arose, Willkie asked that nothing be done with the idea until after the election. But he suffered a heart attack late in August and on October 8, at the age of fifty-two, he died after another series of heart attacks.[19]

A more immediate problem faced Roosevelt: the nomination of a vice president. The concerns and ugly rumors about his health ought to have made this a top priority with him, yet he seemed strangely indifferent. In 1940 he had fought hard to get Henry Wallace on the ticket. Wallace made a spirited effort to get the nomination again, but Roosevelt gave him no help. Saying, "I am just not going to go through a convention like 1940 again," he left the decision up to the delegates. Rosenman had the unhappy task of telling Wallace that the president would not support his candidacy, but his mission failed and the job was bounced back to Roosevelt. Byrnes was eager for the position and the front-runner, but Roosevelt did not support him either. On the evening of July 11 a small group of Democratic politicos gathered at the White House with Roosevelt to make the decision. It was a hot, muggy evening, everyone was in shirtsleeves, and the president seemed listless and content to let others take the lead.[20]

Roosevelt had two requisites for the nominee: He had to be loyal to the New Deal, and he should be younger, given Dewey's relative youth. Both requirements ruled Byrnes out, and hardly any of the bosses wanted Wallace. Sam Rayburn was rejected, and Barkley was too old. Roosevelt suggested William O. Douglas, but no one wanted him. The conversation kept coming back to Harry Truman. Roosevelt spoke well of him and worried only about his age. No one had any significant fault to find with him and there was much to praise. Little or no discussion occurred about Truman's qualifications to be president, or those of anyone else, possibly because it was too delicate a topic with Roosevelt sitting there. Truman, who had said repeatedly he did not want the job, became the party's choice. Wallace, who made one of the speeches nominating Roosevelt, took his snub with grace and class.[21]

Much of the confusion over the nomination derived from Roosevelt's chronic weakness of not wanting to hurt the feelings of old friends. Instead he promised support to several of them, or left them with the impression that he had, and could not deliver. The discarding of Wallace wounded liberals, some deeply. They regarded him as a man of high principles, the most enlightened member of Roosevelt's cabinet. But he was also an aloof figure with few close friends among either professional politicos or labor leaders. "His has been a regrettable personal tragedy," wrote Drury. "Like so many others, he knows now what it means to be a politically dispensable friend of Franklin Roosevelt."[22]

A NEW ELEMENT entered the political arena that season. The Smith-Connally Act contained a provision restricting money contributions to political parties by labor unions. Alarmed by the Democratic losses and low voter turnout in 1942, the CIO in July 1943 created the first Political Action Committee (PAC). Although it would be avowedly nonpartisan, everyone knew its purpose was to support Roosevelt and New Deal candidates. Phil Murray and Sidney Hillman concocted the organization, and Hillman returned to the national stage by becoming its chairman and director. The member unions agreed to give the PAC $700,000, which hostile papers soon exaggerated into $7 million. Shrewdly Hillman tried to give the organization a broad appeal. "We are calling for a dynamic program to make full production possible after this war," he insisted. ". . . This is not a 'labor program.'" To the membership he exhorted,

"Let's quit blaming the politicians and face the responsibility of full citizenship. Let's become politicians ourselves."[23]

To get around Smith-Connally, Hillman formed a second organization with no official connection to PAC but with himself as head. Ultimately PAC got only $600,000 from the unions, but in the minds of its enemies it was wallowing in cash and trying to buy the election. Hillman did put an army of canvassers in the field to get out the vote and backed them with a blizzard of pamphlets, leaflets, and stickers. *Time* called Hillman "the most important politician at the Democratic convention." During the tussle over the vice presidency, the phrase "clear it with Sidney" was overheard and conveyed to Arthur Krock of the *New York Times*. It was to be echoed again and again during the campaign, magnified by the usual distortions into a fantasy that Hillman—and therefore labor—had pulled the strings getting Truman nominated and was dominating the campaign.[24]

PAC had no such power but did make its influence felt. New voter registration jumped throughout the country, especially in cities. In the spring primaries several candidates opposed by labor went down to defeat, and three, including the despised Martin Dies, chose not to run again. When Dies charged that PAC had spent $250,000 to "get him," Hillman retorted, "We haven't spent 7 cents to beat Dies." Only one defeat, in Alabama, could be clearly attributed to PAC's efforts. Nevertheless, Kiplinger's warned that the "CIO Political Action Committee (Hillman) must now be recognized as a major force in elections. It makes the claim that it is bipartisan, but actually it is pro-Roosevelt, pro his foreign policy, pro New Deal." *Time* called PAC's attempt to convert at least some of CIO's 5 million members into political activists "something unique in American labor, and in American history. It is the first sophisticated, thoroughly professional entry of labor into politics . . . the most formidable pressure group yet devised by labor—a pressure group backed with money, brains and an army of willing workers."[25]

"Will the CIO capture the Democratic Party?" asked an article written by an anti-Communist founder of the American Labor Party. Roosevelt was not about to let that happen, but he welcomed PAC's help in a campaign that grew even nastier than that of 1940. The president had vowed again to remain aloof from the campaign. He was weary, haggard, and drawn, partly from his loss of weight. Dewey was young, vigorous, and a master of misstatement. He waded in early with trips around the country making speeches, mocking the "tired old men" of the administration, and ridiculing the constant bickering within its ranks that reached a peak in August with the fall of Nelson and resignation of Wilson.[26]

On July 21 Roosevelt left for a trip to Hawaii and Alaska to discuss war strategy, greet the troops, and inspect installations. At Pearl Harbor he met with Douglas MacArthur and Chester Nimitz, alarmed his Secret Service men by touring Oahu in an open car surrounded by citizens, many of them of Japanese ancestry, and did something well out of character. At an Oahu hospital he asked to be wheeled slowly through all the wards occupied by men who had lost one or more limbs. Only once, many years before, had he allowed himself to be seen publicly in a wheelchair; pictures showed him either standing with his braces locked or seated. He wanted to show the veterans that a cripple could rise above his handicap, that a good life still awaited them. At each bed he offered his usual cheery smile and a few words. As he departed, Rosenman thought he was close to tears, something he had never seen before in the president.[27]

On his way to Alaska Roosevelt received news that Missy LeHand had died. Although he said little, everyone knew the news affected him deeply. On August 12 he gave a speech from the deck of a destroyer to a mass of workers at the naval yard in Bremerton, Washington, and a nationwide radio audience. He donned his braces for the first time in months, unaware that his weight loss made them not fit properly, and he had trouble keeping his balance. A strong wind increased his insecurity. The speech came off poorly, and Roosevelt suffered an angina attack while delivering it. Somehow he got through the speech and then collapsed in the captain's quarters. Listeners knew nothing of the attack but found his voice and delivery shockingly different. Tales of the speech, coupled with an unfortunate photo taken of him in San Diego just before his departure for Hawaii, fed the Dewey campaign theme of a tired, listless old man unfit for another term.[28]

Five days after the speech Roosevelt returned to the White House after an absence of thirty-five days. Dewey declined to comment on what he called "Mr. Roosevelt's holiday." The next day the president held his first news conference since announcing his candidacy and met with Truman for the first time since his nomination. The reporters found him thin and careworn but lightly tanned and rested. On August 29, at another news conference, he surprised them by announcing plans to give a political speech at a dinner of the Teamsters Union. In September he journeyed to Quebec to meet again with Churchill, who was so concerned about his appearance that he went to see Dr. McIntire. The president was fine, McIntire told him. "With all my heart I hope so," said the prime minister. "We cannot have anything happen to that man."[29]

After the conference Roosevelt brought Churchill back to Hyde Park for a couple of days. On his last night there they discussed the new bomb being developed. The scientists at Los Alamos had predicted that a bomb could be ready by August 1945. Admiral Leahy thought the project not worth the cost or resources. Roosevelt and Churchill agreed that the bomb might bring the

Japanese to their knees. Churchill was adamant that the Russians not be told about it. When Roosevelt returned to Washington in late September, he found a group of anxious Democratic Party leaders. Dewey's campaign was slick and smooth, filled with misrepresentations and what Rosenman delicately called "distortions of the truth." The Republicans hammered away at their familiar themes of a government run by tired old men who coddled labor, regimented agriculture, burdened the people with high taxes, and were destroying the free enterprise system in the process.[30]

As early as July 1942 Bill Hassett had noted that "the Boss and W.W. [Willkie] have this in common: they both hate Ham Fish and Tom Dewey." Even the ugly campaign of 1940 did not in Roosevelt's view match the meanness of this one. Merriman Smith, whom Sherwood called "a notoriously accurate reporter," described Roosevelt's attitude toward Dewey as one of "unvarnished contempt."[31]

One falsehood in particular caught Roosevelt's attention. Some Republican congressmen were circulating a story that on Roosevelt's trip home from Alaska Fala had inadvertently been left behind, and a large sum of taxpayer money was wasted in sending a destroyer back to pick up the dog. Papers hostile to Roosevelt pounced gleefully on the story and gave it wide currency. The Teamsters speech marked Roosevelt's entry into the campaign. Rosenman drafted most of the speech, but the president as usual added paragraphs of his own, including one about the Fala falsehood that would forever label it as the "Fala speech." Still unable to manage his braces properly, he agreed reluctantly to deliver the talk from a sitting position. Much depended on it going well and injecting some excitement into the campaign.[32]

"I never saw President Roosevelt in better form than he was that evening," said Rosenman afterward. He had a friendly audience, the kind that brought out the best in him. In his best manner he heaped ridicule on Republican arguments and charges, drawing howls of delight and applause. One excited Teamster pounded a silver bread tray with a soup ladle to show his approval; another smashed glasses with a wine bottle. "The President accused the Republicans of being liars, cheats and swindlers," noted Merriman Smith. "And the teamsters went wild." They went even wilder when Roosevelt, in a voice dripping with his best mock indignation, said, "These Republican leaders have not been content with attacks on me, or my wife, or on my sons. No, not content with that, they now include my little dog, Fala. Well, of course I don't resent attacks, and my family doesn't resent attacks, but Fala *does* resent them."[33]

Hassett called his performance "magnificent." Rosenman thought it jolted the campaign out of its rut. A member of the Democratic National Committee said wryly that it provided a new slogan for headquarters: "The race is between Roosevelt's dog and Dewey's goat." To refute charges that he was too sick to campaign or serve again, Roosevelt took some bold—some thought foolhardy—chances. Scheduled to give a speech in New York City on October 21, he arranged to tour four of the five boroughs in an open car beforehand, stopping in each one for a short talk. For most of his career he had had the luck of good weather for every outdoor activity. This time he faced a cold, steady, bone-chilling rain. Everyone urged him to cancel the tour, but he refused. In proving that he was not "a dying man," groaned Smith, "he nearly killed off his staff and the reporters with him."[34]

With a special heater under his legs in the car, wearing a flannel undersuit, his body covered by a fur robe and his heavy navy cape, the president endured the four-hour tour. The staff, Secret Service, and reporters were all soaked to the skin. Despite the weather, large crowds cheered him all along the route. In Brooklyn he visited the Army Yard and Navy Yard before moving to Ebbets Field. By then the rain was beating down relentlessly, the butt end of a hurricane. Ignoring McIntire's pleas that he close the car's top, Roosevelt threw off his cape, pulled himself up, and hobbled to a lectern behind second base. Standing bareheaded in the rain, his big smile unwavering, he made a few remarks, then pulled into a Coast Guard motor pool to change clothes without leaving the car before going on to Queens. It was a tour de force in every sense. The speech that evening went brilliantly, and, unlike his staff, Roosevelt showed no ill effects from his soaking. "No trace of a cold," said a relieved Hassett, "not even a sniffle ... He's madder than hell, his Dutch is up, and nothing will stop him now."[35]

The bad weather followed Roosevelt through the rest of the campaign, which featured major speeches in Philadelphia, Chicago, and Boston. In Philadelphia he spoke to a shivering crowd of 40,000 while sitting hatless in his car at Shibe Park. The car was driven up a ramp, and a board holding microphones was placed across the president's lap. In Chicago a capacity crowd of 110,000 filled Soldier Field, and an estimated 150,000 people outside waited eagerly to cheer him. There too he opened with a blast of sarcasm at the Republicans before outlining his vision of the future once the war was won. "If anyone feels that my faith in our ability to provide 60 million peacetime jobs is fantastic," he cried, "let them remember that some people said the same thing about my demand in 1940 for 50,000 airplanes."[36]

"The Big Boss brisk as a bee," reported Hassett happily, "brimming with health and spirits ... not the slightest ill effect from his strenuous swing into seven states with exposure to rain and all kinds of bad weather." But Andrew Jackson Higgins, who delivered more than twenty-nine speeches in a four-state swing on Roosevelt's behalf, had a very different impression. "My God, the president looks ghastly," he confided to his public relations man. "There's no doubt in my mind that Truman will be president within the next year."[37]

The Boston speech at Fenway Park also went well, and Roosevelt headed back to Hyde Park, where on election eve he made his traditional "neighborhood" tour: a five-hour, eighty-mile excursion through Dutchess, Orange, and Ulster counties to greet his friends and sometimes his foes. On election eve at 10:45 he made his usual nonpolitical broadcast to the nation. Roosevelt wanted badly to crush the "All-American Boy," as his circle called Dewey. He thought Dewey had run a campaign that was deceitful and dishonest, full of innuendoes, lies, half-truths, and distortions. Near the end he seized the offensive by charging that the administration was filled with and influenced by Communist sympathizers.[38]

"Actually," said *Newsweek*, "Dewey did not wage a campaign; it was a prosecution." However, he had neither the record, the popularity, nor the charisma to match that of Roosevelt, who answered the charges effectively in his speeches. Nor could Dewey overcome the fact that the war was going well. Paris was liberated on August 25, and American troops crossed the German frontier on September 11. By late October Belgium and Luxembourg had been freed and Holland entered. The British had invaded the Greek mainland, and the Russians had entered Romania and signed an armistice with Finland. Landings were made on Leyte Island in the Philippines, and the navy won the decisive battle of Leyte Gulf. Against this tide of victory Dewey could not prevail. Even worse for him, the voter turnout exceeded all expectations. Roosevelt won in something short of a landslide. Although his popular vote dropped from 27.2 million in 1940 to 25.6 million, Dewey could muster only 22 million. The electoral vote, however, ran 432 to 99 for Roosevelt. Dewey won only twelve states, most of them in the Midwest.[39]

"The graceless Dewey," recorded Hassett, "at 3:16 A.M. (Wednesday) broadcast an admission of defeat, but sent no message to the victor." Roosevelt sent him a wire thanking him for the statement. When he said good night to Hassett and started upstairs, he said of Dewey, "I still think he is a son of a bitch." For himself, Hassett was glad to be done with the election. "No one was surprised when the trend was early toward the President," he wrote. "How could it be otherwise after such a slimy campaign conducted by sinister forces, while the world was in conflagration?"[40]

Opinions divided over how major a role PAC had played in Roosevelt's victory, but the president took care to express his gratitude for its help. "It was a great campaign," he wrote Hillman, "and nobody knows better than I do how much you contributed to its success . . . I send you no condolences for the licks you took in the campaign. You and I and Fala have seen what happened to the people who gave them."[41]

* * *

IN JUNE, FOLLOWING the Normandy invasion, the sweet scent of victory finally drifted into Wall Street. For nearly the entire war the market had wallowed in the doldrums, unable to muster much in the way of rallies or trading volume. For a few days in June 1942 it rose four points but on a volume of only half a million shares on its biggest day. "What Became of the Stock Market?" asked one brokerage partner who thought the war had ignored the Street. After five years of decline, a start toward a bull market occurred in February 1943, spurred not by the usual inside money but by a flurry of buying by small investors. The action was confined mostly to lower-priced shares, what the Street called "cats and dogs." Between November 1942 and March 1943 the Dow Jones Industrial Average rose from 114 to 130; in May prices hit three-year highs and volume already exceeded the whole of 1942.[42]

Foreign securities also underwent a modest boom, a trend, said *Time*, that reflected "not only ebullient hopes of Allied victory but also tacit faith in the establishment of a workable world economy afterward." By July investors were picking up blue chip stocks as well amid rumors of a fairly quick end to the war. But when Italy surrendered, the market went down, and by September the Dow Jones stood at 138, less then seven points above its August 1939 low. *Time* concluded that investors were still suffering from "a 1930-style persecution complex." In November it fell another three points despite rumors of peace prospects and an impending opening of the long-awaited second front. Then in March 1944 the Dow Jones reached a six-month high after three straight days in which trading exceeded a million shares.[43]

On the eve of D-day the Dow Jones hit 142.24, a new high for the year. Some 245 stocks, many of them blue chips, hit new highs, and the "peace" stocks, laggards for so long, began outpacing "war" stocks. A similar burst of optimism fueled the London markets, which also hit wartime peaks. Once the landing proved successful, trading boomed into an upward surge that carried the Dow Jones to 147.28, its highest level since May 10, 1940, when the Nazi invasion started a downward slide. Brokers gleefully recorded two days of trading over 2 million shares. *Time* attributed the bull market to "a buying ripple, which had turned into a tidal wave under the fair, strong wind of cheering war news. The Street seemed confident that the end of the war was in sight." Small buyers were again jumping into the market, and "Wall Street was marching happily home from the war." If Wall Street believed the end was near, could victory be far behind?[44]

IT WAS A huge secret to keep, involving as it did thousands of people scattered over several sites. Yet somehow it was kept. "The amount of bare-faced lying that was done in Washington in those days is beyond estimate," said

James Conant. "Military secrets of all sorts were closely guarded. One just didn't ask an old friend whom one met at the Cosmos Club what he was doing."[45]

Every year Stimson and Bush trekked to Capitol Hill and briefed a small group of congressional leaders on the project. Then, when the matter came up before an appropriations committee, one of them would vouch for the project and the funds would be provided with no questions asked. "There was never a hitch," said Bush. "There was never the slightest leak of secret information. There was never an instance of a member of Congress prying into the affair."[46]

For scientists, engineers, and workers alike the Manhattan Project was an ordeal, a trial made worse by the fact that the vast majority of them knew nothing about what they were making or why. Few if any of the hundreds, even thousands of organizations involved wanted to participate. For many of them the risks were enormous and the reward, if any, unknown. Bureaus and departments pushed industrialists ruthlessly to get what they needed without saying why they needed it. Resources on a gigantic scale were being swallowed by some gigantic maw from which nothing ever seemed to emerge. Thousands of disparate pieces were being created for some giant mosaic of unknown design and purpose.[47]

The results were tremendously important but very uncertain, yet the work went steadily forward. At Westinghouse the Lamp Division Laboratories in Bloomfield, New Jersey, had been working for some time on purifying metallic uranium when, in the spring of 1941, some physicists asked whether they could get about twenty-two pounds of pure uranium in bulk. "We thought we could do it," said one Westinghouse researcher, "but it would take the efforts of several men for three months." After they got it done in that time, Arthur Compton called and asked, "How pure is your uranium?" Pretty pure, came the reply. "How soon can you make us three tons?"[48]

The Westinghouse men gulped and said they had no idea how long it would take. They scrambled frantically to figure out how and where to do it. They had no building large and safe enough for work on that scale, and no time to build one. Nor did they have apparatus enough. In desperation they bought all the garbage cans in Bloomfield and set them in long rows for the electrolytic process, using automobile jacks for hoisting gear. By August 1942 a newly created division was producing 300 pounds of uranium a day and shipping it to Chicago as fast as it was ready. The plant beat the delivery date in the contract, enabling the Chicago pile to make its first test. In the process Westinghouse also brought the cost of the material down from its original $750 a pound to $7.34. Then researchers at Iowa State College discovered a simpler, cheaper method for producing uranium of sufficient purity, and the electrolytic process was dropped.[49]

Like General Electric and many other companies, Westinghouse piled its work for the project on top of its heavy load of other war goods. Every division of the company, even the repair shops, had to be ready to make some new device without knowing what it was for. Special purchasing and expediting departments were set up to handle this work. For the electromagnetic process experiments alone the company produced nearly $53.3 million in special equipment and nearly half again that amount in standard items. In 1944 the chairman and president spent a day at Oak Ridge to see how the company's products were faring. They came away impressed but mystified. "We looked through all the labyrinth of pipes, ducts and cells and 'what-not' making up the eight or nine plants in which no manufacturing was being done so far as could be seen," the chairman reported. ". . . We came out of the plants without seeing anything in the way of results of the processes which were being carried on. We were told, however, that the plants were operating successfully."[50]

They were. An enormous complex of buildings arose at Oak Ridge to pursue the three remaining horses in the race, the centrifuge process having been abandoned in November 1942. The electromagnetic separation of isotopes, which E. O. Lawrence had developed, was the least efficient and most costly, but it was a proven process, and facilities for it could be built in stages. The project required an enormous amount of material, including 120 tons of scarce copper. Silver could be substituted for copper. Since the government owned the plant, the silver could be borrowed from the Treasury and returned after the war. Nichols approached Daniel Bell, assistant secretary of the treasury, who asked how much he needed. Six thousand tons, Nichols replied.[51]

"How many troy ounces is that?" asked Bell.

"I don't know how many troy ounces we need," said Nichols impatiently, "but I know I need six thousand tons—that is a definite quantity. What difference does it make how we express the quantity?"

"Young man, you may think of silver in tons," replied Bell stiffly, "but the Treasury will always think of silver in troy ounces."[52]

In the end Nichols obtained 14,700 tons—or 400 million troy ounces—of silver, which was melted down and cast into large ingots before being shipped to Allis-Chalmers in Milwaukee for more processing. The electromagnetic separation plant, known as Y-12, required much more than silver. Its design called for five oval Alpha units that became known as racetracks because of their shape and two Beta racetracks for final processing. In September 1943, seven months after construction began, Groves approved the addition of four more racetracks labeled Alpha II. In May Lawrence himself got his first glimpse of the project. Standing atop a ridge where he could look down on the plant, he said in awe, "When you see the magnitude of that operation there, it sobers you up . . . Just from the size of the thing, you can see that a thousand people would just be lost in this place . . . It's going to be an awful job to get those racetracks into operation on schedule. We must do it."[53]

Lawrence was right; it was an awful job. The process took place in devices called calutrons set in tanks. Each racetrack, 122 feet long, 77 feet wide, and 15 feet high, contained ninety-six of the tanks in which uranium atoms encountered a vacuum under the influence of electric and magnetic fields that separated U-238 and U-235 atoms, which were collected in special cavities and then removed. In all the huge plant required 22,000 operators to run the control boards. Most were Tennessee mountain girls trained by the contractor, Tennessee Eastman, and had only a high school education. The training material gave each operator only enough information to do her task without saying anything about the end result. At first Lawrence and a team of his scientists manned the controls to work out bugs before turning them over to the girls. This also gave the scientists firsthand experience for finding improvements.[54]

As the work progressed, Nichols noticed from the data that the girls seemed to be outperforming the scientists. Lawrence said this was because the men were experimenting with ways to improve production. He accepted a challenge from Nichols for a race between the PhD's and the girls. Nichols won the bet and explained that the girls were trained like soldiers "to do or not to do—not to reason why, while the scientists could not resist investigating every little fluctuation in the dial readings."[55]

Groves took a large gamble in expanding the investment in Y-12, and he got meager returns. The first racetrack began tests in October 1943 and immediately encountered technical problems that slowed progress for months. Meanwhile, in July Oppenheimer reported that, according to revised calculations by his scientists, three times more U-235 would be needed for a bomb than originally estimated. By July 1944 four Alpha tracks were operating but produced only a fraction of the material needed. Months before, it had become clear to the MPC that a combination of the processes would be needed to produce the necessary amount of material. A reviewing committee had concluded early that gaseous diffusion was the most direct process for isotope separation, but it also used a completely novel method. Nevertheless, in December 1942 the MPC agreed to build a full-scale plant known as K-25. For Groves it was one more giant gamble on an untried process. Compared to Y-12, Nichols considered it "by far more difficult to organize, coordinate, and expedite."[56]

The project struggled from the start. Work on the huge K-25 building did not start until October 1943; the pilot plant was ready in April 1944. Most of the delays came from technical problems in the process that had yet to be solved. The whole diffusion process depended on the creation of membranes or barriers that had to be porous, uniform, and robust. It also had to be capable of large-scale production and able to maintain its qualities over a long period of operation. For months researchers scrambled desperately to develop a suitable barrier. Ultimately Groves made the bold decision to go with an untried but promising barrier. By June 1944 construction costs on the K-25 complex had soared to $281 million and still no reliable barrier had been created. Not until late in the year was the barrier conundrum solved and work expedited on getting K-25 into production.[57]

The thermal-diffusion project, which had been around since 1940, did not look promising as an independent process. Using a long, vertical, externally cooled tube with a hot concentric cylinder inside, it separated isotopes on the principle that hot gases tended to rise and cool ones to fall. The outer wall was cooled by circulating water, the inner one heated by high-pressure steam. However, the process required an incredible amount of steam, a thousand pounds per square inch, and Groves thought the cost would be prohibitive. For a year little was done with it. Then, in June 1944, Oppenheimer suggested to Groves that the process might be used as a first step to enrich the product just slightly and use it as feed material for the other processes. "Just why no one had thought of it at least a year earlier I cannot explain," admitted Groves, "but not one of us had." Later he was even more blunt. "Dr. Oppenheimer . . . suddenly told me that we had [made] a terrible scientific blunder," he said. "I think he was right. It is one of the things that I regret the most in the whole course of the operation."[58]

Within days Groves moved to get a thermal-diffusion plant under way. After considering several sites he settled on one near the powerhouse for the K-25 plant at Oak Ridge. It could provide plenty of steam, and K-25 could use the product as feed material. The basic equipment consisted of 102 separation columns arranged together as an operating unit called a rack. Each column was a 48-foot vertical pipe, one made of nickel surrounded by another made of copper with the latter encased in a water jacket contained within a four-inch galvanized pipe. Three groups of seven racks each, a total of 2,142 columns, made up the whole arrangement. Groves wanted the plant completed in ninety days and it was, but the rushed construction led to steam leaks and other difficulties that took until January 1945 to fix.[59]

During 1944 it had become painfully clear that no one of these processes could produce sufficient material for a bomb in a reasonable length of time and that production could be expedited by using them in combination. The only other option was that mysterious substance, plutonium, which remained a wild card in that so little was known about it. The Chicago triumph of

December 2, 1942, proved that a controlled reaction in plutonium could be achieved, but not that plutonium could be produced on a large scale. Nor did it answer the key question of whether a bomb made with plutonium would actually explode. The reactor used a moderator to slow the neutrons, but a bomb would have no moderator and the neutrons would be fast moving.[60]

The Chicago reactor was but a pilot pile for a larger experimental version to be built at Oak Ridge. The plant was referred to as the semi-works because the larger model would itself serve as a pilot for a much larger pile at Hanford, where actual production would take place. The Chicago scientists, still resentful that DuPont seemed to be taking over the project, wanted the mid-sized pilot located at Argonne, where, Arthur Compton insisted, the risk was relatively small. Groves and Nichols thought otherwise and further outraged the scientists by having DuPont build the facility at Oak Ridge. Compton argued that Chicago should manage the facility but was dissuaded by Conant and others. In March 1943 work began on a 112-acre site at Oak Ridge for the X-10 pile site. By November the reactor was up and running smoothly; a few weeks later it turned out its first uranium slugs, which were sent to the chemical plant.[61]

The new pile, or reactor as it was coming to be called, was a massive square of graphite 24 feet on each side, weighing 1,500 tons and surrounded by 7 feet of high-density concrete as a radiation shield. Cooling it posed an immediate problem. Four methods were studied, using helium, air, water, and heavy water. For Oak Ridge air cooling would be used to get it up and running in the shortest possible time, but that method would not do for a much larger facility. It was decided to use helium at Hanford, but within three months Groves and the scientists had changed their preference to water cooling as cheaper and easier to design and build. In March 1944 X-10 produced its first gram of plutonium, which was dispatched to Los Alamos for experiments there.[62]

Construction of the huge Hanford complex got under way in the summer of 1943 and continued into 1945. The place was barren scrubland swept by sandstorms and forlorn in its isolation; the inmates called the swirling dust "termination powder." With great difficulty thousands of workers were lured there to live in trailers and barracks by promises of good pay, excellent food, all one could eat, and little else. Obtaining the needed equipment and supplies proved even harder and required yet another round of priority battles. The WMC helped recruit workers with the necessary skills to build three giant piles, three chemical separation plants, water treatment plants with enough capacity to serve a city of a million people, and all the supporting facilities, barracks, dining halls, and other buildings needed to sustain a workforce that peaked around 44,900 people.[63]

Hanford was a beast, and by the end of June 1944 it was only half finished. Through the long construction ordeal there and elsewhere Groves drove everyone, including himself, mercilessly in his abrasive, sarcastic manner. "I heard only criticism of every aspect of the work," Colonel Marshall said to him after one inspection tour. "Don't you ever praise anyone for a job well done, or a good idea for improving things?" Groves shook his head. "I don't believe in it," he said. "No matter how well something is being done, it can always be done better and faster."[64]

Construction of the first reactor began in February 1944 and, after much difficulty, was completed in September. On the twenty-seventh the control rods were withdrawn to begin production. After three hours the power level began dropping, and soon afterward the reactor shut down completely. It was started again and shut down again, leaving the scientists puzzled. Frantic efforts to determine the cause finally fixed on xenon 135, a "poison" isotope with a half-life of 9.4 hours that was absorbing a substantial number of the neutrons. Fortunately, DuPont had insisted on a conservative approach to construction that provided space for a much larger load of uranium in case it might be needed. By filling more tubes with uranium slugs the xenon problem was overcome, but production would be delayed. By December the second reactor was ready for operation. All 2,004 tubes in its pile were loaded and passed all critical tests. Both reactors ran successfully when fully loaded, and production of plutonium began at last.[65]

IN OCTOBER 1944 an assembling line at the Westinghouse plant in Mansfield, Ohio, proudly showed off the first irons the appliance division had made since 1942. They would be priced at the prewar figure of $8.75, and more goods such as vacuum cleaners, aluminum pots and pans, and bedsprings would soon follow. They were the first fruit of Nelson's spot authorization plan, and already WPB had approved 940 applications to make civilian articles, though in small quantities. Altogether they provided consumers with only a taste, albeit a welcome one, of the goods expected to flow after V-E Day.[66]

On December 7, 1944, the third anniversary of Pearl Harbor, Macy's set a new sales record for itself. Americans went on yet another shopping spree for the Christmas season, but the buying had been going on all year. Higher taxes on luxury items such as jewelry, handbags, luggage, cosmetics, perfumes, and furs dented enthusiasm only on the highest-priced items. Big cities and boom towns registered gains of 20 percent or more in sales, with some stores climbing 50 percent and beyond. Many reported their best pre-Christmas trade ever. A Portland, Oregon, department store dropped all holiday advertising and was still jammed with customers. In Atlanta a lead-ing department store put out twenty dozen nightgowns for $3.98 each at noon and sold out by 2:00 P.M. Boston stores complained of having plenty of cus-tomers and merchandise but too little help.[67]

Cheaper goods disappeared quickly and in some cases had been almost impossible to find for months. Retail sales in 1943 had hit the highest dollar mark on record at $63.3 billion, and some manufacturers shifted from cheaper goods to more profitable expensive items. Before the war 59 percent of Amer-ican women paid less than $5 for a street dress. Coats could be had for less than $12 and cotton housedresses for $1.60. However, by the end of 1943 only 42 of the 124 manufacturers of $4.98 street dresses still made them. Of 286 makers of women's coats for under $12, only 8 continued in that price line. A mere 6 manufacturers still produced housedresses below $1.60 compared to 43 a year earlier. Inflation, rising labor costs, and difficulty in getting raw material meant higher prices for lower-quality goods.[68]

Nevertheless, the holiday buying spree rolled merrily on, running "like a payday crap game," as *Time* put it. A 72-ounce mug of Worth's *Dans la Nuit* perfume flew off counters despite a $1,000 price tag. Handbags sold well at $100 each, and customers "reached for absurdly priced costume jewelry as eagerly as pygmy tribesmen bartering for trade beads." Popular gifts for men ranged from $150 cigarette lighters to $25 neckties. When some shortages grew severe, Mr. Black stood ready to accommodate those looking for scarce or rationed items. "People want to spend money," said one pleased store man-ager, "and if they can't spend it on textiles they'll spend it on furniture; or . . . we'll find something else for them."[69]

Amusements and resorts continued to thrive. People crowded the few horse and dog tracks still open and bet record amounts. California had only one racetrack in operation, but its legal daily handle averaged $420,000 a day, and illegal betting "through bartenders, barbers, elevator-men and pool-rooms" was estimated as high as $10 million a day. Altogether the wagering at track pari-mutuel machines exceeded $1 billion during 1944. Betting in other sports, especially college basketball, would lead to a major scandal in the winter of 1945. The movie industry prospered; people flocked to the theaters as one of the easiest, cheapest, and most enjoyable amusements available all year long.[70]

As early as 1942 novelist Philip Wylie saw what was happening. "Our war aims remain nebulous, we are told," he wrote, "because nobody has yet hit upon a plan for the postwar world which satisfies the majority of people on this all-consuming problem of goods . . . To many it hardly seems worth-while fighting to live until they can be assured that their percolators will live, along with their cars, synthetic roofing, and disposable diapers." American companies of all kinds adjusted their advertising accordingly. Early in the war, when many firms had little or nothing to sell consumers, their ads kept the company name before the public by detailing their role in the war effort. "Pontiac Reports to the Nation on Arms Production," read one automobile ad with its actual output figures dutifully blacked out but the story of its achievement intact. "From the highways of peace to the skyways of war," said Studebaker, which made engines for B-17s.[71]

"Every American expects two things of American industry," observed Raymond Moley in July 1942. "First, it's to produce the goods necessary to win the war; second, to produce, when the war is won, the goods necessary to maintain American standards of living." Goodyear and B. F. Goodrich gave readers a primer on synthetic rubber to prepare the ground for postwar tires. Willys promoted its Jeep, while Nash-Kelvinator described the airplane engines it made with the slogan "A refrigerator and an automobile go to war!" Hart, Schaffner & Marx depicted soldiers as "America's best-dressed man" whose uniform required "the wool off the backs of 26 sheep per year." Westinghouse provided numerous examples of its "making Electricity work for Victory." Armour detailed a typical week's menu enjoyed by the army, adding that "not one man in ten ate as nourishing, well balanced meals at home as he does in the U.S. Armed Forces today." Florsheim reminded readers that "every *extra* month and every *added* mile you get out of your shoes mean more leather for our fighting men."[72]

Advertisers spent $450 million in 1940, $469 million in 1941, and dropped only to $440 million in 1943. Many remembered some well-known firms that had stopped advertising during World War I and suffered dearly afterward. By 1943 the sweet scent of victory, while still faint, prompted an increasing number of companies to shift their emphasis toward the postwar pot of gold that awaited consumers at the war's end. "When the fight is won," promised Philco, "you may look to Philco for leadership, again, in the peacetime application of the miracles which its laboratories have achieved for war." Many coupled their message with an appeal to buy war bonds and stamps. Savings built this way, emphasized General Electric, would result in "after victory— the home you have always wanted!" When the war was won, the company promised, "the new skills and techniques they have developed in the production of *things for fighting* will result in ever finer G. E. *servants for better living.*"[73]

By 1944 the swing to the promise of a better life permeated ads. Revere Copper and Brass showed a Detroit victory garden with the brand name of an automobile above each planting. "A new car!" the ad enthused. "To us Americans, the thrill of those words baffles description. There's a heady fragrance like wine's in the very idea of driving once more across the bosom of the continent." A Scripps Howard survey revealed that a majority of the women polled expected "drastic improvements, immediately following the war . . . in radios, autos, electric refrigerators, electric irons, toasters . . . washing machines, furniture, kitchen cabinets, lighting and heating equipment." After the war Carrier promised "no miracles. *Except the miracle of air conditioning itself* . . . broadened to touch the daily lives of men and women everywhere." Kelvinator assured readers that "we believe your hope for a new and finer home can and will come true" and that the company would "build more and finer electrical appliances than we have ever built before."[74]

Then, without warning in mid-December, the sweet scent of victory turned sour. On the morning of December 16 the Germans launched a massive attack in the Ardennes forests, catching the unprepared Americans completely by surprise, and sent the thinly manned line reeling backward with severe casualties. The attack had been planned to coincide with heavy overcast skies that kept Allied planes on the ground and helpless to contribute. One historian called the Allied failure to anticipate some kind of possible offensive "the most notorious intelligence disaster of the war," one that "derived chiefly from over-confidence." As German tanks and infantry rolled deeper into Luxembourg and Belgium, the American high command scrambled frantically to heal the breach in its lines and retaliate. The Battle of the Bulge had begun, and American planes remained grounded for a full week. During the first five days the Germans destroyed 300 American tanks and took 25,000 prisoners.[75]

News of the attack alarmed Stimson, who had been complaining for weeks about the shortage of ammunition, especially for artillery. "The public has paid no attention to our shortage," he grumbled, "and the fact that the war wasn't over and have thus caused shortage of ammunition. Then as soon as that became known they got scared and were thinking too much of it." Four days before the German attack Patterson argued in a report that no limit should be put on the production of ammunition and no consideration given to when the war might end. The attack gave the War Department added muscle in its campaign to push production still higher and improve the manpower shortfall with a national service law. Stimson also realized privately that failure of the German offensive would likely shorten the war because of the losses incurred by them, but he did not voice that belief publicly.[76]

Patterson welcomed the blow given by the Germans to excessive American optimism over the war's end. "I am sure we will now get more production," he wrote a friend. "The 'reconversion boys' have had their day, and are singing very low." He was right. The spot authorization order was suspended for ninety days in critical labor areas. Nelson's hope for gradual reconversion was dead.[77]

In December, too, Sewell Avery came back to haunt the president and the

War Department. On November 28 Roosevelt had gone to Warm Springs for his first extended visit there since Pearl Harbor. He stayed until December 17, handling all his business by mail or phone and enduring vile cold and rainy weather most of the time. After his return he remained in Washington less than a week before leaving to spend the holidays at Hyde Park. Avery's latest rebellion took place while he was away from Washington.[78]

A strike on the ninth against the Montgomery Ward store in Detroit precipitated another confrontation. As he had in April, Avery refused to obey a WLB directive to renew CIO union contracts providing for maintenance of union membership, dues check-off, grievance machinery, arbitration of disputes, and wage increases. Somervell begged Stimson to persuade the president not to turn Montgomery Ward over to the army again. Stimson said he had done his best short of insubordination, but Roosevelt would not be moved. "There is no doubt in my mind that if the Company gets away with its decision not to obey the War Labor Board's orders," the president wrote Stimson, "it will seriously affect the whole war munitions production in Detroit. Somebody has to do something about it . . . I am sorry but there is literally no other organization which can run the business except the Quartermaster Corps."[79]

Stimson talked to Byrnes but got nowhere. After the cabinet meeting on December 22 he pleaded his case to the president, Byrnes, William Davis of the WLB, Biddle, and Fred Vinson. In a session that Stimson called "long and hot" everyone sided against him even though he said he could not honestly certify Montgomery Ward as an essential war industry. The problem, said Byrnes and the others, was that if Montgomery Ward was not handled vigorously, a wave of strikes would sweep the country. Roosevelt agreed with this argument. On the twenty-seventh he issued an executive order seizing the company's properties. "We cannot allow Montgomery Ward & Co.," he declared, "to set aside the wartime policies of the United States Government just because Mr. Sewell Avery does not approve of the Government's procedure for handling labor disputes."[80]

The April takeover minidrama was replayed, this time with more finesse. Avery again refused to yield or leave his office. Instead of carting him out, General Joseph Bryan politely read him the order and occupied another office two doors down the hall, leaving Avery to stew in his own office with nothing to do. Bryan tactfully stationed not armed soldiers but a WAAC lieutenant outside his door. The army installed its own switchboard and used the company auditorium for its staff. To Avery's chagrin, the government did not return control of Montgomery Ward to its officers until after the war's end, and in June 1945 the court upheld the president's constitutional power to seize the plants.[81]

Labor unrest had been building all fall. At Willow Run 2,000 workers quit for one day in protest over the transfer of twenty riveters. Wildcat coal strikes broke out, and other unions strained to break the Little Steel formula. "The motivating force," declared *Newsweek*, "is the certain knowledge that a return to the 40-hour week and loss of fat overtime checks are ahead. Labor leaders make no bones about that. They want to maintain as much of the present purchasing power as possible." Attempts to unionize workers at Oak Ridge required an appeal to the leaders' patriotism to defer action lest it delay the project. In November a dispute between two unions in one small factory spread to forty-eight other war plants, prompting Patterson to charge the union's leader with "conduct equivalent to treason . . . Your strikes . . . represent no honest grievance . . . You are striking our fighting men from the rear."[82]

Patterson demanded that the strikes end. When they did not, Roosevelt ordered the army to take over eight of the plants. The next day union chief Matthew Smith ordered the strikers back to work. A month later the surprise German offensive fueled the determination of Patterson, Stimson, and Byrnes to snap the nation out of its peace reverie and back to what they deemed the reality of a long, hard push to victory.[83]

1945: The Year of Triumph

CHAPTER 33

THE FEAR OF FALTERING

Just as soon as news of these victories comes, everybody wants to put on his coat and stop working including Congress. I never had a more vivid viewpoint of some of the curious characteristics of our noble people in the United States that have no more notion that they are in a war or the sacrifices which are involved or needed,— that is, the great bulk of them do not—just so many children.

—HENRY STIMSON [1]

The most dearly loved and most bitterly hated man in our day, perhaps in American history.

—WILLIAM HASSETT [2]

Stalin shuddered at the thought. Churchill wept. Political enemies said, "We knew it was coming." Political allies said, "What will happen to us now?" The people seemed to agree that it was a national, and yes, an international catastrophe. They were frightened. The Great White Father was gone. What was going to happen to the war?

—MERRIMAN SMITH [3]

BY FRIDAY, DECEMBER 22, THE worst of the crisis in Belgium had passed. The weather cleared that weekend, allowing American planes to go aloft in record numbers and pound German positions. The brilliant maneuver by George Patton to wheel his Third Army units toward Bastogne also relieved pressure, although more hard fighting lay ahead. Even before the German attack Byrnes, Stimson, and Patterson had expressed strong feelings about what they considered the waning American concentration on winning the war. After a series of conferences on manpower in early November, Byrnes released a letter warning that "while a shortage of material and weapons exists in relatively few programs it is sufficient, if not speedily overcome, to prolong the war." Those few programs included heavy bombers, heavy artillery and ammunition, trucks, and radar. Too many skilled workers in these areas were switching jobs to civilian industries, he said, adding that "much of the manpower trouble is due to the mistaken belief of some people that the war is about over. Two hundred thousand able-bodied men, willing to do hard work, could break the bottleneck in the critical programs and shorten the war."[4]

Stimson and Patterson shared the manpower concern. The army had nearly 1.9 million fighting men in England and France alone, and casualties were piling up. On December 7 Patterson revealed publicly that the army had changed its policy and was now sending eighteen-year-olds to the front. It had little choice; by October 40 percent of its draftees were under nineteen. The army also announced that more men in the twenty-six to thirty-seven age group would be drafted to replace men released to work in critical war programs. "The meaning of the statement was plain," said *Newsweek*. "Men between 26 and 37 would either fight or work." Too many men deferred for jobs in critical industries were leaving those positions and not informing their draft boards. To emphasize the point, WMC agents swooped down on Denver's posh Wolhurst Saddle Club, lined up the employees for questioning, and ordered five of them to report for jobs in defense plants.[5]

To the delight of Stimson and Patterson, authorized reconversion production was cut by more than half. In their view manpower was short, supplies were short, and the supply of nurses was critically low. "There are a lot of able-bodied young men in industry that could be very well replaced by older men and there are a great many in non-war industries who ought to be in the Army anyhow," insisted Stimson. "So we think we can use the Selective Service Act which is the only power left in our hands to force these men into production by threatening to put them into the Army if they don't go into a better industry." He also wanted a new interpretation of the Tydings Amendment. None of this would solve the nurse shortage; the only solution was some form of compulsory service, which brought him back once again to a national service law. For his part Byrnes ordered Lewis Hershey to investigate the large number of men between eighteen and twenty-six who were playing professional sports.[6]

In his State of the Union address on January 6, Roosevelt lined up solidly with Stimson and Patterson. He urged that nurses be drafted, that the 4-F pool of 4 million men be drafted for use in some capacity, and that a national service law be enacted. The existing supply of nurses was adequate, he said, but far too few had volunteered for military duty. As a result, field hospitals were understaffed and more than a thousand nurses were hospitalized, many from overwork. As for those leaving critical jobs for civilian employment, he said sternly, "There is an old and true saying that the Lord hates a quitter. And this Nation must pay for all those who leave their essential jobs for non-essential reasons. And that payment must be made with the life's blood of our sons."[7]

The "get tough" attitude extended beyond manpower. Ickes reminded everyone of an alarming coal shortage, prompting Stimson and Forrestal to issue conservation orders for all military installations. WPB froze all civilian goods production until further notice. Chester Bowles announced a sharp tightening of rationing rules. Byrnes issued an order closing all horse and dog racetracks "until war conditions permit" to "prevent the use of critical materials, services and transportation in the operation of the tracks." Bill Hassett applauded the move as "long overdue to end what for months and months has been a national scandal." In February Byrnes took a more drastic step by imposing a midnight curfew on all places of entertainment throughout the country. "Our aim, of course," he explained, "was to save any further drain on coal, electricity and particularly manpower." Few people saw it that way. "Intended in part to make the nation acutely conscious of war's grim realities," observed *Newsweek*, "the Byrnes damper had succeeded in adding a new category of grumbling."[8]

The savings in all of Byrnes's categories proved negligible, and the curfew caused other problems. Nightclubs and bars in large cities saw their earnings drop. In New York, which swarmed with military personnel on leave, another issue arose. "The 'dumping' on the streets at midnight of thousands of service men—and women—with nowhere to go," said the *New York Times*, "has had a more deleterious effect on war morale . . . than any good that the 12 o'clock closing could possibly have been meant to accomplish." The editor of a liberal Episcopal biweekly denounced the curfew as "a destroyer of public morals, a breeding ground for vice and gangsterism, and a spur to lawlessness." Mayor Fiorello La Guardia challenged Byrnes's authority to issue such an order and said the city's nightspots could stay open until 1:00 A.M. Byrnes responded by getting the army and navy to issue an order that any club failing to meet the curfew would be placed off-limits for military personnel.[9]

The press release on the curfew opened by saying, "We must convince our fighting forces that the home front is prepared to sacrifice for their support." *Time* countered that the "remedy was worse than whatever disease it was supposed to cure." However, on the very same page of the magazine could be found a picture of a dead marine on the beach at Iwo Jima, a toll of the casualties of that bloody fight—4,189 dead, 15,308 wounded, and 441 missing—and the plea of a distraught wife or mother, one of many received by the navy. "Please, for God's sake, stop sending our finest youth to be murdered on places like Iwo Jima," she wrote. "It is too much for boys to stand, too much for mothers and homes to take. It is driving some mothers crazy. Why can't objectives be accomplished some other way. It is most inhuman and awful—stop, stop!"[10]

James Forrestal took such letters seriously and in this instance penned a reply. The relentless firebombing of Japan was under way, and Iwo Jima offered wounded or fuel-short B-29s a haven on their return. Already more than forty had found refuge there. Of this aspect Forrestal said nothing. Instead, after explaining briefly why such sacrifice was necessary, he concluded by saying simply, "There is no short cut or easy way. I wish there were."[11]

LIKE THE MEN fighting overseas, the administration soldiered on, taking its casualties along with its triumphs. On November 27 Cordell Hull, after lying abed at the Bethesda Naval Hospital for five weeks, sorrowfully resigned as secretary of state and was replaced by his undersecretary, the ubiquitous Edward Stettinius, whom *Fortune* called "a young man of great personal charm and energy, yet without technical qualifications and of indeterminate political philosophy." Stimson, worried about his own faltering energy, asked Harry Hopkins whether the president "might well want to get a younger man now to finish up with." Hopkins assured him that quite the opposite was true, that with Hull gone Stimson was the only man in the cabinet with national stature. The president not only valued his friendship and advice, Hopkins added, but wanted him to be as frank as he always had been. Hopkins himself was in poor shape, struggling as ever to harness his waning strength for the tasks ahead.[12]

The most pressing questions about health concerned the president. Opinions varied from day to day and sometimes during the day, depending on what time someone saw him. Frances Perkins recalled that within a few hours he could go "from looking pretty well to looking very badly." On one occasion two senators long friendly with the president came to see him in back-to-back appointments. When Joe O'Mahoney emerged from his meeting, he told Frank Maloney that Roosevelt "was absolutely terrific, telling stories, being funny and charming." Maloney went in and received a blank stare when Roosevelt gazed up at him. The senator realized with a start that the president had no idea who he was. Maloney ran out to tell Pa Watson, thinking the president had suffered a stroke. "Don't worry," said Watson. "He'll come out of it. He always does." Maloney returned to the president's office and was greeted warmly and treated to a lively conversation.[13]

The inauguration on January 20 was like few others in American history. Roosevelt insisted that all of his dozen grandchildren be present, but for personal and political reasons he also required it to be a small, low-key affair. It was held not on the Capitol steps as usual but on the South Porch of the White House. He dispensed with the traditional ceremony; there would be no bands, military units, or big floats. When a reporter inquired about the lack of a parade, Roosevelt replied, "Who is there here to parade?" It was his first wartime inauguration, and he wanted a solemn affair to save money, materials, and manpower. "Dog catchers have taken office with more pomp and ceremony," noted the Secret Service chief. On a bitterly cold day Roosevelt stood on the snowy ground without overcoat or hat to deliver the shortest inaugural address in history. His State of the Union message on the sixth had been the longest in American history, fully 8,000 words; the inaugural lasted less than five minutes and was solemn, even poignant, in tone.[14]

"It was deeply moving to watch him standing there in the cold winter air," recalled Sam Rosenman. ". . . Oblivious of the people standing in front of him or the people all over the world who were listening to him, he seemed to me to be offering a prayer . . . that all the peoples of the world, and their leaders, be endowed with the patience and faith that could abolish war." Other listeners were less convinced. A cynical Allen Drury called it "suitably innocuous, attempting to appeal to a moral righteousness events long since turned into a wan mockery." Two days later Roosevelt slipped out of Washington in a veil of secrecy to begin his long journey to the Yalta Conference.[15]

MAKING ONE CHANGE gave Roosevelt a mixture of pleasure and poetic justice. He had tolerated but never liked Jesse Jones, and he had to do something for Henry Wallace, who had campaigned vigorously for him despite his disappointment at being dumped from the ticket. The president resolved both matters by making Wallace the new secretary of commerce and head of RFC. Jones was furious, the more so at being ousted in favor of his nemesis. Wallace had told Roosevelt he wanted the post; after one meeting just before Christmas he asked the president what he should say to the press. "Tell them," quipped Roosevelt, "we focused particular attention on reforestation in Iran." Nothing was made public until inauguration day, January 20, when Roosevelt finally informed Jones by letter and in person of his fate. After their meeting Jones dashed off a caustic letter to the president, resigned his two major positions, and released the correspondence to the press before Roosevelt could even announce the change.[16]

The letters created a sensation. "Of course Jones has behaved horribly," Eleanor Roosevelt wrote her husband, "but I guess he's the kind of dog you should have ousted the day after the election and given him the reasons." By then the president was on a ship heading for the Yalta Conference and could offer Wallace no help. Conservatives in Congress yelped in protest and vowed to block Wallace's confirmation. "All hell has broken loose," observed Allen Drury of the Senate, where the New Dealers and the conservative "friends of Jesse" formed their battle lines. Walter George introduced a compromise bill to remove all the loan agencies from Commerce and return them to an independent federal loan administrator, a post Jones still held. The Commerce Committee hearings made it clear that Wallace would not be confirmed unless the George bill passed first. The committee emphasized the point by voting 14–5 against confirmation and 15–4 in favor of the George bill.[17]

The fight dragged on until February 1, when the Senate, after some maneuvering, got the George bill on the floor first and approved it 74–12. The vote on Wallace was delayed until Roosevelt could sign the George bill, which he did on March 1, whereupon the Senate confirmed Wallace 56–32. Meanwhile, the long-dormant national service issue awoke in Congress again, thanks in part to Roosevelt's endorsement of it in his January 6 message. The House opened hearings on the May bill, often called 4-F legislation, which sought to compel men in that category to get or stay in war jobs or be drafted. Stimson feared that too many manpower bills would cause a loss of focus on the most important one and allow the enemies of each one to oppose them all. Byrnes did not help by supporting the May bill in the belief that the old Austin-Wadsworth bill had no chance of passage. Stimson thought the May bill a poor substitute.[18]

Ever expedient, Byrnes offered the homey observation "If you can't ride a horse, ride a mule; if you can't ride a mule, ride a cow." Stimson regarded the May bill as more a dog, but conceded that news from the battlefield was working against him. The Battle of the Bulge had resulted in a German rout with enormous losses, and American troops were moving forward again while the Russians kept pressing onward from the east. Opposition ranging from the National Association of Manufacturers to the unions lined up against any compulsory bill. Allen Drury, who loathed any compulsory bill, chronicled the long congressional fight over the issue with a mixture of astuteness and disdain. The tactics of the military especially outraged him, as they had Nelson and Catton.[19]

Despite the amount of opposition, the House passed the substitute bill on February 1 after only four days of debate and sent it on to the Senate, where it received a less cordial reception. Letters, speeches, briefings, and tours flowed from the War Department in support of the bill. Patterson scolded the nation to "quit trimming the rose bushes and start fighting the fire which is burning the barn down . . . In modern warfare, volunteers are not enough, either on the battle front or on the home front . . . It is time to decide whether we are going to fight the war with one hand tied behind our backs or . . . with everything we have." Early in February the press exposed the army's tactics. Patterson issued a statement demanding a national service bill. The War Department then pressured *Stars and Stripes* to publish an editorial on the need for one. The wire services gave the editorial widespread coverage in the papers, whereupon Patterson went before a congressional committee to talk about the effect on "the morale of the boys at the front." Unfortunately for the army, someone leaked the process to the press.[20]

Stimson added his voice to the fight. On Byrnes's advice he reluctantly lent support to the May bill and on February 18 delivered a strong radio speech in support of passage. The newspapers applauded it, but resentment grew on the Hill and elsewhere. A disgusted Drury called it a "strange speech, playing with emotions so violent that he probably has no conception at all of what he is doing. In a deliberately divisive address, which could have been no better designed to turn the country against Congress had Goebbels himself contrived it, he has come forth with a desperate wail for the manpower bill. The Stimson speech sounded hysterical, and it may have been. At any rate it attempted to sir up the most bitter passions among the families of the men in the services, and among the men themselves. Oversimplified, glaring, dangerous, and false, the arguments it used were familiar."[21]

Drury thought Stimson's speech had the effect of killing the May bill. Two days later the Senate committee voted 12–6 to drop the bill in favor of a substitute version that included amendments by Austin and Tydings along with what Drury called "vast, unprecedented powers" for Byrnes. Even Stimson called it "a bad bill, a very bad bill, but it is a bill out in the open, and they can't sputter the whole subject in committee any longer." He conceded that there existed "very strong feeling in the Senate and in fact through the Congress against any compulsion on labor." Something else had crept into the opposition as well—a growing concern over the increasing role and power of the military in affairs normally decided by civilians. When debate on the bill opened, Albert "Happy" Chandler of Kentucky lambasted "the opportunism of the military." Joseph O'Mahoney said acidly that "if the word goes out to the boys at the front that the democratic system has failed and the government has had to apply Fascist methods to the folks back home, then nothing could be worse for morale."[22]

McNutt and his friends had capitalized on this growing resentment to nudge the WMC back into a major position on handling manpower. The substitute bill, partly the work of Senator Harley Kilgore of West Virginia, struck down so much of the original national service bill that Patterson denounced it as "absolutely worthless." The debate dragged on into March, bogged down in the usual miasma of rhetoric and amendments. On March 8 the substitute bill finally passed the Senate 63–16, but the struggle in joint committee to produce a final version lasted until April 3, when the Senate voted 46–29 against the conference compromise bill. National service was finally dead. "Forty-six Senators," wrote an exultant Drury, "decided today that the country should not go under a dictatorship."[23]

As March came on, the fear of faltering did not ease. WPB cut all non-military allotments of materials for April through June and postponed spot authorization in tight labor areas for another ninety days. Urgent and increased military orders were scheduled for shells, special-purpose steel, pipe, and tubing. All reconversion planning except token work for V-E Day was dropped. Concerned about a drop in steel production, WPB set up a new emergency steel committee under Hiland Batcheller. The air force announced that a new jet combat fighter had gone into production at Lockheed. Although it kept most details secret, the P-80, or Shooting Star, was reputed to fly at speeds close to that of sound. A lighter frame, enlarged fuel tanks, and a new method of reducing its fuel consumption gave the plane a pursuit range of 600 miles at ceilings above 40,000 feet, thanks to a pressurized cabin and the lack of a propeller. Unlike the 100-octane-guzzling regular planes, the P-80 ran on kerosene, and its engine could be replaced in fifteen minutes compared to an average of nine hours for a standard reciprocating engine.[24]

Despite the military's efforts to place the blame for the shortage of ammunition elsewhere, it belonged squarely on their own shoulders. Beginning in January 1944, ASF had ordered sharp cutbacks in production to avoid excess supplies. Some facilities were diverted to other programs such as fertilizers, synthetic rubber, and aviation gasoline. Some ordnance officers thought this policy a mistake and pointed to low stocks of 240 mm ammunition and the high rate of usage. "This type ammunition is so large," wrote General Roswell Hardy, chief of the Ammunition Division, "that facilities for its manufacture are very limited in extent, and the time required to reach production amounts to about eight months." His warning went unheeded.[25]

The Italian campaign, which consumed huge quantities of ammunition, convinced ASF that the cutback policy was a mistake, a view that was reinforced by the enormous expenditures of shells after D-day. More bombs were also needed because of stepped-up air operations. Some plants already shut down had to be reopened and refitted with huge forging presses, countless gages, jigs, fixtures, and machine tools. New facilities were also built at a cost of $203 million to expand output. The tremendous production capacity so laboriously built up in 1941–42 and then reduced sharply in 1943 had to be built up yet again. Manpower shortages led to the creation of recruiting cara-vans that toured the country in search of workers. More women were hired, and soldiers who were skilled machinists or toolmakers were furloughed to help out. By March 1945 3,066 enlisted men were working in the ordnance plants.[26]

Still the demand for more ammunition increased. In December 1944 Ord-nance received orders to increase its monthly output of shells for 155 mm, 90 mm, 57 mm, and 105 mm guns by 50 percent and the same amount for 60 mm and 81 mm. mortars. A month later came directives to expand pro-duction of ammunition for 75 mm howitzers and field guns and the 37 mm antitank gun as well as to produce 355,300 rounds of the new armor-piercing ammunition with tungsten carbide cores for a variety of guns. The directives meant a $682 million expansion of facilities. During the first four months of 1945 expenditures for heavy artillery ammunition hit record levels; by June's end procurement during fiscal 1945 topped $5 billion and 7 million tons of ammunition. The frantic effort to boost production had succeeded, though at heavy cost.[27]

Union leaders, growing ever more restive, continued their assault on the Little Steel formula. The soft-coal producers began their contract talks on March 1 and were greeted by John L. Lewis with a list of eighteen "adjust-ments" he desired for his men and a new demand that the operators pay his union a royalty of 10 cents on every ton of soft coal mined in the nation. A Philadelphia paper accused him of "brandishing a coal shovel over the heads of the American people again," to which Lewis responded with his hope that "the public and Government will not be inconvenienced through stoppage or loss of tonnage vital to . . . our war program." The operators protested that Lewis's demands could cost up to $400 million a year and add 65 to 67 cents a ton to the price of coal. Even worse, if the royalty was granted, the anthracite miners and every other union would soon demand the same concession.[28]

The coal crisis grew worse despite record output simply because the de-mand kept increasing. The soft-coal miners produced a record high of more than 619 million net tons in 1944 compared to 395 million in 1939. The anthra-cite miners dug out 64 million tons in 1944 compared to 51.5 million five years earlier. For all the furor Lewis generated in his perpetual fighting with the administration and the mine operators, the miners got the job done—a fact too often overlooked by the headlines and political posturers.[29]

Detroit had its own nest of labor squabbles. The auto companies and the UAW bickered constantly over management's complaint that labor was try-ing to usurp its functions. When Chrysler fired eight airplane gear cutters at its huge Dodge plant, 13,500 workers walked out, stopping work on B-29 parts, rocket shells, trucks, tank transmissions, and antiaircraft guns. The union ignored demands from the army and WLB to return to work and submit to mediation. A meeting to redress grievances degenerated into a half-hour fistfight. On Mack Avenue the Briggs Manufacturing Company fired seven union shop stewards accused of fomenting fifty-seven strikes, prompting 5,800 workers to walk out in the company's 161st wartime strike. At River Rouge 1,100 employees struck for five hours over a grievance and then went back to work. "Like the Hatfields and the McCoys," quipped *Time*, "Detroit's labor and management seem to find a certain sporting sense of satisfaction in settling their differences the hard way."[30]

Even the food supply felt the pressure. On March 4 OPA imposed its tightest rationing yet on meat and canned goods as the military increased its buying by 15 percent and meat production dropped 31 percent below the February 1944 level. The squeeze extended to vegetables as well. WFA officials groused privately about army overbuying to no effect. The restrictions seemed incongruous with continuing worries about possible surpluses after V-E Day. In the grain belt, a race was on between the supply of freight cars and the spring rains. An immense amount of grain, nearly twice the normal supply, lay in piles along the tracks waiting to be picked up, its moisture content rising steadily. Spoilage threatened to wipe out as much as a billion bushels of corn, 237 million bushels of wheat, and a large tonnage of sorghums, oats, barley, and rye.[31]

WPB also cut the quota of truck and bus tires for civilian use 50 percent below the number requested by ODT. The government's tire program was out of balance because of a shortage not of rubber but of carbon black filler, used to increase strength and elasticity in synthetic tires. A typical synthetic tire consisted of about 50 percent rubber, 30 percent cord, and 20 percent carbon black. So rapidly had the production of synthetic rubber grown that it outran the supply of both cord and carbon black. Elsewhere industrial users of sugar, except for ice-cream and jam makers, had their quotas sliced to 65 percent of prewar amounts. Restaurants, bakers, and soft-drink makers were told to use up their inventories and then operate on a hand-to-mouth basis.[32]

The Great Scare campaign got the War Department pretty much everything it had wanted except a national service law. Production of key items was ramped up yet again, reconversion was put on ice, and the fear of faltering did much to sober the public mood and reorient it to the task at hand. Huge military orders for boots, shoes, textiles, and a host of other items poured into factories. "By spring," observed Bruce Catton, "it suddenly appeared that there would be less for the civilian economy to operate on, in the summer and fall of 1945, than at any previous stage in the war ... The great scare campaign had made it certain that nothing could be done, either by government or by business, in the direction of reconversion until after the defeat of Germany."³³

IRA SMITH HAD seen a lot of presidents, eight to be exact, since starting work at the White House in 1897. Now he was its oldest employee in terms of service. In his current job he sorted the 2,000 to 10,000 letters that poured into the White House daily. Fifteen boxes were allotted to this president, two to his wife, and one each to his aides, each one with a simple, handwritten tag under it. Earlier presidents made do with a handful of secretaries; as late as 1939 the Congressional Directory needed only a single page to list the entire White House staff. By 1944 the president employed 687 people directly and required thirteen pages of small type in the directory. A new wing was added to the White House in 1942 to house the growing staff and was too small even before it was completed.³⁴

Harry Hopkins and Sam Rosenman remained the president's closest advisers and troubleshooters. Harold Smith, the budget director, acted as business manager for the enormous enterprise of war. The unimaginative Admiral Leahy served as chief of staff and Jimmy Byrnes as watchdog of domestic policies. Steve Early, the last of Roosevelt's three original secretaries, handled the media, and Ross McIntire tended to the president's health, although Howard Bruenn had largely supplanted him in practice. Grace Tully had replaced Missy LeHand as Roosevelt's personal secretary. Jonathan Daniels functioned as one of five administrative assistants, and Bill Hassett took charge of correspondence. Admiral Wilson Brown ran the White House map room and acted as naval aide.³⁵

The genial Pa Watson had been a loyal and dedicated secretary and guardian of the office door, but he was gone, dead of a cerebral hemorrhage on the voyage back from Yalta. "I shall miss him almost more than I can express," said Roosevelt when told the news. For days afterward the president scarcely left his cabin except to eat and watch movies in the evening. "Many people in Washington considered him merely a jovial companion to the President," noted Rosenman. "He was much more. Like Missy, he had an uncanny instinct for distinguishing between the fake and the genuine in human beings and human conduct . . . He served as eyes and ears for Roosevelt in many places in Washington that Roosevelt could not himself cover . . . His was the kind of loyalty that is met with very seldom in human affairs, and practically never in political life."³⁶

Roosevelt had lost many of the people close to him, especially his mother, Louis Howe, his first political adviser, and Missy LeHand, but, as Rosenman saw, "in his weakened and tired condition, the death of Watson seemed to have a more depressing effect on him than the death of any of the others." After their return to Washington Roosevelt attended Watson's funeral at Arlington with Eleanor and Anna but did not leave his car amid a heavy downpour of cold rain. "The President has come home in the pink of condition—hasn't looked better in a year," observed Hassett. Others did not agree. The Yalta ordeal had exhausted him more than the long voyage home could repair. His diet had caused him to lose even more weight. Rosenman, who came aboard ship when it stopped at Algiers, had not seen Roosevelt for a month and was depressed by his appearance. "He had lost a great deal more weight," he recalled; "he was listless and apparently uninterested in conversation—he was all burnt out."[37]

Lord Moran, who had last seen Roosevelt at the Quebec meeting with Churchill, was shocked at how much he had failed. "To a doctor's eye," he wrote, "he has all the symptoms of hardening of the arteries of the brain in an advanced state so that I give him only a few months to live." Averell Harriman agreed that "the signs of deterioration seemed to me unmistakable."[38]

At home the political pundits had been debating whether Roosevelt had veered to the right or whether any vestige of his old liberalism still remained. Before his departure he allowed as how he was "going down the line a little left of center." Neither his appointments nor his measures sent to Congress gave a clear sign one way or the other. What label, for example, could be applied to his request for a national service law? The influence of the military and men like Byrnes argued for one side, the replacing of Jesse Jones with Wallace the other. "Mr. Roosevelt's expediencies and compromises," complained one exasperated supporter, "his postponements of questions and evasions of issues are coming home to plague him from a dozen places . . . Yet still unrepentantly he wisecracks, he postures, he ducks, he does everything but come clean and tell the country what he is up to."[39]

On March 1 Roosevelt went to the Capitol to give a joint session of Congress his report on the Yalta Conference. An overflow crowd was startled to see him roll down the aisle in his wheelchair, the first time he had done so instead of entering on crutches or someone's arm. Rather than stand at the lectern above the well, he settled into a soft chair in front of a small table below the dais. No longer did he feel the need to deceive the public about his physical affliction. "I hope that you will pardon me for this unusual posture of sitting down during the presentation of what I want to say," he explained, "but I know that you will realize that it makes it a lot easier for me not to have to carry about ten pounds of steel around on the bottom of my legs; and also because of the fact that I have just completed a fourteen-thousand-mile trip."[40]

A long round of applause gave him the answer. Frances Perkins, seated in the front row with the rest of the cabinet, was deeply moved. "It was the first reference he had ever made to his incapacity," she recalled later, "and he did it in the most charming way." She thought he was saying, in effect, I'm a crippled man, something he had never said before and which nobody dared mention in his presence. Now, seated before the body he had constantly fought with during the war, he admitted his frailty. "He had to bring himself to full humility to say it before Congress," said Perkins. In that moment a deception so artfully practiced for twelve years with help from the press corps, which never took pictures of him in his wheelchair or being lifted from or into his car, was revealed and forever discarded.[41]

The speech was long, lasting an hour, and Roosevelt ad-libbed at some length during it, which was so rare it startled Hassett. Drury, ever critical, thought the president looked tired and drawn, and the found the speech "a long, rambling, rather lifeless affair, delivered in a rambling and rather lifeless fashion." Everybody he talked to seemed disappointed that it contained nothing new. "Once again," he concluded, "the man who makes foreign policy had a chance to convince the men who can break it, and once again he had lost it." Hassett agreed that it was not "a particularly good speech," yet the Congress received it well and applauded it strongly. Hearing a recording of it over the radio that evening, Hassett decided it sounded better.[42]

Stimson thought it made a good impression despite covering "some very ticklish questions about which there was a great difference of opinion." To his eyes the president looked well but tired and thin, and not as lively as usual. "I have been a little bit troubled," he admitted, "because the expression on his face has changed somewhat and he looks older." The president's performance disturbed even the ever-loyal Sammy the Rose. "I was dismayed at the halting, ineffective manner of delivery," he confessed. "He ad-libbed a great deal—as frequently as I had ever heard him. Some of his extemporaneous remarks were wholly irrelevant, and some of them almost bordered on the ridiculous." The next morning after the speech Rosenman, about to leave for a mission in London, stopped at the White House to say good-bye to the president and ask if he had any further instructions.[43]

"The only further instructions I have for you, Sam," Roosevelt replied, "are these. It is very rainy and wet in London the early part of March. Be sure to take your rubbers with you."

They were the last words Rosenman heard him speak.[44]

ON MARCH 15 Stimson hurried to get his notes together before meeting with Roosevelt to discuss an S-1 matter. The president had received a memo warning about the extravagance of the matter and urging that a group of outside scientists look into it because of rumors that Bush and Conant had "sold the President a lemon on the subject." Stimson thought the memo silly and showed Roosevelt a list of the scientists involved that included four Nobel winners and virtually every physicist of standing. His reassurance eased the president's mind even as the inmates at Los Alamos continued to struggle with the last and most difficult phase of the project, creating a bomb that would actually work.[45]

Groves never wavered in his belief that Oppenheimer was the best man to get this job done. He was bright, quick, astute, and charismatic, and he faced an enormous task. The scientists, engineers, and technicians lured to Los Alamos, most of them from urban settings, were even more isolated than workers at any of the other Manhattan installations. They were organized into specialized research and technical divisions and groups dedicated to two basic tasks: solving the theoretical and experimental problems of making a fission bomb, and figuring out the complex ordnance and engineering issues involved in designing and building the weapon. They also had to learn how to get along with each other and with the military, who comprised the second major group at the place. Most of the civilian participants balked at being part of or directed by the military. Oppenheimer emerged as the glue that Groves hoped would hold so prickly a set of egos together long enough to create an unprecedented weapon.[46]

Life on "the Hill," as its residents called Los Alamos, was never easy. The housing, always viewed as temporary, was inferior to that of Oak Ridge or Hanford, shopping facilities were limited in the nearby area, and a thirty-mile trip to Santa Fe had to traverse a rough mountain road. During the first winter the water supply ran short. However, the mountain scenery was magnificent, side trips could be made to cave dwellings and Indian pueblos, and skiing and other winter sports could be enjoyed. "The people were young," said Arthur Compton, who visited Los Alamos several times, "and life was a great adventure." They were also incredibly bright. "Never, I suppose," added Compton, "has there been gathered together in one place for so long a period of time so large a group of competent men of science. Ideas originated and developed with startling speed. Equipment that ordinarily requires years for building was here constructed in months."[47]

By the fall of 1943 the facilities and basic organization were in place and the scientists absorbed in a variety of research programs. Oppenheimer, Groves, Conant, and other project leaders dug into the problem of finding the most workable design for an atomic weapon. Two approaches seemed feasible, one utilizing a gun-type device with plutonium and the other called implosion, suggested in April 1943 by physicist Seth Neddermeyer. Implosion involved surrounding a hollow sphere of plutonium or U-235 with a high explosive that, when detonated, forced all the nuclear material inward toward the center of the sphere, where it became a supercritical explosive mass. For this to happen, however, the implosion had to be exactly symmetrical, pushing all the nuclear material inward at the same moment; otherwise it would not form the necessary compact ball. A gun design seemed the better risk since so much was already known about manufacturing and firing artillery.[48]

Most of the physicists doubted that implosion could be made to work. "Neddermeyer faced stiff opposition from Oppenheimer and, I think, Fermi and Bethe," said one of the physicists, John Manley. How could a shock wave be made symmetrical? How could the core be kept from squirting out in every direction like water when squeezed between the hands? "Nobody . . . really took [implosion] very seriously," added Manley. But no possibility could be overlooked. Privately Oppenheimer told Neddermeyer, "This will have to be looked into," and made him group leader for experiments in implosion. However, he worked under Captain William Parsons, which guaranteed ongoing friction.[49]

Dismissing Neddermeyer's work as "the Beer-Can Experiment," Parsons, an experienced gunnery officer, led the team designing a workable gun using either U-235 or plutonium. Work went forward on a plutonium gun-type known as Thin Man. An old ranch nearby was acquired for use as a firing range to test components, using a 3-inch naval antiaircraft gun. Although progress was made on the design, the lack of plutonium retarded crucial experiments with it. No one yet knew how much fissionable material would be required for an effective weapon. Both U-235 and Pu-239 had to be converted into metal of the needed purity and configuration before they could be used in a weapon. The fear of predetonation, resulting in a harmless fizzle rather than an explosion, haunted all the research. It could be caused by the presence of too many stray neutrons or by the supercritical mass coming together too slowly or both combined.[50]

While others focused on a gun design, Oppenheimer fretted over the lack of progress in implosion. Neddermeyer still had not found a way to create shots symmetrical enough to release enough energy for a bomb. In July 1943 Oppenheimer wrote the brilliant Hungarian mathematician and physicist John von Neumann, who had been studying shock waves for NDRC. "We are in what can only be described as a desperate need of your help," he said frankly, and invited von Neumann to "come if possible as a permanent, and let me assure you, honored member of our staff." After some negotiating von Neumann agreed to work on theoretical problems in Washington but make visits to Los Alamos. His arrival there in September for two weeks proved decisive in redirecting the implosion program.[51]

Von Neumann was truly a prodigy. At the age of six he could joke with his father in classical Greek. Thanks to his photographic memory he could recite whole chapters of books. His experiments had convinced him that if certain mechanical problems could be solved, an implosion bomb using more explosives would require less active material of a much lower purity to go critical. If he was correct, precious months could be saved in developing the weapon. He also suggested that the charges be arranged not in a cylindrical shell like Thin Man but in a spherical configuration around the active material. The suggestions, recalled one team leader, "woke everybody up . . . Johnny . . . was a very resourceful man, at least twenty years ahead of his time." Oppenheimer, Hans Bethe, and Edward Teller all agreed that an implosion bomb could be a far more efficient weapon than any gun. They also realized that a deeper technical grasp of high explosives was crucial to success.[52]

Conversations with Edward Teller confirmed for von Neumann that an implosion bomb posed less risk of predetonation, which meant it should be more reliable and might be built more quickly. Fast implosion also meant a smaller bomb. A big gun bomb would measure an estimated two feet in diameter and seventeen feet long; an implosion bomb could be less than five feet in diameter and just over nine feet long—"a man-sized egg with tail fins," as Richard Rhodes described it.[53]

In November Groves and Conant endorsed the decision to expand the implosion program. Looking back on the experience, Conant admitted to being "impressed by the narrowness which separated success from disaster in the undertaking to make one type of bomb." Construction began on some needed new testing facilities, and Conant persuaded chemist George Kistiakowsky, an explosives expert, to join the staff at Los Alamos. "I didn't want to," admitted Kistiakowsky, "partly because I didn't think the bomb would be ready in time and I was interested in helping win the war." His unwillingness gave him "a wonderful opportunity to act as a reluctant bride throughout the life of the project, which helped at times." In February 1944 the MPC informed Roosevelt that "there is a chance, and a fair one, if a process involving the use of a minimum amount of material proves feasible, that the first bomb can be produced in the late fall of 1944."[54]

When Kistiakowsky arrived in late January, he found recurring clashes of egos as well as friction between the scientists and the military men. After a few weeks he concluded that his position was untenable. "I was essentially in the middle trying to make sense of the efforts of two men who were at each other's throats," he recalled. "One was Captain Parsons who tried to run his division the way it is done in military establishments—very conservative. The other was, of course, Seth Neddermeyer, who was the exact opposite of Parsons, working away in a little corner. The two never agreed about anything and they certainly didn't want me interfering." But Kistiakowsky persisted, if only because he, like the others, never lost sight of what was at stake. "Every one of us," said Teller, who threatened to leave at one point and was dissuaded by Oppenheimer, "considered the present war and the completion of the A-bomb as the problems to which we wanted to contribute the most."[55]

The work went slowly. The theoreticians still did not know what occurred within the imploding mass and so could not predict the results of an implosion or determine how to make the assembly symmetrical. They struggled to find a means of measuring what took place inside a violent reaction during an instant so brief that human senses could not record it. Through the winter they experimented with intricate electronic and photographic techniques. While this research proceeded, work continued on both the gun and implosion methods. In February the arrival of several new IBM machines made it possible to solve equations that had defied hand calculations. But little progress was made through the spring, and the gun method looked to be the surest if not the most satisfactory option.[56]

Then a major problem developed with plutonium. As early as March 1943 Glenn Seaborg had suggested that a new isotope, Pu-240, might form in the production piles. When Emilio Segrè tested the first samples of plutonium from Oak Ridge in April 1944, he confirmed Seaborg's suspicion. This indicated that the much larger uranium slugs at Hanford would likely convert even more Pu-239 into Pu-240 and that neutron emission by spontaneous fission would exceed the specification for plutonium by several hundred times, making it impossible to explode Hanford plutonium by any existing gun method. Of necessity emphasis shifted back to implosion, which Neddermeyer had continued doggedly to pursue despite the lack of interest in it. At a July meeting the decision was made to suspend work on the gun-type bomb and concentrate on implosion.[57]

The decision forced an unhappy Groves to present General Marshall with a revised timetable for the production of a bomb. If research on implosion succeeded, a weapon might be available between March and June 1945; if it fell short, a gun-type of lesser destructive effect, using uranium, could be ready by August 1945. This meant that in all likelihood the bomb would be used against Japan rather than Germany even though its origins were rooted in a race against German scientists. Later in the year Groves approved the modification of a B-29, a plane never intended for use in Europe, to carry out the mission. Even these projections amounted to an act of faith by Groves and Conant. In the summer of 1944 the key questions remained unanswered: Could enough active material, uranium or plutonium, of sufficient purity be produced for a bomb? Could a gun-type bomb deliver enough destructive capacity to warrant its use? Most basic of all, could the riddles plaguing the researchers on implosion be unraveled in time to create a workable weapon?[58]

Here, as elsewhere, the fear of faltering drove everyone to redoubled efforts.

Early in July Oppenheimer enacted a sweeping reorganization at Los Alamos that, among other changes, put Kistiakowsky and Robert Bacher in charge of implosion and moved Parsons to what he did best, overseeing ordnance, assembly, delivery, and engineering. Enrico Fermi became associate director of the key research and theoretical divisions and all nuclear physics problems. The Governing Board was abolished and all housekeeping issues assigned to an Administrative Board, leaving a new Technical Board free to concentrate on the major scientific questions. These and other changes enabled the divisions to launch a major push on implosion.[59]

Despite dogged suspicions about his leftist background, Oppenheimer provided superb leadership with a calm outward demeanor. Teller called him "probably the best lab director I have ever seen because of the great mobility of his mind, because of his successful effort to know about practically everything important invented in the laboratory, and also because of his unusual psychological insight into other people which, in the company of physicists, was very much the exception." Hans Bethe marveled that Oppenheimer "knew and understood everything that went on in the laboratory, whether it was chemistry or theoretical physics or machine shop. He could keep it all in his head and coordinate it. It was clear also at Los Alamos that he was intellectually superior to us. He understood immediately when he heard anything, and fitted it into the general scheme of things and drew the right conclusions. There was just nobody else in that laboratory who came even close to him."[60]

That fall the emphasis of necessity began shifting from research to development and production. Components had to be manufactured and specifications determined. The uranium and plutonium from Oak Ridge and Hanford had to be worked into proper shapes, and high-explosive castings produced for the implosion research. More trained people were needed for the shops, the laboratories, and the explosives plant. An accelerated effort to find an implosion design, code-named Fat Man, resulted in a version utilizing explosive lenses and an electric detonator to create a spherical shape. In July 1944 von Neumann had come up with a shape for the lenses, but producing them for tests proved fiendishly difficult. During the tests, Kistiakowsky recalled, "well over twenty thousand castings were delivered to the firing sites, while the number of castings rejected because of poor quality or destroyed for other reasons is several times this figure."[61]

While their testing continued, Oppenheimer pursued the alternative path. He had canceled work on a plutonium gun and concentrated efforts on one using U-235. The new version had to be configured into a bomb that could be delivered by a plane. Oppenheimer put Lieutenant Commander A. Francis Birch in charge of all the work. A Harvard geophysicist, Birch was knowledgeable in physics, electronics, and mechanical design. His calm, mature personality kept the work running smoothly. In December 1944 Groves, worried about the uncertainties surrounding implosion, asked Oppenheimer to give the gun program higher priority than Fat Man. He wanted all research and development on the gun finished by July 1, 1945, the expected date when enough uranium and plutonium would be available for actual weapons.[62]

That same month Oppenheimer approved a new design for the weapon, which acquired the code name Little Boy. In February 1945 Birch's group completed and tested the uranium gadget design. Plans were made to ship the gadget to a military base where it would be readied for combat use. By then it was obvious that the first available weapon would be a uranium bomb; the implosion project had made impressive progress but still lacked clear direction in terms of choosing between two competing designs. Lacking the resources to pursue both and come even close to the deadline, Oppenheimer chose one. Later in February Groves came to Los Alamos and agreed with Oppenheimer that the design had to be frozen and developed to the final stages. All hands mobilized to push it through to final testing in the project and at the place Oppenheimer had named Trinity.[63]

AFTER ROOSEVELT'S RETURN from Yalta no one doubted that Anna had become the gatekeeper for her father, inheriting the duty performed by Missy LeHand, Harry Hopkins, and, much earlier, Louis Howe, the president's political mentor. "Control of access has passed to Anna Roosevelt Boettiger," wrote John Chamberlain, "the long-legged, energetic and handsome eldest child" who was a "free-speaking, free-cursing" woman once called by Jim Farley "the most politically savvy of all the Roosevelt children." In that role, Chamberlain added, "Daddy's girl has her work cut out for her, running Daddy."[64]

On the evening of March 24 Franklin and Eleanor took the train to Hyde Park. The president, desperately tired, went to bed as soon as he got on board, but on Sunday afternoon, sitting with Eleanor, he talked eagerly of future plans in the old way that she loved. He wanted her to accompany him to the opening session of the United Nations, a cause to which he had devoted enormous time and energy. Later, in May or June, he wanted her to join him in visiting London, Holland, and the battlefields. The European war, he confided, would be over in May. Though pleased by his enthusiasm, so rarely seen of late, she could not ignore the obvious signs of decline. That weekend he didn't want to drive his car and asked her to drive instead, something he had never done before, and he even asked her to mix the cocktails.[65]

The war news continued to be positive. Waves of bombers devastated both Germany and Japan mercilessly. In the Pacific American forces had recaptured

Bataan and Corregidor, and the flag had been hoisted over Iwo Jima. In Europe American troops had captured the bridge at Remagen and were pouring into Germany. The end of the long ordeal in Europe seemed within sight, but fortress Japan remained an imposing obstacle that by most estimates could cost the United States half a million or more casualties to storm unless some other way could be found to induce the Japanese to surrender. The best hope in that regard lay in the highly secret doings of S-1.

Roosevelt returned to Washington on March 29 but left by train that same afternoon for what was expected to be a two-week stay in Warm Springs. It was a beautiful spring day with the wisteria in full bloom on the south portico of the White House and the cherry blossoms out in full force. Roosevelt took with him Margaret Suckley, Laura Delano, and two other friends, Howard Bruenn, Grace Tully, Dorothy Brady, Bill Hassett, Alice Winegar, and Louise Hachmeister (or Hackie, as she was known) from his staff, and the usual three news service representatives, Merriman Smith, Bob Nixon, and Harold Oliver, who were not to write any stories until their return. Anna had planned to go, but her son fell sick at the last minute and had to be hospitalized. Tully noticed that the Hyde Park interlude "had failed to erase any of the fatigue from his face" and that he looked drawn and gray. Everyone, Roosevelt most of all, looked forward to a quiet, pleasant, restful time garnished with southern hospitality.[66]

When the train pulled into the tiny Warm Springs depot at 2:00 P.M. on Good Friday, the station agent recalled, "the President was the worst looking man I ever saw who was still alive." Secret Service agent Mike Reilly usually had strong help from Roosevelt in his transfer to the car, but this time he struggled because the president was "absolutely dead weight." Reilly placed his hopes in the restorative power of Warm Springs for the president. "I always felt," he said later, "he looked upon it as a miraculous source of strength and health." That evening Hassett had a chat with Bruenn and startled the doctor by saying abruptly, "He is slipping away from us and no earthly power can keep him here."[67]

"Why do you think so?" asked Bruenn.

"I have talked this way with no one else save one," said Hassett. "To all the staff, to the family, and with the Boss himself I have maintained the bluff; but I am convinced that there is no help for him." The talk got more serious and emotional as Hassett recited his reasons. His old zest was fading; he talked less about the things that had always engaged him—Hyde Park stories, politics, books, pictures. The bold stroke of his signature had become feeble and faint. Yes, the Boss was in a precarious position, Bruenn conceded, but his condition was not hopeless. Hassett was not persuaded and maintained that "the Boss is leaving us."[68]

The next day Roosevelt signed a mass of documents from the mail pouch and his staff, including a letter accepting Jimmy Byrnes's resignation as director of OWMR. When Hassett mentioned that it was a loss to the government, the president agreed, saying, "Yes, it's too bad some people are so primadonnaish." His appearance shocked Hassett and alarmed Bruenn as well. On Easter Sunday Hassett recalled the same day six years earlier when Roosevelt left Warm Springs with the parting crack, "I'll be back in the fall if we don't have a war."[69]

The days passed easily with a minimum of intrusion other than a visit from President Sergio Osmeña of the Philippines. The weather cooperated nicely, and the countryside was ablaze with spring foliage. On Tuesday, April 10, Roosevelt said he would happily attend an old-fashioned Georgia barbecue to be given two days later. He would arrive around 4:30 and request not barbecue but some old-fashioned Brunswick stew. That afternoon Merriman Smith was out on a ride atop a balky horse when he encountered the president's car. As the car moved slowly past Smith, Roosevelt bowed solemnly and said, "Heigh-O, Silver!" Smith smiled. "His voice was wonderful," he recalled, "and resonant. It sounded like the Roosevelt of old."[70]

On the evening of April 11 Morgenthau, who was en route from Washington to Florida to see his ill wife, stopped in Warm Springs to visit the president. "I was terribly shocked when I saw him," he confided to his diary, "and I found that he had aged terrifically and looked very haggard. His hands shook so that he started to knock the glasses over, and I had to hold each glass as he poured out the cocktail." After two drinks Roosevelt seemed better, but his memory was poor and he confused names. "I was in agony watching him," he admitted. He stayed for dinner, then took his leave.[71]

Next morning the president sat in bed reading the *Atlanta Constitution* while waiting for the big-city papers. The headlines told him that American troops were only 57 miles from Berlin and 115 miles from meeting the Russians and that a large wave of B-29s had bombed Tokyo in daylight. By noontime, when Hassett arrived with the delayed mail pouch, Roosevelt was dressed and sitting in his favorite leather chair chatting with his two cousins, Margaret and Laura, and the love of his life, Lucy Rutherfurd, while Elizabeth Shoumatoff, an artist commissioned by Lucy, stood at her easel working on a portrait of him. The mail was heavy, and the president decided to start signing a batch of appointments and awards, interrupted by Shoumatoff asking him to turn this way or that. Hassett took the signed documents and left.[72]

The president looked at his watch. It was one o'clock. "We've got just fifteen minutes more," he announced to Shoumatoff. The houseboy was setting the table for lunch. Margaret Suckley sat crocheting, Laura Delano filled vases with flowers, and Lucy Rutherfurd sat watching Roosevelt, who made a little joke to her and continued reading his papers while lighting a cigarette. Just before the fifteen minutes expired, Roosevelt suddenly passed his right hand over his forehead in a strange, jerky manner. His head went forward; his left hand moved to his temple and then to the back of his neck. "I have a terrific pain in the back of my head," he said, then slumped forward. With difficulty the president was moved to his bed, still unconscious. Bruenn, who was sunning himself at the pool, was summoned. Once arrived, he cut away Roosevelt's clothing and injected papaverine and amyl nitrate before phoning McIntire in Washington. Rutherfurd and Shoumatoff slipped quietly out.[73]

Hassett returned to the cottage unaware of the crisis. The president's heavy, labored breathing convinced him that there was no hope. "All you could hear was breathing," recalled a maid who was present. "It was kind of like—deep, steady, long gasps." Grace Tully sat in a corner softly mouthing a prayer. The breathing grew more tortured, then stopped. Hurriedly Bruenn injected Adrenalin into the heart muscle, but to no avail. At 3:35 P.M. he pronounced the president dead. Merriman Smith and his colleagues were summoned from the barbecue and rushed to the cottage. When Hassett gave them the news, they scrambled to the telephones.[74]

In Washington Eleanor Roosevelt was at a charity event concert when summoned urgently to the White House. Anna was with her son at the hospital when the news came. Harry Truman had just adjourned the Senate and was in Sam Rayburn's office about to enjoy a bourbon and water when he received a message to call Steve Early at the White House. Early told him to come there at once. He arrived about 5:25 P.M. and was taken to Eleanor's study. She put her arm gently on his shoulder and said, "Harry, the President is dead." The news staggered Truman. "Is there anything I can do for you?" he said at last. "Is there anything we can do for *you*?" she replied. "For you are the one in trouble now."[75]

While talking at home with Lord Halifax, the British ambassador, Stimson received a message asking him to be at the White House in fifteen minutes. Halifax drove him to the White House gate, and Stimson went inside to find the cabinet and vice president gathered in the cabinet room. Truman broke the news of Roosevelt's death to them and assured them that he would, with their help, carry on the president's policies. After some time Chief Justice Harlan Stone arrived and swore in the new president. It was 7:09 P.M. when he finished.[76]

Grief spread across the nation and the globe like a bursting storm cloud. "I felt as if I had been struck a physical blow," Churchill said later, ". . . and I was overpowered by a sense of deep and irreparable loss." Ambassador Averell Harriman in Moscow drove to the Kremlin to inform Stalin and reported that he appeared to be deeply moved. The strangest response of all came from Tokyo, where a radio announcer read the death bulletin followed by special music "in honor of the passing of a great man."[77]

Those who believed in omens and portents noted duly that the next day was Friday the thirteenth.

DEATH NO LESS than life forged a final indelible link between Roosevelt and the greatest of his predecessors. He died on April 12 and Lincoln on April 15, exactly eighty years apart. Lincoln had lived just long enough to witness victory in his great war; Roosevelt fell short of that prize by mere weeks on one front and months on the other. Despite how weary and wasted Roosevelt had looked in recent months—as had Lincoln by the war's end—the news of his death hit most people with almost as great a shock as Lincoln's assassination. The headlines read "ROOSEVELT DEAD," mourned Allen Drury. "We read them; and we could not believe it. We read them again; and we could not believe it. We had helped write the great story; still we could not believe it."[78]

Lincoln had said more than once that he wondered whether he would ever see Springfield again. Roosevelt had said nine months before his death, "All that is within me cries out to go back to my home on the Hudson River." Both men got their wish to go home again, but not in the manner they had hoped.[79]

Both presidents were honored by a long train trip that allowed the nation to express its deep outpouring of grief. Lincoln's last journey carried him home to Springfield, Illinois, Roosevelt's to Hyde Park with a stop in Washington for the funeral. The trip back from Warm Springs was, in Merriman Smith's words, "sad and slow." Along the entire route thousands of people, black and white of all ages, even whole choirs, lined the tracks to pay their respects. The heavy bronze coffin sat atop a special cradle so that it could be seen through the window as the train chugged slowly along the 800-mile journey to Washington. Arriving on a bright, beautiful morning, the coffin was placed atop a caisson drawn by six white horses for the trip down Pennsylvania Avenue to the White House. The enormous crowds were well behaved and steeped in sorrow. "It was a processional of terrible simplicity," wrote William S. White, "and a march too solemn for tears."[80]

The funeral in the East Room began at 4:00 P.M. on the fourteenth before an overflow crowd of dignitaries. Robert Sherwood was sitting in a small gilt chair on the far right when he felt a hand on his shoulder. Harry Hopkins had risen from his sickbed in Rochester, Minnesota, and flown to Washington in time for the ceremony. "He himself looked like death," thought Sherwood, "the skin of his face a dreadful cold white with apparently no flesh left under it. I believed that he now had nothing to live for, that his life had ended with

Roosevelt's." The morning after Roosevelt's death Hopkins had called Sherwood from Minnesota and told him, "You and I have something great that we can take with us all the rest of our lives. It's a great realization. Because we know it's *true* what so many people believed about him and what made them love him. He never let them down."[81]

At ten that evening the coffin was returned to the train for the trip to Hyde Park. The special train, carrying the cabinet, Supreme Court justices, military leaders, other officials, Roosevelt friends, and reporters, was so long and heavy that the crew struggled to get it started. When a coupling broke for the third time, a newsman remarked, "The Republicans have always known that it would be difficult to get Roosevelt out of Washington." Finally it got under way. Along that route, too, large crowds gathered beside the track. "I'll never forget that train trip," said Anna later. She had been given her father's stateroom. "All night I sat on the foot of that berth and watched the people who had come to see the train pass by. There were little children, fathers, grandparents. They were there at 11 at night, at 2 in the morning, at 4—at all hours during that long night."[82]

The train arrived the next morning, and another cortege accompanied the coffin up the hillside to the rose garden. William Plog, who had tended the old family place for nearly fifty years, had supervised the digging of the grave. Another brief and dignified service was held for the family and the dignitaries who had come up on the train. Seven West Point cadets fired three volleys; after each one Fala barked and a child whimpered. Then it was over, and most of the mourners boarded the train for the trip back to Washington and the uncertainty, the renewed fear of faltering, that would meet them there.[83]

Everything had happened so fast that most people could not absorb the transition. "All this very strange," admitted Hassett. "Worked with F. D. R. in the hilltop cottage at Warm Springs last Thursday. Today—Monday—he sleeps in the rose garden at Hyde Park."[84]

That same Monday Stimson penned a letter to Eleanor Roosevelt praising his late chief in words that might have served as a fitting epitaph. "He was an ideal war Commander-in-Chief," Stimson wrote. "His vision of the broad problems of the strategy of the war was sound and accurate, and his relations to his military advisers and commanders were admirably correct. In the execution of their duties he gave them freedom, backed them up, and held them responsible. In all these particulars he seems to me to have been our greatest war President. And his courage and cheeriness in times of great emergency won for him the loyalty and affection of all who served under him."[85]

EPILOGUE: THE PAYOFF

The most important things in this war are machines... The United States ... is a country of machines.
— JOSEPH STALIN [1]

You and I were brought up to think cynically of patriotism... I hated everything in music, books, movies, etc. that stressed love of country. That was for the yokels ... Maybe I was right—I don't know. One thing I AM sure of—a thing this war has taught me—I love my country and I'm not ashamed to admit it anymore... I am proud of the men of my generation. Brought up like you and I in false prosperity and then degrading depression, they have overcome these handicaps. And shown the world that America has something the world can never take away from us—a determination to keep our way of life... It still is the one force that won the war—the thing the enemy never believed we had.
— MARJORIE HASELTON TO HER HUSBAND IN CHINA [2]

Over the radio yesterday... I heard the starting of another war! All about how the U.S. was developing new and secret weapons and how we should keep our secrets from the Russians! One was Winston Churchill; another was the head of the Army Air Forces! Talk like that is a betrayal of those who died or were wounded in this war and of those who are working to make it possible for nations to live in peace with each other!
— CONNIE HOPE JONES TO HER FIANCÉ [3]

ON HIS FIRST DAY AS PRESIDENT HARRY Truman broke his first precedent by going up to the Hill for lunch. Congress was his milieu, and he wanted to assure its leaders in person of his strong desire for cooperation. After lunch he spotted some newsmen waiting outside an office and shook hands with them. "I don't know if you boys pray," he said, "but if you do, please pray God to help me carry this load." A captain in the last war, he was the first soldier to occupy the White House since Theodore Roosevelt. The lessons of that war, with its horrendous waste and stupidities, still lodged firmly in his memory. "Harry Truman is a man of distinct limitations," observed *Time*, "especially in experience in high-level politics. He knows his limitations . . . He is no theorist. In his Administration there are likely to be few innovations and little experimentation . . . He hates the palace politics that sometimes marred the Roosevelt Administration."[4]

Henry Stimson had left Washington with Groves on April 10 for his first visit to Oak Ridge. That afternoon and the next morning he toured and had explained to him what he called "the largest and most extraordinary scientific experiment in history." He was the first outsider to breach the secrecy of its work and was equally impressed by "the creation of an orderly and well governed city" where none had existed before. Although Groves had done his job well, Stimson realized its limitations. "It has this unique peculiarity," he observed, "that, although every prophesy thus far has been fulfilled by the development and we can see that success is 99% assured, yet only by the first actual war trial of the weapon can the actual certainly be fixed." He returned to Washington on the eleventh; a day later the world changed, and his enhanced knowledge of S-1 took on a fresh urgency.[5]

The first cabinet meeting was a revelation to Stimson. The new president impressed him with his brisk, no-nonsense approach to everything, the "promptness and snappiness with which Truman took up each matter and decided it." The amount of work, of catching up on matters he knew only a little about, overwhelmed Truman the first several days after taking office, but he kept at it in his dogged, efficient manner. Not until April 25 did he find time to meet with Stimson on a matter of special importance. Stimson handed him a memorandum of just over two pages he had written and waited while the president read it. The opening sentence caught his attention at once: "Within four months we shall in all probability have completed the most terrible weapon ever known in human history, one bomb of which could destroy a city."[6]

Truman had been aware of S-1 since November 1941, when Roosevelt put him on the advisory committee for questions relating to nuclear fission. He had followed developments but not in great detail because details had not been forthcoming. Now Stimson briefed him not on the bomb itself but on its implications for future relations with other powers, most notably the Russians. Already Great Britain shared in knowledge of the program; should it be disclosed to others? "The world in its present state of moral advancement compared with its technical development would be eventually at the mercy of such a weapon," Stimson stressed. "In other words, modern civilization might be completely destroyed."[7]

Groves then joined the meeting and handed Truman a twenty-four-page report on the status of the Manhattan Project, the process and problems. Stimson thought it "very much interested him" even though Truman, besieged with matters to deal with, bridled at having to read so detailed a report. Groves said he had condensed it as much as possible. "This is a big project," he added. Truman indicated his complete agreement with the project, thanked them, and recalled the time when, as chairman of the Trumann Committee, he insisted on investigating what all the money going to S-1 was being spent on. Stimson had fended him off, and Truman said he understood now why the project had been kept so secret.[8]

Overwhelmed though he was by the vast responsibilities thrust so suddenly upon him, the new president made it clear that he was determined to meet them. There would be no faltering, no backing away from the policies Roosevelt had laid down, no hesitation in carrying out whatever must be done. Victory would be pursued relentlessly, a decision made on where and how to use the bomb once it was ready, and nothing short of unconditional surrender accepted in either theater. Plans for the United Nations, one of Roosevelt's most cherished projects, would go forward. Production would be maintained as long as necessary and reconversion embraced once the enemy was vanquished.

Truman would, of course, do things in his own way and in his own style. Unlike Roosevelt, he was nothing if not methodical. He could not be the charismatic father figure Roosevelt had been or the master charmer and politician who, for many younger Americans, had been the only president they had ever known. As a senator Truman took pride in his work and the long hours he put in, usually from seven in the morning to seven at night. Of his colleagues he estimated that thirty to forty "worked like Trojans," another fifteen to twenty worked fairly well, and the rest did little if anything. Now he was alone in a job where there were many helping hands of varying ability, but no one could share the responsibilities. Reporters who were accustomed to arriving at the White House at 10:00 A.M. or later for Roosevelt found they had to be on duty by 8:00 A.M. for the new man. "Stick with me," Truman told them smiling, "and I'll make men of you yet."[9]

The White House staff and Secret Service struggled to adjust to a radically different tempo. Roosevelt had been their boss but also their prisoner, unable to go anywhere without their assistance. "Now," said one Secret Service agent, "here's a guy, you had to move when he moved. And he *moved fast*! He was a whiz, just like that! He'd go—*and went*! And you had to go with him. So, we had to revise our thinking, and the whole strategy of the place changed because of his ability to be in movement and motion."[10]

But Truman learned quickly that he too was a prisoner in another way.

One day he decided to go at noon to his bank, a few blocks from the White House. Without warning he put on his hat and went out the door with the Secret Service men hustling to keep up. The result was a traffic jam that lasted half an hour. The president of the United States discovered that he could not simply go to the bank or anywhere else on his own. The bank, or anything else, would have to come to him. Like it or not, he was not and could not be just an ordinary guy any longer.[11]

WITHIN A SHORT time Truman began reshaping the administration to suit his own needs and tastes. On his second day in office he replaced Jesse Jones as federal loan administrator with John W. Snyder. Postmaster General Frank Walker gave way to Robert E. Hannegan, Labor Secretary Frances Perkins to Lewis B. Schwellenbach, Attorney General Francis Biddle to Thomas C. Clark, and Secretary of Agriculture Claude Wickard to Clinton P. Anderson, all effective June 30. In July Fred Vinson took over as treasury secretary in place of the much-abused Henry Morgenthau, and Jimmy Byrnes returned to power as secretary of state in place of Edward Stettinius. This last change was especially important in that under existing law the presidency passed to the secretary of state should Truman die. Ickes, Stimson, Morgenthau, and Wallace all stayed on past the end of the war. So did Sam Rosenman, who had originally thought to quit but reconsidered. Steve Early left in favor of Charles G. Ross, and Matthew J. Connelly, who had served as Truman's secretary when he was vice president, took on the job of appointment secretary and confidential assistant.[12]

In July 1944 the JCS had approved the notion of invading Japan by October 1, 1945. After the Yalta Conference, however, debate began over whether it might be better, and less costly, to encircle Japan and defeat her by a war of attrition. In April the JCS reaffirmed its preference for an early invasion and calculated that about thirty-six divisions, or 1.5 million men, would be needed for an assault expected to incur heavy casualties. On May 8, six days after the formal surrender of the German forces in Italy, Truman celebrated his sixty-first birthday by announcing the surrender of Germany. The two-front war had become a one-front war, but the problems of subduing Japan remained staggering.[13]

Transferring the European war machine to the Pacific was a colossal logistical problem. The distance from Europe to Manila via the Panama Canal was about 14,000 miles, with Tokyo another 1,900 miles away. Some seventy combat divisions were in Europe. It took fifteen Liberty ships to move the equipment of a single armored division and seventy-five trains to move it overland to a port. For equipment and supplies, the distance required three

ships to do the work one had managed in the European theater. The best estimates figured it would take six months to shift ground forces from Europe to
the Pacific. Everyone sensed that Japan was as thoroughly beaten as Germany, but the diehard resistance of her troops on the conquered islands made
it equally clear that her people would defend their homeland to the death.[14]

THE PAYOFF FOR victory, and the ugliest new face of war, came together in
1945. On the night of February 13 some 1,400 aircraft, mostly bombers,
dropped nearly 650,000 incendiaries along with high explosives on Dresden,
Germany, creating a firestorm visible 200 miles away, utterly devastating the
city, and killing some 25,000 people. In the Pacific thousands of American
troops gave their lives to capture hitherto insignificant islands needed as
bases for B-29s to attack Japan. By the end of 1944 high-altitude bombing by
the vaunted B-29s had accomplished little in destroying targets. In January
1945 General Curtis LeMay took charge of the B-29 attacks and devised a bold
new tactic: Instead of high-altitude attacks, the planes would come in at only
5,000 to 7,000 feet and drop incendiary bombs on Tokyo's mostly wood and
paper structures. The B-29s would be stripped of armaments except for the
tail gun in order to increase the bomb load.[15]

LeMay could attempt this because Tokyo's defenses lacked suitable antiaircraft guns for shooting at low-level bombing. Attacking at night would render
Japanese fighters impotent because, intelligence told the general, they didn't
have airborne radar units. In March 334 B-29s carrying 2,000 tons of incendiaries flew over Tokyo and inflicted what a bombardier called "the most
terrifying thing I've ever known." The bombs created a firestorm, then a wall
of fire called a conflagration that obliterated nearly sixteen square miles of
the city and killed more than 100,000 people. No structure in the target area
escaped damage. The heat boiled the water in some canals where people had
jumped to avoid the fire. Buoyed by the results, LeMay sent his planes to fire-
bomb Nagoya, Osaka, and Kobe. In ten days the B-29s destroyed a total of
thirty-two square miles of Japan's four largest cities, killing at least 150,000
people and likely tens of thousands more.[16]

"No matter how you slice it, you're going to kill an awful lot of civilians,"
LeMay wrote later. "Thousands and thousands. But, if you don't destroy the
Japanese industry, we're going to have to invade Japan. And how many Americans will be killed in an invasion of Japan? Five hundred thousand seems to
be the lowest estimate . . . We're at war with Japan. We were attacked by Japan. Do you want to kill Japanese, or would you rather have Americans killed?"
The firebombings paused because LeMay literally ran out of incendiaries,
but he believed strongly that he had found the key to forcing the Japanese to

surrender. Once resupplied, his planes proceeded to devastate more cities, yet the Japanese refused to give up. Then, in May, the general learned for the first time of another weapon that could be employed by a special squadron of B-29s built for just this mission.[17]

Little Boy was at last ready to be deployed and likely to work. The gun mechanism was inefficient, even wasteful, but U-235 was less sensitive and demanding than plutonium. Unlike implosion, it required no more tests. At Los Alamos the scientists and staff worked furiously to prepare for Trinity, the decisive test for Fat Man. As the test date neared, the lead scientists did a very American thing: They formed a pool with a dollar entry fee on what the explosive yield would be. The guesses ranged from a cynical zero to Teller's optimistic 45,000 tons TNT equivalent. A storm threatened to delay the test but passed through just in time.[18]

At 5:30 A.M. on July 16 the firing circuits closed and thirty-two detonators fired simultaneously. "Suddenly, there was an enormous flash of light," said Isidor Rabi, "the brightest light I have ever seen or that I think anyone has seen. It blasted; it pounced; it bored its way right through you. It was a vision which was seen with more than the eye. It was seen to last forever. You would wish it would stop; altogether it lasted about two seconds. Finally it was over, diminishing, and we looked toward the place where the bomb had been; there was an enormous ball of fire which grew and grew and it rolled as it grew; it went up into the air, in yellow flashes and into scarlet and green. It looked menacing. It seemed to come toward one. A new thing had just been born; a new control; a new understanding of man, which man had acquired over nature."[19]

Implosion worked, and reactions ranged from elation to horror at what had been created. Oppenheimer recalled a line from the Bhagavad Gita: "Now I am become Death, the destroyer of worlds." Kenneth Bainbridge, the Trinity Project director, had a more prosaic but equally apropos response: "Now we are all sons of bitches." Rabi, who had come late to the betting pool and had to take the figure of 18,000 tons, won the bet. The blast measured out at 18.6 kilotons. Five days later a British physicist who studied blast effects for the Target Committee calculated that a comparable bomb "would reduce a city of three or four hundred thousand people to nothing but a sink for disaster relief, bandages, and hospitals." Theory had become terrifying reality.[20]

At about the same time of the Trinity blast, the gun assembly for Little Boy was being loaded aboard the heavy cruiser *Indianapolis* for its ten-day voyage to Tinian. By July 31 the bomb was ready for use, but an approaching storm delayed the mission. Six days later Little Boy, looking in the words of a crew member like "an elongated trash can with fins," was loaded aboard the B-29 *Enola Gay*. It was 10.5 feet long, only 29 inches in diameter, and weighed 9,700 pounds. Once over Hiroshima, the lone plane encountered no fighters or flak. The bomb dropped and detonated with a force equivalent to 12,500 tons of TNT.[21]

"I don't believe anyone ever expected to look at a sight quite like that," said Captain Robert Lewis, the second in command of the plane. "Where we had seen a clear city two minutes before, we could now no longer see the city. We could see smoke and fires creeping up the sides of the mountains." Later he admitted, "If I live a hundred years, I'll never quite get these few minutes out of my mind." Another crew member added, "If you want to describe it as something you are familiar with, a pot of boiling black oil . . . I thought: Thank God the war is over and I don't have to get shot at any more. I can go home."[22]

But it was not quite over. The Japanese military still refused to submit to what they deemed the dishonor of unconditional surrender. Fat Man's components had already arrived at Tinian and were being assembled in case they were needed. Three days after the obliteration of Hiroshima a B-29 named *Bock's Car* took off with Fat Man nestled in its bomb bay. Heavy ground haze clouded over the primary target, the Kokura Arsenal on the north coast of Kyushu, forcing the crew to the secondary, the port city of Nagasaki. Clouds obscured the city; the bomb would have to be dropped by radar or dumped into the ocean. A brief opening in the clouds provided an aiming point, and Fat Man was released. It exploded 1,650 feet above the city's steep slopes with a force later estimated at 22 kilotons. However, because the steep hills contained the explosion, it actually caused less damage and loss of life than did Little Boy.[23]

Two cities had been blown out of existence with an estimated 80,000 killed at Hiroshima and 45,000 at Nagasaki, figures that continued to climb for years from radiation poisoning. Unspeakable suffering had been unleashed. Groves informed Marshall that a second Fat Man could be ready for shipping to Tinian by August 12 or 13, but it was not needed. On August 14 Japan formally surrendered. "If it had gone on any longer," said a Japanese writer of the bombing, "there would have been nothing to do but go mad." The war was over at last, and Americans had been spared the steep cost of invading Japan. America had shown the full range of its industrial and technological might as well as its vast reservoir of resources and brainpower, domestic and imported. History had never witnessed so great and destructive an assembly of military and productive power.[24]

Wild and jubilant celebrations erupted all across the nation. For civilians and returning soldiers alike, the future held a wide array of promises as well as perils. America's role in the world would never be the same, relations with the Soviet Union had yet to be worked out, and the infant United Nations remained a work barely in progress. The bureaucratic apparatus of wartime would be dismantled with measured haste, and the contentious process of reconversion launched in earnest. The tearing down would prove far more complex than the building up. Many still feared the return of depression, while others predicted unprecedented prosperity fueled by the huge level of savings and deferred consumer demand for all kinds of goods.

Even before the bombs were dropped, the exodus had begun at Willow Run, a place with neither a past nor a future but merely a temporary present. Edsel Ford himself had labeled it "as expendable as a battleship." The plant had been built and equipped for war, a special purpose needing special tools. In that sense it represented on a grand scale hundreds of plants across the country. The first 15,000 departees, 60 percent of them men, received personal interviews. Some 1,600 workers were immediately referred to other jobs. Only 30 percent of the 3,000 women were offered other jobs, and most refused because of the type of work involved. An amazing 45 percent of the people left to go back home without even applying for unemployment compensation, 30 percent of them heading back to their home state.[25]

Jim Bone of Tennessee said he was disgusted and happy to leave. "Damned sick and tired I am of being called a hillbilly," he growled. "You make more money here. Sure! But they bleed all hell out of you as fast as you make it"— "they" being the landlords, storekeepers, restaurant owners, gamblers, and other camp followers. Teddy Davies of Mississippi disagreed and planned to stay on in Detroit. "The wife likes it here," he said. "She likes the indoor plumbing, and the kids like the schools. We'll stay as long as we can." They were two of 8,000 so-called white trash who were supposed to breed crime and low morals at Willow Run. Yet they lived three years in war housing without committing a single felony and worked long hours without complaint. Now they all faced an uncertain future, as did millions of other workers who had left home to find work in the war plants.[26]

What did it all mean, and what would come of it all? Thousands of words poured out on these subjects from pundits, participants, and loved ones alike. Lucile Wilson, a schoolteacher in Everett, Washington, wrote to her son, stationed in the Pacific, "There are many things that will make you ask yourself this question, 'Is it all for naught?' from time to time. I've asked myself this question for you many times. I'm sure every mother has done the same . . . Millions of veterans and home folks intelligently asking this question may bring great post war changes. This is the hope of the *future*."[27]

The future turned out to be far kinder than expected. The depression did not return, and the high savings rate during the war, coupled with the lack of many big-ticket items such as cars and appliances, unleashed a torrent of consumer spending that, together with continued military spending, brought the return of prosperity to a population long starved for it. An unprecedented birth rate spawned a baby boom and with it a powerful economic stimulus. Housing developments sprang up across the nation, giving birth to the suburbs that would become the standard cliché of the 1950s. At the same time, the long-sought goal of world peace remained as elusive as ever. Although Roosevelt's cherished dream of the United Nations was realized, the organization was helpless to prevent or curb the rising tensions that spawned the Cold War. The arms race generated new and ever more deadly weapons that kept international relations unstable and the threat of new wars ever present. Even Willow Run found a future producing automobiles, though not for Ford. It turned out cars for Henry Kaiser and later General Motors as well as C-119 transport planes.[28]

Even in the delirium of victory some people, while deliriously grateful for the war's end, could not help but wonder what would follow it. Few matched in poignancy and hope the sentiments expressed by Rose McClain, who lived in Snoqualmie Falls, Washington. Her words echoed those of every mother down through the ages who had endured the horrors of war. "Today I cried and thanked God for the end of this war," she wrote her husband, Charles, who was with the navy in the Pacific, "and I shall continue to pray that this shall be the end of war for all time. That our children will learn kindness, patience, honesty, and the depth of love and trust we have learned from all this, with out the tragedy of war. That they shall never know hate, selfishness and death from such as this has been."[29]

It was a consummation devoutly to be wished, and continues to be wished for down through another seventy-five years of ceaseless wars and suffering.

NOTES

PROLOGUE: THE WORLD UNRAVELING—AGAIN

1. Quoted in Geoffrey Perrett, *Days of Sadness, Years of Triumph: The American People, 1939–1945* (New York, 1973), 27–28.

2. Unless otherwise indicated, this section is drawn from Maury Klein, *The Power Makers* (New York, 2008), 444–52.

3. Steven Zaloga and Victor Madej, *The Polish Campaign, 1939* (New York, 1985), 106–41.

4. Donald M. Nelson, *Arsenal of Democracy: The Story of American War Production* (New York, 1946), 25.

5. Harold G. Vatter, *The U.S. Economy in World War II* (New York, 1985), 3.

6. Nelson, *Arsenal of Democracy*, 26.

7. For a good brief summary of the postwar world, see Michael C. C. Adams, *The Best War Ever: America and World War II* (Baltimore, 1994), 20–42.

8. Ibid., 24.

9. Ibid., 30.

10. Harold L. Ickes, *The Secret Diary of Harold L. Ickes* (New York, 1953–54), January 27, 1940, 113.

11. Keith E. Eiler, *Mobilizing America: Robert P. Patterson and the War Effort, 1940–1945* (Ithaca, 1997), 307.

12. Manfred Jonas, *Isolationism in America, 1935–1941* (Ithaca, 1966), 150–51.

13. Ibid., 136–46; Charles A. Beard, *The Devil Theory of War* (New York, 1936), 11–29; Bernard M. Baruch, *Baruch: The Public Years* (New York, 1960), 269.

14. Robert H. Connery, *The Navy and the Industrial Mobilization in World War II* (Princeton, 1951), 266.

15. Jonas, *Isolationism in America*, 159–66.

16. Robert E. Sherwood, *Roosevelt and Hopkins* (New York, 1948), 129–30, 152–53.

17. Ibid., 130–32.

18. Jonas, *Isolationism in America*, 150; United States Bureau of the Budget, *The United States at War* (Washington, 1946), 9–10; Richard M. Ketchum, *The Borrowed Years, 1938–1941: America on the Way to War* (New York, 1989), 9–10.

19. Kiplinger Washington Editors, *Kiplinger's Looking Ahead: 70 Years of Forecasts from the Kiplinger Washington Letter* (Washington, 1993), 51, hereafter cited as *Kiplinger Letter*.

20. Ibid., 52–54. All emphases are in the original.

21. Sherwood, *Roosevelt and Hopkins*, 127–28; Samuel I. Rosenman, *Working with Roosevelt* (New York, 1952), 167.

22. Sherwood, *Roosevelt and Hopkins*, 125, 131.

23. Ibid., 134; Ketchum, *Borrowed Years*, 227; Budget Bureau, *United States at War*, 18; *Newsweek*, February 5, 1940, 42.

24. Ketchum, *Borrowed Years*, 227–28.

25. Budget Bureau, *United States at War*, 12–14.

26. Ibid., 14–15; David Robertson, *Sly and Able: A Political Biography of James F. Byrnes* (New York, 1994), 290; Paul A. C. Koistinen, *Arsenal of World War II: The Political Economy of American Warfare, 1940–1945* (Lawrence, Kan., 2004), 15; Eliot Janeway, *The Struggle for Survival* (New York, 1968 [1951]), 37. Through a rare Military Order in July 1939, Roosevelt transferred the army and navy chiefs of staff, the Aeronautical Board, the Joint Economy Board, and the Army-Navy Munitions Board from the War and Navy departments to his direct supervision as commander in chief.

27. Sherwood, *Roosevelt and Hopkins*, 209.

28. Koistinen, *Arsenal of World War II*, 15; Janeway, *Struggle for Survival*, 38.

29. See, for example, Ketchum, *Borrowed Years*, 224–25.

30. Budget Bureau, *United States at War*, 18–19; Nelson, *Arsenal of Democracy*, 71.

31. Sherwood, *Roosevelt and Hopkins*, 139.

32. Ibid., 141.

33. *Time*, June 24, 1940, 20; Ketchum, *Borrowed Years*, 339–51.

34. Doris Kearns Goodwin, *No Ordinary Time* (New York, 1994), 63–64.

35. *Time*, June 24, 1940, 20; *Life*, May 27, 1940, 30.

36. Sherwood, *Roosevelt and Hopkins*, 142; Goodwin, *No Ordinary Time*, 64.

37. Nelson, *Arsenal of Democracy*, 76.

38. Ibid., 45.

39. *Life*, May 27, 1940, 30.

CHAPTER 1. THE MAN AND THE HOUR

1. Burnham Finney, *Arsenal of Democracy: How Industry Builds Our Defense* (New York, 1941), 3, 5.

2. Budget Bureau, *United States at War*, 20.

3. Eric Larrabee, *Commander in Chief: Franklin Delano Roosevelt, His Lieutenants, and Their War* (New York, 1987), 644.

4. Goodwin, *No Ordinary Time*, 13–18; *Time*, May 20, 1940, 16.

5. Goodwin, *No Ordinary Time*, 13–18; *Time*, June 10, 1940, 17.

6. Goodwin, *No Ordinary Time*, 17; *Time*, June 10, 1940, 17; Sherwood, *Roosevelt and Hopkins*, 206.

7. *Time*, June 10, 1940, 18; Sherwood, *Roosevelt and Hopkins*, 9.

8. James L. Tyson, "The War Industries Board, 1917–1918," 16. This brief account can be found as a supplement to the September 1940 issue of *Fortune*. For a fuller account of WIB, see Bernard Baruch, *American Industry in the War* (New York, 1941).

9. R. Elberton Smith, *The Army and Economic Mobilization* (Washington, 1991), 73–92; Eiler, *Mobilizing America*, 3–4; Nelson, *Arsenal of Democracy*, 91; Budget Bureau, *United States at War*, 22; United States Civilian Production Administration, *Industrial Mobilization for War: History of the War Production Board and Predecessor Agencies 1940–1945* (Washington, 1947), 1:3–6, hereafter cited as CPA, *Industrial Mobilization for War*.

10. Baruch, *Public Years*, 272–73.

11. Ibid., 274–76; Smith, *Army and Economic Mobilization*, 98–99; Janeway, *Struggle for Survival*, 39.

12. Janeway, *Struggle for Survival*, 44–49; Budget Bureau, *United States at War*, 16; Vatter, *U.S. Economy in World War II*, 33, 45.

13. Janeway, *Struggle for Survival*, 50–55; Smith, *Army and Economic Mobilization*, 100; Richard Polenberg, *War and Society: The United States, 1941–1945* (Philadelphia, 1972), 6; Vatter, *U.S. Economy in World War II*, 45; Bruce Catton, *The War Lords of Washington* (New York, 1948), 101–3; CPA, *Industrial Mobilization for War*, 6–11.

14. Janeway, *Struggle for Survival*, 54–62; Sherwood, *Roosevelt and Hopkins*, 280.

15. Smith, *Army and Economic Mobilization*, 100–102; Janeway, *Struggle for Survival*, 62–65; Polenberg, *War and Society*, 6.

16. For the German experience, see Richard Overy, *Why the Allies Won* (New York, 1995), 198–200.

17. Koistinen, *Arsenal of World War II*, 16.

18. W. M. Kiplinger, *Washington Is Like That* (New York, 1942), 435–41; Rosenman, *Working with Roosevelt*, 214; Forrest C. Pogue, *George C. Marshall: Ordeal and Hope* (New York, 1966), 20.

19. Kiplinger, *Washington Is Like That*, 436, 439; Ketchum, *Borrowed Years*, 460–62; Sherwood, *Roosevelt and Hopkins*, 105–10, 170–71.

20. Sherwood, *Roosevelt and Hopkins*, 1–2. Sherwood's fine book offers the fullest and most revealing portrait of their relationship.

21. Ibid., 92–93, 112–22; George McJimsey, *Harry Hopkins: Ally of the Poor and Defender of Democracy* (Cambridge, Mass., 1987), 118, 126–28; *Look*, June 27, 1944, 21–25; *Time*, January 22, 1945, 17–20.

22. Kiplinger, *Washington Is Like That*, 14.

23. Rosenman, *Working with Roosevelt*, 193; Ickes, *Diary*, June 9, 1940, 203; Franklin D. Roosevelt, *F.D.R.: His Personal Letters, 1928–1945* (New York, 1950), 993; Sherwood, *Roosevelt and Hopkins*, 169–70.

24. Ickes, *Diary*, January 21, January 27, and February 17, 1940, 107, 117, 139.

25. Sherwood, *Roosevelt and Hopkins*, 170, 172.

26. Ickes, *Diary*, April 13 and May 12, 1940, 163, 174–75.

27. *Time*, May 27, 1940, 17–18.

28. Ibid.

29. Ibid., 18; *New York Times*, May 10 and May 11, 1940.

30. Franklin D. Roosevelt, *The Public Papers and Addresses of Franklin D. Roosevelt*, 13 vols. (New York, 1928–45), 9:198–202; *Newsweek*, May 27, 1940, 32–35; *Time*, May 27, 1940, 20; Koistinen, *Arsenal of World War II*, 59; Budget Bureau, *United States at War*, 22; CPA, *Industrial Mobilization for War*, 18–38.

31. Budget Bureau, *United States at War*, 23; *Time*, June 10, 1940, 19; Polenberg, *War and Society*, 7.

32. Rosenman, *Working with Roosevelt*, 195–96.

33. Roosevelt, *Public Papers and Addresses*, 9:230–42.

34. Catton, *War Lords*, 21; Nelson, *Arsenal of Democracy*, 66.

35. Roosevelt, *Personal Letters*, 1037–38; Nelson, *Arsenal of Democracy*, 77–78; Pogue, *Ordeal and Hope*, 51.

36. Ickes, *Diary*, June 2, 1940, 191; McJimsey, *Hopkins*, 129; Goodwin, *No Ordinary Time*, 37.

37. Ickes, *Diary*, June 12, 1940, 206–7; Goodwin, *No Ordinary Time*, 20.

38. Ickes, *Diary*, June 12, 1940, 206–7.

39. Ibid., October 7, 1940, 344; Goodwin, *No Ordinary Time*, 23; Ketchum, *Borrowed Years*, 537–38.

40. Ickes, *Diary*, May 19, 1940, 180; *Time*, June 3, 1940, 11.

41. *Newsweek*, June 17, 1940, 32; Goodwin, *No Ordinary Time*, 67–68.

42. *Newsweek*, June 17, 1940, 32; Roosevelt, *Public Papers and Addresses*, 9:263–64; Diary of Henry L. Stimson, December 29, 1940, Yale University Library. I used a microfilm version of the diary in the University of Rhode Island library.

43. *Time*, June 17, 1940, 13.

44. Ickes, *Diary*, June 23, 1940, 214; Henry L. Stimson and McGeorge Bundy, *On Active Service in Peace and War* (New York, 1948), 323–24; Stimson diary, June 25, 1940.

45. Kiplinger, *Washington Is Like That*, 436–38; Ketchum, *Borrowed Years*, 422–23.

46. Ickes, *Diary*, June 2, 1940, 196; Roosevelt, *Personal Letters*, 1041; Kiplinger, *Washington Is Like That*, 449; Stimson diary, June 25, 1940; Elting E. Morison, *Turmoil and Tradition: A Study of the Life and Times of Henry L. Stimson* (New York, 2003), 477; *Saturday Evening Post*, September 5, 1942, 12–13, 59–60, 62.

47. Baruch, *Public Years*, 277; *Newsweek*, August 5, 1940.

48. Ickes, *Diary*, February 4 and May 19, 1940, 120, 178; *Time*, July 1, 1940, 61.

49. *Time*, June 24, 1940, 20–21; Ketchum, *Borrowed Years*, 356.

50. Sherwood, *Roosevelt and Hopkins*, 150; *Look*, June 4, 1940, 8; Cabell Phillips, *The 1940s: Decade of Triumph and Trouble* (New York, 1975), 16–43.

51. *Look*, June 4, 1940, 8; Ickes, *Diary*, June 29, 1940, 220–21; Steve Neal, *Dark Horse: A Biography of Wendell Willkie* (Garden City, N.Y., 1984), 66–121.

52. Sherwood, *Roosevelt and Hopkins*, 176–77.

53. Ibid., 178–79.

54. Roosevelt, *Public Papers and Addresses*, 9:293–302; *Time*, July 29, 1940, 9–10.

CHAPTER 2. THE WHEREWITHAL OF WAR

1. Janeway, *Struggle for Survival*, 59.

2. Ibid., 80.

3. *Harper's*, August 1940, 227.

4. Unless otherwise indicated, this account of Baruch's early life is drawn from Margaret Coit, *Mr. Baruch* (Boston, 1957), 1–222. See also *Time*, June 28, 1943, 16–19.

5. Coit, *Baruch*, 137.

6. Ibid., 167–68.

7. Ibid., 208; *Fortune*, October 1940, 166.

8. Coit, *Baruch*, 209–411; Baruch, *Public Years*, 217–36.

9. Baruch, *Public Years*, 237–43; Coit, *Baruch*, 412–62.

10. John Kenneth Galbraith, *A Life in Our Times: Memoirs* (Boston, 1981), 130; Rosenman, *Working with Roosevelt*, 231, 335; Eleanor Roosevelt, *This I Remember* (New York, 1949), 256; Coit, *Baruch*, 500.

11. I. F. Stone, *The War Years, 1939–1945* (Boston, 1988), 150–51.

12. Goodwin, *No Ordinary Time*, 412.

13. *Saturday Evening Post*, June 22, 1940, 28.

14. *Time*, May 12, 1941, 16; Galbraith, *A Life in Our Times*, 130; Coit, *Baruch*, 317–18.

15. Janeway, *Struggle for Survival*, 82.

16. I. F. Stone, *Business as Usual: The First Year of Defense* (New York, 1941), 14–15.

17. Godfrey Hodgson, *The Colonel: The Life and Wars of Henry Stimson, 1867–1950* (New York, 1990), 224.

18. Nelson, *Arsenal of Democracy*, 31–32.

19. *Time*, June 17, 1940, 78, and September 2, 1940, 19.

20. Eliot Janeway, "Exit Exports, Enter Boom," *Harper's*, September 1940, 354.

21. *Newsweek*, February 5, 1940, 42, February 12, 1940, 46, February 19, 1940, 58, and March 11, 1940, 54; *Saturday Evening Post*, April 20, 1940, 26.

22. Frederick Lewis Allen, "The Lesson of 1917," *Harper's*, September 1940, 344–46.

23. Ibid., 345, 349.

24. *Time*, June 3, 1940, 65; Tyson, "War Industries Board," 1, 11–16.

25. Tyson, "War Industries Board," 15.

26. Ibid., 7–15; *Time*, June 3, 1940, 65.

27. Allen, "Lesson of 1917," 353.

28. Tyson, "War Industries Board," 5–6.

29. Janeway, *Struggle for Survival*, 58.

30. *Time*, January 15, 1940, 16; *Newsweek*, January 15, 1940, 12–14.

31. *Newsweek*, January 22, 1940, 11–14, and February 26, 1940, 17.

32. *Newsweek*, February 26, 1940, 18; Pogue, *Ordeal and Hope*, 26–27.

33. Pogue, *Ordeal and Hope*, 27–28; Baruch, *Public Years*, 278.

34. Pogue, *Ordeal and Hope*, 28–29.

35. Ibid., 30–31; Norman Beasley, *Knudsen: A Biography* (New York, 1947), 228.

36. Roosevelt, *Public Papers and Addresses*, 9:198–205; *Time*, May 27, 1940, 19–21; *Newsweek*, May 27, 1940, 32–35.

37. Roosevelt, *Public Papers and Addresses*, 9:250–52; *Newsweek*, May 27, 1940, 56, 68, and June 3, 1940, 30, 32.

38. Roosevelt, *Public Papers and Addresses*, 9:286–91; *Saturday Evening Post*, August 31, 1940, 28.

39. Vatter, *U.S. Economy in World War II*, 106.

40. Koistinen, *Arsenal of World War II*, 432; *Time*, June 10, 1940, 20; *Newsweek*, July 8, 1940, 44–45.

41. Roosevelt, *Public Papers and Addresses*, 9:276; *Newsweek*, July 15, 1940, 48, 51; *Time*, July 15, 1940, 12, 14, and August 19, 1940, 72, 74.

42. *Time*, August 19, 1940, 74–76, and September 30, 1940, 16; *Newsweek*, August 26, 1940, 8; Stimson diary, August 22 and 23, 1940.

43. *Newsweek*, October 14, 1940, 52.

44. Finney, *Arsenal of Democracy*, 6–7.

45. Ibid., 7–8.

46. Ibid., 9–34.

47. Ibid., 34–35.

48. *Time*, May 27, 1940, 18–19.

49. Ketchum, *Borrowed Years*, 542.

50. Ibid., 539, 542; Stimson diary, August 8, 1940.

51. Eiler, *Mobilizing America*, 43; Goodwin, *No Ordinary Time*, 23.

52. *Look*, February 13, 1940, 28; *Time*, May 6, 1940, 20; Eiler, *Mobilizing America*, 43–44, 116–18; Nelson, *Arsenal of Democracy*, 41–42.

53. Goodwin, *No Ordinary Time*, 52.

54. Ibid.; Ketchum, *Borrowed Years*, 543–44.

55. Eiler, *Mobilizing America*, 44; *Newsweek*, July 15, 1940, 14.

56. *Newsweek*, June 3, 1940, 59, 61, June 17, 1940, 69, and July 15, 1940, 14.

57. Ketchum, *Borrowed Years*, 539–40.

58. Connery, *Navy and Industrial Mobilization*, 55–57, 130–31.

59. Ibid., 88.

60. James MacGregor Burns, *Roosevelt: The Soldier of Freedom* (New York, 1970), 14.

CHAPTER 3. THE POSSIBILITIES OF PRODUCTION

1. Perrett, *Days of Sadness*, 67.

2. Raymond Clapper, *Watching the World* (New York, 1944), 266.

3. Charles E. Sorensen, *My Forty Years with Ford* (New York, 1956), 273.

4. *Saturday Evening Post*, May 18, 1940, 20–21, 74–76, 78; Francis Walton, *Miracle of World War II: How American Industry Made Victory Possible* (New York, 1956), 216–17.

5. *Time*, August 26, 1940, 53, and October 28, 1940, 72; Wayne G. Broehl, *Precision Valley: The Machine Tool Companies of Springfield, Vermont* (Englewood Cliffs, N.J., 1959), 155.

6. Walton, *Miracle of World War II*, 216–17.

7. Ibid., 216; Finney, *Arsenal of Democracy*, 54.

8. *Saturday Evening Post*, May 18, 1940, 20–21.

9. Finney, *Arsenal of Democracy*, 9.

10. *Time*, August 26, 1940, 53. For more background detail, see Harless D. Wagoner, *The U.S. Machine Tool Industry from 1900 to 1950* (Cambridge, Mass., 1968).

11. Walton, *Miracle of World War II*, 218–20.

12. Wagoner, *U.S. Machine Tool Industry*, 150–57; Broehl, *Precision Valley*, 171–74; *Saturday Evening Post*, May 18, 1940, 75–76.

13. *Saturday Evening Post*, October 5, 1940, 26.

14. Connery, *Navy and Industrial Mobilization*, 115–16.

15. *Life*, May 27, 1940, 83–84.

16. *Newsweek*, April 29, 1940, 54–55.

17. Unless otherwise indicated, this section is drawn from *Saturday Evening Post*, February 24, 1940, 18–19, 39, 42, 44.

18. *Time*, May 6, 1940, 75, and June 10, 1940, 80; *Life*, May 27, 1940, 89–90; Gerald T. White, *Billions for Defense: Government Financing by the Defense Plant Corporation During World War II* (University, Ala., 1980), 19.

19. *Newsweek*, July 8, 1940, 48; *Fortune*, August 1940, 51–52.

20. *Fortune*, August 1940, 52–53.

21. Ibid., 50–53.

22. Ibid., 89; Ickes, *Diary*, January 27, 1940, 117.

23. *Fortune*, July 1940, 50–51, 143–44. The article gives more detail on the advantages of the liquid-cooled engine.

24. *Fortune*, August 1940, 90; *Time*, August 12, 1940, 16; *Look*, August 27, 1940, 8–12.

25. *Newsweek*, June 10, 1940, 58–59, June 17, 1940, 60, and November 4, 1940, 35; *Time*, July 1, 1940, 61, July 8, 1940, 60, and October 7, 1940, 71; Nelson, *Arsenal of Democracy*, 80; Sorensen, *My Forty Years with Ford*, 274–76; Beasley, *Knudsen*, 264–67.

26. Nelson, *Arsenal of Democracy*, 226–27.

27. Stimson diary, July 24, 1940; *Time*, October 7, 1940, 72.

28. This section is drawn from *Saturday Evening Post*, August 21, 1941, 14–15.

29. Ickes, *Diary*, May 20, 1940, 73; *Newsweek*, April 1, 1940, 47.

30. *Time*, May 20, 1940, 73–74, 76. The navy's eight yards were located in Boston, New York, Philadelphia, Norfolk, Charleston, Portsmouth, New Hampshire, Mare Island (California), and Puget Sound.

31. *Newsweek*, July 1, 1940, 49–50. Workers did not object to toiling more than forty hours a week; the issue was whether they should be paid time-and-a-half for any extra hours. Unions fought vigorously to keep that privilege.

32. *Time*, December 16, 1940, 86–87.

33. *Time*, June 17, 1940, 75–76.

34. Ibid.

35. *Time*, December 16, 1940, 86–87.

36. *Fortune*, October 1940, 154, and March 1942, 85–87, 126, 129–30, 132–33, 135; *Saturday Evening Post*, January 31, 1942, 9–10.

37. *Newsweek*, September 2, 1940, 28.

38. *Newsweek*, June 3, 1940, 55; Ickes, *Diary*, May 12, 1940, 175; Koistinen, *Arsenal of World War II*, 116.

39. Budget Bureau, *United States at War*, 26–27; Koistinen, *Arsenal of World War II*, 116–17; *Look*, January 28, 1941, 26; White, *Billions for Defense*, 11–18; *Fortune*, December 1941, 91; *Saturday Evening Post*, November 30, 1940, 9–11, 88–90, 92, and December 7, 1940, 29, 107–8, 110, 112, 115–16. The two *Post* articles are a detailed profile of Jones by Samuel Lubell.

40. *Saturday Evening Post*, November 30, 1940, 11.

41. *Saturday Evening Post*, December 7, 1940, 107–8; Kiplinger, *Washington Is Like That*, 439.

42. Ickes, *Diary*, September 8, 1940, 314; *Newsweek*, July 8, 1940, 54.

43. *Newsweek*, November 11, 1942, 71–72.

44. *Newsweek*, September 2, 1940, 28; *Time*, August 19, 1940, 20; *Fortune*, March 1942, 129–30, 133.

45. *Newsweek*, September 2, 1940, 28–29; *Time*, May 20, 1940, 73; *Fortune*, October 1940, 162, and March 1942, 126, 129; *Harper's*, November 1941, 566. For nylon's story, see *Fortune*, July 1940, 57–60, 114, 116.

46. *Time*, May 20, 1940, 73; *Fortune*, August 1940, 71; *Harper's*, September 1940, 363; Vernon Herbert and Attilio Bisio, *Synthetic Rubber: A Project That Had to Succeed* (Westport, Conn., 1985), ix.

47. Frank A. Howard, *Buna Rubber: The Birth of an Industry* (New York, 1947), 65; *Fortune*, August 1940, 71.

48. Howard, *Buna Rubber*, 6–9; *Fortune*, August 1940, 71, 112; *Harper's*, September 1940, 362.

49. *Harper's*, September 1940, 363–68.

50. Koistinen, *Arsenal of World War II*, 139; *Time*, February 5, 1940, 51–53, and April 8, 1940, 71.

51. *Time*, August 5, 1940, 59–60.

52. *Time*, September 23, 1940, 65–66.

53. Nelson, *Arsenal of Democracy*, 39–40.

54. Roosevelt, *Public Papers and Addresses*, 9:290; Pogue, *Ordeal and Hope*, 56–57.

55. Stimson diary, July 10, 1940; Pogue, *Ordeal and Hope*, 57–58. Pogue offers a brief account of the bill's origins; see also Ketchum, *Borrowed Years*, 561–64.

56. *Newsweek*, August 5, 1940, 13; *Look*, September 10, 1940, 4.

57. *Newsweek*, August 5, 1940, 13–16; Stimson diary, July 16, 1940.

58. Ketchum, *Borrowed Years*, 564; Roosevelt, *Public Papers and Addresses*, 9:317–21.

59. *Time*, August 12, 1940, 11–13.

60. Roosevelt, *Public Papers and Addresses*, 9:313–14, 431–34; Pogue, *Ordeal and Hope*, 62–63; *Newsweek*, September 23, 1940, 30–31.

61. *Harper's*, July 1940, 116.

62. *Time*, July 22, 1940, 48.

63. *Time*, June 24, 1940, 19, and July 22, 1940, 48.

64. *Fortune*, November 1940, 66; Matthew Josephson, *Sidney Hillman: Statesman of American Labor* (Garden City, N.Y., 1952), 510–11.

65. *Fortune*, November 1940, 66; *Look*, January 28, 1941, 15.

66. *Fortune*, November 1940, 66–67, 70.

CHAPTER 4. THE ONUS OF ORGANIZATION

1. Ickes, *Diary*, June 2, 1940, 194.

2. *Saturday Evening Post*, June 29, 1940, 26.

3. *Harper's*, July 1940, 116.

4. Stimson diary, July 19, July 23, and July 30, 1940.

5. Rosenman, *Working with Roosevelt*, 204; Kiplinger, *Washington Is Like That*, 97; Goodwin, *No Ordinary Time*, 138.

6. *Time*, June 3, 1940, 31; *Harper's*, October 1940, 493; Koistinen, *Arsenal of World War II*, 18; *Newsweek*, June 10, 1940, 31. The NDAC was technically a reconstituted civilian advisory commission to the Council of National Defense, created in 1916 and composed of the secretaries of the War, Navy, Interior, Commerce, Agriculture, and Labor departments.

7. *Newsweek*, June 10, 1940, 56, 58–61; Beasley, *Knudsen*, 238; Ickes, *Diary*, June 2, 1940, 194; Goodwin, *No Ordinary Time*, 56–57; Koistinen, *Arsenal of World War II*, 19–20.

8. Beasley, *Knudsen*, 1–233, 246; Kiplinger, *Washington Is Like That*, 445–46.

9. Beasley, *Knudsen*, 57–68; David Hounshell, *From the American System to Mass Production, 1800–1932* (Baltimore, 1984), 217–61. Hounshell provides a detailed and insightful explanation of Ford's role in the origin and development of mass production.

10. Kiplinger, *Washington Is Like That*, 444–45.

11. Ibid., 443–45; *Fortune*, November 1940, 70, 149; *Look*, January 28, 1941, 14–16; Josephson, *Hillman*, 17–460.

12. Josephson, *Hillman*, 79.

13. Ickes, *Diary*, June 2, June 5, June 12, and June 15, 1940, 195–96, 200, 207–9.

14. Koistinen, *Arsenal of World War II*, 22–23.

15. Ibid., 21.

16. Ibid., 23–24.

17. Ibid., 24–27.

18. Nelson, *Arsenal of Democracy*, 58–59.

19. Ibid., 59–61; *Fortune*, November 1941, 153.

20. Nelson, *Arsenal of Democracy*, 60–64; *Fortune*, November 1940, 86.

21. Nelson, *Arsenal of Democracy*, 64.

22. Ibid., 67–68.

23. Ibid., 68, 72–75.

24. Ibid., 75–76.

25. *Fortune*, November 1940, 156.

26. Nelson, *Arsenal of Democracy*, 83–84.

27. Ibid., 84.

28. Eiler, *Mobilizing America*, 80; Koistinen, *Arsenal of World War II*, 33–39.

29. Smith, *Army and Economic Mobilization*, 39–40; Koistinen, *Arsenal of World War II*, 39–40; *Look*, May 29, 1945, 21–25.

30. Smith, *Army and Economic Mobilization*, 39–43.

31. Ibid., 48–53.

32. Ibid., 67–70; *Harper's*, July 1940, 115.

33. Smith, *Army and Economic Mobilization*, 70–72. The four basic forms were contract for supplies (fixed price), contract for construction (fixed price), evaluated-fee construction contract, and adjusted-compensation contract.

34. Ibid., 55–61.

35. Stimson diary, July 25, 1940; *Time*, June 17, 1940, 17.

36. *Newsweek*, July 22, 1940, 48–49, and July 29, 1940, 46.

37. Koistinen, *Arsenal of World War II*, 49.

38. Ibid., 49–50; Nelson, *Arsenal of Democracy*, 99–100.

39. Nelson, *Arsenal of Democracy*, 100–101; Koistinen, *Arsenal of World War II*, 50; *Fortune*, November 1941, 158; *Newsweek*, October 20, 1941, 43.

40. Nelson, *Arsenal of Democracy*, 101–4.

41. Koistinen, *Arsenal of World War II*, 50, 53.

42. Nelson, *Arsenal of Democracy*, 106; *Newsweek*, July 29, 1940, 47.

43. Nelson, *Arsenal of Democracy*, 106; Koistinen, *Arsenal of World War II*, 54.

44. *Fortune*, October 1940, 58; Smith, *Army and Economic Mobilization*, 456–60. See also chapter 2.

45. Ickes, *Diary*, August 10, 1940, 296, and September 8, 1940, 315; Stone, *Business as Usual*, 157.

46. Goodwin, *No Ordinary Time*, 156–58.

47. *Newsweek*, July 22, 1940, 55; *Harper's*, October 1940, 499–500, 502.

48. *Newsweek*, August 19, 1940, 30; *Fortune*, October 1940, 58, 150; Stimson diary, September 7 and September 30, 1940.

49. Stimson diary, August 2, August 6, and August 26, 1940.

50. Ibid., September 10, September 11, and September 19, 1940.

51. Ibid., September 13, September 16, September 17, and October 1, 1940; *Time*, September 23, 1940, 18; Morison, *Turmoil and Tradition*, 490. No evidence of sabotage was found.

52. *Fortune*, October 1940, 150, 156; Koistinen, *Arsenal of World War II*, 54.

53. Fortune, October 1940, 166; Nelson, *Arsenal of Democracy*, 90–91.

54. Roosevelt, *Personal Letters*, 1058–59.

55. *Fortune*, April 1942, 63; *Time*, May 26, 1941, 58.

56. *Fortune*, April 1942, 64.

57. *Time*, March 31, 1941, 59–60.

58. *Fortune*, April 1942, 65.

59. Peter Galison and Bruce Hevly, eds., *Big Science: The Growth of Large-Scale Research* (Stanford, 1992), 155.

60. Ibid., 155–56.

61. G. Pascal Zachary, *Endless Frontier: Vannevar Bush, Engineer of the American Century* (New York, 1997), 11–54. Bush's unusual first name was the last name of a lifelong friend of his father.

62. Ibid., 55–72.

63. Ibid., 73–102.

64. Ibid., 102–6.

65. Ibid., 107–10; Sherwood, *Roosevelt and Hopkins*, 154.

66. Sherwood, *Roosevelt and Hopkins*, 154; Zachary, *Endless Frontier*, 111–13. The other members were General George V. Strong, Admiral Harold G. Bowen, Professor Richard C. Tolman, and Conway P. Coe, the commissioner of patents.

67. Vannevar Bush, *Pieces of the Action* (New York, 1970), 31–32.

68. Sherwood, *Roosevelt and Hopkins*, 155; Irvin Stewart, *Organizing Scientific Research for War: The Administrative History of the Office of Scientific Research and Development* (Boston, 1948), 7–8.

69. James B. Conant, *My Several Lives: Memoirs of a Social Inventor* (New York, 1970), 236; Zachary, *Endless Frontier*, 114–15.

70. *Time*, May 26, 1941, 58, 60; Zachary, *Endless Frontier*, 115–17.

71. *Time*, May 26, 1942, 61; Zachary, *Endless Frontier*, 118.

72. This account is drawn from *Fortune*, March 1945, 130–33.

CHAPTER 5. MAKING HASTE SLOWLY

1. Budget Bureau, *United States at War*, 25–26.

2. *Saturday Evening Post*, January 4, 1941, 26.

3. Catton, *War Lords*, 28.

4. *Time*, July 15, 1940, 59–60, and July 22, 1940, 67; Beasley, *Knudsen*, 265–66.

5. Finney, *Arsenal of Democracy*, 45; *Time*, August 5, 1940, 17. The version in *Time* is somewhat different.

6. *Time*, August 5, 1940, 18; Beasley, *Knudsen*, 247–48.

7. Beasley, *Knudsen*, 256–57.

8. *Newsweek*, October 14, 1940, 13.

9. *Time*, June 24, 1940, 80, and August 5, 1940, 18–19.

10. *Newsweek*, July 29, 1940, 52–53.

11. *Time*, July 1, 1940, 61, and September 30, 1940, 65.

12. *Time*, September 30, 1940, 65.

13. *Newsweek*, August 12, 1940, 25–26; Koistinen, *Arsenal of World War II*, 51–52; Walter W. Wilcox, *The Farmer in the Second World War* (Ames, Iowa, 1947), 337–38.

14. Koistinen, *Arsenal of World War II*, 51–52, has more detail on this dispute.

15. Ibid., 54–57; *Time*, September 2, 1940, 19–20. Koistinen provides details on the two forms of financing facilities.

16. *Newsweek*, August 26, 1940, 29.

17. *Fortune*, November 1941, 156.

18. *Saturday Evening Post*, November 30, 1940, 26.

19. Ketchum, *Borrowed Years*, 475–76, 496.

20. Ibid.; Neal, *Dark Horse*, 139–40.

21. Ketchum, *Borrowed Years*, 476–77.

22. Ibid., 477–80. Ketchum errs in placing the cabinet meeting after Pershing's speech rather than before it. Details on the transaction and relevant documents on it are in Roosevelt, *Public Papers and Addresses*, 9:391–407.

23. Stimson diary, July 24, July 26, and August 7, 1940; Ickes, *Diary*, September 28, 1940, 339.

24. Stimson diary, July 31, August 7, August 8, August 21, August 23, August 26, and September 16, 1940.

25. Ibid., September 17, October 9, and October 16, 1940; Ickes, *Diary*, October 7, 1940, 346–47.

26. Stimson diary, October 16, 1940.

27. *Time*, July 22, 1940, 16; Ickes, *Diary*, September 8, 1940, 312.

28. *Kiplinger Letter*, June 8, June 15, August 30, September 7, and October 12, 1940. All emphases are in the original.

29. *Newsweek*, September 9, 1940, 40; Budget Bureau, *United States at War*, 37; *Saturday Evening Post*, October 19, 1940, 26.

30. Roosevelt, *Personal Letters*, 1046–47; *Time*, October 28, 1940, 11.

31. Roosevelt, *Personal Letters*, 1072.

32. Sherwood, *Roosevelt and Hopkins*, 184–85; Ketchum, *Borrowed Years*, 439–40, 515–16; Neal, *Dark Horse*, 142–43.

33. Sherwood, *Roosevelt and Hopkins*, 185–87; Ketchum, *Borrowed Years*, 515–16; Neal, *Dark Horse*, 144–49; Clapper, *Watching the World*, 159–61.

34. Sherwood, *Roosevelt and Hopkins*, 188.

35. Ibid., 189–91; Ketchum, *Borrowed Years*, 523–25.

36. *Time*, November 4, 1941, 18; Ketchum, *Borrowed Years*, 517; Sherwood, *Roosevelt and Hopkins*, 192–93; Neal, *Dark Horse*, 169–72; Ickes, *Diary*, February 4, 1940, 121.

37. Ketchum, *Borrowed Years*, 518–19; Sherwood, *Roosevelt and Hopkins*, 193–95; Neal, *Dark Horse*, 157–74; Ickes, *Diary*, November 5, 1940, 361.

38. Sherwood, *Roosevelt and Hopkins*, 195–98; Ketchum, *Borrowed Years*, 525.

39. Sherwood, *Roosevelt and Hopkins*, 200–201; Neal, *Dark Horse*, 176.

40. Roosevelt, *Personal Letters*, 1078.

41. Rosenman, *Working with Roosevelt*, 261.

42. Budget Bureau, *United States at War*, 37; Stimson diary, September 16, September 25, October 2, and October 4, 1940.

43. Stimson diary, September 27, October 10 and October 15, 1940; *Time*, October 21, 1940, 23.

44. Goodwin, *No Ordinary Time*, 165–67; *Time*, October 28, 1940, 19.

45. Goodwin, *No Ordinary Time*, 168–70; Stimson diary, September 27, 1940.

46. Stimson diary, October 22, October 23, and October 28, 1940; *Time*, October 21, 1940, 23, and October 28, 1940, 19; Goodwin, *No Ordinary Time*, 169.

47. Stimson diary, December 11 and December 19, 1940; *Time*, October 21, 1940, 23; Eiler, *Mobilizing America*, 48–49.

48. Stimson diary, October 16, 1940.

49. *Time*, November 4, 1940, 67–68.

50. Ickes, *Diary*, December 21, 1940, 393; Stimson diary, December 14, 1940.

51. Stimson diary, December 14, 1940.

52. *Time*, December 9, 1940, 20.

53. *Time*, December 23, 1940, 14–15; *Newsweek*, December 23, 1940, 31–33, 35.

54. Stimson diary, December 17, 1940.

55. Koistinen, *Arsenal of World War II*, 68–69.

56. Stimson diary, December 17 and December 18, 1940.

57. Ibid., December 18, 1940.

58. Ibid., December 18–20, 1940; *Newsweek*, December 30, 1940, 22–23.

59. Roosevelt, *Public Papers and Addresses*, 9:622–25.

60. Ibid., 625–31.

61. "Memorandum of conference of December 21, 1940—First preliminary meeting of Messrs. Knox, Knudsen, Hillman, and Stimson," in Stimson diary, December 21, 1940.

62. *Newsweek*, December 30, 1940, 22.

63. *Time*, December 23, 1940, 9; Sherwood, *Roosevelt and Hopkins*, 222.

64. Ickes, *Diary*, November 23, 1940, 373.

65. Sherwood, *Roosevelt and Hopkins*, 223–24; Warren F. Kimball, ed., *Churchill and Roosevelt: The Complete Correspondence* (Princeton, 1984), 1:102–9.

66. Sherwood, *Roosevelt and Hopkins*, 224; Kimball, *Complete Correspondence*, 1:102–9.

67. *Time*, December 23, 1940, 9.

68. Roosevelt, *Public Papers and Addresses*, 9:606–8.

69. Ibid., 9:632; Sherwood, *Roosevelt and Hopkins*, 225–26.

70. Sherwood, *Roosevelt and Hopkins*, 225–28; Rosenman, *Working with Roosevelt*, 258–62.

71. *Time*, January 6, 1941, 9.

72. Ibid.

73. The entire text is found in Roosevelt, *Public Papers and Addresses*, 9:633–44.

74. *Newsweek*, January 6, 1941, 14–15; Stimson diary, December 29, 1940; Goodwin, *No Ordinary Time*, 195–96.

75. Goodwin, *No Ordinary Time*, 196.

76. *Newsweek*, January 6, 1941, 30.

CHAPTER 6. A HOUSE DIVIDED

1. Nelson, *Arsenal of Democracy*, 139.

2. Roosevelt, *Public Papers and Addresses*, 9:651.

3. *Time*, December 2, 1940, 15.

4. Roosevelt, *Public Papers and Addresses*, 9:645–63; *Newsweek*, January 13, 1941, 13–16.

5. Roosevelt, *Public Papers and Addresses*, 9:679–94; *Newsweek*, January, 20, 1941, 15–16; Nelson, *Arsenal of Democracy*, 117; Max Freedman, annotator, *Roosevelt and Frankfurter: Their Correspondence, 1928–1945* (Boston, 1967), 582.

6. Sherwood, *Roosevelt and Hopkins*, 224, 228; *Time*, January 20, 1941, 15.

7. *Time*, January 20, 1941, 15–16; *Newsweek*, January 20, 1941, 15–17. *Newsweek* includes the full text of the bill.

8. Wayne S. Cole, *America First: The Battle Against Intervention, 1940–1941* (Madison, Wisc., 1953), 3–42, 46; Roosevelt, *Public Papers and Addresses*, 9:711–12.

9. Cole, *America First*, 43–50; *Newsweek*, February 3, 1941, 13–15, February 10, 1941, 13–14, February 17, 1941, 17–19, February 24, 1941, 17–18, March 10, 1941, 15, and March 17, 1941, 17–18; *Time*, February 24, 1941, 18, and March 24, 1941, 15; Roosevelt, *Public Papers and Addresses*, 10:51–52; Rosenman, *Working with Roosevelt*, 256.

10. *Look*, January 28, 1941, 4–5; *Time*, February 24, 1941, 15; *Newsweek*, March 24, 1941, 17–18.

11. *Newsweek*, January 27, 1941, 13–14; *Time*, January 27, 1941, 11–12.

12. *Time*, January 27, 1941, 11–12.

13. *Newsweek*, January 6, 1941, 30.

14. *Newsweek*, October 28, 1940, 36; *Saturday Evening Post*, December 21, 1940, 26.

15. *Newsweek*, June 10, 1940, 64–65; Koistinen, *Arsenal of World War II*, 403–5.

16. Koistinen, *Arsenal of World War II*, 403; *Time*, April 29, 1940, 18; *Fortune*, November 1940, 155.

17. Stimson diary, October 2, 1940; *Newsweek*, October 7, 1940, 37.

18. *Newsweek*, October 14, 1940, 76; *Time*, October 14, 1940, 30–31.

19. *Newsweek*, November 18, 1940, 45–46, and December 2, 1940, 33–34; *Time*, December 2, 1940, 15–16.

20. *Newsweek*, December 2, 1940, 34, 36; *Time*, December 2, 1940, 16.

21. Clapper, *Watching the World*, 218–22.

22. Byron Fairchild and Jonathan Grossman, *The Army and Industrial Manpower* (Washington, 1959), 57–58.

23. Ibid., 58–59; *Time*, November 25, 1940, 25; Stimson diary, November 26, 1940.

24. Koistinen, *Arsenal of World War II*, 406–7; Eiler, *Mobilizing America*, 164; *Newsweek*, December 9, 1940, 32; *Time*, December 9, 1940, 16; Fairchild and Grossman, *Army and Industrial Manpower*, 58–60; *Los Angeles Times*, November 19–27, 1940; Stimson diary, November 26, 1940.

25. *Time*, January 27, 1941, 16–17.

26. Ibid., 18.

27. *Time*, December 9, 1940, 16, and December 16, 1940, 23; Ickes, *Diary*, November 5, 1940, 360; Stimson diary, November 26, 1940; *Newsweek*, December 9, 1940, 32, and January 13, 1941, 44.

28. Stimson diary, December 28, 1940, and January 2, 1941; Eiler, *Mobilizing America*, 156.

29. Vatter, *U.S. Economy in World War II*, 45; Robert H. Zieger, *The CIO, 1935–1955* (Chapel Hill, 1995), 113–15.

30. Zieger, *CIO*, 115.

31. Ibid., 116–19.

32. David M. Kennedy, *Freedom from Fear* (New York, 1999), 639.

33. *Time*, March 3, 1941, 17; *Newsweek*, January 13, 1941, 60; Stimson diary, January 18, February 1, February 27, and February 28, 1941.

34. Clapper, *Watching the World*, 219–21.

35. Fairchild and Grossman, *Army and Industrial Manpower*, 61–62.

36. Ibid., 65; Stimson diary, March 7, 1941; *Time*, March 10, 15–16; Ickes, *Diary*, April 12, 1941, 472–73.

37. Fairchild and Grossman, *Army and Industrial Manpower*, 65; Stimson diary, March 19, 1941; *Time*, March 24, 1941, 17; *Newsweek*, March 24, 1941, 36.

38. Stimson diary, March 19, 1941; *Time*, March 24, 1941, 17, and March 31, 1941, 14–15.

39. *Newsweek*, March 24, 1941, 36–37, April 7, 1941, 36–37, and April 14, 1941, 46; *Time*, March 31, 1941, 15, and April 7, 1941, 20–22; Stimson diary, April 2, 1941; Zieger, *CIO*, 126–27; Roosevelt, *Public Papers and Addresses*, 10:76–80.

40. Stimson diary, April 2 and April 4, 1941.

41. *Time*, April 14, 1941, 21; *Newsweek*, April 14, 1941, 44; Zieger, *CIO*, 122–23.

42. *Time*, April 14, 1941, 21, April 21, 1941, 24, and June 30, 1941, 14; *Newsweek*, April 14, 1941, 44, April 21, 1941, 34–35, and June 30, 1941, 34, 37; Zieger, *CIO*, 123–25.

43. Zieger, *CIO*, 127–29.

44. Stimson diary, May 26 and May 28, 1941; Roosevelt, *Public Papers and Addresses*, 10:142–43, 176–77, 181–95.

45. Zieger, *CIO*, 129; Stimson diary, June 6, 1941. Emphasis is in the original. Those at the meeting included J. H. Kindelberger, president of North American, Knox, Patterson, Hillman, Forrestal, Knudsen, Francis Biddle, the solicitor general, and John Lord O'Brian, general counsel of OPM.

46. Ickes, *Diary*, June 8, 1941, 536.

47. Zieger, *CIO*, 129; Stimson diary, June 6, June 8, and June 9, 1941; Ickes, *Diary*, June 8, 1941, 535–36; *Time*, June 16, 1941, 15; *Newsweek*, June 16, 1941, 34.

48. Stimson diary, June 9–12, 1941; Roosevelt, *Public Papers and Addresses*, 10:205–9.

49. *Time*, June 16, 1941, 15, June 30, 1941, 13–14, and July 7, 1941, 13; Stimson diary, July 2, 1941; Zieger, *CIO*, 129–30.

50. *Fortune*, August 1941, 61.

51. *Time*, July 7, 1941, 15, July 28, 1941, 14, August 18, 1941, 14, September 1, 1941, 17, September 29, 1941, 17, and October 20, 1941, 21–22; *Newsweek*, July 28, 1941, 40, September 1, 1941, 30, and September 15, 1941, 36.

52. Fairchild and Grossman, *Army and Industrial Manpower*, 68–69.

53. Goodwin, *No Ordinary Time*, 225; Roosevelt, *Personal Letters*, 1218–19.

54. *Saturday Evening Post*, June 7, 1941, 28.

55. The early history of the CIO is well covered in Zieger, *CIO*, 6–92. The 600,000-member figure is taken from *Fortune*, August 1941, 126.

56. Zieger, *CIO*, 93–102.

57. Ibid., 103–11.

58. Ibid., 112–37.

59. Fairchild and Grossman, *Army and Industrial Manpower*, 66–67; Ickes, *Diary*, April 12 and April 26, 1941, 476–77, 489; *Time*, June 23, 1941, 15.

60. *Newsweek*, November 3, 1941, 40–41; *Time*, November 3, 1941, 13–14; Stimson diary, November 11, 1941.

61. *Time*, November 3, 1941, 14, and November 10, 1941, 19; *Newsweek*, November 10, 1941, 50, 52; Roosevelt, *Public Papers and Addresses*, 10:435–38. The November 10 issue of *Time* has a good sample of the political cartoons.

62. *Newsweek*, November 24, 1941, 42, 44; *Time*, November 24, 1941, 20–21; Stimson diary, November 11, 1941.

63. *Newsweek*, November 24, 1941, 42, 44; *Time*, November 24, 1941, 20–21; Ickes, *Diary*, November 15, 1941, 642; Roosevelt, *Public Papers and Addresses*, 10:490–95.

64. *Newsweek*, November 24, 1941, 42, and December 1, 1941, 46; Stimson diary, November 13 and November 14, 1941.

65. Ickes, *Diary*, November 15 and November 23, 1941, 642–43, 650; Stimson diary, No-

vember 14, November 15, and November 23, 1941; *Newsweek*, December 1, 1941, 46–47. The three-man board consisted of Lewis, Fairless, and the director of the United States Concili-ation Service.

66. Fairchild and Grossman, *Army and Industrial Manpower*, 67; *Time*, November 10, 1941, 20–21, and November 24, 1941, 21–22; *Newsweek*, November 17, 1941, 42, 44.

67. Budget Bureau, *United States at War*, 190–92; *Fortune*, March 1942, 70–72. 166–70, 172, 174, 176.

CHAPTER 7. TO HAVE AND HAVE NOT

1. *Kiplinger Letter*, January 25, 1941, 65. Emphasis is in original.

2. Nelson, *Arsenal of Democracy*, 153.

3. *Life*, July 14, 1941, quoted in William L. O'Neill, *A Democracy at War* (New York, 1993), 29.

4. *Newsweek*, June 9, 1941, 13–16.

5. Ibid.

6. Roosevelt, *Public Papers and Addresses*, 10:181–82. For the entire talk and proclama-tion, see ibid., 10:181–95.

7. Goodwin, *No Ordinary Time*, 239.

8. *Newsweek*, June 9, 1941, 17–18.

9. Clapper, *Watching the World*, 274–76.

10. Burns, *Soldier of Freedom*, 101; *Time*, June 23, 1941, 13.

11. Stone, *Business as Usual*, 15; Koistinen, *Arsenal of World War II*, 76.

12. Roosevelt, *Public Papers and Addresses*, 9:679–89; *Time*, February 24, 1941, 23, and March 17, 1941, 77; Koistinen, *Arsenal of World War II*, 76–77, 130; CPA, *Industrial Mobiliza-tion for War*, 96–99.

13. CPA, *Industrial Mobilization for War*, 95–98; Koistinen, *Arsenal of World War II*, 81.

14. Koistinen, *Arsenal of World War II*, 82; CPA, *Industrial Mobilization for War*, 98.

15. David Novick, Melvin Anshen, and W. C. Truppner, *Wartime Production Controls* (New York, 1949), 8.

16. Ibid., 7–9.

17. Ibid.

18. Ibid., 3; Baruch, *Public Years*, 283.

19. Nelson, *Arsenal of Democracy*, 108.

20. Ibid., 108–9; Eiler, *Mobilizing America*, 59.

21. Nelson, *Arsenal of Democracy*, 111–12; Stimson diary, November 26, 1940.

22. Nelson, *Arsenal of Democracy*, 112–15.

23. Koistinen, *Arsenal of World War II*, 66–67, 175–77; Eiler, *Mobilizing America*, 83–85.

24. Novick et al., *Wartime Production Controls*, 36–59; Janeway, *Struggle for Survival*, 198.

25. Novick et al., *Wartime Production Controls*, 57; Stone, *Business as Usual*, 59–61; *For-tune*, May 1941, 145.

26. Koistinen, *Arsenal of World War II*, 136; *Fortune*, May 1941, 145.

27. *Time*, January 6, 1941, 15.

28. *Fortune*, May 1941, 67–68; Stone, *Business as Usual*, 61–62.

29. Goodwin, *No Ordinary Time*, 259; Ickes, *Diary*, February 16, 1941, 431; *Time*, March 24, 1941, 76.

30. Stone, *Business as Usual*, 53–54; *Time*, January 6, 1941, 15; Koistinen, *Arsenal of World War II*, 136–37; Eiler, *Mobilizing America*, 177.

31. Stone, *Business as Usual*, 49–50, 70–71; *Newsweek*, March 17, 1941, 43.

32. Stone, *Business as Usual*, 50–52, 74; *Time*, March 24, 1941, 76, 78, May 26, 1941, 21, and June 9, 1941, 24.

33. *Time*, March 24, 1941, 76, 78; *Fortune*, May 1941, 68; *Newsweek*, March 17, 1941, 43; Ickes, *Diary*, February 2, 1941, 420–24.

34. Ickes, *Diary*, February 16 and February 22, 1941, 431–34; *Fortune*, May 1941, 68; *Time*, May 26, 1941, 21.

35. Ickes, *Diary*, March 1 and July 20, 1941, 446, 578; *Time*, March 24, 1941, 78, and June 2, 1941, 20.

36. *Time*, September 1, 1941, 76.

37. Mark S. Foster, *Henry J. Kaiser: Builder in the Modern American West* (Austin, 1989), 196–97; *Fortune*, May 1941, 68, 142.

38. Foster, *Kaiser*, 197–98; *Fortune*, May 1941, 145; *Saturday Evening Post*, June 7, 1941, 124; *Time*, March 3, 1941, 67.

39. Koistinen, *Arsenal of World War II*, 141.

40. *Time*, November 25, 1941, 88–89, and December 16, 1941, 77–78.

41. *Newsweek*, January 6, 1941, 10, February 10, 1941, 37–38, 43, and June 30, 1941, 64; *Time*, January 20, 1941, 67–68, and February 10, 1941, 57–58; *Fortune*, August 1941, 166. For a summary of steel's role during the war years, see *Fortune*, May 1945, 121–24, 241–42, 244, 246, 248, 251–52.

42. *Time*, March 10, 1941, 77–78, 80; *Fortune*, April 1941, 70–72; Stone, *Business as Usual*, 149.

43. Koistinen, *Arsenal of World War II*, 141–42; *Time*, June 2, 1941, 69.

44. Koistinen, *Arsenal of World War II*, 142–43; *Time*, June 2, 1941, 69, and June 16, 1941, 74, 76, 78; Stone, *Business as Usual*, 150.

45. Stimson diary, January 7 and January 8, 1941; *Saturday Evening Post*, August 26, 1941, 33, and September 13, 1941, 13, 78–79.

46. Galbraith, *A Life in Our Times*, 106.

47. *Time*, May 12, 1941, 19.

48. *Saturday Evening Post*, September 13, 1941, 78; Ickes, *Diary*, August 3, 1941, 591.

49. *Saturday Evening Post*, September 13, 1941, 79–82; *Time*, May 12, 1941, 18–19.

50. *Saturday Evening Post*, September 13, 1941, 83–84.

51. Ibid., 84, 86; Stone, *Business as Usual*, 131; *Time*, May 12, 1941, 16–17.

52. Roosevelt, *Public Papers and Addresses*, 10:99–105; Stimson diary, April 3, 1941; *Saturday Evening Post*, April 12, 1941, 9–11, 122–25, 128, 130, 132; CPA, *Industrial Mobilization for War*, 102–3.

53. Roosevelt, *Public Papers and Addresses*, 10:105–6; *Time*, April 28, 1941, 73–74.

54. *Time*, April 28, 1941, 73.

55. *Time*, October 14, 1940, 97; *Kiplinger Letter*, July 19, 1940, 66.

56. Beasley, *Knudsen*, 312–13; Goodwin, *No Ordinary Time*, 232; Stone, *War Years*, 61; *Time*, May 19, 1941, 89–90.

57. Stone, *War Years*, 60–61.

58. *Time*, March 10, 1941, 15; Stimson diary, May 12 and May 29, 1941.

59. *Fortune*, November 1941, 69.

60. Ickes, *Diary*, July 27, 1941, 589; Stimson diary, June 17, 1941; Beasley, *Knudsen*, 270; Nelson, *Arsenal of Democracy*, 218; *Newsweek*, July 28, 1941, 35–36.

61. Nelson, *Arsenal of Democracy*, 219–20; Christy Borth, *Masters of Mass Production* (Indianapolis, 1945), 69–71.

62. Sorensen, *My Forty Years at Ford*, 278–80.

63. Ibid., 281–83.

64. Nelson, *Arsenal of Democracy*, 223; *Time*, July 14, 1941, 59–60, 62, and September 1, 1941, 73.

65. *Time*, September 8, 1941, 33.

66. *Newsweek*, September 22, 1941, 30, 35.

67. *Newsweek*, October 13, 1941, 34; *Time*, November 11, 1940, 65; *Fortune*, November 1941, 70.

68. This section is drawn from *Fortune*, November 1941, 76, 78–83, 124, 126, 128, 194–97, 199.

69. *Newsweek*, December 1, 1941, 14; Ickes, *Diary*, November 6, 1941, 635.

70. Goodwin, *No Ordinary Time*, 233–34; *Time*, April 14, 1941, 17; *Newsweek*, April 21, 1941, 17–19.

71. *Newsweek*, April 21, 1941, 17; *Time*, May 5, 1941, 17.

CHAPTER 8. GETTING SHIPSHAPE

1. *Time*, May 19, 1941, 21.

2. Frederic C. Lane, *Ships for Victory: A History of Shipbuilding Under the U.S. Maritime Commission in World War II* (Baltimore, 1951), vii.

3. Arthur Herman, *Freedom's Forge: How American Business Produced Victory in World War II* (New York, 2012), 133.

4. Lane, *Ships for Victory*, 40.

5. Ibid., 12–14; *Time*, March 31, 1941, 12.

6. Lane, *Ships for Victory*, 12–14.

7. *Time*, March 31, 1941, 12; *Newsweek*, March 3, 1941, 36, 38. *Newsweek* contains a list of individual shipping companies and the foreign markets they served.

8. *Time*, January 13, 1941, 14, and March 31, 1941, 12; *Newsweek*, January 13, 1941, 39.

9. *Fortune*, July 1941, 116; *Time*, January 13, 1941, 14; *Newsweek*, January 13, 1941, 39; Lane, *Ships for Victory*, 43; Martin Middlebrook, *Convoy* (New York, 1977), 8; Roosevelt, *Public Papers and Addresses*, 9:645–47.

10. Roosevelt, *Public Papers and Addresses*, 9:647; Lane, *Ships for Victory*, 44; *Time*, January 13, 1941, 14.

11. Lane, *Ships for Victory*, 45; *Fortune*, July 1941, 119.

12. Lane, *Ships for Victory*, 43; *Time*, March 31, 1941, 12; *Fortune*, July 1941, 41; Roosevelt, *Public Papers and Addresses*, 10:94–96; *Newsweek*, April 1941, 15–17.

13. Lane, *Ships for Victory*, 46–51; *Newsweek*, March 31, 1941, 40, 42.

14. Lane, *Ships for Victory*, 52–53; *Newsweek*, March 31, 1941, 40, 42; *Fortune*, July 1941, 121. Bethlehem was the other big West Coast operator.

15. Lane, *Ships for Victory*, 53–54; Foster, *Kaiser*, 46–47; *Fortune*, July 1941, 122. Foster lists the members of the consortium.

16. *Fortune*, July 1941, 124.

17. Foster, *Kaiser*, 6–23; Albert P. Heiner, *Henry J. Kaiser, Western Colossus* (San Francisco, 1991), 1–20. See also *Fortune*, September 1943, 147–49, 249–50, 252, 255, 258, 261.

18. Foster, *Kaiser*, 24–43.

19. Ibid., 44–61.

20. Ibid., 57, 61–66; *Fortune*, September 1943, 222.

21. Foster, *Kaiser*, 66; *Fortune*, September 1943, 220.

22. Foster, *Kaiser*, 68–69.

23. Ibid., 69–70; *Fortune*, July 1941, 122; Lane, *Ships for Victory*, 41–42.

24. Foster, *Kaiser*, 70–71.

25. *Fortune*, July 1941, 111, 120; Lane, *Ships for Victory*, 72–73.

26. *Fortune*, July 1941, 111, 120; Lane, *Ships for Victory*, 72–73; *Time*, September 28, 1942, 22.

27. *Fortune*, July 1941, 111; Lane, *Ships for Victory*, 73; *Time*, September 28, 1942, 21.

28. *Fortune*, July 1941, 114, 116, 119; Lane, *Ships for Victory*, 74–77. Lane provides considerable detail on the comparison and technical differences between the designs.

29. Lane, *Ships for Victory*, 67–68, 80–89; *Newsweek*, September 8, 1941, 47.

30. Lane, *Ships for Victory*, 88–89; Nelson, *Arsenal of Democracy*, 245; Budget Bureau, *United States at War*, 136–39.

31. Lane, *Ships for Victory*, 83–85.

32. *Fortune*, July 1941, 119; Lane, *Ships for Victory*, 572.

33. *Fortune*, July 1941, 119–20.

34. Ibid., 40, 119; Budget Bureau, *United States at War*, 136, 138.

35. Foster, *Kaiser*, 70. Unless otherwise indicated, this section is drawn from ibid., 70–74.

36. Heiner, *Kaiser*, 43–44; Herman, *Freedom's Forge*, 48.

37. Gerald D. Nash, *The American West Transformed: The Impact of the Second World War* (Bloomington, 1985), 69; Heiner, *Kaiser*, 121–22.

38. Heiner, *Kaiser*, 122.

39. Ibid., 122–24.

40. Ibid., 122.

41. *Time*, May 12, 1941, 83–84.

42. *Newsweek*, June 16, 1941, 38.

43. Ibid., September 8, 1941, 48, 50; *Time*, September 15, 1941, 37.

44. *Newsweek*, September 8, 1941, 47, 50; *Fortune*, July 1941, 116; Koistinen, *Arsenal of World War II*, 61.

45. Jerry E. Strahan, *Andrew Jackson Higgins and the Boats That Won World War II* (Baton Rouge, 1994), 1, 10. Unless otherwise indicated, this section is drawn from ibid., 1–93. See also *Saturday Evening Post*, July 11, 1942, 60–61, and *Fortune*, July 1943, 101–2, 212, 214, 216.

46. Strahan, *Higgins*, 76.

47. Ibid., 64.

48. Ibid., 93.

CHAPTER 9. THE SEASON OF DISCONTENT

1. *Fortune*, August 1941, 170.

2. *Saturday Evening Post*, October 4, 1941, 40, 43.

3. *Time*, August 18, 1941, 29.

4. William Klingaman, *1941: Our Lives in a World on the Edge* (New York, 1988), 323.

5. Ickes, *Diary*, May 10, 1941, 511, May 17, 1941, 514, and June 8, 1941, 531; Stimson diary, June 30, 1941.

6. Klingaman, *1941*, 279–84, 328–32.

7. *Saturday Evening Post*, October 4, 1941, 43; *Fortune*, August 1941, 166–67.

8. *Time*, May 19, 1941, 21–23, and July 28, 1941, 28.

9. *Fortune*, July 1941, 68–70, 146–48.

10. *Newsweek*, June 2, 1941, 38, and August 11, 1941, 44.

11. *Look*, September 9, 1941, 26.

12. *Saturday Evening Post*, July 12, 1941, 26; *Fortune*, August 1941, 43.

13. *Fortune*, August 1941, 51–52. *Fortune* devoted its entire 175-page August issue to the American war effort and its effects on the nation. For a summary of its contents, see *Time*, August 18, 1941, 27–30, 32.

14. *Fortune*, August 1941, 53–54.

15. Goodwin, *No Ordinary Time*, 235–36; *Time*, May 19, 1941, 15; Ickes, *Diary*, May 10, 1941, 511; Sherwood, *Roosevelt and Hopkins*, 293.

16. Ickes, *Diary*, April 20, 1941, 479–80, and April 26, 1941, 487.

17. *Time*, May 19, 1941, 15–16; Stimson diary, May 19, 1941.

18. *Time*, May 19, 1941, 16; Ickes, *Diary*, May 10, 1941, 511, and May 25, 1941, 520.

19. Frances Perkins, *The Roosevelt I Knew* (New York, 1946), 359–60.

20. *Time*, March 19, 1941, 14, 16.

21. Stimson diary, October 22, October 24, and November 21, 1941.

22. *Fortune*, August 1941, 52.

23. *Fortune*, April 1941, 36, 40; Koistinen, *Arsenal of World War II*, 86–87.

24. Koistinen, *Arsenal of World War II*, 87–90; CPA, *Industrial Mobilization for War*, 100–1.

25. CPA, *Industrial Mobilization for War*, 102–3, 108.

26. *Fortune*, April 1941, 40.

27. Ibid.; Eiler, *Mobilizing America*, 85–86; *Time*, July 7, 1941, 30.

28. CPA, *Industrial Mobilization for War*, 105–7.

29. *Time*, July 14, 1941, 59, 62–63.

30. *Time*, July 28, 1941, 63–64, and August 4, 1941, 66–67; *Newsweek*, July 7, 1941, 9, July 28, 1941, 35, and August 4, 1941, 34, 36; CPA, *Industrial Mobilization for War*, 107.

31. Nelson, *Arsenal of Democracy*, 141–42, 149.

32. Eiler, *Mobilizing America*, 90; Ickes, *Diary*, June 15, 1941, 541, and June 22, 1941, 544.

33. *Newsweek*, August 4, 1941, 34, August 25, 1941, 7, and September 8, 1941, 42; Koistinen, *Arsenal of World War II*, 98; *Time*, August 18, 1941, 42; Budget Bureau, *United States at War*, 73–74; Ickes, *Diary*, August 27, 1941, 602. For the meeting of Roosevelt and Churchill, see Burns, *Soldier of Freedom*, 125–31, and Goodwin, *No Ordinary Time*, 262–67.

34. Roosevelt, *Public Papers and Addresses*, 10:355–57.

35. Budget Bureau, *United States at War*, 77; Roosevelt, *Public Papers and Addresses*, 10:349–53; *Newsweek*, October 27, 1941, 11; Ickes, *Diary*, September 5, 1941, 607, and September 20, 1941, 620; Nelson, *Arsenal of Democracy*, 159.

36. Stimson diary, August 15, 1941.

37. *Newsweek*, September 8, 1941, 42, 45; Koistinen, *Arsenal of World War II*, 182; Nelson, *Arsenal of Democracy*, 156, 159; *Time*, September 8, 1941, 12, and December 8, 1941, 79; Sherwood, *Roosevelt and Hopkins*, 376–77.

38. *Newsweek*, September 8, 1941, 42, 45, and September 15, 1941, 31–32; *Time*, September 8, 1941, 12, and September 15, 1941, 67; Koistinen, *Arsenal of World War II*, 99, 182–83.

39. Koistinen, *Arsenal of World War II*, 182–83.

40. *Time*, September 8, 1941, 12; *Newsweek*, October 6, 1941, 9; Nelson, *Arsenal of Democracy*, 160–62. Nelson reprints the full text of the statement.

41. Nelson, *Arsenal of Democracy*, 162–63.

42. Ibid., 163–64.

43. Ibid., 164. Emphasis is in the original.

44. Budget Bureau, *United States at War*, 80; Connery, *Navy and Industrial Mobilization*, 179–80.

45. Budget Bureau, *United States at War*, 80–81; *Time*, September 22, 1941, 71.

46. Burns, *Soldier of Freedom*, 112; Connery, *Navy and Industrial Mobilization*, 106–7.

47. Burns, *Soldier of Freedom*, 113–14; Sherwood, *Roosevelt and Hopkins*, 323–29.

48. Ickes, *Diary*, August 3, 1941, 592; John Morton Blum, *From the Morgenthau Diaries: Years of Urgency, 1938–1941* (Boston, 1965), 264; Stimson diary, August 4, 1941. There is a conflict of dates in the sources. Morgenthau puts the cabinet meeting on August 4, Ickes on August 1. Stimson, writing on Monday the fourth, speaks of the meeting in retrospect. Since the cabinet met on Friday, August 1 seems to be the correct date.

49. Blum, *Years of Urgency*, 264; Stimson diary, August 4, 1941.

50. *Newsweek*, September 15, 1941, 31–32; *Time*, September 22, 1941, 71, and October 20, 1941, 92.

51. Nelson, *Arsenal of Democracy*, 167–70.

52. Ibid., 170–73; Koistinen, *Arsenal of World War II*, 185; *Time*, October 20, 1941, 92; Novick et al., *Wartime Production Controls*, 292.

53. Janeway, *Struggle for Survival*, 205; Catton, *War Lords*, 47; Nelson, *Arsenal of Democracy*, 160, 163.

54. Koistinen, *Arsenal of World War II*, 85, 186; Stimson diary, November 12, 1941.

55. Baruch, *Public Years*, 283; Ickes, *Diary*, December 21, 1940, 393.

56. Beasley, *Knudsen*, 288–89.

57. Ibid., 289.

58. Stimson diary, August 4, 1941.

59. Nelson, *Arsenal of Democracy*, 177–78.

60. Koistinen, *Arsenal of World War II*, 101; Eiler, *Mobilizing America*, 82–84.

61. Beasley, *Knudsen*, 324–25.

62. Donald H. Riddle, *The Truman Committee* (New Brunswick, N.J., 1964), 12–15; *Time*, March 8, 1943, 13–15.

63. Riddle, *Truman Committee*, 7–15; *Newsweek*, February 24, 1941, 44.

64. Riddle, *Truman Committee*, 17.

65. Ibid., 22–26.

66. Ibid., 28, 32, 37.

67. Ibid., 58–65.

68. Ibid., 64–66.

69. Nelson, *Arsenal of Democracy*, 120.

70. *Fortune*, August 1941, 170, 172. Emphasis is in the original.

71. Sherwood, *Roosevelt and Hopkins*, 366–67; Pogue, *Ordeal and Hope*, 145–46.

72. Sherwood, *Roosevelt and Hopkins*, 366; Stimson diary, June 21, 1941.

73. Pogue, *Ordeal and Hope*, 147–48; Stimson diary, July 11, 1941.

74. *Time*, October 13, 1941, 38; *Newsweek*, October 20, 1941, 35; Ickes, *Diary*, July 12, 1941, 576–77; Stimson diary, October 9, 1941; Roosevelt, *Public Papers and Addresses*, 10:272–77, 414–16. For a comparison of how World War II draftees compared with those of the Civil War and World War I, see *Harper's*, October 1941, 546–52.

75. Pogue, *Ordeal and Hope*, 149–51; Cole, *America First*, 100–103; *Time*, July 28, 1941, 32.

76. *Newsweek*, August 18, 1941, 15–16; *Time*, August 18, 1941, 12; Pogue, *Ordeal and Hope*, 153–54; Stimson diary, August 13, 1941.

77. *Newsweek*, August 25, 1941, 31; Sherwood, *Roosevelt and Hopkins*, 367.

CHAPTER 10. MATERIAL GAINS AND LOSSES

1. Nelson, *Arsenal of Democracy*, 37.

2. *Saturday Evening Post*, October 4, 1941, 14.

3. *Fortune*, August 1941, 54.

4. Ibid., 42, 52; *Newsweek*, September 8, 1941, 41; *Look*, September 9, 1941, 26; *Saturday Evening Post*, October 4, 1941, 43.

5. *Time*, May 26, 1941, 83. The survey is found in *Fortune*, August 1941, 66–69, 124.

6. *Newsweek*, February 24, 1941, 49.

7. *Newsweek*, March 3, 1941, 30, 32, 34, and March 10, 1941, 40.

8. *Newsweek*, March 31, 1941, 12, May 12, 1941, 47, July 7, 1941, 41, and September 8, 1941, 53; *Time*, May 19, 1941, 92.

9. *Time*, September 29, 1941, 39–40, 42, and October 13, 1941, 49, 74.

10. *Newsweek*, November 10, 1941, 56, 58; *Saturday Evening Post*, November 15, 1941, 38.

11. This section is drawn from *Saturday Evening Post*, November 15, 1941, 38, 87, 89, 91–92, 94.

12. Harold Ickes, *Fightin' Oil* (New York, 1943), 6; John W. Frey and H. Chandler Ide, eds., *A History of the Petroleum Administration for War* (Washington, 1946), 10, hereafter cited as *PAW*.

13. Chandler and Ide, *PAW*, 9–11.

14. *Time*, May 13, 1940, 89–90.

15. Chandler and Ide, *PAW*, 83–84; *Time*, May 26, 1941, 83–84.

16. Chandler and Ide, *PAW*, 11–12, 56.

17. Nelson, *Arsenal of Democracy*, 98; Roosevelt, *Public Papers and Addresses*, 10:196; Ickes, *Fightin' Oil*, vii.

18. Roosevelt, *Public Papers and Addresses*, 10:196; Ickes, *Diary*, May 30, 1941, 529–30.

19. Chandler and Ide, *PAW*, 12; *Newsweek*, June 9, 1941, 40, and June 23, 1941, 68.

20. Ickes, *Diary*, July 19, 1940, 236, and June 8, 1941, 532; *Newsweek*, June 9, 1941, 40.

21. *Saturday Evening Post*, January 4, 1941, 27, 47–50.

22. *Newsweek*, September 2, 1940, 36, March 10, 1941, 12, and July 7, 1941, 36; *Time*, July 28, 1941, 66.

23. Ickes, *Diary*, May 30, 1941, 528; *Time*, July 28, 1941, 66, 68; T. H. Watkins, *Righteous Pilgrim: The Life and Times of Harold L. Ickes* (New York, 1990), 707.

24. Ickes, *Diary*, June 6, 1941, 537, 539.

25. Ibid., June 22, 1941, 543–44; Watkins, *Righteous Pilgrim*, 707–8.

26. Ickes, *Diary*, June 22, 1941, 546, and June 28, 1941, 553–57. The latter pages contain copies of both letters.

27. Ibid., June 22, 1941, 548, June 28, 1941, 553, 557–60, and July 5, 1941, 560–66. Here too the letters are reproduced.

28. Ibid., June 22, 1941, 547–48, July 5, 1941, 567–68, and August 3, 1941, 591–92; Roosevelt, *Personal Letters*, 1173–74.

29. Ickes, *Diary*, March 15, 1941, 461; *Newsweek*, June 23, 1941, 68, and July 7, 1941, 36.

30. Stimson diary, September 15, 1941.

31. *Time*, July 28, 1941, 66, 68; Ickes, *Diary*, September 20, 1941, 612.

32. *Newsweek*, August 4, 1941, 37, and August 11, 1941, 43; *Time*, August 25, 1941, 15; Ickes, *Diary*, July 5, 1941, 562, July 12, 1941, 572–73, August 9, 1941, 596–97, and August 27, 1941, 599–600.

33. Watkins, *Righteous Pilgrim*, 717–18; Ickes, *Diary*, October 12, 1941, 622–24, and October 25, 1941, 632–33.

34. Ickes, *Diary*, October 18, 1941, 630–31, and October 25, 1941, 633–34.

35. Watkins, *Righteous Pilgrim*, 716; Ickes, *Diary*, August 29, 1941, 607.

36. Ickes, *Diary*, September 19, 1941, 608–9, and September 20, 1941, 609–12.

37. Ibid., October 18, 1941, 629.

38. *Newsweek*, March 17, 1941, 40, 43; *Time*, March 31, 1941, 9–10. The Boulder and Shasta dams were somewhat higher than Grand Coulee but not nearly as long.

39. *Newsweek*, March 17, 1941, 40, 43; *Time*, March 31, 1941, 9–10; Foster, *Kaiser*, 62–64.

40. *Time*, June 2, 1941, 75–76; *Newsweek*, June 9, 1941, 40.

41. *Time*, June 16, 1941, 73; *Fortune*, August 1941, 62.

42. *Fortune*, August 1941, 62; David Woodbury, *Battlefronts of Industry: Westinghouse in World War II* (New York, 1948), 161–62.

43. Ickes, *Diary*, July 20, 1941, 579–80; *Time*, July 28, 1941, 70.

44. Ickes, *Diary*, July 20, 1941, 580, and July 27, 1941, 586–87; *Time*, November 17, 1941, 15.

45. Ickes, *Diary*, August 27, 1941, 602, August 28, 1941, 605, and November 9, 1941, 639–40; *Newsweek*, November 17, 1941, 50; *Time*, November 17, 1941, 15; Roosevelt, *Public Papers and Addresses*, 10:470–74.

46. Ickes, *Diary*, November 30, 1941, 652–53.

47. *Time*, September 8, 1941, 50, and November 24, 1941, 98–99; *Newsweek*, April 7, 1941, 67.

48. Walton, *Miracle of World War II*, 45–46; Jesse Jones with Edward Angly, *Fifty Billion Dollars: My Thirteen Years with the RFC* (New York, 1951), 396–98. To avoid a bidding war, Jones got the rubber companies to agree to let the RFC buy all the rubber and sell it to them at cost plus transportation.

49. Herbert and Bisio, *Synthetic Rubber*, 17; Vatter, *U.S. Economy in World War II*, 28; Jones, *Fifty Billion Dollars*, 399; Janeway, *Struggle for Survival*, 65–67. For a brief history of the control of rubber prices, see Howard, *Buna Rubber*, 4–9.

50. Marquis Childs, *I Write from Washington* (New York, 1942), 268.

51. *Fortune*, August 1941, 112, 118.

52. Ibid., 118; Charles S. Popple, *Standard Oil Company (New Jersey) in World War II* (New York, 1952), 50–54.

53. Howard, *Buna Rubber*, 116–23; Popple, *Standard Oil*, 57–58.

54. Jones, *Fifty Billion Dollars*, 403–5; Popple, *Standard Oil*, 61.

55. *Fortune*, August 1941, 71.

56. *Harper's*, September 1940, 368.

57. *Time*, April 15, 1940, 87, June 17, 1940, 51, 69–70, and July 29, 1940, 34; *Newsweek*, August 12, 1940, 36; *Life*, October 21, 1940, 5.

58. *Time*, April 15, 1940, 88; Howard, *Buna Rubber*, 92–101; Popple, *Standard Oil*, 56.

59. *Newsweek*, April 29, 1940, 61, and August 12, 1940, 36–37; *Time*, July 29, 1940, 34; Howard, *Buna Rubber*, 124–31.

60. Howard, *Buna Rubber*, 131–35.

61. Ibid., 136–43; Herbert and Bisio, *Synthetic Rubber*, 48.

62. Howard, *Buna Rubber*, 136–45; Popple, *Standard Oil*, 56–58.

63. Howard, *Buna Rubber*, 146–49.

64. Ibid., 148–58; Herbert and Bisio, *Synthetic Rubber*, 52–57; Popple, *Standard Oil*, 58–59; *Time*, September 22, 1941, 77.

CHAPTER 11. THE BUSINESS OF WAR

1. *Saturday Evening Post*, January 13, 1940, 12.

2. *Time*, January 6, 1941, 15.

3. *Saturday Evening Post*, January 18, 1941, 13, 76.

4. This section is drawn from *Fortune*, September 1941, 87–88, 90–92, 158–62.

5. For more detail, see Maury Klein, "The Boys Who Stayed Behind," in James I. Robertson Jr. and Richard M. McMurry, *Rank and File: Civil War Essays in Honor of Bell Irvin Wiley* (San Rafael, Calif., 1976), 137–56. The Drew quotation is on p. 149.

6. *Saturday Evening Post*, January, 13, 1940, 12. For the conclusions of Senator Gerald P. Nye's committee, see *Report of the Special Committee on Investigation of the Munitions Industry*, 74th Cong., 2nd Sess., February 24, 1936, 3–13.

7. Ibid.; *Time*, September 16, 1940, 79.

8. *Time*, September 16, 1941, 79.

9. Roosevelt, *Personal Letters*, 1181; Roy G. Blakey and Gladys C. Blakey, "The Revenue Act of 1941," *American Economic Review* 31, no. 4 (December 1941): 809–22; *Newsweek*, October 6, 1941, 45. The Blakeys provide full details on the act's provisions, *Newsweek* an illustrated explanation of how the act would affect individual taxpayers.

10. *Newsweek*, October 6, 1941, 38.

11. *Fortune*, December 1941, 207.

12. *Fortune*, January 29, 1940, 59; *Newsweek*, March 18, 1940, 64, and March 25, 1940, 54.

13. *Time*, June 24, 1940, 78, December 9, 1940, 76, and March 17, 1941, 78; *Newsweek*, March 25, 1940, 54.

14. *Newsweek*, March 25, 1940, 54, and September 9, 1940, 42; *Time*, June 3, 1940, 69, July 29, 1940, 52, and December 9, 1940, 78.

15. *Newsweek*, July 14, 1941, 40.

16. *Newsweek*, October 20, 1941, 46.

17. *Harper's*, November 1941, 567–69.

18. *Newsweek*, June 24, 1940, 54, and September 16, 1940, 42; *Harper's*, September 1940, 360.

19. *Newsweek*, October 21, 1940, 34, and September 8, 1941, 40; *Time*, March 17, 1941, 77–78.

20. *Time*, November 10, 1941, 86; *Newsweek*, November 10, 1941, 55.

21. *Harper's*, November 1941, 561–63.

22. *Fortune*, November 1941, 200–202, 204; *Look*, November 1941, 22; *Time*, March 30, 1941, 70.

23. *Time*, June 30, 1941, 70, 72.

24. *Newsweek*, October 13, 1941, 52, and October 27, 1941, 40; *Time*, October 27, 1941, 81–82.

25. Unless otherwise indicated, this section is drawn from *Saturday Evening Post*, March 15, 1941, 12–13, 98, 100, 102.

26. *Time*, February 17, 1941, 75.

27. Ibid., 75–76, 78.

28. Ibid., 76, 79–80.

29. *Newsweek*, June 30, 1941, 7, and November 18, 1940, 36.

30. *Time*, August 18, 1941, 36–37.

31. Ibid., 37–38; Koistinen, *Arsenal of World War II*, 37–38.

32. *Saturday Evening Post*, January 18, 1941, 12–13.

33. Finney, *Arsenal of Democracy*, 30–31.

34. *Saturday Evening Post*, January 18, 1941, 13; *Time*, May 17, 1941, 21; Eiler, *Mobilizing America*, 121–22.

35. *Saturday Evening Post*, January 18, 1941, 73, and May 31, 1941, 13.

36. *Saturday Evening Post*, May 31, 1941, 12–13, 99–102; *Time*, August 4, 1941, 32.

37. *Saturday Evening Post*, May 31, 1941, 100.

38. Ibid., 101.

39. Ibid., 101–2.

40. *Time*, August 4, 1941, 32, November 10, 1941, 36, and December 8, 1941, 68.

41. *Time*, August, 4, 1941, 32, October 27, 1941, 38, November 10, 1941, 36, and December 8, 1941, 68; Nelson, *Arsenal of Democracy*, 52.

42. *Time*, June 16, 1941, 19–20, and October 27, 1941, 38; Eiler, *Mobilizing America*, 123.

43. *Time*, November 10, 1941, 36; Woodbury, *Battlefronts of Industry*, 62–63.

44. Discussion of the stabilizer is drawn from Woodbury, *Battlefronts of Industry*, 63–71, which also includes a photograph of Hanna and his device.

45. Ibid., 76.

46. *Fortune*, November 1941, 66.

47. *Saturday Evening Post*, January 18, 1941, 13, 72.

48. *Newsweek*, October 13, 1941, 52.

49. *Fortune*, November 1941, 69, 184.

50. Roosevelt, *Personal Letters*, 997; Nash, *American West Transformed*, 32–33; Janeway, *Struggle for Survival*, 197.

51. Nelson, *Arsenal of Democracy*, 176; Koistinen, *Arsenal of World War II*, 170; *Newsweek*, January 12, 1942, 8; *Saturday Evening Post*, May 2, 1942, 18.

52. *Look*, December 2, 1941, 17; *Time*, November 17, 1941, 77; Eiler, *Mobilizing America*, 207; Catton, *War Lords*, 36–37. Odlum's wife, Jacqueline Cochran, had the distinction of being the first woman to fly a bomber across the Atlantic. See *Newsweek*, June 30, 1941, 37.

53. *Saturday Evening Post*, October 25, 1941, 106; *Look*, November 4, 1941, 23; *Fortune*, August 1941, 168.

54. *Harper's*, February 1942, 271.

55. Finney, *Arsenal of Democracy*, 76.

56. Unless otherwise indicated, this account of Laucks is drawn from *Saturday Evening Post*, October 25, 1941, 106, 108.

57. *Fortune*, April 1942, 91, 153.

58. Ibid., 89–90.

59. Ibid., 153.

60. *Newsweek*, October 12, 1942, 69.

CHAPTER 12. THE RUSH OF EVENTS

1. *Saturday Evening Post*, May 10, 1941, 28.

2. *Time*, July 28, 1941, 28.

3. *Fortune*, August 1941, 43.

4. *Saturday Evening Post*, May 17, 1941, 10, and June 7, 1941, 28.

5. *Harper's*, August 1941, 292–93.

6. Harry C. Thomson and Lida Mayo, *The Ordnance Department: Procurement and Supply* (Washington, 1960), 45–46. Emphasis is in original.

7. Jim Lacey, *Keep from All Thoughtful Men: How U.S. Economists Won World War II* (Annapolis, 2011), 26.

8. *Newsweek*, September 8, 1941, 41.

9. *Newsweek*, September 22, 1941, 36.

10. Connery, *Navy and Industrial Mobilization*, 167–69.

11. *Saturday Evening Post*, October 4, 1941, 36.

12. *Time*, August 18, 1941, 30, 32.

13. This section is drawn from *Harper's*, April 1942, 481–86.

14. *Newsweek*, June 23, 1941, 13–16; Roosevelt, *Public Papers and Addresses*, 10:227–30.

15. *Fortune*, April 1941, 102–4, 135–36, August 1941, 75–78, and October 1941, 105–8. The *Fortune* polls were conducted by Elmo Roper.

16. *Time*, July 28, 1941, 11, and August 11, 1941, 52.

17. *Look*, June 3, 1941, 4.

18. *Time*, May 12, 1941, 38, 40, and July 28, 1941, 20; *Newsweek*, May 5, 1941, 21, June 2, 1941, 13–15, and June 30, 1941, 11–13.

19. Roosevelt, *Personal Letters*, 1174; Ickes, *Diary*, July 5, 1941, 567, July 20, 1941, 583, and August 3, 1941, 591; *Newsweek*, August 4, 1941, 11–13, 18–19, and August 11, 1941, 15–17; *Time*, August 4, 1941, 11, 61–62.

20. *Time*, September 22, 1941, 24; Ickes, *Diary*, September 20, 1941, 617.

21. Nelson, *Arsenal of Democracy*, 127–30; CPA, *Industrial Mobilization for War*, 133; Lacey, *Keep from All Thoughtful Men*, 27–29.

22. Nelson, *Arsenal of Democracy*, 130–32; Lacey, *Keep from All Thoughtful Men*, 29–31. For example, to Americans a "car" was an automobile, while to the British it was an armored vehicle. The difference equated to more than 3 tons of steel.

23. Nelson, *Arsenal of Democracy*, 132–34.

24. Ibid., 134–35.

25. Ibid., 135–37.

26. Ibid., 137; CPA, *Industrial Mobilization for War*, 133.

27. Catton, *War Lords*, 49; Nelson, *Arsenal of Democracy*, 204.

28. Quoted in Lacey, *Keep from All Thoughtful Men*, 84.

29. Catton, *War Lords*, 49–50.

30. Lacey, *Keep from All Thoughtful Men*, 86–92.

31. John E. Brigante, *The Feasibility Dispute: Determination of War Production Objectives for 1942 and 1943* (Washington, 1950), 23–28; CPA, *Industrial Mobilization for War*, 140.

32. Catton, *War Lords*, 50.

33. *Kiplinger Letter*, 66; Roosevelt, *Personal Letters*, 1156.

34. *Life*, August 18, 1941, 17.

35. Goodwin, *No Ordinary Time*, 268; *Newsweek*, September 8, 1941, 76; *Look*, September 23, 1941, 14.

36. *Harper's*, November 1941, 669; *Look*, November 18, 1941, 33.

37. *Time*, May 19, 1941, 22; *Newsweek*, May 26, 1941, 80, and August 4, 1941, 30; *Saturday Evening Post*, July 12, 1941, 26.

38. *Newsweek*, August 11, 1941, 35.

39. Ibid.

40. *Newsweek*, August 18, 1941, 38, 40, and September 22, 1941, 36; Ickes, *Diary*, November 6, 1941, 635.

41. Goodwin, *No Ordinary Time*, 272–74.

42. *Time*, September 15, 1941, 11–12, and September 22, 1941, 11; Roosevelt, *Public Papers and Addresses*, 10:384–92.

43. *Time*, July 14, 1941, 11, and August 4, 1941, 11; *Newsweek*, September 1, 1941, 9; Roosevelt, *Public Papers and Addresses*, 10:328–29.

44. Roosevelt, *Public Papers and Addresses*, 10:335, 369, 406–13; *Time*, September 8, 1941, 9; *Newsweek*, September 1, 1941, 11, and October 6, 1941, 13–14.

45. *Newsweek*, September 8, 1941, 9, 16–17, and October 27, 1941, 26–28; *Time*, September 8, 1941, 10, September 22, 1941, 24, 27–28, October 17, 1941, 30–31, and November 3, 1941, 23–25.

46. Ickes, *Diary*, October 18, 1941, 629–30; Roosevelt, *Public Papers and Addresses*, 10:445–46; *Newsweek*, November 3, 1941, 13.

47. Ickes, *Diary*, May 25, 1941, 523; Roosevelt, *Public Papers and Addresses*, 10:438; *Newsweek*, November 3, 1941, 13, and November 10, 1941, 19–21.

48. *Newsweek*, November 10, 1941, 21, and November 17, 1941, 17; *Time*, November 17, 1941, 27.

49. *Time*, November 24, 1941, 26, 30; *Newsweek*, November 24, 1941, 17–19; Stimson diary, November 13, 1941.

50. *Time*, October 27, 1941, 81–82, 84–86, 88.

51. *Time*, November 10, 1941, 17, and December 1, 1941, 13–14; *Newsweek*, November 24, 1941, 24; *Kiplinger Letter*, November 8, 1941, 67. Emphasis is in the original.

52. Stimson diary, November 25, 1941; Goodwin, *No Ordinary Time*, 286.

53. Stimson diary, November 27 and November 28, 1941.

54. *New York Times*, November 30, 1941; A. Merriman Smith, *Thank You, Mr. President: A White House Notebook* (New York, 1946), 107–8.

55. Smith, *Thank You, Mr. President*, 108–11; *Newsweek*, November 24, 1941, 24–26, and December 8, 1941, 14, 17–19; *Time*, December 1, 1941, 21, and December 8, 1941, 15–16, 27–28; Stimson diary, December 1, 1941.

56. Stimson diary, December 1, 1941.

57. Ickes, *Diary*, November 30, 1941, 656–57; Stimson diary, December 6, 1941; Roosevelt, *Public Papers and Addresses*, 10:511–13; Larrabee, *Commander in Chief*, 95.

58. David Brinkley, *Washington Goes to War* (New York, 1988), 84; Smith, *Thank You, Mr. President*, 117–18.

59. Stimson diary, December 7, 1941; Sherwood, *Roosevelt and Hopkins*, 430–31.

60. *Newsweek*, December 15, 1941, 18; Smith, *Thank You, Mr. President*, 111–16; Ickes, *Diary*, December 14, 1941, 661.

61. Galbraith, *A Life in Our Times*, 146.

62. Ibid., 146–47.

63. Ickes, *Diary*, December 14, 1941, 661–62; Stimson diary, December 7, 1941; Goodwin, *No Ordinary Time*, 289–90.

64. Goodwin, *No Ordinary Time*, 292.

65. Ickes, *Diary*, December 14, 1941, 662–64; Stimson diary, December 7, 1941.

66. Ickes, *Diary*, December 14, 1941, 662; Stimson diary, December 7, 1941; *Newsweek*, December 15, 1941, 18; Goodwin, *No Ordinary Time*, 292–93.

67. Stimson diary, December 7, 1941; Goodwin, *No Ordinary Time*, 294.

68. *Time*, December 15, 1941, 18–19; Roosevelt, *Public Papers and Addresses*, 10:514–16, 532–33.

69. Sherwood, *Roosevelt and Hopkins*, 430; Roosevelt, *Public Papers and Addresses*, 10:516–31; Cole, *America First*, 189–99; Stimson diary, December 8 and December 9, 1941.

70. Stimson diary, December 9, 1941; Eiler, *Mobilizing America*, 230.

CHAPTER 13. FIRST REACTIONS

1. Richard Lingeman, *Don't You Know There's a War On?* (New York, 2003 [1970]), 2–3.

2. Nelson, *Arsenal of Democracy*, 371–72.

3. Ibid., 93.

4. Roosevelt, *Public Papers and Addresses*, 10:522–30.

5. Unless otherwise indicated, this section is drawn from Lingeman, *Don't You Know*, 25–33.

6. Ibid., 169.

7. Ibid., 26–30; Goodwin, *No Ordinary Time*, 298; Childs, *I Write from Washington*, 243; Kenneth S. Davis, *FDR: The War President, 1940–1943* (New York, 2000), 353; Roosevelt, *This I Remember*, 249.

8. Goodwin, *No Ordinary Time*, 299; Davis, *FDR: The War President*, 353.

9. Roosevelt, *Public Papers and Addresses*, 10:533–36, 539–54, 563–80.

10. Ibid., 11:3–4; Sherwood, *Roosevelt and Hopkins*, 439–73; Burns, *Soldier of Freedom*, 179–90; Pogue, *Ordeal and Hope*, 261–88; Davis, *FDR: The War President*, 361–74, 379–93.

11. Sherwood, *Roosevelt and Hopkins*, 473–74; Davis, *FDR: The War President*, 393–94.

12. Nelson, *Arsenal of Democracy*, 185–86.

13. Sherwood, *Roosevelt and Hopkins*, 473–74; Roosevelt, *Public Papers and Addresses*, 11:37; CPA, *Industrial Mobilization for War*, 277–81.

14. Roosevelt, *Public Papers and Addresses*, 11:23–24.

15. Beasley, *Knudsen*, 334–37.

16. Ibid., 338–42; Jones, *Fifty Billion Dollars*, 272.

17. Stimson diary, January 6, 1942.

18. Sherwood, *Roosevelt and Hopkins*, 474–75.

19. Ibid., 476.

20. Ibid., 475; Nelson, *Arsenal of Democracy*, 13.

21. The account of this meeting is drawn from Nelson, *Arsenal of Democracy*, 13–21. It differs in two important details from Hopkins's version in Sherwood, *Roosevelt and Hopkins*, 475. Hopkins says he was present at the meeting; Nelson makes no mention of him. Hopkins says he briefed Nelson on what was coming a few hours before the meeting; Nelson portrays the whole business as a complete surprise to him. Other evidence suggests that Hopkins was present.

22. Nelson, *Arsenal of Democracy*, 196–97; Lacey, *Keep from All Thoughtful Men*, 71.

23. Janeway, *Struggle for Survival*, 223; Jones, *Fifty Billion Dollars*, 272–73. Beasley, *Knudsen*, 342, has Jones merely telephoning Knudsen.

24. Jones, *Fifty Billion Dollars*, 272–73; Beasley, *Knudsen*, 342–43; Stimson diary, January 15, 1942.

25. *Time*, August 10, 1942, 21–22.

26. Roosevelt, *Public Papers and Addresses*, 11:54–56; *Baltimore Sun*, January 15, 1942; *Newsweek*, January 26, 1942, 40; CPA, *Industrial Mobilization for War*, 208.

27. *Newsweek*, January 26, 1942, 40, 42.

28. *Newsweek*, January 19, 1942, 42–43; Roosevelt, *Public Papers and Addresses*, 11:42–46.

29. Roosevelt, *Public Papers and Addresses*, 11:67–73, 75; Budget Bureau, *United States at War*, 239–48.

30. Roosevelt, *Public Papers and Addresses*, 11:67; Budget Bureau, *United States at War*, 239–41.

31. Budget Bureau, *United States at War*, 241; *Newsweek*, January 19, 1942, 48; Roosevelt, *Public Papers and Addresses*, 11:68.

32. Roosevelt, *Public Papers and Addresses*, 11:62–67, 83–89; Budget Bureau, *United States at War*, 150–52; *Newsweek*, February 23, 1942, 42.

33. This scene is drawn from Nelson, *Arsenal of Democracy*, 187–89.

34. Burns, *Soldier of Freedom*, 203–10; Davis, *FDR: The War President*, 403.

35. Davis, *FDR: The War President*, 404–5.

36. Ibid., 405–6.

37. Sherwood, *Roosevelt and Hopkins*, 498.

38. Ibid.

39. Burns, *Soldier of Freedom*, 209–11.

40. Ibid., 213; Goodwin, *No Ordinary Time*, 319.

41. This summary is drawn from Roosevelt, *Public Papers and Addresses*, 11:105–17.

42. Ibid.; Goodwin, *No Ordinary Time*, 320.

43. Rosenman, *Working with Roosevelt*, 11.

44. Burns, *Soldier of Freedom*, 213.

45. Nelson, *Arsenal of Democracy*, 195–96; *Newsweek*, February 2, 1942, 42; Goodwin, *No Ordinary Time*, 314.

46. *Newsweek*, February 16, 1942, 44; Josephson, *Hillman*, 572–73.

47. Nelson, *Arsenal of Democracy*, 203–4; Koistinen, *Arsenal of World War II*, 195–96; *Newsweek*, February 2, 1942, 42. In the organizational hierarchy a division contained several branches, which were composed of sections, and the sections of units. See Frank L. Walton, *Thread of Victory* (New York, 1945), 11.

48. Nelson, *Arsenal of Democracy*, 204–5; Koistinen, *Arsenal of World War II*, 198–99, 304; Brigante, *Feasibility Dispute*, 10.

49. Nelson, *Arsenal of Democracy*, 205; CPA, *Industrial Mobilization for War*, 209; *Newsweek*, March 2, 1942, 38.

50. Nelson, *Arsenal of Democracy*, 208. Emphasis is in the original.

51. Ibid., xvii.

52. Baruch, *Public Years*, 294–95.

53. Nelson, *Arsenal of Democracy*, 198; Novick et al., *Wartime Production Controls*, 386.

54. Nelson, *Arsenal of Democracy*, 199–201; CPA, *Industrial Mobilization for War*, 212.

55. Nelson, *Arsenal of Democracy*, 200.

56. Nelson, *Arsenal of Democracy*, 198; Catton, *War Lords*, 115; Herman Miles Somers, *Presidential Agency: OWMR* (New York, 1969 [1950]), 111. What Nelson did was place one of his own men in the office of both Patterson and Forrestal and delegate the contract-clearance authority to them. See Connery, *Navy and Industrial Mobilization*, 140–41.

57. Janeway, *Struggle for Survival*, 151–52; Novick et al., *Wartime Production Controls*, 384, 389.

58. Koistinen, *Arsenal of World War II*, 218–19.

59. Pogue, *Ordeal and Hope*, 289–94.

60. Ibid., 294–97; Roosevelt, *Public Papers and Addresses*, 11:140–42; Smith, *Army and Economic Mobilization*, 112. Although the Army Services of Supply was not renamed Army Service Forces until March 1943, the latter term will be used throughout to minimize confusion. The Army Air Corps had become the Army Air Forces in June 1941.

61. John Kennedy Ohl, *Supplying the Troops: General Somervell and American Logistics in WWII* (DeKalb, Ill,, 1994), 9–11.

62. Ibid., 12–54; *Saturday Evening Post*, July 11, 1942, 56.

63. Koistinen, *Arsenal of World War II*, 223–26; Lacey, *Keep from All Thoughtful Men*, 83–84; *Newsweek*, December 7, 1945, 48.

64. Smith, *Army and Economic Mobilization*, 145–54.

65. Koistinen, *Arsenal of World War II*, 227–33.

66. Ibid., 236–43.

67. CPA, *Industrial Mobilization for War*, 213–14; Nelson, *Arsenal of Democracy*, 272–76. Nelson reprints the agreement.

68. Novick et al., *Wartime Production Controls*, 384–85.

69. CPA, *Industrial Mobilization for War*, 216–17; Connery, *Navy and Industrial Mobilization*, 143–44.

70. CPA, *Industrial Mobilization for War*, 218–19.

71. Ibid., 210–11; Budget Bureau, *United States at War*, 121.

CHAPTER 14. A SEA OF TROUBLES

1. *Fortune*, May 1942, 65.

2. Goodwin, *No Ordinary Time*, 368.

3. *Fortune*, May 1942, 68.

4. This section is drawn from *Saturday Evening Post*, July 4, 1942, 20–21, 79–81.

5. Middlebrook, *Convoy*, 15–18.

6. Nelson, *Arsenal of Democracy*, 246; *Newsweek*, February 23, 1942, 42.

7. Budget Bureau, *United States at War*, 142–43.

8. *Saturday Evening Post*, August 21, 1943, 15, 101.

9. Ibid.

10. *Newsweek*, March 23, 1942, 10; *Fortune*, May 1942, 65, 68, 70, 170.

11. Strahan, *Higgins*, 99–100; Lane, *Ships for Victory*, 185–86.

12. Lane, *Ships for Victory*, 187–90; *Newsweek*, March 30, 1942, 49–50.

13. *Newsweek*, May 4, 1942, 68.

14. This section is drawn from *Harper's*, March 1943, 337–46.

15. *Newsweek*, May 13, 1942, 17, and June 1, 1942, 54; *Fortune*, May 1942, 65–67; *Saturday Evening Post*, July 11, 1942, 9; *Time*, July 6, 1942, 15.

16. *Fortune*, May 1942, 68, 166. Deadweight tonnage refers to the actual storage capacity of vessels, gross tonnage to their overall weight.

17. Ibid., 69–70, 162.

18. Ibid., 165; Foster, *Kaiser*, 70–71, 74–75; Lane, *Ships for Victory*, 218–20.

19. *Fortune*, May 1942, 167, 169–70; *Harper's*, August 1942, 327; Walton, *Miracle of World War II*, 74.

20. Walton, *Miracle of World War II*, 80–81.

21. *Harper's*, August 1942, 322–23; Lane, *Ships for Victory*, 217–19.

22. *Harper's*, August 1942, 328; Foster, *Kaiser*, 83–84.

23. *Harper's*, August 1942, 326–27; Walton, *Miracle of World War II*, 75, 80; Foster, *Kaiser*, 84.

24. *Time*, October 5, 1942, 61, 63.

25. Heiner, *Kaiser*, 128.

26. Ibid., 61; *Newsweek*, November 23, 1942, 60; Foster, *Kaiser*, 84–85.

27. *Time*, September 7, 1942, 89; Clapper, *Watching the World*, 293–94.

28. Lane, *Ships for Victory*, 90–100. Lane includes details of the dispute over fees.

29. *Time*, September 28, 1942, 20.

30. Ibid., 20–21.

31. Ibid., 21–22.

32. Alistair Cooke, *The American Home Front, 1941–1942* (New York, 2006), 161.

33. Ibid., 161–62.

34. Ibid., 160–62.

35. This section is drawn from *Time*, November 16, 1942, 90, 92.

36. For the role of GE and Westinghouse in the development of electricity, see Klein, *Power Makers*.

37. John Anderson Miller, *Men and Volts at War: The Story of General Electric in World War II* (New York, 1947), 12–14.

38. Ibid., 6, 14–15.

39. Ibid., 8, 16.

40. Ibid., 8–9, 36–43.

41. Ibid., 36, 48–49.

42. Ibid., 49–51.

43. Ibid., 30–32.

44. Woodbury, *Battlefronts of Industry*, 124–25.

45. The torpedo story is drawn from ibid., 111–17.

46. This section is drawn from ibid., 128–35.

47. This section is drawn from *Time*, September 28, 1942, 19.

CHAPTER 15. THE MANPOWER MUDDLE

1. *Fortune*, April 1942, 73.

2. *Look*, July 14, 1942, 15.

3. *Time*, October 5, 1942, 22.

4. Eiler, *Mobilizing America*, 282–83.

5. *Fortune*, April 1942, 72–73.

6. Ibid., 74; *Harper's*, April 1942, 460.

7. *Fortune*, April 1942, 74.

8. Eiler, *Mobilizing America*, 292–93.

9. *Harper's*, April 1942, 460–61.

10. *Fortune*, April 1942, 74; Eiler, *Mobilizing America*, 283–84; Roosevelt, *Public Papers and Addresses*, 11:204–5.

11. Eiler, *Mobilizing America*, 283; *Harper's*, April 1942, 466; Josephson, *Hillman*, 572–73.

12. Josephson, *Hillman*, 573–75; Budget Bureau, *United States at War*, 182.

13. Budget Bureau, *United States at War*, 182–83; Eiler, *Mobilizing America*, 285.

14. Budget Bureau, *United States at War*, 183.

15. Josephson, *Hillman*, 575–79.

16. Ibid., 579–83.

17. Ibid., 583–86.

18. Roosevelt, *Public Papers and Addresses*, 11:200–204; Budget Bureau, *United States at War*, 183–84; *Newsweek*, April 27, 1942, 44.

19. *Newsweek*, April 27, 1942, 44; Kiplinger, *Washington Is Like That*, 443–44.

20. Budget Bureau, *United States at War*, 177–78; *Newsweek*, May 11, 1942, 53–54.

21. *Newsweek*, May 11, 1942, 54; *Look*, June 16, 1942, 18–19, and July 14, 1942, 15.

22. Budget Bureau, *United States at War*, 178.

23. Ibid., 178–79.

24. Stimson diary, January 7 and January 15, 1942; *Newsweek*, February 16, 1942, 28; Eiler, *Mobilizing America*, 249.

25. *Newsweek*, March 30, 1942, 25–26, and May 4, 1942, 31.

26. Eiler, *Mobilizing America*, 249–50; *Newsweek*, March 30, 1942, 25–26, and May 11, 1942, 33.

27. *Newsweek*, July 13, 1942, 36, and September 21, 1942, 85–86; Eiler, *Mobilizing America*, 250.

28. Ickes, *Diary*, July 12, 1941, 576, and October 12, 1941, 626–27.

29. Eiler, *Mobilizing America*, 254–55.

30. *Newsweek*, June 29, 1942, 36; *Time*, July 20, 1942, 58.

31. *Harper's*, July 1942, 121–25.

32. *Newsweek*, July 6, 1942, 34–35, and July 13, 1942, 36; Eiler, *Mobilizing America*, 293–95.

33. Eiler, *Mobilizing America*, 256–57.

34. Ibid., 293–94.

35. *Time*, July 20, 1942, 58–59; *Newsweek*, July 27, 1942, 34.

36. Roger Daniels, *Concentration Camps USA: Japanese Americans and World War II*

(New York, 1972), 1–7; *Harper's*, October 1942, 493; John Morton Blum, *V Was for Victory: Politics and American Culture During World War II* (New York, 1976), 156.

37. Daniels, *Concentration Camps USA*, 8–26.

38. Ibid., 35.

39. Stimson diary, February 3, 1942.

40. Ibid., February 10, 1942; Blum, *V Was for Victory*, 157–58. Unless otherwise indicated, this account is drawn from Daniels, *Concentration Camps USA*, 44–74, and Peter Irons, *Justice at War* (New York, 1983), 3–103, both of which include a wealth of detail on the decision to evacuate the Japanese Americans.

41. Francis B. Biddle, *In Brief Authority* (Garden City, N.Y., 1962), 184–85, 205, 207; Stimson and Bundy, *On Active Service*, 342–43.

42. Stimson diary, February 11, 1942.

43. Ibid.; Biddle, *In Brief Authority*, 219, 226.

44. Davis, *FDR: The War President*, 419, 424–25; Blum, *V Was for Victory*, 159. The order was general in scope but was utilized only against Japanese Americans.

45. Davis, *FDR: The War President*, 425.

46. Ibid., 426–27; Roosevelt, *Public Papers and Addresses*, 11:174–76. On April 1 Eisenhower wrote Claude Wickard, "I feel most deeply that when the war is over and we consider calmly this unprecedented migration of 120,000 people, we as Americans are going to regret the avoidable injustices that may have been done." Daniels, *Concentration Camps USA*, 91.

47. Daniels, *Concentration Camps USA*, 74–90; Davis, *FDR: The War President*, 427; Vatter, *U.S. Economy in World War II*, 135; Blum, *V Was for Victory*, 160.

48. Daniels, *Concentration Camps USA*, 7–8; Lingeman, *Don't You Know*, 337. The American Civil Liberties Union called it "the worst single wholesale violation of civil rights of American citizens in our history." Biddle, *In Brief Authority*, 213.

49. Stimson diary, July 7, 1942.

50. Goodwin, *No Ordinary Time*, 323.

51. *Newsweek*, March 16, 1942, 15; *Fortune*, June 1942, 77.

52. Ickes, *Diary*, May 17, 1941, 516; *Harper's*, April 1942, 545.

53. Nash, *American West Transformed*, 91; *Harper's*, April 1942, 545, 551.

54. *Fortune*, June 1942, 79.

55. Zieger, *CIO*, 154; Lingeman, *Don't You Know*, 162–63.

56. Zieger, *CIO*, 155–56.

57. *Fortune*, June 1942, 157.

58. Fairchild and Grossman, *Army and Industrial Manpower*, 157–60.

59. Goodwin, *No Ordinary Time*, 370.

60. Ibid.

61. Fairchild and Grossman, *Army and Industrial Manpower*, 169.

62. Ibid., 169–70; Polenberg, *War and Society*, 146.

63. *Newsweek*, January 12, 1942, 23–24.

64. *Newsweek*, March 30, 1942, 33–34, July 27, 1942, 29–30, and August 3, 1942, 27–28.

65. *Newsweek*, March 16, 1942, 44–45; Polenberg, *War and Society*, 147; Fairchild and Grossman, *Army and Industrial Manpower*, 170.

66. *Look*, May 5, 1942, 40–43.

67. Fairchild and Grossman, *Army and Industrial Manpower*, 170; *Saturday Evening Post*, May 30, 1942, 31.

68. *Look*, June 30, 1942, 21–22, 24.

69. Goodwin, *No Ordinary Time*, 367. For Inez Sauer, see www.unctv.org/warbonds/sauer.

70. Ibid., 369; *Newsweek*, June 22, 1942, 48.

CHAPTER 16. INTRAMURAL WARS

1. Koistinen, *Arsenal of World War II*, 191–92.

2. Janeway, *Struggle for Survival*, 226, 228.

3. Budget Bureau, *United States at War*, 393.

4. *Saturday Evening Post*, June 6, 1942, 100.

5. *Newsweek*, February 16, 1942, 44.

6. Budget Bureau, *United States at War*, 382.

7. Catton, *War Lords*, 111–13.

8. Ibid.

9. *Newsweek*, January 19, 1942, 38.

10. Eiler, *Mobilizing America*, 327.

11. Riddle, *Truman Committee*, 41–43, 71–73; Koistinen, *Arsenal of World War II*, 199–200. For the rules and limitations, see Nelson, *Arsenal of Democracy*, 333–34.

12. Nelson, *Arsenal of Democracy*, 331–33, 382; Catton, *War Lords*, 117.

13. CPA, *Industrial Mobilization for War*, 232–33.

14. Catton, *War Lords*, 117–22.

15. This episode is drawn from Walton, *Thread of Victory*, 11–21.

16. Roosevelt, *Personal Letters*, 1230; Rosenman, *Working with Roosevelt*, 454.

17. Ickes, *Diary*, July 27, 1941, 589.

18. Roger Burlingame, *Don't Let Them Scare You: The Life and Times of Elmer Davis* (Philadelphia, 1961), 184.

19. *Newsweek*, June 22, 1942, 30; Roosevelt, *Public Papers and Addresses*, 11:425–29. For the organization of OFF, see Budget Bureau, *United States at War*, 215.

20. *Newsweek*, June 22, 1942, 30; Budget Bureau, *United States at War*, 91–92.

21. Budget Bureau, *United States at War*, 203–8; Roosevelt, *Public Papers and Addresses*, 10:574–79. Roosevelt announced the new agency and Price's appointment on December 16; the executive order creating it came three days later.

22. Budget Bureau, *United States at War*, 209–10; Stimson diary, February 25, 1942; *Newsweek*, April 13, 1942, 32, and April 27, 1942, 55.

23. Blum, *V Was for Victory*, 23–26.

24. Budget Bureau, *United States at War*, 211. Horton reported to Mellett, who reported directly to the president in OEM.

25. Catton, *War Lords*, 53.

26. Ibid., 68–73.

27. Budget Bureau, *United States at War*, 213–17.

28. Roosevelt, *Personal Letters*, 1230.

29. Catton, *War Lords*, 83–88.

30. Ibid.

31. Ibid., 89.

32. *Newsweek*, April 13, 1942, 32; Budget Bureau, *United States at War*, 220–23; Roosevelt,

Public Papers and Addresses, 11:274–81. The latter two sources both give details on the problems that had to be resolved.

33. Roosevelt, *Public Papers and Addresses*, 11:274–77, 283–87; Budget Bureau, *United States at War*, 223–27. The three branches were Domestic, Policy and Development, and Overseas.

34. Burlingame, *Don't Let Them Scare You*, 194–95.

35. Ibid., 186; Stimson diary, June 17, 1942; *Newsweek*, April 13, 1942, 32, April 27, 1942, 55, and June 22, 1942, 30.

36. Blum, *V Was for Victory*, 26–27.

37. Ibid.

38. Ibid., 27–31.

39. *Newsweek*, January 12, 1942, 31–32, and February 9, 1942, 42.

40. *Harper's*, May 1942, 646. For a different version of the Reuther plan episode, see Catton, *War Lords*, 91–99.

41. *Newsweek*, January 19, 1942, 42.

42. *Harper's*, May 1942, 646–47; *Fortune*, March 1942, 63.

43. Nelson, *Arsenal of Democracy*, 319–22.

44. *Harper's*, May 1942, 647–49. For a somewhat different version of this episode, see Janeway, *Struggle for Survival*, 170–75.

45. *Harper's*, May 1942, 649–51; CPA, *Industrial Mobilization for War*, 187–88.

46. Nelson, *Arsenal of Democracy*, 317–18; Catton, *War Lords*, 91.

47. *Harper's*, May 1942, 652–53; Catton, *War Lords*, 105; *Newsweek*, January 19, 1942, 40.

48. Catton, *War Lords*, 106–7; *Time*, January 19, 1942, 10.

49. Catton, *War Lords*, 107–10.

50. Ibid., 103–4.

51. Ibid., 104–5.

52. Ibid., 99; Janeway, *Struggle for Survival*, 176; *Newsweek*, January 26, 1942, 46; *Harper's*, May 1942, 653–54.

53. Catton, *War Lords*, 108; Nelson, *Arsenal of Democracy*, 318.

54. Nelson, *Arsenal of Democracy*, 318–19; *Newsweek*, March 23, 1942, 38; *Fortune*, May 1942, 146.

55. Nelson, *Arsenal of Democracy*, 322–23.

56. Ibid., 324–25.

57. Koistinen, *Arsenal of World War II*, 275–76.

58. Ibid., 276–77.

59. Nelson, *Arsenal of Democracy*, 201–2.

60. Ibid., 283, 338; CPA, *Industrial Mobilization for War*, 313–14.

61. Nelson, *Arsenal of Democracy*, 376; Polenberg, *War and Society*, 11; Koistinen, *Arsenal of World War II*, 278–79; *Fortune*, February 1942, 61, 150, 152–54.

62. *Fortune*, January 1942, 123; *Newsweek*, March 23, 1942, 38.

63. CPA, *Industrial Mobilization for War*, 317–18.

64. Novick et al., *Wartime Production Controls*, 68–75, 344–45; Koistinen, *Arsenal of World War II*, 277; CPA, *Industrial Mobilization for War*, 320. For an explanation of M orders, see chapter 7. Curtailment orders reduced but did not stop entirely the production of an item.

65. *Newsweek*, March 16, 1942, 48.

66. Ibid., 48, 52, and February 16, 1942, 59.

67. *Newsweek*, February 16, 1942, 59, and March 16, 1942, 48, 52.

68. *Newsweek*, June 15, 1942, 42.

69. Ibid., 42, 46.

70. Ibid.; Catton, *War Lords*, 108.

71. This story is drawn from *Time*, November 6, 1943, 21.

CHAPTER 17. THE FEASIBILITY FOLLIES

1. Kennedy, *Freedom from Fear*, 626-27.

2. Budget Bureau, *United States at War*, 301-2.

3. *Fortune*, March 1942, 59.

4. Ibid.

5. Koistinen, *Arsenal of World War II*, 303. Lacey, *Keep from All Thoughtful Men*, 137-45, provides a thoughtful and succinct discussion of the feasibility concept.

6. Budget Bureau, *United States at War*, 299; Eiler, *Mobilizing America*, 336.

7. CPA, *Industrial Mobilization for War*, 275; Koistinen, *Arsenal of World War II*, 305; Budget Bureau, *United States at War*, 299-301.

8. Eiler, *Mobilizing America*, 336-37; *Newsweek*, January 19, 1942, 38.

9. Smith, *Army and Economic Mobilization*, 154.

10. Brigante, *Feasibility Dispute*, 10, 33-34.

11. Lacey, *Keep from All Thoughtful Men*, 40-43.

12. Brigante, *Feasibility Dispute*, 34-43; Koistinen, *Arsenal of World War II*, 303-6. For a digested version of Kuznets's study, see Lacey, *Keep from All Thoughtful Men*, 146-57.

13. Koistinen, *Arsenal of World War II*, 306-7; Eiler, *Mobilizing America*, 348-49; Brigante, *Feasibility Dispute*, 43-56; Lacey, *Keep from All Thoughtful Men*, 96-103.

14. Brigante, *Feasibility Dispute*, 57-60; Eiler, *Mobilizing America*, 349; CPA, *Industrial Mobilization for War*, 294-95.

15. Novick et al., *Wartime Production Controls*, 105-6.

16. Novick et al., *Wartime Production Controls*, 35-75, treats these developments in detail. For the M and P orders, see chapter 7.

17. Ibid., 76-97; Smith, *Army and Economic Mobilization*, 556.

18. Novick et al., *Wartime Production Controls*, 97-104; Smith, *Army and Economic Mobilization*, 556-57.

19. Eiler, *Mobilizing America*, 337; CPA, *Industrial Mobilization for War*, 216-17.

20. CPA, *Industrial Mobilization for War*, 217-19; Koistinen, *Arsenal of World War II*, 314; Connery, *Navy and Industrial Mobilization*, 154-63. Connery asserts that "ANMB wanted more civilian control, not less; it wanted Mr. Nelson to exercise his authority more, rather than less, extensively."

21. CPA, *Industrial Mobilization for War*, 294-96; Koistinen, *Arsenal of World War II*, 314-16; Nelson, *Arsenal of Democracy*, 364.

22. CPA, *Industrial Mobilization for War*, 296-98; Koistinen, *Arsenal of World War II*, 315-16; Connery, *Navy and Industrial Mobilization*, 172; Nelson, *Arsenal of Democracy*, 364.

23. CPA, *Industrial Mobilization for War*, 298-99; Koistinen, *Arsenal of World War II*, 316-17; Smith, *Army and Economic Mobilization*, 557.

24. Smith, *Army and Economic Mobilization*, 557-58; Eiler, *Mobilizing America*, 338-39.

The fullest description of PRP is in Novick et al., *Wartime Production Controls*, 105–37. See also Budget Bureau, *United States at War*, 119–20.

25. Koistinen, *Arsenal of World War II*, 318–19; Smith, *Army and Economic Mobilization*, 558.

26. Novick et al., *Wartime Production Controls*, 105–6, 110; Koistinen, *Arsenal of World War II*, 319; Smith, *Army and Economic Mobilization*, 559–60.

27. Eiler, *Mobilizing America*, 339–42; Novick et al., *Wartime Production Controls*, 136–37.

28. Somers, *Presidential Agency*, 31.

29. Budget Bureau, *United States at War*, 120–22; Vatter, *U.S. Economy in World War II*, 67.

30. CPA, *Industrial Mobilization for War*, 249–50.

31. *Newsweek*, July 20, 1942, 50, 53.

32. CPA, *Industrial Mobilization for War*, 248–51; Koistinen, *Arsenal of World War II*, 204–5; Budget Bureau, *United States at War*, 122–23.

33. Koistinen, *Arsenal of World War II*, 204–5; CPA, *Industrial Mobilization for War*, 251–52; Budget Bureau, *United States at War*, 122–23.

34. CPA, *Industrial Mobilization for War*, 252–53; Koistinen, *Arsenal of World War II*, 205–6.

35. This section is drawn from *Fortune*, March 1942, 59–62, 179–84.

36. CPA, *Industrial Mobilization for War*, 282–84; Koistinen, *Arsenal of World War II*, 307–8.

37. CPA, *Industrial Mobilization for War*, 284–85; Brigante, *Feasibility Dispute*, 61–68; Lacey, *Keep from All Thoughtful Men*, 104–6. Brigante and Lacey include more detail on the contents of the Kuznets report.

38. CPA, *Industrial Mobilization for War*, 285–87; Brigante, *Feasibility Dispute*, 69–73; Koistinen, *Arsenal of World War II*, 308–9.

39. CPA, *Industrial Mobilization for War*, 286–87; Koistinen, *Arsenal of World War II*, 309; Lacey, *Keep from All Thoughtful Men*, 106–7; Eiler, *Mobilizing America*, 352–53.

40. Brigante, *Feasibility Dispute*, 74–83; Koistinen, *Arsenal of World War II*, 310–11; CPA, *Industrial Mobilization for War*, 287, Ohl, *Supplying the Troops*, 77–78; Lacey, *Keep from All Thoughtful Men*, 108–9, 183–85; Eiler, *Mobilizing America*, 352–54. Brigante and Lacey include the text of Somervell's reply.

41. Brigante, *Feasibility Dispute*, 83–86; Lacey, *Keep from All Thoughtful Men*, 108–9, 183–85; Ohl, *Supplying the Troops*, 78–79; Koistinen, *Arsenal of World War II*, 311.

42. Brigante, *Feasibility Dispute*, 87–91; Koistinen, *Arsenal of World War II*, 311; Lacey, *Keep from All Thoughtful Men*, 109–10. Brigante includes the text of Marshall's letter.

43. The fullest source for the meeting and its background is Brigante, *Feasibility Dispute*, 87–96. It is authoritative but has no documentation. The best secondary accounts lean heavily on it. See Smith, *Army and Economic Mobilization*, 155; Ohl, *Supplying the Troops*, 80–81; Koistinen, *Arsenal of World War II*, 311–12; Eiler, *Mobilizing America*, 354–55; Lacey, *Keep from All Thoughtful Men*, 109–12, 173–82. Lacey, 192–201, contains the minutes of the meeting.

44. Brigante, *Feasibility Dispute*, 97–104; Lacey, *Keep from All Thoughtful Men*, 113–14; Ohl, *Supplying the Troops*, 81–82; Eiler, *Mobilizing America*, 355.

45. Brigante, *Feasibility Dispute*, 104–6; Ohl, *Supplying the Troops*, 81–82; Eiler, *Mobilizing America*, 355–56; Koistinen, *Arsenal of World War II*, 312–13.

46. Roosevelt, *Public Papers and Addresses*, 11:331–34; *Newsweek*, August 31, 1942, 28; *Time*, August 23, 1943, 22.

47. CPA, *Industrial Mobilization for War*, 507; Stimson diary, July 19 and July 20, 1942.

48. Stimson diary, July 22 and July 25, 1942.

49. *Newsweek*, August 24, 1942, 54, and August 31, 1942, 68.

50. *Time*, September 7, 1942, 24.

51. *Time*, August 17, 1942, 69–71.

52. CPA, *Industrial Mobilization for War*, 462–72; Smith, *Army and Economic Mobilization*, 558–64; Ohl, *Supplying the Troops*, 84; Eiler, *Mobilizing America*, 356–57; *Newsweek*, September 7, 1942, 62; *Time*, December 28, 1942, 66.

53. Nelson, *Arsenal of Democracy*, 382; Stimson diary, August 27 and September 10, 1942. Some confusion results from the fact that the war effort included no less than three Charles E. Wilsons: Charles Edward Wilson of GE, Charles Erwin Wilson of GM, and Charles Eben Wilson of Worthington Pump & Machinery. See *Time*, September 28, 1942, 17.

54. Stimson diary, September 10, September 11, September 17, and September 18, 1942; Nelson, *Arsenal of Democracy*, 382–83; CPA, *Industrial Mobilization for War*, 507–8.

55. CPA, *Industrial Mobilization for War*, 508–9; Eiler, *Mobilizing America*, 357; *Time*, September 28, 1942, 17–18; *Newsweek*, September 28, 1942, 58–59.

56. Nelson, *Arsenal of Democracy*, 386–7; *Time*, September 28, 1942, 18.

57. *Time*, September 28, 1942, 18, and December 13, 1943, 21.

CHAPTER 18. OLD FRANK COMES TO CALL

1. *Saturday Evening Post*, July 11, 1942, 84.

2. Catton, *War Lords*, 151.

3. Ickes, *Diary*, June 8, 1941, 537–38.

4. Unless otherwise indicated, this section is drawn from Roosevelt, *Public Papers and Addresses*, 11:384–96; Goodwin, *No Ordinary Time*, 360–74; Smith, *Thank You, Mr. President*, 49–56; Davis, *FDR: The War President*, 611–22; *Time*, October 12, 1942, 15–17; and *Newsweek*, October 12, 1942, 42, 45–46. The first source listed contains Roosevelt's complete itinerary for the trip. The three newsmen were Douglas Cornell for Associated Press, Merriman Smith for United Press, and J. William Theis for International News Service.

5. Sorensen, *My Forty Years with Ford*, 292–94.

6. Ibid., 294–97.

7. Strahan, *Higgins*, 143–45.

8. Davis, *FDR: The War President*, 620–21.

9. Perkins, *Roosevelt I Knew*, 375–76.

10. Roosevelt, *Public Papers and Addresses*, 11:392–95.

11. Ibid., 11:379–80; Popple, *Standard Oil*, 3. For the earlier episode on rubber, see chapter 10.

12. Nelson, *Arsenal of Democracy*, 291–95; Catton, *War Lords*, 153.

13. Eiler, *Mobilizing America*, 263; Nelson, *Arsenal of Democracy*, 294, 296; Catton, *War Lords*, 154–55; *Fortune*, June 1942, 95–96.

14. Galbraith, *A Life in Our Times*, 155; *Newsweek*, February 23, 1942, 10, and March 16, 1942, 55, 57; Catton, *War Lords*, 152.

15. Eiler, *Mobilizing America*, 264–65.

16. Ibid., 265; Catton, *War Lords*, 155.

17. *Newsweek*, May 18, 1942, 40; Nelson, *Arsenal of Democracy*, 302–3; Catton, *War Lords*, 155–56.

18. *Newsweek*, May 18, 1942, 40–41, and May 25, 1942, 27–28; Catton, *War Lords*, 156–58; Eiler, *Mobilizing America*, 266–67. Emphasis is in original.

19. Nelson, *Arsenal of Democracy*, 303; Catton, *War Lords*, 157–59.

20. Nelson, *Arsenal of Democracy*, 304; Catton, *War Lords*, 161–62. Nelson wrongly gave August 1 as the date for the meeting.

21. Catton, *War Lords*, 162–63; Roosevelt, *Public Papers and Addresses*, 11:263–68, 270–74. Emphasis is in the original.

22. Catton, *War Lords*, 162–63; *Newsweek*, July 13, 1942, 46; *Time*, July 6, 1942, 65; Eiler, *Mobilizing America*, 268–69; Roosevelt, *Public Papers and Addresses*, 11:273–74. The estimates of the amount collected vary widely; I have used Rosenman's figure.

23. Eiler, *Mobilizing America*, 268–69.

24. Catton, *War Lords*, 164.

25. *Newsweek*, June 8, 1942, 42, 44.

26. *Newsweek*, April 27, 1942, 50, and June 1, 1942, 46, 48; *Time*, July 20, 1943, 18–19; CPA, *Industrial Mobilization for War*, 377–78; Nelson, *Arsenal of Democracy*, 296–97; Popple, *Standard Oil*, 62–63.

27. Koistinen, *Arsenal of World War II*, 155–56; Nelson, *Arsenal of Democracy*, 297; *Newsweek*, August 3, 1942, 44, 46.

28. Eiler, *Mobilizing America*, 269–70; Nelson, *Arsenal of Democracy*, 297; Roosevelt, *Public Papers and Addresses*, 11:312–20; Baruch, *Public Years*, 302–4; Catton, *War Lords*, 172–73; Rosenman, *Working with Roosevelt*, 336.

29. Baruch, *Public Years*, 304–5; Howard, *Buna Rubber*, 212–14.

30. Roosevelt, *Public Papers and Addresses*, 11:321. The text of the report's general findings can be found in Howard, *Buna Rubber*, 215–20.

31. Roosevelt, *Public Papers and Addresses*, 11:379–80; Catton, *War Lords*, 174; *Newsweek*, September 21, 1942, 58, 60, 62; *Fortune*, November 1942, 98–99, 227.

32. Roosevelt, *Public Papers and Addresses*, 11:379–80. For a more detailed background on Jeffers, see Maury Klein, *Union Pacific: The Rebirth, 1897–1969* (New York, 1989).

33. Catton, *War Lords*, 177.

34. Ibid., 169.

35. Lane, *Ships for Victory*, 177; Chester Wardlow, *The Transportation Corps: Responsibilities, Organization, and Operations* (Washington, 1951), 149; O'Neill, *Democracy at War*, 145–46; Frey and Ide, *PAW*, 88.

36. Frey and Ide, *PAW*, 428–29.

37. *Time*, April 22 1940, 86–87, and September 9, 1940, 75; *Newsweek*, July 8, 1940, 54; *Harper's*, February 1941, 308–9.

38. *Harper's*, February 1941, 310–11; *Newsweek*, April 21, 1941, 41–42; *Time*, May 5, 1941, 78, 80; Janeway, *Struggle for Survival*, 79.

39. *Time*, May 5, 1941, 78, 80, and July 21, 1941, 67–68; Nelson, *Arsenal of Democracy*, 146–47. "Bad order" cars are those out of service and in need of repairs or refurbishing.

40. Janeway, *Struggle for Survival*, 141–42.

41. *Time*, September 29, 1941, 73–75, and November 10, 1941, 78, 80; *Newsweek*, October 20, 1942, 56; Budget Bureau, *United States at War*, 160–61. Contrary to the name, transconti-

nental railroads did not reach from coast to coast; no American railroad ever did. Most ran from the Missouri River to the West Coast, although the Atchison, Topeka & Santa Fe reached from Chicago to California.

42. *Fortune*, June 1942, 84–85. A 1 percent grade is a rise of one foot in a hundred.

43. Ibid., November 1942, 121; Roosevelt, *Public Papers and Addresses*, 10:567–73; Budget Bureau, *United States at War*, 158. Another executive order on May 2, 1942, extended the agency's jurisdiction to "all rubber-borne transport."

44. Budget Bureau, *United States at War*, 159–62; *Fortune*, November 1942, 121–22, 181, 186.

45. Association of American Railroads, *An Outline of 1942 Work and the Activities Contemplated by the Various Departments of the Association During the Year 1943* (Washington, November 1942), 20–28, copy in author's possession; *Fortune*, November 1942, 186. A unit train consists entirely of one commodity such as coal, oil, grain, or produce.

46. *Newsweek*, July 13, 1942, 49–50; *Fortune*, November 1942, 186.

47. *Fortune*, November 1942, 124–25.

48. Nash, *American West Transformed*, 10.

49. Unless otherwise indicated, this section is drawn from *Fortune*, June 1942, 82–88, 147–48, 150, 152, 154.

50. Nash, *American West Transformed*, 110.

CHAPTER 19. GENERAL MAX TAKES COMMAND

1. William D. Hassett, *Off the Record with F. D. R.* (New Brunswick, N.J., 1958), 115.

2. Wilcox, *Farmer in the Second World War*, 117.

3. *Fortune*, July 1942, 60.

4. Budget Bureau, *United States at War*, 239–40.

5. *Fortune*, August 1941, 57.

6. Roosevelt, *Public Papers and Addresses*, 10:284–89, 11:67–73, 75–76; Budget Bureau, *United States at War*, 240. See also chapter 13. For an explanation of the 110-percent-of-parity issue, see Wilcox, *Farmer in the Second World War*, 121–23.

7. Wilcox, *Farmer in the Second World War*, 6–9.

8. Ibid., 118–21; Budget Bureau, *United States at War*, 242–47; *Time*, October 5, 1942, 19.

9. Budget Bureau, *United States at War*, 248–50; Wilcox, *Farmer in the Second World War*, 124–25.

10. Budget Bureau, *United States at War*, 250–51; Roosevelt, *Public Papers and Addresses*, 11:224–25; Rosenman, *Working with Roosevelt*, 333–34; Blum, *Years of Urgency*, 34–38.

11. Budget Bureau, *United States at War*, 251–53; Roosevelt, *Public Papers and Addresses*, 11:225; Rosenman, *Working with Roosevelt*, 334–35.

12. Roosevelt, *Public Papers and Addresses*, 11:216–24; Budget Bureau, *United States at War*, 253–54; Wilcox, *Farmer in the Second World War*, 125; Rosenman, *Working with Roosevelt*, 337–44.

13. Roosevelt, *Public Papers and Addresses*, 11:227–38.

14. Rosenman, *Working with Roosevelt*, 340.

15. Budget Bureau, *United States at War*, 254; Galbraith, *A Life in Our Times*, 165; *Newsweek*, April 20, 1942, 44.

16. *Newsweek*, May 4, 1942, 42, 44, and May 11, 1942, 58; *Fortune*, July 1942, 60.

17. *Harper's*, July 1943, 116, 118.

18. *Newsweek*, May 11, 1942, 48, June 1, 1942, 51, and June 22, 1942, 56–57.

19. *Fortune*, July 1942, 60, 116, 118.

20. Ibid., 116, 151; *Newsweek*, May 11, 1942, 48; Budget Bureau, *United States at War*, 256.

21. Budget Bureau, *United States at War*, 255–57; *Time*, July 13, 1942, 16; *Newsweek*, July 13, 1942, 44–45.

22. *Newsweek*, July 13, 1942, 44–45; *Time*, July 20, 1942, 14.

23. *Fortune*, June 1943, 156–60, 187–88, 191–92, 194, 196.

24. *Time*, July 20, 1942, 14; *Newsweek*, October 11, 1943, 59.

25. Budget Bureau, *United States at War*, 249–50, 262–63.

26. Ibid., 196–97.

27. Ibid., 197–98; Joel Seidman, *American Labor from Defense to Reconversion* (Chicago, 1953), 109–13; *Newsweek*, July 27, 1942, 46, 48. "Little Steel" referred to the companies below the giant United States Steel, notably Bethlehem, Republic, Youngstown, and Inland.

28. Seidman, *American Labor*, 115–16; *Newsweek*, July 27, 1942, 46, 48; *Time*, July 13, 1942, 73.

29. *Time*, July 13, 1942, 73–74, 76, and August 3, 1942, 13; *Newsweek*, July 27, 1942, 48.

30. *Newsweek*, August 10, 1942, 42–43. Emphasis is in the original.

31. *Newsweek*, June 15, 1942, 32; *Time*, August 3, 1942, 14; Budget Bureau, *United States at War*, 265; Clapper, *Watching the World*, 200.

32. *Time*, August 3, 1942, 13; *Newsweek*, June 22, 1942, 56, and August 24, 1942, 49–50.

33. Budget Bureau, *United States at War*, 259–61.

34. Ibid., 265–66.

35. Roosevelt, *Public Papers and Addresses*, 11:356–68; *Newsweek*, September 14, 1942, 54.

36. Roosevelt, *Public Papers and Addresses*, 11:368–71.

37. Ibid., 11:371–77.

38. Budget Bureau, *United States at War*, 267–70; *Newsweek*, September 14, 1942, 54–55, September 21, 1942, 70–72, and October 5, 1942, 27–28; *Time*, October 12, 1942, 18. The new act was an amendment of the Price Control Act.

39. Roosevelt, *Public Papers and Addresses*, 11:396–407; *Time*, October 12, 1942, 18, and January 11, 1943, 18–20; *Newsweek*, October 12, 1942, 58, 60, 63–64; Blum, *Years of Urgency*, 43–45.

40. Roosevelt, *Public Papers and Addresses*, 11:407; *Newsweek*, October 12, 1942, 70; Catton, *War Lords*, 203; *Time*, October 12, 1942, 18; *Look*, October 19, 1943, 34, 36, 38.

41. Budget Bureau, *United States at War*, 164–66; Lingeman, *Don't You Know*, 239; *Newsweek*, January 26, 1942, 12, and May 18, 1942, 40–41.

42. Lingeman, *Don't You Know*, 241–43.

43. Ibid., 239; *Newsweek*, May 18, 1942, 40–41, and May 25, 1942, 27–28; *Time*, July 6, 1942, 54; *Saturday Evening Post*, August 8, 1942, 16–17, 47–48.

44. Lingeman, *Don't You Know*, 244; *Newsweek*, February 9, 1942, 50, and May 18, 1942, 40–41; *Kiplinger Letter*, April 25, 1942, 70. Emphasis is in original.

45. *Fortune*, February 1942, 87–89; Lingeman, *Don't You Know*, 234.

46. Polenberg, *War and Society*, 32; Lingeman, *Don't You Know*, 246; *Newsweek*, September 7, 1942, 66, and November 2, 1942, 36; *Time*, July 13, 1942, 82, November 2, 1942, 24, and November 9, 1942, 22.

47. *Time*, September 7, 1942, 27–28.

48. *Time*, September 14, 1942, 79–80; *Newsweek*, September 14, 1942, 63, and November 2, 1942, 36; *Kiplinger Letter*, September 5, 1942, 70.

49. *Newsweek*, September 21, 1942, 51, and October 5, 1942, 54.

50. *Newsweek*, May 25, 1942, 52, and October 5, 1942, 57; Roosevelt, *Public Papers and Addresses*, 11:361.

51. *Newsweek*, June 1, 1942, 28, October 5, 1942, 34, 36, and December 7, 1941, 31; *Time*, October 5, 1942, 26.

52. *Time*, November 30, 1942, 20; *Newsweek*, December 7, 1942, 31, 34.

53. *Time*, September 7, 1942, 28, and November 9, 1942, 22; Lingeman, *Don't You Know*, 235; Phillips, *1940s*, 86–87.

54. *Time*, November 2, 1942, 22; *Fortune*, December 1942, 123.

55. *Newsweek*, December 14, 1942, 48, and December 28, 1942, 26–27.

56. Ibid., September 7, 1942, 62; Galbraith, *A Life in Our Times*, 172.

CHAPTER 20. MIXED SIGNALS

1. Clapper, *Watching the World*, 97.

2. *Saturday Evening Post*, October 24, 1942, 108.

3. *Newsweek*, November 30, 1942, 55.

4. Roosevelt, *Public Papers and Addresses*, 11:445–46.

5. Polenberg, *War and Society*, 188–93; Zieger, *CIO*, 180.

6. Polenberg, *War and Society*, 188–89; Goodwin, *No Ordinary Time*, 385; Wilcox, *Farmer in the Second World War*, 128; Hassett, *Off the Record*, 134.

7. Hassett, *Off the Record*, 130, 132; Clapper, *Watching the World*, 91.

8. Clapper, *Watching the World*, 172.

9. Ibid., 197; *Newsweek*, November 2, 1942, 54; John Morton Blum, *From the Morgenthau Diaries: Years of War, 1941–1945* (Boston, 1967), 48. For the debate over the tax bill, see *Newsweek*, March 9, 1942, 40–42, March 16, 1942, 56, April 20, 1942, 54, May 18, 1942, 44, June 22, 1942, 58, July 27, 1942, 56, August 24, 1942, 56, and October 19, 1942, 58, 60, 64; *Time*, July 27, 1942, 72, September 7, 1942, 92–93, and September 21, 1942, 12; *Saturday Evening Post*, September 12, 1942, 120.

10. Randolph E. Paul, *Taxation in the United States* (Boston, 1954), 249–325; Kennedy, *Freedom from Fear*, 624. The exemption for dependents was also lowered from $400 to $350. The new law also introduced deductions for medical expenses.

11. Koistinen, *Arsenal of World War II*, 430; Budget Bureau, *United States at War*, 259.

12. *Newsweek*, April 20, 1942, 54, May 18, 1942, 44, June 22, 1942, 58, and November 2, 1942, 56.

13. *Newsweek*, May 24, 1943, 30; *Fortune*, September 1942, 94–95, 178, 182. The *Fortune* article by Ruml outlines the details of his plan. For a profile of Ruml, see *Fortune*, March 1945, 135–38, 170, 172, 174, 176, 179–80.

14. *Fortune*, September 1942, 94; *Newsweek*, August 31, 1942, 54; Blum, *Years of War*, 49.

15. Blum, *Years of War*, 49–51; *Saturday Evening Post*, September 26, 1942, 116.

16. Roosevelt, *Personal Letters*, 1352.

17. Blum, *Years of War*, 51.

18. *Look*, September 22, 1942, 18.

19. Ibid., 19, 22.

20. This section is drawn from *Saturday Evening Post*, October 3, 1942, 20–21, 94. See also *Newsweek*, August 17, 1942, 58.

21. *Time*, October 26, 1942, 81.

22. Vatter, *U.S. Economy in World War II*, 51.

23. Wilcox, *Farmer in the Second World War*, 10–11, 14–16. For an account of the Dust Bowl, see Donald Worster, *Dust Bowl* (New York, 1979).

24. Wilcox, *Farmer in the Second World War*, 15–19, 304.

25. Budget Bureau, *United States at War*, 321–22, 338.

26. *Saturday Evening Post*, October 24, 1942, 108.

27. Budget Bureau, *United States at War*, 326–31.

28. Ibid., 326–30.

29. Ibid., 331–36; Wilcox, *Farmer in the Second World War*, 352–53.

30. Budget Bureau, *United States at War*, 335–36; Roosevelt, *Personal Letters*, 1357.

31. Roosevelt, *Public Papers and Addresses*, 11:517–29.

32. *Look*, December 15, 1942, 20–23.

33. This episode is drawn from *Time*, October 12, 1942, 22.

34. *Time*, September 14, 1942, 80, 82; *Newsweek*, June 15, 1942, 50; *Saturday Evening Post*, December 12, 1942, 116; Stimson diary, October 20 and October 23, 1942.

35. *Fortune*, October 1942, 200, 202; *Newsweek*, August 3, 1942, 51–52; *Time*, August 10, 1942, 75.

36. *Fortune*, October 1942, 200; Nelson, *Arsenal of Democracy*, 355–56.

37. Koistinen, *Arsenal of World War II*, 142–44; *Fortune*, October 1942, 87; *Newsweek*, May 11, 1942, 57.

38. *Newsweek*, October 26, 1942, 63.

39. *Newsweek*, June 8, 1942, 72, and October 26, 1942, 63–64; *Time*, July 27, 1942, 52–53.

40. *Time*, October 5, 1942, 26; *Newsweek*, October 26, 1942, 63–64; *Fortune*, October 1942, 208.

41. *Fortune*, October 1942, 208; *Newsweek*, August 3, 1942, 49, and August 17, 1942, 50–51; Strahan, *Higgins*, 108–11; *Saturday Evening Post*, August 21, 1943, 102; *Time*, July 20, 1942, 57, and November 2, 1942, 61. The latter article lists the advantages and disadvantages of sponge iron.

42. Strahan, *Higgins*, 111–15; *Fortune*, October 1942, 210; *Saturday Evening Post*, August 21, 1943, 102.

43. Koistinen, *Arsenal of World War II*, 320; Novick et al., *Wartime Production Controls*, 4–5.

44. Koistinen, *Arsenal of World War II*, 320–21; Novick et al., *Wartime Production Controls*, 5.

45. Novick et al., *Wartime Production Controls*, 129, 138–63. Novick includes a detailed description of the various alternatives to PRP put forward and debated.

46. Ibid., 140.

47. Ibid., 140–48.

48. Ibid., 124, 163, 177–78.

49. Ibid., 164, 177–78; Koistinen, *Arsenal of World War II*, 326–27.

50. This section is drawn from *Fortune*, September 1942, 89–92, 154, 156, 158, 160, 162, and *Time*, March 8, 1943, 68–69.

51. *Newsweek*, March 23, 1942, 46.

52. Unless otherwise indicated, this section is drawn from *Fortune*, April 1942, 79–81, 114, 116.

53. Sorensen, *My Forty Years with Ford*, 282.

54. Ibid., 279; Walton, *Miracle of World War II*, 307–9.

55. Unless otherwise indicated, this section is drawn from *Saturday Evening Post*, November 21, 1942, 17, 37, 39, and *Look*, August 25, 1942, 11, 13–15.

56. *Newsweek*, April 13, 1942, 55.

CHAPTER 21. CITY OF PAPER

1. Lingeman, *Don't You Know*, 112.

2. Novick et al., *Wartime Production Controls*, 380–81. Emphasis is in the original.

3. Sherwood, *Roosevelt and Hopkins*, 700.

4. Coit, *Baruch*, 503.

5. *Harper's*, October 1943, 419, 426, and December 1941, 58; Kiplinger, *Washington Is Like That*, 402, 460; Brinkley, *Washington Goes to War*, 9–11.

6. *Esquire*, March 1940, 33, 150, 152–53.

7. Brinkley, *Washington Goes to War*, 13.

8. Ibid., 12–13, 24, 107.

9. Ibid., 18–21, 78; *Harper's*, December 1941, 51, 54–55.

10. Brinkley, *Washington Goes to War*, 23, 76–77, 91–92.

11. Ibid., 107–8, 119–20; Lingeman, *Don't You Know*, 74; Walton, *Miracle of World War II*, 18; *Harper's*, December 1941, 50.

12. Lingeman, *Don't You Know*, 99–100; *Newsweek*, September 28, 1942, 35; *Harper's*, December 1941, 51.

13. Lingeman, *Don't You Know*, 101; Brinkley, *Washington Goes to War*, 113; Blum, *V Was for Victory*, 92–93.

14. Brinkley, *Washington Goes to War*, 112.

15. Galbraith, *A Life in Our Times*, 178.

16. Ibid., 179–80; *Time*, December 21, 1942, 20.

17. *Time*, December 28, 1942, 13; Galbraith, *A Life in Our Times*, 180–81; *Newsweek*, December 28, 1942, 27–28; Stone, *War Years*, 143.

18. Roosevelt, *Public Papers and Addresses*, 11:421.

19. *Time*, October 5, 1942, 22.

20. See, for example, *Time*, September 7, 1942, 26.

21. *Newsweek*, August 10, 1942, 33, September 14, 1942, 62–63, and September 28, 54; *Business Week*, November 7, 1942, 104; *Time*, October 5, 1942, 22; Koistinen, *Arsenal of World War II*, 373.

22. *Time*, September 28, 1942, 24; Eiler, *Mobilizing America*, 296–97; George Q. Flynn, *The Mess in Washington: Manpower Mobilization in World War II* (Westport, Conn., 1979), 26–27.

23. Flynn, *Mess in Washington*, 27; Stimson diary, September 16, September 17, and October 19, 1942.

24. Stimson diary, October 19–23, 1942.

25. Ibid., November 4, November 5, November 7, and November 11, 1942; *Newsweek*, November 9, 1942, 50, 52, and November 23, 1942, 30–31; Koistinen, *Arsenal of World War II*, 375. The memo is dated November 5 and included in the diary.

26. Flynn, *Mess in Washington*, 29–33; *Newsweek*, December 7, 1942, 34, 36, and December 14, 1942, 62; *Time*, December 14, 1942, 28–29.

27. Stimson diary, December 11, 1942; Stimson and Bundy, *On Active Service*, 481.

28. Stimson diary, November 29 to December 10, 1942; *Time*, December 21, 1942, 22.

29. *Newsweek*, September 14, 1942, 35, 38, September 21, 1942, 46, October 26, 1942, 33, 36, November 2, 1942, 32–33, and December 21, 1942, 27–28; *Fortune*, November 1942, 96–97; *Time*, September 14, 1942, 18, and December 7, 1942, 25–26; Stimson and Bundy, *On Active Service*, 473–75.

30. Fairchild and Grossman, *Army and Industrial Manpower*, 47–49.

31. Ibid., 50–52; Koistinen, *Arsenal of World War II*, 374; Stimson and Bundy, *On Active Service*, 476–80; Flynn, *Mess in Washington*, 188–91. The special committee consisted of Baruch, Hopkins, Admiral William D. Leahy, and Rosenman.

32. Hassett, *Off the Record*, 160.

33. *Newsweek*, June 22, 1942, 34.

34. *Fortune*, March 1943, 91.

35. Ibid., 93–94; *Newsweek*, November 3, 1942, 42.

36. Connery, *Navy and Industrial Mobilization*, 174.

37. *Newsweek*, November 3, 1942, 42, and March 1, 1942, 54; Robert C. Perez and Edward F. Willett, *The Will to Win: A Biography of Ferdinand Eberstadt* (Westport, Conn., 1989), 6; *Fortune*, March 1943, 93.

38. *Newsweek*, November 16, 1942, 66, 68; *Time*, November 9, 1942, 19; Coit, *Baruch*, 508; Novick et al., *Wartime Production Controls*, 163–70; Koistinen, *Arsenal of World War II*, 322.

39. Koistinen, *Arsenal of World War II*, 322–23; Novick et al., *Wartime Production Controls*, 170–93. Novick has the most detailed analysis of CMP, Koistinen the most succinct. For Wilson's aircraft unit, see *Newsweek*, November 30, 1942, 64.

40. Koistinen, *Arsenal of World War II*, 323.

41. Ibid., 323–25; CPA, *Industrial Mobilization for War*, 262–63; Budget Bureau, *United States at War*, 304–6; Novick et al., *Wartime Production Controls*, 167. For the basic structure of WPB, see Walton, *Thread of Victory*, 11–21.

42. Novick et al., *Wartime Production Controls*, 268.

43. Catton, *War Lords*, 242–43; *Time*, December 13, 1943, 21–23.

44. Koistinen, *Arsenal of World War II*, 328–29; *Fortune*, March 1943, 92.

45. Budget Bureau, *United States at War*, 317–18.

46. Koistinen, *Arsenal of World War II*, 329–30; Eiler, *Mobilizing America*, 360–61; Nelson, *Arsenal of Democracy*, 382–83.

47. Stimson diary, November 23, 1942.

48. Ibid., November 25, 1942; Eiler, *Mobilizing America*, 360–61; *Fortune*, March 1943, 93.

49. Stimson diary, November 25, 1942.

50. Ibid., November 26, 1942.

51. Nelson, *Arsenal of Democracy*, 384.

52. Ibid., 384–85; *Fortune*, March 1943, 93; Coit, *Baruch*, 509. Coit's account of this episode is based largely on an interview with Eberstadt himself.

53. Nelson, *Arsenal of Democracy*, 386–87; Stimson diary, November 26–28, 1942.

54. Koistinen, *Arsenal of World War II*, 330–32; *Time*, December 21, 1942, 21.

55. *Fortune*, March 1943, 92–93; CPA, *Industrial Mobilization for War*, 264; *Newsweek*, November 30, 1942, 64, and February 15, 1943, 57.

56. Stimson diary, January 1 and January 6, 1943; *Time*, January 25, 1943, 17. The synthetic rubber plants and the refineries producing 100-octane gas both used heat and pressure processes that required boilers, hundreds of valves, condensers, pumps, gages, and other instruments.

57. Klein, *Union Pacific: The Rebirth*, 402, 422–23; Stimson diary, January 1, January 2, and January 5, 1943.

58. James F. Byrnes, *All in One Lifetime* (New York, 1958), 169–70.

59. Stimson diary, January 9 and January 19, 1943; *Time*, February 8, 1943, 15, and February 15, 1943, 16–17; *Newsweek*, February 8, 1943, 33; Byrnes, *All in One Lifetime*, 169–71.

60. *Time*, February 8, 1943, 15, and February 15, 1943, 16–17; *Newsweek*, February 8, 1943, 33–34; Stimson diary, January 20, January 23, and January 28, 1943.

61. Budget Bureau, *United States at War*, 318; *Time*, February 15, 1943, 77, and December 13, 1943, 22; *Newsweek*, February 15, 1943, 57; Stimson diary, February 6, 1943. The divisions transferred to Wilson were shipbuilding, industrial equipment, tools, automotive, safety and technical supplies, aluminum and magnesium, and facilities bureau.

62. Byrnes, *All in One Lifetime*, 171–72; Koistinen, *Arsenal of World War II*, 333; *Newsweek*, March 1, 1943, 54; Baruch, *Public Years*, 313.

63. Coit, *Baruch*, 510.

64. Byrnes, *All in One Lifetime*, 172–73; Koistinen, *Arsenal of World War II*, 334; Stimson diary, February 6, 1943.

65. Baruch, *Public Years*, 312–14. Emphasis is in original.

66. Coit, *Baruch*, 509.

67. Baruch, *Public Years*, 312–14.

68. Ibid., 314; Byrnes, *All in One Lifetime*, 172–73. The letter in Baruch's version contains a typo—"benn" instead of "been"—that is not in Byrnes's version. Baruch attributed it to the haste in which the letter was written.

69. Baruch, *Public Years*, 316–17; Coit, *Baruch*, 511–12.

70. Nelson, *Arsenal of Democracy*, 388–89; Eiler, *Mobilizing America*, 365–67; Koistinen, *Arsenal of World War II*, 334; *Time*, March 1, 1943, 10–11; *Newsweek*, March 1, 1943, 54, 56. These accounts conflict over the timing of events but not over their substance. For a somewhat different version, see Catton, *War Lords*, 205–6.

71. Budget Bureau, *United States at War*, 319.

72. Baruch, *Public Years*, 317–18; Sherwood, *Roosevelt and Hopkins*, 700; Coit, *Baruch*, 512. See also Stimson diary, February 18, February 22, and February 24, 1943.

73. Koistinen, *Arsenal of World War II*, 334; Stimson diary, May 4, 1943; *Time*, December 13, 1943, 22.

74. Koistinen, *Arsenal of World War II*, 334–39; Lacey, *Keep from All Thoughtul Men*, 115.

75. Stone, *War Years*, 151–52.

CHAPTER 22. THE STUFF OF VICTORY

1. Ickes, *Fightin' Oil*, 7.

2. Frey and Ide, *PAW*, 293.

3. Ickes, *Fightin' Oil*, 15.

4. Ibid., 70, 74.

5. Ibid., 4–5; Frey and Ide, *PAW*, 1.

6. Koistinen, *Arsenal of World War II*, 259; Frey and Ide, *PAW*, 14–15; Budget Bureau, *United States at War*, 282–83.

7. Koistinen, *Arsenal of World War II*, 259–60; Frey and Ide, *PAW*, 15.

8. Koistinen, *Arsenal of World War II*, 260; *Fortune*, September 1942, 30, 32.

9. *Newsweek*, April 6, 1942, 46, 48; *Time*, August 31, 1942, 83; Frey and Ide, *PAW*, 56; Henrietta Larson, Evelyn H. Knowlton, and Charles S. Popple, *History of Standard Oil Company (New Jersey): New Horizons, 1927–1950* (New York, 1971), 428–52.

10. Roosevelt, *Public Papers and Addresses*, 11:496–504; Budget Bureau, *United States at War*, 287–92; Koistinen, *Arsenal of World War II*, 260–61; Frey and Ide, *PAW*, 44–45.

11. For more detail on these products and by-products, see Popple, *Standard Oil*, 97–130.

12. Ibid., 12–13; George Sweet Gibb and Evelyn H. Knowlton, *Standard Oil Company (New Jersey): The Resurgent Years, 1911–1927* (New York, 1956), 115–16; Larson et al., *New Horizons*, 166–67. Cracking involved some process to decompose chemically (or "crack") certain hydrocarbons into lighter fractions to increase yields.

13. Popple, *Standard Oil*, 13–15; Larson et al., *New Horizons*, 167–69.

14. Larson et al., *New Horizons*, 153–55.

15. Popple, *Standard Oil*, 11, 97.

16. Ibid., 98–102.

17. Ibid., 102–111.

18. *Harper's*, February 1942, 287–88; Larson et al., *New Horizons*, 161; Howard, *Buna Rubber*, 51. Midgley worked under Charles Kettering in GM's research laboratory.

19. *Harper's*, February 1942, 289–91; *Fortune*, June 1943, 156. Octane is a measure of combustion characteristics of a fuel under a specified set of conditions.

20. Howard, *Buna Rubber*, 51–52.

21. Ibid., 52–54; *Fortune*, June 1943, 156; Larson et al., *New Horizons*, 161–63; Popple, *Standard Oil*, 21–22. Shell got into the business at the urging of its aviation manager, an aeronautical engineer named Jimmy Doolittle, who gained more fame as a flyer.

22. *Fortune*, June 1943, 170, 172; Larson et al., *New Horizons*, 163–65; Popple, *Standard Oil*, 22–25.

23. Popple, *Standard Oil*, 25–30. For Walt Disney's illuminating popular explanation of 100-octane gas, see *Look*, January 11, 1944, 30–31.

24. Popple, *Standard Oil*, 27–28; *Oil and Gas Journal*, September 10, 1942, 71–72; Office of Petroleum Coordinator, "100-Octane Aviation Gasoline: Report to the Supply Priorities and Allocations Board," November 18, 1941, 1–2, copy in author's possession, hereafter abbreviated as CAP.

25. Popple, *Standard Oil*, 31–32; *Oil and Gas Journal*, January 2, 1941, 29, and February 6, 1941, 20; Bruce K. Brown memorandum, March 6, 1942, CAP.

26. *Oil and Gas Journal*, February 6, 1941, 20; Ickes to attached list of oil company presidents, July 26, 1941, CAP; Minutes of the Petroleum Industry Committee for National Defense, August 20, 1941, 10, CAP; Petroleum Coordinator for National Defense, "Recommendation No. 8," August 23, 1941, CAP.

27. Davies to Knox, September 6, 1941, CAP; Chester F. Smith to Robert H. Colley, October 9, 1941, CAP; Davies to Nelson, October 11, 1941, CAP.

28. Office of Petroleum Coordinator, "100-Octane Aviation Gasoline: Report to the Supply Priorities and Allocations Board," November 18, 1941, 3–13, CAP; Popple, *Standard Oil*,

33–37; Office of Petroleum Coordinator, "Recommendation No. 16," December 9, 1941, 1–5, CAP; Davies to J. S. Knowlson, February 17, 1942, CAP; Frey and Ide, *PAW*, 197–98.

29. Office of Petroleum Coordinator, "100-Octane Aviation Gasoline: Report to the Supply Priorities and Allocations Board," December 15, 1941, 1–9, CAP; Davies to WPB?, January 17, 1942, CAP; James Forrestal to Jesse Jones, January 19, 1942, CAP; Jones to Davies, January 21 and January 28, 1942, CAP; Davies to Jones, January 23 and February 7, 1942, CAP; George H. Hill Jr. to Jones, January 24 and January 26, 1942, CAP; Jones to Forrestal, January 27, 1942, CAP; Popple, *Standard Oil*, 37.

30. Frey and Ide, *PAW*, 198–99; Ickes, *Fightin' Oil*, 76; Office of Petroleum Coordinator, "100-Octane Gasoline: Report to the War Production Board," March 16, 1942, 2, CAP, hereafter cited as "100-Octane Report."

31. "100-Octane Report," March 16, 1942, 7, April 20, 1942, 3, and May 29, 1942, 5–6; Patterson to Davies, March 6, 1942, CAP; Davies to Patterson, March 9, 1942, CAP; Robert B. Cragin memorandum, July 9, 1942, CAP.

32. *Oil and Gas Journal*, September 10, 1942, 71; "100 Octane Report," September 9, 1942, 5–6, and October 15, 1942, 3–4; Max B. Miller to Eberstadt, September 30, 1942, CAP; Davies to Eberstadt, October 6, 1942, CAP.

33. Nelson to Ickes, December 4, 1942, CAP; "100 Octane Report," December 15, 1942, 6–7, and June 10, 1943, 6–8, 22; E. D. Cumming to George H. Mettam, July 9, 1943, CAP; Cumming to Chester F. Smith, August 16, 1943, CAP; Miller to Mettam, November 19, 1943, CAP. Cumming was PAW's director of refining.

34. Frey and Ide, *PAW*, 82–83; Popple, *Standard Oil*, 131.

35. Larson et al., *New Horizons*, 524–25, 530; Lingeman, *Don't You Know*, 43.

36. Budget Bureau, *United States at War*, 155–56; Ickes, *Fightin' Oil*, 24–27.

37. Frey and Ide, *PAW*, 90; Popple, *Standard Oil*, 143–44.

38. Budget Bureau, *United States at War*, 162; Ickes, *Fightin' Oil*, 26–27, 34; Frey and Ide, *PAW*, 90.

39. Popple, *Standard Oil*, 146–47; Frey and Ide, *PAW*, 102, 105.

40. *Newsweek*, May 4, 1942, 10, and June 22, 1942, 52, 54; Popple, *Standard Oil*, 148, 150.

41. Frey and Ide, *PAW*, 104–6; Popple, *Standard Oil*, 151–53; Ickes, *Fightin' Oil*, 31–32; *Time*, November 9, 1942, 21.

42. Frey and Ide, *PAW*, 107–9; Woodbury, *Battlefronts of Industry*, 171–72; *Time*, February 1, 1943, 13–14, and July 26, 1943, 24.

43. Frey and Ide, *PAW*, 5, 106.

44. *Time*, November 27, 1944, 79–80; *Fortune*, January 1945, 127–28.

45. *Newsweek*, December 28, 1942, 12, January 25, 1943, 25, February 22, 1943, 12, and June 14, 1943, 14; *Time*, January 18, 1943, 22, February 1, 1943, 13, and May 31, 1943, 42.

46. *Time*, August 31, 1942, 71–72, October 19, 1942, 85–86, and May 3, 1943, 79; *Newsweek*, January 4, 1943, 42, 44.

47. *Newsweek*, April 19, 1943, 14, June 7, 1943, 14, August 2, 1943, 33–34, and September 16, 1943, 16; *Time*, July 5, 1943, 19, July 26, 1943, 24, and September 13, 1943, 81.

48. *Time*, November 1, 1943, 54, 56, 58; *Saturday Evening Post*, November 20, 1943, 16.

49. *Harper's*, December 1942, 68–69. For a clever explanation of how synthetic rubber was made, see "Disney Has Donald Duck Explain About Synthetic Rubber," *Look*, May 18, 1943, 70–74. Disney made a number of these brief but informative explanatory articles for the magazine.

50. Howard, *Buna Rubber*, 221–22.

51. Ibid., 174–76.

52. Ibid., 182–83; Larson et al., *New Horizons*, 507. The 805,000 tons was divided as follows: 705,000 tons of Jersey Standard's Buna-S, 60,000 tons of Jersey's Butyl, and 40,000 tons of DuPont's neoprene.

53. Howard, *Buna Rubber*, 182–84; Larson et al., *New Horizons*, 509–10; *Harper's*, December 1942, 73–74.

54. Howard, *Buna Rubber*, 197–200; *Harper's*, December 1942, 69–70.

55. *Harper's*, December 1942, 71–72; *Time*, September 14, 1942, 79, and April 21, 1943, 56.

56. Koistinen, *Arsenal of World War II*, 154–56; *Newsweek*, August 3, 1942, 44, 46–47, and September 21, 1942, 60.

57. *New York Times*, June 6, 1943.

58. *New York Herald Tribune,* October 13, 1942. Unless otherwise indicated, this section is drawn from Klein, *Union Pacific: The Rebirth*, 384–426.

59. *Time*, September 28, 1942, 71, and October 19, 1942, 17; *Newsweek*, March 22, 1943, 11; Howard, *Buna Rubber*, 224.

60. *Time*, October 19, 1942, 17, and January 25, 1943, 17; Klein, *Union Pacific: The Rebirth*, 422–23; Eiler, *Mobilizing America*, 272–73.

61. Eiler, *Mobilizing America*, 273–79; Stimson diary, April 28, 1943; *Newsweek*, May 3, 1943, 34.

62. *Time*, April 26, 1943, 17, and May 3, 1943, 22–23.

63. Eiler, *Mobilizing America*, 279–81; Stimson diary, May 4 and May 10, 1943; *New York Times*, May 4, 1943.

64. *Time*, April 12, 1943, 84; Klein, *Union Pacific: The Rebirth*, 424.

65. Klein, *Union Pacific: The Rebirth*, 424.

66. *Time*, May 31, 1942, 82–84; Popple, *Standard Oil*, 65–66; Koistinen, *Arsenal of World War II*, 156–57.

67. Polenberg, *War and Society*, 18; Budget Bureau, *United States at War*, 296; Vatter, *U.S. Economy in World War II*, 29; Koistinen, *Arsenal of World War II*, 157.

68. Eiler, *Mobilizing America*, 281.

CHAPTER 23. WEAPONS OF MASS PRODUCTION

1. Woodbury, *Battlefronts of Industry*, 27–28.

2. *Newsweek*, January 15, 1945, 26, 29.

3. Kennedy, *Freedom from Fear*, 648–49.

4. Roosevelt, *Public Papers and Addresses*, 11:36; Alan S. Milward, *War, Economy, and Society, 1939–1945* (Berkeley, 1977), 186.

5. Kennedy, *Freedom from Fear*, 619; Overy, *Why the Allies Won*, 201.

6. Overy, *Why the Allies Won*, 201–2.

7. Ibid., 203–4; Albert Speer, *Inside the Third Reich* (New York, 1970), 208–13.

8. Overy, *Why the Allies Won*, 224–25; Finney, *Arsenal of Democracy*, 140.

9. Milward, *War, Economy, and Society*, 67.

10. Middlebrook, *Convoy*, 308–23. Middlebrook provides much more detail on the change in weapons and tactics to combat the submarines. The gist of his book is an account

of the fortunes of one Atlantic convoy, told in fascinating detail from both the Allied and German perspectives.

11. Koistinen, *Arsenal of World War II*, 331–32; *Fortune*, May 1943, 95, 97. The *Fortune* article lists fifteen main claimant agencies and twenty-four most critical common components.

12. *Fortune*, May 1943, 95–96; Novick et al., *Wartime Production Controls*, 274–84.

13. *Fortune*, 95–97, 162.

14. Ibid., 162, 164, 166.

15. Miller, *Men and Volts*, 4; Overy, *Why the Allies Won*, 331–32; Kennedy, *Freedom from Fear*, 655.

16. Wesley Frank Craven and James Lea Cate, *The Army Air Forces in World War II* (Chicago, 1955), 6:350, 352–53; Peter Darman, *World War II Stats and Facts* (New York, 2009), 245.

17. Darman, *World War II Stats and Facts*, 244; Kennedy, *Freedom from Fear*, 655.

18. Connery, *Navy and Industrial Mobilization*, 3; Darman, *World War II Stats and Facts*, 246; Kennedy, *Freedom from Fear*, 655. Here, as elsewhere, the figures for total production vary widely among sources and cannot be reconciled. For the navy I have used Connery's figures, which are taken from the Annual Report of the Secretary of the Navy for fiscal 1945.

19. Miller, *Men and Volts*, 108–9, 114–15.

20. *Newsweek*, January 24, 1944, 97–98, 100–102; *Time*, July 10, 1944, 84, and September 11, 1944, 65.

21. Eiler, *Mobilizing America*, 127.

22. *Look*, February 13, 1940, 28, and October 7, 1940, 18, 20–22; *Time*, May 6, 1940, 20, November 11, 1940, 21, January 20, 1941, 22, March 24, 1941, 20–21, September 15, 1941, 32, and October 27, 1941, 38.

23. O'Neill, *Democracy at War*, 350–53; Max Hastings, *Armageddon: The Battle for Germany, 1944–1945* (New York, 2004), 85–86; *Newsweek*, January 15, 1945, 26. For those too young to remember, the Ronson was a popular cigarette lighter.

24. Miller, *Men and Volts*, 105–8; Hastings, *Armageddon*, 84, 86.

25. Popple, *Standard Oil*, 97–113.

26. Vatter, *U.S. Economy in World War II*, 60–61.

27. *Newsweek*, November 1, 1943, 62, 64.

28. Miller, *Men and Volts*, 234–37.

29. *Fortune*, March 1942, 69.

30. Ibid., 156, 159.

31. Miller, *Men and Volts*, 240–44.

32. Ibid., 6, 248, 251; ibid., 246–51, contains a broad list of products made by each GE factory.

33. Woodbury, *Battlefronts of Industry*, 55–57.

34. Ibid., 57–58.

35. Ibid., 40–43.

36. Ibid., 39, 44–45.

37. Ibid., 38–39.

38. Ibid., 218–20.

39. Ibid., 222–26.

40. This section on Cutler-Hammer is drawn from *Fortune*, August 1942, 96–98, 142, 144, 147–48, 150.

41. Except where indicated, this section on Jack & Heintz is drawn from *Harper's*, May 1943, 556–64, and *Fortune*, January 1944, 97–99, 209–10, 213–14, 216.

42. *Time*, December 14, 1942, 91–92.

43. *Fortune*, July 1942, 110.

44. *Time*, November 3, 1941, 31, and June 28, 1943, 84, 86; Stimson diary, April 14, 1942.

45. *Time*, November 3, 1941, 31; *Look*, April 7, 1942, 36; *Newsweek*, January, 4, 1943, 46.

46. *Newsweek*, March 1, 1943, 59, March 22, 1943, 12, and March 29, 1943, 50; *Time*, March 15, 1943, 70, and May 10, 1943, 81.

47. *Newsweek*, March 29, 1943, 50, and September 6, 1943, 78, 81; *Time*, May 10, 1943, 81, July 12, 1943, 84–86, and October 18, 1943, 77; Foster, *Kaiser*, 185–86.

48. *Time*, October 4, 1943, 80, October 18, 1943, 77, and November 1, 1943, 86, 88; *Newsweek*, October 4, 1943, 85, and December 6, 1943, 85; Heiner, *Western Colossus*, 160–65.

49. *Time*, April 19, 1943, 25–26; *Fortune*, February 1943, 112–13, 208, 210; David L. Lewis, *The Public Image of Henry Ford* (Detroit, 1976), 347–51, 537–38; Robert Lacey, *Ford: The Men and the Machine* (Boston, 1986), 392. In 1943 Chrysler topped Willow Run by opening a plant to make aircraft engines with a mammoth floor space of 6.43 million square feet, but it received much less publicity.

50. Keith Sward, *The Legend of Henry Ford* (New York, 1968 [1948]), 433–34.

51. Ibid., 441–42.

52. Sorensen, *My Forty Years with Ford*, 298–99.

53. Charles A. Lindbergh, *The Wartime Journals of Charles A. Lindbergh* (New York, 1970), July 27, 1942, 682; Beasley, *Knudsen*, 287–88. Emphasis is in original.

54. Craven and Cate, *Army Air Forces in World War II*, 6:334–37.

55. The following section is drawn from Sward, *Legend of Henry Ford*, 430–41.

56. Ibid., 444; Lacey, *Ford*, 393–98; Sorensen, *My Forty Years with Ford*, 301–24.

57. Sward, *Legend of Henry Ford*, 445–49.

58. Ibid., 449; Lacey, *Ford*, 412.

59. *Time*, April 19, 1943, 25.

CHAPTER 24. THE NEW WEST

1. *Fortune*, July 1942, 91.

2. Ibid., 88.

3. Burlingame, *Don't Let Them Scare You*, 209.

4. *Fortune*, July 1942, 90; Nash, *American West Transformed*, 3–5.

5. *Newsweek*, June 22, 1942, 46; Nash, *American West Transformed*, 38.

6. *Fortune*, July 1942, 91, and February 1945, 130–33, 258–61; *Newsweek*, June 22, 1942, 46; Foster, *Kaiser*, 94–95.

7. *Newsweek*, July 22, 1942, 46, 48; Nash, *American West Transformed*, 25.

8. Gerald D. Nash, *World War II and the West: Reshaping the Economy* (Lincoln, Neb., 1990), 5.

9. Ibid., 5–6; Nash, *American West Transformed*, 17, 24–25.

10. Nash, *American West Transformed*, 68; *Newsweek*, July 22, 1942, 48, 50; Lingeman, *Don't You Know*, 88–89.

11. *Time*, December 28, 1942, 65; Stephen B. Adams, *Mr. Kaiser Goes to Washington: The Rise of a Government Entrepreneur* (Chapel Hill, 1997), 108–9.

12. Foster, *Kaiser*, 92–96; Heiner, *Western Colossus*, 170–76; Adams, *Kaiser Goes to Washington*, 100–101.

13. Walton, *Miracle of World War II*, 421; Heiner, *Western Colossus*, 173–75.

14. *Saturday Evening Post*, June 7, 1941, 10–11.

15. Jones, *Fifty Billion Dollars*, 331–32; Foster, *Kaiser*, 197–99; Heiner, *Western Colossus*, 112–13.

16. Foster, *Kaiser*, 179–82; *Time*, August 17, 1942, 15–16; *Newsweek*, August 17, 1942, 57–58.

17. Foster, *Kaiser*, 179–84; Jones, *Fifty Billion Dollars*, 335–36; *Time*, November 8, 1943, 83; Adams, *Kaiser Goes to Washington*, 123–43.

18. Adams, *Kaiser Goes to Washington*, 11–12, 62, 68, 88, 107–16.

19. Ibid., 124; Foster, *Kaiser*, 117.

20. *Fortune*, January 1943, 79; *Newsweek*, October 18, 1943, 68, 70.

21. Ibid.; Nelson, *Arsenal of Democracy*, 403.

22. *Fortune*, January 1943, 201; *Saturday Evening Post*, October 9, 1943, 24.

23. *Time*, January 11, 1943, 73; *Newsweek*, March 8, 1943, 53–54, 56; Eiler, *Mobilizing America*, 370; *Fortune*, January 1943, 192, and March 1943, 104.

24. Eiler, *Mobilizing America*, 371; *Time*, January 11, 1943, 74; *Fortune*, March 1943, 105. Emphasis is in the original.

25. Eiler, *Mobilizing America*, 372; *Newsweek*, April 26, 1943, 26; *Fortune*, January 1943, 80; Nash, *American West Transformed*, 39; Fairchild and Grossman, *Army and Industrial Manpower*, 135–36.

26. Nash, *American West Transformed*, 39.

27. Ibid., 58.

28. Wilcox, *Farmer in the Second World War*, 85–89.

29. *Fortune*, January 1943, 194, 196; Nash, *American West Transformed*, 41.

30. *Fortune*, January 1943, 196, 198; *Saturday Evening Post*, October 9, 1943, 24; Fairchild and Grossman, *Army and Industrial Manpower*, 219.

31. Fairchild and Grossman, *Army and Industrial Manpower*, 219–20; Koistinen, *Arsenal of World War II*, 390–91, *Newsweek*, January 4, 1943, 26–28; Flynn, *Mess in Washington*, 80–81.

32. Fairchild and Grossman, *Army and Industrial Manpower*, 220–21, 225; Eiler, *Mobilizing America*, 390–92; Koistinen, *Arsenal of World War II*, 395–96; Flynn, *Mess in Washington*, 82–84; *Time*, February 15, 1943, 20; *Look*, February 23, 1943, 19; *Newsweek*, March 15, 1943, 25–26.

33. Fairchild and Grossman, *Army and Industrial Manpower*, 225–30; *Fortune*, January 1943, 201; *Newsweek*, February 8, 1943, 45, and February 15, 1943, 25–26; *Time*, March 8, 1943, 31; Stimson diary, July 7, 1943.

34. Roosevelt, *Public Papers and Addresses*, 12:69–71; CPA, *Industrial Mobilization for War*, 703–4.

35. *Time*, February 1, 1943, 16.

36. Ibid., 75–76, and February 15, 1943, 20.

37. Fairchild and Grossman, *Army and Industrial Manpower*, 171–72; *Newsweek*, April 26, 1943, 58.

38. *Time*, March 8, 1943, 51, April 19, 1943, 27; *Newsweek*, March 22, 1943, 42, April 12, 1943, 41, April 19, 1943, 34, 36, 38, and August 23, 1943, 35, 38.

39. *Newsweek*, August 23, 1943, 35; Eiler, *Mobilizing America*, 381, 483; Fairchild and Grossman, *Army and Industrial Manpower*, 131–32.

40. Fairchild and Grossman, *Army and Industrial Manpower*, 132; Eiler, *Mobilizing America*, 380–81.

41. *Time*, September 27, 1943, 84, 86; CPA, *Industrial Mobilization for War*, 705–7. For a profile of Rosenberg, see *Saturday Evening Post*, October 16, 1943, 25, 77–78, 80.

42. CPA, *Industrial Mobilization for War*, 707–11; Eiler, *Mobilizing America*, 381–82; Somers, *Presidential Agency*, 145–49; *Newsweek*, September 13, 1943, 62, 64. The most detailed description of the report is in Budget Bureau, *United States at War*, 439–44. *Newsweek* has a good summary of the plan's main provisions.

43. Eiler, *Mobilizing America*, 381–84; Fairchild and Grossman, *Army and Industrial Manpower*, 147–49; Somers, *Presidential Agency*, 149–52.

44. Budget Bureau, *United States at War*, 442–44. For reactions to the plan, see *Newsweek*, December 6, 1943, 78–79, 81.

45. *Newsweek*, September 27, 1943, 42; *Saturday Evening Post*, October 7, 1943, 24.

46. Nash, *American West Transformed*, 41.

47. *Time*, September 27, 1943, 86–87.

48. *Time*, December 6, 1943, 21, and December 20, 1943, 15–16; *Newsweek*, November 29, 1943, 47; Budget Bureau, *United States at War*, 446–47.

49. Marilynn S. Johnson, *The Second Gold Rush: Oakland and the East Bay in World War II* (Berkeley, 1993), 7, 30, 83; Nash, *American West Transformed*, 56–58.

50. Nash, *American West Transformed*, 58–60.

51. Ibid., 62–69.

52. Ibid., 69–70.

53. Ibid., 75–77; *Newsweek*, November 16, 1942, 71, and November 1, 1943, 64; *Time*, November 23, 1942, 27.

54. Nash, *American West Transformed*, 78–79.

55. Ibid., 79–81.

56. Ibid., 80.

57. Ibid., 84–87.

CHAPTER 25. IRONING OUT THE WRINKLES

1. Janeway, *Struggle for Survival*, 44.

2. Goodwin, *No Ordinary Time*, 204.

3. Roosevelt, *Personal Letters*, 1463.

4. Perkins, *Roosevelt I Knew*, 360; Blum, *V Was for Victory*, 118.

5. Stone, *War Years*, 134; Budget Bureau, *United States at War*, 281–82, 298.

6. Janeway, *Struggle for Survival*, 216.

7. Somers, *Presidential Agency*, 43; Roosevelt, *Public Papers and Addresses*, 12:234–35; Budget Bureau, *United States at War*, 391–97.

8. Roosevelt, *Public Papers and Addresses*, 12:232–34.

9. Ibid., 12:233; Somers, *Presidential Agency*, 1, 47; *Time*, November 30, 1942, 21.

10. *Newsweek*, June 7, 1943, 29–31; *Time*, June 7, 1943, 22; Somers, *Presidential Agency*, 51.

11. Hassett, *Off the Record*, 170.

12. Somers, *Presidential Agency*, 52–54, 143–54; Koistinen, *Arsenal of World War II*, 363. Nelson was something of an exception; his book lavishes praise on many of his associates but barely mentions Byrnes and says nothing of their relationship.

13. Byrnes, *All in One Lifetime*, 186–87; Stimson diary, May 28, June 1, and June 8, 1943.

14. Stimson diary, July 2, 1943; Byrnes, *All in One Lifetime*, 187; Koistinen, *Arsenal of World War II*, 363–64.

15. Koistinen, *Arsenal of World War II*, 364–65; Byrnes, *All in One Lifetime*, 187; *Time*, September 20, 1943, 21.

16. Koistinen, *Arsenal of World War II*, 365–67; Byrnes, *All in One Lifetime*, 187–88.

17. *Newsweek*, July 19, 1943, 88.

18. *Newsweek*, July 5, 1943, 31, and July 12, 1943, 31; Roosevelt, *Public Papers and Addresses*, 11:528–29.

19. Roosevelt, *Public Papers and Addresses*, 10:291–97; Jones, *Fifty Billion Dollars*, 485–86, 490. The board was originally named the Economic Defense Board, but Pearl Harbor led to its being renamed the BEW on December 17, 1941. The fullest account of this episode is in John C. Culver and John Hyde, *American Dreamer: A Life of Henry Wallace* (New York, 2000), 271–313.

20. Culver and Hyde, *American Dreamer*, 272.

21. Ibid., 172–73; Jones, *Fifty Billion Dollars*, 491.

22. Jones, *Fifty Billion Dollars*, 486–87.

23. Stone, *War Years*, 168–69; *Time*, July 12, 1943, 19.

24. Jones, *Fifty Billion Dollars*, 492–95; *Time*, July 12, 1943, 19–21; *Newsweek*, July 12, 1943, 31–32. Wallace's complete statement is reprinted in Jones, 556–72.

25. *Time*, July 12, 1943, 20; *Newsweek*, July 19, 1943, 50. Jones, *Fifty Billion Dollars*, 572–88, reprints his complete reply.

26. Sherwood, *Roosevelt and Hopkins*, 740.

27. Jones, *Fifty Billion Dollars*, 495–98; Byrnes, *All in One Lifetime*, 192–93; Hassett, *Off the Record*, 183.

28. Byrnes, *All in One Lifetime*, 193; Roosevelt, *Public Papers and Addresses*, 12:298–303.

29. Hassett, *Off the Record*, 190–91; Byrnes, *All in One Lifetime*, 193–94; Roosevelt, *Public Papers and Addresses*, 12:299–300.

30. Jones, *Fifty Billion Dollars*, 503–6; *Newsweek*, July 26, 1943, 36, 38; *Time*, July 26, 1943, 19.

31. *Newsweek*, July 26, 1943, 40; *Time*, July 26, 1943, 19, and August 2, 1943, 19–20.

32. Blum, *Years of War*, 48.

33. *Time*, January 25, 1943, 19–20.

34. Ibid.

35. Ibid., 18, 20.

36. Clapper, *Watching the World*, 235–36. For George, see *Saturday Evening Post*, May 19, 1945, 22–23, 39, 41–42, 44.

37. Blum, *Years of War*, 52–59.

38. Ibid., 58–59; *Newsweek*, May 24, 1943, 30, 33; Paul, *Taxation in the United States*, 326–49.

39. *Newsweek*, January 18, 1943, 54, February 8, 1943, 70, February 22, 1943, 58, 60, and March 22, 1943, 56; *Look*, February 23, 1943, 26–27; *Saturday Evening Post*, March 13, 1943, 108; *Time*, March 15, 1943, 63–64.

40. *Time*, April 12, 1943, 52.

41. *Newsweek*, March 22, 1943, 54, 57, April 5, 1943, 36, 39, and April 12, 1943, 50; Blum, *Years of War*, 241–43.

42. *Newsweek*, May 17, 1943, 28, 31, 62; *Time*, May 24, 1943, 13–14; Blum, *Years of War*, 241–43.

43. *Newsweek*, June 7, 1943, 40, 42, 44, and June 28, 1943, 50; Blum, *Years of War*, 241–43.

44. *Newsweek*, June 28, 1943, 50. For the spending tax, see *Fortune*, March 1943, 81, 206, 208.

45. *Time*, February 1, 1943, 80, 82; *Fortune*, March 1943, 200.

46. Roosevelt, *Public Papers and Addresses*, 12:154.

47. *Time*, February 8, 1943, 18, and February 22, 1943, 18–19; *Newsweek*, February 8, 1943, 56, 58, and March 8, 1943, 14; *Fortune*, May 1943, 80; Budget Bureau, *United States at War*, 387.

48. Budget Bureau, *United States at War*, 386; *Newsweek*, February 22, 1943, 55–56; *Time*, February 22, 1943, 19.

49. *Newsweek*, February 15, 1943, 62; *Fortune*, March 1943, 200.

50. *Newsweek*, December 28, 1943, 58; *Time*, March 22, 1943, 14; *Harper's*, July 1943, 126.

51. *Newsweek*, April 12, 1943, 34; *Harper's*, July 1943, 127; Galbraith, *A Life in Our Times*, 185–86.

52. Galbraith, *A Life in Our Times*, 189; *Newsweek*, June 7, 1943, 31; *Time*, June 7, 1943, 25; *Harper's*, July 1943, 127.

53. Budget Bureau, *United States at War*, 387–89; Roosevelt, *Public Papers and Addresses*, 12:135–43; *Newsweek*, April 19, 1943, 31–32; *Time*, April 19, 1943, 21–22.

54. Roosevelt, *Public Papers and Addresses*, 12:148–55; *Newsweek*, April 19, 1943, 31–32; *Time*, April 19, 1943, 21–22.

55. *Newsweek*, February 8, 1943, 56, 58; *Time*, April 19, 1943, 22; *Fortune*, May 1943, 79–80.

56. *Fortune*, May 1943, 198, 200; *Time*, May 3, 1943, 21; *Newsweek*, May 3, 1943, 48, 51; Stimson diary, April 29, 1943.

57. *Fortune*, September 1943, 107–9, 236, 238, 240, 242, 244, 246; *Time*, May 10, 1943, 19–21, and August 2, 1943, 21; *Newsweek*, May 10, 1943, 32, 34, 36, and June 14, 1943, 66; Budget Bureau, *United States at War*, 389.

58. *Newsweek*, May 10, 1943, 34.

59. *Newsweek*, March 29, 1943, 44, and July 5, 1943, 64, 66, 69; *Time*, June 21, 1943, 19; *Fortune*, September 1943, 109, 236; Zieger, *CIO*, 180; Roosevelt, *Public Papers and Addresses*, 12:268–72.

60. *Newsweek*, June 7, 1943, 62, 64, June 14, 1943, 66, and June 28, 1943, 77–78; *Time*, May 17, 1943, 23, June 7, 1943, 23, and June 28, 1943, 20.

61. *Newsweek*, November 8, 1943, 54, 56; *Fortune*, July 1943, 64, 90; *Time*, July 5, 1943, 15.

62. Wilcox, *Farmer in the Second World War*, 255–56.

63. Ibid., 258; *Time*, May 17, 1943, 75; *Newsweek*, May 17, 1943, 32, 34; Budget Bureau, *United States at War*, 389–91.

64. Wilcox, *Farmer in the Second World War*, 254–57; *Time*, May 17, 1943, 75; *Newsweek*, May 17, 1943, 34.

65. *Time*, May 17, 1943, 75; *Newsweek*, May 31, 1943, 65, and November 29, 1943, 37; Budget Bureau, *United States at War*, 391; *Fortune*, September 1943, 105.

66. *Time*, May 24, 1943, 88, 90, and June 7, 1943, 25.

67. *Time*, June 7, 1943, 25, and July 26, 1943, 20–21; *Harper's*, July 1943, 115; *Newsweek*, June 7, 1943, 31, 74, and July 26, 1943, 48.

68. *Newsweek*, August 9, 1943, 46, 48, September 27, 1943, 48, and November 1, 1943, 53; *Time*, August 30, 1943, 22.

69. Koistinen, *Arsenal of World War II*, 426–27; *Newsweek*, September 27, 1943, 58, 60; *Saturday Evening Post*, July 24, 1943, 96.

70. *Time*, December 6, 1943, 19.

71. Clapper, *Watching the World*, 294–95; *Saturday Evening Post*, December 11, 1943, 116; Stone, *War Years*, 192.

CHAPTER 26. FEEDING FRENZIES

1. *Time*, March 1, 1943, 11.

2. Burlingame, *Don't Let Them Scare You*, 209.

3. *Saturday Evening Post*, August 14, 1943, 106.

4. *Fortune*, December 1943, 74.

5. *Saturday Evening Post*, January 30, 1943, 22, 72, 74.

6. Ibid., 74, 92.

7. *Time*, December 21, 1942, 19; *Newsweek*, January 18, 1943, 46, 48.

8. This account of the Schneiters is drawn from *Look*, February 23, 1943, 21–25.

9. This account is drawn from *Harper's*, June 1943, 86.

10. *Time*, March 29, 1943, 9.

11. Ibid. and April 5, 1943, 12.

12. *Look*, April 6, 1943, 61.

13. This account is drawn from *Harper's*, June 1943, 86–90.

14. Ibid., 121; *Time*, May 31, 1943, 38.

15. *Newsweek*, June 21, 1943, 68–69.

16. *Look*, March 9, 1943, 44–45.

17. Wilcox, *Farmer in the Second World War*, 135–36, 140; *Newsweek*, May 3, 1943, 12, and October 4, 1943, 59.

18. Wilcox, *Farmer in the Second World War*, 136–43; *Newsweek*, June 14, 1943, 38, 40, and October 4, 1943, 59.

19. *Fortune*, April 1943, 89.

20. Ibid., 89–91.

21. Ibid., 195–98.

22. Ibid., 198.

23. *Time*, February 8, 1943, 17.

24. *Time*, March 1, 1943, 11–12.

25. *Saturday Evening Post*, August 14, 1943, 20–21.

26. Ibid., 21, 106.

27. *Newsweek*, May 17, 1943, 58, 61.

28. *Newsweek*, July 5, 1943, 69–70, and July 19, 1943, 58, 61; *Time*, July 5, 1943, 20–21.

29. *Newsweek*, July 5, 1943, 70, 72.

30. Ibid., 72.

31. Ibid., 78; Roosevelt, *Public Papers and Addresses*, 11:517–29; Wilcox, *Farmer in the Second World War*, 354.

32. *Time*, March 1, 1943, 11–12; *Newsweek*, January 4, 1943, 12.

33. Budget Bureau, *United States at War*, 360–61, 365; Roosevelt, *Public Papers and Addresses*, 11:528–29; Wilcox, *Farmer in the Second World War*, 354, 360; *Newsweek*, April 5, 1943, 48. The new agency was created by executive order on March 26 and received the name

War Food Administration along with greatly broadened powers by another executive order on April 19.

34. *Newsweek*, April 5, 1943, 48, 50, 52.

35. *Newsweek*, July 12, 1943, 44; Roosevelt, *Public Papers and Addresses*, 12:272–76; Wilcox, *Farmer in the Second World War*, 354–55, 360; *Time*, June 28, 1943, 13.

36. *Time*, April 12, 1943, 20–21.

37. This account is drawn from *Saturday Evening Post*, January 16, 1943, 16, 60, 62. See also *Look*, June 29, 1943, 21–25.

38. *Newsweek*, January 4, 1943, 50; *Time*, April 19, 1943, 81–82.

39. *Time*, April 19, 1943, 81–82.

40. *Newsweek*, June 28, 1943, 68, 70, 72.

41. Ibid.

42. Ibid.

43. *Time*, June 28, 1943, 13–14, and July 5, 1943, 20.

44. *Time*, July 19, 1943, 18–19; *Newsweek*, June 28, 1943, 32, 35, 38.

45. *Newsweek*, July 5, 1943, 74; *Time*, August 9, 1943, 46–48.

46. *Time*, August 2, 1943, 86; *Newsweek*, August 2, 1943, 63.

47. *Time*, August 30, 1943, 20–21, September 13, 1943, 24, September 27, 1943, 70, 72, and October 25, 1943, 80, 82.

48. *Saturday Evening Post*, February 6, 1943, 12–13, 68; *Time*, February 8, 1943, 16.

49. Wilcox, *Farmer in the Second World War*, 63–67, 200, 209–10, 216.

50. Ibid., 70; *Newsweek*, November 5, 1943, 64, 67, and November 22, 1943, 68; Roosevelt, *Public Papers and Addresses*, 12:469.

51. This description is drawn from Rosenman, *Working with Roosevelt*, 1–3.

52. *Newsweek*, September 27, 1943, 46.

53. Roosevelt, *Public Papers and Addresses*, 12:496–97; Rosenman, *Working with Roosevelt*, 395–97.

54. Rosenman, *Working with Roosevelt*, 397; Roosevelt, *Public Papers and Addresses*, 12:466; Hassett, *Off the Record*, 218.

55. The entire speech is in Roosevelt, *Public Papers and Addresses*, 12:466–96.

56. Ibid., 12:484, 490.

57. *Newsweek*, November 8, 1943, 49, and December 20, 1943, 66; *Time*, November 8, 1943, 13.

CHAPTER 27. THE SLIDING SCALE OF SACRIFICE

1. *Newsweek*, March 1, 1943, 34.

2. Stone, *War Years*, 191.

3. *Saturday Evening Post*, January 22, 1944, 92.

4. O'Neill, *Democracy at War*, 249. According to O'Neill, this was the mother of historian Stephen E. Ambrose.

5. Childs, *I Write from Washington*, 290.

6. Blum, *V Was for Victory*, 16.

7. Eiler, *Mobilizing America*, 266, 404, 468–69; Lingeman, *Don't You Know*, 130; Goodwin, *No Ordinary Time*, 317.

8. Blum, *V Was for Victory*, 96–97.

9. Ibid., 16, 91–94; Polenberg, *War and Society*, 132; Vatter, *U.S. Economy in World War II*, 20.

10. Clapper, *Watching the World*, 100, 102, 315–16.

11. *Look*, January 26, 1943, 12.

12. *Saturday Evening Post*, July 25, 1942, 22, 49, 53–54; *Time*, December 21, 1942, 94–95.

13. *Newsweek*, February 1, 1943, 25–26, April 19, 1943, 38–41, and August 2, 1943, 36; *Time*, April 19, 1943, 23; *Saturday Evening Post*, July 25, 1942, 54; *Look*, March 9, 1943, 19–21.

14. *Saturday Evening Post*, July 25, 1943, 54.

15. *Look*, June 1, 1943, 12.

16. Lingeman, *Don't You Know*, 254–55.

17. Ibid., 255; Wilcox, *Farmer in the Second World War*, 267; *Newsweek*, January 11, 1943, 27–28.

18. Lingeman, *Don't You Know*, 255–57; *Newsweek*, March 22, 1943, 38.

19. *Newsweek*, July 12, 1943, 57–58.

20. Lingeman, *Don't You Know*, 257–58; *Time*, January 4, 1943, 17.

21. Lingeman, *Don't You Know*, 254; *Newsweek*, January 11, 1943, 27, 54.

22. *Newsweek*, January 11, 1943, 14.

23. *Time*, April 26, 1943, 21; Lingeman, *Don't You Know*, 260–61; Goodwin, *No Ordinary Time*, 316.

24. *Newsweek*, July 12, 1943, 58, 61, and July 26, 1943, 48; *Time*, August 3, 1943, 82, 84.

25. *Newsweek*, January 18, 1943, 28–30; *Time*, February 8, 1943, 73.

26. *Time*, January 4, 1943, 40, January 11, 1943, 71, August 23, 1943, 88, and November 29, 1943, 55; *Newsweek*, January 11, 1943, 58.

27. *Newsweek*, February 15, 1943, 36, 39; *Time*, March 8, 1943, 18.

28. *Newsweek*, March 15, 1943, 29–30, 32.

29. *Saturday Evening Post*, April 24, 1943, 19.

30. This section is drawn from John Barber and Mark Harrison, *The Soviet Home Front, 1941–1945* (London, 1991), 77–93.

31. Burlingame, *Don't Let Them Scare You*, 198.

32. Ibid., 19–174; *Time*, March 15, 1943, 13–15.

33. *Newsweek*, June 22, 1942, 30, and July 20, 1942, 70–71.

34. *Newsweek*, December 7, 1942, 98; Catton, *War Lords*, 190.

35. *Newsweek*, July 20, 1942, 71, and January 25, 1943, 26; Burlingame, *Don't Let Them Scare You*, 197; Blum, *V Was for Victory*, 34–35.

36. Blum, *V Was for Victory*, 35–36.

37. Ibid., 32–33; *Newsweek*, November 2, 1942, 79.

38. Burlingame, *Don't Let Them Scare You*, 211–14; Blum, *V Was for Victory*, 38; *Time*, March 15, 1943, 13. The latter source has a sample page of the Roosevelt biography.

39. Burlingame, *Don't Let Them Scare You*, 212–13; Budget Bureau, *United States at War*, 229; *Newsweek*, May 3, 1943, 61; *Time*, April 19, 1943, 25.

40. Burlingame, *Don't Let Them Scare You*, 214–15; Budget Bureau, *United States at War*, 229; Blum, *V Was for Victory*, 38–39; *Time*, April 19, 1943, 25.

41. Blum, *V Was for Victory*, 38–39; Burlingame, *Don't Let Them Scare You*, 214–15; *Time*, April 9, 1943, 25. The sources have three different versions of the poster's text; I have used the one from *Time* as the earliest.

42. *Time*, April 19, 1943, 25, and July 5, 1943, 66; *Newsweek*, June 28, 1943, 44, 46; Budget

Bureau, *United States at War*, 229–30; Burlingame, *Don't Let Them Scare You*, 216–17; Blum, *V Was for Victory*, 39–45.

43. *Time*, September 13, 1943, 50.

44. Blum, *V Was for Victory*, 11, 46.

45. *Time*, August 31, 1942, 23; Polenberg, *War and Society*, 126.

46. *Newsweek*, May 17, 1943, 36; Lingeman, *Don't You Know*, 325; Blum, *V Was for Victory*, 190–91; Burlingame, *Don't Let Them Scare You*, 210.

47. Lingeman, *Don't You Know*, 164; Nash, *American West Transformed*, 89; Fairchild and Grossman, *Army and Industrial Manpower*, 160; *Harper's*, November 1943, 489–90.

48. Alan Clive, *State of War: Michigan in World War II* (Ann Arbor, 1979), 36, 179–80.

49. *Newsweek*, July 5, 1943, 36; Polenberg, *War and Society*, 127; *Harper's*, November 1943, 493–94.

50. Clive, *State of War*, 144–46; Blum, *V Was for Victory*, 200–201.

51. Clive, *State of War*, 146–50; Blum, *V Was for Victory*, 201–2.

52. Blum, *V Was for Victory*, 202; Lingeman, *Don't You Know*, 324; *Harper's*, November 1943, 488, 493; Clive, *State of War*, 155–56.

53. *Harper's*, November 1943, 492; Clive, *State of War*, 157–58.

54. Blum, *V Was for Victory*, 202–3; Lingeman, *Don't You Know*, 326–27; Clive, *State of War*, 158–59; *Newsweek*, June 28, 1943, 42, 44, and July 5, 1943, 38; *Harper's*, November 1943, 495.

55. Blum, *V Was for Victory*, 203; Lingeman, *Don't You Know*, 327; *Harper's*, November 1943, 495–96; Clive, *State of War*, 158–59.

56. Blum, *V Was for Victory*, 203–4; Lingeman, *Don't You Know*, 327–28; Clive, *State of War*, 159–60; *Newsweek*, July 5, 1943, 38.

57. Stimson diary, June 21, 1943; Hassett, *Off the Record*, 181; Blum, *V Was for Victory*, 204; Lingeman, *Don't You Know*, 327–28; Clive, *State of War*, 160–61; Goodwin, *No Ordinary Time*, 445–46; *Newsweek*, July 5, 1943, 38, 40; *Time*, August 23, 1943, 20–21; *Harper's*, November 1943, 496–98.

58. *Newsweek*, July 5, 1943, 35–36, 40; Stimson diary, June 24, 1943.

59. Goodwin, *No Ordinary Time*, 444; Lingeman, *Don't You Know*, 329; *Time*, August 9, 1943, 19.

60. Nash, *American West Transformed*, 111–14; Lingeman, *Don't You Know*, 333. Lingeman includes the lyrics to the song. For more detail and some illustrations of zoot suits, see Walton, *Thread of Victory*, 124–32.

61. Nash, *American West Transformed*, 114–15; Lingeman, *Don't You Know*, 333; *Newsweek*, June 21, 1943, 35–36, 38, 40.

62. Nash, *American West Transformed*, 115–17; *Newsweek*, June 21, 1943, 35–36, 38, 40.

63. Nash, *American West Transformed*, 117–18; *Time*, June 21, 1943, 18–19.

64. *Time*, August 16, 1943, 21–22, and November 29, 1943, 21; *Newsweek*, June 21, 1943, 35–36, 38, 40.

65. *Time*, December 20, 1943, 18; *Newsweek*, November 15, 1943, 54, 58.

66. *Time*, December 20, 1943, 18.

67. *Newsweek*, September 13, 1943, 18.

68. *Newsweek*, April 6, 1942, 30.

69. *Look*, May 5, 1942, 18–21.

70. *Look*, April 6, 1943, 36, 38.

71. *Look*, May 4, 1943, 19.

72. *Time*, August 2, 1943, 24; *Newsweek*, October 11, 1943, 40.

73. *Newsweek*, October 11, 1943, 40, 43–44.

CHAPTER 28. THE WINTER OF DISCONNECT

1. *Newsweek*, December 27, 1943, 39.

2. Stimson diary, March 20, 1944.

3. Clapper, *Watching the World*, 131.

4. *Newsweek*, July 19, 1943, 52, 54, August 2, 1943, 54, 56, August 16, 1943, 60, 62, August 30, 1943, 66, September 6, 1943, 52, September 20, 1943, 78, 81, and October 4, 1943, 46, 48; *Time*, August 2, 1943, 21, August 9, 1943, 20, and September 27, 1943, 79; *Look*, August 24, 1943, 28–29.

5. *Time*, October 25, 1943, 21, November 8, 1943, 14, and November 15, 1943, 17–18; *Newsweek*, November 8, 1943, 54, 56.

6. *Newsweek*, November 15, 1943, 60, 62; *Time*, October 11, 1943, 16, November 1, 1943, 19–20, November 15, 1943, 17–18, and December 12, 1943, 21.

7. Hassett, *Off the Record*, 227.

8. Roosevelt, *Public Papers and Addresses*, 12:567–68; Stimson diary, December 23, 1943; *Newsweek*, December 27, 1943, 34, 37. The engineers and the trainmen agreed to accept Roosevelt as arbitrator and to abide by his decision; the enginemen and firemen, switchmen, and conductors refused.

9. Stimson diary, December 31, 1943; *Newsweek*, January 17, 1944, 34; Byrnes, *All in One Lifetime*, 201; Eiler, *Mobilizing America*, 387.

10. Stimson diary, December 24, December 25, and December 27, 1943.

11. Ibid., December 27 and December 28, 1943; Byrnes, *All in One Lifetime*, 200; Roosevelt, *Public Papers and Addresses*, 12:563–69; *Time*, January 3, 1944, 13.

12. Roosevelt, *Public Papers and Addresses*, 12:568–69; *Time*, January 3, 1944, 13, and January 31, 1944, 17; *Newsweek*, January 10, 1944, 52, 54, 56, and January 31, 1944, 50, 52, 54; *Fortune*, February 1944, 166.

13. *Time*, January 31, 1944, 17–18, and April 3, 1944, 22; *Newsweek*, February 21, 1944, 69, March 20, 1944, 66, March 27, 1944, 72, and April 10, 1944, 60, 62.

14. *Newsweek*, January 10, 1944, 37–38; *Time*, January 24, 1944, 61.

15. *Newsweek*, January 10, 1944, 37–38.

16. Ibid.; CPA, *Industrial Mobilization for War*, 775; Flynn, *Mess in Washington*, 231.

17. *Saturday Evening Post*, February 19, 1944, 104; Flynn, *Mess in Washington*, 86–87; Rosenman, *Working with Roosevelt*, 419–21.

18. Rosenman, *Working with Roosevelt*, 417–23; Flynn, *Mess in Washington*, 86–88; Roosevelt, *Public Papers and Addresses*, 13:43–44. Hopkins was ill and unable to work on the speech.

19. Rosenman, *Working with Roosevelt*, 417; Roosevelt, *Public Papers and Addresses*, 13:32–34; *Newsweek*, January 24, 1944, 34, 37.

20. Roosevelt, *Public Papers and Addresses*, 13:35–39.

21. Ibid., 13:40–42; Stimson diary, January 11, 1944; Stimson and Bundy, *On Active Duty*, 483–85; Fairchild and Grossman, *Army and Industrial Manpower*, 234–36.

22. Fairchild and Grossman, *Army and Industrial Manpower*, 236–37; Allen Drury, *A Senate Journal, 1943–1945* (New York, 1963), 53.

23. *Saturday Evening Post*, September 18, 1943, 15.

24. *Newsweek*, July 13, 1942, 64, and September 7, 1942, 74.

25. *Time*, March 29, 1943, 42, and September 25, 1944, 64.

26. *Time*, September 6, 1943, 42; *Newsweek*, September 13, 1943, 98.

27. *Saturday Evening Post*, November 27, 1943, 112; *Time*, February 14, 1944, 71.

28. *Newsweek*, September 21, 1942, 85–86, and January 24, 1944, 68, 71.

29. *Newsweek*, September 14, 1942, 84.

30. *Time*, September 28, 1942, 67.

31. *Time*, October 26, 1942, 81–82, and February 15, 1943, 89; *Newsweek*, May 4, 1942, 59.

32. *Time*, October 26, 1942, 82; *Newsweek*, November 23, 1942, 72, and December 14, 1942, 98–99.

33. *Time*, November 21, 1942, 88; *Fortune*, December 1942, 178; *Newsweek*, December 28, 1942, 60.

34. *Newsweek*, December 28, 1942, 60; *Time*, December 28, 1942, 55.

35. Stimson diary, February 3, 1943; *Newsweek*, January 25, 1943, 55; *Time*, February 15, 1943, 89–90.

36. *Time*, February 15, 1943, 89–90; *Newsweek*, February 22, 1943, 68, 71.

37. *Newsweek*, May 3, 1943, 62, 64; *Time*, July 19, 1943, 60, 62.

38. Ibid.

39. *Time*, December 28, 1942, 55–56, February 15, 1943, 89, and July 12, 1943, 74–75; *Newsweek*, January 4, 1943, 68, and August 2, 1943, 72.

40. Stimson diary, November 5, 1943.

41. Ibid., November 6 and November 30, 1943; *Newsweek*, February 14, 1944, 95, and March 13, 1944, 101, 103; *Time*, February 28, 1944, 65, and March 13, 1944, 72; Blum, *V Was for Victory*, 143.

42. *Time*, September 25, 1944, 64.

43. Ibid.

44. Clapper, *Watching the World*, 131–32; Catton, *War Lords*, 184.

45. Lingeman, *Don't You Know*, 344; *Kiplinger Letter*, 70, 72. Emphasis is in the original.

46. Roosevelt, *Public Papers and Addresses*, 11:505–16; Koistinen, *Arsenal of World War II*, 441; Polenberg, *War and Society*, 79; Clapper, *Watching the World*, 131; *Newsweek*, March 22, 1943, 27–28, 31–32, 34, 36, and August 9, 1943, 36, 38, 40; *Time*, July 10, 1944, 22.

47. Catton, *War Lords*, 182–83.

48. Roosevelt, *Public Papers and Addresses*, 11:569–75; *Newsweek*, January 3, 1944, 32–33.

49. Roosevelt, *Public Papers and Addresses*, 11:574–75.

50. Ibid., 13:41–42; *Newsweek*, January 24, 1944, 34, 37; Polenberg, *War and Society*, 73.

51. Burns, *Soldier of Freedom*, 424.

52. *Time*, February 7, 1944, 16.

53. *Time*, February 21, 1944, 19; *Newsweek*, February 28, 1944, 69–70.

54. *Newsweek*, October 11, 1943, 64, 66, 68, 70, and October 18, 1943, 72, 75; *Time*, October 18, 1943, 21–23; Vatter, *U.S. Economy in World War II*, 109.

55. *Time*, October 18, 1943, 21–23; *Newsweek*, October 18, 1943, 66, 68, 70, and November 22, 1943, 54, 56.

56. *Saturday Evening Post*, February 5, 1944, 96; *Time*, November 8, 1943, 16–17; *Newsweek*, January 31, 1944, 56, 59, and February 14, 1944, 40, 42; Roosevelt, *Public Papers and Addresses*, 13:80–83.

57. Blum, *Years of War*, 75–76.

58. Roosevelt, *Public Papers and Addresses*, 13:80, 82; Hassett, *Off the Record*, 235; Drury, *Senate Journal*, 85–86.

59. Burns, *Soldier of Freedom*, 426–27.

60. Ibid., 429–33; *Time*, April 10, 1944, 17.

61. Burns, *Soldier of Freedom*, 434–36; Blum, *Years of War*, 75–76; Drury, *Senate Journal*, 11, 86–97; *Time*, March 6, 1944, 17–20; *Newsweek*, March 6, 1944, 33–36, 39–40.

62. Hassett, *Off the Record*, 235–37; Burns, *Soldier of Freedom*, 436–37.

63. Burns, *Soldier of Freedom*, 437; Rosenman, *Working with Roosevelt*, 273; *Time*, March 6, 1944, 20.

64. Blum, *Years of War*, 76–77.

65. Goodwin, *No Ordinary Time*, 33–34; Perkins, *Roosevelt I Knew*, 66.

66. Rosenman, *Working with Roosevelt*, 150–51.

67. Ibid., 151; Goodwin, *No Ordinary Time*, 36.

68. Clapper, *Watching the World*, 91–92; Ickes, *Diary*, 577, 580.

69. Goodwin, *No Ordinary Time*, 72, 385; Hassett, *Off the Record*, 146.

70. Rosenman, *Working with Roosevelt*, 350; Hassett, *Off the Record*, 45, 114.

71. Rosenman, *Working with Roosevelt*, 350–56.

72. Burns, *Soldier of Freedom*, 447–48; Goodwin, *No Ordinary Time*, 488–90.

73. Goodwin, *No Ordinary Time*, 488–92; Burns, *Soldier of Freedom*, 448.

74. Burns, *Soldier of Freedom*, 448; Roosevelt, *Personal Letters*, 1499; Goodwin, *No Ordinary Time*, 491–93; Smith, *Thank You, Mr. President*, 133–34; Hassett, *Off the Record*, 239–40; Jim Bishop, *FDR's Last Year* (New York, 1974), 2–3.

75. Hassett, *Off the Record*, 241; Bishop, *FDR's Last Year*, 4–5; Goodwin, *No Ordinary Time*, 493–94.

76. Bishop, *FDR's Last Year*, 4–6; Goodwin, *No Ordinary Time*, 494–95; Burns, *Soldier of Freedom*, 449.

77. Bishop, *FDR's Last Year*, 4–10; Goodwin, *No Ordinary Time*, 495–97.

78. Bishop, *FDR's Last Year*, 10.

79. Ibid., 18; Goodwin, *No Ordinary Time*, 497; Baruch, *Public Years*, 335–36; Burns, *Soldier of Freedom*, 449–50; *Time*, April 10, 1944, 17; *Newsweek*, April 10, 1944, 28.

80. Bishop, *FDR's Last Year*, 25–26; Goodwin, *No Ordinary Time*, 497–98; Smith, *Thank You, Mr. President*, 135–40; Hassett, *Off the Record*, 241; *Time*, May 15, 1944, 11.

81. Goodwin, *No Ordinary Time*, 498; Hassett, *Off the Record*, 241–42.

82. Smith, *Thank You, Mr. President*, 141; Stimson diary, April 28, 1944; Hassett, *Off the Record*, 242–43; *Time*, May 8, 1944, 11, and May 15, 1944, 13.

83. *Kiplinger Letter*, 75; Nelson, *Arsenal of Democracy*, 15.

84. *Time*, May 15, 1944, 17, and May 22, 1944, 17; *Newsweek*, May 15, 1944, 33–34; Goodwin, *No Ordinary Time*, 499, 502; Baruch, *Public Years*, 336–37.

85. *Newsweek*, February 14, 1944, 52, 68, 70; *Time*, February 14, 1944, 44, 46. For a profile of Clapper by his wife, see *Look*, June 13, 1944, 34, 36, 38, 40, and June 27, 1944, 30, 32, 35, 37.

86. *Newsweek*, February 14, 1944, 68, 70; *Time*, February 14, 1944, 44, 46.

87. *Newsweek*, February 7, 1944, 77–78, and February 14, 1944, 52.

88. *Newsweek*, February 7, 1944, 78, and February 14, 1944, 52, 70.

CHAPTER 29. THE CHANGING FACE OF WAR

1. Woodbury, *Battlefronts of Industry*, 2.

2. *Newsweek*, June 26, 1944, 34.

3. Woodbury, *Battlefronts of Industry*, 312.

4. Kennedy, *Freedom from Fear*, 631.

5. Stimson diary, December 23, 1943, and January 12, 1944.

6. Miller, *Men and Volts*, 116–20.

7. Smith, *Army and Economic Mobilization*, 28.

8. Woodbury, *Battlefronts of Industry*, 244–48; Thomson and Mayo, *Ordnance Department*, 123–24. In Army parlance, according to Woodbury, "fuze" referred to a mechanical device that detonated a bomb, while "fuse" was the trail of powder that carried the fire from the initiating cap to the main explosive.

9. Woodbury, *Battlefronts of Industry*, 92–94.

10. Ibid., 92–100.

11. Miller, *Men and Volts*, 156–63.

12. Ibid., 132–34; Woodbury, *Battlefronts of Industry*, 100.

13. Woodbury, *Battlefronts of Industry*, 101–3; Miller, *Men and Volts*, 134–35.

14. Miller, *Men and Volts*, 135–36; Woodbury, *Battlefronts of Industry*, 105–6.

15. Stimson and Bundy, *On Active Service*, 508–14; Morison, *Turmoil and Tradition*, 561–80; Middlebrook, *Convoy*, 309–18; Zachary, *Endless Frontier*, 166–74.

16. Miller, *Men and Volts*, 136–38.

17. Ibid., 138; *Time*, September 11, 1944, 79; Zachary, *Endless Frontier*, 166–88.

18. Miller, *Men and Volts*, 139–40.

19. Ibid., 140–41.

20. Ibid., 141–42.

21. Ibid., 144–46; Woodbury, *Battlefronts of Industry*, 107–8.

22. Miller, *Men and Volts*, 145–46; Woodbury, *Battlefronts of Industry*, 26, 80–81, 107–8; Nelson, *Arsenal of Democracy*, 260–69.

23. *Fortune*, October 1944, 180, 182; Steve Birdsall, *Saga of the Superfortress: The Dramatic Story of the B-29 and the Twentieth Air Force* (Garden City, N.Y., 1980), 3–5; Goodwin, *No Ordinary Time*, 531. For more detail on both the B-17 and B-29, see Robert Redding and Bill Yenne, *Boeing: Planemaker to the World* (Greenwich, Conn., 1983), 75–109.

24. Birdsall, *Saga of the Superfortress*, 2–3; *Fortune*, October 1944, 180.

25. *Fortune*, October 1944, 159–60; Goodwin, *No Ordinary Time*, 367.

26. Redding and Yenne, *Boeing*, 82–87, 92; Paul E. Eden and Soph Moeng, eds., *Aircraft Anatomy of World War II* (London, 2003), 17; *Fortune*, October 1944, 180, 182.

27. *Fortune*, October 1944, 180, 182; Birdsall, *Saga of the Superfortress*, 3–5; Jacob Vander Meulen, *Building the B-29* (Washington, 1995), 13–16.

28. Birdsall, *Saga of the Superfortress*, 5–7; Vander Meulen, *Building the B-29*, 17; Walton, *Miracle of World War II*, 404–5.

29. Miller, *Men and Volts*, 85–86; Vander Meulen, *Building the B-29*, 17.

30. Miller, *Men and Volts*, 72–77.

31. Birdsall, *Saga of the Superfortress*, 10–13; *Fortune*, October 1944, 180.

32. Birdsall, *Saga of the Superfortress*, 13–16.

33. Ibid., 16–25; *Time*, June 26, 1944, 63.

34. Birdsall, *Saga of the Superfortress*, 26–44; *Time*, January 17, 1944, 88.

35. Birdsall, *Saga of the Superfortress*, 52–58; *Newsweek*, June 26, 1944, 34–36; *Time*, June 26, 1944, 63.

36. Birdsall, *Saga of the Superfortress*, 56–58; *Newsweek*, June 26, 1944, 34.

37. *Fortune*, October 1944, 160.

38. Richard G. Hewlett and Oscar E. Anderson Jr., *The New World, 1939–1946* (University Park, Pa., 1962), 16–22; Vincent C. Jones, *Manhattan: The Army and the Atomic Bomb* (Washington, 1985), 12–15; Richard Rhodes, *The Making of the Atomic Bomb* (New York, 1986), 303–38; Burns, *Soldier of Freedom*, 249–50; Bush, *Pieces of the Action*, 34.

39. Hewlett and Anderson, *New World*, 25; Bush, *Pieces of the Action*, 44–45, 59; Jones, *Manhattan*, 26–28; Zachary, *Endless Frontier*, 129–30; Conant, *My Several Lives*, 272–73; James G. Hershberg, *James B. Conant* (New York, 1993), 147–48.

40. Zachary, *Endless Frontier*, 196–97; Jones, *Manhattan*, 30–31; Rhodes, *Making of the Atomic Bomb*, 377–79; Alwyn McKay, *The Making of the Atomic Age* (New York, 1984), 52–61; Hewlett and Anderson, *New World*, 42–43.

41. Rhodes, *Making of the Atomic Bomb*, 374–87; Hewlett and Anderson, *New World*, 45–49; Culver and Hyde, *American Dreamer*, 267–68.

42. Zachary, *Endless Frontier*, 197; Rhodes, *Making of the Atomic Bomb*, 379; McKay, *Making of the Atomic Age*, 101.

43. Arthur C. Compton, *Atomic Quest* (New York, 1956), 69–70, 78. Compton lists the members of the original S-1 committee.

44. Hewlett and Anderson, *New World*, 52.

45. Bush, *Pieces of the Action*, 61; Zachary, *Endless Frontier*, 201; Leslie R. Groves, *Now It Can Be Told: The Story of the Manhattan Project* (New York, 1962), 10; Jones, *Manhattan*, 37–41.

46. K. D. Nichols, *The Road to Trinity* (New York, 1987), 40; Jones, *Manhattan*, 40–44; Lenore Fine and Jesse A. Remington, *The Corps of Engineers: Construction in the United States* (Washington, 1972), 651–52; Hewlett and Anderson, *New World*, 73–74; Jones, *Manhattan*, 41–44.

47. Hewlett and Anderson, *New World*, 27–35; McKay, *Making of the Atomic Age*, 1–52. McKay provides a good brief summary of the scientific background.

48. Compton, *Atomic Quest*, 87–88. Deuterium, the hydrogen isotope of atomic mass 2, was the best moderating material next to hydrogen, but both are gases. For use as a moderator it was combined with oxygen to form heavy water or with carbon to form heavy paraffin.

49. Ibid., 70–71; Conant, *My Several Lives*, 282.

50. Jones, *Manhattan*, 35–39; Nichols, *Road to Trinity*, 32; Compton, *Atomic Quest*, 75–76, 86.

51. Conant, *My Several Lives*, 285; Hewlett and Anderson, *New World*, 69–71. Murphree was director of research for the Standard Oil Development Company.

52. Compton, *Atomic Quest*, 69; Hewlett and Anderson, *New World*, 74–76; Fine and Remington, *Corps of Engineers*, 653.

53. Hewlett and Anderson, *New World*, 77–80; Nichols, *Road to Trinity*, 36–39; Groves, *Now It Can Be Told*, 11–18.

54. Hewlett and Anderson, *New World*, 81–82; Jones, *Manhattan*, 71–75; Groves, *Now It Can Be Told*, 3–4, 20.

55. Nichols, *Road to Trinity*, 107–8; Rhodes, *Making of the Atomic Bomb*, 425–26. Nichols added, "If I had to do my part of the atomic bomb project over again and had the privilege of picking my boss I would pick General Groves."

56. Stimson diary, September 23, 1942; Groves, *Now It Can Be Told*, 4–5, 20–25; Jones, *Manhattan*, 76–77; Zachary, *Endless Frontier*, 202; Jones, *Manhattan*, 73–77.

57. Groves, *Now It Can Be Told*, 24–26; Jones, *Manhattan*, 78–82; Compton, *Atomic Quest*, 154–56; Charles W. Johnson and Charles O. Jackson, *City Behind a Fence: Oak Ridge, Tennessee, 1942–1946* (Knoxville, 1981), 6–8. Estimates of the land acquired vary from 52,000 to 56,000 acres; ultimately Oak Ridge contained 59,000 acres.

58. Johnson and Jackson, *City Behind a Fence*, 14–17, 49, 168–69.

59. Ibid., 51–52; Hewlett and Anderson, *New World*, 116–19.

60. Johnson and Jackson, *City Behind a Fence*, 51–52.

61. Hewlett and Anderson, *New World*, 227; Fine and Remington, *Corps of Engineers*, 664; Groves, *Now It Can Be Told*, 61.

62. Fine and Remington, *Corps of Engineers*, 664–65; Jones, *Manhattan*, 82–85; Hewlett and Anderson, *New World*, 229–30; Groves, *Now It Can Be Told*, 64–67.

63. Fine and Remington, *Corps of Engineers*, 664–65; Jones, *Manhattan*, 85–88, 328–31; Jon Hunner, *Inventing Los Alamos: The Growth of an Atomic Community* (Norman, Okla., 2004), 29–32, 41.

64. Fine and Remington, *Corps of Engineers*, 667–68; Jones, *Manhattan*, 108–11; Groves, *Now It Can Be Told*, 41, 69–78; Hewlett and Anderson, *New World*, 188–90.

65. Groves, *Now It Can Be Told*, 82–83.

66. Hunner, *Inventing Los Alamos*, 4–5, 7, 23.

67. Ibid., 38–43; Jones, *Manhattan*, 95–101.

68. Hunner, *Inventing Los Alamos*, 43–46, 58–59; Fine and Remington, *Corps of Engineers*, 666; Hewlett and Anderson, *New World*, 106–8, 186–88; Nichols, *Road to Trinity*, 84–85; Compton, *Atomic Quest*, 132–34. For legal reasons the contract stipulated a fee of $1. After the war, DuPont sought an early release from the contract and was obliged to return 33 cents to the government.

69. Compton, *Atomic Quest*, 136–38; Rhodes, *Making of the Atomic Bomb*, 429–32.

70. Rhodes, *Making of the Atomic Bomb*, 433–36; Hewlett and Anderson, *New World*, 111–12; Enrico Fermi, *Collected Papers* (Chicago, 1962), 269–70.

71. Compton, *Atomic Quest*, 139–42; Jones, *Manhattan*, 102–4.

72. Compton, *Atomic Quest*, 142–43; Jones, *Manhattan*, 104; Rhodes, *Making of the Atomic Bomb*, 436–40. Rhodes has the fullest and best account of the day's events.

73. Compton, *Atomic Quest*, 144–45.

CHAPTER 30. DAYS OF RECKONING

1. Catton, *War Lords*, 211.

2. Stone, *War Years*, 236–37.

3. Goodwin, *No Ordinary Time*, 558.

4. Ibid., 505; Grace Tully, *F.D.R.: My Boss* (New York, 1949), 265; Roosevelt, *Public Papers and Addresses*, 13:147–52, 155.

5. Max Hastings, *Overlord: D-Day and the Battle for Normandy* (New York, 1984), 80; Strahan, *Higgins*, 220; Goodwin, *No Ordinary Time*, 505–6.

6. Goodwin, *No Ordinary Time*, 509–10; Roosevelt, *Public Papers and Addresses*, 13:154–60; Stone, *War Years*, 236.

7. Rosenman, *Working with Roosevelt*, 433; Stone, *War Years*, 236.

8. Stone, *War Years*, 236; Roosevelt, *Public Papers and Addresses*, 13:159–60.

9. Ernie Pyle, *Brave Men* (New York, 1945), 358, 360.

10. Goodwin, *No Ordinary Time*, 511; Pyle, *Brave Men*, 366–67.

11. Pyle, *Brave Men*, 367, 369.

12. Polenberg, *War and Society*, 140; Koistinen, *Arsenal of World War II*, 38–39; Kennedy, *Freedom from Fear*, 653–54; Nelson, *Arsenal of Democracy*, 237.

13. *Time*, January 10, 1944, 88.

14. Ibid., 88–90.

15. Ibid., 88.

16. *Time*, May 29, 1944, 84; *Newsweek*, June 12, 1944, 54, 56.

17. CPA, *Industrial Mobilization for War*, 737; Koistinen, *Arsenal of World War II*, 455.

18. Foster, *Kaiser*, 128; Nelson, *Arsenal of Democracy*, 391–92.

19. *Newsweek*, March 1, 1943, 24–25, 62; *Time*, September 6, 1943, 75–76, 78, 80.

20. Nelson, *Arsenal of Democracy*, 391; Catton, *War Lords*, 196, 200.

21. *Newsweek*, August 23, 1943, 50; Koistinen, *Arsenal of World War II*, 447–48; Somers, *Presidential Agency*, 175–76; Roosevelt, *Public Papers and Addresses*, 12:432–33; Flynn, *Mess in Washington*, 233.

22. Somers, *Presidential Agency*, 176, 179; Flynn, *Mess in Washington*, 234–37; *Saturday Evening Post*, November 6, 1943, 112.

23. Fairchild and Grossman, *Army and Industrial Manpower*, 120–21; *Newsweek*, November 20, 1943, 58, 61. The other five plants closed were in St. Louis, Denver, Milwaukee, Cincinnati, and Lowell, Massachusetts.

24. *Newsweek*, November 20, 1943, 61; *Saturday Evening Post*, November 6, 1943, 112.

25. Catton, *War Lords*, 214–15.

26. Ibid., 217. Emphasis is in original.

27. Nelson, *Arsenal of Democracy*, 392; Koistinen, *Arsenal of World War II*, 449, 453–54; CPA, *Industrial Mobilization for War*, 733–34.

28. Koistinen, *Arsenal of World War II*, 453–54, 458–59; Nelson, *Arsenal of Democracy*, 395–97; CPA, *Industrial Mobilization for War*, 734; Somers, *Presidential Agency*, 183–84.

29. Catton, *War Lords*, 235–36; Koistinen, *Arsenal of World War II*, 449–50, 454.

30. Budget Bureau, *United States at War*, 482; Somers, *Presidential Agency*, 176–78; Koistinen, *Arsenal of World War II*, 450–51; Baruch, *Public Years*, 331–33.

31. Roosevelt, *Public Papers and Addresses*, 13:75–79; Budget Bureau, *United States at War*, 486–87; Koistinen, *Arsenal of World War II*, 451, 462–64; Baruch, *Public Years*, 333; Nelson, *Arsenal of Democracy*, 394, 396–99; Catton, *War Lords*, 229.

32. *Newsweek*, March 13, 1944, 67; Stimson diary, March 13, 1944.

33. Stimson diary, March 22, 1944.

34. Ibid., March 27 and March 31, 1944; CPA, *Industrial Mobilization for War*, 736; Koistinen, *Arsenal of World War II*, 454–55.

35. CPA, *Industrial Mobilization for War*, 737–38; Koistinen, *Arsenal of World War II*, 455–56.

36. Koistinen, *Arsenal of World War II*, 457; Catton, *War Lords*, 245–47.

37. Catton, *War Lords*, 232–33; Koistinen, *Arsenal of World War II*, 456.

38. CPA, *Industrial Mobilization for War*, 801; Nelson, *Arsenal of Democracy*, 401–2; Budget Bureau, *United States at War*, 487; Somers, *Presidential Agency*, 186–87;

39. Nelson, *Arsenal of Democracy*, 402.

40. Ibid., 409–10; Koistinen, *Arsenal of World War II*, 473–74; CPA, *Industrial Mobilization for War*, 802–4; Budget Bureau, *United States at War*, 488; Somers, *Presidential Agency*,

187–88. Byrnes makes no mention of this episode in his chapter on reconversion in his memoirs.

41. CPA, *Industrial Mobilization for War*, 803–5; Somers, *Presidential Agency*, 187–88; Koistinen, *Arsenal of World War II*, 451, 472–73; Nelson, *Arsenal of Democracy*, 411.

42. Koistinen, *Arsenal of World War II*, 473–74; CPA, *Industrial Mobilization for War*, 805–6; Byrnes, *All in One Lifetime*, 238.

43. Koistinen, *Arsenal of World War II*, 475; Nelson, *Arsenal of Democracy*, 399; Catton, *War Lords*, 231–32. "The services simply were not open to argument," said Catton. ". . . Neither facts nor logic made any impression."

44. Nelson, *Arsenal of Democracy*, 410–11; Koistinen, *Arsenal of World War II*, 475–76.

45. Catton, *War Lords*, 262–70; CPA, *Industrial Mobilization for War*, 806–7; *Newsweek*, August 28, 1944, 64, 66.

46. Koistinen, *Arsenal of World War II*, 476. Other sources lack some of the details provided here.

47. Catton, *War Lords*, 281–82; Nelson, *Arsenal of Democracy*, 413–14; Koistinen, *Arsenal of World War II*, 476–77. Catton has the fullest account of this meeting; Nelson handles it gingerly and avoids detail. The accounts differ on some details. I have tended to follow Catton, who was apparently at the meeting.

48. Nelson, *Arsenal of Democracy*, 414–15. See also Stimson diary, August 24, 1944, for his version of events and dislike of Nelson.

49. Roosevelt, *Public Papers and Addresses*, 13:302–7; Somers, *Presidential Agency*, 76–78.

50. Catton, *War Lords*, 284, 286; *Time*, October 9, 1944, 17.

51. Nelson, *Arsenal of Democracy*, 402–3; Koistinen, *Arsenal of World War II*, 392.

52. Nelson, *Arsenal of Democracy*, 403–5.

53. CPA, *Industrial Mobilization for War*, 844–45.

54. *Newsweek*, March 13, 1944, 66–67; *Time*, September 4, 1944, 78.

55. CPA, *Industrial Mobilization for War*, 837–41; Fairchild and Grossman, *Army and Industrial Manpower*, 179–96.

56. *Saturday Evening Post*, September 6, 1943, 16–17; *Time*, June 21, 1943, 36.

57. Ibid.

58. *Time*, March 27, 1944, 65; Stimson diary, February 18, 1944.

59. Stimson diary, February 18, March 10, and March 13, 1944; Roosevelt, *Public Papers and Addresses*, 13:89–90; Eiler, *Mobilizing America*, 397–98; Budget Bureau, *United States at War*, 447–48.

60. Stimson diary, March 13, 1944; CPA, *Industrial Mobilization for War*, 845; Eiler, *Mobilizing America*, 398; *Time*, March 27, 1944, 65.

61. CPA, *Industrial Mobilization for War*, 845–46; *Newsweek*, March 6, 1944, 48; Eiler, *Mobilizing America*, 399.

62. *Time*, March 27, 1944, 65; Stimson diary, March 13 and March 15, 1944; *Newsweek*, March 27, 1944, 42.

63. Eiler, *Mobilizing America*, 399; CPA, *Industrial Mobilization for War*, 846–47; Budget Bureau, *United States at War*, 448–49; Stimson diary, March 22 and March 24, 1944.

64. Stimson diary, March 27, 1944; Budget Bureau, *United States at War*, 449; Somers, *Presidential Agency*, 161–64; *Time*, April 10, 1944, 18; CPA, *Industrial Mobilization for War*, 846–47. The latter source lists the industries defined as critical.

65. Somers, *Presidential Agency*, 158, 163–64.

66. *Time*, April 10, 1944, 18; *Saturday Evening Post*, May 13, 1944, 112. Bard replaced Forrestal as undersecretary when the latter replaced Knox as secretary.

67. *Time*, May 22, 1944, 66.

68. *Time*, June 12, 1941, 14; Somers, *Presidential Agency*, 154–57; CPA, *Industrial Mobilization for War*, 844–45, 848–53. The last two sources contain details on the directive's contents and the struggle that followed.

69. *Newsweek*, December 18, 1944, 40, 42.

CHAPTER 31. LIFE IN THE DAYS OF

1. O'Neill, *Democracy at War*, 247.

2. *Look*, May 5, 1942, 44.

3. *Saturday Evening Post*, April 3, 1943, 104.

4. *Time*, July 26, 1943, 25.

5. This profile is drawn from *Look*, May 5, 1942, 44–49. Mrs. Winnebald's first name was never given.

6. This profile is drawn from *Look*, June 15, 1943, 25–28.

7. *Look*, December 14, 1943, 23–25.

8. *Look*, January 26, 1943, 21; *Time*, December 21, 1942, 23.

9. *Look*, January 26, 1943, 20–23, and October 19, 1943, 14, 16, 18; *Time*, November 23, 1942, 25, November 30, 1942, 24, and December 27, 1943, 63; *Fortune*, February 1943, 99; *Saturday Evening Post*, April 29, 1944, 12.

10. *Saturday Evening Post*, April 29, 1943, 12; *Harper's*, September 1943, 289–91.

11. *Harper's*, September 1943, 290–93.

12. Ibid., 293–95.

13. Ibid., 295–96.

14. *Saturday Evening Post*, December 25, 1943, 22–23, 58–59.

15. Ibid., 59.

16. This profile is drawn from *Fortune*, July 1944, 248.

17. Wilcox, *Farmer in the Second World War*, 76.

18. This profile is drawn from *Saturday Evening Post*, August 12, 1944, 24–25, 90–91.

19. *Time*, May 8, 1944, 12.

20. Polenberg, *War and Society*, 171–72.

21. *Time*, April 24, 1944, 79, and May 8, 1944, 12–13; Stimson diary, April 14, 1944; Seidman, *American Labor*, 105–6, 147.

22. Stimson diary, April 14, April 29, and May 2, 1944; *Newsweek*, May 8, 1944, 66; *Time*, April 24, 1944, 79. The April 14 entry includes Stimson's memo to Byrnes; the April 29 entry has Byrnes's reply.

23. Stimson diary, April 14, April 29, and May 1, 1944; Roosevelt, *Public Papers and Addresses*, 13:122–25, 452–53.

24. *Newsweek*, May 8, 1944, 62, 64, 66; *Time*, May 8, 1944, 11–12; Seidman, *American Labor*, 147–48.

25. *Newsweek*, May 8, 1944, 70, and May 22, 1944, 68, 70; *Time*, May 15, 1944, 11–12; Stimson diary, May 22, 1944.

26. Hassett, *Off the Record*, 245.

27. This section is drawn from *Saturday Evening Post*, May 6, 1944, 34, 102.

28. *Newsweek*, December 6, 1943, 64, 66.

29. Ibid.

30. *Newsweek*, August 2, 1943, 63.

31. Except where indicated, this section is drawn from *Saturday Evening Post*, October 10, 1942, 20–21, 105–6.

32. *Saturday Evening Post*, April 10, 1943, 24, 82–83.

33. *Time*, March 20, 1944, 22; *Newsweek*, November 9, 1942, 27–29.

34. *Time*, April 12, 1943, 25; *Newsweek*, April 12, 1943, 44, and May 8, 1944, 31.

35. *Time*, March 20, 1944, 66, 68.

36. *Look*, June 1, 1943, 21–25.

37. *Time*, August 17, 1942, 58; *Newsweek*, September 7, 1942, 46–47.

38. *Time*, August 31, 1942, 47.

39. "Death on the Working Front," *Fortune*, July 1942, 1. This was a supplement to the regular issue of *Fortune*.

40. *Harper's*, November 1942, 602–3; *Time*, November 9, 1942, 57–58; *Newsweek*, November 9, 1942, 62.

41. *Newsweek*, September 7, 1942, 47, and August 23, 1943, 46; *Time*, April 26, 1943, 46, *Time*, November 22, 1943, 90, 93.

42. *Newsweek*, October 16, 1944, 74, 77–78.

43. Ibid.; *Saturday Evening Post*, January 27, 1945, 34.

44. *Saturday Evening Post*, January 27, 1945, 34, 39, 41–42.

45. Ibid.

46. *Time*, October 26, 1942, 104, June 7, 1943, 68–69, August 30, 1943, 44, 46, and May 15, 1944, 61–62, 64, 66, 68; *Newsweek*, August 30, 1943, 68, 70. The May 15 *Time* article has a good summary of the historical development of penicillin. For Walt Disney's marvelous illustrated explanation of sulfa drugs, see *Look*, April 4, 1944, 38–39.

47. *Time*, May 15, 1944, 61–62, 64, 66, 68.

48. *Newsweek*, August 30, 1943, 68, 70, December 27, 1943, 16, September 4, 1944, 20, and March 26, 1945, 93; *Time*, May 15, 1944, 61–62, 64, 66, 68, and February 26, 1945, 58.

49. *Newsweek*, January 5, 1942, 45–47, May 15, 1944, 71–72, and June 12, 1944, 96; *Time*, May 15, 1944, 44, August 7, 1944, 66, and January 29, 1945, 66.

50. *Time*, August 23, 1943, 66, 68, August 14, 1944, 56, September 4, 1944, 71, and September 25, 1944, 44; *Newsweek*, July 24, 1944, 78.

CHAPTER 32. THE SWEET SCENT OF VICTORY

1. *Time*, July 17, 1944, 17.

2. Clapper, *Watching the World*, 68.

3. *Time*, July 24, 1944, 18.

4. Wilcox, *Farmer in the Second World War*, 279; *Time*, December 18, 1944, 20; Koistinen, *Arsenal of World War II*, 481; CPA, *Industrial Mobilization for War*, 743.

5. *Harper's*, June 1944, 1; *Time*, July 17, 1944, 17–18.

6. *Harper's*, June 1944, 10.

7. *Saturday Evening Post*, September 30, 1944, 17, 109–10.

8. *Look*, January 11, 1944, 15, and January 9, 1945, 21; *Time*, May 15, 1944, 14; *Newsweek*,

March 6, 1944, 74, 76, May 29, 1944, 59, and September 25, 1944, 69; *Fortune*, May 1944, 58; *Harper's*, May 1944, 541.

9. *Harper's*, May 1944, 542–43; *Saturday Evening Post*, May 20, 1944, 112; *Newsweek*, May 29, 1944, 56; *Time*, July 31, 1944, 79.

10. *Saturday Evening Post*, September 9, 1944, 112; *Newsweek*, October 2, 1944, 72, October 9, 1944, 68, 70, and December 4, 1944, 22.

11. The Walls' story is drawn from *Time*, August 14, 1944, 81–82, 84.

12. Adams, *Mr. Kaiser Goes to Washington*, 156; Blum, *V Was for Victory*, 221, 260–61.

13. Blum, *V Was for Victory*, 260–61; Roosevelt, *Public Papers and Addresses*, 13:180–85; Goodwin, *No Ordinary Time*, 512; *Time*, April 3, 1944, 23–24.

14. Blum, *V Was for Victory*, 222, 250.

15. Ibid., 250–52; Roosevelt, *Public Papers and Addresses*, 13:111–16. The latter source includes a detailed explanation of the two bills by Rosenman. The struggle in Congress can be followed in detail in Drury, *Senate Journal*, 15–112.

16. Clapper, *Watching the World*, 176, 183.

17. Goodwin, *No Ordinary Time*, 516–21, 524; Hassett, *Off the Record*, 260–61; Smith, *Thank You, Mr. President*, 145–46; *Newsweek*, July 24, 1944, 39–40.

18. Drury, *Senate Journal*, 216; Neal, *Dark Horse*, 299–307.

19. Rosenman, *Working with Roosevelt*, 463–70; Neal, *Dark Horse*, 308–21; Hassett, *Off the Record*, 276; *Newsweek*, October 16, 1944, 38, 40; *Time*, October 16, 1944, 21–25.

20. Rosenman, *Working with Roosevelt*, 444–45; David McCullough, *Truman* (New York, 1992), 299–300.

21. Rosenman, *Working with Roosevelt*, 444–51; McCullough, *Truman*, 300–304; Culver and Hyde, *American Dreamer*, 356–66; Drury, *Senate Journal*, 219–21; Josephson, *Hillman*, 615–25; *Newsweek*, July 31, 1944, 25–28. The accounts of Rosenman and McCullough as to Roosevelt's view of Truman differ sharply.

22. Josephson, *Hillman*, 615; Drury, *Senate Journal*, 220.

23. Josephson, *Hillman*, 594–600, 607; Zieger, *CIO*, 177–81; Lingeman, *Don't You Know*, 347; *Saturday Evening Post*, August 26, 1944, 23, 98.

24. Josephson, *Hillman*, 618, 626–28; *Time*, July 24, 1944, 18–20; *Saturday Evening Post*, August 26, 1944, 100.

25. Josephson, *Hillman*, 629; *Newsweek*, June 12, 1944, 30–31; *Kiplinger Letter*, 75; *Time*, May 29, 1944, 20, and July 24, 1944, 18–20; *Look*, September 5, 1944, 74.

26. *Saturday Evening Post*, August 26, 1944, 22–23, 98–102; Rosenman, *Working with Roosevelt*, 471.

27. Rosenman, *Working with Roosevelt*, 455–59; Goodwin, *No Ordinary Time*, 532–33. For a calendar of Roosevelt's schedule, see Hassett, *Off the Record*, 264–65.

28. Rosenman, *Working with Roosevelt*, 453, 459–62; Goodwin, *No Ordinary Time*, 534–37; Hassett, *Off the Record*, 265.

29. Hassett, *Off the Record*, 265–68; *Time*, August 28, 1944, 16; Goodwin, *No Ordinary Time*, 541–45.

30. Hassett, *Off the Record*, 270–72; Goodwin, *No Ordinary Time*, 545–47; Rosenman, *Working with Roosevelt*, 472.

31. Hassett, *Off the Record*, 87; Sherwood, *Roosevelt and Hopkins*, 829; Smith, *Thank You, Mr. President*, 145.

32. Rosenman, *Working with Roosevelt*, 472–74; Goodwin, *No Ordinary Time*, 546–47.

33. Rosenman, *Working with Roosevelt*, 473–77; Goodwin, *No Ordinary Time*, 547–48; Smith, *Thank You, Mr. President*, 154–55.

34. Hassett, *Off the Record*, 273, 278; Rosenman, *Working with Roosevelt*, 478–82; Smith, *Thank You, Mr. President*, 155.

35. Smith, *Thank You, Mr. President*, 155–56; Hassett, *Off the Record*, 278–82; Rosenman, *Working with Roosevelt*, 482–86; Goodwin, *No Ordinary Time*, 549–51.

36. Smith, *Thank You, Mr. President*, 156; Hassett, *Off the Record*, 282–86; Rosenman, *Working with Roosevelt*, 486–98; Sherwood, *Roosevelt and Hopkins*, 828; *Newsweek*, October 23, 1944, 40, 42; *Time*, November 6, 1944, 17–18.

37. Hassett, *Off the Record*, 287; Strahan, *Higgins*, 238.

38. Hassett, *Off the Record*, 290; Smith, *Thank You, Mr. President*, 145; Rosenman, *Working with Roosevelt*, 493–505; Blum, *V Was for Victory*, 294–98; Sherwood, *Roosevelt and Hopkins*, 823–24.

39. Hassett, *Off the Record*, 270, 277; *Time*, November 13, 1944, 19–20, and November 20, 1944, 20; *Newsweek*, November 13, 1944, 2–5; Joseph Nathan Kane, *Facts About the Presidents* (New York, 1989), 198.

40. Hassett, *Off the Record*, 293–94.

41. *Time*, November 20, 1944, 20–21; Roosevelt, *Personal Letters*, 1557.

42. *Newsweek*, June 15, 1942, 54, February 22, 1943, 63, 65, March 1, 1943, 12, March 15, 1943, 67, and May 24, 1943, 58, 60, 62; *Fortune*, December 1942, 126; *Time*, May 24, 1944, 85. Stocks selling under $5 a share were deemed cats and dogs.

43. *Time*, July 12, 1943, 77, September 20, 1943, 79, November 15, 1943, 79, and March 20, 1944, 79.

44. *Time*, June 12, 1944, 85–86, and June 26, 1944, 86; *Newsweek*, July 17, 1944, 12.

45. Conant, *My Several Lives*, 297.

46. Bush, *Pieces of the Action*, 133.

47. Woodbury, *Battlefronts of Industry*, 292–93.

48. Ibid., 299–302.

49. Ibid., 302–6; Hewlett and Anderson, *New World*, 87–88.

50. Woodbury, *Battlefronts of Industry*, 306–12.

51. Jones, *Manhattan*, 117–19; Nichols, *Road to Trinity*, 42.

52. Nichols, *Road to Trinity*, 42.

53. Ibid. 42, 85–90; Groves, *Now It Can Be Told*, 107–9; Jones, *Manhattan*, 126–40; Hewlett and Anderson, *New World*, 152–54; Rhodes, *Making of the Atomic Bomb*, 487–90. After recovery, only .035 of 1 percent of the silver was lost.

54. McKay, *Making of the Atomic Age*, 71–73; Jones, *Manhattan*, 52–53; Nichols, *Road to Trinity*, 131.

55. Nichols, *Road to Trinity*, 131.

56. Hewlett and Anderson, *New World*, 30–32, 96–98, 120, 155–67; Jones, *Manhattan*, 142–48; Rhodes, *Making of the Atomic Bomb*, 492–94; Groves, *Now It Can Be Told*, 111; Nichols, *Road to Trinity*, 90. A good photograph of the Alpha I racetrack is in Hewlett and Anderson, *New World*, opposite p. 163.

57. Jones, *Manhattan*, 154–71; Hewlett and Anderson, *New World*, 120–41; Rhodes, *Making of the Atomic Bomb*, 493–96; Groves, *Now It Can Be Told*, 111–19; McKay, *Making of the Atomic Age*, 73–76; Nichols, *Road to Trinity*, 90–98.

58. Hewlett and Anderson, *New World*, 168–72; Groves, *Now It Can Be Told*, 119–20; Rhodes, *Making of the Atomic Bomb*, 552–53.

59. Groves, *Now It Can Be Told*, 120–23; Hewlett and Anderson, *New World*, 172–73; Jones, *Manhattan*, 171–83.

60. Groves, *Now It Can Be Told*, 54–55.

61. Hewlett and Anderson, *New World*, 190–91, 200–201, 207–10; Nichols, *Road to Trinity*, 77–79; Jones, *Manhattan*, 204–8; Compton, *Atomic Quest*, 184; McKay, *Making of the Atomic Age*, 86. The original pile at Stagg Field was shut down and its components used in a new, larger pile at Argonne.

62. Groves, *Now It Can Be Told*, 41, 78–82; Hewlett and Anderson, *New World*, 193–98; Rhodes, *Making of the Atomic Bomb*, 497–98; Nichols, *Road to Trinity*, 133–34.

63. Hewlett and Anderson, *New World*, 214–26; Rhodes, *Making of the Atomic Bomb*, 499–500; Groves, *Now It Can Be Told*, 78–93; Nichols, *Road to Trinity*, 136.

64. Hewlett and Anderson, *New World*, 226; Nichols, *Road to Trinity*, 102.

65. Hewlett and Anderson, *New World*, 304–8; Compton, *Atomic Quest*, 191–92; Rhodes, *Making of the Atomic Bomb*, 556–60; Nichols, *Road to Trinity*, 140–41.

66. *Time*, October 30, 1944, 85.

67. Blum, *V Was for Victory*, 98; *Newsweek*, December 11, 1944, 70, 72.

68. *Time*, February 21, 1944, 79; *Newsweek*, November 8, 1943, 67–68.

69. *Time*, November 27, 1944, 21–22; Blum, *V Was for Victory*, 98.

70. Blum, *V Was for Victory*, 95–97.

71. Ibid., 99–100; Philip Wylie, *Generation of Vipers* (New York, 1942), 223; *Look*, June 16, 1942, 21; *Saturday Evening Post*, August 1, 1942, front ad. Every major magazine abounds with other examples.

72. *Newsweek*, July 20, 1944, 72, and November 30, 1942, 27; *Time*, August 3, 1942, 10, August 31, 1942, 14, and November 9, 1942, 9; *Look*, August 25, 1942, 5, 7; *Saturday Evening Post*, October 24, 1942, front ad, September 26, 1942, front ad, October 31, 1942, front ad, and January 30, 1943, 2. Emphasis is in the original.

73. *Time*, March 22, 1943, 68, and February 7, 1944, 94; *Saturday Evening Post*, April 24, 1943, 3; *Look*, February 23, 1943, 2, and November 30, 1943, 5. Emphasis is in the original.

74. *Newsweek*, March 20, 1944, 56, and April 10, 1944, 9; *Saturday Evening Post*, October 21, 1944, 74; *Look*, December 26, 1944, 2. Emphasis is in the original.

75. Hastings, *Armageddon*, 198–237, describes the battle in good detail. The quotation is from p. 199.

76. Stimson diary, November 30, December 13, December 17, and December 20, 1944.

77. Eiler, *Mobilizing America*, 413; CPA, *Industrial Mobilization for War*, 719; *Newsweek*, December 18, 1944, 66, 68, and December 25, 1944, 56; *Time*, January 8, 1945, 72–74, 76.

78. Hassett, *Off the Record*, 299–308.

79. *Newsweek*, January 8, 1945, 56; Roosevelt, *Public Papers and Addresses*, 13:452–53; Stimson diary, December 20, 1944; Roosevelt, *Personal Letters*, 1563–64.

80. Stimson diary, December 22, 1944; Roosevelt, *Public Papers and Addresses*, 13:446–52.

81. *Newsweek*, January 8, 1945, 56, 58; *Time*, January 8, 1945, 14; Roosevelt, *Public Papers and Addresses*, 13:453.

82. *Newsweek*, September 18, 1944, 79, September 25, 1944, 66, 68, and November 27,

1944, 68, 70; *Time*, September 18, 1944, 15–16, October 23, 1944, 18, and November 13, 1944, 25; Byrnes, *All in One Lifetime*, 248; Johnson and Jackson, *City Behind a Fence*, 177, 179.

83. *Time*, November 13, 1944, 25.

CHAPTER 33. THE FEAR OF FALTERING

1. Stimson diary, January 15, 1945.
2. Hassett, *Off the Record*, 280.
3. Smith, *Thank You, Mr. President*, 175.
4. Hastings, *Armageddon*, 222–23; Byrnes, *All in One Lifetime*, 246; *Time*, March 19, 1945, 77–78.
5. Stimson diary, January 5, 1945; *Newsweek*, December 18, 1944, 40, 42; *Time*, January 18, 1945, 15, and January 29, 1945, 21–22.
6. Stimson diary, December 20, December 22, and December 31, 1944; Byrnes, *All in One Lifetime*, 250; *Time*, January 15, 1945, 19.
7. Roosevelt, *Public Papers and Addresses*, 13:483–517; *Newsweek*, January 15, 1945, 62, 64. The first reference includes the text of a radio address Roosevelt gave at 10:00 P.M. that same evening giving the essence of his message.
8. Stimson diary, January 5, 1945; Hassett, *Off the Record*, 306; Byrnes, *All in One Lifetime*, 250–51; *Newsweek*, January 1, 1945, 31–32, and March 26, 1945, 44; *Time*, January 1, 1945, 11.
9. *Newsweek*, March 5, 1945, 40, 42, and March 26, 1945, 44, 46; *Time*, March 5, 1945, 18; and March 26, 1945, 17–18; *New York Times*, March 14, 1945; Byrnes, *All in One Lifetime*, 251.
10. Byrnes, *All in One Lifetime*, 251; *Time*, March 26, 1945, 17.
11. *Time*, March 26, 1945, 17.
12. Stimson diary, November 27 and December 12, 1944; Sherwood, *Roosevelt and Hopkins*, 835–36; *Fortune*, March 1945, 109; *Time*, December 4, 1944, 17, and December 11, 1945, 19–23.
13. Goodwin, *No Ordinary Time*, 570–71.
14. Ibid., 572; Rosenman, *Working with Roosevelt*, 516–17; Hassett, *Off the Record*, 312; *Newsweek*, January 15, 1945, 30.
15. Rosenman, *Working with Roosevelt*, 517; Drury, *Senate Journal*, 344; Hassett, *Off the Record*, 313.
16. Culver and Hyde, *American Dreamer*, 372–79; Jones, *Fifty Billion Dollars*, 508–10.
17. Goodwin, *No Ordinary Time*, 575; Stimson diary, January 22, 1945; Drury, *Senate Journal*, 345–51; *Newsweek*, February 5, 1945, 38.
18. Eiler, *Mobilizing America*, 418–19; Drury, *Senate Journal*, 345–51, 363; Stimson diary, January 10 and January 15, 1945.
19. Eiler, *Mobilizing America*, 417; Stimson diary, January 15, 1945; Drury, *Senate Journal*, 356–406.
20. Eiler, *Mobilizing America*, 419; Drury, *Senate Journal*, 360.
21. Stimson diary, January 15, February 13, February 15, and February 18, 1945; *Newsweek*, February 26, 1945, 52, 54; *Time*, February 26, 1945, 16–17; Drury, *Senate Journal*, 365.
22. Drury, *Senate Journal*, 356–61, 366–670; Stimson diary, February 22, 1945; *Newsweek*, March 19, 1945, 48; Eiler, *Mobilizing America*, 419–20.
23. *Time*, April 16, 1945, 21–22; Drury, *Senate Journal*, 369–87, 392–406.
24. *Newsweek*, March 12, 1945, 72; *Time*, March 12, 1945, 24.
25. Thomson and Mayo, *Ordnance Department*, 144.

26. Ibid., 144–46.

27. Ibid., 146–50.

28. *Newsweek*, March 5, 1945, 68, 70, and March 12, 1945, 70, 72; *Time*, March 12, 1945, 23, and April 9, 1945, 18.

29. Koistinen, *Arsenal of World War II*, 265.

30. *Time*, March 12, 1945, 23–24; *Newsweek*, March 12, 1945, 70.

31. *Newsweek*, March 12, 1945, 73–74.

32. *Newsweek*, March 19, 1945, 72, 74.

33. Catton, *War Lords*, 295–97.

34. *Look*, July 25, 1944, 21–27.

35. Ibid.

36. *Newsweek*, March 12, 1945, 50; Rosenman, *Working with Roosevelt*, 523–24; Hassett, *Off the Record*, 316.

37. Rosenman, *Working with Roosevelt*, 522, 524; Hassett, *Off the Record*, 316–17.

38. Goodwin, *No Ordinary Time*, 585.

39. *Newsweek*, January 1, 1945, 30–31; *Look*, January 23, 1945, 28–29; *Fortune*, March 1945, 109–19; *Time*, January 8, 1945, 13.

40. Rosenman, *Working with Roosevelt*, 527–28; Goodwin, *No Ordinary Time*, 586.

41. Goodwin, *No Ordinary Time*, 586; Drury, *Senate Journal*, 371.

42. Drury, *Senate Journal*, 373; Hassett, *Off the Record*, 318–19.

43. Stimson diary, March 1 and March 3, 1945; Rosenman, *Working with Roosevelt*, 527, 539.

44. Rosenman, *Working with Roosevelt*, 539–40.

45. Stimson diary, March 15, 1945.

46. Jones, *Manhattan*, 503; McKay, *Making of the Atomic Age*, 92–93; Hewlett and Anderson, *New World*, 227–39.

47. Compton, *Atomic Quest*, 212–13.

48. Jones, *Manhattan*, 503–4; Hewlett and Anderson, *New World*, 245, 312; McKay, *Making of the Atomic Age*, 97; Rhodes, *Making of the Atomic Bomb*, 486–87; Conant, *My Several Lives*, 292–93.

49. Rhodes, *Making of the Atomic Bomb*, 466–67.

50. Ibid., 479; Hewlett and Anderson, *New World*, 245, 250; McKay, *Making of the Atomic Age*, 95; Lillian Hoddeson, Paul W. Henriksen, Roger A. Meade, and Catherine Westfall, *Critical Assembly: A Technical History of Los Alamos During the Oppenheimer Years, 1943–1945* (New York, 1993), 111–28.

51. Hewlett and Anderson, *New World*, 246; Jones, *Manhattan*, 506; Hoddeson et al., *Critical Assembly*, 129–31.

52. Hoddeson et al., *Critical Assembly*, 130–32; Rhodes, *Making of the Atomic Bomb*, 107, 479–80.

53. Rhodes, *Making of the Atomic Bomb*, 480.

54. Hoddeson et al., *Critical Assembly*, 133–40; Conant, *My Several Lives*, 293; Hewlett and Anderson, *New World*, 247–48; Jones, *Manhattan*, 506–7; Rhodes, *Making of the Atomic Bomb*, 542.

55. Rhodes, *Making of the Atomic Bomb*, 542–43, 546.

56. Hewlett and Anderson, *New World*, 247–49; Hoddeson et al., *Critical Assembly*, 133–45; Jones, *Manhattan*, 507–8; Rhodes, *Making of the Atomic Bomb*, 573–77.

57. Hewlett and Anderson, *New World*, 251–52; McKay, *Making of the Atomic Age*, 96–97;

Jones, *Manhattan*, 508–9; Hoddeson et al., *Critical Assembly*, 228–44. The meeting, led by Conant, included Oppenheimer, Compton, Fermi, Groves, Nichols, and Charles A. Thomas, the coordinator of active material purification research.

58. Hewlett and Anderson, *New World*, 252–53; Jones, *Manhattan*, 509.

59. Hewlett and Anderson, *New World*, 310–11; Hoddeson et al., *Critical Assembly*, 245–48.

60. Rhodes, *Making of the Atomic Bomb*, 570.

61. Ibid., 573–77; Hewlett and Anderson, *New World*, 318–19; Hoddeson et al., *Critical Assembly*, 293–97.

62. Hoddeson et al., *Critical Assembly*, 249–55.

63. Ibid., 249–58; Hewlett and Anderson, *New World*, 317–18; Rhodes, *Making of the Atomic Bomb*, 571–72.

64. *Life*, March 6, 1945, 96, 100, 108; Goodwin, *No Ordinary Time*, 588–89; Hassett, *Off the Record*, 323–24.

65. Goodwin, *No Ordinary Time*, 595–97; Hassett, *Off the Record*, 326.

66. Hassett, *Off the Record*, 327; Tully, *F.D.R.*, 356; Goodwin, *No Ordinary Time*, 598.

67. Goodwin, *No Ordinary Time*, 598–99; Hassett, *Off the Record*, 327–28.

68. Hassett, *Off the Record*, 328–29.

69. Ibid., 329.

70. Ibid., 330–32; Smith, *Thank You, Mr. President*, 186.

71. Blum, *Years of War*, 416–19.

72. Hassett, *Off the Record*, 333–34; Burns, *Soldier of Freedom*, 599–600; Goodwin, *No Ordinary Time*, 601–2.

73. This scene is drawn from Burns, *Soldier of Freedom*, 600–601; Goodwin, *No Ordinary Time*, 602–3; Hassett, *Off the Record*, 335–36.

74. Smith, *Thank You, Mr. President*, 178–83.

75. Goodwin, *No Ordinary Time*, 603–4; *Time*, April 23, 1945, 21–23; Drury, *Senate Journal*, 410; Harry S. Truman, *Memoirs: Year of Decisions* (Garden City, N.Y., 1955), 4–6.

76. Stimson diary, April 12, 1945; Truman, *Year of Decisions*, 7–8; *Newsweek*, April 23, 1945, 26–27.

77. Goodwin, *No Ordinary Time*, 605; Burns, *Soldier of Freedom*, 601.

78. Drury, *Senate Journal*, 412.

79. Burns, *Soldier of Freedom*, 612.

80. Hassett, *Off the Record*, 338–41; Smith, *Thank You, Mr. President*, 189–98; Burns, *Soldier of Freedom*, 601–12; Goodwin, *No Ordinary Time*, 611–13; Stimson diary, April 14, 1945.

81. Sherwood, *Roosevelt and Hopkins*, 880–81. Emphasis is in original.

82. Smith, *Thank You, Mr. President*, 199; Hassett, *Off the Record*, 343–46; Truman, *Year of Decisions*, 35–36; Goodwin, *No Ordinary Time*, 615; Stimson diary, April 14, 1945.

83. Hassett, *Off the Record*, 343–46; Goodwin, *No Ordinary Time*, 615.

84. Hassett, *Off the Record*, 347.

85. Stimson to Eleanor Roosevelt, April 16, 1945, in Stimson diary, April 16, 1945.

EPILOGUE: THE PAYOFF

1. Kennedy, *Freedom from Fear*, 615.

2. Judy Barrett Litoff and David C. Smith, eds., *Since You Went Away* (New York, 1991), 276–77.

3. Ibid., 279.

4. *Time*, April 23, 1945, 21–23.

5. Stimson diary, April 6–11, 1945.

6. Ibid., April 18, April 20–22, and April 25, 1945. The memorandum can be found with the April 25 entry.

7. McCullough, *Truman*, 376–78; Stimson memorandum, April 25, 1945, in Stimson diary of that date.

8. Stimson diary, April 25, 1945; Truman, *Year of Decisions*, 87; McCullough, *Truman*, 377–78; Rhodes, *Making of the Atomic Bomb*, 623–26.

9. Truman, *Year of Decisions*, 146; McCullough, *Truman*, 363.

10. McCullough, *Truman*, 364.

11. Ibid.

12. Truman, *Year of Decisions*, 321–28; McCullough, *Truman*, 357; Kane, *Facts About the Presidents*, 209; *Look*, August 21, 1945, 44–45.

13. Groves, *Now It Can Be Told*, 263–64; Stimson diary, May 2, May 7, and May 8, 1945; Truman, *Year of Decisions*, 199–206; *Time*, May 14, 1945, 17–22.

14. *Newsweek*, April 9, 1945, 38, 40–41, May 14, 1945, 45, and May 21, 1945, 33–38; *Time*, May 21, 1945, 17; *Fortune*, June 1945, 117–21, 275, 277, 279, 281.

15. Rhodes, *Making of the Atomic Bomb*, 591–96.

16. Ibid., 597–600.

17. Ibid., 596; Birdsall, *Saga of the Superfortress*, 263–64.

18. This story is told in absorbing detail in Rhodes, *Making of the Atomic Bomb*, 651–78.

19. Ibid., 672.

20. Ibid., 673–78.

21. Ibid., 678, 699–711.

22. Ibid., 710–11; *Newsweek*, August 13, 1945, 30, 33.

23. Rhodes, *Making of the Atomic Bomb*, 736–40.

24. Ibid., 733–46; *Newsweek*, August 20, 1945, 19–21. For comparative figures on the casualties and discussion of the differences, see Jones, *Manhattan*, 545–48.

25. *Saturday Evening Post*, August 4, 1945, 20, 109–10.

26. Ibid.

27. Litoff and Smith, *Since You Went Away*, 267. Emphasis is in the original.

28. For photographs of the cars and transports on the Willow Run assembly line, see the photo insert in Foster, *Kaiser*.

29. Litoff and Smith, *Since You Went Away*, 272–73.

BIBLIOGRAPHY

GENERAL

Adams, Michael C. C. *The Best War Ever: America and World War II* (Baltimore, 1994).

Baldwin, Hanson. *The Crucial Years: 1939–1941* (New York, 1976).

Basch, Antonin. *The New Economic Warfare* (New York, 1941).

Blum, John Morton. *V Was for Victory* (New York, 1976).

Boyan, Edwin. *Handbook of War Production* (New York, 1942).

Brokaw, Tom. *The Greatest Generation* (New York, 1998).

Buchanan, A. Russell. *The United States in World War II.* 2 vols. (New York, 1964).

Burnham, James. *The Managerial Revolution* (New York, 1941).

Catton, Bruce. *The War Lords of Washington* (New York, 1948).

Clive, Alan. *State of War: Michigan in World War II* (Ann Arbor, 1976).

Darman, Peter. *World War II: Stats and Facts* (New York, 2009).

Dear, I. C. B. *The Oxford Companion to the Second World War* (New York, 1995).

Divine, Robert. *Reluctant Belligerent: American Entry into World War II* (New York, 1987).

Dobson, Alan P. *US Wartime Aid to Britain, 1940–1946* (New York, 1986).

Ellis, John. *World War II: A Statistical Survey* (New York, 1993).

Finney, Burnham. *Arsenal of Democracy: How Industry Builds Our Defense* (New York, 1941).

Gregory, Ross. *America 1941: A Nation at the Crossroads* (New York, 1989).

Gropman, Alan, ed. *The Big "L": American Logistics in World War II* (Washington, 1997).

Hastings, Max. *Overlord: D-Day and the Battle for Normandy* (New York, 1984).

Herman, Arthur. *Freedom's Forge: How American Business Produced Victory in World War II* (New York, 2012).

Hooks, Gregory. *Forging the Industrial-Military Complex: World War II's Battle of the Potomac* (Urbana, Ill., 1991).

Hounshell, David. *From the American System to Mass Production, 1800–1932* (Baltimore, 1984).

Janeway, Eliot. *Struggle for Survival* (New Haven, 1951).

Jeffries, John W. *Wartime America: The World War II Home Front* (Chicago, 1986).

Kennedy, David M. *Freedom from Fear* (New York, 1999).

Ketchum, Richard M. *The Borrowed Years, 1938–1941: America on the Way to War* (New York, 1989).

Kimball, Warren F. *The Most Unsordid Act: Lend-Lease, 1939–1941* (Baltimore, 1969).

Kiplinger, W. M. *Washington Is Like That* (New York, 1942).

Kiplinger Washington Editors. *Kiplinger's Looking Ahead: 70 Years of Forecasts from the Kiplinger Washington Letter* (Washington, 1993).

Klingaman, William K. *1941* (New York, 1988).

Koistinen, Paul A. C. *Planning War, Pursuing Peace: The Political Economy of American Warfare, 1920–1939* (Lawrence, Kans., 1998).

———. *Arsenal of World War II: The Political Economy of American Warfare, 1939–1945* (Lawrence, Kans., 2004).

Lacey, Jim. *Keep from All Thoughtful Men: How U.S. Economists Won World War II* (Annapolis, 2011).

Langer, William L., and S. Everett Gleason. *The Undeclared War, 1940–1941* (New York, 1953).

Maddox, Robert F. *The War Within World War II: The United States and International Cartels* (Westport, Conn., 2001).

Milward, Alan S. *War, Economy, and Society* (Berkeley, 1977).

Nash, Gerald D. *The American West Transformed: The Impact of the Second World War* (Bloomington, 1985).

———. *World War II and the West: Reshaping the Economy* (Lincoln, Neb., 1990).

Novick, David, Melvin Anshen, and W. C. Truppner. *Wartime Production Controls* (New York, 1949).

O'Neill, William L. *A Democracy at War: America's Fight at Home and Abroad in World War II* (New York, 1993).

Overy, Richard. *Why the Allies Won* (New York, 1995).

Phillips, Cabell. *The 1940s: Decade of Triumph and Trouble* (New York, 1975).

Pyle, Ernie. *Brave Men* (New York, 1944).

Schlesinger, Arthur M., Jr. *The Age of Roosevelt: The Politics of Upheaval* (Boston, 1960), vol. 3.

Sparrow, Bartholomew H. *From the Outside In: World War II and the American State* (Princeton, 1996).

Speer, Albert. *Inside the Third Reich* (New York, 1970).

Stein, Arthur A. *The Nation at War* (Baltimore, 1980).

Tooze, Alan. *Wages of Destruction: The Making and Breaking of the Nazi Economy* (New York, 2008).

Winkler, Allan M. *Home Front U.S.A.: America During World War II* (Wheeling, Ill., 2000).

Wylie, Philip. *Generation of Vipers* (New York, 1942).

SOCIETY

Abrams, Ray H., ed. *The American Family in World War Two*. Annals of the American Academy of Political and Social Science. Vol. 229 (Philadelphia, 1943).

Adams, Leonard P. *Wartime Manpower Mobilization: A Study of World War II Experience in the Buffalo-Niagara Area* (Ithaca, 1951).

Anderson, Karen. *Wartime Women: Sex Roles, Family Relations and the Status of Women During World War II* (Westport, 1981).

Baker, Benjamin. *Wartime Food Production and Procurement* (New York, 1951).

Bentley, Amy. *Eating for Victory: Food Rationing and the Politics of Domesticity* (Urbana, Ill., 1998).

Bush, Vannevar. *Science—the Endless Frontier: A Report to the President* (Washington, 1945).

Bush, Vannevar et al. *Scientists Face the World of 1942* (New Brunswick, N. J., 1942).

Cantril, Hadley. *Public Opinion, 1935–1946* (Princeton, N.J., 1951).

Clinard, Marshall B. *The Black Market: A Study in White Collar Crime* (New York, 1952).

Colean, Miles L. *American Housing: Problems and Prospects* (New York, 1944).

Cooke, Alistair. *The American Home Front, 1941–1942* (New York, 2006).

Costello, John. *Virtue Under Fire: How World War II Changed Our Social and Sexual Attitudes* (Boston, 1985).

Daniels, Roger. *Concentration Camps USA: Japanese-Americans and World War II* (New York, 1970).

———. *The Decision to Evacuate the Japanese* (New York, 1972).

Dryer, Sherman S. *Radio in Wartime* (New York, 1942).

Estes, Winston. *Homefront* (New York, 1976).

Furnas, J. C. *How America Lives* (New York, 1941).

Gallup, George. *The Gallup Polls: Public Opinion, 1935–1971.* Vol. 1. (New York, 1972).

Genung, Albert B. *Food Policies During World War Two* (Ithaca, 1951).

Girdner, Audrie, and Anne Loftis. *The Great Betrayal: The Evacuation of the Japanese Americans During World War II* (New York, 1969).

Gluck, Sherna Berger. *Rosie the Riveter Revisited: Women, the War, and Social Change* (Boston, 1987). RIC

Goodman, Jack, ed. *While You Were Gone: A Report of Wartime Life in the US* (New York, 1946).

Gruenberg, Sidonie M. *The Family in a World at War* (New York, 1942).

Harris, Mark Jonathan et al. *The Home Front* (New York, 1984).

Hartmann, Susan M. *The Home Front and Beyond: American Women in the 1940s* (Boston, 1982).

Hoehling, A. A. *The Week Before Pearl Harbor* (New York, 1963).

Hoopes, Roy. *Americans Remember the Home Front: An Oral Narrative of the World War II Years in America* (New York, 1992).

Hunner, Jon. *Inventing Los Alamos: The Growth of an Atomic Community* (Norman, Okla., 2004).

Irons, Peter. *Justice at War: The Story of the Japanese-American Internment Cases* (New York, 1983).

Jeffries, John W. *Testing the Roosevelt Coalition: Connecticut Society and Politics in the Era of World War II* (Knoxville, 1979).

Johnson, Marilynn S. *The Second Gold Rush: Oakland and the East Bay in World War II* (Berkeley, 1993).

Jones, Ken D., and Arthur F. McClure. *Hollywood at War: The American Motion Picture and World War II* (New York, 1973).

Kandel, I. L. *The Impact of the War upon American Education* (Chapel Hill, 1948).

Kryder, Daniel. *Divided Arsenal: Race and the American State During World War II* (New York, 2000).

Lingeman, Richard. *Don't You Know There's a War On? The American Home Front, 1941–1945* (New York, 1970).

Litoff, Judy B., and David C. Smith. *Since You Went Away: World War II Letters from American Women on the Home Front* (New York, 1991).

McWilliams, Carey. *Prejudice: Japanese Americans, Symbol of Racial Intolerance* (Boston, 1944).

Merrill, Francis E. *Social Problems on the Home Front* (New York, 1948).

Merton, Robert K. *Mass Persuasion: The Social Psychology of a War Bond Drive* (New York, 1946).

Milkman, Ruth. *The Dynamics of Gender at Work: Job Discrimination by Sex During World War II* (Chicago, 1987).

Myrdal, Gunnar. *An American Dilemma*. 2 vols. (New York, 1944).

Nielander, William A. *Wartime Food Rationing* (Baltimore, 1947).

O'Brien, Kenneth Paul, and Lynn Hudson Parson, eds. *The Home-Front War: World War II and American Society* (Westport, Conn., 1995).

Perrett, Geoffrey. *Days of Sadness, Years of Triumph: The American People, 1939–1945* (Baltimore, 1979).

Polenberg, Richard. *War and Society: The United States, 1941–1945* (Philadelphia, 1972).

———. *One Nation Divisible: Class, Race and Ethnicity in the US Since 1938* (New York, 1980).

Shogan, Robert, and Tom Craig. *The Detroit Race Riots* (Philadelphia, 1964).

Sibley, Mulford Q., and Philip E. Jacob. *Conscription of Conscience: The American State and the Conscientious Objector 1940–1947* (Ithaca, 1952).

Stone, I. F. *Business as Usual: The First Year of Defense* (New York, 1941).

———. *The War Years, 1939–1945* (Boston, 1988).

Tuttle, William M., Jr. *Daddy's Gone to War: The Second World War in the Lives of America's Children* (New York, 1993).

Wynn, Neil A. *The Afro-American and the Second World War* (New York, 1975).

WEAPONS AND MATERIALS

Baggott, Jim. *The First War of Physics: The Secret History of the Atom Bomb, 1939–1949* (New York, 2010).

Baldwin, Hanson W. *The Price of Power* (New York, 1948).

Barnes, G. M. *Weapons of World War II* (New York, 1947).

Birdsall, Steve. *Saga of the Superfortress* (Garden City, N.Y., 1980).

Bunker, John Gorley. *Liberty Ships: The Ugly Ducklings of World War II* (Annapolis, 1972).

Bush, Vannevar. *Modern Arms and Free Men* (New York, 1949).

———. *Pieces of the Action* (New York, 1970).

Cardin, Martin. *Flying Forts* (New York, 1968).

Clark, Ronald W. *The Birth of the Bomb* (New York, 1961).

Compton, Arthur H. *Atomic Quest* (New York, 1956).

Conant, Jennet. *Tuxedo Park: A Wall Street Tycoon and the Secret Palace of Science that Changed the Course of World War II* (New York, 2002).

Craven, Wesley F., and James L. Cate, eds. *The Army Air Forces in World War II: Men and Planes* (Chicago, 1955).

Eden, Paul E., and Soph Moeng, eds. *Aircraft Anatomy of World War II* (London, 2003).

Gillie, Mildred H. *Forging the Thunderbolt* (Harrisburg, 1947).

Groves, Leslie. *Now It Can Be Told: The Story of the Manhattan Project* (New York, 1962).

Hewlett, Richard G., and Oscar E. Anderson. *The New World, 1939–1946* (University Park, Pa., 1962).

Hoddeson, Lillian, Paul W. Henriksen, Roger A. Meade, and Catherine Westfall. *Critical Assembly: A Technical History of Los Alamos During the Oppenheimer Years, 1943–1945* (New York, 1993).

Hughes, Jeff. *The Manhattan Project* (New York, 2002).

Hyde, Charles K. *Copper for America: The United States Copper Industry from Colonial Times to the 1990s* (Tucson, 1998).

Johnson, Charles W., and Charles O. Jackson. *City Behind a Fence: Oak Ridge, Tennessee, 1942–1946* (Knoxville, 1981).

Jones, Vincent C. *Manhattan: The Army and the Atomic Bomb* (Washington, 1985).

Kinzie, George R. *Copper Policies of the War Production Board and Predecessor Agencies, May 1940 to November 1945* (Washington, 1947).

Laurence, William L. *Dawn over Zero: The Story of the Atomic Bomb* (New York, 1946).

McKay, Alwyn. *The Making of the Atomic Age* (New York, 1984).

Middlebrook, Martin. *Convoy* (New York, 1977).

Nichols, K. D. *The Road to Trinity* (New York, 1987).

Rhodes, Richard. *The Making of the Atomic Bomb* (New York, 1986).

Sawyer, L. A., and W. H. Mitchell, *The Liberty Ships* (New York, 1970).

Schwartz, Stephen I., ed. *Atomic Audit: The Costs and Consequences of U.S. Nuclear Weapons since 1940* (Washington, 1998).

Stewart, Irvin. *Organizing Scientific Research for War: The Administrative History of the Office of Scientific Research and Development* (Boston, 1948).

Taylor, Frank J., and Lawton Wright. *Democracy's Air Arsenal* (New York, 1947).

Vander Meulen, Jacob. *Building the B-29* (Washington, 1995).

POLITICS, AGENCIES

Adler, Selig. *The Isolationist Impulse* (New York, 1957).

Bean, Jonathan J. *Beyond the Broker State: Federal Policies toward Small Business, 1936–1961* (Chapel Hill, 1996).

Brigante, John E. *The Feasibility Dispute: Determination of War Production Objectives for 1942 and 1943* (Washington, 1950).

Brinkley, Alan. *The End of Reform: New Deal Liberalism in Recession and War* (New York, 1995).

Brinkley, David. *Washington Goes to War* (New York, 1988).

Cole, Wayne S. *America First: The Battle Against Intervention, 1940–1941* (Madison, Wisc., 1953).

Connery, Robert H. *The Navy and the Industrial Mobilization in World War II* (Princeton, 1951).

Dickinson, Matthew J. *Bitter Harvest: FDR, Presidential Power, and the Growth of the Presidential Branch* (New York, 1997).

Drummond, Jones. *The Role of the Office of Civilian Requirements in the Office of Production Management of the War Production Board, January 1941 to November 1945*, Historical Reports on War Administration, War Production Board, Special Study No. 20, Civilian Production Administration (Washington, 1946).

Drury, Allen. *A Senate Journal, 1943–1945* (New York, 1963).

Durr, Clifford. *Early History of the Defense Plant Corporation* (Washington, 1950).

Fine, Lenore, and Jess A. Remington. *The Corps of Engineers: Construction in the United States* (Washington, 1972).

Fleming, Thomas. *The New Dealers' War: Franklin D. Roosevelt and the War Within World War II* (New York, 2001).

Flynn, George Q. *The Mess in Washington: Manpower Mobilization in World War II* (Westport, Conn., 1966).

Grundstein, Nathan D. *Presidential Delegation of Authority in Wartime* (Pittsburgh, 1961).

Holley, Irving Brinton, Jr. *Buying Aircraft: Materiel Procurement for the Army Air Forces* (Washington, 1964).

Irons, Peter H. *The New Deal Lawyers* (Princeton, 1982).

Jonas, Manfred. *Isolationism in America, 1939–1945* (Ithaca, 1966).

Jones, Jesse. *Fifty Billion Dollars: My Thirteen Years with the Reconstruction Finance Corporation, 1932–1945* (New York, 1951).

Manning, Thomas G. *The Office of Price Administration: A World War II Agency of Control* (New York, 1960).

Mansfield, Harvey et al. *A Short History of the OPA* (Washington, 1948).

McAleer, James A. *Dollar-a-Year and without Compensation Personnel Policies of the War Production Board and Predecessor Agencies, August 1939 to November 1945* (Washington, 1946).

McCauley, Maryclair. *Concentration of Civilian Production by the War Production Board, September 1941 to April 1943* (Washington, 1946).

McGrane, Reginald C. *The Facilities and Construction Program of the War Production Board and Predecessor Agencies, May 1940 to May 1945* (Washington, 1945).

Novick, David, Melvin Anshen, and W. C. Truppner. *Wartime Production Controls* (New York, 1949).

Ogden, August R. *The Dies Committee, 1938–1943* (Washington, 1944).

Ohl, John Kennedy. *Supplying the Troops: General Somervell and American Logistics in WWII* (DeKalb, Ill., 1994).

Riddle, Donald H. *The Truman Committee: A Study in Congressional Responsibility* (New Brunswick, N.J., 1964).

Rowland, Buford. *U.S. Navy Bureau of Ordnance in World War II* (Washington, 1952).

Ruml, Beardsley. *Tomorrow's Business* (New York, 1945).

Smith, A. Merriman. *Thank You, Mr. President: A White House Notebook* (New York, 1946).

Somers, Herman Miles. *Presidential Agency OWMR* (New York, 1969).

Stoughton, Bradley. *History of the Tools Division, War Production Board* (New York, 1949).

Sullivan, Lawrence. *Bureaucracy Runs Amuck* (Indianapolis, 1944).

Thompson, Victor A. *The Regulatory Process in OPA Rationing* (New York, 1950).

Thomson, Harry C., and Lida Mayo. *The Ordnance Department: Procurement and Supply* (Washington, 1960).

United States Bureau of the Budget. *The United States at War* (Washington, 1946).

United States Civilian Production Administration. *Industrial Mobilization for War: History of the War Production Board and Predecessor Agencies, 1940–1945* (Washington, 1947).

Waddell, Brian. *The War Against the New Deal: World War II and American Democracy* (DeKalb, Ill., 2001).

Walton, Frank L. *The Thread of Victory* (New York, 1945).

Wardlow, Chester. *The Transportation Corps: Responsibilities, Organization, and Operations* (Washington, 1951).

Warken, Philip W. *A History of the National Resources Planning Board* (New York, 1979).

White, Gerald T. *Billions for Defense: Government Financing by the Defense Plant Corporation during World War II* (University, Ala., 1982).

Wiltse, Charles M. *Aluminum Policies of the War Production Board and Predecessor Agencies* (Washington, 1946).

Winkler, Allan M. *The Politics of Propaganda: The Office of War Information, 1942–1945* (New Haven, 1978).

Witney, Fred. *Wartime Experiences of the National Labor Relations Board* (Urbana, 1949).

Young, R. A. *Congressional Politics in the Second World War* (New York, 1956).

ECONOMY

Abrahamson, James L. *The American Home Front* (Washington, 1983).

Chandler, Lester V. *Inflation in the United States, 1940–1948* (New York, 1951).

Chandler, Lester V., and Donald H. Wallace, eds. *Economic Mobilization and Stabilization: Selected Materials on the Economics of War and Defense* (New York, 1951).

Cref, John R. *A Survey of the American Economy, 1940–1946* (New York, 1947).

Crum, William L., et al. *Fiscal Planning for Total War* (New York, 1942).

Eckes, Alfred E., Jr. *The United States and the Global Struggle for Minerals* (Austin, 1979).

Fearon, Peter. *War, Prosperity and Depression: The U.S. Economy 1917–45* (Oxford, Eng., 1987).

Gordon, David L. *The Hidden Weapon: The Story of Economic Warfare* (New York, 1947).

Harris, Seymour. *Economics of American Defense* (New York, 1941).

———. *Prices and Related Controls in the United States* (New York, 1945).

Hitch, Charles J. *America's Economic Strength* (New York, 1942).

Koistinen, Paul A. C. *The Hammer and the Sword: Labor, the Military, and Industrial Mobilization, 1920–1945* (New York, 1979).

Kuznets, Simon. *National Product in Wartime* (New York, 1945).

Lacey, Jim. *Keep from All Thoughtful Men: How U.S. Economists Won World War II* (Annapolis, 2011).

Lampman, Robert J. *The Share of the Top Wealth-Holders in National Wealth, 1922–1956* (Princeton, 1962).

Murray, Philip. *Living Costs in World War II, 1941–1944* (Washington, 1944).

Nugent, Rolf. *Guns, Planes, and Your Pocketbook* (New York, 1941).

Paul, Randolph. *Taxation in the United States* (Boston, 1954).

Smith, R. Elberton. *The Army and Economic Mobilization* (Washington, 1991).

Stein, Emanuel. *Our Wartime Economy: Government, Production, Finance* (New York, 1942).

———. *War Economics* (New York, 1942).

Steiner, George. *Economic Problems of War* (New York, 1942).

Vatter, Harold G. *The U.S. Economy in World War II* (New York, 1985).

INDUSTRIES

Archibald, Katherine. *Wartime Shipyard: A Study in Social Disunity* (Berkeley, 1947).

Arrington, Leonard J., and Anthony Cluff. *Federally Financed Industrial Plants Constructed in Utah during World War II* (Logan, Utah, 1969).

———. *The Defense Industry of Utah* (Logan, Utah, 1965).

Automobile Manufacturing Association. *Freedom's Arsenal: The Story of the Automotive Council for War Production* (Detroit, 1950).

Baker, Helen. *Women in War Industries* (Princeton, 1942).

Baruch, Bernard. *American Industry in the War* (New York, 1941).

Boeing Company. *Pedigree of Champions: Boeing Since 1916* (Seattle, 1977).

Borth, Christy. *Masters of Mass Production* (Indianapolis, 1945).

Broehl, Wayne. *Precision Valley: The Machine Tool Companies of Springfield, Vermont* (Englewood Cliffs, N.J., 1959).

Carr, Lowell J., and James E. Stermer. *Willow Run* (New York, 1952).

Collins, Tom. *Flying Fortress: The Story of Boeing.* (New York, 1943).

Cunningham, William G. *The Aircraft Industry: A Study of Industrial Location* (Berkeley, 1951).

Fairchild, Byron, and Jonathan Grossman. *The Army and Industrial Manpower* (Washington, 1959).

Frey, John W., and H. Chandler Ide. *A History of the Petroleum Administration for War, 1941–1945* (Washington, 1946).

Gorter, Wytze, and George H. Hildebrand. *The Pacific Coast Maritime Shipping Industry, 1930–1948.* 2 vols. (Berkeley, 1952–54).

Grether, Ewald T. *The Steel and Steel Using Industries of California* (Berkeley, 1946).

Heath, Jim F. "American War Mobilization and the Use of Small Manufacturers, 1939–1943," *Business History Review* (Autumn, 1972) 46: 294–319.

Herbert, Vernon, and Attilio Bisio. *Synthetic Rubber: A Project that Had to Succeed* (Westport, Conn., 1985).

Hinton, Harold B. *Air Victory: The Men and the Machines* (New York, 1948).

Howard, Frank A. *Buna Rubber: The Birth of an Industry* (New York, 1947).

Ickes, Harold L. *Fightin' Oil* (New York, 1943).

Jensen, G. Granville. *The Aluminum Industry of the Northwest* (Corvallis, Ore., 1950).

Lane, Frederic C. *Ships for Victory: A History of Shipbuilding Under the U.S. Maritime Commission in World War II* (Baltimore, 1951).

Larson, Henrietta, Evelyn H. Knowlton, and Charles S. Popple. *New Horizons: History of Standard Oil Company (New Jersey), 1927–1950* (New York, 1971).

Lauderbaugh, Richard A. *American Steel Makers and the Coming of the Second World War* (Ann Arbor, 1980).

Lilley, Tom, et al. *Problems of Accelerating Aircraft Production During World War II* (Cambridge, Mass., 1946).

McQuaid, Kim. *Big Business and Presidential Power from FDR to Reagan* (New York, 1982).

Miller, John Anderson. *Men and Volts at War: The Story of General Electric in World War II* (New York, 1947).

Mitchell, C. Bradford. *Every Kind of Shipwork: A History of Todd Shipyards Corporation, 1916–1981* (New York, 1981).

Morris, Peter J. T. *The American Synthetic Rubber Research Program* (Philadelphia, 1989).

National Industrial Conference Board. *America's War Effort: Objectives, Resources, Progress* (New York, 1942).

Novick, David, and George Steiner. *Wartime Industrial Statistics* (Champaign-Urbana, Ill., 1949).

Popple, Charles Sterling. *Standard Oil Company (New Jersey) in World War II* (New York, 1952).

Rae, John B. *Climb to Greatness: The American Aircraft Industry, 1920–1960* (Cambridge, Mass., 1968).

Redding, Robert, and Bill Yenne. *Boeing: Planemaker to the World* (Greenwich, Conn., 1983).

Sill, Van Rensselaer. *American Miracle: the Story of War Construction around the World* (New York, 1947).

Thruelesen, Richard. *The Grumman Story* (New York, 1976).

Tuttle, William M. "The Birth of an Industry: The Synthetic Rubber 'Mess' in World War II," *Technology and Culture* (January 1981) 1:35:67.

Wagoner, Harless D. *The U.S. Machine Tool Industry from 1900 to 1950* (Cambridge, Mass., 1968).

Walton, Francis. *Miracle of World War II: How American Industry Made Victory Possible* (New York, 1956).

Ward, James. *The Fall of the Packard Motor Company* (Stanford, 1995).

Whitehead, Don. *The Dow Story: The History of the Dow Chemical Company* (New York, 1968).

Woodbury, David. *Battlefronts of Industry: Westinghouse in World War II* (New York, 1948).

AGRICULTURE

Gold, Bela. *Wartime Economic Planning in Agriculture* (New York, 1968).

Schultz, Theodore W. *Agriculture in an Unstable Economy* (New York, 1945).

Wilcox, Walter W. *The Farmer in the Second World War* (Ames, Ia., 1947).

Wilcox, Walter W., and Willard W. Cochrane. *Economics of American Agriculture* (Englewood Cliffs, N.J., 1960).

LABOR

Atleson, James. *Labor and the Wartime State: Labor Relations and Law During World War II* (Urbana, Ill., 1998).

Gregory, Chester. *Women in Defense Work During World War II: An Analysis of the Labor Problem* (Jericho, N.Y., 1974).

Harris, John H. *The Right to Manage: Industrial Relations Policies of American Business in the 1940s* (Madison, Wisc., 1982).

Isserman, Maurice. *Which Side Were You On? The American Communist Party During the Second World War* (Middletown, Conn., 1982).

Jacoby, Sanford M. "Union-Management Cooperation in the United States During World War II," in Melvin Dubovsky, ed., *Technological Change and Worker Movements in the Modern World* (Beverly Hills, 1985).

Kesselman, Amy. *Fleeting Opportunities: Women Shipyard Workers in Portland and Vancouver during World War II and Reconversion* (Albany, 1990).

Lichtenstein, Nelson. *Labor's War at Home: The CIO in World War II* (New York, 1982).

Purcell, Richard J. *Labor Policies of the National Defense Advisory Commission and the Office of Production Management, May 1940 to April 1942*, Historical Reports on War Administration, War Production Board (Washington, 1946).

Richards, Allan R. *War Labor Boards in the Field* (Chapel Hill, 1953).

Seidman, Joel. *American Labor: From Defense to Reconversion* (Chicago, 1953).

Swafford, Rosa I. *Wartime Record of Strikes and Lockouts, 1940–1945* (Washington, 1946).

Zieger, Robert H. *The CIO, 1935–1955* (Chapel Hill, 1995).

BIOGRAPHY, AUTOBIOGRAPHY, MEMOIRS

Acheson, Dean. *Present at the Creation: My Years in the State Department* (New York, 1969).

Adams, Henry H. *Harry Hopkins: A Biography* (New York, 1977).

Adams, Stephen B. *Mr. Kaiser Goes to Washington: The Rise of a Government Entrepreneur* (Chapel Hill, 1997).

Albion, Robert G., and Robert H. Connery. *Forrestal and the Navy* (New York, 1962).

Alinsky, Saul. *John L. Lewis: An Unauthorized Biography* (New York, 1949).

Anderson, Jervis. *A. Philip Randolph: A Biographical Portrait* (New York, 1973).

Barnard, Ellsworth. *Wendell Willkie: Fighter for Freedom* (Marquette, 1966).

Baruch, Bernard M. *My Own Story* (New York, 1957).

———. *Baruch: The Public Years* (New York, 1960).

Baughman, James L. *Henry R. Luce and the Rise of the American News Media* (Boston, 1987).

Beasley, Norman. *Knudsen: A Biography* (New York, 1947).

Biddle, Francis B. *In Brief Authority* (Garden City, N.Y., 1962).

Bishop, Jim. *FDR's Last Year* (New York, 1974).

Blake, I. George. *Paul V. McNutt: Portrait of a Hoosier Statesman* (Indianapolis, 1966).

Blum, John Morton. *Years of Urgency, 1938–1941: From the Morgenthau Diaries* (Boston, 1965).

———. *Years of War, 1941–1945: From the Morgenthau Diaries* (Boston, 1967).

———, ed. *The Price of Vision: The Diary of Henry A. Wallace, 1942–1946* (Boston, 1973).

Bowles, Chester. *Promises to Keep: My Years in Public Life* (New York, 1971).

Buhite, Russell D., and David W. Levy, eds. *FDR's Fireside Chats* (Norman, Okla., 1992).

Burlingame, Roger. *Don't Let Them Scare You: The Life and Times of Elmer Davis* (Philadelphia, 1961).

Burns, James McGregor. *The Lion and the Fox* (New York, 1971).

———. *Roosevelt: The Soldier of Freedom* (New York, 1972).

Bush, Vannevar. *Pieces of the Action* (New York, 1970).

Byrnes, James F. *All in One Lifetime* (New York, 1958).

———. *Speaking Frankly* (New York, 1947).

Childs, Marquis. *I Write from Washington* (New York, 1942).

Clapper, Raymond. *Watching the World* (New York, 1944).

Clawson, Angela. *Shipyard Diary of a Woman Welder* (New York, 1944).

Clifford, Clark, with Richard Holbrooke. *Counsel to the President: A Memoir* (New York, 1991).

Coit, Margaret. *Mr. Baruch* (Boston, 1957).

Cole, Wayne S. *Charles A. Lindbergh and the Battle Against America Intervention in World War II* (New York, 1974).

———. *Senator Gerald P. Nye and American Foreign Policy* (Minneapolis, 1962).

Conant, James B. *My Several Lives: Memoir of a Social Inventor* (New York, 1970).

Cousins, Norman, and J. Garry Clifford, eds. *Memoirs of a Man: Grenville Clark* (New York, 1975).

Cray, Ed. *General of the Army: George C. Marshall, Soldier and Statesman* (New York, 1990).

Culver, John C., and John Hyde. *American Dreamer: A Life of Henry Wallace* (New York, 2000).

Current, Richard N. *Secretary Stimson: A Study in Statecraft* (New Brunswick, N.J., 1954).

Dallek, Robert. *Franklin D. Roosevelt and American Foreign Policy, 1932–1945* (New York, 1981).

Davis, Kenneth S. *FDR: The War President, 1940–1943: A History* (New York, 2000).

Dorwart, Jeffery M. *Eberstadt and Forrestal: A National Security Partnership, 1909–1949* (College Station, Tex., 1991).

Dubofsky, Melvyn, and Warren Van Tine. *John L. Lewis: A Biography* (New York, 1977).

Dunne, Gerald T. *Grenville Clark: Public Citizen* (New York, 1986).

Eccles, Marriner. *Beckoning Frontiers* (New York, 1951).

Eiler, Keith E. *Mobilizing America: Robert P. Patterson and the War Effort, 1940–1945* (Ithaca, 1997).

Eisenhower, Dwight D. *Crusade in Europe* (Garden City, N.Y., 1948).

Ermenc, Joseph, ed. *Atomic Bomb Scientists: Memoirs, 1939–1945* (Westport, Conn., 1989).

Farley, James. *The Roosevelt Years* (New York, 1948).

Fields, Alonzo. *My 21 Years in the White House* (New York, 1961).

Flynn, George Q. *Lewis B. Hershey: Mr. Selective Service* (Chapel Hill, 1985).

Foster, Mark S. *Henry J. Kaiser: Builder in the Modern American West* (Austin, 1989).

———. "Giant of the West: Henry J. Kaiser and Regional Industrialization, 1930–1950," *Business History Review* 59 (Spring 1985): 1–23.

Fraser, Steven. *Labor Will Rule: Sidney Hillman and the Rise of American Labor* (New York, 1991).

Freidel, Frank. *Franklin D. Roosevelt: A Rendezvous with Destiny* (Boston, 1990).

Galbraith, John Kenneth. *A Life in Our Times: Memoirs* (Boston, 1981).

Goodwin, Doris Kearns. *No Ordinary Time: Franklin and Eleanor Roosevelt: The Home Front in World War II* (New York, 1994).

Gould, Jean, and Lorena Hickok. *Walter Reuther: Labor's Rugged Individualist* (New York, 1972).

Grant, James. *Bernard M. Baruch: The Adventures of a Wall Street Legend* (New York, 1983).

Hand, Samuel B. *Counsel and Advise: A Political Biography of Samuel I. Rosenman* (New York 1979).

Hassett, William D. *Off the Record with F.D.R.* (New Brunswick, N.J., 1958).

Heiner, Albert J. *Henry J. Kaiser: Western Colossus* (San Francisco, 1991).

Henderson, Richard B. *Maury Maverick: A Political Biography* (Austin, 1970).

Hershberg, James G. *James B. Conant: Harvard to Hiroshima and the Making of the Nuclear Age* (New York, 1993).

Herzstein, Robert E. *Henry R. Luce: A Political Portrait of the Man Who Created the American Century* (New York, 1994).

Hodgson, Godfrey. *The Colonel: The Life and Wars of Henry Stimson, 1867–1950* (New York, 1990).

Hoopes, Townsend, and Douglas Brinkley. *Driven Patriot: The Life and Times of James Forrestal* (New York, 1992).

Hull, Cordell. *The Memoirs of Cordell Hull* (New York, 1948).

Hyman, Sidney. *Marriner S. Eccles: Private Entrepreneur and Public Servant* (Palo Alto, 1976).

Ickes, Harold. *The Secret Diary of Harold L. Ickes.* 3 vols. (New York, 1953–54).

Johnston, Marjorie, ed. *The Cosmos of Arthur Holly Compton* (New York, 1967).

Josephson, Matthew, and Hannah Josephson. *Sidney Hillman: Statesman of American Labor* (New York, 1952).

Kikuchi, Charles. *Kikuchi Diary: Chronicle from an American Concentration Camp* (Urbana, Ill., 1973).

Kimball, Warren F. *The Juggler: Franklin Roosevelt as Wartime Statesman* (Princeton, 1991).

Kimball, Warren F., ed. *Churchill & Roosevelt: The Complete Correspondence,* 3 vols. (Princeton, 1984).

Lacey, Robert. *Ford: The Man and the Machine* (Boston, 1986).

Larrabee, Eric. *Commander in Chief: Franklin Delano Roosevelt, His Lieutenants, and Their War* (New York, 1987).

Lash, Joseph P., ed. *From the Diaries of Felix Frankfurter* (New York, 1975).

Lawrence, David. *Diary of a Washington Correspondent* (New York, 1942).

Leahy, William D. *I Was There* (New York, 1950).

Levin, Linda Lotridge. *The Making of FDR: The Story of Stephen T. Early, America's First Modern Press Secretary* (Amherst, N.Y., 2008).

Lewis, David L. *The Public Image of Henry Ford: An American Folk Hero and His Company* (Detroit, 1976).

Lindbergh, Anne Morrow. *War Within and Without: Diaries and Letters, 1939–1944* (New York, 1980).

Lindbergh, Charles A. *The Wartime Journals of Charles A. Lindbergh* (New York, 1970).

McCullough, David. *Truman* (New York, 1992).

McJimsey, George. *Harry Hopkins: Ally of the Poor and Defender of Democracy* (Cambridge, Mass., 1987).

Morgan, Ted. *FDR: A Biography* (New York, 1985).

Morison, Elting E. *Turmoil and Tradition: A Study of the Life and Times of Henry L. Stimson* (Boston, 2003 [1960]).

Neal, Steve. *Dark Horse: A Biography of Wendell Willkie* (Garden City, N.Y., 1984).

Nelson, Donald M. *Arsenal of Democracy* (New York, 1946).

Perez, Robert C. *The Will to Win: A Biography of Ferdinand Eberstadt* (Westport, Conn., 1989).

Perkins, Frances. *The Roosevelt I Knew* (New York, 1946).

Pogue, Forrest C. *George C. Marshall.* 4 vols. (New York, 1966).

Robertson, David. *Sly and Able: A Political Biography of James F. Byrnes* (New York, 1994).

Roosevelt, Eleanor. *This I Remember* (New York, 1949).

Roosevelt, Franklin D. *Complete Presidential Press Conference of Franklin D. Roosevelt.* 25 vols. (New York, 1972).

———. *F.D.R.: His Personal Letters, 1928–1945.* 4 vols. (New York, 1950).

———. *Roosevelt and Frankfurter: Their Correspondence, 1928–1945* (Boston, 1967).

———. *Public Papers and Addresses of President Franklin D. Roosevelt.* 13 vols (New York, 1928–1945).

Rosenman, Samuel I. *Working with Roosevelt* (New York, 1952).

Schmitz, David F. *Henry L. Stimson: The First Wise Man* (Wilmington, Del., 2001).

Schwartz, Jordan A. *The Speculator: Bernard M. Baruch in Washington, 1917–1965* (Chapel Hill, 1981).

Sevareid, Eric. *Not So Wild a Dream* (New York, 1979).

Sherwood, Robert E. *Roosevelt and Hopkins, an Intimate History* (New York, 1948).

Sorensen, Charles, and William Samuelson. *My Forty Years with Ford* (New York, 1950).

Steel, Ronald. *Walter Lippmann and the American Century* (New York, 1981).

Stettinius, Edward R. *The Diaries of Edward R. Stettinius, Jr., 1943–1946*. Edited by Thomas M. Campell and George C. Herring (New York, 1975).

Stimson, Henry L., and McGeorge Bundy. *On Active Service in Peace and War* (New York, 1948).

Stoler, Mark A. *George C. Marshall: Soldier-Statesman of the American Century* (Boston, 1989).

Strahan, Jerry E. *Andrew Jackson Huggins and the Boats That Won World War II* (Baton Rouge, 1994).

Terkel, Studs. *The Good War* (New York, 1984).

Timmons, Bascom. *Jesse H. Jones: The Man and the Statesman* (New York, 1956).

Truman, Harry. *Memoirs: Year of Decision* (Garden City, N.Y., 1955).

Tully, Grace. *F.D.R. My Boss* (New York, 1949).

Wallace, Henry A. *The Price of Vision: The Diary of Henry A. Wallace, 1942–1946* (Boston, 1973).

Watkins, T. H. *Righteous Pilgrim: The Life and Times of Harold L. Ickes, 1874–1952* (New York, 1990).

Zachary, G. Pascal. *Endless Frontier: Vannevar Bush, Engineer of the American Century* (New York, 1997).

RECONVERSION

Harris, Seymour E., ed. *Economic Reconstruction* (New York, 1946).

Kaiser, Henry J. *Management Looks at the Postwar World* (New York, 1943).

Kaplan, A.D.H. *The Liquidation of War Production* (New York, 1944).

Peltason, Jack W. *The Reconversion Controversy* (New York, 1950).

Wright, Chester. *Economic Problems of War and Its Aftermath* (Chicago, 1942).

GOVERNMENT DOCUMENTS

Bureau of Demobilization, Civilian Production Administration. *Minutes of the Advisory Commission to the Council of National Defense*, Historical Reports on War Administration, War Production Board, Documentary Publication No. 2 (Washington, 1946).

Bureau of Demobilization, Civilian Production Administration. *Minutes of the Council of the Office of Production Management*, Historical Reports on War Administration, War Production Board, Documentary Publication No. 2 (Washington, 1946).

United States Bureau of the Census, *Historical Statistics of the United States from Colonial Times to 1970*. 2 vols. (Washington, 1975).

United States Civilian Production Administration. *Industrial Mobilization for War: History of the War Production Board and Predecessor Agencies, 1940–1945*. vol. 1. (Washington, 1947).

United States Civilian Production Administration. *War Industrial Facilities Authorized July 1940–August 1945* (Washington, 1946).

United States Senate, Report 480, 77 Cong., 2nd sess., pt. 5, January 15, 1942.

United States Senate Special Committee to Investigate the National Defense Program, *Hearings*, 77 Cong., 1st sess., 1941 (Washington, 1941).

United States Senate Special Committee to Investigate the National Defense Program, *Hearings*, 78 Cong., 1st sess., 1941 (Washington, 1943).

United States Senate Special Committee to Investigate the National Defense Program, Additional Report, 78 Cong., 1st sess., pt. 10.

United States Senate Special Committee to Investigate the National Defense Program, *Higgins Contracts*, 77 Cong., 2nd sess., 1942 (Washington, 1942).

United States Senate Special Committee to Investigate the National Defense Program, Report No. 10, pt. 12.

United States Senate Special Committee to Investigate the National Defense Program, *Report on Steel*, 78 Cong., 1st sess., Report No. 10, pt. 3, February 4, 1943.

INDEX

ABOUT THE AUTHOR

Maury Klein is the author of many books, including *The Life and Legend of Jay Gould; Days of Defiance: Sumter, Secession, and the Coming of the Civil War; Rainbow's End: The Crash of 1929;* and *The Power Makers: Steam, Electricity, and the Men Who Invented Modern America.* He is professor emeritus of history at the University of Rhode Island.